Karaoke with Jean

KARAOKE SONGBOOK SORTED BY TITLE

Enjoy the show!

Copyright 2016
Paperback Pushers
ISBN-13: 978-1505370614
ISBN-10: 1505370612

SONG TITLE	ARTIST	#	TYPE
21	Hayes, Hunter	45-94	KV
1976	Jackson, Alan	49-182	KV
#9 Dream	Lennon, John	30-291	RS
#Selfie	Chainsmokers	43-288	ASK
#Selfie	Chainsmokers	43-187	SBI
03 Bonnie & Clyde	Jay-Z & Beyonce	25-459	MM
03 Bonnie & Clyde	Jay-Z & Knowles	32-48	THM
03 Bonnie & Clyde - Duet	Knowles & Jay-Z	32-48	THM
1 2 3 4	Plain White T's	36-386	SC
1 Thing	Amerie feat. Eve	23-308	CB
1-2-3	Miami Sound Mach	11-111	DK
1-2-3	Miami Sound Mach	17-738	PT
1-2-3	Miami Sound Mach	17-178	SC
1-2-3 Red Light	1910 Fruitgum Co.	22-448	SC
1, 2 Step	Ciara & Missy Elliott	37-98	SC
10 Days Late	Third Eye Blind	14-490	SC
10 Out Of 10	Lou, Louchie	12-395	PHM
10,000 Towns	Eli Young Band	44-381	BKD
100 Percent Chance Of Rain	Morris, Gary	34-266	CB
100 Years	Five For Fighting	20-572	CB
100 Years From Now	Lewis & The News	47-190	SC
100% Chance Of Rain	Morris, Gary	5-534	SC
100% Pure Love	Crystal Waters	13-293	P
100% Pure Love	Crystal Waters	2-467	SC
11	Pope, Cassadee	44-135	ASK
12:51	Strokes	19-761	PHM
15 Minutes	Atkins, Rodney	37-50	CB
15 Minutes Of Shame	Cook, Kristy Lee	36-213	PHM
16th Avenue	Dalton, Lacy J.	14-319	SC
17	Cross Can Ragweed	18-597	ST
17 Again	Gilbert, Brantley	44-196	KCD
18 And Life	Skid Row	23-59	MH
18 Days	Saving Abel	36-384	SC
18 Yellow Roses	Darin, Bobby	4-216	SC
18 Yellow Roses	Darin, Bobby	30-762	SF
18 Yellow Roses	Robbins, Marty	44-70	KV
19 Somethin'	Wills, Mark	34-379	CB
19 You And Me	Dan + Shay	43-188	SBI
1969	Stegall, Keith	4-132	SC
1973 (Radio Vers)	Blunt, James	49-907	SC
1979	Smashing Pumpkins	34-356	CB
1979	Smashing Pumpkins	13-603	P
1979	Smashing Pumpkins	4-176	SC
1982	Travis, Randy	1-391	CB
1982	Travis, Randy	8-699	SAV
1985	Bowling For Soup	20-551	PHM
1994	Aldean, Jason	44-203	KV
1999	Prince	12-809	P
19th Nervous Breakdown	Rolling Stones	19-756	LE
19th Nervous Breakdown	Rolling Stones	14-403	PT
2 Become 1	Spice Girls	21-547	PHM
2001 Space Odessey	First Edition	10-354	KC
21 Questions	50 Cent & Dogg	25-712	MM
21 Questions	50 Cent & Nate Dogg	32-276	THM

SONG TITLE	ARTIST	#	TYPE
24 Hours At A Time	Marshall Tucker Ban	9-383	AH
24 Hours At A Time	Marshall Tucker Ban	13-770	SGB
24/7	Edmunds, Kevin	5-896	SC
25 Miles	Starr, Edwin	25-277	MM
25 Minutes To Go	Cash, Johnny	21-608	SF
25 Or 6 To 4	Chicago	13-219	P
26 Cents	Wilkinsons	8-745	CB
26 Cents	Wilkinsons	22-810	ST
26 Miles	Four Preps	9-735	SAV
29 Nights	Leigh, Danni	8-936	CB
3 A.M.	Matchbox 20	7-706	PHM
3 Things	Mraz, Jason	47-304	KV
30 Days In The Hole	Humble Pie	5-590	SC
32 Flavors	Davis, Alana	5-186	SC
35 MPH Town	Keith, Toby	46-301	BKD
3AM	Trainor, Meghan	45-145	DCK
4 + 20	Crosby, Stills, Nash & Young	46-175	SC
4 In The Morning	Stefani, Gwen	30-565	CB
4 Minutes	Madonna	48-592	DK
4 Seasons Of Lonliness	Boyz II Men	7-700	PHM
4 To 1 In Atlanta	Byrd, Tracy	22-902	ST
409	Beach Boys	3-557	SC
455 Rocket	Mattea, Kathy	14-659	CB
455 Rocket	Mattea, Kathy	22-407	CHM
455 Rocket	Mattea, Kathy	7-431	MM
4th Of July	Jennings, Shooter	22-340	CB
5-1-5-0	Bentley, Dierks	39-43	ASK
5-4-3-2-1	Mann, Manfred	10-644	SF
50 Ways To Get Bin Laden	Parody	49-307	RD
50 Ways To Leave Your Lover	Simon & Garfunkel	23-636	BS
50 Ways To Leave Your Lover	Simon, Paul	2-144	SC
50 Ways To Say Goodbye	Train	48-266	KV
50,000 Names	Jones, George	20-585	CB
50,000 Names	Jones, George	16-697	ST
50,000 Names	O'Hara, Jamie	2-428	SC
50,000 Pounds Of Bananas	Chapin, Harry	21-519	SC
500 Miles	Peter, Paul & Mary	12-573	P
500 Miles Away From Home	Bare, Bobby	18-267	CB
57 Chevrolet	Spears, Billie Jo	47-591	KV
57 Chevrolet	Spears, Billie Jo	47-590	MRE
59th Street Bridge Song	Simon & Garfunkel	23-634	BS
6 Underground	Sneaker Pimps	10-110	SC
6-8-12	McKnight, Brian	19-834	SGB
60 Minute Man	Ward & Dominos	2-82	SC
634-5789 Soulville USA	Blues Brothers	35-78	CB
6345-789	Blues Brothers	29-153	ZM
65 Love Affair	Davis, Paul	16-158	SC
6th Avenue Heartache	Wallflowers	24-120	SC
7	Prince	12-761	P
7 Days	David, Craig	25-89	MM
7 Rooms Of Gloom	Four Tops	34-32	CB

SONG TITLE	ARTIST	#	TYPE
7 Whole Days	Braxton, Toni	13-609	P
7 Years	Graham, Lukas	48-792	DCK
7/11	Beyonce	48-328	MRH
8 X 10	Anderson, Bill	20-785	CB
80's Ladies	Oslin, K.T.	6-742	MM
80's Ladies	Oslin, K.T.	2-615	SC
800 Pound Jesus	Sawyer Brown	23-373	SC
88 Lines About 44 Women **	Nails	30-672	RSX
88 Lines About 44 Women **	Nails	23-16	SC
8th Of November	Big & Rich	30-90	CB
8th World Wonder	Locke, Kimberly	20-357	PHM
8th World Wonder	Locke, Kimberly	36-325	PS
9 To 5	Parton, Dolly	8-544	CB
9 To 5	Parton, Dolly	26-307	DK
9 To 5	Parton, Dolly	12-690	P
911	Feat & Blige	14-45	THM
93 Million Miles	Mraz, Jason	47-303	KV
96 Tears	? & the Mysterians	3-284	MM
98.6	Keith	9-705	SAV
98.6	Keith	5-514	SC
99 Luftballoons	Nena	11-685	DK
99 Red Balloons	Nena	4-532	SC
99 Times	Voegele, Kate	36-298	PHM
99.9% Sure	McComas, Brian	25-567	MM
99.9% Sure	McComas, Brian	19-10	ST
99.9% Sure	McComas, Brian	32-195	THM
99.9% Sure (I've Never Been...)	McComas, Brian	34-395	CB
A Tisket A Tasket	Fitzgerald, Ella	9-819	SAV
A-11	Paycheck, Johnny	22-40	CB
A-11	Paycheck, Johnny	5-102	SC
A-Ok	McCoy, Neal	38-245	PHN
A.D.I.D.A.S.	Killer Mike & Big Boi	32-165	THM
A.M.	Young, Chris	47-934	BKD
Aaron's Party Come And Get It	Carter, Aaron	16-249	TT
ABC	Jackson Five	11-411	DK
ABC's Of Love the	Lymon, Frankie	30-526	LE
Abilene	Hamilton, George IV	8-782	CB
Abilene	Hamilton, George IV	8-663	SAV
Abilene	Hamilton, George IV	2-630	SC
About You Now	Cosgrove, Amanda	36-288	PHM
About You Now (Radio Vers)	Sugababes	49-888	SC
Above And Beyond	Owens, Buck	46-101	KWD
Above The Clouds	Amber	21-719	TT
Abracadabra	Miller, Steve	23-631	BS
Abracadabra	Steve Miller Band	33-307	CB
Abraham Martin & John	Dion	33-254	CB
Abraham Martin & John	Dion	3-13	SC
Absence Of Fear	Jewel	19-355	PS
Absence Of The Heart	Carter, Deana	10-145	SC
Absence Of The Heart	Carter, Deana	22-669	ST
Absolutely (Story of a Girl)	Nine Days	35-219	CB
Absolutely (Story of a Girl)	Nine Days	14-466	SC

SONG TITLE	ARTIST	#	TYPE
Absolutely (Story of a Girl)	Nine Days	15-784	THM
Absolutely Not	Cox, Deborah	25-216	MM
Absolutely Nothing	Houser, Randy	39-90	PHN
Ac-Cent-Tchu-Ate The Positive	Crosby, Bing	21-8	CB
Ac-Cent-Tchu-Ate The Positive	Mercer, Johnny	4-188	SC
Accidental Racist	Paisley, Brad	43-455	ASK
Accidentally In Love	Counting Crows	23-557	MM
Ace In The Hole	Strait, George	28-78	DK
Ace In The Hole	Strait, George	20-399	MH
Ace Of Spades	Motorhead	21-757	SC
Aces	Bogguss, Suzy	1-559	CB
Aces	Bogguss, Suzy	6-117	MM
Aces	Bogguss, Suzy	2-705	SC
Aching Breaking Heart	Dolan, Joe	49-140	SRK
Achy Breaky Heart	Cyrus, Billy Ray	11-784	DK
Achy Breaky Heart	Cyrus, Billy Ray	6-106	MM
Achy Breaky Heart	Cyrus, Billy Ray	12-432	P
Achy Breaky Heart (Parody)	Yankovic, Weird Al	15-349	MM
Acquiesce	Oasis	16-215	MM
Across The Alley From The Alamo	Wills, Bob	45-693	OZP
Across The Universe	Apple, Fiona	16-210	MM
Across The Universe	Beatles	7-522	SAV
Act A Fool	Ludacris	32-310	THM
Act A Fool (Radio Version) **	Ludacris	21-797	SC
Act Naturally	Beatles	16-656	DK
Act Naturally	Owens, Buck	8-35	CB
Act Naturally	Owens, Buck	17-297	NA
Act Naturally	Owens, Buck	13-456	P
Adalida	Strait, George	1-247	CB
Adalida	Strait, George	2-697	SC
Adalida	Strait, George	22-877	ST
Adam & Evil	Presley, Elvis	25-494	MM
Adam's Chanuka Song **	Sandler, Adam	16-642	MM
Add It Up **	Violent Femmes	5-544	SC
Addams Family TV Theme	Mizzy, Vic	16-280	TT
Addams Family TV Theme	TV Themes	2-162	SC
Addicted	Clarkson, Kelly	47-687	CB
Addicted	Iglesias, Enrique	19-664	CB
Addicted	Saving Abel	36-528	CB
Addicted	Seals, Dan	14-424	SC
Addicted	Shelton, Blake	38-212	PHN
Addicted To A Dollar	Stone, Doug	20-603	CB
Addicted To A Dollar	Stone, Doug	6-501	MM
Addicted To Love	Palmer, Robert	12-821	P
Addicted To Love	Palmer, Robert	5-118	SC
Addicted To Love	Palmer, Robert	10-534	SF
Addicted To Love	Turner, Tina	10-427	LE
Addicted To Spuds	Yankovic, Weird Al	49-837	SC
Address In The Stars	Caitlin & Will	37-47	CB

SONG TITLE	ARTIST	#	TYPE
Adia	McLachlan, Sarah	14-187	CB
Adia	McLachlan, Sarah	10-133	SC
Adia	McLachlan, Sarah	29-239	ZM
Adios Amigo	Reeves, Jim	8-564	CB
Adios Amigo	Reeves, Jim	3-832	LG
Adios Amigo	Reeves, Jim	5-371	SC
Adore	Prince	49-828	KV
Adore You	Cyrus, Miley	42-20	ASK
Adore You	Cyrus, Miley	43-163	PHM
Aeroplane	Red Hot Chili Peppe	4-604	SC
Africa	Toto	7-91	MM
Africa	Toto	14-636	SC
After A Kiss	Tillis, Pam	14-697	CB
After A Kiss	Tillis, Pam	5-730	SC
After A Kiss	Tillis, Pam	22-508	ST
After All	Bruce, Ed	29-692	SC
After All	Cetera & Cher	6-338	MM
After All	Cetera & Cher	14-52	RS
After All	James, Brett	18-803	ST
After All	James, Brett	32-193	THM
After All The Good Is Gone	Twitty, Conway	8-835	CB
After Closing Time	Houston & Mandrell	9-588	SAV
After Midnight	Clapton, Eric	33-267	CB
After Midnight	Clapton, Eric	17-69	DK
After Midnight	Clapton, Eric	15-54	LE
After Midnight	Clapton, Eric	12-708	P
After The Fire Is Gone - duet	Twitty & Lynn	48-242	CB
After The Glitter Fades	Nicks, Stevie	16-126	SC
After The Gold Rush	Young, Neil	37-72	SC
After The Lights Go Out	VanShelton, Ricky	8-548	CB
After The Love	McKnight, Brian	18-484	NU
After The Love Has Gone	Earth Wind & Fire	4-381	SC
After The Lovin'	Humperdinck, E.	37-156	CB
After The Lovin'	Humperdinck, E.	26-484	DK
After The Lovin'	Humperdinck, E.	6-438	MM
After The Lovin'	Humperdinck, E.	2-201	SC
After The Music Stopped	Owen, Jake	44-393	ASK
After The Storm Blows Through	Maddie & Tae	46-5	DCK
After The Thrill Is Gone	Eagles	15-704	LE
After You've Gone	Jolson, Al	29-473	LE
After You've Gone	Jolson, Al	12-942	PS
After You've Gone	Standard	27-427	DK
Afternoon Delight	Starland Vocal Band	11-394	DK
Afternoons & Coffee Spoons	Crash Test Dummies	30-773	SF
Agadoo	Black Lace	16-369	SF
Again	Alice In Chains	4-334	SC
Again	Day, Doris	45-581	OZP
Again	Jackson, Janet	2-118	SC
Again	Kravitz, Lenny	23-258	HS
Again	Kravitz, Lenny	16-473	MH
Again	Torme, Mel	4-184	SC
Again Tonight	Mellencamp, John	19-97	PS

SONG TITLE	ARTIST	#	TYPE
Against All Odds	Carey, Mariah	19-831	SGB
Against All Odds	Collins, Phil	44-7	CBEP
Against The Grain	Brooks, Garth	12-109	DK
Against The Grain	Brooks, Garth	6-272	MM
Against The Wind	Seger, Bob	10-173	UK
Ah Leah	Iris, Donnie	6-27	SC
Ah My Hawaii	Couch, Danny	6-830	MM
Ahab The Arab	Stevens, Ray	16-487	CB
Ahab The Arab	Stevens, Ray	15-347	MM
Ain;t No Grave	Cash, Johnny	45-663	BBH
Ain't 2 Proud 2 Beg	TLC	34-115	CB
Ain't Back Yet	Chesney, Kenny	37-312	CB
Ain't Easy	Farley, Rachel	41-52	PHN
Ain't Even Done With The Night	Mellencamp, John	5-307	SC
Ain't Goin Down on Brokeback Mrn	Nelson, Willie	49-291	FMK
Ain't Goin' Down	Brooks, Garth	1-217	CB
Ain't Goin' Down	Brooks, Garth	6-404	MM
Ain't Good Enough For You	Springsteen, Bruce	49-103	CDG
Ain't Got No Home	Henry, C. Frogman	5-644	SC
Ain't Got Nothin' But The Blues	Fitzgerald, Ella	47-517	VH
Ain't Got Nothin' But The Blues	Ford, Robin	19-794	SGB
Ain't Got Nothin' On Us	Montgomery, J M	24-280	SC
Ain't Got Nothing On Us	Montgomery, J M	14-218	CB
Ain't Got Time To Rock No Baby	Morgan, Lorrie	47-781	SRK
Ain't Had No Lovin'	Smith, Connie	8-387	CB
Ain't Had No Lovin'	Smith, Connie	14-332	SC
Ain't Hurtin' Nobody	Prine, John	23-524	CB
Ain't It Amazing	Williams, Don	45-221	DFK
Ain't It Funny	Lopez, Jennifer	33-393	CB
Ain't It Funny	Lopez, Jennifer	25-81	MM
Ain't It Funny How Time Slips Away	Nelson, Willie	9-457	SAV
Ain't It Just Like You	Keith, Toby	47-157	CB
Ain't Misbehavin'	Bruce, Tommy	10-613	SF
Ain't Misbehavin'	Jazz Standard	47-717	VH
Ain't Much Left Of Loving You	Montana, Randy	49-30	KVD
Ain't My Day To Care	Bomshel	30-88	CB
Ain't No Mountain High Enough	Gaye & Terrell	11-112	DK
Ain't No Mountain High Enough	Ross, Diana	15-359	LE
Ain't No Other Man	Aguilera, Christina	30-724	SF
Ain't No Particular Way	Twain, Shania	45-530	CB
Ain't No Stoppin' Us Now	McFadden&Whitehead	7-491	MM
Ain't No Sunshine	Cocker, Joe	49-536	KVD
Ain't No Sunshine	Withers, Bill	33-273	CB
Ain't No Sunshine	Withers, Bill	17-137	DK
Ain't No Sunshine	Withers, Bill	13-143	P
Ain't No Way	Franklin, Aretha	9-660	SAV
Ain't No Way	Labelle & Blige	29-316	PHM

SONG TITLE	ARTIST	#	TYPE
Ain't No Way To Treat A Lady	Reddy, Helen	16-156	SC
Ain't No Woman (Like The One...)	Four Tops	26-436	DK
Ain't No Woman Like The One I Got	Four Tops	35-113	CB
Ain't Nobody	Khan, Chaka	15-43	SS
Ain't Nobody Gonna Take That From	Raye, Collin	16-165	CB
Ain't Nobody Gonna Take That From	Raye, Collin	15-680	ST
Ain't Nobody Gonna Take That From Me	Nichols, Joe	47-571	PS
Ain't Nobody Gonna Take That From..	Raye, Collin	25-8	MM
Ain't Nobody Here But Us Chickens	Various Artists	47-757	SRK
Ain't Nobody's Business	Ford & Starr	22-211	CB
Ain't Nobody's Business	Witherspoon,Jimmy	15-314	SC
Ain't Nobody's Business But My Own	Ford & Starr	49-375	CB
Ain't Nobody's Business If I Do	Holiday, Billie	49-474	MM
Ain't Nothin' But a Cloud	Roger Springer Band	8-980	CB
Ain't Nothin' But A She Thing	Salt 'N Pepa	49-321	CB
Ain't Nothin' Like The Real Thing	Gaye & Terrell	6-240	MM
Ain't Nothin' Like The Real Thing	Gaye & Terrell	4-38	SC
Ain't Nothin' Shakin'	Craddock, Billy C	46-648	CB
Ain't Nothing 'Bout You	Brooks & Dunn	14-833	ST
Ain't Nothing But A House Party	J. Geils Band	46-325	SC
Ain't Nothing Going On But The Rent	Guthrie, Gwen	48-777	P
Ain't She Something Else	Twitty, Conway	4-817	SC
Ain't She Sweet	Sinatra, Frank	34-441	CB
Ain't That A Bitch	Watson, Johnny "Guitar"	36-137	SGB
Ain't That A Kick In The Head	Martin, Dean	23-71	MM
Ain't That A Shame	Domino, Fats	11-254	DK
Ain't That A Shame	Domino, Fats	12-731	P
Ain't That A Shame	Four Seasons	45-798	SBI
Ain't That Just The Way	McNeal, Lutricia	7-716	PHM
Ain't That Lonely Yet	Yoakam, Dwight	12-465	P
Ain't That Lonely Yet	Yoakam, Dwight	2-336	SC
Ain't That Lovin' You Baby	Presley, Elvis	7-126	MM
Ain't That Lovin' You Baby	Presley, Elvis	14-816	THM
Ain't That Peculiar	Gaye, Marvin	17-156	DK
Ain't Too Proud To Beg	Temptations	16-839	DK
Ain't Too Proud To Beg	Temptations	4-691	SC
Ain't Wastin' Good Whiskey On You	Trick Pony	23-468	CB
Ain't Wastin' Good	Trick Pony	29-850	SC

SONG TITLE	ARTIST	#	TYPE
Whiskey On You			
Ain't Wastin' Time No More	Allman Brothers	13-771	SGB
Ain't We Got Fun	Miller, Mitch	23-538	CB
Ain't We Got Fun	Standard	35-23	CB
Ain't What It Used To Be	Mullins, Megan	29-584	CB
Ain't Worth The Whiskey	Swindell, Cole	44-287	KCD
Ain't You Even Gonna Cry	Brown, Jim Ed	47-772	SRK
Ain't Your Dog No More	Cyrus, Billy Ray	4-112	SC
Air Force One	Nelly	32-85	THM
Air Force Ones	Nelly	25-461	MM
Air Force Ones	Nelly/Kyjuan/Ali/Le	32-85	THM
Air Guitar	McBusted	48-330	MRH
Air That I Breathe	Hollies	44-358	LG
Air That I Breathe the	Lang, k.d.	47-167	KV
Airborne Cowboy	LeDoux, Chris	23-491	CB
Airstream Song	Lambert, Miranda	46-258	KV
Al Di La - Spanish	Vale, Jerry	49-211	MM
Alabam	Cowboy Copas	8-711	CB
Alabama	Cross Can Ragweed	23-12	CB
Alabama Jubilee	Foley, Red	34-186	CB
Alabama Kinda Girl	Powers, Summerlyn	41-90	PHN
Alabama Song	Doors	18-653	SO
Alabama Song	Moorer, Allison	8-244	CB
Albuquerque	Sons Of The Desert	8-978	CB
Alcohol	Barenaked Ladies	30-625	RS
Alcohol	Paisley, Brad	23-134	CB
Alejandro	Lady Gaga	38-184	CB
Alexander's Ragtime Band	Andrew Sisters	2-250	SC
Alexander's Ragtime Band	Standard	27-463	DK
Alfie	Warwick, Dionne	11-314	DK
Alfie	Warwick, Dionne	13-163	P
Alibis	Lawrence, Tracy	1-574	CB
Alibis	Lawrence, Tracy	12-76	DK
Alibis	Lawrence, Tracy	10-757	JVC
Alibis	Lawrence, Tracy	6-310	MM
Alibis	Lawrence, Tracy	12-463	P
Alice In Wonderland	Sedaka, Neil	45-357	CB
Alice's Restaurant	Guthrie, Arlo	7-353	MM
Alimony	Bare, Bobby	45-734	VH
Alimony	Yankovic, Weird Al	49-846	SGB
Alison (My Aim Is True)	Costello, Elvis	9-327	AG
Alive	Lopez, Jennifer	18-356	CB
Alive	Lopez, Jennifer	18-410	MM
Alive	Lopez, Jennifer	18-142	PHM
Alive	P. O. D.	16-308	TT
Alive	Pearl Jam	9-292	RS
Alive And Kicking	Simple Minds	9-692	SAV
Alive And Kicking	Simple Minds	5-479	SC
All About Soul	Joel, Billy	2-228	SC
All About That Bass	Trainor, Meghan	45-1	ASK
All About Tonight	Shelton, Blake	37-332	CB
All Alone Am I	Lee, Brenda	30-326	CB
All Alone Am I	Lee, Brenda	22-442	SC

SONG TITLE	ARTIST	#	TYPE
All Along	Blessed Union/Soul	24-55	SC
All Along	Blessed Union/Soul	7-574	THM
All Along The Watchtower	Hendrix, Jimi	19-277	SGB
All Alright	Zac Brown Band	44-161	BKD
All American Boy	Bare, Bobby	18-278	CB
All American Girl	Underwood, Carrie	37-14	CB
All American Nightmare	Hinder	48-633	CB
All Around Cowboy	Robbins, Marty	45-680	SRK
All Around Me	Flyleaf	36-510	CB
All Around The World	Stansfield, Lisa	17-95	DK
All Around The World	Stansfield, Lisa	6-166	MM
All Around The World	Stansfield, Lisa	16-539	P
All At Once	Houston, Whitney	48-636	SAV
All Because Of You	Houston, Marques	23-309	CB
All Because Of You	U2	22-366	CB
All By Myself	Carmen, Eric	11-333	DK
All By Myself	Dion, Celine	15-112	BS
All Comes Floodin' Down	McComas, Brian	30-199	CB
All Cried Out	Allure & 112	20-122	PHM
All Cried Out	Lisa Lisa & Cult J	11-592	DK
All Cried Out	Moyet, Allison	11-28	PX
All Day & All Of The Night	Kinks	13-165	P
All Day & All Of The Night	Kinks	5-226	SC
All Day Long	Currington, Billy	46-297	BKD
All Eyez On Me	Monica	18-430	CB
All Fired Up	Benatar, Pat	24-432	SC
All Fired Up	Seals, Dan	4-117	SC
All For Love	Adams&Sting&Stewart	8-608	TT
All For Love	Stewart & Sting	18-481	NU
All For The Love Of A Girl	Horton, Johnny	18-628	PS
All For The Love Of A Girl	King, Claude	47-921	SSK
All For You	Jackson, Janet	35-230	CB
All For You	Jackson, Janet	15-452	PHM
All For You	Jackson, Janet	16-112	PRT
All For You	Jackson, Janet	18-505	TT
All For You	Sister Hazel	33-364	CB
All Good Things (Come to an End)	Furtado, Nelly	30-497	CB
All His Children	Pride, Charley	47-437	CB
All I Ask	Adele	46-87	DCK
All I Ask For Anymore	Adkins, Trace	37-57	CB
All I Ask Of You	Phantom Of Opera	6-316	MM
All I Ask Of You	Streisand, Barbra	49-562	PRS
All I Can Be Is A Sweet Memory	Raye, Collin	1-121	CB
All I Do Is Dream Of You	Buble, Michael	40-88	PS
All I Do Is Dream Of You	Reynolds, Debbie	45-71	OZP
All I Do Is Love Her	Bonamy, James	7-583	CHM
All I Do Is Love Her	Bonamy, James	4-591	SC
All I Ever Need Is You	Rogers & West	13-532	P
All I Ever Need Is You	Rogers & West	9-568	SAV

SONG TITLE	ARTIST	#	TYPE
All I Ever Need Is You	Rogers & West	5-438	SC
All I Ever Need Is You	Sonny & Cher	6-239	MM
All I Ever Need Is You	Sonny & Cher	14-65	RS
All I Ever Need Is You	Sonny & Cher	15-133	SGB
All I Ever Wanted	Clarkson, Kelly	47-692	CB
All I Ever Wanted	Wicks, Chuck	36-413	CB
All I Give A Darn About Is You	Perry, Keith	4-623	SC
All I Have	Chapman, Beth Niels	29-325	PS
All I Have	Lopez & LL Cool J	20-458	CB
All I Have	Lopez & LL Cool J	32-96	THM
All I Have	Lopez w LL Cool J	32-96	THM
All I Have To Do Is Dream	Everly Brothers	11-400	DK
All I have To Do Is Dream	Everly Brothers	3-321	MH
All I Have To Do Is Dream	Everly Brothers	7-315	MM
All I Have To Do Is Dream	Everly Brothers	13-49	P
All I Have To Do Is Dream	Everly Brothers	3-338	PS
All I Have To Do Is Dream	Everly Brothers	9-458	SAV
All I Have To Do Is Dream	Everly Brothers	14-551	SC
All I Have To Give	Backstreet Boys	18-712	MM
All I Have To Give	Backstreet Boys	7-802	PHT
All I Have To Offer You Is Me	Pride, Charley	8-360	CB
All I Have To Offer You Is Me	Pride, Charley	14-336	SC
All I Know	Screaming Trees	24-116	SC
All I Know	Simon & Garfunkel	15-397	DM
All I Need	Air	30-780	SF
All I Need	Temptations	14-897	DK
All I Need Is A Heart	Nichols, Joe	47-573	PS
All I Need Is A Miracle	Mike & Mechanics	24-62	SC
All I Need To Know	Chesney, Kenny	1-317	CB
All I Need To Know	Chesney, Kenny	7-24	MM
All I Needed Was Rain	Presley, Elvis	25-495	MM
All I Really Want To Do	Byrds	47-555	LC
All I Really Want To Do	Cher	47-674	LE
All I See	Williams, Christoph	18-393	SAV
All I Wanna Do	Crow, Sheryl	19-569	MH
All I Wanna Do	Crow, Sheryl	6-641	MM
All I Wanna Do	Crow, Sheryl	29-664	RS
All I Wanna Do Is Make Love To You	Heart	14-633	SC
All I Want	Hoffs, Susanna	24-551	SC
All I Want	Toad&Wet Sprocket	13-240	P
All I Want For Christmas Is You - xmas	Mandrell, Louise	45-256	CB
All I Want Is A Life	McGraw, Tim	1-533	CB
All I Want Is Everything	McCready, Mindy	14-700	CB
All I Want Is Everything	McCready, Mindy	19-234	SC
All I Want To Do	Sugarland	36-591	CB
All In The Family	TV Themes	2-161	SC

SONG TITLE	ARTIST	#	TYPE
All In The Suit That You Wear	Stone Temple Pilots	23-270	THM
All Is Fair In Love	Streisand, Barbra	49-546	PS
All Is Fair In Love And War	Milsap, Ronnie	24-8	SC
All Jacked Up	Wilson, Gretchen	23-408	CB
All Jacked Up	Wilson, Gretchen	36-376	SC
All Jokes Aside	Williams, Hank Jr.	14-735	CB
All Just To Get To You	Green, Pat	47-125	PHN
All Kinds Of Kinds	Lambert, Miranda	41-46	ASK
All Lit Up In Love	Murphy, David Lee	4-838	SC
All My Ex's Live In Texas	Strait, George	1-257	CB
All My Ex's Live In Texas	Strait, George	13-378	P
All My Ex's Live In Texas	Strait, George	9-431	SAV
All My Ex's Live In Texas	Strait, George	3-373	SC
All My Friends Say	Bryan, Luke	30-256	CB
All My Hard Times	Drusky, Roy	20-755	CB
All My Life	Foo Fighters	23-153	PHM
All My Life	K-Ci & JoJo	10-22	SC
All My Life	Rogers, Kenny	5-672	SC
All My Life	Ronstadt & Neville	11-821	DK
All My Life	Ronstadt & Neville	6-236	MM
All My Life	Ronstadt & Neville	12-890	P
All My Life	Witter, Jim	8-925	CB
All My Love	Led Zeppelin	5-876	SC
All My Loving	Beatles	11-127	DK
All My Loving	Beatles	12-739	P
All My Loving	Beatles	7-548	SAV
All My Loving	Beatles	29-342	SC
All My Rowdy Friends/Comin…	Williams, Hank Jr.	16-682	C2C
All My Rowdy Friends/Comin…	Williams, Hank Jr.	13-467	P
All My Rowdy Friends/Settled..	Williams, Hank Jr.	2-122	SC
All My Trials	Baez, Joan	46-465	SBI
All Night Long	Buckcherry	48-474	CB
All Night Long	Montgomery Gentry	14-138	CB
All Night Long	Montgomery Gentry	14-15	CHM
All Night Long	Montgomery Gentry	10-263	SC
All Night Long	Montgomery Gentry	22-573	ST
All Night Long	Montgomery Gentry	14-36	THM
All Night Long	Richie, Lionel	10-398	LE
All Night Long	Walsh, Joe	17-512	SC
All Night Long - All Night	Richie, Lionel	13-200	P
All Night Long (All Night)	Richie, Lionel	43-367	CB
All Of Me	Buble, Michael	40-84	PS
All Of Me	Holiday, Billie	49-459	MM
All Of Me	Legend, John	45-2	KV
All Of Me	Nelson, Willie	16-589	MM
All Of Me	Sinatra, Frank	15-398	NK
All Of Me	Sinatra, Frank	21-212	SGB
All Of Me	Standard	27-422	DK
All Of My Life	Carpenters	45-803	KV
All Of My Life	Collins, Phil	44-16	SBI
All Or Nothin At All	Sinatra, Frank	9-234	PT
All Or Nothing	Cher	14-68	RS

SONG TITLE	ARTIST	#	TYPE
All Or Nothing	O-Town	15-460	PHM
All Or Nothing	O-Town	18-543	TT
All Or Nothing At All	Dorsey, Jimmy	47-32	PS
All Out Of Love	Air Supply	18-121	DK
All Out Of Love	Air Supply	9-786	SAV
All Over Again	Cash, Johnny	29-765	CB
All Over Again	Cash, Johnny	43-418	SRK
All Over But The Shouting	Shenandoah	7-198	MM
All Over But The Shouting	Shenandoah	4-203	SC
All Over Me	Rich, Charlie	5-199	SC
All Over Me	Shelton, Blake	25-64	MM
All Over Me	Shelton, Blake	15-854	ST
All Over Me	Turner, Josh	38-129	CB
All Over The Road	Corbin, Easton	44-269	KCDC
All Over You	Live	17-354	DK
All Revved Up With No Place To Go	Meat Loaf	37-78	SC
All Right	Young, Faron	20-732	CB
All Right Now	Free	17-88	DK
All Right Now	Free	20-309	MH
All Right Now	Free	12-774	P
All Right Okay You Win	Bennett & Krall	25-670	MM
All Roads Lead To You	Wariner, Steve	14-257	SC
All She Wants To Do Is Dance	Henley, Don	15-707	LE
All Shook Up	Presley, Elvis	11-158	DK
All Shook Up	Presley, Elvis	13-97	P
All Shook Up	Presley, Elvis	9-804	SAV
All Shook Up	Presley, Elvis	2-594	SC
All Shook Up	Presley, Elvis	14-738	THM
All Star	Smash Mouth	29-169	MH
All Star	Smash Mouth	7-873	PHM
All Stars	Blush	39-127	PHM
All Summer Long	Beach Boys	46-494	NT
All Summer Long	Kid Rock	36-467	CB
All That Heaven Will Allow	Mavericks	2-776	SC
All That Matters Anymore	Parnell, Lee Roy	8-409	CB
All That Matters Anymore	Parnell, Lee Roy	22-778	ST
All That She Wants	Ace Of Base	12-244	DK
All That She Wants	Ace Of Base	6-408	MM
All That She Wants	Ace Of Base	9-269	SC
All That She Wants	Ace Of Base	8-614	TT
All That's Left	Thrice	23-187	PHM
All That's Left For You To Do Is Leave	Lambert, Miranda	45-308	KV
All The Fun	Overstreet, Paul	14-686	CB
All The Gold In California	Gatlin, Larry	33-43	CB
All The Gold In California	Gatlins	6-768	MM
All The Gold In California	Gatlins	13-327	P
All The Good Ones Are	Tillis, Pam	1-461	CB

SONG TITLE	ARTIST	#	TYPE
Gone			
All The Good Ones Are Gone	Tillis, Pam	7-621	CHM
All The Love In The World	Corrs	49-191	SBI
All The Love In The World	Warwick, Dionne	48-763	P
All The Man That I Need	Houston, Whitney	21-459	CB
All The Man That I Need	Houston, Whitney	12-248	DK
All The Man That I Need	Houston, Whitney	13-204	P
All The Right Moves	OneRepublic	44-139	BKD
All The Small Things	Blink 182	16-185	PHM
All The Things She Said	T.A.T.U.	25-541	MM
All The Things She Said	T.A.T.U.	18-608	PHM
All The Things She Said	T.A.T.U.	23-340	SC
All The Things You Are	Vaughn, Sarah	12-533	P
All The Time	Greene, Jack	43-338	CB
All The Time	Greene, Jack	4-312	SC
All The Way	Sinatra, Frank	11-306	DK
All The Way	Sinatra, Frank	10-715	JVC
All The Way	Sinatra, Frank	20-757	KB
All The Way	Sinatra, Frank	12-521	P
All The Way	Sinatra, Frank	16-416	PR
All The Way	Sinatra, Frank	21-226	SGB
All These Things	Stampley, Joe	5-760	SC
All These Things That I've Done	Killers	30-226	PHM
All Things Bright And Beautiful	Uncle Mac	48-764	P
All Things Considered	Yankee Grey	19-201	CB
All Things Considered	Yankee Grey	10-215	SC
All Things Considered	Yankee Grey	22-495	ST
All This Love	DeBarge	24-334	SC
All This Love	Lost Trailors	47-209	CB
All Those Years Ago	Harrison, George	24-67	SC
All Through The Night	Lauper, Cyndi	33-319	CB
All Through The Night	Lauper, Cyndi	16-163	SC
All Tied Up	McDowell, Ronnie	5-535	SC
All Time High	Coolidge, Rita	9-69	SC
All We Are	Nathanson, Matthew	36-274	PHM
All We Ever Find	McGraw, Tim	49-75	ZPA
All Wrapped Up In Christmas	Lawrence, Tracy	48-382	CB
All You Ever	Hayes, Hunter	39-69	PHN
All You ever Do Is Bring/Down	Mavericks	3-652	SC
All You Get From Love is a Love Song	Carpenters	44-357	ZMPA
All You Had To Do Was Stay	Swift, Taylor	48-301	KV
All You Need Is Love	Beatles	16-744	DK
All You Wanted	Branch, Michelle	25-84	MM
All Your Life	Band Perry	40-37	CB
Alleghany Moon	Page, Patti	2-245	SC
Allegheny Moon	Page, Patti	3-365	MH
Allentown	Joel, Billy	17-463	SC
Alley Cat the - DANCE #	Welk, Lawrence	22-389	SC
Alley Oop	Hollywood Argyles	29-832	SC

SONG TITLE	ARTIST	#	TYPE
Almost	Bowling For Soup	22-360	CB
Almost	Presley, Elvis	25-757	MM
Almost A Memory Now	Blackhawk	4-202	SC
Almost Always True	Presley, Elvis	25-107	MM
Almost Doesn't Count	Wills, Mark	9-405	CB
Almost Doesn't Count	Wills, Mark	13-830	CHM
Almost Doesn't Count	Brandy	8-218	PHT
Almost Doesn't Count	Wills, Mark	19-253	CSZ
Almost Easy (Radio Version)	Avenged Sevenfold	37-139	SC
Almost Goodbye	Chesnutt, Mark	1-354	CB
Almost Goodbye	Chesnutt, Mark	2-819	SC
Almost Grown	Berry, Chuck	46-229	DCK
Almost Home	Carpenter, M C	22-431	ST
Almost Home	Morgan, Craig	34-362	CB
Almost Home	Morgan, Craig	18-474	ST
Almost Home	Morgan, Craig	32-224	THM
Almost Jamaica	Bellamy Brothers	44-76	SRK
Almost Like A Song	Milsap, Ronnie	17-295	NA
Almost Like Being In Love	Sinatra, Frank	21-227	SGB
Almost Over You	Easton, Sheena	20-47	SC
Almost Over You	McCann, Lila	8-411	CB
Almost Over You	McCann, Lila	7-739	CHM
Almost Over You	McCann, Lila	22-784	ST
Almost Paradise	Reno & Wilson	17-333	DK
Almost Persuaded	Houston, David	8-427	CB
Almost Persuaded	Houston, David	13-514	P
Almost Persuaded	Houston, David	9-617	SAV
Almost Persuaded	Wynette, Tammy	49-354	CB
Almost There	Lettermen	48-531	L1
Almost There	Nolen, Gabbie	16-707	ST
Aloha Oe	Williams Andy	15-399	NK
Alone	Bee Gees	48-689	KB
Alone	Heart	11-388	DK
Alone	Heart	13-157	P
Alone Again	O'Sullivan, Gilbert	4-384	SC
Alone And Forsaken	Williams, Hank Sr.	45-704	CB
Alone I Break	Korn	32-74	THM
Alone With You	Al B. Sure!	18-488	SAV
Alone With You	Owen, Jake	38-210	PHN
Alone With You	Young, Faron	8-797	CB
Alone With You	Young, Faron	3-594	SC
Along Came Jones	Coasters	6-687	MM
Along Came Jones	Stevens, Ray	16-496	CB
Along Came Jones **	Coasters	23-23	SC
Along Comes A Woman	Chicago	24-197	SC
Along Comes Mary	Association	21-529	SC
Along Comes Mary	Rufus	4-512	SC
Alphabet Street	Prince	23-328	CB
Already Callin' You Mine	Parmalee	49-657	BKD
Already Gone	Clarkson, Kelly	47-690	CB
Already Gone	Eagles	2-257	SC
Already Gone	Sugarland	36-223	PHM
Already Gone	Tucker, Tanya	38-9	CB
Already It's Heaven	Houston, David	48-188	CB
Alright	Rucker, Darius	36-48	PT

SONG TITLE	ARTIST	#	TYPE
Alright Already	Stewart, Larry	2-332	SC
Alright I'll Sign The Papers	Morgan, George	46-20	SSK
Alright Ok You Win	Jazz Standard	47-718	VH
Always	Air Supply	46-401	SBI
Always	Atlantic Starr	6-344	MM
Always	Bon Jovi	28-448	DK
Always	Bon Jovi	2-472	SC
Always	Cline, Patsy	22-184	CB
Always	Cline, Patsy	6-732	MM
Always	Cline, Patsy	5-162	SC
Always	Saliva	18-831	THM
Always - duet	Atlantic Starr	35-193	CB
Always A Woman	Joel, Billy	16-139	LE
Always A Woman	Stewart, Larry	7-424	MM
Always a Woman	Stewart, Larry	4-621	SC
Always And Forever	Heatwave	2-272	SC
Always And Forever	Vandross, Luther	10-19	SC
Always Be My Baby	Carey, Mariah	34-90	CB
Always Be My Baby	Carey, Mariah	19-577	MH
Always Be My Baby	Carey, Mariah	21-139	SC
Always Come Back To Your ...	Mumba, Samantha	18-506	TT
Always Have Always Will	Fricke, Janie	29-652	SC
Always Have Always Will	Shenandoah	3-623	SC
Always Late (With Your Kisses)	Yoakam, Dwight	49-685	CB
Always Late With Your Kisses	Frizzell, Lefty	19-483	CB
Always Late With Your Kisses	Frizzell, Lefty	7-151	MM
Always Late With Your Kisses	Frizzell, Lefty	4-810	SC
Always Look On The Bright Side	Monty Python	15-141	SC
Always Never The Same	Strait, George	38-153	CB
Always On My Mind	Monro, Matt	11-57	PT
Always On My Mind	Nelson, Willie	8-14	CB
Always On My Mind	Nelson, Willie	11-143	DK
Always On My Mind	Nelson, Willie	13-433	P
Always On My Mind	Presley, Elvis	18-439	KC
Always Sixteen	Cyrus, Billy Ray	22-15	CB
Always Something There To Remind	Naked Eyes	18-362	AH
Always Something There To Remind	Naked Eyes	29-291	SC
Always Somewhere	Scorpions	49-99	KVD
Always The Love Song	Eli Young Band	44-202	CB
Always The Love Song	Eli Young Band	36-225	PHM
Always Tomorrow	Estefan, Gloria	17-749	PT
Always Wanting You	Haggard, Merle	22-238	CB
Always Was	Tippin, Aaron	15-611	ST
Always Will	Judd, Wynonna	8-104	CB
Always You	Paige, Jennifer	5-784	SC
Alyssa Lies	Carroll, Jason M.	30-169	CB
Alyssa Lies	Carroll, Jason M.	30-169	CB
Am I Blue	Ronstadt, Linda	49-208	MM
Am I Blue	Standard	9-468	SAV

SONG TITLE	ARTIST	#	TYPE
Am I Blue	Strait, George	16-584	SC
Am I Ever Gonna See You Again	Angels	46-438	CK
Am I Losing You	Milsap, Ronnie	47-271	CB
Am I Losing You	Reeves, Jim	8-785	CB
Am I Losing You	Reeves, Jim	3-841	LG
Am I That Easy To Forget	Davis, Skeeter	34-201	CB
Am I That Easy To Forget	Humperdinck, E.	37-158	CB
Am I That Easy To Forget	Humperdinck, E.	48-393	ZMV
Am I That Easy To Forget	Reeves, Jim	45-266	VH
Am I The Only One	Bentley, Dierks	44-382	BKD
Am I The Only One	Bentley, Dierks	37-354	CB
Am I The Only One	Dixie Chicks	16-653	RS
Amanda	Boston	35-183	CB
Amanda	Boston	16-598	MM
Amanda	Jennings, Waylon	22-152	CK
Amanda	Jennings, Waylon	12-448	P
Amanda	Williams, Don	35-364	CB
Amanda	Williams, Don	8-627	SAV
Amapola	Sinatra, Frank	45-582	OZP
Amarillo	Jackson, Alan	47-774	SRK
Amarillo By Morning	Strait, George	1-241	CB
Amarillo By Morning	Strait, George	13-453	P
Amarillo Sky	Aldean, Jason	30-107	CB
Amazed	Lonestar	19-196	CB
Amazed	Lonestar	7-882	CHT
Amazed	Lonestar	14-606	SC
Amazing	Kelley, Josh	25-652	MM
Amazing	Kelley, Josh	32-247	THM
Amazing Grace	Mavericks	6-591	MM
Amazing Grace	Presley, Elvis	30-376	SC
Amazing Love	Pride, Charley	43-203	CB
Amazing Love	Pride, Charley	6-80	SC
Amen	Kid Rock	36-475	CB
Amen Kind Of Love	Singletary, Daryle	7-580	CHM
Amen Kind Of Love	Singletary, Daryle	7-377	MM
Amen Kind Of Love	Singletary, Daryle	4-508	SC
America	Deuce	39-100	PHM
America	Diamond, Neil	20-161	BCI
America	Diamond, Neil	30-679	LE
America	Diamond, Neil	13-296	P
America	Jennings, Waylon	22-145	CK
America	Jennings, Waylon	20-666	SC
America	Razorlight	46-420	SF
America	Simon & Garfunkel	49-763	LG
America First	Haggard, Merle	49-170	SC
America The Beautiful	Charles, Ray	20-162	BCI
America The Beautiful	Patriotic	44-43	PT
America The Beautiful	Standard	23-219	SM
America the Beautiful - Patriotic	Standard	34-436	CB
America The Beautiful/Battle Hymn o	Standard	20-164	BCI
America Will Always	Travis, Randy	20-577	CB

SONG TITLE	ARTIST	#	TYPE
Stand			
America Will Survive - patriotic	Williams, Hank Jr.	34-365	CB
America's Sweetheart	King, Elle	46-123	BKD
American Bad Ass (Radio Version) **	Kid Rock	14-487	SC
American Bandstand	TV Themes	2-164	SC
American Boy - duet	Estelle & Kanye West	48-591	DK
American By God's Amazing Grace	Stricklin, Luke	23-469	CB
American Child	Vassar, Phil	25-231	MM
American Child	Vassar, Phil	17-568	ST
American City Suite	Cashman & West	15-754	AMS
American Country Love Song	Owen, Jake	49-4	DCK
American Girl	Petty & Heartbreake	2-474	SC
American Girls	Counting Crows	18-425	CB
American Honey	Lady Antebellum	36-55	PT
American Honky Tonk Bar Assn.	Brooks, Garth	6-376	MM
American Honky-Tonk Bar Assn.	Brooks, Garth	2-409	SC
American Idiot	Green Day	20-558	PHM
American Kids	Chesney, Kenny	44-272	SBI
American Kids	Chesney, Kenny	44-337	SSC
American Life	Madonna	20-524	CB
American Life	Madonna	25-589	MM
American Life	Madonna	32-242	THM
American Made	Oak Ridge Boys	23-493	CB
American Made	Oak Ridge Boys	26-598	DK
American Made	Oak Ridge Boys	13-404	P
American Made	Oak Ridge Boys	29-657	SC
American Pie	Madonna	15-298	CB
American Pie	Madonna	15-324	PHM
American Pie	McLean, Don	11-716	DK
American Radio	Carolina Rain	36-195	PHM
American Ride	Keith, Toby	38-157	CB
American Soldier	Keith, Toby	20-271	SC
American Soldier	Keith, Toby	19-700	ST
American Trilogy	Presley, Elvis	2-582	SC
American Way the	Williams, Hank Jr.	16-683	C2C
American Woman	Guess Who	11-132	DK
American Woman	Guess Who	7-45	MM
American Woman	Guess Who	12-862	P
American Woman	Kravitz, Lenny	8-529	PHT
American Woman	Kravitz, Lenny	16-192	THM
Americana	Bandy, Moe	19-499	CB
Americana	Bandy, Moe	5-155	SC
Americana Gold	Patin, Rick	41-101	PHN
Americans the	Mellencamp, John	30-451	CB
Americans the	Mellencamp, John	45-426	CB
Americans the - Patriotic	Mellencamp, John	30-451	CB
Amie	Pure Prairie League	9-328	AG
Amie	Pure Prairie League	26-368	DK
Amigo's Guitar	Wells, Kitty	20-644	SC
Amish Paradise **	Yankovic, Weird Al	23-20	SC
Amnesia	Blake & Brian	8-105	CB

SONG TITLE	ARTIST	#	TYPE
Amnesia	Chumbawamba	10-140	SC
Amnesia	Fabulous T-Birds	48-610	MM
Among My Souvenirs	Francis, Connie	8-825	CB
Among My Souvenirs	Francis, Connie	3-510	SC
Among My Souvenirs	Robbins, Marty	4-812	SC
Among The Missing	McDonald&Mattea	8-914	CB
Amos Moses	Reed, Jerry	20-723	SC
Amy's Back In Austin	Little Texas	6-708	MM
Amy's Back In Austin	Little Texas	17-282	NA
Amy's Back In Austin	Little Texas	3-533	SC
An American Child - Patriotic	Vassar, Phil	34-381	CB
An American Trilogy	Presley, Elvis	20-157	BCI
An Angel	Kelly Family	49-717	KV
An Easier Affair	Michael, George	30-735	CB
An Easier Affair	Michael, George	30-735	SF
An Old Fashioned Love Song	Three Dog Night	11-636	DK
An Old Fashioned Love Song	Three Dog Night	13-302	P
An Unusual Kiss	Etheridge, Melissa	47-71	SC
Ana's Song	Silverchair	8-507	PHT
Analyse	Cranberries	25-23	MM
Anchor	Cave In	32-294	THM
Anchors Away	Patriotic	44-39	PT
And I Love Her	Beatles	11-128	DK
And I Love Her	Beatles	13-61	P
And I Love You So	Bassey, Shirley	46-478	LGK
And I Love You So	Como, Perry	26-474	DK
And I Love You So	Como, Perry	13-547	LE
And I Love You So	Como, Perry	12-507	P
And I Love You So	McLean, Don	21-507	SC
And I Love You So	Monro, Matt	11-63	PT
And It Stoned Me	Morrison, Van	23-601	BS
And It Stoned Me	Morrison, Van	15-728	SI
And She Said (2006 Mets Anthem)	Prata, Lucas	30-63	PHM
And She Was	Talking Heads	12-788	P
And So It Goes	Joel, Billy	12-271	DK
And So It Goes	Williams, Don	39-88	PHN
And So It Goes	Williams, Don	45-215	PHN
And Still	McEntire, Reba	1-819	CB
And Still	McEntire, Reba	6-813	MM
And Still	McEntire, Reba	2-833	SC
And The Angels Sing	Fitzgerald, Ella	45-583	OZP
And The Beat Goes On	Whispers	15-39	SS
And The Cradle Will Rock	Van Halen	13-618	LE
And The Crowd Goes Wild	Wills, Mark	35-429	CB
And The Crowd Goes Wild	Wills, Mark	25-697	MM
And The Crowd Goes Wild	Wills, Mark	19-365	ST
And The Crowd Goes Wild	Wills, Mark	32-376	THM
And The Grass Won't Pay No Mind	Diamond, Neil	30-498	THM

SONG TITLE	ARTIST	#	TYPE
And The Radio Played	Lady Antebellum	44-160	BKD
And The Sun Will Shine	Bee Gees	48-687	FMK
And The Wheels Turn	Cannon, Melanie	36-278	PHM
And Then	Drake, Dusty	49-857	SC
And When I Die	Blood Sweat &Tears	11-256	DK
And When I Die	Blood Sweat &Tears	13-233	P
Andante	Abba	46-218	FUN
Angel	Aerosmith	4-319	SC
Angel	Aerosmith	13-669	SGB
Angel	Corrs	49-189	MRH
Angel	Madonna	24-65	SC
Angel	McLachlan, Sarah	14-186	CB
Angel	McLachlan, Sarah	28-188	DK
Angel	McLachlan, Sarah	7-781	PHT
Angel	McLachlan, Sarah	13-702	SGB
Angel	McLachlan, Sarah	29-241	ZM
Angel	Perez, Amanda	34-156	CB
Angel	Perez, Amanda	20-629	NS
Angel	Perez, Amanda	18-770	PHM
Angel	Richie, Lionel	45-525	BSK
Angel	Richie, Lionel	47-450	CB
Angel	Shaggy	12-391	PHM
Angel	Shaggy	18-544	TT
Angel	Shaggy & Rayvon	16-483	MH
Angel	Stewart, Rod	14-850	LE
Angel Baby	Rosie & Originals	6-144	MM
Angel Baby	Rosie & Originals	5-523	SC
Angel Boy	McGraw, Tim	25-72	MM
Angel Boy	McGraw, Tim	16-330	ST
Angel Eyes	Abba	19-85	MM
Angel Eyes	Jeff Healy Band	9-341	AH
Angel Eyes	Jeff Healy Band	34-98	CB
Angel Eyes	Love And Theft	38-252	PHN
Angel Eyes	Standard	13-634	SGB
Angel Flying Too Close/Ground	Nelson, Willie	8-199	CB
Angel Flying Too Close/Ground	Nelson, Willie	4-541	SC
Angel From Montgomery	Prine, John	23-534	CB
Angel In Blue Jeans	Train	48-267	KV
Angel In Disguise	Conley, E.T.	47-605	CB
Angel In My Eyes	Montgomery, J M	14-215	CB
Angel In My Eyes	Montgomery, J M	22-655	ST
Angel Of Death the	Williams, Hank Sr.	37-198	CB
Angel Of Harlem	Secada, Jon	6-409	MM
Angel Of Harlem	U2	17-471	SC
Angel Of Mine	McLachlan, Sarah	48-186	SC
Angel Of Mine	Monica	16-212	MM
Angel Of Mine	Monica	7-795	PHT
Angel Of Mine	Monica	16-396	PR
Angel Of The Morning	Newton, Juice	16-724	DK
Angel Of The Morning	Newton, Juice	9-571	SAV
Angel Of The Morning	Rush, Merilee	49-449	MM
Angel Standing By	Jewel	36-335	SC
Angel's Hands	Atkins, Rodney	30-552	CB
Angela Jones	Cox, Michael	29-816	SF
Angelia	Marx, Richard	14-584	SC

SONG TITLE	ARTIST	#	TYPE
Angeline Is Coming Home	Badlees	24-54	SC
Angels	Simpson, Jessica	23-566	MM
Angels	Travis, Randy	23-124	CB
Angels	Travis, Randy	29-510	SC
Angels	Travis, Randy	29-609	ST
Angels	Williams, Robbie	8-517	PHT
Angels Among Us	Alabama	1-24	CB
Angels Among Us	Alabama	2-538	SC
Angels And Alcohol	Jackson, Alan	45-338	KRG
Angels Cried the - duet	Jackson & Krauss	49-175	CB
Angels Don't Lie	Reeves, Jim	44-245	SRK
Angels Fly Away	Durrance, Eric	36-229	PHM
Angels In Waiting	Cochran, Tammy	33-144	CB
Angels In Waiting	Cochran, Tammy	9-869	ST
Angels Listened In	Crests	6-680	MM
Angels Listened In	Crests	4-247	SC
Angels Of The Silences	Counting Crows	24-555	SC
Angels Working Overtime	Carter, Deana	7-864	CHT
Angels Working Overtime	Carter, Deana	14-603	SC
Angels Working Overtime	Carter, Deana	22-744	ST
Angels Would Fall	Etheridge, Melissa	8-515	PHT
Angie	Rolling Stones	19-750	LE
Angie	Rolling Stones	14-393	PT
Angie Baby	Reddy, Helen	16-822	DK
Angry All The Time	McGraw & Hill	15-600	ST
Angry All The Time	McGraw, Tim	29-348	CB
Angry American (Courtesy of...)	Keith, Toby	33-164	CB
Angry Johnny	Poe	24-296	SC
Animal	Pearl Jam	9-306	RS
Animal Song	Savage Garden	7-846	PHM
Animal Song	Savage Garden	13-714	SGB
Anita You're Dreaming	Jennings, Waylon	45-191	SRK
Ann Don't Go Runnin'	Overstreet, Paul	5-564	SC
Anna Marie	Reeves, Jim	40-123	CB
Anna Marie	Reeves, Jim	49-747	KRG
Anna Molly	Incubus	37-111	SC
Annie's Song	Denver, John	11-614	DK
Annie's Song	Denver, John	36-142	LE
Annie's Song	Denver, John	10-507	SF
Anniversary	Tony! Toni! Tone!	2-232	SC
Anniversary Song	Clooney, Rosemary	15-400	MM
Anniversary Song	Jolson, Al	11-300	DK
Anniversary Song	Jolson, Al	12-509	P
Anniversary Song	Shore, Dinah	27-410	DK
Anonymous	Valentino w Timbaland	30-584	CB
Anonymous	Valentino, Bobby	30-564	CB
Another	Drusky, Roy	20-743	CB
Another Again	Legend, John	45-295	CB
Another Brick In The Wall	Class Of 99	16-206	PHT
Another Brick In The Wall	Pink Floyd	3-449	SC

SONG TITLE	ARTIST	#	TYPE
Another Day Goes By	Dakota Moon	14-281	MM
Another Day In Paradise	Collins, Phil	44-6	CBEP
Another Dumb Blonde	Hoku	15-297	CB
Another Good Reason Not To Drink	Jackson, Alan	40-99	CB
Another Goodbye	Fargo, Donna	48-666	SC
Another Lonely Song	Wynette, Tammy	49-359	CB
Another Lonely Song	Wynette, Tammy	9-589	SAV
Another Man Loved Me Last Night	Lynn, Loretta	48-253	VH
Another Nine Minutes	Yankee Grey	22-475	ST
Another One Bites The Dust	Queen	12-334	DK
Another One Rides The Bus	Yankovic, Weird Al	49-845	SGB
Another Perfect Day	American HiFi	18-400	MM
Another Perfect Day	Blake & Brian	4-827	SC
Another Place Another Time	Lewis, Jerry Lee	47-195	CB
Another Place To Fall	Tunstall, K.T.	30-704	SF
Another Postcard (Chimps)	Barenaked Ladies	32-430	THM
Another Rock & Roll Christmas	Glitter, Gary	45-780	SF
Another Sad Love Song	Braxton, Toni	34-118	CB
Another Sad Love Song	Braxton, Toni	6-412	MM
Another Sad Love Song	Braxton, Toni	18-817	PS
Another Saturday Night	Buffett, Jimmy	46-137	SC
Another Saturday Night	Cooke, Sam	46-639	PS
Another Saturday Night	Stevens, Cat	23-655	BS
Another Saturday Night	Stevens, Cat	13-583	NU
Another Side	Sawyer Brown	8-404	CB
Another Side	Sawyer Brown	46-244	CB
Another Side	Sawyer Brown	22-771	ST
Another Side Of You	Nichols, Joe	30-454	CB
Another Sleepless Night	Clanton, Jimmy	47-564	DCK
Another Sleepless Night	Murray, Anne	13-408	P
Another Somebody Done Somebody	Thomas, B.J.	36-153	LE
Another Somebody Done Somebody	Thomas, B.J.	13-430	P
Another Somebody Done Somebody..	Thomas, B.J.	11-669	DK
Another Somebody Done Somebody…	Thomas, B.J.	5-23	SC
Another Sunday In The South	Lambert, Miranda	45-282	BKD
Another Tear Falls	McDaniels, Gene	49-122	DFK
Another Time Another Place	Humperdinck, E.	37-160	CB
Another Try	Turner & Yearwood	36-432	CB
Another Try	Turner, Josh	48-609	DK
Another Year Of Love	Greenwood, Lee	47-130	MM
Another You	Kersh, David	14-653	CB
Another You	Kersh, David	22-408	CHM
Another You	Rich, John	48-705	BKD
Another You Another Me	Seals, Brady	4-452	SC
Answer Is Yes the	Wright, Michelle	4-622	SC

SONG TITLE	ARTIST	#	TYPE
Answer Me My Love	Cole, Nat "King"	28-511	DK
Answer Me My Love	Cole, Nat "King"	34-12	CB
Answer Me My Love	Thompson, Hank	48-578	DK
Answer The Phone	Sugar Ray	33-386	CB
Answer The Phone	Sugar Ray	25-32	MM
Anthem the	Good Charlotte	35-281	CB
Anthem the	Good Charlotte	32-143	THM
Anticipation	Simon, Carly	4-50	SC
Anticipation Blues	Ford, Tenn Ernie	22-207	CB
Any Day Now	Milsap, Ronnie	11-743	DK
Any Day Now	Milsap, Ronnie	13-425	P
Any Man Of Mine	Twain, Shania	1-511	CB
Any Man Of Mine	Twain, Shania	7-436	MM
Any Man Of Mine	Twain, Shania	2-773	SC
Any Old Wind That Blows	Cash, Johnny	29-560	CB
Any Old Wind That Blows	Cash, Johnny	6-82	SC
Any Place Is Paradise	Presley, Elvis	14-817	THM
Any Time Any Place	Jackson, Janet	15-445	CB
Any Way At All	Summer, Donna	14-882	SC
Any Way You Want It	Dave Clark Five	45-82	OZP
Any Way You Want It	Journey	4-871	SC
Any Way You Want Me	Presley, Elvis	14-739	THM
Anymore	Drusky, Roy	20-744	CB
Anymore	Tritt, Travis	1-661	CB
Anyone At All	King, Carole	43-451	MM
Anyone Could Fall In Love W/You	Presley, Elvis	25-485	MM
Anyone Else	Raye, Collin	19-199	CB
Anyone Else	Raye, Collin	7-853	CHT
Anyone Else	Raye, Collin	22-712	ST
Anyone Who Had A Heart	Black, Cilla	48-781	P
Anyone Who Had A Heart	Vandross, Luther	48-286	KV
Anyone Who Had A Heart	Warwick, Dionne	13-324	P
Anyone Who Had A Heart	Warwick, Dionne	4-249	SC
Anyone Who Isn't Me Tonight	Rogers & West	15-233	CB
Anything	JoJo	30-488	CB
Anything	SWV	12-250	DK
Anything But Down	Crow, Sheryl	28-192	DK
Anything But Down	Crow, Sheryl	29-667	RS
Anything But Down	Crow, Sheryl	10-51	SC
Anything But Mine	Chesney, Kenny	23-5	CB
Anything Can Happen	Eder, Linda	17-441	PS
Anything For You	Estefan, Gloria	17-746	PT
Anything For Your Love	Clapton, Eric	13-797	SGB
Anything Goes	Florida Georgia Line	45-136	BKD
Anything Goes	Houser, Randy	36-599	CB
Anything Goes	Houser, Randy	36-198	PHM
Anything Goes	Sinatra, Frank	14-268	MM
Anything Like Me	Paisley, Brad	37-339	CB
Anything That's Part Of You	Presley, Elvis	7-131	MM

SONG TITLE	ARTIST	#	TYPE
Anything You Can Do	Annie Get Your Gun	19-585	SC
Anything's Better Than Feelin'/Blue	McBride, Martina	8-896	CB
Anytime	Arnold, Eddy	19-638	CB
Anytime	Arnold, Eddy	17-626	THM
Anytime	Cline, Patsy	16-359	CB
Anytime You Need A Friend	Carey, Mariah	2-236	SC
Anyway	McBride, Martina	30-200	CB
Anyway Anyhow Anywhere	Who	28-142	DK
Anyway Anyhow Anywhere	Who	19-735	LE
Anyway That You Want Me	Troggs	37-275	CMC
Anyway You Want Me	Presley, Elvis	7-134	MM
Anywhere But Here	Kershaw, Sammy	2-355	SC
Anywhere But Here	Long, Brice	23-483	CB
Anywhere For You	Backstreet Boys	18-703	MM
Anywhere For You	Backstreet Boys	30-415	THM
Anywhere There's A Jukebox	Bailey, Razzy	29-390	CB
Anywhere With You	Owen, Jake	45-397	BKD
Anywhere You Want To Go	Santana	49-883	SF
Apartment # 9	Wynette, Tammy	8-381	CB
Apartment #9	Paycheck, Johnny	45-212	SSK
Ape Man	Kinks	48-175	LE
Apologize	Timbaland feat One Republic	36-453	CB
Apologize	Timbaland feat One Republic	30-589	PHM
Applejack	Parton, Dolly	34-318	CB
Applejack	Parton, Dolly	2-518	SC
Apples Peaches Pumpkin Pie	Jay & Techniques	35-86	CB
April Love	Boone, Pat	11-205	DK
April Love	Boone, Pat	9-557	SAV
April Showers	Crosby, Bing	29-474	LE
Aqualung	Tull, Jethro	26-336	DK
Aquarius	5th Dimension	11-337	DK
Archies the - TV theme	Archies	46-440	SC
Are The Good Times Really Over	Haggard, Merle	37-178	CB
Are The Good Times Really Over	Haggard, Merle	12-90	DK
Are We In Trouble Now	Travis, Randy	7-334	MM
Are We in Trouble Now	Travis, Randy	4-392	SC
Are You Ever Gonna Love Me	Brooks & Dunn	14-687	CB
Are You Ever Gonna Love Me	Dunn, Holly	2-358	SC
Are You Experienced	Hendrix, Jimi	28-198	DK
Are You Gonna Be My Girl	Jet	20-540	CB
Are You Gonna Be My Girl	Jet	19-855	PHM
Are You Gonna Kiss Me Or Not	Thompson Square	37-199	AS

SONG TITLE	ARTIST	#	TYPE
Are You Happy Baby	West, Dottie	29-785	CB
Are You Happy Baby	West, Dottie	14-322	SC
Are You Happy Now	Branch, Michelle	34-165	CB
Are You Happy Now	Branch, Michelle	25-621	MM
Are You Happy Now	Branch, Michelle	23-338	SC
Are You Happy Now	Branch, Michelle	32-284	THM
Are You Jimmy Ray	Ray, Jimmy	5-190	SC
Are You Lonesome Tonight	Presley, Elvis	12-65	DK
Are You Lonesome Tonight	Presley, Elvis	25-758	MM
Are You Lonesome Tonight	Presley, Elvis	13-111	P
Are You Lonesome Tonight	Presley, Elvis	2-603	SC
Are You Lonesome Tonight	Presley, Elvis	14-740	THM
Are You Lovin' Me Like I'm...	Milsap, Ronnie	38-124	CB
Are You Ready For The Country	Jennings, Waylon	22-144	CK
Are You Ready For The Sex **	Gleaming Spires	15-7	SC
Are You Sure - duet	Musgraves & Nelson	49-93	FMK
Are You Sure Hank Done It This Way	Alabama	46-245	CB
Are You Sure Hank Done It This Way	Jennings, Waylon	1-617	CB
Are You Sure Hank Done It This Way	Jennings, Waylon	22-143	CK
Are You Sure Hank Done It This Way	Jennings, Waylon	4-309	SC
Are You Teasing Me	Smith, Carl	22-109	CB
Are You That Somebody	Aaliyah	7-783	PHT
Are You With Me	Corbin, Easton	45-392	BKD
Are Your Eyes Still Blue	McAnally, Shane	8-982	CB
Are Your Eyes Still Blue	McAnally, Shane	22-381	ST
Area Codes **	Ludacris	18-545	TT
Arlington	Adkins, Trace	23-287	CB
Arlington	Adkins, Trace	29-605	ST
Armageddon It	Def Leppard	3-518	SC
Arms Of Mary	Everly Brothers	45-550	OZP
Arms Of The One Who Loves You	Xscape	10-144	SC
Around The World	ATC	12-393	PHM
Around The World	Cole, Nat "King"	46-374	ZM
Around The World	Crosby, Bing	29-481	LE
Around The World	Hilton, Ronnie	10-600	SF
Around The World	Monro, Matt	18-100	PS
Around The World	Monro, Matt	9-215	SO
Art Of Losing the	American Hi-Fi	32-145	THM
Arthur's Theme	Cross, Christopher	16-812	DK
Artificial Flowers	Darin, Bobby	23-356	PS
Artificial Flowers	Darin, Bobby	47-11	PS
As Any Fool Can See	Lawrence, Tracy	1-579	CB
As Any Fool Can See	Lawrence, Tracy	6-710	MM
As Any Fool Can See	Lawrence, Tracy	17-279	NA
As Good As I Once Was	Keith, Toby	23-133	CB
As Good As New	Abba	19-76	MM

SONG TITLE	ARTIST	#	TYPE
As I Am	Cyrus, Miley	36-77	WD
As If	Evans, Sara	30-470	CB
As Lone As You Follow	Fleetwood Mac	47-912	LE
As Long As He Needs Me	Bassey, Shirley	46-485	SF
As Long As He Needs Me	Oliver	15-401	MM
As Long As He Needs Me - show	Oliver	48-788	MM
As Long As I Live - Duet	Foley, Red & Kitty Wells	43-362	CB
As Long As I Live - duet	Wells & Foley	48-201	CB
As Long As I'm Rockin' With You	Conlee, John	47-617	CB
As Long As It Matters	Gin Blossoms	4-670	SC
As Long As We Got Each Other	Thomas&Springfield	9-828	SAV
As Long As We Got Each Other - duet	Thomas & Springfield	47-599	SAV
As Long As You Belong To Me	Dunn, Holly	6-190	MM
As Long As You Love Me	Backstreet Boys	18-714	MM
As Long As You Love Me	Backstreet Boys	7-708	PHM
As Long As You Love Me	Backstreet Boys	10-135	SC
As She's Walking Away - duet	Zac Brown Band & Alan Jackson	37-344	CB
As She's Walking Away - duet	Zac Brown Band & Jackson	46-79	CB
As Tears Go By	Rolling Stones	19-751	LE
As The Honky Tonk Turns	Chesnutt, Mark	3-576	SC
As Time Goes By	Como, Perry	16-789	DK
As Time Goes By	Como, Perry	13-542	LE
As Time Goes By	Durante, Jimmy	3-121	KB
As Time Goes By	Murray, Anne	49-928	KVD
As Time Goes By	Simon, Carly	18-67	MM
As Time Goes By	Streisand, Barbra	49-561	MM
As Time Goes By	Vallee, Rudy	12-516	P
As Usual	Lee, Brenda	45-454	ZM
As We Lay	Murdock, Shirley	5-470	SC
As You Turn Away	Lady Antebellum	47-925	KV
Ascension (Don't Ever Wonder)	Maxwell	24-240	SC
Ashes By Now	Womack, Lee Ann	14-121	CB
Ashes By Now	Womack, Lee Ann	22-571	ST
Ashes By Now	Womack, Lee Ann	14-31	THM
Ashes Of Love	Desert Rose Band	8-621	SAV
Ask Me Why	Beatles	9-642	SAV
Asking Us To Dance	Mattea, Kathy	49-29	KCD
Asking Us To Dance	Mattea, Kathy	17-229	NA
Asphalt Cowboy	Shelton, Blake	47-447	KV
Asshole **	Leary, Denis	30-658	RSX
At 17	Ian, Janis	19-162	SGB
At Last	Adams, Oleta	17-432	KC
At Last	Dion, Celine	25-679	MM
At Last	Dion, Celine	19-19	PS

SONG TITLE	ARTIST	#	TYPE
At Last	James, Etta	23-359	CR
At Last	James, Etta	15-402	JTG
At Last	James, Etta	19-610	MH
At Last	James, Etta	21-693	PS
At Last	James, Etta	36-359	SC
At Long Last Love	Sinatra, Frank	14-273	MM
At Mail Call Today	Autry, Gene	22-174	CB
At My Front Door	El Dorados	14-456	SC
At Night I Pray	Wild Orchid	24-543	SC
At The Beginning	Anastasia	17-652	PR
At The Beginning	Lewis & Marx	10-114	SC
At The Club	Drifters	45-898	SF
At The End Of The Day	Coffey, Kelly	34-366	CB
At The End Of The Day	Coffey, Kelly	25-354	MM
At The End Of The Day	Coffey, Kelly	18-132	ST
At The Hop	Danny & Juniors	17-51	DK
At The Hop	Danny & Juniors	13-255	P
At The Sound Of The Tone	Schneider, John	5-774	SC
At The Stars	Better Than Ezra	7-811	PHT
At This Moment	Buble, Michael	40-87	PS
At This Moment	Vella, Billy	9-829	SAV
At This Moment	Vera & Beaters	35-194	CB
At This Moment	Vera & Beaters	11-653	DK
At This Moment	Vera & Beaters	20-317	MH
At This Moment	Vera & Beaters	12-833	P
Atomic	Blondie	49-130	LG
Atomic Dog	Clinton, George	14-354	MH
Attitude	Judd, Wynonna	29-21	CB
Attitude Adjustment	Williams, Hank Jr.	16-681	C2C
Auctioneer	Van Dyke, Leroy	8-720	CB
Auctioneer	Van Dyke, Leroy	5-364	SC
Audrey	Bread	46-528	PR
Auld Lang Syne	New Years Eve	21-472	DK
Auld Lang Syne	New Years Eve	14-520	SC
Auld Lang Syne	Standard	14-308	MM
Aun Existe Amor	Dion, Celine	19-25	PS
Austin	Shelton, Blake	33-140	CB
Austin	Shelton, Blake	15-100	ST
Authority Song	Mellencamp, John	21-434	LE
Authority Song	Mellencamp, John	45-413	LE
Authority Song	Mellencamp, John	21-427	SC
Automatic	Lambert, Miranda	43-124	ASK
Automatic	Pointer Sisters	17-43	DK
Autumn Almanac	Kinks	48-174	LE
Autumn Leaves	Standard	15-403	SGB
Autumn Of My Life	Goldsboro, Bobby	4-219	SC
Aw Naw	Young, Chris	40-55	ASK
Awake	Groban, Josh	36-447	CB
Away From Me	Puddle Of Mud	23-269	THM
Away From The Sun	3 Doors Down	20-530	CB
Away In A Manger - xmas	Cash, Johnny	45-37	SC
Away In A Manger - xmas	Wiggles	45-241	WIG
Awesome GOD	Mullins, Rich	35-320	CB
Awful Beautiful Day	Worley, Darryl	20-490	ST

SONG TITLE	ARTIST	#	TYPE
Awful Beautiful Life	Worley, Darryl	23-11	CB
Awful Beautiful Life	Worley, Darryl	21-656	SC
B-A-B-Y	Thomas, Carla	7-70	MM
B-A-B-Y	Thomas, Carla	12-715	P
B-B-Burnin' Up With Love	Rabbitt, Eddie	5-329	SC
Baba O'Reilly	Who	10-481	DA
Babalu (Spanish)	Arnaz, Desi	49-19	KV
Babe	Styx	11-192	DK
Babel	Mumford & Sons	39-126	PHM
Babies Makin' Babies	Lambert, Miranda	49-923	KVD
Babooshka	Bush, Kate	48-753	P
Baby	Bieber, Justin	36-57	ASK
Baby Ain't Rockin' Me Right	Nesler, Mark	8-926	CB
Baby Baby	Grant, Amy	21-462	CB
Baby Baby	Grant, Amy	18-764	PS
Baby Baby	Rich, Charlie	8-424	CB
Baby Baby Baby	TLC	33-342	CB
Baby Baby Baby	TLC	12-747	P
Baby Baby Don't Cry	Robinson & Miracles	27-269	DK
Baby Baby I Know You're A Lady	Houston, David	13-533	P
Baby Baby I Know You're A Lady	Houston, David	6-7	SC
Baby Be My Love Song	Corbin, Easton	45-410	BKD
Baby Be My Love Song	Corbin, Easton	46-642	SSC
Baby Blue	Jones, Jiggley	41-102	PHN
Baby Blue	Strait, George	34-278	CB
Baby Blue	Strait, George	2-510	SC
Baby Boy	Beyonce feat Sean Paul	35-272	CB
Baby Boy	Knowles & Paul	25-715	MM
Baby Boy	Knowles & Paul	21-787	SC
Baby Boy - Duet	Knowles & Paul	32-382	THM
Baby Can I Hold You	Chapman, Tracy	44-190	MRE
Baby Come Back	Equals	12-652	P
Baby Come Back	Player	12-153	DK
Baby Come Back	Player	4-48	SC
Baby Come Over	Mumba, Samantha	18-507	TT
Baby Come To Me	Ingram & Austin	11-406	DK
Baby Come To Me	Ingram & Austin	6-238	MM
Baby Come To Me	Ingram & Austin	21-604	SF
Baby Come To Me	Ingram & Austin	9-207	SO
Baby Did A Bad Bad Thing	Isaak, Chris	8-511	PHT
Baby Did A Bad Bad Thing	Isaak, Chris	22-496	ST
Baby Doll	Green, Pat	22-319	CB
Baby Don't Care	Holly, Buddy	3-210	LG
Baby Don't Get Hooked On Me	Davis, Mac	23-509	CB
Baby Don't Get Hooked On Me	Davis, Mac	17-16	DK
Baby Don't Go	Cher	15-125	SGB
Baby Don't Go	Sonny & Cher	14-57	RS
Baby Don't Go - duet	Yoakam & Crow	49-692	DFK
Baby Don't You Break	Shepard, Vonda	8-225	PHT

SONG TITLE	ARTIST	#	TYPE
My Heart Slow			
Baby Don't You Break My Heart Slow	Shepard, Vonda	16-193	THM
Baby Face	Darin, Bobby	47-10	MM
Baby Face	Lewis, Ted	21-6	SC
Baby Face	Standard	11-758	DK
Baby Girl	Sugarland	35-449	CB
Baby Girl	Sugarland	30-232	RS
Baby Girl	Sugarland	20-491	ST
Baby Got Back	Sir Mix-A-Lot	33-440	CB
Baby Got Back **	Sir Mix-A-Lot	12-1	DK
Baby Got Back **	Sir Mix-A-Lot	2-178	SC
Baby Hold On	Money, Eddie	15-180	MH
Baby I Don't Care	Holly, Buddy	11-39	PX
Baby I Don't Care	Presley, Elvis	2-604	SC
Baby I Lied	Allen, Deborah	20-679	SC
Baby I Lied	Brown, Shannon	25-58	MM
Baby I Lied	Brown, Shannon	16-107	ST
Baby I Love You	Kim, Andy	47-407	DFK
Baby I Love You	Lopez, Jennifer	19-647	CB
Baby I Love You	Lopez, Jennifer	21-795	SC
Baby I Love Your Way	Big Mountain	34-116	CB
Baby I Love Your Way	Frampton, Peter	24-209	SC
Baby I Love Your Way	Gin Blossoms	12-241	DK
Baby I Need Your Lovin'	Four Tops	16-797	DK
Baby I Need Your Lovin'	Four Tops	12-634	P
Baby I Need Your Loving	Rivers, Johnny	47-366	LE
Baby I'm A Want You	Bread	12-316	DK
Baby I'm A Want You	Bread	9-717	SAV
Baby I'm A Want You	Newton, Wayne	16-722	DK
Baby I'm A Want You	Newton, Wayne	47-319	MM
Baby I'm In Love	Thalia	19-655	CB
Baby I'm Yours	Lewis, Barbara	26-100	DK
Baby I'm Yours	Lewis, Barbara	3-362	MH
Baby I'm Yours	Lewis, Barbara	3-288	MM
Baby I'm Yours	Lewis, Barbara	12-907	P
Baby It's Cold Outside	Lady Antebellum	45-775	KV
Baby It's Cold Outside	Martin, Dean	23-72	MM
Baby It's You	Shirelles	15-404	MM
Baby Jane	Stewart, Rod	14-848	LE
Baby Let's Play House	Presley, Elvis	43-240	MM
Baby Likes To Rock It	Tractors	30-107	CB
Baby Likes To Rock It	Tractors	17-255	NA
Baby Likes To Rock It	Tractors	2-450	SC
Baby Love	Mother's Finest	24-431	SC
Baby Love	Ross, Diana	15-363	LE
Baby Love	Supremes	11-119	DK
Baby Love	Supremes	9-311	STR
Baby Luv	Groove Theory	24-176	SC
Baby Mama	Fantasia	22-369	CB
Baby Mine	Midler, Bette	45-916	KV
Baby Now That I've Found You	Foundations	7-473	MM
Baby Now That I've Found You	Foundations	3-134	SC
Baby Now That I've Found You	Foundations	10-594	SF

SONG TITLE	ARTIST	#	TYPE
Baby Now That I've Found You	Krauss & Union Station	34-322	CB
Baby Now That I've Found You	Krauss, Alison	8-893	CB
Baby Now That I've Found You	Krauss, Alison	6-824	MM
Baby One More Time	Spears, Britney	13-557	LE
Baby One More Time	Spears, Britney	13-706	SGB
Baby Please Don't Go	Morrison, Van	23-595	BS
Baby Please Don't Go	Them	10-640	SF
Baby Step Back	Lightfoot, Gordon	43-492	SK
Baby That's Cold	Gosdin, Vern	48-431	VH
Baby the	Shelton, Blake	34-353	CB
Baby the	Shelton, Blake	25-416	MM
Baby the	Shelton, Blake	18-463	ST
Baby the	Shelton, Blake	32-40	THM
Baby The Rain Must Fall	Yarbrough, Glenn	7-74	MM
Baby We're Really In Love	Williams, Hank Sr.	14-229	CB
Baby What A Big Surprise	Chicago	35-135	CB
Baby What A Big Surprise	Chicago	17-508	SC
Baby What About You	Gayle, Crystal	49-634	CB
Baby What You Want Me To Do	Presley, Elvis	45-612	HM
Baby You Are My Lady	Jackson, Freddie	17-509	SC
Baby You're Something	Conlee, John	5-570	SC
Baby You've Got What It Takes	Benton&Washington	6-684	MM
Baby's Gone	Twitty, Conway	48-239	CB
Baby's Gone Blues	McEntire, Reba	4-468	SC
Baby's Got Her Blue Jeans On	McDaniel, Mel	35-390	CB
Baby's Got Her Blue Jeans On	McDaniel, Mel	17-402	DK
Baby's Got Her Blue Jeans On	McDaniel, Mel	7-113	MM
Baby's Got Her Blue Jeans On	McDaniel, Mel	12-447	P
Baby's Got Her Blue Jeans On	McDaniel, Mel	3-597	SC
Baby's Gotten Good At Goodbye	Strait, George	8-167	CB
Baby's Gotten Good At Goodbye	Strait, George	4-553	SC
Babylon	Gray, David	16-482	MH
Bachelor Boy	Cliff, Richard	48-759	P
Back 2 Good	Matchbox 20	33-359	CB
Back At One	McKnight, Brian	5-786	SC
Back At One	Wills, Mark	5-829	SC
Back At One	Wills, Mark	22-515	ST
Back Door Man **	Doors	15-5	SC
Back Door Man **	Doors	18-641	SO
Back For Good	Take That	28-445	DK
Back Here	BB Mak	13-841	PHM
Back Here	BB Mak	14-476	SC
Back Here	BB Mak	18-546	TT
Back Home Again	Denver, John	36-150	LE

SONG TITLE	ARTIST	#	TYPE
Back Home Again	Denver, John	4-820	SC
Back In Baby's Arms	Cline, Patsy	6-721	MM
Back In Baby's Arms	Cline, Patsy	22-256	SC
Back In Black	AC/DC	13-753	SGB
Back In Love Again	LFO	14-359	MH
Back In My Arms Again	Chesney, Kenny	1-321	CB
Back In My Arms Again	Supremes	17-358	DK
Back In My Younger Days	Williams, Don	45-223	CB
Back In The Arms Of Love	Greene, Jack	43-343	CB
Back In The Day	Downday	41-89	PHN
Back In The Doghouse Again	Stevens, Ray	16-498	CB
Back In The High Life Again	Winwood, Steve	33-318	CB
Back In The High Life Again	Winwood, Steve	29-267	SC
Back In The Saddle	Aerosmith	12-772	P
Back In The Saddle	Berg, Martraca	8-408	CB
Back In The Saddle	Berg, Martraca	7-735	CHM
Back In The Saddle	Berg, Martraca	22-777	ST
Back In The Saddle Again	Autry, Gene	12-284	DK
Back In The Saddle Again	Autry, Gene	5-430	SC
Back In The U.S.S.R.	Beatles	16-842	DK
Back In The U.S.S.R.	Beatles	12-725	P
Back In The USA	Berry, Chuck	46-231	SRK
Back In Time	Lewis & The News	47-189	KV
Back In Your Arms Again	Morgan, Lorrie	1-342	CB
Back In Your Arms Again	Morgan, Lorrie	7-90	MM
Back In Your Own Backyard	Andrew Sisters	46-425	KV
Back In Your Own Backyard	Jolson, Al	12-934	PS
Back Of The Bottom Drawer	Wright, Chely	20-259	PHM
Back Of The Bottom Drawer	Wright, Chely	20-332	ST
Back Of Your Hand the	Yoakam, Dwight	49-681	SC
Back Off Bitch **	Guns & Roses	23-113	SC
Back On My Feet Again	Babys	5-143	SC
Back On My Mind Again	Milsap, Ronnie	8-209	CB
Back On My Mind Again	Milsap, Ronnie	5-400	SC
Back On The Chain Gang	Pretenders	13-209	P
Back On The Chain Gang	Pretenders	24-451	SC
Back On The Chain Gang	Wright, Gary	4-526	SC
Back Side Of Thirty	Conlee, John	9-502	SAV
Back Stabbers	O'Jays	16-765	DK
Back Stabbers	O'Jays	16-561	P
Back Stabbers	O'Jays	9-752	SAV
Back Street Affair	Pierce, Webb	8-794	CB
Back That Thang Up	Juvenile&Little Way	14-448	SC

SONG TITLE	ARTIST	#	TYPE
Back That Thing Up	Moore, Justin	38-120	CB
Back To Black	Winehouse, Amy	37-142	SC
Back To Good	Matchbox 20	16-217	MM
Back To Life	Soul II Soul	12-383	DK
Back To The Barrooms Again	Haggard, Merle	29-447	DK
Back To The Cave	Ford, Lita	21-778	SC
Back To The Hotel	N2 Deep	28-394	DK
Back To You	Adams, Bryan	23-448	CB
Back To You	Adams, Bryan	15-405	SC
Back To Your Heart	Backstreet Boys	10-206	SC
Back Together Again	Flack & Hathaway	12-850	P
Back Up Buddy	Smith, Carl	22-115	CB
Back When	McGraw, Tim	22-62	CB
Back When	McGraw, Tim	20-502	ST
Back When	Potts, MC	4-162	SC
Back When I Knew It All	Montgomery Gentry	36-412	CB
Back Where I Come From	Chesney, Kenny	48-81	CB
Back Where We Belong	Skaggs, Ricky	4-227	SC
Backroad Song	Smith, Granger	47-488	DCK
Backroad Song	Smith, Granger	48-697	KRG
Backroads	VanShelton, Ricky	8-557	CB
Backseat Of A Greyhound Bus	Evans, Sara	29-549	CB
Backseat Of A Greyhound Bus	Evans, Sara	25-562	MM
Backseat Of A Greyhound Bus	Evans, Sara	18-793	ST
Backseat Of A Greyhound Bus	Evans, Sara	32-189	THM
Backseat Serenade	All Time Low	39-125	PHM
Backside Of Thirty	Conlee, John	8-829	CB
Backstabbers	O'Jays	9-223	PT
Backstage	Pitney, Gene	47-526	ZM
Backstreets	Springsteen, Bruce	20-241	LE
Backwater	Meat Puppets	15-768	NU
Backwoods	Moore, Justin	43-310	CB
Backwoods Boogie	Alabama	49-674	KCD
Bad	Jackson, Michael	35-191	CB
Bad	Jackson, Michael	11-190	DK
Bad	U2	30-69	CB
Bad	U2	30-69	SC
Bad Angel - duet	Bentley, Lambert & Johnson	37-351	CB
Bad Bad Boy	Nazareth	30-740	SF
Bad Bad Leroy Brown	Croce, Jim	17-374	DK
Bad Bad Leroy Brown	Croce, Jim	13-135	P
Bad Blood	Sedaka, Neil	9-170	SO
Bad Blood	Swift, Taylor	48-298	KV
Bad Boys	Miami Sound Mach	17-171	SC
Bad Case Of Loving You	Palmer, Robert	11-517	DK
Bad Case Of Loving You	Palmer, Robert	17-521	SC
Bad Day	Fuel	33-418	CB
Bad Day	Fuel	18-397	MM
Bad Day To Let You Go	White, Bryan	8-467	CB
Bad Dog No Biscuit	Norwood, Daron	22-876	ST
Bad For Me	Peck, Danielle	30-534	CB

SONG TITLE	ARTIST	#	TYPE
Bad For Us	Little Texas	48-100	MM
Bad Girls	Summer, Donna	11-209	DK
Bad Girls	Summer, Donna	4-529	SC
Bad Goodbye a	Black & Wynonna	8-115	CB
Bad Goodbye a	Black & Wynonna	30-5	MM
Bad Goodbye a	Black & Wynonna	12-396	P
Bad Goodbye a	Black & Wynonna	30-437	THM
Bad Is Bad	Lewis & The News	47-193	SC
Bad Little Boy - xmas	Stevens, Ray	47-903	CB
Bad Luck	Melvin & Bluenotes	10-498	DA
Bad Man	Kelly, R.	20-7	SGB
Bad Medicine	Bon Jovi	21-713	CB
Bad Medicine	Bon Jovi	26-101	DK
Bad Moon Risin'	CCR	11-363	DK
Bad Moon Risin'	CCR	7-44	MM
Bad Moon Risin'	CCR	5-351	SC
Bad Reputation	Jett, Joan	35-202	CB
Bad Romance	Lady Gaga	38-188	CB
Bad Things	Everett, Jace	29-24	CB
Bad Things	Everett, Jace	23-460	ST
Bad Time	Grand Funk RR	3-520	SC
Bad To Me	Kramer & Dacotas	10-560	SF
Bad To Me	Kramer, Billy J.	20-37	SC
Bad To The Bone	Thorogood, George	20-146	KB
Bad To The Bone	Thorogood, George	15-171	MH
Bad To The Bone	Thorogood, George	21-563	MM
Bad Touch the	Bloodhound Gang	16-232	PHM
Baddest Boots	Keith, Toby	47-161	CB
Badge	Clapton, Eric	13-805	SGB
Badlands	Springsteen, Bruce	17-611	LE
Badly Bent	Tractors	2-766	SC
Bag Lady	Badu, Erykah	23-257	HS
Bag Lady	Badu, Erykah	25-690	MM
Baggage Claim	Lambert, Miranda	44-130	ASK
Bailamos	Iglesias, Enrique	35-215	CB
Bailamos	Iglesias, Enrique	29-168	MH
Bailamos	Iglesias, Enrique	8-503	PHT
Bait A Hook	Moore, Justin	38-115	CB
Baker Street	Rafferty, Gerry	29-265	SC
Ball And Chain	Joplin, Janis	15-221	LE
Ball And Chain	Overstreet, Paul	29-769	CB
Ball And Chain	Overstreet, Paul	12-57	DK
Ball And Chain	Overstreet, Paul	10-781	JVC
Ball And Chain	Overstreet, Paul	9-531	SAV
Ball And Chain - Nashville	Britton & Chase	45-476	KVD
Ball Of Confusion	Temptations	11-775	DK
Ballad of a Dog Named Stains **	Peters, Red	37-93	SC
Ballad Of A Teenage Queen	Cash, Johnny	14-240	CB
Ballad Of A Teenage Queen	Cash, Johnny	21-579	SC
Ballad Of Billy The Kid	Joel, Billy	46-173	SC
Ballad Of Chassey Lain	Bloodhound	20-4	SGB
Ballad Of Curtis Lowe	Lynyrd Skynyrd	5-256	SC
Ballad Of Curtis Lowe	Lynyrd Skynyrd	19-816	SGB

SONG TITLE	ARTIST	#	TYPE
Ballad Of Davy Crockett	Ford, Tenn Ernie	22-209	CB
Ballad Of Dwight Fry	Alice Cooper	16-453	SGB
Ballad Of Easy Rider	Byrds	47-553	KV
Ballad Of Forty Dollars	Hall, Tom T.	18-283	CB
Ballad Of Ira Hayes the	Cash, Johnny	29-726	CB
Ballad Of Ira Hayes the	Cash, Johnny	21-588	SC
Ballad Of Jed Clampett - TV	Flatt & Scruggs	33-222	CB
Ballad Of The Alamo	Robbins, Marty	44-54	KV
Ballad Of The Blue Cyclone (Rasslin	Stevens, Ray	16-495	CB
Ballad Of The Green Beret	Sadler, Ssgt Barry	20-71	SC
Ballerina	Cole, Nat "King"	29-458	LE
Ballerina Girl	Richie, Lionel	47-456	LE
Ballroom Blitz	Sweet	12-347	DK
Bama Breeze	Buffett, Jimmy	46-136	ST
Banana Pancakes	Johnson, Jack	48-704	BKD
Banana Splits	Dickies	48-769	P
Band Of Gold	Cherry, Don	22-449	SC
Band Of Gold	Locke, Kimberly	49-903	SC
Band Of Gold	Payne, Freda	26-230	DK
Band Of Gold	Payne, Freda	13-191	P
Band On The Run	McCartney & Wings	17-406	DK
Band On The Run	McCartney & Wings	14-578	SC
Band On The Run	McCartney, Paul	48-562	DK
Bandages	Hot Hot Heat	32-293	THM
Banditos	Refreshments	24-289	SC
Bandstand Boogie	Manilow, Barry	29-111	CB
Bandy The Rodeo Clown	Bandy, Moe	19-501	CB
Bang A Gong (Get It On)	Power Station	5-106	SC
Bang A Gong (Get It On)	T. Rex	13-229	P
Bang And Blame	REM	16-620	MM
Bang And Blame	REM	13-607	P
Bang Bang	Cher	14-61	RS
Bang Bang	Cher	15-126	SGB
Bang Bang	Sinatra, Nancy	49-756	LGK
Bang Bang Bang	Nitty Gritty Dirt Band	49-379	CB
Bang The Drum All Day	Rundgren, Todd	2-553	SC
Bang Them Sticks	Trainor, Meghan	45-146	KCD
Banjo	Rascal Flatts	48-503	KVD
Banks Of The Ohio	Baez, Joan	46-463	KVD
Bar Room Buddies	Haggard & Eastwood	22-234	CB
Barbara Ann	Beach Boys	5-496	BS
Barbara Ann	Beach Boys	33-257	CB
Barbara Ann	Beach Boys	17-46	DK
Barbed Wire & Roses	PinMonkey	25-238	MM
Barbed Wire & Roses	PinMonkey	16-708	ST
Barbie Girl	Aqua	13-568	LE
Barefoot And Crazy	Ingram, Jack	37-42	CB
Barefoot Blue Jean Night	Owen, Jake	37-215	AS
Barefoot In The Grass	Isaacs, Sonya	14-118	CB
Barefootin'	Jackson w Buffett	40-15	SD
Barely Breathing	Sheik, Duncan	15-476	SC
Barenaked	Hewitt, Jennifer Lo	25-308	MM

SONG TITLE	ARTIST	#	TYPE
Barenaked	Hewitt, Jennifer Lo	18-346	PHM
Bargain Store the	Parton, Dolly	4-786	SC
Barlight	Robison, Charlie	8-921	CB
Barracuda	Heart	17-511	SC
Barstool Mountain	Bandy, Moe	19-508	CB
Bartender	Lady Antebellum	44-201	SBIG
Bartender (It's So Easy)	Sugar Ray	19-592	CB
Bartender (Radio Vers)	T-Pain & Akon	37-109	SC
Bartender Song (aka Sittin' At a Bar	Rehab & Hank Jr.	43-376	CB
Bartender's Blues	Jones, George	15-821	CB
Bartender's Blues	Jones, George	6-771	MM
Bartenders, Barstools & Barmaids	Bentley, Dierks	45-48	TBR
Basics Of Life	4Him	35-319	CB
Basin Street Blues	Jazz Standard	47-520	VH
Basket Case	Green Day	19-285	SGB
Bat Country	Avenged Sevenfold	29-257	SC
Bat Dance	Prince	49-835	SAV
Bat Out Of Hell - Halloween	Meat Loaf	45-141	LE
Battery	Metallica	47-257	SBI
Battle Hymn Of Love the	Mattea & O'Brien	1-198	CB
Battle Hymn Of Love the	Mattea & O'Brien	2-305	SC
Battle Hymn Of The Republic	Patriotic	44-48	PT
Battle Of Kokamonga	Homer & Jethro	15-348	MM
Battle Of New Orleans the	Horton, Johnny	6-523	MM
Battle Of New Orleans the	Horton, Johnny	13-127	P
Battle Of New Orleans the	Horton, Johnny	18-625	PS
Battlefield	Sparks, Jordin	36-25	PT
Bawitdaba	Kid Rock	36-345	SC
Bay Bay A (Radio Vers)	Hurricane Chris	49-887	SC
Be Alright	Bieber, Justin	48-628	KVD
Be Bop A Lula	Everly Brothers	45-865	VH
Be Bop A Lula	Holly, Buddy	47-879	PS
Be Bop A Lula	Vincent, Gene	11-399	DK
Be Bop A Lula	Vincent, Gene	7-256	MM
Be Bop Baby	Nelson, Ricky	21-708	CB
Be Bop Santa Claus - xmas	Gonzales, Babs	45-245	CB
Be By Myself	Roth, Asher feat Cee-Lo	36-299	PHM
Be Careful	Martin & Madonna	9-128	PS
Be Careful	Martin & Madonna	13-730	SGB
Be Good Johnny	Men At Work	47-251	KV
Be Honest With Me	Aurty, Gene	45-658	OZP
Be Like That	3 Doors Down	33-373	CB
Be Like That	3 Doors Down	18-402	MM
Be Like That	3 Doors Down	16-309	TT
Be My Baby	Ronettes	35-57	CB
Be My Baby Tonight	Montgomery, J M	14-207	CB
Be My Baby Tonight	Montgomery, J M	12-483	P
Be My Baby Tonight	Montgomery, J M	2-219	SC
Be My Girl	Lettermen	48-534	L1

SONG TITLE	ARTIST	#	TYPE
Be My Guest	Domino, Fats	45-732	VH
Be My Love	Lanza, Mario	9-748	SAV
Be My Lover	Alice Cooper	16-450	SGB
Be My Yoko Ono	Barenaked Ladies	30-626	RS
Be Near Me	ABC	18-382	SAV
Be Near Me	ABC	5-604	SC
Be That Way	McBride, Martina	8-864	CB
Be There For My Baby	Lee, Johnny	5-771	SC
Be True To Your School	Beach Boys	5-497	BS
Be With You	Bangles	46-469	CB
Be With You	Iglesias, Enrique	14-176	CB
Be With You	Iglesias, Enrique	29-167	MH
Be With You	Iglesias, Enrique	16-237	PHM
Be Without You	Blige, Mary J.	48-601	DK
Beaches Of Cheyenne	Brooks, Garth	7-166	MM
Beaches Of Cheyenne	Brooks, Garth	4-152	SC
Beachin'	Owen, Jake	44-18	KCDC
Beast Of Burden	Rolling Stones	18-20	LE
Beast Of Burden	Rolling Stones	14-397	PT
Beat Goes On	Sonny & Cher	35-62	CB
Beat Goes On the	Sonny & Cher	11-543	DK
Beat Goes On the	Sonny & Cher	13-257	P
Beat Goes On the	Sonny & Cher	14-55	RS
Beat Goes On the	Sonny & Cher	9-661	SAV
Beat Goes On the	Sonny & Cher	15-127	SGB
Beat It	Jackson, Michael	33-306	CB
Beat It	Jackson, Michael	17-19	DK
Beat It	Jackson, Michael	12-755	P
Beat Me Daddy 8 To The Bar	Andrew Sisters	46-429	KV
Beat Of A Heart	Smyth, Patty	24-426	SC
Beat Of The Music	Eldridge, Brett	43-136	PHN
Beat On The Brat	Ramones	45-85	SC
Beatin' It In	McCoy, Neal	14-794	ST
Beauitful Woman	Rich, Charlie	19-430	SC
Beautiful	10 Years	36-499	CB
Beautiful	Aguilera, Christina	25-424	MM
Beautiful	Aguilera, Christina	18-603	PHM
Beautiful	King, Carole	16-882	DK
Beautiful	Lightfoot, Gordon	43-494	SK
Beautiful	Snoop Dogg, Pharrell, Wilson	32-315	THM
Beautiful - All That You Are	Rogers, Kenny	16-166	CB
Beautiful (All That You Can Be)	Rogers, Kenny	15-675	ST
Beautiful As U	All-4-One	18-355	CB
Beautiful Brown Eyes	Standard	17-398	DK
Beautiful Day	Marley, Ziggy	25-388	MM
Beautiful Day	U2	23-264	HS
Beautiful Day	U2	16-479	MH
Beautiful Day	U2	30-78	SC
Beautiful Day	U2	18-547	TT
Beutiful Dreamer	Foster, Stephen	46-290	CB
Beautiful Dreamer	Orbison, Roy	47-343	DFK
Beautiful Dreamer	Standard	11-493	DK

SONG TITLE	ARTIST	#	TYPE
Beautiful Drug	Zac Brown Band	49-418	BKD
Beautiful Drug (Instrumental)	Zac Brown Band	47-705	BKD
Beautiful Every Time	Brice, Lee	45-549	CB
Beautiful Girl	INXS	4-276	SC
Beautiful Girls	Van Halen	10-488	DA
Beautiful Goodbye	Hanson, Jennifer	34-354	CB
Beautiful Goodbye	Hanson, Jennifer	25-415	MM
Beautiful Goodbye	Hanson, Jennifer	18-210	ST
Beautiful In My Eyes	Kadison, Joshua	29-324	PS
Beautiful In My Eyes	Kadison, Joshua	2-223	SC
Beautiful Liar	Beyonce & Shakira	30-485	CB
Beautiful Loser	Seger, Bob	20-73	SC
Beautiful Mess	Diamond Rio	25-191	MM
Beautiful Mess	Diamond Rio	16-701	ST
Beautiful Mess a	Mraz, Jason	47-305	KV
Beautiful Morning a	Rascals	3-17	SC
Beautiful Noise	Diamond, Neil	30-683	LE
Beautiful People	Sharp, Kevin	15-864	ST
Beautiful Soul	McCartney, Jesse	22-370	CB
Beautiful Soul	McCartney, Jesse	30-742	SF
Beautiful Stranger	Keith, Toby	49-675	KCD
Beautiful Stranger	Madonna	8-101	PHT
Beautiful Sunday	Boone, Debbie	9-370	MG
Beautiful Swimmers	Buffett, Jimmy	46-152	PS
Beautiful Wreck	Mullins, Shawn	29-218	PHM
Beauty And The Beast	Dion & Bryson	9-213	SC
Beauty And The Beast	Dion, Celine	15-108	BS
Beauty Is In the Eye of the Beerholder	Harvey, Adam	47-491	CKA
Beauty Is Only Skin Deep	Temptations	12-84	DK
Beauty School Drop Out	Avalon, Frankie	9-278	SC
Beauty's In The Eye Of The Beerhold	Chuck Wagon&Wheels	14-725	CB
Because	Dave Clark Five	12-654	P
Because I Got High	Afroman	16-377	SGB
Because I Love You (Postman Song)	Stevie B	28-117	DK
Because I Want You	Placebo	30-702	SF
Because Of Love	Jackson, Janet	2-112	SC
Because Of You	98 Degrees	16-222	MM
Because Of You	98 Degrees	15-371	SKG
Because Of You	Bennett, Tony	17-364	DK
Because Of You	Boyce Avenue	46-60	KV
Because Of You	Clarkson, Kelly	29-254	SC
Because Of You	James, Sonny	48-469	DKM
Because Of You	McEntire&Clarkson	30-464	CB
Because Of You	Nickelback	22-348	CB
Because Of You	Standard	47-822	DK
Because Of You - duet	McEntire & Clarkson	30-464	CB
Because Of Your Love	Chesney, Kenny	48-90	CB
Because The Night	10,000 Maniacs	2-111	SC
Because The Night	Smyth, Patty	7-489	MM
Because You Love Me	Dion, Celine	15-111	BS
Because You Love Me	Dion, Celine	19-568	MH
Because You Love Me	Messina, Jo Dee	8-858	CB

SONG TITLE	ARTIST	#	TYPE
Because You Love Me	Messina, Jo Dee	22-375	ST
Because You Loved Me	Dion, Celine	14-197	CB
Bed Of Roses	Bon Jovi	12-37	DK
Bed Of Roses	Bon Jovi	18-548	TT
Bed Of Roses	Statler Brothers	19-390	CB
Bed Of Roses	Statler Brothers	5-822	SC
Bed Of Roses	Tucker, Tanya	45-123	THM
Bed That You Made the	Duncan, Whitney	48-707	BKD
Bed You Made For Me the	Highway 101	9-514	SAV
Bed You Made For Me the	Highway 101	5-17	SC
Bedrock Twitch	B-52's	46-455	SBI
Bedroom Eyes	McDowell, Ronny	45-675	DCK
Beds Are Burning	Midnight Oil	17-74	DK
Bedshaped	Keane	21-690	Z
Bedtime Story	Wynette, Tammy	49-356	CB
Been Down So Long	Doors	13-647	SGB
Been There	Black & Wariner	22-473	ST
Been There - duet	Black & Wariner	30-419	THM
Been There Done That	Bryan, Luke	45-322	SSC
Been There Drunk That	Seals, Brady	47-581	PHN
Been To Canaan	King, Carole	43-444	CB
Beep **	Pussycat Dolle w Will I Am	48-600	DK
Beep Beep	Playmates	5-635	SC
Beer & Bones	Montgomery, J M	6-526	MM
Beer & Bones	Montgomery, J M	2-412	SC
Beer Bait And Ammo	Kershaw, Sammy	22-1	CB
Beer Barrel Polka	Andrew Sisters	2-62	SC
Beer Barrel Polka	Standard	27-448	DK
Beer Barrel Polka	Standard	7-412	MM
Beer Barrel Polka	Vinton, Bobby	21-20	CB
Beer Drinkers & Hell Raisers	ZZ Top	13-766	SGB
Beer For My Horses	Keith, Toby	19-48	ST
Beer For My Horses	Keith, Toby	32-227	THM
Beer For My Horses	Keith, Toby w/Nelso	25-451	MM
Beer For My Horses - duet	Keith & Nelson	34-391	CB
Beer In Mexico	Chesney, Kenny	29-589	CB
Beer In Mexico	Chesney, Kenny	29-501	SC
Beer In The Headlights	Bryan, Luke	45-480	ASK
Beer Man	Williams, Trent	20-346	ST
Beer Man	Wilmon, Trent	47-494	CB
Beer Money	Moore, Kip	45-633	SBI
Beer On The Table	Thompson, Josh	36-316	PHM
Beer Run	Brooks & Jones	16-4	ST
Beer Run - Duet	Brooks & Jones	33-141	CB
Beer Thirty	Brooks & Dunn	5-828	SC
Beer Thirty	Brooks & Dunn	22-514	ST
Beer With Jesus	Rhett, Thomas	45-440	SBI
Beers Ago	Keith, Toby	38-218	PHN
Before He Cheats	Underwood, Carrie	29-202	CB
Before He Cheats	Underwood, Carrie	30-98	PHM
Before He Cheats	Underwood, Carrie	29-847	SC
Before He Kissed Me	Brokop, Lisa	7-201	MM

SONG TITLE	ARTIST	#	TYPE
Before He Kissed Me	Brokop, Lisa	4-238	SC
Before i Knew Better	Martin, Brad	33-159	CB
Before I Knew Better	Martin, Brad	25-240	MM
Before I Knew Better	Martin, Brad	16-431	ST
Before I Met You	McEntire, Reba	1-818	CB
Before I'm Ever Over You	Greenwood, Lee	47-131	SC
Before I'm Over You	Lynn, Loretta	48-249	CB
Before My Time	Conlee, John	47-620	CB
Before The Next Teardrop Falls	Fender, Freddie	29-784	CB
Before The Parade Passes	Streisand, Barbra	49-547	PS
Before The Ring On Your Finger Turn	West, Dottie	5-841	SC
Before You Accuse Me	Clapton, Eric	20-133	KB
Before You Accuse Me	Clapton, Eric	14-601	SC
Before You Go	Owens, Buck	3-909	CB
Before You Kill Us All	Travis, Randy	6-496	MM
Before You Kill Us All	Travis, Randy	2-209	SC
Before Your Love	Clarkson, Kelly	25-332	MM
Before Your Love	Clarkson, Kelly	36-363	SC
Before Your Love	Clarkson, Kelly	32-102	THM
Begging To You	Robbins, Marty	3-238	CB
Begging To You	Robbins, Marty	22-245	SC
Begin Again	Swift, Taylor	44-326	SSC
Begin The Beguine	Fitzgerald, Ella	12-554	P
Begin The Beguine	Shaw, Artie	11-761	DK
Begin The Beguine	Shaw, Artie	10-710	JVC
Behind Blue Eyes	Who	19-736	LE
Behind Blue Eyes	Who	37-69	SC
Behind Closed Doors	Diffie, Joe	10-163	SC
Behind Closed Doors	Rich, Charlie	15-823	CB
Behind Closed Doors	Rich, Charlie	17-5	DK
Behind Closed Doors	Rich, Charlie	8-624	SAV
Behind His Last Goodbye	Morgan, Lorrie	49-119	SC
Behind The Tear	James, Sonny	19-468	CB
Behind The Tear	James, Sonny	5-583	SC
Behind These Hazel Eyes	Clarkson, Kelly	30-134	PT
Behind Those Eyes	3 Doors Down	47-652	CB
Bei Mir Bist Du Schon	Andrew Sisters	12-569	P
Bei Mir Bist Du Schon	Andrew Sisters	9-563	SAV
Bei Mir Bist Du Schon	Gorme, Steve&Eydie	15-842	MM
Bein' Alive And Livin'	Morgan, Craig	48-282	PHN
Bein' Happy	Taff, Russ	6-847	MM
Being Alive	Sondheim, Stephen	17-778	PS
Being Alive	Streisand, Barbra	49-569	PS
Being Drunk's A Lot Like Loving You	Chesney, Kenny	47-580	CB
Being With You	Robinson, Smokey	16-796	DK
Being With You	Robinson, Smokey	36-108	JTG
Believe	Brooks & Dunn	23-482	CB
Believe	Brooks & Dunn	49-898	SC
Believe	Cher	28-4	DK
Believe	Cher	7-841	PHM
Believe	Cher	14-47	RS

SONG TITLE	ARTIST	#	TYPE
Believe	Groban, Josh	48-47	CB
Believe	John, Elton	12-75	DK
Believe	Staind	36-537	CB
Believe In Life	Clapton, Eric	15-819	CB
Believe In Life	Clapton, Eric	18-404	MM
Believe In Love	Scorpions	49-101	KVD
Believe In Yourself	The Wiz	49-434	SDK
Believe Me Baby I Lied	Yearwood, Trisha	1-639	CB
Believe Me Baby I Lied	Yearwood, Trisha	7-335	MM
Believe Me Baby I Lied	Yearwood, Trisha	4-406	SC
Believe What You Say	Nelson, Ricky	21-709	CB
Believers	Nichols, Joe	37-40	CB
Bell Bottom Blues	Derek & Dominos	28-206	DK
Bell Bottom Blues	Derek & Dominos	20-72	SC
Bella Donna	Nicks, Stevie	47-896	LE
Bella Luna	Mraz, Jason	47-300	KV
Belleau Woods	Brooks, Garth	8-228	CB
Bells the	Color Me Badd	15-760	NU
Bend It Until It Breaks	Anderson, John	22-853	ST
Bend Me Shape Me	American Breed	7-65	MM
Bend Me Shape Me	American Breed	14-337	SC
Bend Me Shape Me	American Breed	10-639	SF
Bend Until It Breaks	Anderson, John	20-113	CB
Bend Until It Breaks	Anderson, John	6-711	MM
Bend Until It Breaks	Anderson, John	17-280	NA
Bend Until It Breaks	Anderson, John	2-572	SC
Beneath Still Waters	Harris, EmmyLou	1-226	CB
Beneath Still Waters	Harris, EmmyLou	4-794	SC
Bennie & The Jets	John, Elton	11-92	DK
Bennie & The Jets	John, Elton	12-680	P
Bent	Matchbox 20	33-408	CB
Bent	Matchbox 20	13-837	PHM
Bent	Matchbox 20	14-469	SC
Bernadette	Four Tops	26-520	DK
Besame Mucho	Beatles	44-121	KV
Best Day Of My Life the	Strait, George	22-527	ST
Best Day the	Swift, Taylor	43-173	CB
Best Days	Cotton, Graham	48-595	DK
Best For Last	Adele	44-171	KV
Best I Can the	Perez, Chris	8-532	PHT
Best I Ever Had	Allan, Gary	23-280	CB
Best Is Yet To Come	Hinder	48-630	CB
Best Is Yet To Come the	Seals, Brady	8-984	CB
Best Is Yet To Come the	Wilson, Nancy	23-348	MM
Best Man the	Larsen, Blaine	23-139	CB
Best Night Ever - duet	Gloriana	43-237	ASK
Best Of Both Worlds the	Montana, Hannah	36-66	WD
Best Of Intentions	Tritt, Travis	14-92	CB
Best Of Intentions	Tritt, Travis	13-862	CHM
Best Of Intentions	Tritt, Travis	19-212	CSZ
Best Of Intentions	Tritt, Travis	22-567	ST
Best Of Love the	Bolton, Michael	10-115	SC
Best Of My Love	Brooks & Dunn	1-85	CB
Best Of My Love	Eagles	7-549	BS
Best Of My Love	Eagles	6-422	MM
Best Of My Love	Eagles	2-263	SC
Best Of My Love	Emotions	11-290	DK

SONG TITLE	ARTIST	#	TYPE
Best Of My Love	Emotions	12-706	P
Best Of My Love	Emotions	5-107	SC
Best Of Times	Styx	47-379	LE
Best Of You	Foo Fighters	23-307	CB
Best Seat In The House	Lo Cash Cowboys	44-279	KCDC
Best That You Can Do	Arthur's Theme	6-889	MM
Best the	Turner, Tina	10-431	LE
Best Thing That Ever Happened To Me	Knight & Pips	13-315	P
Best Thing That Ever Happened To Me	Knight & Pips	2-446	SC
Best Things In Life Are Free	Vandross, Luther	48-291	LE
Best Year Of My Life the	Rabbitt, Eddie	5-325	SC
Best Years Of My Life	Ross, Diana	15-360	LE
Bet Your Heart On Me	Lee, Johnny	47-174	SC
Betch By Golly Wow	Stylistics	9-830	SAV
Beth	Kiss	14-558	AH
Beth	Kiss	10-36	SC
Bette Davis Eyes	Carnes, Kim	2-148	SC
Better As A Memory	Chesney, Kenny	36-427	CB
Better Be Good To Me	Turner, Tina	11-376	DK
Better Be Good To Me	Turner, Tina	10-426	LE
Better Beer	Nicole, Erica	41-55	PHN
Better Beer	Nicole, Erica	47-503	PHN
Better Call Saul	Brown, Junior	47-545	SF
Better Class Of Losers	Travis, Randy	17-148	DK
Better Class Of Losers	Travis, Randy	6-204	MM
Better Days	Citizen King	7-894	PHT
Better Dig Two	Band Perry	40-38	ASK
Better Get To Livin'	Parton, Dolly	30-581	CB
Better I Don't	Janson, Chris	45-379	ASK
Better In Boots	Farr, Tyler	47-928	BKD
Better In The Long Run	Lambert, Miranda	46-267	KV
Better In Time	Lewis, Leona	36-529	CB
Better Life	Urban, Keith	23-413	CB
Better Life	Urban, Keith	29-606	ST
Better Love Next Time	Dr. Hook	21-506	SC
Better Love Next Time a	Haggard, Merle	8-326	CB
Better Man	Morrison, James	38-268	ZM
Better Man	Pearl Jam	9-300	RS
Better Man	Pearl Jam	3-499	SC
Better Man	Warren Brothers	8-352	CB
Better Man a	Black, Clint	1-106	CB
Better Man a	Black, Clint	13-523	P
Better Man a	Black, Clint	8-691	SAV
Better Man Better Off	Lawrence, Tracy	14-654	CB
Better Man Better Off	Lawrence, Tracy	22-406	CHM
Better Not Tell Her	Simon, Carly	49-152	CB
Better Off Alive	Train	48-263	KV
Better Off Alone	DeeJay, Alice	30-630	THM
Better Place Than This	Byrd, Tracy	30-439	CB
Better Than I Used To Be	McGraw, Tim	47-763	SRK
Better Than It Used To Be	Akins, Rhett	8-305	CB
Better Than It Was	Fastball	47-86	CB

21

SONG TITLE	ARTIST	#	TYPE
Better Than Me	Hinder	30-494	CB
Better Things To Do	Clark, Terri	19-302	MH
Better Things To Do	Clark, Terri	6-822	MM
Better To Dream Of You	Carpenter, M C	47-665	CB
Better When I'm Dancing	Trainor, Meghan	46-11	BKD
Better Your Heart Than Mine	Yearwood, Trisha	6-473	MM
Better Your Heart Than Mine	Yearwood, Trisha	2-708	SC
Bettin' Forever On You	Toliver, Tony	24-152	SC
Betty And Dupree	Willis, Chuck	49-734	SRK
Betty Lou's Getting Out	Seger, Bob	10-179	UK
Betty Lou's Got A New Pair Of Shoes	Cafferty, John	45-162	KV
Betty's Bein' Bad	Sawyer Brown	29-695	SC
Betty's Got A Bass Boat	Tillis, Pam	1-462	CB
Betty's Got A Bass Boat	Tillis, Pam	4-504	SC
Between A Rock And A Heartache	Greenwood, Lee	47-128	CB
Between An Old Memory & Me	Tritt, Travis	2-537	SC
Between An Old Memory & Me	Tritt, Travis	22-854	ST
Between Blue Eyes And Jeans	Twitty, Conway	4-549	SC
Between Now And Forever	White, Bryan	7-234	MM
Between Raisin' Hell & Amazing...	Big & Rich	30-549	CB
Between The Devil And Me	Jackson, Alan	1-57	CB
Between The Devil And Me	Jackson, Alan	22-653	ST
Between The Sheets	Isley Brothers	18-489	SAV
Between The Two Of Them	Alabama	4-106	SC
Between The Two Of Them	Tucker, Tanya	1-613	CB
Between The Two Of Them	Tucker, Tanya	2-649	SC
Beverly Hillbillies	TV Themes	2-152	SC
Beverly Hills	Weezer	23-318	CB
Bewildered	Brown, James	29-146	LE
Bewitched Bothered & Bewildered	Baker, Anita	9-792	SAV
Bewitched Bothered & Bewildered	Day, Doris	48-138	ZMP
Beyond The Gray Sky	311	23-273	THM
Beyond The Sea	Darin, Bobby	7-185	MM
Beyond The Sea	Darin, Bobby	12-506	P
Beyond The Sea	Royal Crown Revue	15-212	AMS
Beyond The Sunset	Standard	12-70	DK
BFD	Mattea, Kathy	14-908	CB
BFD	Mattea, Kathy	22-568	ST
Bible Belt	Tritt, Travis	24-88	SC
Bible On The Dash	Lund, Corb	39-89	PHN
Bible Song	Evans, Sara	29-509	SC
Bicycle Race	Queen	20-77	SC
Big Bad John	Dean, Jimmy	8-787	CB

SONG TITLE	ARTIST	#	TYPE
Big Bad John	Dean, Jimmy	9-471	SAV
Big Ball In Cowtown a	Wills, Bob	20-702	CB
Big Balls **	AC/DC	5-551	SC
Big Bang Theory Theme Song	Barenaked Ladies	49-751	KV
Big Battle	Cash, Johnny	45-688	BAT
Big Big Love	lang, k.d.	8-891	CB
Big Big World	Emilia	7-797	PHT
Big Black Man (With Vocals)	Full Monty	36-132	SGB
Big Blue Note	Keith, Toby	23-463	CB
Big Boss Man	King, B.B.	20-136	KB
Big Boss Man	Reed, Jimmy	7-220	MM
Big Boss Man	Rich, Charlie	8-441	CB
Big Bottom **	Spinal Tap	23-18	SC
Big Casino	Jimmy Eat World	49-889	SC
Big City	Haggard, Merle	1-364	CB
Big City	Haggard, Merle	11-432	DK
Big City Nights	Scorpions	49-97	SC
Big Deal	Rimes, LeAnn	5-800	SC
Big Deal	Rimes, LeAnn	22-503	ST
Big Dog Daddy	Keith, Toby	40-28	SC
Big Dreams In A Small Town	Restless Heart	1-412	CB
Big Dreams In A Small Town	Restless Heart	5-674	SC
Big Fat Bitch **	Zac Brown Band	43-473	KV
Big Four Poster Bed	Lee, Brenda	30-330	CB
Big Fun	Gap Band	48-278	SFM
Big Girls Don't Cry	Fergie	30-568	CB
Big Girls Don't Cry	Four Seasons	35-41	CB
Big Girls Don't Cry	Four Seasons	16-840	DK
Big Girls Don't Cry	Four Seasons	13-120	P
Big Girls Don't Cry	Four Seasons	4-10	SC
Big Green Tractor	Aldean, Jason	37-55	CB
Big Guitar	Blackhawk	4-394	SC
Big Guitar	Blackhawk	22-894	ST
Big Heart	Crowell, Rodney	17-247	NA
Big Hunk Of Love	Presley, Elvis	14-768	THM
Big In Vegas	Owens, Buck	5-843	SC
Big Iron	Robbins, Marty	3-227	CB
Big Iron	Robbins, Marty	7-107	MM
Big Iron	Robbins, Marty	4-311	SC
Big Iron Horses	Restless Heart	24-3	SC
Big Love	Byrd, Tracy	1-549	CB
Big Love	Byrd, Tracy	4-462	SC
Big Love	Fleetwood Mac	47-911	LE
Big Love Big Heartache	Presley, Elvis	25-99	MM
Big Machine	Goo Goo Dolls	18-431	CB
Big Machine	Goo Goo Dolls	25-316	MM
Big Man In Town	Four Seasons	43-436	LG
Big Me	Foo Fighters	34-124	CB
Big Me	Foo Fighters	4-664	SC
Big Money	Brooks, Garth	18-10	CB
Big Ol' Truck	Keith, Toby	1-691	CB
Big Ol' Truck	Keith, Toby	6-820	MM
Big Ol' Truck	Keith, Toby	3-423	SC

SONG TITLE	ARTIST	#	TYPE
Big Ole Blew	McDaniel, Mel	4-821	SC
Big One the	Strait, George	6-663	MM
Big One the	Strait, George	2-487	SC
Big Picture	Brokop, Lisa	23-300	CB
Big Poppa **	Notorious B.I.G.	25-470	MM
Big River	Cash, Johnny	29-741	CB
Big River	Cash, Johnny	5-844	SC
Big Rock Candy Mountain	Hartford, John	49-327	CB
Big Rock Candy Mountain	Ives, Burl	44-5	SF
Big Shot	Joel, Billy	6-553	MM
Big Shot	Joel, Billy	17-518	SC
Big Spender	Bassey, Shirley	11-19	PX
Big Spender	Lee, Peggy	47-179	KV
Big Star	Chesney, Kenny	29-423	CB
Big Star	Chesney, Kenny	25-440	MM
Big Star	Chesney, Kenny	18-779	ST
Big Star	Chesney, Kenny	32-116	THM
Big Sur	Thrills	21-606	SF
Big Sweet John - parody	Colter, Ben	45-287	BS
Big Ten Inch Record **	Aerosmith	2-184	SC
Big Time	Adkins, Trace	7-765	CHM
Big Time	Big & Rich	22-24	CB
Big Time	Eder, Linda	16-715	PS
Big Train From Memphis	Fogerty, John	49-104	CDG
Big Wheels In The Moonlight	Seals, Dan	48-103	CB
Big Wind	Wagoner, Porter	19-310	CB
Big Yellow Taxi	Counting Crows	20-470	CB
Big Yellow Taxi	Counting Crows	32-137	THM
Big Yellow Taxi	Grant, Amy	3-430	SC
Big Yellow Taxi	Grant, Amy	19-346	STP
Big Yellow Taxi	Mitchell, Joni	12-101	DK
Big Yellow Taxi	Mitchell, Joni	29-273	SC
Bigbooty	Nelson, Willie	47-733	SRK
Bigger Fish To Fry	Boy Howdy	2-741	SC
Bigger Than My Body	Mayer, John	19-646	CB
Bigger Than My Body	Mayer, John	20-221	MM
Bigger Than My Body	Mayer, John	32-395	THM
Bigger Than The Beatles	Diffie, Joe	1-284	CB
Bigger Than The Beatles	Diffie, Joe	7-178	MM
Bigger Than The Beatles	Diffie, Joe	3-660	SC
Biggest Part Of Me	Ambrosia	29-645	SC
Biggest Part Of Me	Doobie Brothers	47-29	TT
Biker Chick	Messina, Jo Dee	30-530	CB
Biker Chick	Messina, Jo Dee	30-530	CB
Bill Bailey Won't You Please Come	Darin, Bobby	12-653	P
Bill Bailey Won't You Please Come..	Cline, Patsy	22-185	CB
Bill Bailey Won't You Please Come..	Standard	27-458	DK
Bill's Laundromat Bar & Grill	Confederate RR	7-79	MM
Billie Jean	Jackson, Michael	17-20	DK
Billie Jean	Jackson, Michael	14-356	MH
Billion Dollar Babies	Alice Cooper	16-447	SGB

SONG TITLE	ARTIST	#	TYPE
Billion Dollar Babies	Cooper, Alice	37-65	SC
Billionaire - duet	McCoy, T. & Bruno Mars	38-235	CB
Bills Bills Bills	Destiny's Child	13-564	LE
Bills Bills Bills	Destiny's Child	8-505	PHT
Bills Bills Bills	Destiny's Child	10-201	SC
Bills Bills Bills	Destiny's Child	13-775	SGB
Billy Bayou	Reeves, Jim	40-124	CK
Billy Bayou	Reeves, Jim	4-866	SC
Billy Don't Be A Hero	Donaldson, Bo	16-157	SC
Billy Don't Be A Hero	Paper Lace	47-541	ZM
Billy S.	Sweetnam, S.	32-282	THM
Billy The Kid	Dean, Billy	2-614	SC
Billy's Got His Beer Goggles On	McCoy, Neal	23-286	CB
Bimbo	Reeves, Jim	8-574	CB
Bimbo # 5 (Mambo #5 Parody)	Parody	15-339	MM
Bird Dog	Everly Brothers	11-546	DK
Bird Song a	Edwards, Meredith	15-333	CB
Bird the	Reed, Jerry	21-471	SC
Birds And The Bees the	Akens, Jewel	17-108	DK
Birds And The Bees the	Akens, Jewel	13-269	P
Birds And The Bees the	Akens, Jewel	3-267	SC
Birds And The Bees the	Lewis & Playboys	48-560	DK
Birmingham	Marshall, Amanda	24-363	SC
Birmingham Bounce	Foley, Red	43-366	CB
Birmingham Turnaround the	Whitley, Keith	49-401	KVD
Birth Of The Blues	Jazz Standard	47-519	VH
Birth Of The Blues the	Davis, Sammy Jr.	15-849	MM
Birthday	Beatles	17-63	DK
Birthday	Beatles	19-135	KC
Birthday	Beatles	12-870	P
Biscuits	Musgraves, Kacey	45-314	KV
Bitch **	Brooks, Meredith	10-93	SC
Bitch **	Rolling Stones	18-23	LE
Bitch Is Back the **	John, Elton	6-490	MM
Bitch Is Back the **	John, Elton	2-380	SC
Bits & Pieces	Dave Clark Five	10-648	SF
Bitter Bad	Melanie	45-609	OZP
Bitter End a	Dodd, Deryl	8-939	CB
Bitter End a	Dodd, Deryl	22-721	ST
Bitter Green	Lightfoot, Gordon	43-491	SK
Bizarre Love Triangle	New Order	6-31	SC
BJ The DJ	Jackson, Stonewall	8-715	CB
BJ The DJ	Jackson, Stonewall	5-103	SC
Black	Pearl Jam	9-303	RS
Black	Pearl Jam	24-139	SC
Black & White	Moody Blues	17-519	SC
Black & White	Three Dog Night	24-328	SC
Black And Gold	Adele	44-176	KV
Black Balloon	Goo Goo Dolls	33-368	CB
Black Balloon	Goo Goo Dolls	16-190	THM
Black Betty	Jones, Tom	49-269	DFK
Black Betty	Ram Jam Band	4-565	SC
Black Coffee	Dalton, Lacy J.	4-73	SC

23

SONG TITLE	ARTIST	#	TYPE
Black Coffee	Lee, Peggy	47-178	KV
Black Dog	Led Zeppelin	4-558	SC
Black Friday	Steely Dan	15-382	RS
Black Hills Of Dakota the	Day, Doris	48-136	ZMP
Black Hole Sun	Soundgarden	30-744	SF
Black Horse And The Cherry Tree	Tunstall, K.T.	29-276	PHM
Black Is Black	Los Bravos	11-596	DK
Black Is Black	Los Bravos	5-178	SC
Black Magic Woman	Santana	17-119	DK
Black Magic Woman (Radio Version)	Santana	5-878	SC
Black Night	Black Sabbath	45-113	ZM
Black Or White	Jackson, Michael	21-456	CB
Black Or White	Jackson, Michael	28-111	DK
Black Or White	Jackson, Michael	6-180	MM
Black Or White	Jackson, Michael	12-804	P
Black Roses - Nashville	Bowen, Clare	45-461	BKD
Black Sheep	Anderson, John	13-515	P
Black Sheep	Anderson, John	5-620	SC
Black Suits Comin'	Smith, Will	18-216	CB
Black Suits Comin'	Smith, Will	25-255	MM
Black Suits Comin'	Smith, Will	18-144	PHM
Black Tears	Aldean, Jason	45-277	BKD
Black Tears	Aldean, Jason	44-291	BKD
Black Velvet	Lee, Robin	6-620	MM
Black Velvet	Lee, Robin	17-304	NA
Black Velvet	Lee, Robin	4-63	SC
Black Velvet	Myles, Alannah	26-299	DK
Black Velvet	Myles, Alannah	6-171	MM
Black Velvet	Tedeschi, Susan	17-457	AMS
Black Water	Doobie Brothers	29-82	CB
Black Water	Doobie Brothers	11-662	DK
Black Water	Doobie Brothers	13-6	P
Black Water	Doobie Brothers	9-772	SAV
Blackberry	Black Crowes	24-545	SC
Blackbird	Beatles	13-106	P
Blackboard Of My Heart	Thompson, Hank	19-327	CB
Blackout	(HED) Planet Earth	32-183	THM
Blame Canada	South Park	15-340	MM
Blame It On Mama	Jenkins	20-260	PHM
Blame It On Mama	Jenkins	20-347	ST
Blame It On Me	Womack, Lee Ann	48-484	CKC
Blame It On My Youth	Standard	15-407	SGB
Blame It On Texas	Chesnutt, Mark	8-845	CB
Blame It On The Boogie	Jacksons	30-789	SF
Blame It On The Bossanova	Gorme, Eydie	11-257	DK
Blame It On The Fire In My Heart	Bellamy Brothers	45-301	DCK
Blame It On The Mistletoe	Keith, Toby	48-486	CKC
Blame It On Your Heart	Loveless, Patty	1-721	CB
Blame it On Your Heart	Loveless, Patty	6-301	MM
Blame It On Your Heart	Loveless, Patty	12-467	P
Blame It On Your Heart	Loveless, Patty	2-520	SC
Blank Space	Swift, Taylor	48-308	MRH

SONG TITLE	ARTIST	#	TYPE
Blanket On The Ground	Spears, Billie Jo	33-17	CB
Blanket On The Ground	Spears, Billie Jo	10-505	SF
Blaze Of Glory	Bon Jovi	17-110	DK
Blaze Of Glory	Bon Jovi	13-210	P
Bleeding Love	Lewis, Leona	36-446	CB
Bless The Broken Road	Rascal Flatts	22-93	CB
Bless The Broken Road	Rascal Flatts	21-657	SC
Blessed	Aguilera, Christina	14-491	SC
Blessed	John, Elton	13-596	P
Blessed	John, Elton	4-679	SC
Blessed	Lampa, Rachael	34-423	CB
Blessed	McBride, Martina	29-533	CB
Blessed	McBride, Martina	25-63	MM
Blessed	McBride, Martina	16-30	ST
Blessed Are The Believers	Murray, Anne	11-11	PL
Blessed Are The Believers	Murray, Anne	6-77	SC
Blessed Hellride the	Black Label Society	19-856	PHM
Blinded (When I See You)	Third Eye Blind	25-630	MM
Blinded (When I See You)	Third Eye Blind	32-285	THM
Blinded By The Light	Mann, Manfred	3-455	SC
Blinded By The Light	Springsteen, Bruce	20-249	LE
Blink Of An Eye	Ricochet	8-126	CB
Blink Of An Eye	Ricochet	22-644	ST
Blistered	Cash, Johnny	29-752	CB
Blitzkrieg Bop	Ramones	45-84	SC
Blizzard the	Reeves, Jim	45-259	OZP
Blob the - Halloween	Five Blobs	45-121	SC
Blockbuster	Sweet	48-761	P
Blood Brothers	Bryan, Luke	45-427	YBK
Blood Red & Going Down	Tucker, Tanya	13-458	P
Bloody Mary Morning	Nelson, Willie	5-757	SC
Blossom Fell a	Cole, Nat "King"	29-454	LE
Blow Me **	Peters, Red	30-661	RSX
Blow Me **	Peters, Red	5-548	SC
Blow Me A Kiss **	Bob & Tom Band	37-89	SC
Blowin' In The Wind	Dylan, Bob	29-98	CB
Blowin' In The Wind	Peter, Paul & Mary	11-470	DK
Blowin' In The Wind	Peter, Paul & Mary	7-357	MM
Blowin' In The Wind	Peter, Paul & Mary	9-120	PS
Blowin' In The Wind	Peter, Paul & Mary	29-836	SC
Blowin' Me Up	Dub, DF	18-773	PHM
Blowin' Me Up (With Her Love)	Chasez, JC	32-132	THM
Blowin' Smoke	Musgraves, Kacey	41-47	ASK
Blowin' Smoke	Musgraves, Kacey	45-315	ASK
Blown Away	Underwood, Carrie	39-34	ASK
Blue	Rimes, LeAnn	1-286	CB
Blue	Rimes, LeAnn	7-442	MM
Blue	Rimes, LeAnn	4-372	SC
Blue	Rimes, LeAnn	22-892	ST
Blue (Da Da Dee)	Eiffel 65	5-887	SC
Blue (Da Da Dee)	Eiffel 85	34-145	CB
Blue Angel	Orbison, Roy	35-37	CB

SONG TITLE	ARTIST	#	TYPE
Blue Angel	Orbison, Roy	9-191	SO
Blue Bandana	Niemann, Jerrod	47-326	BKD
Blue Bayou	Anderson, Lynn	47-651	SFI
Blue Bayou	Charles, Ray	46-579	KV
Blue Bayou	Orbison, Roy	33-243	CB
Blue Bayou	Orbison, Roy	9-192	SO
Blue Bayou	Ronstadt, Linda	16-767	DK
Blue Bayou	Ronstadt, Linda	9-3	MH
Blue Bayou	Ronstadt, Linda	12-736	P
Blue Bayou	Ronstadt, Linda	10-4	SC
Blue Blue Day	Gibson, Don	3-595	SC
Blue Boy	Reeves, Jim	8-820	CB
Blue Boy	Reeves, Jim	40-125	CK
Blue Boy	Reeves, Jim	5-575	SC
Blue California	Bellamy Brothers	47-744	SRK
Blue Canary	Shore, Dinah	15-408	NK
Blue Clear Sky	Strait, George	7-227	MM
Blue Clear Sky	Strait, George	22-878	ST
Blue Collar Dollar	Engvall, Foxworthy & Stuart	47-62	CB
Blue Collar Dollar	Foxworthy&Engvall	9-422	CB
Blue Collar Man (Long Nights)	Styx	5-592	SC
Blue Denim	Nicks, Stevie	47-900	SC
Blue Eyes Blue	Clapton, Eric	5-783	SC
Blue Eyes Crying In The Rain	Nelson, Willie	15-66	CB
Blue Eyes Crying In The Rain	Nelson, Willie	17-2	DK
Blue Eyes Crying In The Rain	Nelson, Willie	8-707	SAV
Blue Eyes Crying In The Rain	Nelson, Willie	3-638	SC
Blue Eyes Crying In The Rain	Presley, Elvis	25-92	MM
Blue Eyes Crying In The Rain	UB40	49-929	KVD
Blue Eyes Crying In The Rain	Whittaker, Roger	13-586	PL
Blue Hawaii	Presley, Elvis	12-111	DK
Blue Jean Blues	ZZ Top	13-768	SGB
Blue Jean Bop	Vincent, Gene	49-232	DFK
Blue Kentucky Girl	Harris, EmmyLou	8-275	CB
Blue Kentucky Girl	Harris, EmmyLou	11-708	DK
Blue Kentucky Girl	Harris, EmmyLou	13-421	P
Blue Kentucky Girl	Lynn, Loretta	8-385	CB
Blue Memories	Loveless, Patty	1-716	CB
Blue Monday	Domino, Fats	9-741	SAV
Blue Money	Morrison, Van	23-607	BS
Blue Money	Morrison, Van	15-733	SI
Blue Moon	Bennett, Tony	34-445	CB
Blue Moon	Holy, Steve	14-712	CB
Blue Moon	Holy, Steve	19-254	CSZ
Blue Moon	Marcels	16-828	DK
Blue Moon	Marcels	6-152	MM
Blue Moon	Marcels	13-79	P
Blue Moon	Standard	35-32	CB
Blue Moon	Torme, Mel	9-737	SAV

SONG TITLE	ARTIST	#	TYPE
Blue Moon Nights	Fogerty, John	48-650	DCK
Blue Moon Of Kentucky	Cline, Patsy	2-628	SC
Blue Moon Of Kentucky	Harris, EmmyLou	6-735	MM
Blue Moon Of Kentucky	Monroe, Bill	8-249	CB
Blue Moon Of Kentucky	Presley, Elvis	12-189	DK
Blue Moon Of Kentucky	Yoakam, Dwight	49-700	KV
Blue Moon With Heartache	Cash, Roseanne	14-255	SC
Blue Morning Blue Day	Foreigner	16-599	MM
Blue On Black	Shepherd, Kenny	21-558	PHM
Blue On Blue	Vinton, Bobby	11-368	DK
Blue On Blue	Vinton, Bobby	4-35	SC
Blue Ridge Mountain Song	Jackson, Alan	49-14	KV
Blue Ridge Mountain Song	Jackson, Alan	45-104	KV
Blue Rose the	Tillis, Pam	1-454	CB
Blue Side Of Lonesome	Reeves, Jim	8-573	CB
Blue Side Of Town the	Loveless, Patty	1-708	CB
Blue Side the	Gayle, Crystal	48-498	CKC
Blue Skies	Cassidy, Eva	25-675	MM
Blue Skies	Minelli, Liza	49-221	ASK
Blue Skies	Nelson, Willie	35-380	CB
Blue Skies	Nelson, Willie	13-451	P
Blue Skirt Waltz	Waltz Favorites	29-810	SSR
Blue Skirt Waltz - w/Words	Polka Favorites	29-864	SSR
Blue Suede Shoes	Perkins, Carl	33-227	CB
Blue Suede Shoes	Perkins, Carl	8-648	SAV
Blue Suede Shoes	Presley, Elvis	15-272	DK
Blue Suede Shoes	Presley, Elvis	12-657	P
Blue Suede Shoes	Presley, Elvis	4-703	SC
Blue Suede Shoes	Presley, Elvis	14-741	THM
Blue Train the	Ronstadt, Linda	14-875	SC
Blue Velvet	Vinton, Bobby	33-240	CB
Blue Velvet	Vinton, Bobby	9-892	DK
Blue Velvet	Vinton, Bobby	13-101	P
Blueberry Hill	Armstrong, Louis	9-560	SAV
Blueberry Hill	Domino, Fats	11-313	DK
Blueberry Hill	Domino, Fats	14-554	SC
Blueberry Hill	Presley, Elvis	43-241	MM
Bluebird Of Happiness	Standard	47-829	PS
Bluebird the	Murray, Anne	38-4	SC
Bluer Than Blue	Johnson, Michael	20-44	SC
Blues Brothers Medley No 1	Blues Brothers	29-164	ZM
Blues Brothers Medley No 2	Blues Brothers	29-165	ZM
Blues For Dixie	Asleep at the Wheel	24-124	SC
Blues In The Night	Shore, Dinah	11-580	DK
Blues In The Night	Shore, Dinah	47-721	DKM
Blues In The Night	Shore, Dinah	4-347	SC
Blues In The Night	Standard	47-818	DK
Blues Man the	Jackson, Alan	13-806	CHM
Blues Man the	Jackson, Alan	19-256	CSZ
Blues Man the	Jackson, Alan	6-63	SC
Blues Plus Booze (Mean I Lose)	Jackson, Stonewall	46-38	SSK

SONG TITLE	ARTIST	#	TYPE
Bluest Eyes In Texas	Restless Heart	1-406	CB
Bluest Eyes In Texas	Restless Heart	12-427	P
Blurry	Puddle Of Mud	33-426	CB
Blurry	Puddle Of Mud	25-145	MM
Blurry	Puddle Of Mud	16-310	TT
Bo Diddley	Diddley, Bo	6-690	MM
Bo Diddley	Holly, Buddy	3-212	LG
Bo Diddley	Holly, Buddy	11-38	PX
Boardwalk Angel	Royal, Billy Joe	47-371	VH
Boat Drinks	Buffett, Jimmy	42-17	SC
Boat On The River	Styx	47-378	KV
Bob Wills Is Still The King	Jennings, Waylon	22-142	CK
Bobbie Ann Mason	Trevino, Rick	3-415	SC
Bobbie Sue	Oak Ridge Boys	23-494	CB
Bobbie Sue	Oak Ridge Boys	9-508	SAV
Bobbie Sue	Oak Ridge Boys	5-665	SC
Bobby Sox To Stockings	Avalon, Frankie	46-449	LE
Bobby's Girl	Blaine, Marcie	10-327	KC
Bobby's Girl	Blaine, Marcie	9-288	SC
Bodhisattva	Steely Dan	15-396	RS
Bodies	Drowning Pool	16-311	TT
Body & Soul	Baker, Anita	27-306	DK
Body And Soul	Baker, Anita	13-611	P
Body And Soul	Bennett, Tony	10-712	JVC
Body To Body	Cher	21-720	TT
Bohemian Rhapsody	Queen	26-347	DK
Bohemian Rhapsody	Queen	9-677	SAV
Bonaparte's Retreat	Cramer, Floyd	45-579	OZP
Bones	Allan, Gary	43-190	ASK
Bones	Little Big Town	30-201	CB
Boney Maronie	Valens, Richie	45-433	SRK
Bonfire	Morgan, Craig	37-53	CB
Bony Moronie	Williams, Larry	6-686	MM
Bony Moronie	Williams, Larry	11-53	PX
Bony Moronie	Williams, Larry	4-244	SC
Boogie Back To Texas	Asleep At The Wheel	45-863	VH
Boogie Down	Kendricks, Eddie	14-899	DK
Boogie Fever	Sylvers	27-577	DK
Boogie Fever	Sylvers	2-494	SC
Boogie Grass Band	Twitty, Conway	20-660	SC
Boogie Man the	Black, Clint	43-263	CB
Boogie Man the	Black, Clint	20-344	ST
Boogie Nights	Heatwave	14-362	MH
Boogie Nights	Heatwave	15-33	SS
Boogie On Reggae Woman	Wonder, Stevie	11-825	DK
Boogie Oogie Oogie	Taste Of Honey	17-130	DK
Boogie Oogie Oogie	Taste Of Honey	15-42	SS
Boogie Wonderland	Earth Wind & Fire	11-378	DK
Boogie Woogie Bugle Boy	Andrew Sisters	11-581	DK
Boogie Woogie Bugle Boy	Andrew Sisters	12-532	P
Boogie Woogie Bugle Boy	Andrew Sisters	2-238	SC
Boogie Woogie Bugle Boy	Midler, Bette	45-912	CB

SONG TITLE	ARTIST	#	TYPE
Boogie Woogie Bugle Boy	Midler, Bette	45-922	LE
Boogie Woogie Country Man	Lewis, Jerry Lee	47-813	SRK
Boogie Woogie Fiddle Country Blues	Charlie Daniels Band	5-406	SC
Boogie Woogie Fiddle Country Blues	Charlie Daniels Band	37-287	SC
Boogie Woogie Santa Claus - xmas	Page, Patti	45-248	CB
Book Of Love	Monotones	35-6	CB
Book Of Love	Monotones	3-467	SC
Book Of Love the	Air Supply	46-403	SBI
Boom Bang-A-Bang	Lulu	49-54	ZVS
Boom Boom	Animals	12-28	DK
Boom Boom	Travers, Pat	3-614	SC
Boom Boom (Let's Go Back..) **	Lekakis, Paul	15-1	SC
Boom Boom Boom	Hooker, John Lee	20-137	KB
Boom Boom Boom	Hooker, John Lee	7-46	MM
Boom Boom Boom	Hooker, John Lee	15-319	SC
Boombox	Marano, Laura	49-863	DCK
Boondocks	Little Big Town	23-283	CB
Boondocks	Little Big Town	29-503	SC
Boot Scootin' Boogie	Brooks & Dunn	1-79	CB
Boot Scootin' Boogie	Brooks & Dunn	26-325	DK
Boot Scootin' Boogie	Brooks & Dunn	10-762	JVC
Boot Scootin' Boogie	Brooks & Dunn	13-379	P
Boots And Wings	Lambert, Miranda	46-273	KCD
Boots On	Houser, Randy	45-552	AC
Bootylicious	Destiny's Child	18-394	MM
Bootylicious	Destiny's Child	18-508	TT
Bop	Seals, Dan	38-43	CB
Bop	Seals, Dan	6-756	MM
Bop	Seals, Dan	8-692	SAV
Bop To Be	Swan, Billy	47-539	VH
Borderline	Madonna	11-807	DK
Borderline	Madonna	21-154	LE
Borderline	Madonna	14-637	SC
Born Again	Monro, Matt	11-55	PT
Born Country	Alabama	4-436	BS
Born Country	Alabama	33-103	CB
Born Country	Alabama	12-195	DK
Born Country	Alabama	6-196	MM
Born Country	Alabama	5-417	SC
Born Free	Born Free	12-30	DK
Born Free	Kid Rock	37-269	CB
Born Free	Williams, Andy	13-553	LE
Born In A High Wind	Sheppard, T.G.	16-366	CB
Born In The Dark	Stone, Doug	7-148	MM
Born in The Dark	Stone, Doug	3-572	SC
Born In The USA	Springsteen, Bruce	17-615	LE
Born In The USA	Springsteen, Bruce	30-4	MM
Born On The Bayou	CCR	48-366	SC
Born On The Wind	Orbison, Roy	38-51	ZM
Born To Be Alive	Hernandez, Patrick	18-368	AH
Born To Be Alive	Hernandez, Patrick	15-697	LE
Born To Be Blue	Judds	6-537	MM

SONG TITLE	ARTIST	#	TYPE
Born To Be My Baby	Bon Jovi	21-718	CB
Born To Be My Baby	Bon Jovi	11-753	DK
Born To Be Wild	Steppenwolf	11-352	DK
Born To Be Wild	Steppenwolf	6-139	MM
Born To Be Wild	Steppenwolf	13-39	P
Born To Be Wild	Steppenwolf	2-44	SC
Born To Be With You	James, Sonny	19-473	CB
Born To Boogie	Williams, Hank Jr.	6-754	MM
Born To Boogie	Williams, Hank Jr.	13-405	P
Born To Die	Del Rey, Lana	49-72	ZPC
Born To Fly	Evans, Sara	14-91	CB
Born To Fly	Evans, Sara	22-561	ST
Born To Hand Jive	Sha-Na-Na	14-585	SC
Born To Hand Jive - Grease	Grease	49-425	SDK
Born To Lose	Charles, Ray	12-188	DK
Born To Love You	Collie, Mark	2-350	SC
Born To Make You Happy	Spears, Britney	13-559	LE
Born To Run	Harris, EmmyLou	19-447	SC
Born To Run	Springsteen, Bruce	17-607	LE
Born To Run	Springsteen, Bruce	3-454	SC
Born Too Late	Ponytails	7-293	MM
Born Under A Bad Sign	King, Albert	20-135	KB
Born Under A Bad Sign	King, Albert	15-309	SC
Borrowed	Rimes, LeAnn	39-83	PHN
Borrowed Angel	Dennis, Wesley	2-771	SC
Boss	5th Harmony	48-329	MRH
Boss the	Ross, Diana	15-366	LE
Bossa Nova Baby	Presley, Elvis	8-583	CB
Bossa Nova Baby	Presley, Elvis	4-712	SC
Both Sides Now	Collins, Judy	11-630	DK
Both Sides Of Goodbye	Williams, Hank Jr.	4-149	SC
Both Sides Of The Story	Collins, Phil	44-21	SC
Both To Each Other (Friends & Lovers)	Rabbitt & Newton-John	48-39	CB
Bother	Stone Sour	25-431	MM
Bottle Bottle	Brown, Jim Ed	45-691	BAT
Bottle Let Me Down the	Haggard, Merle	8-313	CB
Bottle Of Wine	Fireballs	2-403	SC
Bottle Of Wine And Patsy Cline	Thornton, Marsha	45-508	CB
Bottle Takes Effect	Reeves, Jim	45-262	VH
Bottle Up Lightning	Lady Antebellum	38-111	KV
Bottom Of A Bottle	Smile Empty Soul	32-290	THM
Bottoms Up	Gilbert, Brantley	43-129	ASK
Bottoms Up	Gilbert, Brantley	46-604	BKD
Bottoms Up	Gilbert, Brantley	46-605	KVD
Bottoms Up	Gilbert, Brantley	46-603	PHN
Bounce	Cab the	36-289	PHM
Bounce	Carter, Aaron	16-250	TT
Bouncing Off The Ceiling	A-Teens	18-549	TT
Bouquet Of Roses	Arnold, Eddy	3-673	CB
Bouquet Of Roses	Arnold, Eddy	15-409	NK
Bouquet Of Roses	Arnold, Eddy	17-625	THM
Box the	Travis, Randy	4-64	SC

SONG TITLE	ARTIST	#	TYPE
Box the	Travis, Randy	22-855	ST
Boxer the	Simon & Garfunkel	5-310	SC
Boy (I Need You)	Carey, Mariah	20-464	CB
Boy From New York City the	Ad Libs	19-607	MH
Boy From New York City the	Ad Libs	3-297	MM
Boy From New York City the	Manhattan Transfer	26-330	DK
Boy Is Mine the	Brandy & Monica	21-560	PHM
Boy Is Mine the	Monica & Brandy	13-685	SGB
Boy Like Me, A Girl Like You a	Presley, Elvis	25-98	MM
Boy Like You a	Trick Pony	34-401	CB
Boy Like You a	Trick Pony	25-573	MM
Boy Like You a	Trick Pony	18-798	ST
Boy Like You a	Trick Pony	32-230	THM
Boy Named Sue a	Cash, Johnny	14-238	CB
Boy Named Sue a	Cash, Johnny	6-516	MM
Boy Named Sue a	Cash, Johnny	21-583	SC
Boy Oh Boy	Wilkinsons	8-956	CB
Boy Oh Boy	Wilkinsons	22-676	ST
Boy's Cry	Kane, Eden	10-614	SF
Boyfriend	RaeLynn	48-471	BKD
Boyfriend	Simpson, Ashlee	30-143	PT
Boys	Spears, Britney	34-152	CB
Boys	Spears, Britney	25-304	MM
Boys 'Round Here	Shelton, Blake	43-254	ASK
Boys 'Round Here	Shelton, Blake	43-261	KCD
Boys And Me the	Sawyer Brown	17-164	JVC
Boys Are Back In Town the	Bus Boys	13-660	SGB
Boys Are Back In Town the	Loveless, Patty	17-488	CB
Boys Boys Boys	Lady Gaga	38-189	PS
Boys Do Fall In Love	Gibb, Robin	49-27	SBI
Boys From The South	Pistol Annies	44-152	BKD
Boys Like Girls	Hero/Heroine	37-143	SC
Boys Like Girls	Thunder	36-531	CB
Boys Of Fall the	Chesney, Kenny	37-341	CB
Boys Of Summer	Ataris	25-664	MM
Boys Of Summer the	Ataris	32-327	THM
Boys Of Summer the	Henley, Don	48-151	LE
Boys Round Here	Blake Shelton w Pistol Annies	40-54	ASK
Boys Will Be Boys	Backstreet Boys	30-409	THM
Boyz In The Hood	Dynamite Hack	19-837	SGB
Brady Bunch	TV Themes	2-155	SC
Brady Bunch the	TV Themes	27-404	DK
Brain Stew	Green Day	4-175	SC
Brand New Day	The Wiz	49-433	SDK
Brand New Girlfriend	Holy, Steve	29-198	CB
Brand New Key	Melanie	11-597	DK
Brand New Key	Melanie	4-755	SC
Brand New Man	Brooks & Dunn	1-76	CB
Brand New Man	Brooks & Dunn	12-419	P
Brand New Me a	Springfield, Dusty	11-404	DK
Branded Man	Haggard, Merle	1-367	CB

SONG TITLE	ARTIST	#	TYPE
Branded Man	Haggard, Merle	4-724	SC
Brandy (You're A Fine Girl)	Looking Glass	11-702	DK
Brandy (You're A Fine Girl)	Looking Glass	12-704	P
Brass In Pocket **	Pretenders	5-112	SC
Brass Monkey	Beastie Boys	14-440	SC
Brave	Bareillas, Sara	48-209	KV
Brave Honest Beautiful - duet	5th Harmony & Trainor	48-440	KCD
Brazil	Dorsey, Jimmy	47-33	PS
Brazil	Sinatra, Frank	28-508	DK
Bread & Butter	Newbeats	6-865	MM
Bread & Butter	Newbeats	4-700	SC
Break Down Here	Roberts, Julie	35-432	CB
Break Down Here	Roberts, Julie	30-13	SC
Break Down Here	Roberts, Julie	20-330	ST
Break In The Storm	Great Divide	8-868	CB
Break It Back Down	Green, Pat	45-622	DCK
Break It Down Again	Tears For Fears	16-630	MM
Break It Off	Rihanna	30-260	CB
Break It Off	Rihanna feat Sean Paul	36-97	CB
Break It To Me Gently	Lee, Brenda	30-328	CB
Break It To Me Gently	Newton, Juice	5-22	SC
Break It To Me Gently	Newton, Juice	8-600	TT
Break Me	Jewel	18-218	CB
Break Me	Jewel	25-197	MM
Break My Stride	Wilder, Matthew	4-58	SC
Break On Me	Urban, Keith	48-1	KCD
Break On Me	Urban, Keith	48-738	KV
Break On Me - instrumental	Urban, Keith	48-746	BKD
Break On Through	Doors	34-50	CB
Break On Through	Doors	18-642	SO
Break Out	Swing Out Sister	20-83	SC
Break The Ice	Spears, Britney	36-473	CB
Break These Chains	Allen, Deborah	17-253	NA
Break Up To Make Up	Stylistics	49-455	MM
Break Up With Him	Old Dominion	45-455	BKD
Break Up With Him (Inst)	Old Dominion	49-794	BKD
Breakaway	Clarkson, Kelly	20-543	PHM
Breakaway	Clarkson, Kelly	30-712	SF
Breakdown	Johnson, Jack	29-281	PHM
Breakdown Dead Ahead	Scaggs, Boz	46-318	SC
Breakfast In America	Supertramp	5-587	SC
Breakfast In America	Supertramp	30-754	SF
Breakfast In Birmingham	Murphy, David Lee	48-99	MM
Breakin' Dishes	Rihanna	36-105	CB
Breaking All The Rules	She Moves	5-188	SC
Breaking Point	Moody Blues	45-586	OZP
Breaking The Law	Judas Priest	5-489	SC
Breaking Up Is Hard To Do	Sedaka, Neil	11-268	DK
Breaking Up Is Hard To Do	Sedaka, Neil	12-743	P
Breaking Up Is Hard To Do	Sedaka, Neil	9-168	SO

SONG TITLE	ARTIST	#	TYPE
Breaking Up Is Hard To Do (Slow V)	Sedaka, Neil	5-480	SC
Breaking Your Own Heart	Clarkson, Kelly	47-695	KV
Breakout	Foo Fighters	48-228	SC
Breakup Song	Greg Kihn Band	9-342	AH
Breakup Song	Greg Kihn Band	21-398	SC
Breakup Song	Kihn, Greg	18-578	TT
Breath	Pearl Jam	9-299	RS
Breath Of Life	Florence & Machine	39-113	PHM
Breath You Take the	Strait, George	38-140	CB
Breathe	Branch, Michelle	19-657	CB
Breathe	Branch, Michelle	32-428	THM
Breathe	Cantrell & Paul	25-718	MM
Breathe	Cantrell, Blu	34-144	CB
Breathe	Etheridge, Melissa	20-359	PHM
Breathe	Fabolous	37-99	SC
Breathe	Hill, Faith	22-371	ST
Breathe	Sixpence None The	34-139	CB
Breathe	St. James, Rebecca	35-306	CB
Breathe	Swift, Taylor	43-169	ASK
Breathe	Top Loader	16-312	TT
Breathe (2am)	Nalick, Anna	30-154	PT
Breathe Again	Braxton, Toni	12-131	DK
Breathe Again	Braxton, Toni	16-551	P
Breathe Again	Braxton, Toni	18-816	PS
Breathe In Breathe Out	Kearney, Mat	49-886	SC
Breathe Stretch Shake	Mase & P Diddy	30-809	PHM
Breathe You In	Bentley, Dierks	45-164	PHN
Breathe Your Name	Sixpence None The	25-429	MM
Breathe Your Name	Sixpence None The	18-587	NS
Breathe Your Name	Sixpence None the	32-25	THM
Breathing	Lifehouse	35-237	CB
Breathing	Lifehouse	25-78	MM
Breathless	Corrs	20-621	CB
Breathless	Corrs	14-41	THM
Breathless	Corrs	18-510	TT
Breathless	Jackson, Wanda	46-55	SSK
Breathless	Lewis, Jerry Lee	5-455	SC
Breathless	Presley, Elvis	43-242	PSJT
Breathless	River Road	9-397	CB
Brian Wilson	Barenaked Ladies	5-748	SC
Brian Wilson - 2000 Vers	Barenaked Ladies	30-615	RS
Brian Wilson - Original Vers	Barenaked Ladies	30-627	RS
Brick	Ben Folds Five	5-193	SC
Brick House	Commodores	14-363	MH
Brick House	Richie, Lionel	10-387	LE
Bride the	Trick Pony	30-803	PHM
Bride the	Trick Pony	20-472	ST
Bridge Of Sighs	Trower, Robin	18-257	DK
Bridge Over Troubled Water	Aiken, Clay	19-546	SC
Bridge Over Troubled Water	Murray, Anne	46-13	CKC
Bridge Over Troubled Water	Rimes, LeAnn	1-298	CB
Bridge Over Troubled	Simon & Garfunkel	23-635	BS

SONG TITLE	ARTIST	#	TYPE
Water			
Bridge Over Troubled Water	Simon & Garfunkel	10-367	KC
Bridge Over Troubled Water	Simon & Garfunkel	21-242	SC
Bridge That Just Won't Burn	Twitty, Conway	6-76	SC
Bridge Washed Out the	Mack, Warner	15-85	CB
Bridge Washed Out the	Mack, Warner	4-805	SC
Bright Lights	Matchbox 20	19-651	CB
Bright Lights	Matchbox 20	20-224	MM
Bright Lights	Matchbox 20	32-393	THM
Bright Lights And Country Music	Anderson, Bill	5-420	SC
Bright Lights Big City	James, Sonny	19-477	CB
Bright Lights Big City	James, Sonny	29-651	SC
Bright Side Of The Road	Morrison, Van	23-592	BS
Bright Side Of The Road	Morrison, Van	15-722	SI
Brighter Than Sunshine	Aqualung	30-283	SC
Brighter Than The Sun	Cailliat, Colbie	48-222	PHM
Brilliant Disguise	Springsteen, Bruce	17-613	LE
Bring Back Your Lovin' To Me	Conley, E.T.	47-601	CB
Bring It All For My Baby	Lewis & The News	9-790	SAV
Bring It All To Me	Blaque & N'Sync	15-774	BS
Bring It All To Me	Blaque & N'Sync	15-296	CB
Bring It All To Me	Blaque & N'Sync	5-898	SC
Bring It On Home	Little Big Town	29-193	CB
Bring it On Home To Me	Animals	43-423	EZH
Bring It On Home To Me	Animals	37-273	ZM
Bring It On Home To Me	Cooke, Sam	46-640	RB
Bring It On Home To Me	Gilley, Mickey	16-175	THM
Bring It On Home To Me	Williamson, Sonny	14-596	SC
Bring Me Down	Lambert, Miranda	23-118	CB
Bring Me Down	Lambert, Miranda	23-381	SC
Bring Me Some Water	Etheridge, Melissa	4-540	SC
Bring Me Sunshine	Nelson, Willie	47-515	VH
Bring Me To Life	Evanescence	20-514	CB
Bring Me To Life	Evanescence	25-584	MM
Bring Me To Life	Evanescence	32-178	THM
Bring On The Rain	Messina, Jo Dee	33-132	CB
Bring On The Rain	Messina, Jo Dee	15-852	ST
Bring Out The Elvis	Hill, Faith	14-724	CB
Bringin' It Back	Presley, Elvis	25-741	MM
Bringin' On The Heartbreak	Def Leppard	23-47	MH
Britches	Presley, Elvis	45-613	HM
Broadway	Goo Goo Dolls	35-223	CB
Broadway Baby	Sondheim, Stephen	17-770	PS
Broadway Baby - show	Dames At Sea	48-784	MM
Broken	Childs, Andy	24-79	SC
Broken	Haun, Lindsey	30-176	CB
Broken	Lifehouse	36-503	CB
Broken Arrow	Script	39-122	PHM
Broken Down In Tiny Pieces	Craddock, Billy C	4-825	SC
Broken Hearted Me	Murray, Anne	29-788	CB
Broken Hearted Me	Murray, Anne	11-12	PL

SONG TITLE	ARTIST	#	TYPE
Broken Hearted Me	Murray, Anne	9-831	SAV
Broken Hearted Me	Murray, Anne	5-25	SC
Broken Lady	Gatlin, Larry	34-221	CB
Broken Lady	Gatlins	13-516	P
Broken Lady	Gatlins	8-688	SAV
Broken Promised Land	Chesnutt, Mark	1-350	CB
Broken Road	Crittenden, Melodie	8-406	CB
Broken Road	Crittenden, Melodie	7-733	CHM
Broken Strings - duet	Morrison, James	38-274	EK
Broken Trust	Lee, Brenda	30-335	CB
Broken Vow	Groban, Josh	43-305	CB
Broken Wing a	McBride, Martina	1-387	CB
Broken Wing a	McBride, Martina	22-645	ST
Broken Wings	Mr. Mister	11-658	DK
Broken Wings	Mr. Mister	12-819	P
Brokenhearted - duet	Brandy	34-123	CB
Brokenheartsville	Nichols, Joe	34-370	CB
Brokenheartsville	Nichols, Joe	25-413	MM
Brokenheartsville	Nichols, Joe	18-450	ST
Brokenheartsville	Nichols, Joe	32-42	THM
Brotha (Part II)	Stone, Keys & Eve	25-686	MM
Brother Jukebox	Chesnutt, Mark	8-848	CB
Brother Jukebox	Chesnutt, Mark	20-398	MH
Brother Jukebox	Chesnutt, Mark	17-212	NA
Brother Louie	Stories	11-382	DK
Brother Louie	Stories	2-441	SC
Brother Love's Travelin' Salvation Show	Diamond, Neil	7-530	AH
Brother Love's Travelin' Salvation Show	Diamond, Neil	18-689	PS
Brother Love's Travelin' Salvation Show	Diamond, Neil	24-698	SC
Brother Love's Travelin' Salvation Show	Diamond, Neil	30-499	THM
Brothers	Bates, Greg	39-75	PHN
Brothers	Brody, Dean	36-275	PHM
Brown Eyed Girl	Morrison, Van	23-597	BS
Brown Eyed Girl	Morrison, Van	17-339	DK
Brown Eyed Girl	Morrison, Van	13-254	P
Brown Eyed Girl	Steel Pulse	25-386	MM
Brown Eyed Handsome Man	Berry, Chuck	46-227	SC
Brown Eyed Handsome Man	Holly, Buddy	3-217	LG
Brown Eyed Handsome Man	Holly, Buddy	11-35	PX
Brown Eyed Handsome Man	Holly, Buddy	10-641	SF
Brown Skin	India.Arie	25-687	MM
Brown Sugar	Rolling Stones	19-759	LE
Brown Sugar	Rolling Stones	14-391	PT
Bruises	Train	48-265	KV
Bubba Hyde	Diamond Rio	1-173	CB
Bubba Hyde	Diamond Rio	6-707	MM
Bubba Hyde	Diamond Rio	4-65	SC
Bubba Shot The Jukebox	Chesnutt, Mark	8-846	CB
Bubba Shot The	Chesnutt, Mark	10-761	JVC

29

SONG TITLE	ARTIST	#	TYPE
Jukebox			
Bubba Shot The Jukebox	Chesnutt, Mark	6-112	MM
Bubblegoose **	Wycliff	13-724	SGB
Bubbles In My Beer	Wills, Bob	20-691	CB
Bubbles In My Beer	Wills, Bob	47-496	CB
Bubbletoes	Johnson, J	32-63	THM
Bubbly	Caillat, Colbie	30-591	PHM
Bubbly	Caillat, Colbie	37-16	PS
Buck These Haggard Blues	Big House	14-727	CB
Buckaroo	Womack, Lee Ann	34-326	CB
Buckaroo	Womack, Lee Ann	7-748	CHM
Buffalo Gals	Standard	27-415	DK
Bug the	Carpenter, M C	6-389	MM
Bug the	Carpenter, M C	15-164	THM
Buicks To The Moon	Jackson, Alan	44-81	PS
Build Me Up Buttercup	Foundations	12-47	DK
Building A Mystery	McLachlan, Sarah	14-189	CB
Building A Mystery	McLachlan, Sarah	15-461	SC
Building Bridges	Brooks & Dunn	29-593	CB
Built For Blue Jeans	Dean, Tyler	30-118	CB
Built For Blue Jeans	Tyler, Dean	30-118	CB
Bull And The Beaver the	Haggard & Williams	5-445	SC
Bullet With Butterfly Wings	Smashing Pumpkins	28-442	DK
Bullets	Creed	18-295	CB
Bullets	Editors	30-748	SF
Bullets In The Gun	Keith, Toby	38-162	PHM
Bullett With Butterfly Wings	Smashing Pumpkins	34-141	CB
Bullitproof	Pacifier	32-110	THM
Bump 'N Grind	Kelly, R.	2-473	SC
Bump Bump Bump	B2K & P Diddy	32-122	THM
Bump Bump Bump	P. Diddy	32-122	THM
Bumper Of My SUV the	Wright, Chely	22-102	CB
Bumpin' The Night	Florida Georgia Line	46-99	SBI
Buncha Girls a	Ballard, Frankie	37-352	CB
Bundle Of Nerves	Mellons, Ken	8-852	CB
Bungle In The Jungle	Tull, Jethro	14-559	AH
Bungle In The Jungle	Tull, Jethro	12-329	DK
Bungle In The Jungle	Tull, Jethro	20-313	MH
Bungle In The Jungle	Tull, Jethro	17-513	SC
Bunny Hop the - DANCE #	Anthony, Ray	22-387	SC
Burdening My Mind	Soundgarden	24-112	SC
Burgers And Fries	Pride, Charley	3-790	CB
Burgers And Fries	Pride, Charley	5-32	SC
Buried Myself Alive	Used	32-179	THM
Buried Treasure	Rogers, Kenny	3-175	CB
Burn	Goulding, Ellie	43-183	ASK
Burn	Messina, Jo Dee	14-146	CB
Burn	Messina, Jo Dee	22-456	ST
Burn	Messina, Jo Dee	14-32	THM
Burn Down The Trailer Park	Cyrus, Billy Ray	14-788	ST
Burn Me Down	Stuart, Marty	3-640	SC
Burn One Down	Black, Clint	30-422	THM

SONG TITLE	ARTIST	#	TYPE
Burn One Down For Me	Black, Clint	1-116	CB
Burn One Down For Me	Black, Clint	6-121	MM
Burn These Memories Down	Moore, Lathan	41-87	PHN
Burnin' It Down	Aldean, Jason	44-320	SBI
Burnin' The Roadhouse Down	Wariner w/Brooks	22-826	ST
Burnin' The Roadhouse Down	Wariner, Steve	8-738	CB
Burnin' Up	Jonas Brothers	36-488	CB
Burning A Hole In My Mind	Smith, Connie	48-95	CB
Burning Bridges	Campbell, Glen	47-525	VH
Burning Bridges	OneRepublic	47-334	KV
Burning Down The House	Talking Heads	11-623	DK
Burning Down The House	Talking Heads	12-787	P
Burning Down The House	Talking Heads	29-260	SC
Burning House	Cam	45-409	BKD
Burning Love	Judd, Wynonna	48-318	KV
Burning Love	Presley, Elvis	11-148	DK
Burning Love	Presley, Elvis	12-677	P
Burning Love	Presley, Elvis	2-584	SC
Burning Love	Presley, Elvis	14-769	THM
Burning Memories	Price, Ray	44-218	DFK
Burning Old Memories	Mattea, Kathy	4-74	SC
Bury Me Beneath The Willow	White, Clarence	45-685	VH
Bury The Shovel	Walker, Clay	1-99	CB
Bury The Shovel	Walker, Clay	4-463	SC
Bus Stop	Hollies	17-359	DK
Bus Stop	Hollies	44-364	LG
Bus Stop	Hollies	19-101	SAV
Bushel And A Peck	Guys And Dolls	49-773	PS
Bust A Move	Young MC	34-136	CB
Bust A Move	Young MC	11-496	DK
Bust A Move	Young MC	16-531	P
Busted	Charles, Ray	46-576	JVC
Busted	Conlee, John	17-400	DK
Busted	Conlee, John	17-303	NA
Busted	Conlee, John	5-124	SC
Busy Being Fabulous	Eagles	49-708	ST
Busy Man	Cyrus, Billy Ray	8-859	CB
Busy Man	Cyrus, Billy Ray	22-700	ST
But Anyway	Blues Traveler	33-335	CB
But Anyway	Blues Traveler	24-47	SC
But Beautiful	Streisand, Barbra	49-605	PS
But For The Grace Of God	Urban, Keith	14-124	CB
But For The Grace Of God	Urban, Keith	14-16	CHM
But For The Grace Of God	Urban, Keith	19-217	CSZ
But I Do	Henry, C. Frogman	7-303	MM
But I Do	Henry, C. Frogman	11-47	PX
But I Do	Henry, C. Frogman	4-252	SC

30

SONG TITLE	ARTIST	#	TYPE
But I Do Love You	Anka, Paul	46-594	DCK
But I Do Love You	Rimes, LeAnn	30-444	CB
But I Do Love You	Rimes, LeAnn	14-837	ST
But I Will	Hill, Faith	15-681	CB
But I Will	Hill, Faith	6-594	MM
But I Will	Hill, Faith	17-223	NA
But I Will	Hill, Faith	2-315	SC
But It's Alright	Lewis & The News	6-640	MM
But It's Better If You Do	Panic at the Disco	30-58	PHM
But Not For Me	Baker, Chet	9-793	SAV
But Not For Me	Connick, Harry Jr.	3-124	KB
But Not For Me	Connick, Harry Jr.	19-715	PS
But Not For Me	Newton, Wayne	47-316	LE
But She Loves Me	Whittaker, Roger	13-593	PL
But The World Goes 'Round	Garland, Judy	48-274	LE
But You Know I Love You	Parton, Dolly	38-40	SC
But You Love Me Daddy	Reeves, Jim	49-741	DCK
But You Love Me Daddy	Reeves, Jim	44-240	DCK
Butterflies	Jackson, Michael	25-76	MM
Butterflies	Jackson, Michael	16-76	ST
Butterfly	Carey, Mariah	7-695	PHM
Butterfly	Crazy Town	34-121	CB
Butterfly	Crazy Town	16-475	MH
Butterfly	Crazy Town	12-392	PHM
Butterfly	Crazy Town	16-111	PRT
Butterfly	Crazy Town	18-550	TT
Butterfly Kisses	Carlisle, Bob	10-20	SC
Butterfly Kisses	Carson, Jeff	22-599	ST
Butterfly Kisses	Raybon Brothers	16-577	SC
Butterfly Kisses (Country Version)	Carlisle, Bob	7-636	CHM
Buttons	Pussycat Dolls w Snoop Dogg	30-734	SF
Buttons And Bows	Shore, Dinah	17-399	DK
Buttons And Bows	Shore, Dinah	21-17	SC
Buy Me A Boat	Janson, Chris	45-28	BKD
Buy Me A Boat (Inst)	Janson, Chris	49-738	BKD
Buy Me A Rose	Rogers, Kenny	5-836	SC
Buy Me A Rose	Rogers, Kenny	22-521	ST
Buy Me A Rose	Vandross, Luther	46-200	SC
Buzz Back	Rice, Chase	45-623	PHN
Buzzkill	Bryan, Luke	44-328	SSC
By My Side	Morgan & Randall	8-123	CB
By My Side	Morgan & Randall	7-251	MM
By My Side	Morgan, Lorrie	22-888	ST
By The Book	Peterson, Michael	22-692	ST
By The Light Of The Silvery Moon	Day, Doris	48-144	SFD
By The Light Of The Silvery Moon	Miller, Mitch	23-540	CB
By The Time I Get To Phoenix	Campbell, Glen	16-869	DK
By The Time I Get To Phoenix	Campbell, Glen	13-447	P
By The Time This Night Is Over	Bryson w/Kenny G..	2-268	SC

SONG TITLE	ARTIST	#	TYPE
By The Time This Night Is Over	Bryson, Peabo	6-369	MM
By The time This Night Is Over	Bryson, Peabo	9-214	SO
By The Way	Red Hot Chili Peppe	25-342	MM
By The Way She's Lookin'	Hunter, Jesse	24-346	SC
By Your Side	Sade	20-618	CB
By Your Side	Sade	30-779	SF
Bye Bye	Carey, Mariah	36-483	CB
Bye Bye	Messina, Jo Dee	8-236	CB
Bye Bye	Messina, Jo Dee	22-759	ST
Bye Bye Baby (Baby Goodbye)	Four Seasons	43-434	LG
Bye Bye Blackbird	Miller, Mitch	23-541	CB
Bye Bye Blackbird	Newton, Wayne	47-311	LE
Bye Bye Bye	N'Sync	20-427	CB
Bye Bye Bye	N'Sync	29-170	MH
Bye Bye Love	Charles, Ray	46-573	CB
Bye Bye Love	Everly Brothers	17-343	DK
Bye Bye Love	Everly Brothers	7-295	MM
Bye Bye Love	Everly Brothers	13-77	P
Bye Bye Love	Everly Brothers	3-334	PS
Bye Bye Love	Everly Brothers	19-104	SAV
Bye Bye Love	Simon & Garfunkel	49-767	LG
C C Rider	Presley, Elvis	14-770	THM
C.O.U.N.T.R.Y.	LoCash Cowboys	49-530	ZP
C'Est La Vie	B*Witched	7-845	PHM
C'Est La Vie	Berry, Chuck	11-43	PX
C'Est La Vie	Seger, Bob	5-305	SC
C'Est La Vie	Twain, Shania	23-429	CB
C'Mon	Mario	18-771	PHM
C'mon And Swim - DANCE #	Freeman, Bobby	22-397	SC
C'Mon C'Mon	Crow, Sheryl	25-436	MM
C'mon C'mon	Crow, Sheryl	18-609	PHM
C'Mon C'Mon	Crow, Sheryl	29-677	RS
C'Mon Everybody	Cochran, Eddie	27-494	DK
C'Mon!	Anderson, Keith	36-220	PHM
Cab	Train	29-278	PHM
Cab Driver	Mills Brothers	47-261	AH
Cab Driver (Quartet)	Standard	10-474	MG
Cab Driver (Solo)	Standard	10-464	MG
Cabaret	Armstrong, Louis	46-445	PS
Cabaret	Minelli, Liza	49-224	MM
Cable Car (Over My Head)	Fray	30-282	SC
Cabo San Lucas	Keith, Toby	45-67	DFK
Cactus In A Coffee Can	Kilgore, Jerry	14-79	CB
Cadillac Cadillac	Train	48-269	ZPC
Cadillac Land	Springsteen, Bruce	20-240	LE
Cadillac Ranch	LeDoux, Chris	17-165	JVC
Cadillac Style	Kershaw, Sammy	1-466	CB
Cadillac Style	Kershaw, Sammy	13-512	P
Cadillac Tears	Denney, Kevin	25-295	MM
Cadillac Tears	Denney, Kevin	17-582	ST
Café On The Corner	Sawyer Brown	5-31	SC
Cain's Blood	4 Runner	6-809	MM

SONG TITLE	ARTIST	#	TYPE
Cain's Blood	4 Runner	2-826	SC
Caisson's Song	Patriotic	44-41	PT
Cajun - Cajun Baby	Williams, Hank Jr.	49-387	SC
Cajun - Cajun Hoedown	McDawn, Karen	49-386	VH
Cajun - Cajun Moon	Skaggs, Ricky	49-388	SC
Cajun - Cajun Queen	O'Neil, Todd	49-389	CB
Cajun - Cajun Twist	Randy & the Rockets	49-403	SCK
Cajun - Loving Cajun Style	Rich, Don	49-404	SCK
Cajun - Mona Lisa	Cajun	49-405	SCK
Cajun - Tee Na Na	Cajun	49-293	GS
Cajun Baby	Williams, Hank Jr.	49-387	SC
Cajun Hoedown	McDawn, Karen	45-870	VH
Cajun Moon	Skaggs, Ricky	20-22	SC
Cajun Moon	Skaggs, Ricky	49-388	SC
Cajun Queen	O'Neil, Todd	49-389	CB
Cajun Twist	Randy & the Rockets	49-403	SCK
Cake By The Ocean	DNCE	49-658	BKD
Caldonia	King, B.B.	14-591	SC
Calendar Girl	Sedaka, Neil	26-417	DK
Calendar Girl	Sedaka, Neil	14-346	SC
Calendar Girl	Sedaka, Neil	9-164	SO
California Dreamin'	Mamas & Papas	11-351	DK
California Dreamin'	Mamas & Papas	6-156	MM
California Dreamin'	Mamas & Papas	13-54	P
California Dreamin'	Mamas & Papas	9-115	PS
California Girls	Beach Boys	5-498	BS
California Girls	Beach Boys	16-758	DK
California Girls	Wilson, Gretchen	30-82	CB
California Here I Come	Jolson, Al	29-469	LE
California Here I Come	Jolson, Al	12-935	PS
California Nights	Gore, Lesley	4-715	SC
California Promises	Buffett, Jimmy	47-793	SRK
California Sun	Riviera's	12-663	P
Californication	Red Hot Chili Peppe	15-430	PHM
Californication	Red Hot Chili Peppe	19-606	SGB
Call And Answer	Barenaked Ladies	34-131	CB
Call And Answer	Barenaked Ladies	7-890	PHT
Call And Answer	Barenaked Ladies	30-622	RS
Call Me	Blondie	15-412	DK
Call Me	Blondie	24-558	SC
Call Me Crazy	Lost Trailers	29-579	CB
Call Me Crazy	VanShelton, Ricky	14-144	CB
Call Me Irresponsible	Sinatra, Frank	15-462	DK
Call Me Irresponsible	Standard	47-821	DK
Call Me Maybe	Boyce Avenue	46-95	KV
Call Me Maybe	Jepson, Carly Rae	39-44	ASK
Call Me Red	Brandt, Lindsay	41-83	PHN
Call Me The Breeze	Lynyrd Skynyrd	5-257	SC
Call Me The Breeze	Lynyrd Skynyrd	19-807	SGB
Call Me The Breeze	Mayer, John	42-15	PHM
Call Me When You're Sober	Evanescense	47-873	CB
Call Me When You're Sober	Evanescense	48-602	DK

SONG TITLE	ARTIST	#	TYPE
Call My Job	King, Albert	19-800	SGB
Call My Name	Prince	49-823	CB
Call Of The Wild the	Tippin, Aaron	2-703	SC
Call On Me	Tucker, Tanya	38-10	CB
Call the	Backstreet Boys	12-387	PHM
Call the - duet	Brooks & Yearwood	48-346	KV
Call The Man	Dion, Celine	15-116	BS
Callin' Baton Rouge	Brooks, Garth	20-410	MH
Callin' Baton Rouge	Brooks, Garth	2-704	SC
Calling All Angels	Train	19-596	CB
Calling All Angels	Train	25-622	MM
Calling All Angels	Train	32-281	THM
Calling All Girls	ATL	32-423	THM
Calling Me - duet	Rogers & Henley	30-348	CB
Calling Occupants Of Interplanetary...	Carpenters	45-804	LE
Calling Out Your Name	Nail, Jimmy	47-706	DCK
Calling You	Streisand, Barbra	49-611	PS
Calling You	Williams, Hank Sr.	37-197	CB
Calypso	Denver, John	36-146	LE
Came Here To Forget	Shelton, Blake	49-370	BKD
Came Here To Forget	Shelton, Blake	49-3	DCK
Camouflage	Paisley, Brad	45-58	KST
Camouflage	Paisley, Brad	44-314	SBI
Can Anybody Hear Me	Diamond, Neil	47-416	PS
Can I Come Home	Bellamy Brothers	24-129	SC
Can I Come Over Tonight	Wariner, Steve	8-931	CB
Can I Count On You	McBride & The Ride	2-613	SC
Can I Get A...	Jay-Z&Amil&Ja-Rule	14-445	SC
Can I Get your Number	No Authority	15-451	PHM
Can I See You Tonight	Tucker, Tanya	5-56	SC
Can I Steal A Little Love	Sinatra, Frank	10-721	JVC
Can I Steal A Little Love	Sinatra, Frank	49-484	MM
Can I Trust You With My Heart	Tritt, Travis	1-662	CB
Can I Trust You With My Heart	Tritt, Travis	17-386	DK
Can I Trust You With My Heart	Tritt, Travis	6-222	MM
Can U Help Me	Usher	34-172	CB
Can We	SWV	10-91	SC
Can We Talk	Campbell, Tevin	28-116	DK
Can You Feel It	Family Force 5	38-251	PHM
Can You Feel The Love Tonight	John, Elton	11-67	JTG
Can You Feel The Love Tonight	Lion King	20-185	Z
Can You Find It In Your Heart	Bennett, Tony	25-258	MM
Can You Hear Me Now	Sawyer Brown	17-576	ST
Can You Hear Me When I Talk To U	Gearing, Ashley	25-650	MM
Can You Hear Me When I Talk To U	Gearing, Ashley	19-177	ST
Can You Hear Me When I Talk To You	Gearing, Ashley	32-341	THM
Can You Read My Mind	McGovern, Maureen	7-184	MM

SONG TITLE	ARTIST	#	TYPE
Can't Be Really Gone	McGraw, Tim	1-532	CB
Can't Be Really Gone	McGraw, Tim	7-173	MM
Can't Be Really Gone	McGraw, Tim	3-627	SC
Can't Believe	Evans, Faith	18-511	TT
Can't Break It To My Heart	Lawrence, Tracy	6-400	MM
Can't Buy Me Love	Beatles	11-87	DK
Can't Buy Me Love	Beatles	13-80	P
Can't Cry Anymore	Crow, Sheryl	29-668	RS
Can't Even Get The Blues	McEntire, Reba	1-783	CB
Can't Even Get The Blues	McEntire, Reba	13-412	P
Can't Even Get The Blues	McEntire, Reba	5-30	SC
Can't Fight The Moonlight	Rimes, LeAnn	14-131	CB
Can't Fight This Feeling	REO Soeedwagon	29-297	SC
Can't Fight This Feeling	REO Speedwagon	20-294	CB
Can't Find My Way Back Home	Blind Faith	10-479	DA
Can't Get By Without You	Real Thing	10-544	SF
Can't Get Enough	Loveless, Patty	1-729	CB
Can't Get Enough	Loveless, Patty	22-726	ST
Can't Get Enough Of You	Smash Mouth	7-772	PHT
Can't Get Enough Of You Baby	Smash Mouth	34-147	CB
Can't Get Enough Of Your Love	Dayne, Taylor	24-150	SC
Can't Get Enough Of Your Love	White, Barry	35-118	CB
Can't Get Enough Of Your Love	White, Barry	6-566	MM
Can't Get Enough Of Your Love	White, Barry	16-553	P
Can't Get Enough Of Your Love	White, Barry	4-758	SC
Can't Get It Out Of My Head	ELO	17-514	SC
Can't Get Nowhere	Tractors	17-480	CB
Can't Get Used To Losing You	Williams, Andy	12-29	DK
Can't Get Used To Losing You	Williams, Andy	2-199	SC
Can't Get You Out Of My Head	Minogue, Kylie	33-430	CB
Can't Get You Out Of My Head	Minogue, Kylie	25-142	MM
Can't Get You Out Of My Head	Minogue, Kylie	21-721	TT
Can't Help Falling In Love	Presley, Elvis	12-86	DK
Can't Help Falling In Love	Presley, Elvis	2-605	SC
Can't Help Falling In Love	Presley, Elvis	14-742	THM
Can't Hold Us Down **	Aguilera & Lil Kim	21-796	SC
Can't Keep A Good Man	Alabama	1-11	CB

SONG TITLE	ARTIST	#	TYPE
Down			
Can't Keep A Good Man Down	Alabama	5-152	SC
Can't Keep It In	Stevens, Cat	23-646	BS
Can't Keep It In	Stevens, Cat	13-574	NU
Can't Let Go	Adele	49-6	DCK
Can't Let Go	Carey, Mariah	9-662	SAV
Can't Let Go	Monroe, Ashley	48-737	VH
Can't No Body Love You Like I Do	Judd, Wynonna	22-523	ST
Can't Nobody	Rowland, Kelly	34-173	CB
Can't Nobody	Rowland, Kelly	19-348	STP
Can't Nobody	Rowland, Kelly	32-166	THM
Can't Run From Yourself	Tucker, Tanya	38-11	CB
Can't Smile Without You	Carpenters	44-350	KV
Can't Smile Without You	Manilow, Barry	29-115	CB
Can't Smile Without you	Manilow, Barry	11-689	DK
Can't Smile Without You	Manilow, Barry	6-547	MM
Can't Smile Without You	Manilow, Barry	13-151	P
Can't Smile Without You	Manilow, Barry	9-78	PS
Can't Stay Away From You	Estefan, Gloria	30-1	PT
Can't Stop	Red Hot Chili Peppe	20-456	CB
Can't Stop	Red Hot Chili Peppe	23-170	PHM
Can't Stop Dancin'	Captain & Tennille	46-554	CB
Can't Stop Fallin' Into Love	Cheap Trick	17-82	DK
Can't Stop Fallin' Into Love	Cheap Trick	9-678	SAV
Can't Stop Loving You	Collins, Phil	25-398	MM
Can't Stop Loving You	Collins, Phil	23-339	SC
Can't Stop My Heart From Loving You	Neville, Aaron	14-870	SC
Can't Stop Myself From Loving You	Loveless, Patty	1-719	CB
Can't Stop Myself From Loving You	Loveless, Patty	2-709	SC
Can't Stop Thinkin' 'Bout You	Ricochet	10-167	SC
Can't Stop Thinking 'Bout That	Ricochet	22-708	ST
Can't Stop This Thing We Started	Adams, Bryan	21-465	CB
Can't Stop This Thing We Started	Adams, Bryan	16-408	PR
Can't Take My Eyes Off Of You	Hill, Lauryn	19-723	CB
Can't Take My Eyes Off Of You	Valli, Frankie	11-335	DK
Can't Take My Eyes Off Of You	Valli, Frankie	9-37	MM
Can't Take My Eyes Off You	Lady Antebellum	46-85	BKD
Can't Take My Eyes Off You	Williams, Andy	49-42	ZVS
Can't Take That Away From Me	Newton, Wayne	47-313	LE
Can't Tell Me Nothin'	Cotter, Brad	22-70	CB
Can't Turn Back The Years	Collins, Phil	44-20	SC

SONG TITLE	ARTIST	#	TYPE
Can't Turn You Loose	Blues Brothers	38-30	TT
Can't Turn You Loose (Live)	Redding, Otis	46-163	SC
Can't We Be Friends	Ronstadt, Linda	9-832	SAV
Can't We Talk It Over In Bed	Newton-John, Olivia	18-391	SAV
Can't We Try - duet	Sheppard & Hill	35-313	CB
Can't You Hear My Heartbeat	Herman's Hermits	12-194	DK
Can't You Hear My Heartbeat	Herman's Hermits	30-776	SF
Can't You See	Humperdinck, E.	49-260	DFK
Can't You See	Jennings, Waylon	22-146	CK
Can't You See	Marshall Tucker Ban	9-323	AG
Can't You See	Marshall Tucker Ban	18-153	CB
Can't You See	Marshall Tucker Ban	3-611	SC
Can't You See	Marshall Tucker Ban	13-761	SGB
Can't You See	Marshall Tucker Band	47-559	SC
Can't You See That She's Mine	Dave Clark Five	45-81	LE
Can't You See That She's Mine	Dave Clark Five	43-214	SC
Can't You Tell	Diamond Rio	23-399	CB
Can't You Tell	Diamond Rio	30-11	SC
Can't Break It To My Heart	Lawrence, Tracy	1-575	CB
Can't Buy Me Love	Beatles	9-643	SAV
Can't Help Calling Your Name	Sellers, Jason	9-391	CB
Can't Stop Now	Keane	21-688	Z
Can't Take My Eyes Off Of You	Hill, Lauryn	13-672	SGB
Can't You See	Marshall Tucker Ban	20-311	MH
Canadian RR Trilogy	Lightfoot, Gordon	43-496	SK
Candida	Orlando & Dawn	3-245	LG
Candida	Orlando & Dawn	21-809	SC
Candle In The Wind	John, Elton	33-327	CB
Candle In The Wind	John, Elton	11-295	DK
Candle In The Wind	John, Elton	16-521	P
Candle In The Wind	John, Elton	2-378	SC
Candy Cane Christmas	Rucker, Darius	45-769	CK
Candy Everybody Wants	10,000 Maniacs	12-112	DK
Candy Girl	Four Seasons	22-441	SC
Candy Kisses	Morgan, George	19-842	CB
Candy Kisses	Morgan, George	8-664	SAV
Candy Man	Davis, Sammy Jr.	34-5	CB
Candy Man	Orbison, Roy	9-193	SO
Candy Man	Poole & Tremeloes	10-657	SF
Candy Man the	Davis, Sammy Jr.	11-311	DK
Candy Man the	Davis, Sammy Jr.	20-760	KB
Cannonball	Breeders	5-738	SC
Cannonball (Remix)	Rice, Damien	20-355	PHM
Captain Jack	Joel, Billy	15-751	AMS
Captain Jack	Joel, Billy	21-517	SC
Captive Heart	Selena	23-569	MM
Captive Heart	Selena	21-451	PS
Car the	Carson, Jeff	3-564	SC

SONG TITLE	ARTIST	#	TYPE
Car Wash	Aguilera & Elliott	20-554	PHM
Car Wash	Rose Royce	11-405	DK
Car Wash	Rose Royce	3-559	SC
Cara Mia	Jay & Americans	7-32	MM
Cara Mia	Jay & Americans	14-375	PS
Cara Mia	Jay & Americans	4-245	SC
Caramel	City High	20-613	CB
Caravan	Morrison, Van	17-534	SC
Card Carrying Fool	Travis, Randy	47-767	SRK
Carefree Highway	Lightfoot, Gordon	2-791	SC
Carefree Highway	Lightfoot, Gordon	43-487	SK
Careless	RaeLynn	48-398	DCK
Careless Whisper	Wham!	16-721	DK
Careless Whisper	Wham!	13-206	P
Careless Whisper	Wham!	24-66	SC
Caribbean Queen	Ocean, Billy	11-591	DK
Carlene	Vassar, Phil	8-895	CB
Carlene	Vassar, Phil	5-837	SC
Carlene	Vassar, Phil	22-538	ST
Carmelita	Yoakam, Dwight	45-854	VH
Carnival	Merchant, Natalie	34-129	CB
Carnival	Merchant, Natalie	10-681	HE
Carnival	Merchant, Natalie	19-578	MH
Carnival	Merchant, Natalie	18-35	PS
Carnival	Merchant, Natalie	3-491	SC
Carnival Is Over the	Seekers	10-664	SF
Carol	Berry, Chuck	12-337	DK
Carol	Rolling Stones	12-152	DK
Carol Of The Bells	Christmas	45-747	CB
Carolina	Parmalee	44-216	KCDC
Carolina In My Mind	Taylor, James	10-66	SC
Carolina In The Morning	Martin, Dean	21-2	CB
Carolina In The Pines	Murphy, Michael M	3-621	SC
Carolina Kind the	Lucas, Lauren	23-297	CB
Carolyn	Haggard, Merle	22-237	CB
Carolyn	Haggard, Merle	12-15	DK
Carribean Disco Show - Day-O	Lobo	46-333	FMG
Carrie	Europe	29-302	SC
Carrie Anne	Hollies	3-131	SC
Carried Away	Strait, George	1-249	CB
Carried Away	Strait, George	7-275	MM
Carried Away	Strait, George	4-364	SC
Carried Away	Strait, George	22-893	ST
Carroll County Accident	Wagoner, Porter	19-309	CB
Carry Me Back To Old Virginny	Standard	47-826	JVC
Carry On	Green, Pat	25-11	MM
Carry On	Green, Pat	16-12	ST
Carry On - WN	Crosby Stills & Nash	48-61	SC
Carry On Wayward Son	Kansas	4-47	SC
Carry Your Load	King, Carole	43-445	CB
Carrying Your Love With Me	Strait, George	1-264	CB
Carrying Your Love With Me	Strait, George	7-638	CHM

SONG TITLE	ARTIST	#	TYPE
Carrying Your Love With Me	Strait, George	10-97	SC
Carrying Your Love With Me	Strait, George	22-597	ST
Case Of The Ex	Mya	15-431	PHM
Casey Jones	Grateful Dead	2-750	SC
Casper The Friendly Ghost - Halloween	TV Themes	45-119	SC
Castaway	Zac Brown Band	46-69	KV
Castles In The Air	McLean, Don	37-66	SC
Castles In The Sky	Dahl, Ian Van	21-722	TT
Cat Scratch Fever	Nugent, Ted	14-560	AH
Cat Scratch Fever	Nugent, Ted	35-128	CB
Cat Scratch Fever	Nugent, Ted	20-316	MH
Cat's In The Cradle	Cash, Johnny	45-89	SBI
Cat's In The Cradle	Chapin, Harry	6-445	MM
Cat's In The Cradle	Chapin, Harry	13-172	P
Cat's In The Cradle	Skaggs, Ricky	7-246	MM
Cat's In The Cradle	Ugly Kid Joe	23-100	SC
Catch A Falling Star	Como, Perry	13-543	LE
Catch A Falling Star	Como, Perry	20-776	PS
Catch A Falling Star	Como, Perry	2-198	SC
Catch A Little Raindrop	King, Claude	47-917	SSK
Catch A Wave	Beach Boys	5-510	BS
Catch Me (I'm Falling)	Pretty Poison	17-23	DK
Catch Me While I'm Sleeping	Pink	20-533	CB
Catch Us If You Can	Dave Clark Five	45-80	LC
Catfish John	Nitty Gritty Dirt Band	49-290	FMK
Cathy's Clown	Everly Brothers	11-506	DK
Cathy's Clown	Everly Brothers	13-76	P
Cathy's Clown	Everly Brothers	3-337	PS
Cathy's Clown	Judds	9-447	SAV
Cathy's Clown	McEntire, Reba	17-302	NA
Cats In The Cradle	Cash, Johnny	43-406	DCK
Cats In The Kettle - parody	Parody	46-567	RDK
Cattle Call	Arnold, Eddy	19-30	CB
Cattle Call	Arnold, Eddy	4-259	SC
Cattle Call	Arnold, Eddy	17-628	THM
Caught A Lite Sneeze	Amos, Tori	4-667	SC
Caught In The Rain	Revis	32-252	THM
Caught Up	Usher	22-342	CB
Caught Up In The Rapture	Baker, Anita	12-884	P
Caught Up In the Rapture	Baker, Anita	4-299	SC
Caught Up In You	38 Special	18-155	CB
Caught Up In You	38 Special	7-465	MM
Caught Up In You	38 Special	2-530	SC
Cause I'm A Blonde	Brown, Julie	15-138	SC
CC Water Back	Haggard & Jones	22-232	CB
CC Water Back	Haggard, Merle	43-52	CB
Cecelia	Simon & Garfunkel	5-304	SC
Cecelia	Suggs	25-381	MM
Celebrate	Three Dog Night	35-91	CB
Celebrate	Three Dog Night	5-597	SC

SONG TITLE	ARTIST	#	TYPE
Celebration	Kool & The Gang	16-874	DK
Celebration	Kool & The Gang	16-530	P
Celebration	Kool & The Gang	9-663	SAV
Celebrity	Paisley, Brad	34-394	CB
Celebrity	Paisley, Brad	25-568	MM
Celebrity	Paisley, Brad	19-5	ST
Celebrity	Paisley, Brad	32-260	THM
Celluloid Heroes	Kinks	48-183	SC
Centerfield	Fogerty, John	21-575	SC
Centerfold	J. Geils Band	27-201	DK
Centerfold	J. Geils Band	13-12	P
Ceremony the	Wynette & Jones	9-591	SAV
Certain Kind Of Fool	Eagles	49-83	ZPA
Certain Smile	Mathis, Johnny	9-736	SAV
Certain Smile a	Mathis, Johnny	29-460	LE
Cha Cha Slide	D J Casper	45-75	CK
Chain Gang	Cooke, Sam	46-634	SC
Chain Of Fools	Franklin, Aretha	26-477	DK
Chain Of Fools	Franklin, Aretha	36-160	JT
Chain Of Fools	Franklin, Aretha	19-612	MH
Chain Of Fools	Franklin, Aretha	12-722	P
Chain Of Fools	Franklin, Aretha	9-664	SAV
Chain Of Love the	Walker, Clay	8-897	CB
Chain Of Love the	Walker, Clay	13-827	CHM
Chain Of Love the	Walker, Clay	5-839	SC
Chain the	Fleetwood Mac	29-272	SC
Chains	Arena, Tina	14-903	SC
Chains	Beatles	11-260	DK
Chains	Cookies	9-707	SAV
Chains	Loveless, Patty	1-712	CB
Chains	Loveless, Patty	9-505	SAV
Chains	Loveless, Patty	2-811	SC
Chains Of Gold	Sweethearts/Rodeo	19-425	SC
Chains Of Love	Clovers	10-274	SS
Chains Of Love	Erasure	16-526	P
Chains Of Love	Gilley, Mickey	16-178	THM
Chainsaw	Band Perry	43-142	KV
Chair the	Strait, George	8-161	CB
Chair the	Strait, George	8-694	SAV
Champagne	Cavo	36-304	PHM
Champagne Jam	Atlanta Rhythm Sec	7-464	MM
Champagne Supernova	Oasis	43-112	SC
Chance a	Chesney, Kenny	8-124	CB
Chance a	Chesney, Kenny	22-656	ST
Chance Of Lovin' You	Conley, Earl Thomas	5-823	SC
Chance the	Roberts, Julie	22-89	CB
Chance the	Roberts, Julie	21-655	SC
Chance To Be A Hero a	Humperdinck, E.	49-261	DFK
Chances	Air Supply	46-399	CB
Chances	Five For Fighting	42-29	PHM
Chances Are	Mathis, Johnny	29-465	LE
Chances Are	Mathis, Johnny	10-458	MG
Chances Are	Mathis, Johnny	2-848	SC
Chances Are	Womack, Lee Ann	49-408	BKD
Chances Are - duet	Seger & McBride	46-342	MM
Chances Are (Inst)	Womack, Lee Ann	49-409	BKD
Change	Sons Of The Desert	13-825	CHM

35

SONG TITLE	ARTIST	#	TYPE
Change	Swift, Taylor	43-174	CB
Change	Waite, John	37-67	SC
Change	Warren Brothers	23-489	CB
Change My Mind	Berry, John	7-325	MM
Change My Mind	Berry, John	24-153	SC
Change Of Heart	Carmen, Eric	9-774	SAV
Change Of Heart	Judds	1-142	CB
Change Of Heart	Judds	2-618	SC
Change the	Brooks, Garth	20-103	CB
Change the	Brooks, Garth	7-179	MM
Change the	Brooks, Garth	22-891	ST
Change The World	Clapton, Eric	33-388	CB
Change The World	Clapton, Eric	28-202	DK
Change The World	Clapton, Eric	13-803	SGB
Change Would Do You Good	Crow, Sheryl	10-52	SC
Change Would Do You Good a	Crow, Sheryl	29-671	RS
Change Your Mind	Sister Hazel	33-378	CB
Change Your Mind	Sister Hazel	15-640	THM
Changes **	2 Pac	25-471	MM
Changes In Latitude Changes In..	Buffett, Jimmy	6-426	MM
Changes In Latitude, Changes In Attitude	Croce, Jim	48-465	LE
Changes In Latitude...	Buffett, Jimmy	33-287	CB
Changing Partners	Page, Patti	11-455	DK
Chantilly Lace	Big Bopper	3-315	MH
Chantilly Lace	Big Bopper	6-137	MM
Chantilly Lace	Big Bopper	2-48	SC
Chantilly Lace	Lewis, Jerry Lee	47-202	EK
Chapel Of Love (Going To The...)	Dixie Cups	10-336	KC
Charlene	Hamilton, Anthony	30-813	PHM
Charlie Brown	Coasters	17-107	DK
Charlie Brown	Coasters	13-270	P
Charlie Brown	Coasters	29-829	SC
Charlie Brown's Parents	Dishwalla	24-541	SC
Charlie's Angel	Tillis, Mel	48-101	FMK
Charlie's Shoes	Walker, Billy	5-223	SC
Charm Attack	Naess, Leona	13-845	PHM
Charro	Presley, Elvis	25-491	MM
Chase A Little Love	LoCash Cowboys	49-527	KCD
Chasin' Girls	Atkins, Rodney	37-325	CB
Chasin' That Neon Rainbow	Jackson, Alan	1-33	CB
Chasin' That Neon Rainbow	Jackson, Alan	12-421	P
Chasin' You Around	Sugar Ray	19-670	CB
Chasing Amy	James, Brett	25-188	MM
Chasing Amy	James, Brett	16-696	ST
Chasing Cars	Snow Patrol	30-261	CB
Chasing Cars	Snow Patrol	30-61	PHM
Chasing Cars	Snow Patrol	30-726	SF
Chasing Pavements	Adele	38-180	SC
Chatanooga Choo Choo	Glen Miller Orchestra	34-435	CB
Chattahoochee	Jackson, Alan	26-494	DK

SONG TITLE	ARTIST	#	TYPE
Chattahoochie	Jackson, Alan	1-42	CB
Chattahoochie	Jackson, Alan	6-302	MM
Chattahoochie	Jackson, Alan	12-461	P
Chattanooga Choo Choo	Andrew Sisters	46-426	KV
Chattanooga Choo Choo	Miller & Orchestra	21-3	CB
Chattanooga Choo Choo	Miller, Glen	12-530	P
Chattanooga Dog	Hall, Tom T.	45-341	BSP
Chattanoogie Shoe Shine	Foley, Red	8-718	CB
Chattanoogie Shoe Shine	Foley, Red	4-796	SC
Cheap Love	Newton, Juice	6-746	MM
Cheap Seats	Alabama	1-23	CB
Cheap Seats	Alabama	6-585	MM
Cheap Sunglasses	ZZ Top	16-150	SC
Cheap Whiskey	McBride, Martina	6-108	MM
Cheap Whiskey	McBride, Martina	2-404	SC
Cheaper To Keep Her	Fowler, Kevin	48-708	BKD
Cheaper To Keep Her	Taylor, Johnnie	24-344	SC
Cheated On Me	DeGraw, Gavin	36-535	CB
Cheater Cheater	Joey & Rory	45-812	CB
Cheatin'	Evans, Sara	29-18	CB
Cheatin'	Evans, Sara	23-453	ST
Cheatin' On Her Heart	Carson, Jeff	8-235	CB
Check It Out	Mellencamp, John	45-420	CB
Check On It	Beyonce	48-387	DKM
Check On It	Beyonce w Slim Thug	30-158	PT
Check Yes Or No	Strait, George	1-248	CB
Check Yes Or No	Strait, George	7-136	MM
Cheek To Cheek	Astaire, Fred	12-539	P
Cheek To Cheek	Standard	47-832	SC
Cheers	TV Themes	2-170	SC
Cheeseburger In Paradise	Buffett, Jimmy	6-424	MM
Cheeseburger In Paradise	Buffett, Jimmy	2-137	SC
Chemicals Between Us the	Bush	5-794	SC
Cherish	Association	11-634	DK
Cherish	Association	9-695	SAV
Cherish	Madonna	12-851	P
Cherokee Boogie	BR5-49	7-380	MM
Cherokee Boogie	BR5-49	4-506	SC
Cherokee Fiddle	Lee, Johnny	47-173	SC
Cherokee Highway	Western Flyer	2-734	SC
Cherokee Maiden	Asleep at the Wheel	14-737	CB
Cherokee Maiden	Haggard, Merle	15-71	CB
Cherry Bomb	Mellencamp, John	19-91	PS
Cherry Bomb	Mellencamp, John	21-415	SC
Cherry Cherry	Diamond, Neil	7-531	AH
Cherry Cherry	Diamond, Neil	18-686	PS
Cherry Cherry	Diamond, Neil	24-700	SC
Cherry Hill Park	Royal, Billy Joe	6-782	MM
Cherry Pie	Warrant	5-485	SC
Cherry Pie **	Warrant	23-51	MH
Chevy Van	Johns, Sammy	14-561	AH
Chevy Van	Johns, Sammy	20-46	SC

SONG TITLE	ARTIST	#	TYPE
Chewy Chewy	Ohio Express	16-665	LC
Chicago	Sinatra, Frank	34-11	CB
Chicago	Sinatra, Frank	11-567	DK
Chicago	Sinatra, Frank	18-70	MM
Chicago	Sinatra, Frank	9-236	PT
Chicago	Sinatra, Frank	21-229	SGB
Chicago (That Toddlin' Town)	Sinatra, Frank	28-503	DK
Chick A Boom	Dewdrop, Daddy	4-83	SC
Chick Magnet	MXPX	45-590	OZP
Chicken & Biscuits - duet	Ford & Otto	47-506	CB
Chicken Dance - music only	Polka Favorites	29-867	SSR
Chicken Dance the - DANCE #	Standard	22-390	SC
Chicken Every Sunday	Bare, Bobby	18-277	CB
Chicken Fried	Zac Brown Band	36-615	CB
Chicken Fried	Zac Brown Band	36-199	PHM
Chicken Truck	Anderson, John	5-43	SC
Chicks Dig It	Cagle, Chris	34-416	CB
Chicks Dig It	Cagle, Chris	25-642	MM
Chicks Dig It	Cagle, Chris	19-267	ST
Chicks Dig It	Cagle, Chris	32-338	THM
Chico Time	Chico	30-701	CB
Chico Time	Chico	30-701	SF
Chidren Will Listen	Streisand, Barbra	49-554	KKS
Child Is Born a	Standard	15-464	SGB
Childhood	Jackson, Michael	3-488	SC
Children Will Listen	Sondheim, Stephen	17-780	PS
Chill Factor	Haggard, Merle	29-449	DK
Chill Of An Early Fall	Strait, George	8-173	CB
Chill Of An Early Fall	Strait, George	3-649	SC
Chill Of An Early Fall a	Strait, George	9-542	SAV
Chillin'	Larsen, Blaine	37-338	CB
Chillin' It	Swindell, Cole	40-58	ASK
China Grove	Doobie Brothers	29-78	CB
China Grove	Doobie Brothers	15-170	MH
China Grove	Doobie Brothers	13-30	P
Chipmunk Song the	Seville, David & Chipmunks	49-126	TU
Chiquitita	Abba	7-497	MM
Chirpy Chirpy Cheep Cheep	Middle of the Road	16-373	SF
Chiseled In Stone	Gosdin, Vern	8-690	SAV
Chitty Chitty Bang Bang	Chitty Chitty Bang	9-809	SAV
Chocolate Salty Balls **	Chef	5-541	SC
Chocolate Salty Balls **	Chef	13-721	SGB
Choices	Jones, George	14-630	SC
Choices	Jones, George	22-436	ST
Choo Choo Ch' Boogie	Haley & Comets	49-533	KRG
Choo Choo Ch'Boogie	King, B.B.	45-367	DFK
Christmas Blues	Canned Heat	45-762	CB
Christmas Card a	Stone, Doug	45-751	CB
Christmas Cookies	Strait, George	45-754	CB
Christmas Guest	Grandpa Jones	45-789	DW
Christmas Guest	McEntire, Reba	45-767	CB
Christmas In Dixie	Alabama	35-321	CB

SONG TITLE	ARTIST	#	TYPE
Christmas In Heaven	McCreery, Scotty	45-638	KV
Christmas In Killarney	Day, Dennis	45-771	THX
Christmas In Prison	Prine, John	46-284	CB
Christmas Island - xmas	Buffett, Jimmy	45-251	SC
Christmas Like Mama Used To Make It	Byrd, Tracy	45-768	CB
Christmas Long Ago	Echelons	45-766	CB
Christmas Lullaby	Streisand, Barbra	49-588	PS
Christmas Memories	Streisand, Barbra	49-589	PS
Christmas Rock	Keith, Toby	45-752	CB
Christmas To Remember a	Rogers & Parton	18-721	CB
Christmas Wish	Vee, Bobby	45-788	TB
Christmas Without You	Parton & Rogers	8-85	CB
Christmas Wrapping	Waitresses	45-743	SC
Chrome	Adkins, Trace	34-390	CB
Chrome	Adkins, Trace	25-357	MM
Chrome	Adkins, Trace	18-336	ST
Chrome	Adkins, Trace	32-4	THM
Chrome Plated Heart	Etheridge, Melissa	5-678	SC
Chug A Lug	Miller, Roger	22-274	CB
Chug A Lug	Miller, Roger	2-405	SC
Chug All Night	Eagles	44-92	LG
Church Bells	Underwood, Carrie	49-11	KV
Church Of The Poison Mind	Culture Club	46-652	SF
Church On Cumberland Road	Shenandoah	14-692	CB
Church Pew Or Barstool	Aldean, Jason	47-712	BKD
Church, A Courtroom And Then Goodbye a	Cline, Patsy	45-485	CB
Cigarettes And Coffee Blues	Frizzell, Lefty	46-16	SSK
Cincinnati Ohio	Smith, Connie	8-269	CB
Cinderella	Gill, Vince	4-551	SC
Cinderella Rockafella	Ofarim, Esther & Ab	10-637	SF
Cinnamon Girl	Young, Neil	5-879	SC
Circle	Streisand, Barbra	49-614	PS
Circle In The Sand	Carlisle, Belinda	5-603	SC
Circle Is Small (I Can See It In,,)	Lightfoot, Gordon	21-805	SC
Circle Of Friends	Ball, David	7-277	MM
Circle Of Love	Walker, Tamara	34-413	CB
Circle Of One	Adams, Oleta	46-383	SC
Circle Too Small	Lightfoot, Gordon	43-478	SK
Circles	Kramer, Jana	48-197	BKD
Circles	Sawyer Brown	16-104	ST
Circus Leaving Town	Claypool, Philip	46-625	SC
Cisco Kid the	War	12-171	DK
Cisco Kid the	War	4-57	SC
Citizen Soldier	3 Doors Down	36-511	CB
Citizen Soldier	3 Doors Down	36-291	PHM
City Lights	Gilley, Mickey	22-226	CB
City Lights	McGraw, Tim	45-285	BKD
City Lights	McGraw, Tim	44-285	KCDC
City Lights	Minelli, Liza	49-218	LG
City Lights	Price, Ray	8-382	CB

37

SONG TITLE	ARTIST	#	TYPE
City Of Love	McBride, Martina	29-541	CB
City Of Love	McBride, Martina	20-263	SC
City Of New Orleans	Guthrie, Arlo	9-361	MG
City Of New Orleans	Nelson, Willie	1-630	CB
City Of New Orleans	Nelson, Willie	8-708	SAV
City Of New Orleans	Nelson, Willie	14-317	SC
City Of New Orleans	Prine, John	47-596	KV
City Put The Country Back In Me	McCoy, Neal	1-855	CB
City Put The Country Back In Me	McCoy, Neal	6-675	MM
City Put The Country Back In Me	McCoy, Neal	17-220	NA
City Put The Country Back In Me	McCoy, Neal	2-394	SC
City Streets	King, Carole	43-2	KV
Clapping Song	Ellis, Shirley	47-91	P
Clarity	Mayer, John	20-563	CB
Class Of ' 57	Statler Brothers	19-387	CB
Class Reunion (That Used To Be Us)	Lonestar	22-26	CB
Claudette	Everly Brothers	38-21	ZM
Claudette	Orbison, Roy	38-52	ZM
Claudette	Yoakam, Dwight	4-836	SC
Clean	Swift, Taylor	48-300	KV
Clean Up Woman	Wright, Betty	24-343	SC
Clean Up Your Own Back Yard	Presley, Elvis	8-591	CB
Cleaning Out My Closet **	Eminem	25-458	MM
Cleaning This Gun	Atkins, Rodney	30-573	CB
Cledus The Karaoke King	Judd, Cledus T.	16-515	CB
Clementine	Darin, Bobby	23-357	PS
Clementine	Kids	10-297	SC
Clementine	Miller, Mitch	45-923	CB
Clementine	Standard	11-479	DK
Clementine	Standard	23-222	SM
Cleopatra Queen Of Denial	Tillis, Pam	1-457	CB
Cleopatra Queen Of Denial	Tillis, Pam	26-574	DK
Cleopatra Queen of Denial	Tillis, Pam	2-30	SC
Cleveland Rocks	Hunter, Ian	37-73	SC
Climb Every Mountain	Bassey, Shirley	46-480	P
Climb That Hill	Petty & Heartbreake	4-606	SC
Climb That Mountain High	McEntire, Reba	6-819	MM
Clint Eastwood	Gorillaz	16-313	TT
Clint Eastwood	James-Decker, Jessie	48-460	BKD
Clint Eastwood (Radio Version)	Gorillaz	16-87	SC
Clock Don't Stop	Underwood, Carrie	49-641	KV
Clocks	Coldplay	35-283	CB
Clocks	Coldplay	25-542	MM
Clocks	Coldplay	23-162	PHM
Clocks	Coldplay	23-335	SC

SONG TITLE	ARTIST	#	TYPE
Clockwork	Corbin, Easton	44-280	KCDC
Close Enough To Perfect	Alabama	1-4	CB
Close Enough To Perfect	Alabama	4-486	SC
Close My Eyes Forever	Osbourne & Ford	23-427	SC
Close The Door	Pendergrass, Teddy	15-719	LE
Close To The Borderline	Joel, Billy	45-580	OZP
Close To You	Carpenters	16-740	DK
Close To You	Carpenters	12-829	P
Close To You	Carpenters	10-538	SF
Close To You	Maxi Priest	11-678	DK
Close To You	Maxi Priest	5-342	SC
Close Up The Honky Tonks	Foster, Radney	47-99	SSK
Close Up The Honky Tonks	Owens, Buck	46-108	KVD
Close Up The Honky Tonks	Yoakam, Dwight	49-697	KV
Close Your Eyes	Parmalee	44-198	KCDC
Close Your Eyes	Trainor, Meghan	45-55	BKD
Closer	Ashton, Susan	8-898	CB
Closer	Messina, Jo Dee	14-142	CB
Closer	Ne-Yo	36-458	CB
Closer **	Nine Inch Nails	5-545	SC
Closer **	Nine Inch Nails	13-729	SGB
Closer I Get To You	Flack, Roberta	47-90	MM
Closer I Get To You the	Knowles&Vandross	21-791	SC
Closer Than Close	Bryson, Peabo	24-265	SC
Closer To Fine	Indigo Girls	14-638	SC
Closer To Heaven	Mason, Mila	8-298	CB
Closer To Heaven	Mason, Mila	22-774	ST
Closer To Love	Kearney, Mat	36-297	PHM
Closer To Me	Outfield	45-371	OZP
Closer You Get the	Alabama	13-429	P
Closer You Get the	Alabama	9-434	SAV
Closing Time	Foster, Radney	47-96	SC
Closing Time	Semisonic	10-142	SC
Closure	Chevelle	19-851	PHM
Cloud Nine	Temptations	12-83	DK
Clouds	Nail, David	45-561	KV
Clown In Your Rodeo	Mattea, Kathy	2-666	SC
Clown the	Twitty, Conway	14-312	SC
Club At The End Of The Street	John, Elton	2-373	SC
Club Can't Handle Me	Flo Rida	45-654	KV
Clumsy	Fergie	46-321	SC
Clumsy	Our Lady Peace	5-273	SC
Clyde	Jennings, Waylon	45-171	SC
Coal Miner's Daughter	Lynn, Loretta	11-426	DK
Coal Miner's Daughter	Lynn, Loretta	13-357	P
Coal Miner's Daughter	Lynn, Loretta	8-706	SAV
Coalmine	Evans, Sara	29-575	CB
Coast Is Clear the	Emerick, Scotty	20-334	ST
Coast Is Clear the	Lawrence, Tracy	22-640	ST
Coastal	Chesney, Kenny	48-74	BKD
Coat Of Many Colors	Parton, Dolly	8-533	CB
Coat Of Many Colors	Twain & Krauss	20-270	SC

SONG TITLE	ARTIST	#	TYPE
Coat Of Many Colors	Twain, Shania	19-712	ST
Coca Cola Cowboy	Tillis, Mel	19-465	CB
Coca Cola Cowboy	Tillis, Mel	5-37	SC
Cocaine	Browne, Jackson	23-612	BS
Cocaine	Clapton, Eric	9-343	AH
Cocaine	Clapton, Eric	28-204	DK
Cocaine	Clapton, Eric	15-53	LE
Cocaine	Clapton, Eric	20-310	MH
Cocaine	Clapton, Eric	2-139	SC
Cocaine Blues	Cash, Johnny	37-218	SF
Cochise	Audio Slave	20-465	CB
Cochise	Audio Slave	23-145	PHM
Cocky **	Kid Rock	36-346	SC
Cocoanut Woman	Belafonte, Harry	46-506	LE
Coconut	Nilsson, Harry	6-868	MM
Coconut	Nilsson, Harry	12-861	P
Coconut	Nilsson, Harry	5-642	SC
Coffee Song the	Andrew Sisters	48-641	KV
Cold	Crossfade	30-614	PHM
Cold	McComb, Jeremy	36-281	PHM
Cold (But I'm Still Here - Radio)	Blue, Evans	30-281	SC
Cold (But I'm Still Here)	Evans Blue	30-281	SC
Cold And Empty	Kid Rock	49-511	PHM
Cold As Ice	Foreigner	13-13	P
Cold As Stone - duet	Lady Antebellum	47-870	KV
Cold As You Say	Swift, Taylor	36-83	BM
Cold Beer - duet	Ford & Johnson	47-493	CB
Cold Beer And A Fishing Pole	Wilmon, Trent	47-495	CB
Cold Beer Conversations	Strait, George	45-389	BKD
Cold Beer With Your Name On It	Thompson, Josh	41-96	PHN
Cold Coffee Morning	Randall, Jon	8-951	CB
Cold Cold Heart	Jones, Norah	19-184	Z
Cold Cold Heart	Williams, Hank Sr.	11-187	DK
Cold Cold Heart	Williams, Hank Sr.	13-436	P
Cold Cold Heart	Williams, Hank Sr.	8-635	SAV
Cold Cold Heart	Williams, Hank Sr.	5-101	SC
Cold Day in July	Dixie Chicks	8-903	CB
Cold Day In July	Dixie Chicks	30-597	RS
Cold Day In July	Dixie Chicks	22-542	ST
Cold Hard Facts Of Life	Wagoner, Porter	19-307	CB
Cold Hard Facts Of Life	Wagoner, Porter	5-699	SC
Cold Hard Truth the	Jones, George	14-701	CB
Cold Hard Truth the	Jones, George	5-832	SC
Cold Hearted	Abdul, Paula	14-583	SC
Cold Hearted	Zac Brown Band	46-62	FTX
Cold One	Church, Eric	46-621	SBI
Cold One Comin' On	Montgomery Gentry	25-4	MM
Cold One Comin' On	Montgomery Gentry	15-670	ST
Cold Outside	Big House	7-613	CHM
Cold Outside	Big House	7-423	MM
Cold Shot	Vaughn, Stevie Ray	7-212	MM
Cold Shot	Vaughn, Stevie Ray	13-765	SGB
Cold Shoulder	Adele	38-228	CB

SONG TITLE	ARTIST	#	TYPE
Cold Sweat	Brown, James	29-145	LE
Cold Turkey	Lennon, John	30-298	RS
Colder Weather	Zac Brown Band	37-201	AS
Collide - duet	Kid Rock & Crow	38-204	FTX
Color Of Love the	Boyz II Men	18-221	CB
Color Of Love the	Boyz II Men	25-220	MM
Color Of Roses the	Morgan, Lorrie	49-120	SC
Color Of The Night	Christy, Lauren	16-628	MM
Colors And Numbers	Spartz, Doug	2-669	SC
Colour My World	Chicago	13-220	P
Colour My World	Chicago	2-841	SC
Colour Of Love the	Ocean, Billy	22-921	SC
Colour Of My Love	Dion, Celine	15-117	BS
Combine Harvester (Brand New..)	Wurzels	44-63	STTW
Come	Jain	48-644	KV
Come	Transmatic	25-86	MM
Come & Stay With Me	Faithfull, Marianne	10-659	SF
Come A Little Bit Closer	Jay & Americans	11-638	DK
Come A Little Bit Closer	Jay & Americans	6-162	MM
Come A Little Bit Closer	Jay & Americans	13-88	P
Come A Little Bit Closer	Jay & Americans	14-374	PS
Come A Little Closer	Bentley, Dierks	23-409	CB
Come A Little Closer	Bentley, Dierks	29-506	SC
Come A Little Closer	Bentley, Dierks	29-604	ST
Come A Little Closer	McCann, Lila	15-101	ST
Come A Little Closer	Williams, Don	45-220	DCK
Come And Get It	Badfinger	15-747	SC
Come And Get Your Love	Redbone	11-294	DK
Come And Talk To Me	Jodeci	9-686	SAV
Come As You Are	Knight, Beverly	30-775	SF
Come Away With Me	Jones, Norah	35-249	CB
Come Away With Me	Jones, Norah	25-406	MM
Come Away With Me	Jones, Norah	36-362	SC
Come Away With Me	Jones, Norah	19-337	STP
Come Away With Me	Jones, Norah	32-133	THM
Come Away With Me	Jones, Norah	19-186	Z
Come Back To Me	Monro, Matt	18-107	PS
Come Back When It Ain't Rainin'	Yearwood, Trisha	48-337	SC
Come Back When You Grow Up	Vee, Bobby	5-232	SC
Come Clean	Duff, Hillary	20-566	CB
Come Close To Me	Common & Blige	32-88	THM
Come Close To Me	Common Feat&Blige	20-515	CB
Come Cryin' To Me	Lonestar	7-643	CHM
Come Cryin' To Me	Lonestar	10-102	SC
Come Cryin' To Me	Lonestar	22-602	ST
Come Dance With Me	Jay & Americans	14-371	PS
Come Dance With Me	Sinatra, Frank	49-505	MM
Come Dancing	Kinks	3-619	SC
Come Down In Time	John, Elton	48-396	DCK
Come Early Morning	Williams, Don	5-201	SC
Come Fly With Me	Sinatra, Frank	9-249	PT
Come Fly With Me	Sinatra, Frank	21-211	SGB
Come Friday	Tippin, Aaron	23-293	CB

SONG TITLE	ARTIST	#	TYPE
Come From The Heart	Mattea, Kathy	1-187	CB
Come From The Heart	Mattea, Kathy	3-645	SC
Come Get It Bae	Williams, Pharrell	49-74	ZPC
Come Go With Me	Del Vikings	33-233	CB
Come Go With Me	Del Vikings	25-553	MM
Come Go With Me	Del Vikings	15-463	P
Come Go With Me	Expose	24-208	SC
Come Home Soon	SheDaisy	20-447	ST
Come In From The Rain	Captain & Tennille	46-590	CB
Come In From The Rain	Manchester,Melissa	14-586	SC
Come In From The Rain	Monro, Matt	11-59	PT
Come In Our Of The World	Tucker, Tanya	24-134	SC
Come In Out Of The Pain	Stone, Doug	20-597	CB
Come In Stranger	Cash, Johnny	29-564	CB
Come Into My World	Minogue, Kylie	25-402	MM
Come Into My World	Minogue, Kylie	32-95	THM
Come Live With Me & Be My Love	Clark, Roy	9-578	SAV
Come Monday	Buffett, Jimmy	6-421	MM
Come Monday	Buffett, Jimmy	12-694	P
Come Next Monday	Oslin, K.T.	6-618	MM
Come Next Monday	Oslin, K.T.	12-420	P
Come Next Monday	Oslin, K.T.	9-443	SAV
Come Next Monday	Oslin, K.T.	2-809	SC
Come On	White, Barry	46-196	SC
Come On And Get My Love	Nobb, D.	9-680	SAV
Come On Back	Carter, Carlene	2-616	SC
Come On Come On	Carpenter, M C	8-883	CB
Come On Come On	Carpenter, M C	12-469	P
Come On Down	TLC	15-425	CB
Come On Down To My Boat	Every Mother's Son	4-255	SC
Come On Eileen	Midnight Runners	29-11	MH
Come On Get Happy	Partridge Family	34-418	CB
Come On Get Higher	Nathanson, Marr	49-856	SC
Come On Get Higher	Nathanson, Matthew	36-237	PHM
Come On In	Oak Ridge Boys	9-573	SAV
Come On Let's Go	Los Lobos	47-208	SBI
Come On Let's Go	Valens, Richie	12-744	P
Come On Over	Aguilera, Christina	15-438	PHM
Come On Over	Aguilera, Christina	20-6	SGB
Come On Over	Simpson, Jessica	36-605	CB
Come On Over	Twain, Shania	8-6	CB
Come On Over	Twain, Shania	5-797	SC
Come On Over	Twain, Shania	22-499	ST
Come On Over (Radio Version)	Aguilera, Christina	14-501	SC
Come On Over To My Place	Drifters	45-900	SF
Come On Rain	Holy, Steve	30-250	CB
Come On-A-My Place	Clooney, Rosemary	4-187	SC
Come Out And Play	Offspring	5-749	SC
Come Over	Aaliyah	20-522	CB
Come Over	Aaliyah & Tank	32-352	THM
Come Over	Chesney, Kenny	39-27	ASK
Come Rain Or Come	Garland, Judy	28-103	DK

SONG TITLE	ARTIST	#	TYPE
Shine			
Come Rain Or Come Shine	Garland, Judy	12-541	P
Come Rain Or Come Shine	Lee, Peggy	49-935	SC
Come Rain Or Come Shine	Standard	9-833	SAV
Come Sail Away	Cartman, Eric	13-716	SGB
Come Sail Away	Styx	16-600	MM
Come Sail Away	Styx	17-516	SC
Come Saturday Morning	Sandpipers	11-348	DK
Come See About Me	Ross, Diana	48-548	DK
Come See About Me	Supremes	14-889	DK
Come See About Me	Supremes	12-630	P
Come See About Me	Supremes	4-13	SC
Come See Me And Come Lonely	West, Dottie	15-231	CB
Come See Me And Come Lonely	West, Dottie	47-815	SRK
Come Softly To Me	Fleetwoods	27-505	DK
Come Softly To Me	Fleetwoods	12-898	P
Come Some Rainy Day	Judd, Wynonna	8-227	CB
Come Some Rainy Day	Judd, Wynonna	10-122	SC
Come Some Rainy Day	Judd, Wynonna	22-752	ST
Come Sundown	Bare, Bobby	18-275	CB
Come Sundown	Kristofferson, Kris	45-199	DCK
Come Sundown	Kristofferson, Kris	47-750	SRK
Come To Bed	Wilson, Gretchen	30-170	CB
Come To Me	Raitt, Bonnie	10-767	JVC
Come To My Window	Etheridge, Melissa	19-574	MH
Come To My Window	Etheridge, Melissa	6-637	MM
Come To My Window	Etheridge, Melissa	13-292	P
Come To My Window	Etheridge, Melissa	10-238	PS
Come To My Window	Etheridge, Melissa	9-271	SC
Come to Poppa	Seger, Bob	19-276	SGB
Come Together	Beatles	11-193	DK
Come Together	Beatles	11-72	JTG
Come Together	Beatles	12-914	P
Come Together	Beatles	9-645	SAV
Come Together	Third Day	34-420	CB
Come What May	Moulin Rouge	19-121	PR
Come What May	Moulin Rouge	18-664	PS
Come With Me	Jennings, Waylon	29-781	CB
Comedians the	Orbison, Roy	45-596	OZP
Comedown	Bush	24-749	SC
Comfortably Numb	Pink Floyd	16-248	AMS
Comfortably Numb	Pink Floyd	2-755	SC
Comfortably Numb	Scissor Sisters	29-221	ZM
Comin' Around	Thompson, Josh	45-563	BKD
Comin' Down	Dudley, Dave	43-298	CB
Comin' From Where I'm From	Hamilton, Anthony	32-425	THM
Comin' In And Out Of Your Life	Streisand, Barbra	49-543	MM
Comin' To Your City	Big & Rich	23-467	CB
Coming Around Again	Simon, Carly	4-388	SC
Coming Back For You	Harling, Keith	8-758	CB
Coming Home	James-Decker,	48-459	BKD

40

SONG TITLE	ARTIST	#	TYPE
	Jessie		
Coming Home Soldier	Vinton, Bobby	46-33	SSK
Coming On Strong	Lee, Brenda	49-7	DCK
Coming On Strong	Lee, Brenda	45-733	VH
Coming Out Of The Dark	Estefan, Gloria	17-743	PT
Coming Undone	Korn	49-890	SC
Coming Up	McCartney & Wings	28-327	DK
Coming Up Short Again	Perfect Stranger	9-390	CB
Commitment	Rimes, LeAnn	1-292	CB
Commitment	Rimes, LeAnn	22-782	ST
Common Man	Conlee, John	33-77	CB
Commotion	CCR	48-363	CB
Company	Bieber, Justin	48-622	DCK
Company Time	Davis, Linda	6-509	MM
Company Time	Davis, Linda	2-132	SC
Company's Comin'	Wagoner, Porter	19-318	CB
Compass	Lady Antebellum	43-93	HM
Completely	Bolton, Michael	12-168	DK
Completely	Bolton, Michael	2-110	SC
Completely	Bolton, Michael	8-610	TT
Completely	Day, Jennifer	36-358	SC
Completely	Diamond Rio	19-704	ST
Complicated	Johnson, Carolyn D.	33-157	CB
Complicated	Johnson, Carolyn D.	14-843	ST
Complicated	Lavigne, Avril	33-432	CB
Complicated	Lavigne, Avril	25-302	MM
Complicated	Lavigne, Avril	18-145	PHM
Conceived	Orton, Beth	29-275	PHM
Concrete And Clay	Unit 4 Plus 2	10-615	SF
Concrete Angel	McBride, Martina	29-530	CB
Concrete Angel	McBride, Martina	25-420	MM
Concrete Angel	McBride, Martina	18-462	ST
Concrete Angel	McBride, Martina	32-79	THM
Confession	Florida Georgia Line	48-733	BKD
Confession (Inst)	Florida Georgia Line	49-413	BKD
Confidence Man	Jeff Healy Band	9-373	AH
Confidence Man	Jeff Healy Band	19-797	SGB
Confused	Campbell, Tevin	9-843	SAV
Conga	Estefan & Miami Sound	34-79	CB
Conga	Estefan, Gloria	17-741	PT
Connected At The Heart	Ricochet	8-412	CB
Consider Me Gone	McEntire, Reba	36-37	PT
Consider Yourself	Oliver	12-179	DK
Constant Craving	lang, k.d.	8-889	CB
Constant Craving	lang, k.d.	6-367	MM
Constant Craving	lang, k.d.	13-238	P
Constant Craving	lang, k.d.	9-265	SC
Constantly	Cross Can Ragweed	19-694	ST
Consume Me	DC Talk	34-424	CB
Continental Trailways Blues	Earle, Steve	46-176	CB
Control	Jackson, Janet	11-227	DK
Control	Jackson, Janet	12-752	P
Control	Puddle Of Mud	16-314	TT
Conversation the - duet	Williams & Jennings	45-186	KV
Convoy	McCall, C.W.	8-21	CB

SONG TITLE	ARTIST	#	TYPE
Convoy	McCall, C.W.	6-870	MM
Cool	Stefani, Gwen	23-312	SC
Cool Change	Little River Band	18-303	SC
Cool Jerk	Capitols	35-83	CB
Cool Jerk	Capitols	3-580	SC
Cool Me Down	Jenai	18-791	ST
Cool Night	Davis, Paul	15-743	SC
Cool To Be A Fool	Nichols, Joe	35-439	CB
Cool To Be A Fool	Nichols, Joe	19-531	ST
Cool Water	Sons Of Pioneers	12-305	DK
Cool Water	Sons Of Pioneers	5-424	SC
Cooler Than Me	Posner, Mike	40-47	CB
Cop Car	Urban, Keith	43-168	PHN
Copacabana	Manilow, Barry	29-107	CB
Copacabana	Manilow, Barry	17-56	DK
Copacabana	Manilow, Barry	9-76	PS
Copacabana	Manilow, Barry	9-771	SAV
Copacabana	Manilow, Barry	10-541	SF
Copperhead Road	Earle, Steve	45-951	KV
Copperline	Taylor, James	45-544	SC
Corina Corina	Nelson, Willie	46-90	SSK
Corn Fed	Brown, Shannon	23-484	CB
Corn Fed	Brown, Shannon	23-459	ST
Corn Star	Morgan, Craig	30-28	ASK
Corner Of My Life the	Anderson, Bill	20-796	CB
Corner Of My Life the	Anderson, Bill	5-249	SC
Cornflake Girl	Amos, Tori	5-343	SC
Coronary Life	Judd, Cledus T.	16-506	CB
Corrina Corrina	Peterson, Ray	9-702	SAV
Corrina Corrina	Turner, Joe	20-59	SC
Corrina Corrina	Turner, Joe	17-325	SS
Cosmic Girl	Oquai, James	21-598	SF
Cost Of Livin'	Dunn, Ronnie	38-223	FTX
Cotton Eye Joe	Rednex	24-437	SC
Cotton Eye Joe - DANCE #	Rednex	22-386	SC
Cotton Fields	CCR	19-103	SAV
Cotton Fields	Highwaymen	16-357	CB
Cotton Fields	Standard	11-473	DK
Cotton Jenny	Lightfoot, Gordon	43-115	SK
Cotton Jenny	Murray, Anne	11-7	PL
Cottonfields	Beach Boys	46-489	KV
Could I Have This Dance	Murray, Anne	17-123	DK
Could I Have This Dance	Murray, Anne	6-762	MM
Could I Have This Dance	Murray, Anne	13-355	P
Could I Have This Dance	Murray, Anne	11-3	PL
Could I Have This Dance	Murray, Anne	9-517	SAV
Could I Have This Kiss Forever	Houston & Iglesias	14-478	SC
Could I Have This Kiss Forever	Houston & Iglesias	15-636	THM
Could I Have This Kiss Forever	Iglesias & Houston	20-119	PHM
Could It Be	Worsham, Charles	41-95	PHN
Could It Be Any Harder	Calling	18-427	CB
Could It Be I'm Falling In Love	Detroit Spinners	9-753	SAV

SONG TITLE	ARTIST	#	TYPE
Could It Be I'm Falling In Love	Spinners	28-113	DK
Could It Be Magic	Manilow, Barry	29-112	CB
Could It Be Magic	Manilow, Barry	18-49	MM
Could It Be Magic	Summer, Donna	15-204	LE
Could She Be Mine	Osmond, Donny	47-868	ZP
Could This Be Love	Lopez, Jennifer	23-327	CB
Could This Be Love	Lopez, Jennifer	23-576	MM
Could You Be Loved	Marley, Bob	25-391	MM
Could've Been	Tiffany	12-4	DK
Could've Been	Tiffany	4-296	SC
Could've Been Me	Cyrus, Billy Ray	10-756	JVC
Could've Been Me	Cyrus, Billy Ray	3-641	SC
Couldn't Get it Right	Climax Blues Band	4-876	SC
Couldn't Have Said It Better	Meat Loaf	46-304	SC
Couldn't Have Said It Better - duet	Meat Loaf	45-524	SC
Couldn't Last A Moment	Raye, Collin	13-809	CHM
Couldn't Last A Moment	Raye, Collin	23-374	SC
Couldn't Stand The Weather	Vaughn, Stevie Ray	46-310	SC
Count Me In	Carter, Deana	14-655	CB
Count Me In	Carter, Deana	7-617	CHM
Count Me In	Lewis & Playboys	43-31	CB
Count Me In	Lewis & Playboys	7-41	MM
Count On Me	Houston & Winans	14-902	SC
Count On Me	Jefferson Starship	24-201	SC
Count On Me	Starship	15-225	LE
Count Your Blessings Instead Of Sheep	Crosby, Bing	21-15	CB
Counting Blue Cars	Dishwalla	7-573	THM
Counting Stars	OneRepublic	44-90	ASK
Counting Stars	OneRepublic	45-3	KV
Counting The Days	Collective Soul	30-819	CB
Counting The Days	Collective Soul	30-819	PHM
Country	Diffie, Joe	4-237	SC
Country	Pitney, Mo	48-757	KCD
Country 'Til I Die	Anderson, John	2-460	SC
Country Ain't Country	Tritt, Travis	25-523	MM
Country Ain't Country	Tritt, Travis	18-788	ST
Country Ain't Country	Tritt, Travis	32-156	THM
Country Ain't Never Been Pretty	Cam	49-753	KV
Country And Cold Cans	Bentley, Dierks	45-49	ASK
Country As A Boy Can Be	Seals, Brady	45-829	VH
Country Boy	Dickens, Little Jimmy	14-914	SC
Country Boy	Dickens, Little Jimmy	45-336	SC
Country Boy	Jackson, Alan	36-222	PHM
Country Boy	Lewis, Aaron	48-770	BKD
Country Boy	Skaggs, Ricky	33-88	CB
Country Boy	Skaggs, Ricky	11-799	DK
Country Boy	Skaggs, Ricky	5-409	SC
Country Boy Can Survive - (Y2K)	Brock, Chad	8-909	CB

SONG TITLE	ARTIST	#	TYPE
Country Boy Can Survive a	Williams, Hank Jr.	13-382	P
Country Boy Can Survive Y2K	Brock, Chad	22-537	ST
Country Boy In Me	Outshyne	38-255	PHN
Country Boy You Got /Feet In LA	Campbell, Glen	15-68	CB
Country Boy You Got /Feet In LA	Campbell, Glen	5-412	SC
Country Boy You Got Your...	Campbell, Glen	33-34	CB
Country Bumpkin	Smith, Cal	15-834	CB
Country Bumpkin	Smith, Cal	4-303	SC
Country By The Grace Of God	Cagle, Chris	16-703	ST
Country Club	Tritt, Travis	1-663	CB
Country Comes To Town	Keith, Toby	14-716	CB
Country Comes To Town	Keith, Toby	13-833	CHM
Country Comes To Town	Keith, Toby	19-246	CSZ
Country Comes To Town	Keith, Toby	38-159	SC
Country Crazy	Little Texas	4-103	SC
Country Down To My Soul	Parnell, Lee Roy	49-255	DFK
Country Folks Livin' Loud	Lost Trailers	37-285	PHM
Country Girl	Chasez, JC	18-772	PHM
Country Girl	DF Dub	32-159	THM
Country Girl	Young, Faron	20-735	CB
Country Girl Shake It For Me	Bryan, Luke	37-202	AS
Country Girls	Hobbs, Becky	8-759	CB
Country Girls	Schneider, John	5-415	SC
Country Grammar (Hot....)	Nelly	14-495	SC
Country Hall Of Fame	Locklin, Hank	37-283	CB
Country In My Genes	Lynn, Loretta	14-95	CB
Country Is	Hall, Tom T.	15-65	CB
Country Is	Hall, Tom T.	5-416	SC
Country Junction	Ford, Tenn Ernie	5-410	SC
Country Man	Bryan, Luke	36-582	CB
Country Man	Bryan, Luke	36-214	PHM
Country Memories	Lewis, Jerry Lee	47-799	SRK
Country Music Is Here To Stay	Husky, Ferlin	22-260	CB
Country Music Is Here To Stay	Husky, Ferlin	5-375	SC
Country Music Love Song	Bomshel	37-286	SC
Country Must Be Country Wide	Gilbert, Brantley	38-87	CB
Country Must Be Country Wide	Gilbert, Brantley	46-157	CB
Country Nation	Paisley, Brad	49-879	DCK
Country On The Radio	Shelton, Blake	47-444	ASK
Country Road	Taylor, James	11-272	DK
Country Rock Star	Marcel	25-233	MM
Country Rock Star	Marcel	17-570	ST
Country Star	Green, Pat	47-122	CB
Country State Of Mind	Williams, Hank Jr.	8-206	CB

SONG TITLE	ARTIST	#	TYPE
Country State Of Mind	Williams, Hank Jr.	5-411	SC
Country Sunshine	West, Dottie	8-795	CB
Country Sunshine	West, Dottie	13-494	P
Country Sunshine	West, Dottie	5-418	SC
Country Thang	Ford, Colt w Davidson	38-119	CB
Country Thang	Montgomery, J M	18-787	ST
Country Thang	Montgomery, J M	32-152	THM
County Fair	LeDoux, Chris	14-731	CB
County Fair	Lonestar	22-77	CB
Couple Days Off	Lewis & The News	47-185	CB
Courtest Of The Red White & Blue	Keith, Toby	33-164	CB
Courtesy Of The Red White & Blue	Keith, Toby	17-564	ST
Courtesy Of The Red, White & Blue	Keith, Toby	25-236	MM
Cover Girl	New Kids On Block	11-514	DK
Cover Me	Springsteen, Bruce	20-252	LE
Cover Of The Rolling Stone	Dr. Hook	15-174	MH
Cover Of The Rolling Stone	Dr. Hook	7-453	MM
Cover Of The Rolling Stone	Dr. Hook	2-138	SC
Cover You In Kisses	Montgomery, J M	14-217	CB
Cover You In Kisses	Montgomery, J M	5-300	SC
Cover You In Kisses	Raye, Collin	22-795	ST
Cow Patti	Stafford, Jim	15-145	SC
Coward Of The County	Rogers, Kenny	3-168	CB
Coward Of The County	Rogers, Kenny	11-746	DK
Coward Of The County	Rogers, Kenny	48-129	SC
Cowboy	Kid Rock	10-221	SC
Cowboy Band	Dean, Billy	6-595	MM
Cowboy Band	Dean, Billy	17-251	NA
Cowboy Beat	Bellamy Brothers	6-755	MM
Cowboy Boogie	Travis, Randy	6-760	MM
Cowboy Boots	Dudley, Dave	43-291	CB
Cowboy Boots	Mackelmore & Lewis	43-456	ASK
Cowboy Cadillac	Brooks, Garth	48-351	MM
Cowboy Cadillac	Confederate RR	8-946	CB
Cowboy Cadillac	Confederate RR	14-607	SC
Cowboy Cassanova	Underwood, Carrie	36-50	PT
Cowboy In Me	McGraw, Tim	16-95	ST
Cowboy In Me the	McGraw, Tim	25-61	MM
Cowboy In The Continental Suit	Robbins, Marty	48-16	CB
Cowboy Love	Montgomery, J M	7-174	MM
Cowboy Love	Montgomery, J M	3-661	SC
Cowboy Movies	Jennings, Waylon	24-132	SC
Cowboy Rides Away the	Strait, George	4-543	SC
Cowboy Take Me Away	Dixie Chicks	20-210	CB
Cowboy Take Me Away	Dixie Chicks	30-598	RS
Cowboy Take Me Away	Dixie Chicks	22-513	ST
Cowboy Up & Party Down	Warren, Darren	38-102	PHM
Cowboy Way	Anthony, Derek	42-9	PHN
Cowboy's Sweetheart	Rimes, LeAnn	12-928	CB

SONG TITLE	ARTIST	#	TYPE
Cowboy's Work Is Never Done	Sonny & Cher	14-48	RS
Cowboy's Work Is Never Done - duet	Cher	47-678	RSZ
Cowboys And Angels	Brooks, Garth	15-465	SC
Cowboys And Angels	Lynch, Dustin	44-129	ASK
Cowboys And Clowns	Milsap, Ronnie	47-270	CB
Cowboys Don't Cry	Norwood, Daron	3-42	SC
Cowboys Don't Shoot Straight	Wynette, Tammy	49-357	CB
Cowboys Like Us	Strait, George	25-703	MM
Cowboys Like Us	Strait, George	19-362	ST
Cowboys Like Us	Strait, George	32-377	THM
Cowboys To Girls	Intruders	6-55	SC
Cowgirl	Farr, Tyler	44-388	BKD
Cowgirl And The Dandy	Lee, Brenda	30-334	CB
Cowgirls	Harvick, Kerry	22-86	CB
Cracker Jack Diamond	Raybon, Marty	6-69	SC
Crackers	Mandrell, Barbara	33-33	CB
Crackers	Mandrell, Barbara	5-49	SC
Cracklin' Rosie	Diamond, Neil	7-532	AH
Cracklin' Rosie	Diamond, Neil	30-677	LE
Cracklin' Rosie	Diamond, Neil	24-692	SC
Cracklin' Rosie	Diamond, Neil	30-500	THM
Cradle Of Love	Idol, Billy	12-165	DK
Cradle Of Love	Idol, Billy	12-779	P
Crank That (Soulja Boy)	Soulja Boy Tell 'Em	37-110	SC
Crash And Burn	Rhett, Thomas	45-296	SBI
Crash And Burn	Savage Garden	14-178	CB
Crash Boom Bang	Roxette	29-133	ST
Crash Course In The Blues	Wariner, Steve	3-50	SC
Crash Here Tonight	Keith, Toby	30-46	CB
Crash Into Me	Dave Matthews Band	49-451	MM
Crash My Party	Bryan, Luke	40-60	ASL
Crawdad Song, the	Standard	44-51	KV
Crawfish	Presley, Elvis	25-761	MM
Crawlin'	Linkin Park	16-381	SGB
Crawling Back	Orbison, Roy	47-339	PG
Crawling In The Dark	Hoobastank	49-315	CB
Crazy	Barkley, Gnarls	30-606	SF
Crazy	Cline, Patsy	16-864	DK
Crazy	Cline, Patsy	6-725	MM
Crazy	Cline, Patsy	8-667	SAV
Crazy	Cline, Patsy	10-506	SF
Crazy	Iglesias, Julio	47-560	LE
Crazy	Javier	32-314	THM
Crazy	K-Ci & JoJo	18-551	TT
Crazy	Rogers, Kenny	3-176	CB
Crazy	Wilson, Gretchen	41-72	PHN
Crazy 'Bout You Baby	Cyrus, Billy Ray	9-870	ST
Crazy (James Michael Mix)	Morrisette, Alanis	29-246	SC
Crazy (You Drive Me)	Spears, Britney	8-279	PHT
Crazy Arms	Cline, Patsy	6-749	MM
Crazy Arms	Cline, Patsy	13-448	P
Crazy Arms	Price, Ray	15-828	CB

SONG TITLE	ARTIST	#	TYPE
Crazy Arms	Price, Ray	12-88	DK
Crazy Arms	Price, Ray	10-749	JVC
Crazy Arms	Price, Ray	5-222	SC
Crazy Beat	Blur	32-251	THM
Crazy Bitch **	Buckcherry	30-656	RSX
Crazy Blue Eyes	Dalton, Lacy J.	45-827	OZP
Crazy Days	Gregory, Adam	36-612	CB
Crazy Downtown **	Sherman, Allan	23-17	SC
Crazy Dreams	Underwood, Carrie	37-6	CB
Crazy Ex-Girlfriend	Lambert, Miranda	30-194	CB
Crazy For This Girl	Evan & Jaron	16-485	MH
Crazy For You	Adele	44-170	KV
Crazy For You	Madonna	20-295	CB
Crazy For You	Madonna	21-153	LE
Crazy For You	Madonna	9-2	MH
Crazy For You	Madonna	13-216	P
Crazy For You	Madonna	4-853	SC
Crazy For You	N'Sync	15-781	BS
Crazy For You	N'Sync	20-438	CB
Crazy For Your Love	Exile	11-428	DK
Crazy From The Heart	Bellamy Brothers	45-299	CDG
Crazy Girl	Eli Young Band	37-220	CB
Crazy He Calls Me	Streisand, Barbra	49-383	PS
Crazy Heart	Williams, Hank Sr.	14-227	CB
Crazy Horses	Osmonds	47-849	MFK
Crazy In Love	Beyonce	30-168	CB
Crazy In Love	Beyonce feat Jay-Z	19-597	CB
Crazy In Love	Jay-Z & Beyonce	25-653	MM
Crazy In Love	Twitty, Conway	43-202	CB
Crazy In Love - Duet	Knowles & Jay-Z	32-307	THM
Crazy In The Night	Carnes, Kim	5-473	SC
Crazy Kind Of Love Thing	Kinleys	19-566	CB
Crazy Life	Rushlow, Tim	15-610	ST
Crazy Little Thing Called Love	Buble, Michael	30-177	LE
Crazy Little Thing Called Love	Queen	11-625	DK
Crazy Little Thing Called Love	Queen	12-835	P
Crazy Little Thing Called Love	Yoakam, Dwight	8-969	CB
Crazy Little Thing Called Love	Yoakam, Dwight	7-879	CHT
Crazy Little Thing Called Love	Yoakam, Dwight	14-626	SC
Crazy Love	Anka, Paul	45-584	OZP
Crazy Love	Buble, Michael	40-86	PS
Crazy Love	McKnight, Brian	14-879	SC
Crazy Love	Morrison, Van	5-873	SC
Crazy Love	Neville, Aaron	24-366	SC
Crazy Love	Poco	5-387	SC
Crazy Me	Rogers, Kenny	48-412	DFK
Crazy On You	Heart	48-160	LE
Crazy One More Time	Moore, Kip	45-634	PHN
Crazy Over You	Foster & Lloyd	5-621	SC
Crazy Possessive	Battaglia, Kaci	36-300	PHM
Crazy Town	Aldean, Jason	37-327	PHM

SONG TITLE	ARTIST	#	TYPE
Crazy Train	Osbourne, Ozzy	23-424	SC
Crazy Train	Osbourne, Ozzy	13-745	SGB
Crazy Women	Rimes, LeAnn	38-109	CB
Cream **	Prince	21-466	CB
Cream **	Prince	15-12	SC
Creatures (For A While)	311	23-175	PHM
Credit	Trainor, Meghan	45-150	KVD
Creep	Radiohead	13-241	P
Creep	TLC	16-624	MM
Creepin'	Church, Eric	46-616	ASK
Creepin' In	Parton & Jones, N.	20-479	ST
Creeque Alley	Mamas & Papas	14-452	SC
Crime Of Passion	VanShelton, Ricky	20-658	SC
Crimson And Clover	James & Shondells	11-418	DK
Crimson And Clover	James & Shondells	12-868	P
Crimson And Clover	James & Shondells	4-704	SC
Crimson And Clover	Jett, Joan	16-640	MM
Crocodile Rock	John, Elton	11-123	DK
Crocodile Rock	John, Elton	12-823	P
Crocodile Tears	Parnell, Lee Roy	49-273	CB
Crooked Teeth	Death Cab for Cutie	29-219	PHM
Cross My Broken Heart	Bogguss, Suzy	1-556	CB
Cross My Heart	Parton, Dolly	4-139	SC
Cross-Tie Walker	CCR	48-372	KV
Crossfire	Bellamy Brothers	45-297	KV
Crossfire	Vaughn, Stevie Ray	20-138	KB
Crossfire	Vaughn, Stevie Ray	7-214	MM
Crossroads	Chapman, Tracy	44-192	SBI
Crossroads	Clapton, Eric	20-147	KB
Crossroads	Cream	15-19	SC
Crosstown Traffic	Hendrix, Jimi	10-475	DA
Crowd the	Orbison, Roy	38-53	ZM
Crucify	Amos, Tori	6-34	SC
Cruel Summer	Bananarama	17-520	SC
Cruise	Florida Georgia Line	44-131	ASK
Cruisin'	D'Angelo	4-680	SC
Cruisin'	Lewis & Paltrow	14-22	THM
Cruisin'	Robinson, Smokey	27-268	DK
Crumblin' Down	Mellencamp, John	21-433	LE
Crumblin' Down	Mellencamp, John	19-96	PS
Crumblin' Down	Mellencamp, John	20-78	SC
Crunchy Granola Suite (Hot August Night)	Diamond, Neil	47-411	BHK
Crush	Archuleta, David	36-494	CB
Crush	Archuleta, David	36-233	PHM
Crush	Dave Matthews Band	14-287	MM
Crush	McCann, Lila	10-212	SC
Crush	McCann, Lila	22-435	ST
Crush	Moore, Mandy	15-809	CB
Crush	Moore, Mandy	23-590	PHM
Crush	Paige, Jennifer	28-187	DK
Crushin' It	Paisley, Brad	45-39	BKD
Crusin'	Robinson, Smokey	3-558	SC
Cry	Anderson, Lynn	47-641	CB
Cry	Gayle, Crystal	34-261	CB
Cry	Gayle, Crystal	13-498	P

SONG TITLE	ARTIST	#	TYPE
Cry	Hill, Faith	33-187	CB
Cry	Hill, Faith	25-336	MM
Cry	Hill, Faith	18-203	ST
Cry	Moore, Mandy	25-88	MM
Cry	Ray, Johnnie	12-309	DK
Cry	Ray, Johnnie	7-297	MM
Cry	Ray, Johnnie	18-621	PS
Cry	Ray, Johnnie	4-185	SC
Cry Baby	Joplin, Janis	28-199	DK
Cry Baby	Joplin, Janis	7-482	MM
Cry Baby	Mimms & Enchanters	5-515	SC
Cry Cry Cry	Cash, Johnny	29-567	CB
Cry Cry Cry	Highway 101	34-280	CB
Cry Cry Darling	Nelson, Willie	38-75	PS
Cry Like A Baby	Box Tops	11-338	DK
Cry Me A River	Buble, Michael	40-83	PS
Cry Me A River	Cocker, Joe	21-442	LE
Cry Me A River	London, Julie	11-579	DK
Cry Me A River	London, Julie	12-564	P
Cry Me A River	London, Julie	4-355	SC
Cry Me A River	Standard	9-795	SAV
Cry Me A River	Standard	19-788	SGB
Cry Me A River	Streisand, Barbra	49-469	MM
Cry Me A River	Streisand, Barbra	49-215	MM
Cry Me A River	Timberlake, Justin	25-423	MM
Cry Me A River	Timberlake, Justin	18-605	PHM
Cry Of The Wild Goose	Ford, Tenn Ernie	5-219	SC
Cry Of The Wild Goose	Laine, Frankie	18-613	PS
Cry Of The Wild Goose the	Ford, Tenn Ernie	22-206	CB
Cry On The Shoulder Of The Road	McBride, Martina	1-382	CB
Cry On The Shoulder Of The Road	McBride, Martina	7-592	CHM
Cry On The Shoulder Of The Road	McBride, Martina	7-429	MM
Cry On The Shoulder Of The Road	McBride, Martina	3-568	SC
Cry With You	Hayes, Hunter	39-73	PHN
Cry Wolf	A-Ha	46-240	SFM
Cry Wolf	Shaw, Victoria	6-580	MM
Crybaby	Carey, Mariah	15-634	THM
Cryin'	Aerosmith	18-479	NU
Cryin'	Vixen	19-558	SC
Cryin' Days	Mullins, Megan	30-446	CB
Cryin' Days	Mullins, Megan	30-446	CB
Cryin' For Me	Keith, Toby	38-156	AC
Cryin' Game	Evans, Sara	8-733	CB
Cryin' Game	Evans, Sara	5-296	SC
Cryin' Game	Evans, Sara	22-832	ST
Cryin' In My Sleep	Reeves, Jim	44-256	DFK
Cryin' Time	Charles, Ray	12-173	DK
Cryin' Time	Morgan, Lorrie	3-47	SC
Crying	Jay & Americans	14-373	PS
Crying	McLean, Don	47-247	CB
Crying	Orbison, Roy	17-26	DK
Crying	Orbison, Roy	14-553	SC

SONG TITLE	ARTIST	#	TYPE
Crying	Orbison, Roy	10-508	SF
Crying	Orbison, Roy	9-182	SO
Crying At The Discoteque	Alcazar	21-723	TT
Crying Game the	Boy George	12-151	DK
Crying Game the	Boy George	24-140	SC
Crying In The Chapel	Presley, Elvis	11-609	DK
Crying In The Chapel	Presley, Elvis	13-99	P
Crying In The Chapel	Presley, Elvis	9-796	SAV
Crying In The Chapel	Presley, Elvis	30-378	SC
Crying In The Chapel	Presley, Elvis	14-798	THM
Crying In The Rain	Everly Brothers	38-17	CB
Crying In The Rain	King, Carole	43-453	UB
Crying My Heart Out Over You	Skaggs, Ricky	49-632	CB
Crying Out For Me	Mario	36-487	CB
Crying Time	Orbison, Roy	47-732	SRK
Crying Time	Owens, Buck	46-102	VH
Crying, Waiting, Hoping	Holly, Buddy	47-889	ZM
Crystal Ball	Styx	47-381	SC
Crystal Blue Persuasion	James & Shondells	33-260	CB
Crystal Blue Persuasion	James & Shondells	12-134	DK
Crystal Chandeliers	Pride, Charley	8-802	CB
Cult Of Personality	Living Colour	27-206	DK
Cum On Feel The Noize	Quiet Riot	12-93	DK
Cup Of Life	Martin, Ricky	33-365	CB
Cup Of Life, the	Martin, Ricky	9-130	PS
Cups (When I'm Gone)	Kendrick, Anna	42-13	PHM
Cups (You're Gonna Miss Me...)	Pitch Perfect	44-116	KV
Curbside Prophet	Mraz, Jason	23-556	MM
Curiosity	Jepsen, Carly Rae	49-111	SBI
Cut Both Ways	Estefan, Gloria	17-742	PT
Cut Me Off	Perfect Stranger	4-889	SC
Cut Me Some Slack	Janson, Chris	41-98	PHN
Cut Me Some Slack	Janson, Chris	45-380	PHN
Cutie Pie	One Way	14-364	MH
Cuzz You're So Sweet	Husky, Ferlin	22-266	CB
Da Butt **	E.U.	2-189	SC
Da Doo Ron Ron	Crystals	3-359	MH
Da Doo Ron Ron	Crystals	25-174	MM
Da Doo Ron Ron	Crystals	9-283	SC
Daddy And Home	Tucker, Tanya	45-124	THM
Daddy Doesn't Pray Anymore	Stapleton, Chris	49-788	DCK
Daddy Don't You Walk So Fast	Newton, Wayne	47-307	LE
Daddy Frank The Guitar Man	Haggard, Merle	8-316	CB
Daddy Frank The Guitar Man	Haggard, Merle	7-120	MM
Daddy Had A Cadillac, & Mama Got A C...	Yates, Billy	48-712	CB
Daddy Never Was The Cadillac Kind	Confederate RR	2-221	SC
Daddy Sang Bass	Cash & Carter	11-836	DK
Daddy Sang Bass	Cash, Johnny	21-581	SC
Daddy What If	Bare, Bobby Jr & Sr	18-268	CB

SONG TITLE	ARTIST	#	TYPE
Daddy Won't Sell The Farm	Montgomery Gentry	8-911	CB
Daddy Won't Sell The Farm	Montgomery Gentry	22-516	ST
Daddy's Come Around	Overstreet, Paul	29-768	CB
Daddy's Come Around	Overstreet, Paul	12-41	DK
Daddy's Drinking Up Our Xmas	Trailer Trash	46-286	CB
Daddy's Hands	Dunn, Holly	26-359	DK
Daddy's Hands	Dunn, Holly	13-383	P
Daddy's Hands	Dunn, Holly	8-696	SAV
Daddy's Home	Shep & Limelights	35-47	CB
Daddy's Home	Shep & Limelights	3-296	MM
Daddy's Home	Shep & Limelights	3-581	SC
Daddy's Last Letter the	Ritter, Tex	20-716	CB
Daddy's Little Girl	Martino, Al	29-493	LE
Daddy's Little Girl	Martino, Al	2-63	SC
Daddy's Little Girl	Standard	19-789	SGB
Daddy's Money	Ricochet	7-240	MM
Daddy's Money	Ricochet	22-887	ST
Daisy	Halfway To Hazard	30-445	CB
Daisy A Day	Strunk, Judd	49-252	DFK
Daisy Jane	America	20-96	SC
Dallas	Jackson, Alan	1-37	CB
Dallas	Jackson, Alan	6-206	MM
Dallas	Jackson, Alan	2-706	SC
Dallas Days And Fort Worth Nights	LeDoux, Chris	3-636	SC
Damaged	TLC	25-580	MM
Damaged	TLC	19-345	STP
Damaged	TLC	32-233	THM
Damn Right	Clark, Terri	29-184	CB
Damn Right I Got The Blues	Guy, Buddy	20-139	KB
Damn! - duet	Youngbloodz & Lil Jon	32-422	THM
Damned If I Do (Darned If..)	All Time Low	36-307	PHM
Dance	Twister Alley	6-752	MM
Dance (While the Music Still Goes On)	Abba	49-303	LRT
Dance Again - duet	Lopez & Pitbull	40-10	BH
Dance And Shout	Shaggy	15-442	PHM
Dance Dance	Fall Out Boy	30-147	PT
Dance Dance Dance	Beach Boys	5-499	BS
Dance Dance Dance	Chic	9-754	SAV
Dance Dance Dance	Miller, Steve	23-629	BS
Dance For Me	Sisquo	18-552	TT
Dance Hall Days	Wang Chung	29-638	SC
Dance In The Boat	Kinleys	19-567	CB
Dance Into The Light	Collins, Phil	24-367	SC
Dance Little Jean	Nitty Gritty Dirt Band	5-858	SC
Dance Naked	Mellencamp, John	19-94	PS
Dance On Little Girl	Anka, Paul	4-224	SC
Dance the	Brooks, Garth	1-213	CB
Dance the	Brooks, Garth	17-349	DK
Dance the	Brooks, Garth	6-275	MM

SONG TITLE	ARTIST	#	TYPE
Dance the	Brooks, Garth	13-325	P
Dance the	Brooks, Garth	2-675	SC
Dance the	Rockwell	18-536	TT
Dance This Mess Around	B-52's	46-454	KV
Dance To The Music	Sly & Family Stone	35-76	CB
Dance With Me	Drifters	45-896	RB
Dance With Me	Morgan, Debelah	14-505	SC
Dance With Me	Morgan, Debelah	18-512	TT
Dance With Me	Orleans	2-863	SC
Dance With Me Henry (The Wall)	Gibbs, Georgia	33-236	CB
Dance With Me Just One More Time	Rodriguez, Johnny	8-841	CB
Dance With Me Molly	Whitley, Keith	47-742	SRK
Dance With My Father	Coffey, Kelly	20-475	ST
Dance With My Father	Dion, Celine	29-212	PHM
Dance With My Father	Vandross, Luther	20-376	HP
Dance With My Father	Vandross, Luther	25-659	MM
Dance With My Father	Vandross, Luther	19-539	SC
Dance With My Father	Vandross, Luther	32-388	THM
Dance With The One That Brought You	Twain, Shania	3-644	SC
Dancin'	Guy	9-332	PS
Dancin'	Guy	5-899	SC
Dancin' Cowboys	Bellamy Brothers	14-430	SC
Dancin' On The Boulevard	Alabama	22-601	ST
Dancin' Shaggin' On The Boulevard	Alabama	1-26	CB
Dancin' Shaggin' On The Boulevard	Alabama	7-655	CHM
Dancing Away With My Heart	Lady Antebellum	46-295	BKD
Dancing Away With My Heart - duet	Lady Antebellum	46-80	BKD
Dancing Barefoot	Moorer, Allison	49-206	CB
Dancing In The Dark	Springsteen, Bruce	17-608	LE
Dancing In The Dark	Springsteen, Bruce	3-486	SC
Dancing In The Moonlight	King Harvest	27-578	DK
Dancing In The Moonlight	King Harvest	9-368	MG
Dancing In The Moonlight	King Harvest	9-714	SAV
Dancing In The Street	Mamas & Papas	47-215	KV
Dancing In The Street	Martha & Vandellas	11-126	DK
Dancing In The Street	Martha & Vandellas	3-355	MH
Dancing In The Street	Martha & Vandellas	12-632	P
Dancing In The Street	Van Halen	13-617	LE
Dancing Machine	Jackson Five	49-316	CB
Dancing On The Ceiling	Richie, Lionel	34-84	CB
Dancing On The Ceiling	Richie, Lionel	11-537	DK
Dancing On The Ceiling	Richie, Lionel	10-391	LE
Dancing On The Ceiling	Richie, Lionel	14-573	SC
Dancing Queen	Abba	11-518	DK
Dancing Queen	Abba	7-496	MM
Dancing The Night Away	Amazing Rhythm Aces	45-836	VH

SONG TITLE	ARTIST	#	TYPE
Dancing With A Man	Carrington, Rodney	15-147	SC
Dancing With Myself	Idol, Billy	12-124	DK
Dancing With Myself	Idol, Billy	13-212	P
Dancing Your Memory Away	McClain, Charley	38-41	SC
Dancy's Dream	Restless Heart	4-67	SC
Dandy	Herman's Hermits	4-222	SC
Dang Me	Miller, Roger	8-293	CB
Dang Me	Miller, Roger	11-764	DK
Dang Me	Miller, Roger	6-774	MM
Dang Me	Miller, Roger	17-287	NA
Dang Me	Miller, Roger	13-483	P
Dang Me	Miller, Roger	9-521	SAV
Danger Ahead	Tucker, Tanya	38-12	CB
Danger Zone	Loggins & Messina	48-567	DK
Danger Zone	Loggins, Kenny	28-319	DK
Dangerous	Roxette	18-247	DK
Dangerous Game	3 Doors Down	47-658	CB
Dangerous Type	Letters To Cleo	4-339	SC
Daniel	John, Elton	16-849	DK
Daniel	John, Elton	3-241	LG
Daniel	John, Elton	12-679	P
Daniel	John, Elton	9-655	SAV
Daniel	John, Elton	2-376	SC
Daniel	Wilson Phillips	24-259	SC
Daniel Boone	TV Themes	2-165	SC
Danke Schoen	Newton, Wayne	12-529	P
Danke Schoen	Newton, Wayne	9-314	STR
Danny Boy	Standard	17-346	DK
Danny's Dream	Restless Heart	1-407	CB
Danny's Song	Loggins, Kenny	9-329	AG
Danny's Song	Murray, Anne	8-448	CB
Danny's Song	Swon Brothers	44-212	DCK
Dare To Dream	Messina, Jo Dee	25-232	MM
Dare To Dream	Messina, Jo Dee	16-700	ST
Dark End Of The Street	Flying Burrito Bros	11-440	DK
Dark Hollow	Monroe, Bill	8-251	CB
Dark Horse	Mason, Mila	22-403	CHM
Dark Lady	Cher	11-654	DK
Dark Lady	Cher	14-56	RS
Dark Lady	Cher	15-132	SGB
Dark Moon	Isaak, Chris	24-244	SC
Darktown Strutters Ball	Monte, Lou	9-744	SAV
Darlene	Brown T. Graham	34-279	CB
Darlene	Brown, T. Graham	5-777	SC
Darlin'	Backstreet Boys	18-706	MM
Darlin'	Beach Boys	46-174	SC
Darlin'	Miller, Frankie	44-57	SF
Darling Be Home Soon	Lovin' Spoonful	47-212	LE
Darling Je Vous Aime Beaucoup	Cole, Nat "King"	46-347	CB
Darling Nikki **	Prince	5-543	SC
Darlington County	Springsteen, Bruce	20-248	LE
Darned If I Don't Danged If I Do	Shenandoah	1-494	CB
Darned If I Don't Danged If I Do	Shenandoah	2-746	SC

SONG TITLE	ARTIST	#	TYPE
Daughter	Pearl Jam	9-295	RS
Dawn	Four Seasons	4-716	SC
Dawn (Go Away)	Four Seasons	33-247	CB
Day After Day	Badfinger	12-705	P
Day After Day	Badfinger	29-293	SC
Day Before You Came the	Abba	46-217	FUN
Day By Day	Sinatra, Frank	28-504	DK
Day By Day	Standard	12-67	DK
Day Drinking	Little Big Town	44-324	SSC
Day I Stop Loving You the	Adams, Oleta	46-382	SC
Day In Day Out	Kersh, David	22-608	ST
Day In The Life a	Beatles	17-64	DK
Day In The Life Of A Fool a	Jones, Jack	29-485	LE
Day Job	Gin Blossoms	24-744	SC
Day O (Banana Boat Song)	Belafonte, Harry	12-97	DK
Day O (Banana Boat Song)	Belafonte, Harry	13-60	P
Day She Left Tulsa the	Hayes, Wade	8-142	CB
Day She Left Tulsa the	Hayes, Wade	7-736	CHM
Day She Left Tulsa the	Hayes, Wade	22-423	ST
Day That Never Comes the	Metallica	47-256	SBI
Day Too Soon	Sia	37-151	SC
Day Tripper	Beatles	16-801	DK
Day Tripper	Beatles	12-912	P
Daybreak	Manilow, Barry	29-113	CB
Daydream	Lovin' Spoonful	47-210	CB
Daydream Believer	Monkees	16-748	DK
Daydream Believer	Monkees	9-648	SAV
Daydream Believer	Monkees	14-556	SC
Daydream Believer	Murray, Anne	38-5	SC
Daydreamer	Adele	38-229	CB
Daydreams About Night Things	Milsap, Ronnie	15-63	CB
Daydreams About Night Things	Milsap, Ronnie	8-683	SAV
Daylight Katy	Lightfoot, Gordon	43-490	SK
Days	Kinks	48-181	LE
Days Go By	Dirty Vegas	18-149	PHM
Days Go By	Urban, Keith	20-444	ST
Days Like These	Ian, Janis	24-28	SC
Days Like This	Proctor, Rachel	36-366	CB
Days Like This	Proctor, Rachel	25-617	MM
Days Like This	Proctor, Rachel	19-67	ST
Days Like This	Proctor, Rachel	32-371	THM
Days Of America	Blackhawk	16-40	ST
Days Of Gold	Owen, Jake	45-641	ASK
Days Of Our Lives	Otto, James	20-275	SC
Days Of Our Lives	Otto, James	19-686	ST
Days Of Thunder	Wills, Mark	30-467	CB
Days Of Wine And Roses	Standard	13-627	SGB
Days Of Wine And Roses	Williams, Andy	33-214	CB

SONG TITLE	ARTIST	#	TYPE
Days Of Wine And Roses	Williams, Andy	27-393	DK
Days Of Wine And Roses	Williams, Andy	13-555	LE
Days Of Wine And Roses	Williams, Andy	12-553	P
Daysleeper	REM	16-214	MM
Daytime Friends	Rogers, Kenny	4-643	SC
Daytime Friends & Nighttime Lovers	Rogers, Kenny	3-169	CB
Dayum Baby	Florida Georgia Line	47-92	ASK
Dazed And Confused	Led Zeppelin	19-274	SGB
Deacon Blues	Steely Dan	13-16	P
Deacon Blues	Steely Dan	15-390	RS
Dead Babies	Alice Cooper	16-454	SGB
Dead End Street	Kinks	48-178	LE
Dead Flowers	Lambert, Miranda	46-252	CB
Dead Man's Curve	Jan & Dean	34-17	CB
Dead Man's Curve	Jan & Dean	4-250	SC
Dead Man's Party - Halloween	Oingo Boingo	45-118	SC
Dead Ringer	Bentley, Stephanie	4-500	SC
Dead Skunk	Wainwright, Loudin	2-789	SC
Deadbeat Club	B-52's	46-453	DK
Deadwood Stage the	Day, Doris	48-137	ZMP
Deadwood Stage the - show	Calamity Jane	49-852	SGB
Deal	Hall, Tom T.	18-285	CB
Deal the	Dalton, Lacy J.	45-825	VH
Dear Abby	Prine, John	23-525	CB
Dear Brother	Williams, Hank Sr.	37-188	CB
Dear Diamond	Lambert, Miranda	44-396	KV
Dear Future Husband	Trainor, Meghan	45-142	ASK
Dear God	Cline, Patsy	45-487	CB
Dear Heart	Lettermen	48-519	L1
Dear Heart	Williams, Andy	33-216	CB
Dear Hearts And Gentle People	Crosby, Bing	9-546	SAV
Dear Hearts And Gentle People	Reeves, Jim	44-265	OZP
Dear John	Williams, Hank Sr.	14-225	CB
Dear John	Williams, Hank Sr.	34-187	CB
Dear John Letter	Shepard, Jeanne	8-771	CB
Dear Lie	TLC	15-423	CB
Dear Mama	2 Pac	28-218	DK
Dear Me	Morgan, Lorrie	1-331	CB
Dear Me	Morgan, Lorrie	2-623	SC
Dear No One	Kelly, Tori	48-649	DCK
Dear Santa	McGraw, Tim	47-238	CB
Dear Uncle Sam	Lynn, Loretta	5-849	SC
Dearly Beloved	Lettermen	48-533	L1
Debbie	B-52's	46-456	SC
December	Collective Soul	3-496	SC
December 1963	Four Seasons	10-539	SF
December 1963 (Oh What A Night)	Four Seasons	11-789	DK
Deck Of Cards	Ritter, Tex	20-714	CB
Dede Dinah	Avalon, Frankie	5-462	SC

SONG TITLE	ARTIST	#	TYPE
Dedicated Follower Of Fashion	Kinks	48-180	LE
Dedicated To The One I Love	Mamas & Papas	9-116	PS
Dedicated To The One I Love	Shirelles	3-283	MM
Dedicated To The One I Love	Shirelles	4-14	SC
Deep Dark Water	Reeves, Jim	44-258	DFK
Deep Down	Tillis, Pam	7-139	MM
Deep Down	Tillis, Pam	3-565	SC
Deep In The Heart Of Texas	Crosby, Bing	29-409	CB
Deep In The Heart Of Texas	Crosby, Bing	29-477	LE
Deep In The Heart Of Texas	Crosby, Bing	4-354	SC
Deep In The Heart Of Texas	Standard	27-464	DK
Deep Inside of You	Third Eye Blind	33-421	CB
Deep Inside Of You	Third Eye Blind	14-498	SC
Deep River Woman	Richie, Lionel	33-316	CB
Deep the	Moody Blues	45-587	OZP
Deep Water	Smith, Carl	8-649	SAV
Deeper And Deeper	Madonna	6-101	MM
Deeper Love a	Civilles & Cole	9-841	SAV
Deeper Love a	Franklin, Aretha	36-161	JT
Deeper Than That	Shenandoah	4-401	SC
Deeper Than The Holler	Travis, Randy	1-401	CB
Deeper Than The Holler	Travis, Randy	13-328	P
Deer Slayer	Stevens, Ray	47-904	TU
Defy You	Offspring	30-647	THM
Delaware	Como, Perry	49-40	ZVS
Delia's Gone	Jennings, Waylon	46-52	SSK
Delicious Surprise (I Believe It)	Messina, Jo Dee	23-285	CB
Delicious Surprise (I Believe)	Messina, Jo Dee	29-603	ST
Delilah	Jones, Tom	12-9	DK
Delirious	Prince	12-794	P
Delirious	Prince	5-611	SC
Della And The Dealer	Axton, Hoyt	44-62	HM
Delta Dawn	Reddy, Helen	11-191	DK
Delta Dawn	Reddy, Helen	13-441	P
Delta Dawn	Reddy, Helen	9-844	SAV
Delta Dawn	Tucker, Tanya	8-15	CB
Delta Dawn	Tucker, Tanya	7-112	MM
Delta Dawn	Tucker, Tanya	8-679	SAV
Denis Denis	Blondie	49-131	LG
Denise	Randy & Rainbows	5-169	SC
Der Kommissar	After The Fire	29-15	MH
Desert Rose	Sting	15-635	THM
Desert Rose	Sting	18-553	TT
Desert Rose (Radio Version)	Sting	14-481	SC
Designated Drinker	Jackson & Strait	40-100	CB
Designated Drinker	Jackson & Strait	16-327	ST
Desire	U2	11-766	DK

SONG TITLE	ARTIST	#	TYPE
Desire	U2	30-70	SC
Desire	U2	30-759	SF
Desiree	Diamond, Neil	47-420	PS
Desperado	Alice Cooper	16-445	SGB
Desperado	Black, Clint	1-828	CB
Desperado	Black, Clint	30-423	THM
Desperado	Cash, Johnny	43-409	KCA
Desperado	Eagles	7-560	BS
Desperado	Eagles	2-255	SC
Desperado Love	Twitty, Conway	49-347	CB
Desperado Love	Twitty, Conway	2-632	SC
Desperados Waiting For A Train	Highwaymen	48-407	DFK
Desperately	Strait, George	19-762	ST
Desperation	Lambert, Miranda	46-265	KV
Destination Unknown	Sanz, Victor	14-145	CB
Destiny	Richie, Lionel	47-455	LE
Detroit Breakdown	J. Geils Band	17-472	SC
Detroit City	Bare, Bobby	15-78	CB
Detroit City	Bare, Bobby	17-162	DK
Detroit City	Bare, Bobby	8-620	SAV
Detroit City	Jones, Tom	15-466	JTG
Detroit Rock City	Kiss	10-39	SC
Deuce	Kiss	10-37	SC
Devil And The Cross	Halfway To Hazard	36-575	CB
Devil In A Sleeping Bag	Nelson, Willie	46-36	SSK
Devil In Disguise	Presley, Elvis	17-549	DK
Devil In Disguise	Presley, Elvis	2-583	SC
Devil In The Bottle	Sheppard, T.G.	20-661	SC
Devil Inside	Inxs	34-95	CB
Devil Named Music the	Stapleton, Chris	49-650	KV
Devil Or Angel	Clovers	25-559	MM
Devil Or Angel	Vee, Bobby	13-104	P
Devil To Pay the	Cash, Johnny	49-283	BAT
Devil Went Down To Georgia	Charlie Daniels Band	7-451	MM
Devil Went Down To Georgia	Charlie Daniels Band	13-540	P
Devil Went Down To Georgia	Charlie Daniels Band	2-15	SC
Devil Went Down To Georgia	Charlie Daniels Band	8-596	TT
Devil Went Down To Georgia	Zac Brown Band	48-642	KV
Devil With a Blue Dress On	Ryder & Detroit Whe	11-445	DK
Devil Woman	Richards, Cliff	9-775	SAV
Devil Woman	Robbins, Marty	3-225	CB
Devil Woman	Robbins, Marty	17-383	DK
Devil Woman	Robbins, Marty	7-155	MM
Devil Woman	Robbins, Marty	8-672	SAV
Devil Woman	Robbins, Marty	5-95	SC
Devil's Right Hand the	Earle, Steve	45-954	KV
Devoted To You	Everly Brothers	38-18	CB
Devoted To You	Simon, Carly	49-157	LG
Diamond Girl	Seals & Croft	12-350	DK
Diamond Girl	Seals & Croft	17-560	PR
Diamond Girl	Seals & Croft	3-473	SC

SONG TITLE	ARTIST	#	TYPE
Diamond Rings & Old Barstools - duet	McGraw & Dunn, C	45-43	BKD
Diamonds And Guns	Transplants	23-169	PHM
Diamonds And Pearls	Prince	23-329	CB
Diamonds And Rust	Baez, Joan	46-462	SC
Diamonds Are A Girl's Best Friend	Monroe, Marilyn	2-251	SC
Diamonds Are A Girl's Best Friend	Monroe, Marilyn	19-776	SGB
Diamonds Are Forever	Bassey, Shirley	9-71	SC
Diana	Anka, Paul	33-235	CB
Diana	Anka, Paul	27-500	DK
Diana	Anka, Paul	13-124	P
Diana	Anka, Paul	9-171	SO
Diana	One Direction	43-180	ASK
Diane	Bruce, Ed	14-260	SC
Diary	Bread	9-720	SAV
Diary	Bread	5-612	SC
Diary	Keys, Alicia	35-253	CB
Diary the	Sedaka, Neil	45-356	CB
Dibs	Ballerini, Kelsea	45-386	BKD
Did I Shave My Back For This	Judd, Cledus T.	16-513	CB
Did I Shave My Legs For This	Carter, Deana	33-133	CB
Did I Shave My Legs For This	Carter, Deana	22-412	ST
Did It For The Girl	Bates, Jeff	44-149	BKD
Did It In A Minute - WN	Hall & Oates	48-62	CB
Did You Ever Have To Make Up Your Mind	Lovin' Spoonful	3-19	SC
Did You Ever See A Dream Walking	Crosby, Bing	29-420	CB
Didn't Have You	Montana, Billy	2-736	SC
Didn't I	Montgomery Gentry	16-684	ST
Didn't I	Proctor, Rachel	19-705	ST
Didn't I Blow Your Mind	Delfonics	9-797	SAV
Didn't We	Sinatra, Frank	9-253	PT
Didn't We Almost Have It All	Houston, Whitney	43-373	CB
Didn't We Love	Walker, Tamara	14-128	CB
Die A Happy Man	Rhett, Thomas	45-442	BKD
Die Another Day	Madonna	25-394	MM
Die Another Day	Madonna	18-582	NS
Die Another Day	Madonna	32-20	THM
Die Die My Darling	Metallica	47-258	SC
Die Of A Broken Heart	Urban, Keith	20-385	ST
Diet Mountain Dew	Del Ray, Lana	44-108	KV
Differences	Ginuwine	35-264	CB
Differences	Ginuwine	16-82	ST
Different Breed	Carter's Chord	36-196	PHM
Different Colors	Walk The Moon	48-414	BKD
Different Drum	Ronstadt, Linda	12-323	DK
Different Drum	Ronstadt, Linda	13-304	P
Different Drum	Ronstadt, Linda	9-696	SAV
Different Kind Of Fine	Zac Brown Band	43-472	CB
Different Kind Of Flower a	Price, Ray	45-736	VH

49

SONG TITLE	ARTIST	#	TYPE
Different Kind Of Love Song	Cher	47-671	CB
Different Kind Of Pain a	Cold	29-277	PHM
Different Point Of View	Ferrell, Rick	17-481	CB
Different World a	Covington, Bucky	30-310	CB
Difficult Kind the	Crow, Sheryl	8-521	PHT
Difficult Thing the	Crow, Sheryl	29-673	RS
Dig In	Kravitz, Lenny	25-33	MM
Diggin' On You	TLC	15-422	CB
Diggin' Up Bones	Travis, Randy	1-393	CB
Diggin' Up Bones	Travis, Randy	11-437	DK
Diggin' Up Bones	Travis, Randy	8-700	SAV
Diggy Liggy Lo	Cajun Classic	45-725	VH
Diggy Liggy Lo	Kershaw, Doug	44-53	KV
Dilemma	Nelly & Rowland, K.	25-457	MM
Dilemma - duet	Nelly & Rowland	33-433	CB
Dim All The Lights	Summer, Donna	17-58	DK
Dim All The Lights	Summer, Donna	15-207	LE
Dim Lights Thick Smoke And...	Yoakam, Dwight	49-698	KV
Dime Store Cowgirl	Musgraves, Kacey	45-316	KRG
Dimming Of The Day	Raitt, Bonnie	45-858	VH
Dinah Moe Humm **	Zappa, Frank	2-729	SC
Dindi	Cole, Natalie	48-643	KV
Ding Dong Daddy Of The D Car Line	Cherry Poppin Daddy	13-693	SGB
Ding Dong Daddy Of The D Car Line	Cherry Poppin' Daddys	49-797	SGB
Ding Dong Merrily On High - xmas	Christmas	45-14	KV
Ding Dong The Witch Is Dead - Show	Wizard Of Oz	33-219	CB
Dinner For One Please James	Cole, Nat "King"	46-372	SBI
Dinner With Delores	Prince	49-833	KV
Dinosaur	Williams, Hank Jr.	45-694	TBR
Dirt	Florida Georgia Line	44-319	SBI
Dirt Off Your Shoulder **	Jay-Z	23-249	THM
Dirt Road Anthem	Aldean, Jason	37-231	CB
Dirt Road Diary	Bryan, Luke	46-376	ASK
Dirt Road the	Sawyer Brown	2-353	SC
Dirty	Aguilera, Christina	18-338	PHM
Dirty Boogie the	Brian Setzer Orch	46-530	KV
Dirty Deeds Done Dirt Cheap	AC/DC	4-556	SC
Dirty Deeds Done With Sheep	Rivers, Bob	45-933	ZP
Dirty Deeds, Done Dirt Cheap	Jett, Joan	43-388	PS
Dirty Girl	Clark, Terri	30-353	CB
Dirty Laundry	Henley, Don	48-148	AH
Dirty Laundry	Underwood, Carrie	49-719	KV
Dirty Little Secret	McLachlan, Sarah	29-240	ZM
Dirty Love	Zappa, Frank	10-484	DA
Dirty Man	Stone, Joss	43-119	ZMP
Dirty Mind	Williams, Hank Jr.	16-676	C2C
Dirty Polka **	Dirty Polka Band	30-667	RSX
Dirty White Boy	Foreigner	13-748	SGB

SONG TITLE	ARTIST	#	TYPE
Dirty Work	Steely Dan	15-394	RS
Dis-Satisfied	Anderson & Howard	20-797	CB
Dis-Satisfied - duet	Anderson & Howard	40-75	CB
Disappear	Hoobastank	20-26	PHM
Disappear - Nashville	Panettiere, Hayden	45-466	BKD
Disco Duck - Part 1	Dees & Idiots	23-28	SC
Disco Inferno	Trammps	9-226	PT
Disco Inferno	Trammps	20-368	SC
Disco Inferno (Radio Vers)	50 Cent	37-102	SC
Disco Lady	Taylor, Johnnie	17-138	DK
Disco Nights	G.Q.	18-366	AH
Disease	Matchbox 20	25-395	MM
Disease	Matchbox 20	18-583	NS
Disease	Matchbox 20	32-22	THM
Dissident	Pearl Jam	9-297	RS
Distance the	Evan & Jaron	33-406	CB
Distant Drums	Reeves, Jim	8-575	CB
Distant Drums	Reeves, Jim	3-826	LG
Distant Drums	Reeves, Jim	13-520	P
Distant Drums	Reeves, Jim	9-620	SAV
Disturbia	Rihanna	36-104	CB
Ditmas	Mumford & Sons	48-433	BKD
Divers Do It Deeper	Coe, David Allan	18-323	CB
DIVORCE	Wynette, Tammy	15-824	CB
DIVORCE	Wynette, Tammy	16-737	DK
DIVORCE	Wynette, Tammy	10-746	JVC
DIVORCE	Wynette, Tammy	13-417	P
DIVORCE	Wynette, Tammy	8-675	SAV
DIVORCE	Wynette, Tammy	3-377	SC
Divorce Me C.O.D.	Travis, Merle	19-623	CB
Divorce Me C.O.D.	Wariner, Steve	5-220	SC
Divorce Sale the	Wynette, Tammy	45-670	DCK
Dixie	Standard	26-500	DK
Dixie	Standard	2-65	SC
Dixie	Standard	23-227	SM
Dixie Chicken	Brooks, Garth	1-220	CB
Dixie Chicken	Little Feat	12-25	DK
Dixie Fried	Perkins, Carl	5-42	SC
Dixie Highway	Jackson, Alan	45-106	KV
Dixie Lullaby	Green, Pat	47-124	NSC
Dixie On My Mind	Williams, Hank Jr.	16-672	C2C
Dixie Road	Greenwood, Lee	11-744	DK
Dixie Rose Deluxe's Honky Tonk...	Willmon, Trent	23-402	CB
Dixie Rose's Deluxe Honky Tonk..	Wilmon, Trent	20-494	ST
Dixieland Delight	Alabama	4-438	BS
Dixieland Delight	Alabama	1-5	CB
Dizzy	Goo Goo Dolls	34-59	CB
Dizzy	Roe, Tommy	11-601	DK
Dizzy	Roe, Tommy	6-783	MM
DJ Tonight	Rascal Flatts	44-288	KCDC
Do I	Bryan, Luke	45-479	AC
Do I Have To Cry For You	Carter, Nick	18-607	PHM

SONG TITLE	ARTIST	#	TYPE
Do I Have To Say The Words	Adams, Bryan	23-441	CB
Do I Love You (Yes In Every Way)	Fargo, Donna	48-665	CB
Do I Love You Enough	Ricochet	9-400	CB
Do I Make You Proud	Hicks, Taylor	30-151	PT
Do It Again	Beach Boys	46-502	ZM
Do It Again	Steely Dan	11-500	DK
Do It Again	Steely Dan	15-169	MH
Do It Again	Steely Dan	15-384	RS
Do It Again	Steely Dan	20-52	SC
Do It Again	Steely Dan	10-540	SF
Do It For Love	Hall & Oates	18-416	MM
Do It Like This	Rice, Chase	49-663	BKD
Do It Till Your Satisfied	B.T. Express	11-386	DK
Do It To Me	Richie, Lionel	43-369	CB
Do It With Madonna	Androids	32-250	THM
Do Me	Poison	17-368	DK
Do Me **	Bell Biv Devoe	28-399	DK
Do Me **	Bell Biv Devoe	5-552	SC
Do Me Baby	Prince	49-831	SC
Do Me With Love	Fricke, Janie	34-247	CB
Do Not Disturb	Presley, Elvis	25-113	MM
Do Nothin' 'Til You Hear From Me	Ellington, Duke	12-567	P
Do Right	Davis, Paul	48-613	SC
Do Right	Jimmy's Chickens	8-530	PHT
Do Right Woman Do Right Man	Franklin, Aretha	11-293	DK
Do That	Baby & P Diddy	32-129	THM
Do That To Me One More Time	Captain & Tennille	11-522	DK
Do That To Me One More Time	Captain & Tennille	2-866	SC
Do The Conga	Black Lace	49-49	ZVS
Do The Dog	Thomas, Rufus	47-611	RB
Do The Holey Pokey	Kids	33-197	CB
Do Wacka Do	Miller, Roger	22-285	CB
Do Wah Diddy Diddy	Mann, Manfred	26-329	DK
Do Wah Diddy Diddy	Mann, Manfred	3-289	MM
Do Wah Diddy Diddy	Mann, Manfred	13-75	P
Do We Still	Lynne, Rockie	30-86	CB
Do What You Do Do Well	Miller, Ned	49-227	DFK
Do What You Gotta Do	Brooks, Garth	23-363	SC
Do What You Gotta Do	Brooks, Garth	22-471	ST
Do What You Have To Do	McLachlan, Sarah	43-3	SC
Do Ya	Oslin, K.T.	29-69	CB
Do Ya Think I'm Sexy	Stewart, Rod	35-139	CB
Do Ya Think I'm Sexy	Stewart, Rod	16-735	DK
Do Ya Think I'm Sexy	Stewart, Rod	25-597	MM
Do Ya Think I'm Sexy	Stewart, Rod	9-651	SAV
Do You Believe In Love	Lewis & The News	47-184	CB
Do You Believe In Magic	Lovin' Spoonful	11-666	DK
Do You Believe Me Now	Gosdin, Vern	19-444	SC
Do You Call My Name	Ra	23-167	PHM
Do You Ever Fool Around	Stampley, Joe	43-302	CB

SONG TITLE	ARTIST	#	TYPE
Do You Know	Robyn	21-550	PHM
Do You Know (Ping-Pong Song)	Iglesias, Enrique	30-560	CB
Do You Know (Ping-Pong Song)	Iglesias, Enrique	46-317	SC
Do You Know The Way To San Jose	Warwick, Dionne	11-216	DK
Do You Know The Way To San Jose	Warwick, Dionne	3-360	MH
Do You Know The Way To San Jose	Warwick, Dionne	4-698	SC
Do You Know What I Mean	Michaels, Lee	29-274	SC
Do You Know Where You're Goin' To	Ross, Diana	11-266	DK
Do you Know Where You're Goin' To	Ross, Diana	4-53	SC
Do You Know Where Your Man Is	Tillis, Pam	6-393	MM
Do You Know Who I Am	Presley, Elvis	25-319	MM
Do You Know You Are My Sunshine	Statler Brothers	19-380	CB
Do You Know You Are My Sunshine	Statler Brothers	4-270	SC
Do You Love As Good As You Look	Bellamy Brothers	33-67	CB
Do You Love As Good As You Look	Bellamy Brothers	13-460	P
Do You Love As Good As You Look	Bellamy Brothers	5-616	SC
Do You Love Me	Blues Brothers	29-162	ZM
Do You Love Me	Contours	16-791	DK
Do You Love Me	Dave Clark Five	45-78	CB
Do You Love Me	Dave Clark Five	49-776	SC
Do You Love Me	Fiddler On The Roof	19-585	SC
Do You Love Me	Poole & Tremeloes	10-563	SF
Do You Love Me Just Say Yes	Highway 101	5-752	SC
Do You Miss Me	Enriquez, Jocelyn	24-553	SC
Do You Really Want Me	Robyn	10-136	SC
Do You Really Want To Hurt Me	Culture Club	18-492	SAV
Do You Really Want To Hurt Me	Culture Club	5-120	SC
Do You Remember	Collins, Phil	44-9	LG
Do You Remember These	Statler Brothers	19-379	CB
Do You Remember These	Statler Brothers	4-583	SC
Do You Sleep	Loeb, Lisa	14-202	CB
Do You Sleep	Loeb, Lisa	24-743	SC
Do You Still Want To Buy Me That...	Morgan, Lorrie	19-709	ST
Do You Think About Me	Underwood, Carrie	39-29	KV
Do you Think About Us	Total	4-615	SC
Do You Wanna Dance	98 Degrees	15-375	SKG
Do You Wanna Dance	Beach Boys	46-493	LE
Do You Wanna Dance	Freeman, Bobby	7-287	MM
Do You Wanna Dance	Freeman, Bobby	13-51	P
Do You Wanna Dance	Rivers, Johnny	47-368	KBR

SONG TITLE	ARTIST	#	TYPE
Do You Wanna Go To Heaven	Sheppard, T.G.	34-242	CB
Do You Wanna Go To Heaven	Sheppard, T.G.	4-651	SC
Do You Wanna Make Something Of It	Messina, Jo Dee	24-646	SC
Do You Wanna Make Something...	Messina, Jo Dee	7-394	MM
Do You Wanna Touch Me...	Jett, Joan	15-8	SC
Do You Want Fries With That	McGraw, Tim	23-277	CB
Do You Want To Build A Snowman - Frozen	Bell, Kristen	43-186	ASK
Do You Want To Know A Secret	Beatles	11-250	DK
Do You Want To Know A Secret	Beatles	13-259	P
Do You Want To Know A Secret	Beatles	29-339	SC
Do You Wish It Was Me	Aldean, Jason	44-292	BKD
DOA	Foo Fighters	48-225	SC
Dock Of The Bay	Redding, Otis	17-39	DK
Dock Of The Bay	Redding, Otis	12-641	P
Dock Of The Bay	Redding, Otis	19-105	SAV
Dock Of The Bay	Redding, Otis	2-85	SC
Doctor My Eyes	Browne, Jackson	17-180	SC
Doctor the	Doobie Brothers	29-77	CB
Does Anybody Really Know..	Chicago	4-878	SC
Does Anybody Really Know...	Chicago	34-37	CB
Does Ft. Worth Ever Cross Your Mind	Strait, George	1-242	CB
Does Ft. Worth Ever Cross Your Mind	Strait, George	9-518	SAV
Does He Love You	McEntire & Davis	1-808	CB
Does He Love You	McEntire & Davis	6-399	MM
Does My Ring Burn Your Finger	Womack, Lee Ann	25-66	MM
Does My Ring Burn Your Finger	Womack, Lee Ann	16-32	ST
Does My Ring Hurt Your Finger	Pride, Charley	8-422	CB
Does That Blue Moon Ever Shine On You	Keith, Toby	1-692	CB
Does That Blue Moon Ever Shine On You	Keith, Toby	7-208	MM
Does That Blue Moon Ever Shine On You	Keith, Toby	4-210	SC
Does Your Chewing Gum Lose It's Flavor...	Donegan, Lonnie	6-514	MM
Does Your Mother Know	Abba	7-498	MM
Doesn't Really Matter	Jackson, Janet	33-379	CB
Doesn't Really Matter	Jackson, Janet	14-6	PHM
Doesn't Really Matter	Jackson, Janet	15-413	PS
Doesn't Really Matter	Jackson, Janet	20-10	SGB
Doesn't Really Matter	Janet	30-641	THM
Dog & Butterfly	Heart	24-680	SC
Dog River Blues	Jackson, Alan	45-103	DFK

SONG TITLE	ARTIST	#	TYPE
Doggie In The Window	Page, Patti	33-213	CB
Doin' It All For My Baby	Lewis & The News	11-329	DK
Doin' It Right	Azar, Steve	23-284	CB
Doin' My Time	Cash, Johnny	43-412	SRK
Doin' What Comes Natur'ly	Shore, Dinah	2-243	SC
Doin' What She Likes	Shelton, Blake	43-135	PHN
Doing It All For My Baby	Lewis & The News	33-321	CB
Dollar the	Johnson, Jamey	23-473	CB
Dollar the	Johnson, Jamey	29-854	SC
Dollar Wine Dance	Standard	49-464	MM
Dollar's Worth Of Pennies a	Roe, Tommy	48-114	CB
Domestic Light And Cold	Bentley, Dierks	23-466	CB
Dominique	Reynolds, Debbie	45-70	CB
Domino	Morrison, Van	23-603	BS
Domino	Morrison, Van	4-844	SC
Domino Theory the	Wariner, Steve	1-497	CB
Don Henley Must Die	Mojo Nixon	15-142	SC
Don Juan D' Bubba	Williams, Hank Jr.	4-429	SC
Don Quixote	Eder, Linda	16-714	PS
Don Quixote	Lightfoot, Gordon	43-493	SK
Don't	Currington, Billy	36-606	CB
Don't	Jewel	36-332	SC
Don't	Presley, Elvis	14-743	THM
Don't	Twain, Shania	22-18	CB
Don't	Twain, Shania	21-654	SC
Don't Ask Me How I Know	Pinson, Bobby	22-312	CB
Don't Ask Me No Questions	Lynyrd Skynyrd	5-263	SC
Don't Ask Me No Questions	Lynyrd Skynyrd	19-814	SGB
Don't Ask Me No Questions	Williams, Hank Jr.	45-207	CZC
Don't Ask Me Why	Eder, Linda	17-442	PS
Don't Ask Me Why	Eurythmics	47-77	SBI
Don't Ask Me Why	Presley, Elvis	8-579	CB
Don't Ask Me Why I'm Going To Texas	Asleep At The Wheel	45-862	VH
Don't Be Angry	Fargo, Donna	48-661	CB
Don't Be Angry	Jackson, Stonewall	8-788	CB
Don't Be Angry	Jackson, Stonewall	5-221	SC
Don't Be Cruel	Brown, Bobby	11-315	DK
Don't Be Cruel	Brown, Bobby	13-198	P
Don't Be Cruel	Cheap Trick	48-543	DK
Don't Be Cruel	Judds	5-401	SC
Don't Be Cruel	Presley, Elvis	11-99	DK
Don't Be Cruel	Presley, Elvis	19-98	SAV
Don't Be Cruel	Presley, Elvis	2-587	SC
Don't Be Cruel	Presley, Elvis	14-744	THM
Don't Be Stupid	Twain, Shania	8-140	CB
Don't Be Stupid (You Know I Love..)	Twain, Shania	22-410	ST
Don't Believe Everything You Think	Brice, Lee	49-92	PHN
Don't Believe My Heart	Tucker, Tanya	19-429	SC

SONG TITLE	ARTIST	#	TYPE
Can Stand...			
Don't Blink	Chesney, Kenny	30-576	CB
Don't Bother Me	Beatles	9-641	SAV
Don't Break My Heart Again	Green, Pat	22-100	CB
Don't Break My Heart Again	Green, Pat	20-504	ST
Don't Break The Heart That Loves U	Francis, Connie	8-816	CB
Don't Break The Heart That Loves U	Francis, Connie	4-218	SC
Don't Bring Lulu	Provine, D.	29-822	SF
Don't Bring Me Down	Animals	15-467	LE
Don't Bring Me Down	ELO	16-597	MM
Don't Call Him A Cowboy	Twitty, Conway	43-193	CB
Don't Call It Love	Parton, Dolly	49-336	CB
Don't Call Us We'll Call You	Sugarloaf&Corbetta	5-586	SC
Don't Cha	Pussycat Dolls	23-315	CB
Don't Cha	Pussycat Dolls	30-132	PT
Don't Cha (Radio Vers)	Pussycat Dolls w Rhymes	37-103	SC
Don't Cheat in Our Hometown	Skaggs, Ricky	4-547	SC
Don't Close Your Eyes	Kix	6-30	SC
Don't Close Your Eyes	Whitley, Keith	11-738	DK
Don't Come Cryin' To Me	Gill, Vince	8-355	CB
Don't Come Cryin' To Me	Gill, Vince	7-823	CHT
Don't Come Cryin' To Me	Gill, Vince	22-715	ST
Don't Come Home A-Drinkin'	Lynn, Loretta	8-46	CB
Don't Come Home A-Drinkin'	Lynn, Loretta	6-739	MM
Don't Come Home A-Drinkin'	Lynn, Loretta	13-406	P
Don't Come the Cowboy With Me	Willis, Kelly	49-735	TU
Don't Cross The River	America	46-414	CB
Don't Cross The River	Brooks, Garth	48-357	SC
Don't Cry (Original)	Guns & Roses	6-29	SC
Don't Cry Baby	James, Etta	21-695	PS
Don't Cry Daddy	Presley, Elvis	17-548	DK
Don't Cry Daddy	Presley, Elvis	2-599	SC
Don't Cry For Me Argentina	Madonna	21-161	LE
Don't Cry Joni	Twitty, Conway	8-799	CB
Don't Cry Out Loud	Manchester,Melissa	15-468	MM
Don't Do Me Like That	Petty & Heartbreake	12-792	P
Don't Do Me No Good	Wilson, Gretchen	36-608	CB
Don't Dream It's Over	Crowded House	4-880	SC
Don't Dream It's Over	Sixpence None The	25-538	MM
Don't Dream It's Over	Sixpence None The	32-171	THM
Don't Expect Me To Be Your Friend	Lobo	46-330	SC
Don't Fall In Love With A Dreamer	Rogers & Carnes	17-152	DK
Don't Fall In Love With A Dreamer	Rogers & Carnes	2-303	SC

SONG TITLE	ARTIST	#	TYPE
Don't Fear The Reaper	Blue Oyster Cult	34-48	CB
Don't Fear The Reaper	Blue Oyster Cult	11-512	DK
Don't Fear The Reaper	Blue Oyster Cult	7-494	MM
Don't Fear The Reaper	Blue Oyster Cult	14-647	SC
Don't Fence Me In	Autry, Gene	22-173	CB
Don't Fence Me In	Miller & Orchestra	21-18	SC
Don't Fence Me In	Miller, Mitch	43-225	CB
Don't Fence Me In	Seeger, Pete	7-347	MM
Don't Fence Me In	Standard	10-471	MG
Don't Fence Me In	White, Lari	16-645	MM
Don't Fight The Feelings Of Love	Pride, Charley	47-439	CB
Don't Forbid Me	Boone, Pat	12-646	P
Don't Forget Me When I'm Gone	Glass Tiger	21-752	MH
Don't Forget To Dance	Kinks	48-176	LE
Don't Forget To Remember Me	Underwood, Carrie	30-119	AS
Don't Forget To Remember Me	Underwood, Carrie	29-364	CB
Don't Get Around Much Anymore	Cole, Nat "King"	46-354	SC
Don't Get Around Much Anymore	Connick, Harry Jr.	19-716	PS
Don't Get Around Much Anymore	Fitzgerald, Ella	12-549	P
Don't Get Around Much Anymore	Sinatra, Frank	9-241	PT
Don't Get Me Started	Akins, Rhett	7-232	MM
Don't Get Me Started	Akins, Rhett	22-885	ST
Don't Get Me Wrong	Pretenders	24-563	SC
Don't Give It To Him	Puckett & Union Gap	4-213	SC
Don't Give Up On Us	Brennan&McDonald	21-622	SF
Don't Give Up On Us Baby	Soul, David	2-557	SC
Don't Go Away	Oasis	7-688	PHM
Don't Go Away Mad	Buckcherry	48-472	CB
Don't Go Breakin' My Heart	Herndon & Tucker	19-711	ST
Don't Go Breakin' My Heart	John, E & Dee, Kiki	6-334	MM
Don't Go Breakin' My Heart	John, E & Dee, Kiki	13-253	P
Don't Go Breakin' My Heart	John, E & Dee, Kiki	4-757	SC
Don't Go Breakin' My Heart	John, E & Rupaul	4-278	SC
Don't Go Out	Tucker & Brown	2-346	SC
Don't Go To Strangers	Brown, T. Graham	47-550	SC
Don't Hang Around Me Anymore	Autry, Gene	22-175	CB
Don't Happen Twice	Chesney, Kenny	29-432	CB
Don't Hate Me For Lovin' You	Bates, Jeff	36-588	CB
Don't It	Currington, Billy	45-44	BKD
Don't It Make My Brown Eyes Blue	Gayle, Crystal	8-20	CB
Don't It Make My Brown Eyes Blue	Gayle, Crystal	16-746	DK

SONG TITLE	ARTIST	#	TYPE
Don't It Make My Brown Eyes Blue	Gayle, Crystal	13-358	P
Don't It Make My Brown Eyes Blue	Gayle, Crystal	9-597	SAV
Don't It Make My Brown Eyes Blue	Gayle, Crystal	10-512	SF
Don't It Make You Lonely	Twitty, Conway	4-120	SC
Don't It Make You Wanna Go Home	South, Joe	7-163	MM
Don't Just Stand There	Smith, Carl	22-108	CB
Don't Just Stand There	Smith, Carl	6-8	SC
Don't Keep Me Hangin' On	James, Sonny	19-474	CB
Don't Know Much	Ronstadt & Neville	6-337	MM
Don't Know What You Got (Till It's.	Cinderella	23-54	MH
Don't Know What You Got (Till It's)	Cinderella	24-676	SC
Don't Know Why	Jones, Norah	33-436	CB
Don't Know Why	Jones, Norah	18-421	MM
Don't Know Why	Jones, Norah	32-50	THM
Don't Know Why	Jones, Norah	19-182	Z
Don't Laugh At me	Wills, Mark	8-748	CB
Don't Laugh At Me	Wills, Mark	22-816	ST
Don't Leave Home	Dido	29-237	ZM
Don't Leave Me Now	Presley, Elvis	7-123	MM
Don't Leave Me This Way	Houston, Thelma	35-133	CB
Don't Leave Me This Way	Houston, Thelma	16-833	DK
Don't Leave, I Think I Love You	Keith, Toby	47-160	CB
Don't Let Go	McDowell, Ronnie	47-233	CB
Don't Let Go	Tillis & Bryce	9-593	SAV
Don't Let Go (Love)	En Vogue	4-602	SC
Don't Let Him Steal Your Heart	Collins, Phil	44-23	SD
Don't Let It End	Styx	47-380	LE
Don't Let It End	Styx	47-384	SC
Don't Let It Go To Waste	Willis, Matt	49-732	MRE
Don't Let Me Be Lonely	Band Perry	44-336	SSC
Don't Let Me Be Lonely Tonight	Taylor, James	33-289	CB
Don't Let Me Be Lonely Tonight	Taylor, James	10-72	SC
Don't Let Me Be Misunderstood	Animals	11-553	DK
Don't Let Me Be Misunderstood	Animals	15-49	LE
Don't Let Me Be Misunderstood	Animals	13-232	P
Don't Let Me Be Misunderstood	Animals	19-102	SAV
Don't Let Me Be Misunderstood	Animals	5-180	SC
Don't Let Me Be The Last To Know	Spears, Britney	15-455	PHM
Don't Let Me Cross Over	Butler, Carl	8-719	CB
Don't Let Me Cross Over	Butler, Carl	4-257	SC
Don't Let Me Cross Over	Reeves, Jim	45-270	DCK

SONG TITLE	ARTIST	#	TYPE
Don't Let Me Cross Over - duet	Butler, Carl & Pearl	35-332	CB
Don't Let Me Down	Beatles	20-195	SC
Don't Let Me Down	Sisters Wade	8-900	CB
Don't Let Me Get Me	Pink	25-213	MM
Don't Let Our Love Start Slippin'	Gill, Vince	6-216	MM
Don't Let Our Love Start Slippin'..	Gill, Vince	1-592	CB
Don't Let Our Love Start Slippin'..	Gill, Vince	8-603	TT
Don't Let The Stars Get In Your Eye	Como, Perry	25-267	MM
Don't Let The Stars Get In Your Eye	Como, Perry	20-779	PS
Don't Let The Stars Get In Your Eye	Como, Perry	10-607	SF
Don't Let The Sun Catch You Cryin'	Gerry & Pacemakers	12-325	DK
Don't Let The Sun Go Down On Me	John, Elton	6-98	MM
Don't Let The Sun Go Down On Me	John, Elton	13-310	P
Don't Let The Sun So Down On Me	John, Elton	17-552	DK
Don't Lie	Adkins, Trace	10-229	SC
Don't Lie	Adkins, Trace	22-376	ST
Don't Like This Bar (Parody)	C, Al	38-281	ALC
Don't Live A Lie	Autry, Gene	22-176	CB
Don't Look Back	Boston	5-595	SC
Don't Look Back	Morris, Gary	9-624	SAV
Don't Look Back	Temptations	49-859	DCK
Don't Look Now (It Ain't You Or Me)	CCR	48-369	KV
Don't Look Now **	Carrington, Rodney	44-98	SC
Don't Lose My Number	Collins, Phil	21-600	SF
Don't Love Make A Diamond Shine	Byrd, Tracy	1-551	CB
Don't Love Make A Diamond Shine	Byrd, Tracy	7-644	CHM
Don't Love Make A Diamond Shine	Byrd, Tracy	10-104	SC
Don't Love you No More	Craig, David	30-774	SF
Don't Love You No More (I'm Sorry)	David, Craig	30-774	SF
Don't Make It Easy For Me	Conley, Earl Thomas	12-473	P
Don't Make It Easy For Me	Conley, Earl Thomas	5-772	SC
Don't Make It So Hard On Me	Sam & Dave	9-755	SAV
Don't Make Me	Shelton, Blake	45-333	ASK
Don't Make Me	Shelton, Blake	30-166	CB
Don't Make Me Beg	Holy, Steve	5-809	SC
Don't Make Me Beg	Holy, Steve	22-520	ST
Don't Make Me Come Over There...	Strait, George	14-130	CB
Don't Make Me Come Over There...	Strait, George	22-584	ST

SONG TITLE	ARTIST	#	TYPE
Don't Make Me Over	Diamond, Neil	47-424	PS
Don't Make Me Over	Warwick, Dionne	20-58	SC
Don't Make Me Wait For Love	Kenny G	49-746	KRG
Don't Matter (Radio Vers)	Akon	37-123	SC
Don't Mess With Bill	Marvalettes	11-774	DK
Don't Mess With Bill	Marvalettes	25-172	MM
Don't Mess With Bill	Wells, Mary	49-452	MM
Don't Mess With My Toot Toot	Nelson, Willie	47-759	SRK
Don't Nobody Bring Me No Bad News	The Wiz	49-438	SDK
Don't Phunk With My Heart	Black Eyed Peas	23-321	CB
Don't Play That Song	Franklin, Aretha	17-102	DK
Don't Play That Song	King, Ben E.	4-217	SC
Don't Pull Your Love	Hamilton/Frank/Reyn	17-113	DK
Don't Pull Your Love	Hamilton/Frank/Reyn	13-70	P
Don't Pull Your Love	Hamilton/Frank/Reyn	4-841	SC
Don't Rain On My Parade	Funny Girl	49-440	MM
Don't Rain On My Parade	Streisand, Barbra	26-372	DK
Don't Rob Another Man's Castle	Arnold, Eddy	19-843	CB
Don't Rock The Jukebox	Jackson, Alan	1-35	CB
Don't Rock The Jukebox	Jackson, Alan	12-21	DK
Don't Rock The Jukebox	Jackson, Alan	6-118	MM
Don't Rock The Jukebox	Jackson, Alan	13-329	P
Don't Say Goodbye	Rubio, Paulina	17-593	PHM
Don't Say Goodbye Girl	Campbell, Tevin	29-135	ST
Don't Say Goodnight Pt. 1	Isley Brothers	17-320	SS
Don't Say Goodnight Pt. 2	Isley Brothers	17-321	SS
Don't Say Nothin' About My Baby	Cookies	20-64	SC
Don't Say You Love Me	M2M	16-186	PHM
Don't Set Me Free	Charles, Ray	46-582	LE
Don't She Look Good	Anderson, Bill	20-792	CB
Don't Shed A Tear	Carrack, Paul	12-376	DK
Don't Sleep In The Subway	Clark, Petula	9-87	PS
Don't Sleep In The Subway	Clark, Petula	20-63	SC
Don't Speak	No Doubt	15-411	SC
Don't Squeeze My Sharmon	Walker, Charlie	46-39	SSK
Don't Stand So Close To Me	Police	46-114	SC
Don't Stand Too Close To Me	Police	20-42	SC
Don't Stay Away Till Love Grows…	Frizzell, Lefty	19-493	CB
Don't Stop	Fleetwood Mac	17-390	DK
Don't Stop	Fleetwood Mac	10-31	SC
Don't Stop	Hayes, Wade	6-814	MM
Don't Stop	Hayes, Wade	3-422	SC

SONG TITLE	ARTIST	#	TYPE
Don't Stop Believin'	Journey	4-82	SC
Don't Stop Dancing	Creed	25-432	MM
Don't Stop Dancing	Creed	32-64	THM
Don't Stop In My World	Morgan, Lorrie	4-419	SC
Don't Stop The Music	Rihanna	36-468	CB
Don't Stop Till You Get Enough	Jackson, Michael	28-112	DK
Don't Stop Till You Get Enough	Jackson, Michael	36-120	JTG
Don't Stop Till You Get Enough	Jackson, Michael	7-92	MM
Don't Take Away My Heaven	Neville, Aaron	12-125	DK
Don't Take Her She's All I Got	Byrd, Tracy	14-649	CB
Don't Take Her She's All I Got	Byrd, Tracy	7-589	CHM
Don't Take Her She's All I Got	Byrd, Tracy	7-435	MM
Don't Take Her She's All I Got	Paycheck, Johnny	45-211	SBI
Don't Take It Away	Twitty, Conway	8-824	CB
Don't Take The Girl	McGraw, Tim	1-527	CB
Don't Take The Girl	McGraw, Tim	6-573	MM
Don't Take The Girl	McGraw, Tim	2-218	SC
Don't Take Your Guns To Town	Cash, Johnny	14-243	CB
Don't Take Your Guns To Town	Cash, Johnny	21-586	SC
Don't Talk To Strangers	Springfield, Rick	24-75	SC
Don't Tell Her	Dugan, Jeff	8-941	CB
Don't Tell Me	Lavigne, Avril	20-568	CB
Don't Tell Me	Madonna	17-715	THM
Don't Tell Me	Womack, Lee Ann	22-517	ST
Don't Tell Me Goodnight	Lobo	21-806	SC
Don't Tell Me What To Do	Tillis, Pam	1-451	CB
Don't Tell Me What To Do	Tillis, Pam	10-782	JVC
Don't Tell Me What To Do	Tillis, Pam	2-105	SC
Don't Tell Me You Love Me	Night Ranger	12-780	P
Don't Tell Me You Love Me	Night Ranger	5-488	SC
Don't The Girls All Get Prettier At Closing Time	Gilley, Mickey	8-48	CB
Don't The Girls All Get Prettier At Closing Time	Gilley, Mickey	7-416	MM
Don't Think I Can't Love You	Owen, Jake	45-643	ASK
Don't Think I Don't Think About It	Rucker, Darius	47-374	CB
Don't Think I'm Not	Kandi	15-448	PHM
Don't Think Twice	Four Seasons	43-435	LG
Don't Think Twice	Presley, Elvis	25-743	MM
Don't Think Twice It's All Right	Dylan, Bob	29-99	CB
Don't Think Twice It's Alright	Clapton, Eric	19-795	SGB

55

SONG TITLE	ARTIST	#	TYPE
Don't Throw It All Away	Bee Gees	48-681	CB
Don't Toss Us Away	Loveless, Patty	1-709	CB
Don't Toss Us Away	Loveless, Patty	2-612	SC
Don't Touch Me	Seely, Jeannie	8-389	CB
Don't Touch Me There	McEntire, Reba	6-202	MM
Don't Touch Me There **	Tubes	15-6	SC
Don't Touch My Willie	Fowler, Kevin	29-613	ST
Don't Trust Me	3OH!3	36-284	PHM
Don't Try To Own Me	Wright, Gary	24-17	SC
Don't Turn Around	Ace Of Base	6-632	MM
Don't Turn Off The Light	Iglesias, Enrique	18-414	MM
Don't Wanna Lose You	Richie, Lionel	47-458	LE
Don't Wanna Try	Frankie J	21-636	CB
Don't Wanna Try	Frankie, J	32-237	THM
Don't Want To Be A Fool	Vandross, Luther	48-292	MM
Don't Want To Lose You Now	Estefan, Gloria	49-461	MM
Don't Waste My Time	Little Big Town	25-190	MM
Don't Waste My Time	Little Big Town	16-690	ST
Don't Waste Your Heart	Dixie Chicks	8-905	CB
Don't Waste Your Heart	Dixie Chicks	30-599	RS
Don't Waste Your Time	Clarkson, Kelly	47-688	CB
Don't We All Have The Right	VanShelton, Ricky	34-285	CB
Don't We All Have The Right	VanShelton, Ricky	8-558	CB
Don't We All Have The Right	VanShelton, Ricky	5-526	SC
Don't Worry	Robbins, Marty	8-287	CB
Don't Worry	Robbins, Marty	2-631	SC
Don't Worry 'Bout A Thing	SheDaisy	22-20	CB
Don't Worry 'Bout Me	Clooney, Rosemary	11-456	DK
Don't Worry Baby	Beach Boys	5-901	BS
Don't Worry Baby	Beach Boys	11-652	DK
Don't Worry Baby	Beach Boys	13-118	P
Don't Worry Be Happy	McFerrin, Bobby	26-309	DK
Don't Ya	Eldridge, Brett	47-433	SSC
Don't You Ever Get Tired Of...	Milsap, Ronnie	1-447	CB
Don't You Forget About Me	Simple Minds	11-392	DK
Don't You Forget About Me	Simple Minds	16-58	SC
Don't You Forget It	Lewis, Glenn	25-214	MM
Don't You Know You're Beautiful	Pickler, Kellie	36-598	CB
Don't You Remember	Adele	44-167	KV
Don't You Think This Outlaw Thing Has...	Jennings, Waylon	45-178	TU
Don't You Wanna Stay - duet	Aldean & Clarkson	37-208	AS
Don't You Want Me	Watley, Jodi	11-767	DK
Don't You Want Me	Watley, Jodi	20-55	SC
Don't You Worry 'Bout A Thing	Wonder, Stevie	17-338	DK
Done	Band Perry	40-39	ASK
Done	Band Perry	40-18	PHN
Done Too Soon	Diamond, Neil	48-413	DFK

SONG TITLE	ARTIST	#	TYPE
Donna	Valens, Richie	35-15	CB
Donna	Valens, Richie	12-742	P
Donna Donna	Baez, Joan	46-466	JVC
Donna The Prima Donna	Dion	20-28	SC
Doo Doo Doo Heartbreaker	Rolling Stones	20-201	SC
Doo Wah Days	Gilley, Mickey	47-778	SRK
Doo Wap (That Thing)	Hill, Lauryn	16-201	PHT
Doo Wop (That Thing)	Hill, Lauryn	19-725	CB
Doo Wop (That Thing)	Hill, Lauryn	28-219	DK
Doo Wop (That Thing)	Hill, Lauryn	25-682	MM
Doo Wop (That Thing)	Hill, Lauryn	21-611	SF
Doo Wop (That Thing)	Hill, Lauryn	13-679	SGB
Dooley	Dillards	46-192	SC
Doolin-Dalton	Eagles	49-82	ZPA
Door Is Always Open the	Jennings, Waylon	47-753	SRK
Door Is Still Open To My Heart	Bennett, Tony	10-407	LE
Door the	Jones, George	8-341	CB
Door the	Jones, George	4-822	SC
Doraville	Atlanta Rhythm Sec	7-93	MM
Dosed	Red Hot Chili Peppe	32-331	THM
Double D Cups - parody	Judd, Cledus T.	47-874	HM
Double Dutch Bus	Smith, Frankie	14-361	MH
Double Shot Of My Baby's Love	Swingin' Medallions	13-268	P
Double Vision	Foreigner	17-79	DK
Double Wide Paradise	Keith, Toby	1-693	CB
Double Wide Paradise	Keith, Toby	5-292	SC
Double Wide Paradise	Kershaw, Sammy	22-797	ST
Dov L' Amor	Cher	47-677	PS
Down	311	6-41	SC
Down	Lambert, Miranda	46-270	QH
Down	Moke	32-109	THM
Down	Motograter	23-189	PHM
Down	Socialburn	23-154	PHM
Down And Out	Randy Rogers Band	29-48	CB
Down And Out	Strait, George	5-318	SC
Down At The Roadside Inn	Al Dexter & Troopers	46-411	CB
Down At The Twist & Shout	Carpenter, M C	1-421	CB
Down At The Twist & Shout	Carpenter, M C	12-19	DK
Down At The Twist & Shout	Carpenter, M C	13-508	P
Down At The Twist & Shout	Carpenter, M C	2-9	SC
Down At The Twist & Shout	Carpenter, M C	15-163	THM
Down Boys	Warrant	6-28	SC
Down By he Riverside	Standard	27-446	DK
Down By The Lasy River	Osmonds	47-864	ZP
Down By The Old Mill Stream	Miller, Mitch	23-543	CB
Down By The Water	Harvey, P.J.	19-549	SC
Down Came A Blackbird	McCann, Lila	7-656	CHM
Down Came The World	Jennings, Waylon	45-187	SRK

SONG TITLE	ARTIST	#	TYPE
Down For A Get Down	Thompson, Josh	45-281	BKD
Down Home	Alabama	4-439	BS
Down Home	Alabama	13-397	P
Down Home	Alabama	9-475	SAV
Down Home Blues	King, Freddy	7-224	MM
Down In Flames	Blackhawk	2-646	SC
Down In Mexico	Coasters	43-83	VH
Down In Mississippi	Sugarland	29-370	CB
Down In Mississippi	Sugarland	30-236	RS
Down In My Heart	Standard	46-292	CB
Down In Tennessee	Chesnutt, Mark	6-846	MM
Down In Tennessee	Chesnutt, Mark	3-420	SC
Down In The Boondocks	Royal, Billy Joe	6-791	MM
Down In The Boondocks	Royal, Billy Joe	5-97	SC
Down In The Valley	Ives, Burl	43-440	CB
Down Louisiana Way	Strait, George	49-228	DFK
Down Low (Nobody Has To Know)	Kelly, R.	49-517	CB
Down On Me	Joplin, Janis	15-220	LE
Down On My Knees	Bread	46-526	CB
Down On My Knees	Yearwood, Trisha	6-381	MM
Down On The Beach Tonight	Drifters	45-894	MFK
Down On The Corner	CCR	33-262	CB
Down On The Corner	CCR	11-339	DK
Down On The Corner	CCR	15-172	MH
Down On The Corner	CCR	5-347	SC
Down On The Farm	McGraw, Tim	1-528	CB
Down On The Farm	McGraw, Tim	6-613	MM
Down On The Farm	McGraw, Tim	2-480	SC
Down On The Rio Grande	Rodriguez, Johnny	22-59	CB
Down So Long	Jewel	19-356	PS
Down The Road	Chesney, Kenny	45-384	BKD
Down The Road	Chesney, Kenny	36-259	PHM
Down The Trail Of Achin' Hearts	Snow, Hank	22-125	CB
Down This Road	Wrights	22-27	CB
Down To My Last Broken Heart	Fricke, Janie	19-420	SC
Down To My Last Cigarette	lang, k.d.	6-740	MM
Down To My Last Teardrop	Tucker, Tanya	16-343	CB
Down to My Last Teardrop	Tucker, Tanya	13-384	P
Down under	Men At Work	34-76	CB
Down Under	Men At Work	16-739	DK
Down Under	Men At Work	12-763	P
Down Under	Men At Work	5-386	SC
Down We Go	Marshall Tucker Band	47-225	DCK
Down With The Sickness **	Disturbed	16-315	TT
Downfall	Matchbox 20	20-542	CB
Downside Of Growing Up	Maddie & Tae	49-754	KVD
Downtime	Messina, Jo Dee	15-94	ST

SONG TITLE	ARTIST	#	TYPE
Downtime	Vaughn, Tyrone	38-248	PHN
Downtown	Clark, Petula	6-350	MM
Downtown	Clark, Petula	9-84	PS
Downtown	Clark, Petula	10-661	SF
Downtown	Lady Antebellum	46-83	BKD
Downtown Train	Stewart, Rod	22-922	SC
Dozen Red Roses A	Graham, Terry	7-623	CHM
Dr. Feelgood	Motley Crue	23-52	MH
Drag City	Jan & Dean	3-556	SC
Drag Me Down	One Direction	48-446	KCD
Draggin' The Line	James & Shondells	9-344	AH
Draggin' The Line	James & Shondells	20-321	MH
Draggin' The Line	James, Tommy	29-285	SC
Draw Me A Map	Bentley, Dierks	37-345	PHM
Draw The Line	Aerosmith	5-70	SC
Dream	Day, Doris	9-798	SAV
Dream	Martin, Dean	23-79	MM
Dream A Little Dream Of Me	Elliot, Cass	49-513	MM
Dream A Little Dream Of Me	Mamas & Papas	9-117	PS
Dream A Little Dream Of Me	Mamas & Papas	19-152	SGB
Dream Baby	Campbell, Glen	8-453	CB
Dream Baby	Dalton, Lacy J.	45-823	KC
Dream Baby	Orbison, Roy	9-595	SAV
Dream Baby	Orbison, Roy	9-185	SO
Dream Big	Shupe&Rubberband	23-126	CB
Dream Lover	Craddock, Billy C	46-647	CB
Dream Lover	Darin, Bobby	11-629	DK
Dream Lover - duet	Tucker & Campbell	49-655	KV
Dream Of Me	Gosdin, Vern	47-120	CB
Dream On	Aerosmith	33-302	CB
Dream On	Aerosmith	12-709	P
Dream On	Depeche Mode	33-377	CB
Dream On Texas Ladies	Montgomery, J M	4-142	SC
Dream Police	Cheap Trick	9-725	SAV
Dream Walkin'	Keith, Toby	8-296	CB
Dream Weaver	Wright, Gary	35-134	CB
Dream Weaver	Wright, Gary	13-11	P
Dream You (All I Can Do)	Orbison, Roy	47-346	PS
Dreamboat	Cogan, Alma	10-608	SF
Dreamboat Annie	Heart	24-568	SC
Dreamer the	Shelton, Blake	39-2	CB
Dreamin'	Rambler	9-408	CB
Dreaming	Blondie	15-745	SC
Dreaming Of You	Selena	19-582	MH
Dreaming Of You	Selena	21-452	PS
Dreaming Of You	Selena	15-471	THM
Dreaming With My Eyes Wide Open	Walker, Clay	1-93	CB
Dreaming With My Eyes Wide Open	Walker, Clay	12-186	DK
Dreaming With My Eyes Wide Open	Walker, Clay	6-600	MM
Dreaming With My Eyes Wide Open	Walker, Clay	17-239	NA
Dreaming With My Eyes	Walker, Clay	2-325	SC

SONG TITLE	ARTIST	#	TYPE
Wide Open			
Dreamlover	Carey, Mariah	6-420	MM
Dreamlover	Carey, Mariah	17-172	SC
Dreams	Allman Brothers Band	45-589	OZP
Dreams	Ashanti	20-628	NS
Dreams	Chesney, Kenny	48-85	CB
Dreams	Corrs	49-196	SF
Dreams	DeGarmo, Diana	20-553	PHM
Dreams	Fleetwood Mac	7-47	MM
Dreams	Fleetwood Mac	12-699	P
Dreams	Fleetwood Mac	10-28	SC
Dreams	Hatchett, Molly	9-375	AH
Dreams	Hatchett, Molly	13-772	SGB
Dreams	Van Halen	21-771	SC
Dreams Of The Everyday Housewife	Campbell, Glen	9-616	SAV
Dreams Of The Everyday Housewife	Campbell, Glen	5-434	SC
Dreams To Remember	Redding, Otis	47-361	MM
Dress Blues	Zac Brown Band	46-76	BKD
Dress You Up	Madonna	28-345	DK
Dress You Up	Madonna	21-156	LE
Drift Away	Gray, Dobie	2-440	SC
Drift Away	Uncle Kracker	25-532	MM
Drift Away	Uncle Kracker	19-342	STP
Drift Away	Uncle Kracker w Gray	32-245	THM
Drift Off To Dream	Tritt, Travis	1-664	CB
Drifter	Sylvia	20-23	SC
Drifting Too Far From The Shore	Monroe, Bill	47-296	CB
Drink In My Hand	Church, Eric	44-211	CB
Drink Myself Single	Sweeney, Sunny	45-271	DCK
Drink On It	Shelton, Blake	38-278	AS
Drink Swear Steal & Lie	Peterson, Michael	7-632	CHM
Drink Swear Steal & Lie	Peterson, Michael	22-604	ST
Drink To That All Night	Niemann, Jerrod	43-138	ASK
Drinkin'	Beard, Kendall	42-6	PHN
Drinkin' And Dreamin'	Jennings, Waylon	22-141	CK
Drinkin' And Dreamin'	Jennings, Waylon	20-653	SC
Drinkin' Beer & Wasting Bullets	Bryan, Luke	43-13	BKD
Drinkin' Blues	Winter, Johnny	49-677	SC
Drinkin' Bone	Byrd, Tracy	25-700	MM
Drinkin' Bone	Byrd, Tracy	19-363	ST
Drinkin' Bone	Byrd, Tracy	32-378	THM
Drinkin' Buddy	Bamford, Gord	44-85	KV
Drinkin' Champagne	Strait, George	2-411	SC
Drinkin' Dark Whiskey	Allan, Gary	45-872	VH
Drinkin' In My Sunday Dress	Haynes, Susan	29-52	CB
Drinkin' In My Sunday Dress	Haynes, Susan	29-710	ST
Drinkin' Me Lonely	Young, Chris	30-24	CB
Drinkin' My Baby Goodbye	Charlie Daniels Band	43-19	CB
Drinkin' My Baby	Charlie Daniels	7-410	MM

SONG TITLE	ARTIST	#	TYPE
Goodbye	Band		
Drinkin' My Baby Goodbye	Charlie Daniels Band	5-242	SC
Drinkin' My Baby Off My Mind	Rabbitt, Eddie	15-74	CB
Drinkin' My Baby Off My Mind	Rabbitt, Eddie	3-382	SC
Drinkin' My Way Back Home	Watson, Gene	14-675	CB
Drinkin' Songs & Other Logic	Black, Clint	29-203	CB
Drinkin' Thing	Stewart, Gary	14-313	SC
Drinkin' Town With A Football Problem	Currington, Billy	45-273	KCD
Drinkin' Wine	Lewis, Jerry Lee	7-408	MM
Drinking Bone	Byrd, Tracy	35-421	CB
Drinking Champagne	Nelson, Willie	38-76	PS
Drinking Champagne	Strait, George	1-244	CB
Drinking Champagne	Strait, George	8-601	TT
Drinking Class	Brice, Lee	49-202	BKD
Drinking Class	Lee, Brice	45-47	BKD
Drinking Man	Strait, George	39-35	ASK
Drinking Song the	Bob & Tom	44-74	KV
Drinking Wine (Spo Dee O Dee)	Lewis, Jerry Lee	33-27	CB
Drinks After Work	Keith, Toby	44-303	ASK
Drip Drop	Dion	5-230	SC
Drive	Cars	11-659	DK
Drive	Cars	13-192	P
Drive	Cars	14-643	SC
Drive	Incubus	35-239	CB
Drive	Incubus	16-387	SGB
Drive	Wariner, Steve	1-505	CB
Drive (For Daddy Gene)	Jackson, Alan	33-167	CB
Drive (For Daddy Gene)	Jackson, Alan	25-133	MM
Drive (For Daddy Gene)	Jackson, Alan	16-426	ST
Drive By	Train	46-191	BHK
Drive By	Train	48-261	FTX
Drive Me Wild	Sawyer Brown	7-831	CHT
Drive Me Wild	Sawyer Brown	22-720	ST
Drive My Car	Beatles	12-720	P
Drive My Car	Beatles	20-196	SC
Drive Myself Crazy	N'Sync	15-777	BS
Drive On	Cash, Johnny	24-349	SC
Drive On	Cash, Johnny	49-743	SC
Drive South	Bogguss, Suzy	1-561	CB
Drive South	Bogguss, Suzy	6-224	MM
Drive South	Bogguss, Suzy	12-456	P
Driver's Seat	Sniff 'N The Tears	5-679	SC
Drivin' And Cryin'	Wariner, Steve	1-503	CB
Drivin' And Cryin'	Wariner, Steve	3-45	SC
Drivin' My Life Away	Rabbitt, Eddie	11-723	DK
Drivin' My Life Away	Rabbitt, Eddie	13-438	P
Drivin' Nails In My Coffin	Tubb, Ernest	22-306	CB
Driving Around Song	Ford, Colt	47-505	ASK
Driving Home For Christmas	Rea, Chris	45-778	ZM
Driving Into The Sun	Austin, Sherrie	20-174	ST

SONG TITLE	ARTIST	#	TYPE
Driving With the Brakes On	Amitri, Del	30-793	SF
Driving With The Brakes On	Del Amitri	30-793	SF
Drop It Like It's Hot (Radio Vers)	Snoop Dogg w Pharrell	37-94	SC
Dropkick Me Jesus	Bare, Bobby	6-78	SC
Drops Of Jupiter	Train	15-810	CB
Drops Of Jupiter	Train	16-477	MH
Drops Of Jupiter	Train	21-609	SF
Drops Of Jupiter	Train	16-388	SGB
Drops Of Jupiter	Train	15-303	THM
Drops Of Jupiter	Train	18-554	TT
Drown In My Own Tears	Charles, Ray	46-570	CB
Drown In My Own Tears	Charles, Ray	46-210	SC
Drowning	Backstreet Boys	33-389	CB
Drowning	Backstreet Boys	25-34	MM
Drowning	Backstreet Boys	16-305	PHM
Drowning	Backstreet Boys	16-90	SC
Drowning	Crazy Town	32-72	THM
Drowning Shadows	Smith, Sam	45-395	DCK
Drugs Or Jesus	McGraw, Tim	22-19	CB
Drunk Americans	Keith, Toby	45-66	BKD
Drunk Chicks	Seven	36-373	SC
Drunk In The Morning	Graham, Lukas	48-791	KV
Drunk Last Night	Eli Young Band	43-88	HM
Drunk On A Plane	Bentley, Dierks	46-232	PHN
Drunk On A Plane	Bryan, Luke	44-183	SBIG
Drunk On You	Bryan, Luke	44-1	ASK
Drunk On You	Bryan, Luke	46-294	BKD
Drunk On Your Love	Eldridge, Brett	49-661	BKD
Drunk On Your Love	Eldridge, Brett	47-707	DCK
Drunk On Your Love	Eldridge, Brett	48-450	KCD
Drunken Lullabies	Flogging Molly	48-614	SC
Drunker Than Me	Tomlinson, Trent	29-22	CB
Drunker Than Me	Tomlinson, Trent	29-505	SC
Drunker Than Me	Tomlinson, Trent	23-462	ST
Dry Town	Lambert, Miranda	45-431	KV
Du Hast (English Version)	Rammstein	21-761	SC
Duck And Run	3 Doors Down	34-161	CB
Dude	Beene Man&Ms Thing	20-550	PHM
Dude (Looks Like A Lady)	Aerosmith	43-211	SC
Duet - 03 Bonnie & Clyde	Jay-Z & Knowles	32-48	THM
Duet - 03 Bonnie & Clyde	Knowles & Jay-Z	32-48	THM
Duet - 21 Questions	50 Cent & Dogg	25-712	MM
Duet - 911	Feat & Blige	14-45	THM
Duet - A Bad Goodbye	Black & Wynonna	30-5	MM
Duet - A Bad Goodbye	Black & Wynonna	30-437	THM
Duet - After All	Cher & Cetera	6-338	MM
Duet - After All	Cher & Cetera	14-52	RS
Duet - After Closing Time	Mandrell & Houston	9-588	SAV
Duet - After The Fire Is Gone	Twitty & Lynn	48-242	CB
Duet - Afternoon Delight	Starland Local	11-394	DK

SONG TITLE	ARTIST	#	TYPE
Duet - Ain't No Mountain High Enoug	Gaye & Terrell	11-112	DK
Duet - Ain't Nobody's Business But.	Ford & Starr	22-211	CB
Duet - Ain't Nobody's Business But...	Ford & Starr	49-375	CB
Duet - Ain't Nothin' Like the Real	Gaye & Terrell	6-240	MM
Duet - Ain't Nothin' Like the Real	Gaye & Terrell	4-38	SC
Duet - All Cried Out	Allure & 112	20-122	PHM
Duet - All Cried Out	Lisa Lisa & Cult J	11-592	DK
Duet - All For Love	Adams&Sting&Stewar	8-608	TT
Duet - All For Love	Stewart & Sting	18-481	NU
Duet - All I Ask Of You	Phantom Of Opera	6-316	MM
Duet - All I Ever Need Is You	Rogers & West	13-532	P
Duet - All I Ever Need Is You	Rogers & West	9-568	SAV
Duet - All I Ever Need Is You	Rogers & West	5-438	SC
Duet - All I Ever Need Is You	Sonny & Cher	6-239	MM
Duet - All I Ever Need Is You	Sonny & Cher	14-65	RS
Duet - All I Ever Need Is You	Sonny & Cher	15-133	SGB
Duet - All I Have	Lopez & LL Cool J	20-458	CB
Duet - All I Have	Lopez & LL Cool J	32-96	THM
Duet - All In The Family	TV Themes	2-161	SC
Duet - All My Life	Ronstadt & Neville	11-821	DK
Duet - All My Life	Ronstadt & Neville	6-236	MM
Duet - All My Life	Ronstadt & Neville	12-890	P
Duet - All Right Okay You Win	Bennett & Krall	25-670	MM
Duet - Almost Paradise	Reno & Wilson	17-333	DK
Duet - Always	Atlantic Starr	35-193	CB
Duet - Always	Atlantic Starr	28-105	DK
Duet - Always	Atlantic Starr	6-344	MM
Duet - American Boy	Estelle & Kanye West	48-591	DK
Duet - Among The Missing	McDonald&Mattea	8-914	CB
Duet - Angel	Shaggy & Rayvon	16-483	MH
Duet - Angels Cried the	Jackson & Krauss	49-175	CB
Duet - Angry All The Time	McGraw & Hill	15-600	ST
Duet - Anyone Who Isn't Me Tonight	Rogers & West	15-233	CB
Duet - Are You That Somebody	Aaliyah	7-783	PHT
Duet - As Long As I Live	Foley, Red & Kitty Wells	43-362	CB
Duet - As Long As I Love	Wells & Foley	48-201	CB
Duet - As Long As We Got Each Other	Thomas & Springfield	47-599	SAV
Duet - As Long As We Got Each Other	Thomas&Springfield	9-828	SAV
Duet - As She's Walking	Zac Brown Band &	37-344	CB

SONG TITLE	ARTIST	#	TYPE
Away	Alan Jackson		
Duet - As She's Walking Away	Zac Brown Band & Jackson	46-79	CB
Duet - At The Beginning	Lewis & Marx	10-114	SC
Duet - Baby Boy	Knowles & Paul	25-715	MM
Duet - Baby Boy	Knowles & Paul	21-787	SC
Duet - Baby Boy	Knowles & Paul	32-382	THM
Duet - Baby Come To Me	Austin & Ingram	11-406	DK
Duet - Baby Come To Me	Ingram & Austin	6-238	MM
Duet - Baby Come To Me	Ingram & Austin	21-604	SF
Duet - Baby Come To Me	Ingram & Austin	9-207	SO
Duet - Baby Don't Go	Sonny & Cher	14-57	RS
Duet - Baby Don't Go	Yoakam & Crow	49-692	DFK
Duet - Baby You've got What it Take	Benton&Washington	6-684	MM
Duet - Back Together Again	Flack & Hathaway	12-850	P
Duet - Bad Goodbye a	Black & Wynonna	8-115	CB
Duet - Bad Goodbye a	Black & Wynonna	12-396	P
Duet - Bar Room Buddies	Haggard & Eastwood	22-234	CB
Duet - Barbie Girl	Aqua	13-568	LE
Duet - Bartender Song (aka Sittin at..	Rehab & Hank Jr.	43-376	CB
Duet - Battle Hymn Of Love the	Mattea & O'Brien	1-190	CB
Duet - Battle Hymn Of Love the	Mattea & O'Brien	2-305	SC
Duet - Be Careful	Martin & Madonna	9-128	PS
Duet - Be Careful	Martin & Madonna	13-730	SGB
Duet - Beat Goes On the	Sonny & Cher	11-543	DK
Duet - Beat Goes On the	Sonny & Cher	13-257	P
Duet - Beat Goes On the	Sonny & Cher	14-55	RS
Duet - Beat Goes On the	Sonny & Cher	9-661	SAV
Duet - Beat Goes On the	Sonny & Cher	15-127	SGB
Duet - Beautiful Liar	Beyonce & Shakira	30-485	CB
Duet - Beauty & The Beast	Dion & Bryson	9-213	SO
Duet - Because Of You	McEntire & Clarkson	30-464	CB
Duet - Because Of You	McEntire&Clarkson	30-464	CB
Duet - Becha Can't Do It Like Me **	D4L	29-252	SC
Duet - Been There	Black & Wariner	30-419	THM
Duet - Beer For My Horses	Keith & Nelson	23-391	CB
Duet - Beer Run	Brooks & Jones	33-141	CB
Duet - Bei Mir Mist Du Shoen	Gorme, Steve&Eydie	15-842	MM
Duet - Best Night Ever	Gloriana	43-237	ASK
Duet - Billionaire	McCoy, T. & Bruno Mars	38-235	CB
Duet - Boogie Wonderland	Earth Wind & Fire	11-378	DK
Duet - Boondocks	Little Big Town	23-283	CB
Duet - Both To Each Other	Rabbitt & Newton-John	48-39	CB
Duet - Boy Is Mine the	Brandy & Monica	21-560	PHM
Duet - Brave Honest Beautiful	5th Harmony & Trainor	48-440	KCD

SONG TITLE	ARTIST	#	TYPE
Duet - Breathe	Cantrell & Paul	25-718	MM
Duet - Bring It All To Me	Blaque & N'Sync	15-774	BS
Duet - Bring It All To Me	Blaque & N'Sync	15-296	CB
Duet - Bring It All To Me	Blaque & N'Sync	5-898	SC
Duet - Broken Strings	Morrison, James	38-274	EX
Duet - Brokenhearted	Brandy	34-123	CB
Duet - Bull & The Beaver the	Haggard & Williams	5-445	SC
Duet - Buttons	Pussycat Dolls&Snoo	30-734	SF
Duet - By My Side	Morgan & Randall	8-123	CB
Duet - By My Side	Morgan & Randall	7-251	MM
Duet - Call the	Brooks & Yearwood	48-346	KV
Duet - Calling Me	Rogers & Henley	30-348	CB
Duet - Can I Get A...	Jay-Z&Amil&Ja-Rule	14-445	SC
Duet - Can't Believe	Evans, Faith	18-511	TT
Duet - Can't Hold Us Down **	Aguilera & Lil Kim	21-796	SC
Duet - Can't We Try	Sheppard & Hill	35-313	CB
Duet - CC Water Back	Haggard & Jones	22-232	CB
Duet - Ceremony the	Wynette & Jones	9-591	SAV
Duet - Chances Are	Seger & McBride	46-342	MM
Duet - Check On It	Beyonce&Slim Thug	30-158	PT
Duet - Chicken & Biscuits	Ford & Otto	47-506	CB
Duet - Cinderella Rockafella	Ofarim, Esther & Ab	10-637	SF
Duet - Clint Eastwood - Radio Vers	Gorillaz	16-87	SC
Duet - Close My Eyes Forever	Ford & Osbourne	29-304	SC
Duet - Close My Eyes Forever	Osbourne & Ford	23-427	SC
Duet - Closer I Get To You	Knowles&Vandross	21-791	SC
Duet - Cold Beer	Ford & Johnson	47-493	CB
Duet - Collide	Kid Rock & Crow	38-204	FTX
Duet - Come Close To Me	Common & Blige	32-88	THM
Duet - Come Close To Me	Common Feat&Blige	20-515	CB
Duet - Come Softly To Me	Fleetwoods	27-505	DK
Duet - Conversation the	Williams & Jennings	45-186	KV
Duet - Could I Have This Kiss Forev	Houston & Iglesias	14-478	SC
Duet - Could I Have This Kiss Forev	Houston & Iglesias	15-636	THM
Duet - Could I Have This Kiss Forev	Iglesias & Houston	20-119	PHM
Duet - Couldn't Have Said It Better	Meat Loaf	45-524	SC
Duet - Count On Me	Houston & Winans	14-902	SC
Duet - Cowboy's Work Is Never Done	Cher	47-678	RSZ
Duet - Cowboy's Work Is Never Done	Sonny & Cher	14-48	RS
Duet - Crazy In Love	Knowles & Jay-Z	32-307	THM
Duet - Creeque Alley	Mamas & Papas	14-452	SC
Duet - Cruisin'	Lewis & Paltrow	14-22	THM

SONG TITLE	ARTIST	#	TYPE
Duet - Daddy What If	Bare, Bobby Sr & Jr	18-268	CB
Duet - Damn!	Youngbloodz & Lil Jon	32-422	THM
Duet - Dance Again	Lopez & Pitbull	40-10	BH
Duet - Dancing Away With My Heart	Lady Antebellum	46-80	BKD
Duet - Dangerous	Roxette	18-247	DK
Duet - Designated Drinker	Jackson & Strait	40-100	CB
Duet - Diamond Rings & Old Barstools	McGraw & Dunn, C	45-43	BKD
Duet - Dilemma	Nelly & Rowland	33-433	CB
Duet - Dirty Polka **	Dirty Polka Band	30-667	RSX
Duet - Dis-Satisfied	Anderson & Howard	20-797	CB
Duet - Disco Duck - Part 1	Dees & Idiots	23-28	SC
Duet - Does He Love You	McEntire & Davis	1-808	CB
Duet - Does He Love You	McEntire & Davis	6-399	MM
Duet - Don't Cry Joni	Twitty, Conway	8-799	CB
Duet - Don't Fall In Love W/Dreamer	Rogers & Carnes	17-152	DK
Duet - Don't Fall in Love W/Dreamer	Rogers & Carnes	2-303	SC
Duet - Don't Fence Me In	Crosby & Andrew S	29-421	CB
Duet - Don't Give Up On Us	Brennan&McDonald	21-622	SF
Duet - Don't Go Breakin' My Heart	Herndon & Tucker	19-711	ST
Duet - Don't Go Breakin' My Heart	John, E & Dee, Kiki	6-334	MM
Duet - Don't Go Breakin' My Heart	John, E & Dee, Kiki	13-252	P
Duet - Don't Go Breakin' My Heart	John, E & Dee, Kiki	4-757	SC
Duet - Don't Go Breakin' My Heart	John, E & Rupaul	4-278	SC
Duet - Don't Go Out	Tucker & Brown	2-346	SC
Duet - Don't Know Much	Ronstadt & Neville	6-337	MM
Duet - Don't Let Go	Tillis & Bryce	9-593	SAV
Duet - Don't Let Me Cross Over	Butler, Carl & Pearl	35-332	CB
Duet - Don't Phunk With My Heart	Black Eyed Peas	23-321	CB
Duet - Don't Touch Me There **	Tubes	15-6	SC
Duet - Don't Waste My Time	Little Big Town	25-190	MM
Duet - Don't You Wanna Stay	Aldean & Clarkson	37-208	AS
Duet - Dream Lover	Tucker & Campbell	49-655	KV
Duet - Dude	Beene Man/Ms Thing	20-550	PHM
Duet - Easy For Me To Say	Black & Hartman	15-851	ST
Duet - Easy Lover	Collins & Baskey	49-310	BC
Duet - Ebony & Ivory	McCartney&Wonder	11-117	DK
Duet - Endless Love	Rabbitt & Gayle	11-459	DK
Duet - Endless Love	Richie & Ross	35-207	CB
Duet - Endless Love	Richie & Ross	26-187	DK
Duet - Endless Love	Richie & Ross	6-230	MM

SONG TITLE	ARTIST	#	TYPE
Duet - Endless Love	Richie & Twain	47-452	KV
Duet - Endless Love	Ross & Richie	15-354	LE
Duet - Endless Love	Ross & Richie	13-203	P
Duet - Energy	Natalie&Baby Bash	23-319	CB
Duet - Every Other Weekend	McEntire & Chesney	49-707	ST
Duet - Every Time Two Fools Collide	West & Rogers	8-117	CB
Duet - Every Time Two Fools Collide	West & Rogers	2-298	SC
Duet - Everyday People	Sly & Family Stone	17-116	DK
Duet - Everyday People	Sly & Family Stone	12-911	P
Duet - Face In The Crowd	Richie & Dosterhuis	47-454	KV
Duet - Face To Face	Alabama	12-79	DK
Duet - Faded Love	Price & Nelson	45-631	ASK
Duet - Far Side Banks Of Jordan	Cash & Carter	47-785	SRK
Duet - Fascination (Keep Feeling)	Human League	24-210	SC
Duet - Father & Son	Cash & Fiona Apple	43-403	SC
Duet - Feel Like A Rock Star	Chesney & McGraw	45-126	BKD
Duet - Feelings	Twitty & Lynn	48-243	CB
Duet - Feels Like A Rock Star	Chesney & McGraw	39-37	ASK
Duet - Feels Like Heaven	Cetera & Kahn	6-103	MM
Duet - Feels Like Home	Malo & McBride	30-257	CB
Duet - Following The Feeling	Bandy & Hobbs	9-577	SAV
Duet - For Loving You	Anderson & Howard	40-65	CB
Duet - For You	Cash & Matthews	37-243	CB
Duet - Freak-A-Zoid	Midnight Star	17-526	SC
Duet - From This Moment On	Twain & White	8-2	CB
Duet - From This Moment On	Twain & White	7-745	CHM
Duet - From This Moment On	Twain & White	14-293	MM
Duet - Frontin'	Farrell & Jay-Z	32-347	THM
Duet - Funny How Time Slips Away	Green & Lovett	26-566	DK
Duet - Game Of Love the	Santana & Branch	18-580	NS
Duet - Game Of Triangles the	Bare & Anderson's	3-709	CB
Duet - Gansta Lovin'	Eve & Keys	18-436	CB
Duet - Gasoline & Matches	Rimes, Rob Thomas, Jeff Beck	41-86	PHN
Duet - Get A Little Dirt On You	Coe & Anderson	18-319	CB
Duet - Get In Line	Barenaked Ladies	30-620	RS
Duet - Get Low **	Lil Jon&Eastside&YY	21-794	SC
Duet - Get Right	Lopez & Fabolous	22-359	CB
Duet - Get Up	Dogg, Nate & Eve	32-126	THM
Duet - Get Up **	Nate Dogg & Eve	32-126	THM
Duet - Gift the	Brickman & Ash	7-710	PHM
Duet - Girl Is Mine the	Jackson&McCartney	17-150	DK
Duet - Girl Is Mine the	Jackson&McCartney	24-205	SC

SONG TITLE	ARTIST	#	TYPE
Duet - Girl Thang	Judd, W & Wynette, T	48-319	MH
Duet - Golden Ring	Jones & Wynette	5-441	SC
Duet - Golden Ring	Wynette & Jones	8-114	CB
Duet - Gone Gone Gone (Done ...	Krauss & Plant	37-116	SC
Duet - Good Life the	Osmond, Donny & Marie	47-850	PHN
Duet - Good Way To Get On My...	Byrd, Tracy	16-263	TT
Duet - Good Year For The Roses	Jones & Jackson	49-184	SC
Duet - Gossip Folks	Elliot, M. & Ludacris	32-127	THM
Duet - Grease Megamix (Rad Vers)	Travolta & Newton-John	20-118	PHM
Duet - Greatest Gift Of All	Rogers & Parton	48-121	CB
Duet - Green Acres	TV Themes	2-156	SC
Duet - Green Eyes	Lawrence & Gorme	25-268	MM
Duet - Guilty	Streisand & Gibb	15-485	MM
Duet - Guitarzan	Stevens, Ray	15-346	MM
Duet - Hairy Christmas	Robertson & Bryan	43-82	ASK
Duet - Happy Trails	Rogers, Roy&Dale	12-116	DK
Duet - Hard To Be A Husband/Wife	Paisley & Wright	14-156	CB
Duet - Hard To Be A Husband/Wife	Paisley & Wright	14-789	ST
Duet - Have You Ever Been Lonely	Reeves & Cline	3-161	CB
Duet - Have You Ever Been Lonely	Reeves & Cline	2-297	SC
Duet - Having My Baby	Anka, Paul & ??	28-252	DK
Duet - He Drinks Tequila	Kershaw & Morgan	30-31	CB
Duet - He Drinks Tequila	Kershaw & Morgan	14-838	ST
Duet - He Drinks Tequila	Kershaw & Morgan	16-267	TT
Duet - He's Sure The Boy I Love	Midler & Love	45-359	KV
Duet - Healing	Judd, W & English	24-80	SC
Duet - Healing	Judd, W & English, M	48-322	SC
Duet - Heart Half Empty	Herndon & Bentley	7-146	MM
Duet - Heart Half Empty	Herndon & Bentley	4-100	SC
Duet - Heart Of America	Benet,McDonald,Judd	29-50	CB
Duet - Heart Won't Lie the	McEntire & Gill	1-806	CB
Duet - Heart Won't Lie the	McEntire & Gill	12-402	P
Duet - Heart Won't Lie the	McEntire & Gill	2-301	SC
Duet - Helping Me Get Over You	Tritt & White	7-670	CHM
Duet - Helping Me Get Over You	Tritt & White	4-840	SC
Duet - Hey Joe Hey Moe	Bandy & Stampley	19-509	CB
Duet - Hey Ma	Cam'ron & Juelz	25-460	MM
Duet - Hey Paula	Paul & Paula	11-529	DK
Duet - Hey Paula	Paul & Paula	2-840	SC
Duet - Highway Don't Care	McGraw & Swift	40-45	ASK

SONG TITLE	ARTIST	#	TYPE
Duet - Hillbilly Bone	Shelton & Adkins	38-84	CB
Duet - Hips Don't Lie	Shakira&Wyclef Jean	30-727	SF
Duet - Hold You Down	Lopez & Fat Joe	33-395	CB
Duet - Holding The Bag	Bandy & Stampley	19-505	CB
Duet - Home Alone Tonight	Bryan & Fairchild	45-822	DCK
Duet - Hopelessly Yours	Greenwood&Bogguss	2-308	SC
Duet - How Do You Keep the Music...	Ingram & Austin	49-463	MM
Duet - How High The Moon	Les Paul/Mary Ford	4-190	SC
Duet - Hunger Strike	Pearl Jam	9-296	RS
Duet - I Call Your Name	Mamas & Papas	49-724	KV
Duet - I Can't Love You Enough	Twitty & Lynn	5-449	SC
Duet - I Don't Believe You Met My..	Louvin Brothers	3-207	SC
Duet - I Don't Wanna Have To Marry	Brown & Cornelius	13-485	P
Duet - I Don't Wanna Have To Marry.	Brown & Cornelius	9-603	SAV
Duet - I Don't Wanna Know	Winans & P. Diddy	20-570	CB
Duet - I Finally Found Someone	Kershaw & Morgan	17-482	CB
Duet - I Finally Found Someone	Streisand & Adams	20-120	PHM
Duet - I Got You	Jennings & Carter	45-170	RCA
Duet - I Got You	Jennings & Colter	22-151	CK
Duet - I Got You	Jennings & Colter	9-621	SAV
Duet - I Got You	Thompson Square	37-228	CB
Duet - I Got You Babe	Sonny & Cher	11-446	DK
Duet - I Got You Babe	Sonny & Cher	14-59	RS
Duet - I Got You Babe	Sonny & Cher	15-121	SGB
Duet - I Hate You Then I Love You	Dion & Pavaratti	17-655	PR
Duet - I Have A Love	Streisand & Mathis	49-540	MM
Duet - I Have A Love (One Hand...)	Mathis & Streisand	6-345	MM
Duet - I Just Came Here To Dance	Frizzell & West	45-411	CB
Duet - I Just Can't Stop Loving You	Jackson, M &	27-276	DK
Duet - I Just Can't Stop Loving You	Jackson, Michael	16-564	P
Duet - I knew You Were Waiting	Franklin & Michael	35-310	CB
Duet - I Knew You Were Waiting For	Franklin & Michael	17-350	DK
Duet - I Love Nascar	Judd & Keith	38-169	SC
Duet - I Love This Life	LoCash	49-529	ZP
Duet - I Made A Promise	Gayle & Rabbitt	2-835	SC
Duet - I Need A Girl	Diddy/P Feat/Usher	17-596	PHM
Duet - I Need You	McGraw & Hill	40-29	SC
Duet - I Need You	McGraw & Hill	46-316	SC
Duet - I Walk The Line	Crowell & Cash, J.	10-154	SC
Duet - I Want To Spend My Life...	Anthony & Arena	20-130	PHM

SONG TITLE	ARTIST	#	TYPE
Duet - I Want To Stay Here	Lawrence & Gorme	29-491	LE
Duet - I Want You	Thalia & Fat Joe	25-719	MM
Duet - I Want You	Thalia & Fat Joe	32-349	THM
Duet - I Was There	Owens & Yoakum	46-104	CB
Duet - I Was There	Yoakam & Owens	49-687	CB
Duet - I Will Always Love You	Parton & Gill	7-78	MM
Duet - I Will Always Love You	Parton & Gill	3-566	SC
Duet - I Will Fall - Nashville	Scott & O'Connor	45-477	KVD
Duet - I Won't Be the One To Let Go	Streisand & Manilow	49-622	ST
Duet - I Won't Take Less Than...	Tucker, Davis, Overstreet	34-276	CB
Duet - I'd Give My Right Nut To....	Driskoll&Womak,Jo	14-10	CHM
Duet - I'd Lie For You	Meat Loaf & Russo	33-352	CB
Duet - I'll Be Missing You	Puff Daddy & Evans	20-125	PHM
Duet - I'll Be There	Carey & Lorenz	11-712	DK
Duet - I'll Be There	Carey & Lorenz	6-94	MM
Duet - I'll Be There	Carey, Mariah	33-345	CB
Duet - I'll Make Love To You	Boyz II Men	12-182	DK
Duet - I'll Never Be Free	Ford & Starr	22-205	CB
Duet - I'll Never Be Free	Ford & Starr	46-193	SC
Duet - I'm Gonna Do Anything	Wills & O'Neal	15-863	ST
Duet - I'm Gonna Make You Love Me	Ross & Temptations	17-100	DK
Duet - I'm Gonna Make You Love Me	Supremes&Temptat	9-765	SAV
Duet - I'm Leavin' It Up To You	Dale & Gale	8-714	CB
Duet - I'm Leaving It All Up To You	Osmond, Donny & Marie	47-858	ZM
Duet - I'm Leaving It Up To You	Dale & Grace	35-336	CB
Duet - I'm Not Gonna Do Anything...	Wills & O'Neal	25-124	MM
Duet - I'm Real	Lopez & Ja Rule	23-586	PHM
Duet - I'm Your Angel	Dion & Kelly, R.	14-195	CB
Duet - I'm Your Angel	Dion & Kelly, R.	20-124	PHM
Duet - I'm Your Angel	Dion, Celine & ?	16-208	MM
Duet - If I Didn't Know Better - Nash	Bowen & Palladio	45-472	KVD
Duet - If I Had $1,000,000	Barenaked Ladies	30-613	RS
Duet - If I Had A $1,000,000	Barenaked Ladies	5-332	SC
Duet - If I Had A Million Dollars	Barenaked Ladies	33-362	CB
Duet - If I Knew Then What I Know..	Rogers, Kenny	6-234	MM
Duet - If I Needed You	Williams & Harris	45-231	CB
Duet - If I Were A Carpenter	Cash & Carter	29-558	CB
Duet - If I Were A Carpenter	Slaughter, Shannon & Heather	41-92	PHN
Duet - If You Ever Leave	Streisand & Gill	15-288	PS

SONG TITLE	ARTIST	#	TYPE
Me			
Duet - If You Ever Leave Me	Streisand & Gill	10-217	SC
Duet - If You Say My Eyes/Beautiful	Jackson & Houston	22-927	SC
Duet - If You See Him/Her	McEntire & B&D	8-97	CB
Duet - If You See Him/Her	McEntire & B&D	7-760	CHM
Duet - In Another's Eyes	Brooks & Yearwood	7-675	CHM
Duet - In Another's Eyes	Brooks & Yearwood	22-625	ST
Duet - Into You	Fabolous & Tamia	32-418	THM
Duet - Into You (Radio Version) **	Fabolous&Ashanti	21-784	SC
Duet - Islands In The Stream	Rogers & Parton	8-111	CB
Duet - Islands In The Stream	Rogers & Parton	16-784	DK
Duet - Islands In The Stream	Rogers & Parton	13-419	P
Duet - Islands In The Stream	Rogers & Parton	2-299	SC
Duet - Islands In The Stream	Rogers & Parton	10-511	SF
Duet - It Had To Be You	Bennett & Underwood	45-949	KV
Duet - It Had To Be You	Streisand & Buble	49-544	CK
Duet - It Should Have Been Love By Now	Mandrell & Greenwood	48-696	CB
Duet - It Takes Two	Gaye & Weston	35-308	CB
Duet - It Takes Two	Weston & Gaye	26-524	DK
Duet - It Wasn't Me	Shaggy & Ricardo	16-471	MH
Duet - It Wasn't Me	Shaggy & Ricardo	16-117	PRT
Duet - It's All About The Benjamins	Puff Daddy & Family	14-442	SC
Duet - It's Five O'Clock Somewhere	Jackson & Buffett	35-427	CB
Duet - It's Five O'Clock Somewhere	Jackson & Buffett	25-636	MM
Duet - It's Five O'Clock Somewhere	Jackson & Buffett	32-334	THM
Duet - It's Hard To Kiss The Lips..	Notorious Cherry Bo	23-404	CB
Duet - It's Hard To Kiss The Lips...	Notorious Cherry Bombs	30-14	SC
Duet - It's Like That	Carey & Snoop&JD	22-365	CB
Duet - It's Such A Small World	Crowell & Cash, R.	5-437	SC
Duet - It's Your Love	McGraw & Hill	7-634	CHM
Duet - Itsy Bitsy Teenie Weenie...	Hyland, Bryan	10-329	KC
Duet - Jackson	Cash & Carter	29-754	CB
Duet - Jackson	Cash & Carter	4-267	SC
Duet - Jackson	Phoenix & Witherspoon	29-855	SC
Duet - Jackson	Phoenix & Witherspoon	29-717	ST
Duet - Jackson (Alan That Is)	Judd, Cledus T.	16-511	CB
Duet - Jimmy Choo	Shyne & Ashanti	30-807	PHM

SONG TITLE	ARTIST	#	TYPE
Duet - Just A Fool	Aguilera & Shelton	43-181	ASK
Duet - Just A Fool	Shelton & Aguilera	47-449	MRH
Duet - Just A Kiss	Lady Antebellum	38-88	AT
Duet - Just Dance	Lady Gaga & O'Donis	38-190	SC
Duet - Just Good Ol' Boys	Bandy & Stampley	19-496	CB
Duet - Just My Imagination	Paltrow & Babyface	49-770	PR
Duet - Just To Satisfy You	Jennings & Nelson	45-176	CB
Duet - Just To Satisfy You	Nelson & Jennings	38-97	CB
Duet - Katie Wants A Fast One	Wariner & Brooks	14-93	CB
Duet - Katie Wants A Fast One	Wariner & Brooks	19-220	CSZ
Duet - Keeping Up With the Joneses	Young & Singleton	20-740	CB
Duet - Keeping Up With The Joneses	Young & Singleton	46-57	CB
Duet - Kick My Ass (Radio Version)	Big & Rich	21-651	SC
Duet - Kiss Kiss	Brown & T-Pain	49-895	SC
Duet - Knee Deep	Zac Brown Band & Buffett	37-216	CB
Duet - Lady Marmalade	Aguilera&Mya&Lil Ki	18-526	TT
Duet - Last Thing On My Mind	Wagoner & Parton	9-613	SAV
Duet - Lay Me Down	Smith, S & Legend	48-441	KCD
Duet - Lead Me On	Twitty & Lynn	5-446	SC
Duet - Leather & Lace	Nicks & Henley	12-378	DK
Duet - Leather & Lace	Nicks & Henley	4-763	SC
Duet - Let It Be Me	Brown & Schmidt	14-881	SC
Duet - Let The Good Times Roll	Shirley & Lee	6-142	MM
Duet - Let The Good Times Roll	Shirley & Lee	4-241	SC
Duet - Let's All Go Down To The River	Paycheck & Miller, J	45-213	CB
Duet - Let's All Go Down To/River	Paycheck & Miller	22-33	CB
Duet - Let's Call The Whole Thing..	Fitzgerald&Armstron	12-489	P
Duet - Let's Face the Music & Dance	Bennett & Lady Gaga	49-720	KV
Duet - Let's Get Over Them Together	Bandy & Hobbs	9-575	SAV
Duet - Let's Make Love	Hill & McGraw	35-335	CB
Duet - Let's Make Love	Hill & McGraw	22-530	ST
Duet - Like I'm Gonna Lose You	Trainor & Legend	45-144	BH
Duet - Like To Get To Know You	Spanky & Our Gang	14-450	SC
Duet - Like We Never Had a Broken..	Brooks & Yearwood	2-304	SC
Duet - Like We Never Loved At All	Hill & McGraw	36-377	SC
Duet - Little Bit Country Little Bit...	Osmond, Donny & Marie	47-861	VH

SONG TITLE	ARTIST	#	TYPE
Duet - Little Man	Sonny & Cher	14-67	RS
Duet - Live This Life	Big & Rich	23-380	SC
Duet - Lonely Tonight	Shelton & Monroe	45-329	CKC
Duet - Long Legged Guitar Pickin'..	Cash & Carter	29-719	CB
Duet - Long Tall Texan	Supernaw/Beach Boys	24-411	SC
Duet - Looking Back To See	Browns	8-717	CB
Duet - Looking Through Your Eyes	Corrs & White	17-667	PR
Duet - Lost Forever In Your Kisses	Parton & Wagoner	4-315	SC
Duet - Louisiana Woman Miss..Man	Twitty & Lynn	8-110	CB
Duet - Love At First Sight	Blige & Method Man	32-346	THM
Duet - Love Can't Ever Get Better	Skaggs & White	5-450	SC
Duet - Love Is	McKnight & Williams	34-113	CB
Duet - Love Is	Williams&McKnight	6-332	MM
Duet - Love Is	Williams&McKnight	12-746	P
Duet - Love Is An Open Door - Frozen	Bell & Fontana	43-189	SBIG
Duet - Love Is No Excuse	Reeves & West, D	45-263	SSK
Duet - Love Is Strange	Mickey & Sylvia	4-243	SC
Duet - Love Is Strange	Rogers & Parton	6-237	MM
Duet - Love Like There's No Tomorrow	Tippin & Tippin	25-450	MM
Duet - Love Shack	B-52's	26-232	DK
Duet - Love Shack	B-52's	16-520	P
Duet - Love Shack	B-52's	2-43	SC
Duet - Love Shack	B-52's	10-525	SF
Duet - Love Train	O'Jays	13-180	P
Duet - Love Will Always Win	Brooks & Yearwood	29-195	CB
Duet - Love Will Always Win	Yearwood & Brooks	49-345	CB
Duet - Macarena the	Los Del Rios	7-567	THM
Duet - Magic Stick	Lil Kim & 50 Cent	32-387	THM
Duet - Make Believe (Till We Can...)	Wells & Foley	48-203	CB
Duet - Make No Mistake She's Mine	Rogers & Milsap	29-74	CB
Duet - Making Up For Lost Time	Gayle & Morris	34-265	CB
Duet - Making Up For Lost Time	Morris & Gayle	49-636	CB
Duet - Mango Tree	Zac Brown Band & Bareillas	48-510	KVD
Duet - Marvin Gaye	Puth & Trainor	45-143	BH
Duet - Maybe	Rogers & Dunn	48-120	CB
Duet - Maybe Not Tonight	Kershaw & Morgan	8-924	CB
Duet - Me And God	Turner & Stanley	30-196	CB
Duet - Me And My Shadow	Sinatra & Davis	49-502	MM
Duet - Meet Me In Montana	Seals & Osmond	8-119	CB

64

SONG TITLE	ARTIST	#	TYPE
Duet - Meet Me In Montana	Seals & Osmond	2-309	SC
Duet - Melting Pot	Blue Mink	10-635	SF
Duet - Mendocino County Line	Nelson & Womack	25-129	MM
Duet - Mendocino County Line	Nelson & Womack	16-332	ST
Duet - Mesmerize	Ja Rule & Ashanti	32-123	THM
Duet - Mochingbird	Taylor & Simon	46-120	SC
Duet - Mockingbird	Keith, Toby&Krystal	21-661	SC
Duet - Mockingbird	Taylor & Simon	13-44	P
Duet - Money Makes the World Go Round	Minelli, Liza	49-223	LG
Duet - Moonglow	Bennett & Lang	29-129	ST
Duet - Morning Side Of The Mountain	Osmond, Donny & Marie	47-845	FMG
Duet - Murder On Music Row	Jackson & Strait	43-68	CB
Duet - Murder On Music Row	Strait & Jackson	34-338	CB
Duet - Music Of My Heart	Estefan & N'Sync	35-315	CB
Duet - Music Of My Heart	N'Sync & Estefan	20-439	CB
Duet - Music Of My Heart	N'Sync & Estefan	8-498	PHT
Duet - Music Of The Night	Streisand & Crawford	49-573	PS
Duet - MY Boo	Usher & Keys	30-805	PHM
Duet - My Elusive Dreams	Twitty & Lynn	48-247	THM
Duet - My Elusive Dreams	Wynette & Houston	7-118	MM
Duet - My Elusive Dreams	Wynette & Houston	4-306	SC
Duet - My Humps	Black Eyed Peas	30-747	SF
Duet - My Kind Of Woman/Man	Gill & Loveless	8-970	CB
Duet - My Kind Of Woman/Man	Gill & Loveless	14-625	SC
Duet - My Love Is The Shhh	Something/People	7-719	PHM
Duet - My World Is Over	Rogers & Duncan	20-480	ST
Duet - Near You	Jones & Wynette	5-447	SC
Duet - Nearness Of You	Fitzgerald & Armstrong	49-723	KV
Duet - Need You Now	Lady Antebellum	36-49	PT
Duet - Needles & Pins	Petty & Nicks	9-853	SAV
Duet - Needles And Pins	Nicks & Perry	47-899	SAV
Duet - Never Mind Me	Big & Rich	29-857	SC
Duet - Next Time I Fall In Love	Cetera & Grant	13-158	P
Duet - Next Time I Fall In Love	Cetera & Grant	9-203	SO
Duet - Next Time I Fall In Love	Grant & Cetera	35-312	CB
Duet - Night Time Is The Right Time	Charles, Ray	35-69	CB
Duet - Nine2Five	Ordinary Boys&Lady	30-710	SF
Duet - No More Tears	Streisand&Summer	10-546	SF
Duet - No More Tears (Enough Is..)	Streisand&Summer	26-95	DK

SONG TITLE	ARTIST	#	TYPE
Duet - No More Tears/Enough is Enou	Streisand&Summer	13-155	P
Duet - No One Will Ever Love You	James & Claybourne	45-473	KVD
Duet - Nobody	Sweat & Cage	20-128	PHM
Duet - Nobody	Sweat & Cage	24-372	SC
Duet - Nobody Loves Me Like U Do	Murray & Loggins	12-118	DK
Duet - Nobody Loves Me Like U Do	Murray & Loggins	11-4	PL
Duet - Nobody Loves Me Like You Do	Murray & Loggins	38-3	CB
Duet - Nobody Wants to be Lonely	Martin & ?	20-123	PHM
Duet - Not Too Much To Ask	Carpenter & Diffie	1-425	CB
Duet - Not Too Much To Ask	Carpenter & Diffie	15-155	THM
Duet - Nothin' On You	B.O.B. & Bruno Mars	38-238	BH
Duet - Nothing Ever Matters	Hill, Lauryn	13-708	SGB
Duet - Nothing In This World	Wyatt & Avant	20-616	CB
Duet - Obsession	Animotion	11-279	DK
Duet - Oh Tonight	Josh Abbott & Musgraves	45-436	CB
Duet - Oklahoma Swing	Gill & McEntire	1-795	CB
Duet - Oklahoma Swing	McEntire & Gill	1-795	CB
Duet - Oklahoma Swing	McEntire & Gill	6-751	MM
Duet - Oklahoma Swing - DANCE	McEntire & Gill	22-390	SC
Duet - Old Habits	Moore & Lambert	44-283	KCDC
Duet - On My Knees	Rich & Fricke	13-479	P
Duet - On My Knees	Rich & Fricke	5-439	SC
Duet - On My Own	Labelle & McDonald	16-725	DK
Duet - On My Own	LaBelle & McDonald	12-832	P
Duet - On The Floor	Lopez & Pitbull	40-11	CB
Duet - One	Blige & U2	30-757	SF
Duet - One By One	Foley, Red & Kitty Wells	43-356	CB
Duet - One By One	Wells & Foley	48-200	CB
Duet - One By One	Wells & Foley	6-4	SC
Duet - One Good Love	Diamond & Jennings	7-235	MM
Duet - One Good Love	Diamond & Jennings	45-172	SC
Duet - One Great Mystery	Lady Antebellum	48-445	KCD
Duet - Opposites Attract	Abdul, Paula	18-241	DK
Duet - Our Kind Of Love	Lady Antebellum	37-336	CB
Duet - Out In The Parking Lot	Paisley & Jackson	48-495	CKC
Duet - Out of Control Raging Fire	Loveless & Tritt	16-43	ST
Duet - Out Of Goodbyes	Maroon 5 & Lady Antebellum	38-239	CB
Duet - Out Of The Rain	Jennings & Colter	45-183	DCK
Duet - Outside	Lewis & Durtz	16-480	MH
Duet - Outta State, Outta	Vallejo, Al & Kendall	42-10	PHN

65

SONG TITLE	ARTIST	#	TYPE
Mind	Beard		
Duet - Over & Over	Nelly & McGraw	22-350	CB
Duet - Pancho & Lefty	Haggard & Nelson	33-78	CB
Duet - Paradise	LL Cool J & Amerie	32-86	THM
Duet - Paradise by the Dashboard..	Meat Loaf	26-328	DK
Duet - Paradise by the Dashboard..	Meat Loaf	20-315	MH
Duet - Paradise by the Dashboard...	Meat Loaf	9-348	AH
Duet - Paradise by the Dashboard...	Meat Loaf	2-31	SC
Duet - Party For Two	Twain & Currington	22-61	CB
Duet - Peaceful World	Mellencamp&India.Ar	25-24	MM
Duet - Peaceful World	Mellencamp&India.Ar	23-97	SC
Duet - People Get Ready	Impressions	27-234	DK
Duet - Pick Me Up On Your Way Down	Haggard & Nelson	49-816	KV
Duet - Pick Me Up On Your Way Down	Haggard, Merle	49-168	KV
Duet - Pick Me Up On Your Way Down	Haggard, Nelson & Price	44-87	KV
Duet - Picture	Crow, Sheryl & Kid Rock	32-10	THM
Duet - Picture	Kid Rock & Crow	18-433	CB
Duet - Picture	Kid Rock & Crow	25-400	MM
Duet - Picture	Kid Rock & Crow	29-666	RS
Duet - Picture	Kid Rock & Crow	32-10	THM
Duet - Piece Of Work	Buffett & Keith	38-168	SC
Duet - Piece Of Work	Keith & Buffett	30-17	SC
Duet - Play The Song	Joey & Rory	45-813	BKD
Duet - Please Don't Stop Loving Me	Wagoner & Parton	5-442	SC
Duet - Please Read The Letter	Plant & Krauss	49-905	SC
Duet - Politically Uncorrect	Haggard & Wilson	49-424	ST
Duet - Politically Uncorrect	Wilson & Haggard	29-199	CB
Duet - Portland Oregon	Lynn & Jack White	48-251	SC
Duet - Promiscuous	Furtado & Timbaland	48-605	DK
Duet - Promiscuous	Furtado&Timbaland	30-146	PT
Duet - Put A Little Love In Your...	Lennox & Green	18-379	SAV
Duet - Put A Little Love in/Heart	Lennox & Green	6-336	MM
Duet - Put Your Hand In The Hand	Ocean	17-27	DK
Duet - Put Your Hand In The Hand	Ocean	24-61	SC
Duet - Rainy Dayz	Blige & Ja Rule	25-225	MM
Duet - Raise The Barn	Urban & Dunn	42-27	CB
Duet - Reach Out In The Darkness	Friend & Lover	6-781	MM
Duet - Real Love	Parton, Dolly	13-394	P
Duet - Reason Why the	Little Big Town	38-220	CB
Duet - Remind Me	Paisley &	37-355	CB

SONG TITLE	ARTIST	#	TYPE
	Underwood		
Duet - Respect Yourself	Staple Singers	27-259	DK
Duet - Respect Yourself	Staple Singers	12-920	P
Duet - Reunited	Peaches & Herb	35-158	CB
Duet - Reunited	Peaches & Herb	13-150	P
Duet - Rich Girl	Stefani & Eve	22-357	CB
Duet - Ride	Rice & Malloy	48-3	BKD
Duet - Right Round	Flo Rida	45-649	B
Duet - Rock Steady	Adams & Raitt	35-314	CB
Duet - Rockin' Years	Parton & Van Shelton	49-338	CB
Duet - Rockin' Years	Parton&VanShelton	8-116	CB
Duet - Rockin' Years	Parton&VanShelton	2-300	SC
Duet - Rollin' (Ballad of Big&Rich)	Big & Rich	23-45	SC
Duet - Rollin' (Ballad Rap Style)	Big & Rich	23-46	SC
Duet - Romeo	Parton, Dolly	8-545	CB
Duet - Romeo & Juliet	Earl & Stacy	9-855	SAV
Duet - Rompe (Radio Version)	Daddy Yankee	29-251	SC
Duet - Runaway Train	John, E & Clapton	24-25	SC
Duet - Sam's Song	Martin, Dean & ?	23-89	MM
Duet - Saturday Love	Cherrelle	12-372	DK
Duet - Say Something	Carey & Snoop Dogg	23-310	CB
Duet - Secret Lovers	Atlantic Starr	2-845	SC
Duet - Send A Message To My Heart	Yoakam & Loveless	49-689	CB
Duet - Separate Lives	Collins & Martin	20-306	CB
Duet - Separate Lives	Collins & Martin	6-235	MM
Duet - September When It Comes	Cash, J. & Cash, R.	37-252	CB
Duet - September When It Comes	Cash, Johnny & Roseann	43-460	CB
Duet - Set The Night To Music	Flack & Priest	6-226	MM
Duet - Sex (I'm A...) **	Berlin	30-671	RSX
Duet - Shake Ya Tail Feather	Nelly, P. Diddy, Lee	32-344	THM
Duet - She Ain't Hooked On Me...	Keith & Haggard	49-778	SC
Duet - Shift Work	Chesney & Strait	30-585	CB
Duet - Shoop	Salt 'N Pepa	16-573	SC
Duet - Short Shorts	Royal Teens	29-830	SC
Duet - Sisters	Clooney, Rosemary & Betty	49-768	MM
Duet - Sisters	Midler & Ronstadt	45-914	HSW
Duet - Slippin' Around	Whiting & Wakely	19-640	CB
Duet - Slippin' Around	Whiting & Wakely	6-3	SC
Duet - Snakes On A Plane	Cobra Starship & Gym...	30-65	PHM
Duet - Soldier	Destiny's Child&Lil	22-343	CB
Duet - Some Velvet Morning	Sinatra, N. & Hazelwood	47-513	VH
Duet - Someone To Love	Jon B with Babyface	3-436	SC
Duet - Something Bad	Lambert & Underwood	44-278	PHN
Duet - Sometimes	Anderson & Turner	40-69	CB

SONG TITLE	ARTIST	#	TYPE
Duet - Sometimes Love Just Ain't...	Smyth & Henley	6-229	MM
Duet - Sometimes Love Just Ain't...	Smyth & Henley	9-674	SAV
Duet - Somewhere in the Vicinity of	Shenandoah/Krauss	17-259	NA
Duet - Somewhere in the Vicinity of	Shenandoah/Krauss	2-822	SC
Duet - Somewhere Out There	Ronstadt & Ingram	11-805	DK
Duet - Somewhere Out There	Ronstadt & Ingram	6-335	MM
Duet - Somewhere Out There	Ronstadt & Ingram	13-185	P
Duet - Somewhere Out There	Ronstadt & Ingram	9-205	SO
Duet - Southern Boy	Charlie Daniels & Tritt	34-557	CB
Duet - Squeeze Me In	Brooks & Yearwood	18-12	CB
Duet - Squeeze Me In	Brooks & Yearwood	25-121	MM
Duet - Steal My Sunshine	Len	33-407	CB
Duet - Steal My Sunshine	Len	8-497	PHT
Duet - Steal My Sunshine	Len	10-205	SC
Duet - Still Holdin' On	Black & McBride	1-840	CB
Duet - Still Holdin' On	Black & McBride	7-639	CHM
Duet - Stop Draggin' my Heart Aroun	Nicks & Petty	13-199	P
Duet - Storms Never Last	Colter & Jennings	44-66	KV
Duet - Storms Never Last	Jennings & Colter	45-185	DCK
Duet - Streets Of Bakersfield	Yoakam & Owens	49-686	CB
Duet - Summer Is Over	McLaughlin & Bareilles	48-734	PHM
Duet - Summer Nights	Newton-John & Travolta	33-253	CB
Duet - Summer Nights	Travolta & Newton-John	12-95	DK
Duet - Summer Nights	Travolta & Newton-John	13-142	P
Duet - Summer Nights	Travolta & Newton-John	9-277	SC
Duet - Summer Nights	Travolta & Newton-John	10-531	SF
Duet - Summertime	Armstrong & Fitzgerald	44-112	KV
Duet - Take Away	Elliott/Tweet/Ginuw	20-614	CB
Duet - Take Me	Wynette & Jones	49-358	CB
Duet - Take Me There	Backstreet & Mia	16-203	PHT
Duet - Take My Hand	Tillis & Bryce	5-448	SC
Duet - Telephone	Lady Gaga & Beyonce	38-194	CB
Duet - Tell Him	Streisand & Dion	7-693	PHM
Duet - Tell Him	Streisand & Dion	10-118	SC
Duet - Tell Me About It	Tucker & McClinton	8-112	CB
Duet - Tell Me About It	Tucker & McClinton	6-527	MM

SONG TITLE	ARTIST	#	TYPE
Duet - Tell Me About It	Tucker & McClinton	2-338	SC
Duet - Tennesse Border #2	Tubb & Foley	22-302	CB
Duet - Tennessee	Arrested Developmen	28-393	DK
Duet - Tennessee Birdwalk	Blanchard&Morgan	8-716	CB
Duet - Thank God I Found You	Carey/Joe/98 Degree	16-183	PHM
Duet - Thank God I Found You	Carey/Joe/98 Degree	17-542	SC
Duet - Thanks For The Memory	Hope, Bob	11-457	DK
Duet - That Lucky Old Sun	Chesney & Nelson	36-241	PHM
Duet - That Old Pair Of Jeans	Fatboy Slim	30-707	SF
Duet - That's How You Know When...	Wariner & Larson	5-443	SC
Duet - That's The Beat Of A Heart	Warrens & Evans	13-862	CHM
Duet - That's The Beat Of A Heart	Warrens & Evans	19-251	CSZ
Duet - That's the Way Love Goes	Haggard & Jewel	49-809	CB
Duet - That's What Friends Are For	Warwick & Friends	9-876	DK
Duet - The "F" Word	Williams & Kid Rock	45-133	SC
Duet - There Ain't No Good Chain..	Cash & Jennings	29-562	CB
Duet - There Ain't No Good Chain...	Cash & Jennings	20-663	SC
Duet - These Are The Days of/ Life	Stansfield & Mic	18-235	DK
Duet - They Just Can't Stop It	Spinners	17-142	DK
Duet - Think Of You	Young & Pope	48-2	BKD
Duet - This Bottle In My Hand	Coe & Jones	18-322	CB
Duet - This Bottle In My Hand	Coe & Jones	48-425	CB
Duet - This Old Heart Of Mine	Stewart, Rod	6-233	MM
Duet - This Song's For You	Joey & Rory	45-815	CB
Duet - Three's Company	TV Themes	2-174	SC
Duet - Till A Tear Becomes A Rose	Whitley & Morgan	8-118	CB
Duet - Till a Tear Becomes a Rose	Whitley & Morgan	2-302	SC
Duet - Till I Can Make It On My Own	Rogers & West	15-234	CB
Duet - Till I Loved You	Streisand & Johnson	49-539	CB
Duet - Till You Do Me Right	After 7	3-433	SC
Duet - Time Of My Life the	Medley & Warnes	6-333	MM
Duet - Time's A Wastin'	Cash & Carter	49-294	HKC
Duet - Timeless	Clarkson & Guari	25-633	MM
Duet - Tired Of Lovin'	Raye & Eakes	14-82	CB

SONG TITLE	ARTIST	#	TYPE
This Way			
Duet - To All The Girls I've Loved	Nelson & Iglesias	9-204	SO
Duet - To All The Girls I've Loved.	Nelson & Iglesias	16-848	DK
Duet - To All The Girls I've Loved.	Nelson & Iglesias	13-183	P
Duet - To All the Girls I've Loved...	Iglesias & Nelson	35-333	CB
Duet - To Me	Greenwood&Mandre ll	2-307	SC
Duet - Together (Wherever We Go)	Lawrence & Gorme	25-257	MM
Duet - Tonight	Wood & Beymer	11-795	DK
Duet - Tonight I Celebrate My Love.	Bryson & Flack	6-228	MM
Duet - Tonight I Celebrate My Love.	Bryson & Flack	9-211	SO
Duet - Tonight I Celebrate..	Bryson & Flack	35-311	CB
Duet - Tonight is Right for Lovin**	Chef & Meatloaf	13-720	SGB
Duet - Too Close	Next	21-561	PHM
Duet - Too Drunk To Karaoke	Keith & Buffett	41-44	ASK
Duet - Too Much Too Little Too Late	Mathis & Williams	11-460	DK
Duet - Too Much Too Little Too Late	Mathis & Williams	6-341	MM
Duet - Too Much Too Little Too Late	Mathis & Williams	13-156	P
Duet - Too Much Too Little Too...	Mathis & Williams	35-309	CB
Duet - Trip Around The Sun	Buffett & McBride	22-65	CB
Duet - Trip Around The Sun	Buffett & McBride	30-7	SC
Duet - Trip Around The Sun	Buffett & McBride	20-506	ST
Duet - True Love	Crosby & Kelly	29-417	CB
Duet - True Love	John, E & Dee, Kiki	24-148	SC
Duet - Tubthumping	Chumbawamba	7-692	PHM
Duet - Two Sleepy People	Martin & Renaud	23-76	MM
Duet - U Got The Look	Prince & Easton	23-332	CB
Duet - Unforgettable	Cole, Nat & Natalie	12-127	DK
Duet - United We Stand	Brotherhood Of Man	33-271	CB
Duet - Up Where We Belong	Cocker & Warnes	26-138	DK
Duet - Up Where We Belong	Cocker & Warnes	6-227	MM
Duet - Up Where We Belong	Cocker & Warnes	13-190	P
Duet - Up Where We Belong	Mellencamp & ?	21-437	LE
Duet - Voices That Care	Multi-Voice	18-682	PR
Duet - Walk Softly	Dixie Chicks&Skaggs	14-158	CB
Duet - Walkaway Joe	Yearwood & Diffie	8-121	CB
Duet - Wanted You More	Lady Antebellum	46-81	BKD

SONG TITLE	ARTIST	#	TYPE
Duet - Way I Are the	Timbaland & Keri Hilson	37-152	SC
Duet - We Loved It Away	Jones & Wynette	49-374	CB
Duet - We Were Us	Lambert & Urban	46-249	ASK
Duet - We Were Us	Urban & Lambert	43-87	PHN
Duet - We've Got Tonight	Rogers & Easton	15-578	MM
Duet - We're Gonna Hold On	Jones & Wynette	8-122	CB
Duet - What A Wonderful World	Bennett & Lang	45-518	SC
Duet - What Are We Doin' In Love	Rogers & West	5-436	SC
Duet - What Have I Done To Deserve	Pet Shop Boys	17-529	SC
Duet - What If I Said	Cochran & Wariner	8-143	CB
Duet - What If I Said	Cochran & Wariner	22-761	ST
Duet - What Kind Of Fool	Streisand & Gibb	15-579	MM
Duet - What Kind Of Fool	Streisand & Gibb	49-608	PS
Duet - What Now My Love	Sinatra & Franklin	15-580	MM
Duet - What's Goin' On	All Star Tribute	25-45	MM
Duet - What's Goin' On	All Star Tribute	16-81	ST
Duet - When I Fall In Love	Cole, Nat & Natalie	24-548	SC
Duet - When I Fall In Love	Dion & Griffin	12-239	DK
Duet - When I Fall In Love	Dion & Griffin	6-331	MM
Duet - When I Look Into Your Heart	Gill & Grant	9-871	ST
Duet - When I Said I Do	Black & Hartman	30-420	THM
Duet - When I Said I Do	Black & Hartman-Bla	30-420	THM
Duet - When I'm Gone	Joey & Rory	45-817	BKD
Duet - When The Right One Comes Along	Bowen & Palladio	45-471	KVD
Duet - When The Stars Go Blue	Corrs & Bond	18-413	MM
Duet - When The Sun Goes Down	Chesney & Uncle Kracker	35-445	CB
Duet - When You Tell Me That You...	Iglesias & Parton	49-771	PS
Duet - Whenever Forever Comes	Parton & Raye	2-310	SC
Duet - Whenever I Call You Friend	Loggins & Nicks	11-292	DK
Duet - Whenever I Call You Friend	Loggins & Nicks	13-159	P
Duet - Where Are You	Simpson & Lachey	20-127	PHM
Duet - Where We Both Say Goodbye	Britt, C & John, E.	23-135	CB
Duet - Where We Both Say...	Britt & Elton John	36-379	SC
Duet - Where You Are	Simpson & Lachey	14-183	CB
Duet - Where You Are	Simpson & Lachey	20-127	PH
Duet - Where Your Road Leads	Brooks & Yearwood	22-667	ST
Duet - Whiskey Ain't Workin' Anymor	Tritt & Stuart	2-410	SC
Duet - Whiskey Lullaby	Paisley & Krauss	20-323	ST
Duet - Who Says You	Bon Jovi & Nettles	29-41	CB

SONG TITLE	ARTIST	#	TYPE
Can't Go Home			
Duet - Who Says You Can't Go Home	Bon Jovi & Nettles	30-242	RS
Duet - Who Says You Can't Go Home	Nettles & Bon Jovi	30-242	RS
Duet - Whole New World a	Bryson & LaBelle	17-424	KC
Duet - Whole New World a	Bryson & LaBelle	9-208	SO
Duet - Wild As The Wind	Brooks & Yearwood	8-871	CB
Duet - Wild As The Wind	Brooks & Yearwood	10-165	SC
Duet - Wild Child	Chesney & Potter	45-46	BKD
Duet - Wild Night	Mellencamp&Ndege'oc	21-423	SC
Duet - Wild Side Of Life	Jennings & Colter	45-195	SSK
Duet - Will You Marry Me	Alabama	15-98	ST
Duet - Willingly	Nelson & Collie	38-96	CB
Duet - Wish I Didn't Have To Miss U	Greene & Seely	5-444	SC
Duet - With You I'm Born Again	Preston & Syretta	12-23	DK
Duet - With You I'm Born Again	Preston & Syretta	10-675	HE
Duet - Wooden Ships - WN	Crosby Stills & Nash	48-56	SC
Duet - Workin' Mans Blues	Diamond Rio,Warner	2-643	SC
Duet - Written In The Stars	John, E & Rimes	16-204	PHT
Duet - Written In The Stars	John, E & Rimes	13-712	SGB
Duet - Wrong Side Of Sober	Ryan & Daniels	49-920	KVD
Duet - Wrong Song - Nashville	James & Barnes	45-470	KVD
Duet - Yeah	Usher/Lil Jon/Ludac	23-253	THM
Duet - Yellow Rose Of Texas	Lee & Brody	49-645	VH
Duet - Yes I'm Ready	Desario & KC	35-79	CB
Duet - Yes I'm Ready	Desario & KC	12-384	DK
Duet - Yes Mr. Peters	Drusky & Mitchell	20-742	CB
Duet - Yes Mr. Peters	Drusky & Mitchell	9-611	SAV
Duet - Yesterday's Wine	Haggard & Jones	22-242	CB
Duet - You Ain't Dolly & You Ain't...	Shelton & Monroe	49-522	BKD
Duet - You Ain't Dolly... (Inst)	Shelton & Monroe	49-523	BKD
Duet - You And I	Rabbitt & Gayle	8-109	CB
Duet - You And I	Rabbitt & Gayle	26-369	DK
Duet - You And I	Rabbitt & Gayle	6-231	MM
Duet - You And I	Rabbitt & Gayle	13-197	P
Duet - You And I	Rabbitt & Gayle	2-306	SC
Duet - You And Me	Wells & Foley	48-202	CB
Duet - You Can Have Her	Jones & Paycheck	9-584	SAV
Duet - You Can Have Her	Paycheck & Jones	45-214	SAV
Duet - You Don't Bring Me Flowers	Diamond&Streisand	30-512	THM
Duet - You Don't Bring Me Flowers	Streisand&Diamond	7-547	AH
Duet - You Don't Bring	Streisand&Diamond	18-51	MM

SONG TITLE	ARTIST	#	TYPE
Me Flowers			
Duet - You Don't Bring Me Flowers	Streisand&Diamond	9-206	SO
Duet - You Don't Have To Be A Star	McCoo & Davis Jr.	17-140	DK
Duet - You Don't Know Me	Cassidy & Gray	25-673	MM
Duet - You're All I Need To Get By	Gaye & Terrell	11-829	DK
Duet - You're Always On My Mind	SWV	12-249	DK
Duet - You're Havin' My Baby	Anka, Paul & ??	15-595	DK
Duet - You're The One That I Want	Travolta & Newton-John	11-172	DK
Duet - You're The One That I Want	Travolta & Newton-John	6-339	MM
Duet - You're The One That I Want	Travolta & Newton-John	9-280	SC
Duet - You're The Reason God Made	Frizzell & West	2-311	SC
Duet - You're The Reason God Made..	Frizzell & West	8-120	CB
Duet - You're The Reason God Made..	Frizzell & West	13-522	P
Duet - You're the Reason Our Kids..	Jones & McClinton	14-160	CB
Duet - You've Got Your Troubles	Blanchard&Morgan	9-590	SAV
Duet- I Know What You Want	Busta Rhymes, Carey, Flipmo	32-311	THM
Duke Of Earl	Chandler, Gene	11-467	DK
Duke Of Earl	Chandler, Gene	13-260	P
Duke Of Earl	Chandler, Gene	2-56	SC
Dukes Of Hazzard Theme	Jennings, Waylon	22-147	CK
Dum Dum	Lee, Brenda	4-710	SC
Dumas Walker	Kentucky HH	2-27	SC
Dumb Girls	Woodward, Lucy	20-526	CB
Dumb Girls	Woodward, Lucy	32-139	THM
Duncan	Simon & Garfunkel	15-469	DM
Dungaree Doll	Fisher, Eddie	7-294	MM
Durham Town	Whittaker, Roger	13-587	PL
Dust	Eli Young Band	44-205	DCK
Dust	Eli Young Band	44-325	SSC
Dust In The Wind	Kansas	11-327	DK
Dust In The Wind	Scorpions	49-102	CDG
Dust On The Bottle	Murphy, David Lee	6-850	MM
Dustland Fairytale a	Killers	36-310	PHM
E I E I O Polka - w/Words	Polka Favorites	29-858	SSR
E I E I O Polka (Let's Have a Party	Polka Favorites	29-804	SSR
E Lei Ka Lei Lei	Ho, Don	6-831	MM
E-BAY	Yankovic, Weird Al	37-82	SC
E-Bow The Letter	REM	24-295	SC
E.N.H.	Cyrus, Miley	36-75	WD
Each Day Gets Better	Legend, John	36-464	CB
Each Minute Seems Like A Million..	Arnold, Eddy	6-9	SC
Eagle	Abba	46-219	FUN

SONG TITLE	ARTIST	#	TYPE
Eagle Over Angel	Brother Phelps	4-115	SC
Eagle the	Jennings, Waylon	20-582	CB
Eagle the	Jennings, Waylon	45-1`73	CB
Eagle the - Americana	Jennings, Waylon	36-340	CB
Eagle When She Flies	Parton, Dolly	3-639	SC
Eagles And Horses	Denver, John	48-404	DCK
Earache My Eye	Cheech & Chong	37-88	SC
Early In The Morning	Gap Band	14-366	MH
Early In The Morning	Holly, Buddy	3-222	LG
Early Morning Rain	Lightfoot, Gordon	43-486	SK
Earrings Song the	Wilson, Gretchen	37-41	CB
Earth Angel	Penguins	35-3	CB
Earth Angel	Penguins	7-313	MM
Earth Angel	Penguins	13-112	P
Earth Angel	Penguins	9-18	PS
Earth The Sun The Rain the	Color Me Badd	4-338	SC
Earthbound	Crowell, Rodney	19-710	ST
Ease My Troubled Mind	Ricochet	7-593	CHM
Ease On Down The Road	Jackson, M & Ross	9-834	SAV
Ease On Down The Road	Multi-Voice	18-685	PR
Ease On Down The Road	The Wiz	49-435	SDK
Easier Said Than Done	Essex	6-149	MM
Easier Said Than Done	Essex	4-32	SC
Easier Said Than Done	Foster, Radney	2-328	SC
East Bound And Down	Reed, Jerry	8-25	CB
East Bound And Down	Reed, Jerry	20-724	SC
Easter - Peter Cottontail	Autry, Gene	45-660	DCK
Easy	Commodores	11-699	DK
Easy	Commodores	10-364	KC
Easy	Richie, Lionel	10-392	LE
Easy As Pie	Craddock, Billy C	5-34	SC
Easy Come Easy Go	Sherman, Bobby	21-800	SC
Easy Come Easy Go	Strait, George	8-175	CB
Easy Come Easy Go	Strait, George	6-391	MM
Easy Come Easy Go	Strait, George	2-508	SC
Easy Does It	Hot Apple Pie	29-373	CB
Easy For Me To Say	Black & Hartman	15-851	ST
Easy Livin'	Heep, Uriah	29-636	SC
Easy Living	Lambert, Miranda	45-956	KV
Easy Lover	Collins, Phil	44-25	TOS
Easy Lover - duet	Collins & Baskey	49-310	BC
Easy Lovin'	Hart, Freddie	12-89	DK
Easy Lovin'	Hart, Freddie	8-633	SAV
Easy Lovin'	Hart, Freddie	5-27	SC
Easy Loving	Hart, Freddie	35-360	CB
Easy Makin' Love	Harling, Keith	9-424	CB
Easy On The Eyes	Arnold, Eddy	45-569	CB
Easy Part's Over the	Pride, Charley	47-436	CB
Easy To Be Hard	Three Dog Night	34-28	CB
Eat Drink & Be Merry	Wagoner, Porter	19-311	CB
Eat Drink & Be Merry	Wagoner, Porter	5-38	SC
Eat It	Yankovic, Weird Al	6-512	MM
Eat It	Yankovic, Weird Al	12-597	P
Eat The Rich	Krokus	23-105	SC
Ebb Tide	Hamilton, Roy	9-738	SAV
Ebb Tide	Righteous Brothers	11-232	DK

SONG TITLE	ARTIST	#	TYPE
Ebb Tide	Righteous Brothers	3-332	PS
Ebb Tide	Righteous Brothers	9-316	STR
Ebony And Ivory	McCartney&Wonder	11-117	DK
Ebony Eyes	Everly Brothers	38-22	CB
Edelweiss	Sound Of Music	10-45	SC
Edge Of A Broken Heart	Vixen	24-435	SC
Edge Of Glory	Lady Gaga	38-185	CB
Edge Of Seventeen	Nicks, Stevie	16-125	SC
Ego	Beyonce	36-293	PHM
Eight Days A Week	Beatles	16-732	DK
Eight Days A Week	Beatles	3-322	MH
Eight Days A Week	Beatles	29-345	SC
Eight Miles High	Byrds	2-759	SC
Eight Second Ride	Owen, Jake	37-59	CB
Eight Second Ride (Inst)	Owen, Jake	49-391	DCK
Eighteen Wheels & A Dozen Roses	Mattea, Kathy	1-184	CB
Eighteen Wheels & A Dozen Roses	Mattea, Kathy	13-413	P
Eighteen Wheels & A Dozen Roses	Mattea, Kathy	9-432	SAV
Eighteen Wheels & A Dozen Roses	Mattea, Kathy	2-16	SC
El Cerrito Place	Chesney, Kenny	39-65	PHN
El Condor Pasa	Simon & Garfunkel	23-641	BS
El Paso	Robbins, Marty	7-160	MM
El Paso	Robbins, Marty	13-449	P
El Paso	Robbins, Marty	8-673	SAV
El Paso	Robbins, Marty	4-582	SC
El Paso (Long Version)	Robbins, Marty	3-232	CB
El Paso City	Robbins, Marty	3-236	CB
Elderly Woman Behind The Counter	Pearl Jam	9-304	RS
Eleanor Rigby	Beatles	11-166	DK
Eleanor Rigby	Beatles	13-234	P
Electric Blue	Icehouse	11-321	DK
Electric Slide (Electric Boogie)	Griffiths, Marcia	22-392	SC
Electrical Storm	U2	23-150	PHM
Elenore	Turtles	12-869	P
Elenore	Turtles	20-60	SC
Elephant Love Medley	Moulin Rouge	19-120	PR
Elevation	U2	48-311	SC
Eleven Roses	Williams, Hank Jr.	4-814	SC
Elisabeth	Gilman, Billy	16-13	ST
Elizabeth	Statler Brothers	19-383	CB
Elizabeth	Statler Brothers	5-569	SC
Elusive Butterfly	Lind, Bob	11-362	DK
Elusive Butterfly	Lind, Bob	9-845	SAV
Elvira	Oak Ridge Boys	8-264	CB
Elvira	Oak Ridge Boys	11-221	DK
Elvira	Oak Ridge Boys	6-764	MM
Elvira	Oak Ridge Boys	13-352	P
Elvira	Oak Ridge Boys	9-438	SAV
Elvis & Andy	Confederate RR	6-615	MM
Elvis & Andy	Confederate RR	2-360	SC
Embraceable You	Adams, Oleta	23-343	MM
Embraceable You	Cole, Nat "King"	9-799	SAV

SONG TITLE	ARTIST	#	TYPE
Embraceable You	Fitzgerald, Ella	12-502	P
Emily	Streisand, Barbra	49-603	PS
Emotion	Bee Gees	48-692	ZMP
Emotion	Destiny's Child	25-18	MM
Emotion	Sang, Samantha	11-326	DK
Emotional Girl	Clark, Terri	7-588	CHM
Emotional Love	Mellencamp, John	45-422	SC
Emotional Rescue	Rolling Stones	18-24	LE
Emotional Rollercoaster	Green, V.	32-164	THM
Emotionally Yours	O'Jays	10-679	HE
Emotions	Lee, Brenda	11-603	DK
Emotions	Newton, Juice	17-291	NA
Empathy	Morrisette, Alanis	39-120	PHM
Emptiest Arms In The World	Haggard, Merle	17-382	DK
Emptiest Arms In The World the	Haggard, Merle	37-171	CB
Empty Arms	Hunter, Ivory Joe	17-329	SS
Empty Arms	James, Sonny	19-476	CB
Empty Heart	Potter, Grace	48-703	BKD
End Of The Innocence	Henley, Don	48-156	ZMP
End Of The Road	Boyz II Men	6-411	MM
End Of The World	Carpenters	45-801	DKM
End Of The World	Davis, Skeeter	43-323	CB
End Of The World	Herman's Hermits	47-136	LE
End Of The World	Lee, Brenda	45-453	SAV
End Of The World the	Davis, Skeeter	17-1	DK
End Of The World the	Davis, Skeeter	6-164	MM
End Of The World the	Davis, Skeeter	13-428	P
End Of The World the	Paige, Allison	9-429	CB
End Of Time	Band Perry	45-56	BKD
End Of Time	Band Perry	48-108	KV
End the	Doors	18-655	SO
Endless Love	Rabbitt & Gayle	11-459	DK
Endless Love	Richie & Ross	26-187	DK
Endless Love	Richie & Ross	15-354	LE
Endless Love	Richie & Ross	13-203	P
Endless Love	Richie, Lionel	10-397	LE
Endless Love - duet	Richie & Ross	35-207	CB
Endless Love - duet	Richie & Twain	47-452	KV
Endless Sleep	Reynolds, Judy	9-751	SAV
Endless Summer Nights	Marx, Richard	34-96	CB
Endless Summer Nights	Marx, Richard	15-792	SC
Endlessly	Benton, Brook	4-214	SC
Endlessly	Benton, Brook	10-258	SS
Endlessly	James, Sonny	19-475	CB
Enemy	Days Of The New	5-785	SC
Enemy	Sevendust	19-760	PHM
Energy	Hilson, Keri	36-527	CB
Energy	Natalie&Baby Bash	23-319	CB
Engine Engine # 9	Miller, Roger	8-421	CB
Engine Engine # 9	Miller, Roger	4-305	SC
England 2 Columbia 0	MacColl, Kirsty	30-787	SF
England Swings	Miller, Roger	22-280	CB
England Swings	Miller, Roger	22-451	SC
Enid	Barenaked Ladies	30-623	RS
Enjoy Yourself	Currington, Billy	48-214	KV

SONG TITLE	ARTIST	#	TYPE
Enormous P#n#s	Da Vinci's Notebook	37-92	SC
Enough	McEntire, Reba	45-406	BKD
Enough Of A Woman	Wynette, Tammy	45-668	DCK
Enough Of Me	Etheridge, Melissa	47-64	MM
Enough Of Me	Etheridge, Melissa	49-423	SC
Enter Sandman	Metallica	13-626	LE
Entertainer the	Joel, Billy	12-275	DK
Entertainer the	Joel, Billy	16-141	LE
Epiphany	Staind	21-650	CB
Escapade	Jackson, Janet	15-415	PS
Escape	Iglesias, Enrique	25-136	MM
Escape (the Pina Colada Song)	Holmes, Rupert	11-211	DK
Escape (the Pina Colada Song)	Holmes, Rupert	4-765	SC
Escape (the Pina Coloda Song)	Holmes, Rupert	35-155	CB
ESP	Bee Gees	9-777	SAV
Eternal Flame	Bangles	12-812	P
Eternally	Humperdinck, E.	49-262	DFK
Eugene You Genius	White, Bryan	6-669	MM
Eve Of Destruction	McGuire, Barry	21-201	DK
Eve Of Destruction	McGuire, Barry	10-355	KC
Even Better Than The Real Thing	U2	30-66	SC
Even Flow	Pearl Jam	9-291	RS
Even God Must Get The Blues	Messina, Jo Dee	23-362	SC
Even If I Tried	Emilio	4-102	SC
Even If It Breaks Your Heart	Eli Young Band	44-298	PHN
Even It Up	Heart	4-530	SC
Even Now	Manilow, Barry	29-116	CB
Even Now	Manilow, Barry	6-551	MM
Even Now	Manilow, Barry	9-79	PS
Even The Man In The Moon Is Cryin	Collie, Mark	17-163	JVC
Even The Man In The Moon Is Cryin'	Collie, Mark	2-334	SC
Even The Nights Are Better	Air Supply	46-393	SC
Even The Stars Fell For You	Urban, Keith	42-22	ASK
Even Then	Montgomery, J M	15-336	CB
Even Though	Pierce, Webb	29-399	CB
Ever Changing Woman	Brother Phelps	2-422	SC
Ever Never Loving You	Bruce, Ed	19-449	SC
Ever The Same	Thomas, Rob	47-609	CB
Evergreen	Streisand, Barbra	12-879	P
Everlasting Love	Estefan, Gloria	26-338	DK
Everlasting Love	Estefan, Gloria	16-635	MM
Everlasting Love	Estefan, Gloria	29-127	ST
Everlasting Love	Jones, Howard	21-738	MH
Everlasting Love	Love Affair	10-584	SF
Everlong	Foo Fighters	6-40	SC
Evert Morning	Sugar Ray	16-199	PHT
Every 1's A Winner	Hot Chocolate	17-71	DK
Every Beat Of My Heart	Knight & Pips	7-66	MM

SONG TITLE	ARTIST	#	TYPE
Every Beat Of My Heart	Stewart, Rod	14-855	LE
Every Breath I Take	Pitney, Gene	9-846	SAV
Every Breath I Take	Pitney, Gene	9-178	SO
Every Breath You Take	Police	35-153	CB
Every Bulb In The House Is Blown	Judd, Cledus T.	16-512	CB
Every Day	McLean, Don	47-248	SBI
Every Day	Rascal Flatts	36-577	CB
Every Day I Have The Blues	King, B.B.	46-308	SC
Every Fool Has A Rainbow	Haggard, Merle	49-805	CB
Every Friday Afternoon	Morgan, Craig	25-705	MM
Every Friday Afternoon	Morgan, Craig	19-268	ST
Every Friday Afternoon	Morgan, Craig	32-411	THM
Every Heart Should Have One	Pride, Charley	43-208	CB
Every Heartbeat	Grant, Amy	6-102	MM
Every Light In The House Is On	Adkins, Trace	4-435	SC
Every Little Step	Brown, Bobby	12-844	P
Every Little Thing	Carter, Deana	19-301	MH
Every Little Thing	O'Neal, Jamie	34-399	CB
Every Little Thing	O'Neal, Jamie	19-61	ST
Every Little Thing She Does	Lonestar	48-478	CKC
Every Little Thing She Does	Police	4-376	SC
Every Little Thing She Does is Magic	Police	34-51	CB
Every Little Whisper	Wariner, Steve	8-221	CB
Every Little Whisper	Wariner, Steve	22-690	ST
Every Man For Himself	McCoy, Neal	14-108	CB
Every Man For Himself	McCoy, Neal	22-574	ST
Every Mile A Memory	Bentley, Dierks	30-22	CB
Every Now And Then	Jackson, Alan	45-107	KV
Every Once In Awhile	Blackhawk	6-579	MM
Every Other Weekend	McEntire & Ewing	36-581	CB
Every Other Weekend - duet	McEntire & Chesney	49-707	ST
Every River	Brooks & Dunn	25-358	MM
Every River	Brooks & Dunn	18-205	ST
Every Rose Has It's Thorn	Poison	9-372	AH
Every Rose Has It's Thorn	Poison	20-322	MH
Every Rose Has It's Thorn	Poison	24-196	SC
Every Rose Has It's Thorn	Poison	13-746	SGB
Every Second	Raye, Collin	1-123	CB
Every Second	Raye, Collin	26-529	DK
Every Second	Raye, Collin	6-122	MM
Every Second	Raye, Collin	2-509	SC
Every Storm (Runs Out Of Rain)	Allan, Gary	47-711	BKD
Every Teardrop Is A Waterfall	Coldplay	48-257	MRH
Every Time	Jackson, Janet	15-414	PS

SONG TITLE	ARTIST	#	TYPE
Every Time	Tillis, Pam	8-191	CB
Every Time I Get Around	Murphy, David Lee	7-230	MM
Every Time I Get Around You	Murphy, David Lee	22-883	ST
Every Time I Hear Your Name	Anderson, Keith	29-44	CB
Every Time I Hear Your Name	Anderson, Keith	29-711	ST
Every Time I Think Of You	Babys	3-133	SC
Every Time I'm With You	Seal	48-395	DCK
Every Time My Heart Calls	Berry, John	4-196	SC
Every Time She Passes By	Ducas, George	4-368	SC
Every Time Two Fools Collide	Rogers & West	8-117	CB
Every Time Two Fools Collide	Rogers & West	2-298	SC
Every Time You Go Away	Young, Paul	20-300	CB
Every Time You Go Away	Young, Paul	16-814	DK
Every Time You Go Away	Young, Paul	13-35	P
Every Time You Go Away	Young, Paul	4-322	SC
Every Woman In The World	Air Supply	46-392	SC
Every Word I Write	West, Dottie	15-229	CB
Every Year Every Christmas	Vandross, Luther	45-772	KV
Everybody	Backstreet Boys	18-713	MM
Everybody	Backstreet Boys	10-129	SC
Everybody	Roe, Tommy	4-251	SC
Everybody	Urban, Keith	30-550	CB
Everybody Have Fun Tonight	Wang Chung	26-272	DK
Everybody Have Fun Tonight	Wang Chung	15-799	SC
Everybody Knows	Dave Clark Five	45-83	ZMP
Everybody Knows	Dixie Chicks	29-596	CB
Everybody Knows	Henley, Don	48-153	SBI
Everybody Knows	Yearwood, Trisha	1-640	CB
Everybody Knows	Yearwood, Trisha	16-661	CHM
Everybody Knows	Yearwood, Trisha	24-649	SC
Everybody Loves A Clown	Lewis & Playboys	3-18	SC
Everybody Loves A Lover	Day, Doris	34-10	CB
Everybody Loves A Lover	Day, Doris	9-93	PS
Everybody Loves A Lover	Day, Doris	5-1	SC
Everybody Loves a Rain Song	Thomas, B.J.	38-44	GMG
Everybody Loves A Rain Song	Thomas, B.J.	9-570	SAV
Everybody Loves Me But You	Lee, Brenda	45-905	CB

SONG TITLE	ARTIST	#	TYPE
Everybody Loves Somebody	Martin, Dean	11-309	DK
Everybody Loves Somebody	Martin, Dean	20-758	KB
Everybody Loves Somebody	Martin, Dean	10-405	LE
Everybody Loves Somebody	Martin, Dean	23-65	MM
Everybody Loves Somebody	Martin, Dean	12-505	P
Everybody Loves Somebody	Martin, Dean	2-205	SC
Everybody Loves To Cha Cha Cha	Cooke, Sam	46-641	RB
Everybody Makes Mistakes	Dalton, Lacy J.	5-630	SC
Everybody Needs Somebody	Blues Brothers	38-31	SF
Everybody Needs Somebody	Blues Brothers	29-156	ZM
Everybody Plays The Fool	Main Ingredient	35-200	CB
Everybody Plays The Fool	Main Ingredient	22-934	SC
Everybody Says Don't	Sondheim, Stephen	17-783	PS
Everybody Says Don't	Streisand, Barbra	49-559	PS
Everybody Talks	Neon Trees	39-30	PHM
Everybody Wants	Lawson, Shannon	20-257	PHM
Everybody Wants To Go To Heaven	Chesney, Kenny	36-212	PHM
Everybody Wants To Go To Heaven	Krauss, Alison	49-712	VH
Everybody Wants To Rule The World	Tears For Fears	20-292	CB
Everybody Wants To Rule The World	Tears For Fears	13-253	P
Everybody Wants To Rule The World	Tears For Fears	5-150	SC
Everybody's Everything	Santana	21-514	SC
Everybody's Fool	Evanescence	20-562	CB
Everybody's Free	Luhrmann, Baz	7-849	PHM
Everybody's Gone To War	Pallot, Nerina	30-708	SF
Everybody's Gonna Be Happy	Kinks	48-184	ZMJ
Everybody's Got A Vice	Dalley, Amy	30-251	CB
Everybody's Got Somebody But Me	Hayes, Hunter	43-91	HM
Everybody's Got Something To Hide	Beatles	47-770	SRK
Everybody's Gotta Grow Up	Sons Of The Desert	14-84	CB
Everybody's Had The Blues	Haggard, Merle	8-322	CB
Everybody's Had The Blues	Haggard, Merle	49-804	CB
Everybody's Makin' It But Me	Dr. Hook	47-48	SFM
Everybody's Somebody's Fool	Francis, Connie	11-271	DK
Everybody's Talkin'	Nillson	11-541	DK

SONG TITLE	ARTIST	#	TYPE
Everybody's Talkin'	Nillson	12-915	P
Everybody's Trying To Be My Baby	Beatles	44-118	KV
Everyday	Collins, Phil	2-117	SC
Everyday	Dave Matthews Band	36-135	SGB
Everyday	Dave Matthews Band	16-85	ST
Everyday	Holly, Buddy	12-175	DK
Everyday	Holly, Buddy	3-220	LG
Everyday	Oak Ridge Boys	23-506	CB
Everyday	Taylor, James	45-535	OZP
Everyday America	Sugarland	30-457	CB
Everyday Angel	Foster, Radney	49-28	KCD
Everyday Angel	Foster, Radney	18-211	ST
Everyday Girl	Dean, Roxie	19-535	ST
Everyday I Have The Blues	Allman Brothers	7-219	MM
Everyday I Write The Book	Costello, Elvis	16-59	SC
Everyday Is A Winding Road	Crow, Sheryl	29-670	RS
Everyday Is A Winding Road	Crow, Sheryl	10-49	SC
Everyday Is A Winding Road	Crow, Sheryl	19-160	SGB
Everyday Is Like Sunday	Pretenders	14-884	SC
Everyday People	Sly & Family Stone	17-116	DK
Everyday People	Sly & Family Stone	12-911	P
Everyone	Socialburn	32-330	THM
Everything	Andrews, Jessica	36-276	PHM
Everything	Buble, Michael	30-489	CB
Everything	Buble, Michael	37-119	SC
Everything	Jackson, Janet	6-413	MM
Everything	Stereo Fuse	18-611	PHM
Everything	Streisand, Barbra	47-847	FMG
Everything About You	Ugly Kid Joe	13-747	SGB
Everything But You	Moore, Kip	45-635	PHN
Everything Changes	Little Big Town	18-135	ST
Everything From Jesus To Jack Daniels	Hall, Tom T.	45-838	VH
Everything Happens To Me	Standard	15-472	SGB
Everything I Do I Do It For You	Adams, Bryan	21-454	CB
Everything I Do I Do It For You	Adams, Bryan	11-71	JTG
Everything I Do I Do It For You	Adams, Bryan	6-93	MM
Everything I Love	Jackson, Alan	1-54	CB
Everything I Love	Jackson, Alan	7-587	CHM
Everything I Love	Jackson, Alan	24-656	SC
Everything I Own	Boy George	46-522	P
Everything I Own	Bread	34-39	CB
Everything I Own	Bread	11-230	DK
Everything I Own	Bread	16-541	P
Everything I Own	Bread	9-724	SAV
Everything I Own	N'Sync	15-773	BS
Everything I Own	Tippin, Aaron	4-366	SC

SONG TITLE	ARTIST	#	TYPE
Everything I Own	Tippin, Aaron	22-900	ST
Everything I Shouldn't Be Thinkin' About	Thompson Square	47-35	BKD
Everything I Used To Be	Chris Weaver Band	41-69	PHN
Everything Is Beautiful	Stevens, Ray	8-45	CB
Everything Is Beautiful	Stevens, Ray	22-926	SC
Everything Is Everything	Hill, Lauryn	25-695	MM
Everything Is Fine	Turner, Josh	36-227	PHM
Everything She Wants	Wham!	20-298	CB
Everything She Wants	Wham!	28-337	DK
Everything She Wants	Wham!	16-522	P
Everything She Wants	Wham!	4-847	SC
Everything That Glitters Is Not Gol	Seals, Dan	4-554	SC
Everything There Is To Know	Wills, Mark	10-266	SC
Everything Tonite	Lyons, Elizabeth	41-80	PHN
Everything You Want	Vertical Horizon	16-234	PHM
Everything You Want (Radio Vers)	Vertical Horizon	5-893	SC
Everything Your Heart Desires - WN	Hall & Oates	48-63	CB
Everything Zen	Bush	5-745	SC
Everything's Changed	Lonestar	22-812	ST
Everything's Coming Up Roses	Merman, Ethel	7-191	MM
Everything's Magic	Angels & Airwaves	37-141	SC
Everything's The Same	Swan, Billy	47-540	VH
Everytime I Close My Eyes	Babyface	15-473	SC
Everytime I Close My Eyes	Backstreet Boys	30-410	THM
Everytime I Cry	Clark, Terri	34-330	CB
Everytime I Cry	Clark, Terri	7-852	CHT
Everytime I Cry	Clark, Terri	22-713	ST
Everytime I Hear That Mellow Sax	Brian Setzer Orch	46-533	MM
Everytime I Roll The Dice	LeDoux, Chris	2-104	SC
Everytime You Cross My Mind	Bailey, Razzy	29-387	CB
Everytime You Go	3 Doors Down	47-656	CB
Everytime You Go Away	McKnight, Brian	22-368	CB
Everytime You Touch Me	Rich, Charlie	4-577	SC
Everytime You Touch Me...	Rich, Charlie	34-228	CB
Everywhere	Branch, Michelle	15-815	CB
Everywhere	Branch, Michelle	23-589	PHM
Everywhere	Fleetwood Mac	47-913	SBI
Everywhere	McGraw, Tim	12-927	CB
Everywhere	McGraw, Tim	7-680	CHM
Everywhere	McGraw, Tim	4-837	SC
Everywhere	McGraw, Tim	22-611	ST
Everywhere I Go	Mullins, Shawn	14-24	THM
Everywhere You Look	Jepsen, Carly Rae	49-792	BKD
Evidence	Tedeschi, Susan	29-216	PHM
Evil On Your Mind	Howard, Jan	8-789	CB
Evil Ways	Santana	11-831	DK
Evil Woman	ELO	16-596	MM

SONG TITLE	ARTIST	#	TYPE
Ex Factor	Hill, Lauryn	25-688	MM
Ex Old Man	Kelly, Kristen	39-36	ASK
Ex-Factor	Hill, Lauryn	19-724	CB
Ex-Factor	Hill, Lauryn	28-220	DK
Ex-Factor	Hill, Lauryn	7-821	PHM
Ex-Factor	Hill, Lauryn	13-675	SGB
Ex's & Oh's	King, Elle	46-121	BKD
Except For Monday	Morgan, Lorrie	1-338	CB
Except For Monday	Morgan, Lorrie	13-400	P
Excerpt From A Teenage Opera	West, Keith	10-647	SF
Excuse Me I Think I've Got A Hearta	Owens, Buck	14-330	SC
Exhale (Shoop Shoop)	Houston, Whitney	19-583	MH
Exodus Song	Boone, Pat	9-558	SAV
Exodus Song	Williams, Andy	46-283	UBS
Express Yourself	Madonna	21-158	LE
Express Yourself	Madonna	9-665	SAV
Expression	Salt-N-Pepa	37-68	SC
Expressway To Your Heart	Soul Survivor	28-109	DK
Expressway To Your Heart	Soul Survivor	9-835	SAV
Extra Ordinary	Better Than Ezra	23-94	SC
Extraordinary	Phair, Liz	20-573	CB
Eye In The Sky	Parsons Project	11-118	DK
Eye In The Sky	Parsons Project	9-785	SAV
Eye Of The Tiger	Anka, Paul	44-113	KV
Eye Of The Tiger	Survivor	20-365	SC
Eyes Of A Child the	Cline, Patsy	6-731	MM
Eyes Of A New York Woman	Thomas, B.J.	5-211	SC
Eyes Of A New York Woman the	Thomas, B.J.	36-155	LE
Eyes of Waylon	Williams, Hank Jr.	16-674	C2C
Eyes Open	Swift, Taylor	39-45	ASK
Eyes Without a Face	Idol, Billy	4-879	SC
F Troop	TV Themes	2-159	SC
F### Her Gently **	Tenacious D	37-91	SC
Fa Fa Fa Fa Fa (Sad Song)	Redding, Otis	46-162	SC
Fa Fa Fa Fa Fa Fa	Redding, Otis	47-357	LE
Face In The Crowd - duet	Richie & Dosterhuis	47-454	KV
Face To Face	Alabama	12-79	DK
Face To Face	Brooks, Garth	48-344	JVC
Face To The Wall	Young, Faron	20-738	CB
Fade	Staind	16-316	TT
Fade Away	Springsteen, Bruce	20-251	LE
Fade Into You - Nashville	O'Connor & Scott	45-469	KVD
Fade My Shade Of Black the	Statesboro Revue	41-68	PHN
Fade To Black	Metallica	21-764	SC
Faded	Cascada	36-234	PHM
Faded	Soul Decision	35-225	CB
Faded	Soul Decision w Thrust	30-640	THM
Faded (Radio Version)	Soul Decision	14-508	SC
Faded Love	Cline, Patsy	6-730	MM

SONG TITLE	ARTIST	#	TYPE
Faded Love	Cline, Patsy	2-636	SC
Faded Love	Wills, Bob	20-699	CB
Faded Love	Wills, Bob	17-366	DK
Faded Love	Wills, Bob	8-647	SAV
Faded Love - duet	Price & Nelson	45-631	ASK
Fading Like A Flower	Roxette	18-495	SAV
Fair Shake	Foster & Lloyd	20-280	SC
Faith	Big House	5-289	SC
Faith	Michael, George	28-311	DK
Faith	Michael, George	12-750	P
Faith	Michael, George	29-288	SC
Faith In Me Faith In You	Stone, Doug	2-663	SC
Faith In You	Wariner, Steve	13-834	CHM
Faith In You	Wariner, Steve	19-257	CSZ
Faith Of The Heart	Ashton, Susan	8-916	CB
Faith Of The Heart	Ashton, Susan	7-856	CHT
Faith Of The Heart	Stewart, Rod	7-813	PHT
Faith To Fall Back On	Hayes, Hunter	39-84	PHN
Faithfully	Berry, John	22-620	ST
Faithless Love	Campbell, Glen	19-433	SC
Faithless Love	Ronstadt, Linda	9-487	SAV
Fall	Bieber, Justin	48-627	KVD
Fall	Walker, Clay	30-449	CB
Fall Back Down	Rancid	32-403	THM
Fall In Love	Chesney, Kenny	1-316	CB
Fall In Love	Chesney, Kenny	2-689	SC
Fall In Love Again	Money, Eddie	47-285	SC
Fall Into Me	Emerson Drive	25-301	MM
Fall Into Me	Emerson Drive	18-131	ST
Fall Reaching	Ward, Chris	24-160	SC
Fall To Pieces	Velvet Revolver	22-354	CB
Fallen	McLachlan, Sarah	35-274	CB
Fallen	McLachlan, Sarah	32-431	THM
Fallen	McLachlan, Sarah	29-244	ZM
Fallen	Mya	19-667	CB
Fallen Star a	Husky, Ferlin	22-267	CB
Fallen Star a	Newman, Jimmy	4-807	SC
Fallen Star a	Noble, Nick	10-751	JVC
Fallen Star a	Reeves, Jim	49-803	VH
Fallin'	Keys, Alicia	35-228	CB
Fallin'	Keys, Alicia	23-585	PHM
Fallin'	Keys, Alicia	16-379	SGB
Fallin'	Keys, Alicia	18-513	TT
Fallin' Again	Alabama	26-558	DK
Fallin' For You	Caillat, Colbie	36-302	PHM
Fallin' For You For Years	Twitty, Conway	43-197	CB
Fallin' In Love	Hamilton/Frank/Reyn	2-849	SC
Fallin' Never Felt So Good	Camp, Shawn	9-625	SAV
Fallin' Never Felt So Good	Chesnutt, Mark	9-413	CB
Falling	Hogan, Brooks,Stacks	36-309	PHM
Falling	Jordan, Montell	24-552	SC
Falling	Nettles, Jennifer	44-277	PHN
Falling	Orbison, Roy	38-54	ZM

SONG TITLE	ARTIST	#	TYPE
Falling Again	Williams, Don	45-217	SC
Falling For The First Time	Barenaked Ladies	18-405	MM
Falling For The First Time	Barenaked Ladies	23-99	SC
Falling In Love	Sylvia	45-925	SC
Falling Into You	Dion, Celine	24-232	SC
Falling Into You	Whiskey Falls	36-566	CB
Falling Out Of Love	McEntire, Reba	1-799	CB
Falling Out Of Love	McEntire, Reba	10-779	JVC
Falling Slowly	Groban, Josh	48-645	KV
Falling Up	Etheridge, Melissa	39-105	PHM
Falls Apart	Sugar Ray	9-337	PS
Falls Apart	Sugar Ray	5-890	SC
Falls On Me	Fuel	20-565	CB
Falls On Me	Fuel	23-174	PHM
Fame	Cara, Irene	11-343	DK
Fame	Cara, Irene	9-4	MH
Fame	Cara, Irene	18-57	MM
Fame And Fortune	Presley, Elvis	7-132	MM
Familiar Pain	Restless Heart	1-413	CB
Family Affair	Blige, Mary J.	33-399	CB
Family Affair	Blige, Mary J.	25-35	MM
Family Affair	Sly & Family Stone	33-272	CB
Family Affair	Sly & Family Stone	11-671	DK
Family Affair	Sly & Family Stone	9-756	SAV
Family Is Family	Musgraves, Kacey	45-318	KV
Family Man	Campbell, Craig	37-346	CB
Family Man	Hall & Oates	9-199	SO
Family Portrait	Pink	35-244	CB
Family Portrait	Pink	32-24	THM
Family Portrait **	Pink	25-428	MM
Family Tradition	Williams, Hank Jr.	7-109	MM
Family Tradition	Williams, Hank Jr.	13-333	P
Family Tradition	Williams, Hank Jr.	2-123	SC
Family Tree	Parnell, Lee Roy	49-278	CB
Family Tree	Worley, Darryl	25-411	MM
Family Tree	Worley, Darryl	18-448	ST
Family Tree	Worley, Darryl	32-39	THM
Family Tree	Worley, Darryl	32-39	THM
Famous Final Scene the	Seger, Bob	10-178	UK
Famous In A Small Town	Lambert, Miranda	30-359	CB
Famous Last Words Of A Fool	Strait, George	8-166	CB
Fanatic	Green, V.	32-309	THM
Fanatic	Heart	39-129	PHM
Fancy	McEntire, Reba	1-796	CB
Fancy	McEntire, Reba	13-478	P
Fancy	McEntire, Reba	2-390	SC
Fancy Free	Oak Ridge Boys	23-505	CB
Fanny (Be Tender With My Love)	Bee Gees	48-690	P
Fantasy	Aldo Nova	35-209	CB
Fantasy	Aldo Nova	5-492	SC
Far Away	Nickelback	46-315	SC
Far Away Places	Crosby, Bing	4-186	SC
Far From Over	Stallone, Frank	27-395	DK

SONG TITLE	ARTIST	#	TYPE
Far Side Banks Of Jordan - duet	Cash & Carter	47-785	SRK
Farewell Angelina	Baez, Joan	46-461	SBI
Farewell Party	Watson, Gene	8-830	CB
Farewell Party	Watson, Gene	14-314	SC
Farmer's Daughter	Atkins, Rodney	37-329	CB
Farmer's Daughter	Haggard, Merle	8-314	CB
Farther	Outspoken	32-148	THM
Farther Along	Presley, Elvis	25-509	MM
Fascinated	Company B	18-376	AH
Fascination	Cole, Nat "King"	46-373	TU
Fascination	Cole, Natalie	18-245	DK
Fascination (Keep Feeling)	Human League	24-210	SC
Fast As You	Yoakam, Dwight	2-345	SC
Fast As You Can - Radio Version	Apple, Fiona	17-537	SC
Fast Car	Chapman, Tracy	9-320	AG
Fast Car	Chapman, Tracy	9-5	MH
Fast Car	Chapman, Tracy	21-620	SF
Fast Car	Chapman, Tracy	19-158	SGB
Fast Cars And Freedom	Rascal Flatts	22-329	CB
Fast Lanes & Country Roads	Mandrell, Barbara	5-407	SC
Fast Love	Michael, George	4-342	SC
Fast Movin' Train	Restless Heart	14-690	CB
Fast Movin' Train	Restless Heart	3-647	SC
Faster Horses	Hall, Tom T.	8-439	CB
Fastest Girl In Town	Lambert, Miranda	39-31	ASK
Fat	Yankovic, Weird Al	49-843	SGB
Fat Bottomed Girls **	Queen	2-725	SC
Fat Lip	Sum 41	16-383	SGB
Fat Man In The Bathtub	Little Feat	47-207	SC
Father & Daughter	Simon, Paul	25-437	MM
Father & Son	Stevens, Cat	13-580	NU
Father & Son - Duet	Cash & Fiona Apple	43-403	SC
Father And Son	Stevens, Cat	23-652	BS
Father Christmas - xmas	Kinks	45-250	SC
Father Figure	Michael, George	11-660	DK
Father Figure	Michael, George	12-751	P
Father Of Mine	Everclear	7-792	PHT
Father To Son	Collins, Phil	44-17	SBI
Favorite State Of Mind	Gracin , Josh	29-366	CB
Fear Of A Broken Heart	Jefferson, Paul	7-326	MM
Fear Of A Broken Heart	Jefferson, Paul	24-158	SC
Fear Of Being Alone the	McEntire, Reba	1-821	CB
Fear Of Being Alone the	McEntire, Reba	4-505	SC
Fearless	Cailliat, Colbie	48-221	KV
Fearless	Swift, Taylor	38-131	CB
Fearless Love	Etheridge, Melissa	47-66	PHM
February Song	Groban, Josh	43-304	CB
Feed Jake	Pirates of Mississi	13-381	P
Feed My Frankenstein	Alice Cooper	16-448	SGB
Feed The Fire	Bodeans	18-480	NU
Feed The Fire	Murray, Anne	38-2	CB
Feel	Matchbox 20	19-600	CB
Feel	Matchbox 20	32-369	THM

SONG TITLE	ARTIST	#	TYPE
Feel	Williams, Robbie	25-533	MM
Feel Alright	Earle, Steve	46-185	SC
Feel Good Inc (Radio Vers)	Gorillaz	37-108	SC
Feel Good Time	Pink	25-656	MM
Feel Good Time	Pink & Orbit	34-164	CB
Feel Good Time	Pink & Orbit	32-320	THM
Feel Good Time	Pink/Feat/Orbit	19-595	CB
Feel Like A Number	Seger, Bob	46-345	SC
Feel Like A Rock Star - duet	Chesney & McGraw	45-126	BKD
Feel Like Fallin'	Ricochet	20-454	ST
Feel Like Makin' Love	Bad Company	2-143	SC
Feel Like Makin' Love	Claypool, Philip	7-81	MM
Feel Like Makin' Love	Gerblansky, Ned	13-722	SGB
Feel Like Making Love	Flack, Roberta	11-627	DK
Feel My Way To You	Restless Heart	20-496	ST
Feel That Again	Aldean, Jason	44-134	ASK
Feel That Fire	Bentley, Dierks	36-221	PHM
Feel The Tide	Mumford & Sons	39-115	PHM
Feel Your Love Tonight	Van Halen	13-642	SGB
Feelin' Alright	Cocker, Joe	12-918	P
Feelin' Groovy	Simon & Garfunkel	15-474	DM
Feelin' It	McCreery, Scotty	44-136	ASK
Feelin' It	McCreery, Scotty	45-45	BKD
Feelin' Like That a	Allan, Gary	30-193	CB
Feelin' So Good	Lopez, Jennifer	15-295	CB
Feelin' So Good	Lopez, Jennifer	5-895	SC
Feelin' The Feelin'	Bellamy Brothers	44-75	KV
Feelin' The Same Way	Jones, Norah	25-672	MM
Feelin' The Same Way	Jones, Norah	32-241	THM
Feelin' The Same Way	Jones, Norah	19-185	Z
Feeling Alright	Cocker, Joe	21-440	LE
Feeling Alright	Lewis & The News	47-192	SC
Feeling Good	Buble, Michael	38-175	CB
Feeling Good	Darin, Bobby	48-646	KV
Feeling So Good	Lopez, Jennifer	23-582	MM
Feeling Tonight	Pickler, Kellie	48-701	BKD
Feeling Way Too Damn Good	Nickelback	23-554	MM
Feeling Way Too Damn Good	Nickelback	45-811	SC
Feelings	Albert, Morris	26-262	DK
Feelings	Albert, Morris	2-195	SC
Feelings - duet	Twitty & Lynn	48-243	CB
Feelings Show	Caillat, Colbie	37-20	PS
Feels Just Like It Should	Green, Pat	30-91	CB
Feels Like A Rock Star - duet	Chesney & McGraw	39-37	ASK
Feels Like Fire	Santana & Dido	32-134	THM
Feels Like Heaven	Cetera & Kahn	6-103	MM
Feels Like Home	Rimes, LeAnn	14-291	MM
Feels Like Home - duet	Malo & McBride	30-257	CB
Feels Like Love	Chamandy, Chantal	36-180	PHM
Feels Like Love	Gill, Vince	14-722	CB
Feels Like Love	Gill, Vince	13-850	CHM
Feels Like Love	Gill, Vince	19-213	CSZ

SONG TITLE	ARTIST	#	TYPE
Feels Like Today	Rascal Flatts	20-445	ST
Feels Like Tonight	Daughtry	36-448	CB
Feels So Right	Alabama	34-262	CB
Feels So Right	Alabama	13-377	P
Feels So Right	Eagle Eye Cherry	18-299	CB
Feels So Right	Eagle Eye Cherry	25-90	MM
Felt Good On My Lips	McGraw, Tim	37-347	SC
Female Bonding	James, Brett	6-812	MM
Fergalicious **	Fergie	48-235	DKM
Fernando	Abba	7-506	MM
Fernando	Muriel's Wedding	6-900	MM
Ferry Cross The Mersey	Gerry & Pacemakers	11-287	DK
Fever	Buble, Michael	30-178	LE
Fever	Lee, Peggy	26-331	DK
Fever	Lee, Peggy	10-324	KC
Fever	Lee, Peggy	23-352	MM
Fever	Lee, Peggy	4-192	SC
Fever	Presley, Elvis	18-443	KC
Fever the	Brooks, Garth	4-20	SC
Few Good Things Remain a	Mattea, Kathy	6-737	MM
Few Good Things Remain, a	Mattea, Kathy	1-191	CB
Few More Rednecks (What the World..)	Charlie Daniels Band	46-608	CB
Few Old Country Boys a	Travis & Jones	9-483	SAV
Few Questions a	Walker, Clay	34-409	CB
Few Questions a	Walker, Clay	25-615	MM
Few Questions a	Walker, Clay	19-62	ST
Few Questions a	Walker, Clay	32-301	THM
Few Short Years a	Herndon, Ty	17-591	ST
Fez the	Steely Dan	15-395	RS
Fields Of Gold	Sting	6-368	MM
Fiesta	Kelly, R.	18-555	TT
Fifteen	Swift, Taylor	37-28	CB
Fifteen Beers Ago	Cleveland, Mel	47-499	HM
Fifteen Years Ago	Twitty, Conway	4-575	SC
Fight Fire With Fire	Kansas	37-70	SC
Fight Like A Girl	Bomshel	37-31	CB
Fight Song	Platten, Rachel	48-146	BKD
Fight The Power	Isley Brothers	2-503	SC
Fighter	Aguilera, Christina	25-578	MM
Fighter	Aguilera, Christina	19-338	STP
Fighter	Aguilera, Christina	32-206	THM
Fightin' For	Cross Can Ragweed	23-476	CB
Fightin' Side Of Me the	Haggard, Merle	8-312	CB
Fightin' Side Of Me the	Haggard, Merle	4-633	SC
Figured You Out	Nickelback	19-668	CB
Figured You Out	Nickelback	23-272	THM
Filipino Baby	Tubb, Ernest	8-443	CB
Fill Me In	David, Craig	15-816	CB
Fill My Little World	Feeling	30-713	SF
Filthy/Gorgeous **	Scissor Sisters	29-226	ZM
Finally	Fergie	36-491	CB
Finally	Fergie	46-323	SC
Finally	Peniston, CeCe	17-367	DK
Finally	Sheppard, T.G.	3-249	CB

SONG TITLE	ARTIST	#	TYPE
Finally	Sheppard, T.G.	13-473	P
Find A Way To My Heart	Collins, Phil	44-12	PSJT
Find Me A Man	Braxton, Toni	18-820	PS
Find My Way Back To My Heart	Krauss, Alison	7-620	CHM
Find Out What's Happenin'	Presley, Elvis	25-744	MM
Find Out What's Happening	Tucker, Tanya	1-614	CB
Find Out What's Happening	Tucker, Tanya	2-828	SC
Find Out Who Your Friends Are	Lawrence, Tracy	30-43	CB
Find The Cost Of Freedom - WN	Crosby Stills & Nash	48-58	SC
Finders Are Keepers	Williams, Hank Jr.	19-422	SC
Finding My Way Back Home	Womack, Lee Ann	30-106	CB
Fine Line	Little Big Town	36-592	CB
Fine Line	Little Big Town	36-207	PHM
Fine Line a	Montgomery Gentry	17-475	TT
Fine Tune	Lambert, Miranda	46-254	KV
Finger Poppin' Time	Ballard & Midnights	4-223	SC
Finger Poppin' Time	Ballard & Midnights	10-242	SS
Fingerprints	Cline, Patsy	45-484	CB
Fingertips Pt. 2	Wonder, Stevie	10-734	JVC
Finish What We Started	Diamond Rio	6-816	MM
Finish What We Started	Diamond Rio	3-546	SC
Fins	Buffett, Jimmy	42-18	SC
Fire	Ohio Players	35-126	CB
Fire	Ohio Players	12-707	P
Fire	Pointer Sisters	3-445	SC
Fire	Springsteen, Bruce	20-245	LE
Fire - Halloween	Crazy World of Arthur Brown	45-114	SC
Fire & Rain	Taylor, James	11-236	DK
Fire & Rain	Taylor, James	6-423	MM
Fire & Rain	Taylor, James	10-69	SC
Fire & Smoke	Conley, Earl Thomas	4-815	SC
Fire And Ice	Benatar, Pat	9-12	MH
Fire And Ice	Benatar, Pat	19-156	SGB
Fire And Smoke	Conley, Earl Thomas	33-68	CB
Fire Away	Stapleton, Chris	46-134	FMK
Fire Away	Stapleton, Chris	48-671	KVD
Fire Down Below	Seger, Bob	46-340	AH
Fire Escape	Fastball	47-85	MM
Fire I Can't Put Out a	Strait, George	8-171	CB
Fire I Can't Put Out a	Strait, George	24-77	SC
Fire In The Night	Alabama	4-440	BS
Fire In The Night	Alabama	1-8	CB
Fire Lake	Seger, Bob	10-176	UK
Fire On The Mountain	Marshall Tucker Ban	18-161	CB
Firecracker	Loeb, Lisa	14-203	CB
Firecracker	Turner, Josh	30-533	CB
Firefly	Bennett, Tony	10-415	LE
Fireman the	Strait, George	8-164	CB
Fireman the	Strait, George	4-484	SC
Fireproof	Pillar	32-255	THM

SONG TITLE	ARTIST	#	TYPE
First Cut Is The Deepest the	Crow, Sheryl	21-633	CB
First Cut Is The Deepest the	Crow, Sheryl	29-663	RS
First Cut Is The Deepest the	Stewart, Rod	14-852	LE
First Date	Blink 182	35-266	CB
First I Look At The Purse	J. Geils Band	46-326	SC
First Kiss	Kid Rock	45-17	KVD
First Love	Adele	46-2	KV
First Night	Monica	33-372	CB
First Noel the	Underwood, Carrie	45-783	KV
First Steo the	Byrd, Tracy	20-112	CB
First Step the	Byrd, Tracy	17-266	NA
First Step the	Byrd, Tracy	2-548	SC
First Step the	Byrd, Tracy	22-852	ST
First Time	Lifehouse	30-562	CB
First Time	Lifehouse	37-113	SC
First Time Ever I Saw Your Face	Flack, Roberta	11-124	DK
First Time Ever I Saw Your Face	Flack, Roberta	5-114	SC
First Time Ever I Saw Your Face	Presley, Elvis	25-325	MM
First Time For Everything	Little Texas	12-400	P
First Time the	Hart, Freddie	45-842	VH
First Time the	Surface	2-270	SC
First To Never Know	Roberts, Julie	29-58	CB
First Year Blues	Williams, Hank Sr.	45-698	CB
Fish	Campbell, Craig	40-6	CB
Fish Ain't Bitin'	Murphy, David Lee	3-544	SC
Fish Heads	Barnes & Barnes	5-636	SC
Fishin' In The Dark	Nitty Gritty Dirt Band	8-13	CB
Fishin' In The Dark	Nitty Gritty Dirt Band	10-683	HE
Fishin' In The Dark	Nitty Gritty Dirt Band	5-253	SC
Fishing In The Dark	Nitty Gritty Dirt Band	35-391	CB
Fist City	Lynn, Loretta	11-430	DK
Fist City	Lynn, Loretta	5-574	SC
Five Brothers	Robbins, Marty	48-28	VH
Five Dollar Fine	LeDoux, Chris	4-625	SC
Five Feet High And Rising	Cash, Johnny	14-245	CB
Five Foot Two Eyes Of Blue	Miller, Mitch	23-542	CB
Five Foot Two Eyes Of Blue	Standard	35-18	CB
Five Minutes	Morgan, Lorrie	1-334	CB
Five Minutes	Morgan, Lorrie	26-584	DK
Five Minutes	Morgan, Lorrie	2-389	SC
Five More Hours	Gabe Dixon Band	36-256	PHM
Five O'Clock World	Vogues	3-25	SC
Five Pennies Saints the	Kaye, Danny	48-467	TDS
Fix	Lane, Chris	49-789	BKD
Fix You	Coldplay	48-256	SC

SONG TITLE	ARTIST	#	TYPE
Fixer Upper - Frozen	Frozen	46-381	DIS
Flagpole Sitta	Danger, Harvey	7-769	PHT
Flagpole Sitta	Harbey Danger	10-139	SC
Flake	Johnson, Jack	25-310	MM
Flame the	Cheap Trick	4-883	SC
Flame Thrower	J. Geils Band	37-74	SC
Flaming Star	Presley, Elvis	8-580	CB
Flash Light	Parliament	14-365	MH
Flashdance (What A Feeling)	Cara, Irene	11-265	DK
Flat On The Floor	Elam, Katrina	30-349	CB
Flat On The Floor	Underwood, Carrie	37-2	CB
Flesh And Blood	Cash, Johnny	14-248	CB
Flesh For Fantasy	Joel, Billy	47-147	LE
Flies On The Butter	Judd, Wynonna	19-767	ST
Flintstones	TV Themes	2-164	SC
Flip Flop Summer	Chesney, Kenny	30-529	CB
Flirtin' With Disaster	Hatchett, Molly	7-461	MM
Flirtin' With Disaster	Hatchett, Molly	16-149	SC
Float On	Floaters	16-557	P
Float On	Modest Mouse	23-564	MM
Floetic	Floetry	32-12	THM
Flood	Jars Of Clay	7-571	THM
Flora-Bama	Chesney, Kenny	45-129	BKD
Flowers	Paisley, Brad	36-375	SC
Flowers	Yates, Billy	7-641	CHM
Flowers	Yates, Billy	22-607	ST
Flowers In The Rain	Move	10-642	SF
Flowers In Your Hair	Lumineers	48-422	ASK
Flowers Mean Forgiveness	Sinatra, Frank	10-722	JVC
Flowers On The Wall	Heatherly, Eric	6-70	SC
Flowers On The Wall	Statler Brothers	19-378	CB
Flowers On The Wall	Statler Brothers	11-782	DK
Flowers On The Wall	Statler Brothers	12-468	P
Flowers On The Wall	Statler Brothers	9-442	SAV
Flowers On The Wall	Statler Brothers	5-93	SC
Fly	Duff, Hillary	20-552	PHM
Fly	Maddie & Tae	45-42	BKD
Fly	PinMonkey	18-456	ST
Fly	Sugar Ray	30-221	PHM
Fly (The Angel Song)	Wilkinsons	8-242	CB
Fly (The Angel Song)	Wilkinsons	22-687	ST
Fly Away	Denver, John	36-149	LE
Fly Away	Kravitz, Lenny	11-69	JTG
Fly Away	Kravitz, Lenny	7-801	PHT
Fly Away	Kravitz, Lenny	13-710	SGB
Fly Away	Sugarland	30-237	RS
Fly Away Again	Dudley, Dave	47-53	CB
Fly Away From Here	Dropline	21-646	MM
Fly By Night	Rush	5-883	SC
Fly From The Inside	Shinedown	32-254	THM
Fly Like An Eagle	Miller, Steve	23-627	BS
Fly Like An Eagle	Seal	4-612	SC
Fly Like An Eagle	Steve Miller Band	35-129	CB
Fly Like An Eagle	Steve Miller Band	10-361	KC
Fly Like An Eagle	Steve Miller Band	3-530	SC

SONG TITLE	ARTIST	#	TYPE
Fly Me To The Moon	Bennett, Tony	28-502	DK
Fly Me To The Moon	Day, Doris	46-276	KV
Fly Me To The Moon	Lee, Brenda	15-475	CMC
Fly Me To The Moon	Sinatra, Frank	21-215	SGB
Fly To The Angels	Slaughter	24-689	SC
Fly With Me	98 Degrees	15-377	SKG
Flying High Again	Osbourne, Ozzy	23-426	SC
Flying Without Wings	Studdard, Ruben	34-150	CB
Flying Without Wings	Studdard, Ruben	25-635	MM
Flying Without Wings	Studdard, Ruben	32-317	THM
FM (No Static At All)	Steely Dan	15-393	RS
Foggy Day a	Bennett, Tony	10-411	LE
Foggy Day In London Town	Buble, Michael	38-178	PS
Foggy River	Walker, Charlie	45-833	VH
Folk Singer the	Roe, Tommy	48-113	CB
Folks Like Us	Montgomery Gentry	48-702	BKD
Follow Me	Denver, John	15-620	THM
Follow Me	Uncle Kracker	35-241	CB
Follow Me	Uncle Kracker	16-472	MH
Follow Me	Uncle Kracker	15-300	THM
Follow Me	Uncle Kracker	18-556	TT
Follow Me Home	Sugababes	30-715	SF
Follow That Dream	Presley, Elvis	8-581	CB
Follow You Down	Gin Blossoms	33-361	CB
Follow You Follow Me	Genesis	21-798	SC
Follow Your Arrow	Musgraves, Kacey	49-94	BKD
Follow Your Arrow	Musgraves, Kacey	45-309	KV
Following Rita	Train	48-262	KV
Following The Feeling	Bandy & Hobbs	9-577	SAV
Folsum Prison Blues	Cash, Johnny	14-234	CB
Folsum Prison Blues	Cash, Johnny	17-161	DK
Folsum Prison Blues	Cash, Johnny	13-424	P
Folsum Prison Blues	Cash, Johnny	21-580	SC
Folsum Prison Blues (Faster Vers)	Cash, Johnny	29-735	CB
Fool	Rea, Chris	3-448	SC
Fool #1	Lee, Brenda	16-367	CB
Fool #1	Lee, Brenda	4-304	SC
Fool For The City	Foghat	5-599	SC
Fool For Your Love	Gilley, Mickey	22-217	CB
Fool Hearted Memory	Strait, George	8-162	CB
Fool Hearted Memory	Strait, George	4-819	SC
Fool I'm A Woman	Evans, Sara	29-548	CB
Fool I'm A Woman	Evans, Sara	7-867	CHT
Fool I'm A Woman	Evans, Sara	22-741	ST
Fool Me	Anderson, Lynn	47-645	CB
Fool On The Hill the	Beatles	28-456	DK
Fool On The Hill the	Beatles	12-919	P
Fool Such As I a	Presley, Elvis	11-606	DK
Fool Such As I a	Presley, Elvis	14-753	THM
Fool Such As I a	Snow, Hank	8-652	SAV
Fool That I Am	Adele	38-230	CB
Fool the	Clark, Sanford	5-846	SC
Fool the	Presley, Elvis	25-742	MM
Fool the	Womack, Lee Ann	35-412	CB
Fool the	Womack, Lee Ann	7-659	CHM

SONG TITLE	ARTIST	#	TYPE
Fool To Cry	Rolling Stones	18-29	LE
Fool's Gold	Greenwood, Lee	5-626	SC
Fool's Paradise	Holly, Buddy	47-888	ZM
Fool's Paradise	Reeves, Jim	44-239	DCK
Fooled Around & Fell In Love	Bishop, Elvin	35-386	CB
Fooled Around And Fell In Love	Bishop, Elvin	18-151	CB
Fooled Around And Fell In Love	Bishop, Elvin	7-459	MM
Fooled Around And Fell In Love	Bishop, Elvin	16-528	P
Foolin'	Def Leppard	5-484	SC
Foolin'	Rodriguez, Johnny	22-60	CB
Foolin' Around	Cline, Patsy	43-176	CB
Fooling Yourself	Styx	47-385	SC
Foolish	Ashanti	18-297	CB
Foolish	Ashanti	25-215	MM
Foolish Games	Jewel	19-357	PS
Foolish Games	Jewel	36-334	SC
Foolish Heart	Perry, S	35-179	CB
Foolish Little Girl	Shirelles	48-374	LE
Foolish Pride	Browns	47-544	DFK
Foolish Pride	Tritt, Travis	6-592	MM
Foolish Pride	Tritt, Travis	2-217	SC
Fools Fall In Love	Drifters	45-884	VH
Fools Fall In Love	Presley, Elvis	25-106	MM
Fools Rush In	Benton, Brook	10-234	SS
Fools Rush In	Nelson, Ricky	38-99	ZM
Footloose	Loggins, Kenny	26-139	DK
Footloose	Loggins, Kenny	12-828	P
Footloose	Shelton, Blake	47-448	KV
Footprints In The Snow	Wiseman, Mac	8-258	CB
Footstompin' Music	Grand Funk RR	20-89	SC
For A Boy	RaeLynn	48-470	BKD
For A Change	McCoy, Neal	1-842	CB
For A Change	McCoy, Neal	6-720	MM
For A Change	McCoy, Neal	17-278	NA
For A Change	McCoy, Neal	2-645	SC
For A Little While	McGraw, Tim	1-540	CB
For A Little While	McGraw, Tim	22-682	ST
For A Minute There	Paycheck, Johnny	22-41	CB
For A Minute There	Paycheck, Johnny	45-210	CB
For All The Wrong Reasons	Bellamy Brothers	4-811	SC
For All We Know	Bassey, Shirley	46-481	PS
For All We Know	Carpenters	35-68	CB
For All We Know	Carpenters	11-683	DK
For All We Know	Cole, Nat "King"	46-358	LE
For All We Know	Streisand, Barbra	24-18	SC
For Future Generations - Gospel	4Him	34-428	CB
For He's A Jolly Good Fellow	Standard	34-437	CB
For Herself	McEntire, Reba	1-804	CB
For Herself	McEntire, Reba	7-142	MM
For Lack Of Better Words	Restless Heart	10-152	SC

SONG TITLE	ARTIST	#	TYPE
For Lovin Me/Did She Mention My Name	Lightfoot, Gordon	43-477	SK
For Loving You	Anderson, Bill	46-213	CB
For Loving You - duet	Anderson & Howard	40-65	CB
For Me And My Gal	Reminiscing Series	3-32	SC
For Me And My Gal	Standard	23-223	SM
For My Broken Heart	McEntire, Reba	1-800	CB
For My Broken Heart	McEntire, Reba	19-298	MH
For My Broken Heart	McEntire, Reba	2-793	SC
For My Wedding	Henley, Don	14-154	CB
For No One	Beatles	7-525	SAV
For Once In My Life	Carr, Vicki	6-443	MM
For Once In My Life	Connick, Harry Jr.	48-504	KVD
For Once In My Life	Wonder, Stevie	11-732	DK
For Once In My Life	Wonder, Stevie	4-692	SC
For Once In My Life (80th Live)	Sinatra, Frank	49-500	MM
For Reasons I've Forgotten	Yearwood, Trisha	48-342	THM
For Sentimental Reasons	Cole, Nat "King"	28-515	DK
For Sentimental Reasons	Cole, Nat "King"	12-880	P
For Sentimental Reasons	Cole, Nat "King"	4-360	SC
For The Cool In You	Babyface	13-608	P
For The First Time	Chesney, Kenny	30-34	CB
For The First Time	Loggins, Kenny	10-23	SC
For The First Time In Forever	Frozen	46-377	DIS
For The Girl Who Has Everything	N'Sync	15-770	BS
For The Girl Who Has Everything	N'Sync	20-441	CB
For The Good Times	Cash, Johnny	49-295	HKC
For The Good Times	Cash, Johnny	43-407	KCA
For The Good Times	Green, Al	46-160	SC
For The Good Times	Kristofferson, Kris	45-200	DCK
For The Good Times	Little Willies	38-262	PHN
For The Good Times	Price, Ray	8-357	CB
For The Good Times	Price, Ray	26-256	DK
For The Good Times	Price, Ray	7-159	MM
For The Good Times	Price, Ray	8-676	SAV
For The Longest Time	Joel, Billy	33-312	CB
For The Love Of Money	O'Jays	9-758	SAV
For The Love Of You	Hill, Jordan	7-575	THM
For The Movies	Buckcherry	8-531	PHT
For The Movies	Buckcherry	5-787	SC
For The Movies	Buckcherry	48-475	SC
For These Times	McBride, Martina	30-578	CB
For Today	Pride & Ketchum	4-110	SC
For What It's Worth	Buffalo Springfield	17-122	DK
For What It's Worth	Buffalo Springfield	12-909	P
For What It's Worth	Buffalo Springfield	9-666	SAV
For You	Cash, Johnny	43-382	CKC
For You	Otto, James	36-603	CB
For You	Otto, James	36-211	PHM
For You	Outfield	45-372	KV

SONG TITLE	ARTIST	#	TYPE
For You	Staind	33-437	CB
For You	Staind	32-212	THM
For You	Urban, Keith	39-32	PHM
For You - duet	Cash & Matthews	37-243	CB
For You I Will	Tippin, Aaron	22-693	ST
For Your Eyes Only	Easton, Sheena	33-324	CB
For Your Eyes Only	Easton, Sheena	28-295	DK
For Your Eyes Only	Easton, Sheena	9-70	SC
For Your Love	Townsend, Ed	6-262	MM
For Your Love	Townsend, Ed	9-739	SAV
For Your Love	Yardbirds	11-258	DK
For Your Love	Yardbirds	13-226	P
Fore She Was Mama	Walker, Clay	30-174	CB
Forever	Brown, Chris	36-469	CB
Forever	Kiss	23-103	SC
Forever (Radio Version)	Kid Rock	16-91	SC
Forever Again	Watson, Gene	14-676	CB
Forever And Always	Frizzell, Lefty	19-495	CB
Forever And Always	Swift, Taylor	43-172	ASK
Forever And Ever Amen	Travis, Randy	1-395	CB
Forever And Ever Amen	Travis, Randy	12-105	DK
Forever And Ever Amen	Travis, Randy	13-361	P
Forever And For Always	Twain, Shania	34-359	CB
Forever And For Always	Twain, Shania	25-613	MM
Forever And For Always	Twain, Shania	19-46	ST
Forever And For Always	Twain, Shania	32-232	THM
Forever Everyday	Womack, Lee Ann	25-412	MM
Forever Everyday	Womack, Lee Ann	18-451	ST
Forever Everyday	Womack, Lee Ann	32-43	THM
Forever For Now	Connick, Harry Jr.	19-719	PS
Forever In Blue Jeans	Diamond, Neil	7-533	AH
Forever In Blue Jeans	Diamond, Neil	30-678	LE
Forever Kind Of Love	Vee, Bobby	47-844	DCK
Forever Love	McEntire, Reba	8-743	CB
Forever Love	McEntire, Reba	22-808	ST
Forever Lovers	Davis, Mac	23-520	CB
Forever Loving You	Rich, John	15-102	ST
Forever Man	Moore, Lathan	39-94	PHN
Forever Mine Nevermind	Band Perry	44-389	ASK
Forever Mine Nevermind	Band Perry	41-53	PHN
Forever More	Johnson, Puff	4-678	SC
Forever My Lady	Al B. Sure!	18-503	SAV
Forever Together	Travis, Randy	2-396	SC
Forever Works For Me	McCoy, Neal	9-388	CB
Forever Works For Me	McCoy, Neal	13-832	CHM
Forever Works For Me	McCoy, Neal	19-259	CSZ
Forever Young	Cash, Johnny	45-90	SB
Forever Young	Cash, Johnny	43-420	SBI
Forever Young	Dylan, Bob	29-103	CB
Forever Young	Stewart, Rod	11-70	JTG
Forever's As Far As I'll Go	Alabama	4-441	BS
Forever's As Far As I'll Go	Alabama	17-293	NA
Forever's As Far As I'll Go	Alabama	9-461	SAV
Forever's As Far As I'll	Alabama	2-401	SC

SONG TITLE	ARTIST	#	TYPE
Go			
Forget About Me	Bellamy Brothers	45-303	KV
Forget About Us	McGraw, Tim	47-240	CB
Forget Domani	Sinatra, Frank	49-487	MM
Forget Him	Rydell, Bobby	47-475	SC
Forget Me Never	Presley, Elvis	25-328	MM
Forget Me Not	Kane, Eden	29-823	SF
Forget Me Nots	Rushen, Patrice	18-371	AH
Forgive	Howard, Rebecca L	33-189	CB
Forgive	Howard, Rebecca L	25-237	MM
Forgive	Howard, Rebecca L	17-574	ST
Forgiveness	Shaw, Victoria	6-805	MM
Forgiveness	Shaw, Victoria	2-834	SC
Forgiving You Was Easy	Nelson, Willie	4-655	SC
Fortunate	CCR	17-29	DK
Fortunate	Maxwell	7-848	PHM
Fortunate Son	CCR	5-358	SC
Fortune Faded	Red Hot Chili Peppe	23-268	THM
Forty Hour Week	Alabama	4-442	BS
Forty Hour Week	Alabama	1-10	CB
Foul Play	Cray, Robert	7-218	MM
Found Out About You	Gin Blossoms	35-208	CB
Found Out About You	Gin Blossoms	12-240	DK
Found Out About You	Gin Blossoms	18-476	NU
Foundations (Radio Vers)	Nash, Kate	37-147	SC
Fountain Of Love	Presley, Elvis	25-115	MM
Four Strong Winds	Bare, Bobby	18-270	CB
Four To One In Atlanta	Byrd, Tracy	20-104	CB
Four Walls	Reeves, Jim	8-572	CB
Four Walls	Reeves, Jim	40-122	CK
Four Walls	Reeves, Jim	3-834	LG
Four Walls	Reeves, Jim	3-596	SC
Four Wheel Drive	BTO	46-550	CB
Four Wheel Drive	Montgomery, J M	19-181	ST
Fourteen Carat Mind	Watson, Gene	14-664	CB
Fourteen Carat Mind	Watson, Gene	2-633	SC
Fourteen Minutes Old	Stone, Doug	20-592	CB
Fourteen Minutes Old	Stone, Doug	6-617	MM
Fox On The Run	Country Gentlemen	8-256	CB
Fox On The Run	Hall, Tom T.	18-279	CB
Fox On The Run	Zac Brown Band	43-469	KV
Foxy Lady	Hendrix, Jimi	28-194	DK
Framed	Coasters	6-681	MM
Framed	Valens, Richie	45-677	DCK
Frankie & Johnny	Cash, Johnny	43-401	KV
Frankie & Johnny	Presley, Elvis	46-42	SSK
Frankie & Johnny	Standard	11-476	DK
Frantic	O'Neal, Jamie	25-285	MM
Frantic	O'Neal. Jamie	16-427	ST
Fraulein	Helms, Bobby	34-2	CB
Fraulein	Helms, Bobby	5-582	SC
Freak-A-Zoid	Midnight Star	17-526	SC
Freakin' At The Freakers Ball	Dr. Hook	47-40	SC
Freaks Come Out At Night	Whodini	17-530	SC

SONG TITLE	ARTIST	#	TYPE
Freaks Like Me	Nichols, Joe	48-6	KCD
Fred	Carrington, Rodney	44-102	SC
Freddy My Love	Bullens, Cindy	10-14	SC
Free	Conway, Liana	39-80	PHN
Free	Mya	12-394	PHM
Free	Phish	24-634	SC
Free	Powerman 5000	32-253	THM
Free	Secada, John	36-179	PHM
Free	Train	48-270	SC
Free	Zac Brown Band	37-335	CB
Free Again	Streisand, Barbra	49-209	MM
Free Again	Streisand, Barbra	49-576	PS
Free And Easy Down the Road I Go	Bentley, Dierks	30-453	CB
Free Bird	Lynyrd Skynyrd	18-152	CB
Free Bird	Lynyrd Skynyrd	12-692	P
Free Bird	Lynyrd Skynyrd	5-267	SC
Free Bird	Lynyrd Skynyrd	13-774	SGB
Free For All	Nugent, Ted	4-560	SC
Free Man In Paris	Mitchell, Joni	16-63	SC
Free Me	Stone, Joss	43-117	CB
Free Ride	Edgar Winter Group	34-46	CB
Free Ride	Edgar Winter Group	16-594	MM
Free Ride	Edgar Winter Group	29-295	SC
Free To Decide	Cranberries	24-108	SC
Free Your Mind	En Vogue	16-571	SC
Freedom	Judd, Wynonna	8-863	CB
Freedom	McCartney, Paul	33-391	CB
Freedom	Sutherland, Christy	22-74	CB
Freedom	Wham!	11-648	DK
Freedom	Wham!	21-607	SF
Freedom (NYC Version)	McCartney, Paul	16-94	SC
Freedom 90	Michael, George	11-804	DK
Freedom Isn't Free	Ricochet	20-584	CB
Freedom Isn't Free - Patriotic	Ricochet	36-342	CB
Freeway Of Love	Franklin, Aretha	34-33	CB
Freeway Of Love	Franklin, Aretha	36-162	JT
Freeway Of Love	Franklin, Aretha	4-877	SC
Freeze	Pay The Girl	32-138	THM
Freeze Frame	J. Geils Band	3-521	SC
Freight Train Boogie	Nelson, Willie	38-77	PS
French Foreign Legion	Sinatra, Frank	49-495	MM
Fresh	Kool & the Gang	39-5	CB
Friday Night	Darkness	29-227	ZM
Friday Night	Gilbert, Brantley	44-158	BKD
Friday Night	Lady Antebellum	38-253	PHN
Friday Night	Paslay, Eric	43-278	ASK
Friday Night Blues	Conlee, John	17-296	NA
Friday Night Blues	Conlee, John	5-163	SC
Friday Night Stampede	Western Flyer	7-23	MM
Friday On My Mind	Easybeats	14-463	SC
Friend Lover Wife	Paycheck, Johnny	22-35	CB
Friend Lover Wife	Paycheck, Johnny	19-445	SC
Friend Lover Woman Wife	Davis, Mac	23-518	CB
Friend of The Devil	Grateful Dead	9-321	AG

SONG TITLE	ARTIST	#	TYPE
Friend To Me a	Brooks, Garth	48-354	PC
Friendly Beast the - xmas	Christmas	45-12	KV
Friendly Persuasion	Boone, Pat	10-601	SF
Friends	Bailey, Razzy	29-377	CB
Friends	John, Elton	2-382	SC
Friends	Midler, Bette	45-913	CB
Friends	Montgomery, J M	14-212	CB
Friends	Montgomery, J M	7-381	MM
Friends	Montgomery, J M	4-590	SC
Friends & Lovers	Loring & Anderson	15-477	CMC
Friends Don't Drive Friends To Dr..	Dodd, Deryl	7-386	MM
Friends Don't Drive Friends To Drink	Dodd, Deryl	4-586	SC
Friends In Low Places	Brooks, Garth	1-214	CB
Friends In Low Places	Brooks, Garth	11-802	DK
Friends In Low Places	Brooks, Garth	6-273	MM
Friends In Low Places	Brooks, Garth	12-433	P
Friends In Low Places (Live Version	Brooks, Garth	2-672	SC
Friends Never Say Goodbye	John, Elton	14-25	THM
From A Distance	Midler, Bette	26-233	DK
From A Distance	Midler, Bette	12-875	P
From A Jack To A King	Miller, Ned	2-129	SC
From A Jack To A King	VanShelton, Ricky	33-98	CB
From A Jack To A King	VanShelton, Ricky	14-680	CB
From A Lover To A Friend	McCartney & Wings	25-36	MM
From A Lover To A Friend	McCartney, Paul	16-92	SC
From A Moving Train	America	46-421	SC
From Graceland to the Promised...	Haggard, Merle	37-175	CB
From Here To Eternity	Peterson, Michael	22-647	ST
From Hillbilly Heaven to Honky-Tonk	Chesney, Kenny	8-137	CB
From Me To You	Beatles	15-478	MM
From Me To You	Beatles	29-333	SC
From Me To You	Ian, Janis	29-266	SC
From Now On All My Friends Are...	Drusky, Roy	20-751	CB
From Paris To Berlin	Inferno	30-706	SF
From Russia With Love	Monro, Matt	9-63	SC
From The Beginning	Emerson Lake Palmer	4-84	SC
From The Bottom Of My Broken Heart	Spears, Britney	15-294	CB
From The Bottom Of My Broken Heart	Spears, Britney	13-560	LE
From The Inside Out	Davis, Linda	8-950	CB
From The Underworld	Heard	10-645	SF
From This Moment On	Sinatra, Frank	14-265	MM
From This Moment On	Twain & White	8-2	CB
From This Moment On	Twain & White	7-745	CHM
From This Moment On	Twain & White	14-293	MM
From This Moment On	Twain, Shania	15-625	PHM
From Where I Stand	Bogguss, Suzy	8-869	CB

SONG TITLE	ARTIST	#	TYPE
From Where I Stand	Bogguss, Suzy	10-155	SC
From Where I Stand	Richey, Kim	7-238	MM
From Where I'm Sitting	Allan, Gary	10-82	SC
From Your Knees	King, Matt	8-961	CB
Front Porch Thing	Little Big Town	40-25	PHM
Frontin'	Pharrell & Jay Z	25-717	MM
Frontin' - duet	Farrell & Jay-Z	32-347	THM
Frosty The Snowman	Autry, Gene	45-659	DKM
Frozen	Madonna	21-148	LE
Fruit Cakes	Buffett, Jimmy	46-130	SC
Fruitcake Makes Me Puke	Engvall, Bill	47-61	CB
Fuel	Metallica	47-259	SC
Fuel To The Flame	Davis, Skeeter	43-332	CB
Fugitive the	Haggard, Merle	8-315	CB
Fugitive the	Haggard, Merle	4-732	SC
Full Circle	Parton, Dolly	8-822	CB
Full Deck Of Cards	Darling, Helen	4-588	SC
Full Force Gale	Morrison, Van	23-600	BS
Full Force Gale	Morrison, Van	15-727	SI
Full Moon	Brandy	18-224	CB
Full Moon	Brandy	17-600	PHM
Full Time Job	Wilson, Gretchen	29-508	SC
Full Time Job a	Arnold, Eddy	45-570	CB
Fun Fun Fun	Beach Boys	5-500	BS
Fun Fun Fun	Beach Boys	11-632	DK
Fun Fun Fun	Beach Boys	12-669	P
Fun Fun Fun	Beach Boys	4-41	SC
Fun Of Your Love the	Day, Jennifer	13-816	CHM
Fun Of Your Love the	Day, Jennifer	22-481	ST
Funeral For A Friend/Lover	John, Elton	9-381	AH
Funk #49	Walsh, Joe	15-710	LE
Funky Broadway	Wilson Pickett	11-792	DK
Funky Broadway	Wilson Pickett	17-330	SS
Funky Cold Medina	Tone-Loc	33-438	CB
Funky Cold Medina	Tone-Loc	12-110	DK
Funky Cold Medina	Tone-Loc	16-542	P
Funky Cold Medina	Tone-Loc	2-183	SC
Funky Junky the	Charlie Daniels Band	43-272	CB
Funky Nassau	Blues Brothers	38-33	TT
Funky Town	Pseudo Echo	33-323	CB
Funkytown	Lipps Inc.	18-365	AH
Funkytown	Lipps Inc.	18-244	DK
Funkytown	Lipps Inc.	9-14	MH
Funkytown	Lipps Inc.	20-372	SC
Funny	Kelly, Tori	48-677	DCK
Funny Face	Fargo, Donna	12-410	P
Funny Face	Fargo, Donna	8-629	SAV
Funny Familiar Forgotten Feelings	Humperdinck, E.	48-515	LE
Funny How Love Can Be	Ivy League	10-616	SF
Funny How Time Slips Away	Eldridge, Jimmy	10-747	JVC
Funny How Time Slips Away	Green & Lovett	26-566	DK
Funny Way Of Laughing	Ives, Burl	10-748	JVC

SONG TITLE	ARTIST	#	TYPE
Further On Up The Road	Cash, Johnny	49-282	BAT
Future Has Arrived the	All American Rejects	30-495	CB
Future Has Arrived the	All-American Reject	30-496	CB
G.N.O. Girls Night Out	Cyrus, Miley	36-73	WD
G.R.I.T.S.	Gilbert, Brantley	44-300	BKD
Galaxy Song	Monty Python	15-144	SC
Gale Song	Lumineers	48-421	SBI
Galveston	Campbell, Glen	35-66	CB
Galveston	Campbell, Glen	12-300	DK
Galway Girl	Earle, Steve	46-181	KV
Gambler the	Brady, Johnny	49-860	DCK
Gambler the	Rogers, Kenny	3-164	CB
Gambler the	Rogers, Kenny	11-617	DK
Gambler the	Rogers, Kenny	19-134	KC
Gambler the	Rogers, Kenny	7-157	MM
Gambler the	Rogers, Kenny	8-655	SAV
Gamblin' Man	Donegan, Lonnie	10-596	SF
Game Of Love	Santana & Branch	25-392	MM
Game Of Love	Santana feat M. Branch	35-242	CB
Game Of Love the	Branch & Santana	32-21	THM
Game Of Love the	Branch, Michelle	32-21	THM
Game Of Love the	Fontana, Wayne	11-356	DK
Game Of Love the	Fontana, Wayne	13-89	P
Game Of Love the	Santana & Branch	18-580	NS
Game Of Triangles the	Bare & Anderson's	3-709	CB
Game Of Triangles the	Bare, Bobby	18-276	CB
Games	Bryan, Luke	45-29	BKD
Games People Play	Cliff, Jimmy	46-630	HSW
Games People Play	South, Joe	6-784	MM
Games People Play	South, Joe	3-262	SC
Games People Play	Weller, Freddie	8-634	SAV
Games People Play the	South, Joe	33-263	CB
Games That Daddies Play	Twitty, Conway	43-198	CB
Gang That Sang Heart Of My Heart	Four Aces	9-746	SAV
Gansta Lovin'	Eve & Keys	18-436	CB
Gansta' Lovin'	Keys, Alicia & Eve	25-467	MM
Gansta's Paradise	Coolio	34-120	CB
Ganster Of Love	Winter, Johnny	49-678	VH
Garden Party	Nelson, Ricky	21-699	CB
Garden Party	Nelson, Ricky	26-510	DK
Garden the	Gosdin, Vern	47-114	CB
Gasoline & Matches - duet	Rimes, Rob Thomas, Jeff Beck	41-86	PHN
Gasoline Alley Bred	Hollies	44-376	ZM
Gee Baby Ain't I Good To You	Cole, Nat "King"	46-364	PS
Gee Whiz	Thomas, Carla	35-38	CB
Gee Whiz Look At His Eyes	Thomas, Carla	12-902	P
Geek In The Pink	Mraz, Jason	47-306	PHM
Geisha Girl	Locklin, Hank	5-695	SC
Generation Landslide	Alice Cooper	16-443	SGB
Genie In A Bottle	Aguilera, Christina	13-571	LE
Genie In A Bottle	Aguilera, Christina	8-196	PHT

SONG TITLE	ARTIST	#	TYPE
Genie In A Bottle	Aguilera, Christina	10-187	SC
Genie In A Bottle	Aguilera, Christina	13-778	SGB
Gentle On My Mind	Campbell, Glen	17-14	DK
Gentle On My Mind	Campbell, Glen	13-418	P
Gentle On My Mind	Campbell, Glen	8-657	SAV
Gentle On My Mind	Martin, Dean	10-588	SF
Gentle On My Mind	Presley, Elvis	25-100	MM
Gentle Rain	Streisand, Barbra	49-593	PS
Gentleman	PSY	43-457	ASK
Gently Breathe	Sosoreny, Greg	41-84	PHN
Genuine	Orrico, Stacie	35-304	CB
Genuine Rednecks	Murphy, David Lee	7-430	MM
George (And The North Woods)	Dudley, Dave	43-297	CB
Georgia	Johnson, Carolyn D.	14-136	CB
Georgia	Johnson, Carolyn D.	22-577	ST
Georgia	Johnson, Carolyn D.	14-35	THM
Georgia	Scaggs, Boz	46-319	SC
Georgia In A Jug	Shelton, Blake	38-113	AT
Georgia Keeps Pullin On My Ring	Twitty, Conway	43-195	CB
Georgia On My Mind	Buble, Michael	40-85	PS
Georgia On My Mind	Charles, Ray	12-145	DK
Georgia On My Mind	Charles, Ray	19-779	SGB
Georgia Rain	Yearwood, Trisha	23-127	CB
Georgie Porgie	Standard	47-833	SDK
Georgy Girl	Seekers	16-810	DK
Georgy Girl	Seekers	9-836	SAV
Gertcha	Chas & Dave	30-745	SF
Get A Job	Silhouettes	15-479	MM
Get A Leg Up	Mellencamp, John	5-741	SC
Get A Little Dirt On You	Coe & Anderson	18-319	CB
Get Back	Beatles	11-180	DK
Get Back	Beatles	13-47	P
Get Back	Beatles	7-528	SAV
Get Back On That Pony	LeDoux, Chris	10-780	JVC
Get Busy	Paul, Sean	25-722	MM
Get Busy	Paul, Sean	32-238	THM
Get Closer	Seals & Croft	12-351	DK
Get Closer	Seals & Croft	20-362	SC
Get Down	Backstreet Boys	30-416	THM
Get Down (You're The One...)	Backstreet Boys	18-707	MM
Get Down Get Down	Simon, Joe	17-105	DK
Get Down On It	Kool & The Gang	14-357	MH
Get Down On It	Kool & The Gang	15-36	SS
Get Down Saturday Night	Cheetam, Oliver	15-702	LE
Get Down Tonight	KC & Sunshine Band	13-251	P
Get Down Tonight	KC & Sunshine Band	2-501	SC
Get Drunk And Be Somebody	Keith, Toby	29-182	CB
Get Drunk And Be Somebody	Keith, Toby	29-851	SC
Get Drunk And Be Somebody	Keith, Toby	29-706	ST

SONG TITLE	ARTIST	#	TYPE
Get Happy	Garland, Judy	43-379	PS
Get Happy	Minelli, Liza	49-220	MFK
Get Happy	Sinatra, Frank	14-272	MM
Get Here	Adams, Oleta	17-426	KC
Get Here	Adams, Oleta	19-570	MH
Get Here	Adams, Oleta	12-876	P
Get In Line	Barenaked Ladies	16-181	PHM
Get In Line - Duet	Barenaked Ladies	30-620	RS
Get In Line (Solo Verses)	Barenaked Ladies	30-628	RS
Get Into Reggae Cowboy	Bellamy Brothers	44-72	KV
Get It Daddy	Sleeper Agent	38-243	PHM
Get It Like You Like It	Harper, Ben	36-188	PHM
Get It On Tonight	Jordan, Montell	15-328	PHM
Get It On Tonight	Jordan, Montell	5-897	SC
Get It Right Next Time	Rafferty, Gerry	21-803	SC
Get It While You Can	Joplin, Janis	15-223	LE
Get Low **	Lil Jon&Eastside&YY	21-794	SC
Get Me Bodied	Beyonce	30-559	CB
Get Me Some Of That	Rhett, Thomas	43-137	ASK
Get My Drink On	Keith, Toby	36-422	CB
Get Off	Prince	49-834	LG
Get Off Of My Cloud	Rolling Stones	19-850	LE
Get Off Of My Cloud	Rolling Stones	14-400	PT
Get Off On The Pain	Allan, Gary	37-333	CB
Get On Up	Esquires	6-57	SC
Get On Up	Jodeci	4-685	SC
Get On Your Boots	U2	48-315	SF
Get On Your Feet	Estefan, Gloria	23-574	MM
Get On Your Feet	Estefan, Gloria	17-740	PT
Get On Your Feet	Estefan, Gloria	30-756	SF
Get On Your Feet	Estefan, Gloria	30-758	SF
Get Out Of My Car	Keith, Toby	44-145	BKD
Get Out Of This House	Colvin, Shawn	4-608	SC
Get Outta My Dreams Get Into My..	Ocean, Billy	3-547	SC
Get Outta My Way	Carolina Rain	30-94	CB
Get Over It	Eagles	7-550	BS
Get Over It	Eagles	43-113	LG
Get Over Yourself	SheDaisy	25-184	MM
Get Over Yourself	SheDaisy	16-685	ST
Get Ready	Rare Earth	11-646	DK
Get Ready	Temptations	4-42	SC
Get Rhythm	Cash, Johnny	29-568	CB
Get Rhythm	Cash, Johnny	4-858	SC
Get Rhythm	Skaggs, Ricky	12-485	P
Get Right	Lopez & Fabolous	22-359	CB
Get Stoned (Radio Version)	Hinder	30-279	SC
Get The Funk Out	Extreme	5-74	SC
Get The Party Started	Bassey, Shirley	46-479	MRH
Get The Party Started	Pink	25-87	MM
Get The Party Started	Pink	16-73	ST
Get To Me	Lady Antebellum	46-82	BKD
Get To Me	Train	37-315	THM
Get To You	Morrison, James	38-273	MH
Get Together	Youngbloods	34-49	CB

SONG TITLE	ARTIST	#	TYPE
Get Together	Youngbloods	11-828	DK
Get Up - duet	Dogg, Nate & Eve	32-126	THM
Get Up **	Nate Dogg & Eve	32-126	THM
Get Up Offa That Thing	Brown, James	29-140	LE
Get What You Got Comin'	Van Zant	15-307	THM
Get Your Freak On	Elliot, Missy	18-514	TT
Get Your Hands Off My Woman **	Darkness	29-231	ZM
Get Your Shine On	Florida Georgia Line	44-273	ASK
Getaway	Earth Wind & Fire	11-264	DK
Getaway Car	Jenkins	23-400	CB
Getaway Car	Jenkins	20-508	ST
Getcha Back	Beach Boys	46-487	CB
Getcha Some	Keith, Toby	8-190	CB
Getcha Some	Keith, Toby	10-147	SC
Getcha Some	Keith, Toby	22-672	ST
Gets Me Through	Osbourne, Ozzy	16-317	TT
Gettin' In The Mood	Brian Setzer Orch	46-534	MM
Gettin' You Home (Black Dress)	Young, Chris	37-32	CB
Getting Back To You	Dern, Daisy	25-68	MM
Getting In The Way	Scott, Jill	20-620	CB
Getting Jiggy Wit' It	Smith, Will	13-686	SGB
Getting There	Clark, Terri	29-349	CB
Getting There	Clark, Terri	15-612	ST
Getting To Me	Willis, Kelly	49-729	DCK
Getting' In The Way	Scott, Jill	25-693	MM
Getting' Jiggy Wit It	Smith, Will	10-130	SC
Ghost In This House	Shenandoah	1-484	CB
Ghost In This House	Shenandoah	2-625	SC
Ghost Riders In The Sky	Cash, Johnny	29-563	CB
Ghost Riders In The Sky	Cash, Johnny	13-509	P
Ghost Riders In The Sky	Cash, Johnny	5-210	SC
Ghost Riders In The Sky	Outlaws	48-656	SC
Ghost Riders In The Sky	Sons Of Pioneers	8-434	CB
Ghost Riders In The Sky (Fast)	Monroe, Vaughn	48-542	DK
Ghost Town	Owen, Jake	45-639	ASK
Ghost Town - Halloween	Specials	45-115	ZM
Ghostbusters	Parker, Ray Jr.	2-73	SC
Ghostbusters	Parker, Ray Jr.	16-281	TT
Giddy Up	N'Sync	15-779	BS
Gift Of Love the	Midler, Bette	45-941	PC
Gift the	Brickman & Ash	7-710	PHM
Gift the	Raye, Collin	10-783	JVC
Gift the	Raye, Collin	22-417	ST
Giggle	Grant, Amy	49-34	SHER
Gigolette	Orbison, Roy	47-338	HM
Gilligan's Island	TV Themes	27-401	DK
Gilligan's Island	TV Themes	2-160	SC
Gilly Gilly Ossenfeffer	Four Lads	21-597	SF
Gimme All Your Lovin'	ZZ Top	13-208	P
Gimme Back My Bullets	Lynyrd Skynyrd	19-810	SGB
Gimme Gimme Gimme	Abba	7-499	MM
Gimme Gimme Good Lovin'	Crazy Elephant	9-363	MG

SONG TITLE	ARTIST	#	TYPE
Gimme Gimme Good Lovin'	Crazy Elephant	4-212	SC
Gimme Little Sign	Wood, Brenton	27-285	DK
Gimme Little Sign	Wood, Brenton	5-460	SC
Gimme Shelter	Rolling Stones	18-15	LE
Gimme Some Love	Gina G.	21-553	PHM
Gimme Some Love	Gina G.	10-106	SC
Gimme Some Lovin'	Blues Brothers	16-162	SC
Gimme Some Lovin'	Blues Brothers	29-163	ZM
Gimme Some Lovin'	Davis, Spencer	49-460	MM
Gimme Some Lovin'	Spencer Davis Grp	15-480	SC
Gimme Some More	Busta Rhymes	28-221	DK
Gimme That Girl	Nichols, Joe	38-125	CB
Gimme The Light	Paul S	32-90	THM
Gimme The Light	Paul, Sean	32-90	THM
Gimme Three Steps	Lynyrd Skynyrd	18-160	CB
Gimme Three Steps	Lynyrd Skynyrd	7-456	MM
Gimme Three Steps	Lynyrd Skynyrd	5-269	SC
Gimme Three Steps	Lynyrd Skynyrd	19-806	SGB
Gimme Your Money Please	BTO	46-546	CB
Gin & Juice	Snoop Doggy Dogg	25-473	MM
Gin & Juice	Snoop Doggy Dogg	14-447	SC
Gina	Mathis, Johnny	49-322	CB
Girl	Beatles	7-512	SAV
Girl All The Bad Guys Want	Bowling For Soup	20-461	CB
Girl All The Bad Guys Want	Bowling For Soup	20-624	NS
Girl Crush	Little Big Town	45-6	KV
Girl Crush (Inst)	Little Big Town	49-737	BKD
Girl From Ipanema the	Getz & Gilberto	12-518	P
Girl I Never Loved the	Presley, Elvis	25-488	MM
Girl I Used To Know a	Jackson, Wanda	20-646	SC
Girl I Used To Know a	Jones, George	19-403	SC
Girl I'm Gonna Miss You	Milli Vanilli	33-329	CB
Girl I'm Gonna Miss You	Milli Vanilli	11-495	DK
Girl In A Country Song	Maddie & Tae	45-111	BKD
Girl In Love	English, Robin	25-52	MM
Girl In Your Truck Song	Rose, Maggie	47-714	BKD
Girl Is Mine the	Jackson&McCartney	17-150	DK
Girl Is Mine the	Jackson&McCartney	24-205	SC
Girl Like Me	Lambert, Miranda	46-253	KV
Girl Like You a	Ketchum, Hal	8-178	CB
Girl Like You a	Smithereens	9-842	SAV
Girl Like You a	Smithereens	5-610	SC
Girl Like You a	Young Rascals	3-461	SC
Girl Most Likely the	Riley, Jeannie C	49-230	DFK
Girl Next Door	Deggs, Cole & Lonesome	30-555	CB
Girl Next Door	Roberts, Julie	30-20	CB
Girl Next Door (Inst)	Clark, Brandi	49-791	BKD
Girl Next Door (Radio Version)	Saving Jane	30-273	SC
Girl Of Mine	Presley, Elvis	25-753	MM
Girl On The Billboard	Reeves, Del	3-899	CB
Girl On The Billboard	Reeves, Del	12-34	DK
Girl On The Billboard	Road Hammers	36-205	PHM

SONG TITLE	ARTIST	#	TYPE
Girl On TV	LFO	16-182	PHM
Girl Talk	TLC	32-92	THM
Girl Talk **	TLC	25-468	MM
Girl Thang - duet	Judd, W & Wynette, T	48-319	MH
Girl Watcher	O'Kaysions	35-72	CB
Girl Watcher	O'Kaysions	27-328	DK
Girl Watcher	O'Kaysions	3-255	SC
Girl With Gardenias In Her Hair the	Robbins, Marty	48-15	CB
Girl You Know It's True	Milli Vanilli	11-587	DK
Girl You Left Me For the	Carter, Deana	23-123	CB
Girl You Think I Am the	Underwood, Carrie	49-12	KV
Girl You'll Be A Woman Soon	Diamond, Neil	7-534	AH
Girl You'll Be A Woman Soon	Diamond, Neil	30-680	LE
Girl You'll Be A Woman Soon	Diamond, Neil	13-299	P
Girl You'll Be A Woman Soon	Diamond, Neil	24-705	SC
Girl's Gone Wild	Tritt, Travis	35-436	CB
Girl's Gone Wild	Tritt, Travis	20-341	ST
Girl's Gotta Do a	McCready, Mindy	7-614	CHM
Girl's Night Out	Judds	1-143	CB
Girlfriend	B2K	32-196	THM
Girlfriend	Billie	17-24	DK
Girlfriend	Brown, Bobby	16-563	P
Girlfriend	Darkness	30-755	SF
Girlfriend	Lavigne, Avril	30-487	CB
Girlfriend	N'Sync	20-436	CB
Girlfriend	N'Sync	25-150	MM
Girlfriend	Pebbles	12-848	P
Girls	Lambert, Miranda	45-632	BKD
Girls	Nizlopi	30-692	SF
Girls And Boys	Good Charlotte	25-655	MM
Girls And Boys	Good Charlotte	32-396	THM
Girls Chase Boys	Michaelson, Ingrid	45-4	KV
Girls Don't Tell Me	Beach Boys	46-496	NT
Girls Girls Girls	Motley Crue	7-484	MM
Girls Girls Girls	Motley Crue	5-75	SC
Girls In Bikinis	Brice, Lee	48-735	DCK
Girls In Leather Have Fun	Parody	49-309	WMP
Girls Just Want To Have Fun	Lauper, Cyndi	11-389	DK
Girls Just Want To Have Fun	Lauper, Cyndi	9-8	MH
Girls Just Want To Have Fun	Lauper, Cyndi	16-534	P
Girls Lie Too	Clark, Terri	35-434	CB
Girls Lie Too	Clark, Terri	20-339	ST
Girls Night Out	Judds	13-330	P
Girls Night Out	Judds	2-101	SC
Girls Of Summer the	McCoy, Neal	1-844	CB
Girls Of Summer the	McCoy, Neal	10-196	SC
Girls Of Summer the	McCoy, Neal	22-434	ST
Girls Of Summer the	McCoy, Neal	16-194	THM

SONG TITLE	ARTIST	#	TYPE
Girls On The Beach	Beach Boys	46-497	NT
Girls With Guitars	Judd, Wynonna	1-654	CB
Girls With Guitars	Judd, Wynonna	6-586	MM
Girls With Guitars	Judd, Wynonna	2-324	SC
Girls Women And Ladies	Bruce, Ed	46-538	SC
Give A Little Bit	Goo Goo Dolls	22-352	CB
Give A Little Bit	Supertramp	6-492	MM
Give A Little Bit	Supertramp	12-790	P
Give A Little Bit	Supertramp	29-269	SC
Give A Little Love	Jones, Tom	49-270	DFK
Give a Little Love	Judds	1-144	CB
Give A Little Love	Judds	12-58	DK
Give A Little Love	Judds	9-503	SAV
Give A Little Whistle	Standard	21-10	SC
Give Him A Great Big Kiss	Shangri-Las	6-655	MM
Give It All We Got Tonight	Strait, George	44-154	BKD
Give It Away	Strait, George	30-15	CB
Give It Time	BTO	46-547	CB
Give It Time	Lindell, Eric	36-183	PHM
Give It To Me	J. Geils Band	10-486	DA
Give It To Me Baby **	James, Rick	15-3	SC
Give It To Me Straight	Currington, Billy	45-274	DCK
Give It Up Or Let Me Go	Dixie Chicks	16-652	RS
Give Me A Reason	Corrs	49-199	SF
Give Me Back My Home Town	Church, Eric	43-125	ASK
Give Me Back My Wig	Vaughn, Stevie Ray	46-31	SSK
Give Me Forever I Do	Tesh, John	10-18	SC
Give Me His Last Chance	Cartwright, Lionel	9-626	SAV
Give Me Just A Little More Time	Chairman of Board	12-139	DK
Give Me Just A Little More Time	Chairman of Board	4-705	SC
Give Me Just One Night	98 Degrees	14-4	PHM
Give Me More More More	Frizzell, Lefty	19-491	CB
Give Me More More More	Frizzell, Lefty	5-421	SC
Give Me One More Chance	Exile	33-80	CB
Give Me One More Chance	Exile	11-721	DK
Give Me One More Chance	Exile	20-279	SC
Give Me One More Shot	Alabama	2-648	SC
Give Me One More Shot	Alabama	22-869	ST
Give Me One Reason	Chapman, Tracy	14-906	SC
Give Me One Reason	Tedeschi, Susan	17-458	AMS
Give Me Some Wheels	Bogguss, Suzy	4-362	SC
Give Me Some Wheels	Bogguss, Suzy	22-903	ST
Give Me The Night	Benson, George	9-52	MM
Give Me The Night	Benson, George	14-639	SC
Give Me The Simple Life	Tyrell, Steve	30-191	LE
Give Me Wings	Johnson, Michael	34-275	CB
Give Me Wings	Johnson, Michael	11-706	DK
Give Me Wings	Johnson, Michael	20-14	SC
Give My Heart To You	Cyrus, Billy Ray	14-612	SC
Give My Heart To You	Cyrus, Billy Ray	22-746	ST

SONG TITLE	ARTIST	#	TYPE
Give My Love To Rose	Cash, Johnny	29-565	CB
Give My Love To Rose	Cash, Johnny	21-584	SC
Give My Regards To Broadway	Yankee Doodle Dandy	49-442	MM
Give Myself A Party	Gibson, Don	43-287	CB
Give Myself To You	Train	48-268	THM
Give Peace A Chance	Lennon, John	30-293	RS
Give Peace A Chance	Plastic Ono Band	34-26	CB
Gives You Hell	All American Rejects	36-253	PHM
Givin' It Up For Your Love	McClinton, Delbert	2-565	SC
Givin' Up **	Darkness	29-232	ZM
Givin' Water To A Drowning Man	Parnell, Lee Roy	7-282	MM
Givin' Water To A Drowning Man	Parnell, Lee Roy	22-898	ST
Giving Him Something He Can Feel	En Vogue	12-749	P
Giving You The Best That I Got	Baker, Anita	2-280	SC
Glad All Over	Dave Clark Five	45-76	LE
Glamorous	Fergie	48-234	CB
Glamorous Life	Sheila E	24-429	SC
Glass	Thompson Square	38-277	AS
Gloria	Branigan, Laura	26-324	DK
Gloria	Branigan, Laura	4-536	SC
Gloria	Cadillacs	35-163	CB
Gloria	Cadillacs	25-558	MM
Gloria	Morrison, Van	23-593	BS
Gloria	Morrison, Van	21-198	DK
Gloria	Morrison, Van	12-925	P
Gloria	Shadows Of Knight	27-560	DK
Glorified G	Pearl Jam	9-302	RS
Glory Days	Springsteen, Bruce	17-620	LE
Glory Of Love	Cetera, Peter	11-78	JTG
Glory Of Love	Midler, Bette	16-757	DK
Glory Of Love	Roommates	13-263	P
Glory Road	Diamond, Neil	47-410	BHK
Gloryland	Hall, Daryl	9-200	SO
Gloryland	Thomas, Keni	23-488	CB
Glow	Alien Ant Farm	32-441	THM
Go	Pearl Jam	9-293	RS
Go All The Way	Raspberries	2-722	SC
Go Away	Morgan, Lorrie	1-345	CB
Go Away	Morgan, Lorrie	7-665	CHM
Go Away Little Girl	Lawrence, Steve	16-807	DK
Go Away Little Girl	Lawrence, Steve	29-492	LE
Go Away Little Girl	Osmond, Donny	33-274	CB
Go Back	Tennison, Chalee	14-168	CB
Go Back	Tennison, Chalee	22-468	ST
Go Boy Go	Smith, Carl	22-116	CB
Go Deep	Jackson, Janet	15-444	CB
Go Deep	Jackson, Janet	15-626	PHM
Go Deep	Jackson, Janet	15-416	PS
Go Easy On Me	McCann, Lila	22-323	CB
Go Go Go	Orbison, Roy	47-347	PS
Go Home	Holy, Steve	22-339	CB

SONG TITLE	ARTIST	#	TYPE
Go Now	Moody Blues	20-97	SC
Go Now	Moody Blues	10-573	SF
Go On	Strait, George	14-101	CB
Go On	Strait, George	13-857	CHM
Go On	Strait, George	19-209	CSZ
Go Rest High On That Mountain	Gill, Vince	1-595	CB
Go Rest High On That Mountain	Gill, Vince	7-150	MM
Go Santa Go - xmas	Wiggles	45-239	WIG
Go Tell It On The Mountain	Standard	10-247	SC
Go To Sleep	Radiohead	32-440	THM
Go Where You Wanna Go	5th Dimension	48-92	LE
Go With Her	Keith, Toby	23-33	SC
Go Your Own Way	Fleetwood Mac	33-290	CB
Go Your Own Way	Fleetwood Mac	10-32	SC
Go Your Own Way	Fleetwood Mac	10-542	SF
Go-Go 'Round	Lightfoot, Gordon	43-482	SK
God Bless America	Dion, Celine	16-299	PHM
God Bless America	Patriotic	44-36	PT
God Bless America	Rimes, LeAnn	1-299	CB
God Bless America	Smith, Kate	11-571	DK
God Bless America	Standard	20-160	BCI
God Bless America - Patriotic	Standard	33-209	CB
God Bless America Again	Spencer, Kevin	48-668	VH
God Bless The Child	Blood Sweat &Tears	19-129	KC
God Bless The Child	Holiday, Billie	6-569	MM
God Bless The Child	Twain, Shania	1-518	CB
God Bless The Child	Twain, Shania	24-650	SC
God Bless The USA	Greenwood, Lee	20-156	BCI
God Bless The USA	Greenwood, Lee	13-410	P
God Bless The USA	Greenwood, Lee	2-22	SC
God Blessed Texas	Little Texas	12-460	P
God Blessed Texas	Little Texas	2-28	SC
God Don't Make Mistakes	O'Neal, Jamie	30-357	CB
God Family And Country	Morgan, Craig	17-474	THM
God Gave Me Everything	Jagger, Mick	16-89	SC
GOD Gave Me You	Shelton, Blake	38-89	CB
God Gave Me You	White, Bryan	5-827	SC
God Gave Rock & Roll To You	Kiss	13-653	SGB
God Love Her	Keith, Toby	36-239	PHM
God Made Girls	RaeLynn	48-417	KV
God Must Be Busy	Brooks & Dunn	36-550	CB
God Must Have Spent	Alabama	8-958	CB
God Must Have Spent	Alabama	7-880	CHT
God Must Have Spent	N'Sync	15-776	BS
God Must Have Spent	N'Sync	20-430	CB
God Must Have Spent	N'Sync	11-64	JTG
God Must Have Spent	N'Sync	7-789	PHT
God Must Have Spent	N'Sync	13-788	SGB
God Must Really Love Me	Morgan, Craig	48-279	CB

SONG TITLE	ARTIST	#	TYPE
God Only Cries	Diamond Rio	29-576	CB
God Only Knows	Beach Boys	17-544	DK
God Put A Smile Upon Your Face	Coldplay	32-442	THM
God's Country USA	Hummon, Marcus	7-202	MM
God's Gonna Cut You Down	Cash, Johnny	45-36	SC
God's Gonna Cut You Down - Gospel	Cash, Johnny	37-244	CB
God's Hands	Cash, Johnny	47-806	SRK
God's Own Drunk	Buffett, Jimmy	7-417	MM
God's Own Drunk	Buffett, Jimmy	46-151	MM
God's Will	McBride, Martina	23-10	CB
God's Will	McBride, Martina	20-265	SC
Godspeed (Sweet Dreams)	Dixie Chicks	34-351	CB
Godspeed (Sweet Dreams)	Dixie Chicks	25-644	MM
Godspeed (Sweet Dreams)	Dixie Chicks	19-172	ST
Godspeed (Sweet Dreams)	Dixie Chicks	32-306	THM
Goes Down Easy	Van Zant	30-587	CB
Goes Good With Beer	Montgomery, J M	23-391	CB
Goes Good With Beer	Montgomery, J M	30-798	PHM
Goes Good With Beer	Montgomery, J M	20-495	ST
Goin' Crazy	Roth, David Lee	47-467	CB
Goin' Down Hill	Anderson, John	14-252	SC
Goin' Goin' Gone	Thrasher Shiver	4-426	SC
Goin' Gone	Mattea, Kathy	1-183	CB
Goin' Gone	Mattea, Kathy	6-747	MM
Goin' Gone	Mattea, Kathy	5-19	SC
Goin' Home	Osmonds	47-859	ZM
Goin' Out Of My Head	Lettermen	48-526	L1
Goin' Out Of My Head	Little Anthony	30-514	LE
Goin' Steady	Young, Faron	20-729	CB
Goin' Steady	Young, Faron	9-847	SAV
Goin' Steady	Young, Faron	5-664	SC
Goin' Through The Big "D"	Chesnutt, Mark	8-847	CB
Goin' Through The Big "D"	Chesnutt, Mark	3-369	SC
Goin' Through The Big "D"	Chesnutt, Mark	33-116	CB
Going Down In Flames	3 Doors Down	47-659	SBI
Going Away	Clark Family Exp.	17-571	ST
Going Back To Miami	Blues Brothers	38-34	SBII
Going Down To Liverpool	Bangles	46-473	SF
Going Going Gone	Greenwood, Lee	4-492	SC
Going Going Gone	McCoy, Neal	1-845	CB
Going Going Gone	McCoy, Neal	4-400	SC
Going Gone	Whitley, Keith	11-739	DK
Going In Circles	Vandross, Luther	48-295	SC
Going Nowhere	Judd, Wynonna	22-565	ST
Going Out Like That	McEntire, Reba	45-405	BKD
Going Out Of My Head	Anthony & Imperials	17-35	DK
Going Out Of My Head	Anthony & Imperials	6-678	MM

SONG TITLE	ARTIST	#	TYPE
Going Out Of My Head	Anthony & Imperials	4-254	SC
Going Out Tonight	Carpenter, M C	6-630	MM
Going Out Tonight	Carpenter, M C	2-797	SC
Going Out Tonight	Carpenter, M C	15-159	THM
Going To A Go-Go	Robinson, Smokey	11-201	DK
Going Under	Evanescence	19-593	CB
Going Under	Evanescence	32-363	THM
Going Where The Lonely Go	Haggard, Merle	22-241	CB
Going Where The Lonely Go	Haggard, Merle	19-412	SC
Gold	Prince	49-827	KV
Gold Digger (Radio Vers)	West, Kanye & Foxx	37-95	SC
Gold Digger **	West & Foxx	30-138	PT
Gold Digger **	West, Kanye	30-138	PT
Gold Dust Woman	Fleetwood Mac	5-467	SC
Gold Dust Woman	Hole	24-227	SC
Gold Rush Is Over the	Snow, Hank	22-126	CB
Gold Rush Is Over the	Snow, Hank	5-700	SC
Golden Coins	Presley, Elvis	25-489	MM
Golden Earrings	Lee, Peggy	47-180	KV
Golden Eye	Turner, Tina	10-425	LE
Golden Eye	Turner, Tina	9-68	SC
Golden Ring	Wynette & Jones	8-114	CB
Golden Ring	Wynette & Jones	5-441	SC
Golden Rocket the	Snow, Hank	22-123	CB
Golden Rocket the	Snow, Hank	5-576	SC
Golden Touch	Razorlight	30-738	SF
Golden Years	Dunn, Holly	6-225	MM
Goldfinger	Bassey, Shirley	12-649	P
Goldfinger	Bassey, Shirley	9-60	SC
Gone	Husky, Ferlin	8-773	CB
Gone	Husky, Ferlin	4-867	SC
Gone	Montgomery Gentry	22-95	CB
Gone	Montgomery Gentry	23-34	SC
Gone	N'Sync	20-432	CB
Gone	N'Sync	25-30	MM
Gone	Yoakam, Dwight	4-163	SC
Gone As A Girl Can Get	Strait, George	1-259	CB
Gone As A Girl Can Get	Strait, George	49-276	CB
Gone Country	Jackson, Alan	2-577	SC
Gone Crazy	Jackson, Alan	8-394	CB
Gone Crazy	Jackson, Alan	7-851	CHT
Gone Crazy	Jackson, Alan	22-723	ST
Gone Daddy Gone	Barkley, Gnarls	30-59	PHM
Gone Either Way	Scott, Ray	29-371	CB
Gone From Love Too Long	Wilkinson, Amanda	22-3	CB
Gone From Love Too Long	Wilkinson, Amanda	19-695	ST
Gone Gone Gone	Phillips, Phillip	39-102	ASK
Gone Gone Gone (Done... - duet	Krauss & Plant	37-116	SC
Gone Out Of My Mind	Diamond Rio	4-141	SC
Gone Out Of My Mind	Stone, Doug	8-492	CB
Gone To Carolina	Jennings, Shooter	30-54	CB
Gonna	Shelton, Blake	45-40	BKD

SONG TITLE	ARTIST	#	TYPE
Gonna Build A Big Fence Around TX	Autry, Gene	22-172	CB
Gonna Buy Me A Dog	Monkees	47-779	SRK
Gonna Come Back As A Country Song	Jackson, Alan	39-60	PHN
Gonna Die Young	Bentley, Dierks	45-166	PHN
Gonna Find Me A Bluebird	Rainwater, Marvin	5-584	SC
Gonna Get A Life	Chesnutt, Mark	1-357	CB
Gonna Get A Life	Chesnutt, Mark	2-659	SC
Gonna Get Along Without You Now	Davis, Skeeter	43-329	CB
Gonna Go Huntin' Tonight	Williams, Hank Jr.	16-680	C2C
Gonna Have A Party	Alabama	17-314	NA
Gonna Know We Were Here	Aldean, Jason	45-100	BK
Gonna Make You Sweat	C&C Music Factory	33-341	CB
Gonna Make You Sweat	C&C Music Factory	21-458	CB
Gonna Wanna Tonight	Rice, Chase	45-63	DCK
Good	Better Than Ezra	3-489	SC
Good As Gone	Little Big Town	30-108	CB
Good As I Was To You	Morgan, Lorrie	14-651	CB
Good As I Was To You	Morgan, Lorrie	7-590	CHM
Good As I Was To You	Morgan, Lorrie	7-432	MM
Good As I Was To You	Morgan, Lorrie	4-617	SC
Good As You Were Bad	Kramer, Jana	44-165	BKD
Good At Startin' Fires	Shelton, Blake	36-277	PHM
Good Boys	Blondie	49-139	TU
Good Day	Jewel	36-192	PHM
Good Day In Hell	Eagles	44-105	ZMP
Good Day To Run a	Worley, Darryl	14-143	CB
Good Day To Run a	Worley, Darryl	14-13	CHM
Good Day To Run a	Worley, Darryl	19-223	CSZ
Good Day To Run a	Worley, Darryl	22-582	ST
Good Directions	Currington, Billy	30-162	CB
Good Enough	McLachlan, Sarah	14-191	CB
Good Enough	McLachlan, Sarah	16-627	MM
Good Feeling	Flo Rida	45-653	MRH
Good For Me	Grant, Amy	16-623	MM
Good For Me	Seger, Bob	10-180	UK
Good Friday	Black Crowes	24-58	SC
Good Friend And A Glass Of Wine	Rimes, LeAnn	36-396	CB
Good Girl	Underwood, Carrie	44-206	MRH
Good Girls Go To Heaven	Brooks & Dunn	17-476	TT
Good Golly Miss Molly	CCR	48-362	ASK
Good Golly Miss Molly	Little Richard	3-313	MH
Good Golly Miss Molly	Little Richard	6-165	MM
Good Golly Miss Molly	Little Richard	3-470	SC
Good Good Lovin'	McComas, Brian	29-585	CB
Good Hearted Woman	Jennings & Nelson	11-151	DK
Good Hearted Woman	Jennings, Waylon	8-18	CB
Good Hearted Woman	Jennings, Waylon	12-425	P
Good Hearted Woman	Merritt,Tift	22-325	CB
Good Hearted Woman a	Haggard, Merle	49-822	SRK
Good Hearted Woman a	Jennings, Waylon	22-136	CK

SONG TITLE	ARTIST	#	TYPE
Good Idea Tomorrow	Dodd, Deryl	8-934	CB
Good Idea Tomorrow	Dodd, Deryl	14-608	SC
Good Intentions	Toad&Wet Sprocket	15-482	THM
Good Kind Of Crazy	Dalley, Amy	30-355	CB
Good Kind the	Wreckers	30-316	CB
Good Left Undone the	Rise Against	37-140	SC
Good Left Undone the	Rise Against	49-900	SC
Good Life the	Bennett, Tony	10-413	LE
Good Life the	OneRepublic	47-332	CB
Good Life the	Robison, Bruce	19-230	SC
Good Life the - duet	Osmond, Donny & Marie	47-850	PHN
Good Little Girls	Blue County	19-678	ST
Good Lord Willing	Little Big Town	47-206	CB
Good Lovin'	Rascals	48-588	DK
Good Lovin'	Wynette, Tammy	13-534	P
Good Lovin'	Wynette, Tammy	9-602	SAV
Good Lovin'	Young Rascals	35-58	CB
Good Lovin'	Young Rascals	11-690	DK
Good Lovin' Gone Bad	Bad Company	4-562	SC
Good Luck Charm	Presley, Elvis	3-314	MH
Good Luck Charm	Presley, Elvis	13-98	P
Good Luck Charm	Presley, Elvis	2-598	SC
Good Man a	Emerson Drive	29-583	CB
Good Moring Self	Reeves, Jim	45-724	VH
Good Morning Beautiful	Holy, Steve	16-167	CB
Good Morning Beautiful	Holy, Steve	15-678	ST
Good Morning Heartache	Holiday, Billie	49-467	MM
Good Morning Heartache	Standard	13-639	SGB
Good Mother	Arden, Jann	24-550	SC
Good Ol' Boys	Jennings, Waylon	1-618	CB
Good Ol' Boys	Jennings, Waylon	4-721	SC
Good Ol' Boys Like Me	Williams, Don	5-198	SC
Good Ol' Fashioned Love	Byrd, Tracy	8-129	CB
Good Ol' Fashioned Love	Byrd, Tracy	22-633	ST
Good Old Fashioned Lover Boy	Queen	49-80	ZPA
Good Ole Days	Vassar, Phil	23-289	CB
Good Ole Days	Vassar, Phil	29-607	ST
Good People	Bates, Jeff	23-298	CB
Good Ride Cowboy	Brooks, Garth	23-449	ST
Good Run Of Bad Luck a	Black, Clint	1-827	CB
Good Run Of Bad Luck a	Black, Clint	30-6	MM
Good Stuff the	Chesney, Kenny	29-425	CB
Good Stuff the	Chesney, Kenny	25-230	MM
Good Stuff the	Chesney, Kenny	17-567	ST
Good Thing	Fine Young Cannibal	14-562	AH
Good Thing	Revere & Raiders	11-559	DK
Good Things	Houston, David	48-192	CB
Good Time	Jackson, Alan	36-389	CB
Good Time Charlie	King, Albert	19-793	SGB
Good Time Charlie's Got The Blues	O'Keefe, Danny	9-500	SAV

SONG TITLE	ARTIST	#	TYPE
Good Times	Andrews, Jessica	25-706	MM
Good Times	Andrews, Jessica	19-269	ST
Good Times	Chic	27-300	DK
Good Times	Chic	9-759	SAV
Good Times	Cochran, Anita	9-426	CB
Good Times	Jones, Jack	17-336	DK
Good Times	Pope, Cassadee	49-669	BKD
Good Times	Seals, Dan	48-104	CB
Good Timin'	Beach Boys	46-488	DK
Good Timin'	Jones, Jimmy	11-364	DK
Good Timin'	Jones, Jimmy	29-815	SF
Good To Be Alive	Trainor, Meghan	48-449	KCD
Good To Go	Corbett, John	29-211	CB
Good To Go	Steele, Jeffrey	17-587	ST
Good To Go To Mexico	Keith, Toby	47-158	CB
Good Vibrations	Beach Boys	5-501	BS
Good Vibrations	Beach Boys	33-242	CB
Good Vibrations	Beach Boys	11-812	DK
Good Vibrations	Beach Boys	12-856	P
Good Vibrations	Mark, Marky	6-176	MM
Good Way To Get On My Bad Side	Byrd & Chesnutt	9-868	ST
Good Way To Get On My Bad Side	Byrd, Tracy	16-263	TT
Good Woman Blues	Tillis, Mel	19-458	CB
Good Woman's Love a	Reed, Jerry	20-721	SC
Good Year For The Roses a	Jones, George	4-637	SC
Good Year For The Roses a - duet	Jones & Jackson	49-184	SC
Goodbye	Air Supply	46-400	SBI
Goodbye	Harris, EmmyLou	46-278	KV
Goodbye Comes Hard For Me	Haggard, Merle	49-818	SSK
Goodbye Cruel World	Darren, James	7-37	MM
Goodbye Cruel World	Darren, James	5-457	SC
Goodbye Earl	Dixie Chicks	14-177	CB
Goodbye Earl	Dixie Chicks	13-811	CHM
Goodbye Earl	Dixie Chicks	30-600	RS
Goodbye Earl	Dixie Chicks	5-801	SC
Goodbye Earl	Dixie Chicks	16-264	TT
Goodbye England's Rose (Diana)	John, Elton	12-933	CB
Goodbye For Now	Streisand, Barbra	49-612	PS
Goodbye In Her Eyes	Zac Brown Band	43-155	ASK
Goodbye In Her Eyes	Zac Brown Band	43-462	SBI
Goodbye Is All We Have	Krauss, Alison	23-487	CB
Goodbye Is All We Have	Krauss, Alison	29-616	ST
Goodbye Is The Wrong Way	Hayes, Wade	9-425	CB
Goodbye Little Darlin'	Cash, Johnny	43-416	SRK
Goodbye On A Bad Day	Lawson, Shannon	30-386	CB
Goodbye On A Bad Day	Lawson, Shannon	25-227	MM
Goodbye On A Bad Day	Lawson, Shannon	16-432	ST
Goodbye Says It All	Blackhawk	6-474	MM
Goodbye Squirrel (Parody)	Judd, Cledus T.	16-265	TT
Goodbye Squirrell	Judd, Cledus T.	44-308	SBI

89

SONG TITLE	ARTIST	#	TYPE
Goodbye Time	Shelton, Blake	22-30	CB
Goodbye Time	Twitty, Conway	5-868	SC
Goodbye To Love	Carpenters	44-349	JVC
Goodbye To Romance	Osbourne, Ozzy	13-754	SGB
Goodbye To You	Branch, Michelle	18-438	CB
Goodbye To You	Branch, Michelle	25-309	MM
Goodbye To You	Scandal	5-314	SC
Goodbye Town	Lady Antebellum	43-143	BK3 D
Goodbye Yellow Brick Road	Bareilles, Sara	49-643	KV
Goodbye Yellow Brick Road	John, Elton	11-208	DK
Goodbye Yellow Brick Road	John, Elton	12-822	P
Goodbye Yellow Brick Road	John, Elton	9-656	SAV
Goodbye Yellow Brick Road	John, Elton	5-377	SC
Goodbye Yellow Brick Road (Live)	Bareilles, Sara	49-15	KV
Goodbye Yellow Brock Road	John, Elton	34-29	CB
Goodbye's All We Got Left	Earle, Steve	46-178	CB
Goodbye's The Saddes Word	Dion, Celine	19-26	PS
Goodies	Ciara & Petey Pablo	37-105	SC
Goodnight	Bogguss, Suzy	14-707	CB
Goodnight	Bogguss, Suzy	10-231	SC
Goodnight	Orbison, Roy	38-55	CB
Goodnight And Goodbye	Jonas Brothers	36-538	WD
Goodnight Irene	Weavers	8-419	CB
Goodnight Kiss	Houser, Randy	43-144	ASK
Goodnight My Love	Connick, Harry Jr.	30-186	LE
Goodnight My Love	Standard	10-460	MG
Goodnight Sweetheart	Crosby, Bing	29-410	CB
Goodnight Sweetheart	Kersh, David	4-421	SC
Goodnight Sweetheart	Spaniels	12-673	P
Goodnight Sweetheart	Spaniels	2-75	SC
Goody Goody	Lymon & Teenagers	6-146	MM
Goody Goody	Lymon & Teenagers	4-221	SC
Goody Goody	Lymon, Frankie	30-522	LE
Goody Two Shoes	Adam Ant	21-742	MH
Goosey Goosey Gander	Standard	47-834	SDK
Gorilla	Mars, Bruno	47-219	KV
Gospel - Abide With Me	Gospel	12-203	DK
Gospel - Alas And Did My Saviour...	Broadman Hymnal	21-82	SX
Gospel - All Hail The Power	Broadman Hymnal	21-84	SX
Gospel - Amazing Grace	Broadman Hymnal	21-60	SX
Gospel - Amazing Grace	Gospel	11-477	DK
Gospel - Amazing Grace	Presley, Elvis	30-376	SC
Gospel - Angel Of Death the	Williams, Hank Sr.	37-198	CB
Gospel - Are You Washed In The...	Broadman Hymnal	21-49	SX
Gospel - At The Cross	Broadman Hymnal	21-50	SX

SONG TITLE	ARTIST	#	TYPE
Gospel - Awesome GOD	Mullins, Rich	35-320	CB
Gospel - Banner Of The Cross the	Broadman Hymnal	21-30	SX
Gospel - Basics Of Life	4HIM	35-319	CB
Gospel - Battle Hymn Of/Republic	Gospel	12-219	DK
Gospel - Beautiful Isle Of Somewher	Gospel	12-218	DK
Gospel - Beluah Land	Squire Parsons	16-603	CB
Gospel - Bible Tells Me So	Gospel	12-221	DK
Gospel - Big House	Audio Adrenaline	20-151	KB
Gospel - Blessed Assurance	Broadman Hymnal	21-55	SX
Gospel - Blessed Assurance	Gospel	12-228	DK
Gospel - Blessed Assurance	Southern Gospel	16-617	CB
Gospel - Blessed Be The Name	Broadman Hymnal	21-92	SX
Gospel - Blood Will Never Lose It's	Southern Gospel	16-612	CB
Gospel - Both Sides Of The Road	Southern Gospel	16-15	SX
Gospel - Brethren We Have Met To...	Broadman Hymnal	21-70	SX
Gospel - Brighten The Corner	Gospel	12-237	DK
Gospel - Bringing In The Sheaves	Broadman Hymnal	21-103	SX
Gospel - Bringing In The Sheaves	Gospel	12-223	DK
Gospel - By And By	Presley, Elvis	25-510	MM
Gospel - Calling You	Williams, Hank Sr.	37-197	CB
Gospel - Champion Of Love	Cathedrals	16-16	SX
Gospel - Christ Receiveth Sinful Me	Broadman Hymnal	21-51	SX
Gospel - Christ the Lord Is Risen..	Broadman Hymnal	21-116	SX
Gospel - Close To Thee	Broadman Hymnal	21-74	SX
Gospel - Come Thou Fount	Broadman Hymnal	21-66	SX
Gospel - Crying In The Chapel	Presley, Elvis	43-99	CB
Gospel - Crying In The Chapel	Presley, Elvis	6-694	MM
Gospel - Crying In The Chapel	Presley, Elvis	30-378	SC
Gospel - Dear Brother	Williams, Hank Sr.	37-188	CB
Gospel - Dear God	Cline, Patsy	43-107	CB
Gospel - Dry Bones	Cathedrals	16-17	SX
Gospel - Face To Face	Broadman Hymnal	21-46	SX
Gospel - Fairest Lord Jesus	Broadman Hymnal	21-73	SX
Gospel - Farther Along	Southern Gospel	16-18	SX
Gospel - Flood	Jars Of Clay	20-150	KB
Gospel - Flow Gently Sweet Afton	Gospel	12-213	DK
Gospel - Footsteps Of	Broadman Hymnal	21-75	SX

SONG TITLE	ARTIST	#	TYPE
Jesus			
Gospel - For Future Generations	4Him	34-428	CB
Gospel - Give Me That Old Time Reli	Gospel	12-224	DK
Gospel - Glory To His Name	Broadman Hymnal	21-65	SX
Gospel - Go Down Moses	Gospel	12-233	DK
Gospel - Go Tell It On The Mountain	Gospel	12-204	DK
Gospel - Go Tell It On The Mountain	Gospel	12-647	P
Gospel - God	St. James, Rebecca\	20-149	KB
Gospel - God On The Mountain	Southern Gospel	16-19	SX
Gospel - God's Gonna Cut You Down	Cash, Johnny	37-244	CB
Gospel - Good Christain Friends Rej	Standard	15-481	SC
Gospel - Greater Is He	Long, Janna	34-429	CB
Gospel - Hallelujah Square	Sego's	16-20	SX
Gospel - Have Faith In God	Broadman Hymnal	21-27	SX
Gospel - Have Thine Own Way Lord	Broadman Hymnal	21-85	SX
Gospel - He Keeps Me Singing	Broadman Hymnal	21-106	SX
Gospel - He Loves Me	Southern Gospel	16-604	CB
Gospel - He Touched Me	Presley, Elvis	33-201	CB
Gospel - He's a Mighty Good Friend	Fairchild, Barbara	47-84	VHG
Gospel - He's Got The Whole World	Gospel	12-225	DK
Gospel - Heavenly Sunlight	Broadman Hymnal	21-54	SX
Gospel - Here They Come	Broadman Hymnal	21-132	SX
Gospel - Higher Ground	Broadman Hymnal	21-89	SX
Gospel - His Hand In Mine	Presley, Elvis	30-384	SC
Gospel - His Way With Thee	Broadman Hymnal	21-56	SX
Gospel - Hold Bible Book Divine	Broadman Hymnal	21-79	SX
Gospel - Holy Holy Holy	Broadman Hymnal	21-21	SX
Gospel - House Of Gold	Williams, Hank Sr.	37-191	CB
Gospel - How About Your Heart	Broadman Hymnal	21-118	SX
Gospel - How Can You Refuse HIM Now	Williams, Hank Sr.	37-189	CB
Gospel - How Firm A Foundation	Broadman Hymnal	21-71	SX
Gospel - How Great Thou Art	Gospel	12-205	DK
Gospel - How Great Thou Art	Lynn, Loretta	47-635	CB
Gospel - How Great Thou Art	Presley, Elvis	6-693	MM
Gospel - How Great	Presley, Elvis	30-373	SC

SONG TITLE	ARTIST	#	TYPE
Thou Art			
Gospel - How Great Thou Art	Presley, Elvis	14-800	THM
Gospel - I Am Resolved	Broadman Hymnal	21-45	SX
Gospel - I Am Thine Oh Lord	Broadman Hymnal	21-28	SX
Gospel - I Believe	Presley, Elvis	6-692	MM
Gospel - I Believe	Presley, Elvis	30-375	SC
Gospel - I Can't Even Walk	Southern Gospel	16-21	SX
Gospel - I Dreamed About Mama...	Williams, Hank Sr.	37-186	CB
Gospel - I Love To Tell The Story	Broadman Hymnal	21-104	SX
Gospel - I Love To Tell The Story	Gospel	12-229	DK
Gospel - I Love To Tell The Story	Jackson, Alan	43-109	CB
Gospel - I Need Thee Every Hour	Broadman Hymnal	21-68	SX
Gospel - I Need Thee Every Hour	Gospel	12-209	DK
Gospel - I Saw The Light	Southern Gospel	16-605	CB
Gospel - I Saw The Light	Williams, Hank Sr.	37-185	CB
Gospel - I Talk To Jesus Every Day	Cash, Johnny	49-714	VH
Gospel - I Was Glad When They...	Broadman Hymnal	21-113	SX
Gospel - I Will Sing the Wondrous..	Broadman Hymnal	21-105	SX
Gospel - I'll Fly Away	Gospel	33-202	CB
Gospel - I'll Fly Away	Gospel	12-217	DK
Gospel - I'll Fly Away	Southern Gospel	16-22	SX
Gospel - I'll Have A New Body	Williams, Hank Sr.	37-196	CB
Gospel - I'm Standing On The Solid.	Southern Gospel	16-23	SX
Gospel - I've Found A New Way	Broadman Hymnal	21-115	SX
Gospel - If Jesus Said It	Broadman Hymnal	21-125	SX
Gospel - If We Never Meet Again	Presley, Elvis	43-111	CB
Gospel - In Christ	Big Daddy Weave	34-430	CB
Gospel - In My Father's House	Presley, Elvis	6-695	MM
Gospel - In My Father's House	Presley, Elvis	14-804	THM
Gospel - In The Garden	Gospel	12-207	DK
Gospel - In The Garden	Lynn, Loretta	47-633	CB
Gospel - In The Garden	Southern Gospel	16-606	CB
Gospel - In The Shelter Of His Arms	Broadman Hymnal	21-121	SX
Gospel - In The sweet By & By	Broadman Hymnal	21-100	SX
Gospel - In The Sweet By & By	Gospel	12-227	DK
Gospel - In The Sweet Bye and Bye	Lynn, Loretta	47-634	CB
Gospel - Inside Out	Jensen, Gordon	16-24	SX
Gospel - It Is No Secret	Gospel	12-234	DK

SONG TITLE	ARTIST	#	TYPE
What God..			
Gospel - It Is Well With My Soul	Broadman Hymnal	21-37	SX
Gospel - It's So Sweet To Trust...	Jackson, Alan	43-98	CB
Gospel - Jesus Is Calling	Broadman Hymnal	21-29	SX
Gospel - Jesus Is Coming Soon	Gospel	12-208	DK
Gospel - Jesus Loves Me	Broadman Hymnal	21-112	SX
Gospel - Jesus Loves Me	Gospel	12-201	DK
Gospel - Jesus Loves the Little Chi	Broadman Hymnal	21-114	SX
Gospel - Jesus Loves the Little...	Kids	33-198	CB
Gospel - Jesus Paid It All	Broadman Hymnal	21-86	SX
Gospel - Jesus Remembered Me	Williams, Hank Sr.	37-190	CB
Gospel - Jesus Saves	Broadman Hymnal	21-24	SX
Gospel - Jesus the Very Thought of.	Broadman Hymnal	21-80	SX
Gospel - John The Relevation	Southern Gospel	16-25	SX
Gospel - Joshua Fit The Battle	Presley, Elvis	30-381	SC
Gospel - Just A Closer Walk W/Thee	Gospel	12-222	DK
Gospel - Just A Closer Walk W/Thee	Southern Gospel	16-607	CB
Gospel - Just A Closer Walk With Thee	Cline, Patsy	45-493	CB
Gospel - Just A Closer Walk With Thee	Lynn, Loretta	47-631	CB
Gospel - Just A Little Talk w/Jesus	Southern Gospel	16-608	CB
Gospel - Just As I Am	Broadman Hymnal	21-61	SX
Gospel - Keep Walkin'	Broadman Hymnal	21-124	SX
Gospel - King Of Eternity	Southern Gospel	16-613	CB
Gospel - Known Only To Him	Presley, Elvis	30-382	SC
Gospel - Last Mile of the Day the	Broadman Hymnal	21-129	SX
Gospel - Lead Me Guide Me	Presley, Elvis	6-696	MM
Gospel - Lead Me Guide Me	Presley, Elvis	30-377	SC
Gospel - Lead Me Guide Me	Presley, Elvis	14-822	THM
Gospel - Lead On O Eternal King	Broadman Hymnal	21-78	SX
Gospel - Leaning On The Everlasting	Broadman Hymnal	21-91	SX
Gospel - Leaning on the Everlasting..	Jackson, Alan	43-104	CB
Gospel - Let The Lord's Light Beam	Broadman Hymnal	21-87	SX
Gospel - Let Us Pray	Presley, Elvis	14-805	THM
Gospel - Lily Of The Valley	Gospel	12-230	DK

SONG TITLE	ARTIST	#	TYPE
Gospel - Little Brown Church In The	Gospel	12-210	DK
Gospel - Live The Life	Smith, Michael W.	20-152	KB
Gospel - Lord Of The Dance	Chapman, Steven C	20-148	KB
Gospel - Lord's Prayer the	Gospel	12-220	DK
Gospel - Love Lifted Me	Broadman Hymnal	21-101	SX
Gospel - Make Me A Channel of Bless	Broadman Hymnal	21-31	SX
Gospel - Mansion Over the Hilltop	Presley, Elvis	6-699	MM
Gospel - Mansion Over The Hilltop	Presley, Elvis	14-806	THM
Gospel - Me And Jesus - VR	Hall, Tom T.	49-711	VH
Gospel - Medley ('68 Comeback Sp)	Presley, Elvis	25-500	MM
Gospel - Michael Row The Boat Ashor	Highwaymen	16-756	DK
Gospel - My Jesus I Love Thee	Broadman Hymnal	21-57	SX
Gospel - My Sweet Lord	Harrison, George	33-270	CB
Gospel - Near The Cross	Broadman Hymnal	21-97	SX
Gospel - Nearer My God To Thee	Broadman Hymnal	21-72	SX
Gospel - Nearer My God To Thee	Broadman Hymnal	21-90	SX
Gospel - Nearer My God To Thee	Gospel	12-206	DK
Gospel - Nothing But The Blood	Broadman Hymnal	21-110	SX
Gospel - Nothing Can Compare	Broadman Hymnal	21-117	SX
Gospel - Oh Buddah	Imperials	16-29	SX
Gospel - Oh Say But I'm Glad	Broadman Hymnal	21-128	SX
Gospel - Old Rivers	Brennan, Walter	43-105	CB
Gospel - Old Rugged Cross the	Broadman Hymnal	21-36	SX
Gospel - Old Rugged Cross the	Gospel	12-236	DK
Gospel - Old Time Way	Southern Gospel	16-609	CB
Gospel - On Eagles Wings	Amerson, Steve	49-716	VH
Gospel - On Eagles Wings	Bondi, Renee	49-715	VH
Gospel - On Jordan's Stormy Banks	Broadman Hymnal	21-83	SX
Gospel - One Day At A Time	Gospel	33-203	CB
Gospel - One Day At A Time	Southern Gospel	16-610	CB
Gospel - Only Believe	Broadman Hymnal	21-98	SX
Gospel - Only Trust Him	Broadman Hymnal	21-69	SX
Gospel - Onward Christian Soldiers	Broadman Hymnal	21-26	SX
Gospel - Onward Christian Soldiers	Gospel	12-200	DK
Gospel - Other Side Of Jordan the	Broadman Hymnal	21-119	SX

SONG TITLE	ARTIST	#	TYPE
Gospel - Pass Me Not	Broadman Hymnal	21-76	SX
Gospel - Peace In The Valley	Gospel	12-235	DK
Gospel - Peace In The Valley	Presley, Elvis	30-374	SC
Gospel - Peace Of Prayer	Broadman Hymnal	21-131	SX
Gospel - Place In This World	Smith, Michael W	35-317	CB
Gospel - Praise Him All Ye Little C	Broadman Hymnal	21-111	SX
Gospel - Praise Him Praise Him	Broadman Hymnal	21-102	SX
Gospel - Precious Lord	Presley, Elvis	6-701	MM
Gospel - Precious Memories	Gospel	12-215	DK
Gospel - Precious Memories	Lynn, Loretta	43-97	CB
Gospel - Prodigal Son the	Williams, Hank Sr.	37-193	CB
Gospel - Promised Land the	Presley, Elvis	6-698	MM
Gospel - Promised Land the	Presley, Elvis	14-810	THM
Gospel - Ready To Go Home	Williams, Hank Sr.	37-184	CB
Gospel - Redeemed	Broadman Hymnal	21-41	SX
Gospel - Redeemer	Mullen, Nicole C	35-318	CB
Gospel - Rescue The Perishing	Broadman Hymnal	21-39	SX
Gospel - Rest Of Heaven the	Broadman Hymnal	21-38	SX
Gospel - Revive Us Again	Broadman Hymnal	21-58	SX
Gospel - Rock Of Ages	Broadman Hymnal	21-63	SX
Gospel - Rock Of Ages	Gospel	12-199	DK
Gospel - Sailing Away	Southern Gospel	16-611	CB
Gospel - Saved Saved	Broadman Hymnal	21-99	SX
Gospel - Saviour Like a Shepherd ..	Broadman Hymnal	21-23	SX
Gospel - Send The Light	Broadman Hymnal	21-53	SX
Gospel - Shake A Hand	Presley, Elvis	6-700	MM
Gospel - Shall We Gather At The Riv	Broadman Hymnal	21-109	SX
Gospel - Shine	Newsboys	20-154	KB
Gospel - Shine	Parton, Dolly	43-110	CB
Gospel - Since I Have Been Redeemed	Broadman Hymnal	21-48	SX
Gospel - Sing Sing Sing	Williams, Hank Sr.	37-293	CB
Gospel - Soemthing Within Me	Take 6	13-114	P
Gospel - Softly And Tenderly	Broadman Hymnal	21-44	SX
Gospel - Softly And Tenderly	Southern Gospel	16-26	SX
Gospel - Solid Rock the	Broadman Hymnal	21-42	SX
Gospel - Somebody Bigger Than You..	Presley, Elvis	14-809	THM
Gospel - Somebody Bigger Than...	Presley, Elvis	6-702	MM

SONG TITLE	ARTIST	#	TYPE
Gospel - Someone To Talk To	Chuck Wagon Gang	16-27	SX
Gospel - Stand Up Stand Up for Jesu	Broadman Hymnal	21-25	SX
Gospel - Standing On The Promises	Broadman Hymnal	21-52	SX
Gospel - Standing On The Promises	Gospel	12-232	DK
Gospel - Standing On The Promises	Southern Gospel	16-28	SX
Gospel - Steady On	Point Of Grace	20-153	KB
Gospel - Sweet Hour Of Prayer	Broadman Hymnal	21-88	SX
Gospel - Sweet Hour Of Prayer	Gospel	12-212	DK
Gospel - Swing Down Sweet Chariot	Presley, Elvis	30-380	SC
Gospel - Swing Low Sweet Chariot	Standard	11-481	DK
Gospel - Swing Low Sweet Chariot	Standard	21-621	SF
Gospel - Take My Hand Precious Lord	Gospel	12-214	DK
Gospel - Take My Hand Precious Lord	Presley, Elvis	30-386	SC
Gospel - Take My Life & Let It Be..	Broadman Hymnal	21-64	SX
Gospel - Take the Name of Jesus...	Broadman Hymnal	21-108	SX
Gospel - Take Time To Be Holy	Broadman Hymnal	21-96	SX
Gospel - Tell It To Jesus	Broadman Hymnal	21-47	SX
Gospel - Testify To Love	Avalon	20-155	KB
Gospel - Thank GOD	Williams, Hank Sr.	37-192	CB
Gospel - Thanks To Calvary	Broadman Hymnal	21-123	SX
Gospel - the City	Watson, Gene	43-100	CB
Gospel - the Old Rugged Cross	Lynn, Loretta	43-101	CB
Gospel - the Seeker	Parton, Dolly	43-96	CB
Gospel - There Is a Name I Love To	Broadman Hymnal	21-94	SX
Gospel - There Shall Be Showers Of.	Broadman Hymnal	21-43	SX
Gospel - There's A God Somewhere	Broadman Hymnal	21-130	SX
Gospel - Thy Burdens Are Greater...	Williams, Hank Sr.	37-194	CB
Gospel - Till The Storm Passes By	Broadman Hymnal	21-126	SX
Gospel - Tis So Sweet To Trust In J	Broadman Hymnal	21-95	SX
Gospel - To The Work	Broadman Hymnal	21-33	SX
Gospel - Tramp On The Street the	Williams, Hank Sr.	37-195	CB
Gospel - Trust And Obey	Broadman Hymnal	21-107	SX
Gospel - Uncloudy Day the	Broadman Hymnal	21-40	SX
Gospel - Wait For the Light To Shine	Gospel	49-713	VH
Gospel - Warm Kind of	Jensen, Gordon	16-614	CB

SONG TITLE	ARTIST	#	TYPE
Family Feelin			
Gospel - Way That He Loves the	Broadman Hymnal	21-120	SX
Gospel - Wayfaring Stranger	Harris, Emmylou	43-102	CB
Gospel - We Call On Him	Presley, Elvis	25-512	MM
Gospel - We Shall Overcome	Jackson, Mahalia	33-211	CB
Gospel - We're Marching To Zion	Broadman Hymnal	21-22	SX
Gospel - What a Friend We Have In Jesus	Lynn, Loretta	43-106	CB
Gospel - What A Friend We Have In..	Broadman Hymnal	21-59	SX
Gospel - What A Friend We Have In..	Gospel	12-226	DK
Gospel - When God Dips His Love…	Broadman Hymnal	21-127	SX
Gospel - When I See Jesus	Broadman Hymnal	21-122	SX
Gospel - When I Survey the Wondrous	Broadman Hymnal	21-67	SX
Gospel - When The Roll Is Called Up	Gospel	12-211	DK
Gospel - When The Saints Go Marchin	Armstrong, Louis	11-480	DK
Gospel - When They Ring Those…	Gospel	12-231	DK
Gospel - When We All Get To Heaven	Broadman Hymnal	21-93	SX
Gospel - Where Could I Go	Presley, Elvis	43-108	CB
Gospel - Where Could I Go But To…	Presley, Elvis	30-379	SC
Gospel - Where He Leads Me	Broadman Hymnal	21-62	SX
Gospel - Where No One Stands Alone	Presley, Elvis	6-704	MM
Gospel - Where No One Stands Alone	Presley, Elvis	14-811	THM
Gospel - Where Would I Be	Southern Gospel	16-615	CB
Gospel - Where Would I Go	Presley, Elvis	6-697	MM
Gospel - Whispering Hope	Gospel	12-216	DK
Gospel - Who Am I	Presley, Elvis	6-703	MM
Gospel - Who Am I	Presley, Elvis	30-383	SC
Gospel - Who Am I	Presley, Elvis	14-812	THM
Gospel - Who Is On The Lord's Side	Broadman Hymnal	21-32	SX
Gospel - Will Jesus Find Us Watchin	Broadman Hymnal	21-34	SX
Gospel - Will The Circle Be Unbroke	Standard	11-478	DK
Gospel - Will the Circle Be Unbroken	Lynn, Loretta	47-636	CB
Gospel - Will the Circle be unbroken	Martin, Jimmy	33-204	CB
Gospel - Wings Of A Dove	Gospel	12-202	DK

SONG TITLE	ARTIST	#	TYPE
Gospel - Without Him	Presley, Elvis	14-813	THM
Gospel - Wonderful Words Of Life	Broadman Hymnal	21-77	SX
Gospel - Work For The Night Is Comi	Broadman Hymnal	21-81	SX
Gospel - Working On The Building	Presley, Elvis	30-385	SC
Gospel - Ye Must Be Born Again	Broadman Hymnal	21-35	SX
Gospel - You Gave Me A Mountain	Presley, Elvis	6-705	MM
Gospel - You Gave Me A Mountain	Presley, Elvis	14-814	THM
Gospel - You'll Never Walk Alone	Presley, Elvis	6-691	MM
Gospel - You'll Never Walk Alone	Presley, Elvis	30-372	SC
Gospel - You'll Never Walk Alone	Presley, Elvis	14-815	THM
Gospel - You're My GOD	Valasquez, Jaci	34-427	CB
Gospel According To Luke	Ewing, Skip	3-74	SC
Gossip Folks - duet	Elliot, M. & Ludacris	32-127	THM
Got A Good Day	Johnson, Carolyn D.	30-363	CB
Got A Little Crazy	Chesney, Kenny	48-88	CB
Got My Heart Set On You	Conlee, John	29-690	SC
Got My Mind Set On You	Harrison, George	14-563	AH
Got My Mojo Workin'	Muddy Waters	15-313	SC
Got No Reason Now For Going Home	Watson, Gene	14-677	CB
Got No Reason Now For Going Home	Watson, Gene	5-780	SC
Got To Get You Into My Life	Earth Wind & Fire	11-284	DK
Got To Give It Uo	Gaye, Marvin	22-933	SC
Got To Give It Up	Gaye, Marvin	36-113	JTG
Got To Give It Up	Gaye, Marvin	15-703	LE
Gotham City	Kelly, R.	34-128	CB
Gotham City	Kelly, R.	10-109	SC
Gots Ta Be	B2K	18-227	CB
Gotta Be Somebody	Nickelback	45-810	SC
Gotta Get Away	Offspring	6-39	SC
Gotta Serve Somebody	Dylan, Bob	40-30	SC
Gotta Tell You	Mumba, Samantha	14-39	THM
Gotta Tell You	Mumba, Samantha	18-515	TT
Grab Your Balls We're Going Bowling	Polka Favorites	29-812	SSR
Grab Your Balls We're… - w/Words	Polka Favorites	29-866	SSR
Graduation (Friends Forever)	Vitamin C	14-185	CB
Graduation (Friends Forever)	Vitamin C	19-825	SGB
Grain Of Salt	Keith, Toby	48-430	VH
Grand Illusion the	Styx	47-382	SC
Grand Tour the	Jones, George	8-280	CB
Grand Tour the	Jones, George	7-116	MM
Grand Tour the	Jones, George	9-574	SAV
Grand Tour the	Jones, George	5-666	SC

SONG TITLE	ARTIST	#	TYPE
Grand Tour the	Neville, Aaron	2-617	SC
Grandfather's Clock	Standard	11-484	DK
Grandma	Wilson, Gretchen	41-76	PHN
Grandma Harp	Haggard, Merle	8-842	CB
Grandma's Feather Bed	Denver, John	49-235	DFK
Grandpa (Tell Me 'Bout The...)	Judds	1-136	CB
Grandpa (Tell Me 'Bout The...)	Judds	11-202	DK
Grandpa (Tell Me 'Bout The...)	Judds	13-360	P
Grandpa Got Runned Over/John Deere	Judd, Cledus T.	16-514	CB
Grandpa Told Me So	Chesney, Kenny	1-320	CB
Grandpa Told Me So	Chesney, Kenny	3-653	SC
Grandpa Was A Carpenter	Prine, John	23-528	CB
Grapefruit Diet	Yankovic, Weird Al	49-848	SGB
Grapefruit Juicy Fruit	Buffett, Jimmy	46-139	SC
Grass Is Greener the	Lee, Brenda	45-888	VH
Gravedigger	Nelson, Willie	49-709	ST
Gravitational Pull	LeDoux, Chris	7-250	MM
Gravity Is A Bitch	Lambert, Miranda	45-946	KV
Grease	Bee Gees	9-779	SAV
Grease	Valli, Frankie	9-276	SC
Grease Megamix (Radio Version)	Travolta & Newton-John	20-118	PHM
Greased Lightnin'	Grease	49-430	SDK
Greased Lightning	Travolta, John	9-274	SC
Great Balls Of Fire	Lewis, Jerry Lee	11-164	DK
Great Balls Of Fire	Lewis, Jerry Lee	12-894	P
Great Balls Of Fire	Lewis, Jerry Lee	9-501	SAV
Great Compromise the	Prine, John	23-537	CB
Great Defenders the	Greenwood, Lee	47-132	SC
Great Disguise a	McBride, Martina	4-393	SC
Great Divide	Hornsby, Bruce	14-290	MM
Great Pretender the	Platters	12-366	DK
Great Pretender the	Platters	7-310	MM
Great Pretender the	Platters	2-79	SC
Great Speckled Bird	Acuff, Roy	8-417	CB
Great Speckled Bird	Acuff, Roy	11-819	DK
Great To Be A Man	Carrington, Rodney	44-101	SC
Greatest American Hero	TV Themes	2-176	SC
Greatest Gift Of All - duet	Rogers & Parton	48-121	CB
Greatest Love Of All	Houston, Whitney	11-263	DK
Greatest Love Of All	Houston, Whitney	17-431	KC
Greatest Love Of All	Houston, Whitney	9-1	MH
Greatest Love Of All	Houston, Whitney	6-349	MM
Greatest Love Of All	Houston, Whitney	12-676	P
Greatest Love the	Dion, Celine	19-28	PS
Greatest Man I Never Knew	McEntire, Reba	33-110	Cb
Greatest Man I Never Knew	McEntire, Reba	6-209	MM
Greatest Man I Never Knew	McEntire, Reba	2-807	SC
Greatest Performance Of	Bassey, Shirley	46-477	KV

SONG TITLE	ARTIST	#	TYPE
My Life			
Greatest the	Rogers, Kenny	3-167	CB
Greatest the	Rogers, Kenny	7-883	CHT
Greatest the	Rogers, Kenny	14-615	SC
Greed	Godsmack	16-382	SGB
Greeks Don't Want No Freaks	Eagles	49-85	ZPA
Green Acres	TV Themes	2-156	SC
Green Dolphin Street	Eckstine, Billy	15-483	SGB
Green Door the	Lowe, Jim	3-504	SC
Green Eyed Lady	Sugarloaf	19-133	KC
Green Eyed Lady	Sugarloaf	9-366	MG
Green Eyed Lady	Sugarloaf	2-783	SC
Green Eyes	Coldplay	48-259	SBI
Green Eyes	Lawrence & Gorme	25-268	MM
Green Grass And High Tides	Outlaws	48-657	CB
Green Green	Brothers Four	15-484	CMC
Green Green Grass Of Home	Humperdinck, E.	11-471	DK
Green Green Grass Of Home	Jones, Tom	12-494	P
Green Green Grass Of Home	Jones, Tom	10-582	SF
Green Green Grass Of Home	Wagoner, Porter	19-319	CB
Green Leaves Of Summer	Brothers Four	18-168	DK
Green Light	Legend, John w Andre 3000	36-512	CB
Green Manalishi (W/2-Pronged Crown)	Judas Priest	21-760	SC
Green River	CCR	34-21	CB
Green River	CCR	17-28	DK
Green River	CCR	13-230	P
Green River	CCR	5-350	SC
Green River	Fogerty, John	48-652	DCK
Green Tambourine	Lemon Pipers	11-113	DK
Greenback Dollar	Kingston Trip	47-754	SRK
Greenfields	Brothers Four	18-166	DK
Greensleeves	Standard	11-474	DK
Greyhound Bound For Nowhere	Lambert, Miranda	46-251	CB
Greystone Chapel	Cash, Johnny	43-32	HM
Grillz	Nelly	30-699	SF
Grits Ain't Groceries	Little Milton	21-576	SC
Groove Is In The Heart	Dee-Lite	10-493	DA
Groove Is In The Heart	Dee-Lite	5-340	SC
Groove With Me Tonight	MDO	10-224	SC
Groovin'	Rascals	3-256	SC
Groovin'	Young Rascals	35-63	CB
Groovin'	Young Rascals	11-93	DK
Groovin'	Young Rascals	13-115	P
Groovy Kind Of Love	Diamond, Neil	47-421	PS
Groovy Kind Of Love a	Collins, Phil	11-225	DK
Groovy Kind Of Love a	Collins, Phil	21-743	MH
Groovy Kind Of Love a	Mindbenders	10-610	SF
Groovy Situation	Chandler, Gene	5-119	SC

SONG TITLE	ARTIST	#	TYPE
Ground Beneath Her Feet the	U2	48-310	MM
Grow Old With Me	Campbell, Glen	49-266	DFK
Grow Old With Me	Carpenter, M C	1-434	CB
Grow Young With You	McCabe, Coley	6-73	SC
Growing Older But Not Up	Buffett, Jimmy	46-150	ZM
Growing On Me	Pure 13	21-623	SF
Grown Men Don't Cry	McGraw, Tim	9-860	ST
Grown Men Don't Cry	McGraw, Tim	16-266	TT
Grown-Up Christmas List	Streisand, Barbra	49-591	PS
GTO	Ronny & Daytonas	3-551	SC
Guardian	Morrisette, Alanis	39-114	PHM
Guess Things Happen That Way	Cash, Johnny	14-241	CB
Guess Things Happen That Way	Cash, Johnny	21-593	SC
Guess What	Johnson, S	32-124	THM
Guilty	Raitt, Bonnie	46-129	SC
Guilty	Streisand & Gibb	15-485	MM
Guilty	Warren Brothers	22-694	ST
Guilty In Here	Lambert, Miranda	46-261	KV
Guinevere	Eli Young Band	47-59	CB
Guitar Man	Bread	4-325	SC
Guitar Singer	Crossin' Dixon	30-540	CB
Guitar Town	Earle, Steve	11-779	DK
Guitars And Tiki Bars	Chesney, Kenny	22-16	CB
Guitars Cadillacs	Yoakam, Dwight	6-536	MM
Guitars Cadillacs	Yoakam, Dwight	13-452	P
Guitarzan	Stevens, Ray	16-492	CB
Guitarzan	Stevens, Ray	15-346	MM
Gunpowder & Lead	Lambert, Miranda	36-571	CB
Guns Made America Great	Pinkard & Bowden	15-148	SC
Gunslinger	Fogerty, John	48-655	KV
Guy Is Just A Guy a	Day, Doris	48-132	SC
Guy Like Me	Green, Pat	19-702	ST
Guy Walks Into A Bar a	Farr, Tyler	45-672	BKD
Guys Do It All The Time	McCready, Mindy	4-391	SC
Guys Like Me	Church, Eric	30-314	CB
Gypsies Tramps & Thieves	Cher	17-115	DK
Gypsies Tramps & Thieves	Cher	14-60	RS
Gypsies Tramps & Thieves	Cher	2-445	SC
Gypsies Tramps & Thieves	Cher	15-131	SGB
Gypsy	Fleetwood Mac	10-29	SC
Gypsy	Nicks, Stevie	47-898	PS
Gypsy Cried the	Christie, Lou	6-649	MM
Gypsy Woman	Hyland, Bryan	7-257	MM
H.O.L.Y.	Florida Georgia Line	49-858	DCK
Had A Dream (For The Heart)	Judds	19-437	SC
Haggard	Rhyder, Brandon	42-2	PHN
Hail Hail	Pearl Jam	9-301	RS

SONG TITLE	ARTIST	#	TYPE
Hail Hail The Gang's All Here	Kaufman, Irving	34-443	CB
Hair	Cowsills	11-794	DK
Hair - show	Mills, Frank	49-264	SC
Hair Keeps Falling Off My Head - parody	Parody	47-614	WMP
Hair Of The Dog	Nazareth	10-483	DA
Haircut Song the	Stevens, Ray	16-491	CB
Haircut Song the	Stevens, Ray	15-139	SC
Hairy Christmas	Robertson & Bryan	43-82	ASK
Half A Heart Tattoo	Hanson, Jennifer	25-698	MM
Half A Heart Tattoo	Hanson, Jennifer	19-366	ST
Half A Heart Tattoo	Hanson, Jennifer	32-379	THM
Half A Man	Baxley, Tori	23-141	CB
Half A Man	Smith, Anthony	18-799	ST
Half A Man	Smith, Anthony	32-153	THM
Half A Mind	Nelson, Willie	47-758	SRK
Half A Mind	Tubb, Ernest	45-710	VH
Half As Much	Cline, Patsy	45-496	RCA
Half As Much	Williams, Hank Sr.	14-219	CB
Half As Much	Williams, Hank Sr.	8-636	SAV
Half Breed	Cher	34-20	CB
Half Breed	Cher	11-687	DK
Half Breed	Cher	14-58	RS
Half Breed	Cher	15-134	SGB
Half Broken Heart	Cam	48-750	BKD
Half Broken Heart (Inst)	Cam	49-412	BKD
Half Enough	Morgan, Lorrie	6-383	MM
Half Heaven Half Heartache	Pitney, Gene	4-225	SC
Half Of My Mistakes	Foster, Radney	47-98	ST
Half The Man	Black, Clint	1-829	CB
Half The Way	Gayle, Crystal	48-496	CKC
Half The Way	Gayle, Crystal	46-111	SC
Half Way Up	Black, Clint	1-830	CB
Halfcrazy	Musiq	35-262	CB
Halfcrazy	Musiq	18-148	PHM
Halfway Down	Loveless, Patty	1-726	CB
Halfway Down	Loveless, Patty	6-842	MM
Halfway Down	Loveless, Patty	3-421	SC
Halfway Home Café	Skaggs, Ricky	18-215	ST
Halfway To Paradise	Fury, Billy	10-554	SF
Halfway To Paradise	Vinton, Bobby	49-88	SAV
Hallelujah	lang, k.d.	41-43	PS
Hallelujah	Wainwright, Rufus	44-306	SC
Hallelujah - xmas	Gayle, Crystal	45-254	CB
Halleujah I Love Her So	Charles, Ray	9-534	SAV
Halloween - Bat Out Of Hell	Meat Loaf	45-141	LE
Halloween - Black Night	Black Sabbath	45-113	ZM
Halloween - Blob the	Five Blobs	45-121	SC
Halloween - Casper the Friendly Ghost	TV Themes	45-119	SC
Halloween - Dead Man's Party	Oingo Boingo	45-118	SC
Halloween - Fire	Crazy World of Arthur Brown	45-114	SC
Halloween - Ghost Town	Specials	45-115	ZM

SONG TITLE	ARTIST	#	TYPE
Halloween - Ghostbusters	Parker, Ray Jr.	11-262	DK
Halloween - Ghostbusters	Parker, Ray Jr.	2-73	SC
Halloween - Ghostbusters	Parker, Ray Jr.	16-281	TT
Halloween - Haunted House	Lewis, Jerry Lee	45-140	OZP
Halloween - Haunted House	Simmons, "Jumpin" Gene	45-117	SC
Halloween - Haunted House Of Rock	Whodini	45-139	GGZ
Halloween - Hell Raiser	Sweet	45-116	SF
Halloween - Helter Skelter	Beatles	45-120	SC
Halloween - I Put A Spell On You	CCR	16-282	TT
Halloween - I'm Gonna Haunt You	Schneider, Fred	16-283	TT
Halloween - Jack O Lantern Jump	Halloween Songs	45-102	KV
Halloween - Journey to the Center..	Dukes, Amboy	16-284	TT
Halloween - Living Dead Girl	Zombie, Rob	45-323	SC
Halloween - Monster in my Pants	Schneider, Fred	16-285	TT
Halloween - Monster Mash	Pickett, Bobby	11-566	DK
Halloween - Monster Mash	Pickett, Bobby	2-72	SC
Halloween - Monster Mash	Pickett, Bobby	16-286	TT
Halloween - One Wild Night	Bon Jovi	16-287	TT
Halloween - Purple People Eater	Wooley, Sheb	16-288	TT
Halloween - Rent	Rent	45-122	PS
Halloween - Skeleton Dance	Halloween Songs	45-101	KV
Halloween - Spooky	Classics IV	16-289	TT
Halloween - Theme from Musters	Munster's Theme	16-290	TT
Halloween - This Is Halloween	Nightmare B4 Christmas	45-196	HM
Halloween - Thriller	Jackson, Michael	16-292	TT
Halloween - To Hell With The Devil	Stryper	16-294	TT
Halloween - Twilight Zone Music	Golden Earring	16-295	TT
Halloween - Werewolves Of London	Zevon, Warren	16-296	TT
Halo	Beyonce	36-29	PT
Hand in My Pocket	Morrisette, Alanis	18-41	PS
Hand Me Down World	Guess Who	5-591	SC
Hand Of Fate	Sons Of The Desert	22-422	ST
Hand Prints On The Wall	Rogers, Kenny	19-685	ST
Handful Of Water	Tennison, Chalee	5-727	SC
Handle With Care	Traveling Wilburys	30-764	SF
Hands	Jewel	28-189	DK

SONG TITLE	ARTIST	#	TYPE
Hands	Jewel	19-358	PS
Hands	Jewel	13-678	SGB
Hands Clean	Morrisette, Alanis	25-139	MM
Hands Down	Dashboard Confessional	23-188	PHM
Hands Down	Dashboard Confessional	32-404	THM
Hands Of A Working Man	Herndon, Ty	8-878	CB
Hands Of A Working Man	Herndon, Ty	7-830	CHT
Hands Of A Working Man	Herndon, Ty	22-703	ST
Hands On You	Florida Georgia Line	43-238	ASK
Hands To Heaven	Breathe	16-67	SC
Hands Up	Ottawan	49-457	MM
Hands Up	TLC	32-161	THM
Handy Man	Jones, Jimmy	5-170	SC
Handy Man	Presley, Elvis	43-243	PSJT
Handy Man	Taylor, James	11-345	DK
Handy Man	Taylor, James	6-431	MM
Hang In There Superman	Ketchum, Hal	4-399	SC
Hang On Sloopy	McCoy's	17-155	DK
Hang On Sloopy	McCoy's	6-138	MM
Hang On Sloopy	McCoys	35-52	CB
Hang On To Your Heart	Exile	17-15	DK
Hang On To Your Love	Sade	10-503	DA
Hangin' Around	Whites	8-705	SAV
Hangin' In	Tucker, Tanya	1-612	CB
Hangin' In	Tucker, Tanya	6-597	MM
Hangin' In	Tucker, Tanya	2-795	SC
Hangin' In & Hangin' On	Ball, David	7-328	MM
Hangin' In & Hangin' On	Ball, David	24-151	SC
Hangin' On	McCready, Rich	4-154	SC
Hangin' Tough	New Kids On Block	11-515	DK
Hanginaround	Counting Crows	18-701	CB
Hanginaround	Counting Crows	8-527	PHT
Hanginaround	Counting Crows	17-541	SC
Hanging By A Moment	Lifehouse	15-808	CB
Hanging By A Moment	Lifehouse	16-470	MH
Hanging By A Moment	Lifehouse	16-113	PRT
Hanging By A Moment	Lifehouse	18-557	TT
Hanging On The Telephone	Blondie	49-129	CB
Hanging Tough	New Kids On Block	31-110	CB
Hanging Tree the	Robbins, Marty	45-679	VHM
Hank	Williams, Hank Jr.	16-677	C2C
Hank	Wills, Mark	29-594	CB
Hank Williams Junior Junior	Coe, David Allan	18-321	CB
Hank Williams You Wrote My Life	Bandy, Moe	3-688	CB
Hanky Panky	James & Shondells	11-813	DK
Hanky Panky	James & Shondells	6-140	MM
Hanky Panky	Madonna	6-179	MM
Hanky Panky	Madonna	15-11	SC
Hannah Jane	Hootie & Blowfish	13-597	P
Hannah Jane	Hootie & Blowfish	4-689	SC

SONG TITLE	ARTIST	#	TYPE
Happening the	Ross, Diana	48-545	DK
Happening the	Supremes	14-885	DK
Happiest Girl In The Whole USA	Fargo, Donna	15-833	CB
Happiest Girl In The Whole USA	Fargo, Donna	13-388	P
Happiness Is A Warm Gun	Beatles	10-491	DA
Happiness Of Having You the	Pride, Charley	40-119	CB
Happy	Sister Hazel	5-184	SC
Happy	Williams, Pharrell	43-177	SF
Happy Anniversary	Little River Band	18-308	SC
Happy Birthday	Lynn, Loretta	47-629	CB
Happy Birthday (Short Vers)	Standard	35-45	CB
Happy Birthday Darlin'	Twitty, Conway	29-777	CB
Happy Birthday Darling	Twitty, Conway	4-767	SC
Happy Birthday Dear Heartache	Mandrell, Barbara	5-46	SC
Happy Birthday Sweet Sixteen	Sedaka, Neil	11-253	DK
Happy Birthday Sweet Sixteen	Sedaka, Neil	12-740	P
Happy Birthday Sweet Sixteen	Sedaka, Neil	9-165	SO
Happy Birthday To Me	Locklin, Hank	44-213	CB
Happy Birthday To You	Standard	11-585	DK
Happy Birthday To You	Standard	12-607	P
Happy Days	TV Themes	2-172	SC
Happy Days Are Here Again	Standard	35-21	CB
Happy Days Are Here Again	Standard	12-570	P
Happy Days Are Here Again	Streisand, Barbra	15-841	MM
Happy Ending	Presley, Elvis	25-769	MM
Happy Endings	Brice, Lee	36-560	CB
Happy Endings	Brice, Lee	49-38	SC
Happy Ever After	Brown, T. Graham	47-551	SC
Happy Ever After Love	Dr. Hook	47-52	ZM
Happy Girl	McBride, Martina	8-102	CB
Happy Girl	McBride, Martina	7-764	CHM
Happy Happy Birthday Baby	Tune Weavers	4-211	SC
Happy Happy Birthday Baby	Tune Weavers	30-777	SF
Happy Happy Birthday Darling	Milsap, Ronnie	47-272	CB
Happy Jack	Who	28-143	DK
Happy Jack	Who	19-731	LE
Happy New Year	Abba	19-81	MM
Happy People (Radio Vers)	Kelly, R.	49-531	SC
Happy Song the	Redding, Otis	47-359	LE
Happy State Of Mind	Anderson, Bill	20-789	CB
Happy Together	Turtles	17-67	DK
Happy Trails	Rogers, Roy	8-435	CB
Happy Trails	Rogers, Roy	2-166	SC

SONG TITLE	ARTIST	#	TYPE
Happy Trails	Rogers, Roy&Dale	12-116	DK
Happy Xmas - The War Is Over	Lennon, John	30-305	RS
Happy Xmas (The War Is Over)	Lennon, John	3-389	SC
Harbor Lights	Platters	16-803	DK
Harbor Lights	Platters	9-554	SAV
Harbor Lights	Scaggs, Boz	15-749	AMS
Hard Call To Make	Harter, J. Michael	18-136	ST
Hard Candy Christmas	Parton, Dolly	35-330	CB
Hard Day's Night a	Beatles	11-176	DK
Hard Day's Night a	Beatles	13-48	P
Hard Day's Night a	Beatles	7-519	SAV
Hard Days & Honky Tonk Nights	Conley, E.T.	47-776	SRK
Hard Habit To Break	Chicago	12-816	P
Hard Hat & A Hammer	Jackson, Alan	49-178	CB
Hard Headed Woman	Presley, Elvis	14-745	THM
Hard Headed Woman	Stevens, Cat	23-647	BS
Hard Headed Woman	Stevens, Cat	13-575	NU
Hard Knocks	Presley, Elvis	25-498	MM
Hard Livin'	Whitley, Keith	14-422	SC
Hard Luck Woman	Brooks, Garth	48-349	MM
Hard Luck Woman	Kiss	10-33	SC
Hard Man To Love	Fowler, Kevin	49-91	YBK
Hard Rock Bottom Of My Heart	Travis, Randy	1-404	CB
Hard Rock Bottom Of My Heart	Travis, Randy	26-549	DK
Hard Rock Bottom Of My Heart	Travis, Randy	12-437	P
Hard Rock Hallelujah	Lord!	30-711	SF
Hard Secret To Keep a	Chesnutt, Mark	23-120	CB
Hard Staying Sober	Lambert, Miranda	46-263	KV
Hard Sun	Vedder, Eddie	37-121	SC
Hard Times	Dalton, Lacy J.	5-627	SC
Hard Times (No One Knows)	Charles, Ray	46-572	CB
Hard To Be A Hippie	Nelson, Willie	45-328	KV
Hard To Be A Husband/Wife	Paisley & Wright	14-156	CB
Hard To Be A Husband/Wife	Paisley & Wright	14-789	ST
Hard To Be Humble	Davis, Mac	10-480	DA
Hard To Handle	Black Crowes	34-104	CB
Hard To Handle	Black Crowes	5-336	SC
Hard To Handle	Redding, Otis	47-356	LE
Hard To Hold On To	Mellencamp, John	45-421	OZP
Hard To Love	Brice, Lee	45-547	ASK
Hard Way the	Black, Clint	30-432	THM
Hard Way the	Carpenter, M C	6-306	MM
Hard Way the	Carpenter, M C	2-810	SC
Hard Way the	Carpenter, M C	15-156	THM
Hard Way the	Hill, Faith	15-682	CB
Hard Workin' Man	Brooks & Dunn	1-81	CB
Hard Workin' Man	Brooks & Dunn	6-315	MM
Harder Cards	Rogers, Kenny	16-704	ST
Harder They Come the	Cliff, Jimmy	46-633	HSW

SONG TITLE	ARTIST	#	TYPE
Harder They Come the	Cliff, Jimmy	12-702	P
Harder To Breathe	Maroon 5	35-294	CB
Harder To Breathe	Maroon 5	25-585	MM
Harder To Breathe	Maroon 5	32-323	THM
Harder To Breathe	Maroon 5	21-682	Z
Hardest Button To Button	White Stripes	23-185	PHM
Hardest Part the	Coldplay	30-275	SC
Hardest Part the	Coldplay	30-694	SF
Hardest Thing the	98 Degrees	29-174	MH
Hardest Thing the	98 Degrees	7-847	PHM
Hardest Thing the	98 Degrees	13-780	SGB
Hardest Thing the	98 Degrees	15-370	SKG
Hark The Herald Angels Sing	Robbins, Marty	48-23	CB
Hark The Herald Angels Sing	Underwood, Carrie	45-784	KV
Harlem Shuffle	Rolling Stones	16-868	DK
Harlem Shuffle	Rolling Stones	14-394	PT
Harold's Super Service	Haggard, Merle	46-17	SSK
Harper Valley PTA	Riley, Jeannie C.	16-846	DK
Harper Valley PTA	Riley, Jeannie C.	3-361	MH
Harper Valley PTA	Riley, Jeannie C.	9-462	SAV
Harper Valley PTA	Riley, Jeannie C.	2-130	SC
Has Anybody Seen Amy	Wiggins, J & A	17-240	NA
Has Anybody Seen Amy	Wiggins, J & A	2-484	SC
Has Anybody Seen My Gypsy Rose	Newton, Wayne	47-318	LE
Has Anybody Seen My Sweet Gypsy Ros	Orlando & Dawn	3-243	LG
Hashpipe	Weezer	16-380	SGB
Hasta Manana	Abba	19-82	MM
Hate That I Love You	Rihanna feat Ne-Yo	36-100	CB
Hate That I Love You	Rihanna w Ne-Yo	36-100	CB
Hate To Say I Told You So	Hives	18-437	CB
Hats Off To Larry	Del Shannon	6-647	MM
Hauled Off And Kissed Me	Holy, Steve	39-66	PHN
Haunted Heart	Kershaw, Sammy	20-406	MH
Haunted House - Halloween	Lewis, Jerry Lee	45-140	OZP
Haunted House - Halloween	Simmons, "Jumpin" Gene	45-117	SC
Haunted House Of Rock - Halloween	Whodini	45-139	GGZ
Havana	Eder, Linda	17-436	PS
Have A Cigar	Pink Floyd	20-98	SC
Have A Heart	Raitt, Bonnie	11-641	DK
Have A Heart	Raitt, Bonnie	10-772	JVC
Have A Little Faith	Houston, David	5-431	SC
Have A Little Faith In Me	Moore, Mandy	32-434	THM
Have A Nice Day	Stereophonics	25-79	MM
Have Fun Go Mad	Blair	5-272	SC
Have I Got A Deal For You	McEntire, Reba	1-811	CB
Have I Got A Deal For You	McEntire, Reba	17-299	NA
Have I Told You Lately	Autry, Gene	33-4	CB

SONG TITLE	ARTIST	#	TYPE
Have I Told You Lately	Morrison, Van	23-596	BS
Have I Told You Lately	Morrison, Van	15-724	SI
Have I Told You Lately	Reeves, Jim	44-227	EZC
Have I Told You Lately	Stewart, Rod	14-859	LE
Have I Told You Lately	Stewart, Rod	10-17	SC
Have I Told You Lately	Whittaker, Roger	13-591	PL
Have I Told You Lately That I Love	Ritter, Tex	20-712	CB
Have I Told You Lately That I Love	Stewart, Rod	25-599	MM
Have Mercy	Judds	1-137	CB
Have Mercy	Judds	11-707	DK
Have Mercy	Judds	12-470	P
Have Mercy	Judds	9-507	SAV
Have We Forgotten What Love Is	Bernard, Crystal	7-425	MM
Have We Forgotten What Love Is	Bernard, Crystal	4-616	SC
Have You Ever	Brandy	28-213	DK
Have You Ever Been In Love	Dion, Celine	34-158	CB
Have You Ever Been In Love	Dion, Celine	25-624	MM
Have You Ever Been In Love	Dion, Celine	19-15	PS
Have You Ever Been Lonely	Cline, Patsy	22-186	CB
Have You Ever Been Lonely	Cline, Patsy	13-319	P
Have You Ever Been Lonely	Reeves & Cline	3-161	CB
Have You Ever Been Lonely	Reeves & Cline	2-297	SC
Have You Ever Been Lonely	Tubb, Ernest	8-393	CB
Have You Ever Loved A Woman	Clapton, Eric	13-799	SGB
Have You Ever Really Loved a Woman	Adams, Bryan	23-443	CB
Have You Ever Really Loved a Woman	Adams, Bryan	14-877	SC
Have You Ever Seen The Rain	CCR	35-104	CB
Have You Ever Seen The Rain	CCR	11-465	DK
Have You Ever Seen The Rain	CCR	6-793	MM
Have You Ever Seen The Rain	CCR	12-865	P
Have You Ever Seen The Rain	CCR	5-353	SC
Have You Forgotten	Worley, Darryl	25-561	MM
Have You Forgotten	Worley, Darryl	19-3	ST
Have You Forgotten	Worley, Darryl	32-186	THM
Have You Forgotten - Patriotic	Worley, Darryl	34-407	CB
Have You Heard	Duprees	6-258	MM
Have You Never Been Mellow	Newton-John, Olivia	33-283	CB
Have You Never Been	Newton-John, Olivia	11-122	DK

99

SONG TITLE	ARTIST	#	TYPE
Mellow			
Have You Never Been Mellow	Newton-John, Olivia	4-751	SC
Have You Seen Her	Chi-Lites	16-565	P
Have You Seen Me Lately	Counting Crows	18-698	CB
Have Yourself a Merry Little Xmas	Carpenters	44-338	CB
Haven't Got Time For The Pain	Simon, Carly	12-703	P
Haven't Met You Yet	Buble, Michael	38-176	CB
Having A Party	Cooke, Sam	46-636	LE
Having A Party	Stewart, Rod	14-858	LE
Having My Baby	Anka, Paul	9-173	SO
Hawaii - Aloha Oe	Williams, Andy	15-399	NK
Hawaii - Blue Hawaii	Presley, Elvis	12-111	DK
Hawaii - E Lei Ka Lei Lei	Ho, Don	6-831	MM
Hawaii - Hawaiian Wedding Song	Ho, Don	6-834	MM
Hawaii - Honolulu City Lights	Beamer,Keola/Kapono	6-839	MM
Hawaii - I'll Remember	Ho, Don	6-836	MM
Hawaii - Ku'Uipo/Bora Bora	Ho, Don	6-838	MM
Hawaii - Lovely Hula Hands	Beamer,Keola/Kapono	6-833	MM
Hawaii - Lover's Prayer	Ho, Don	6-828	MM
Hawaii - Molokai	Ho, Don	6-827	MM
Hawaii - My Hawaii	Krush	6-832	MM
Hawaii - Naturally	Kalapana	6-840	MM
Hawaii - Pua Carnation	Ho, Don	6-837	MM
Hawaii - Sweet Someone	Ho, Don	6-835	MM
Hawaii - Tiny Bubbles	Ho, Don	6-826	MM
Hawaiian Sunset	Presley, Elvis	25-496	MM
Hawaiian War Chant	Ames Brothers	9-749	SAV
Hawaiian Wedding Song	Ho, Don	6-834	MM
Hawaiian Wedding Song	Presley, Elvis	14-771	THM
Haywire	Turner, Josh	44-296	BKD
Hazy Shade Of Winter	Bangles	46-471	LE
Hazy Shade Of Winter	Simon & Garfunkel	49-761	LG
He Ain't Country	King, Claude	47-923	SSK
He Ain't Heavy He's My Brother	Diamond, Neil	30-676	LE
He Ain't Heavy He's My Brother	Diamond, Neil	24-203	SC
He Ain't Heavy, He's My Brother	Hollies	12-321	DK
He Ain't Worth Missing	Keith, Toby	6-384	MM
He Believed	Tippin, Aaron	30-202	CB
He Called Me Baby	Cline, Patsy	22-187	CB
He Called Me Baby	Cline, Patsy	6-729	MM
He Can Only Hold Her	Winehouse, Amy	49-58	ZVS
He Didn't Have To Be	Paisley, Brad	19-202	CB
He Didn't Have to Be	Paisley, Brad	19-228	SC
He Didn't Have To Be	Paisley, Brad	22-377	ST
He Don't Love You Like I Love You	Orlando & Dawn	35-132	CB
He Don't Love You Like I Love You	Orlando & Dawn	11-523	DK

SONG TITLE	ARTIST	#	TYPE
He Drinks Tequila	Kershaw & Morgan	30-31	CB
He Drinks Tequila	Kershaw & Morgan	14-838	ST
He Drinks Tequila	Kershaw & Morgan	16-267	TT
He Drinks Tequila - duet	Kershaw & Morgan	30-31	CB
He Gets That From Me	McEntire, Reba	22-64	CB
He Gets That From Me	McEntire, Reba	20-503	ST
He Got You	Milsap, Ronnie	47-273	CB
He Is Your Brother	Abba	46-220	FUN
He Keeps Me In One Piece	Reeves, Julie	8-965	CB
He Left A Lot To Be Desired	Ricochet	7-660	CHM
He Left A Lot To Be Desired	Ricochet	10-103	SC
He Loves Her All The Way	Wynette, Tammy	6-767	MM
He Loves Me	Scott, Jill	25-691	MM
He Loves U Not	Dream	33-447	CB
He Loves U Not	Dream	16-122	PRT
He Loves U Not	Dream	14-43	THM
He Oughta Know That By Now	Womack, Lee Ann	23-119	CB
He Oughta Know That By Now	Womack, Lee Ann	23-390	SC
He Says The Same Things To Me	Davis, Skeeter	43-335	CB
He Stopped Loving Her Today	Jones, George	12-33	DK
He Stopped Loving Her Today	Jones, George	13-363	P
He Stopped Loving Her Today	Jones, George	9-515	SAV
He Talks To Me	Morgan, Lorrie	1-335	CB
He Talks To Me	Morgan, Lorrie	19-293	MH
He Talks To Me	Morgan, Lorrie	6-622	MM
He Talks To Me	Morgan, Lorrie	9-476	SAV
He Thinks He'll Keep Her	Carpenter, M C	1-424	CB
He Thinks He'll Keep Her	Carpenter, M C	6-452	MM
He Thinks He'll Keep Her	Carpenter, M C	2-816	SC
He Thinks He'll Keep Her	Carpenter, M C	15-152	THM
He Thinks I Still Care	Murray, Anne	11-13	PL
He Thinks I Still Care	Murray, Anne	4-790	SC
He Touched Me	Streisand, Barbra	49-558	LG
He Walked On Water	Travis, Randy	1-405	CB
He Walked On Water	Travis, Randy	20-397	MH
He Walked On Water	Travis, Randy	2-362	SC
He Was A Friend Of Mine	Nelson, Willie	47-743	SRK
He Wasn't Man Enough	Braxton, Toni	14-181	CB
He Wasn't Man Enough	Braxton, Toni	14-5	PHM
He Wasn't Man Enough	Braxton, Toni	14-471	SC
He Wasn't Man Enough	Braxton, Toni	18-516	TT
He Went To Paris	Buffett, Jimmy	46-142	SC
He Will She Knows	Rogers, Kenny	14-911	CB
He Will She Knows	Rogers, Kenny	22-563	ST
He Won't Go	Adele	40-31	KV
He Would Be Sixteen	Wright, Michelle	6-214	MM
He'd Never Seen Julie Cry	Messina, Jo Dee	10-87	SC

SONG TITLE	ARTIST	#	TYPE
He'll Be Back	Womack, Lee Ann	48-482	CKC
He'll Have To Go	Presley, Elvis	25-329	MM
He'll Have To Go	Reeves, Jim	15-831	CB
He'll Have To Go	Reeves, Jim	40-128	CK
He'll Have To Go	Reeves, Jim	3-839	LG
He'll Have To Go	Reeves, Jim	13-370	P
He'll Have To Go	Reeves, Jim	9-610	SAV
He'll Have To Stay	Smith, Connie	49-298	KST
He's A Good Ol' Boy	Wright, Chely	6-672	MM
He's A Good Ol' Boy	Wright, Chely	17-213	NA
He's A Good Ol' Boy	Wright, Chely	3-48	SC
He's A Heartache	Fricke, Janie	9-627	SAV
He's A Heartache Lookin' For A	Fricke, Janie	13-519	P
He's A Heartache Lookin' For A...	Fricke, Janie	5-21	SC
He's A Mighty Good Friend - gospel	Fairchild, Barbara	47-84	VHG
He's A Rebel	Crystals	11-200	DK
He's A Rebel	Crystals	19-620	MH
He's A Rebel	Crystals	7-42	MM
He's A Rebel	Crystals	9-803	SAV
He's A Rebel	Crystals	4-11	SC
He's Alive	Parton, Dolly	24-5	SC
He's Back And I'm Blue	Desert Rose Band	5-759	SC
He's Funny That Way	Holiday, Billie	15-486	MM
He's Got The Whole World	Kids	33-450	CB
He's Got You	Brooks & Dunn	22-666	ST
He's In Town	Rockin' Berries	10-617	SF
He's My Rock	Lee, Brenda	30-332	CB
He's My Weakness	Reeves, Ronna	3-39	SC
He's On The Way Home	Toliver, Tony	4-629	SC
He's So Fine	Chiffons	10-333	KC
He's Sure The Boy I Love	Crystals	45-593	OZP
He's Sure The Boy I Love - duet	Midler & Love	45-359	KV
He's The Wizard	The Wiz	49-436	SDK
Head Full Of Dreams	Coldplay	48-415	BKD
Head On Collision	New Found Glory	32-106	THM
Head Over Boots	Pardi, Jon	47-399	BKD
Head Over Boots (Inst)	Pardi, Jon	49-417	BKD
Head Over Feet	Morrisette, Alanis	24-174	SC
Head Over Heels	Abba	19-78	MM
Head Over Heels	Go-Go's	20-86	SC
Head Over Heels	Tears For Fears	29-10	MH
Head Shoulders Knees & Toes	Kids	49-351	CB
Head To Toe	Lisa Lisa & Cult J	11-317	DK
Headache Tomorrow, Heartache Tonight	Gilley, Mickey	22-216	CB
Headache Tomorrow, Heartache Tonight	Gilley, Mickey	16-173	THM
Headed For The Future	Diamond, Neil	30-501	THM
Headful Of Ghosts	Bush	30-649	THM
Heads Carolina Tails California	Messina, Jo Dee	4-135	SC

SONG TITLE	ARTIST	#	TYPE
Headstrong	Trapt	19-598	CB
Heal The World	Jackson, Michael	6-105	MM
Healing	Judd, W & English	24-80	SC
Healing - duet	Judd, W & English, M	48-322	SC
Healing Hands	Great Plains	4-432	SC
Healing Hands	John, Elton	2-381	SC
Healing Kind the	Seals, Dan	4-18	SC
Hear Me In The Harmony	Connick, Harry Jr.	24-369	SC
Heard It In A Love Song	Marshall Tucker Ban	2-528	SC
Heard It Through The Grapevine	CCR	48-361	THM
Heart & Soul	Standard	27-462	DK
Heart And Soul	Cleftones	48-390	KRG
Heart And Soul	Four Aces	4-358	SC
Heart And Soul	Lewis & The News	11-101	DK
Heart And Soul	Lewis, Huey	48-572	DK
Heart Attack	Newton-John, Olivia	5-680	SC
Heart Full Of Love	Arnold, Eddy	19-841	CB
Heart Full Of Soul	Yardbirds	20-66	SC
Heart Half Empty	Herndon & Bentley	7-146	MM
Heart Half Empty	Herndon & Bentley	4-100	SC
Heart Healer	Tillis, Mel	19-459	CB
Heart Hold On	Buffalo Club	8-146	CB
Heart Hold On	Buffalo Club	22-662	ST
Heart Is A Lonely Hunter	McEntire, Reba	6-717	MM
Heart Is A Lonely Hunter	McEntire, Reba	2-642	SC
Heart Is A Lonely Hunter	McEntire, Reba	22-864	ST
Heart Is Right	Carter, Carlene	49-759	KRG
Heart Like Mine	Lambert, Miranda	37-223	CB
Heart Of A Lonely Girl	Bentley, Dierks	45-165	PHN
Heart Of Dixie	Bradbery, Danielle	43-90	HM
Heart Of Glass	Blondie	17-151	DK
Heart Of Gold	Young, Neil	17-68	DK
Heart Of Gold	Young, Neil	15-168	MH
Heart Of Gold	Young, Neil	5-138	SC
Heart Of Rock & Roll	Lewis & The News	16-811	DK
Heart Of Rock N Roll	Lewis & The News	35-171	CB
Heart Of Rome	Presley, Elvis	25-745	MM
Heart Of Stone	Cher	15-130	SGB
Heart Of Stone	Yoakam, Dwight	4-898	SC
Heart Of The Matter	Henley, Don	48-150	LE
Heart Of The Night	Poco	49-267	SC
Heart Over Mind	Morgan, Lorrie	6-674	MM
Heart Over Mind	Morgan, Lorrie	3-46	SC
Heart Over Mind	Tillis, Mel	19-452	CB
Heart Shaped Box	Nirvana	24-145	SC
Heart To Heart	Denver, John	15-618	THM
Heart To Heart Talk	Wills, Bob	20-694	CB
Heart Trouble	McBride, Martina	1-379	CB
Heart Trouble	McBride, Martina	2-541	SC
Heart Trouble	Wariner, Steve	5-326	SC
Heart With A 4-Wheel Drive	4 Runner	6-854	MM
Heart Won't Lie the	McEntire & Gill	1-806	CB
Heart Won't Lie the	McEntire & Gill	12-402	P
Heart Won't Lie the	McEntire & Gill	2-301	SC

101

SONG TITLE	ARTIST	#	TYPE
Heart Won't Lie the	McEntire, Reba	6-129	MM
Heart You Break May Be Your Own the	Cline, Patsy	45-488	CB
Heartache	Bogguss, Suzy	1-562	CB
Heartache	Orbison, Roy	47-342	DCK
Heartache Avenue	Maisonettes	30-746	SF
Heartache Tonight	Eagles	7-551	BS
Heartache Tonight	Eagles	6-430	MM
Heartache Tonight	Eagles	2-259	SC
Heartaches	Cline, Patsy	3-183	CB
Heartaches By The Number	Price, Ray	8-274	CB
Heartaches By The Number	Price, Ray	12-301	DK
Heartaches By The Number	Price, Ray	17-301	NA
Heartaches By The Number	Price, Ray	8-677	SAV
Heartaches By The Number	Yoakam, Dwight	49-699	KV
Heartbeat	Holly, Buddy	3-224	LG
Heartbeat	Underwood, Carrie	45-463	BKD
Heartbeat In the Darkness	Williams, Don	5-197	SC
Heartbeats Accelerating	Ronstadt, Linda	16-361	CB
Heartbreak Highway	Whitley, Keith	49-497	CB
Heartbreak Hill	Harris, EmmyLou	1-228	CB
Heartbreak Hotel	Fargo, Donna	8-807	CB
Heartbreak Hotel	Houston, Whitney	7-806	PHT
Heartbreak Hotel	Houston, Whitney	13-673	SGB
Heartbreak Hotel	Houston,Feat,Evan	7-817	PHM
Heartbreak Hotel	Houston/Evans/Price	28-191	DK
Heartbreak Hotel	Presley, Elvis	11-604	DK
Heartbreak Hotel	Presley, Elvis	2-610	SC
Heartbreak Radio	Orbison, Roy	47-348	RDK
Heartbreak Town	Dixie Chicks	8-906	CB
Heartbreak Town	Dixie Chicks	30-601	RS
Heartbreak Town	Dixie Chicks	15-599	ST
Heartbreak USA	Wells, Kitty	8-778	CB
Heartbreak USA	Wells, Kitty	4-748	SC
Heartbreak Woman	Presley, Elvis	14-746	THM
Heartbreaker	Benatar, Pat	12-769	P
Heartbreaker	Benatar, Pat	4-528	SC
Heartbreaker	Parton, Dolly	8-540	CB
Heartbreaker	Parton, Dolly	13-493	P
Heartbreaker	Warwick, Dionne	12-373	DK
Heartbroke	Skaggs, Ricky	8-202	CB
Heartbroke	Skaggs, Ricky	8-701	SAV
Heartbroke Every Day	Lonestar	22-402	CHM
Heartbroke Every Day	Lonestar	7-396	MM
Heartbroke Out Of My Mind	Brooks & Dunn	1-83	CB
Heartland	Strait, George	1-250	CB
Heartland	Strait, George	20-400	MH
Heartland	Strait, George	6-125	MM
Heartland	Strait, George	2-803	SC
Heartless	West, Kanye	36-267	PHM

SONG TITLE	ARTIST	#	TYPE
Heartlight	Diamond, Neil	30-690	LE
Heartlight	Diamond, Neil	24-696	SC
Hearts Are Gonna Roll	Ketchum, Hal	12-466	P
Hearts Are Gonna Roll	Ketchum, Hal	2-341	SC
Hearts Aren't Made To Break	Greenwood, Lee	20-19	SC
Hearts Desire	Parnell, Lee Roy	49-281	SC
Hearts Fall	McCain, Edwin	18-407	MM
Hearts In Armor	Yearwood, Trisha	48-339	SC
Hearts Of Stone	Fontane Sisters	33-234	CB
Hearts Of Stone	Fontane Sisters	5-78	SC
Hearts On Fire	Cafferty, John	30-768	SF
Hearts On Fire	Cafferty, John	45-161	SFM
Hearts On Fire	Rabbitt, Eddie	14-320	SC
Heartspark Dollar Sign	Everclear	4-331	SC
Heat Is On the	Frey, Glenn	26-142	DK
Heat Is On the	Frey, Glenn	5-111	SC
Heat It Up	98 Degrees	15-378	SKG
Heat Of The Moment	Asia	4-321	SC
Heat Of The Night	Adams, Bryan	23-438	CB
Heat Wave	Martha & Vandellas	16-743	DK
Heat Wave	Martha & Vandellas	12-633	P
Heat Wave	Ronstadt, Linda	22-924	SC
Heather Honey	Roe, Tommy	48-111	CB
Heather's Wail	Herndon, Ty	16-106	ST
Heatwave (Love Is Like A)	Collins, Phil	44-32	SB
Heaven	Adams, Bryan	23-436	CB
Heaven	Adams, Bryan	11-154	DK
Heaven	Adams, Bryan	16-549	P
Heaven	Live	19-649	CB
Heaven	Live	25-628	MM
Heaven	Live	32-397	THM
Heaven	Los Lonely Boys	22-67	CB
Heaven	Owen, Jake	49-186	SBI
Heaven	Warrant	24-207	SC
Heaven (Disco Version)	DJ Sammy&Yanou	21-724	TT
Heaven Bound	Petrone, Shawna	8-737	CB
Heaven Bound	Shenandoah	1-495	CB
Heaven Bound	Shenandoah	7-28	MM
Heaven Can Wait	Meat Loaf	6-488	MM
Heaven Can Wait	Meat Loaf	30-765	SF
Heaven Help Me	Judd, Wynonna	19-532	ST
Heaven Help Me	Wynonna	32-416	THM
Heaven Help My Heart	Judd, Wynonna	1-656	CB
Heaven Help My Heart	Judd, Wynonna	7-243	MM
Heaven In My Woman's Eyes	Byrd, Tracy	20-109	CB
Heaven In My Woman's Eyes	Byrd, Tracy	4-91	SC
Heaven Is A Place On Earth	Carlisle, Belinda	18-239	DK
Heaven Is A Place On Earth	Carlisle, Belinda	16-547	P
Heaven Knows	Grass Roots	45-157	SC
Heaven Must Be Missing An Angel	Tavares	24-338	SC
Heaven Only Knows	Harris, EmmyLou	8-827	CB

SONG TITLE	ARTIST	#	TYPE
Heaven Only Knows	Harris, EmmyLou	6-748	MM
Heaven Says Hello	James, Sonny	19-472	CB
Heaven Says Hello	James, Sonny	5-694	SC
Heaven Sent	Cole, Keyshia	36-534	CB
Heaven Sent Me You	Montgomery, J M	4-415	SC
Heaven's Just A Sin Away	Kendalls	3-593	SC
Heaven's Just A Sin Away	Willis, Kelly	6-531	MM
Heaven's What I Feel	Estefan, Gloria	23-572	MM
Heavenly Bodies	Conley, Earl Thomas	29-701	SC
Heavenly Sunshine	Husky, Ferlin	22-271	CB
Heavy Is The Head	Zac Brown Band & Cornell	46-78	KV
Heavy Liftin'	Shelton, Blake	25-611	MM
Heavy Liftin'	Shelton, Blake	19-84	ST
Heavy Things	Phish	15-787	THM
Hell	Squirrel Nut Zipper	10-92	SC
Hell	Squirrel Nut Zipper	13-689	SGB
Hell and High Water	Brown, T. Graham	20-286	SC
Hell Is For Children	Benatar, Pat	9-376	AH
Hell Is For Children	Benatar, Pat	9-10	MH
Hell Is For Children	Benatar, Pat	19-548	SC
Hell Is For Children	Benatar, Pat	19-151	SGB
Hell No	Keith, Toby	38-163	SC
Hell Of A Night	Lynch, Dustin	47-930	BKD
Hell On Heels	Pistol Annie's	38-207	AS
Hell On The Heart	Church, Eric	46-619	CB
Hell Raiser - Halloween	Sweet	45-116	SF
Hell Raisin' Heat Of The Summer	Florida Georgia Line	47-94	ASK
Hell Song the	Sum 41	32-216	THM
Hell Yeah	Ginuwine w Baby	32-162	THM
Hell Yeah	Montgomery Gentry	34-415	CB
Hell Yeah	Montgomery Gentry	25-696	MM
Hell Yeah	Montgomery Gentry	19-265	ST
Hell Yeah	Montgomery Gentry	32-375	THM
Hell Yeah I Like Beer	Fowler, Kevin	47-500	JRM
Hella Good	No Doubt	18-348	CB
Hella Good	No Doubt	18-411	MM
Hello	Adele	45-291	DCK
Hello	Adele	49-128	SBI
Hello	Anka, Paul	49-246	DFK
Hello	Richie, Lionel	11-536	DK
Hello	Richie, Lionel	10-384	LE
Hello	Richie, Lionel	13-201	P
Hello	Sugarland	30-233	RS
Hello Again	Diamond, Neil	7-535	AH
Hello Again	Diamond, Neil	24-702	SC
Hello Again	Diamond, Neil	30-502	THM
Hello Beautiful	Jonas Brothers	36-539	WD
Hello Cruel World	Ducas, George	2-768	SC
Hello Darlin'	Twitty, Conway	1-151	CB
Hello Darlin'	Twitty, Conway	26-373	DK
Hello Darlin'	Twitty, Conway	13-462	P
Hello Detroit	Davis, Sammy Jr.	45-608	OZP
Hello Dolly	Armstrong, Louis	12-107	DK

SONG TITLE	ARTIST	#	TYPE
Hello Dolly	Armstrong, Louis	12-510	P
Hello Dolly	Streisand, Barbra	49-572	PS
Hello God	Haggard, Marty	4-627	SC
Hello God	Parton, Dolly	32-46	THM
Hello Goodbye	Beatles	16-726	DK
Hello Goodbye	Beatles	13-95	P
Hello Goodbye	Beatles	9-644	SAV
Hello Happiness	Drifters	45-901	SF
Hello Hello I'm Back Again	Glitter, Gary	49-147	SF
Hello Hooray	Alice Cooper	16-452	SGB
Hello I Love You	Doors	35-65	CB
Hello I Love You	Doors	3-14	SC
Hello I Love You	Doors	18-643	SO
Hello In There	Prine, John	23-529	CB
Hello It's Me	Rundgren, Todd	11-341	DK
Hello Josephine	Domino, Fats	44-110	KV
Hello L-O-V-E	Montgomery, J M	7-863	CHT
Hello L-O-V-E	Montgomery, J M	22-740	ST
Hello Love	Snow, Hank	22-131	CB
Hello Love	Snow, Hank	5-561	SC
Hello Mary Lou	Nelson, Ricky	21-698	CB
Hello Mary Lou	Nelson, Ricky	12-135	DK
Hello Mary Lou	Nelson, Ricky	9-480	SAV
Hello Mary Lou	Nelson, Ricky	10-509	SF
Hello Mr. Heartache	Dixie Chicks	20-213	CB
Hello Mr. Heartache	Dixie Chicks	30-602	RS
Hello Muddah Hello Faddah	Sherman, Allen	6-513	MM
Hello Muddah Hello Faddah	Sherman, Allen	5-638	SC
Hello Stranger	Lewis, Barbara	25-168	MM
Hello Summertime	Goldsboro, Bobby	45-879	VH
Hello Trouble	Desert Rose Band	9-497	SAV
Hello Trouble Come On In	Owens, Buck	46-107	CB
Hello Walls	Young, Faron	20-736	CB
Hello Walls	Young, Faron	17-298	NA
Hello Walls	Young, Faron	13-492	P
Hello Walls	Young, Faron	8-632	SAV
Hello World	Lady Antebellum	37-232	CB
Hells Bells	AC/DC	13-743	SGB
Helluva Life	Ballard, Frankie	43-16	KCDC
Help	Beatles	16-760	DK
Help	Beatles	15-489	SC
Help Is On The Way	Little River Band	18-307	SC
Help Me	Mitchell, Joni	9-330	AG
Help Me	Mitchell, Joni	2-787	SC
Help Me Hold On	Tritt, Travis	1-666	CB
Help Me Hold On	Tritt, Travis	11-717	DK
Help Me Make It Through The Night	Baez, Joan	46-459	KV
Help Me Make It Through The Night	Kristofferson, Kris	45-208	PT
Help Me Make It Through The Night	McBride, Martina	29-37	CB
Help Me Make It Through	Smith, Sammi	17-154	DK

103

SONG TITLE	ARTIST	#	TYPE
The Night			
Help Me Make It Through The Night	Smith, Sammi	9-594	SAV
Help Me Make It Thru The Yard	Pinkard & Bowden	21-543	SC
Help Me Rhonda	Beach Boys	5-502	BS
Help Me Rhonda	Beach Boys	11-233	DK
Help Me Understand	Adkins, Trace	25-194	MM
Help Me Understand	Adkins, Trace	16-331	ST
Help Pour Out The Rain	Jewell, Buddy	34-402	CB
Help Pour Out The Rain	Jewell, Buddy	25-638	MM
Help Pour Out The Rain	Jewell, Buddy	19-70	ST
Help Pour Out The Rain	Jewell, Buddy	32-296	THM
Help Somebody	Van Zant	22-332	CB
Help Stamp Out Lonliness	Jackson, Stonewall	49-284	BFK
Help Yourself	Jones, Tom	15-488	MM
Help!	Beatles	35-53	CB
Helping Me Get Over You	Tritt & White	7-670	CHM
Helping Me Get Over You	Tritt & White	4-840	SC
Helpless	Lang, k.d.	47-169	PHR
Helplessly Hopelessly	Andrews, Jessica	29-352	CB
Helplessly Hopelessly	Andrews, Jessica	15-186	ST
Helplessly Hopelessly - WN	Crosby Stills & Nash	48-59	SC
Helter Skelter - Halloween	Beatles	45-120	SC
Hemmorage In My Hands	Fuel	35-245	CB
Hemmorage In My Hands	Fuel	15-428	PHM
Hemmorage In My Hands	Fuel	18-558	TT
Henry Cartrights Prayer & Produce	Tomlinson, Trent	37-54	CB
Her	Tippin, Aaron	22-437	ST
Her Diamonds	Thomas, Rob	36-296	PHM
Her Eyes	Monahan, Pat	49-891	SC
Her Man	Allan, Gary	4-424	SC
Her Name Is ...	Jones, George	14-253	SC
Her Royal Majesty	Darren, James	14-458	SC
Her Strut	Seger, Bob	43-210	SC
Her Town Too	Taylor, James	45-537	RSZ
Here And Now	Letters To Cleo	24-750	SC
Here And Now	Vandross, Luther	28-107	DK
Here And Now	Vandross, Luther	6-437	MM
Here And Now	Vandross, Luther	13-205	P
Here And Now	Vandross, Luther	2-276	SC
Here By Me	3 Doors Down	47-653	CB
Here Come The Reindeer - xmas	Wiggles	45-238	WIG
Here Come Those Tears Again	Browne, Jackson	23-616	BS
Here Come Those Tears Again	Browne, Jackson	7-94	MM
Here Comes Goodbye	Rascal Flatts	48-709	BKD
Here Comes Heaven	Arnold, Eddy	19-43	CB

SONG TITLE	ARTIST	#	TYPE
Here Comes My Baby	Mavericks	5-831	SC
Here Comes My Baby	West, Dottie	33-22	CB
Here Comes My Baby	West, Dottie	8-383	CB
Here Comes My Baby Back Again	Price, Ray	47-790	SRK
Here Comes My Girl	Petty & Heartbreake	13-17	P
Here Comes Santa Claus	Autry, Gene	45-661	KKS
Here Comes Summer	LoCash Cowboys	49-528	CB
Here Comes That Feeling	Lee, Brenda	45-908	EZ
Here Comes That Rainy Day Feeling	Dave Clark Five	3-858	SC
Here Comes That Song Again	Orbison, Roy	38-62	AT
Here Comes The Freedom Train	Haggard, Merle	8-456	CB
Here Comes The Hotstepper	Ini Kamoze	2-724	SC
Here Comes The Hurt Again	Gilley, Mickey	5-870	SC
Here Comes The Night	Morrison, Van	23-602	BS
Here Comes The Night	Morrison, Van	15-729	SI
Here Comes The Night	Them	10-574	SF
Here Comes The Rain	Mavericks	7-144	MM
Here Comes The Rain Again	Eurythmics	13-294	P
Here Comes The Rain Again	Lennox, Annie	17-724	PS
Here Comes The Sun	Beatles	33-264	CB
Here Comes The Sun	Beatles	7-520	SAV
Here Comes The Sun	Havens, Richie	3-620	SC
Here Comes The Thunder	Hicks, Tim	47-509	DCK
Here Comes Trouble Again	Willis, Bruce	49-726	HGK
Here For A Good Time	Strait, George	38-86	AT
Here For The Party	Wilson, Gretchen	35-446	CB
Here For The Party	Wilson, Gretchen	20-443	ST
Here I Am	Adams, Bryan	18-418	MM
Here I Am	Loveless, Patty	1-724	CB
Here I Am	Loveless, Patty	17-270	NA
Here I Am	Loveless, Patty	2-547	SC
Here I Am (Just When I)	Air Supply	46-394	SC
Here I Am Again	Lynn, Loretta	48-250	CB
Here I Am Come And Take Me	UB40	12-20	DK
Here I Am I'm Drunk Again	Bandy, Moe	19-510	CB
Here I Go Again	Hollies	17-86	DK
Here I Go Again	Hollies	10-646	SF
Here I Go Again	Morgan, Lorrie	14-695	CB
Here I Go Again	Morgan, Lorrie	5-723	SC
Here I Go Again	Whitesnake	13-37	P
Here In Frisco	Haggard, Merle	49-880	DCK
Here In My Heart	Martino, Al	4-191	SC
Here In The Real World	Jackson, Alan	14-678	CB
Here Is Gone	Goo Goo Dolls	34-149	CB
Here Is Gone	Goo Goo Dolls	25-199	MM
Here There And	Beatles	11-108	DK

SONG TITLE	ARTIST	#	TYPE
Everywhere			
Here There And Everywhere	Beatles	7-514	SAV
Here There and Everywhere	Dion, Celine	14-193	CB
Here There And Everywhere	Dion, Celine	16-218	MM
Here There And Everywhere	Lettermen	48-539	PIX
Here We Are	Alabama	4-443	BS
Here We Are	Alabama	1-16	CB
Here We Are	Alabama	12-475	P
Here We Are	Estefan, Gloria	17-744	PT
Here We Go	N'Sync	15-782	BS
Here We Go Again	Charles, Ray	4-246	SC
Here We Go Again	Franklin, Aretha	36-163	JT
Here We Go Again	Lovato, Demi	36-23	PT
Here With Me	Dido	18-517	TT
Here Without You	3 Doors Down	20-222	MM
Here Without You	3 Doors Down	32-365	THM
Here Without You	Boyce Avenue	46-59	KV
Here You Come Again	Parton, Dolly	8-537	CB
Here You Come Again	Parton, Dolly	11-291	DK
Here You Come Again	Parton, Dolly	12-681	P
Here You Come Again	Parton, Dolly	9-600	SAV
Here's A Quarter Call Someone Who	Tritt, Travis	1-667	CB
Here's A Quarter Call Someone Who	Tritt, Travis	26-288	DK
Here's A Quarter Call Someone Who	Tritt, Travis	6-184	MM
Here's A Quarter Call Someone Who	Tritt, Travis	13-380	P
Here's Some Love	Tucker, Tanya	1-606	CB
Here's Some Love	Tucker, Tanya	9-583	SAV
Here's Some Love	Tucker, Tanya	14-262	SC
Here's That Rainy Day	Sinatra, Frank	15-490	SGB
Here's That Rainy Day	Streisand, Barbra	49-597	PS
Here's To Life	Streisand, Barbra	49-598	PS
Here's To The Good Times	Florida Georgia Line	45-154	ASK
Here's To The Night	Eve 6	18-559	TT
Here's To You	Rascal Flatts	23-278	CB
Here's Your Sign	Engvall & Tritt	14-648	CB
Here's A Quarter Call Someone Who	Tritt, Travis	9-488	SAV
Hero	Carey, Mariah	19-571	MH
Hero	Carey, Mariah	6-406	MM
Hero	Carey, Mariah	9-268	SC
Hero	Eder, Linda	17-766	PS
Hero	Iglesias, Enrique	33-398	CB
Hero	Iglesias, Enrique	16-301	PHM
Hero	Kroeger & Scott	18-217	CB
Hero	Kroeger & Scott	18-409	MM
Hero (Fast Version)	Iglesias, Enrique	25-21	MM
Hero Of The Day	Metallica	47-252	AH
Hero Takes A Fall	Bangles	46-472	SF
Hero/Heroine	Boys Like Girls	37-143	SC

SONG TITLE	ARTIST	#	TYPE
Heroes	Overstreet, Paul	29-770	CB
Heroes	Wallflowers	16-231	PHM
Heroes And Friends	Travis, Randy	20-588	CB
Heroes And Friends	Travis, Randy	3-646	SC
Heroes And Villians	Beach Boys	46-500	SC
Hey	Iglesias, Julio	47-561	MM
Hey 19	Steely Dan	15-383	RS
Hey Baby	Cannel, Bruce	6-154	MM
Hey Baby	Channel, Bruce	14-348	SC
Hey Baby	No Doubt	33-401	CB
Hey Baby	Nugent, Ted	10-482	DA
Hey Baby	Nugent, Ted	10-740	JVC
Hey Baby (Drop It To the Floor)	Pitbull w T-Pain	40-14	PHM
Hey Baby Que Paso	Texas Tornados	44-78	KV
Hey Baby They're Playing Our Song	Buckinghams	20-34	SC
Hey Bartender	Blues Brothers	20-142	KB
Hey Bartender	Blues Brothers	19-804	SGB
Hey Bartender	Blues Brothers	29-161	ZM
Hey Bartender	Lee, Johnny	2-408	SC
Hey Big Spender	Sweet Charity	15-492	MM
Hey Cinderella	Bogguss, Suzy	1-565	CB
Hey Cinderella	Bogguss, Suzy	6-454	MM
Hey Cinderella	Bogguss, Suzy	2-96	SC
Hey Girl	Currington, Billy	40-57	ASK
Hey Girl	Legend, John w Estelle	38-265	PHM
Hey Girls This Is Earl I Didn't Die	Craft, Paul "Earl"	14-159	CB
Hey Good Lookin'	Buffett, Jimmy	46-293	CB
Hey Good Lookin'	Buffett/Black/Chesn	20-395	ST
Hey Good Lookin'	Williams, Hank Sr.	16-752	DK
Hey Good Lookin'	Williams, Hank Sr.	7-156	MM
Hey Good Lookin'	Williams, Hank Sr.	13-434	P
Hey Good Lookin'	Williams, Hank Sr.	8-637	SAV
Hey Hey We're The Monkees	Monkees	35-59	CB
Hey Hey We're The Monkees	Monkees	27-403	DK
Hey Hey We're The Monkees	Monkees	15-491	MM
Hey Jealous Lover	Sinatra, Frank	49-503	MM
Hey Jealousy	Gin Blossoms	34-58	CB
Hey Jealousy	Gin Blossoms	13-236	P
Hey Joe	Hendrix, Jimi	11-667	DK
Hey Joe	Smith, Carl	22-114	CB
Hey Joe	Smith, Carl	5-852	SC
Hey Joe Hey Moe	Bandy & Stanpley	19-509	CB
Hey Joe Hey Moe - duet	Bandy & Stampley	34-245	CB
Hey Jude	Beatles	16-830	DK
Hey Jude	Presley, Elvis	25-760	MM
Hey Leonardo	Blessed Union/Soul	7-893	PHT
Hey Little Cobra	Rip Chords	3-548	SC
Hey Little Girl	Clark, Dee	9-734	SAV
Hey Little Girl	Presley, Elvis	43-244	PSJT
Hey Little Girl	Professor Longhair	17-319	SS
Hey Little Girl	Syndicate of Sound	10-492	DA

SONG TITLE	ARTIST	#	TYPE
Hey Little Girl	Syndicate of Sound	10-649	SF
Hey Little One	Campbell, Glen	47-803	SRK
Hey Loretta	Lynn, Loretta	5-566	SC
Hey Lover	LL Cool J	4-681	SC
Hey Ma	Cam'ron & Juelz	25-460	MM
Hey Man Nice Shot	Filter	5-742	SC
Hey Man Nice Shot (Album Version)	Filter	21-762	SC
Hey Mr. Cottonpicker	Ford, Tenn Ernie	8-432	CB
Hey Mr. Cottonpicker	Ford, Tenn Ernie	18-618	PS
Hey Mr. DJ	Backstreet Boys	30-417	THM
Hey Mr. DJ (Keep Playing...)	Backstreet Boys	18-705	MM
Hey Mr. President	Warren Brothers	19-51	ST
Hey Mr. President	Warren Brothers	32-231	THM
Hey Pachuco	Royal Crown Revue	13-691	SGB
Hey Paula	Paul & Paula	11-529	DK
Hey Paula	Paul & Paula	2-840	SC
Hey Porter	Cash, Johnny	29-731	CB
Hey Pretty Girl	Moore, Kip	44-330	SSC
Hey Soul Sister	Train	37-316	PHM
Hey Stoopid	Alice Cooper	21-779	SC
Hey There	Davis, Sammy Jr.	7-193	MM
Hey There	Davis, Sammy Jr.	10-603	SF
Hey There	Grace, Stephanie	39-56	PHN
Hey There Delilah	Plain White T's	48-599	DK
Hey There Lonely Boy	Ruby & Romantics	7-38	MM
Hey There Lonely Girl	Holman, Eddie	35-73	CB
Hey There Lonely Girl	Holman, Eddie	26-104	DK
Hey Tonight	CCR	5-357	SC
Hey Ya!	Outkast	20-528	CB
Hey Ya!	Outkast	20-231	MM
Hey You	BTO	46-540	CB
Hey You	Pink Floyd	5-881	SC
Hi Dee Ho That Old Sweet Roll	Blood Sweat &Tears	9-728	SAV
Hi Dee Ho That Old Sweet Roll	Blood Sweat &Tears	5-615	SC
Hi Heel Sneakers	Cross Section	30-784	SF
Hi Hi Hi	McCartney & Wings	12-81	DK
Hi Hi Hi	McCartney, Paul	48-565	DK
Hi LiLi Hi Lo	Caron, Leslie	9-827	SAV
Hicktown	Aldean, Jason	23-117	CB
Hicktown	Ford, Tenn Ernie	22-210	CB
Hidden Agenda	Craig, David	34-169	CB
Hidden Agenda	Craig, David	32-173	THM
Hidden Agenda	David, Craig	18-775	PHM
Hidden Angels	David, Craig	20-459	CB
Hidden Away	Groban, Josh	48-48	CB
Hidden Heroes	Fairchild, Barbara	47-83	DWG
Hide Away	Daya	48-619	BKD
Hiding My Heart	Adele	44-174	KV
High And Dry	Chesney, Kenny	48-80	CB
High Cotton	Alabama	46-243	CB
High Enough	Damn Yankees	34-57	CB
High Hopes	Sinatra, Frank	12-198	DK
High Hopes	Sinatra, Frank	10-716	JVC

SONG TITLE	ARTIST	#	TYPE
High Hopes	Sinatra, Frank	12-490	P
High Hopes	Sinatra, Frank	9-238	PT
High Hopes	Sinatra, Frank	4-349	SC
High Hopes	Standard	35-24	CB
High Lonesome	Hughes, Judd	20-453	ST
High Lonesome Sound	Gill, Vince	7-241	MM
High Lonesome Sound	Gill, Vince	22-882	ST
High Low And In Between	Wills, Mark	7-383	MM
High Low And In Between	Wills, Mark	24-655	SC
High Maintenance Woman	Keith, Toby	30-336	CB
High Noon	Ritter, Tex	45-567	TOS
High On Love	Loveless, Patty	8-729	CB
High On Love	Loveless, Patty	5-298	SC
High On Love	Loveless, Patty	22-796	ST
High Powered Love	Harris, EmmyLou	1-230	CB
High Powered Love	Harris, EmmyLou	4-472	SC
High Road the	Stone, Joss	44-162	BKD
High School Confidential	Lewis, Jerry Lee	47-204	SC
High Sierra	Ronstadt, Linda	6-855	MM
High Tech Redneck	Jones, George	8-337	CB
High Tech Redneck	Jones, George	6-757	MM
High Time	Musgraves, Kacey	45-435	ZM
High Time We Went	Cocker, Joe	48-540	DK
High Tone Woman	Strait, George	29-33	CB
Higher	Creed	14-174	CB
Higher	Creed	5-793	SC
Higher	Creed	15-786	THM
Higher And Higher	Coolidge, Rita	15-493	DK
Higher And Higher	Wilson, Jackie	12-753	P
Higher Ground	Franklin, Aretha	13-87	P
Higher Ground	Streisand, Barbra	49-616	PS
Higher Ground	Streisand, Barbra	5-280	SC
Higher Ground	UB40	25-387	MM
Higher Ground	Wonder, Stevie	24-336	SC
Higher Love	Winwood, Steve	4-378	SC
Higher Window	Groban, Josh	48-50	KVD
Highway 20 Ride	Zac Brown Band	38-126	CB
Highway 40 Blues	Skaggs, Ricky	8-702	SAV
Highway Don't Care - duet	McGraw & Swift	40-45	ASK
Highway Patrol	Brown, Junior	40-76	CB
Highway Robbery	Tucker, Tanya	1-608	CB
Highway Star	Deep Purple	4-568	SC
Highway To Hell	Texas Lightning	49-922	KVD
Highwayman	Highwaymen	11-711	DK
Hillbillies	Hot Apple Pie	22-330	CB
Hillbilly Bone - duet	Shelton & Adkins	38-84	CB
Hillbilly Deluxe	Brooks & Dunn	30-192	CB
Hillbilly Fever	Dickens, Little Jimmy	8-770	CB
Hillbilly Fever	Dickens, Little Jimmy	45-335	CBEP
Hillbilly Girl With The Blues	Dalton, Lacy J.	29-689	SC
Hillbilly Heart	Rodriguez, Johnny	22-56	CB

SONG TITLE	ARTIST	#	TYPE
Hillbilly Highway	Earle, Steve	46-177	CB
Hillbilly Nation	Cowboy Crush	29-205	CB
Hillbilly Rap	McCoy, Neal	7-341	MM
Hillbilly Rap	McCoy, Neal	24-154	SC
Hillbilly Rock	Stuart, Marty	17-219	NA
Hillbilly Shoes	Montgomery Gentry	8-938	CB
Hip Hop Hooray	Naughty By Nature	16-572	SC
Hip Hop To Honky Tonk	Judd, Cledus T.	16-510	CB
Hip To Be Square	Lewis & The News	16-793	DK
Hip To Be Square	Lewis, Huey	48-571	DK
Hip To My Heart	Band Perry	37-331	CB
Hippy Chick	Soho	30-771	SF
Hippy Hippy Shake	Georgia Satellites	34-117	CB
Hippy Hippy Shake	Swinging Blue Jeans	5-179	SC
Hips Don't Lie	Shakira w Jean Wyclef	30-727	SF
Hips Don't Lie	Shakira&Wyclef Jean	30-727	SF
His Hand In Mine	Presley, Elvis	30-384	SC
His Kinda Money (My Kinda Love)	Church, Eric	46-618	CB
His Latest Flame (Marie's the Name)	Presley, Elvis	2-611	SC
His Memory	Western Flyer	4-21	SC
Hit 'Em Up Style	Blue Cantrell	33-410	CB
Hit 'Em Up Style	Cantrell, Blu	15-807	CB
Hit 'Em Up Style	Cantrell, Blu	23-584	PHM
Hit 'Em Up Style	Cantrell, Blu	16-389	SGB
Hit 'Em Up Style	Cantrell, Blu	18-518	TT
Hit Me Off	New Edition	24-291	SC
Hit Me With Your Best Shot	Benatar, Pat	16-870	DK
Hit Me With Your Best Shot	Benatar, Pat	13-283	P
Hit Me With Your Best Shot	Benatar, Pat	2-150	SC
Hit That	Offspring	20-567	CB
Hit The Freeway	Braxton & Loon	32-18	THM
Hit The Freeway	Braxton, Toni	32-18	THM
Hit The Ground Runnin'	Urban, Keith	46-155	KV
Hit The Road Jack	Charles, Ray	10-671	HE
Hit The Road Jack	Charles, Ray	2-52	SC
Hit The Road Jack	Horn, S.	23-349	MM
Hitchin' A Ride	Vanity Fare	9-801	SAV
Ho Hey	Lumineers	48-418	BKD
Ho Ho Ho And A Bottle Of Rum	Buffett, Jimmy	46-144	SC
Hog Wild	Williams, Hank Jr.	2-690	SC
Hokey Cokey	Black Lace	49-53	ZVS
Hold A Woman	Covington, Bucky	39-63	PHN
Hold Back The Water	BTO	46-543	CB
Hold Me	Fleetwood Mac	4-85	SC
Hold Me	Fleetwood Mac	10-571	SF
Hold Me	Lee, Brenda	45-364	OZP
Hold Me	Oslin, K.T.	4-785	SC
Hold Me Now	Thompson Twins	2-846	SC
Hold Me Thrill Me Kiss	Carter, Mel	6-257	MM

SONG TITLE	ARTIST	#	TYPE
Me			
Hold Me Thrill Me Kiss Me	Carter, Mel	2-60	SC
Hold Me Thrill Me Kiss Me	Mathis, Johnny	9-740	SAV
Hold Me Thrill Me Kiss Me Kill Me	U2	30-73	SC
Hold My Beer	Pritchett, Aaron	45-678	DCK
Hold My Hand	Hootie & Blowfish	21-134	CB
Hold My Hand	Hootie & Blowfish	28-422	DK
Hold My Hand	Hootie & Blowfish	2-475	SC
Hold My Hand	Hootie & Blowfish	29-126	ST
Hold My Heart	Bareillas, Sara	48-208	KV
Hold On	Buble, Michael	38-174	CB
Hold On	Buble, Michael	40-89	PS
Hold On	Cailliat, Colbie	48-219	KV
Hold On	Jonas Brothers	36-455	CB
Hold On	McLachlan, Sarah	29-132	ST
Hold On	Tunstall, K.T.	30-593	PHM
Hold On	Tunstall, K.T.	37-112	SC
Hold On	Walters, Jamie	3-438	SC
Hold On	Wilson Phillips	11-694	DK
Hold On	Wilson Phillips	12-748	P
Hold On I'm A Comin'	Sam & Dave	26-201	DK
Hold On I'm Coming	Sam & Dave	35-81	CB
Hold On I'm Coming	Sam & Dave	12-726	P
Hold On I'm Coming	Sam & Dave	3-261	SC
Hold On Loosely	38 Special	2-527	SC
Hold On Loosely	38 Special	13-767	SGB
Hold On Tight	ELO	5-685	SC
Hold On To Me	Montgomery, J M	8-212	CB
Hold On To Me	Montgomery, J M	22-670	ST
Hold On To The Nights	Marx, Richard	35-195	CB
Hold On To The Nights	Marx, Richard	21-746	MH
Hold That Thought	Wicks, Chuck	48-453	CB
Hold The Dream	Firehouse	24-21	SC
Hold Tight Hold Tight	Andrew Sisters	46-428	KV
Hold You Down - duet	Lopez & Fat Joe	33-395	CB
Holdin'	Diamond Rio	1-176	CB
Holdin'	Diamond Rio	7-585	CHM
Holdin'	Diamond Rio	22-912	ST
Holdin' A Good Hand	Greenwood, Lee	6-619	MM
Holdin' Heaven	Byrd, Tracy	1-541	CB
Holdin' Heaven	Byrd, Tracy	2-354	SC
Holdin' Heaven	Byrd, Tracy	8-602	TT
Holdin' On To Something	Carson, Jeff	4-209	SC
Holdin' On To Yesterday	Ambrosia	17-535	SC
Holding Back The Years	Simply Red	11-120	DK
Holding Back The Years	Simply Red	12-826	P
Holding Her And Loving You	Conley, Earl Thomas	33-72	CB
Holding Her And Loving You	Conley, Earl Thomas	16-582	SC
Holding My Own	Darkness	29-230	ZM
Holding On	Winwood, Steve	34-99	CB
Holding On To You	Lambert, Miranda	46-272	BKD
Holding Out For A Hero	Tyler, Bonnie	11-422	DK

SONG TITLE	ARTIST	#	TYPE
Holding Pattern	Brown, Junior	40-79	CB
Holding The Bag	Bandy & Stampley	19-505	CB
Holding Things Together	Haggard, Merle	44-55	KV
Hole Hearted	Extreme	17-352	DK
Hole In A Bottle	Smith, Canaan	49-673	KCD
Hole In My Head	Dixie Chicks	14-730	CB
Hole In My Head	Dixie Chicks	30-603	RS
Hole In My Heart	Blackhawk	7-674	CHM
Hole In The Wall	Jackson, Alan	46-300	BKD
Hole In The Wall	Jackson, Alan	47-746	SRK
Hole In The World	Eagles	32-353	THM
Hole the	Travis, Randy	8-728	CB
Hole the	Travis, Randy	22-803	ST
Holes In The Floor Of Heaven	Raye, Collin	22-783	ST
Holes In The Floor Of Heaven	Wariner, Steve	8-473	CB
Holiday	Bee Gees	12-7	DK
Holiday	Bee Gees	17-503	LE
Holiday	Madonna	13-25	P
Holiday In My Head	Smash Mouth	18-286	CB
Holiday In My Head	Smash Mouth	25-143	MM
Hollaback Girl **	Stefani, Gwen	30-130	PT
Holler Back	Lost Trailers	36-590	CB
Hollow	Kelly, Tori	48-640	KV
Holly Holy	Diamond, Neil	7-536	AH
Holly Holy	Diamond, Neil	30-682	LE
Holly Holy	Diamond, Neil	13-297	P
Holly Holy	Diamond, Neil	18-695	PS
Holly Holy	Diamond, Neil	24-693	SC
Holly Leaves And Christmas Trees	Presley, Elvis	45-777	CB
Hollywood	Buble, Michael	38-173	CB
Hollywood	Madonna	19-605	CB
Hollywood	Madonna	25-634	MM
Hollywood	Madonna	32-318	THM
Hollywood	Rufus&Chaka Kahn	17-469	SC
Hollywood Nights	Seger, Bob	15-175	MH
Holy Cow	Dorsey, Lee	47-36	SF
Holy Diver	Dio, Ronnie James	5-483	SC
Holy Is The Lamb - xmas	Adams, Oleta	46-391	PR
Holy Water	Big & Rich	22-103	CB
Holywood Nights	Seger, Bob	10-174	UK
Home	Bentley, Dierks	38-216	ASK
Home	Buble, Michael	30-179	LE
Home	Daughtry	30-484	CB
Home	Jackson, Alan	1-52	CB
Home	Jackson, Alan	7-242	MM
Home	McGraw, Tim	47-244	CB
Home	Phillips, Phillip	39-99	ASK
Home	Reeves, Jim	40-126	CK
Home	Reeves, Jim	5-94	SC
Home	Ross, Diana	15-368	LE
Home	Shelton, Blake	36-416	CB
Home	The Wiz	49-432	SDK
Home Again	King, Carole	43-452	MM
Home Ain't Where His	Twain, Shania	4-893	SC

SONG TITLE	ARTIST	#	TYPE
Heart Is..			
Home Ain't Where His Heart Is...	Twain, Shania	1-517	CB
Home Ain't Where His Heart Is...	Twain, Shania	7-441	MM
Home Alone Tonight - duet	Bryan & Fairchild	45-822	DCK
Home Improvement	Strait, George	38-142	CB
Home In My Heart	Church, Claudia	8-480	CB
Home Of The Blues	Cash, Johnny	29-722	CB
Home Of The Blues	Cash, Johnny	47-720	CB
Home On The Range	Kids	10-303	SC
Home On The Range	Standard	11-494	DK
Home On The Range	Standard	23-221	SM
Home Sweet Home	Moore, Justin	49-304	KRG
Home Sweet Home	Motley Crue	24-685	SC
Home Sweet Home	Underwood, Carrie	37-35	CB
Home Sweet Home	Underwood, Carrie	36-381	SC
Home To Stay	Groban, Josh	48-43	CB
Home To You	Montgomery, J M	22-430	ST
Homeboy	Church, Eric	46-620	CB
Homebreaker	Davis, Skeeter	43-333	CB
Homecoming	Hall, Tom T.	45-928	SSK
Homecoming ' 63	Whitley, Keith	8-697	SAV
Homecoming ' 63	Whitley, Keith	19-446	SC
Homecoming Queen's Got A Gun	Brown, Julie	5-639	SC
Homegrown Honey	Rucker, Darius	47-375	SSC
Homeland	Rogers, Kenny	20-581	CB
Homeland	Rogers, Kenny	16-37	ST
Homeland - patriotic	Rogers, Kenny	36-337	CB
Hometown Glory	Adele	38-231	CB
Hometown Honeymoon	Alabama	1-21	CB
Hometown Honeymoon	Alabama	6-395	MM
Hometown Honeymoon	Alabama	9-629	SAV
Hometown Honeymoon	Alabama	2-805	SC
Homeward Bound	Simon & Garfunkel	23-642	BS
Homeward Bound	Simon & Garfunkel	15-494	DM
Homewrecker	Wilson, Gretchen	22-311	CB
Honestly	Rimes, LeAnn	7-440	MM
Honestly	Stryper	23-111	SC
Honestly	Zwan	23-163	PHM
Honesty	Joel, Billy	12-277	DK
Honesty	Joel, Billy	16-517	P
Honesty (Write Me A List)	Atkins, Rodney	30-36	CB
Honesty (Write Me A List)	Atkins, Rodney	19-273	ST
Honesty (Write Me A List)	Atkins, Rodney	32-337	THM
Honey	Goldsboro, Bobby	35-98	CB
Honey	Goldsboro, Bobby	11-95	DK
Honey	Goldsboro, Bobby	10-750	JVC
Honey	Goldsboro, Bobby	12-645	P
Honey	Goldsboro, Bobby	4-702	SC
Honey Bee	Shelton, Blake	37-206	AS
Honey Come Back	Campbell, Glen	5-36	SC
Honey Do	Buffett, Jimmy	46-147	TU

SONG TITLE	ARTIST	#	TYPE
Honey Do You Think It's Wrong	Al Dexter & Troopers	46-408	CB
Honey Don't	Perkins, Carl	11-611	DK
Honey Don't	Walsh & Earle	24-350	SC
Honey Honey	Abba	19-75	MM
Honey I Do	Campbell, Stacy D.	6-853	MM
Honey I Do	Campbell, Stacy D.	3-563	SC
Honey I'm Home	Twain, Shania	8-3	CB
Honey I'm Home	Twain, Shania	22-824	ST
Honey Love	Drifters	17-323	SS
Honey Open That Door	Skaggs, Ricky	33-82	CB
Honey Open That Door	Skaggs, Ricky	4-485	SC
Honey You Don't Know My Mind	Martin, Jimmy	8-252	CB
Honeycomb	Rodgers, Jimmie	11-206	DK
Honeymoon Feelin'	Clark, Roy	5-160	SC
Honeysuckle Rose	Standard	12-32	DK
Honeysuckle Sweet	Alexander, Jessi	20-345	ST
Honk If You Honky-Tonk	Strait, George	38-143	CB
Honky Cat	John, Elton	15-179	MH
Honky Tonk America	Kershaw, Sammy	1-479	CB
Honky Tonk America	Kershaw, Sammy	22-813	ST
Honky Tonk Attitude	Diffie, Joe	1-277	CB
Honky Tonk Attitude	Diffie, Joe	6-313	MM
Honky Tonk Baby	Highway 101	6-193	MM
Honky Tonk Baby	Ricochet	8-757	CB
Honky Tonk Baby	Ricochet	22-834	ST
Honky Tonk Badonkadonk	Adkins, Trace	23-470	CB
Honky Tonk Badonkadonk	Adkins, Trace	23-376	SC
Honky Tonk Blues	Pirates Of Mississippi	47-567	NT
Honky Tonk Blues	Pride, Charley	38-122	CB
Honky Tonk Blues	Williams, Hank Sr.	14-220	CB
Honky Tonk Blues	Williams, Hank Sr.	9-489	SAV
Honky Tonk Crowd	Anderson, John	6-81	SC
Honky Tonk Crowd	Trevino, Rick	16-593	MM
Honky Tonk Girl	Cash, Johnny	45-665	HSK
Honky Tonk Girl	Lynn, Loretta	47-624	CB
Honky Tonk Girl	Thompson, Hank	19-330	CB
Honky Tonk Healin'	Ball, David	7-86	MM
Honky Tonk Heart	Highway 101	14-318	SC
Honky Tonk Heroes	Jennings, Waylon	45-174	CB
Honky Tonk Man	Horton, Johnny	17-11	DK
Honky Tonk Man	Horton, Johnny	14-325	SC
Honky Tonk Man	Yoakam, Dwight	20-652	SC
Honky Tonk Merry Go Round	Cline, Patsy	45-489	CB
Honky Tonk Mona Lisa	Hummon, Marcus	4-397	SC
Honky Tonk Moon	Travis, Randy	1-400	CB
Honky Tonk Music	Axton, Hoyt	46-452	VH
Honky Tonk Myself To Death	Jones, George	8-342	CB
Honky Tonk Myself To Death	Jones, George	4-136	SC
Honky Tonk Song	Jones, George	4-456	SC
Honky Tonk Song	Pierce, Webb	29-398	CB

SONG TITLE	ARTIST	#	TYPE
Honky Tonk Songs	Parton, Dolly	8-768	CB
Honky Tonk Truth	Brooks & Dunn	7-676	CHM
Honky Tonk Truth	Brooks & Dunn	22-627	ST
Honky Tonk U	Keith, Toby	22-17	CB
Honky Tonk Wine	Gilley, Mickey	5-44	SC
Honky Tonk Woman	Lewis, Jerry Lee	47-814	SRK
Honky Tonk Woman	Rolling Stones	19-849	LE
Honky Tonk Woman	Rolling Stones	14-398	PT
Honky Tonkin'	Williams, Hank Jr.	9-455	SAV
Honky Tonkin'	Williams, Hank Jr.	2-414	SC
Honky Tonkin'	Williams, Hank Sr.	22-307	CB
Honky Tonkin' Fool	Supernaw, Doug	4-471	SC
Honolulu City Lights	Beamer,Keola/Kapona	6-839	MM
Honolulu Lulu	Jan & Dean	45-602	OZP
Honor Bound	Conley, Earl Thomas	5-529	SC
Hoochie Coochie Man	Muddy Waters	27-238	DK
Hoochie Coochie Man	Muddy Waters	7-221	MM
Hook	Blues Traveler	34-119	CB
Hook	Blues Traveler	24-746	SC
Hooked On A Feeling	Thomas, B.J.	35-106	CB
Hooked On A Feeling	Thomas, B.J.	11-255	DK
Hooked On A Feeling	Thomas, B.J.	36-157	LE
Hooked On A Feeling	Thomas, B.J.	13-174	P
Hooked On Music	Davis, Mac	23-511	CB
Hooked On Music	Davis, Mac	19-426	SC
Hooray For Hazel (Where Were You...)	Roe, Tommy	48-119	DCK
Hope On The Rocks	Keith, Toby	40-46	ASK
Hope On The Rocks	Keith, Toby	40-19	PHN
Hope You Get Lonely	Swindell, Cole	44-268	PHN
Hope You Get Lonely Tonight	Swindell, Cole	45-393	KCDC
Hope You're Feelin' Me Like I'm...	Pride, Charley	4-585	SC
Hopeless	Farris, Dionne	9-97	PS
Hopelessly Devoted To You	Grease	49-427	SDK
Hopelessly Devoted To You	Newton-John, Olivia	15-273	DK
Hopelessly Devoted To You	Newton-John, Olivia	9-273	SC
Hopelessly Devoted To You	Newton-John, Olivia	10-521	SF
Hopelessly Yours	Greenwood&Bogguss	2-308	SC
Horizon Has Been Defeated the	Johnson, J.	32-257	THM
Horizontal Bop the **	Seger, Bob	2-731	SC
Horse To Mexico	Triggs, Trini	8-933	CB
Horse With No Name	America	16-774	DK
Horse With No Name	America	7-485	MM
Horse With No Name a	America	35-109	CB
Horsepower	LeDoux, Chris	20-178	ST
Hot	Lavigne, Avril	37-120	SC
Hot 'N Cold	Perry, Katy	38-195	SC
Hot And Tipsy	Lyric	32-278	THM
Hot Blooded	Foreigner	35-136	CB

SONG TITLE	ARTIST	#	TYPE
Hot Blooded	Foreigner	13-284	P
Hot Child In The City	Benatar, Pat	35-138	CB
Hot Child In The City	Benatar, Pat	11-417	DK
Hot Child In The City	Gilder, Nick	28-267	DK
Hot Child In The City	Gilder, Nick	4-761	SC
Hot Country And Single	Dillon, Dean	4-473	SC
Hot Diggity	Como, Perry	13-541	LE
Hot Diggity	Como, Perry	20-778	PS
Hot Diggity	Como, Perry	3-509	SC
Hot For Teacher	Van Halen	5-62	SC
Hot Fun In The Summertime	Sly & Family Stone	12-63	DK
Hot Fun In The Summertime	Sly & Family Stone	13-606	P
Hot Girls In Love	Loverboy	18-498	SAV
Hot Girls In Love	Loverboy	5-144	SC
Hot Hot Hot	Poindexter, Buster	33-437	CB
Hot Hot Hot	Poindexter, Buster	12-113	DK
Hot In Here	Nelly	25-306	MM
Hot In Here	Nelly	18-146	PHM
Hot In The City	Joel, Billy	47-144	BSP
Hot In The City	Joel, Billy	47-148	LE
Hot Legs	Stewart, Rod	16-151	SC
Hot Line	Sylvers	11-383	DK
Hot Line	Sylvers	2-495	SC
Hot Mama	Adkins, Trace	35-448	CB
Hot Mama	Adkins, Trace	19-529	ST
Hot N' Cold	Perry, Katy	36-536	CB
Hot Pants	Brown, James	29-142	LE
Hot Rod Lincoln	Commander Cody	3-553	SC
Hot Stuff	Summer, Donna	35-154	CB
Hot Stuff	Summer, Donna	16-781	DK
Hot Stuff	Summer, Donna	2-506	SC
Hotel California	Eagles	7-552	BS
Hotel California	Eagles	6-428	MM
Hotel California	Eagles	2-264	SC
Hotel Room Service	Pitbull	40-12	BH
Hotel Whiskey	Williams, Hank Jr.	16-362	CB
Hottest Thing In Town	Shaver, Billy Joe	45-839	VH
Hound Dog	Presley, Elvis	11-189	DK
Hound Dog	Presley, Elvis	3-317	MH
Hound Dog	Presley, Elvis	12-729	P
Hound Dog	Presley, Elvis	2-600	SC
Hound Dog	Presley, Elvis	14-747	THM
House I Live In the (What is...)	Sinatra, Frank	49-489	MM
House Is Not a Home a	Vandross, Luther	14-574	SC
House Is Rockin'	Vaughn, Stevie Ray	7-213	MM
House Like That	Chapman, Donovan	30-311	CB
House Of Cards	Carpenter, M C	8-885	CB
House Of Cards	Carpenter, M C	4-70	SC
House Of Cards	Carpenter, M C	15-158	THM
House Of Cash	Strait, George	49-420	CB
House Of Love	Grant, Amy	18-769	PS
House Of The Rising Sun	Animals	11-354	DK
House Of The Rising Sun	Animals	15-46	LE

SONG TITLE	ARTIST	#	TYPE
Sun			
House Of The Rising Sun	Animals	13-168	P
House Of The Rising Sun	Animals	29-834	SC
House Party	Hunt, Sam	45-23	BKD
House Rules the	Kane, Christian	43-84	PHN
House That Built Me the	Lambert, Miranda	36-54	PT
House With No Curtains	Jackson, Alan	8-238	CB
House With No Curtains	Jackson, Alan	7-724	CHM
House Without Windows	Orbison, Roy	38-63	PS
Houston	Martin, Dean	23-84	MM
Houston (Means I'm One Day Closer	Gatlins	13-484	P
Houston Solution	Milsap, Ronnie	1-448	CB
How 'Bout Them Cowgirls	Strait, George	30-544	CB
How 'Bout You	Church, Eric	29-194	CB
How 'Bout You Don't	Lost Trailers	36-244	PHM
How A CowgirL Says Goodbye	Lawrence, Tracy	1-585	CB
How A Cowgirl Says Goodbye	Lawrence, Tracy	7-642	CHM
How About That	Faith, A.	29-817	SF
How About You	Sinatra, Frank	9-257	PT
How About You	Staind	23-274	THM
How Am I Doin	Bentley, Dierks	20-386	ST
How Am I Doin'	Bentley, Dierks	30-796	PHM
How Am I Doin'	Bentley, Dierks	21-663	SC
How Am I Supposed To Live w/o You	Bolton, Michael	17-109	DK
How Am I Supposed To Live w/o You	Bolton, Michael	18-502	SAV
How Am I Supposed To Live...	Bolton, Michael	33-338	CB
How Bad Do You Want It	McGraw, Tim	23-40	SC
How Bizarre	OMC	15-495	SC
How Can I Be Sure	Lynne, Shelby	49-915	SC
How Can I Be Sure	Young Rascals	3-462	SC
How Can I Face Tomorrow	Cline, Patsy	45-495	CB
How Can I Forget	Isaacs, Sonya	14-166	CB
How Can I Help You Say Goodbye	Loveless, Patty	1-722	CB
How Can I Help You Say Goodbye	Loveless, Patty	19-296	MH
How Can I Help You Say Goodbye	Loveless, Patty	6-503	MM
How Can I Help You Say Goodbye	Loveless, Patty	2-207	SC
How Can I Live	Ill Nino	23-186	PHM
How Can I Make You Love Me	Davis, Linda	4-467	SC
How Can I Meet Her	Everly Brothers	45-551	DCK
How Can I Tell Her About You	Lobo	46-332	AH
How Can I Unlove You	Anderson, Lynn	13-503	P
How Can This Happen To Me	Simple Plan	23-320	CB

SONG TITLE	ARTIST	#	TYPE
How Can You Mend A Broken Heart	Bee Gees	11-674	DK
How Can You Mend A Broken Heart	Bee Gees	17-504	LE
How Can You Mend A Broken Heart	Bee Gees	13-162	P
How Can You Mend A Broken Heart	Bee Gees	2-432	SC
How Can You Mend A Broken Heart	Buble, Michael	30-180	LE
How Come	Morrison, James	38-269	ZM
How Come How Long	Babyface	21-552	PHM
How Come You Don't Call Me	Keys, Alicia	18-352	CB
How Come You Don't Call Me	Keys, Alicia	25-211	MM
How Come You Don't Call Me	Keys, Alicia	17-594	PHM
How Cool Is That	Griggs, Andy	15-335	CB
How Cool Is That	Griggs, Andy	15-191	ST
How Could An Angel Break A Heart	Braxton, Toni	18-822	PS
How Could An Angel Break A Heart	Braxton, Toni	15-496	SC
How Could I	Anthony, Marc	17-736	PS
How Could I Want More	Spears, Jamie Lynn	44-276	PHN
How Country Feels	Houser, Randy	45-321	SBI
How Deep Is The Ocean	Sinatra, Frank	14-277	MM
How Deep is Your Love	Bee Gees	11-84	DK
How Deep Is Your Love	Bee Gees	11-76	JTG
How Deep Is Your Love	Bee Gees	17-492	LE
How Deep Is Your Love	Bee Gees	9-653	SAV
How Deep Is Your Love	Bee Gees	2-843	SC
How Deep Is Your Love	Portrait	3-501	SC
How Do	Carpenter, M C	47-666	CB
How Do I Breathe	Mario	30-486	CB
How Do I Deal	Hewitt, Jennifer Lo	7-798	PHT
How Do I Get There	Carter, Deana	7-667	CHM
How Do I Get There	Carter, Deana	4-831	SC
How Do I Get There	Carter, Deana	22-612	ST
How Do I Just Stop	McDonald, Richie	36-279	PHM
How Do I Let Go	Brokop, Lisa	8-487	CB
How Do I Live	Rimes, LeAnn	22-600	ST
How Do I Live	Yearwood, Trisha	1-641	CB
How Do I Live	Yearwood, Trisha	7-635	CHM
How Do I Live (Pop Mix)	Rimes, LeAnn	21-548	PHM
How Do I Love Her	Chapmen, Stacy	32-398	THM
How Do I Make You	Ronstadt, Linda	10-8	SC
How Do I Turn You On	Milsap, Ronnie	5-563	SC
How Do U Want It **	2 Pac	25-474	MM
How Do You Do It	Gerry & Pacemakers	48-778	P
How Do You Do It	Reed, Jerry	3-810	SC
How Do You Fall In Love	Alabama	8-755	CB
How Do You Get That Lonely	Larsen, Blaine	23-6	CB
How Do You Get That Lonely	Larsen, Blaine	21-658	SC
How Do You Keep the Music Playing	Ingram & Austin	49-463	MM

SONG TITLE	ARTIST	#	TYPE
How Do You Keep The Music Playing	Sinatra, Frank	9-239	PT
How Do You Keep the Music Playing	Streisand, Barbra	49-604	PS
How Do You Like Me Now	Keith, Toby	8-907	CB
How Do You Like Me Now	Keith, Toby	22-534	ST
How Do You Milk A Cow	Judd, Cledus T.	16-505	CB
How Do You Sleep	McCartney, Jesse	36-286	PHM
How Do You Sleep At Night	Hayes, Wade	8-754	CB
How Do You Sleep At Night	Hayes, Wade	22-678	ST
How Far	McBride, Martina	29-537	CB
How Far	McBride, Martina	20-337	ST
How Far To Waco	Dunn, Ronnie	45-236	SRK
How Far We've Gone	Matchbox 20	49-892	SC
How Forever Feels	Chesney, Kenny	8-875	CB
How Forever Feels	Chesney, Kenny	22-714	ST
How Gone Is Goodbye	Tillis, Pam	17-166	JVC
How Great Thou Art	Lynn, Loretta	47-635	CB
How Great Thou Art	Presley, Elvis	30-373	SC
How High The Moon	Fitzgerald, Ella	12-550	P
How High The Moon	Les Paul/Mary Ford	4-190	SC
How I Beat Shaq	Carter, Aaron	16-253	TT
How I Feel	Flo Rida	45-648	SBI
How I Feel	McBride, Martina	30-455	CB
How I Got To Be This Way	Moore, Justin	38-112	CB
How I Got To Memphis	Bare, Bobby	18-273	CB
How I Love Them Old Songs	Thompson, Sue	49-393	VH
How I Love You	Humperdinck, E.	49-258	DFK
How Insensitive	Sinatra, Frank	15-497	SGB
How Long	Ace	3-452	SC
How Long	Ace	10-545	SF
How Long	White, Bryan	14-127	CB
How Long	White, Bryan	22-464	ST
How Long Gone	Brooks & Dunn	8-742	CB
How Long Gone	Brooks & Dunn	22-809	ST
How Long Has This Been Going On	Lee, Peggy	47-177	KV
How Many Days	Ingram, Jack	5-830	SC
How Many Tears	Vee, Bobby	49-64	ZVS
How Many Times	Franklin, Aretha	36-164	JT
How Many Times How Many Lies	Pussycat Dolls	30-263	CB
How Many Ways	Braxton, Toni	2-471	SC
How Much I Feel	Ambrosia	17-563	PR
How Much Is That Doggy In The...	Kids	12-263	DK
How Much Longer	Sisters Wade	10-214	SC
How Much More Can She Stand	Twitty, Conway	48-240	CB
How Sweet It Is	Gaye, Marvin	36-114	JTG
How Sweet It Is To Be Loved By You	Gaye, Marvin	4-40	SC
How Sweet It is To Be	Taylor, James	9-882	DK

SONG TITLE	ARTIST	#	TYPE
Loved By You			
How Sweet It Is To Be Loved By You	Taylor, James	6-434	MM
How Sweet It Is To Be Loved By You	Taylor, James	12-635	P
How To Be A Country Star	Statler Brothers	19-389	CB
How To Deal	Frankie J	23-313	CB
How To Save A Life	Fray	36-191	PHM
How To Touch A Girl	JoJo	30-262	CB
How Was I To Know	McEntire, Reba	1-813	CB
How Was I To Know	McEntire, Reba	7-586	CHM
How Was I To Know	Montgomery, J M	14-214	CB
How Was I To Know	Montgomery, J M	7-658	CHM
How We Do (Radio Vers)	Game & 50 Cent	37-100	SC
How Will I Know	Houston, Whitney	16-745	DK
How Will I Know	Houston, Whitney	12-825	P
How You Gonna Act Like That	Tyrese	20-521	CB
How You Gonna Act Like That	Tyrese	32-272	THM
How You Live (Turn Up The Music)	Point of Grace	36-589	CB
How You Remind Me	Nickelback	35-243	CB
How Your Love Makes Me Feel	Diamond Rio	7-664	CHM
How Your Love Makes Me Feel	Diamond Rio	22-619	ST
How'd I Wind Up In Jamaica	Byrd, Tracy	20-256	PHM
How'd I Wind Up In Jamaica	Byrd, Tracy	20-336	ST
How's It Going To Be	Third Eye Blind	35-210	CB
How's It Going To Be	Third Eye Blind	7-707	PHM
How's It Going To Be	Third Eye Blind	5-187	SC
How's The Radio Know	Tippin, Aaron	7-389	MM
How's The Radio Know	Tippin, Aaron	4-594	SC
How's The World Treating You	Krauss, Alison	19-774	ST
How's The World Treating You	Presley, Elvis	25-327	MM
How's The World Treating You	Reeves, Jim	44-251	SRK
How's Your Whole....Family **	Peters, Red	5-549	SC
How's Your Whole...Family **	Peters, Red	30-663	RSX
Howlin' At The Moon	Williams, Hank Sr.	14-226	CB
Hucklebuck the	Checker, Chubby	4-708	SC
Hully Gully (Baby) - DANCE #	Olympics	22-398	SC
Human	Human League	33-313	CB
Human	Human League	16-866	DK
Human	Killers	36-273	PHM
Human	Perry, Christina	43-184	ASK
Human	Stewart, Rod	16-254	TT
Human Beings	Van Halen	4-333	SC
Human Nature	Jackson, Michael	12-375	DK
Human Touch	Springsteen, Bruce	20-247	LE

SONG TITLE	ARTIST	#	TYPE
Human Wheels	Mellencamp, John	4-283	SC
Humble And Kind	McGraw, Tim	48-678	BKD
Hummingbird	Seals & Croft	47-484	DCK
Humpty Dance	Digital Underground	25-475	MM
Humpty Dance	Digital Underground	5-344	SC
Humpty Dumpty Heart	Thompson, Hank	19-321	CB
Hundred Dollar Lady	Bruce, Ed	48-410	DFK
Hundred Pounds Of Clay	McDaniels, Gene	10-325	KC
Hundred Pounds Of Clay	McDaniels, Gene	5-89	SC
Hunger Strike	Pearl Jam	9-296	RS
Hunger the	Holy, Steve	22-586	ST
Hungover And Hard Up	Church, Eric	48-7	KCD
Hungry Eyes	Carmen, Eric	46-563	MM
Hungry Eyes	Haggard, Merle	1-374	CB
Hungry Eyes	Haggard, Merle	5-33	SC
Hungry Heart	Springsteen, Bruce	17-610	LE
Hungry Like The Wolf	Duran Duran	35-169	CB
Hungry Like The Wolf	Duran Duran	11-539	DK
Hunter	Dido	15-818	CB
Hunter	Dido	18-408	MM
Hunter	Dido	18-519	TT
Huntin' Fishin' & Lovin' Everyday	Bryan, Luke	48-110	DCK
Hurdy Gurdy Man	Donovan	27-110	DK
Hurdy Gurdy Man	Donovan	5-234	SC
Hurricane	Carter, Carlene	2-660	SC
Hurricane	Dylan, Bob	29-104	CB
Hurry Home	Carroll, Jason M.	36-317	PHM
Hurry Sundown	McBride & The Ride	2-711	SC
Hurry Sundown	Outlaws	48-658	CB
Hurt	Cash, Johnny	29-733	CB
Hurt	Cash, Johnny	21-590	SC
Hurt	Cash, Johnny	19-14	ST
Hurt	Cash, Johnny	32-219	THM
Hurt	Presley, Elvis	18-445	KC
Hurt	Presley, Elvis	14-772	THM
Hurt By Love	Bodeans	24-636	SC
Hurt Me	Rimes, LeAnn	7-437	MM
Hurt Me	Rimes, LeAnn	4-896	SC
Hurt Me Bad In A Real Good Way	Loveless, Patty	1-717	CB
Hurt Me Bad In A Real Good Way	Loveless, Patty	13-331	P
Hurt So Bad	Lettermen	48-523	L1
Hurt So Bad	Little Anthony	35-54	CB
Hurt So Bad	Little Anthony	30-515	LE
Hurt So Bad	Ronstadt, Linda	11-182	DK
Hurt the	Stevens, Cat	23-656	BS
Hurt the	Stevens, Cat	13-584	NU
Hurtin's All Over the	Smith, Connie	15-80	CB
Hurting Each Other	Carpenters	33-265	CB
Hurting Each Other	Carpenters	11-684	DK
Hurting Each Other	Carpenters	45-802	DKM
Hurting Each Other	Carpenters	2-434	SC
Hurts Like Heaven	Coldplay	39-103	PHM
Hurts So Good	Mellencamp, John	34-66	CB
Hurts So Good	Mellencamp, John	21-430	LE

SONG TITLE	ARTIST	#	TYPE
Hurts So Good	Mellencamp, John	19-93	PS
Hurts So Good	Mellencamp, John	4-328	SC
Hurts To Think	Lambert, Miranda	45-674	DCK
Husbands & Wives	Brooks & Dunn	10-151	SC
Husbands & Wives	Brooks & Dunn	22-668	ST
Husbands & Wives	Miller, Roger	22-281	CB
Husbands & Wives	Miller, Roger	6-11	SC
Hush	Deep Purple	11-444	DK
Hush	Deep Purple	6-792	MM
Hush (Pop Mix)	LL Cool J	20-276	PHM
Hush Hush	Pussycat Dolls	36-295	PHM
Hypnotize **	Notorious B.I.G.	25-476	MM
Hypnotize The Moon	Walker, Clay	1-98	CB
Hypnotize The Moon	Walker, Clay	4-92	SC
Hypnotized	Fleetwood Mac	13-648	SGB
I Ain't Ever Satisfied	Peters, Gretchen	4-404	SC
I Ain't Goin' Down	Twain, Shania	45-526	CB
I Ain't Goin' Peacefully	Williams, Hank Jr.	45-696	VH
I Ain't Got No Business Doin...	Bailey, Razzy	29-384	CB
I Ain't Got Nobody	Wills, Bob	20-698	CB
I Ain't Living Long Like This	Jennings, Waylon	6-84	SC
I Ain't Never	Brooks, Garth	4-260	SC
I Ain't Never	Pierce, Webb	29-394	CB
I Ain't Never	Pierce, Webb	4-861	SC
I Ain't Never	Tillis, Mel	19-451	CB
I Ain't Never	Tillis, Mel	4-642	SC
I Ain't No Quitter	Boyd, Craig Wayne	39-61	PHN
I Ain't No Quitter	Twain, Shania	23-116	CB
I Ain't No Quitter	Twain, Shania	23-37	SC
I Ain't Scared	Carolina Rain	22-87	CB
I Ain't Superstitious	Jeff Beck Group	15-24	SC
I Ain't The One	Lynyrd Skynyrd	19-809	SGB
I Ain't Your Mama	Dotson, Amber	23-477	CB
I Alone	Live	3-498	SC
I Already Do	Wright, Chely	8-472	CB
I Always Get Lucky With You	Jones, George	5-396	SC
I Always Liked That Best	Thompson, Cyndi	33-160	CB
I Always Liked That Best	Thompson, Cyndi	25-50	MM
I Always Liked That Best	Thompson, Cyndi	16-2	ST
I Am	Train	37-317	SC
I Am	Train	15-790	THM
I Am A Man Of Constant Sorrow	Soggy Bottom Boys	30-35	CB
I Am A Man Of Constant Sorrow	Soggy Bottom Boys	9-873	ST
I Am A Pilgrim	Travis, Merle	45-692	CB
I Am A Rock	Simon & Garfunkel	15-499	DM
I Am A Saint	Chesnutt, Mark	22-98	CB
I Am A Simple Man	VanShelton, Ricky	8-549	CB
I Am A Simple Man	VanShelton, Ricky	17-146	DK
I Am A Simple Man	VanShelton, Ricky	2-397	SC
I Am An Island	Haggard, Merle	49-821	SC
I Am An Island	Haggard, Merle	49-169	SC
I Am I Said	Diamond, Neil	7-537	AH

SONG TITLE	ARTIST	#	TYPE
I Am I Said	Diamond, Neil	30-674	LE
I Am I Said	Diamond, Neil	30-503	THM
I Am Invincible	Pope, Cassadee	49-668	BKD
I Am Made Of You	Martin, Ricky	9-140	PS
I Am Made Of You	Martin, Ricky	13-732	SGB
I Am Mine	Pearl Jam	18-824	THM
I Am Santa Claus	Rivers, Bob	45-745	SC
I Am That Man	Brooks & Dunn	4-365	SC
I Am The Beat	Look	30-782	SF
I Am The Highway	Audio Slave	20-534	CB
I Am The Music Man	Black Lace	49-50	ZVS
I Am The Walrus	Beatles	21-510	SC
I Am The Working Man	Drake, Dusty	22-72	CB
I Am Who I Am	Dunn, Holly	2-691	SC
I Am Woman	Reddy, Helen	16-751	DK
I Am Woman	Reddy, Helen	2-436	SC
I Apologize	Baker, Anita	29-128	ST
I Beg Of You	Presley, Elvis	14-754	THM
I Believe	Barrino, Fantasia	23-563	MM
I Believe	Diamond Rio	34-367	CB
I Believe	Diamond Rio	25-442	MM
I Believe	Diamond Rio	18-461	ST
I Believe	Diamond Rio	32-45	THM
I Believe	Presley, Elvis	18-832	KC
I Believe	Presley, Elvis	30-375	SC
I Believe	Presley, Elvis	14-801	THM
I Believe	Rimes, LeAnn	25-80	MM
I Believe	Strait, George	40-59	ASK
I Believe	Strait, George	41-97	PHN
I Believe	Streisand, Barbra	49-618	PS
I Believe	Wynette, Tammy	49-362	CB
I Believe I Can Fly	Kelly, R.	11-77	JTG
I Believe I Can Fly	Kelly, R.	24-637	SC
I Believe I Can Fly	Space Jam	18-178	DK
I Believe In A Thing Called Love	Darkness	29-228	ZM
I Believe In America	LeDoux, Chris	20-586	CB
I Believe In Happy Endings	Diamond, Neil	47-423	THM
I Believe In Love	Paula Cole Band	5-795	SC
I Believe In Music	Davis, Mac	23-519	CB
I Believe In Music	Davis, Mac	11-781	DK
I Believe In Music	Davis, Mac	12-830	P
I Believe In Music	Gallery	47-568	MKP
I Believe In Santa Claus	Parton & Rogers	8-73	CB
I Believe In Santa Claus - duet	Rogers & Parton	48-122	CB
I Believe In You	Lewis, Jerry Lee	47-802	SRK
I Believe In You	Tillis, Mel	3-862	CB
I Believe In You	Tillis, Mel	5-753	SC
I Believe In You	Williams, Don	13-407	P
I Believe In You	Williams, Don	9-848	SAV
I Believe In You And Me	Houston, Whitney	49-312	BC
I Believe the South is Gonna Rise	Tucker, Tanya	38-13	CB
I Believe To My Soul	Charles, Ray	46-581	LE
I Belong To You	Braxton, Toni	16-619	MM

113

SONG TITLE	ARTIST	#	TYPE
I Belong To You	Kravitz, Lenny	16-239	PHM
I Bet You Look Good On the Dance...	Arctic Monkeys	30-287	SC
I Brake For Brunettes	Akins, Rhett	6-713	MM
I Brake For Brunettes	Akins, Rhett	22-856	ST
I Break Things	Erika Jo	23-137	CB
I Breathe In I Breathe Out	Cagle, Chris	33-143	CB
I Breathe In I Breathe Out	Cagle, Chris	25-51	MM
I Breathe In I Breathe Out	Cagle, Chris	15-859	ST
I Broke It I'll Fix It	River Road	16-580	SC
I Built This Wall	Hayes, Amber	39-77	PHM
I Call It Love	Richie, Lionel	30-271	CB
I Call It Love	Richie, Lionel	36-189	PHM
I Call Your Name	Beatles	11-552	DK
I Call Your Name - duet	Mamas & Papas	49-724	KV
I Came Straight To You	Randall, Jon	2-827	SC
I Can	Nas	25-720	MM
I Can	Nas	32-239	THM
I Can Bring Her Back	Mellons, Ken	2-650	SC
I Can Buy My Own Roses	Morgan, Lorrie	4-599	SC
I Can Do This	McCann, Lila	23-306	CB
I Can Dream About You	Hartman, Dan	35-172	CB
I Can Dream About You	Hartman, Dan	17-559	PR
I Can Dream About You	Hartman, Dan	9-687	SAV
I Can Give You Love Like That	Steele, Jeffrey	17-487	CB
I Can Hear Music	Beach Boys	46-501	SC
I Can Help	Presley, Elvis	25-752	MM
I Can Help	Swan, Billy	17-415	DK
I Can Help	Swan, Billy	9-596	SAV
I Can Love You Better	Dixie Chicks	35-414	CB
I Can Love You Better	Dixie Chicks	10-63	SC
I Can Love You Better	Dixie Chicks	22-760	ST
I Can Love You Like That	All-4-One	3-428	SC
I Can Love You Like That	Montgomery, J M	14-208	CB
I Can Love You Like That	Montgomery, J M	2-688	SC
I Can Make It Better	Vandross, Luther	24-644	SC
I Can Make It With You	Pozo Seco Singers	20-35	SC
I Can Mend Your Broken Heart	Gibson, Don	43-285	CB
I Can Only Imagine	Carson, Jeff	19-179	ST
I Can Only Imagine	Mercy Me	35-305	CB
I Can Only Imagine	Mercy Me	32-286	THM
I Can Only Imagine	MercyMe	20-380	HP
I Can See An Angel	Cline, Patsy	45-492	CB
I Can See Arkansas	Murray, Anne	11-15	PL
I Can See Clearly Now	Cliff, Jimmy	16-575	SC
I Can See Clearly Now	Cliff, Jimmy	8-607	TT
I Can See Clearly Now	Nash, Johnny	35-111	CB
I Can See Clearly Now	Nash, Johnny	17-410	DK
I Can See Clearly Now	Osmond, Donny	47-865	ZP
I Can See For Miles	Who	28-144	DK
I Can See For Miles	Who	19-729	LE
I Can See For Miles	Who	3-129	SC

SONG TITLE	ARTIST	#	TYPE
I Can See You Smile	Estefan, Gloria	23-575	MM
I Can Sleep When I'm Dead	Carroll, Jason M.	36-418	CB
I Can Still Feel You	Raye, Collin	8-98	CB
I can Still Feel You	Raye, Collin	5-294	SC
I Can Still Make Cheyenne	Strait, George	1-265	CB
I Can Still Make Cheyenne	Strait, George	4-464	SC
I Can Take It From There	Young, Chris	47-933	BKD
I Can Tell By The Way You Dance	Gosdin, Vern	33-83	CB
I Can Tell By The Way You Dance	Gosdin, Vern	4-555	SC
I Can Wait Forever	Air Supply	46-587	CB
I Can't Be Bothered	Lambert, Miranda	46-266	KV
I Can't Be Myself	Haggard, Merle	37-173	CB
I Can't Be Your Friend	Rushlow	19-64	ST
I Can't Be Your Friend	Rushlow	32-372	THM
I Can't Believe It's Me	Lynne, Rockie	36-572	CB
I Can't Believe That You've Stopped...	Pride, Charley	47-434	CB
I Can't Change The World	Paisley, Brad	47-710	BKD
I Can't Change The World	Paisley, Brad	43-15	KCDC
I Can't Dance	Collins, Phil	44-26	AH
I Can't Do That Anymore	Hill, Faith	15-683	CB
I Can't Do That Anymore	Hill, Faith	7-382	MM
I Can't Do That Anymore	Hill, Faith	4-600	SC
I Can't Drive 55	Hagar, Sammy	3-555	SC
I Can't Explain	Who	19-742	LE
I Can't Feel You Anymore	Lynn, Loretta	43-233	CB
I Can't Fight this Feeling	Hobbs, Becky	4-114	SC
I Can't Forget You	Cline, Patsy	45-491	CB
I Can't Get Close Enough	Exile	29-659	SC
I Can't Get Enough Of You	Bailey, Razzy	29-382	CB
I Can't Get Next To You	Temptations	17-128	DK
I Can't Get Over You	Brooks & Dunn	22-710	ST
I Can't Get Started	Standard	11-834	DK
I Can't Give You Anything But Love	Garland, Judy	48-276	MM
I Can't Give You Anything But Love	Lee, Peggy	49-926	KVD
I Can't Go For That	Hall & Oates	3-524	SC
I Can't Go For That (No Can Do)	Hall & Oates	33-309	CB
I Can't Hear The Music	Lynn, Loretta	47-627	CB
I Can't Help It If I'm Still In...	Williams, Hank Sr.	16-754	DK
I Can't Help It If I'm Still In...	Williams, Hank Sr.	8-638	SAV
I Can't Help It If I'm Still In...	Williams, Hank Sr.	5-98	SC
I Can't Help Myself	Four Tops	11-102	DK
I Can't Help Myself	Four Tops	2-86	SC

SONG TITLE	ARTIST	#	TYPE
I Can't Help Myself	Martins	22-12	CB
I Can't Help Myself	Rabbitt, Eddie	48-34	CB
I Can't Help You Now	Raitt, Bonnie	25-210	MM
I Can't Help You, I'm Falling Too	Davis, Skeeter	15-92	CB
I Can't Hold Back	Survivor	24-688	SC
I Can't Let Go	Hollies	44-368	ZM
I Can't Lie To Me	Davidson, Clay	14-111	CB
I Can't Lie To Me	Davidson, Clay	19-225	CSZ
I Can't Lie To Me	Davidson, Clay	22-556	ST
I Can't Love You Anymore	Nichols, Gary	30-198	CB
I Can't Love You Back	Corbin, Easton	43-150	CB
I Can't Love You Back	Corbin, Easton	38-105	CB
I Can't Love You Enough	Twitty & Lynn	5-449	SC
I Can't Make You Love Me	Adele	38-237	CB
I Can't Make You Love Me	Raitt, Bonnie	6-97	MM
I Can't Quit (I've Gone Too Far)	Robbins, Marty	48-29	VH
I Can't Quit You Baby	Led Zeppelin	15-22	SC
I Can't Reach Her Anymore	Kershaw, Sammy	1-470	CB
I Can't Reach Her Anymore	Kershaw, Sammy	6-479	MM
I Can't See Nobody	Bee Gees	48-682	DFK
I Can't Sleep	Walker, Clay	19-703	ST
I Can't Sleep Baby	Kelly, R.	49-521	SC
I Can't Stay Mad At You	Davis, Skeeter	43-336	CB
I Can't Stop	Osmonds	47-854	SFM
I Can't Stop Loving You	Charles, Ray	35-48	CB
I Can't Stop Loving You	Charles, Ray	16-805	DK
I Can't Stop Loving You	Charles, Ray	13-349	P
I Can't Stop Loving You	Charles, Ray	2-269	SC
I Can't Stop Loving You	Husky, Ferlin	22-269	CB
I Can't Stop Loving You	Wells, Kitty	34-194	CB
I Can't Stop Loving You	Wells, Kitty	47-390	CB
I Can't Take You Anywhere	Emerick, Scotty	25-707	MM
I Can't Take You Anywhere	Emerick, Scotty	19-271	ST
I Can't Tell the Bottom From the Top	Hollies	44-374	ZPK
I Can't Tell You Why	Eagles	7-562	BS
I Can't Tell You Why	Eagles	2-266	SC
I Can't Turn You Loose	Redding, Otis	47-362	PS
I Can't Understand	Yearwood, Trisha	24-122	SC
I Can't Unlove You	Rogers, Kenny	29-42	CB
I Can't Unlove You	Rogers, Kenny	29-712	ST
I Can't Wait	Nicks, Stevie	16-128	SC
I Can't Wait Any Longer	Anderson, Bill	5-813	SC
I Can't Win For Losing You	Conley, Earl Thomas	4-493	SC
I Can't Get Over You	Brooks & Dunn	8-350	CB
I Can't Make You Love Me	Raitt, Bonnie	10-765	JVC
I Care	Hall, Tom T.	18-282	CB
I Care	Hall, Tom T.	29-700	SC

SONG TITLE	ARTIST	#	TYPE
I Cheated Me Right Out Of You	Bandy, Moe	19-497	CB
I Cheated Me Right Out Of You	Bandy, Moe	4-645	SC
I Cheated On A Good Woman	Craddock, Billy C	5-764	SC
I Choose You	Bareillas, Sara	48-210	KV
I Close My Eyes And Count To Ten	Springfield, Dusty	10-636	SF
I Could	Locke, Kimberly	29-315	PHM
I Could Fall In Love	Selena	21-449	PS
I Could Get Used To This Lovin' Thing	Jackson, Alan	45-105	KV
I Could Get Used To You	Exile	17-365	DK
I Could Have Danced All Night	Andrews, Julie	19-107	SAV
I Could Have Danced All Night	Syms, Sylvia	12-556	P
I Could Kick Your Ass	Moore, Justin	44-383	BKD
I Could Never Love You Enough	McComas, Brian	16-689	ST
I Could Never Take the Place of Your Man	Prince	49-826	KV
I Could Never Take The Place Of...	Knight, Jordan	8-520	PHT
I Could Never Take The Place Of...	Knight, Jordan	10-199	SC
I Could Not Ask For More	Evans, Sara	29-545	CB
I Could Not Ask For More	Evans, Sara	14-835	ST
I Could Not Ask For More	McCain, Edwin	49-508	PHC
I Could Write A Book	Connick, Harry Jr.	19-722	PS
I Couldn't Be Me Without You	Rodriguez, Johnny	22-54	CB
I Couldn't Keep From Cryin'	Robbins, Marty	48-19	CB
I Couldn't Leave You If I Tried	Crowell, Rodney	12-40	DK
I Couldn't Leave You If I Tried	Crowell, Rodney	5-255	SC
I Couldn't Live Without Your Love	Clark, Petula	6-53	SC
I Couldn't See You Leaving	Twitty, Conway	43-199	CB
I Count The Minutes	Martin, Ricky	9-139	PS
I Count The Minutes	Martin, Ricky	13-733	SGB
I Count The Tears	Drifters	45-895	MM
I Cried A Tear	Baker, Laverne	17-318	SS
I Cried All The Way To The Altar	Cline, Patsy	45-486	CB
I Cried My Last Tear	Doe, Ernie K.	45-577	OZP
I Cross My Heart	Strait, George	1-245	CB
I Cross My Heart	Strait, George	6-110	MM
I Cross My Heart	Strait, George	12-434	P
I Cross My Heart	Strait, George	2-12	SC
I Cry	Cochran, Anita	16-35	ST
I Cry	Cochran, Tammy	25-74	MM
I Cry	Flo Rida	45-650	MRH

SONG TITLE	ARTIST	#	TYPE
I Dare You	Shinedown	30-284	SC
I Did It	Dave Matthews Band	35-246	CB
I Did It	Dave Matthews Band	16-481	MH
I Didn't Mean To Turn You On	Palmer, Robert	11-226	DK
I Didn't Mean To Turn You On	Palmer, Robert	21-745	MH
I Didn't Know My Own Strength	Morgan, Lorrie	6-807	MM
I Didn't Know My Own Strength	Morgan, Lorrie	2-762	SC
I Dig Rock & Roll Music	Peter, Paul & Mary	5-167	SC
I Dig Rock And Roll Music	Mamas & Papas	47-218	ST
I Disappear	Metallica	14-492	SC
I Do	98 Degrees	7-703	PHM
I Do	Brandt, Paul	7-330	MM
I Do	Brandt, Paul	4-454	SC
I Do	Caillat, Colbie	37-262	CB
I Do	J. Geils Band	46-329	SC
I Do	Loeb, Lisa	14-199	CB
I Do	Loeb, Lisa	10-117	SC
I Do	Toya	35-232	CB
I Do (Cherish You)	98 Degrees	29-179	MH
I Do (Cherish You)	98 Degrees	8-500	PHT
I Do (Cherish You)	98 Degrees	10-204	SC
I Do (Cherish You)	98 Degrees	13-789	SGB
I Do (Cherish You)	98 Degrees	15-369	SKG
I Do (Cherish You)	Wills, Mark	8-410	CB
I Do (Cherish You)	Wills, Mark	22-787	ST
I Do But Do I	Arminger, Katie	38-90	PHM
I Do I Do I Do I Do I Do	Abba	7-500	MM
I Do My Swinging At Home	Houston, David	14-433	SC
I Do Not Hook Up	Clarkson, Kelly	47-691	CB
I Do Now	Andrews, Jessica	14-728	CB
I Don't	Peck, Danielle	29-31	CB
I Don't Believe In Goodbye	Sawyer Brown	2-670	SC
I Don't Believe You've Met My...	Louvin Brothers	3-207	SC
I Don't Care	Owens, Buck	3-200	SC
I Don't Care	Pierce, Webb	29-393	CB
I Don't Care	Pierce, Webb	6-773	MM
I Don't Care	Skaggs, Ricky	34-252	CB
I Don't Care (Just As Long As...)	Owens, Buck	34-206	CB
I Don't Care Anymore	Collins, Phil	44-10	LG
I Don't Dance	Brice, Lee	43-145	SBIG
I Don't Do Lonely Well	Wicks, Chuck	48-451	KCD
I Don't Even Know Your Name	Jackson, Alan	1-50	CB
I Don't Even Know Your Name	Jackson, Alan	2-829	SC
I Don't Fall In Love So Easy	Crowell, Rodney	24-14	SC
I Don't Feel Like Loving	Wilson, Gretchen	29-23	CB

SONG TITLE	ARTIST	#	TYPE
You Today			
I Don't Feel Like Loving You Today	Wilson, Gretchen	23-452	ST
I Don't Feel This Way Anymore	Leigh, Danni	14-736	CB
I Don't Have The Heart	Ingram, Jack	33-340	CB
I Don't Have The Heart	Ingram, James	2-273	SC
I Don't Have To Be Me 'Til Monday	Azar, Steve	16-42	ST
I Don't Have To Be Me Till Monday	Azar, Steve	25-56	MM
I Don't Have To Wonder	Brooks, Garth	9-407	CB
I Don't Hurt Anymore	Snow, Hank	22-128	CB
I Don't Hurt Anymore	Snow, Hank	4-806	SC
I Don't Know	Dennis, Wesley	2-701	SC
I Don't Know	Williams, Hank III	14-841	ST
I Don't Know A Thing About Love	Twitty, Conway	2-364	SC
I Don't Know How Love Starts	Walker, Clay	24-241	SC
I Don't Know If I'm Coming Home	Mudhog	30-557	CB
I Don't Know What She Said...	Larsen, Blaine	29-715	ST
I Don't Know Where To Start	Rabbitt, Eddie	48-40	CB
I Don't Know Why (I Just Do)	Robbins, Marty	48-27	VH
I Don't Know Why But I Do	Henry, C. Frogman	3-300	MM
I Don't Know Why I Love You But I Do	Pride, Charley	47-440	FMK
I Don't Know Why You Don't Want Me	Cash, Roseanne	5-818	SC
I Don't Like To Sleep Alone	Anka, Paul	9-174	SO
I Don't Look Good Naked Anymore - F	Snake Oil Willie Band	45-325	CK
I Don't Look Good Naked Anymore - M	Snake Oil Willie Band	45-324	DFK
I Don't Love You Like That	Jypsi	36-573	CB
I Don't Need To Tell You I'm Pretty	Mumba, Samantha	15-813	CB
I Don't Need You	Rogers, Kenny	4-778	SC
I Don't Need Your Rockin' Chair	Jones, George	33-115	CB
I Don't Need Your Rockin' Chair	Jones, George	2-641	SC
I Don't Paint Myself Into Corners	Howard, Rebecca L	14-87	CB
I Don't Paint Myself Into Corners	Howard, Rebecca L	25-296	MM
I Don't Paint Myself Into Corners	Yearwood, Trisha	18-130	ST
I Don't Remember Loving You	Conlee, John	20-283	SC
I Don't See Me In Your Eyes Anymore	Reeves, Jim	44-246	SRK
I Don't Think I Will	Bonamy, James	7-279	MM
I Don't Think I Will	Bonamy, James	4-367	SC

SONG TITLE	ARTIST	#	TYPE
I Don't Think She's In Love Anymore	Pride, Charley	40-107	CB
I Don't Wanna Be Alone	Shai	4-344	SC
I Don't Wanna Cry	Carey, Mariah	21-463	CB
I Don't Wanna Cry	Gatlin, Larry	47-103	CB
I Don't Wanna Fight	Turner, Tina	27-310	DK
I Don't Wanna Fight	Turner, Tina	10-429	LE
I Don't Wanna Fight	Turner, Tina	6-363	MM
I Don't Wanna Fight	Turner, Tina	13-23	P
I Don't Wanna Go On With You Like	John, Elton	6-545	MM
I Don't Wanna Go On With You Like..	John, Elton	2-372	SC
I Don't Wanna Have To Marry You	Brown & Cornelius	13-485	P
I Don't Wanna Have To Marry You	Brown & Cornelius	9-603	SAV
I Don't Wanna Kiss You Goodnight	LFO	14-172	CB
I Don't Wanna Kiss You Goodnight	LFO	16-235	PHM
I Don't Wanna Kiss You Goodnight	LFO	14-479	SC
I Don't Wanna Know	New Found Glory	22-355	CB
I Don't Wanna Know	Winans & P Diddy	20-570	CB
I Don't Wanna Live Without Your..	Chicago	17-77	DK
I Don't Wanna Lose You	Turner, Tina	10-424	LE
I Don't Wanna Lose Your Love	Santana/Los Lonely	29-279	PHM
I Don't Wanna Play House	Wynette, Tammy	33-3	CB
I Don't Wanna Play House	Wynette, Tammy	4-265	SC
I Don't Want Anything To Change	Raitt, Bonnie	29-217	PHM
I Don't Want This Night To End	Bryan, Luke	38-117	CB
I Don't Want To	Braxton, Toni	10-692	HH
I Don't Want To	Monroe, Ashley	30-109	CB
I Don't Want To Be	DeGraw, Gavin	20-193	PHM
I Don't Want To Be A Memory	Exile	17-12	DK
I Don't Want To Be A Memory	Exile	16-585	SC
I Don't Want To Be Alone Tonight	Dr. Hook	47-46	SFM
I Don't Want To Be Right	Ingram, Luther	7-476	MM
I Don't Want To Be Tied	Presley, Elvis	25-486	MM
I Don't Want To Get Hurt	Summer, Donna	15-200	LE
I Don't Want To Go On Without You	John, Elton	17-553	DK
I Don't Want To Live Without You	Foreigner	17-80	DK
I Don't Want To Lose You	Jackson, Freddie	17-131	DK
I Don't Want To Miss A Thing	Aerosmith	34-130	CB
I Don't Want To Miss A Thing	Aerosmith	21-556	PHM

SONG TITLE	ARTIST	#	TYPE
I Don't Want To Miss A Thing	Chesnutt, Mark	8-865	CB
I Don't Want To Miss A Thing	Chesnutt, Mark	10-166	SC
I Don't Want To Miss A Thing	Chesnutt, Mark	22-702	ST
I Don't Want To Spoil The Party	Cash, Roseanne	7-115	MM
I Don't Want To Talk About It	Stewart, Rod	14-851	LE
I Don't Want To Wait	Cole, Paula	49-509	PHG
I Don't Want To Wait	Cole, Paula	15-501	SC
I Don't Want You To Go	Johnson, Carolyn D.	34-339	CB
I Don't Want You To Go	Johnson, Carolyn D.	25-70	MM
I Don't Want You To Go	Johnson, Carolyn D.	16-96	ST
I Don't Wanta	Cline, Patsy	45-482	CB
I Don't Know A Thing About Love	Twitty, Conway	1-163	CB
I Don't Think Love Ought To Be That	McEntire, Reba	5-863	SC
I Dream Of Women Like You	McDowell, Ronnie	47-228	CB
I Dreamed A Dream	Minelli, Liza	49-216	KH
I Dreamed About Mama Last Night	Williams, Hank Sr.	37-186	CB
I Dreamed Of A Hillbilly Heaven	Ritter, Tex	20-717	CB
I Dreamed Of A Hillbilly Heaven	Ritter, Tex	4-301	SC
I Drink Alone	Thorogood, George	43-9	CB
I Drink Alone	Thorogood, George	20-320	MH
I Drive Myself Crazy	N'Sync	20-435	CB
I Drive Myself Crazy	N'Sync	29-173	MH
I Drive Your Truck	Brice, Lee	43-191	ASK
I Drove All Night	Dion, Celine	20-460	CB
I Drove All Night	Dion, Celine	25-531	MM
I Drove All Night	Dion, Celine	20-626	NS
I Drove All Night	Dion, Celine	18-774	PHM
I Drove All Night	Lauper, Cyndi	5-688	SC
I Drove All Night	Orbison, Roy	38-56	SF
I Drove All Night	Pinmonkey	25-421	MM
I Drove All Night	PinMonkey	18-330	ST
I Drove Her To Dallas	England, Tyler	10-271	CB
I Fall To Pieces	Cline, Patsy	16-763	DK
I Fall To Pieces	Cline, Patsy	6-733	MM
I Fall To Pieces	Cline, Patsy	13-344	P
I Fall To Pieces	Cline, Patsy	2-11	SC
I Feel Better All Over	Husky, Ferlin	22-264	CB
I Feel Better All Over	Husky, Ferlin	5-428	SC
I Feel Fine	Beatles	37-272	CB
I Feel Fine	Beatles	11-133	DK
I Feel Fine	Beatles	29-336	SC
I Feel For You	Khan, Chaka	16-875	DK
I Feel Free	Cream	5-882	SC
I Feel Like Loving You Again	Sheppard, T.G.	3-248	CB
I Feel Love	Summer, Donna	15-203	LE
I Feel Loved	Depeche Mode	16-318	TT
I Feel Lucky	Carpenter, M C	1-422	CB

SONG TITLE	ARTIST	#	TYPE
I Feel Lucky	Carpenter, M C	6-113	MM
I Feel Lucky	Carpenter, M C	15-150	THM
I Feel The Earth Move	King, Carole	26-337	DK
I Feel The Earth Move	King, Carole	13-303	P
I Feel The Earth Move	King, Carole	19-166	SGB
I Feel Your Love Tonight	Van Halen	19-136	SGB
I Fell	Seals, Brady	5-297	SC
I Fell In Love	Carter, Carlene	6-529	MM
I Fell In Love Again Last Night	Forrester Sisters	12-406	P
I Fell The Earth Move	Martika	18-497	SAV
I Finally Found Someone	Kershaw & Morgan	17-483	CB
I Finally Found Someone	Streisand & Adams	20-120	PHM
I Finally Found Someone	Up Close&Personal	18-184	DK
I Forget You Every Day	Haggard, Merle	49-820	SSK
I Forgot More Than You'll Ever Know	Davis Sisters	13-389	P
I Forgot To Be Your Love	Idol, Billy	13-211	P
I Forgot To Remember	Presley, Elvis	14-755	THM
I Fought The Law	Bobby Fuller Four	11-366	DK
I Fought The Law	Bobby Fuller Four	13-123	P
I Fought The Law	Bobby Fuller Four	9-464	SAV
I Found A Boy	Adele	44-173	KV
I Found A Million Dollar Baby	Cole, Nat "King"	46-366	PS
I Found Someone	Cher	11-323	DK
I Found Someone	Cher	14-62	RS
I Found Someone	Cher	15-120	SGB
I Found Sunshine	Chilites	35-116	CB
I Get A Kick Out Of You	Sinatra, Frank	17-381	DK
I Get A Kick Out Of You	Sinatra, Frank	14-270	MM
I Get A Kick Out Of You	Sinatra, Frank	12-560	P
I Get A Kick Out Of You	Sinatra, Frank	21-213	SGB
I Get Along Without You Very Well	Sinatra, Frank	49-506	MM
I Get Around	Beach Boys	5-503	BS
I Get Around	Beach Boys	33-252	CB
I Get Around	Beach Boys	11-398	DK
I Get Around	Beach Boys	12-867	P
I Get Ideas	Martin, Tony	4-183	SC
I Get Lonely	Jackson, Janet	15-443	CB
I Get Lonely	Jackson, Janet	15-417	PS
I Get The Fever	Anderson, Bill	20-786	CB
I Get The Fever	Anderson, Bill	5-96	SC
I Get To	Blue County	30-203	CB
I Get To	Blue County	30-203	CB
I Get Weak	Carlisle, Belinda	11-283	DK
I Get Weak	Carlisle, Belinda	5-146	SC
I Give You To His Heart	Krauss, Alison	10-158	SC
I Go Back	Chesney, Kenny	29-430	CB
I Go Back	Chesney, Kenny	20-382	ST
I Go Blind	Hootie & Blowfish	4-170	SC
I Go Crazy	Davis, Paul	18-52	MM
I Go Crazy	Davis, Paul	13-154	P
I Go To Extremes	Joel, Billy	12-268	DK
I Go To Extremes	Joel, Billy	16-144	LE

SONG TITLE	ARTIST	#	TYPE
I Go To Extremes	Joel, Billy	16-518	P
I Got A Car	Strait, George	42-21	ASK
I Got A Feelin'	Currington, Billy	43-316	CB
I Got A Feelin'	Currington, Billy	19-766	ST
I Got A Feeling I'm Falling - show	Ain't Misbehavin'	48-790	MM
I Got A Feeling In My Body	Presley, Elvis	25-746	MM
I Got A Million Of 'Em	McDowell, Ronnie	47-229	CB
I Got A Name	Croce, Jim	7-48	MM
I Got A Name	Croce, Jim	9-535	SAV
I Got A Woman	Charles, Ray	27-230	DK
I Got A Woman	Charles, Ray	46-575	DKM
I Got A Woman	Presley, Elvis	7-133	MM
I Got Dreams	Wariner, Steve	14-259	SC
I Got Drunk	Montgomery Gentry	46-201	SC
I Got ID	Pearl Jam	9-308	RS
I Got It Bad	Campbell, Tevin	24-297	SC
I Got It Honest	Tippin, Aaron	2-714	SC
I Got Loaded	Peppermint Harris	2-406	SC
I Got Mexico	Raven, Eddy	4-649	SC
I Got More	Deggs, Cole & Lonesome	30-313	CB
I Got My Game On	Adkins, Trace	30-543	CB
I Got Nerve	Montana, Hannah	36-65	WD
I Got Rhythm	Darin, Bobby	47-5	KV
I Got Rhythm	Garland, Judy	48-272	KV
I Got Rhythm	Happenings	16-855	DK
I Got Spurs That Jingle Jangle Jingle	Ritter, Tex	45-568	DCK
I Got Stripes	Cash, Johnny	29-766	CB
I Got Stripes	Cash, Johnny	6-5	SC
I Got Stung	Presley, Elvis	14-756	THM
I Got The Boy	Kramer, Jana	48-198	BKD
I Got The Feelin' (Oh No No)	Diamond, Neil	47-418	MM
I Got The Feeling	Amazing Rhythm Aces	45-835	VH
I Got The Feeling	Brown, James	29-139	LE
I Got The Hoss	Tillis, Mel	19-460	CB
I Got You	Jennings & Colter	22-151	CK
I Got You	Jennings & Colter	9-621	SAV
I Got You	Morgan, Craig	29-38	CB
I Got You	Shenandoah	1-485	CB
I Got You	Yoakam, Dwight	49-684	SC
I Got You - duet	Jennings & Carter	45-170	RCA
I Got You - duet	Thompson Square	37-228	CB
I Got You Babe	Sonny & Cher	11-446	DK
I Got You Babe	Sonny & Cher	14-59	RS
I Got You Babe	Sonny & Cher	15-121	SGB
I Got You I Feel Good	Brown, James	14-564	AH
I Got You I Feel Good	Brown, James	26-327	DK
I Got You I Feel Good	Brown, James	29-151	LE
I Got You I Feel Good	Brown, James	13-92	P
I Got You I Feel Good	Brown, James	2-38	SC
I Got Your Country Right Here	Wilson, Gretchen	37-340	CB
I Gotta Get Drunk	Nelson, Willie	45-849	VH

SONG TITLE	ARTIST	#	TYPE
I Gotta Get To You	Strait, George	38-144	CB
I Gotta Know	Presley, Elvis	7-127	MM
I Guess I'm Crazy	Reeves, Jim	15-82	CB
I Guess I'm Crazy	Reeves, Jim	12-71	DK
I Guess I'm Crazy	Reeves, Jim	14-334	SC
I Guess That's Why They Call It The Blues	John, Elton	17-554	DK
I Guess That's Why They Call It The Blues	John, Elton	13-312	P
I Guess That's Why They Call It The Blues	John, Elton	2-379	SC
I Guess You Had To Be There	Morgan, Lorrie	6-309	MM
I Had A Beautiful Time	Haggard, Merle	44-73	KV
I Had No Right	PM Dawn	7-785	PHT
I Had One One Time	Turner, Josh	49-229	DFK
I Had The Craziest Dream	Sinatra, Frank	9-248	PT
I Hang My Head And Cry	Autry, Gene	22-171	CB
I Hate Everything	Strait, George	30-797	PHM
I Hate Everything	Strait, George	20-485	ST
I Hate Everything About You	Three Days Grace	20-575	CB
I Hate Everything About You	Three Days Grace	35-287	CB
I Hate Everything About You	Three Days Grace	23-176	PHM
I Hate Myself For Losing You	Clarkson, Kelly	47-693	KV
I Hate Myself For Loving You	Jett, Joan	18-385	SAV
I Hate Myself For Loving You	Jett, Joan	5-315	SC
I Hate U	Prince	4-687	SC
I Hate You Then I Love You	Dion & Pavaratti	17-655	PR
I Have A Dream	Abba	7-501	MM
I Have A Love - duet	Streisand & Mathis	49-540	MM
I Have A Love (One Hand One Heart)	Mathis & Streisand	6-345	MM
I Have But One Heart	Martino, Al	46-209	SC
I Have Loved You Girl (But Not Like This	Conley, E.T.	47-606	SC
I Have To Surrender	Herndon, Ty	8-131	CB
I Have To Surrender	Herndon, Ty	22-642	ST
I Haven't Found It Yet	Darling, Helen	4-122	SC
I Haven't Played This Song In Years	Diamond, Neil	30-504	THM
I Haven't Stopped Dancing Yet	Pat And Mick	49-925	KVD
I Hear A Symphony	Ross, Diana	48-547	DK
I Hear A Symphony	Supremes	14-888	DK
I Hear a Symphony	Supremes	4-43	SC
I Hear Little Rock Calling	Husky, Ferlin	45-565	SSK
I Hear You Knockin'	Lewis, Smiley	13-266	P
I Hear You Knockin'	Lewis, Smiley	5-459	SC
I Hear You Knockin'	Storm, Gale	17-72	DK
I Hear You Knocking	Judd, Wynonna	48-317	CB
I Hear Your Voice	Richie, Lionel	16-209	MM

SONG TITLE	ARTIST	#	TYPE
I Heard A Heart Break Last Night	Reeves, Jim	44-257	DFK
I Heard A Rumour	Bananarama	17-149	DK
I Heard It Through The Grapevine	Gaye, Marvin	16-778	DK
I Heard It Through the Grapevine	Gaye, Marvin	36-118	JTG
I Heard It Through The Grapevine	Gaye, Marvin	12-627	P
I Heard It Through The Grapevine	Gaye, Marvin	2-77	SC
I Heard That Lonesome Whistle Blow	Cash, Johnny	29-742	CB
I Heard The Bells On Christmas Day	Gatlin, Larry	47-100	CB
I Heard The Bells On Xmas Day - xmas	Gatlin, Larry	45-253	CB
I Heard The Bluebirds Sing	Robbins, Marty	48-25	DCK
I Heard The Bluebirds Sing	Robbins, Marty	47-786	SRK
I Heart Question Mark	Swift, Taylor	44-141	BKD
I Hold On	Bentley, Dierks	41-48	ASK
I Honestly Love You	Newton-John, Olivia	11-183	DK
I Honestly Love You	Newton-John, Olivia	12-685	P
I Honestly Love You	Newton-John, Olivia	2-442	SC
I Hope	Dixie Chicks	29-29	CB
I Hope	Dixie Chicks	23-461	ST
I Hope Heaven Has A Honky Tonk	Lawrence, Tracy	48-379	CB
I Hope It Rains	Kramer, Jana	48-194	KCD
I Hope You Dance	Womack, Lee Ann	13-821	CHM
I Hope You Find It	Cher	47-680	KV
I Hung It Up	Brown, Junior	40-81	CB
I John	Presley, Elvis	25-511	MM
I Just Call You Mine	McBride, Martina	37-39	CB
I Just Called To Say I Love You	Wonder, Stevie	35-173	CB
I Just Called To Say I Love You	Wonder, Stevie	11-644	DK
I Just Came Back (From a War)	Worley, Darryl	30-172	CB
I Just Came Here To Dance - duet	Frizzell & West	45-411	CB
I Just Came In To Get My Baby Out Of..	Young, Faron	46-53	SSK
I Just Can't Be True	Pierce, Webb	29-404	CB
I Just Can't Get Her Out Of My Mind	Rodriguez, Johnny	22-50	CB
I Just Can't Get Her Out Of My Mind	Rodriguez, Johnny	5-667	SC
I Just Can't Go On Dying Like This	Strait, George	42-12	PHN
I Just Can't Help Believing	Thomas, B.J.	36-152	LE
I Just Can't Live A Lie	Underwood, Carrie	30-120	AS
I Just Can't Stop Loving You	Jackson, M &	27-276	DK
I Just Can't Stop Loving You	Jackson, Michael	15-503	CMC

119

SONG TITLE	ARTIST	#	TYPE
I Just Can't Stop Loving You	Jackson, Michael	16-564	P
I Just Died In Your Arms	Cutting Crew	33-350	CB
I Just Dies in Your Arms	Cutting Crew	5-389	SC
I Just Don't Have A Heart	Cliff, Richard	48-767	P
I Just Fall In Love Again	Murray, Anne	11-598	DK
I Just Fall In Love Again	Murray, Anne	11-16	PL
I Just Had To Hear Your Voice	Adams, Oleta	46-390	HKC
I Just Might Be	Morgan, Lorrie	7-323	MM
I Just Might Be	Morgan, Lorrie	24-163	SC
I Just Wanna Be Loved	Culture Club	47-1	SF
I Just Wanna Be Mad	Clark, Terri	33-193	CB
I Just Wanna Be Mad	Clark, Terri	25-352	MM
I Just Wanna Be Mad	Clark, Terri	18-209	ST
I Just Wanna Dance With You	Strait, George	7-740	CHM
I Just Wanna Live	Good Charlotte	22-356	CB
I Just Wanna Stop	Vannelli, Gino	17-561	PR
I Just Wanna Stop	Vannelli, Gino	4-59	SC
I Just Want To Be With You	N'Sync	15-769	BS
I Just Want To Be Your Everything	Bee Gees	11-441	DK
I Just Want To Be Your Everything	Gibb, Andy	27-574	DK
I Just Want To Be Your Everything	Gibb, Andy	2-851	SC
I Just Want To Celebrate	Rare Earth	16-407	PR
I Just Want To Dance With You	Strait, George	1-251	CB
I Just Want To Love You	Rabbitt, Eddie	48-36	CB
I Just Want To Make Love	Foghat	18-259	DK
I Just Want To Make Love	Foghat	4-570	SC
I Just Want To Make Love To You	James, Etta	19-561	SC
I Just Want You To Know	Rose, Amy	40-24	PHN
I Just Wanted You To Know	Chesnutt, Mark	1-355	CB
I Just Wanted You To Know	Chesnutt, Mark	2-93	SC
I Just Wish You Were Someone I Loved	Gatlins	47-105	CB
I Keep Coming Back	Bailey, Razzy	29-378	CB
I Keep Coming Back	Gracin, Josh	30-171	CB
I Keep Forgettin'	McDonald, Michael	4-383	SC
I Keep Looking	Evans, Sara	29-550	CB
I Keep Looking	Evans, Sara	25-181	MM
I Keep Looking	Evans, Sara	16-430	ST
I Kept On Loving You	Carpenters	44-342	OZP
I Kiss Your Hand Madame	Crosby, Bing	9-547	SAV
I Kissed A Girl	Perry, Katy	36-496	CB
I Kissed A Girl	Sobule, Jill	3-500	SC
I Knew I Loved You	Savage Garden	5-791	SC
I Knew The Bride	Lowe, Nick	19-139	SGB

SONG TITLE	ARTIST	#	TYPE
I Knew You That Way	Bryan, Luke	45-430	CK
I Knew You Were Trouble	Swift, Taylor	42-33	ASK
I Knew You Were Waiting	Franklin & Michael	35-310	CB
I Knew You Were Waiting	Franklin & Michael	17-350	DK
I Knew You Were Waiting	Franklin, Aretha	48-551	DK
I Knew You When	Adams, Oleta	46-384	PS
I Knew You When	South, Joe	16-648	JTG
I Know	Farris, Dionne	28-408	DK
I Know	Farris, Dionne	14-874	SC
I Know	Farris, Dionne	29-125	ST
I Know	George, Barbara	6-150	MM
I Know	Vandross, Luther	48-324	SC
I Know A Heartache When I See One	Warnes, Jennifer	33-308	CB
I Know A Little	Kershaw, Sammy	24-6	SC
I Know A Little	Lynyrd Skynyrd	19-820	SGB
I Know A Place	Clark, Petula	9-88	PS
I Know How He Feels	McEntire, Reba	1-794	CB
I Know How The River Feels	Diamond Rio	8-957	CB
I Know How The River Feels	McAlyster	10-272	CB
I Know How To Love You Well	McGraw, Tim	49-77	ZPA
I Know I'm Losing You	Temptations	26-515	DK
I Know One	Pride, Charley	6-12	SC
I Know Places	Swift, Taylor	48-299	KV
I Know She Still Loves Me	Strait, George	4-17	SC
I Know So	Newton, Wayne	47-794	SRK
I Know That's Right	Raye, Collin	29-59	CB
I Know There's Something Goin' On	Frida	18-494	SAV
I Know There's Something Goin' On	Frida	5-608	SC
I Know What Boys Like	Waitresses	15-14	SC
I Know What You Want	Busta Rhymes, Carey, Flipmo	32-311	THM
I Know Where I'm Going	Judds	1-138	CB
I Know Where I'm Going	Judds	4-789	SC
I Know Where It's At	All Saints	7-716	PHM
I Know Where Love Lives	Ketchum, Hal	12-424	P
I Know Who Holds Tomorrow	Rimes, LeAnn	1-300	CB
I Know Why The River Runs	Womack, Lee Ann	48-480	CKC
I Know You Better Than That	Goldsboro, Bobby	49-648	DFK
I Know You Want Me (Calle Ocho)	Pitbull	40-13	PHM
I Know You're Out There	Moody Blues	20-87	SC
I Learned About Love	Al Dexter & Troopers	19-624	CB
I Learned From The Best	Houston, Whitney	16-180	PHM
I Left My Heart In San	Bennett, Tony	16-728	DK

SONG TITLE	ARTIST	#	TYPE
Francisco			
I Left My Heart In San Francisco	Bennett, Tony	10-410	LE
I Left My Heart In San Francisco	Bennett, Tony	12-519	P
I Left My Heart In San Francisco	Bennett, Tony	2-192	SC
I Left Something Turned On At Home	Adkins, Trace	7-640	CHM
I Left Something Turned On At Home	Adkins, Trace	10-88	SC
I Let A Song Go Out Of My Heart	Fitzgerald, Ella	12-563	P
I Let Her Lie	Singletary, Daryle	7-26	MM
I Let Her Lie	Singletary, Daryle	3-655	SC
I Let The Stars Get In My Eyes	Hill, Goldie	8-775	CB
I Lie In The Bed I Make	Brother Cane	10-143	SC
I Like Beer	Hall, Tom T.	8-447	CB
I Like Beer	Hall, Tom T.	7-409	MM
I Like Beer	Hall, Tom T.	3-603	SC
I Like Dreamin'	Nolan, Kenny	22-925	SC
I Like Girls That Drink Beer	Keith, Toby	39-18	SB
I Like It	Gerry & Pacemakers	10-562	SF
I Like It	Iglesias w Pitbull	40-9	BH
I Like It I Love It	McGraw, Tim	1-531	CB
I Like It I Love It	McGraw, Tim	6-844	MM
I Like It Like That	Dave Clark Five	45-79	LC
I Like It Like That	Kenner, Chris	3-585	SC
I Like Queers	Parody	47-875	ZP
I Like The Sound Of That	Rascal Flatts	44-289	KCDC
I Like You A Lot	Owen, Jake	43-131	ASK
I Look At You	Strait, George	38-145	CB
I Lost It	Chesney, Kenny	29-434	CB
I Lost It	Chesney, Kenny	19-218	CSZ
I Lost On Jeopardy	Yankovic, Weird Al	49-842	SC
I Love	Hall, Tom T.	8-43	CB
I Love	Hall, Tom T.	5-402	SC
I Love A Rainy Night	Rabbitt, Eddie	17-7	DK
I Love A Rainy Night	Rabbitt, Eddie	13-439	P
I Love Her She Hates Me	Worley, Darryl	23-415	CB
I Love How You Love Me	Campbell, Glen	34-255	CB
I Love How You Love Me	Paris Sisters	12-562	P
I Love How You Love Me	Vinton, Bobby	49-87	LE
I Love L.A.	Newman, Randy	29-270	SC
I Love Music	O'Jays	9-762	SAV
I Love My Baby (My Baby Loves Me)	Miller, Mitch	23-548	CB
I Love My Friend	Rich, Charlie	9-576	SAV
I Love My Friend	Rich, Charlie	5-200	SC
I Love My Life	O'Neal, Jamie	29-46	CB
I Love Nascar - duet	Judd & Keith	38-169	SC
I Love Paris	Sinatra, Frank	11-760	DK
I Love Rock & Roll	Jett, Joan	11-325	DK
I Love Rock & Roll	Jett, Joan	13-3	P
I Love Rock & Roll	Jett, Joan	10-522	SF

SONG TITLE	ARTIST	#	TYPE
I Love Rocky Road	Yankovic, Weird Al	49-838	SC
I Love That I Hate You	Brown, Kane	49-626	BKD
I Love That I Hate You - Inst	Brown, Kane	49-629	BKD
I Love The Blues & the Boogie Woogie	Craddock, Billy C	46-645	CB
I Love The Dead	Alice Cooper	16-441	SGB
I Love The Nightlife	Bridges, Alicia	9-229	PT
I Love The Nightlife	Bridges, Alicia	2-496	SC
I Love The Way You Love Me	Montgomery, J M	14-205	CB
I Love The Way You Love Me	Montgomery, J M	6-385	MM
I Love The Way You Love Me	Montgomery, J M	12-414	P
I Love The Way You Love Me	Montgomery, J M	2-2	SC
I Love This Bar	Keith, Toby	35-422	CB
I Love This Bar	Keith, Toby	25-710	MM
I Love This Bar	Keith, Toby	19-525	ST
I Love This Bar	Keith, Toby	32-414	THM
I Love This Life	LoCash	49-526	BKD
I Love This Life - duet	LoCash	49-529	ZP
I Love To Love	Charles, Tina	11-29	PX
I Love To Tell The Story	Jackson, Alan	49-174	ASK
I Love To Tell The Story	Standard	47-830	SC
I Love You	Evans, Faith	20-617	CB
I Love You	Evans, Faith	25-217	MM
I Love You	McBride, Martina	29-534	CB
I Love You	McBride, Martina	22-485	ST
I Love You 'Cause I Want To	Carter, Carlene	6-743	MM
I Love You A Thousand Ways	Frizzell, Lefty	19-486	CB
I Love You A Thousand Ways	Frizzell, Lefty	5-374	SC
I Love You Always Forever	Lewis, Donna	24-46	SC
I Love You Because	Anka, Paul	5-224	SC
I Love You Because	Payne, Leon	8-666	SAV
I Love You Because	Reeves, Jim	3-827	LG
I Love You Because	Reeves, Jim	10-580	SF
I Love You Because	Tubb, Ernest	8-388	CB
I Love You Because	Whittaker, Roger	13-589	PL
I Love You Came Too Late	McEntire, Joey	7-897	PHT
I Love You Came Too Late	McEntire, Joey	10-188	SC\
I Love You For Sentimental Reasons	Cole, Nat "King"	11-572	DK
I Love You Honey	Cline, Patsy	47-511	VH
I Love You Love Me Love	Glitter, Gary	49-144	SF
I Love You More And More	Bellamy Brothers	45-292	DCK
I Love You More Today	Twitty, Conway	5-100	SC
I Love You So Much It Hurts	Cline, Patsy	22-188	CB
I Love You So Much It	Wakely, Jimmy	19-844	CB

121

SONG TITLE	ARTIST	#	TYPE
Hurts			
I Love You That Much	Sider, Lizzie	41-62	PHN
I Love You This Big	McCreary, Scotty	38-110	CB
I Love You This Much	Wayne, Jimmy	25-708	MM
I Love You This Much	Wayne, Jimmy	19-262	ST
I Love You This Much	Wayne, Jimmy	32-417	THM
I Love You Truly	Standard	10-469	MG
I Love You What Can I Say	Reed, Jerry	20-725	SC
I Love Your Smile	Shanice	13-605	P
I Loved 'Em Every One	Sheppard, T.G.	13-385	P
I Loved Her First	Heartland	30-29	CB
I Made A Promise	Gayle & Rabbitt	2-835	SC
I Made It Through The Rain	Manilow, Barry	29-119	CB
I Made It Through The Rain	Manilow, Barry	9-75	PS
I May Hate Myself In The Morning	Womack, Lee Ann	22-94	CB
I May Never Get To Heaven	Twitty, Conway	4-779	SC
I Me Mine	Beatles	44-119	KV
I Meant Every Word He Said	VanShelton, Ricky	8-550	CB
I Meant Every Word He Said	VanShelton, Ricky	4-68	SC
I Meant To	Cotter, Brad	20-384	ST
I Meant To Do That	Brandt, Paul	7-395	MM
I Meant To Do That	Brandt, Paul	4-628	SC
I Meant To Do That	Brandt, Paul	22-907	ST
I Melt	Rascal Flatts	35-426	CB
I Melt	Rascal Flatts	25-647	MM
I Melt	Rascal Flatts	19-260	ST
I Melt	Rascal Flatts	32-339	THM
I Melt With You	Modern English	9-345	AH
I Met Him On A Sunday	Shirelles	27-499	DK
I Might Even Quit Lovin' You	Chesnutt, Mark	8-471	CB
I Might Even Quit Lovin' You	Chesnutt, Mark	22-786	ST
I Might Just Make It	Jefferson, Paul	7-388	MM
I Miss Her Missing Me	Daniel, Davis	4-118	SC
I Miss Me	Cotter, Brad	22-88	CB
I Miss My Friend	Worley, Darryl	33-171	CB
I Miss My Friend	Worley, Darryl	25-187	MM
I Miss My Friend	Worley, Darryl	16-688	ST
I Miss My Mary	Ketchum, Hal	4-461	SC
I Miss You	Adele	45-819	DCK
I Miss You	Cyrus, Miley	36-78	WD
I Miss You	Hall, Aaron	15-767	NU
I Miss You	Klymaxx	15-796	SC
I Miss You	Presley, Elvis	25-323	MM
I Miss You A Little	Montgomery, J M	14-213	CB
I Miss You A Little	Montgomery, J M	22-404	CHM
I Miss You So	Little Anthony	30-520	LE
I Missed Again	Collins, Phil	44-22	SC
I Missed Me	Reeves, Jim	44-250	SRK
I Must Be Seeing Things	Pitney, Gene	47-527	ZM

SONG TITLE	ARTIST	#	TYPE
I Need A Girl	P Diddy&Feat&Usher	17-596	PHM
I Need A Lover	Mellencamp, John	46-207	SC
I Need A Vacation	Howard, Rebecca L	19-693	ST
I Need Love	N'Sync	15-772	BS
I Need Love	N'Sync	20-437	CB
I Need More Of You	Bellamy Brothers	5-815	SC
I Need My Girl	Shelton, Blake	45-376	BKD
I Need Somebody	Presley, Elvis	25-762	MM
I Need Somebody Bad	Greene, Jack	43-350	CB
I Need To Know	Anthony, Marc	35-248	CB
I Need To Know	Anthony, Marc	29-176	MH
I Need To Know	Anthony, Marc	8-516	PHT
I Need To Know	Anthony, Marc	5-782	SC
I Need To Wake Up	Etheridge, Melissa	47-65	NSP
I Need You	America	4-79	SC
I Need You	Anthony, Marc	25-198	MM
I Need You	Rimes, LeAnn	9-412	CB
I Need You	Rimes, LeAnn	22-549	ST
I Need You	Yearwood, Trisha	22-401	CHM
I Need You - duet	McGraw & Hill	40-29	SC
I Need You - duet	McGraw & Hill	46-316	SC
I Need You All The Time	Blackhawk	6-67	SC
I Never Cry	Alice Cooper	16-446	SGB
I Never Go Around Mirrors	Whitley, Keith	47-766	SRK
I Never Had A Chance	Griggs, Andy	29-56	CB
I Never Knew Lonely	Gill, Vince	3-38	SC
I Never Knew Love	Stone, Doug	20-602	CB
I Never Loved a Man....	Franklin, Aretha	36-165	JT
I Never Loved You Anyway	Corrs	49-195	SF
I Never Met A Woman I Didn't Like	Cox, Don	4-164	SC
I Never Once Stopped Loving You	Smith, Connie	48-93	CB
I Never Picked Cotton	Clark, Roy	5-820	SC
I Never Picked Cotton	Clark, Roy	46-624	SC
I Never Said Goodbye	Humperdinck, E.	37-161	CB
I Never Stopped Lovin' You	Azar, Steve	7-340	MM
I Never Stopped Lovin' You	Azar, Steve	4-398	SC
I Never Told You	Cailliat, Colbie	48-216	CB
I Only Get This Way With You	Trevino, Rick	7-629	CHM
I Only Get This Way With You	Trevino, Rick	10-80	SC
I Only Have Eyes For You	Fitzgerald, Ella	23-350	MM
I Only Have Eyes For You	Flamingos	12-662	P
I Only Have Eyes For You	Flamingos	9-806	SAV
I Only Have Eyes For You	Garfunkel, Art	12-287	DK
I Only Have Eyes For You	Lettermen	48-518	L1
I Only Have Eyes For	Sinatra, Frank	49-718	KV

SONG TITLE	ARTIST	#	TYPE
You			
I Only Have Good Days	Roys	36-219	PHM
I Only Smoke When I Drink	Small Town Pistols	49-742	DCK
I Only Wanna Be With You	Fox, Samantha	35-190	CB
I Only Wanna Be With You	Fox, Samantha	11-697	DK
I Only Wanna Be With You	Fox, Samantha	6-484	MM
I Only Wanna Be With You	Hootie & Blowfish	21-135	CB
I Only Want To Be With You	Bay City Rollers	4-390	SC
I Only Want To Be With You	Springfield, Dusty	5-77	SC
I Only Want To Be With You	Springfield, Dusty	10-651	SF
I Overlooked An Orchid	Frizzell, Lefty	19-484	CB
I Overlooked An Orchid	Gilley, Mickey	22-222	CB
I Overlooked An Orchid	Gilley, Mickey	4-576	SC
I Play The Road	Zac Brown Band	43-467	KV
I Play The Road	Zac Brown Band	38-260	PHN
I Pray For You	Rich, John	14-86	CB
I Prefer The Moonlight	Rogers, Kenny	4-816	SC
I Put A Spell On You	Animals	11-367	DK
I Put A Spell On You	CCR	5-606	SC
I Put A Spell On You	CCR	16-282	TT
I Put A Spell On You	Midler, Bette	45-920	KV
I Put A Spell On You	Sonique	18-520	TT
I Ran (So Far Away)	Flock Of Seagulls	29-7	MH
I Raq And Roll	Black, Clint	34-410	CB
I Really Didn't Mean It	Vandross, Luther	48-325	SFM
I Really Don't Want To Know	Arnold, Eddy	17-17	DK
I Really Don't Want To Know	Arnold, Eddy	9-525	SAV
I Really Don't Want To Know	Arnold, Eddy	5-692	SC
I Really Don't Want To Know	Husky, Ferlin	22-272	CB
I Really Got The Feeling	Parton, Dolly	29-776	CB
I Really Love You	Jepsen, Carly Rae	45-275	BKD
I Recall A Gypsy Woman	Williams, Don	10-519	SF
I Remember	Boyz II Men	4-178	SC
I Remember	Chesney, Kenny	48-77	CB
I Remember	Cole, Keyshia	36-465	CB
I Remember You	Dorsey, Jimmy	15-504	DK
I Run To You	Lady Antebellum	40-2	CB
I Said A Prayer	Tillis, Pam	22-798	ST
I Said A Prayer For You	Tillis, Pam	1-464	CB
I Sang Dixie	Yoakam, Dwight	33-91	CB
I Saved The World Today	Eurythmics	47-80	SF
I Saw GOD Today	Strait, George	36-391	CB
I Saw Her Again	Mamas & Papas	47-217	LE
I Saw Her Standing There	Beatles	16-771	DK
I Saw Her Standing There	Beatles	12-737	P

SONG TITLE	ARTIST	#	TYPE
I Saw Her Standing There	Beatles	29-340	SC
I Saw Her Standing There	Lewis, Jerry Lee	47-203	KV
I Saw Her Standing There	Lewis, Jerry Lee	45-874	VH
I Saw Him Standing There	Tiffany	28-388	DK
I Saw Mommy Kissing Santa Claus	Ronettes	47-589	ZM
I Saw Red	Warrant	24-686	SC
I Saw The Light	Judd, Wynonna	1-647	CB
I Saw The Light	Judd, Wynonna	7-747	CHM
I Saw The Light	Judd, Wynonna	13-506	P
I Saw The Light	Judd, Wynonna	2-511	SC
I Saw The Light	Ketchum, Hal	8-464	CB
I Saw The Light	Williams, Hank Sr.	37-185	CB
I Saw Three Ships - xmas	Christmas	45-13	KV
I Say a Little Prayer	Franklin, Aretha	10-627	SF
I Say A Little Prayer	Warwick, Dionne	16-831	DK
I Say A Little Prayer	Warwick, Dionne	5-464	SC
I Second That Emotion	Robinson, Smokey	16-841	DK
I Second That Emotion	Robinson, Smokey	36-111	JTG
I See It Now	Lawrence, Tracy	1-578	CB
I See It Now	Lawrence, Tracy	17-235	NA
I See It Now	Lawrence, Tracy	2-488	SC
I See Me	Tritt, Travis	22-22	CB
I See The Want To In Your Eyes	Twitty, Conway	43-201	CB
I See You	Bryan, Luke	45-403	BKD
I See Your Smile	Estefan, Gloria	17-750	PT
I Shall Be Released	Band	12-61	DK
I Shall Be Released	Band	46-468	DK
I Shall Not Be Moved	Presley, Elvis	25-513	MM
I Shot Tequila	Parody	47-877	KRZ
I Shot The Sheriff	Clapton, Eric	16-847	DK
I Shot The Sheriff	Clapton, Eric	15-55	LE
I Shot The Sheriff	Clapton, Eric	13-166	P
I Should Be	Hill, D	32-56	THM
I Should Be Sleeping	Emerson Drive	34-348	CB
I Should Be Sleeping	Emerson Drive	25-67	MM
I Should Be Sleeping	Emerson Drive	16-102	ST
I Should Care	Cole, Nat "King"	45-603	OZP
I Should Have Been True	Mavericks	22-858	ST
I Should Have Known Better	Beatles	11-550	DK
I Should Have Known Better	Beatles	13-62	P
I Should've Known	Crittenden, Melodie	5-291	SC
I Showed Her	O-Town	20-627	NS
I Sing For Joy	Williams, Don	48-672	DCK
I Smoke I Drink	Mr. Magic	30-808	PHM
I Started A Joke	Bee Gees	17-491	LE
I Still Believe	Carey, Mariah	16-200	PHT
I Still Believe	Richie, Lionel	47-451	PHN
I Still Believe In Fairytales	Wynette, Tammy	49-363	CB

SONG TITLE	ARTIST	#	TYPE
I Still Believe In You	Desert Rose Band	5-531	SC
I Still Believe In you	Gill, Vince	1-591	CB
I Still Believe In You	Gill, Vince	12-476	P
I Still Believe In You	Gill, Vince	3-642	SC
I Still Can't Say Goodbye	Atkins, Chet	46-448	DFK
I Still Haven't Found What I'm Look	U2	17-147	DK
I Still Haven't Found What I'm Look	U2	13-274	P
I Still Like Bologna	Jackson, Alan	36-313	PHM
I Still Love You	702	32-234	THM
I Still Miss Someone	McBride, Martina	29-190	CB
I Still Miss Someone	McBride, Martina	29-844	SC
I Still Miss You	Anderson, Keith	36-415	CB
I Still Write Your Name In The Snow	Atkins, Chet	18-487	SC
I Sure Can Smell The Rain	Blackhawk	2-418	SC
I Surrender	Dion, Celine	19-20	PS
I Swear	All-4-One	34-133	CB
I Swear	All-4-One	26-314	DK
I Swear	All-4-One	13-289	P
I Swear	All-4-One	2-226	SC
I Swear	Montgomery, J M	14-206	CB
I Swear	Montgomery, J M	6-451	MM
I Take A Lot Of Pride	Haggard, Merle	22-229	CB
I Take A Lot Of Pride In What I Am	Haggard, Merle	43-49	CB
I Take A Lot Of Pride In What I Am	Haggard, Merle	4-727	SC
I Take My Chances	Carpenter, M C	8-884	CB
I Take My Chances	Carpenter, M C	6-572	MM
I Take My Chances	Carpenter, M C	15-153	THM
I Talk To Jesus Every Day	Cash, Johnny	49-714	VH
I Tell It Like It Used To Be	Brown, T. Graham	9-526	SAV
I Thank The Lord For The Nighttime	Diamond, Neil	30-684	LE
I Thank You	Sam & Dave	7-258	MM
I Thank You	Sam & Dave	12-727	P
I Think About It All The Time	Berry, John	7-18	MM
I Think About It All The Time	Berry, John	3-425	SC
I Think About You	Raye, Collin	1-134	CB
I Think About You	Raye, Collin	4-200	SC
I Think I Love You	Partridge Family	33-269	CB
I Think I Love You	Partridge Family	11-336	DK
I Think I Love You	Partridge Family	13-9	P
I Think I Love You Too Much	Jeff Healy Band	17-96	DK
I Think I'll Just Stay Here & Drink	Haggard, Merle	8-317	CB
I Think I'll Just Stay Here & Drink	Haggard, Merle	17-10	DK
I Think I'll Just Stay Here & Drink	Haggard, Merle	13-386	P
I Think I'm A Clone Now	Yankovic, Weird Al	15-342	MM

SONG TITLE	ARTIST	#	TYPE
I Think I'm In Love	Simpson, Jessica	33-420	CB
I Think I'm In Love With You	Simpson, Jessica	14-482	SC
I Think I'm In Love With You	Simpson, Jessica	19-835	SGB
I Think I'm In Love With You	Simpson, Jessica	15-637	THM
I Think I'm Paranoid	Garbage	19-553	SC
I Think Of You	Corbin, Easton	41-54	PHN
I Think The World Needs A Drink	Clark, Terri	22-76	CB
I Think We're Alone Now	James & Shondells	20-65	SC
I Think We're On To Something	Emilio	4-375	SC
I Think We're On To Something	Emilio	7-285	MM
I Think You're Beautiful	Dalley, Amy	19-537	ST
I Think You're Beautiful	Minor, Shane	23-367	SC
I Think You're Beautiful	Minor, Shane	22-476	ST
I Thought It Was You	Stone, Doug	20-595	CB
I Thought It Was You	Stone, Doug	3-643	SC
I Threw Away The Rose	Haggard, Merle	8-370	CB
I Told You So	Travis, Randy	1-399	CB
I Told You So	Travis, Randy	35-398	CB
I Told You So	Travis, Randy	11-424	DK
I Told You So	Travis, Randy	5-123	SC
I Told You So	Underwood, Carrie	37-5	CB
I Told You So	Urban, Keith	30-438	CB
I Took A Pill In Ibiza	Posner, Mike	49-930	MRH
I Touch Myself	Divinyls	30-662	RSX
I Touch Myself **	Divinyls	18-255	DK
I Touch Myself **	Divinyls	2-190	SC
I Try	Gray, Macy	14-173	CB
I Try	Gray, Macy	13-567	LE
I Try	Gray, Macy	15-327	PHM
I Try To Think About Elvis	Loveless, Patty	1-723	CB
I Try To Think About Elvis	Loveless, Patty	6-662	MM
I Try To Think About Elvis	Loveless, Patty	2-453	SC
I Turn To You	Aguilera, Christina	14-175	CB
I Turn To You	Aguilera, Christina	13-570	LE
I Turn To You	Aguilera, Christina	10-219	SC
I Turn To You	Melanie C	23-262	HS
I Understand	Dorsey, Jimmy	47-31	PS
I Understand	Valli, June	9-745	SAV
I Walk Alone	Cher	47-686	SBI
I Walk Alone	Robbins, Marty	3-233	CB
I Walk Alone	Robbins, Marty	20-636	SC
I Walk The Line	Cash, Johnny	14-236	CB
I Walk The Line	Cash, Johnny	11-763	DK
I Walk The Line	Cash, Johnny	13-365	P
I Walk The Line	Cash, Johnny	9-481	SAV
I Walk The Line	Cash, Johnny	21-589	SC
I Walk The Line	Crowell & Cash, J.	10-154	SC
I Wanna Be Around	Bennett, Tony	10-414	LE
I Wanna Be Around	Bennett, Tony	18-69	MM

SONG TITLE	ARTIST	#	TYPE
I Wanna Be Bad	Ford, Willa	18-406	MM
I Wanna Be Down	Brandy	33-348	CB
I Wanna Be Free	Monkees	47-293	ABS
I Wanna Be Loved	Andrew Sisters	46-422	CB
I Wanna Be Loved By You	Kane, Helen	12-544	P
I Wanna Be Sedated	Ramones	16-456	MH
I Wanna Be Sedated	Ramones	21-411	SC
I Wanna Be Seduced	Lee, Peggy	45-850	VH
I Wanna Be With You	Backstreet Boys	30-411	THM
I Wanna Be With You	Moore, Mandy	35-222	CB
I Wanna Be With You	Moore, Mandy	30-636	THM
I Wanna Be With You	Moore, Mandy	18-521	TT
I Wanna Be Your Lover	Prince	7-95	MM
I Wanna Believe	Loveless, Patty	20-393	ST
I Wanna Dance With Somebody	Houston, Whitney	11-135	DK
I Wanna Dance With Somebody	Houston, Whitney	13-188	P
I Wanna Dance With You	Rabbitt, Eddie	11-423	DK
I Wanna Die	Lambert, Miranda	46-260	KV
I Wanna Do It All	Clark, Terri	35-423	CB
I Wanna Do It All	Clark, Terri	25-709	MM
I Wanna Do It All	Clark, Terri	19-370	ST
I Wanna Do It All	Clark, Terri	32-412	THM
I Wanna Fall In Love	McCann, Lila	35-415	CB
I Wanna Fall In Love	McCann, Lila	22-649	ST
I Wanna Feel That Way Again	Byrd, Tracy	8-734	CB
I Wanna Feel That Way Again	Byrd, Tracy	5-293	SC
I Wanna Feel That Way Again	Byrd, Tracy	22-814	ST
I Wanna Go Back	Money, Eddie	47-286	SC
I Wanna Go Too Far	Yearwood, Trisha	6-849	MM
I Wanna Go Too Far	Yearwood, Trisha	3-417	SC
I Wanna Have Some Fun	Fox, Samantha	15-10	SC
I Wanna Know	Joe	35-231	CB
I Wanna Know	Joe	16-123	PRT
I Wanna Know	Joe	15-633	THM
I Wanna Love	Campbell, Glen	48-490	CKC
I Wanna Love Him So Bad	Jelly Beans	6-47	SC
I Wanna Love You Forever	Simpson, Jessica	8-523	PHT
I Wanna Love You Forever	Simpson, Jessica	17-538	SC
I Wanna Make You Close Your Eyes	Bentley, Dierks	49-376	CB
I Wanna Make You Close Your Eyes	Bentley, Dierks	45-167	SF
I Wanna Make You Cry	Bates, Jeff	19-775	ST
I Wanna Play House With You	Arnold, Eddy	44-222	CKC
I Wanna Remember This	Davis, Linda	8-493	CB
I Wanna Remember This	Davis, Linda	22-817	ST
I Wanna Say Yes	Mandrell, Louise	20-678	SC
I Wanna Sex You Up	Color Me Badd	34-105	CB
I Wanna Sex You Up **	Color Me Badd	2-718	SC

SONG TITLE	ARTIST	#	TYPE
I Wanna Talk About Me	Keith, Toby	33-137	CB
I Wanna Talk About Me	Keith, Toby	25-1	MM
I Wanna Talk About Me	Keith, Toby	15-669	ST
I Want A Cowboy	Elam, Katrina	22-29	CB
I Want A Man	Lace	14-705	CB
I Want A Man	Lace	5-733	SC
I Want A Man	Lace	22-494	ST
I Want A New Drug	Lewis & The News	34-77	CB
I Want A New Drug	Lewis & The News	2-748	SC
I Want A New Duck	Yankovic, Weird Al	49-849	SGB
I Want Candy	Bow Wow Wow	24-430	SC
I Want Candy	Carter, Aaron	16-255	TT
I Want Crazy	Hayes, Hunter	40-51	ASK
I Want It That Way	Backstreet Boys	29-175	MH
I Want It That Way	Backstreet Boys	18-711	MM
I Want It That Way	Backstreet Boys	7-896	PHT
I Want It That Way	Backstreet Boys	13-779	SGB
I Want Love	John, Elton	25-19	MM
I Want Love	John, Elton	16-84	ST
I Want More	Eder, Linda	17-443	PS
I Want My Baby Back	Chesnutt, Mark	18-331	ST
I Want My Goodbye Back	Herndon, Ty	7-16	MM
I Want My Life Back	Covington, Bucky	39-52	CB
I Want My Money Back	Kershaw, Sammy	25-526	MM
I Want My Money Back	Kershaw, Sammy	18-789	ST
I Want My Money Back	Kershaw, Sammy	32-151	THM
I Want To Be In Love	Etheridge, Melissa	23-98	SC
I Want To Be In Love	Manchester, Melissa	18-396	MM
I Want To Be Loved Like That	Shenandoah	1-491	CB
I Want To Be Loved Like That	Shenandoah	2-8	SC
I Want To Be Sure	Autry, Gene	22-177	CB
I Want To Be Wanted	Lee, Brenda	5-81	SC
I Want To Be Wanted	Lee, Brenda	30-795	SF
I Want To Be With You Always	Avalon, Frankie	5-225	SC
I Want To Be With You Always	Frizzell, Lefty	3-735	CB
I Want To Be Your Girlfriend	Carpenter, M C	7-434	MM
I Want To Be Your Man	Roger	48-590	DK
I Want To Be Your Man	Troutman, Roger	11-407	DK
I Want To Come Over	Etherdige, Melissa	19-164	SGB
I Want To Come Over	Etheridge, Melissa	10-235	PS
I Want To Come Over	Etheridge, Melissa	4-180	SC
I Want To Give It All	Air Supply	46-589	CB
I Want To Go With You	Arnold, Eddy	19-34	CB
I Want To Go With You	Arnold, Eddy	4-797	SC
I Want To Hold Your Hand	Beatles	29-346	SC
I Want To Know	Wills, Mark	14-135	CB
I Want To Know What Love Is	Foreigner	20-293	CB
I Want To Know What Love Is	Foreigner	11-82	DK
I Want To Know What	Foreigner	13-286	P

125

SONG TITLE	ARTIST	#	TYPE
Love Is			
I Want To Know What Love Is	Foreigner	9-202	SO
I Want To Know You Before We Make Love	Twitty, Conway	48-244	CB
I Want To Live	Gracin, Josh	35-450	CB
I Want To Live	Gracin, Josh	20-261	PHM
I Want To Live	Gracin, Josh	20-333	ST
I Want To Live	Spacehog	15-306	THM
I Want To Spend My Life With You	Anthony & Arena	20-130	PHM
I Want To Take You Higher	Turner, Ike & Tina	15-505	CMC
I Want To Walk You Home	Domino, Fats	9-742	SAV
I Want To Walk You Home	Domino, Fats	22-452	SC
I Want Us Back	Morgan, Craig	30-33	CB
I Want You	Inspiral Carpets	30-770	SF
I Want You	Thalia & Fat Joe	25-719	MM
I Want You	Thalia feat Fat Joe	19-603	CB
I Want You - Duet	Thalia & Fat Joe	32-349	THM
I Want You Back	Bananarama	48-782	P
I Want You Back	Jackson Five	11-377	DK
I Want You Back	N'Sync	15-778	BS
I Want You Back	N'Sync	20-433	CB
I Want You Bad	Robison, Charlie	15-103	ST
I Want You Bad & That Ain't Good	Raye, Collin	1-125	CB
I Want You Bad & That Ain't Good	Raye, Collin	6-221	MM
I Want You I Need You I Love You	Presley, Elvis	11-608	DK
I Want You I Need You I Love You	Presley, Elvis	2-597	SC
I Want You I Need You I Love You	Presley, Elvis	14-748	THM
I Want You To Be My Girl	Lymon, Frankie	30-523	LE
I Want You To Need Me	Dion, Celine	13-838	PHM
I Want You To Want Me	Cheap Trick	13-19	P
I Want You To Want Me	Yoakam, Dwight	15-334	CB
I Want You To Want Me	Yoakam, Dwight	15-193	ST
I Want Your Sex **	Michael, George	17-94	DK
I Want Your Sex **	Michael, George	21-748	MH
I Want Your Sex **	Michael, George	5-550	SC
I Was	McCoy, Neal	8-920	CB
I Was	McCoy, Neal	22-731	ST
I Was Blown Away	Tillis, Pam	2-661	SC
I Was Blown Away	Tillis, Pam	22-868	ST
I Was Country When Country Wasn't	Mandrell, Barbara	13-457	P
I Was Country When Country Wasn't C	Mandrell, Barbara	11-745	DK
I Was Here	Lady Antebellum	37-56	CB
I Was Made To Love Her	Wonder, Stevie	15-714	LE
I Was The One	Presley, Elvis	14-749	THM
I Was There - duet	Owens & Yoakum	46-104	CB
I Was There - duet	Yoakam & Owens	49-687	CB
I Was Wrong	Social Distortion	24-546	SC

SONG TITLE	ARTIST	#	TYPE
I Watched It All On My Radio	Cartwright, Lionel	9-456	SAV
I Wear your Love	Angelle, Lisa	5-722	SC
I Went Out Of My Way To Make...	Drusky, Roy	20-750	CB
I Went To Your Wedding	Page, Patti	12-16	DK
I Went To Your Wedding	Snow, Hank	22-132	CB
I Who Have Nothing	Jones, Tom	18-44	MM
I Who Have Nothing	King, Ben E.	10-737	JVC
I Will	Taylor, Ben	14-880	SC
I Will	Wayne, Jimmy	36-245	PHM
I Will Always Love You	Houston, Whitney	17-385	DK
I Will Always Love You	Houston, Whitney	6-91	MM
I Will Always Love You	Houston, Whitney	12-873	P
I Will Always Love You	Houston, Whitney	29-326	PS
I Will Always Love You	Parton & Gill	7-78	MM
I Will Always Love You	Parton & Gill	3-566	SC
I Will Always Love You	Parton, Dolly	17-300	NA
I Will Always Love You	Parton, Dolly	2-14	SC
I Will Be	McCann, Lila	8-908	CB
I Will Be Right There	All-4-One	5-790	SC
I Will Be There	Seals, Dan	6-88	SC
I Will Be There For You	Andrews, Jessica	8-930	CB
I Will Buy You A New Life	Everclear	7-774	PHT
I Will Buy You A New Life	Everclear	10-137	SC
I Will Carry You	Aiken, Clay	20-544	PHM
I Will Carry You	Aiken, Clay	36-321	PS
I Will Come To You	Hanson	7-697	PHM
I Will Fall - Nashville - duet	Scott & O'Connor	45-477	KVD
I Will Follow	U2	30-68	SC
I Will Follow Him	March, Peggy	7-73	MM
I Will Follow Him	March, Peggy	4-36	SC
I Will Get There	Boyz II Men	7-820	PHM
I Will Go With You	Summer, Donna	15-198	LE
I Will Hold My Ground	Worley, Darryl	22-10	CB
I Will Hold My Ground	Worley, Darryl	19-692	ST
I Will If You Will	Berry, John	7-633	CHM
I Will Leave The Light On	Sawyer Brown	4-197	SC
I Will Love Again	Fabian, Lara	15-639	THM
I Will Love You	Angelle, Lisa	14-842	ST
I Will Love You	Angelle, Lisa	15-216	THM
I Will Never let You Know - Nashville	Bowen & Palladio	45-467	BKD
I Will Not Go Quietly	Henley, Don	48-158	ZMP
I Will Remember You	Grant, Amy	18-765	PS
I Will Remember You	McLachlan, Sarah	8-182	PHT
I Will Remember You	McLachlan, Sarah	4-662	SC
I Will Remember You	McLachlan, Sarah	13-790	SGB
I Will Stand	Chesney, Kenny	8-764	CB
I Will Stand	Chesney, Kenny	22-827	ST
I Will Survive	Gaynor, Gloria	11-89	DK
I Will Survive	Gaynor, Gloria	12-834	P
I Will Survive	Gaynor, Gloria	9-224	PT
I Will Survive	Gaynor, Gloria	19-165	SGB
I Will Survive	Wild Horses	16-39	ST

SONG TITLE	ARTIST	#	TYPE
I Will Survive/Funkytown Medley	Selena	23-570	MM
I Will Wait	Mumford & Sons	39-123	PHM
I Will....But	SheDaisy	13-810	CHM
I Wish	Kelly, R	35-252	CB
I Wish	Messina, Jo Dee	25-701	MM
I Wish	Messina, Jo Dee	19-263	ST
I Wish	Messina, Jo Dee	32-380	THM
I Wish	Wonder, Stevie	15-716	LE
I Wish (Radio Version)	Thomas, Carl	14-504	SC
I Wish I Could Break Your Heart	Pope, Cassadee	44-304	SBI
I Wish I Could Have Been There	Anderson, John	20-404	MH
I Wish I Didn't Miss You	Stone, Angie	25-224	MM
I Wish I Had Never Met Sunshine	Autry, Gene	22-182	CB
I Wish I Was 18 Again	Price, Ray	45-343	BSP
I Wish I Was A Punk Rocker	Thom, Sandi	30-709	SF
I Wish I Was Eighteen Again	Burns, George	44-58	KV
I Wish I Was Still In Your Dreams	Twitty, Conway	48-241	CB
I Wish I Wasn't	Headley, H.	32-275	THM
I Wish I Were In Love Again	Sinatra, Frank	14-275	MM
I Wish It Would Rain	Collins, Phil	44-14	PSJT
I Wish It Would Rain	Temptations	14-896	DK
I Wish That I Could Hurt That Way Again	Brown, T. Graham	47-549	SAV
I Wish That I Could Hurt That Way..	Lee, Brenda	9-435	SAV
I Wish You Love	Martin, Dean	23-92	MM
I Wish You Love	Wilson, Nancy	15-506	MM
I Wish You Were Here	Incubus	33-400	CB
I Wish You Were Here	Incubus	16-319	TT
I Wish You'd Stay	Paisley, Brad	25-414	MM
I Wish You'd Stay	Paisley, Brad	18-202	ST
I Won't Be The One To Let Go	Streisand & Manilow	49-622	ST
I Won't Come In While He's There	Reeves, Jim	3-829	LG
I Won't Dance	Sinatra, Frank	14-267	MM
I Won't Die Alone	Lynne, Shelby	23-417	CB
I Won't Forget You	Poison	6-16	SC
I Won't Forget You	Reeves, Jim	3-837	LG
I Won't Give Up	Kramer, Jana	48-195	PHN
I Won't Give Up	Mraz, Jason	44-384	BKD
I Won't Go Hunting With You Jake	Dean, Jimmy	47-19	BFK
I Won't Go On And On	Prather, Colt	20-331	ST
I Won't Have The Heart	Walker, Clay	4-235	SC
I Won't Hold You Back	Toto	20-99	SC
I Won't Last A Day Without You	Carpenters	33-286	CB
I Won't Last A Day Without You	Carpenters	4-848	SC
I Won't Let You Go	Morrison, james	38-267	ZM

SONG TITLE	ARTIST	#	TYPE
I Won't Lie	Brown, Shannon	8-853	CB
I Won't Mention It Again	Price, Ray	8-284	CB
I Won't Need You Anymore	Travis, Randy	1-396	CB
I Won't Need You Anymore	Travis, Randy	9-520	SAV
I Won't Need You Anymore	Travis, Randy	5-661	SC
I Won't Say Goodbye	Elam, Katrina	20-478	ST
I Won't Stand In Your Way	Stray Cats	48-166	KV
I Won't Take Less Than... - duet	Tucker, Davis, Overstreet	34-276	CB
I Won't Tell A Soul	Puth, Charlie	47-576	KV
I Wonder	Pickler, Kellie	30-341	CB
I Wonder Could I Love There Anymore	Pride, Charley	3-793	CB
I Wonder Do You Think Of Me	Whitley, Keith	4-654	SC
I Wonder Do You Think Of Me	Whitley, Keith	8-595	TT
I Wonder If I Ever Said Goodbye	Rodriguez, Johnny	22-55	CB
I Wonder If They Ever Think Of Me	Haggard, Merle	37-170	CB
I Wonder What She's Doin' Tonight	Boyce, Tommy	49-744	KRG
I Wonder What Would Happen	Chapin, Harry	46-565	KV
I Wonder where You Are Tonight	Whitley, Keith	49-402	KVD
I Wonder Why	Dion & Belmonts	47-20	LE
I Would	Jolie & The Wanted	14-155	CB
I Would	Vassar, Phil	36-607	CB
I Would	Vassar, Phil	36-209	PHM
I Would Cry	Dalley, Amy	23-3	CB
I Would Die For U	Prince	12-810	P
I Would Do Anything For Love	Meat Loaf	28-428	DK
I Would Have Loved You Anyway	Yearwood, Trisha	9-861	ST
I Wouldn't Be A Man	Dean, Billy	7-398	MM
I Wouldn't Be A Man	Dean, Billy	4-618	SC
I Wouldn't Be A Man	Dean, Billy	22-911	ST
I Wouldn't Be A Man	Turner, Josh	38-104	CB
I Wouldn't Change You If I Could	Skaggs, Ricky	4-652	SC
I Wouldn't Have Missed It For The..	Milsap, Ronnie	17-411	DK
I Wouldn't Have Missed It For The..	Milsap, Ronnie	12-446	P
I Wouldn't Know	McEntire, Reba	9-336	PS
I Wouldn't Tell You No Lies	Tractors	8-948	CB
I Wouldn't Tell You No Lies	Tractors	14-627	SC
I Wouldn't Want To Live If You...	Williams, Don	8-836	CB
I Wouldn't Want To Live...	Williams, Don	4-773	SC

SONG TITLE	ARTIST	#	TYPE
I Write The Songs	Manilow, Barry	29-109	CB
I Write The Songs	Manilow, Barry	16-759	DK
I Write The Songs	Manilow, Barry	9-77	PS
I-95 Asshole Song **	August & Spur of th	30-660	RSX
I-95 Asshole Song **	August & Spur of th	2-180	SC
I'd Be A Legend In My Time	Milsap, Ronnie	1-437	CB
I'd Be A Legend In My Time	Milsap, Ronnie	4-269	SC
I'd Be Better Off In A Pine Box	Stone, Doug	20-591	CB
I'd Be Better Off In A Pine Box	Stone, Doug	9-453	SAV
I'd Be Lyin'	Cagle, Chris	19-768	ST
I'd Die Without You	Dawn, P.M.	13-247	P
I'd Die Without You	P.M. Dawn	47-351	SC
I'd Do Anything	Simple Plan	35-300	CB
I'd Do Anything For Love	Meat Loaf	6-407	MM
I'd Fall In Love Tonight	Whittaker, Roger	13-592	PL
I'd Give My Right Nut To Save…	Driskoll&Womak,Jo	14-10	CHM
I'd Lie For You	Meat Loaf	15-507	THM
I'd Lie For You - duet	Meat Loaf & Russo	33-352	CB
I'd Like To Have That One Back	Strait, George	1-260	CB
I'd Like To Have That One Back	Strait, George	2-808	SC
I'd Like To Teach The World To Sing	Multi-Voice	11-544	DK
I'd Like To Teach The World To Sing	Multi-Voice	18-684	PR
I'd Like To Teach the World to Sing	New Seekers	28-237	DK
I'd Love To Knock the Hell Out Of You	Williams, Hank Jr.	47-594	CB
I'd Love To Lay You Down	Singletary, Daryle	18-454	ST
I'd Love To Lay You Down	Twitty, Conway	1-160	CB
I'd Love To Lay You Down	Twitty, Conway	4-658	SC
I'd Love You All Over Again	Jackson, Alan	1-34	CB
I'd Love You All Over Again	Jackson, Alan	2-387	SC
I'd Love You To Want Me	Lobo	11-396	DK
I'd Love You To Want Me	Lobo	2-433	SC
I'd Never Find Another You	Fury, Billy	10-557	SF
I'd Rather Die Young	Cash, Johnny	43-415	SRK
I'd Rather Leave While I'm In Love	Coolidge, Rita	10-517	SF
I'd Rather Love You	Pride, Charley	43-205	CB
I'd Rather Miss You	Little Texas	2-620	SC
I'd Rather Ride Around With You	McEntire, Reba	1-815	CB
I'd Rather Ride Around With You	McEntire, Reba	7-625	CHM
I'd Rather Ride Around With You	McEntire, Reba	10-81	SC

SONG TITLE	ARTIST	#	TYPE
I'd Really Love To See You Tonight	Carmen, Eric	11-334	DK
I'd Really Love To See You Tonight	England Dan&Coley	28-230	DK
I'd Really Love To See You Tonight	Seals, Dan	4-151	SC
I'd Still Have You	Pierce, John	29-207	CB
I'd Still Have You	Pierce, John	29-713	ST
I'd Surrender All	Travis, Randy	2-419	SC
I'd Trade All Of My Tomorrows	Robbins, Marty	45-868	VH
I'd Want It To Be Yours	Moore, Justin	45-646	BKD
I'll Always Be Right There	Adams, Bryan	23-444	CB
I'll Always Be Your Fraulein	Wells, Kitty	48-204	SSK
I'll Always Come Back	Oslin, K.T.	33-49	CB
I'll Always Love You	Dayne, Taylor	13-160	P
I'll Always Love You	Dayne, Taylor	29-292	SC
I'll Always Love You	Martin, Dean	23-75	MM
I'll Be	McCain, Edwin	10-21	SC
I'll Be	McEntire, Reba	13-808	CHM
I'll Be	McEntire, Reba	6-64	SC
I'll Be Alright Without You	Journey	17-536	SC
I'll Be Around	Sawyer Brown	19-373	ST
I'll Be Around	Spinners	16-559	P
I'll Be Around	Spinners	5-613	SC
I'll Be Coming Back For You	Sheppard, T.G.	20-18	SC
I'll Be Doggone	Gaye, Marvin	12-62	DK
I'll Be Here	Tuesdays	21-559	PHM
I'll Be Home	Boone, Pat	9-559	SAV
I'll Be Home	Flamingos	10-256	SS
I'll Be Home	Trainor, Meghan	48-513	KVD
I'll Be Home For Christmas	Streisand, Barbra	49-590	PS
I'll Be Leaving Alone	Pride, Charley	3-789	CB
I'll Be Loving You	Greenwood, Lee	47-127	CB
I'll Be Loving You Forever	New Kids On Block	9-688	SAV
I'll Be Missing You	Puff Daddy& Evans	20-125	PHM
I'll Be Right Here Lovin' You	Travis, Randy	14-99	CB
I'll Be Seeing You	Sinatra, Frank	9-259	PT
I'll Be There	Carey & Lorenz	11-713	DK
I'll Be There	Carey & Lorenz	6-94	MM
I'll Be There	Jackson Five	49-317	CB
I'll Be There	Presley, Elvis	25-116	MM
I'll Be There	Price, Ray	3-786	CB
I'll Be There - duet	Carey, Mariah	30-345	CB
I'll Be There (When You Get Lonely)	Price, Ray	45-629	PSJ
I'll Be There For You	Bon Jovi	21-715	CB
I'll Be There For You	Boyce Avenue	46-93	KV
I'll Be There For You	Rembrandts	12-238	DK
I'll Be There For You	Rembrandts	3-440	SC
I'll Be There For You	Rogers, Kenny	48-125	SC
I'll Be True To You	Oak Ridge Boys	23-504	CB

SONG TITLE	ARTIST	#	TYPE
I'll Be True To You	Oak Ridge Boys	4-636	SC
I'll Be Waiting	Adele	39-19	KV
I'll Be Waiting	Kravitz, Lenny	49-902	SC
I'll Be With You In Apple Blossom Time	Andrew Sisters	46-430	KV
I'll Be Your Baby Tonight	Murray, Anne	11-9	PL
I'll Be Your Shelter	Dayne, Taylor	12-798	P
I'll Come Back As Another Woman	Tucker, Tanya	16-351	CB
I'll Come Back As Another Woman	Tucker, Tanya	9-445	SAV
I'll Come Running	Smith, Connie	5-842	SC
I'll Die Tryin'	Lonestar	29-57	CB
I'll Do It All Over Again	Gayle, Crystal	29-619	CB
I'll Fly Away	Reeves, Jim	44-266	OZP
I'll Fly Away - Gospel	Gospel	33-202	CB
I'll Fly With You	Agostino, Gigi	16-307	PHM
I'll Forget You	Eder, Linda	17-444	PS
I'll Get By	Money, Eddie	4-274	SC
I'll Get Even With You	Rimes, LeAnn	4-592	SC
I'll Get Over You	Gayle, Crystal	15-73	CB
I'll Get Over You	Gayle, Crystal	5-48	SC
I'll Go Crazy	Brown, James	14-598	SC
I'll Go Crazy	Griggs, Andy	19-203	CB
I'll Go Crazy	Griggs, Andy	10-213	SC
I'll Go Crazy	Griggs, Andy	22-488	ST
I'll Go Down Loving You	Shenandoah	2-423	SC
I'll Go Down Swinging	Wagoner, Porter	19-316	CB
I'll Go On Alone	Robbins, Marty	5-365	SC
I'll Go On Loving You	Jackson, Alan	8-767	CB
I'll Go On Loving You	Jackson, Alan	22-821	ST
I'll Go Steppin' Too	Flatt & Scruggs	8-259	CB
I'll Go To My Grave Lovin' You	Statler Brothers	19-376	CB
I'll Go To My Grave Lovin' You	Statler Brothers	4-632	SC
I'll Have To Say I Love You...	Croce, Jim	33-292	CB
I'll Have To Say I Love You...	Croce, Jim	3-479	SC
I'll Hold You In My Heart	Arnold, Eddy	19-629	CB
I'll Hold You In My Heart	Arnold, Eddy	3-599	SC
I'll Hold You In My Heart	Arnold, Eddy	17-627	THM
I'll Just Hold On	Shelton, Blake	45-331	AC
I'll Leave This World Loving You	VanShelton, Ricky	8-560	CB
I'll Leave This World Loving You	VanShelton, Ricky	9-527	SAV
I'll Make Love To You	Boyz II Men	12-182	DK
I'll Make Love To You	Boyz II Men	6-642	MM
I'll Make Love To You	Boyz II Men	33-376	CB
I'll Need Someone To Hold Me When	Fricke, Janie	7-165	MM
I'll Never Be Free	Ford & Starr	22-205	CB
I'll Never Be Free - Duet	Ford & Starr	46-193	SC
I'll Never Break Your Heart	Backstreet Boys	11-65	JTG
I'll Never Break Your Heart	Backstreet Boys	18-710	MM

SONG TITLE	ARTIST	#	TYPE
I'll Never Break Your Heart	Backstreet Boys	7-770	PHT
I'll Never Do Better Than You	Canyon, George	22-73	CB
I'll Never Fall In Love	Jones, Tom	35-94	CB
I'll Never Fall In Love Again	Gentry, Bobbie	48-223	SF
I'll Never Fall In Love Again	Jones, Tom	27-552	DK
I'll Never Fall In Love Again	Jones, Tom	4-346	SC
I'll Never Fall In Love Again	Jones, Tom	10-628	SF
I'll Never Fall In Love Again	Warwick, Dionne	16-802	DK
I'll Never Fall In Love Again	Warwick, Dionne	30-750	SF
I'll Never Find Another You	James, Sonny	19-469	CB
I'll Never Find Another You	James, Sonny	5-705	SC
I'll Never Find Another You	Seekers	10-590	SF
I'll Never Forgive My Heart	Brooks & Dunn	1-89	CB
I'll Never Forgive My Heart	Brooks & Dunn	17-256	NA
I'll Never Forgive My Heart	Brooks & Dunn	2-448	SC
I'll Never Get Out Of This World Al	Williams, Hank Sr.	14-228	CB
I'll Never Get Out Of This World Al	Williams, Hank Sr.	6-15	SC
I'll Never Get Over You	Kid & Pirates	29-818	SF
I'll Never Get Over You Getting...	Expose	28-409	DK
I'll Never Get Over You Getting...	Expose	6-362	MM
I'll Never Get Over You Getting...	Wilson Phillips	12-73	DK
I'll Never Know	Presley, Elvis	25-324	MM
I'll Never Let You Go (Angel Eyes)	Steelheart	24-690	SC
I'll Never Pass This Way Again	Lawrence, Tracy	8-220	CB
I'll Never Smile Again	Sinatra, Frank	11-570	DK
I'll Never Smile Again	Sinatra, Frank	10-719	JVC
I'll Never Stand In Your Way	Presley, Elvis	45-616	HM
I'll Never Stop Loving You	J'Son	24-53	SC
I'll Never Stop Loving You	Morris, Gary	20-20	SC
I'll Play For You	Seals & Croft	47-483	SC
I'll Remember	Ho, Don	6-836	MM
I'll Remember	Madonna	21-160	LE
I'll Remember	Madonna	2-225	SC
I'll Remember April	Day, Doris	45-594	OZP
I'll Sail My Ship Alone	Mullican, Moon	5-579	SC
I'll Sail My Ship Alone	Russell, Leon	45-686	VH

129

SONG TITLE	ARTIST	#	TYPE
I'll See Him Through	Wynette, Tammy	4-745	SC
I'll See You In My Dreams	Boone, Pat	45-595	OZP
I'll Share My World With You	Jones, George	6-14	SC
I'll Sing About Mine	Josh Abbot Band	40-26	PHM
I'll Stand By You	Pretenders	6-643	MM
I'll Stand By You	Pretenders	2-470	SC
I'll Stand By You	Underwood, Carrie	30-473	CB
I'll Stick Around	Foo Fighters	48-226	SC
I'll Still Be Loving You	Reid, Mike	9-448	SAV
I'll Still Be Loving You	Restless Heart	1-416	CB
I'll Still Love You More	Yearwood, Trisha	14-619	SC
I'll Still Love You More	Yearwood, Trisha	22-739	ST
I'll Stop Loving You	Reid, Mike	9-541	SAV
I'll Take Care Of You	Dixie Chicks	16-651	RS
I'll Take Love Over Money	Tippin, Aaron	25-229	MM
I'll Take Love Over Money	Tippin, Aaron	16-711	ST
I'll Take Romance	Gorme, Eydie	25-271	MM
I'll Take Romance	Monro, Matt	20-765	KB
I'll Take Romance	Monro, Matt	18-104	PS
I'll Take That As A Yes (Hot Tub)	Vassar, Phil	23-8	CB
I'll Take The Memories	Morgan, Lorrie	49-116	CB
I'll Take Today	Allan, Gary	22-706	ST
I'll Take You There	General Public	15-765	NU
I'll Take You There	Staple Singers	2-443	SC
I'll Take You Where The Music Is Playing	Drifters	45-886	VH
I'll Think Of A Reason Later	Womack, Lee Ann	8-879	CB
I'll Think Of A Reason Later	Womack, Lee Ann	22-711	ST
I'll Think Of Something	Chesnutt, Mark	2-333	SC
I'll Try	Jackson, Alan	1-51	CB
I'll Try	Jackson, Alan	7-249	MM
I'll Try	Jackson, Alan	4-125	SC
I'll Try A Little Bit Harder	Fargo, Donna	48-660	CB
I'll Try Anything	Dotson, Amber	22-314	CB
I'll Tumble 4 Ya	Culture Club	46-650	SC
I'll Wait For You	Carr, Vicki	46-564	MM
I'll Wait For You	Nichols, Joe	30-50	CB
I'll Wait For You Dear	Al Dexter & Troopers	46-405	CB
I'm A Believer	Diamond, Neil	18-688	PS
I'm A Believer	Monkees	9-646	SAV
I'm A Believer	Smash Mouth	18-399	MM
I'm A Believer	Smash Mouth	16-392	SGB
I'm A Better Man	Humperdinck, E.	37-167	CB
I'm A Boy	Who	28-149	DK
I'm A Boy	Who	19-741	LE
I'm A Cowboy	Engvall, Bill	8-213	CB
I'm A Cowboy	Engvall, Bill	49-176	CB
I'm A Fool To Want You	Streisand, Barbra	49-382	PS
I'm A Freak	Iglesias & Pitbull	43-269	SF
I'm A Girl Watcher	O'Kaysions	12-667	P

SONG TITLE	ARTIST	#	TYPE
I'm A Keeper	Band Perry	44-390	KV
I'm A King Bee	Harpo, Slim	14-599	SC
I'm A Long Gone Daddy	Williams, Hank Sr.	14-230	CB
I'm A Loser	Beatles	20-198	SC
I'm A Lover (Not A Fighter)	Davis, Skeeter	43-331	CB
I'm A Man	Yardbirds	14-461	SC
I'm A Mean Ol' Lion	The Wiz	49-437	SDK
I'm A Nut	Miller, Roger	15-350	MM
I'm A Nut	Pullins, Larry	5-851	SC
I'm A Ramblin' Man	Jennings, Waylon	1-619	CB
I'm A Ramblin' Man	Jennings, Waylon	22-150	CK
I'm A Slave 4 U	Spears, Britney	35-234	CB
I'm A Slave 4 U	Spears, Britney	25-28	MM
I'm A Slave For You	Spears, Britney	16-304	PHM
I'm A Song (Sing Me)	Sedaka, Neil	45-851	VH
I'm A Stand By My Woman Man	Milsap, Ronnie	1-439	CB
I'm A Stranger Here Myself	Perfect Stranger	4-16	SC
I'm A Survivor	McEntire, Reba	15-668	ST
I'm A Woman	Lee, Peggy	25-668	MM
I'm About To Come Alive	Nail, David	36-619	CB
I'm Afraid This Must Be Love	Eder, Linda	17-445	PS
I'm Against It (Whatever It Is)	Marx, Groucho	48-8	KV
I'm Alive	Chesney, Kenny	48-73	BKD
I'm Alive	Diamond, Neil	30-505	THM
I'm Alive	Dion, Celine	18-228	CB
I'm Alive	Dion, Celine	19-21	PS
I'm Alive	Hollies	10-570	SF
I'm All About It	Houser, Randy	45-555	CB
I'm Already Taken	Wariner, Steve	19-200	CB
I'm Already Taken	Wariner, Steve	22-425	ST
I'm Already There	Lonestar	33-138	CB
I'm Already There	Lonestar	15-93	ST
I'm Already There	Lonestar	16-268	TT
I'm Alright	Loggins, Kenny	34-72	CB
I'm Alright	Loggins, Kenny	14-635	SC
I'm Alright	Messina, Jo Dee	8-489	CB
I'm Always On a Mountain When...	Haggard, Merle	37-180	CB
I'm Always Touched By Your Presence	Blondie	49-132	LG
I'm Amazed	McCann, Lila	23-486	CB
I'm Amazed	McCann, Lila	23-457	ST
I'm An Old Old Man	Frizzell, Lefty	19-494	CB
I'm Bad I'm Nationwide	ZZ Top	13-763	SGB
I'm Beautiful (When I Look In ..Eye	Jolie & The Wanted	15-337	CB
I'm Beginning To Forget You	Reeves, Jim	44-259	DFK
I'm Blue Again	Cline, Patsy	45-514	MM
I'm Coming Home	Cinderella	10-501	DA
I'm Coming Home	Cinderella	10-625	SF
I'm Coming Out	Ross, Diana	9-763	SAV
I'm Coming Over	Young, Chris	45-26	BKD

SONG TITLE	ARTIST	#	TYPE
I'm Crying	Animals	46-439	CB
I'm Diggin' It	Elliott, Alecia	5-798	SC
I'm Done	Messina, Jo Dee	36-433	CB
I'm Down	Beatles	20-197	SC
I'm Down	Beatles	46-127	SC
I'm Down	Hollies	44-373	DCK
I'm Down To My Last "I Love You"	Houston, David	48-191	CB
I'm Down To My Last Cigarette	lang, k.d.	34-321	CB
I'm Down To My Last Cigarette	lang, k.d.	26-571	DK
I'm Eighteen	Alice Cooper	19-144	SGB
I'm Eighteen	Creed	16-207	PHT
I'm Every Woman	Houston, Whitney	11-27	PX
I'm Every Woman	Houston, Whitney	19-551	SC
I'm Forever Blowing Bubbles	Standard	47-819	DK
I'm Free	Secada, Jon	4-281	SC
I'm Free	Who	19-738	LE
I'm From The Country	Byrd, Tracy	8-401	CB
I'm From The Country	Byrd, Tracy	22-770	ST
I'm Getting Better	Reeves, Jim	22-252	SC
I'm Getting Sentimental Over You	Standard	15-502	DK
I'm Getting Used To You	Selena	23-571	MM
I'm Getting Used To You	Selena	21-450	PS
I'm Glad	Lopez, Jennifer	20-520	CB
I'm Glad	Lopez, Jennifer	32-236	THM
I'm Glad You're Here With Me Tonite	Diamond, Neil	24-691	SC
I'm Going Down	Springsteen, Bruce	20-239	LE
I'm Gone	Thompson, Cyndi	25-228	MM
I'm Gone	Thompson, Cyndi	15-856	ST
I'm Gonna Be 500 Miles	Proclaimers	12-242	DK
I'm Gonna Be 500 Miles	Proclaimers	6-414	MM
I'm Gonna Be 500 Miles	Proclaimers	24-149	SC
I'm Gonna Be A Country Girl Again	Spears, Billie Jo	47-510	VH
I'm Gonna Be A Wheel Someday	Domino, Fats	9-743	SAV
I'm Gonna Be Alright	Lopez, Jennifer	17-595	PHM
I'm Gonna Be Somebody	Tritt, Travis	1-665	CB
I'm Gonna Be Strong	Pitney, Gene	9-699	SAV
I'm Gonna Change Everything	Reeves, Jim	22-250	SC
I'm Gonna Do Anything	Wills & O'Neal	15-863	ST
I'm Gonna Follow You	Benatar, Pat	46-513	MH
I'm Gonna Get Married	Price, Lloyd	11-814	DK
I'm Gonna Get Married	Price, Lloyd	10-703	JVC
I'm Gonna Get Married	Price, Lloyd	14-343	SC
I'm Gonna Getcha Good	Twain, Shania	33-191	CB
I'm Gonna Getcha Good	Twain, Shania	25-408	MM
I'm Gonna Getcha Good	Twain, Shania	18-447	ST
I'm Gonna Getcha Good	Twain, Shania	32-38	THM
I'm Gonna Haunt You	Schneider, Fred	16-283	TT
I'm Gonna Hire A Wino	Frizzell, David	16-355	CB
I'm Gonna Hire A Wino	Frizzell, David	7-419	MM

SONG TITLE	ARTIST	#	TYPE
I'm Gonna Hire A Wino	Frizzell, David	13-392	P
I'm Gonna Knock On Your Door	Craddock, Billy C	46-644	CB
I'm Gonna Love You Anyway	Adkins, Trace	14-113	CB
I'm Gonna Love You Anyway	Adkins, Trace	14-12	CHM
I'm Gonna Love You Just A Little...	White, Barry	9-764	SAV
I'm Gonna Love You Through It	McBride, Martina	38-219	CB
I'm Gonna Love You Too	Holly, Buddy	47-882	ZM
I'm Gonna Make You Love Me	Ross & Temptations	17-100	DK
I'm Gonna Make You Love Me	Supremes&Temptation	9-765	SAV
I'm Gonna Miss Her	Paisley, Brad	33-173	CB
I'm Gonna Miss Her	Paisley, Brad	25-182	MM
I'm Gonna Miss Her	Paisley, Brad	16-429	ST
I'm Gonna Sit Right Down & Write...	Sinatra, Frank	14-276	MM
I'm Gonna Sit Right Down & Write...	Williams, Billy	5-518	SC
I'm Gonna Take That Mountain	McEntire, Reba	19-526	ST
I'm Gonna Take That Mountain	McEntire, Reba	32-408	THM
I'm Henry The VIII I Am	Herman's Hermits	11-557	DK
I'm Henry The VIII I Am	Herman's Hermits	6-862	MM
I'm Henry The VIII I Am	Herman's Hermits	9-310	STR
I'm Holdin' On To Love	Twain, Shania	14-85	CB
I'm Holdin' On To Love	Twain, Shania	13-858	CHM
I'm Holdin' On To Love	Twain, Shania	22-557	ST
I'm Holding My Own	Parnell, Lee Roy	6-471	MM
I'm Horny **	Hot 'N Juicy	13-723	SGB
I'm Hurtin'	Orbison, Roy	38-57	ZM
I'm In	Kinleys	14-125	CB
I'm In	Kinleys	22-469	ST
I'm In	Urban, Keith	37-337	CB
I'm In A Hurry And Don't Know Why	Alabama	6-303	MM
I'm In A Hurry And Don't Know Why	Alabama	13-490	P
I'm In A Hurry And Don't Know Why	Alabama	2-814	SC
I'm In Love	Wilson Pickett	10-368	SS
I'm In Love Again	Domino, Fats	9-733	SAV
I'm In Love Again	Domino, Fats	5-239	SC
I'm In Love All Over	McEntire, Reba	1-817	CB
I'm In Love With A Capital U	Diffie, Joe	1-283	CB
I'm In Love With A Capital U	Diffie, Joe	2-836	SC
I'm In Love With A Married Woman	Chesnutt, Mark	25-564	MM
I'm In Love With A Married Woman	Chesnutt, Mark	18-800	ST
I'm In Love With A Married Woman	Chesnutt, Mark	32-157	THM
I'm In Love With Her	Sawyer Brown	16-196	THM

SONG TITLE	ARTIST	#	TYPE
I'm In Love With You	Dean, Billy	19-684	ST
I'm In The Mood	Alabama	17-589	ST
I'm In The Mood	Hooker, John Lee	49-477	MM
I'm In The Mood For Dancing	Nolans	49-51	ZVS
I'm In The Mood For Love	Cole, Nat "King"	28-514	DK
I'm In The Mood For Love	Cole, Natalie	12-156	DK
I'm In The Mood For Love	Eckstine, Billy	12-491	P
I'm In The Mood For Love	Lee, Brenda	45-907	DKM
I'm In The Mood For Love	Streisand, Barbra	49-601	PS
I'm In The Mood For Love	Streisand, Barbra	45-521	SS
I'm Into Something Good	Herman's Hermits	18-258	DK
I'm Into Something Good	Herman's Hermits	13-82	P
I'm Jealous	Twain, Shania	23-430	CB
I'm Just A Country Boy	Williams, Don	4-775	SC
I'm Just A Girl	Carter, Deana	20-216	CB
I'm Just A Girl	Carter, Deana	25-610	MM
I'm Just A Girl	Carter, Deana	19-65	ST
I'm Just A Girl	Carter, Deana	32-303	THM
I'm Just A Singer In A Rock & Roll	Moody Blues	17-507	SC
I'm Just An Old Chunk Of Coal	Anderson, John	44-67	DFK
I'm Just Me	Pride, Charley	38-134	CB
I'm Just Talkin' 'Bout Tonight	Keith, Toby	15-183	ST
I'm Leavin'	Presley, Elvis	25-755	MM
I'm Leavin' It Up To You	Dale & Gale	8-714	CB
I'm Leavin' It Up To You	Dale & Gale	6-268	MM
I'm Leavin' You	Humperdinck, E.	37-162	CB
I'm Leaving	Tippin, Aaron	8-375	CB
I'm Leaving	Tippin, Aaron	7-858	CHT
I'm Leaving	Tippin, Aaron	22-736	ST
I'm Leaving It All Up To You	Fender, Freddie	48-501	CKC
I'm Leaving It All Up To You - duet	Osmond, Donny & Marie	47-858	ZM
I'm Leaving It Up To You - duet	Dale & Grace	35-336	CB
I'm Left You're Right She's Gone	Presley, Elvis	14-757	THM
I'm Like A Bird	Furtado, Nelly	35-236	CB
I'm Like A Bird	Furtado, Nelly	16-114	PRT
I'm Like A Bird	Furtado, Nelly	18-522	TT
I'm Like A Lawyer	Fall Out Boy	30-595	PHM
I'm Looking Over A 4-Leaf Clover	Miller, Mitch	23-544	CB
I'm Losing My Mind Over You	Al Dexter & Troopers	38-37	CB
I'm Lost Without You	Al Dexter & Troopers	46-407	CB
I'm Lovin' It	Timberlake, Justin	19-666	CB
I'm Missing You	Rogers, Kenny	19-54	ST

SONG TITLE	ARTIST	#	TYPE
I'm Missing You	Rogers, Kenny	32-306	THM
I'm Movin' On	Rascal Flatts	15-858	ST
I'm Movin' On	Snow, Hank	8-791	CB
I'm Movin' On	Snow, Hank	12-407	P
I'm Movin' On	Snow, Hank	9-512	SAV
I'm Moving On	Cash, Roseanne	45-396	DCK
I'm Moving On	Rascal Flatts	33-149	CB
I'm Moving On	Rascal Flatts	25-49	MM
I'm My Own Grandpa	Stevens, Ray	15-343	MM
I'm No Stranger To The Rain	Whitley, Keith	9-510	SAV
I'm No Stranger To The Rain	Whitley, Keith	16-583	SC
I'm Not A Candle In The Wind	Wynette, Tammy	49-355	CB
I'm Not A Fool Anymore	Fender, Freddie	49-292	GS
I'm Not A Girl Not Yet A Woman	Spears, Britney	20-615	CB
I'm Not A Girl Not Yet A Woman	Spears, Britney	25-148	MM
I'm Not A Girl Not Yet A Woman	Spears, Britney	16-93	SC
I'm Not Breakin'	Holy, Steve	25-353	MM
I'm Not Breakin'	Holy, Steve	18-207	ST
I'm Not Breakin'	Holy, Steve	19-349	THM
I'm Not Built That Way	Dean, Billy	4-111	SC
I'm Not Feelin' It No More	Jones, Tom	47-780	SRK
I'm Not Gonna Do Anything	Wills & O'Neal	15-863	ST
I'm Not In Love	10CC	12-122	DK
I'm Not In Love	10CC	7-495	MM
I'm Not In The Mood (To Say No)	Twain, Shania	45-533	CB
I'm Not Lisa	Colter, Jessi	8-204	CB
I'm Not Listening Anymore	Daniel, Davis	4-887	SC
I'm Not Running Anymore	Mellencamp, John	21-414	SC
I'm Not Sayin'/Ribbon Of Darkness	Lightfoot, Gordon	43-489	SK
I'm Not Strong Enough To Say No	Blackhawk	6-841	MM
I'm Not Supposed To Love You Anymor	White, Bryan	4-233	SC
I'm Not That Easy To Forget	Morgan, Lorrie	8-469	CB
I'm Not That Lonely Yet	McEntire, Reba	1-791	CB
I'm Not The Girl	Farris, R.	32-210	THM
I'm Not The Marrying Kind	Presley, Elvis	25-766	MM
I'm Not The Only One	Smith, Sam	44-317	SBI
I'm Not Through Loving You Yet	Twitty, Conway	43-200	CB
I'm Not Your Stepping Stone	Monkees	11-693	DK
I'm Not Your Stepping Stone	Monkees	9-712	SAV
I'm Okay And Getting Better	Royal, Billy Joe	24-128	SC
I'm Old Fashioned	Standard	13-630	SGB

SONG TITLE	ARTIST	#	TYPE
I'm On Fire	Dwight Twilly Band	7-452	MM
I'm On Fire	Springsteen, Bruce	17-609	LE
I'm On Fire	Springsteen, Bruce	17-179	SC
I'm On My Way	Captain & Tennille	46-559	CB
I'm On The Outside (Lookin' In)	Little Anthony	30-517	LE
I'm On The Outside Lookin' In	Anthony & Imperials	10-495	DA
I'm On The Outside Lookin' In	Anthony & Imperials	25-284	MM
I'm One Of You	Williams, Hank Jr.	19-536	ST
I'm One Of You	Williams, Hank Jr.	32-413	THM
I'm Only In It For The Love	Conlee, John	47-618	CB
I'm Only In It For The Love	Conlee, John	46-110	SC
I'm Only Me When I'm With You	Swift, Taylor	36-423	CB
I'm Outta Here	Twain, Shania	7-444	MM
I'm Outta Here	Twain, Shania	3-659	SC
I'm Over You	Whitley, Keith	34-296	CB
I'm Over You	Whitley, Keith	4-545	SC
I'm Playing For You	Milsap, Ronnie	24-78	SC
I'm Popeye The Sailor Man - kids	Kids	49-32	SHER
I'm Ragged But I'm Right	Jones, George	49-644	VH
I'm Ready	Campbell, Tevin	28-443	DK
I'm Ready	Campbell, Tevin	2-234	SC
I'm Ready	Domino, Fats	4-709	SC
I'm Real	Lopez, Jennifer	16-391	SGB
I'm Sensitive	Jewel	36-333	SC
I'm Setting You Free	Amazing Rhythm Aces	47-788	SRK
I'm Setting You Free	Amazing Rhythm Aces	45-834	VH
I'm Sitting On Top Of The World	Jolson, Al	29-470	LE
I'm Sitting On Top Of The World	Jolson, Al	12-936	PS
I'm So Afraid Of Losing You	Pride, Charley	5-698	SC
I'm So Excited	Pointer Sisters	11-374	DK
I'm So Excited	Pointer Sisters	9-221	PT
I'm So Excited	Pointer Sisters	10-523	SF
I'm So Fly	Banks, Lloyd	30-806	PHM
I'm So Happy I Can't Stop Cryin'	Keith, Toby	1-705	CB
I'm So Happy I Can't Stop Cryin'	Keith, Toby w/Sting	22-658	ST
I'm So Into You	SWV	34-126	CB
I'm So Into You	SWV	6-418	MM
I'm So Into You	SWV	13-22	P
I'm So Lonesome I Could Cry	Campbell, Glen	48-489	CKC
I'm So Lonesome I Could Cry	Presley, Elvis	49-445	MM
I'm So Lonesome I Could Cry	Thomas, B.J.	47-388	MM
I'm So Lonesome I Could Cry	Williams, Hank Sr.	18-123	DK

SONG TITLE	ARTIST	#	TYPE
I'm So Lonesome I Could Cry	Williams, Hank Sr.	13-351	P
I'm So Lonesome I Could Cry	Williams, Hank Sr.	8-639	SAV
I'm So Miserable	Cyrus, Billy Ray	39-79	PHN
I'm Sorry	Denver, John	48-487	CKC
I'm Sorry	Denver, John	36-147	LE
I'm Sorry	Denver, John	4-635	SC
I'm Sorry	Lee, Brenda	30-323	CB
I'm Sorry	Lee, Brenda	11-505	DK
I'm Sorry	Lee, Brenda	10-725	JVC
I'm Sorry	Lee, Brenda	3-363	MH
I'm Sorry	Lee, Brenda	12-741	P
I'm Sorry For You My Friend	Bandy, Moe	19-504	CB
I'm Still A Guy	Paisley, Brad	36-401	CB
I'm Still Alive	Yearwood, Trisha	48-340	SC
I'm Still Crazy	Gosdin, Vern	21-630	SC
I'm Still Dancing With You	Hayes, Wade	2-700	SC
I'm Still Here	Reznik, John	23-151	PHM
I'm Still Here	Vertical Horizon	20-228	MM
I'm Still Here (Jim's Theme)	Rzeznik, J	32-27	THM
I'm Still Here (Jim's Theme)	Vertical Horizon	32-27	THM
I'm Still In Love With You	Paul, Sean	23-247	THM
I'm Still Standing	John, Elton	13-309	P
I'm Still Waiting	Jodeci	9-849	SAV
I'm Still Waiting	Ross, Diana	15-365	LE
I'm Strong In Love With You	Stylistics	20-366	SC
I'm Telling You Now	Freddie & Dreamers	11-558	DK
I'm That Kind Of Girl	Loveless, Patty	1-715	CB
I'm That Kind Of Girl	Loveless, Patty	9-473	SAV
I'm That Kind Of Girl	Loveless, Patty	2-21	SC
I'm The Cat	Browne, Jackson	24-229	SC
I'm The Only Hell My Mama Ever Raised	Paycheck, Johnny	22-37	CB
I'm The Only Hell My Mama Ever Raised	Paycheck, Johnny	3-606	SC
I'm The Only One	Etheridge, Melissa	16-625	MM
I'm The Only One	Etheridge, Melissa	13-291	P
I'm The Only One	Etheridge, Melissa	10-236	PS
I'm The Only One	Etheridge, Melissa	2-468	SC
I'm The Only Thing	Twitty, Conway	48-246	SC
I'm Thinking Tonight Of My Blue Eye	Autry, Gene	22-170	CB
I'm Through With Love	Cole, Nat "King"	46-359	MM
I'm Through With Love	Monheit, Jane	25-678	MM
I'm Throwing Rice At The Girl That	Arnold, Eddy	19-643	CB
I'm Tired	Pierce, Webb	29-406	CB
I'm Tired	Williams, Hank Jr.	16-675	C2C
I'm To Blame	Moore, Kip	46-6	DCK
I'm Too Sexy	Right Said Fred	6-168	MM
I'm Too Sexy	Right Said Fred	29-637	SC
I'm Tryin'	Adkins, Trace	33-145	CB

SONG TITLE	ARTIST	#	TYPE
I'm Tryin'	Adkins, Trace	15-608	ST
I'm Waiting For The Day	Beach Boys	45-607	OZP
I'm Walkin'	Domino, Fats	17-136	DK
I'm Walkin'	Domino, Fats	12-665	P
I'm Walkin'	Domino, Fats	4-4	SC
I'm Walking	Nelson, Ricky	38-98	LE
I'm Walking Behind You	Fisher, Eddie	49-46	ZVS
I'm Walking The Dog	Pierce, Webb	29-396	CB
I'm Walking The Dog	Pierce, Webb	49-31	KCD
I'm Wastin' My Tears On You	Ritter, Tex	20-705	CB
I'm Wastin' My Tears On You	Ritter, Tex	5-422	SC
I'm With The Band	Little Big Town	30-579	CB
I'm With You	Lavigne, Avril	35-261	CB
I'm With You	Lavigne, Avril	25-427	MM
I'm With You	Lavigne, Avril	18-604	PHM
I'm Your Angel	Dion & Kelly, R.	14-195	CB
I'm Your Angel	Dion & Kelly, R.	20-124	PHM
I'm Your Angel	Dion, Celine	16-208	MM
I'm Your Baby Tonight	Houston, Whitney	34-89	CB
I'm Your Baby Tonight	Houston, Whitney	11-785	DK
I'm Your Baby Tonight	Houston, Whitney	12-841	P
I'm Your Boogie Man	KC & Sunshine Band	35-146	CB
I'm Your Boogie Man	KC & Sunshine Band	49-314	CB
I'm Your Boogie Man	KC & Sunshine Band	2-493	SC
I'm Your Hoochie Coochie Man	Dixon, Willie	15-322	SC
I'm Your Man	Buble, Michael	38-179	BIP
I'm Your Puppet	Purify, James & Bob	35-80	CB
I'm Your Puppet	Purify,James&Bobby	4-220	SC
I'm Yours	Davis, Linda	8-246	CB
I'm Yours	Davis, Linda	22-704	ST
I'm Yours	Emerald, Caro	48-213	KV
I'm Yours	Mraz, Jason	36-515	CB
I'm Yours	Mraz, Jason	48-593	DK
I've Already Loved You In My Mind	Twitty, Conway	20-277	SC
I've Always Been Crazy	Jennings, Waylon	8-208	CB
I've Always Been Crazy	Jennings, Waylon	22-138	CK
I've Always Been Crazy	Jennings, Waylon	4-640	SC
I've Been Around Enough To Know	Schneider, John	14-316	SC
I've Been Everywhere	Cash, Johnny	43-380	ASK
I've Been Everywhere	Snow, Hank	22-122	CB
I've Been Everywhere	Snow, Hank	8-653	SAV
I've Been Everywhere	Snow, Hank	5-366	SC
I've Been In Love Before	Money, Eddie	47-283	LC
I've Been Lonely Too Long	Rascals	14-344	SC
I've Been Lookin'	Nitty Gritty Dirt Band	5-618	SC
I've Been Loving You So Long	Redding, Otis	6-143	MM
I've Been Thinking	Londonbeat	21-460	CB

SONG TITLE	ARTIST	#	TYPE
About You			
I've Been This Way Before	Diamond, Neil	47-412	DFK
I've Been Workin' On The RR	Kids	34-447	CB
I've Come Awful Close	Thompson, Hank	19-328	CB
I've Come To Expect It From You	Strait, George	8-163	CB
I've Come To Expect It From You	Strait, George	3-650	SC
I've Cried	Gayle, Crystal	5-60	SC
I've Cried My Last Tear For You	VanShelton, Ricky	8-561	CB
I've Cried My Last Tear For You	VanShelton, Ricky	11-718	DK
I've Done Enough Dying Today	Gatlin, Larry	33-51	CB
I've Done Enough Dying Today	Gatlins	8-803	CB
I've Dreamed Of You	Streisand, Barbra	15-285	PS
I've Enjoyed As Much of This as I Can Stand	Reeves, Jim	44-234	DCK
I've Enjoyed As Much Of This As I..	Wagoner, Porter	19-313	CB
I've Forever Blowing Bubbles	Standard	11-584	DK
I've Forgotten How You Feel	Isaacs, Sonya	13-815	CHM
I've Forgotten You	Vincent, Rhonda	23-144	CB
I've Found Someone Of My Own	Free Movement	25-281	MM
I've Got A Crush On You	Ronstadt, Linda	34-8	CB
I've Got A Crush On You	Ronstadt, Linda	12-565	P
I've Got A Crush On You	Streisand, Barbra	49-579	PS
I've Got A Crush On You	Streisand, Barbra	49-381	PS
I've Got A Gal In Kalamazoo	Miller, Glen	12-557	P
I've Got A Life	Eurythmics	47-73	EZ
I've Got A Lovely Bunch Of Coconuts	Griffin, Merv	27-432	DK
I've Got A Lovely Bunch Of Coconuts	Standard	11-583	DK
I've Got A Name	Croce, Jim	34-64	CB
I've Got A New Heartache	Price, Ray	3-779	CB
I've Got A New Heartache	Price, Ray	14-331	SC
I've Got A Picture Of Us On My Mind	Lynn, Loretta	43-236	CB
I've Got A Right To Cry	Barnett, Mandy	14-620	SC
I've Got A Thing About You	Presley, Elvis	14-818	THM
I've Got A Tiger By The Tail	Owens, Buck	8-784	CB
I've Got A Tiger By The Tail	Owens, Buck	12-54	DK
I've Got A Tiger By The Tail	Owens, Buck	6-777	MM
I've Got A Winner In You	Williams, Don	45-225	CB
I've Got A Woman	Presley, Elvis	43-245	PSJT

SONG TITLE	ARTIST	#	TYPE
I've Got Friends That Do	McGraw, Tim	49-313	BC
I've Got Friends That Do	McGraw, Tim	29-574	CB
I've Got It Made	Anderson, John	2-361	SC
I've Got Mine	Frey, Glenn	4-275	SC
I've Got My Love To Keep Me Warm	Martin, Dean	23-78	MM
I've Got Sand In My Shoes	Drifters	45-883	VH
I've Got That Old Feelin'	Krauss, Alison	8-892	CB
I've Got The Music In Me	Dee, Kiki	49-482	MM
I've Got The Music In Me	Jump 5	48-584	DK
I've Got The Music In Me	Kiki Dee Band	18-236	DK
I've Got The Music In Me	Kiki Dee Band	9-727	SAV
I've Got The Music In Me	Kiki Dee Band	4-855	SC
I've Got The World By The Tail	King, Claude	47-920	SSK
I've Got The World On A String	Sinatra, Frank	9-244	PT
I've Got To Get A Message To You	Bee Gees	17-495	LE
I've Got To See You Again	Jones, Norah	25-676	MM
I've Got To See You Again	Jones, Norah	19-190	Z
I've Got To Use My Imagination	Knight & Pips	11-504	Dk
I've Got You	Anthony, Marc	18-223	CB
I've Got You	Anthony, Marc	25-256	MM
I've Got You Under My Skin	Lee, Peggy	9-807	SAV
I've Got You Under My Skin	Sinatra, Frank	16-731	DK
I've Got You Under My Skin	Sinatra, Frank	10-717	JVC
I've Got You Under My Skin	Sinatra, Frank	20-759	KB
I've Got You Under My Skin	Sinatra, Frank	9-261	PT
I've Got You Under My Skin	Standard	35-28	CB
I've Gotta Be Me	Davis, Sammy Jr.	15-508	MM
I've Gotta Be Me	Davis, Sammy Jr.	47-14	MM
I've Gotta Be Me	Davis, Sammy Jr.	19-780	SGB
I've Gotta Be Me	Lawrence, Steve	29-489	LE
I've Had A Beautiful Time	Haggard, Merle	46-23	SSK
I've Heard That Song Before	Boone, Pat	45-828	VH
I've Learned To Live	Tucker, Tanya	24-243	SC
I've Loved And Lost Again	Cline, Patsy	45-515	MM
I've Never Been In Love Before	Guys & Dolls	19-584	SC
I've Never Been In Love Before	Streisand, Barbra	49-548	PS
I've Never Been So Sure	Restless Heart	1-415	CB
I've Never Been To Me	Charlene	12-3	DK
I've Never Been To Me	Monro, Matt	11-56	PT
I've Still Got My Health	Midler, Bette	45-915	KV
I've Thought Of	Singletary, Daryle	10-273	CB

SONG TITLE	ARTIST	#	TYPE
Everything			
I've Told Every Little...	Scott, Linda	3-464	SC
Ice Cream (Live)	McLachlan, Sarah	10-222	SC
Ice Cream (Live)	McLachlan, Sarah	48-164	SC
Ice Cream Man	Van Halen	20-81	SC
Ice Ice Baby	Vanilla Ice	5-334	SC
Ida Red Like To Boogie	Wills, Bob	20-697	CB
Ida Red Like To Boogie	Wills, Bob	45-351	CBE
Ida! Sweet As Apple Cider	Cantor, Eddie	43-217	CB
If	Armstrong, Louis	17-378	DK
If	Bread	35-212	CB
If	Bread	12-318	DK
If	Como, Perry	13-545	LE
If	Como, Perry	20-781	PS
If	Monheit, Jane	25-674	MM
If	Monro, Matt	11-61	PT
If a Man Answers	Keith, Toby	8-913	CB
If A Man Answers	Keith, Toby	22-730	ST
If A Woman Answers	Van Dyke, Leroy	5-429	SC
If Anyone Falls	Nicks, Stevie	16-127	SC
If As We Never Said Goodbye	Streisand, Barbra	49-553	KKS
If Bubba Can Dance I Can Too	Shenandoah	1-492	CB
If Bubba Can Dance I Can Too	Shenandoah	6-498	MM
If Bubba Can Dance I Can Too	Shenandoah	2-208	SC
If Dreams Came True	Boone, Pat	49-263	DFK
If Ever	Denver, John	48-408	DFK
If Ever I Would Leave You	Goulet, Robert	28-102	DK
If Ever I Would Leave You	Goulet, Robert	12-568	P
If Ever You're In My Arms Again	Bryson, Peabo	49-480	MM
If Everyone Cared	Nickelback	30-259	CB
If Everyone Cared	Nickelback	45-809	SC
If George Strait Starts Dancing	Judd, Cledus T.	45-735	VH
If Heartaches Had Wings	Vincent, Rhonda	19-707	ST
If Heaven	Griggs, Andy	22-104	CB
If Heaven	Griggs, Andy	23-42	SC
If Heaven Ain't A Lot Like Dixie	Williams, Hank Jr.	33-71	CB
If Heaven Wasn't So Far Away	Moore, Justin	37-236	CB
If Her Lovin' Don't Kill Me	Anderson, John	30-42	CB
If Her Lovin' Don't Kill Me	Atkins, Rodney	30-42	CB
If Her Lovin' Don't Kill Me	Tippin, Aaron	18-133	ST
If Her Loving Don't Kill Me	Tippin, Aaron	34-346	CB
If Hollywood Don't Need You	Williams, Don	4-548	SC
If I Ain't Got You	Keys, Alicia	20-531	CB

135

SONG TITLE	ARTIST	#	TYPE
If I Ain't Got You	Keys, Alicia	23-250	THM
If I Ain't Got You	Stuart, Marty	16-576	SC
If I Ain't Got You	Yearwood, Trisha	48-334	MM
If I Am	Nine Days	15-433	PHM
If I Can Dream	Presley, Elvis	2-602	SC
If I Can Dream	Presley, Elvis	14-773	THM
If I Can't Have You	Bee Gees	11-249	DK
If I Can't Have You	Bee Gees	9-778	SAV
If I Can't Have You	Bee Gees	10-548	SF
If I Can't Have You	Clarkson, Kelly	47-697	KV
If I Can't Have You	Elliman, Yvonne	2-505	SC
If I Could	Belle, Regina	17-425	KC
If I Could	Belle, Regina	15-509	PS
If I Could	Streisand, Barbra	49-617	PS
If I Could Bottle This Up	Overstreet, Paul	29-773	CB
If I Could Do It All Again	Wilson, Gretchen	37-60	CB
If I Could Fall In Love	Kravitz, Lenny	18-435	CB
If I Could Go	Martinez, Angie	18-345	PHM
If I Could Make A Living	Walker, Clay	1-94	CB
If I Could Make A Living	Walker, Clay	2-485	SC
If I Could Only Fly	Nichols, Joe	47-574	PS
If I Could Only Win Your Love	Harris, EmmyLou	8-282	CB
If I Could Only Win Your Love	Harris, EmmyLou	5-158	SC
If I Could See The World Thru/Eyes.	Cline, Patsy	22-189	CB
If I Could Talk I'd Tell You	Lemonheads	24-645	SC
If I Could Turn Back The Hands..	Kelly, R.	49-516	CB
If I Could Turn Back Time	Cher	11-750	DK
If I Could Turn Back Time	Cher	6-342	MM
If I Could Turn Back Time	Cher	14-49	RS
If I Didn't Care	Platters	45-72	CB
If I Didn't Have A Dime	Pitney, Gene	47-534	SFM
If I Didn't Know Any Better	Krauss & Union Station	36-185	PHM
If I Didn't Know Better - Nashville	Bowen & Palladio	45-472	KVD
If I Didn't Love You	Wariner, Steve	6-387	MM
If I Die Young	Band Perry	44-142	BKD
If I Die Young	Band Perry	40-40	PHN
If I Don't Make It Back	Lawrence, Tracy	29-853	SC
If I Don't Make It Back	Lawrence, Tracy	23-458	ST
If I Don't Make It Back	Lawrence, Tracy	29-45	CB
If I Ever Fall In Love (With a Honky...)	young, Faron	47-737	SRK
If I Ever Leave This World Alive	Flogging Molly	48-618	KV
If I Ever Lose My Faith In You	Sting	24-142	SC
If I Ever Love Again	Norwood, Daron	24-245	SC
If I Fall You're Goin' Down With Me	Dixie Chicks	8-901	CB
If I Fall You're Goin'	Dixie Chicks	30-604	RS

SONG TITLE	ARTIST	#	TYPE
Down With Me			
If I Fall You're Goin' Down With Me	Dixie Chicks	14-832	ST
If I Get Home On Christmas Day	Presley, Elvis	45-761	CB
If I Give My Heart To You	Day, Doris	9-750	SAV
If I Give My Heart To You	Day, Doris	20-70	SC
If I Had $1,000,000	Barenaked Ladies	30-613	RS
If I Had $1,000,000	Barenaked Ladies	5-332	SC
If I Had A Cheatin' Heart	Gregg, Ricky Lynn	24-7	SC
If I Had A Hammer	Peter, Paul & Mary	34-446	CB
If I Had A Hammer	Peter, Paul & Mary	18-162	DK
If I Had A Hammer	Peter, Paul & Mary	7-358	MM
If I Had A Hammer	Peter, Paul & Mary	9-121	PS
If I Had A Hammer	Peter, Paul & Mary	4-697	SC
If I Had A Hammer	Peter, Paul & Mary	10-624	SF
If I Had A Million Dollars - duet	Barenaked Ladies	33-362	CB
If I Had A Nickle (One Thin Dime)	Reddmann & Vale	14-618	SC
If I Had Any Pride Left At All	Berry, John	3-574	SC
If I Had Only Known	McEntire, Reba	6-212	MM
If I Had To Do It All Over Again	Clark, Roy	29-647	SC
If I Had You	Alabama	4-444	BS
If I Had You	Alabama	1-14	CB
If I Had You	Stewart, Rod	16-256	TT
If I Kiss You (Will You Go Away)	Anderson, Lynn	47-637	CB
If I Knew Then What I Know Now	Rogers, Kenny	6-234	MM
If I Knew You Were Comin'	Barton, Eileen	5-83	SC
If I Know Me	Strait, George	8-168	CB
If I Know Me	Strait, George	6-627	MM
If I Know Me	Strait, George	17-244	NA
If I Left It Up To You	Haggard, Merle	45-575	SSK
If I Left You	Willis, Kelly	18-473	ST
If I Lost You	Tritt, Travis	8-177	CB
If I May	Cole, Nat "King"	46-349	CB
If I Needed Someone	Hollies	44-375	ZM
If I Needed You - duet	Williams & Harris	45-231	CB
If I Never See Your Face Again	Maroon 5 feat Rihanna	36-472	CB
If I Never See Your Face Again	Rihanna feat Maroon 5	36-103	CB
If I Never Stop Lovin' You	Kersh, David	22-772	ST
If I Never Stop Loving You	Kersh, David	8-237	CB
If I Never Stop Loving You	Kersh, David	7-732	CHM
If I Never Stop Loving You	Kersh, David	10-128	SC
If I Only Knew	Jones, Tom	15-510	JTG
If I Ruled The World (Imagine That)	Nas	25-477	MM
If I Said You Had A	Bellamy Brothers	8-832	CB

SONG TITLE	ARTIST	#	TYPE
Beautiful Body			
If I Said You Had A Beautiful Body	Bellamy Brothers	12-117	DK
If I Said You Had A Beautiful Body	Bellamy Brothers	13-334	P
If I Said You Had A Beautiful Body	Bellamy Brothers	10-510	SF
If I Talk To Him	Smith, Connie	6-13	SC
If I Told You That	Houston, Whitney	19-832	SGB
If I Wanted To	Etheridge, Melissa	10-237	PS
If I Was A Drinkin' Man	McCoy, Neal	1-847	CB
If I Was A Drinkin' Man	McCoy, Neal	6-851	MM
If I Was Your Girlfriend	Prince	49-825	KV
If I Were A Boy	Beyonce	36-513	CB
If I Were A Boy	Beyonce	36-249	PHM
If I Were A Carpenter	Cash & Carter	29-558	CB
If I Were A Carpenter	Darin, Bobby	7-31	MM
If I Were A Carpenter	Darin, Bobby	10-626	SF
If I Were A Carpenter	Four Tops	43-428	EZC
If I Were A Carpenter	Plant, Robert	24-257	SC
If I Were A Carpenter - duet	Slaughter, Shannon & Heather	41-92	PHN
If I Were The Man You Wanted	Nelson, Willie	45-326	DCK
If I Were You	Clark, Terri	34-327	CB
If I Were You	Clark, Terri	7-196	MM
If I Were You	Clark, Terri	4-207	SC
If I Were You	Hoobastank	30-286	SC
If I Were You	Lang, k.d.	47-171	SC
If I Were You	Raye, Collin	4-72	SC
If I Were Your Woman	Knight & Pips	17-356	DK
If I'd Been The One	38 Special	7-458	MM
If I'm A Fool For Loving You	Presley, Elvis	25-759	MM
If It Ain't Love	Smith, Connie	8-285	CB
If It Don't Come Easy	Tucker, Tanya	16-342	CB
If It Don't Come Easy	Tucker, Tanya	5-18	SC
If It Don't Take Two	Twain, Shania	7-439	MM
If It Feels Good Do It	Dudley, Dave	47-55	CB
If It Hadn't Been For Love	Adele	40-33	KV
If It Hadn't Been For Love	Steeldrivers	49-921	KVD
If It Isn't Love	New Edition	28-336	DK
If It Makes You Happy	Crow, Sheryl	29-672	RS
If It Makes You Happy	Crow, Sheryl	10-56	SC
If It's All The Same To You	Anderson, Bill	20-795	CB
If It's All The Same To You	Anderson, Bill w Howard	40-73	CB
If It's Love	Train	37-318	PHM
If It's Lovin' That You Want	Rihanna	36-95	CB
If It's Lovin' That You Want (Radio	Rihanna	29-259	SC
If Looks Could Kill	Crowell, Rodney	2-348	SC
If Looks Could Kill	Heart	19-552	SC
If Love Had A Face	Bailey, Razzy	29-385	CB
If Love Was A River	Jackson, Alan	49-234	DFK

SONG TITLE	ARTIST	#	TYPE
If Lovin' You Is Wrong I Don't	Mandrell, Barbara	4-781	SC
If Lovin' You Is Wrong I Don't	Stewart, Rod	14-853	LE
If Lovin' You Is Wrong I Don't...	Ingram, Luther	16-562	P
If Loving You Is Wrong	Ingram, James	48-589	DK
If My Heart Had Windows	Loveless, Patty	1-706	CB
If My Heart Had Windows	Loveless, Patty	8-698	SAV
If My Heart Had Wings	Hill, Faith	14-784	ST
If Nobody Believed In You	Nichols, Joe	35-441	CB
If Nobody Believed In You	Nichols, Joe	20-325	ST
If Not You	Dr. Hook	47-43	PSH
If Only (Radio Version)	Hanson	14-486	SC
If Only For One Night	Vandross, Luther	48-323	SC
If Practice Makes Perfect	Rodriguez, Johnny	22-57	CB
If Shania Was Mine	Judd, Cledus T.	16-502	CB
If She Don't Love You	Buffalo Club	14-660	CB
If She Don't Love You	Buffalo Club	22-409	CHM
If She Don't Love You	Buffalo Club	7-433	MM
If She Knew What She Wanted	Bangles	15-734	SC
If She Only Knew	98 Degrees	15-379	SKG
If She Only Knew	Sharp, Kevin	8-744	CB
If She Walked Into My Life	Monro, Matt	18-103	PS
If She Were Any Other Woman	Jewell, Buddy	22-318	CB
If Something Should Happen	Worley, Darryl	22-28	CB
If Teardrops Were Pennies	Smith, Carl	5-362	SC
If That Ain't Country	Coe, David Allan	18-317	CB
If That Ain't Country	Smith, Anthony	33-170	CB
If That Ain't Country	Smith, Anthony	16-710	ST
If The Devil Danced In Empty Pocket	Diffie, Joe	1-272	CB
If The Devil Danced In Empty Pocket	Diffie, Joe	17-370	DK
If The Devil Danced In Empty Pocket	Diffie, Joe	13-403	P
If The Good Die Young	Lawrence, Tracy	1-576	CB
If The Good Die Young	Lawrence, Tracy	20-402	MH
If The Good Die Young	Lawrence, Tracy	17-214	NA
If The House Is Rockin'	Parnell, Lee Roy	49-275	SC
If The Jukebox Took Teardrops	Leigh, Danni	8-187	CB
If The Jukebox Took Teardrops	Royal, Billy Joe	47-373	SRK
If The Rain Must Fall	Morrison, James	38-270	ZM
If The World Had A Front Porch	Lawrence, Tracy	1-581	CB
If The World Had A Front Porch	Lawrence, Tracy	7-20	MM
If There Ain't There Oughta Be	Stuart, Marty	34-414	CB

SONG TITLE	ARTIST	#	TYPE
If There Ain't There Oughta Be	Stuart, Marty	19-375	ST
If There Hadn't Been You	Dean, Billy	17-224	NA
If There Hadn't Been You	Dean, Billy	3-49	SC
If This Is It	Lewis & The News	11-245	DK
If This Is Love	Greene, Jack	43-347	CB
If This Love Should End	Adams, Oleta	46-386	PS
If Today Was Your Last Day	Nickelback	36-20	PT
If Tomorrow Never Comes	Brooks, Garth	1-211	CB
If Tomorrow Never Comes	Brooks, Garth	6-278	MM
If Tomorrow Never Comes	Brooks, Garth	2-673	SC
If Trucks Drank Beer	Error 404 & C J Watson	45-132	DFK
If We Fall In Love Tonight	Stewart, Rod	24-631	SC
If We Make It Through December	Haggard, Merle	17-6	DK
If We Make It Through December	Haggard, Merle	13-459	P
If We Never Meet Again	Presley, Elvis	25-506	MM
If We Were A Movie	Montana, Hannah	36-67	WD
If We're Not Back In Love By Monday	Haggard, Merle	34-233	CB
If We're Not Back In Love By Monday	Haggard, Merle	4-579	SC
If We're Not Back In Love By Monday	Haggard, Merle	8-325	CB
If You Ain't Here To Party	Bryan, Luke	43-279	BKD
If You Ain't Here To Party	Bryan, Luke	45-98	KV
If You Ain't Lovin'	Strait, George	5-317	SC
If You Ain't Lovin'	Young, Faron	7-164	MM
If You Ain't Lovin' You Ain't Livin	Young, Faron	20-730	CB
If You Ain't Lovin' You Ain't Livin'	Strait, George	34-281	CB
If You Asked Me To	Dion, Celine	33-339	CB
If You Asked Me To	Dion, Celine	6-99	MM
If You Came Back From Heaven	Morgan, Lorrie	1-341	CB
If You Came Back From Heaven	Morgan, Lorrie	45-412	CB
If You Came Back From Heaven	Morgan, Lorrie	6-578	MM
If You Can	Cochran, Tammy	9-415	CB
If You Can	Cochran, Tammy	22-566	ST
If You Can Do Anything Else	Strait, George	34-361	CB
If You Can Do Anything Else	Strait, George	14-836	ST
If You Can Live With it	Anderson, Bill	20-793	CB
If You Can Touch Her At All	Nelson, Willie	38-68	CB
If You Can't Be Good, Be Good At It	McCoy, Neal	1-848	CB

SONG TITLE	ARTIST	#	TYPE
If You Can't Be Good, Be Good At It	McCoy, Neal	7-729	CHM
If You Can't Be Good, Be Good At It	McCoy, Neal	22-419	ST
If You Change Your Mind	Cash, Roseanne	12-77	DK
If You Change Your Mind	Cash, Roseanne	5-24	SC
If You Could Only See	Thompson, Cyndi	18-452	ST
If You Could Only See	Tonic	10-112	SC
If You Could Read My Mind	Lightfoot, Gordon	43-25	CBE
If You Could Read My Mind	Lightfoot, Gordon	9-358	MG
If You Could Read My Mind	Lightfoot, Gordon	43-476	SK
If You Could See Me Now	Brown, T. Graham	47-548	CB
If You Didn't Love Me	Stacey, Phil	36-403	CB
If You Don't Come Back	Presley, Elvis	25-763	MM
If You Don't Know Me By Now	Simply Red	19-123	KC
If You Don't Know Me By Now	Simply Red	13-184	P
If You Don't Like Hank Williams	Williams, Hank Jr.	16-678	C2C
If You Don't Start Drinkin' I'm...	Thorogood, George	5-743	SC
If You Ever Change Your Mind	Gayle, Crystal	5-391	SC
If You Ever Did Believe	Nicks, Stevie	16-220	MM
If You Ever Did Believe	Nicks, Stevie	16-132	SC
If You Ever Feel Like Lovin' Me Aga	Walker, Clay	15-605	ST
If You Ever Have Forever In Mind	Gill, Vince	8-724	CB
If You Ever Have Forever In Mind	Gill, Vince	7-763	CHM
If You Ever Have Forever In Mind	Gill, Vince	5-286	SC
If You Ever Have Forever In Mind	Gill, Vince	22-794	ST
If You Ever Leave Me	Streisand & Gill	15-288	PS
If You Ever Leave Me	Streisand & Gill	10-217	SC
If You Ever Leave Me	Streisand, Barbra	49-555	KKS
If You Ever Stop Loving Me	Montgomery Gentry	20-170	ST
If You Ever Went Away	Montgomery, J M	36-282	PHM
If You Go Away	Bassey, Shirley	46-476	KV
If You Gotta Make A Fool Of Some-	Freddie & Dreamers	10-561	SF
If You Had My Love	Lopez, Jennifer	23-322	CB
If You Had My Love	Lopez, Jennifer	13-563	LE
If You Had My Love	Lopez, Jennifer	23-580	MM
If You Had My Love	Lopez, Jennifer	8-189	PHT
If You Had My Love	Lopez, Jennifer	10-181	SC
If You Had My Love	Lopez, Jennifer	13-776	SGB
If You Knew Susie (Like I Know Susie)	Cantor, Eddie	43-215	CB
If You Know What I Mean	Diamond, Neil	30-687	LE
If You Know What I Mean	Diamond, Neil	18-690	PS
If You Leave Me Tonight	Wallace, Jerry	14-323	SC

SONG TITLE	ARTIST	#	TYPE
If You Love Me Let Me Know	Newton-John, Olivia	9-582	SAV
If You Love Me Really Love Me	Lee, Brenda	47-893	SAV
If You Love Me Really Love Me	Lee, Brenda	47-894	SF
If You Love Somebody	Sharp, Kevin	7-677	CHM
If You Love Somebody	Sharp, Kevin	4-832	SC
If You Love Somebody	Sharp, Kevin	22-614	ST
If You Love Somebody Set 'Em Free	Sting	4-316	SC
If You Loved Me	Lawrence, Tracy	4-96	SC
If You Really Love Me	Wonder, Stevie	34-38	CB
If You Say My Eyes R Beautiful	Jackson & Houston	22-927	SC
If You See Him If You See Her	McEntire & B&D	8-97	CB
If You See Him If You See Her	McEntire & B&D	7-760	CHM
If You Talk In Your Sleep	Presley, Elvis	14-819	THM
If You Wanna Be Happy	Soul, Jimmy	17-396	DK
If You Wanna Be Happy	Soul, Jimmy	10-739	JVC
If You Wanna Be Happy	Soul, Jimmy	12-643	P
If You Wanna Be Happy	Soul, Jimmy	2-69	SC
If You Wanna Get To Heaven	Ozark Mtn Daredevil	7-454	MM
If You Wanna Get To Heaven	Ozark Mtn Daredevil	2-536	SC
If You Wanna Touch Her, Ask	Twain, Shania	45-528	ASK
If You Want Me To Go	Diffie, Joe	1-271	CB
If You Want Me To Stay	Sly & Family Stone	10-672	HE
If You Want To Be A Good Girl	Backstreet Boys	30-418	THM
If You Want To Be Good Girl	Backstreet Boys	18-708	MM
If You Want To Find Love	Rogers, Kenny	16-365	CB
If You're Goin' Through Hell	Atkins, Rodney	30-40	CB
If You're Going Through Hell	Atkins, Rodney	29-714	ST
If You're Gone	Matchbox 20	16-476	MH
If You're Gone	Matchbox 20	15-426	PHM
If You're Gonna o Me Wrong Do It Right	Gosdin, Vern	34-258	CB
If You're Gonna o Me Wrong Do It Right	Gosdin, Vern	29-696	SC
If You're Gonna Play In Texas	Alabama	1-7	CB
If You're Gonna Walk I'm Gonna..	Kershaw, Sammy	2-694	SC
If You're Gonna Walk I'm Gonna...	Kershaw, Sammy	1-474	CB
If You're Happy & U Know It	Kids	34-449	CB
If You're Not Gone Too Long	Lynn, Loretta	45-723	VH
If You're Not In It For Love	Twain, Shania	1-513	CB

SONG TITLE	ARTIST	#	TYPE
If You're Not In It For Love	Twain, Shania	7-444	MM
If You're Not In It For Love	Twain, Shania	3-659	SC
If You're Not The One	Bedingfield, Daniel	20-523	CB
If You're Not The One	Bedingfield, Daniel	25-583	MM
If You're Not The One	Bedingfield, Daniel	19-339	STP
If You're Not The One	Bedingfield, Daniel	32-169	THM
If You're Reading This	McGraw, Tim	30-456	CB
If You're Thinkin' You Want A Stran	Strait, George	5-323	SC
If You've Got 10 Minutes	Stampley, Joe	43-301	CB
If You've Got Love	Montgomery, J M	14-210	CB
If You've Got Love	Montgomery, J M	17-250	NA
If You've Got Love	Montgomery, J M	2-459	SC
If You've Got The Money	Nelson, Willie	4-584	SC
If You've Got The Money I've Got...	Frizzell, Lefty	19-481	CB
If You've Got The Money I've Got...	Frizzell, Lefty	7-106	MM
If You've Got The Money I've Got...	Frizzell, Lefty	3-592	SC
If Your Girl Only Knew	Aaliyah	24-300	SC
If Your Heart Ain't Busy Tonight	Tucker, Tanya	1-609	CB
If Your Heart Ain't Busy Tonight	Tucker, Tanya	33-102	CB
If Your Heart Ain't Busy Tonight	Tucker, Tanya	6-187	MM
If Your Heart Ain't Busy Tonight	Tucker, Tanya	3-651	SC
Ignition	Kelly, R	32-49	THM
Ignition	Kelly, R.	25-721	MM
Ignition	Kelly, R.	19-344	STP
Ignition	Kelly, R.	32-49	THM
Iko Iko	Belle Stars	3-527	SC
Iko Iko	Dixie Cups	47-24	SBI
Illegal	McGraw, Tim	47-245	CB
Illegal Smile	Prine, John	23-523	CB
Illegal Smile	Prine, John	2-756	SC
Im In The Mood	Peniston, CeCe	16-626	MM
Image Of A Girl	Safaris	25-167	MM
Image Of Me the	Twitty, Conway	22-248	SC
Imagination	Martin, Dean	23-73	MM
Imagination	Martin, Dean	19-778	SGB
Imagine	Lennon, John	6-157	MM
Imagine	Lennon, John	30-292	RS
Imagine	Lennon, John	9-649	SAV
Imagine That	Cline, Patsy	19-395	SC
Imagine That	Diamond Rio	8-141	CB
Imagine That	Diamond Rio	22-646	ST
Imagine That	Next	32-89	THM
Immigrant Song	Led Zeppelin	12-770	P
Immortality	Bee Gees	48-684	DCK
Impossible Dream the	Goulet, Robert	3-116	KB
Impossible Dream the	Jones, Jack	29-484	LE
Impossible Dream the	Vandross, Luther	48-289	LE
Impossible the	Nichols, Joe	33-174	CB

139

SONG TITLE	ARTIST	#	TYPE
Impossible the	Nichols, Joe	25-192	MM
Impossible the	Nichols, Joe	16-705	ST
Imprint	DoubleDrive	32-296	THM
In A Big Country	Big Country	28-341	DK
In A Big Country	Big Country	18-386	SAV
In A Different Light	Stone, Doug	20-594	CB
In A Gadda Da Vida	Iron Butterfly	9-669	SAV
In A Gadda Da Vida	Iron Butterfly	5-609	SC
In A Heartbeat	Wariner, Steve	8-395	CB
In A Little While	U2	48-312	SC
In A Little While	Uncle Kracker	25-335	MM
In A Little While	Uncle Kracker	18-344	PHM
In A New York Minute	McDowell, Ronnie	34-272	CB
In A New York Minute	McDowell, Ronnie	5-763	SC
In A Real Love	Vassar, Phil	21-660	SC
In A Real Love	Vassar, Phil	20-340	ST
In A Town This Size	Prine, John	47-597	VH
In A Week Or Two	Diamond Rio	1-170	CB
In A Week Or Two	Diamond Rio	2-337	SC
In America	Charlie Daniels Band	46-607	CB
In America - patriotic	Charlie Daniels Band	34-240	CB
In Another World	Diffie, Joe	15-674	ST
In Another's Eyes	Brooks & Yearwood	22-625	ST
In Another's Eyes	Brooks & Yearwood]	7-675	CHM
In Between Dances	Tillis, Pam	1-459	CB
In Between Dances	Tillis, Pam	6-797	MM
In Between Dances	Tillis, Pam	2-831	SC
In Bloom	Nirvana	6-42	SC
In Care Of The Blues	Cline, Patsy	8-819	CB
In Care Of The Blues	Cline, Patsy	45-510	CB
In Crowd the	Gray, Dobie	12-668	P
In Da Club	50 Cent	32-160	THM
In Da Club **	50 Cent	25-724	MM
In Dreams	Orbison, Roy	20-29	SC
In Dreams	Orbison, Roy	9-189	SO
In God We Still Trust	Diamond Rio	29-19	CB
In Heaven There Is No Beer	Clean Living	2-416	SC
In Heaven There Is No Beer - w/Word	Polka Favorites	29-860	SSR
In Heaven There Is No Beer Polka	Polka Favorites	29-806	SSR
In Love	Milsap, Ronnie	47-265	CB
In Love With a Girl	DeGraw, Gavin	36-466	CB
In Love With A Girl	DeGraw, Gavin	49-853	SC
In Love With The Girl	Bryan, Luke	48-109	BKD
In My Car (I'll Be The Driver)	Twain, Shania	45-519	SC
In My Daughter's Eyes	McBride, Martina	29-535	CB
In My Daughter's Eyes	McBride, Martina	19-688	ST
In My Dreams	Dokken	23-49	MH
In My Dreams	Dokken	6-25	SC
In My Dreams	Trevino, Rick	19-374	ST
In My Eyes	Conlee, John	47-615	CB
In My Head	Queens/Stone Age	30-229	PHM
In My High School	Larsen, Blaine	20-392	ST

SONG TITLE	ARTIST	#	TYPE
In My Life	Beatles	16-747	DK
In My Life	Beatles	7-515	SAV
In My Merry Oldsmobile	Crosby, Bing	29-411	CB
In My Next Life	Clark, Terri	36-551	CB
In My Next Life	Haggard, Merle	46-46	SSK
In My Own Backyard	Diffie, Joe	2-216	SC
In My Place	Coldplay	25-307	MM
In My Place	Coldplay	18-588	NS
In My Pocket	Moore, Mandy	21-644	TT
In My Room	Beach Boys	5-902	BS
In No Time At All	Milsap, Ronnie	47-277	CB
In Over My Head	Dr. Hook	47-49	SFM
In Pictures	Alabama	7-137	MM
In Pictures	Alabama	3-543	SC
In Private	Springfield, Dusty	49-239	DFK
In Summer - Frozen	Frozen	46-380	DIS
In The Afterlife	Haggard, Marty	4-423	SC
In The Air Tonight	Collins, Phil	44-11	MH
In The Chapel In The Moonlight	Martin, Dean	23-86	MM
In The City	Eagles	5-880	SC
In the End	Linkin Park	36-136	SGB
In The End	Linkin Park	16-320	TT
In The Garden - gospel	Lynn, Loretta	47-633	CB
In The Ghetto	Merchant, Natalie	8-400	PHT
In The Ghetto	Presley, Elvis	11-342	DK
In The Ghetto	Presley, Elvis	9-709	SAV
In The Ghetto	Presley, Elvis	2-586	SC
In The Good Old Summertime	Crosby, Bing	29-412	CB
In The Halls Of Montezuma	Patriotic	44-42	PT
In The Heart Of A Woman	Cyrus, Billy Ray	9-628	SAV
In The Heart Of A Woman	Cyrus, Billy Ray	2-356	SC
In The Heat Of The Night	Charles, Ray	12-555	P
In The House Of Stone & Light	Page, Martin	28-425	DK
In The Jailhouse Now	Cash, Johnny	43-402	LG
In The Jailhouse Now	Pierce, Webb	15-826	CB
In The Jailhouse Now	Pierce, Webb	4-809	SC
In The Middle Of A Heartache	Jackson, Wanda	19-404	SC
In The Middle Of Nowhere	Springfield, Dusty	10-658	SF
In The Midnight Hour	Wilson Pickett	35-71	CB
In The Midnight Hour	Wilson Pickett	26-446	DK
In The Midnight Hour	Wilson Pickett	13-93	P
In The Midnight Hour	Wilson Pickett	2-83	SC
In The Misty Moonlight	Wallace, Jerry	16-368	CB
In The Mood	Andrew Sisters	46-427	KV
In The Mood	Midler, Bette	45-921	KV
In the Morning	Franklin, Aretha	36-166	JT
In The Morning	Razorlight	30-463	CB
In The Morning	Razorlight	30-731	SF
In The Navy	Village People	45-618	CBE
In The Pines	Monroe, Bill	8-250	CB

SONG TITLE	ARTIST	#	TYPE
In The Shade Of The Old Apple Tree	Mills Brothers	43-219	CB
In the Shade Of the Old Apple Tree	Reminiscing Series	3-28	SC
In The Shape Of A Heart	Browne, Jackson	23-618	BS
In The Still Of The Night	Boyz II Men	34-112	CB
In The Still Of The Night	Five Satins	35-5	CB
In The Still Of The Night	Five Satins	16-738	DK
In The Still Of The Night	Five Satins	7-308	MM
In The Still Of The Night	Five Satins	12-734	P
In The Still Of The Night	Five Satins	9-21	PS
In The Still Of The Night	Whitesnake	5-61	SC
In The Summertime	Hall, Tom T.	45-929	ESS
In The Summertime	Mungo, Jerry	13-321	P
In The Summertime	Shaggy	25-390	MM
In The Sweet Bye And Bye	Lynn, Loretta	47-634	CB
In The Wee Small Hours	Simon, Carly	6-447	MM
In The Wee Small Hours Of The AM	Streisand, Barbra	49-592	PS
In The Year 2525	Zager & Evans	11-832	DK
In These Last Few Days	Gill, Vince	20-335	ST
In This Diary	Ataris	32-222	THM
In This Life	Goodrem, Delta	36-493	CB
In This Life	Kreviazuk, Chantel	25-539	MM
In This Life	Raye, Collin	1-124	CB
In This Life	Raye, Collin	10-760	JVC
In This Little Town	Restless Heart	24-82	SC
In Those Jeans	Ginuwine	32-383	THM
In Those Jeans (Radio Version)	Ginuwine	21-783	SC
In Time	Humperdinck, E.	49-259	DFK
In Times Like These	Mandrell, Barbara	5-50	SC
In Times Like These	Paisley, Brad	30-165	CB
In Walked Love	Expose	2-224	SC
In Your Eyes	Gabriel, Peter	16-247	AMS
In Your Eyes	Minogue, Kylie	21-725	TT
In Your Face	Herndon, Ty	7-207	MM
In Your Face	Herndon, Ty	4-231	SC
In Your Room	Bangles	24-423	SC
In Your Shoes	McLachlan, Sarah	48-163	BKD
Incense & Peppermints	Strawberry Alarm	11-344	DK
Incomplete	Sisquo	23-259	HS
Incomplete	Sisquo	30-646	THM
Incomplete (Radio Version)	Sisquo	14-496	SC
Incredible	Shapeshifters	30-697	SF
Independence	Band Perry	40-41	ASK
Independence Day	McBride, Martina	1-378	CB
Independence Day	McBride, Martina	6-574	MM
Independence Day	McBride, Martina	12-464	P
Independent Woman	Destiny's Child	16-109	PRT
Independent Women	Destiny's Child	35-226	CB
Independent Women Part 1	Destiny's Child	14-21	THM
Indestructible	Four Tops	43-383	CB
Indian In-Laws (Parody)	Judd, Cledus T.	16-270	TT
Indian Lake	Cowsills	14-462	SC
Indian Love Call	Whitman, Slim	5-581	SC
Indian Outlaw	McGraw, Tim	1-526	CB
Indian Outlaw	McGraw, Tim	6-508	MM
Indian Outlaw	McGraw, Tim	2-94	SC
Indian Outlaw	McGraw, Tim	16-269	TT
Indian Reservation	Revere & Raiders	35-107	CB
Indian Reservation	Revere & Raiders	11-700	DK
Indian Reservation (the Lament of..	Revere & Raiders	14-640	SC
Indian Summer	Brooks & Dunn	37-51	CB
Indigo Swing the	Indigo Swing	13-696	SGB
Infinity	Williams, Don	39-97	PHN
Inhale	Stone Sour	32-220	THM
Innamorata	Martin, Dean	10-403	LE
Innamorata	Martin, Dean	23-66	MM
Inner City Blues	Gaye, Marvin	47-723	DK
Innervision	System of a Down	23-159	PHM
Innocence	Buxton, Sarah	30-52	CB
Innocence	Buxton, Sarah	30-100	PHM
Innocent Bystander	Dean, Billy	8-935	CB
Innocent Man	Austin, Sherrie	8-749	CB
Insane In The Brain **	Cypress Hill	25-479	MM
Insane In The Brain **	Cypress Hill	14-436	SC
Insensitive	Arden, Jann	19-581	MH
Insensitive	Arden, Jann	4-672	SC
Inseparable	Cole, Natalie	17-429	KC
Inseparable	Cole, Natalie	7-475	MM
Inseparable	Cole, Natalie	29-329	PS
Inside	Milsap, Ronnie	5-536	SC
Inside	Rothberg, Patti	24-117	SC
Inside Out	Eve 6	7-786	PHT
Inside Out	VanRay	32-135	THM
Inside Out	VonRay	32-135	THM
Inside Out	Yearwood, Trisha	25-57	MM
Inside Out	Yearwood, Trisha	16-33	ST
Inside Your Heaven	Bo Bice	23-317	CB
Inside Your Heaven	Underwood, Carrie	30-121	AS
Inside Your Heaven	Underwood, Carrie	23-282	CB
Inside Your Heaven	Underwood, Carrie	30-141	PT
Inspiration	Murphy, David Lee	22-90	CB
Inspiration Lady	Lightfoot, Gordon	43-475	SK
Instant Karma	Lennon, John	30-294	RS
Instant Karma	Lennon, John	16-65	SC
Instate	Edwards, Kathleen	29-321	PHM
Intentional Heartache	Yoakam, Dwight	49-701	ST
International Harvester	Morgan, Craig	30-574	CB
Interstate	Randy Rogers Band	38-224	CB
Interstate Love Song	Stone Temple Pilots	2-476	SC
Interstate Love Song	Stone Temple Pilots	13-750	SGB
Into My Arms	Nick Cave & Badseeds	44-311	SBI
Into The Fire	Dokken	21-780	SC
Into The Great Wide Open	Petty & Heartbreake	33-343	CB
Into The Groove	Madonna	2-37	SC
Into The Night	Santana feat Chad Kroeger	36-450	CB

SONG TITLE	ARTIST	#	TYPE
Into You	Fabolous & Tamia	32-418	THM
Into You (Radio Version)	Fabolous&Ashanti	21-784	SC
Into Your Arms	Lemonheads	6-43	SC
Intuition	Jewel	25-627	MM
Intution	Jewel	32-280	THM
Invincible (Legend of Billy Jean)	Benatar, Pat	46-125	SC
Invisible	Aiken, Clay	20-532	CB
Invisible	Aiken, Clay	36-320	PS
Invisible	Hayes, Hunter	43-132	PHN
Invisible	Swift, Taylor	36-91	BM
Invisible Man	98 Degrees	15-372	SKG
Invisible Touch	Collins, Phil	44-28	BS
Invisible Touch	Genesis	35-166	CB
Invitation To The Blues	Price, Ray	8-420	CB
Invitation To The Blues	Price, Ray	5-104	SC
IOU	Greenwood, Lee	2-637	SC
Iraq And Roll	Black, Clint	19-50	ST
Ireland 99	Brooks, Garth	7-850	CHT
Iris	Goo Goo Dolls	16-224	PHM
Iris	Goo Goo Dolls	5-274	SC
Iris	Goo Goo Dolls	21-595	SF
Irish - Annie Laurie	Mallan, Peter	11-489	DK
Irish - Aye Aye Aye (The Limerick Song)	Irish Songs	48-730	SDK
Irish - Black Velvet Band	Dubliners	21-493	SC
Irish - Danny Boy	Irish Songs	9-142	AH
Irish - Danny Boy	Irish Songs	12-492	P
Irish - Danny Boy	Irish Songs	21-499	SC
Irish - Danny Boy	Irish Songs	23-218	SM
Irish - Daughter Of Rosie O'Grady	Irish Songs	48-726	PS
Irish - Does Your Mother Come From...	Irish Songs	48-727	PS
Irish - Drunken Sailor	Irish Songs	48-721	KV
Irish - Fields Of Atheny	Irish Songs	48-715	DCK
Irish - Foggy Dew	Irish Songs	48-729	PR
Irish - Galway Bay	Piper, Jerry	21-491	SC
Irish - Goodnight Irene	Standard	21-504	SC
Irish - Green Fields Of Ireland	Irish Songs	48-724	KWD
Irish - Harrigan	Irish Songs	9-143	AH
Irish - Harrigan	Irish Songs	23-216	SM
Irish - I'll Take You Home Again...	Irish Songs	9-144	AH
Irish - I'll Take You Home Again...	Irish Songs	21-488	SC
Irish - Irish Heart	Ryan, Derek	48-722	KV
Irish - Irish Washerwoman the	Irish Songs	9-145	AH
Irish - It's A Long Way To Tipperary	Irish Songs	48-716	EZC
Irish - Kerrigan	Irish Songs	9-162	AH
Irish - Kerry Dance the	Irish Songs	9-146	AH
Irish - Lanigan's Ball	Irish Songs	48-731	SF
Irish - Little Bit Of Heaven a	Irish Songs	48-728	PS
Irish - Loch Lamond	Irish Songs	27-438	DK

SONG TITLE	ARTIST	#	TYPE
Irish - Londonderry Air (Old Irish Air)	Irish Songs	48-725	MM
Irish - MacNamara's Band	Irish Songs	9-147	AH
Irish - McNamara's Band	Noonan, Paddy & Gr.	21-492	SC
Irish - Molly Malone	Irish Songs	9-148	AH
Irish - Molly Malone (Cockles...)	Irish Songs	21-496	SC
Irish - Mountains Of Mourne	Irish Songs	48-719	KCD
Irish - My Bonnie	Irish Songs	11-482	DK
Irish - My Wild Irish Rose	Irish Songs	9-149	AH
Irish - My Wild Irish Rose	Irish Songs	2-70	SC
Irish - My Wild Irish Rose	Irish Songs	23-217	SM
Irish - One Irish Rover	Morrison, Van	21-503	SC
Irish - Orange And The Green the	Irish Songs	21-502	SC
Irish - Paddy McGinty's Goat	Irish Songs	48-732	SF
Irish - Peg O' My Heart	Irish Songs	9-150	AH
Irish - Rose Of Tralee the	Irish Songs	9-151	AH
Irish - Rothesay-O	Irish Songs	48-718	LRT
Irish - Seven Drunken Nights	Dubliners	21-494	SC
Irish - St. Patrick's Day	Irish Songs	9-152	AH
Irish - Sweet Rosie O'Grady	Irish Songs	9-153	AH
Irish - There Is A Tavern In The Town	Irish Songs	48-714	DK
Irish - There's Irish In Our Eyes	Matthews, Lee	48-720	KV
Irish - Too Ra Loo Ra Loo Ral	Breen, Ann	21-495	SC
Irish - Too Ra Loo Ra Loo Ral	Irish Songs	9-154	AH
Irish - Too-Ra-Loo Ra-Loo-Ra	Irish Songs	27-436	DK
Irish - Trotting To The Fair	Irish Songs	48-717	LRT
Irish - Unicorn the	Irish Songs	9-155	AH
Irish - Unicorn the	Irish Songs	2-64	SC
Irish - Unicorn the	Irish Songs	21-500	SC
Irish - Wearin' O' The Green	Irish Songs	9-156	AH
Irish - Wearin' O' The Green	Malone & Rapparees	21-489	SC
Irish - When Irish Eyes Are Smiling	Crosby, Bing	29-415	CB
Irish - When Irish Eyes Are Smiling	Irish Songs	9-157	AH
Irish - When Irish Eyes Are Smiling	Irish Songs	12-108	DK
Irish - When Irish Eyes Are Smiling	Irish Songs	2-68	SC
Irish - When Irish Eyes Are Smiling	Irish Songs	23-215	SM
Irish - When Irish Eyes Are Smiling	Various	48-583	DK
Irish - Whiskey In The	Irish Rovers	21-490	SC

SONG TITLE	ARTIST	#	TYPE
Jar			
Irish - Whiskey In The Jar	Irish Songs	9-158	AH
Irish - Whiskey On A Sunday	Irish Rovers	48-723	KV
Irish - Whistling Gypsy Rover	Irish Songs	9-159	AH
Irish - Who Threw the Overalls in..	Irish Songs	9-160	AH
Irish - Wild Rover the	Irish Songs	9-161	AH
Irish - Wild Rover the	Irish Songs	21-498	SC
Ironic	Morrisette, Alanis	18-42	PS
Irreplaceable	Beyonce	30-258	CB
Irresistible	Corrs	49-198	SF
Irresistible	Fall Out Boy	48-435	KCD
Irresistible	Simpson, Jessica	35-220	CB
Irresistible	Simpson, Jessica	18-524	TT
Irresistible Force	Jane's Addiction	38-241	PHM
Irresistible You	England, Ty	24-156	SC
Irresistible You	England, Tyler	7-318	MM
Is Anybody Goin' To San Antone	Pride, Charley	8-273	CB
Is Anybody Goin' To San Antone	Pride, Charley	9-485	SAV
Is Anybody Going To San Antone	Pride, Charley	17-308	NA
Is Anybody Going To San Antone	Pride, Charley	20-12	SC
Is It Cold In Here Or Is It Me	Diffie, Joe	1-274	CB
Is It Cold In Here Or Is It Me	Diffie, Joe	13-409	P
Is It Over Yet	Judd, Wynonna	1-652	CB
Is It Raining At Your House	Gosdin, Vern	47-115	CB
Is It Really Over	Reeves, Jim	8-576	CB
Is It Really Over	Reeves, Jim	40-127	CK
Is It Really Over	Reeves, Jim	3-835	LG
Is It Really Over	Reeves, Jim	5-855	SC
Is It Still Over	Travis, Randy	14-684	CB
Is It Still Over	Travis, Randy	3-371	SC
Is It True	Lee, Brenda	45-911	ZM
Is It Wrong For Loving You	James, Sonny	48-468	GS
Is She Really Going Out With Him	Jackson, Joe	11-657	DK
Is She Really Going Out With Him	Jackson, Joe	5-308	SC
Is She Really Going Out With Him	Sugar Ray	25-662	MM
Is That A Tear	Lawrence, Tracy	7-393	MM
Is That A Tear	Lawrence, Tracy	4-890	SC
Is That All There Is	Lee, Peggy	47-182	PS
Is There A Ghost	Band Of Horses	49-909	SC
Is There Life After Love	Twain, Shania	7-443	MM
Is There Life After Love	Twain, Shania	4-457	SC
Is There Life Out There	McEntire, Reba	1-801	CB
Is There Life Out There	McEntire, Reba	12-403	P
Is There Something I	Duran Duran	17-98	DK

SONG TITLE	ARTIST	#	TYPE
Should Know			
Is This Anyway To Fall	Eder, Linda	17-446	PS
Is This Love	Marley, Bob	12-6	DK
Is This Love	Marley, Bob	25-377	MM
Is This Love	Whitesnake	13-36	P
Island Girl	John, Elton	15-511	CMC
Island Girl	John, Elton	20-364	SC
Island In The Sun	Belafonte, Harry	46-507	LE
Island In The Sun	Belafonte, Harry	48-773	P
Island In The Sun	Weezer	25-37	MM
Island Of Dreams	Seekers	49-63	ZVS
Island Of Dreams	Springfields	29-824	SF
Island Of Lost Souls	Blondie	49-133	LG
Island Of Love	Presley, Elvis	25-112	MM
Island Song	Zac Brown Band	43-471	KV
Island the	Streisand, Barbra	15-289	PS
Islands	Bareilles, Sara	49-22	KV
Islands In The Stream	Bee Gees	17-499	LE
Islands In The Stream	Rogers & Parton	8-111	CB
Islands In The Stream	Rogers & Parton	16-784	DK
Islands In The Stream	Rogers & Parton	13-419	P
Islands In The Stream	Rogers & Parton	2-299	SC
Islands In The Stream	Rogers & Parton	10-511	SF
Isn't It Time	Babys	15-802	SC
Isn't She	Carolina Rain	30-255	CB
Isn't She Lovely	Wonder, Stevie	35-165	CB
Isn't She Lovely	Wonder, Stevie	27-258	DK
Isn't That Everything	Peck, Danielle	30-167	CB
Israelites	Dekker & the Aces	25-385	MM
Istanbul Not Constantinople	They Might B Giants	6-859	MM
Istanbul Not Constantinople	They Might B Giants	15-135	SC
It Should Have Been Love By Now - duet	Mandrell & Greenwood	48-696	CB
It Ain't Cool to Be Crazy Over You	Strait, George	5-330	SC
It Ain't Easy Being Easy	Frickie, Janie	49-633	CB
It Ain't Easy Being Me	Knight, Chris	8-223	CB
It Ain't Me	Warren Brothers	29-350	CB
It Ain't Me Babe	Cash, Johnny	29-730	CB
It Ain't Me Babe	Dylan, Bob	29-101	CB
It Ain't Me Babe	Turtles	7-64	MM
It Ain't My Fault **	Silkk the Shocker	28-28	DK
It Ain't No Big Thing	Presley, Elvis	25-754	MM
It Ain't No Crime	Nichols, Joe	36-395	CB
It Ain't No Crime	Nichols, Joe	47-324	THC
It Ain't Nothin'	Whitley, Keith	14-682	CB
It Ain't Nothin'	Whitley, Keith	6-621	MM
It Ain't Nothing	Whitley, Keith	34-298	CB
It Ain't Over	Kravitz, Lenny	17-331	DK
It Ain't Pretty	Lady Antebellum	46-84	BKD
It Ain't The Whiskey	Allan, Gary	44-156	BKD
It Ain't Yours To Throw Away	Palladio, Sam	44-286	KCD
It Came Out Of The Sky	CCR	48-368	KV
It Comes And Goes	Arnold, Eddy	44-223	DCK

SONG TITLE	ARTIST	#	TYPE
It Could Happen To You	Standard	15-512	SGB
It Couldn't Have Been Any Better	Duncan, Johnny	19-428	SC
It Do Feel Good	Fargo, Donna	5-755	SC
It Doesn't Matter Anymore	Holly, Buddy	17-362	DK
It Doesn't Matter Anymore	Holly, Buddy	3-208	LG
It Don't Feel Like Sinning To Me	Kendalls	5-540	SC
It Don't Happen Twice	Chesney, Kenny	22-589	ST
It Don't Matter To Me	Bread	26-355	DK
It Don't Matter To The Sun	Brooks, Garth	19-227	SC
It Don't Matter To The Sun	Brooks, Garth	22-511	ST
It Don't Mean A Thing	Standard	12-548	P
It Don't Mean I Don't Love You	McHayes	19-9	ST
It Feels So Good	Sonique	20-623	CB
It Feels So Good	Sonique	18-525	TT
It Goes Like This	Rhett, Thomas	45-401	BKD
It Goes Like This	Rhett, Thomas	44-331	SSC
It Goes Like This	Thomas, Rhett	43-14	ASK
It Had To Be You	Charles, Ray	46-583	LE
It Had To Be You	Connick, Harry Jr.	20-764	KB
It Had To Be You	Connick, Harry Jr.	30-188	LE
It Had To Be You	Connick, Harry Jr.	19-713	PS
It Had To Be You - duet	Bennett & Underwood	45-949	KV
It Had To Be You - duet	Streisand & Buble	49-544	CK
It Hit Me Like A Hammer	Lewis & The News	47-186	CB
It Hurts Like Hell	Franklin, Aretha	36-167	JT
It Hurts Like Love	Tucker, Tanya	4-598	SC
It Hurts So Bad	Tedeschi, Susan	17-451	AMS
It Hurts So Bad	Tedeschi, Susan	23-345	MM
It Hurts So Bad	Tedeschi, Susan	15-18	SC
It Hurts So Much	Reeves, Jim	3-836	LG
It Hurts To Be In Love	Pitney, Gene	7-268	MM
It Hurts To Be In Love	Pitney, Gene	5-227	SC
It Is What It Is	Highwaymen	2-742	SC
It Is What It Is	Highwaymen	47-736	SRK
It Is What It Is	Musgraves, Kacey	45-310	KV
It Just Comes Natural	Strait, George	30-163	CB
It Just Don't Feel Like Xmas w/o You	Rihanna	36-107	CB
It Keeps Right On A Hurtin'	Tillotson, Johnny	7-259	MM
It Keeps Right On A-Hurtin'	Presley, Elvis	7-122	MM
It Keeps You Runnin'	Doobie Brothers	29-86	CB
It Makes No Difference Now	Haggard, Merle	46-28	SSK
It Matters To Me	Hill, Faith	15-684	CB
It Matters To Me	Hill, Faith	7-145	MM
It Matters To Me	Hill, Faith	3-632	SC
It Might As Well Be Spring	Cole, Natalie	11-797	DK
It Might As Well Be Spring	Haymes, Dick	4-181	SC

SONG TITLE	ARTIST	#	TYPE
It Might As Well Rain Until September	King, Carole	43-446	LG
It Might Be You	Bishop, Stephen	46-515	MH
It Must Be Him	Carr, Vicki	11-637	DK
It Must Be Him	Carr, Vicki	14-339	SC
It Must Be Love	Herndon, Ty	8-159	CB
It Must Be Love	Herndon, Ty	22-830	ST
It Must Be Love	Jackson, Alan	9-430	CB
It Must Be Love	Jackson, Alan	19-245	CSZ
It Must Be Love	Jackson, Alan	22-546	ST
It Must Be Love	Williams, Don	29-626	CB
It Must Be Love	Williams, Don	5-208	SC
It Must Have Been Love	Roxette	28-419	DK
It Must Have Been Love	Roxette	12-811	P
It Must Have Been Love	Roxette	9-693	SAV
It Must Have Been The Mistletoe	Streisand, Barbra	48-514	KVD
It Never Rains In Southern CA	Gorme, Steve&Eydie	16-749	DK
It Never Rains In Southern CA	Hammond, Albert	5-113	SC
It Only Hurts For A Little While	Smith, Margo	29-779	CB
It Only Hurts When I Cry	Yoakam, Dwight	12-440	P
It Only Hurts When I'm Breathing	Twain, Shania	19-763	ST
It Only Takes A Minute	Dayne, Taylor	11-408	DK
It Only Takes A Minute	Tavares	27-359	DK
It Sure Is Monday	Chesnutt, Mark	8-844	CB
It Sure Is Monday	Chesnutt, Mark	6-761	MM
It Sure Is Monday	Chesnutt, Mark	17-246	NA
It Takes A Little Rain (To Make...)	Oak Ridge Boys	23-496	CB
It Takes A Man	Lines, Aaron	23-302	CB
It Takes One To Know One	Orbison, Roy	47-340	BFK
It Takes People Like You	Owens, Buck	46-106	CB
It Takes Two	Base & DJ Ez Rock	18-370	AH
It Takes Two	Base & DJ Ez Rock	12-177	DK
It Takes Two	Weston & Gaye	26-524	DK
It Takes Two - duet	Gaye & Weston	36-308	CB
It Turns Me Inside Out	Greenwood, Lee	8-686	SAV
It Turns Me Inside Out	Greenwood, Lee	5-29	SC
It Was	Wright, Chely	5-799	SC
It Was	Wright, Chely	22-505	ST
It Was A Good Time	Minelli, Liza	49-222	ASK
It Was A Very Good Year	Sinatra, Frank	11-569	DK
It Was A Very Good Year	Sinatra, Frank	9-260	PT
It Was Almost Like A Song	Milsap, Ronnie	1-440	CB
It Was Almost Like A Song	Milsap, Ronnie	11-620	DK
It Was Always So Easy To Forget	Bandy, Moe	19-507	CB
It Was Always So Easy To Forget	Bandy, Moe	20-284	SC
It Was An Absolutely Finger Lickin'	Bomshel	29-208	CB

144

SONG TITLE	ARTIST	#	TYPE
It Wasn't God Who Made Honky Tonk	Wells, Kitty	7-119	MM
It Wasn't God Who Made HonkyTonk	Wells, Kitty	26-490	DK
It Wasn't Me	Shaggy & Ricardo	16-471	MH
It Wasn't Me	Shaggy & Ricardo	16-117	PRT
It Wasn't Me	Shaggy & Ricardo	18-561	TT
It Will Rain	Mars, Bruno	39-117	SB
It Won't Be Christmas Without You	Brooks & Dunn	45-749	CB
It Won't Be Like This for Long	Rucker, Darius	36-240	PHM
It Won't Be Me	Tucker, Tanya	16-352	CB
It Won't Be Over You	Wariner, Steve	1-504	CB
It Won't Be Over You	Wariner, Steve	6-577	MM
It Works	Alabama	4-131	SC
It Would Be You	Allan, Gary	8-402	CB
It Would Be You	Allan, Gary	7-768	CHM
It Wouldn't Hurt To Have Wings	Chesnutt, Mark	22-455	SC
It Wouldn't Hurt To Have Wings	Chesnutt, Mark	8-849	CB
It'll Be Me	Exile	20-659	SC
It'll Go Away	Denney, K	32-44	THM
It'll Go Away	Denney, Kevin	18-457	ST
It'll Go Away	Denney, Kevin	32-44	THM
It's 5 O'Clock Somewhere - duet	Jackson & Buffett	35-427	CB
It's A Beautiful Morning	Rascals	18-252	DK
It's A Beautiful Thing	Brandt, Paul	14-702	CB
It's A Beautiful Thing	Brandt, Paul	5-810	SC
It's A Beautiful Thing	Brandt, Paul	22-540	ST
It's A Business Doing Pleasure With You	McGraw, Tim	47-236	CB
It's A Cheatin' Situation	Bandy, Moe	19-498	CB
It's A Cheatin' Situation	Bandy, Moe	4-268	SC
It's A Cowboy Lovin' Night	Tucker, Tanya	45-125	THM
It's A Good Day	Lee, Peggy	47-181	KV
It's A Good Thing	Jason & the Long Road	38-225	CB
It's A Great Day To Be A Guy	Judd, Cledus T.	44-307	SBI
It's A Great Day To Be Alive	Tritt, Travis	22-585	ST
It's A Heartache	Trick Pony	22-317	CB
It's A Heartache	Tyler, Bonnie	35-141	CB
It's A Heartache	Tyler, Bonnie	2-554	SC
It's A Little More Like Heaven	Locklin, Hank	5-691	SC
It's A Little Too Late	Chesnutt, Mark	1-358	CB
It's A Little Too Late	Chesnutt, Mark	4-502	SC
It's A Little Too Late	Tucker, Tanya	16-345	CB
It's A Little Too Late	Tucker, Tanya	10-788	JVC
It's A Little Too Late	Tucker, Tanya	6-131	MM
It's A Little Too Late	Tucker, Tanya	12-478	P
It's A Long Lonely Highway	Presley, Elvis	25-117	MM
It's A Love Thing	Urban, Keith	14-693	CB

SONG TITLE	ARTIST	#	TYPE
It's A Love Thing	Urban, Keith	19-229	SC
It's A Love Thing	Urban, Keith	22-535	ST
It's A Man's Man's Man's World	Brown, James	15-308	SC
It's A Matter Of Time	Presley, Elvis	25-751	MM
It's A Miracle	Culture Club	47-4	ZM
It's A Miracle	Manilow, Barry	29-120	CB
It's A Miracle	Manilow, Barry	17-532	SC
It's A Mistake	Men At Work	9-689	SAV
It's A Sin	Anka, Paul	49-244	DFK
It's A Sin	Arnold, Eddy	19-630	CB
It's A Sin	Robbins, Marty	48-18	CB
It's A Sin To Tell A Lie	Bennett, Tony	10-711	JVC
It's A Sin To Tell A Lie	Bennett, Tony	19-99	SAV
It's About Time	Lillix	25-582	MM
It's About Time	Lillix	19-544	SC
It's About Time	Lillix	32-248	THM
It's About Time	Reeves, Julie	8-922	CB
It's All About Him (Moby Edit)	Jackson, Alan	30-547	CB
It's All About The Benjamins	Puff Daddy& Family	14-442	SC
It's All Been Done	Barenaked Ladies	33-366	CB
It's All Been Done	Barenaked Ladies	16-216	MM
It's All Been Done	Barenaked Ladies	7-778	PHT
It's All Been Done	Barenaked Ladies	30-612	RS
It's All Coming Back To Me Now	Dion, Celine	15-118	BS
It's All Coming Back To Me Now	Dion, Celine	4-690	SC
It's All Going To Pot	Haggard, Merle	45-947	KV
It's All Good	Keith, Toby	47-155	CB
It's All Good	Nichols, Joe	47-321	KV
It's All How You Look At It	Lawrence, Tracy	30-801	PHM
It's All How You Look At It	Lawrence, Tracy	20-474	ST
It's All In The Game	Edwards, Tommy	11-737	DK
It's All In The Game	Edwards, Tommy	6-439	MM
It's All In The Movies	Haggard, Merle	8-319	CB
It's All In Your Head	Diamond Rio	1-175	CB
It's All Over But The Crying	Williams, Hank Jr.	49-299	KWC
It's All Over But The Crying	Williams, Hank Jr.	45-695	KWC
It's All Over Now	Rolling Stones	18-18	LE
It's All Right	Impressions	12-716	P
It's All Right With Me	Connick, Harry Jr.	19-721	PS
It's All Right With Me	Sinatra, Frank	9-237	PT
It's All The Same To Me	Cyrus, Billy Ray	7-673	CHM
It's All The Same To Me	Cyrus, Billy Ray	22-624	ST
It's All Too Much	Beatles	20-200	SC
It's All Wrong But It's Alright	Parton, Dolly	8-538	CB
It's All Wrong But It's Alright	Parton, Dolly	5-532	SC
It's All Your Fault	Church, Claudia	19-241	SC
It's Alright	Bare, Bobby	18-271	CB

145

SONG TITLE	ARTIST	#	TYPE
It's Alright Baby's Coming Back	Eurythmics	47-82	SFM
It's Alright To Be A Redneck	Jackson, Alan	15-860	ST
It's Alright With Me	Fitzgerald, Ella	23-351	MM
It's Always Something	Diffie, Joe	33-133	CB
It's Always Something	Diffie, Joe	6-66	SC
It's Always Something	Diffie, Joe	22-477	ST
It's America - Patriotic	Atkins, Rodney	36-261	PHM
It's Been A Great Afternoon	Haggard, Merle	37-181	CB
It's Been A Great Afternoon	Haggard, Merle	11-837	DK
It's Been A Great Afternoon	Haggard, Merle	10-777	JVC
It's Been Awhile	Staind	35-250	CB
It's Been Awhile	Staind	18-395	MM
It's Been Awhile	Staind	16-384	SGB
It's Been So Long	Pierce, Webb	29-400	CB
It's Been So Long Darlin'	Tubb, Ernest	22-293	CB
It's Christmas	Milsap, Ronnie	45-756	CB
It's Easy For You	Presley, Elvis	25-326	MM
It's Five O'Clock Somewhere	Jackson & Buffett	25-636	MM
It's Five O'Clock Somewhere	Jackson & Buffett	19-168	ST
It's Five O'Clock Somewhere - Duet	Jackson & Buffett	32-334	THM
It's Four In The Morning	Young, Faron	4-314	SC
It's Getting Better	Elliot, Cass	49-514	ZM
It's Getting Better All The Time	Brooks & Dunn	23-2	CB
It's Getting Better All The Time	Brooks & Dunn	23-31	SC
It's Goin' Down	X-Ecutioners	18-230	CB
It's Going To Take Some Time	Carpenters	9-718	SAV
It's Going To Take Some Time	Carpenters	20-56	SC
It's Goinna Be A Cold Cold Christmas	Dana	45-591	OZP
It's Gonna Be Me	N'Sync	20-428	CB
It's Gonna Be Me	N'Sync	14-470	SC
It's Gonna Be Me	N'Sync	30-632	THM
It's Gonna Be Me	N'Sync	18-562	TT
It's Gonna Take A Little Bit Longer	Pride, Charley	47-438	CB
It's Gonna Take A Miracle	Williams, Deniece	13-195	P
It's Gonna Take A Miracle	Williams, Deniece	5-384	SC
It's Good To Be King	Petty & Heartbreake	13-601	P
It's Good To Be Me	Parker, Caryl Mack	4-834	SC
It's Good To Be Us	Covington, Bucky	30-556	CB
It's Hard To Be Humble	Davis, Mac	23-508	CB
It's Hard To Be Humble	Davis, Mac	5-629	SC
It's Hard To Kiss The Lips At...	Notorious Cherry Bo	23-404	CB
It's Hard To Kiss The Lips At...	Notorious Cherry Bo	30-14	SC

SONG TITLE	ARTIST	#	TYPE
It's Impossible	Como, Perry	33-217	CB
It's Impossible	Como, Perry	11-299	DK
It's Impossible	Como, Perry	20-774	PS
It's Impossible	Como, Perry	4-352	SC
It's In His Kiss	Everett, Betty	15-514	MM
It's In The Way That You Use It	Clapton, Eric	46-203	SC
It's In Your Eyes	Collins, Phil	44-19	SC
It's Just A Matter Of Time	Benton, Brook	3-516	SC
It's Just A Matter Of Time	Travis, Randy	1-403	CB
It's Just About Time	Cash, Johnny	29-764	CB
It's Just That Way	Jackson, Alan	44-144	BKD
It's Just What We Do	Florida Georgia Line	43-126	ASK
It's Late	Nelson, Ricky	21-700	CB
It's Late	Nelson, Ricky	20-30	SC
It's Like That	Carey&Scoop&JD	22-365	CB
It's Like We Never Said Goodbye	Gayle, Crystal	5-54	SC
It's Lonely Out There	Tillis, Pam	22-901	ST
It's Magic	Day, Doris	34-13	CB
It's Magic	Day, Doris	9-89	PS
It's Me	K-Ci & JoJo	32-53	THM
It's Me Again Margaret	Stevens, Ray	16-490	CB
It's Midnight Cinderella	Brooks, Garth	4-160	SC
It's My Life	Animals	11-277	DK
It's My Life	Animals	15-48	LE
It's My Life	Animals	13-231	P
It's My Life	Anka, Paul	44-114	KV
It's My Life	Bon Jovi	10-665	SF
It's My Life	Bon Jovi	19-836	SGB
It's My Life	Bon Jovi	15-641	THM
It's My Life	Bon Jovi	18-563	TT
It's My Life	No Doubt	19-659	CB
It's My Party	Gore, Lesley	11-114	DK
It's My Party	Gore, Lesley	3-364	MH
It's My Party	Gore, Lesley	12-901	P
It's My Party	Gore, Lesley	9-25	PS
It's My Party	Gore, Lesley	9-284	SC
It's My Time	McBride, Martina	33-154	CB
It's My Time	McBride, Martina	22-588	ST
It's My Time	Ross, Diana	15-362	LE
It's My Time (Waste It If I Want To	Holy, Steve	23-416	CB
It's My Turn	Breelan, Angel	41-81	PHN
It's My Turn	Ross, Diana	6-567	MM
It's Never Easy To Say Goodbye	Judd, Wynonna	48-321	SC
It's Nice To Go Traveling	Sinatra, Frank	49-496	MM
It's No Secret Anymore	Eder, Linda	17-437	PS
It's Not About Blame	Dunn, Holly	3-630	SC
It's Not For Me To Say	Mathis, Johnny	10-467	MG
It's Not Love But It's Not Bad	Haggard, Merle	8-321	CB
It's Not Love But It's Not Bad	Haggard, Merle	5-129	SC
It's Not My Cross To	Allman Brothers	15-16	SC

SONG TITLE	ARTIST	#	TYPE
Bear			
It's Not My Time (I Won't Go)	3 Doors Down	36-439	CB
It's Not OK	Zac Brown Band	46-64	KV
It's Not Over	Chesnutt, Mark	8-232	CB
It's Not Over	Chesnutt, Mark	7-727	CHM
It's Not Over	Chesnutt, Mark	22-755	ST
It's Not Over	Daughtry	30-266	CB
It's Not Over	McEntire, Reba	1-798	CB
It's Not Right But It's Okay	Houston, Whitney	8-327	PHT
It's Not Right But It's Okay	Houston, Whitney	13-677	SGB
It's Not The End Of The World	Emilio	7-168	MM
It's Not The End Of The World	Emilio	4-30	SC
It's Not Unusual	Jones, Tom	13-300	P
It's Now Or Never	Presley, Elvis	11-607	DK
It's Now Or Never	Presley, Elvis	13-65	P
It's Now Or Never	Presley, Elvis	2-590	SC
It's Now Or Never	Presley, Elvis	14-758	THM
It's Only A Paper Moon	Cole, Nat "King"	11-222	DK
It's Only A Paper Moon	Cole, Nat "King"	15-838	MM
It's Only A Paper Moon	Lee, Brenda	48-579	DK
It's Only A Paper Moon	Reeves, Jim	45-260	DKM
It's Only Love	Carpenter, M C	8-873	CB
It's Only Make Believe	Campbell, Glen	11-106	DK
It's Only Make Believe	McDowell, Ronnie	47-231	CB
It's Only Make Believe	Twitty, Conway	8-268	CB
It's Only Make Believe	Twitty, Conway	7-304	MM
It's Only Make Believe	Twitty, Conway	13-420	P
It's Only Monday	Long, Brice	23-299	CB
It's Only Over For You	Tucker, Tanya	16-348	CB
It's Only Over For You	Tucker, Tanya	5-164	SC
It's Only Rock & Roll	Rolling Stones	18-25	LE
It's Only Rock & Roll	Rolling Stones	14-395	PT
It's Over	McCartney, Jesse	36-497	CB
It's Over	Orbison, Roy	9-190	SO
It's Over	Presley, Elvis	7-121	MM
It's Over My Head	Hayes, Wade	22-914	ST
It's Raining Men	Two Tons O' Fun	12-22	DK
It's Raining Men	Weather Girls	20-373	SC
It's Raining On Prom Night	Bullens, Cindy	10-15	SC
It's So Easy	Holly, Buddy	9-884	DK
It's So Easy	Holly, Buddy	12-683	P
It's So Easy	Holly, Buddy	11-32	PX
It's So Easy	Ronstadt, Linda	8-801	CB
It's So Easy	Ronstadt, Linda	11-161	DK
It's So Easy	Ronstadt, Linda	10-3	SC
It's So Hard To Say Goodbye	Boyz II Men	17-427	KC
It's So Hard To Say Goodbye	Boyz II Men	15-515	PS
It's So Hard To Say Goodbye	Mraz, Jason	44-318	SBI
It's Still Rock & Roll To	Joel, Billy	12-274	DK

SONG TITLE	ARTIST	#	TYPE
Me			
It's Still Rock & Roll To Me	Joel, Billy	16-147	LE
It's Still Rock & Roll To Me	Joel, Billy	12-801	P
It's Such A Pretty World Today	Stewart, Wynne	8-670	SAV
It's Such A Small World	Crowell & Cash, R.	5-437	SC
It's The End Of The World	REM	34-60	CB
It's The End Of The World	REM	13-598	P
It's The Little Things	James, Sonny	19-471	CB
It's The Little Things	James, Sonny	14-335	SC
It's The Same Old Shillelagh - Irish	Irish Songs	49-35	SHER
It's The Same Old Song	Four Tops	11-146	DK
It's The Same Old Song	Four Tops	2-78	SC
It's Time	Eder, Linda	16-712	PS
It's Time To Cross That Bridge	Greene, Jack	43-351	CB
It's Time To Cry	Anka, Paul	5-524	SC
It's Too Late	Estefan, Gloria	23-573	MM
It's Too Late	Estefan, Gloria	3-492	SC
It's Too Late	Goldsboro, Bobby	45-604	OZP
It's Too late	King, Carole	11-215	DK
It's Too Late	King, Carole	12-682	P
It's Too Late	King, Carole	19-116	SAV
It's Too Late	Willis, Chuck	17-324	SS
It's Too Late To Turn Back Now	Cornelius Brothers	27-322	DK
It's Too Late To Worry	Messina, Jo Dee	30-17	CB
It's True	Backstreet Boys	15-446	PHM
It's Up To You	Al Dexter & Troopers	46-409	CB
It's Up To You	Nelson, Ricky	21-711	CB
It's Up To You	Nelson, Ricky	15-764	NU
It's Up To You	Nelson, Ricky	5-513	SC
It's What I Am	Montgomery, J M	7-252	MM
It's What I Do	Dean, Billy	4-161	SC
It's Who You Love	Williams, Don	4-474	SC
It's You	Zayn	49-931	MRH
It's You Again	Ewing, Skip	5-775	SC
It's You Again	Exile	12-35	DK
It's You It's You It's You	Dolan, Joe	49-141	SRK
It's Your Call	McEntire, Reba	1-807	CB
It's Your Call	McEntire, Reba	6-128	MM
It's Your Love	McGraw & Hill	7-634	CHM
It's Your Love (Solo)	McGraw, Tim	1-535	CB
It's Your Love (Solo)	McGraw, Tim	7-624	CHM
It's Your Love (Solo)	McGraw, Tim	10-101	SC
It's Your Song	Brooks, Garth	8-850	CB
It's Your Song	Brooks, Garth	22-683	ST
It's Your Thing	Isley Brothers	17-393	DK
It's Your Thing	Isley Brothers	7-49	MM
It's Your Thing	Isley Brothers	12-724	P
It's Your Thing	Isley Brothers	5-453	SC
It's Your Thing	Mercedes	48-554	DK

SONG TITLE	ARTIST	#	TYPE
It's Your World	Robbins, Marty	48-22	CB
It's All In Your Head	Diamond Rio	4-498	SC
It's Four In The Morning	Young, Faron	20-728	CB
It's Impossible	Como, Perry	13-546	LE
Itch the	Vitamin C	35-238	CB
Itchy Twitchy Feeling	Hendricks, Bobby	45-831	VH
Itchycoo Park	Small Faces	13-322	P
Itsy Bitsy Teenie Weenie	Hyland, Bryan	6-867	MM
Itsy Bitsy Teenie Weenie	Hyland, Bryan	12-644	P
Itsy Bitsy Teenie Weenie	Hyland, Bryan	16-376	SF
Itsy Bitsy Teenie Weenie	Price, Ray	45-627	JV
Itsy Bitsy Teenie Weenie...	Hyland, Bryan	10-329	KC
Itsy Bitsy Teenie Weenie...	Hyland, Bryan	4-1	SC
Jack & Diane	Mellencamp, John	21-432	LE
Jack & Diane	Mellencamp, John	6-485	MM
Jack & Diane	Mellencamp, John	19-92	PS
Jack & Diane	Mellencamp, John	21-424	SC
Jack Daniels	Church, Eric	49-525	BKD
Jack Daniels	Lambert, Miranda	44-83	BKD
Jack Daniels If You Please	Coe, David Allan	18-313	CB
Jack O Lantern Jump - Halloween	Halloween Songs	45-102	KV
Jackie Blue	Ozark Mtn Daredevil	7-460	MM
Jackie Blue	Ozark Mtn Daredevil	2-532	SC
Jackie Brown	Mellencamp, John	45-424	SC
Jackson	Cash & Carter	29-754	CB
Jackson	Cash & Carter	4-267	SC
Jackson	Phoenix & Witherspoon	29-855	SC
Jackson	Phoenix & Witherspoon	29-717	ST
Jackson (Alan That Is)	Judd, Cledus T.	16-511	CB
Jacob's Ladder	Lewis & The News	47-187	CB
Jacob's Ladder	Lewis & The News	24-69	SC
Jacob's Ladder	Wills, Mark	4-371	SC
Jaded	Aerosmith	16-474	MH
Jaded	Aerosmith	16-257	TT
Jai Ho (You Are My Destiny)	Pussycat Dolls	44-138	BKD
Jailbreak	Thin Lizzie	5-875	SC
Jailhouse Rock	Presley, Elvis	16-829	DK
Jailhouse Rock	Presley, Elvis	2-606	SC
Jailhouse Rock	Presley, Elvis	14-750	THM
Jalapenos	Bellamy Brothers	45-304	KST
Jam Up & Jelly Tight	Roe, Weller	16-647	JTG
Jamaica Farewell	Belafonte, Harry	46-504	JVC
Jambalaya	Carpenters	44-348	DK
Jambalaya	Williams, Hank Sr.	17-31	DK
Jambalaya	Williams, Hank Sr.	12-745	P
Jambalaya	Williams, Hank Sr.	9-486	SAV
James Dean	Bedingfield, Daniel	18-778	PHM
James Dean	Eagles	36-130	SGB
Jamestown Ferry the	Tucker, Tanya	19-434	SC
Jamie	Parker, Ray Jr.	24-341	SC
Jamie's Cryin'	Van Halen	5-884	SC

SONG TITLE	ARTIST	#	TYPE
Jane	Barenaked Ladies	30-617	RS
Janie Baker's Love Slave	Shenandoah	1-490	CB
Janie Baker's Love Slave	Shenandoah	6-763	MM
Janie's Gone Fishing	Hill, Kim	6-584	MM
Janie's Got A Gun	Aerosmith	43-212	SC
Jazzman	King, Carole	47-716	LE
Jazzman	King, Carole	3-618	SC
Jealous Again	Black Crowes	6-33	SC
Jealous Bone	Loveless, Patty	1-718	CB
Jealous Bone	Loveless, Patty	13-528	P
Jealous Guy	Lennon, John	30-303	RS
Jealous Guy	Roxy Music	13-317	P
Jealous Heart	Locklin, Hank	47-512	VH
Jealous Heart	Ritter, Tex	20-707	CB
Jealous Heart	Ritter, Tex	5-701	SC
Jealous Of The Moon	Nickel Creek	29-215	PHM
Jealousy	Merchant, Natalie	18-39	PS
Jealousy	Wells, Kitty	47-393	CB
Jean	Oliver	12-572	P
Jeanie With The Light Brown Hair	Standard	11-491	DK
Jeans On	Urban, Keith	29-367	CB
Jeepers Creepers	Bennett, Tony	34-442	CB
Jefferson's the	TV Themes	2-173	SC
Jellyhead	Crush	24-237	SC
Jennifer Eccles	Hollies	44-372	ZM
Jenny Come Back	Darling, Helen	7-19	MM
Jenny From The Block	Lopez, Jennifer	18-586	NS
Jenny From The Block	Lopez, Jennifer	32-16	THM
Jenny Jenny	Little Richard	11-88	DK
Jeopardy	Greg Khin Band	5-139	SC
Jeremiah Peabody's Song	Stevens, Ray	6-863	MM
Jeremy	Pearl Jam	33-353	CB
Jeremy	Pearl Jam	9-298	RS
Jersey Girl	Springsteen, Bruce	20-246	LE
Jerusalem	Earle, Steve	46-182	TU
Jesse	Simon, Carly	49-153	CB
Jesse's Girl	Springfield, Rick	16-160	SC
Jesus & Gravity	Parton, Dolly	36-421	CB
Jesus And Bartenders	Singletary, Daryle	30-458	CB
Jesus And Mama	Confederate RR	2-339	SC
Jesus Is Just Alright	Doobie Brothers	29-85	CB
Jesus Is Just Alright	Doobie Brothers	20-50	SC
Jesus Take The Wheel	Underwood, Carrie	30-122	AS
Jesus Take The Wheel	Underwood, Carrie	29-25	CB
Jesus Take The Wheel	Underwood, Carrie	23-450	ST
Jesus Takes A Hand	Haggard, Merle	37-172	CB
Jesus To A Child	Michael, George	11-73	JTG
Jesus To A Child	Michael, George	4-179	SC
Jesus Was A Capricorn	Kristofferson, Kris	45-201	DCK
Jesus Was A Country Boy	Walker, Clay	20-448	ST
Jet	McCartney & Wings	17-557	DK
Jet	McCartney, Paul	21-516	SC
Jet Airliner	Miller, Steve	23-628	BS
Jet Airliner	Steve Miller Band	16-595	MM

SONG TITLE	ARTIST	#	TYPE
Jet City Woman	Queensyrche	18-377	SAV
Jet City Woman	Queensyrche	5-605	SC
Jezebel	Wright, Chely	25-75	MM
Jezebel	Wright, Chely	16-36	ST
Jim And Jack And Hank	Jackson, Alan	45-53	BKD
Jim Dandy	Black Oak Arkansas	18-150	CB
Jimmie Brown the Newsboy	Wiseman, Mac	36-355	CB
Jimmy Buffett Don't Live In Key West	Coe, David Allan	48-426	HC
Jimmy Choo	Shyne & Ashanti	30-807	PHM
Jimmy Crack Corn	Standard	23-229	SM
Jimmy Mack	Martha & Vandellas	16-853	DK
Jimmy's Got A Girlfriend	Wilkinsons	22-480	ST
Jingle Bell Rock	Lee, Brenda	45-904	DMG
Jingle Bells - xmas	Thomas, B.J.	46-96	CB
Jingle Jangle Jingle	Kyser, Kay	4-189	SC
Jive Talkin'	Bee Gees	11-331	DK
Jive Talkin'	Bee Gees	17-506	LE
Jive Talkin'	Bee Gees	9-780	SAV
Jive Talkin'	Bee Gees	20-369	SC
JoAnna	Kool & The Gang	16-558	P
Job Description	Jackson, Alan	4-109	SC
Joe Knows How To Live	Raven, Eddy	29-656	SC
Joey	Concrete Blond	24-566	SC
Jogger the	Bare, Bobby	23-26	SC
Joggers	Bare, Bobby	47-902	DCK
John Cougar, John Deere, John 3:16	Urban, Keith	45-24	BKD
John Deere Green	Diffie, Joe	1-279	CB
John Deere Green	Diffie, Joe	26-539	DK
John Deere Green	Diffie, Joe	6-455	MM
John Deere Tractor	Judds	17-242	NA
John Doe No. 24	Carpenter, M C	2-578	SC
John J. Blanchard	Smith, Anthony	18-332	ST
John J. Blanchard	Smith, Anthony	32-9	THM
John Wayne Walking Away	White, Lari	14-611	SC
Johnny & June	Newfield, Heidi	36-208	PHM
Johnny Angel	Fabares, Shelly	17-125	DK
Johnny Angel	Fabares, Shelly	3-358	MH
Johnny Angel	Fabares, Shelly	13-125	P
Johnny B Goode	Presley, Elvis	43-246	MM
Johnny B. Goode	Berry, Chuck	17-413	DK
Johnny B. Goode	Berry, Chuck	46-600	LE
Johnny B. Goode	Berry, Chuck	46-601	MM
Johnny B. Goode	Berry, Chuck	9-19	PS
Johnny B. Goode	Berry, Chuck	46-226	SC
Johnny B. Goode	Berry, Chuck	17-322	SS
Johnny Cash	Aldean, Jason	30-339	CB
Johnny Cash Junkie	Brooks & Dunn	45-676	DCK
Johnny Come Lately	Earle, Steve	45-953	KV
Johnny Get Angry	Sommers, Joanie	20-62	SC
Johnny Get Your Gun	Gibson Miller Band	24-352	SC
Johnny Guitar	Lee, Peggy	47-176	JVC
Johnny One Time	Lee, Brenda	30-325	CB
Johnny Reb	Horton, Johnny	14-327	SC

SONG TITLE	ARTIST	#	TYPE
Johnny Remember Me	Leyton, John	10-564	SF
Join Together	Who	19-733	LE
JoJo	Boz Scaggs	17-533	SC
Joker the	Lang, k.d.	47-170	SC
Joker the	Miller, Steve	23-626	BS
Joker the	Steve Miller Band	16-779	DK
Joker the	Steve Miller Band	5-313	SC
Jolene	Parton, Dolly	8-535	CB
Jolene	Parton, Dolly	12-80	DK
Jolene	Parton, Dolly	13-443	P
Jolene	Zac Brown Band	43-466	KV
Joli Girl	Robbins, Marty	48-20	CB
Jolly Old Saint Nicholas - xmas	Chicago	45-255	SC
Jones On The Jukebox	Hobbs, Becky	6-533	MM
Jose Quervo	West, Shelly	7-414	MM
Jose Quervo	West, Shelly	2-26	SC
Joshua Fit The Battle	Presley, Elvis	30-381	SC
Josie	Steely Dan	15-392	RS
Journey To The Center Of The Earth	Dukes, Amboy	16-284	TT
Journey To The Center Of The Mind	Amboy Dukes	14-457	SC
Journey To The Past	Aaliyah	10-120	SC
Joy & Pain	EZ-Rock & Rob Base	14-446	SC
Joy And Pain	Hendrix, A.	32-350	THM
Joy To the World	Three Dog Night	11-686	DK
Joy To The World - xmas	Willie, Boxcar	45-257	CB
Joyride	Hanson, Jennifer	30-537	CB
Joyride	Roxette	18-496	SAV
Juanita	Twain, Shania	45-529	CB
Jubilee Street	Nick Cave & the Badseeds	43-80	SF
Judy	Robbins, Marty	48-31	VH
Judy Blue Eyes	Crosby Stills & Nash	7-481	MM
Judy In Disguise	John Fred & Playboy Band	48-582	DK
Judy In Disguise With Glasses	John, Fred	35-99	CB
Judy In Disguise With Glasses	John, Fred	11-561	DK
Judy Judy Judy	Tillotson, Johnny	49-285	CAK
Judy's Turn To Cry	Gore, Lesley	5-7	SC
Jukebox (Don't Put Another Dime...)	Flirts	24-421	SC
Jukebox Blues	Carter, June	49-297	HM
Jukebox In My Mind	Alabama	4-445	BS
Jukebox In My Mind	Alabama	1-17	CB
Jukebox In My Mind	Alabama	6-623	MM
Jukebox In My Mind	Alabama	17-292	NA
Jukebox Junkie	Mellons, Ken	34-313	CB
Jukebox Junkie	Mellons, Ken	6-671	MM
Jukebox Junkie	Mellons, Ken	2-451	SC
Jukebox With A Country Song	Stone, Doug	20-596	CB
Jukebox With A Country Song	Stone, Doug	9-543	SAV

SONG TITLE	ARTIST	#	TYPE
Julia	Twitty, Conway	43-194	CB
Juliet	Four Pennies	10-569	SF
Juliet	Gibb, Robin	49-25	KV
Jump	Anka, Paul	49-243	DFK
Jump	Van Halen	13-615	LE
Jump	Van Halen	2-42	SC
Jump Around	House Of Pain	25-480	MM
Jump Around	House Of Pain	20-90	SC
Jump For My Love	Pointer Sisters	3-478	SC
Jump In Line	Belafonte, Harry	46-508	LE
Jump Jive & Wail	Brian Setzer Orch	7-775	PHT
Jump Jive & Wail	Brian Setzer Orch	13-692	SGB
Jump Off the	Lil Kim w Mr. Cheeks	32-351	THM
Jump Right In	Zac Brown Band	43-470	KV
Jump Then Fall	Swift, Taylor	37-324	CB
Jumper	Third Eye Blind	33-370	CB
Jumper	Third Eye Blind	13-681	SGB
Jumpin' Jack Flash	Rolling Stones	19-758	LE
Jumpin' Jack Flash	Rolling Stones	14-396	PT
Jumpin' Jumpin'	Destiny's Child	34-180	CB
Jumpin' Jumpin'	Destiny's Child	13-566	LE
Jumpin' Jumpin'	Destiny's Child	30-635	THM
Jungle Boogie	Kool & the Gang	39-4	CB
Jungle Love	Fleetwood Mac	4-873	SC
Jungle Love	Miller, Steve	23-620	BS
Jungle Love	Time	16-61	SC
Junior	Mellencamp, John	45-414	SC
Junior's Farm	McCartney & Wings	17-558	DK
Junk Food Junkie	Croce, Jim	5-640	SC
Jupiter	Monica	8-334	PHT
Just A Closer Walk With Thee	Cline, Patsy	45-493	CB
Just A Closer Walk With Thee	Lynn, Loretta	47-631	CB
Just A Dream	Clanton & Rockets	3-513	SC
Just A Dream	Clanton, Jimmy	7-36	MM
Just A Dream	Underwood, Carrie	37-8	CB
Just A Fool - Duet	Aguilera & Shelton	43-181	ASK
Just A Fool - duet	Shelton & Aguilera	47-449	MRH
Just A Gigolo	Roth, David Lee	6-351	MM
Just A Gigolo	Roth, David Lee	12-805	P
Just A Gigolo	Roth, David Lee	2-142	SC
Just A Gigolo	Van Halen	13-619	LE
Just A Girl	Freeman, Adrianna	42-3	PHN
Just A Girl	No Doubt	33-354	CB
Just A Girl	No Doubt	4-169	SC
Just A Kiss - duet	Lady Antebellum	38-88	AT
Just A Little	Liberty X	25-337	MM
Just A Little Bit	Head, Roy &Traits	10-267	SS
Just A Little Bit Better	Herman's Hermits	49-777	SC
Just A Little Bit Better	Herman's Hermits	47-137	SC
Just A Little Lovin'	Arnold, Eddy	19-838	CB
Just A Little Lovin'	Arnold, Eddy	19-398	SC
Just A Little Lovin'	Arnold, Eddy	17-624	THM
Just A Little Too Much	Nelson, Ricky	21-701	CB
Just A Little While	Jackson, Janet	20-529	CB

SONG TITLE	ARTIST	#	TYPE
Just A Little While	Jackson, Janet	20-356	PHM
Just A Sip	Bryan, Luke	40-52	ASK
Just A Sip	Bryan, Luke	45-97	ASK
Just A Song Before I Go	Crosby Stills & Nash	24-74	SC
Just A Touch Of Love (Everyday)	C&C Music Factory	49-917	KVD
Just About Now	Hill, Faith	24-351	SC
Just Add Moonlight	Eli Young Band	45-279	BKD
Just An Old Fashioned Love Song	Three Dog Night	34-54	CB
Just Another Day	Mellencamp, John	45-415	MM
Just Another Day In Paradise	Higgins, Bertie	7-50	MM
Just Another Day In Paradise	Vassar, Phil	14-70	CB
Just Another Day In Paradise	Vassar, Phil	19-214	CSZ
Just Another Dream	Dennis, Cathy	9-679	SAV
Just Another Heartache	Wright, Chely	8-153	CB
Just Another Heartache	Wright, Chely	22-763	ST
Just Another Love	Tucker, Tanya	16-349	CB
Just Another Love	Tucker, Tanya	4-783	SC
Just Another Woman In Love	Murray, Anne	33-39	CB
Just Another Woman In Love	Murray, Anne	12-430	P
Just As I Am	Air Supply	46-398	CB
Just As I Am	VanShelton, Ricky	8-551	CB
Just As Much As Ever	Vinton, Bobby	45-337	BSP
Just Ask Me	Presley, Elvis	14-820	THM
Just Ask Your Heart	Avalon, Frankie	5-525	SC
Just Be A Man About It	Braxton, Toni	14-509	SC
Just Be A Man About It	Braxton, Toni	20-2	SGB
Just Be A Man About It	Braxton, Toni	30-642	THM
Just Because	Baker, Anita	11-538	DK
Just Because	Jane's Addiction	32-326	THM
Just Because	Presley, Elvis	43-247	MM
Just Because	Price, Lloyd	10-699	JVC
Just Because I Love You	Santiago, Lina	24-167	SC
Just Because Polka	Polka Favorites	29-805	SSR
Just Because Polka - w/Words	Polka Favorites	29-859	SSR
Just Between You & Me	Kinleys	19-563	CB
Just Between You & Me	Kinleys	10-121	SC
Just Between You & Me	Kinleys	22-758	ST
Just Between You And Me	April Wine	24-677	SC
Just Between You And Me	Gramm, Lou	18-380	SAV
Just Between You And Me	Pride, Charley	22-257	SC
Just Beyond The Moon	Ritter, Tex	20-718	CB
Just Blew In From the Windy City - show	Day, Doris	48-143	SBI
Just Call Me Hank	Williams, Hank Jr.	48-748	BKD
Just Call Me Lonesome	Arnold, Eddy	45-571	CB
Just Call Me Lonesome	Foster, Radney	12-457	P
Just Call Me Lonesome	Presley, Elvis	25-111	MM
Just Dance - duet	Lady Gaga &	36-1	PT

SONG TITLE	ARTIST	#	TYPE
	O'Donis		
Just Don't Wait Around	Murphy, David Lee	8-152	CB
Just Don't Wait Around	Murphy, David Lee	7-726	CHM
Just Don't Wait Around Til She's...	Murphy, David Lee	22-416	ST
Just Dropped In	Rogers, Kenny	48-124	SC
Just Dropped In...	First Edition	2-754	SC
Just Fine	Blige, Mary J.	36-462	CB
Just Fishin'	Adkins, Trace	40-7	CB
Just For Old Time's Sake	Brown, Jim Ed	9-850	SAV
Just For The Love Of It	Pride, Charley	24-247	SC
Just For Tonight	Williams, Vanessa	6-96	MM
Just For What I Am	Smith, Connie	4-793	SC
Just For You	Husky, Ferlin	22-262	CB
Just Friends	Jonas Brothers	36-541	WD
Just Friends	Winehouse, Amy	49-60	ZVS
Just Get Up And Close The Door	Rodriguez, Johnny	22-51	CB
Just Get Up And Close The Door	Rodriguez, Johnny	21-629	SC
Just Gettin' Started	Aldean, Jason	45-99	BKD
Just Go	Richie, Lionel	47-453	KV
Just Good Ol' Boys	Bandy & Stampley	19-496	CB
Just Got Paid	Kemp, Johnny	18-369	AH
Just Got Started Lovin' You	Otto, James	36-392	CB
Just In Case	Forrester Sisters	33-45	CB
Just In Case	Forrester Sisters	11-425	DK
Just In Case	Forrester Sisters	8-687	SAV
Just In Case	Forrester Sisters	5-28	SC
Just In Case	Milsap, Ronnie	47-276	CB
Just In Time	Bennett, Tony	18-45	MM
Just In Time	Sinatra, Frank	49-256	DFK
Just Let Me Be In Love	Byrd, Tracy	25-15	MM
Just Let Me Be In Love	Byrd, Tracy	15-677	ST
Just Like A Pill	Pink	21-647	CB
Just Like A Pill	Pink	25-315	MM
Just Like A Pill	Pink	18-141	PHM
Just Like A Redneck	Lawson, Shannon	20-482	ST
Just Like A Woman	Dylan, Bob	29-94	CB
Just Like A Woman	Dylan, Bob	12-43	DK
Just Like Eddie	Heinz	10-650	SF
Just Like Fire	Pink	49-864	DCK
Just Like Heaven	Cure	16-569	SC
Just Like Jesse James	Cher	14-63	RS
Just Like Jesse James	Cher	15-129	SGB
Just Like Love	Martin, Brad	18-333	ST
Just Like Me	Revere & Raiders	16-753	DK
Just Like Paradise	Roth, David Lee	34-91	CB
Just Like Romeo & Juliet	Reflections	6-52	SC
Just Like Starting Over	Lennon, John	30-295	RS
Just Like The Weather	Bogguss, Suzy	1-563	CB
Just Like The Weather	Bogguss, Suzy	6-396	MM
Just Like You	Mellencamp, John	45-425	TU
Just Like You	Montana, Hannah	36-70	WD
Just Look At Me	Strait, George	24-10	SC
Just Lucky That Way	Parnell, Lee Roy	49-279	DFK

SONG TITLE	ARTIST	#	TYPE
Just Married	Robbins, Marty	22-254	SC
Just Might (Make Me Believe)	Sugarland	23-474	CB
Just Might (Make Me Believe)	Sugarland	29-856	SC
Just Might Have Her Radio On	Tomlinson, Trent	30-364	CB
Just Might Make Me Believe	Sugarland	30-235	RS
Just My Imagination - duet	Paltrow & Babyface	49-770	PR
Just My Luck	Richey, Kim	3-562	SC
Just Once	Ingram, James	26-365	DK
Just Once	Ingram, James	17-434	KC
Just Once	Ingram, James	6-558	MM
Just Once	Ingram, James	9-210	SO
Just Once	Murphy, David Lee	24-251	SC
Just Once In My Life	Righteous Brothers	15-518	JTG
Just Once In My Life	Righteous Brothers	3-333	PS
Just One	Shaffer, Lisa	30-541	CB
Just One Lifetime	Streisand, Barbra	15-291	PS
Just One Look	Hollies	44-363	LG
Just One Look	Ronstadt, Linda	10-5	SC
Just One Look	Troy, Doris	35-70	CB
Just One Look	Troy, Doris	13-116	P
Just One Look	Troy, Doris	5-461	SC
Just One Look	Troy, Doris	10-568	SF
Just One More	Jones, George	4-800	SC
Just One Night	McBride & The Ride	2-347	SC
Just One Of The Boys	Poe, Michelle	20-391	ST
Just One Of Those Things	Sinatra, Frank	14-264	MM
Just One Smile	Pitney, Gene	47-531	ZM
Just One Time	Gibson, Don	5-423	SC
Just One Time	Smith, Connie	8-843	CB
Just Out Of Reach	Cline, Patsy	45-498	MM
Just Remember I Love You	Firefall	3-450	SC
Just Say Goodbye	VanShelton, Ricky	8-552	CB
Just So You Know	Palmer, H.	32-435	THM
Just Someone I Used To Know	Parton, Dolly	8-534	CB
Just Tell Her Jim Said Hi	Presley, Elvis	14-821	THM
Just The Guy To Do It	Keith, Toby	47-153	AMM
Just The Same	Clark, Terri	7-631	CHM
Just The Same	Clark, Terri	10-99	SC
Just The Same	Clark, Terri	22-605	ST
Just The Same	Monroe, Rick	41-65	PHN
Just The Two Of Us	Smith, Will	7-771	PHT
Just The Two Of Us	Washington, Grover	35-162	CB
Just The Two Of Us	Washington, Grover	12-886	P
Just The Two Of Us	Washington, Grover	2-275	SC
Just The Way You Are	Joel, Billy	12-278	DK
Just The Way You Are	Joel, Billy	11-74	JTG
Just The Way You Are	Joel, Billy	16-132	LE
Just The Way You Are	Joel, Billy	6-440	MM
Just The Way You Are	Mars, Bruno	37-264	CB
Just The Way You Like It	S.O.S. Band	12-382	DK

SONG TITLE	ARTIST	#	TYPE
Just This Side Of Heaven - Hal-lelu	Ketchum, Hal	29-200	CB
Just To Be With You	Passions	25-548	MM
Just To Hear You Say That You Love Me	Hill, Faith	8-486	CB
Just To Hear You Say That You Love Me	Hill, Faith	7-762	CHM
Just To Hear You Say That You Love Me	Hill, Faith	22-793	ST
Just To Prove My Love To You	Coe, David Allan	18-316	CB
Just To Satisfy You - duet	Jennings & Nelson	45-176	CB
Just To Satisfy You - duet	Nelson & Jennings	38-97	CB
Just To See You Smile	McGraw, Tim	1-536	CB
Just To See You Smile	McGraw, Tim	22-751	ST
Just Walkin' In The Rain	Ray, Johnnie	13-90	P
Just Walkin' In The Rain	Ray, Johnnie	18-622	PS
Just Walking In The Rain	Reeves, Jim	45-267	VH
Just What I Do	Trick Pony	34-397	CB
Just What I Do	Trick Pony	25-128	MM
Just What I Do	Trick Pony	16-101	ST
Just What The Dr. Ordered	Nugent, Ted	19-278	SGB
Just When I Needed You Most	Parton, Dolly	7-379	MM
Just When I Needed You Most	Parton, Dolly	4-509	SC
Just When I Needed You Most	Vanwarmer, Randy	35-156	CB
Just When I Needed You Most	Vanwarmer, Randy	2-552	SC
Justify My Love	Madonna	21-455	CB
Ka-Ching!	Twain, Shania	23-431	CB
Kaleidoscope	Script	39-124	PHM
Kansas City	Harrison, Wilbert	35-16	CB
Kansas City	Harrison, Wilbert	11-355	DK
Kansas City	Harrison, Wilbert	6-155	MM
Kansas City (Hey Hey Hey Hey)	Beatles	44-123	KV
Kansas City Lights	Wariner, Steve	8-689	SAV
Kansas City Song	Owens, Buck	46-109	SC
Kansas City Star	Miller, Roger	22-279	CB
Kansas City Star	Miller, Roger	3-195	SC
Karma	Andrews, Jessica	16-334	ST
Karma Chameleon	Culture Club	35-175	CB
Karma Chameleon	Culture Club	29-6	MH
Karma Chameleon	Culture Club	3-523	SC
Kashmir	Led Zeppelin	19-286	SGB
Kate	Cash, Johnny	29-559	CB
Katie Wants A Fast One	Wariner & Brooks	14-93	CB
Katie Wants A Fast One	Wariner & Brooks	19-220	CSZ
Katie Wants A Fast One	Wariner & Brooks	22-559	ST
Katmandu	Seger, Bob	13-651	SGB
Katy Brought My Guitar Back Today	Alabama	24-1	SC
Kaw-Liga	Williams, Hank Jr.	16-671	C2C
Kaw-Liga	Williams, Hank Sr.	11-801	DK

SONG TITLE	ARTIST	#	TYPE
Kaw-Liga	Williams, Hank Sr.	13-435	P
Kaya	Marley, Bob	25-389	MM
Keep Breathing	Michaelson, Ingrid	49-910	SC
Keep Her In Mind	Osmond, Donny	47-863	ZP
Keep It Between The Lines	VanShelton, Ricky	8-553	CB
Keep It Between The Lines	VanShelton, Ricky	6-195	MM
Keep It Loose Keep It Tight	Lee, Amos	29-317	PHM
Keep It To Yourself	Hooker, John Lee	46-26	SSK
Keep It To Yourself	Musgraves, Kacey	45-319	BKD
Keep Me In Mind	Anderson, Lynn	47-642	CB
Keep Me In Mind	Zac Brown Band	38-170	FTX
Keep On Chasing Rainbows	Whittaker, Roger	13-594	PL
Keep On Chooglin'	CCR	48-365	KV
Keep On Dancin'	Gentrys	11-360	DK
Keep On Loving You	REO Speedwagon	11-649	DK
Keep On Loving You	REO Speedwagon	4-756	SC
Keep On Movin'	Soul II Soul	16-540	P
Keep On Rockin'	Confederate RR	8-192	CB
Keep On Rollin'	Richard, Steve	41-85	PHN
Keep On Running	Spencer Davis Grp	10-577	SF
Keep On Smilin'	Wet Willie	18-156	CB
Keep On Smilin'	Wet Willie	7-462	MM
Keep On Smilin'	Wet Willie	2-534	SC
Keep On The Sunny Side	Carter-Cash, June	49-394	SC
Keep On The Sunny Side	Whites	33-224	CB
Keep On Truckin'	Kendricks, Eddie	14-898	DK
Keep The Ball Rollin'	Jay & Techniques	9-698	SAV
Keep The Change	Williams, Hank Jr.	38-211	PHN
Keep Them Kisses Comin'	Campbell, Craig	44-186	KCDC
Keep Your Distance	Loveless, Patty	23-420	CB
Keep Your Hands Off My Baby	Little Eva	5-76	SC
Keep Your Hands To Yourself	Georgia Sattelites	18-159	CB
Keep Your Hands To Yourself	Georgia Sattelites	11-822	DK
Keep Your Hands To Yourself	Georgia Sattelites	20-307	MH
Keep Your Hands To Yourself	Georgia Sattelites	12-793	P
Keeper Of The Flame	Page, Martin	3-494	SC
Keeper Of The Stars	Byrd, Tracy	1-545	CB
Keeper Of The Stars	Byrd, Tracy	2-568	SC
Keeper Of The Stars the	Byrd, Tracy	22-872	ST
Keepin' Up	Alabama	8-867	CB
Keepin' Up	Alabama	22-696	ST
Keeping Our Love Warm	Captain & Tennille	46-556	CB
Keeping The Faith	Joel, Billy	48-9	SC
Keeping Up With The Joneses	Young & Singleton	20-740	CB
Keeping Up With The Joneses - duet	Young & Singleton	46-57	SSK
Keg In The Closet	Chesney, Kenny	23-131	CB
Kenny's Dead **	Master P	13-725	SGB

SONG TITLE	ARTIST	#	TYPE
Kentucky Gambler	Haggard, Merle	16-663	CB
Kentucky Rain	Presley, Elvis	17-550	DK
Kentucky Rain	Presley, Elvis	7-125	MM
Kentucky Rain	Presley, Elvis	2-609	SC
Kentucky Waltz	Monroe, Bill	47-295	CB
Kentucky Woman	Diamond, Neil	7-538	AH
Kentucky Woman	Diamond, Neil	24-699	SC
KentuckyWaltz	Monroe, Bill	49-325	CB
Kerosene	Lambert, Miranda	22-336	CB
Kerosene	Lambert, Miranda	23-387	SC
Ketchup Song the	Las Ketchup	25-396	MM
Ketchup Song the	Las Ketchup	18-585	NS
Ketchup Song the	Las Ketchup	32-23	THM
Kev's Courtin' Song **	Wilson, Kevin Bloody	37-81	SC
Key Largo	Higgins, Bertie	8-828	CB
Key Largo	Higgins, Bertie	18-50	MM
Key West Intermezzo	Mellencamp, John	21-421	SC
Keys In The Mailbox	Mandrell, Barbara	47-775	SRK
Keys In The Mailbox	Owens, Buck	44-52	KV
Keys In The Mailbox	Owens, Buck	45-848	VH
Keys In The Mailbox the	Ward, Damon	37-226	DW
Kick A Little	Little Texas	20-407	MH
Kick A Little	Little Texas	6-665	MM
Kick A Little	Little Texas	2-481	SC
Kick A Little Dirt Around	Shelby, David	41-61	PHN
Kick Down The Door	Middleman, Georgia	14-165	CB
Kick It In The Sticks	Gilbert, Brantley	38-100	CB
Kick It In The Sticks	Gilbert, Brantley	46-158	CB
Kick It Out	Heart	48-161	KV
Kick It Up	Montgomery, J M	17-237	NA
Kick My Ass (Radio Version)	Big & Rich	21-651	SC
Kick The Dust Up	Bryan, Luke	45-41	SSC
Kickin' And Screamin'	Brooks, Garth	4-137	SC
Kickout	Exies	32-291	THM
Kicks	Revere & Raiders	11-273	DK
Kid Charlemagne	Steely Dan	15-389	RS
Kid Stuff	Fairchild, Barbara	29-693	SC
Kiddio	Benton, Brook	12-370	DK
Kids	MGMT	36-301	PHM
Kids - All Around The Mulberry Bush	Kids	23-200	SM
Kids - Alouette	Kids	12-623	P
Kids - Alphabet Song	Kids	12-605	P
Kids - Alphabet Song	Kids	17-193	SC
Kids - Alphabet Song	Kids	23-206	SM
Kids - Ants Go Marching In	Kids	17-185	SC
Kids - B-I-N-G-O	Kids	17-190	SC
Kids - Baa Baa Black Sheep	Kids	12-613	P
Kids - Baa Baa Black Sheep	Kids	17-186	SC
Kids - Baa Baa Black Sheep	Kids	23-202	SM
Kids - Battle Hymn of the Republic	Kids	10-305	SC

SONG TITLE	ARTIST	#	TYPE
Kids - Be Kind to Your Web-Footed..	Kids	10-306	SC
Kids - Billy Boy	Kids	10-298	SC
Kids - Billy Boy	Kids	23-212	SM
Kids - Bolweevil	Kids	10-301	SC
Kids - Boom Boom Ain't It Great	Kids	10-307	SC
Kids - Camptown Races	Kids	10-312	SC
Kids - Candy Man the	Kids	12-602	P
Kids - Chitty Chitty Bang Bang	Kids	12-595	P
Kids - Clapping Song the	Kids	12-624	P
Kids - Clementine	Kids	10-297	SC
Kids - Do The Hokey Pokey	Kids	33-197	CB
Kids - Do Your Ears Hang Low	Kids	16-402	PR
Kids - Do Your Ears Hang Low	Kids	17-184	SC
Kids - Do-Re-Mi	Kids	12-618	P
Kids - Eensy Weensy Spider	Kids	33-448	CB
Kids - Farmer In The Dell	Kids	12-615	P
Kids - Farmer In The Dell	Kids	23-207	SM
Kids - Found A Peanut	Kids	10-294	SC
Kids - Frere Jacques	Kids	12-621	P
Kids - Froggie Went A Courtin'	Kids	10-275	SC
Kids - Georgie Porgie	Kids	10-318	SC
Kids - Happy Talk	Kids	12-603	P
Kids - He's Got The Whole World	Kids	33-450	CB
Kids - He's Got The Whole World	Kids	12-619	P
Kids - Head Shoulders Knees & Toes	Kids	49-351	CB
Kids - Here We Go Loopty Loo	Kids	10-293	SC
Kids - Hey Diddle Diddle	Kids	10-280	SC
Kids - Hey Diddle Diddle	Kids	23-205	SM
Kids - Hickory Dickory Dock	Kids	10-277	SC
Kids - Hickory Dickory Dock	Kids	23-201	SM
Kids - Hokey Pokey	Kids	12-610	P
Kids - Hokey Pokey	Kids	2-71	SC
Kids - Hokey Pokey	Kids	16-371	SF
Kids - Home On The Range	Kids	10-303	SC
Kids - How Much Is That Doggy In Th	Kids	12-263	DK
Kids - Humpty Dumpty	Kids	10-284	SC
Kids - I'm A Little Teapot	Kids	17-187	SC
Kids - I've Been Workin' On the RR	Kids	33-447	CB
Kids - I've Been Working on the RR	Kids	12-265	DK
Kids - I've Been Working on the RR	Kids	17-183	SC
Kids - If You're Happy &	Kids	34-449	CB

153

SONG TITLE	ARTIST	#	TYPE
U Know It			
Kids - If Your Happy & You Know It	Kids	17-198	SC
Kids - It's Raining It's Pouring	Kids	12-598	P
Kids - Jack & Jill	Kids	17-191	SC
Kids - Jeepers Creepers	Kids	12-262	DK
Kids - Jesus Loves The Little Children	Kids	33-198	CB
Kids - Jimmy Crack Corn	Kids	10-311	SC
Kids - John Jacob Jingleheimer Schm	Kids	10-292	SC
Kids - Kum Ba Yah	Kids	10-300	SC
Kids - Little Bo Peep	Kids	17-189	SC
Kids - Little Boy Blue	Kids	10-283	SC
Kids - Little Bunny Foo Foo	Kids	17-195	SC
Kids - Little Jack Horner	Kids	10-278	SC
Kids - Little Miss Muffet	Kids	10-285	SC
Kids - Little White Duck	Kids	35-326	CB
Kids - London Bridge	Kids	12-255	DK
Kids - London Bridge	Kids	12-601	P
Kids - London Bridge	Kids	17-188	SC
Kids - London Bridge	Kids	23-199	SM
Kids - Mary Had A Little Lamb	Kids	35-327	CB
Kids - Mary Had A Little Lamb	Kids	12-252	DK
Kids - Mary Had A Little Lamb	Kids	12-600	P
Kids - Mary Had A Little Lamb	Kids	17-196	SC
Kids - Mary Had A Little Lamb	Kids	23-211	SM
Kids - Mary Mary Quite Contrary	Kids	10-308	SC
Kids - Michael Row the Boat Ashore	Kids	12-596	P
Kids - My Bonnie	Kids	10-321	SC
Kids - Nobody Likes Me	Kids	10-313	SC
Kids - Oh Susanna	Kids	12-611	P
Kids - Oh Susanna	Kids	17-192	SC
Kids - Old Grey Mare	Kids	49-352	CB
Kids - Old King Cole	Kids	10-281	SC
Kids - Old King Cole	Kids	23-208	SM
Kids - Old MacDonald Had a Farm	Kids	12-599	P
Kids - Old MacDonald Had A Farm	Kids	17-194	SC
Kids - On Top Of Old Smokey	Kids	10-310	SC
Kids - On Top Of Old Smoky	Kids	33-199	CB
Kids - On Top Of Spaghetti	Kids	12-606	P
Kids - Paper Of Pins a	Kids	10-317	SC
Kids - Pat A Cake	Kids	10-282	SC
Kids - Pease Porrige Hot	Kids	10-288	SC
Kids - Pick A Bale Of Cotton	Kids	10-304	SC

SONG TITLE	ARTIST	#	TYPE
Kids - Polly Wolly Doodle	Kids	12-256	DK
Kids - Pop Goes The Weasel	Kids	23-204	SM
Kids - Puff The Magic Dragon	Kids	12-264	DK
Kids - Puff The Magic Dragon	Peter, Paul & Mary	33-442	CB
Kids - Put On A Happy Face	Kids	12-259	DK
Kids - Rain Rain Go Away	Kids	10-286	SC
Kids - Ring Around The Rosy	Kids	23-210	SM
Kids - Row Row Row Your Boat	Kids	12-620	P
Kids - Row Row Row Your Boat	Kids	10-290	SC
Kids - Rub A Dub Dub	Kids	10-316	SC
Kids - Sally The Camel	Kids	16-403	PR
Kids - She'll Be Comin' 'Round the	Kids	12-257	DK
Kids - She'll Be Comin' 'Round the.	Kids	10-291	SC
Kids - Simple Simon	Kids	10-315	SC
Kids - Sing A Song of Sixpence	Kids	10-289	SC
Kids - Skip To My Lou	Kids	12-258	DK
Kids - Skip To My Lou	Kids	10-296	SC
Kids - Skip To My Lou	Kids	23-213	SM
Kids - Swanee River	Kids	10-302	SC
Kids - Taps	Kids	10-299	SC
Kids - There Was a Crooked Man	Kids	10-309	SC
Kids - There Was An Old Woman	Kids	10-320	SC
Kids - There's a Hole in the Middle	Kids	10-322	SC
Kids - This Old Man	Kids	12-261	DK
Kids - This Old Man	Kids	12-612	P
Kids - This Old Man	Kids	23-203	SM
Kids - Three Blind Mice	Kids	12-253	DK
Kids - Three Blind Mice	Kids	12-617	P
Kids - Three Blind Mice	Kids	23-214	SM
Kids - Three Little Kittens	Kids	10-287	SC
Kids - Tisket A Tasket a	Kids	10-279	SC
Kids - Tra La La Boom De Ay	Kids	12-260	DK
Kids - Twinkle Twinkle Little Star	Kids	12-254	DK
Kids - Twinkle Twinkle Little Star	Kids	12-622	P
Kids - Twinkle Twinkle Little Star	Kids	17-197	SC
Kids - Twinkle Twinkle Little Star	Kids	23-209	SM
Kids - Ugly Duckling	Kaye, Danny	48-466	SBI
Kids - Wheels On The Bus the	Kids	33-200	CB

SONG TITLE	ARTIST	#	TYPE
Kids - Where Has My Little Dog Gone	Kids	10-276	SC
Kids - Where Is Thumbkin?	Kids	10-319	SC
Kids - Yankee Doodle	Kids	12-604	P
Kids - Yankee Doodle	Kids	10-295	SC
Kids - Yankee Doodle Dandy	Kids	16-401	PR
Kids Are Alright the	Who	19-745	LE
Kids In America	Wilde, Kim	24-422	SC
Kids Of The Baby Boom	Bellamy Brothers	34-274	CB
Kids Of The Future	Jonas Brothers	36-545	WD
Kids Say The Darndest Things	Wynette, Tammy	15-70	CB
Kids Say The Darndest Things	Wynette, Tammy	9-592	SAV
Kids With Guns	Gorillaz	30-767	SF
Kiko And The Lavender Moon	Los Lobos	7-51	MM
Kill Me Now	Rio Grand	30-84	CB
Kill Myself	McGraw, Tim	23-35	SC
Kill The Wabbit	Fudd, Ozzy	47-777	SRK
Killer Queen	Queen	12-333	DK
Killin' Time	Black, Clint	1-107	CB
Killin' Time	Black, Clint	6-208	MM
Killin' Time	Black, Clint	13-398	P
Killin' Time	Black, Clint	30-424	THM
Killing Floor	Howlin' Wolf	20-144	KB
Killing Me Softly	Flack, Roberta	11-521	DK
Killing Me Softly	Fugees	14-905	SC
Killing Me Softly	Hill, Lauryn/Fugees	19-728	CB
Killing Me Softly with Her Song	Holt, John	49-769	MRE
Killing Of Georgie the	Stewart, Rod	14-846	LE
Kind And Generous	Merchant, Natalie	16-226	PHM
Kind Of A Drag	Buckinghams	7-63	MM
Kind Of A Drag	Buckinghams	3-16	SC
Kind Of Love I Can't Forget the	Asleep At The Wheel	46-215	VH
Kind Woman	Poco	49-268	SC
Kindly Keep It Country	Gill, Vince	8-215	CB
Kindly Keep It Country	Gill, Vince	22-685	ST
King Bee/Back Door Man Medley	Marino, Frank	19-798	SGB
King Is Gone the	McDowell, Ronnie	8-458	CB
King Midas In Reverse	Hollies	48-423	DCK
King Of Anything	Bareillas, Sara	48-206	CB
King Of Broken Hearts	Womack, Lee Ann	36-260	PHM
King Of Broken Hearts the	Strait, George	24-121	SC
King Of Fools	Yoakam, Dwight	49-691	CK
King Of New Orleans	Better Than Ezra	4-674	SC
King Of Pain	Police	17-517	SC
King Of The Blues	Moore, Gary	36-134	SGB
King Of The Castle	Jenkins, Matt	23-301	CB
King Of The Mountain	Strait, George	1-266	CB
King Of The Mountain	Strait, George	7-579	CHM
King Of The Mountain	Strait, George	22-909	ST

SONG TITLE	ARTIST	#	TYPE
King Of The Road	Miller, Roger	3-896	CB
King Of The Road	Miller, Roger	17-33	DK
King Of The Road	Miller, Roger	6-769	MM
King Of The Road	Miller, Roger	17-286	NA
King Of The Road	Miller, Roger	12-789	P
King Of The Road	Miller, Roger	14-552	SC
King Of The World	Blackhawk	7-403	MM
King Of The World	Blackhawk	4-624	SC
King Of Wishful Thinking	Go West	16-72	SC
King Tut	Martin, Steve	6-511	MM
King Tut	Martin, Steve	5-634	SC
Kiss	Prince	11-622	DK
Kiss	Prince	12-785	P
Kiss 'Em All	Lace	14-717	CB
Kiss A Girl	Urban, Keith	37-34	CB
Kiss An Angel Good Morning	Pride, Charley	3-796	CB
Kiss An Angel Good Morning	Pride, Charley	12-52	DK
Kiss An Angel Good Morning	Pride, Charley	13-393	P
Kiss And Run	Roe, Tommy	48-115	CB
Kiss And Say Goodbye	Manhattans	16-837	DK
Kiss And Say Goodbye	Manhattans	7-468	MM
Kiss From A Rose	Seal	11-66	JTG
Kiss From A Rose	Seal	3-432	SC
Kiss Goodbye	Little Big Town	37-349	CB
Kiss It And Make It Better	Davis, Mac	23-522	CB
Kiss Kiss	Soleii, Stella	15-456	PHM
Kiss Kiss - duet	Brown & T-Pain	49-895	SC
Kiss Me	Calabrese, Kayla	41-88	PHN
Kiss Me	Fairchild, Shelly	23-291	CB
Kiss Me	Martin, Dean	10-404	LE
Kiss Me	Sixpence None The	35-216	CB
Kiss Me	Sixpence None The	7-807	PHT
Kiss Me	Sixpence None The	13-703	SGB
Kiss Me Deadly	Ford, Lita	28-290	DK
Kiss Me Deadly	Ford, Lita	4-537	SC
Kiss Me Honey Honey Kiss Me	Bassey, Shirley	46-474	EK
Kiss Me I'm Gone	Stuart, Marty	6-499	MM
Kiss Me I'm Gone	Stuart, Marty	2-400	SC
Kiss Me In The Car	Berry, John	2-128	SC
Kiss Me In The Dark	Randy Rogers Band	30-49	CB
Kiss Me In The Rain	Streisand, Barbra	29-268	SC
Kiss Me Now	McCann, Lila	6-71	SC
Kiss Me When I'm Down	Allan, Gary	38-108	CB
Kiss My Country Ass	Akins, Rhett	29-35	CB
Kiss My Country Ass	Shelton, Blake	38-116	CB
Kiss Of Fire	Gibbs, Grant	11-458	DK
Kiss On My List - WN	Hall & Oates	48-64	CB
Kiss The Bride	John, Elton	2-861	SC
Kiss The Rain	Myers, Billie	7-714	PHM
Kiss The Rain	Myers, Billie	5-183	SC
Kiss Them For Me	Siouxsie&Banshees	6-44	SC
Kiss This	Tippin, Aaron	14-69	CB

155

SONG TITLE	ARTIST	#	TYPE
Kiss This	Tippin, Aaron	19-243	CSZ
Kiss To Build A Dream On	Armstrong, Louis	6-450	MM
Kiss Tomorrow Goodbye	Bryan, Luke	45-428	BKD
Kiss Tomorrow Goodbye	Bryan, Luke	44-163	BKD
Kiss You	Aaliyah	20-466	CB
Kiss You All Over	Exile	11-395	DK
Kiss You All Over	Exile	2-838	SC
Kiss You All Over **	Carter, Clarence	2-185	SC
Kiss You In The Morning	Ray, Michael	48-699	BKD
Kiss You There	Dunn, Ronnie	45-235	KCDC
Kiss You Tonight	Nail, David	45-289	BKD
Kiss You Tonight	Nail, Jason	44-294	BKD
Kisses Don't Lie	Smith, Carl	22-120	CB
Kisses Sweeter Than Wine	Rodgers, Jimmie	7-299	MM
Kisses Sweeter Than Wine	Rodgers, Jimmie	3-502	SC
Kissin' Bug Boogie	Ford, Tenn Ernie	8-418	CB
Kissin' Bug Boogie	Ford, Tenn Ernie	18-619	PS
Kissin' Cousins	Presley, Elvis	8-585	CB
Kissin' In The Dark	Drifters	45-889	EZC
Kissin' On The Phone	Anka, Paul	9-551	SAV
Kissin' U	Cosgrove, Miranda	44-143	BKD
Kissin' You	Total	4-341	SC
Kissing A Fool	Buble, Michael	30-181	LE
Kissing A Fool	Michael, George	11-624	DK
Kissing You Goodbye	Jennings, Waylon	45-181	DCK
Kitty	Presidents of USA	5-335	SC
Kizmic Blues	Joplin, Janis	15-222	LE
Knee Deep	Zac Brown Band	43-463	FTX
Knee Deep	Zac Brown Band	43-474	QH
Knee Deep - duet	Zac Brown Band & Buffett	37-216	CB
Knee Deep In The Blues	Robbins, Marty	49-172	CB
Knee Deep In The Blues	Robbins, Marty	48-14	CB
Kneeling Drunkard's Plea	Cash, Johnny	49-289	CWK
Knickin' On Heaven's Door	Guns 'N Roses	46-165	SC
Knock Knock	Monica	19-671	CB
Knock Knock	Monica	32-424	THM
Knock On Wood	Floyd, Eddie	11-501	DK
Knock On Wood	Floyd, Eddie	12-721	P
Knock Three Times	Orlando & Dawn	3-244	LG
Knock Three Times	Orlando & Dawn	13-250	P
Knock Three Times	Orlando & Dawn	8-619	SAV
Knock Three Times	Orlando & Dawn	5-115	SC
Knock Yourself Out	Keith, Toby	47-154	AMM
Knocked Out	Abdul, Paula	12-813	P
Knockin' Boots	Candyman	49-16	KV
Knockin' Da Boots	H-Town	16-568	P
Knockin' On Heaven's Door	Dylan, Bob	29-95	CB
Knockin' On Heaven's Door	Dylan, Bob	12-64	DK
Knockin' On Heaven's	Dylan, Bob	13-175	P

SONG TITLE	ARTIST	#	TYPE
Door			
Knockin' On Heaven's Door	Guns 'N Roses	48-53	SC
Knocking At Your Back Door	Deep Purple	21-753	SC
Knowing Me Knowing You	Abba	7-502	MM
Knowing Me Knowing You	Abba	10-535	SF
Knowing She's There	Dr. Hook	47-51	ZM
Known Only To Him	Presley, Elvis	30-382	SC
Knoxville Girl	Jim & Jesse	33-225	CB
Ko Ko Mo	Beach Boys	5-504	BS
Ko Ko Mo	Beach Boys	18-63	MM
Ko Ko Mo Island	Al Dexter & Troopers	46-410	CB
Kodachrome	Simon & Garfunkel	23-633	BS
Kodachrome	Simon, Paul	9-318	AG
Kodachrome	Simon, Paul	20-318	MH
Kristofferson	McGraw, Tim	36-410	CB
Kryptonite	3 Doors Down	13-844	PHM
Kryptonite	3 Doors Down	18-565	TT
Ku' Uipo/Bora Bora	Ho, Don	6-838	MM
Kung Fu Fighting	Douglas, Carl	16-734	DK
Kung Fu Fighting	Douglas, Carl	4-881	SC
Kyle's Mom's A Bitch **	Cartman, Eric	13-726	SGB
Kyrie	Mr. Mister	21-740	MH
L-O-V-E	Cole, Nat "King"	12-501	P
L-O-V-E	Cole, Nat "King"	19-781	SGB
L-O-V-E	Newton, Wayne	47-308	LE
L.A. Is My Lady	Sinatra, Frank	49-501	MM
L.A. Woman	Doors	18-644	SO
La Bamba	Los Lobos	34-85	CB
La Bamba	Los Lobos	22-395	SC
La Bamba	Valens, Richie	11-171	DK
La Grange	ZZ Top	20-54	SC
La Isla Bonita	Madonna	13-26	P
La La	Simpson, Ashlee	22-353	CB
La La Means I Love You	Delfonics	7-314	MM
La La Means I Love You	Delfonics	12-923	P
LA Song	Hart, Beth	16-188	PHM
La Vie En Rose	Armstrong, Louis	46-446	TU
Labels Or Love	Fergie	48-233	CB
Labor Of Love	Foster, Radney	2-320	SC
Lack Of Communication	Ratt	21-777	SC
Ladies Love Country Boys	Adkins, Trace	30-114	CB
Ladies Love Outlaws	Jennings, Waylon	44-60	KV
Ladies Night	Kool & The Gang	27-571	DK
Ladies Night	Kool & The Gang	12-701	P
Ladies Night	Kool & The Gang	9-761	SAV
Ladies Who Lunch the	Streisand, Barbra	49-577	PS
Lady	Jones, Jack	29-486	LE
Lady	Little River Band	18-304	SC
Lady	Mojo	34-166	CB
Lady	Rogers, Kenny	8-270	CB
Lady	Rogers, Kenny	17-55	DK
Lady	Rogers, Kenny	13-387	P

SONG TITLE	ARTIST	#	TYPE
Lady	Styx	35-125	CB
Lady	Styx	24-64	SC
Lady (You Bring Me Up)	Commodores	16-832	DK
Lady (You Bring Me Up)	Commodores	14-358	MH
Lady (You Bring Me Up)	Commodores	15-44	SS
Lady Blue	Russell, Leon	2-786	SC
Lady Down On Love	Alabama	33-75	CB
Lady Down On Love	Alabama	5-395	SC
Lady Godiva	Peter & Gordon	3-842	SC
Lady In Red	DeBurgh, Chris	34-88	CB
Lady In Red	DeBurgh, Chris	6-346	MM
Lady In Red	DeBurgh, Chris	13-186	P
Lady Is A Tramp the	Sinatra, Frank	34-14	CB
Lady Is A Tramp the	Sinatra, Frank	28-495	DK
Lady is A Tramp the	Sinatra, Frank	20-766	KB
Lady Is A Tramp the	Sinatra, Frank	14-266	MM
Lady Is A Tramp the	Sinatra, Frank	9-250	PT
Lady Is A Tramp the	Sinatra, Frank	13-633	SGB
Lady Lady	Domino, Fats	47-804	SRK
Lady Lay Down	Conlee, John	34-238	CB
Lady Lay Down	Conlee, John	4-813	SC
Lady Like You a	Campbell, Glen	5-161	SC
Lady Love	Rawls, Lou	28-106	DK
Lady Love	Rawls, Lou	9-768	SAV
Lady Love	Trower, Robin	13-652	SGB
Lady Madonna	Beatles	34-68	CB
Lady Madonna	Beatles	16-780	DK
Lady Madonna	Beatles	7-526	SAV
Lady Marmalade	Aguilera&Mya&Lil Ki	15-454	PHM
Lady Marmalade	Aguilera&Mya&Lil Ki	16-110	PRT
Lady Marmalade	LaBelle, Patti	34-27	CB
Lady Marmalade	LaBelle, Patti	11-194	DK
Lady Marmalade	Moulin Rouge	18-665	PS
Lady Oh	Diamond, Neil	47-414	DCK
Lady Picture Show	Stone Temple Pilots	24-633	SC
Lady Soul	Temptations	49-249	DFK
Lady Willpower	Puckett & Union Gap	34-22	CB
Lady Willpower	Puckett & Union Gap	3-24	SC
Lady's Man	Snow, Hank	22-127	CB
Lady's Man	Snow, Hank	5-850	SC
Ladykiller	Maroon 5	39-104	PHM
Laid Back 'N Low Key	Jackson, Alan	44-126	KV
Lambada - Spanish	Kaoma	49-458	MM
Lana	Orbison, Roy	38-58	SF
Lance's Song	Zac Brown Band	46-74	BKD
Land Of 1000 Dances	Wilson Pickett	35-92	CB
Land Of Confusion	Collins, Phil	44-30	BS
Land Of The Living	Tillis, Pam	1-465	CB
Land Of The Living	Tillis, Pam	22-632	ST
Landslide	Dixie Chicks	25-348	MM
Landslide	Dixie Chicks	18-325	ST
Landslide	Fleetwood Mac	10-27	SC
Landslide	Smashing Pumpkins	29-130	ST
Lap Dance Is So Much Better... **	Bloodhound Gang	37-79	SC

SONG TITLE	ARTIST	#	TYPE
Laredo	Cagle, Chris	14-844	ST
Larger Than Life	Backstreet Boys	18-716	MM
Larger Than Life	Backstreet Boys	8-522	PHT
Lasso The Moon	Morris, Gary	45-620	DCK
Last Beautiful Girl	Matchbox 20	25-17	MM
Last But Not Least	Zac Brown Band	46-71	KV
Last Call	Womack, Lee Ann	36-600	CB
Last Call	Womack, Lee Ann	36-206	PHM
Last Cheater's Waltz	Sheppard, T.G.	3-247	CB
Last Cheater's Waltz	Sheppard, T.G.	13-500	P
Last Cheater's Waltz	Sheppard, T.G.	4-581	SC
Last Child	Aerosmith	23-102	SC
Last Cowboy Song the	Bruce, Ed	46-537	KV
Last Dance	Summer, Donna	17-41	DK
Last Dance	Summer, Donna	9-219	PT
Last Dance/The Hustle/On The Radio	Selena	19-161	SGB
Last Day In The Mines	Dudley, Dave	43-292	CB
Last Day Of My Life	Vassar, Phil	29-191	CB
Last Day Of My Life	Vassar, Phil	29-848	SC
Last Dollar (Fly Away)	McGraw, Tim	30-306	CB
Last Fallen Hero	Charlie Daniels Band	46-606	CB
Last Farewell the	Whittaker, Roger	13-585	PL
Last Friday Night	Perry, Katy	38-196	MH
Last Good Time	Flynnville Train	30-441	CB
Last In Line the	DIO	21-755	SC
Last Kiss	Pearl Jam	30-217	PHM
Last Kiss	Pearl Jam	7-889	PHT
Last Kiss	Pearl Jam	9-305	RS
Last Kiss	Pearl Jam	13-777	SGB
Last Kiss	Wilson, J. Frank	2-57	SC
Last Living Cowboy	Keith, Toby	45-65	KV
Last Man Committed	Heatherly, Eric	25-299	MM
Last Man Committed	Heatherly, Eric	17-588	ST
Last Mango In Paris	Buffett, Jimmy	46-146	CKC
Last Minute Late Night	Brown, Kane	49-628	DCK
Last Name	Underwood, Carrie	37-9	CB
Last Night	AZ Yet	24-298	SC
Last Night I Didn't Get To Sleep At All	Fifth Dimension	49-470	MM
Last Night I Didn't Get To Sleep..	5th Dimension	37-71	SC
Last Of A Dying Breed the	McCoy, Neal	29-586	CB
Last Of A Dying Breed the	McCoy, Neal	29-716	ST
Last Of The Singing Cowboys	Marshall Tucker Band	47-224	SC
Last One Standing	Emerson Drive	19-770	ST
Last One To Know the	McEntire, Reba	29-67	CB
Last Pork Chop	Williams, Hank Jr.	45-697	VH
Last Request	Frazier River	4-619	SC
Last Request	Nutini, Paolo	30-786	SF
Last Resort	Eagles	15-705	LE
Last Ride the	Snow, Hank	22-135	CB
Last Song	Bear, Edward	2-781	SC
Last Song the	John, Elton	9-40	MM

SONG TITLE	ARTIST	#	TYPE
Last Ten Years the (Superman)	Rogers, Kenny	48-128	ST
Last Thing I Needed First Thing This Morning	Nelson, Willie	43-28	CB
Last Thing I Needed First Thing This Morning	Nelson, Willie	4-495	SC
Last Thing On My Mind	Diamond, Neil	11-350	DK
Last Thing On My Mind	Wagoner & Parton	9-613	SAV
Last Thing On My Mind the	Loveless, Patty	22-596	ST
Last Thing She Said the	Tyler, Ryan	30-799	PHM
Last Thing She Said the	Tyler, Ryan	20-477	ST
Last Time	Bread	46-523	CB
Last Time	Fuel	18-293	CB
Last Time	Fuel	30-653	THM
Last Time	Rolling Stones	19-755	LE
Last Time I Saw Him	Ross, Diana	18-260	DK
Last Time I Saw Him	Ross, Diana	15-364	LE
Last Time I Saw Him	West, Dottie	15-519	CB
Last Train Running	Whiskey Falls	30-476	CB
Last Train To Clarksville	Monkees	16-768	DK
Last Train To Clarksville	Monkees	12-863	P
Last Train To Clarksville	Monkees	9-647	SAV
Last Train To Clarksville	Monkees	3-471	SC
Last Train To San Fernando	Duncan, Johnny	10-602	SF
Last Waltz the	Humperdinck, E.	37-168	CB
Last Waltz the	Humperdinck, E.	10-468	MG
Last Waltz the	Humperdinck, E.	19-115	SAV
Last Waltz the	Humperdinck, E.	10-583	SF
Last Word In Lonesome Is Me	Arnold, Eddy	19-39	CB
Last Worthless Evening the	Henley, Don	48-157	ZMP
Late To The Party	Musgraves, Kacey	45-366	KV
Lately	Divine	7-793	PHT
Lately	Tyrese	16-191	THM
Lately (Been Dreamin' 'Bout Babies)	Byrd, Tracy	18-465	ST
Lately (Been Dreamin' 'Bout Babies)	Byrd, Tracy	32-78	THM
Later On	Swon Brothers	44-200	BKD
Latino - Acariciame	Limite	17-756	SC
Latino - Amame	Pires, Alexandre	23-235	AI
Latino - Armor Prohibido (Forbidden	Selena	21-444	PS
Latino - Bella She's All I Ever Had	Martin, Ricky	9-135	PS
Latino - Bella She's All I Ever Had	Martin, Ricky	13-731	SGB
Latino - Casi Perfecta	Stuart, Michael	17-793	SC
Latino - Celos	Anthony, Marc	23-234	AI
Latino - Como La Flor (Like a Flowe	Selena	21-448	PS
Latino - Como Tu Mi Quiere A Mi	Limi-T 21	17-794	SC
Latino - Contra La Lorriente	Anthony, Marc	17-806	PS
Latino - Costas Del	Iglesias, Enrique	17-809	PS

SONG TITLE	ARTIST	#	TYPE
Amor			
Latino - Could I Have This Kiss For	Houston & Iglesias	14-478	SC
Latino - Cuando	Arjona, Ricardo	17-787	SC
Latino - Cuando Nadie Me Ve	Sanz, Alejandro	18-2	SC
Latino - Da La Vuelta	Anthony, Marc	17-734	PS
Latino - De Paisano A Paisano	Los Tigres Del Nort	18-1	SC
Latino - Desde Que No Estas	Ruiz, Rey	17-759	SC
Latino - Dimalo (I Need To Know)	Anthony, Marc	17-733	PS
Latino - Dime	Nazario, Ednita	23-242	AI
Latino - Donde Estes (Where Are...)	Selena&Barrio Boys	21-445	PS
Latino - El Coyote	Norteno, Oro	18-3	SC
Latino - El Problema	Arjona, Ricardo	23-231	AI
Latino - El Toro Relajo (Crazy Bull	Selena	21-447	PS
Latino - En La Misma Cama	Liberacion	23-239	AI
Latino - Entra En Mi Vida	Sin Bandera	23-245	AI
Latino - Esperanza	Iglesias, Enrique	17-810	PS
Latino - Fotografia	Juanes & Furtado	23-238	AI
Latino - Gorracho Te Recuerdo	Fernando, Vincente	18-8	PS
Latino - Gozar La Vida	Iglesias, Julio	17-789	SC
Latino - Guatanamera	Sandpipers	11-503	DK
Latino - Heroe	Iglesias, Enrique	23-233	AI
Latino - Imaginame Sin To	Fonsi, Luis	17-788	SC
Latino - Ketchup Song the	Las Ketchup	25-407	MM
Latino - La Bikina	Miguel, Luis	17-791	SC
Latino - La Copa De La Vida	Martin, Ricky	13-734	SGB
Latino - Livin' La Vida Loca	Martin, Ricky	9-134	PS
Latino - Livin' La Vida Loca	Martin, Ricky	13-736	SGB
Latino - Marchate	Gisselle	23-243	AI
Latino - Maria	Martin, Ricky	9-131	PS
Latino - Mauvals Garcon	Adamo, Salvadore	15-528	CMC
Latino - Me Causte Del Cielo	Preciado, Julio	17-753	SC
Latino - Mentiroso	Iglesias, Enrique	23-232	AI
Latino - Mi Primer Amor (Salsa	Laballo, Kevin	18-7	PS
Latino - Muevelo	Ruiz, Rey	17-790	SC
Latino - No Me Ames	Lopez & Anthony	23-237	AI
Latino - No Puedo Olvidar Tu Voz	El Coyote	17-752	SC
Latino - No Sabes Como	Anthony, Marc	17-807	PS
Latino - Oye Mi Canto	Estefan, Gloria	17-745	PT
Latino - Pena De Amor	Puerto Rican Power	23-241	AI
Latino - Pintame	Greapo, Elvis	17-812	PS
Latino - Por Encima Te Todo	Limite	18-6	PS
Latino - Por La Espalda	Banda La Costena	17-755	SC

SONG TITLE	ARTIST	#	TYPE
Latino - Prision De Amor	Los Tigres Del Nort	17-757	SC
Latino - Que So Yo	Enrique, Luis	17-792	SC
Latino - Quemame Los Ojos	Ayala, Ramon y Sus	17-758	SC
Latino - Resumiendo	Montaner, Ricardo	23-244	AI
Latino - Ruelta Rusa	Iglesias, Enrique	17-811	PS
Latino - Secreto De Amor	Sebastian, Joan	17-754	SC
Latino - Si Tu Te A Lejas	Greapo, Elvis	17-813	PS
Latino - Suceden	Anthony, Marc	17-808	PS
Latino - Tal Vez	Martin, Ricky	23-236	AI
Latino - Tombe La Neige	Adamo, Salvadore	15-572	CMC
Latino - Tu Eres Ajena	Herrara, Eddy	23-240	AI
Latino - Tu Solo Tu (You Only You)	Selena	21-446	PS
Latino - Vuelve Junto A Mi	Montero, Pablo	23-246	AI
Latino - Y Dale.....	Limi-T 21	18-4	PS
Latino - Yo Te Amo	Chayanne	18-5	PS
Laugh Laugh	Beau Brummels	5-176	SC
Laughed Until We Cried	Aldean, Jason	30-553	CB
Laughing	Guess Who	12-324	DK
Laughing	Guess Who	5-454	SC
Laughter In The Rain	Sedaka, Neil	11-196	DK
Laughter in The Rain	Sedaka, Neil	9-169	SO
Laura	Scissor Sisters	29-222	ZM
Laura (What's He Got That I Ain't Got)	King, Claude	47-924	SSK
Laura What's He Got That I Ain't Go	Ashley, Leon	13-535	P
Lavender Blue	Turner, Sammy	7-305	MM
Laverne & Shirley	TV Themes	2-163	SC
Laverne & Shirley Theme	TV Themes	27-402	DK
Lawdy Miss Clawdy	Gilley, Mickey	16-176	THM
Lawdy Miss Clawdy	Presley, Elvis	14-774	THM
Lawdy Miss Clawdy	Price, Lloyd	12-371	DK
Lay All Your Love On Me	Abba	19-74	MM
Lay Around And Love On You	White, Lari	8-880	CB
Lay Down Beside Me	Williams, Don	45-228	CB
Lay Down Beside Me	Williams, Don	44-56	CB
Lay Down Sally	Clapton, Eric	11-670	DK
Lay Down Sally	Clapton, Eric	15-56	LE
Lay Down Your Love	4PM	14-876	SC
Lay It Down	Ratt	27-402	DK
Lay It On The Line	Triumph	6-17	SC
Lay It On The Line	Triumph	13-666	SGB
Lay Lady Lay	Dylan, Bob	29-92	CB
Lay Lady Lay	Dylan, Bob	12-44	DK
Lay Lady Lay	Dylan, Bob	13-228	P
Lay Lady Lay	Dylan, Bob	2-855	SC
Lay Low	Shelton, Blake	45-385	BKD
Lay Me Down - duet	Smith, S & Legend	48-441	KCD
Lay Your Hands On Me	Bon Jovi	21-759	SC
Layla	Derek & Dominos	9-371	AH
Layla	Derek & Dominos	15-178	MH
Layla - Electric Version	Clapton, Eric	13-804	SGB

SONG TITLE	ARTIST	#	TYPE
Layla (Slow Version)	Clapton, Eric	15-58	LE
Lazy Days	Spanky & Our Gang	9-710	SAV
Lazy Lady	Domino, Fats	45-853	VH
Lazy Mazy	Monte, Lou	7-289	MM
Lazy River	Darin, Bobby	4-711	SC
Lazy Song the	Mars, Bruno	37-263	CB
Lazy Sunday	Ford, Emile	48-754	P
Le Freak	Chic	11-626	DK
Le Freak	Chic	16-567	P
Le Freak	Chic	20-370	SC
Lead Me Guide Me	Presley, Elvis	30-377	SC
Lead Me Not	White, Lari	2-794	SC
Lead Me On	Nightingale, Maxine	2-563	SC
Lead Me On	Twitty & Lynn	5-446	SC
Lead On	Strait, George	1-262	CB
Lead On	Strait, George	6-806	MM
Lead On	Strait, George	3-416	SC
Leader Of Men	Nickelback	46-314	SC
Leader Of The Gang	Glitter, Gary	49-145	SF
Leader Of The Pack	Shangri-Las	11-777	DK
Leader Of The Pack	Shangri-Las	3-366	MH
Leader Of The Pack	Shangri-Las	6-158	MM
Leader Of The Pack	Shangri-Las	9-282	SC
Leading With Your Heart	Streisand, Barbra	49-615	PS
Lean On Me	Bolton, Michael	46-275	KV
Lean On Me	Nouveau	20-371	SC
Lean On Me	Withers, Bill	16-854	DK
Lean On Me	Withers, Bill	13-107	P
Leap Of Faith	Cartwright, Lionel	13-525	P
Learn The Hard Way	Nickelback	19-347	STP
Learn To Fly	Foo Fighters	33-371	CB
Learn To Fly	Foo Fighters	8-528	PHT
Learn To Fly	Goo Goo Dolls	30-218	PHM
Learned It From The Radio	Rhett, Thomas	49-5	DCK
Learnin' The Blues	Sinatra, Frank	10-714	JVC
Learning As You Go	Trevino, Rick	7-331	MM
Learning As You Go	Trevino, Rick	4-369	SC
Learning As You Go	Trevino, Rick	22-904	ST
Learning How To Bend	Allan, Gary	36-409	CB
Learning The Blues	Sinatra, Frank	35-29	CB
Learning The Game	Holly, Buddy	47-886	ZM
Learning To Live Again	Brooks, Garth	6-308	MM
Learning To Live Again	Brooks, Garth	2-685	SC
Least Complicated	Indigo Girls	4-285	SC
Least Of All You	Osmond, Marie	47-867	ZP
Leather And Lace	Nicks & Henley	12-378	DK
Leather And Lace	Nicks & Henley	4-763	SC
Leave (Get Out)	Jo Jo	23-560	MM
Leave A Little Room For God	Diamond, Neil	30-506	THM
Leave A Tender Moment Alone	Joel, Billy	12-273	DK
Leave A Tender Moment Alone	Joel, Billy	6-555	MM
Leave Him Out Of This	Wariner, Steve	1-500	CB
Leave It Alone	Forrester Sisters	16-590	MM

159

SONG TITLE	ARTIST	#	TYPE
Leave Me Alone	Cantrell, Jerry	24-119	SC
Leave Me Alone (Ruby Red Dress)	Reddy, Helen	28-269	DK
Leave My Mama Out Of This	Holmes, Monty	8-874	CB
Leave My Mama Out Of This	Holmes, Monty	10-160	SC
Leave The Night On	Hunt, Sam	44-321	SBI
Leave The Pieces	Wreckers	29-587	CB
Leave Virginia Alone	Stewart, Rod	3-439	SC
Leave Your Lover	Smith, Sam	44-316	SBI
Leaves That Are Green	Simon & Garfunkel	49-765	LG
Leavin'	McCartney, Jesse	36-445	CB
Leavin'	Tony! Toni! Tone!	15-757	NU
Leavin' And Sayin' Goodbye	Young, Faron	46-54	SSK
Leavin' Louisiana In The Broad Day-	Oak Ridge Boys	23-507	CB
Leavin' On Your Mind	Cline, Patsy	26-509	DK
Leavin' On Your Mind	Cline, Patsy	6-724	MM
Leavin' On Your Mind	Cline, Patsy	2-23	SC
Leavin's Been A Long Time Comin'	Shenandoah	1-489	CB
Leavin's Been A Long Time Comin'	Shenandoah	6-123	MM
Leaving Is The Only Way Out	Twain, Shania	45-534	CB
Leaving Las Vegas	Crow, Sheryl	29-669	RS
Leaving Las Vegas	Crow, Sheryl	17-465	SC
Leaving New York	REM	30-816	PHM
Leaving October	Sons Of The Desert	8-405	CB
Leaving On A Jet Plane	Peter, Paul & Mary	35-101	CB
Leaving On A Jet Plane	Peter, Paul & Mary	11-349	DK
Leaving On A Jet Plane	Peter, Paul & Mary	7-351	MM
Leaving On A Jet Plane	Peter, Paul & Mary	13-149	P
Leaving On A Jet Plane	Peter, Paul & Mary	9-122	PS
Leaving Song the (Pt. 2)	AFI	23-177	PHM
Left To Right	Wells, Kitty	47-394	CB
Legacy	Coty, Neal	14-129	CB
Legacy	Coty, Neal	22-595	ST
Legend In Your Own Time	Simon, Carly	49-151	CB
Legend Of A Mind	Moody Blues	28-139	DK
Legend Of Bonnie & Clyde	Haggard, Merle	37-174	CB
Legend Of Bonnie & Clyde	Haggard, Merle	5-92	SC
Legend Of John Henry's Hammer	Cash, Johnny	43-404	VH
Legend Of Wooley Swamp	Charlie Daniels Band	20-648	SC
Legs	ZZ Top	12-170	DK
Legs	ZZ Top	4-297	SC
Lemon Tree	Lopez, Trini	11-734	DK
Leona	Jackson, Stonewall	46-40	SSK
Les Champs Ulysees	Vidal, Daniele	15-521	CMC
Lesson In Leavin'	Messina, Jo Dee	8-476	CB
Lesson In Leavin'	Messina, Jo Dee	14-621	SC
Lesson In Leavin'	West, Dottie	8-840	CB

SONG TITLE	ARTIST	#	TYPE
Lessons Learned	Lawrence, Tracy	5-835	SC
Lessons Learned	Lawrence, Tracy	22-536	ST
Lessons Learned	Underwood, Carrie	30-123	AS
Let 'Em In	McCartney & Wings	15-756	AMS
Let 'Er Rip	Dixie Chicks	8-756	CB
Let 'Er Rip	Dixie Chicks	10-60	SC
Let Go	Brother Phelps	2-368	SC
Let Her Cry	Hootie & Blowfish	21-137	CB
Let Her Cry	Hootie & Blowfish	28-49	DK
Let Her Go	Boyce Avenue	45-5	KV
Let Her Go & Start Over	Lewis & The News	25-26	MM
Let Him Fly	Dixie Chicks	20-214	CB
Let Him Fly	Dixie Chicks	30-605	RS
Let Him Run Wild	Beach Boys	46-490	KV
Let It Be	Beatles	16-762	DK
Let It Be	Beatles	13-141	P
Let It Be Me	Brown & Schmidt	14-881	SC
Let It Be Me	Campbell, Glen	48-494	CKC
Let It Be Me	Everly Brothers	11-665	DK
Let It Be Me	Nelson, Willie	38-69	SC
Let It Be Me	Raye, Collin	1-126	CB
Let It Be Me	Raye, Collin	4-116	SC
Let It Bleed	Rolling Stones	18-16	LE
Let It Die	Foo Fighters	36-495	CB
Let It Go	Lovato, Demi	43-166	ASK
Let It Go	McGraw, Tim	47-235	CB
Let It Go	Prince	49-830	MM
Let It Go	Strait, George	46-12	BKD
Let It Go	Zac Brown Band	46-66	KV
Let It Go	Zac Brown Band	47-762	SRK
Let It Go - Frozen	Frozen	46-378	DIS
Let It Go - Frozen	Mendel, Idina	45-459	ASK
Let It Grow	Clapton, Eric	13-801	SGB
Let It Out	Hombres	3-26	SC
Let It Rain	Chesnutt, Mark	7-627	CHM
Let It Rain	Clapton, Eric	5-589	SC
Let It Rain	Nail, David	45-557	ASK
Let It Rain	Smith, Michael M	34-426	CB
Let It Ride	BTO	35-121	CB
Let It Ride	BTO	20-91	SC
Let It Rock	Rudolph, Kevin feat Lil Wayne	36-28	PT
Let It Roll	Flo Rida	45-652	MRH
Let It Roll	McDaniel, Mel	5-670	SC
Let It Snow	Buble, Michael	45-739	ZP
Let It Snow	Lady Antebellum	45-741	KVD
Let It Snow	Nichols, Joe	45-740	CB
Let It Snow	Sinatra, Frank	45-738	SFX
Let It Snow	Thomas, B.J.	45-737	CB
Let Love In	Goo Goo Dolls	30-269	CB
Let Love Pass	Hollies	44-377	ZM
Let Me	Green, Pat	36-616	CB
Let Me	Green, Pat	36-200	PHM
Let Me Be Myself	3 Doors Down	36-231	PHM
Let Me Be The One	Blessed Union of Souls	34-159	CB
Let Me Be The One	Carpenters	44-343	OZP

160

SONG TITLE	ARTIST	#	TYPE
Let Me Be The One	Expose	20-43	SC
Let Me Be The One	Locklin, Hank	37-290	CB
Let Me Be The One	Locklin, Hank	5-363	SC
Let Me Be There	Newton-John, Olivia	17-49	DK
Let Me Be There	Newton-John, Olivia	13-346	P
Let Me Be There	Newton-John, Olivia	9-587	SAV
Let Me Be Your Love Pillow	Milsap, Ronnie	47-268	CB
Let Me Be Your Teddy Bear	Presley, Elvis	35-2	CB
Let Me Be Your Teddy Bear	Presley, Elvis	18-118	DK
Let Me Blow Ya Mind	Stefani,Eve & Gwen	18-527	TT
Let Me Call You Sweetheart	Crosby, Bing	29-413	CB
Let Me Call You Sweetheart	Mills Brothers	47-263	P
Let Me Call You Sweetheart	Standard	35-22	CB
Let Me Call You Sweetheart	Standard	11-475	DK
Let Me Call You Sweetheart	Standard	12-535	P
Let Me Call You Sweetheart	Standard	23-224	SM
Let Me Down Easy	Currington, Billy	37-348	CB
Let Me Down Easy	Isaak, Chris	18-351	CB
Let Me Down Easy	Isaak, Chris	25-208	MM
Let Me Fall	Groban, Josh	48-45	CB
Let Me Go	3 Doors Down	22-364	CB
Let Me Go	Kane, Christian	43-85	CB
Let Me Go Lover	Jackson, Wanda	47-798	SRK
Let Me Go Lover	Martin, Dean	23-80	MM
Let Me Go Lover	Page, Patti	3-507	SC
Let Me Go Lover	Snow, Hank	22-129	CB
Let Me Go Lover	Weber, Joan	33-241	CB
Let Me In	Osmonds	47-860	ZM
Let Me In	Sensations	9-285	SC
Let Me In To Your Heart	Carpenter, M C	1-429	CB
Let Me Let Go	Hill, Faith	15-685	CB
Let Me Live In The Light Of His Love	Pride, Charley	47-435	CB
Let Me Love You	Mario	22-358	CB
Let Me Love You	McGraw, Tim	47-241	CB
Let Me Love You	Tonight Da Buzz	21-727	TT
Let Me Love You Tonight	Pure Prairie League	7-457	MM
Let Me Out	Future Leaders of the World	30-815	PHM
Let Me Roll It	McCartney, Paul	15-755	AMS
Let Me See Ya Girl	Swindell, Cole	45-378	BKD
Let Me Sing And I'm Happy	Jolson, Al	12-937	PS
Let Me Tell You About Love	Judds	1-145	CB
Let Me Tell You About Love	Judds	9-441	SAV
Let Me Touch You For Awhile	Krauss, Alison	25-134	MM
Let Me Touch You For Awhile	Krauss, Alison	16-436	ST

SONG TITLE	ARTIST	#	TYPE
Let Me Try Again	Sinatra, Frank	12-493	P
Let My Love Open The Door	Townsend, Pete	20-79	SC
Let Old Mother Nature Have Her Way	Smith, Carl	22-107	CB
Let Old Mother Nature Have Her Way	Smith, Carl	4-803	SC
Let That Pony Run	Tillis, Pam	1-456	CB
Let That Pony Run	Tillis, Pam	19-299	MH
Let That Pony Run	Tillis, Pam	12-422	P
Let The Chips Fall	Pride, Charley	40-116	CB
Let The Cowboy Ride	Dunn, Ronnie	45-233	DFK
Let The Four Winds Blow	Domino, Fats	10-216	SS
Let The Good Times Roll	Charles, Ray	46-574	CB
Let The Good Times Roll	Shirley & Lee	6-143	MM
Let The Good Times Roll	Shirley & Lee	4-241	SC
Let The Good Times Roll	Tucker, Tanya	24-76	SC
Let The Meter Run	Mars, Charlie	39-107	PHM
Let The Music Lift you Under..	McEntire, Reba	1-803	CB
Let The Music Play	Shannon	3-443	SC
Let The Music Play	White, Barry	48-772	P
Let The Rain	Bareillas, Sara	48-212	KV
Let The River Run	Simon, Carly	49-155	CB
Let The Teardrops Fall	Cline, Patsy	45-483	CB
Let Them Be Little	Dean, Billy	22-105	CB
Let Them Be Little	Dean, Billy	20-512	ST
Let There Be Love	Cole, Nat "King"	29-457	LE
Let Your Heart Lead Your Mind	Smokin' Armadillos	4-121	SC
Let Your Love Flow	Bellamy Brothers	15-69	CB
Let Your Love Flow	Bellamy Brothers	13-432	P
Let Your Love Flow	Bellamy Brothers	10-513	SF
Let Your Love Go	Bread	46-524	CB
Let Your Tears Fall	Clarkson, Kelly	48-436	KCD
Let'e Hear It For The Boy	Williams, Deniece	27-295	DK
Let's All Go Down To The River	Paycheck & Miller	22-33	CB
Let's All Go Down To The River - duet	Paycheck & Miller, J	45-213	CB
Let's Be Us Again	Lonestar	35-435	CB
Let's Be Us Again	Lonestar	20-166	ST
Let's Call The Whole Thing Off	Connick, Harry Jr.	19-717	PS
Let's Call The Whole Thing Off	Fitzgerald&Armstron	12-489	P
Let's Chase Each Other 'Round..	Haggard, Merle	7-153	MM
Let's Chase Each Other 'Round...	Haggard, Merle	8-320	CB
Let's Chase Each Other 'Round...	Haggard, Merle	4-660	SC
Let's Dance	Bowie, David	21-749	MH
Let's Dance	Cyrus, Miley	36-74	WD
Let's Dance	Evans, Sara	29-556	CB
Let's Dance	Montez, Chris	13-262	P
Let's Dance	Montez, Chris	5-171	SC

SONG TITLE	ARTIST	#	TYPE
Let's Do It Again	Staple Singers	11-373	DK
Let's Face the Music & Dance	Bennett & Lady Gaga	49-720	KV
Let's Face The Music & Dance	Krall, Diana	23-342	MM
Let's Fall In Love	Sinatra, Frank	9-262	PT
Let's Fall To Pieces Together	Strait, George	2-363	SC
Let's Fight	Thompson Square	47-389	PHN
Let's Forget About It	Loeb, Lisa	14-201	CB
Let's Get Drunk And Fight	Nichols, Joe	47-570	PS
Let's Get It On	Gaye, Marvin	36-115	JTG
Let's Get It On	Palmer, Robert	35-114	CB
Let's Get It On	Palmer, Robert	9-333	PS
Let's Get It On	Prata, Lucas	21-728	TT
Let's Get It Started	Black Eyed Peas	46-205	SC
Let's Get Over Them Together	Bandy & Hobbs	9-575	SAV
Let's Get Rocked	Def Leppard	49-318	CB
Let's Get Rocked	Def Leppard	46-172	SC
Let's Get Started If We're Gonna	Statler Brothers	5-773	SC
Let's Get The Mood Right	Gill, Johnny	24-294	SC
Let's Get Together One Last Time	Wynette, Tammy	49-364	CB
Let's Go All The Way	Jean, Norma	46-19	SSK
Let's Go Crazy	Prince	11-731	DK
Let's Go Crazy	Prince	13-27	P
Let's Go Crazy	Prince	5-472	SC
Let's Go Get Stoned	Charles, Ray	46-306	SC
Let's Go Steady Again	Sedaka, Neil	45-60	CB
Let's Go To Vegas	Hill, Faith	15-686	CB
Let's Go To Vegas	Hill, Faith	7-30	MM
Let's Go Waltzing Together	Denver, Mike	45-806	KV
Let's Groove	Earth Wind & Fire	18-372	AH
Let's Hang On	Four Seasons	20-36	SC
Let's Have A Party	Backstreet Boys	30-412	THM
Let's Hear It For The Boy	Williams, Deniece	7-52	MM
Let's Hear It For The Boy	Williams, Deniece	16-546	P
Let's Jump The Broomstick	Lee, Brenda	29-827	SF
Let's Keep It That Way	Davis, Mac	23-521	CB
Let's Kill Saturday Night	PinMonkey	20-255	PHM
Let's Kill Saturday Night	PinMonkey	20-349	ST
Let's Live A Little	Smith, Carl	22-106	CB
Let's Live For Today	Grass Roots	16-769	DK
Let's Live For Today	Grass Roots	12-650	P
Let's Lock The Door & Throw Away..	Jay & Americans	14-372	PS
Let's Make A Baby King	Judd, Wynonna	6-478	MM
Let's Make A Deal	Dangerman	7-875	PHM
Let's Make A Memory	Orbison, Roy	47-335	BAT
Let's Make A Night To Remember	Adams, Bryan	23-445	CB
Let's Make A Night To Remember	Adams, Bryan	24-226	SC

SONG TITLE	ARTIST	#	TYPE
Let's Make Love	Hill & McGraw	22-530	ST
Let's Make Love - Duet	Hill & McGraw	35-335	CB
Let's Make Sure We Kiss Goodbye	Gill, Vince	23-361	SC
Let's Make Sure We Kiss Goodbye	Gill, Vince	22-483	ST
Let's Ride	Kid Rock	46-61	BKD
Let's Say Goodbye Like....Hello	Tubb, Ernest	22-303	CB
Let's Spend The Night Together	Rolling Stones	19-752	LE
Let's Spend The Night Together	Rolling Stones	17-182	SC
Let's Start Living	Grand, Gil	8-937	CB
Let's Stay Together	Green, Al	11-369	DK
Let's Stay Together	Green, Al	7-467	MM
Let's Stay Together	Green, Al	13-145	P
Let's Stay Together	Turner, Tina	10-423	LE
Let's Stop Talking About It	Frickie, Janie	49-635	CB
Let's Take The Long Way Around the World	Milsap, Ronnie	35-383	CB
Let's Talk About Love	McCready, Mindy	8-243	CB
Let's Talk About Sex **	Salt 'N Pepa	2-191	SC
Let's Talk About Sex **	SWV	12-251	DK
Let's Talk About Us	Presley, Elvis	43-248	PS
Let's Talk Dirty In Hawaiian	Prine, John	46-285	RDK
Let's Think About Living	Luman, Bob	29-826	SF
Let's Try Goodbye	Dalley, Amy	30-466	CB
Let's Turn Back The Years	Jennings, Waylon	46-18	SSK
Let's Twist Again	Checker, Chubby	17-344	DK
Let's Twist Again	Checker, Chubby	13-318	P
Let's Twist Again	Checker, Chubby	5-86	SC
Let's Wait Awhile	Jackson, Janet	2-281	SC
Letter Edged In Black	Reeves, Jim	45-269	STTW
Letter That Johnny Walker Read	Asleep at the Wheel	5-765	SC
Letter the	Box Tops	16-876	DK
Letter the	Box Tops	6-658	MM
Letter the	Box Tops	12-671	P
Letter the	Box Tops	21-572	SF
Letter the	BTO	46-539	CB
Letter the	Cocker, Joe	18-254	DK
Letter the	Cocker, Joe	21-439	LE
Letter the	Cocker, Joe	15-803	SC
Letter the	Daniels, Clint	34-405	CB
Letter the (Almost Home)	Daniels, Clint	19-71	ST
Letter To Me	Paisley, Brad	36-430	CB
Letter To My Heart a	Reeves, Jim	49-649	DFK
Letter To My P#N#S **	Carrington, Rodney	44-100	SC
Letters From Home	Montgomery, J M	20-168	ST
Letters Have No Arms	Tubb, Ernest	4-802	SC
Letters To London	Smith, Granger	47-486	PHN
Lettin' The Night Roll	Moore, Justin	43-141	KCDC

SONG TITLE	ARTIST	#	TYPE
Letting Go	Bogguss, Suzy	1-560	CB
Letting Go	Bogguss, Suzy	6-120	MM
Letting Go	Bogguss, Suzy	12-444	P
Levon	John, Elton	6-548	MM
Levon	John, Elton	2-375	SC
Liar	Profyle	14-26	THM
Liar	Three Dog Night	29-635	SC
Liar Liar	Castaways	20-38	SC
License To Kill	Knight & Pips	9-67	SC
Lick It Up	Kiss	6-26	SC
Licking Stick	Brown, James	29-148	LE
Lido Shuffle	Boz Skaggs	15-176	MH
Lie To Me	Lang, Johnny	5-747	SC
Lie To You For Your Love	Bellamy Brothers	6-85	SC
Life # 9	McBride, Martina	1-377	CB
Life # 9	McBride, Martina	19-292	MH
Life # 9	McBride, Martina	6-459	MM
Life Ain't Always Beautiful	Allan, Gary	29-189	CB
Life Ain't Always Beautiful	Wills, Mark	29-708	ST
Life As We Knew it	Mattea, Kathy	1-186	CB
Life As We Knew It	Mattea, Kathy	7-158	MM
Life At Best	Eli Young Band	47-60	PHN
Life Don't Have To Be So Hard	Lawrence, Tracy	16-8	ST
Life During Wartime	Talking Heads	21-412	SC
Life Gets Away	Black, Clint	3-573	SC
Life Goes On	Little Texas	7-140	MM
Life Goes On	Prosser, James	8-396	CB
Life Goes On	Rimes, LeAnn	34-369	CB
Life Goes On	Rimes, LeAnn	25-339	MM
Life Goes On	Rimes, LeAnn	18-340	PHM
Life Goes On (Pop Version)	Rimes, LeAnn	20-381	HP
Life Happened	Cochran, Tammy	33-195	CB
Life Happened	Cochran, Tammy	25-300	MM
Life Happened	Cochran, Tammy	17-585	ST
Life Has It's Little Ups & Downs	McDowell, Ronnie	47-234	SAV
Life In A Northern Town	Dream Academy	16-245	AMS
Life In A Northern Town	Sugarland/Little Big Town/Owen,J	36-398	CB
Life In Technicolor II	Coldplay	48-255	SC
Life In The Fast Lane	Eagles	7-559	BS
Life In The Fast Lane	Eagles	2-260	SC
Life Is A Highway	LeDoux, Chris	8-964	CB
Life Is A Highway	Rascal Flatts	30-16	CB
Life Is But A Dream	Harptones	25-557	MM
Life Is Good	LFO	18-287	CB
Life Is Good	LFO	16-77	ST
Life Is Worth Living	Bieber, Justin	49-881	DCK
Life Is Worth Living	Bieber, Justin	48-623	DCK
Life Keeps Bringing Me Down	Jackson, Alan	49-183	PHN
Life Keeps Moving On	Adams, Oleta	46-387	PS
Life Of My Own	3 Doors Down	47-662	SBI

SONG TITLE	ARTIST	#	TYPE
Life Story	Streisand, Barbra	49-624	SF
Life Sucks & Then You Die **	Fools	30-657	RSX
Life To Go	Jackson, Stonewall	5-372	SC
Life Turned Her That Way	VanShelton, Ricky	4-659	SC
Life's A Dance	Montgomery, J M	14-204	CB
Life's Highway	Wariner, Steve	13-536	P
Life's Highway	Wariner, Steve	5-20	SC
Life's Just Not The Way It Used To Be	Haggard, Merle	46-43	SSK
Life's Little Ups and Downs	Twitty, Conway	9-504	SAV
Life's Little Ups And Downs	VanShelton, Ricky	8-554	CB
Life's Railway To Heaven	Cline, Patsy	45-494	CB
Life's Railway To Heaven	Dalton, Lacy J.	45-826	VH
Life's Too Short To Love Like That	Hill, Faith	17-268	NA
Lifestyles Of The Not So Rich&Famou	Byrd, Tracy	20-106	CB
Lifestyles Of The Not So Rich&Famou	Byrd, Tracy	6-583	MM
Lifestyles Of The Rich & Famous	Good Charlotte	20-457	CB
Lifestyles Of The Rich & Famous	Good Charlotte	25-434	MM
Lifestyles Of The Rich & Famous	Good Charlotte	18-825	THM
Lift Me Up	Jones, Howard	4-282	SC
Light A Fire	Taylor, Rachel	48-402	DCK
Light In Your Eyes	Crow, Sheryl	29-662	RS
Light In Your Eyes the	Rimes, LeAnn	1-288	CB
Light In Your Eyes the	Rimes, LeAnn	7-615	CHM
Light In Your Eyes the	Rimes, LeAnn	7-445	MM
Light In Your Eyes the	Rimes, LeAnn	24-648	SC
Light My Fire	Bassey, Shirley	46-475	KV
Light My Fire	Doors	2-749	SC
Light My Fire	Doors	18-645	SO
Light Of The Clear Blue Morning the	Parton, Dolly	8-457	CB
Light On	Cook, David	36-250	PHM
Light Up	Styx	2-751	SC
Light Years	Pearl Jam	15-646	THM
Lightening Does The Work	Brock, Chad	8-963	CB
Lighter Shade Of Blue a	Wynette, Tammy	45-721	VH
Lighthouses' Tale the	Nickel Creek	16-336	ST
Lightnin' Strikes	Christie, Lou	34-24	CB
Lightnin' Strikes	Christie, Lou	11-357	DK
Lightnin' Strikes	Christie, Lou	10-666	SF
Lightning	Church, Eric	46-623	ST
Lightning Crashes	Live	13-664	SGB
Lightning Does The Work	Brock, Chad	34-322	CB
Lightning Does The Work	Brock, Chad	14-624	SC
Lights	Journey	14-576	SC
Lights Come On	Aldean, Jason	49-640	DCK

163

SONG TITLE	ARTIST	#	TYPE
Lights Down Low	James-Decker, Jessie	48-448	KCD
Lights Out	Presley, Lisa Marie	25-534	MM
Lights Out	Presley, Lisa Marie	23-334	SC
Lights Out	Presley, Lisa Marie	32-176	THM
Like A Boy	Ciara	30-495	CB
Like A Boy	Clara	30-495	CB
Like A Cowboy	Houser, Randy	45-553	ASK
Like A Prayer	Madonna	6-347	MM
Like A Prayer	Madonna	12-852	P
Like A River	Simon, Carly	49-159	SC
Like A River To The Sea	Wariner, Steve	1-506	CB
Like A Rock	Seger, Bob	35-184	CB
Like A Rolling Stone	Dylan, Bob	29-93	CB
Like A Rolling Stone	Dylan, Bob	11-469	DK
Like A Stone	Audio Slave	25-586	MM
Like A Stone	Audio Slave	32-141	THM
Like A Surgeon	Yankovic, Weird Al	6-525	MM
Like A Virgin	Madonna	11-81	DK
Like A Virgin	Madonna	21-146	LE
Like A Virgin	Madonna	12-675	P
Like A Virgin	Madonna	10-524	SF
Like A Woman	O'Neal, Jamie	36-262	PHM
Like Glue	Paul, Sean	25-716	MM
Like Glue	Paul, Sean	21-786	SC
Like Glue	Paul, Sean	32-389	THM
Like I Can	Smith, Sam	45-137	BHK
Like I Love You	Grant, Amy	18-766	PS
Like I Love You	Timberlake, Justin	25-345	MM
Like I'll Never Love You Again	Underwood, Carrie	47-703	BKD
Like I'm Gonna Lose You - duet]	Trainor & Legend	45-144	BH
Like My Dog	Currington, Billy	38-205	SRK
Like My Mother Does	Lee, Jesse	38-226	CB
Like Red On A Rose	Jackson, Alan	30-47	CB
Like Red On A Rose	Jackson, Slan	30-47	CB
Like Sister And Brother	Drifters	45-902	SF
Like Someone In Love	Standard	13-640	SGB
Like Strangers	Everly Brothers	45-293	DCK
Like The Rain	Black, Clint	4-453	SC
Like The Way I Do	Etheridge, Melissa	9-378	AH
Like The Way I Do	Etheridge, Melissa	7-486	MM
Like The Way I Do	Etheridge, Melissa	19-154	SGB
Like The Weather	10,000 Maniacs	46-234	MM
Like There Ain't No Yesterday	Blackhawk	3-629	SC
Like This	Rowland, K & Eve	30-561	CB
Like This	Rowland, Kelly	30-561	CB
Like To Get To Know You	Spanky & Our Gang	14-450	SC
Like To Love Again	Burnin' Daylight	4-830	SC
Like Water Into Wine	Loveless, Patty	1-731	CB
Like Water Into Wine	Loveless, Patty	22-673	ST
Like We Never Had A Broken Heart	Brooks & Yearwood	2-304	SC
Like We Never Had A Broken Heart	Yearwood, Trisha	1-632	CB

SONG TITLE	ARTIST	#	TYPE
Like We Never Loved At All	Hill, Faith	23-411	CB
Like We Never Loved At All - duet	Hill & McGraw	36-377	SC
Like You'll Never See Me Again	Keys, Alicia	36-449	CB
Like You'll Never See Me Again	Keys, Alicia	49-893	SC
Likes Of Me the	Stuart, Marty	2-698	SC
Limbo Rock - DANCE #	Checker, Chubby	22-440	SC
Limelight	Hush	5-65	SC
Lincoln Avenue	Train	48-264	KV
Lincoln Park Inn	Bare, Bobby	3-704	CB
Lincoln Park Inn	Bare, Bobby	20-285	SC
Linda	Reeves, Jim	44-241	DCK
Linda Lu	Jones, Tom	49-257	DFK
Linda On My Mind	Twitty, Conway	1-155	CB
Linda On My Mind	Twitty, Conway	3-598	SC
Linger	Cranberries	33-351	CB
Linger	Cranberries	13-239	P
Lion Sleeps Tonight the	Tokens	12-129	DK
Lion Sleeps Tonight the	Tokens	3-327	MH
Lion Sleeps Tonight the	Tokens	6-657	MM
Lion Sleeps Tonight the	Tokens	13-58	P
Lips Are Moving	Trainor, Meghan	45-138	BKD
Lips Of An Angel	Hinder	30-264	CB
Lips Of An Angel	Ingram, Jack	30-249	CB
Lipstick	Lynne, Rockie	29-26	CB
Lipstick	Lynne, Rockie	23-456	ST
Lipstick Don't Lie	Collie, Mark	7-236	MM
Lipstick On Your Collar	Francis, Connie	10-729	JVC
Lipstick Promises	Ducas, George	6-706	MM
Lipstick Promises	Ducas, George	17-283	NA
Lipstick Promises	Ducas, George	2-647	SC
Lipstick Promises	Ducas, George	22-857	ST
Liquid Dreams	O-Town	35-254	CB
Liquid Dreams	O-Town	12-390	PHM
Listen People	Herman's Hermits	14-453	SC
Listen They're Playing Our Song	Jennings, Waylon	45-190	KV
Listen To A Country Song	Anderson, Lynn	5-157	SC
Listen To Me	Hollies	44-370	ZM
Listen To Me	Holly, Buddy	3-223	LG
Listen To Me	Holly, Buddy	11-36	PX
Listen To The Falling Rain	Feliciano, Jose	47-808	SRK
Listen To The Music	Doobie Brothers	29-79	CB
Listen To The Music	Doobie Brothers	12-349	DK
Listen To The Music	Doobie Brothers	13-28	P
Listen To The Radio	Mattea, Kathy	17-265	NA
Listen To The Radio	Williams, Don	45-230	CB
Listen To What The Man Said	Wings	35-130	CB
Listen To What The Man Said	Wings	4-76	SC
Listen To Your Heart	D.H.T.	30-145	PT
Listen To Your Heart	Roxette	18-232	DK

SONG TITLE	ARTIST	#	TYPE
Listenin' To The Radio	Wright, Chely	4-24	SC
Lit Up	Buckcherry	48-476	SC
Lithium	Evanescence	30-272	CB
Lithium	Evanescence	30-272	CB
Little Bird	Lennox, Annie	13-246	P
Little Bird	Lennox, Annie	17-728	PS
Little Bit a	Simpson, Jessica	33-384	CB
Little Bit Country Little Bit Rock&Roll	Osmond, Donny & Marie	47-861	VH
Little Bit Gypsy	Pickler, Kellie	41-94	PHN
Little Bit In Love a	Loveless, Patty	1-707	CB
Little Bit Is Better Than Nada a	Texas Tornados	10-693	HH
Little Bit Is Better Than Nada a	Texas Tornados	44-79	KV
Little Bit Me Little Bit You a	Monkees	20-27	SC
Little Bit More	Dr. Hook	48-771	P
Little Bit More	Dr. Hook	47-39	SC
Little Bit O' Soul	Music Explosion	3-590	SC
Little Bit Of Everything	Urban, Keith	45-626	ASK
Little Bit Of Honey	Baker & Myers	24-164	SC
Little Bit Of Life	Morgan, Craig	30-51	CB
Little Bit Of Love	Judd, Wynonna	6-194	MM
Little Bit Of You	Bryant, Chase	49-736	SBI
Little Bit Of You a	Parnell, Lee Roy	7-27	MM
Little Bit Of You a	Parnell, Lee Roy	2-774	SC
Little Bitty	Jackson, Alan	1-53	CB
Little Bitty	Jackson, Alan	4-620	SC
Little Bitty Crack In His Heart	Lovett, Ruby	8-491	CB
Little Bitty Pretty One	Harris, Thurston	3-458	SC
Little Bitty Pretty One	Lymon, Frankie	30-521	LE
Little Bitty Tear a	Ives, Burl	4-258	SC
Little Black Book	Dean, Jimmy	47-18	SRK
Little Blue Dot	Bonamy, James	8-31	CB
Little Brown Jug	Miller, Glen	10-706	JVC
Little By Little	House, James	2-651	SC
Little Cabin Home On The Hill	Stanley, Ralph	49-328	CB
Little Children	Kramer & Dacotas	10-567	SF
Little Christmas Tree	Jackson, Michael	47-478	DCK
Little Darlin'	Diamonds	12-114	DK
Little Darlin'	Diamonds	6-141	MM
Little Darlin'	Diamonds	13-50	P
Little Darlin'	Diamonds	19-100	SAV
Little Darlin' (I Need You(	Doobie Brothers	47-27	PS
Little Deuce Coupe	Beach Boys	5-509	BS
Little Deuce Coupe	Beach Boys	35-40	CB
Little Deuce Coupe	Beach Boys	11-651	DK
Little Deuce Coupe	Beach Boys	13-265	P
Little Deuce Coupe	Beach Boys	3-554	SC
Little Devil	Sedaka, Neil	11-453	DK
Little Drops Of My Heart	Gattis, Keith	7-239	MM
Little Drops Of My Heart	Gattis, Keith	4-234	SC
Little Drummer Boy - xmas	Seger, Bob	46-343	SC
Little Egypt	Coasters	10-698	JVC

SONG TITLE	ARTIST	#	TYPE
Little Favours	Tunstall, K.T.	49-885	SC
Little Folks	Charlie Daniels Band	46-609	CB
Little Gasoline a	Clark, Terri	14-110	CB
Little Georgia Rose	Monroe, Bill	8-262	CB
Little Girl	McEntire, Reba	1-781	CB
Little Girl	McEntire, Reba	24-125	SC
Little Girl Blue	Day, Doris	48-142	LE
Little Girl Blue	Joplin, Janis	49-752	KV
Little Girl Gone	Fargo, Donna	48-659	CB
Little Girl Of Mine	Cleftones	25-179	MM
Little Girl the	Montgomery, J M	14-119	CB
Little Girl the	Montgomery, J M	13-859	CHM
Little Girl the	Montgomery, J M	19-242	CSZ
Little Good News a	Murray, Anne	11-10	PL
Little Goodbyes	SheDaisy	8-333	CB
Little Green Apples	Miller, Roger	22-283	CB
Little Green Apples	Miller, Roger	5-39	SC
Little Green Apples	Smith, O.C. & Page	27-547	DK
Little Green Apples	Smith, O.C.R.	4-242	SC
Little Green Apples	Standard	10-466	MG
Little Honda	Hondells	3-549	SC
Little Houses	Stone, Doug	20-604	CB
Little Houses	Stone, Doug	17-267	NA
Little Houses	Stone, Doug	2-546	SC
Little In Love a	Brandt, Paul	22-660	ST
Little Jeannie	John, Elton	35-151	CB
Little Jeannie	John, Elton	2-384	SC
Little Left Of Center	Travis, Randy	14-710	CB
Little Left Of Center a	Travis, Randy	22-554	ST
Little Less 16 Candles, Little More	Fall Out Boy	30-280	SC
Little Less Conversation	Presley, Elvis	25-303	MM
Little Less Talk Lot More Action	Keith, Toby	1-703	CB
Little Less Talk Lot More Action	Keith, Toby	17-405	DK
Little Less Talk Lot More Action	Keith, Toby	6-461	MM
Little Lies	Fleetwood Mac	4-320	SC
Little Maggie	Stanley, Ralph	8-253	CB
Little Man	Cher	47-685	RSZ
Little Man	Jackson, Alan	34-331	CB
Little Man	Jackson, Alan	10-194	SC
Little Man	Jackson, Alan	22-743	ST
Little Man	Sonny & Cher	14-67	RS
Little Miracles	Vandross, Luther	48-296	SC
Little Miss Can't Be Wrong	Spin Doctors	17-387	DK
Little Miss Honky Tonk	Brooks & Dunn	2-662	SC
Little Miss Honky Tonk	Brooks & Dunn	22-867	ST
Little Miss Honky-Tonk	Brooks & Dunn	1-90	CB
Little Miss Lover	Hendrix, Jimi	10-490	DA
Little Moments	Paisley, Brad	35-431	CB
Little Moments	Paisley, Brad	19-527	ST
Little Moments	Paisley, Brad	32-415	THM
Little More Country Than That	Corbin, Easton	37-230	CB

SONG TITLE	ARTIST	#	TYPE
Little More Love a	Gill, Vince	7-607	CHM
Little More Love a	Gill, Vince	10-78	SC
Little More time With You	Taylor, James	10-65	SC
Little More You a	Little Big Town	30-345	CB
Little Old Lady From Pasadena	Jan & Dean	11-633	DK
Little Old Lady From Pasadena	Jan & Dean	13-66	P
Little Old Lady From Pasadena	Jan & Dean	3-561	SC
Little Old Wine Drinker Me	Martin, Dean	10-400	LE
Little Old Wine Drinker Me	Martin, Dean	23-77	MM
Little Ole Dime	Reeves, Jim	44-230	SRK
Little Past Little Rock a	Womack, Lee Ann	8-761	CB
Little Queenie	Berry, Chuck	46-225	KV
Little Queenie	Rolling Stones	12-130	DK
Little Red Balloon	Cornell, Kristina	30-346	CB
Little Red Book	Drifters	46-199	SC
Little Red Corvette	Prince	11-286	DK
Little Red Corvette	Prince	12-839	P
Little Red Corvette	Prince	3-560	SC
Little Red Corvette	Prince	21-602	SF
Little Red Riding Hood	Sam The Sham & Pharoahs	13-117	P
Little Red Riding Hood	Sam The Sham & Pharoahs	14-345	SC
Little Red Rodeo	Raye, Collin	8-229	CB
Little Red Rodeo	Raye, Collin	10-124	SC
Little Red Rodeo	Raye, Collin	22-756	ST
Little Red Rooster	Dixon, Willie	15-316	SC
Little Red Rooster	Rolling Stones	12-339	DK
Little Red Wagon	Lambert, Miranda	46-268	KV
Little Rock	McEntire, Reba	6-539	MM
Little Rock	McEntire, Reba	3-378	SC
Little Rock	Raye, Collin	1-130	CB
Little Rock	Raye, Collin	12-453	P
Little Rock	Raye, Collin	2-421	SC
Little Saint Nick - Xmas	Beach Boys	33-208	CB
Little Sister	Presley, Elvis	11-177	DK
Little Sister	Presley, Elvis	2-607	SC
Little Sister	Presley, Elvis	14-775	THM
Little Sparrow	Tillotson, Johnny	47-738	SRK
Little Star	Elegants	25-560	MM
Little Star	Elegants	14-349	SC
Little Things	Bush	6-36	SC
Little Things	Goldsboro, Bobby	14-454	SC
Little Things	Tucker, Tanya	14-662	CB
Little Things	Tucker, Tanya	7-616	CHM
Little Things Mean A Lot	Allen, Kitty	19-613	MH
Little Things Mean A Lot	Allen, Kitty	9-747	SAV
Little Things Mean A Lot	McGuire Sisters	46-197	KV
Little Things the	Caillat, Colbie	36-532	CB
Little Things the	Caillat, Colbie	37-17	PS
Little Things the	India.Arie	34-154	CB
Little Tom	Husky, Ferlin	22-265	CB

SONG TITLE	ARTIST	#	TYPE
Little Too Late	Benatar, Par	46-510	MH
Little Too Late a	Keith, Toby	29-590	CB
Little Too Late the	Keith, Toby	38-164	SC
Little Too Not Over You a	Archulets, David	36-287	PHM
Little Ways	Yoakam, Dwight	6-87	SC
Little White Church	Little Big Town	37-328	CB
Little White Cloud That Cried	Ray, Johnnie	3-887	PS
Little Willy	Sweet	15-804	SC
Little Wonders	Thomas, Rob	47-613	THM
Live & Learn	Joe Public	28-441	DK
Live A Lie	Default	32-73	THM
Live A Little	Chesney, Kenny	37-237	CB
Live And Learn	Public, Joe	48-576	DK
Live And Let Die	McCartney & Wings	13-32	P
Live And Let Die	McCartney, Paul	9-61	SC
Live And Let Die - WN	Guns 'N Roses	48-60	SC
Live Fast Love Hard Die Young	Young, Faron	20-731	CB
Live For Loving You	Estefan, Gloria	17-751	PT
Live For Today	3 Doors Down	47-654	CB
Live Forever	Band Perry	45-545	BKD
Live High	Mraz, Jason	47-301	KV
Live Is A Carnival	Band	6-58	SC
Live It Up	Dyllon, Marshall	14-133	CB
Live It Up	Dyllon, Marshall	22-580	ST
Live Laugh Love	Walker, Clay	5-726	SC
Live Laugh Love	Walker, Clay	22-502	ST
Live Like You Were Dying	McGraw, Tim	29-516	CB
Live Like You Were Dying	McGraw, Tim	20-471	ST
Live This Life	Big & Rich	23-380	SC
Live Those Songs	Chesney, Kenny	48-84	CB
Live Those Songs	Chesney, Kenny	45-131	SC
Live To Love Another Day	Urban, Keith	30-80	CB
Live To Tell	Madonna	12-853	P
Live Until I Die	Walker, Clay	1-91	CB
Live Wire	Motley Crue	23-104	SC
Lively Up Yourself	Marley, Bob	25-382	MM
Livin' For The City	Wonder, Stevie	27-267	DK
Livin' For The City	Wonder, Stevie	10-676	HE
Livin' In America	Brown, James	29-149	LE
Livin' La Vida Loca	Martin, Ricky	11-80	JTG
Livin' La Vida Loca	Martin, Ricky	7-870	PHM
Livin' La Vida Loca	Martin, Ricky	9-126	PS
Livin' La Vida Loca	Martin, Ricky	13-735	SGB
Livin' On A Prayer	Bon Jovi	21-714	CB
Livin' On A Prayer	Bon Jovi	28-301	DK
Livin' On Love	Jackson, Alan	1-47	CB
Livin' On Love	Jackson, Alan	20-408	MH
Livin' On Love	Jackson, Alan	6-661	MM
Livin' On Love	Milsap, Ronnie	47-266	CB
Livin' Our Love Song	Carroll, Jason M.	30-442	CB
Livin' Our Love Song	Carroll, Jason M.	30-442	CB
Living & Living Well	Strait, George	25-183	MM

SONG TITLE	ARTIST	#	TYPE
Living And Living Well	Strait, George	33-194	CB
Living And Living Well	Strait, George	16-428	ST
Living Daylights the	A-Ha	9-66	SC
Living Dead Girl - Halloween	Zombie, Rob	45-323	SC
Living Doll	Cliff, Richard	48-765	P
Living For A Song	Johnson, Jamey	39-87	PHN
Living For The Night	Strait, George	37-58	CB
Living In A House Full Of Love	Allan, Gary	8-138	CB
Living In A House Full Of Love	Allan, Gary	22-651	ST
Living In A House Full Of Love	Houston, David	34-209	CB
Living In America	Brown, James	20-163	BCI
Living In America	Brown, James	33-315	CB
Living In America	Brown, James	9-681	SAV
Living In Danger	Ace Of Base	16-622	MM
Living In Fast Forward	Chesney, Kenny	29-32	CB
Living In Fast Forward	Chesney, Kenny	29-500	SC
Living In Fast Forward	Chesney, Kenny	29-704	ST
Living In Sin	Bon Jovi	21-716	CB
Living In The Here And Now	Worley, Darryl	30-356	CB
Living In The Past	Tull, Jethro	20-92	SC
Living Next Door To Alice	Dr. Hook	47-37	BMG
Living Proof	VanShelton, Ricky	9-459	SAV
Living Together	Dalley, Amy	22-82	CB
Living Years the	Mike & Mechanics	34-103	CB
Livingdaylights the	A-Ha	46-241	SC
Livingston Saturday Night	Buffett, Jimmy	46-143	SC
Liza (All The Clouds Float Away)	Jolson, Al	12-938	PS
Liza Jane	Gill, Vince	1-589	CB
Liza Jane	Gill, Vince	13-488	P
Lizzie And The Rainman	Tucker, Tanya	1-605	CB
Lizzie And The Rainman	Tucker, Tanya	5-55	SC
Loaded And Alone	Hinder	48-631	BKD
Local Girls	Milsap, Ronnie	29-368	CB
Lock And Load	Seger, Bob	46-341	MM
Lock Stock & Teardrops	lang, k.d.	18-34	CB
Lock Stock And Teardrops	Miller, Roger	45-342	BSP
Locked Out Of Heaven	Mars, Bruno	47-222	ZP
Locked Up	Akon & Styles P	30-812	PHM
Loco	Murphy, David Lee	35-440	CB
Loco	Murphy, David Lee	19-773	ST
Loco In Acapulco	Four Tops	43-429	EZC
Loco-Motion the	Grand Funk RR	2-40	SC
Loco-Motion the	Little Eva	35-187	CB
Loco-Motion the	Little Eva	23-360	CR
Loco-Motion the	Little Eva	10-733	JVC
Loco-Motion the	Little Eva	3-356	MH
Loco-Motion the	Little Eva	12-636	P
Locomotion the	Star Academy	45-944	KV
Locomotive Breath	Tull, Jethro	12-328	DK

SONG TITLE	ARTIST	#	TYPE
Lodi	CCR	5-356	SC
Lola	Kinks	48-169	LE
Lola	Kinks	48-182	MM
Lola's Love	VanShelton, Ricky	22-861	ST
Lollipop	Chordettes	19-609	MH
Lollipop	Chordettes	9-287	SC
London Bridge (Radio Version)	Fergie	48-232	SC
Lonely	Lawrence, Tracy	14-718	CB
Lonely	Lawrence, Tracy	13-851	CHM
Lonely	Lawrence, Tracy	19-249	CSZ
Lonely (Radio Vers)	Akon	37-106	SC
Lonely Again	Arnold, Eddy	19-41	CB
Lonely Alone	Forrester Sisters	19-432	SC
Lonely And Gone	Montgomery Gentry	19-205	CB
Lonely And Gone	Montgomery Gentry	22-433	ST
Lonely Blue Boy	Twitty, Conway	45-93	HCK
Lonely Boy	Anka, Paul	3-505	SC
Lonely Boy	Gold, Andrew	24-206	SC
Lonely Days	Bee Gees	17-490	LE
Lonely Days	Bee Gees	22-932	SC
Lonely Eyes	Young, Chris	45-377	ASK
Lonely Eyes	Young, Chris	49-782	SSC
Lonely Hearts Club	Spears, Billie Jo	45-720	VH
Lonely Night (Angel Face)	Captain & Tennille	46-552	CB
Lonely Nights	Gilley, Mickey	22-227	CB
Lonely No More	Thomas, Rob	47-607	SC
Lonely Ol' Night	Mellencamp, John	45-419	CB
Lonely People	America	3-529	SC
Lonely Road Of Faith	Kid Rock	18-292	CB
Lonely Road Of Faith	Kid Rock	36-349	SC
Lonely Side Of Love	Loveless, Patty	14-681	CB
Lonely Side Of Love	Loveless, Patty	17-234	NA
Lonely Stranger	Clapton, Eric	13-793	SGB
Lonely Street	Williams, Andy	46-119	SC
Lonely Summer Nights	Stray Cats	48-167	SS
Lonely Teardrops	Wilson, Jackie	2-87	SC
Lonely Teenager	Dion & Belmonts	47-23	SC
Lonely Tonight - duet	Shelton & Monroe	45-329	CKC
Lonely Too Long	Loveless, Patty	1-732	CB
Lonely Too Long	Loveless, Patty	4-434	SC
Lonely Weekends	Jennings, Waylon	45-194	SSK
Lonely Weekends	Lewis, Jerry Lee	47-800	SRK
Lonely Wine	Orbison, Roy	47-344	FMK
Lonely Women Make Beautiful Lovers	Luman, Bob	5-565	SC
Lonely Won't Leave Me Alone	Adkins, Trace	8-32	CB
Lonely Won't Leave Me Alone	Adkins, Trace	7-734	CHM
Lonesome #1	Gibson, Don	43-284	CB
Lonesome 7-7203	Hawkins, Hankshaw	8-713	CB
Lonesome 7-7203	Lynn, Loretta	10-516	SF
Lonesome 77203	Ives, Burl	45-924	OZP
Lonesome Day	Springsteen, Bruce	18-598	ST
Lonesome Day	Springsteen, Bruce	32-28	THM

167

SONG TITLE	ARTIST	#	TYPE
Lonesome Dove the	Brooks, Garth	48-352	PT
Lonesome Loser	Little River Band	18-302	SC
Lonesome Number One	Gibson, Don	5-696	SC
Lonesome On'Ry Mean	Tritt, Travis	19-270	ST
Lonesome Orn'ry & Mean	Jennings, Waylon	26-194	DK
Lonesome Orn'ry & Mean	Jennings, Waylon	45-175	DK
Lonesome Road	Tennison, Chalee	18-458	ST
Lonesome Standard Time	Mattea, Kathy	6-133	MM
Lonesome Town	Nelson, Ricky	21-702	CB
Lonesome Waltz	Reeves, Jim	49-796	VH
Lonesome Whistle	Williams, Hank Sr.	14-232	CB
Lonesome Whistle (I Heard That)	Darin, Bobby	47-751	SRK
Lonestar	Jones, Norah	19-189	Z
Lonestar Beer	Stegal, Rod	47-489	OZP
Long Ago And Far Away	Taylor, James	45-540	CB
Long And Winding Road	Beatles	16-815	DK
Long And Winding Road	Beatles	13-153	P
Long As I Can See The Light	CCR	5-360	SC
Long As I Live	Montgomery, J M	14-211	CB
Long As I Live	Montgomery, J M	4-229	SC
Long Black Limousine	Haggard, Merle	49-819	SSK
Long Black Train	Turner, Josh	19-176	ST
Long Black Train	Turner, Josh	32-302	THM
Long Black Veil	Frizzell, Lefty	19-492	CB
Long Black Veil	Frizzell, Lefty	12-311	DK
Long Cool Woman In A Black Dress	Hollies	9-346	AH
Long Cool Woman in a Black Dress	Hollies	44-365	LG
Long Cool Woman In A Black Dress	Hollies	20-314	MH
Long Day	Matchbox 20	34-127	CB
Long Day	Matchbox 20	24-635	SC
Long Day Is Over the	Jones, Norah	19-193	Z
Long December a	Counting Crows	18-700	CB
Long Distance	Brandy	36-269	PHM
Long Distance Runaround	Yes	20-100	SC
Long Drive	Mraz, Jason	45-284	BKD
Long Gone Lonesome Blues	Williams, Hank Sr.	22-308	CB
Long Goodbye the	Brooks & Dunn	25-59	MM
Long Goodbye the	Brooks & Dunn	15-853	ST
Long Haired Country Boy	Charlie Daniels Band	4-546	SC
Long Haired Country Boy	Charlie Daniels Band	13-762	SGB
Long Haired Redneck	Coe, David Allan	18-311	CB
Long Hard Lesson Learned	Anderson, John	7-204	MM
Long Hard Lesson Learned	Anderson, John	4-239	SC
Long Hard Road	Nitty Gritty Dirt Band	19-413	SC

SONG TITLE	ARTIST	#	TYPE
Long Hard Road	Taff, Russ	20-655	SC
Long Hot Summer	Urban, Keith	38-45	PHM
Long Journey Home	Martin, Jimmy	8-263	CB
Long Legged Guitar Pickin' Man	Cash & Carter	29-719	CB
Long Legged Hannah...	Hunter, Jesse	2-574	SC
Long Line Of Losers	Montgomery Gentry	37-63	CB
Long Live Love	Newton-John, Olivia	49-55	ZVS
Long Live Love	Shaw, Sandie	10-591	SF
Long Lonely Nights	Andrews,L & Hearts	25-173	MM
Long Lonely Nights	McFatter, Clyde	10-337	SS
Long Long Ago	Standard	47-827	JVC
Long Long Texas Road	Drusky, Roy	20-747	CB
Long Long Time	Ronstadt, Linda	10-2	SC
Long Long Way	Jackson, Alan	49-238	DFK
Long Long Way To Go	Collins, Phil	44-15	SBI
Long Night	Corrs	49-201	SF
Long Road To Run	Foo Fighters	49-894	SC
Long Road To Run	Foo Fighters	48-224	SC
Long Run the	Eagles	7-553	BS
Long Run the	Eagles	2-254	SC
Long Shot	Baillie & The Boys	5-568	SC
Long Slow Kisses	Bates, Jeff	22-85	CB
Long Stretch Of Love - duet	Lady Antebellum	48-442	KCD
Long Tall Glasses (I Can Dance)	Sayer, Leo	47-479	SC
Long Tall Sally	Little Richard	15-276	DK
Long Tall Sally	Little Richard	13-57	P
Long Tall Sally	Little Richard	11-51	PX
Long Tall Sally	Little Richard	14-557	SC
Long Tall Sally	Presley, Elvis	18-542	KC
Long Tall Sally	Presley, Elvis	14-759	THM
Long Tall Texan	Supernaw, Doug	4-501	SC
Long Tall Texan	Supernaw/Beach Boys	7-385	MM
Long Tall Texan	Supernaw/Beach Boys	24-411	SC
Long Time	Boston	4-882	SC
Long Time Gone	Crosby Stills & Nash	12-866	P
Long Time Gone	Dixie Chicks	25-287	MM
Long Time Gone	Dixie Chicks	17-578	ST
Long Time Gone	Ritter, Tex	20-710	CB
Long Train Runnin'	Doobie Brothers	29-80	CB
Long Train Runnin'	Doobie Brothers	11-824	DK
Long Train Runnin'	Doobie Brothers	13-29	P
Long Trip Alone	Bentley, Dierks	30-195	CB
Long Walk a	Scott, Jill	33-387	CB
Long Walk a	Scott, Jill	25-683	MM
Long Way 2 Go	Cassie	30-60	PHM
Long Way Around	Eagle Eye Cherry	19-833	SGB
Long Way Around the	Dixie Chicks	30-338	CB
Long Way Down	Goo Goo Dolls	4-671	SC
Long Way To Fall	Parnell, Lee Roy	49-280	DFK
Long Way To Go	Jackson, Alan	49-180	CB
Long Way To Go	Jackson, Alan	49-237	DFK
Long White Cadillac	Yoakam, Dwight	49-682	SC

SONG TITLE	ARTIST	#	TYPE
Longer Boats	Stevens, Cat	46-161	SC
Longer Than	Fogelberg, Dan	10-359	KC
Longer Than	Fogelberg, Dan	9-209	SO
Longest Day the	Anka, Paul	45-598	OZP
Longest Time the	Joel, Billy	16-140	LE
Longest Time the	Joel, Billy	6-543	MM
Longfellow Serenade	Diamond, Neil	7-539	AH
Longfellow Serenade	Diamond, Neil	30-675	LE
Longfellow Serenade	Diamond, Neil	15-748	SC
Longhaired Redneck	Coe, David Allan	5-857	SC
Longneck Bottle	Brooks, Garth	8-151	CB
Longneck Bottle	Brooks, Garth	15-522	SC
Longneck Bottle	Brooks, Garth	22-411	ST
Longnecks Cigarettes	Leigh, Danni	14-170	CB
Longview	Green Day	19-287	SGB
Look At Little Sister	Vaughn, Stevie Ray	13-764	SGB
Look At Me	Holly, Buddy	47-891	ZM
Look At Me I'm Sandra Dee	Newton-John, Olivia	10-16	SC
Look At Me Now	Sixwire	16-709	ST
Look At Me Now	White, Bryan	24-126	SC
Look At Miss Ohio	Lambert, Miranda	46-256	KV
Look At Us	Gill, Vince	1-590	CB
Look At Us	Gill, Vince	9-536	SAV
Look At Us	Morgan, Craig	19-771	ST
Look At Us	Paris, Sarina	34-148	CB
Look At You	Big & Rich	49-781	SSC
Look Heart No Hands	Travis, Randy	10-759	JVC
Look In My Eyes	Chantels	25-178	MM
Look In My Eyes Pretty Woman	Orbison, Roy	47-350	LE
Look Of Love the	ABC	16-455	MH
Look Of Love the	Mendes & Brazil 66	16-733	DK
Look Of Love the	Mendez & Brazil 66	13-53	P
Look the	Roxette	11-513	DK
Look Through Any Window	Hollies	44-360	EK
Look Through My Eyes	Collins, Phil	44-31	KV
Look What Followed Me Home	Ball, David	22-859	ST
Look What The Cat Dragged In	Poison	21-776	SC
Look What They Done To My Song Ma	Melanie	28-261	DK
Look What They've Done To My Song	New Seekers	49-471	MM
Look What Thoughts Will Do	Frizzell, Lefty	19-487	CB
Lookin' For A Good Time	Lady Antebellum	36-601	CB
Lookin' For A Good Time	Lady Antebellum	36-197	PHM
Lookin' For Love	Lee, Johnny	29-629	CB
Lookin' For Love	Lee, Johnny	17-414	DK
Lookin' For Love	Lee, Johnny	12-431	P
Lookin' For Love	Lee, Johnny	8-678	SAV
Lookin' For Love	Sawyer Brown	22-592	ST
Lookin' For Love	Sawyer Brown	16-271	TT
Lookin' For That Girl	McGraw, Tim	43-134	PHN
Lookin' Out For #1	BTO	46-548	CB

SONG TITLE	ARTIST	#	TYPE
Lookin' Out My Back Door	CCR	34-69	CB
Lookin' Out My Back Door	CCR	11-340	DK
Lookin' Out My Back Door	CCR	13-8	P
Lookin' Out My Back Door	CCR	5-346	SC
Looking Back	Cole, Nat "King"	46-350	CB
Looking Back Now	Rose, Maggie	43-185	ASK
Looking Back To See	Browns	8-717	CB
Looking For A Love	J. Geils Band	46-324	SC
Looking For A New Love	Watley, Jodi	33-326	CB
Looking For A New Love	Watley, Jodi	11-787	DK
Looking For A Place To Land	Dakota Moon	24-85	MM
Looking For A Place To Shine - Nashville	Bowen, Clare	45-475	KVD
Looking For A Reason	Little Big Town	29-595	CB
Looking For A Stranger	Benatar, Pat	46-511	MH
Looking For Mr. Right	Jade	18-485	NU
Looking For The Light	Trevino, Rick	2-655	SC
Looking For The Light	Trevino, Rick	22-873	ST
Looking For Tomorrow	Tillis, Mel	45-844	VH
Looking Through The Eyes Of Love	Pitney, Gene	47-529	ZM
Looking Through Your Eyes	Corrs & White	17-667	PR
Looking Through Your Eyes	Rimes, LeAnn	8-725	CB
Looking Through Your Eyes	Twain, Shania	45-527	BS
Looking Up	John, Elton	47-699	DCK
Looks Like We Made It	Manilow, Barry	29-110	CB
Looks Like We Made It	Manilow, Barry	11-635	DK
Looks Like We Made It	Manilow, Barry	9-43	MM
Looks Like We Made it	Manilow, Barry	9-81	PS
Loose Talk	Smith, Carl	22-110	CB
Loose Talk	Smith, Carl	14-333	SC
Loosen Up My Strings	Black, Clint	8-762	CB
Loosen Up My Strings	Black, Clint	22-825	ST
Lord Have Mercy On A Country Boy	Williams, Don	17-353	DK
Lord Have Mercy On The Workin Man	Tritt, Travis	1-669	CB
Lord Have Mercy On The Workin Man	Tritt, Travis	10-755	JVC
Lord Have Mercy On The Workin Man	Tritt, Travis	2-1	SC
Lord Help Me Be The Kind Of Person	Bellamy Brothers	47-760	SRK
Lord I Hope This Day Is Good	Williams, Don	33-74	CB
Lord I Hope This Day Is Good	Williams, Don	3-600	SC
Lord I Hope This Day Is Good	Womack, Lee Ann	48-481	CKC
Lord Is That Me	Greene, Jack	43-349	CB
Lord Knows I'm Drinkin' the	Smith, Carl	8-806	CB

169

SONG TITLE	ARTIST	#	TYPE
Lord Knows I'm Drinking the	Smith, Cal	33-29	CB
Lord Loves The Drinking Man	Chesnutt, Mark	20-451	ST
Lord Mr. Ford	Reed, Jerry	20-722	SC
Lorelei	Styx	47-383	SC
Lose Control	Elliot, Missy	37-104	SC
Lose My Mind	Eldridge, Brett	45-134	SC
Lose Yourself **	Eminem	25-455	MM
Lose Yourself **	Eminem	32-13	THM
Loser	3 Doors Down	15-642	THM
Loser	3 Doors Down	18-566	TT
Losin' Kind Of Love	Dalton, Lacy J.	3-87	SC
Losing Grip	Lavigne, Avril	20-518	CB
Losing Grip	Lavigne, Avril	25-576	MM
Losing Grip	Lavigne, Avril	19-335	STP
Losing Grip	Lavigne, Avril	32-209	THM
Losing My Religion	REM	28-436	DK
Losing My Religion	REM	12-783	P
Losing My Touch	Keith, Toby	47-156	CB
Losing You	Lee, Brenda	47-727	DCK
Losing Your Love	Reeves, Jim	49-800	VH
Losing Your Love	Stewart, Larry	2-644	SC
Losing Your Love	Stewart, Larry	22-860	ST
Lost	Buble, Michael	38-172	SC
Lost	Hill, Faith	30-460	CB
Lost And Found	Brooks & Dunn	1-80	CB
Lost And Found	Brooks & Dunn	6-219	MM
Lost And Found	Brooks & Dunn	12-418	P
Lost Forever In Your Kisses	Parton & Rogers	4-315	SC
Lost Highway	Williams, Hank Sr.	45-700	CB
Lost His Love On Our First Date	Harris, EmmyLou	8-207	CB
Lost In Emotion	Lisa Lisa & Cult J	11-593	DK
Lost In France	Tyler, Bonnie	48-774	P
Lost In Love	Air Supply	35-159	CB
Lost In Love	Air Supply	15-523	CMC
Lost In Love	Air Supply	16-795	DK
Lost In The Feeling	Chesnutt, Mark	14-122	CB
Lost In The Fifties Tonight	Milsap, Ronnie	1-445	CB
Lost In The Fifties Tonight	Milsap, Ronnie	9-482	SAV
Lost In The Fifties Tonight	Milsap, Ronnie	2-10	SC
Lost In The Moment	Big & Rich	30-347	CB
Lost In This Moment (Radio Vers)	Big & Rich	38-208	SC
Lost In You	Brooks, Garth	22-497	ST
Lost In You	Minelli, Liza	8-504	PHT
Lost In Your Eyes	Gibson, Debbie	7-96	MM
Lost In Your Eyes	Jeff Healy Band	4-280	SC
Lost Inside Of You	Streisand, Barbra	49-549	PS
Lost On The Desert	Cash, Johnny	46-21	SSK
Lost Ones	Hill, Lauryn	19-726	CB
Lost Without Your Love	Bread	39-3	CB
Lost You Anyway	Keith, Toby	44-137	BKD

SONG TITLE	ARTIST	#	TYPE
Lost!	Coldplay	36-236	PHM
Lot Of Good	Jennings, Waylon	47-809	SRK
Lot Of Leavin' Left To Do	Bentley, Dierks	22-21	CB
Lot Of Things Different a	Chesney, Kenny	29-424	CB
Lot Of Things Different a	Chesney, Kenny	25-360	MM
Lot Of Things Different a	Chesney, Kenny	18-327	ST
Loud	Big & Rich	30-539	CB
Louie Louie	Kingsmen	11-688	DK
Louie Louie	Kingsmen	13-110	P
Louie Louie	Kingsmen	2-59	SC
Louisiana Hot Sauce	Kershaw, Sammy	14-117	CB
Louisiana Mama	Pitney, Gene	47-537	SAV
Louisiana Moon	Alabama	49-106	CDG
Louisiana Saturday Night	McDaniel, Mel	2-366	SC
Louisiana Woman Mississippi Man	Twitty & Lynn	8-110	CB
LOVE	Cole, Natalie	36-361	SC
Love	Kramer, Jana	48-199	BKD
Love	Lennon, John	30-302	RS
Love & Affection	Nelson	24-683	SC
Love A Little Stronger	Diamond Rio	6-602	MM
Love A Little Stronger	Diamond Rio	2-806	SC
Love Ain't Like That	Hill, Faith	8-328	CB
Love Ain't Like That	Hill, Faith	7-824	CHT
Love Ain't Like That	Hill, Faith	22-709	ST
Love And Marriage	Sinatra, Frank	27-405	DK
Love And Marriage	Sinatra, Frank	2-864	SC
Love And Marriage	Sinatra, Frank	21-218	SGB
Love And Negotiation	Johnson, Carolyn D.	30-48	CB
Love And Understanding	Cher	15-128	SGB
Love At First Sight	Blige & Method Man	32-346	THM
Love At First Sight	Minogue, Kylie	18-226	CB
Love At First Sight	Minogue, Kylie	25-311	MM
Love At First Sight	Minogue, Kylie	21-729	TT
Love At The Five And Dime	Mattea, Kathy	1-181	CB
Love Ballad	Benson, George	12-820	P
Love Bites	Def Leppard	35-189	CB
Love Bites	Def Leppard	4-81	SC
Love Boat the	TV Themes	2-171	SC
Love Boat Theme	Jones, Jack	29-488	LE
Love Bug	Jones, George	8-336	CB
Love Bug	Strait, George	8-174	CB
Love Bug	Strait, George	6-506	MM
Love Bug (Bite Me)	South Sixty Five	14-78	CB
Love By Grace	Fabian, Lara	17-720	THM
Love Calls	Kem	32-421	THM
Love Can Build A Bridge	Judds	1-139	CB
Love Can Build A Bridge	Judds	12-39	DK
Love Can Build A Bridge	Judds	6-203	MM
Love Can't Ever Get Better	Skaggs & White	5-450	SC
Love Changes Everything	Lines, Aaron	25-619	MM
Love Changes Everything	Lines, Aaron	19-53	ST
Love Child	Ross, Diana	35-82	CB

SONG TITLE	ARTIST	#	TYPE
Love Child	Ross, Diana	15-367	LE
Love Child	Ross, Diana	4-520	SC
Love Child	Supremes	11-755	DK
Love Child	Supremes	5-10	SC
Love Come Down	King, Ben E.	11-463	DK
Love Come Down	King, Evelyn C.	27-354	DK
Love Come Down - Pt. 1	King, Evelyn C.	15-40	SS
Love Come Down - Pt. 2	King, Evelyn C.	15-41	SS
Love Coming Down	Presley, Elvis	25-105	MM
Love Didn't Do It	Davis, Linda	6-609	MM
Love Didn't Do It	Davis, Linda	17-238	NA
Love Didn't Do It	Davis, Linda	2-316	SC
Love Don't Care Who's Heart It Brea	Conley, Earl Thomas	12-405	P
Love Don't Cost A Thing	Lopez, Jennifer	16-116	PRT
Love Don't Cost A Thing	Lopez, Jennifer	17-714	THM
Love Don't Live Here	Lady Antebellum	36-559	CB
Love Don't Live Here Anymore	Madonna	14-900	SC
Love Don't Love You Anymore	Vandross, Luther	48-293	MM
Love Don't Run	Holy, Steve	38-106	CB
Love Done Gone	Currington, Billy	43-313	CB
Love Game	Lady Gaga	38-191	SC
Love Gets Me Every Time	Twain, Shania	8-125	CB
Love Gets Me Every Time	Twain, Shania	22-639	ST
Love Gravy **	Chef	13-717	SGB
Love Grows	Edison Lighthouse	4-323	SC
Love Hangover	Ross, Diana	33-297	CB
Love Hangover	Ross, Diana	11-773	DK
Love Happens Like That	McCoy, Neal	8-732	CB
Love Happens Like That	McCoy, Neal	22-818	ST
Love Has No Right	Royal, Billy Joe	29-650	SC
Love Her Madly	Doors	33-277	CB
Love Her Madly	Doors	18-646	SO
Love Hurts	Cher	15-122	SGB
Love Hurts	Incubus	36-272	PHM
Love Hurts	Nazareth	7-490	MM
Love Hurts	Nazareth	3-474	SC
Love Hurts	Orbison, Roy	38-64	PS
Love I Lost the	Melvin & Bluenotes	27-237	DK
Love I Lost the	Melvin & Bluenotes	12-916	P
Love In An Elevator	Aerosmith	2-730	SC
Love In The Club	Usher feat Young Jeezy	36-482	CB
Love In The Dark	Adele	46-86	DCK
Love In The First Degree	Alabama	13-468	P
Love In The First Degree	Alabama	9-479	SAV
Love In The First Degree	Bananarama	48-566	DK
Love In The Hot Afternoon	Watson, Gene	14-667	CB
Love In The Hot Afternoon	Watson, Gene	7-154	MM
Love In This Club	Usher	48-594	DK
Love Is	Elam, Katrina	30-204	CB
Love Is	Williams&McKnight	6-332	MM

SONG TITLE	ARTIST	#	TYPE
Love Is	Williams&McKnight	12-746	P
Love Is - duet	McKnight & Williams	34-113	CB
Love Is A Battlefield	Benatar, Pat	28-282	DK
Love Is A Battlefield	Benatar, Pat	3-613	SC
Love Is A Beautiful Thing	Vassar, Phil	36-404	CB
Love Is A Drug	Jypsi	36-554	CB
Love Is A Gift	Newton-John, Olivia	45-588	OZP
Love Is A Good Thing	Paycheck, Johnny	22-43	CB
Love Is A Losing Game	Winehouse, Amy	49-59	ZVS
Love Is A Many Splendored Thing	Cole, Nat "King"	16-773	DK
Love Is A Many Splendored Thing	Four Aces	48-762	P
Love Is A Many Splendored Thing	Standard	35-30	CB
Love Is A Rose	Ronstadt, Linda	29-631	CB
Love Is A Stranger	Eurythmics	47-76	LE
Love Is A Sweet Thing	Hill, Faith	9-392	CB
Love Is A Wonderful Thing	Bolton, Michael	35-201	CB
Love Is A Wonderful Thing	Bolton, Michael	9-670	SAV
Love Is Alive	Judds	1-146	CB
Love Is Alive	Judds	9-528	SAV
Love is Alive	Wright, Gary	4-56	SC
Love Is All	Anthony, Marc	17-732	PS
Love Is All Around	Troggs	46-312	SC
Love is All Around	Wet Wet Wet	12-181	DK
Love Is All That Matters	Carmen, Eric	46-562	KV
Love Is All That Really Matters	Sharp, Kevin	8-461	CB
Love Is All That Really Matters	Sharp, Kevin	22-792	ST
Love Is Always Seventeen	Gates, David	24-242	SC
Love Is An Open Door - duet - Frozen	Bell & Fontana	43-189	SBIG
Love Is Beautiful a	Bolton, Michael	4-167	SC
Love Is Blue	Williams, Andy	45-605	OZP
Love Is Enough	3 Of Hearts	15-106	ST
Love Is For Giving	Berry, John	8-981	CB
Love Is For Giving	Berry, John	16-197	THM
Love Is Gone	Willis, Chris	49-911	SC
Love Is Here & Now You're Gone	Ross, Diana	48-546	DK
Love Is Here And Now You're Gone	Supremes	14-887	DK
Love Is Here To Stay	Sinatra, Frank	14-274	MM
Love Is In The Air	Young, Paul	9-48	MM
Love Is Just A Four Letter Word	Baez, Joan	49-772	PS
Love Is Just A Game	Gatlin, Larry	47-104	CB
Love Is Like A Butterfly	Parton, Dolly	4-313	SC
Love Is Looking For You	Lambert, Miranda	44-395	KV
Love is My Religion	Marley, Ziggy	36-190	PHM
Love Is No Excuse - duet	Reeves & West, D	45-263	SSK
Love Is On A Roll	Williams, Don	4-491	SC
Love Is Only A Feeling	Darkness	29-229	ZM

171

SONG TITLE	ARTIST	#	TYPE
Love Is Strange	Holly, Buddy	47-883	ZM
Love Is Strange	Mickey & Sylvia	4-243	SC
Love Is Strange	Rogers & Parton	6-237	MM
Love Is Stronger Than Pride	Ricochet	16-660	CHM
Love Is Stronger Than Pride	Ricochet	24-165	SC
Love Is The Answer	England Dan&Coley	15-739	SC
Love Is The Foundation	Lynn, Loretta	47-626	CB
Love Is The Power	Bolton, Michael	4-607	SC
Love Is The Right Place	White, Bryan	7-679	CHM
Love Is The Right Place	White, Bryan	22-615	ST
Love Is Thicker Than Water	Gibb, Andy	11-442	DK
Love Is Thicker Than Water	Gibb, Andy	20-360	SC
Love Lessons	Byrd, Tracy	20-108	CB
Love Lessons	Byrd, Tracy	7-87	MM
Love Lessons	Byrd, Tracy	3-536	SC
Love Letter	Raitt, Bonnie	43-114	SC
Love Letters	Cole, Nat "King"	46-375	ZM
Love Letters	Lambert, Miranda	46-259	KV
Love Letters	Moyet, Allison	11-25	PX
Love Letters	Moyet, Allison	43-86	SF
Love Letters	Presley, Elvis	13-91	P
Love Letters In The Sand	Boone, Pat	35-7	CB
Love Letters In The Sand	Boone, Pat	11-454	DK
Love Letters In The Sand	Boone, Pat	13-69	P
Love Letters In The Sand	Cline, Patsy	45-517	JTG
Love Letters In The Sand	Lettermen	48-537	L1
Love Lies Bleeding	John, Elton	13-670	SGB
Love Like Crazy	Brice, Lee	45-548	CB
Love Like Mine - Nashville	Panettiere, Hayden	45-464	BKD
Love Like Ours	Streisand, Barbra	15-286	PS
Love Like That a	Herndon, Ty	14-73	CB
Love Like That a	Herndon, Ty	22-562	ST
Love Like There's No Tomorrow	Tippin & Tippin	25-450	MM
Love Like There's No Tomorrow	Tippin, Aaron	18-792	ST
Love Like This	Evans, Faith	15-524	SGB
Love Lite	Caldwell, Bobby	24-20	SC
Love Lockdown	West, Kanye	49-906	SC
Love Love Love	Pierce, Webb	4-857	SC
Love Loves A Long Night	Morgan, Craig	48-281	PHN
Love Machine	Robinson, Smokey	46-133	SC
Love Machine (Part 1)	Robinson, Smokey	48-550	DK
Love Machine Part 1	Miracles	17-153	DK
Love Makes The World Go Round	Como, Perry	49-41	ZVS
Love Me	Bieber, Justin	36-58	ASK
Love Me	Presley, Elvis	2-592	SC
Love Me	Raye, Collin	1-122	CB
Love Me	Raye, Collin	6-205	MM
Love Me	Raye, Collin	9-540	SAV
Love Me	Raye, Collin	2-19	SC

SONG TITLE	ARTIST	#	TYPE
Love Me A Litle Bit Longer	Myles, Heather	14-609	SC
Love Me Again	Newman, John	43-162	PHM
Love Me Bad	Durbin, James	38-264	PHM
Love Me Do	Beatles	11-681	DK
Love Me Do	Beatles	12-723	P
Love Me Do	Beatles	29-335	SC
Love Me For A Reason	Osmonds	47-856	ZM
Love Me If You Can	Keith, Toby	30-472	CB
Love Me Like A Man	Raitt, Bonnie	15-21	SC
Love Me Like You Do	Boyce Avenue	48-511	KVD
Love Me Like You Mean It	Ballerini, Kelsea	45-456	SSC
Love Me Like You Used To	Tucker, Tanya	16-340	CB
Love Me Like You Used To	Tucker, Tanya	5-47	SC
Love Me Love Me Love	Mills, Frank	49-251	DFK
Love Me Over Again	Williams, Don	4-776	SC
Love Me Tender	Presley, Elvis	16-723	DK
Love Me Tender	Presley, Elvis	6-260	MM
Love Me Tender	Presley, Elvis	2-591	SC
Love Me Tender	Presley, Elvis	14-760	THM
Love Me Tonight	Jones, Tom	12-655	P
Love Me Tonight	Presley, Elvis	25-317	MM
Love Me Tonight	Williams, Don	4-578	SC
Love Me Two Times	Doors	18-647	SO
Love Me With All Your Heart	Humperdinck, E.	37-163	CB
Love Me With All Your Heart	Williams, Andy	49-212	MM
Love Needs A Heart	Browne, Jackson	23-614	BS
Love Needs A Holiday	McEntire, Reba	29-187	CB
Love Of A Lifetime	Firehouse	16-570	SC
Love Of A Lifetime	Gatlin, Larry	47-110	CB
Love Of A Woman	Tritt, Travis	15-185	ST
Love Of My Life	Kershaw, Sammy	8-139	CB
Love Of My Life	Kershaw, Sammy	22-414	ST
Love Of My Life	McKnight, Brian	33-402	CB
Love Oh Love	Richie, Lionel	47-784	SRK
Love On A Two Way Street	Moments	27-325	DK
Love On a Two Way Street	Moments	25-279	MM
Love On Arrival	Seals, Dan	6-540	MM
Love On The Loose Heart	McBride & The Ride	2-357	SC
Love On The Rocks	Diamond, Neil	7-540	AH
Love On The Rocks	Diamond, Neil	30-681	LE
Love On The Rocks	Diamond, Neil	30-507	THM
Love On Top	Beyonce	48-389	MRH
Love On Your Mind	Xscape	15-758	NU
Love Or Something Like It	Rogers, Kenny	5-768	SC
Love Or The Lack Thereof	Francis, Cleve	2-395	SC
Love Out Loud	Conley, Earl Thomas	34-288	CB
Love Pang	Franklin, Aretha	36-168	JT

SONG TITLE	ARTIST	#	TYPE
Love Plus One	Haircut One Hundred	21-402	SC
Love Potion # 9	Searchers	11-421	DK
Love Potion # 9	Searchers	6-656	MM
Love Potion # 9	Searchers	12-661	P
Love Put A Song In My Heart	Rodriguez, Johnny	22-52	CB
Love Put A Song In My Heart	Rodriguez, Johnny	37-280	SC
Love Rears It's Ugly Head	Living Colour	6-45	SC
Love Remains	Raye, Collin	1-135	CB
Love Remains	Raye, Collin	7-336	MM
Love Remains	Raye, Collin	4-236	SC
Love Remains The Same	Rossdale, Gavin	36-525	CB
Love Remembers	Morgan, Craig	36-594	CB
Love Rollercoaster	Ohio Players	2-504	SC
Love Shack	B-52-s	16-520	P
Love Shack	B-52-s	2-43	SC
Love Shack	B-52-s	10-525	SF
Love She Can't Live Without	Black, Clint	14-74	CB
Love She Can't Live Without	Black, Clint	13-848	CHM
Love She Can't Live Without	Black, Clint	19-255	CSZ
Love Sneakin' Up On You	Raitt, Bonnie	2-113	SC
Love So Right	Bee Gees	17-500	LE
Love Somebody	Maroon 5	44-147	BKD
Love Someone	Mraz, Jason	47-302	KV
Love Someone Like Me	Dunn, Holly	6-744	MM
Love Song	Bareilles, Sara	36-454	CB
Love Song	Bareilles, Sara	37-23	PS
Love Song	Lambert, Miranda	46-248	AC
Love Song	Murray, Anne	15-67	CB
Love Song	Murray, Anne	11-2	PL
Love Song	Murray, Anne	2-638	SC
Love Song	Oak Ridge Boys	47-330	VH
Love Song the	Bates, Jeff	25-520	MM
Love Song the	Bates, Jeff	18-786	ST
Love Song the	Bates, Jeff	32-114	THM
Love Stinks	J. Geils Band	46-586	SC
Love Story	Swift, Taylor	36-5	PT
Love Story	Williams, Andy	13-556	LE
Love Story In The Making	Davis, Linda	7-233	MM
Love Story In The Making	Davis, Linda	4-226	SC
Love Story In The Making a	Davis, Linda	22-886	ST
Love T.K.O.	Pendergrass, Teddy	15-718	LE
Love Takes Care Of Me	Greene, Jack	43-345	CB
Love Takes Time	Carey, Mariah	34-86	CB
Love Talks	McDowell, Ronnie	47-230	CB
Love That We Lost the	Wright, Chely	4-156	SC
Love The One You're With	Stills, Stephen	33-278	CB
Love The One You're	Stills, Stephen	10-356	KC

SONG TITLE	ARTIST	#	TYPE
With			
Love The One You're With	Stills, Stephen	2-784	SC
Love The One You're With	Vandross, Luther	48-285	KV
Love The World Away	Rogers, Kenny	4-772	SC
Love Theme from A Star Is Born	Streisand, Barbra	49-625	TOS
Love Thing	Spice Girls	28-185	SF
Love To Burn	Collie, Mark	16-644	MM
Love To Love You Baby	Summer, Donna	15-201	LE
Love To Love You Baby	Summer, Donna	24-337	SC
Love Touch	Stewart, Rod	48-541	DK
Love Train	O'Jays	35-115	CB
Love Train	O'Jays	26-398	DK
Love Train	O'Jays	13-180	P
Love Train	O'Jays	9-227	PT
Love Train	O'Jays	9-770	SAV
Love Travels	Mattea, Kathy	8-136	CB
Love Travels	Mattea, Kathy	22-635	ST
Love Trip	Kilgore, Jerry	14-696	CB
Love Trip	Kilgore, Jerry	5-724	SC
Love Trip	Kilgore, Jerry	22-384	ST
Love Will Always Win	Brooks & Yearwood	29-195	CB
Love Will Always Win - duet	Yearwood & Brooks	49-345	CB
Love Will Conquer All	Richie, Lionel	47-457	LE
Love Will Find A Way	Pablo Cruise	5-607	SC
Love Will Find It's Way	McEntire, Reba	1-792	CB
Love Will Keep Us Alive	Eagles	17-168	SC
Love Will Keep Us Alive	Eagles	30-752	SF
Love Will Keep Us Together	Captain & Tennille	26-102	DK
Love Will Keep Us Together	Captain & Tennille	9-9	MH
Love Will Keep Us Together	Captain & Tennille	12-831	P
Love Will Lead You Back	Dayne, Taylor	17-92	DK
Love Will Lead You Back	Dayne, Taylor	6-100	MM
Love Will Never Do	Jackson, Janet	21-457	CB
Love Will Never Do	Jackson, Janet	15-418	PS
Love Will Save The Day	Houston, Whitney	43-372	CB
Love Will Set You Free	Humperdinck, E.	49-254	DFK
Love Will Turn You Around	Rogers, Kenny	4-483	SC
Love Without End Amen	Strait, George	1-258	CB
Love Without End Amen	Strait, George	11-705	DK
Love Without End Amen	Strait, George	4-61	SC
Love Without Mercy	Parnell, Lee Roy	49-274	SC
Love Won't Let Me	Cochran, Tammy	18-592	ST
Love Won't Let Me	Cochran, Tammy	32-155	THM
Love Won't Let Me Wait	Harris, Major	28-108	DK
Love Working On You	Montgomery, J M	14-216	CB
Love Working On You	Montgomery, J M	22-781	ST
Love You	Ingram, Jack	30-87	CB
Love You Ain't Seen The Last of Me	Byrd, Tracy	9-410	CB
Love You Ain't Seen The	Byrd, Tracy	13-831	CHM

SONG TITLE	ARTIST	#	TYPE
Last Of Me			
Love You Back	Akins, Rhett	4-499	SC
Love You For A Day	Martin, Ricky	9-132	PS
Love You For A Day	Martin, Ricky	13-737	SGB
Love You Inside Out	Bee Gees	48-680	CB
Love You Inside Out	Bee Gees	48-688	JV
Love You Like That	Smith, Canaan	48-743	KCD
Love You Out Loud	Rascal Flatts	25-515	MM
Love You Out Loud	Rascal Flatts	18-784	ST
Love You Out Loud	Rascal Flatts	32-150	THM
Love You Save the	Rose, Rusty	17-373	DK
Love You With All My Heart	Evans, Sara	36-595	CB
Love Your Love The Most	Church, Eric	44-217	CB
Love Your Man	Joey & Rory	45-816	BKD
Love Yourself	Bieber, Justin	48-621	DCK
Love Yourself	Bieber, Justin	48-629	SF
Love's Been A Little Bit Hard On Me	Newton, Juice	33-42	CB
Love's Been A Little Bit Hard On Me	Newton, Juice	2-136	SC
Love's Gonna Fall Here Tonight	Bailey, Razzy	29-388	CB
Love's Gonna Live Here Again	Owens, Buck	15-81	CB
Love's Gonna Live Here Again	Owens, Buck	12-36	DK
Love's Gonna Make It Alright	Strait, George	38-215	PHN
Love's Got A Hold On You	Jackson, Alan	1-39	CB
Love's Got An Attitude	Dalley, Amy	34-393	CB
Love's Got An Attitude	Dalley, Amy	24-570	MM
Love's Got An Attitude	Dalley, Amy	18-801	ST
Love's Got An Attitude	Dalley, Amy	32-300	THM
Love's Made A Fool Of You	Holly, Buddy	49-81	ZPA
Love's Taken Over	Moore, Chanti	9-851	SAV
Love's The Answer	Tucker, Tanya	14-254	SC
Love's The Only House	McBride, Martina	29-531	CB
Love's The Only House	McBride, Martina	22-524	ST
Love's The Only Voice	Conley, E.T.	47-603	CB
Lovebug	Jonas Brothers	36-518	CB
Loved Too Much	Herndon, Ty	7-628	CHM
Lovefool	Cardigans	24-640	SC
Lovely Hula Hands	Beamer,Keola/Kapona	6-833	MM
Lovely To See You	Moody Blues	28-140	DK
Lover (When You're Near Me)	Streisand, Barbra	49-385	PS
Lover Come Back To Me	Cole, Nat "King"	46-352	SAV
Lover Come Back To Me	Lee, Brenda	45-910	TO
Lover Come Back To Me	Standard	17-363	DK
Lover For Life	Houston, Whitney	48-638	PS
Lover In Me the	Easton, Sheena	16-529	P
Lover Lover	Niemann, Jerrod	47-325	CB
Lover Man	Streisand, Barbra	49-380	PS
Lover Of The Light	Mumford & Sons	39-119	PHM

SONG TITLE	ARTIST	#	TYPE
Lover Please	Etheridge, Melissa	47-63	ASK
Lover Please	McPhatter, Clyde	5-520	SC
Lover Please	Swan, Billy	47-538	VH
Lover's Concerto a	Toys	11-563	DK
Lover's Cross	Croce, Jim	19-351	PS
Lover's Cross	Croce, Jim	29-644	SC
Lover's Groove	Immature	24-288	SC
Lover's Holiday	Change	30-743	SF
Lover's Holiday a	Change	30-743	SF
Lover's Prayer	Ho, Don	6-828	MM
Loverboy	Mariah	35-269	CB
Lovergirl	Marie, Teena	18-374	AH
Lovergirl	Marie, Teena	24-567	SC
Lovers In Japan	Coldplay	36-271	PHM
Loves Me Like A Rock	Simon & Garfunkel	49-762	LG
Loves Me Like A Rock	Simon, Paul	3-615	SC
Lovesick Blues	Cline, Patsy	45-502	KV
Lovesick Blues	Mills & Friend	10-559	SF
Lovesick Blues	Williams, Hank Sr.	19-845	CB
Lovesick Blues	Williams, Hank Sr.	13-367	P
Lovesick Blues	Williams, Hank Sr.	9-622	SAV
Lovesick Blues	Williams, Hank Sr.	5-215	SC
Lovesong	Adele	40-34	ASK
Lovin' A Hurricane	Bogguss, Suzy	1-564	CB
Lovin' All Night	Crowell, Rodney	2-330	SC
Lovin' All Night	Loveless, Patty	35-430	CB
Lovin' All Night	Loveless, Patty	25-641	MM
Lovin' All Night	Loveless, Patty	19-180	ST
Lovin' All Night	Loveless, Patty	32-304	THM
Lovin' Each Day	Keating, Ronan	23-95	SC
Lovin' Her Was Easier	Jennings, Waylon	1-621	CB
Lovin' Her Was Easier (Than Any...	Chesnutt, Mark	49-739	CB
Lovin' Her Was Easier (Than...)	Miller, Roger	22-286	CB
Lovin' On Back Streets	Street, Mel	29-655	SC
Lovin' Touchin' Squeezin'	Journey	15-166	MH
Lovin' Touchin' Squeezin'	Journey	3-531	SC
Lovin' You	Ripperton, Minnie	7-469	MM
Lovin' You	Ripperton, Minnie	22-930	SC
Lovin' You Against My Will	Allan, Gary	9-399	CB
Lovin' You Is Fun	Corbin, Easton	44-392	KV
Loving Arms	Dixie Chicks	8-478	CB
Loving Blind	Black, Clint	1-112	CB
Loving Blind	Black, Clint	12-399	P
Loving Blind	Black, Clint	30-425	THM
Loving Cajun Style	Rich, Don	49-404	SCK
Loving Every Minute	Wills, Mark	15-95	ST
Loving Her Was Easier	Kristofferson, Kris	45-203	DCK
Loving It Up	Bell & James	9-769	SAV
Loving Up A Storm	Bailey, Razzy	29-379	CB
Loving You	Presley, Elvis	15-525	MM
Loving You	Riperton, Minnie	33-279	CB
Loving You Easy	Zac Brown Band	45-51	BKD

SONG TITLE	ARTIST	#	TYPE
Loving You Makes Me A Better Man	Gill, Vince	5-804	SC
Low	Clarkson, Kelly	19-648	CB
Low	Clarkson, Kelly	20-223	MM
Low	Clarkson, Kelly	32-394	THM
Low	Flo Rida	45-647	DKM
Low	Foo Fighters	23-172	PHM
Low Rider	War	4-86	SC
Lowdown	Scaggs, Boz	7-97	MM
Lowspark Of High Heeled Boys	Traffic	13-654	SGB
Lubbock Or Leave It	Dixie Chicks	30-360	CB
Lucille	Everly Brothers	45-866	VH
Lucille	Jennings, Waylon	22-148	CK
Lucille	Little Richard	16-858	DK
Lucille	Little Richard	14-340	SC
Lucille	Rogers, Kenny	8-26	CB
Lucille	Rogers, Kenny	16-871	DK
Lucille	Rogers, Kenny	8-656	SAV
Lucille	Rogers, Kenny	48-130	SC
Lucille (You Won't Do Your Daddy..)	Jennings, Waylon	4-735	SC
Luck Be A Lady	Sinatra, Frank	12-155	DK
Luck Be A Lady	Sinatra, Frank	21-210	SGB
Luck Be A Lady	Streisand, Barbra	49-563	PS
Luckenbach Texas	Jennings, Waylon	1-622	CB
Luckenbach Texas	Jennings, Waylon	22-137	CK
Luckenbach Texas	Jennings, Waylon	17-3	DK
Luckenbach Texas	Jennings, Waylon	13-463	P
Luckenbach Texas	Jennings, Waylon	8-685	SAV
Luckiest Man In The World	McCoy, Neal	18-469	ST
Luckiest Man In The World the	McCoy, Neal	32-7	THM
Lucky	Etheridge, Melissa	47-67	PHR
Lucky	Spears, Britney	14-3	PHM
Lucky	Spears, Britney	14-506	SC
Lucky 4 You (Tonite I'm Just Me)	SheDaisy	22-572	ST
Lucky In Love	Austin, Sherrie	7-663	CHM
Lucky Man	Emerson Lake Palmer	3-519	SC
Lucky Man	Montgomery Gentry	30-337	CB
Lucky Me Lucky You	Parnell, Lee Roy	7-630	CHM
Lucky Moon	Oak Ridge Boys	23-497	CB
Lucky One	Branigan, Laura	16-634	MM
Lucky One	Grant, Amy	6-639	MM
Lucky One the	Hill, Faith	29-192	CB
Lucky One the	Krauss, Alison	25-55	MM
Lucky One the	Krauss, Alison	16-41	ST
Lucky Ones	Del Rey, Lana	49-24	KV
Lucky Star	Madonna	12-847	P
Lucky Strike	Maroon 5	39-111	PHM
Lucy In The Sky With Diamonds	Beatles	33-250	CB
Lucy In The Sky With Diamonds	Beatles	15-274	DK
Lucy In The Sky With Diamonds	Beatles	12-872	P

SONG TITLE	ARTIST	#	TYPE
Lucy In The Sky With Diamonds	Beatles	7-521	SAV
Lucy In The Sky With Diamonds	Beatles	2-761	SC
Luka	Vega, Suzanne	9-324	AG
Luka	Vega, Suzanne	9-13	MH
Lullaby In Blue	Midler, Bette	13-705	SGB
Lullaby Of Birdland	Vaughn, Sarah	10-709	JVC
Lullaby Of Broadway	Andrew Sisters	46-423	EK
Lullaby Of Broadway	Day, Doris	48-141	LE
Lullaby Of Broadway	Standard	11-817	DK
Lullaby Of Broadway	Standard	9-808	SAV
Lullaby Of Clubland	Everything B T Girl	17-718	THM
Lullabye	Mullins, Shawn	14-288	MM
Lullabye	Mullins, Shawn	7-779	PHT
Lullabye	Mullins, Shawn	13-711	SGB
Lullabye Goodnight My Angel	Joel, Billy	12-269	DK
Lullabye Goodnight My Angel	Joel, Billy	2-120	SC
Lumberjack Song	Python, Monty	23-27	SC
Lump	Presidents of USA	24-748	SC
Luther Played The Boogie	Cash, Johnny	22-243	SC
Lydia The Tattooed Lady	Marx, Groucho	47-926	KV
Lyin' Eyes	Eagles	7-554	BS
Lyin' Eyes	Eagles	6-433	MM
Lyin' Eyes	Eagles	2-256	SC
Lyin' In His Arms Again	Forrester Sisters	26-570	DK
Lying In A Moment	Herndon, Ty	7-337	MM
Lynda	Wariner, Steve	29-75	CB
Lynda	Wariner, Steve	5-319	SC
Ma Belle Amie	Tee Set	16-666	LC
Macarena	Los Del Rios	10-684	HE
Macarena	Los Del Rios	7-567	THM
Macarena (Bayside Boyz Mix)	Los Del Rios	13-612	P
Macarena (Female only) - DANCE #	Los Del Rios	22-388	SC
MacArthur Park	Monro, Matt	11-60	PT
MacArthur Park	Summer, Donna	35-148	CB
MacArthur Park	Summer, Donna	11-715	DK
MacArthur Park	Summer, Donna	13-134	P
MacArthur Park	Summer, Donna	4-850	SC
Mach 5	Presidents of USA	24-641	SC
Machinery	Easton, Sheena	15-526	CMC
Macho Man	Village People	35-142	CB
Macho Man	Village People	9-217	PT
Mack The Knife	Armstrong, Louis	46-443	LE
Mack The Knife	Darin, Bobby	11-110	DK
Mack The Knife	Darin, Bobby	7-189	MM
Mad	Dudley, Dave	43-293	CB
Mad About You	Carlisle, Belinda	28-273	DK
Mad About You	Carlisle, Belinda	4-538	SC
Mad Issues	Stone, Angie	25-692	MM
Mad Over You	Crawford, Randy	24-266	SC
Mad Season	Matchbox 20	35-229	CB

SONG TITLE	ARTIST	#	TYPE
Mad Season	Matchbox 20	15-458	PHM
Made For Loving You	Stone, Doug	20-600	CB
Made For Loving You	Stone, Doug	6-311	MM
Made In America - Patriotic	Keith, Toby	38-165	PHM
Made In England	John, Elton	3-437	SC
Made In Japan	Owens, Buck	46-105	CB
Made You Look	Nas	32-51	THM
Madman Across The Water	John, Elton	46-132	SC
Magazine	Christy, Lauren	7-718	PHM
Maggie May	Stewart, Rod	15-177	MH
Maggie May	Stewart, Rod	25-598	MM
Maggie's Farm	Dylan, Bob	29-102	CB
Magic	Coldplay	46-187	BHK
Magic	Newton-John, Olivia	33-275	CB
Magic	Newton-John, Olivia	11-498	DK
Magic	Pilot	15-744	SC
Magic	Thicke, Robin	36-520	CB
Magic Bus	Who	28-145	DK
Magic Bus	Who	19-734	LE
Magic Carpet Ride	Steppenwolf	11-502	DK
Magic Carpet Ride	Steppenwolf	13-227	P
Magic Carpet Ride	Steppenwolf	3-259	SC
Magic Man	Heart	6-489	MM
Magic Man	Heart	12-697	P
Magic Man	Heart	2-147	SC
Magic Moments	Como, Perry	16-411	PR
Magic Power	Triumph	23-106	SC
Magic Stick - Duet	Lil Kim & 50 Cent	32-387	THM
Magic Touch the	Platters	27-219	DK
Maiden's Prayer	Wills, Bob	20-692	CB
Mailman Bring Me No More Blues	Holly, Buddy	45-718	VH
Main Event Fight the	Streisand, Barbra	49-550	PS
Mainstreet	Seger, Bob	20-319	MH
Mainstreet	Seger, Bob	3-451	SC
Mainstreet	Seger, Bob	10-171	UK
Mairzy Doats	Pied Pipers	4-193	SC
Make A Mistake With Me	Paisley, Brad	49-507	PCD
Make A Move	Incubus	30-224	PHM
Make Believe (Till We Can...) - duet	Wells & Foley	48-203	CB
Make Her Fall In Love With Me Song	Strait, George	45-684	VH
Make It Easy On Yourself	Butler & Impression	7-471	MM
Make It Happen	Carey, Mariah	6-173	MM
Make It Like It Was	Belle, Regina	16-552	P
Make It Mine	Mraz, Jason	44-386	CB
Make It Real	Jets	11-390	DK
Make It With You	Bread	11-229	DK
Make It With You	Bread	13-128	P
Make It With You	Carpenters	44-344	OZP
Make Love Easy	Jackson, Freddie	18-486	NU
Make Me Lose Control	Carmen, Eric	11-319	DK
Make Me Wanna	Rhett, Thomas	45-180	SSC
Make Me Your Baby	Lewis, Barbara	20-69	SC

SONG TITLE	ARTIST	#	TYPE
Make Someone Happy	Como, Perry	25-260	MM
Make Someone Happy	Durante, Jimmy	20-769	KB
Make Someone Happy	Standard	9-579	SAV
Make Someone Happy	Streisand, Barbra	49-594	PS
Make That Move	Shalamar	15-38	SS
Make The World Go Away	Arnold, Eddy	19-33	CB
Make The World Go Away	Arnold, Eddy	13-480	P
Make The World Go Away	Arnold, Eddy	8-659	SAV
Make The World Go Away	Arnold, Eddy	2-193	SC
Make The World Go Away	Arnold, Eddy	17-622	THM
Make This Day	Zac Brown Band	46-73	DFK
Make This Day	Zac Brown Band	49-725	KV
Make To World Go Away	Arnold, Eddy	11-434	DK
Make Up In Love	Stone, Doug	19-208	CB
Make Up In Love	Stone, Doug	14-629	SC
Make Up In Love	Stone, Doug	22-490	ST
Make Up Your Mind	Theory of/Deadman	23-168	PHM
Make You Feel My Love	Adele	38-186	CB
Make You Mine	Crossin' Dixon	36-574	CB
Make You Miss Me (Inst)	Hunt, Sam	49-793	K2G
Make Your Own Kind Of Music	Elliot, Cass	49-515	SAV
Make Your Own Kind Of Music	Mamas & Papas	9-706	SAV
Make Yourself Comfortable	Vaughn, Sarah	5-84	SC
Maker Said Take Her the	Alabama	7-345	MM
Maker Said Take Her the	Alabama	4-895	SC
Makes Me Wonder	Maroon 5	30-567	CB
Makes No Sense At All - Nashville	Peeples, Audrey	45-462	BKD
Makeup And Faded Blue Jeans	Haggard, Merle	46-45	SSK
Makin' Plans	Lambert, Miranda	44-394	KV
Makin' This Boy Go Crazy	Scott, Dylan	41-77	PHN
Makin' Up With You	Tennison, Chalee	14-112	CB
Makin' Whoopee	Sinatra, Frank	9-245	PT
Makin' Whoopie	Cole, Nat "King"	46-363	PS
Making Believe	Harris, EmmyLou	8-460	CB
Making Believe	Twitty, Conway	8-665	SAV
Making Believe	Wells, Kitty	13-348	P
Making Believe	Wells, Kitty	14-326	SC
Making Love Out Of Nothing At All	Air Supply	14-580	SC
Making Memories	Standard	10-461	MG
Making Memories Of Us	Urban, Keith	22-327	CB
Making Memories Of Us	Urban, Keith	23-378	SC
Making Up for Lost Time - Duet	Gayle & Morris	34-265	CB
Making Up For Lost Time - duet	Morris & Gayle	49-636	CB
Making Whoopee	Sinatra, Frank	34-4	CB
Mama	Thomas, B.J.	36-154	LE

176

SONG TITLE	ARTIST	#	TYPE
Mama - Spanish	Vale, Jerry	49-210	MM
Mama - xmas	Frizzell, Lefty	46-51	SSK
Mama Can't Buy You Love	John, Elton	9-894	SAV
Mama Don't Forget To Pray	Diamond Rio	1-168	CB
Mama Don't Get Dressed Up For Nothi	Brooks & Dunn	4-465	SC
Mama Don't Let Your Babies Grow...	Jennings, Waylon	22-149	CK
Mama He's Crazy	Judds	1-140	CB
Mama He's Crazy	Judds	13-362	P
Mama He's Crazy	Judds	8-704	SAV
Mama I'm Coming Home	Osbourne, Ozzy	23-421	SC
Mama Knows	Shenandoah	5-559	SC
Mama Knows The Highway	Ketchum, Hal	10-776	JVC
Mama Look At Boo Boo	Belafonte, Harry	6-866	MM
Mama Said	Metallica	47-255	SBI
Mama Said	Shirelles	19-611	MH
Mama Sang A Song	Anderson, Bill	20-784	CB
Mama Told Me Not To Come	Three Dog Night	11-542	DK
Mama Told Me Not To Come	Three Dog Night	15-173	MH
Mama Told Me Not To Come	Three Dog Night	29-284	SC
Mama Tried	Haggard, Merle	8-277	CB
Mama Tried	Haggard, Merle	16-788	DK
Mama Tried	Haggard, Merle	17-306	NA
Mama Tried	Haggard, Merle	13-501	P
Mama Used To Say - Pt. 1	Junior	15-31	SS
Mama Used To Say - Pt. 2	Junior	15-32	SS
Mama's Bible	McDaniel, Mel	49-39	DFK
Mama's Broken Heart	Lambert, Miranda	39-92	PHN
Mama's Never Seen Those Eyes	Forrester Sisters	34-259	CB
Mama's Never Seen Those Eyes	Forrester Sisters	12-472	P
Mamas Don't Let Your Babies Grow	Nelson & Jennings	16-786	DK
Mamas Don't Let Your Babies Grow	Nelson & Jennings	13-359	P
Mamas Don't Let Your Babies Grow..	Nelson & Jennings	9-433	SAV
Mamas Don't Let Your Babies Grow...	Jennings, Waylon	1-623	CB
Mamas Don't Let Your Babies Grow...	Nelson & Jennings	8-22	CB
Mambo #5	Bega, Lou	8-506	PHT
Mambo Italiano	Martin, Dean	23-90	MM
Mambo No 5	Bega, Lou	29-178	MH
Mame	Armstrong, Louis	46-444	LE
Mamma Mia	Abba	7-508	MM
Mamma's Hungry Eyes	Haggard, Merle	49-171	CB
Man Ain't Made Of Stone a	Travis, Randy	5-735	SC
Man Ain't Made Of Stone	Travis, Randy	22-510	ST

SONG TITLE	ARTIST	#	TYPE
a			
Man Comes Around the	Cash, Johnny	43-400	KV
Man Gave Names To All The Animals	Dylan, Bob	47-796	SRK
Man He Was the	Jones, George	16-164	CB
Man Holdin' On A	Herndon, Ty	7-749	CHM
Man I Feel Like A Woman	Twain, Shania	7-861	CHT
Man I Love a	Streisand, Barbra	15-527	MM
Man I Love the	Garland, Judy	48-273	LE
Man I Want To Be the	Young, Chris	36-40	PT
Man In Black	Cash, Johnny	14-235	CB
Man In Black	Cash, Johnny	4-573	SC
Man In Love With You the	Strait, George	1-246	CB
Man In Love With You the	Strait, George	6-605	MM
Man In Love With You the	Strait, George	17-216	NA
Man In Love With You the	Strait, George	2-449	SC
Man In The Mirror	Jackson, Michael	34-102	CB
Man In The Mirror	Jackson, Michael	14-582	SC
Man In White	Cash, Johnny	45-671	DCK
Man Like Me a	Houser, Randy	38-103	CB
Man Like Me a	Houser, Randy	45-556	CB
Man Of Me	Allan, Gary	15-602	ST
Man Of My Word	Raye, Collin	6-673	MM
Man Of My Word	Raye, Collin	3-540	SC
Man Of Steel	Williams, Hank Jr.	16-679	C2C
Man Of The House	Wicks, Chuck	48-455	CB
Man On The Corner	Genesis	37-76	SC
Man On The Flying Trapeze	Standard	9-858	SAV
Man On The Moon	Phillips, Phillip	39-101	ASK
Man On The Moon	REM	12-784	P
Man On The Moon	REM	9-671	SAV
Man Song the	Carrington, Rodney	44-103	SRK
Man That Got Away the	Eder, Linda	17-447	PS
Man That Got Away the	Garland, Judy	7-181	MM
Man That Turned My Mama On	Tucker, Tanya	15-64	CB
Man That Turned My Mama On	Tucker, Tanya	13-338	P
Man This Lonely a	Brooks & Dunn	22-906	ST
Man To Man	Allan, Gary	34-364	CB
Man To Man	Allan, Gary	25-410	MM
Man To Man	Allan, Gary	18-329	ST
Man To Man	Allan, Gary	32-2	THM
Man Who Shot Liberty Valance	Pitney, Gene	20-41	SC
Man Who Shot Liberty Valance	Pitney, Gene	9-179	SO
Man With 18 Wheels a	Womack, Lee Ann	48-479	CKC
Man With The Blues	Nelson, Willie	38-78	PS
Man With The Golden Gun the	Lulu	9-64	SC
Man Without Love a	Humperdinck, E.	37-154	CB
Man! I Feel Like A	Twain, Shania	8-5	CB

177

SONG TITLE	ARTIST	#	TYPE
woman			
Man! I Feel Like A Woman	Twain, Shania	8-519	PHT
Man's Gotta Do a	Brock, Chad	18-139	ST
Manana	Lee, Peggy	47-183	PS
Mandy	Manilow, Barry	29-108	CB
Mandy	Manilow, Barry	13-161	P
Mandy	Manilow, Barry	9-74	PS
ManEater	Hall & Oates	4-327	SC
ManEater	Hall & Oates	9-201	SO
Mango Tree - duet	Zac Brown Band & Bareillas	48-510	KVD
Manhattan Kansas	Fargo, Donna	48-667	VH
Maniac	Sembello, Michael	28-355	DK
Manic Monday	Bangles	12-845	P
Manic Monday	Bangles	4-535	SC
Mannish Boy	Muddy Waters	20-145	KB
Mannish Boy	Muddy Waters	15-27	SC
Mansion On The Hill	Williams, Hank Sr.	8-640	SAV
Mansion You Stole the	Horton, Johnny	4-307	SC
Many A Long & Lonesome Highway	Crowell, Rodney	14-434	SC
Many Rivers To Cross	Cliff, Jimmy	46-628	SC
Many Shades Of Black	Adele	44-177	KV
Marakesh Express - WN	Crosby Stills & Nash	48-55	SC
Margaritaville	Buffett, Jimmy	12-55	DK
Margaritaville	Buffett, Jimmy	20-312	MH
Margaritaville	Buffett, Jimmy	6-429	MM
Margaritaville	Buffett, Jimmy	2-36	SC
Margaritaville	Jackson, Alan	8-899	CB
Margaritaville (With lost verse)	Buffett, Jimmy	49-296	HM
Margie	Reminiscing Series	3-30	SC
Margie's At The Lincoln Park Inn	Bare, Bobby	18-272	CB
Marguerita	Presley, Elvis	25-487	MM
Maria	Blondie	28-193	SF
Maria	Blondie	13-782	SGB
Maria (Shut Up And Kiss Me)	Nelson, Willie	25-297	MM
Maria (Shut Up and Kiss Me)	Nelson, Willie	18-137	ST
Maria Elena	Dorsey, Jimmy	47-34	PS
Maria Elena	Pitney, Gene	47-532	ZM
Maria Maria	Santana	14-182	CB
Marianne	Hilltoppers	9-852	SAV
Marie Laveau	Bare, Bobby	3-700	CB
Marie Laveau	Bare, Bobby	14-311	SC
Marilyn Monroe	Williams, Pharrell	49-73	ZPC
Marina Del Rey	Strait, George	2-367	SC
Mark My Words	Bieber, Justin	48-624	DCK
Marriage Made In Hollywood	Raitt, Bonnie	39-110	PHM
Married But Not To Each Other	Mandrell, Barbara	8-288	CB
Marry For Money	Urban, Keith	46-154	CB
Marry Me	Diamond, Neil	4-395	SC
Marry Me	Train	37-261	PHM

SONG TITLE	ARTIST	#	TYPE
Marry You	Mars, Bruno	38-201	PHM
Marshmallow World a - xmas	Martin, Dean	46-277	KV
Martin	Zac Brown Band	46-65	KV
Marvin Gaye - duet	Puth & Trainor	45-143	BH
Mary	Scissor Sisters	29-223	ZM
Mary	Zac Brown Band	49-242	DFK
Mary	Zac Brown Band	43-464	FTX
Mary Ann	Charles, Ray	46-571	CB
Mary In The Morning	Martino, Al	29-496	LE
Mary Jane's Last Dance	Petty & Heartbreake	18-478	NU
Mary Jane's Last Dance	Petty & Heartbreake	5-331	SC
Mary Lou	Hawkins, Ronnie	5-522	SC
Mary Mary	Monkees	47-292	SC
Mary's In India	Dido	29-235	ZM
Mary's Song (Oh My My My)	Swift, Taylor	36-88	BM
Mary's Vineyard	King, Claude	47-918	SSK
Mashed Potato Time	Sharp, Dee Dee	27-492	DK
Mashed Potato Time - DANCE #	Sharp, Dee Dee	22-393	SC
Masochism Tango the **	Lehrer, Tom	23-21	SC
Mason Dixon Lines	Jennings, Waylon	47-514	VH
Massachusettes (Lights Went Out)	Bee Gees	11-827	DK
Master Blaster (Jammin')	Wonder, Stevie	46-164	SC
Master Of Puppets	Metallica	13-624	LE
Masterplan	Oasis	21-616	SF
Matchbox	Perkins, Carl	11-612	DK
Matches	Kershaw, Sammy	8-462	CB
Matches	Kershaw, Sammy	7-737	CHM
Matches	Kershaw, Sammy	22-788	ST
Matchmaker - show	Fiddler On The Roof	48-785	MM
Material Girl	Madonna	11-274	DK
Material Girl	Madonna	21-147	LE
Matilda	Belafonte, Harry	46-505	KV
Matter Of Time a	Sellers, Jason	8-985	CB
Matter Of Time a	Sellers, Jason	10-209	SC
Matter Of Time a	Sellers, Jason	22-383	ST
Matters Of The Heart	McDonald, Michael	13-600	P
Matthew Mark Luke & Earnhardt	Sellars, Shane	9-872	ST
May The Bird Of Paradise Fly Up...	Dickens, Little Jimmy	8-712	CB
May The Bird Of Paradise Fly Up...	Dickens, Little Jimmy	19-391	SC
Maybe	Barnett, Mandy	7-274	MM
Maybe	Chantels	25-276	MM
Maybe	Iglesias, Enrique	20-469	CB
Maybe - duet	Rogers & Dunn	48-120	CB
Maybe Baby	Holly, Buddy	35-10	CB
Maybe Baby	Holly, Buddy	3-215	LG
Maybe Baby	Holly, Buddy	7-291	MM
Maybe Baby	Holly, Buddy	4-513	SC
Maybe He'll Notice Her Now	McCready, Mindy	34-323	CB
Maybe He'll Notice Her Now	McCready, Mindy	7-390	MM

SONG TITLE	ARTIST	#	TYPE
Maybe He'll Notice Her Now	McCready, Mindy	4-510	SC
Maybe He'll Notice Her Now	McCready, Mindy	22-908	ST
Maybe I Know	Gore, Lesley	4-718	SC
Maybe I Know	Springfield, Dusty	10-728	JVC
Maybe I Mean Yes	Dunn, Holly	6-199	MM
Maybe I'm Amazed	McCartney, Paul	6-493	MM
Maybe I'm Amazed	McCartney, Paul	29-290	SC
Maybe It Was Memphis	Tillis, Pam	1-453	CB
Maybe It Was Memphis	Tillis, Pam	11-806	DK
Maybe It Was Memphis	Tillis, Pam	6-188	MM
Maybe It Was Memphis	Tillis, Pam	13-399	P
Maybe It Was Memphis	Tillis, Pam	4-62	SC
Maybe It's Because I'm A Londoner	Standard	17-397	DK
Maybe Maybe Not	McCready, Mindy	16-335	ST
Maybe Not Tonight	Kershaw & Morgan	8-924	CB
Maybe She'll Get Lonely	Ingram, Jack	36-552	CB
Maybe She's Human	Mattea, Kathy	2-549	SC
Maybe Someday	Lonestar	41-78	PHN
Maybe This Time	Minelli, Liza	49-447	MM
Maybe This Time	Minelli, Liza	49-214	MM
Maybe We Should Just Sleep On It	McGraw, Tim	7-376	MM
Maybe We Should Just Sleep On It	McGraw, Tim	4-458	SC
Maybe You Remember Me Now	Hey Romeo	39-71	PHN
Maybe Your Baby's Got the Blues	Judds	1-147	CB
Maybe Your Baby's Got The Blues	Judds	9-496	SAV
Maybelline	Berry, Chuck	12-48	DK
Maybelline	Berry, Chuck	2-49	SC
Maybelline	Checker, Chubby	48-558	DK
Mayberry	Rascal Flatts	19-701	ST
Mayday	Cam	49-8	KV
McArthur Park	Harris, Richard	19-131	KC
Me	Cole, Paula	49-512	PHM
Me	Cole, Paula	5-192	SC
Me & Bobby McGee	Joplin, Janis	11-140	DK
Me & Bobby McGee	Joplin, Janis	9-309	STR
Me & Bobby McGee	Kristofferson, Kris	13-173	P
Me & Julio Down By The Schoolyard	Simon & Garfunkel	23-637	BS
Me & Julio Down By The Schoolyard	Simon & Garfunkel	15-529	DM
Me & You & A Dog Named Boo	Lobo	17-36	DK
Me & You & A Dog Named Boo	Lobo	7-99	MM
Me And Bobby McGee	Miller, Roger	45-930	VH
Me And Bobby McGee	Pride, Charley	47-441	KV
Me And Charlie Talking	Lambert, Miranda	22-97	CB
Me And Charlie Talking	Lambert, Miranda	23-44	SC
Me And Emily	Proctor, Rachel	20-328	ST
Me And God	Turner & Stanley	30-196	CB
Me And Jesus - VR -	Hall, Tom T.	49-711	VH

SONG TITLE	ARTIST	#	TYPE
Gospel			
Me And Little Andy	Parton, Dolly	8-536	CB
Me And Maxine	Kershaw, Sammy	22-478	ST
Me And Mr. Jones	Winehouse, Amy	49-57	ZVS
Me And Mrs. Jones	Paul, Billy	11-379	DK
Me And Mrs. Jones	Paul, Billy	17-422	KC
Me And My Gang	Rascal Flatts	29-592	CB
Me And My Shadow	Mills Brothers	43-220	CB
Me And My Shadow (Live)	Sinatra & Davis	49-502	MM
Me And Ole CB	Dudley, Dave	43-296	CB
Me And Paul	Nelson, Willie	5-860	SC
Me And The Elephant	Goldsboro, Bobby	44-65	SAV P
Me And You	Chesney, Kenny	1-322	CB
Me And You	Chesney, Kenny	7-338	MM
Me And You	Chesney, Kenny	4-402	SC
Me And You And A Dog Named Boo	Como, Perry	48-561	DK
Me My Heart And I	Gearing, Ashley	38-246	PHN
Me Myself & I	Beyonce	19-661	CB
Me Myself & I	De La Soul	14-441	SC
Me Myself & I	Vitamin C	16-187	PHM
Me Neither	Paisley, Brad	13-835	CHM
Me Neither	Paisley, Brad	23-372	SC
Me Neither	Paisley, Brad	16-272	TT
Me So Horny **	2 Live Crew	5-547	SC
Me Too	Keith, Toby	1-697	CB
Me Too	Keith, Toby	7-581	CHM
Me Too	Keith, Toby	7-400	MM
Me Too	Keith, Toby	22-910	ST
Me Without You	Nettles, Jennifer	43-267	BKD
Me Without You	Nettles, Jennifer	44-282	KCD
Mean	Swift, Taylor	37-210	AS
Mean Mistreater	Grand Funk RR	5-594	SC
Mean Streak	Y & T	23-109	SC
Mean To Me	Eldridge, Brett	45-290	BKD
Mean To Me	Ronstadt, Linda	15-530	MM
Mean Woman Blues	Orbison, Roy	38-59	LE
Meant To Be	Kershaw, Sammy	1-475	CB
Meant To Be	Kershaw, Sammy	7-229	MM
Meant To Live	Switchfoot	19-854	PHM
Meanwhile	Strait, George	8-353	CB
Meanwhile	Strait, George	7-825	CHT
Meanwhile	Strait, George	22-724	ST
Meanwhile Back At Mama's	McGraw, Tim	44-197	KCD
Meanwhile Back At The Ranch	Clark Family Exp.	19-219	CSZ
Measure Of A Man	Ingram, Jack	30-447	CB
Meat And Potato Man	Jackson, Alan	29-347	CB
Meat And Potato Man	Long, Brice	29-598	CB
Mecca	Pitney, Gene	17-470	SC
Medicine	Bethel, Hannah	42-11	PHN
Meet In The Middle	Diamond Rio	1-166	CB
Meet In The Middle	Diamond Rio	26-565	DK
Meet In The Middle	Diamond Rio	13-335	P

SONG TITLE	ARTIST	#	TYPE
Meet In The Middle	Diamond Rio	2-512	SC
Meet Me In Montana	Seals & Osmond	8-119	CB
Meet Me In Montana	Seals & Osmond	2-309	SC
Meet Me In St. Louis Louis	Garland, Judy	16-412	PR
Meet Me In St. Louis Louis	Garland, Judy	9-823	SAV
Meet Me In St. Louis Louis	Reminiscing Series	3-29	SC
Meet Me With Your Black Drawers On	Hardiman, Gloria	14-595	SC
Meet The Flintstones	B-52's	46-458	KV
Meet The Flintstones	TV Themes	12-616	P
Meet Virginia	Train	35-211	CB
Meet Virginia	Train	10-184	SC
Melissa	Allman Brothers	9-326	AG
Melissa	Allman Brothers	13-760	SGB
Mellow Yellow	Donovan	12-161	DK
Melt My Heart To Stone	Adele	44-168	KV
Melting Pot	Blue Mink	10-635	SF
Memories	Presley, Elvis	18-560	KC
Memories Are Made Of This	Martin, Dean	11-573	DK
Memories Are Made Of This	Martin, Dean	10-401	LE
Memories Are Made Of This	Martin, Dean	7-188	MM
Memories Are Made Of This	Reeves, Jim	44-228	SRK
Memories Of You	Sinatra, Frank	45-597	OZP
Memory Like I'm Gonna Be	Tucker, Tanya	25-356	MM
Memory Like I'm Gonna Be	Tucker, Tanya	18-455	ST
Memory Maker	Tillis, Mel	3-865	CB
Memory Making Night	Wiggins, J & A	2-696	SC
Memory Remains the	Metallica	47-253	MH
Memphis	Checker, Chubby	48-557	DK
Memphis	Nail, David	17-573	ST
Memphis	Presley, Elvis	14-823	THM
Memphis	Rivers, Johnny	3-23	SC
Memphis Soul Song	Uncle Kracker	20-234	MM
Memphis Soul Song	Uncle Kracker	32-432	THM
Memphis Tennessee	Berry, Chuck	27-486	DK
Memphis Women & Chicken	Brown, T. Graham	5-833	SC
Men	Forrester Sisters	18-264	DK
Men	Forrester Sisters	6-109	MM
Men	Forrester Sisters	13-390	P
Men	Forrester Sisters	2-126	SC
Men & Mascara	Roberts, Julie	29-578	CB
Men Buy The Drinks, Girls Call The Shots	Holy, Steve	30-459	CB
Men Don't Change	Dalley, Amy	35-428	CB
Men Don't Change	Dalley, Amy	20-172	ST
Men In Black	Smith, Will	10-107	SC
Mending Fences	Restless Heart	9-630	SAV
Mendocino County Line	Nelson & Womack	25-129	MM
Mendocino County Line	Nelson & Womack	16-332	ST

SONG TITLE	ARTIST	#	TYPE
Mendocino Ragazzina	Sir Douglas Quint	13-109	P
Mercedes Benz	Joplin, Janis	34-40	CB
Mercedes Benz	Joplin, Janis	10-673	HE
Mercedes Benz	Joplin, Janis	19-155	SGB
Mercedes Boy	Pebbles	17-25	DK
Mercedes Boy	Pebbles	16-545	P
Mercedes Boy	Pebbles	15-736	SC
Mercury Blues	Jackson, Alan	1-44	CB
Mercury Blues	Jackson, Alan	6-382	MM
Mercy	Duffy	36-452	CB
Mercy Mercy Me	Gaye, Marvin	11-757	DK
Mercy Mercy Me - the Ecology	Gaye, Marvin	14-352	MH
Mercy Seat the	Nick Cave & the Badseeds	43-78	SF
Mermaid the	Bare, Bobby	46-47	SSK
Merry Christmas Alabama	Buffett, Jimmy	46-145	TU
Merry Christmas Everybody	Slade	45-770	SF
Merry Christmas From The Family	Montgomery Gentry	45-750	CB
Merry Christmas Polka	Reeves, Jim	49-288	CON
Merry Christmas To Me	Jackson, Alan	49-177	CB
Merry Christmas Wherever You Are	Strait, George	45-765	CB
Merry Go 'Round	Musgraves, Kacey	43-260	KCD
Mesmerize - duet	Ja Rule & Ashanti	32-123	THM
Mess Around	Charles, Ray	46-569	CB
Mess Of The Blues	Presley, Elvis	47-719	CB
Message of Love	Journey	4-613	SC
Message the	Grand Masters Flash	14-439	SC
Message To Michael	Warwick, Dionne	5-6	SC
Message To My Mother	Williams, Hank Sr.	45-705	CB
Messin' With The Kid	Wells, Junior	15-29	SC
Metal Health	Quiet Riot	23-58	MH
Metal Health	Quiet Riot	5-490	SC
Mexicali Rose	Reeves, Jim	44-232	SRK
Mexican Blackbird	ZZ Top	13-643	SGB
Mexican Joe	Reeves, Jim	8-577	CB
Mexican Radio	Wall Of Voodoo	21-400	SC
Mexico	Taylor, James	17-525	SC
Mexico Tequila And Me	Jackson, Alan	45-21	KVD
Mexicoma	Covington, Bucky	38-78	PHN
Mi Vida Loca	Tillis, Pam	1-458	CB
Mi Vida Loca	Tillis, Pam	17-258	NA
Mi Vida Loca	Tillis, Pam	2-551	SC
Miami	Smith, Will	7-794	PHT
Miami My Amy	Whitley, Keith	5-557	SC
Michael Row The Boat Ashore	Brothers Four	9-821	SAV
Michelle	Beatles	11-139	DK
Michelle	Beatles	13-46	P
Mickey	Basil, Toni	11-328	DK
Mickey	Basil, Toni	16-533	P
Mickey's Monkey	Miracles	17-360	DK
Middle Age Crazy	Lewis, Jerry Lee	34-236	CB
Middle Of Nowhere	Hot Hot Heat	30-225	PHM

SONG TITLE	ARTIST	#	TYPE
Middle Of Nowhere the	McComas, Brian	22-315	CB
Middle Of Nowhere the	McComas, Brian	23-389	SC
Middle Of The Road	Pretenders	24-434	SC
Middle the	Jimmy Eat World	18-349	CB
Middle the	Jimmy Eat World	25-203	MM
Middle the	Jimmy Eat World	30-651	THM
Midnight	Foley, Red	43-355	CB
Midnight Blue	Manchester,Melissa	4-46	SC
Midnight Bottle	Cailliat, Colbie	48-220	KV
Midnight Confession	Grass Roots	7-260	MM
Midnight Girl In A Sunset Town	Sweethearts/Rodeo	6-778	MM
Midnight Girl In A Sunset Town	Sweethearts/Rodeo	5-241	SC
Midnight Hauler	Bailey, Razzy	29-380	CB
Midnight In Montgomery	Jackson, Alan	1-38	CB
Midnight In Montgomery	Jackson, Alan	2-393	SC
Midnight Me & The Blues	Tillis, Mel	14-428	SC
Midnight Oil	Wilson, Gretchen	30-164	CB
Midnight Rider	Allman Brothers	18-157	CB
Midnight Rider	Allman, Greg	12-696	P
Midnight Rider	Nelson & Keith	22-75	CB
Midnight Rider	Nelson w Keith	38-70	CB
Midnight Rider	Nelson, Willie	38-71	CB
Midnight Shift	Holly, Buddy	47-885	ZM
Midnight Special	CCR	33-258	CB
Midnight Special	CCR	13-169	P
Midnight Special	Rivers, Johnny	47-365	JVC
Midnight Train To Georgia	Diamond, Neil	47-415	DCK
Midnight Train To Georgia	Knight & Pips	16-808	DK
Midnight Train To Georgia	Knight & Pips	13-146	P
Midnight Train To Georgia	Knight & Pips	9-228	PT
Midnight Train To Georgia	Knight & Pips	9-791	SAV
Midnight Train To Georgia	Knight & Pips	2-438	SC
Might Have Been	Holy, Steve	36-613	CB
Might Have Been	Holy, Steve	36-280	PHM
Mighty Clouds Of Joy	Thomas, B.J.	21-518	SC
Mighty Love	Spinners	28-114	DK
Mighty Qunin the	Mann, Manfred	5-466	SC
Miles And Miles Of Texas	Asleep At The Wheel	45-861	VH
Miles And Mud Tires	Smith, Granger	42-5	PHN
Miles And Years	Cartwright, Lionel	8-972	CB
Miles Away	Basia	14-865	PS
Miles Away	Winger	24-687	SC
Milk	Garbage	24-642	SC
Milk Cow Blues	Wills, Bob	20-693	CB
Milkcow Blues Boogie	Presley, Elvis	7-129	MM
Milky White Way	Presley, Elvis	25-503	MM
Millennium	Williams, Robbie	11-75	JTG
Millennium	Williams, Robbie	7-892	PHT
Millennium	Williams, Robbie	10-185	SC

SONG TITLE	ARTIST	#	TYPE
Miller's Cave	Bare, Bobby	18-269	CB
Miller's Cave	Snow, Hank	22-247	SC
Million Dollar Bill	Houston, Whitney	48-634	BKD
Million Miles Away	Plimsouls	16-60	SC
Million Years Ago	Adele	45-821	DCK
Millionaire the	Dr. Hook	47-44	SC
Mind Games	Lennon, John	30-290	RS
Mind Of Her Own a	Berry, John	24-347	SC
Mind Your Own Business	Williams, Hank Jr.	9-494	SAV
Mind Your Own Business	Williams, Hank Sr.	14-224	CB
Mine	Kinder, Ryan	42-8	PHN
Mine	Presley, Elvis	25-101	MM
Mine	Swift, Taylor	38-280	CB
Mine All Mine	SheDaisy	25-235	MM
Mine All Mine	SheDaisy	17-569	ST
Mine Would Be You	Shelton, Blake	40-56	ASL
Minerva	Deftones	32-289	THM
Minivan	Hometown News	16-706	ST
Minnie The Moocher	Blues Brothers	29-155	ZM
Minnie The Moocher	Calloway, Cab	12-538	P
Minute By Minute	Doobie Brothers	29-90	CB
Miracle	Houston, Whitney	48-635	MM
Miracle Man	Smokin' Armadillos	4-888	SC
Miracle Of Love	Eurythmics	47-75	KV
Miracles	Jefferson Starship	12-353	DK
Miracles	Williams, Don	45-229	CB
Miracles Music & My Wife	Pride, Charley	47-443	SRK
Mirror In The Bathroom	Beat	49-112	SF
Mirror Mirror	Diamond Rio	1-167	CB
Mirror Mirror	Diamond Rio	2-392	SC
Mirror Mirror	M2M	14-493	SC
Mirror Mirror	M2M	30-634	THM
Mirror Mirror	Ross, Diana	15-358	LE
Misery	Soul Asylum	3-497	SC
Misery & Gin	Haggard, Merle	22-233	CB
Misery And Gin	Haggard, Merle	49-811	CB
Misery Business	Paramore	49-897	SC
Misery Loves Company	Wagoner, Porter	19-306	CB
Misery Loves Company	Wagoner, Porter	5-217	SC
Misled	Dion, Celine	34-138	CB
Misled	Dion, Celine	2-233	SC
Miss America	Styx	5-63	SC
Miss Being Mrs.	Lynn, Loretta	20-449	ST
Miss Chatelaine	lang, k.d.	4-273	SC
Miss Difficult	Cowboy Crush	30-554	CB
Miss Emily's Picture	Conlee, John	5-250	SC
Miss Independence	Ne-Yo	36-509	CB
Miss Independent	Clarkson, Kelly	25-623	MM
Miss Independent	Clarkson, Kelly	36-324	PS
Miss Independent	Clarkson, Kelly	23-337	SC
Miss Independent	Clarkson, Kelly	32-279	THM
Miss Independent	Ne-Yo	49-854	SC
Miss Me Baby	Cagle, Chris	23-295	CB
Miss Me Baby	Cagle, Chris	29-512	SC

SONG TITLE	ARTIST	#	TYPE
Miss Me Baby	Cagle, Chris	29-611	ST
Miss Me Blind	Culture Club	46-651	ST
Miss That Girl	Aldean, Jason	48-669	BKD
Miss You	Aaliyah	34-142	CB
Miss You	Aaliyah	32-58	THM
Miss You	Clapton, Eric	13-795	SGB
Miss You	Rolling Stones	14-399	PT
Miss You	Rucker, Darius	43-164	ASK
Miss You Like Crazy	Cole, Natalie	33-328	CB
Miss You Like Crazy	Cole, Natalie	6-352	MM
Miss You Like Crazy	Cole, Natalie	2-271	SC
Miss You Most At Christmas Time	Carey, Mariah	45-799	SBI
Miss You Much	Jackson, Janet	11-387	DK
Miss You Much	Jackson, Janet	16-544	P
Miss You Nights	Cliff, Richard	48-776	P
Missin' You	Pride, Charley	40-109	CB
Missing Angel	Reeves, Jim	46-214	SF
Missing In Action	Tubb, Ernest	22-304	CB
Missing Missouri	Evans, Sara	30-248	CB
Missing My Baby	Selena	23-568	MM
Missing Years	Little Texas	30-450	CB
Missing You	Brandy/Tamia/Knight	24-234	SC
Missing You	Brooks & Dunn	5-725	SC
Missing You	Brooks & Dunn	22-484	ST
Missing You	Mavericks	4-410	SC
Missing You	Reeves, Jim	8-563	CB
Missing You	Rogers, Kenny	48-126	SC
Missing You	Ross, Diana	15-361	LE
Missing You	Turner, Tina	4-688	SC
Missing You Crazy	Pardi, Jon	47-408	ASK
Missionary Man	Eurythmics	9-886	DK
Missionary Man	Eurythmics	29-296	SC
Mississippi	Foley, Red	43-357	CB
Mississippi Cotton Pickin'...	Pride, Charley	38-121	CB
Mississippi Girl	Hill, Faith	23-279	CB
Mississippi Moon	Anderson, John	20-114	CB
Mississippi Moon	Anderson, John	2-764	SC
Mississippi Queen	Mountain	17-90	DK
Mississippi Squirrel Revival	Stevens, Ray	16-486	CB
Mississippi Squirrel Revival	Stevens, Ray	6-515	MM
Mississippi Squirrel Revival	Stevens, Ray	15-137	SC
Mistletoe	Bieber, Justin	48-625	KVD
Misty	Mathis, Johnny	29-466	LE
Misty	Standard	17-345	DK
Misty	Stevens, Ray	16-493	CB
Misty	Stevens, Ray	4-634	SC
Misty Blue	Arnold, Eddy	44-221	CKC
Misty Blue	Moore, Dorothy	24-335	SC
Misty Blue	Spears, Billie Jo	39-7	CB
Misunderstood	Bon Jovi	20-463	CB
Misunderstood	Bon Jovi	25-433	MM
Mixed Emotions	Rolling Stones	20-206	SC

SONG TITLE	ARTIST	#	TYPE
Mmm Bop	Hanson	33-358	CB
Mmm Bop	Hanson	15-531	SC
Mmm Mmm Mmm Mmm	Crash Test Dummies	12-163	DK
Mmm Mmm Mmm Mmm	Crash Test Dummies	8-605	TT
Mo Money Mo Problems	Notorious BIG/Puff/	25-481	MM
Moanin' The Blues	Williams, Hank Sr.	22-309	CB
Mob Rules the	Black Sabbath	21-765	SC
Mochingbird - duet	Taylor & Simon	46-120	SC
Mockingbird	Foxx, Inez	3-579	SC
Mockingbird	Keith, Toby&Krystal	21-661	SC
Mockingbird	Simon, Carly	49-149	CB
Mockingbird	Taylor & Simon	13-44	P
Mockingbird Hill	Fargo, Donna	48-662	CB
Mockingbird Hill	Page, Patti	2-246	SC
Modern Day Bonnie & Clyde	Tritt, Travis	33-176	CB
Modern Day Bonnie & Clyde	Tritt, Travis	25-126	MM
Modern Day Bonnie & Clyde	Tritt, Travis	16-99	ST
Modern Day Romance	Nitty Gritty Dirt Band	4-650	SC
Modern Love	Bowie, David	20-84	SC
Modern Man	Peterson, Michael	18-213	ST
Mojo Boogie	Winter, Johnny	49-676	DJ
Mojo Boogie	Winter, Johnny	14-597	SC
Molokai	Ho, Don	6-827	MM
Mom	Brooks, Garth	48-348	KV
Mom And Dad's Waltz	Frizzell, Lefty	19-485	CB
Mom And Dad's Waltz	Frizzell, Lefty	7-162	MM
Moment Like This a	Clarkson, Kelly	33-425	CB
Moment Like This a	Clarkson, Kelly	25-333	MM
Moment Like This a	Clarkson, Kelly	18-581	NS
Moment Like This a	Clarkson, Kelly	18-341	PHM
Moment Like This a	Clarkson, Kelly	36-357	SC
Moment Of Weakness	Bif Naked	10-223	SC
Moments	Emerson Drive	30-247	CB
Moments Like This	Lee, Peggy	49-934	PS
Moments To Remember	Four Lads	45-69	JVC
Mommy For A Day	Wells, Kitty	4-737	SC
Mona Lisa	Cole, Nat "King"	11-297	DK
Mona Lisa	Cole, Nat "King"	12-525	P
Mona Lisa - Cajun Style	Cajun	49-405	SCK
Mona Lisa Lost Her Smile	Coe, David Allan	18-312	CB
Mona Lisa Lost Her Smile	Coe, David Allan	14-315	SC
Mona Lisa the	Paisley, Brad	43-152	ASK
Monday Monday	Mamas & Papas	35-96	CB
Monday Monday	Mamas & Papas	11-358	DK
Monday Monday	Mamas & Papas	12-864	P
Monday Monday	Mamas & Papas	9-118	PS
Monday Morning Church	Jackson, Alan	22-81	CB
Monday Morning Church	Jackson, Alan	21-652	SC
Money	Pink Floyd	5-312	SC
Money Burns a Hole In	Martin, Dean	49-647	DFK

SONG TITLE	ARTIST	#	TYPE
My Pocket			
Money Can't Buy It	Eurythmics	47-78	SFG
Money For Nothing	Dire Straits	2-149	SC
Money Greases The Wheels	Husky, Ferlin	22-270	CB
Money Honey	Kingsmen	17-326	SS
Money In The Band	Anderson, John	2-429	SC
Money Makes The World Go Round	Gray, Joel	6-524	MM
Money Makes The World Go Round - duet	Minelli, Liza	49-223	LG
Money Money Money	Abba	15-532	CMC
Money Money Money	Abba	19-72	MM
Money Or Love	Black, Clint	16-434	ST
Money! That's What I Want	Kingsmen	11-179	DK
Money! That's What I Want	Kingsmen	12-637	P
Monkees the	TV Themes	2-169	SC
Monkey	Michael, George	11-677	DK
Monkey In The Middle	Atkins, Rodney	23-14	CB
Monster	Automatic	30-730	SF
Monster Mash	Pickett, Bobby	11-566	DK
Monster Mash	Pickett, Bobby	2-72	SC
Monster Mash	Pickett, Bobby	16-286	TT
Montego Bay	Bloom, Bobby	9-716	SAV
Mony Mony	Idol, Billy	26-290	DK
Mony Mony	James & Shondells	10-331	KC
Mony Mony	James & Shondells	13-207	P
Mood Indigo	Austin, Paul	12-566	P
Moody Blue	Presley, Elvis	17-126	DK
Moody Blue	Presley, Elvis	2-608	SC
Moody Blue	Presley, Elvis	14-824	THM
Moody Manitoba Morning	Five Bells	49-253	DFK
Moody River	Boone, Pat	18-248	DK
Moody River	Boone, Pat	4-357	SC
Moon Is Still Over Her Shoulder the	Johnson, Michael	29-653	SC
Moon Over Georgia the	Shenandoah	1-486	CB
Moon River	Streisand, Barbra	49-609	PS
Moon River	Williams, Andy	11-307	DK
Moon River	Williams, Andy	13-550	LE
Moon River	Williams, Andy	12-514	P
Moon River	Williams, Andy	2-203	SC
Moondance	Buble, Michael	30-182	LE
Moondance	Morrison, Van	23-594	BS
Moondance	Morrison, Van	13-10	P
Moonglow	Goodman, Benny	45-606	OZP
Moonglow	Stewart, Rod	25-594	MM
Moonlight And Roses	Reeves, Jim	3-150	LG
Moonlight Bay	Miller, Mitch	49-331	CB
Moonlight Bay	Standard	11-582	DK
Moonlight Feels Right	Starbuck	7-100	MM
Moonlight Gambler	Laine, Frankie	3-878	PS
Moonlight In Vermont	Vaughn, Sarah	2-249	SC
Moonlight Lady	Iglesias, Julio	47-563	CAK
Moonlight Serenade	Simon, Carly	49-160	ST

SONG TITLE	ARTIST	#	TYPE
Moonlight Serenade	Standard	10-459	MG
Moonlighting	Sayer, Leo	47-482	ZM
Moonshadow	Stevens, Cat	23-648	BS
Moonshadow	Stevens, Cat	13-576	NU
Moonshadow	Stevens, Cat	5-303	SC
Moonshadow Road	Brown, T. Graham	47-546	CB
Moonshine In The Trunk	Paisley, Brad	47-709	BKD
More	Adkins, Trace	13-813	CHM
More	Adkins, Trace	22-482	ST
More	Darin, Bobby	47-8	MM
More	Lynne, Rockie	30-206	CB
More	Newton, Wayne	47-310	LE
More	Sinatra, Frank	13-655	SGB
More	Williams, Andy	13-552	LE
More (Radio Version)	Adkins, Trace	23-369	SC
More And More	Pierce, Webb	29-401	CB
More And More	Pierce, Webb	6-780	MM
More Beautiful Day	McGuinn, Mark	18-140	ST
More Beaver (Parody)	Judd, Cledus T.	16-273	TT
More Boys I Meet the	Underwood, Carrie	37-12	CB
More I Drink the	Shelton, Blake	30-471	CB
More I See You the	Montez, Chris	10-667	SF
More In Love With You	Streisand, Barbra	49-610	PS
More Like Her	Lambert, Miranda	43-377	CB
More Like The Movies	Dr. Hook	47-45	SFM
More Love	Stone, Doug	2-322	SC
More More More Pt. 1	Andrea True Conn.	17-531	SC
More Of A Man	Carrington, Rodney	14-161	CB
More Of A Man	Carrington, Rodney	44-99	SC
More Of You	Stapleton, Chris	49-652	KV
More Of Your Love	Derailers	17-483	CB
More Than A Memory	Brooks, Garth	30-583	CB
More Than A Name On A Wall	Statler Brothers	49-795	DFK
More Than A Woman	Aaliyah	18-291	CB
More Than A Woman	Aaliyah	18-147	PHM
More Than A Woman	Bee Gees	17-501	LE
More Than A Woman	Travares	13-323	P
More Than Everything	Akins, Rhett	8-132	CB
More Than Everything	Akins, Rhett	22-663	ST
More Than Feeling	Boston	16-602	MM
More Than I Can Say	Sayer, Leo	13-31	P
More Than I Can Say	Sayer, Leo	11-50	PX
More Than I Can Say	Sayer, Leo	21-799	SC
More Than I Can Say	Vee, Bobby	49-65	ZVS
More Than Love	Los Lonely Boys	20-557	PHM
More Than Miles	Gilbert, Brantley	42-24	ASK
More Than Miles	Gilbert, Brantley	44-299	SBI
More Than That	Backstreet Boys	18-567	TT
More Than The Eyes Can See	Martino, Al	29-495	LE
More Than This	10,000 Maniacs	46-235	MM
More Than Words	Extreme	21-464	CB
More Than Words	Extreme	12-767	P
More Than You'll Ever Know	Tritt, Travis	1-670	CB
More Than You'll Ever	Tritt, Travis	7-317	MM

SONG TITLE	ARTIST	#	TYPE
Know			
More Than You'll Ever Know	Tritt, Travis	4-899	SC
More To Life	Orrico, Stacie	21-613	SF
More To Life (There's Gotta Be)	Orrico, Stacie	32-358	THM
More To Me	Pride, Charley	40-113	CB
More Today Than Yesterday	Spiral Staircase	9-362	MG
More Today Than Yesterday	Spiral Staircase	7-75	MM
More Trucks Than Cars	Morgan, Craig	48-283	SBI
More Where That Came From	Parton, Dolly	24-135	SC
More You Ignore Me the	Morrissey	6-38	SC
Mornin'	Jareau, Al	48-780	P
Mornin' Ride	Greenwood, Lee	4-550	SC
Morning	Brown, Jim Ed	5-769	SC
Morning After Baby Let Me Down	Lynn, Loretta	47-773	SRK
Morning After the	McGovern, Maureen	17-32	DK
Morning Desire	Rogers, Kenny	4-771	SC
Morning Has Broken	Stevens, Cat	23-654	BS
Morning Has Broken	Stevens, Cat	13-582	NU
Morning Has Broken	Stevens, Cat	2-777	SC
Morning Papers the	Prince	49-832	KV
Morning Papers the	Prince	12-840	P
Morning Side Of The Mountain - duet	Osmond, Donny & Marie	47-845	FMG
Morning Song	Jewel	36-331	SC
Morning Train (9 to 5)	Easton, Sheena	11-131	DK
Morning Train (9 to 5)	Easton, Sheena	9-782	SAV
Morning Wood **	Carrington, Rodney	44-97	SC
Morningside	Bareilles, Sara	37-21	PS
Morningtown Ride	Seekers	49-62	ZVS
Moses Supposes (Tongue Twister)	Kelly, Gene	9-818	SAV
Most Beautiful Girl In The World	Prince	2-121	SC
Most Beautiful Girl the	Jones, Tom	25-270	MM
Most Beautiful Girl the	Rich, Charlie	17-8	DK
Most Beautiful Girl the	Rich, Charlie	13-422	P
Most Beautiful Girl the	Rich, Charlie	9-580	SAV
Most Girls	Pink	34-170	CB
Most Girls	Pink	15-450	PHM
Most Girls	Pink	20-11	SGB
Motel Song the	Stevens, Ray	16-499	CB
Mother	Lennon, John	30-304	RS
Mother And Child Reunion	Simon & Garfunkel	15-534	DM
Mother Freedom	Bread	46-525	CB
Mother I Miss You	Tesh & Dalia	14-280	MM
Mother In Law	Doe, Ernie K.	26-454	DK
Mother In Law	Ernie K Doe	6-521	MM
Mother In Law	Ernie K Doe	2-74	SC
Mother In Law	Herman's Hermits	47-134	DKM
Mother Like Mine	Band Perry	41-58	PHN
Mother Like Mine a	Band Perry	43-458	ASK

SONG TITLE	ARTIST	#	TYPE
Mother Mother	Bonham, Tracy	4-337	SC
Mother Popcorn	Brown, James	29-147	LE
Mother's Day	Pickler, Kellie	38-257	PHN
Mother's Little Helper	Rolling Stones	19-754	LE
Mother's Little Helper	Rolling Stones	14-402	PT
Motherless Child	Clapton, Eric	46-204	SC
Motor City Madhouse	Nugent, Ted	17-473	SC
Motorcycle Cowboy	Haggard, Merle	9-428	CB
Motownphilly	Boyz II Men	33-334	CB
Mountain Dew	Flatt & Scruggs	12-159	DK
Mountain Dew	Grandpa Jones	35-329	CB
Mountain Dew	Jones, Grandpa	8-257	CB
Mountain Dew	Nelson, Willie	17-313	NA
Mountain Music	Alabama	35-387	CB
Mountain Music	Alabama	26-342	DK
Mountain Music	Alabama	13-368	P
Mountain Music	Alabama	2-100	SC
Mountain Of Love	Pride, Charley	3-791	CB
Mountain Of Love	Rivers, Johnny	17-45	DK
Mountain Of Love	Rivers, Johnny	13-103	P
Mountains	Lonestar	30-19	CB
Mountains Of Things	Chapman, Tracy	44-193	SBI
Mouth	Bainbridge, Merrill	10-680	HE
Mouth	Bainbridge, Merrill	24-365	SC
Mouth	Bainbridge, Merrill	19-167	SGB
Move Along	All American Rejects	30-277	SC
Move Along	All-American Reject	30-155	PT
Move Along	All-American Reject	30-277	SC
Move It On Over	Thorogood, George	20-80	SC
Move It On Over	Three Hanks	4-626	SC
Move It On Over	Williams, Hank Sr.	8-641	SAV
Move On	Warren Brothers	14-132	CB
Move On	Warren Brothers	22-463	ST
Move Over	Joplin, Janis	46-311	SC
Move Over	Tedeschi, Susan	17-454	AMS
Move Over Darling	Day, Doris	48-135	ZMP
Move Your Feet	Junior Senior	25-661	MM
Moves Like Jagger	Maroon 5	49-71	ZPC
Movies the	Statler Brothers	8-826	CB
Movin' On	Bad Company	10-489	DA
Movin' On	Haggard, Merle	22-239	CB
Movin' On	Haggard, Merle	13-340	P
Movin' On	Peniston, CeCe	24-290	SC
Movin' Out (Anthony's Song)	Joel, Billy	12-279	DK
Movin' Out (Anthony's Song)	Joel, Billy	16-136	LE
Moving Mountains	Usher	36-530	CB
Moving On Up	M-People	2-227	SC
Moving Out	Comeaux, Amie	24-85	SC
Mr. And Mississippi	Ford, Tenn Ernie	22-203	CB
Mr. Bartender (It's So Easy)	Sugar Ray	25-662	MM
Mr. Bass Man	Cymbal, Johnny	6-660	MM
Mr. Big Stuff	Knight, Jean	35-85	CB
Mr. Big Stuff	Knight, Jean	10-674	HE

SONG TITLE	ARTIST	#	TYPE
Mr. Big Stuff	Light, Jan	6-650	MM
Mr. Blue	Brooks, Garth	48-343	DKM
Mr. Blue	Fleetwoods	11-547	DK
Mr. Blue	Fleetwoods	12-899	P
Mr. Bojangles	Davis, Sammy Jr.	47-16	SC
Mr. Bojangles	Nitty Gritty Dirt Band	7-455	MM
Mr. Bojangles	Nitty Gritty Dirt Band	9-545	SAV
Mr. Brightside	Killers	30-133	PT
Mr. Brownstone	Guns & Roses	5-482	SC
Mr. Custer	Verne, Larry	5-633	SC
Mr. Ed	TV Themes	2-157	SC
Mr. Jones	Counting Crows	18-696	CB
Mr. Lee	Bobbettes	5-236	SC
Mr. Leonardo	Blessed Union/Soul	7-878	PHM
Mr. Lonely	Vinton, Bobby	5-177	SC
Mr. Lovemaker	Paycheck, Johnny	22-39	CB
Mr. Midnight	Brooks, Garth	18-11	CB
Mr. Misunderstood	Church, Eric	46-10	BKD
Mr. Mom	Lonestar	23-398	CB
Mr. Mom	Lonestar	21-662	SC
Mr. Mom	Lonestar	20-489	ST
Mr. Moon	Smith, Carl	22-111	CB
Mr. Moonlight	Beatles	11-452	DK
Mr. Pinstripe Suit	Big Bad Voodoo Dadd	15-209	AMS
Mr. Pitiful	Redding, Otis	47-354	KV
Mr. Policeman	Paisley, Brad	44-88	KV
Mr. Right	Brooks, Garth	20-102	CB
Mr. Roboto	Styx	38-47	SC
Mr. Sandman	Chordettes	33-230	CB
Mr. Sandman	Chordettes	11-833	DK
Mr. Sandman	Chordettes	13-67	P
Mr. Sandman	Harris, EmmyLou	1-234	CB
Mr. Sandman	Harris, EmmyLou	7-110	MM
Mr. Shorty	Robbins, Marty	45-272	SSK
Mr. Spaceman	Byrds	47-554	KV
Mr. Tambourine Man	Byrds	17-44	DK
Mr. Tambourine Man	Byrds	12-860	P
Mr. Vain	Culture Club	47-3	SF
Mr/ Bartender (It's So Easy)	Sugar Ray	32-283	THM
Mrs. Brown You've Got A Lovely..	Herman's Hermits	16-790	DK
Mrs. Brown You've Got A Lovely...	Herman's Hermits	35-55	CB
Mrs. Brown You've Got A Lovely...	Herman's Hermits	9-783	SAV
Mrs. Brown You've Got A Lovely...	Herman's Hermits	5-173	SC
Mrs. Robinson	Simon & Garfunkel	23-643	BS
Mrs. Robinson	Simon & Garfunkel	5-302	SC
Mrs. Steven Rudy	McGuinn, Mark	14-839	ST
Mrs. Steven Rudy	McGuinn, Rudy	33-148	CB
Ms. Jackson	Outkast	25-462	MM
Ms. Jackson	Outkast	18-568	TT
Ms. Jackson	Vines	32-177	THM

SONG TITLE	ARTIST	#	TYPE
Much Too Young To Feel This Damn Ol	Brooks, Garth	6-279	MM
Mud On The Tires	Paisley, Brad	21-653	SC
Mud On The Tires	Paisley, Brad	20-501	ST
Muddy Water	Adkins, Trace	36-215	PHM
Mule Train	Ford, Tenn Ernie	19-846	CB
Mule Train	Ford, Tenn Ernie	3-881	PS
Multiplication	Darin, Bobby	47-7	MFK
Mummer's Dance the	McKennitt, Loreena	7-715	PHM
Mummer's Dance the	McKennitt, Loreena	5-195	SC
Murder On Music Row	Jackson & Strait	43-68	CB
Murder On Music Row	Jackson & Strait	13-829	CHM
Murder On Music Row	Strait & Jackson	19-258	CSZ
Murder On Music Row - duet	Strait & Jackson	34-338	CB
Murder On The Dance Floor	Ellis-Bextor,Sophie	25-346	MM
Music For Love	Mario	36-478	CB
Music Is The Victim **	Scissor Sisters	29-224	ZM
Music Music Music	Brewer, Teresa	35-4	CB
Music Music Music	Brewer, Teresa	4-194	SC
Music Of My Heart	N'Sync & Estefan	20-439	CB
Music Of My Heart	N'Sync & Estefan	8-498	PHT
Music Of My Heart - duet	Estefan & N'Sync	35-315	CB
Music Of The Night - duet	Streisand & Crawford	49-573	PS
Music That Makes Me Dance	Streisand, Barbra	15-287	PS
Music To Watch Girls Go By	Williams, Andy	49-43	ZVS
Music's No Good Without You	Cher	21-730	TT
Muskrat Love	America	46-413	CB
Muskrat Love	Captain & Tennille	34-30	CB
Must Be Doin' Somethin' Right	Currington, Billy	23-142	CB
Must Get Out	Maroon 5	21-684	Z
Must To Avoid a	Herman's Hermits	47-140	ZM
Must've Had A Ball	Jackson, Alan	45-109	SC
Musta Got Lost	J. Geils Band	4-78	SC
Musta Had A Good Time	Parmalee	44-210	BKD
Mustang Burn	Ingram, Jack	14-723	CB
Mustang Sally	Wilson Pickett	26-273	DK
Mustang Sally	Wilson Pickett	6-483	MM
Muzic	M	14-1	PHM
Muzic	M	16-119	PRT
Muzzle	Smashing Pumpkins	24-364	SC
My Angel Is Here	Judd, Wynonna	1-657	CB
My Angel Is Here	Judd, Wynonna	4-363	SC
My Arms Stay Open All Night	Tucker, Tanya	16-347	CB
My Arms Stay Open All Night	Tucker, Tanya	2-813	SC
My Babe	Fabulous T-Birds	48-611	NT
My Babe	Nelson, Ricky	46-37	SSK
My Baby	Lil Romeo	18-569	TT
My Baby	Rimes, LeAnn	7-447	MM
My Baby Just Cares For	Cole, Nat "King"	46-360	MM

185

SONG TITLE	ARTIST	#	TYPE
Me			
My Baby Loves Lovin'	White Plains	20-48	SC
My Baby Loves Me	McBride, Martina	1-376	CB
My Baby Loves Me	McBride, Martina	26-582	DK
My Baby Loves Me	McBride, Martina	6-402	MM
My Baby Thinks He's A Train	Cash, Roseanne	49-631	CB
My Baby You	Anthony, Marc	33-383	CB
My Baby You	Anthony, Marc	15-434	PHM
My Baby's Got Good Timin'	Seals, Dan	5-560	SC
My Baby's Guns & Roses	Gilbert, Brantley	44-281	KCD
My Baby's Lovin'	Singletary, Daryle	8-765	CB
My Back Pages	Byrds	14-459	SC
My Best Friend	McGraw, Tim	5-808	SC
My Best Friend	McGraw, Tim	22-512	ST
My Best Friend's Girl	Cars	13-646	SGB
My Blue Angel	Tippin, Aaron	2-519	SC
My Blue Heaven	Autry, Gene	46-291	CB
My Bologna	Yankovic, Weird Al	49-844	SGB
My Bonnie	Standard	12-608	P
My Boo	Keys, Alicia & Usher	37-97	SC
My Boo - duet	Usher & Keys	30-805	PHM
My Boy	Presley, Elvis	14-825	THM
My Boy Lollipop	Small, Millie	11-511	DK
My Boy Lollipop	Small, Millie	14-338	SC
My Boyfriend's Back	Angels	11-115	DK
My Boyfriend's Back	Angels	10-726	JVC
My Boyfriend's Back	Angels	3-367	MH
My Boyfriend's Back	Angels	6-153	MM
My Boyfriend's Back	Angels	13-84	P
My Boyfriend's Back	Angels	9-289	SC
My Boyfriend's Back	Shirelles	48-373	SGB
My Bucket's Got A Hole In It	Williams, Hank Sr.	22-310	CB
My Cellmate Thinks I'm Sexy	Judd, Cledus T.	35-419	CB
My Cellmate Thinks I'm Sexy	Judd, Cledus T.	14-164	CB
My Cellmate Thinks I'm Sexy	Judd, Cledus T.	15-136	SC
My Cherie Amour	Wonder, Stevie	11-811	DK
My Cherie Amour	Wonder, Stevie	9-46	MM
My Christmas Wish	Montgomery, J M	45-753	CB
My Church	Morris, Maren	48-639	KV
My Church (Inst)	Morris, Maren	49-415	BKD
My Confession	Groban, Josh	48-42	CB
My Country	Easter, Jeff&Sheri	22-11	CB
My Country 'Tis Of Thee	Patriotic	44-38	PT
My Cup Runneth Over	Lettermen	48-517	L1
My Dear Old Friend	Carpenter, M C	47-670	SC
My Dearest Darling	James, Etta	21-696	PS
My Ding A Ling **	Berry, Chuck	2-186	SC
My Ding-A-Ling **	Berry, Chuck	30-666	RSX
My Elusive Butterfly	Campbell, Glen	48-492	CKC
My Elusive Dreams	Rich, Charlie	8-361	CB
My Elusive Dreams	Wynette & Houston	7-118	MM

SONG TITLE	ARTIST	#	TYPE
My Elusive Dreams	Wynette & Houston	4-306	SC
My Elusive Dreams - duet	Twitty & Lynn	48-247	THM
My Everything	98 Degrees	17-717	THM
My Everything	98 Degrees	18-570	TT
My Eyes	Shelton, Blake	44-166	BKD
My Eyes Adored You	Valli, Frankie	12-24	DK
My Eyes Adored You	Valli, Frankie	2-850	SC
My Eyes Can Only See As Far As You	Pride, Charley	43-206	CB
My Father's Eyes	Clapton, Eric	10-131	SC
My Favorite Memory	Haggard, Merle	22-235	CB
My Favorite Memory	Haggard, Merle	12-53	DK
My Favorite Mistake	Crow, Sheryl	29-675	RS
My Favorite Mistake	Crow, Sheryl	10-50	SC
My Favorite S & M Things	Parody	47-876	ZP
My First Last One And Only	Collins, Jim	8-413	CB
My First Night With You	Mya	13-787	SGB
My First Taste Of Texas	Bruce, Ed	5-824	SC
My First Time	Lobo	46-336	SBI
My Foolish Heart	Cole, Nat "King"	46-371	SAV
My Foolish Heart	Martino, Al	29-494	LE
My Foolish Heart	Monheit, Jane	25-671	MM
My Friend	Laine, Frankie	45-601	OZP
My Friends	Red Hot Chili Peppe	15-535	THM
My Friends Are All Gonna...	Haggard, Merle	3-908	CB
My Front Porch Looking In	Lonestar	25-566	MM
My Front Porch Looking In	Lonestar	19-1	ST
My Front Porch Looking In	Lonestar	32-225	THM
My Funny Friend And Me	Sting	17-721	THM
My Funny Valentine	Bennett/Vaught/Sina	16-750	DK
My Funny Valentine	Gaylor, Ruth	12-542	P
My Funny Valentine	Sinatra, Frank	49-483	MM
My Funny Valentine	Streisand, Barbra	49-580	PS
My Gal Sal	Ives, Burl	43-391	CBE P
My Generation	Who	28-146	DK
My Generation	Who	7-53	MM
My Generation	Who	3-857	SC
My Girl	Drifters	45-891	LE
My Girl	Temptations	17-127	DK
My Girl	Temptations	12-625	P
My Girl	Temptations	9-659	SAV
My Girl	Temptations	2-89	SC
My Girl Back Home	South Pacific	17-708	SC
My Girl Bill **	Stafford, Jim	23-25	SC
My Girl Friday	Norwood, Daron	2-832	SC
My Girl Josephine	Domino, Fats	45-845	VH
My Give A Damn's Busted	Messina, Jo Dee	23-7	CB
My Goddess	Exies	32-111	THM
My Grandfather's Clock	Standard	47-840	SFM

SONG TITLE	ARTIST	#	TYPE
My Guy	Wells, Mary	9-880	DK
My Guy	Wells, Mary	10-727	JVC
My Guy	Wells, Mary	3-268	MM
My Hallelujah Song	Hough, Julianne	36-224	PHM
My Hang-Up Is You	Hart, Freddie	12-51	DK
My Hang-Up Is You	Hart, Freddie	19-441	SC
My Happiness	Francis, Connie	20-40	SC
My Happiness	Powderfinger	15-304	THM
My Happiness	Presley, Elvis	25-102	MM
My Happy Ending	Lavigne, Avril	23-555	MM
My Hawaii	Krush	6-832	MM
My Heart	Milsap, Ronnie	11-621	DK
My Heart Belongs To Daddy	Lee, Peggy	25-261	MM
My Heart Belongs To Daddy	Monroe, Marilyn	49-330	CB
My Heart Belongs To Me	Streisand, Barbra	10-497	DA
My Heart Belongs To Only You	Vinton, Bobby	7-261	MM
My Heart Can't Tell You No	Evans, Sara	38-135	PHM
My Heart Can't Tell You No	Stewart, Rod	12-187	DK
My Heart Cracked	Travis, Randy	47-791	SRK
My Heart Cries For You	Standard	10-470	MG
My Heart Has A History	Brandt, Paul	7-199	MM
My Heart Has A Mind Of It's Own	Francis, Connie	5-90	SC
My Heart Is Calling	Houston, Whitney	48-637	PI
My Heart Is Lost To You	Brooks & Dunn	25-226	MM
My Heart Is Lost To You	Brooks & Dunn	16-699	ST
My Heart Is Still Beating	Kinleys	5-721	SC
My Heart Is Still Beating	Kinleys	22-493	ST
My Heart Skips A Beat	Owens, Buck	22-244	SC
My Heart Skips A Beat	Yoakam, Dwight	49-695	DCK
My Heart Wants To Run	Azar, Steve	17-583	ST
My Heart Will Go On	Dion, Celine	15-107	BS
My Heart Will Go On	Dion, Celine	14-194	CB
My Heart Will Go On	Dion, Celine	7-711	PHM
My Heart Will Never Know	Walker, Clay	1-97	CB
My Heart Will Never Know	Walker, Clay	6-800	MM
My Heart Will Never Know	Walker, Clay	2-763	SC
My Hero	Foo Fighters	48-229	SC
My Heroes Have Always Been...	Nelson, Willie	34-241	CB
My Heros Have Always Been Cowboys	Nelson, Willie	13-464	P
My Home Town	Anka, Paul	9-552	SAV
My Home Town	Anka, Paul	14-455	SC
My Home's In Alabama	Alabama	4-446	BS
My Home's In Alabama	Alabama	1-1	CB
My Hometown	Robison, Charlie	5-838	SC
My Hometown	Springsteen, Bruce	35-185	CB
My Hometown	Springsteen, Bruce	17-612	LE
My House	Musgraves, Kacey	45-312	KV

SONG TITLE	ARTIST	#	TYPE
My Humps	Black Eyed Peas	30-139	PT
My Humps	Black Eyed Peas	30-747	SF
My Imagination	Black, Clint	20-497	ST
My Immortal	Evanescence	19-663	CB
My Kind Of Crazy	Anderson, John	4-416	SC
My Kind Of Crazy	Gilbert, Brantley	44-302	DCK
My Kind Of Girl	Monro, Matt	9-181	PS
My Kind Of Girl	Raye, Collin	1-131	CB
My Kind Of Girl	Raye, Collin	34-309	CB
My Kind Of Girl	Raye, Collin	17-263	NA
My Kind Of Girl	Raye, Collin	2-571	SC
My Kind Of Music	Scott, Ray	23-475	CB
My Kind Of Town	Sinatra, Frank	9-233	PT
My Kind Of Town	Sinatra, Frank	21-209	SGB
My Kind Of Town, Chicago Is	Sinatra, Frank	20-768	KB
My Kind of Woman/My Kind of Man	Gill & Loveless	8-970	CB
My Kind of Woman/My Kind of Man	Gill & Loveless	14-625	SC
My Kinda Girl	Babyface	11-730	DK
My Kinda Party	Aldean, Jason	37-343	CB
My Last Date (With You)	Davis, Skeeter	43-326	CB
My Last Name	Bentley, Dierks	22-5	CB
My Last Name	Bentley, Dierks	20-266	SC
My Last Name	Bentley, Dierks	19-676	ST
My Life	Joel, Billy	16-138	LE
My Life	Joel, Billy	5-116	SC
My Life (I'll Throw It Away If I..)	Anderson, Bill	20-790	CB
My Life Throw It Away If I Want To	Anderson, Bill	5-361	SC
My Life Would Suck Without You	Clarkson, Kelly	47-689	CB
My List	Keith, Toby	25-135	MM
My List	Keith, Toby	16-97	ST
My Little Friend	Presley, Elvis	25-118	MM
My Little Girl	McGraw, Tim	30-45	CB
My Little Girl	McGraw, Tim	30-99	PHM
My Little Grass Shack	Standard	9-825	SAV
My Little Town	Simon & Garfunkel	15-536	DM
My Love	Clark, Petula	19-619	MH
My Love	Clark, Petula	9-85	PS
My Love	Clark, Petula	5-12	SC
My Love	James, Sonny	3-770	CB
My Love	Little Texas	10-785	JVC
My Love	Little Texas	6-472	MM
My Love	McCartney & Wings	11-248	DK
My Love	McCartney, Paul	48-563	DK
My Love	Richie, Lionel	43-371	CB
My Love Goes On And On	Cagle, Chris	14-104	CB
My Love Goes On And On	Cagle, Chris	14-17	CHM
My Love Goes On And On	Cagle, Chris	19-226	CSZ
My Love Is Like - Wooh	Mya	32-426	THM
My Love Is Like A Red	Clydesiders	48-766	P

SONG TITLE	ARTIST	#	TYPE
Red Rose			
My Love Is Like... WO!	Mya	25-725	MM
My Love Is Like....WO!	Mya	21-785	SC
My Love Is Like...Wooh	Mya	35-284	CB
My Love Is The Shhh	Something/People	7-719	PHM
My Love Is Your Love	Houston, Whitney	34-134	CB
My Love Is Your Love	Houston, Whitney	8-526	PHT
My Love Sweet Love	LaBelle, Patti	4-332	SC
My Love Will Not Change	Ketchum, Hal	20-450	ST
My Lovin' (You're Never Gonna Get I	En Vogue	6-104	MM
My Loving (You're Never...)	En Vogue	34-108	CB
My Mammy	Jolson, Al	29-472	LE
My Mammy	Jolson, Al	12-939	PS
My Man	Funny Girl	49-441	MM
My Man	Streisand, Barbra	49-448	MM
My Man	Streisand, Barbra	49-564	PS
My Man	Wynette, Tammy	4-749	SC
My Man - show	Funny Girl	48-789	MM
My Maria	Brooks & Dunn	35-409	CB
My Maria	Brooks & Dunn	7-226	MM
My Maria	Brooks & Dunn	22-879	ST
My Maria	Stevenson, B.W.	34-42	CB
My Melody Of Love	Vinton, Bobby	7-43	MM
My Michelle - WN	Guns 'N Roses	48-57	SC
My Mistake	Cam	49-9	FMK
My Mistake	Cam	49-537	KVD
My My My	Gill, Johnny	34-94	CB
My Name	Canyon, George	22-334	CB
My Name Is **	Eminem	25-463	MM
My Next Broken Heart	Brooks & Dunn	1-77	CB
My Next Broken Heart	Brooks & Dunn	13-511	P
My Next Broken Heart	Brooks & Dunn	2-343	SC
My Next Thirty Years	McGraw, Tim	14-708	CB
My Next Thirty Years	McGraw, Tim	19-210	CSZ
My Next Thirty Years	McGraw, Tim	14-28	THM
My Night To Howl	Morgan, Lorrie	6-500	MM
My Night To Howl	Morgan, Lorrie	2-127	SC
My Oh My	Wreckers	30-112	CB
My Old Dog Tray	Standard	47-836	SDK
My Old Friend	McGraw, Tim	23-478	CB
My Old Kentucky Home	Autry, Gene	43-320	CB
My Old Kentucky Home	Smith, Kate	11-492	DK
My Old Man	Atkins, Rodney	30-39	CB
My Old Man	Atkins, Rodney	18-596	ST
My Old Man	Atkins, Rodney	32-84	THM
My Old Piano	Ross, Diana	48-779	P
My Old School	Steely Dan	15-388	RS
My Old Yellow Car	Seals, Dan	46-112	SC
My One True Friend	Midler, Bette	14-279	MM
My One True Friend	Midler, Bette	45-939	MM
My Only Love	Statler Brothers	19-384	CB
My Only Love	Statler Brothers	5-754	SC
My Own Kind Of Hat	Haggard, Merle	37-179	CB
My Own Kind Of Hat	Jackson, Alan	8-912	CB

SONG TITLE	ARTIST	#	TYPE
My Own True Love	Duprees	49-453	MM
My Own Worst Enemy	Lit	7-895	PHT
My Part Of Forever	Paycheck, Johnny	22-44	CB
My Perogative	Brown, Bobby	34-92	CB
My Poor Old Heart	Krauss, Alison	29-49	CB
My Prayer	Platters	11-759	DK
My Prayer	Platters	6-259	MM
My Prayer	Platters	14-347	SC
My Reason For Living	Husky, Ferlin	22-268	CB
My Rifle My Pony And Me	Williams, Don	45-216	SC
My Romance	Standard	13-631	SGB
My Roots Are Showing	Shawanda, Crystal	36-264	PHM
My Sacrifice	Creed	33-404	CB
My Sacrifice	Creed	25-38	MM
My Sacrifice	Creed	16-74	ST
My Same	Adele	44-169	KV
My Second Home	Lawrence, Tracy	2-7	SC
My Selfish Heart	Trainor, Meghan	45-151	KVD
My Sentimental Friend	Herman's Hermits	10-629	SF
My Sharona	Knack	33-301	CB
My Sharona	Knack	6-486	MM
My Sharona	Knack	12-796	P
My Shoes Keep Walking Back To..	Price, Ray	4-863	SC
My Shoes Keep Walking Back To...	Price, Ray	3-774	CB
My Side Of The Street	Steele, Tommy	39-70	PHN
My Sister	McEntire, Reba	22-331	CB
My Sister	McEntire, Reba	23-379	SC
My Songs Know What You Did...	Fall Out Boy	45-446	SS
My Special Angel	Helms, Bobby	33-441	CB
My Special Angel	Helms, Bobby	6-270	MM
My Strongest Weakness	Judd, Wynonna	1-649	CB
My Strongest Weakness	Judd, Wynonna	6-223	MM
My Sweet Lady	Denver, John	29-694	SC
My Sweet Lady	Denver, John	15-613	THM
My Tender Heart	Richie, Lionel	47-462	SBI
My Tennessee Mountain Home	Parton, Dolly	49-333	CB
My Town	Montgomery Gentry	33-177	CN
My Town	Montgomery Gentry	25-293	MM
My Town	Montgomery Gentry	17-584	ST
My True Story	Jive Five	7-270	MM
My Uncle Used to Love....She Died	Miller, Roger	22-287	CB
My Way	Limp Bizkit	15-301	THM
My Way	Paper Lace	47-542	TU
My Way	Presley, Elvis	18-442	KC
My Way	Sinatra, Frank	17-145	DK
My Way	Sinatra, Frank	7-190	MM
My Way	Sinatra, Frank	12-522	P
My Way	Sinatra, Frank	9-242	PT
My Way	Sinatra, Frank	2-202	SC
My Wife Thinks You're Dead	Brown, Junior	40-77	CB
My Wife Thinks You're	Brown, Junior	4-134	SC

SONG TITLE	ARTIST	#	TYPE
Dead			
My Wish	Rascal Flatts	30-110	CB
My Wish	Rascal Flatts	30-97	PHM
My Woman My Woman My Wife	Robbins, Marty	3-235	CB
My Woman My Woman My Wife	Robbins, Marty	8-674	SAV
My Woman's Good To Me	Houston, David	48-193	CB
My World Is Caving In	Van Dyke, Leroy	45-887	VH
My World Is Empty Without You Babe	Supremes	12-102	DK
My World Is Over	Rogers & Duncan	20-480	ST
My Worst Fear	Rascal Flatts	23-395	CB
Mysterious Ways	U2	13-272	P
Mysterious Ways	U2	6-32	SC
Mystery Train	Brian Setzer Orch	46-531	KV
Mystery Train	Presley, Elvis	7-128	MM
Mystery Train - Tiger Man	Presley, Elvis	49-444	MM
Mystery Train Pt. 2	Earle, Steve	46-183	DCK
Na Na Hey Hey Kiss Him Goodbye	Steam	33-446	CB
Na Na Hey Hey Kiss Him Goodbye	Steam	11-664	DK
Na Na Hey Hey Kiss Him Goodbye	Steam	7-54	MM
Na Na Hey Hey Kiss Him Goodbye	Steam	13-94	P
Na Na Hey Hey Kiss Him Goodbye	Steam	9-766	SAV
Na Na Hey Hey Kiss Him Goodbye	Steam	3-260	SC
Nadine (Is It You)	Berry, Chuck	43-438	LG
Nah!	Twain, Shania	22-14	CB
Naive	Kooks	30-753	SF
Naked	Goo Goo Dolls	13-610	P
Naked	Goo Goo Dolls	4-177	SC
Naked To The Pain	Bonamy, James	4-828	SC
Naked Without You	Dayne, Taylor	13-709	SGB
Naked Woman And Beer	Williams, Hank Jr.	9-402	CB
Name Game the	Ellis, Shirley	16-860	DK
Name Game the	Ellis, Shirley	21-573	SC
Name Game the	Fontana, Wayne	21-199	DK
Name Of The Game the	Abba	7-505	MM
Nashville Cats	Lovin' Spoonful	47-213	PRI
Nashville Without You	McGraw, Tim	44-157	BKD
Nasty	Jackson, Janet	27-304	DK
Nasty	Jackson, Janet	15-419	PS
Nasty Girl **	Vanity's	5-546	SC
Natalie	Mars, Bruno	47-221	KV
National Working Woman's Holiday	Kershaw, Sammy	6-589	MM
National Working Woman's Holiday...	Kershaw, Sammy	1-471	CB
Natural Blue (Grammy Version)	Moby	16-258	TT
Natural Born Lovers	Seals, Brady	48-102	SC
Natural Disaster	Zac Brown Band	46-70	KV

SONG TITLE	ARTIST	#	TYPE
Natural High	Bloodstone	25-275	MM
Natural High	Haggard, Merle	22-228	CB
Natural Man	Rawls, Lou	25-272	MM
Natural One	Folk Implosion	4-682	SC
Natural Thing	Doobie Brothers	47-26	KV
Natural Woman	Franklin, Aretha	12-710	P
Natural Woman	Franklin, Aretha	2-267	SC
Natural Woman (You Make Me...)	Franklin, Aretha	25-170	MM
Natural Woman a (You Make Me...)	Franklin, Aretha	26-108	DK
Naturally	Kalapana	6-840	MM
Nature Boy	Cole, Nat "King"	46-353	SAV
Nature Boy	Dion, Celine	19-17	PS
Nature's Law	Embrace	30-691	SF
Naughty Girl	Beyonce	48-385	SC
Naughty Girls Need Love Too	Fox, Samantha	11-534	DK
Naughty Lady Of Shady Lane	Bennett, Tony	10-408	LE
Naughty Naughty	Parr, John	6-22	SC
Navy Blue	Renay, Diane	4-717	SC
Near You	Jones & Wynette	5-447	SC
Near You	Yoakam, Dwight	49-630	DCK
Near You Always	Jewel	36-330	SC
Nearness Of You - duet	Fitzgerald & Armstrong	49-723	KV
Nearness Of You the	Easton, Sheena	18-266	DK
Nearness Of You the	Standard	15-537	DK
Need A Little Taste Of Love	Doobie Brothers	18-392	SAV
Need To Be Next To You	Nash, Leigh	17-719	THM
Need You Now - duet	Lady Antebellum	36-49	PT
Need You Tonight	Inxs	33-325	CB
Need You Tonight	INXS	11-786	DK
Needle & Damage Damage Damage	Young, Neil	15-752	AMS
Needle & The Spoon the	Lynyrd Skynyrd	5-270	SC
Needle & The Spoon the	Lynyrd Skynyrd	19-817	SGB
Needles & Pins	Searchers	11-252	DK
Needles & Pins	Searchers	20-33	SC
Needles And Pins	Petty & Nicks	9-853	SAV
Needles And Pins - duet	Nicks & Petty	47-899	SAV
Negatory Romance	Hall, Tom T.	18-280	CB
Neighbor the	Dixie Chicks	49-916	SC
Neither One Of Us	Knight & Pips	10-677	HE
Neither One Of Us..	Knight & Pips	17-104	DK
Nellie The Elephant	Toy Dolls	16-374	SF
Neon	Young, Chris	38-217	PHN
Neon Light	Shelton, Blake	45-332	ASK
Neon Moon	Brooks & Dunn	1-78	CB
Neon Moon	Brooks & Dunn	13-510	P
Neon Moon	Brooks & Dunn	2-4	SC
Neon Moon	Brooks, Garth	48-358	SC
Neon Moonlight	Martinez, Rosco	15-766	NU
Neon Wishing Well	Ward, Mike	10-85	SC
Nerve the	Strait, George	1-252	CB
Neutron Dance	Pointer Sisters	11-375	DK

189

SONG TITLE	ARTIST	#	TYPE
Never	Heart	20-53	SC
Never	Jaheim	36-504	CB
Never A Time	Collins, Phil	44-27	BS
Never Again	Clarkson, Kelly	30-483	CB
Never Again	Nickelback	46-313	SC
Never Again	Presley, Elvis	25-321	MM
Never Again Again	Womack, Lee Ann	7-619	CHM
Never Again Again	Womack, Lee Ann	10-79	SC
Never Be Anyone Else But You	Nelson, Ricky	21-703	CB
Never Be Anyone Else But You	Nelson, Ricky	6-60	SC
Never Be You	Cash, Roseanne	5-761	SC
Never Been Any Reason	Head East	21-812	SC
Never Been Kissed	Austin, Sherrie	8-959	CB
Never Been Kissed	Austin, Sherrie	14-628	SC
Never Been So Loved	Pride, Charley	3-800	CB
Never Been So Loved	Pride, Charley	4-646	SC
Never Been To Spain	Three Dog Night	2-435	SC
Never Can Say Goodbye	Gaynor, Gloria	11-754	DK
Never Can Say Goodbye	Jackson Five	24-331	SC
Never Comes The Day	Moody Blues	28-141	DK
Never Could Toe The Mark	Jennings, Waylon	45-192	TU
Never Die Young	Taylor, James	45-543	SC
Never Ending	Presley, Elvis	25-119	MM
Never Ending	Rihanna	48-405	DCK
Never Ending Song Of Love	Delaney, Bonnie	9-369	MG
Never Ending Song Of Love	Delaney, Bonnie	9-721	SAV
Never Ending Why	Placebo	48-739	KV
Never Ever	All Saints	16-230	PHM
Never Going Back Again	Fleetwood Mac	17-522	SC
Never Gonna Fall In Love Again	Carmen, Eric	11-416	DK
Never Gonna Feel That Way Again	Chesney, Kenny	48-78	CB
Never Gonna Give You Up	Astley, Rick	11-243	DK
Never Gonna Give You Up	White, Barry	10-678	HE
Never Gonna Leave This Bed	Maroon 5	37-268	PHM
Never Had A Dream Come True	Club 7	18-528	TT
Never Had It So Good	Carpenter, M C	14-685	CB
Never In A Million Tears	Brown, T. Graham	8-975	CB
Never In A Million Tears	Brown, T. Graham	10-191	SC
Never Is Enough	Barenaked Ladies	30-624	RS
Never Keeping Secrets	Babyface	2-235	SC
Never Knew Lonely	Gill, Vince	1-587	CB
Never Knew Love	Adams, Oleta	4-172	SC
Never Knew Love Like This Before	Mills, Stephanie	9-42	MM
Never Leave You - Uh Ooh Uh Ooooh	Lumidee	32-312	THM
Never Let Go	Groban, Josh	48-46	CB
Never Let Me Go	Vandross, Luther	18-482	NU

SONG TITLE	ARTIST	#	TYPE
Never Let You Go	Third Eye Blind	15-323	PHM
Never Love You Enough	Wright, Chely	29-355	CB
Never Love You Enough	Wright, Chely	15-188	ST
Never Mind Me	Big & Rich	29-183	CB
Never Mind Me	Big & Rich	29-857	SC
Never My Love	5th Dimension	48-91	LE
Never My Love	Association	12-312	DK
Never My Love	Association	13-108	P
Never My Love	Association	9-474	SAV
Never Never Gonna Give You Up	White, Barry	6-560	MM
Never Never Never	Bassey, Shirley	46-482	PS
Never On Sunday	Costa, Paul	12-498	P
Never Really Wanted	Paslay, Eriic	43-277	PHN
Never Saw A Miracle	Stigers, Curtis	7-474	MM
Never Say Die	Dixie Chicks	16-650	RS
Never Say Goodbye	Bon Jovi	14-565	AH
Never Should've Let You Go	Hi-Five	4-271	SC
Never The Less	Tyrell, Steve	30-190	LE
Never Too Far	Carey, Mariah	23-583	PHM
Never Too Much	Vandross, Luther	48-288	LE
Never Trust A Woman	Foley, Red	43-364	CB
Never Wanted Nothing More	Chesney, Kenny	30-469	CB
Never Went To Church	Streets	30-718	SF
Nevertheless (I'm In Love With You)	Standard	47-516	VH
New Age Girl	Deadeye Dick	2-719	SC
New Attitude	LaBelle, Patti	28-364	DK
New Attitude	LaBelle, Patti	5-141	SC
New Beginning	Chapman, Tracy	24-239	SC
New Day For You	Basia	14-862	PS
New Day For You	Basia	16-70	SC
New Day Has Come	Dion, Celine	18-300	CB
New Day Has Come	Dion, Celine	19-16	PS
New Day Has Come a	Dion, Celine	25-196	MM
New Favorite	Krauss, Alison	25-417	MM
New Favorite	Krauss, Alison	18-472	ST
New Fool	Krauss, Alison	24-86	sC
New Fool At An Old Game	McEntire, Reba	1-793	CB
New Girl Now	Honeymoon Suite	5-468	SC
New Green Light the	Thompson, Hank	19-323	CB
New Groom Boogie	Al Dexter & Troopers	46-412	CB
New Jolie Blond	Foley, Red	19-631	CB
New Kid In Town	Eagles	7-555	BS
New Kid In Town	Eagles	2-261	SC
New Life a	Eder, Linda	16-720	PS
New Looks From An Old Lover	Thomas, B.J.	9-511	SAV
New Looks From An Old Lover	Thomas, B.J.	5-248	SC
New Looks From An Old Lover	Thomas, B.J.	47-387	SC
New Money	Summer&New Row	14-94	CB
New Mule Skinner Blues	Monroe, Bill	47-294	CB

190

SONG TITLE	ARTIST	#	TYPE
New Orleans	Blues Brothers	38-35	SBII
New Patches	Tillis, Mel	19-464	CB
New Rose	Damned	21-610	SF
New San Antonio Rose	Wills, Bob	5-704	SC
New Sensation	INXS	27-200	DK
New Spanish Two Step	Wills, Bob	19-625	CB
New Strings	Lambert, Miranda	45-33	ASK
New Strings	Lambert, Miranda	29-581	CB
New Tomantics	Swift, Taylor	48-306	KV
New Way Home	Oslin, K.T.	4-148	SC
New Way To Fly	Brooks, Garth	48-360	TU
New Way To Light Up An Old Flame	Diffie, Joe	1-273	CB
New Way To Light Up An Old Flame	Diffie, Joe	20-403	MH
New World In The Morning	Whittaker, Roger	13-590	PL
New Year's Day	U2	30-75	SC
New York Groove	Frehley, Ace	17-468	SC
New York Hold Her Tight	Restless Heart	1-417	CB
New York Minute	Henley, Don	15-708	LE
New York New York	Adams, Ryan	25-39	MM
New York New York	Adams, Ryan	30-652	THM
New York New York	Minelli, Liza	49-217	LG
New York New York	Sinatra, Frank	11-104	DK
New York New York	Sinatra, Frank	20-761	KB
New York New York	Sinatra, Frank	6-355	MM
New York New York	Sinatra, Frank	12-504	P
New York New York	Sinatra, Frank	16-410	PR
New York New York	Sinatra, Frank	9-258	PT
New York New York	Sinatra, Frank	2-194	SC
New York State Of Mind	Joel, Billy	33-298	CB
New York State Of Mind	Joel, Billy	16-133	LE
New York State Of Mind	Streisand, Barbra	46-280	KV
New York's Not My Home	Croce, Jim	48-463	CB
Next Big Thing	Gill, Vince	34-398	CB
Next Big Thing	Gill, Vince	25-452	MM
Next Big Thing	Gill, Vince	18-464	ST
Next Big Thing	Gill, Vince	32-76	THM
Next Door To An Angel	Sedaka, Neil	45-355	CB
Next In Line	Twitty, Conway	4-860	SC
Next In Line	Twitty, Conway	48-245	SC
Next Lifetime	Badu, Erykah	10-90	SC
Next Step the	Collins, Jim	8-145	CB
Next Thing Smokin'	Diffie, Joe	1-276	CB
Next Thing Smokin'	Diffie, Joe	15-538	MM
Next Time I Fall In Love	Cetera & Grant	13-158	P
Next Time I Fall In Love	Cetera & Grant	9-203	SO
Next Time I Fall In Love	Grant, Amy	18-768	PS
Next Time I Fall In Love - duet	Grant & Cetera	35-312	CB
Next Time I Love	Eder, Linda	16-716	PS
Next To You Next To me	Shenandoah	1-483	CB
Next Year	Foo Fighters	48-227	SC
Nice 'N Easy	Sinatra, Frank	21-220	SGB
Nice And Slow	Usher	16-229	PHM

SONG TITLE	ARTIST	#	TYPE
Nice And Slow	Usher	5-194	SC
Nice To Be With You	Gallery	9-365	MG
Nice To Be With You	Gallery	3-20	SC
Nice Work If You Can Get It	Bennett, Tony	7-183	MM
Nice Work If You Can Get It	Sinatra, Frank	14-271	MM
Nick Of Time	Raitt, Bonnie	17-403	DK
Nick Of Time	Raitt, Bonnie	10-773	JVC
Nick Of Time	Raitt, Bonnie	6-359	MM
Nick Of Time	Raitt, Bonnie	12-882	P
Nickajack	River Road	12-930	CB
Nickels & Dimes & Love	Montgomery, J M	49-422	SC
Night And Day	Fitzgerald, Ella	44-117	KV
Night And Day	Sinatra, Frank	42-31	CB
Night And Day	Sinatra, Frank	10-720	JVC
Night And Day	Sinatra, Frank	45-7	KV
Night And Day (Faster Version)	Sinatra, Frank	28-500	DK
Night Before (Life Goes On)	Underwood, Carrie	30-126	AS
Night Before the	Beatles	20-207	SC
Night Birds	Kimes, Royal Wade	19-11	ST
Night Calls	Cocker, Joe	45-621	DCK
Night Changes	One Direction	48-326	MRH
Night Chicago Died the	Paper Lace	9-347	AH
Night Disappear With You	McComas, Brian	16-168	CB
Night Disappear With You	McComas, Brian	25-9	MM
Night Disappear With You	McComas, Brian	15-862	ST
Night Fever	Bee Gees	11-663	DK
Night Fever	Bee Gees	9-654	SAV
Night Fever	Bee Gees	2-497	SC
Night Games	Pride, Charley	3-798	CB
Night Hank Williams Came To Town	Cash, Johnny	43-419	KV
Night Has A Thousand Eyes the	Vee, Bobby	5-166	SC
Night Has A Thousand Eyes the	Vee, Bobby	10-618	SF
Night I Called The Old Man Out	Brooks, Garth	6-629	MM
Night Is Fallin' In My Heart	Diamond Rio	2-543	SC
Night Is Young the	Park, Kyle	39-57	PHN
Night Is Young the	Strait, George	42-7	PHN
Night Life	Price, Ray	3-785	CB
Night Moves	Seger, Bob	2-790	SC
Night Moves	Seger, Bob	10-170	UK
Night Owls the	Little River Band	4-326	SC
Night Shift	Richie, Lionel	16-873	DK
Night Shift	Richie, Lionel	10-395	LE
Night That You'll Never Forget	Love And Theft	49-666	SBI
Night the	Disturbed	36-383	SC
Night The Lights Went Out In GA	Lawrence, Vicki	13-14	P

SONG TITLE	ARTIST	#	TYPE
Night The Lights Went Out in GA	McEntire, Reba	1-802	CB
Night The Lights Went Out In GA	McEntire, Reba	6-191	MM
Night They Drove Old Dixie Down	Baez, Joan	7-348	MM
Night They Drove Old Dixie Down	Baez, Joan	5-383	SC
Night They Drove Old Dixie Down	Band	17-70	DK
Night Time Is The Right Time - duet	Charles, Ray	35-69	CB
Night Time Magic	Gatlin, Larry	47-101	CB
Night To Remember	Diffie, Joe	8-943	CB
Night To Remember	Diffie, Joe	7-868	CHT
Night To Remember a	Diffie, Joe	22-745	ST
Night Train	Aldean, Jason	41-70	ASK
Night Will Only Know the	Brooks, Garth	24-2	SC
Night's On Fire	Nail, David	45-57	BKD
Nightingale	Eagles	49-86	ZPA
Nightingale	Jones, Norah	19-192	Z
Nightingale	King, Carole	43-450	LG
Nightrain - WN	Guns 'N Roses	48-67	KV
Nights	Bruce, Ed	5-154	SC
Nights I Can't Remember, Friends I'll...	Keith, Toby	47-162	CB
Nights In White Satin	Moody Blues	33-284	CB
Nights in White Satin	Moody Blues	12-331	DK
Nights In White Satin	Moody Blues	13-176	P
Nights Like These	Lynns	10-126	SC
Nights Like This	Azar, Steve	4-597	SC
Nights on Broadway	Bee Gees	17-498	LE
Nights' Too Long the	Loveless, Patty	1-714	CB
Nine In The Afternoon	Panic at the Disco	36-463	CB
Nine Pound Hammer	Country Gentlemen	8-254	CB
Nine Pound Hammer	Monroe, Bill	47-297	SC
Nine2Five	Ordinary Boys&Lady	30-710	SF
Nineteen Somethin'	Wills, Mark	25-409	MM
Nineteen Somethin'	Wills, Mark	18-449	ST
Nineteen Somethin'	Wills, Mark	32-6	THM
Ninety Miles An Hour	Snow, Hank	22-130	CB
Nite & Day	Al B. Sure!	28-325	DK
Nite & Day	Holiday, Billie	11-588	DK
Nite And Day	Kasino F	48-569	DK
NO	Trainor, Meghan	49-659	BKD
No Air	Palmer, Rissi	36-620	CB
No Air	Sparls, Jordin feat Chris Brown	36-486	CB
No Alibis	Clapton, Eric	13-796	SGB
No Boundaries	Allen, Chris	36-294	PHM
No Business	Raitt, Bonnie	10-768	JVC
No Doubt About It	McCoy, Neal	1-850	CB
No Doubt About It	McCoy, Neal	26-534	DK
No Doubt About It	McCoy, Neal	10-775	JVC
No Doubt About It	McCoy, Neal	6-469	MM
No Doubt About It	McCoy, Neal	2-426	SC
No Easy Goodbye	South Sixty Five	8-932	CB

SONG TITLE	ARTIST	#	TYPE
No Easy Goodbye	South Sixty Five	14-605	SC
No End In Sight	Elam, Katrina	23-405	CB
No End In Sight	Elam, Katrina	23-43	SC
No End In Sight	Elam, Katrina	20-493	ST
No End To This Road	Restless Heart	8-488	CB
No End To This Road	Restless Heart	5-288	SC
No End To This Road	Restless Heart	22-820	ST
No Excuses	Alice In Chains	30-766	SF
No Fear	Clark, Terri	14-148	CB
No Fear	Clark, Terri	14-786	ST
No Future In The Past	Gill, Vince	1-598	CB
No Future In The Past	Gill, Vince	26-527	DK
No Getting' Over You	Milsap, Ronnie	9-569	SAV
No Good For You	Trainor, Meghan	45-152	KVD
No Help Wanted	Carlisles	39-15	CB
No Hurry	Zac Brown Band	38-279	BKD
No Hurry	Zac Brown Band	45-797	SBI
No Letting Go	Wonder, W.	32-213	THM
No Light No Light	Florence & Machine	38-242	PHM
No Love	Edmunds, Kevin	19-829	SGB
No Love Have I	Dunn, Holly	24-357	SC
No Man In His Wrong Heart	Allan, Gary	8-760	CB
No Man In His Wrong Heart	Allan, Gary	22-829	ST
No Man's Land	Montgomery, J M	7-138	MM
No Matter How High	Oak Ridge Boys	23-498	CB
No Matter What Happens	Streisand, Barbra	49-578	PS
No Mercy	Herndon, Ty	13-836	CHM
No Mercy	Herndon, Ty	23-371	SC
No Mercy	Herndon, Ty	22-532	ST
No Milk Today	Herman's Hermits	47-138	SF
No Mistakes	Smyth, Patty	6-178	MM
No Mistakes	Smyth, Patty	24-146	SC
No More (Baby I'm A Doo Right)	3LW	18-529	TT
No More Drama	Blige, Mary J.	20-612	CB
No More Drama	Blige, Mary J.	25-146	MM
No More Drama	Blige, Mary J.	16-86	ST
No More I Love Yous	Lennox, Annie	16-618	MM
No More I Love Yous	Lennox, Annie	17-722	PS
No More Lies	Michel'le	12-846	P
No More Looking Over My Shoulder	Tritt, Travis	8-354	CB
No More Looking Over My Shoulder	Tritt, Travis	22-719	ST
No More Me And You	Wilkinson, Amanda	23-132	CB
No More Tears	Diaz, Dian	36-181	PHM
No More Tears	Osbourne, Ozzy	23-423	SC
No More Tears - Enough Is Enough	Streisand&Summer	26-95	DK
No More Tears - Enough Is Enough	Streisand&Summer	13-155	P
No More Tears - Enough Is Enough	Streisand&Summer	10-546	SF
No More Tears (Left To Cry)	Gore, Lesley	47-112	DFK
No More Than I Got	Lewis, Jerry Lee	47-801	SRK

SONG TITLE	ARTIST	#	TYPE
No More Words	Berlin	24-561	SC
No News	Lonestar	22-454	SC
No No Song	Starr, Ringo	2-752	SC
No One	Keys, Alicia	36-480	CB
No One Else On Earth	Judd, Wynonna	1-648	CB
No One Else On Earth	Judd, Wynonna	19-294	MH
No One Else On Earth	Judd, Wynonna	6-107	MM
No One Else On Earth	Judd, Wynonna	13-505	P
No One Else On Earth	Judd, Wynonna	2-715	SC
No One Knows	Queens/Stone Age	18-827	THM
No One Knows Who I Am	Eder, Linda	16-719	PS
No One Like You	Scorpions	49-96	SC
No One Mends A Broken Heart	Mandrell, Barbara	5-567	SC
No One Needs To Know	Twain, Shania	1-516	CB
No One Needs To Know	Twain, Shania	7-271	MM
No One Needs To Know	Twain, Shania	22-880	ST
No One To Run With	Allman Brothers	2-535	SC
No One Will Ever Love You - Nashville	James & Claybourne	45-473	KVD
No One'll Ever Love Me	Howard, Rebecca L	22-338	CB
No Ordinary Love	Sade	6-415	MM
No Ordinary Love	Sade	14-867	PS
No Ordinary Man	Byrd, Tracy	20-111	CB
No Other Love	Como, Perry	20-780	PS
No Other Time	Anderson, Lynn	47-646	CB
No Particular Place To Go	Berry, Chuck	11-42	PX
No Particular Place To Go	Berry, Chuck	3-12	SC
No Place Like Home	Middleman, Georgia	14-89	CB
No Place Like Home	Middleman, Georgia	22-578	ST
No Place Like Home	Travis, Randy	1-394	CB
No Place That Far	Evans, Sara	29-553	CB
No Place That Far	Evans, Sara	22-705	ST
No Promises	Ward, Shayne	30-705	SF
No Questions Asked	Fleetwood Mac	47-910	LE
No Rain	Blind Melon	28-401	DK
No Rain	Blind Melon	6-417	MM
No Regrets...Yet	Isaacs, Sonya	22-9	CB
No Regrets...Yet	Isaacs, Sonya	19-697	ST
No Reply	Beatles	11-144	DK
No Scrubs	TLC	7-842	PHM
No Scrubs	TLC	28-222	SF
No Scrubs	TLC	13-704	SGB
No Shame	Bates, Jeff	29-51	CB
No Shoes No Shirt No Problem	Chesney, Kenny	29-426	CB
No Shoes No Shirt No Problem	Chesney, Kenny	25-620	MM
No Shoes No Shirt No Problem	Chesney, Kenny	19-58	ST
No Shoes No Shirt No Problem	Chesney, Kenny	32-297	THM
No Sleep 'Til Brooklyn	Beastie Boys	25-482	MM
No Souveniers	Etheridge, Melissa	15-738	SC
No Substitute/Oh Cathy	Chef	13-718	SGB
Lee **			
No Such Thing	Mayer, John	18-219	CB
No Such Thing	Mayer, John	20-377	HP
No Such Thing	Mayer, John	18-412	MM
No Sugar Tonight/Mother Nature	Guess Who	20-94	SC
No Surrender	Springsteen, Bruce	20-243	LE
No Time	Guess Who	26-363	DK
No Time For Tears	Messina, Jo Dee	9-401	CB
No Time For Tears	Messina, Jo Dee	13-818	CHM
No Time To Kill	Black, Clint	1-119	CB
No Time To Kill	Black, Clint	30-426	THM
No Tomorrow	Orson	30-700	SF
No Way Back	Foo Fighters	30-278	SC
No Way Out	Bogguss, Suzy	1-567	CB
No Way Out	Bogguss, Suzy	4-455	SC
No Yesterday	Montana, Billy	4-26	SC
No. 9 Dreams	Lennon, John	30-291	RS
Nobody	Sweat & Cage	20-128	PHM
Nobody	Sweat & Cage	24-372	SC
Nobody	Sylvia	11-724	DK
Nobody	Sylvia	13-437	P
Nobody But A Fool Would Love You	Smith, Connie	48-97	CB
Nobody But Me	Human Beings	9-359	MG
Nobody But Me	Shelton, Blake	23-407	CB
Nobody But Me	Shelton, Blake	29-845	SC
Nobody But You	Backstreet Boys	30-413	THM
Nobody But You	Clark, Dee	14-342	SC
Nobody But You	Williams, Don	45-218	SC
Nobody Does It Better	Simon, Carly	33-299	CB
Nobody Does It Better	Simon, Carly	11-520	DK
Nobody Does It Better	Simon, Carly	12-881	P
Nobody Does It Better	Simon, Carly	9-57	SC
Nobody Does It Like You	Gomez, Selena	48-399	DCK
Nobody Ever Died Of A Broken Heart	Cowboy Crush	23-128	CB
Nobody Falls Like A Fool	Conley, Earl Thomas	29-783	CB
Nobody Gonna Tell Me What To Do	Van Zant	23-472	CB
Nobody In His Right Mind	Strait, George	5-316	SC
Nobody In His Right Mind...	Strait, George	34-268	CB
Nobody Knows	Sharp, Kevin	7-392	MM
Nobody Knows	Sharp, Kevin	4-589	SC
Nobody Knows	Tony Rich Project	4-168	SC
Nobody Knows You When You're...	Derek & Dominos	15-315	SC
Nobody Likes Sad Songs	Milsap, Ronnie	29-775	CB
Nobody Love	Kelly, Tori	48-648	BKD
Nobody Love Nobody Gets Hurt	Bogguss, Suzy	8-184	CB
Nobody Loves Me Like You Do	Murray & Loggins	12-118	DK
Nobody Loves Me Like You Do	Murray & Loggins	11-4	PL

SONG TITLE	ARTIST	#	TYPE
Nobody Loves Me Like You Do	Murray, Anne	46-15	THM
Nobody Loves Me Like You Do - duet	Murray & Loggins	38-3	CB
Nobody Needs Your Love	Pitney, Gene	47-533	ZM
Nobody To Blame	Stapleton, Chris	47-395	BKD
Nobody Told Me	Lennon, John	7-488	MM
Nobody Told Me	Lennon, John	30-296	RS
Nobody Wants To Be Lonely	Martin & 7	20-123	PHM
Nobody Wins	Foster, Radney	2-622	SC
Nobody Wins	Lee, Brenda	30-327	CB
Nobody Wins	Lee, Brenda	45-450	CB
Nobody's Darlin' But Mine	Haggard, Merle	48-485	CKC
Nobody's Fool	Cinderella	17-87	DK
Nobody's Fool	Cinderella	5-486	SC
Nobody's Fool	Lambert, Miranda	38-259	PHN
Nobody's Fool	Loggins, Kenny	4-318	SC
Nobody's Fool	Reeves, Jim	45-261	VH
Nobody's Fool But Yours	Gill, Vince	49-710	VH
Nobody's Girl	Wright, Michelle	7-342	MM
Nobody's Girl	Wright, Michelle	4-408	SC
Nobody's Gonna Rain On Our Parade	Mattea, Kathy	6-603	MM
Nobody's Got It All	Anderson, John	14-152	CB
Nobody's Home	Black, Clint	1-108	CB
Nobody's Home	Black, Clint	12-164	DK
Nobody's Home	Black, Clint	13-469	P
Nobody's Home	Black, Clint	30-427	THM
Nobody's Home	Lavigne, Avril	20-191	PHM
Nobody's Lonesome For Me	Williams, Hank Sr.	14-233	CB
Nobody's Supposed To Be Here	Cox, Deborah	7-840	PHM
Noise	Chesney, Kenny	49-390	DCK
Norma Jean Riley	Diamond Rio	1-169	CB
Norman - (Lots of backup)	Thompson, Sue	49-302	LRT
Norman (Inst)	Thompson, Sue	49-392	KV
North To Alaska	Horton, Johnny	8-380	CB
North To Alaska	Horton, Johnny	11-835	DK
North To Alaska	Horton, Johnny	18-627	PS
Northern Girl	Clark, Terri	38-1	CB
Northern Redemption	Abrams Brothers	41-60	PHN
Norwegian Wood	Beatles	17-546	DK
Not	Bellamy Brothers	46-50	SSK
Not A Day Goes By	Lonestar	25-130	MM
Not A Day Goes By	Lonestar	16-100	ST
Not A Moment Too Soon	McGraw, Tim	1-529	CB
Not A Moment Too Soon	McGraw, Tim	17-264	NA
Not A Moment Too Soon	McGraw, Tim	2-545	SC
Not A Second Time	Beatles	44-120	KV
Not Broken	Goo Goo Dolls	37-265	PHM
Not Counting You	Brooks, Garth	1-212	CB
Not Counting You	Brooks, Garth	6-280	MM

SONG TITLE	ARTIST	#	TYPE
Not Counting You	Brooks, Garth	2-684	SC
Not Enough Hours In The Night	Supernaw, Doug	7-141	MM
Not Enough Hours In The Night	Supernaw, Doug	3-569	SC
Not Enough Love In The World	Henley, Don	48-149	AH
Not Fade Away	Holly, Buddy	11-37	PX
Not Fade Away	Rolling Stones	11-276	DK
Not Fade Away	Rolling Stones	14-401	PT
Not Falling	Mudvayne	23-156	PHM
Not For You	Pearl Jam	9-307	RS
Not Forgotten You	Willis, Kelly	49-727	CB
Not Fragile	BTO	46-545	CB
Not Going Down	Messina, Jo Dee	29-43	CB
Not Gon' Cry	Blige, Mary J.	4-684	SC
Not Gonna Get Us	T.A.T.U.	32-244	THM
Not Gonna Take You Back	Blazer, Justine	41-67	PHN
Not In Love	Iglesias & Kelis	20-351	PHM
Not Like The Movies	Perry, Katy	38-197	CB
Not On Your Love	Carson, Jeff	6-825	MM
Not On Your Love	Carson, Jeff	3-414	SC
Not Ready To Make Nice	Dixie Chicks	29-376	CB
Not That Different	Raye, Collin	1-133	CB
Not That Different	Raye, Collin	7-175	MM
Not That Different	Raye, Collin	3-654	SC
Not That Kinda Girl	JoJo	22-361	CB
Not Too Much To Ask	Carpenter & Diffie	1-425	CB
Not Too Much To Ask	Carpenter & Diffie	15-155	THM
Not Too Much To Ask	Carpenter, M C	6-134	MM
Not Until The Next Time	Reeves, Jim	3-151	LG
Not While I'm Around	Sondheim, Stephen	17-781	PS
Not While I'm Around	Streisand, Barbra	49-565	PS
Not With My Heart You Don't	Carlson, Paulette	4-466	SC
Note the	Singletary, Daryle	7-728	CHM
Note the	Singletary, Daryle	22-776	ST
Note To Self	Keith, Toby	38-166	SC
Nothin' 'Bout Love Makes Sense	Rimes, LeAnn	22-68	CB
Nothin' 'Bout Love Makes Sense	Rimes, LeAnn	20-507	ST
Nothin' At All	Heart	24-63	SC
Nothin' Better To Do	Rimes, LeAnn	30-462	CB
Nothin' Bout Memphis	Yearwood, Trisha	36-283	PHM
Nothin' But A Good Time	Poison	5-68	SC
Nothin' But A Love Thang	Worley, Darryl	29-602	CB
Nothin' But A Woman	Cray, Robert	7-217	MM
Nothin' But Cowboy Boots	Blue County	23-15	CB
Nothin' But Cowboy Boots	Blue County	43-265	SD
Nothin' But Good	Sears, Dawn	4-475	SC
Nothin' But The Taillights	Black, Clint	1-826	CB
Nothin' But The Taillights	Black, Clint	7-723	CHM

194

SONG TITLE	ARTIST	#	TYPE
Nothin' But The Taillights	Black, Clint	22-613	ST
Nothin' Less Than Love	Buffalo Club	22-634	ST
Nothin' Like You	Dan + Shay	47-397	BKD
Nothin' New Under The Moon	Rimes, LeAnn	8-766	CB
Nothin' New Under The Moon	Rimes, LeAnn	22-822	ST
Nothin' On You - duet	B.O.B. & Bruno Mars	38-238	BH
Nothin' To Die For	McGraw, Tim	36-387	SC
Nothin' To Lose	Gracin, Josh	22-69	CB
Nothin' To Lose	Gracin, Josh	23-36	SC
Nothin' To Lose	Gracin, Josh	20-505	ST
Nothin's Right And Nothin's Left	Reilly, Dee	45-860	VH
Nothing	Yoakam, Dwight	7-143	MM
Nothing	Yoakam, Dwight	3-571	SC
Nothing At All	Santana & Musiq	20-631	NS
Nothing At All	Santana & Musiq	18-777	PHM
Nothing Broken But My Heart	Dion, Celine	34-160	CB
Nothing But The Wheel	Loveless, Patty	1-720	CB
Nothing But The Wheel	Loveless, Patty	6-386	MM
Nothing But Time	Browne, Jackson	23-615	BS
Nothing Can Keep Me From You	Kiss	8-509	PHT
Nothing Catches Jesus by Surprise	Montgomery, J M	23-368	SC
Nothing Catches Jesus By Surprise	Montgomery, J M	22-474	ST
Nothing Compares 2 U	O'Connor, Sinead	28-438	DK
Nothing Compares 2 U	O'Connor, Sinead	6-174	MM
Nothing Compares 2 U	O'Connor, Sinead	12-842	P
Nothing Else Matters	Metallica	13-622	LE
Nothing Else Matters	Metallica	5-736	SC
Nothing Ever Matters	Hill, Lauryn	13-708	SGB
Nothing From Nothing	Preston, Billy	2-439	SC
Nothing I Can Do About It Now	Nelson, Willie	38-72	CB
Nothing In This World	Wyatt & Avant	20-616	CB
Nothing Is Real But The Girl	Blondie	49-134	LG
Nothing Like Us	Bieber, Justin	48-626	KVD
Nothing On But The Radio	Allan, Gary	20-473	ST
Nothing Short Of Dying	Tritt, Travis	1-672	CB
Nothing Short Of Dying	Tritt, Travis	17-369	DK
Nothing Short Of Dying	Tritt, Travis	6-197	MM
Nothing Sure Looked Good On You	Watson, Gene	14-671	CB
Nothing Sure Looked Good On You	Watson, Gene	19-435	SC
Nothing That You Are	Moore, Mandy	37-25	PS
Nothing To Believe In	Cracker	24-59	SC
Nothing To Prove	Lonestar	30-317	CB
Nothing To Prove (Radio Version)	Caroline's Spine	14-472	SC
Nothing's Changed Here	Yoakam, Dwight	49-683	SC
Nothing's Gonna Stop	Starship	7-55	MM

SONG TITLE	ARTIST	#	TYPE
Us			
Nothing's Gonna Stop Us Now	Starship	35-143	CB
Nothing's New	Black, Clint	30-428	THM
Nothing's News	Black, Clint	1-110	CB
Notion	Kings Of Leon	36-306	PHM
Notorious	Duran Duran	28-307	DK
Notorious	Duran Duran	18-381	SAV
November	Emerson Drive	23-401	CB
November Rain	Guns & Roses	6-172	MM
November Rain	Guns & Roses	12-764	P
November Rain	Guns & Roses	23-108	SC
Novocaine For The Soul	Eels	24-361	SC
Now	Andrews, Jessica	36-367	CB
Now And Again	Singletary, Daryle	29-353	CB
Now And Forever	Air Supply	46-588	CB
Now And Forever	King, Carole	24-22	SC
Now And Forever	Marx, Richard	18-477	NU
Now And Forever	Marx, Richard	16-574	SC
Now And Forever (You And Me)	Murray, Anne	14-263	SC
Now I Know	White, Lari	8-881	CB
Now I Know	White, Lari	6-664	MM
Now I Know	White, Lari	2-420	SC
Now I Lay Me Down To Cheat	Coe, David Allan	18-320	CB
Now I'm Here	Queen	49-79	ZPA
Now That I Found You	Clark, Terri	8-463	CB
Now That I Found You	Clark, Terri	7-744	CHM
Now That's All Right With Me	Barnett, Mandy	4-158	SC
Now That's Awesome!	Engvall & Friends	14-162	CB
Now That's Awesome!	Engvall,Bill,Byrd,M	10-264	SC
Now That's Country	Stuart, Marty	5-414	SC
Now the	Carpenters	45-800	SBI
Now You See Me Now You Don't	Womack, Lee Ann	10-197	SC
Now You See Me Now You Don't	Womack, Lee Ann	22-427	ST
Nowhere Bound	Diamond Rio	1-180	CB
Nowhere Bound	Diamond Rio	2-624	SC
Nowhere Fast	Old Dominion	47-398	BKD
Nowhere In The Neighborhood	Everett, Jace	29-375	CB
Nowhere Man	Beatles	11-217	DK
Nowhere Man	Beatles	12-858	P
Nowhere Man	Beatles	7-518	SAV
Nowhere To Go	Etheridge, Melissa	24-51	SC
Nowhere USA	Miller, Dean	4-829	SC
Number One (Call Me)	Tremeloes	10-638	SF
Numbers	Bare, Bobby	45-713	VH
Nutbush City Limits	Turner, Tina	10-419	LE
Nuttin' But A "G" Thang	Dr Dre/Snoop Doggy	14-435	SC
O Holy Night	Underwood, Carrie	45-785	KV
O Mexico	Yearwood, Trisha	24-87	SC
O White Christmas	Little People the	45-795	SC
O.P.P.	Naughty By Nature	25-483	MM
O.P.P.	Naughty By Nature	14-438	SC

195

SONG TITLE	ARTIST	#	TYPE
Ob La Di Ob La Da	Beatles	11-147	DK
Ob La Di Ob La Da	Beatles	46-599	P
Ob La Di Ob La Da	Beatles	7-517	SAV
Ob La Di Ob La Da	Beatles	46-598	SC
Ob La Di Ob La Da	Inner Circle	25-383	MM
Object Of My Affection	Martin, Dean	23-74	MM
Objection	Shakira	18-424	CB
Obsession	Animation	11-279	DK
Obsession (No Es Amor)	Frankie J w Baby Bash	37-96	SC
Ocean Front Property	Strait, George	8-165	CB
Ocean Front Property	Strait, George	9-472	SAV
Ocean Front Property	Strait, George	2-18	SC
Ocean Of Diamonds	Nelson, Willie	38-79	PS
Octopus's Garden	Beatles	20-203	SC
Ode To Billy Joe	Gentry, Bobbie	8-291	CB
Ode To Billy Joe	Gentry, Bobbie	11-401	DK
Ode To Billy Joe	Gentry, Bobbie	13-126	P
Ode To My Car **	Sandler, Adam	13-728	SGB
Of Course I'm Alright	Alabama	22-657	ST
Of Course I'm Right	Alabama	1-29	CB
Off My Rocker	Currington, Billy	43-315	CB
Off The Hillbilly Hook	Trailor Choir	49-17	KV
Off The Hillbilly Hook	Trailor Choir	36-201	PHM
Off The Wall	Jackson, Michael	36-121	JTG
Off To See The Lizard	Buffett, Jimmy	45-846	VH
Officially Missing You	Tamia	32-345	THM
Oh Atlanta	Krauss, Alison	4-27	SC
Oh Atlanta	Little Feat	17-461	SC
Oh Baby Mine	Statler Brothers	19-382	CB
Oh Boy	Holly, Buddy	12-99	DK
Oh Boy	Holly, Buddy	3-213	LG
Oh Boy	Holly, Buddy	6-689	MM
Oh Boy	Holly, Buddy	13-41	P
Oh Boy	Holly, Buddy	3-264	SC
Oh Boy!	Jackson, Wanda	46-56	SSK
Oh Carol	Sedaka, Neil	11-197	DK
Oh Carol	Sedaka, Neil	13-121	P
Oh Carol	Sedaka, Neil	9-166	SO
Oh Daddy	Fleetwood Mac	47-907	DCK
Oh Daddy	Fleetwood Mac	46-116	SC
Oh Darling	Beatles	17-547	DK
Oh Darling	Beatles	13-105	P
Oh Diane	Fleetwood Mac	47-914	SBI
Oh Donna	Valens, Richie	35-15	CB
Oh Girl	Chi-Lites	27-317	DK
Oh Girl	Chi-Lites	12-883	P
Oh Girl	Young, Paul	11-98	DK
Oh Girl	Young, Paul	9-672	SAV
Oh Happy Day	Hawkins, Edwin	11-385	DK
Oh Happy Day	Presley, Elvis	25-514	MM
Oh Happy Day	Williams, BeBe	48-553	DK
Oh How I Miss You Tonight	Reeves, Jim	44-253	DFK
Oh How The Years Go By	Williams, Vanessa	9-98	PS
Oh How The Years Go	Williams, Vanessa	5-181	SC

SONG TITLE	ARTIST	#	TYPE
By			
Oh Little One	Scott, Jack	45-345	BSP
Oh London Bridge	Stafford, Jo	16-792	DK
Oh Lonesome Me	Gibson, Don	8-808	CB
Oh Lonesome Me	Gibson, Don	13-444	P
Oh Lonesome Me	Gibson, Don	8-654	SAV
Oh Lonesome Me	Kentucky HH	8-598	TT
Oh Lonesome You	Yearwood, Trisha	6-135	MM
Oh Look At Me Now	Sinatra, Frank	15-540	SGB
Oh Me Oh My Sweet Baby	Diamond Rio	1-171	CB
Oh Me Oh My Sweet Baby	Diamond Rio	2-370	SC
Oh My My	Starr, Ringo	49-779	SC
Oh My My Can You Boogie	Turner, Ike & Tina	7-61	MM
Oh My Pa Pa	Fisher, Eddie	33-229	CB
Oh My Papa	Fisher, Eddie	7-298	MM
Oh No	Richie, Lionel	10-386	LE
Oh No Not My Baby	Stewart, Rod	14-849	LE
Oh Oh I'm Falling In Love Again	Rodgers, Jimmie	4-518	SC
Oh Pretty Woman	Orbison, Roy	11-181	DK
Oh Pretty Woman	Orbison, Roy	3-326	MH
Oh Pretty Woman	Orbison, Roy	9-465	SAV
Oh Sheila	Ready For The World	35-198	CB
Oh Sheila	Ready for the World	12-380	DK
Oh Superman	Anderson, Lynn	47-648	SF
Oh Susanna	Miller, Mitch	43-395	CB
Oh Susanna	Standard	11-490	DK
Oh Susanna	Standard	23-225	SM
Oh Tonight - duet	Josh Abbott & Musgraves	45-436	CB
Oh Very Young	Stevens, Cat	23-645	BS
Oh Very Young	Stevens, Cat	13-573	NU
Oh What A Night	Dells	3-299	MM
Oh What A Night	Dells	10-207	SS
Oh What A Night	Four Seasons	35-90	CB
Oh What A Night	Four Seasons	10-539	SF
Oh What A Thrill	Mavericks	6-604	MM
Oh What It Did To Me	Tucker, Tanya	16-353	CB
Oh Yeah **	Big Tymers	32-11	THM
Oh Yeah!	Big Timers/Boo/Gott	32-11	THM
Oh You Beautiful Doll	Murphy, George	21-4	SC
Ohio	Crosby Stills & Nash	4-80	SC
Ohio (Come Back To Texas)	Bowling For Soup	23-311	CB
Ok It's Alright With Me	Hutchinson, Eric	36-305	PHM
Okie From Muskogee	Haggard, Merle	1-362	CB
Okie From Muskogee	Haggard, Merle	11-765	DK
Okie From Muskogee	Haggard, Merle	13-374	P
Oklahoma	Gilman, Billy	14-141	CB
Oklahoma	Gilman, Billy	22-581	ST
Oklahoma	Gilman, Billy	14-33	THM
Oklahoma Borderline	Gill, Vince	3-108	SC
Oklahoma Hills	Reeves, Jim	44-263	SSK
Oklahoma Hills	Thompson, Hank	45-727	VH

SONG TITLE	ARTIST	#	TYPE
Oklahoma Sky	Lambert, Miranda	46-255	KV
Oklahoma Swing	Gill & McEntire	1-795	CB
Oklahoma Swing	McEntire & Gill	6-751	MM
Oklahoma Swing	McEntire & Gill	22-390	SC
Ol' 55	Eagles	15-706	LE
Ol' Man River	Standard	17-159	DK
Ol' Red	Rogers, Kenny	48-127	SC
Ol' Red	Shelton, Blake	33-179	CB
Ol' Red	Shelton, Blake	25-239	MM
Ol' Red	Shelton, Blake	16-687	ST
Old 8 X 10	Travis, Randy	1-397	CB
Old Alabama	Paisley & Alabama	46-246	FTX
Old Apartment the	Barenaked Ladies	30-611	RS
Old Blue	Standard	47-837	SDK
Old Bones	Martin, Dean	49-646	DFK
Old Cape Cod	Page, Patti	10-463	MG
Old Cape Cod	Page, Patti	3-512	SC
Old Country	Chesnutt, Mark	6-124	MM
Old Country	Chesnutt, Mark	2-712	SC
Old Devil Moon	Bennett, Tony	10-409	LE
Old Dogs Children & Watermelon Wine	Hall, Tom T.	3-748	CB
Old Dogs Children & Watermelon Wine	Hall, Tom T.	13-482	P
Old Enough To Know Better	Hayes, Wade	6-715	MM
Old Enough To Know Better	Hayes, Wade	17-275	NA
Old Enough To Know Better	Hayes, Wade	2-544	SC
Old Farts Jackasses Steel Guitars &	Hall, Tom T.	45-927	DCK
Old Flame	Alabama	8-23	CB
Old Flame	Alabama	17-311	NA
Old Flames Can't Hold A Candle To U	Parton, Dolly	29-628	CB
Old Flames Can't Hold A Candle To U	Parton, Dolly	8-543	CB
Old Flames Can't Hold A Candle To U	Parton, Dolly	5-662	SC
Old Flames Can't Hold A Candle To U	Parton, Dolly	9-544	SAV
Old Flames Have New Names	Chesnutt, Mark	1-351	CB
Old Flames Have New Names	Chesnutt, Mark	6-534	MM
Old Flames Have New Names	Chesnutt, Mark	2-365	SC
Old Folks At Home	Mills Brothers	43-221	CB
Old Folks At Home - Swanee River	Standard	11-485	DK
Old Grey Mare - kids	Kids	49-352	CB
Old Habits	Moore, Justin	43-178	ASK
Old Habits	Williams, Hank Jr.	37-297	CB
Old Habits - Duet	Moore & Lambert	44-283	KCDC
Old Hippie (The Sequel)	Bellamy Brothers	7-206	MM
Old Hippie Christmas - xmas	Bellamy Brothers	45-306	CB

SONG TITLE	ARTIST	#	TYPE
Old Hometown	Campbell, Glen	9-631	SAV
Old Lamplighter the	Browns	6-54	SC
Old Love	Clapton, Eric	10-485	DA
Old Man And His Horn the	Watson, Gene	29-703	SC
Old Man And Me	Hootie & Blowfish	21-136	CB
Old Man From The Mountain	Haggard, Merle	22-230	CB
Old Man Moses	Newton, Wayne	47-314	LE
Old Pop And An Oak	Rednex	49-20	KV
Old Porch Swing	Watson, Gene	4-140	SC
Old School	Conlee, John	47-622	PCD
Old School	Conlee, John	47-623	SRK
Old School	Wicks, Chuck	48-454	CB
Old Shit	Lambert, Miranda	45-945	KV
Old Slew Foot	Jim & Jesse	8-261	CB
Old Songs the	Manilow, Barry	29-121	CB
Old Stuff the	Brooks, Garth	48-350	MM
Old Tige	Reeves, Jim	44-229	SRK
Old Time Christmas	Strait, George	45-764	CB
Old Time Rock & Roll	Seger, Bob	12-674	P
Old Time Rock & Roll	Seger, Bob	2-39	SC
Old Time Rock & Roll	Seger, Bob	10-526	SF
Old Town New	McGraw, Tim	23-386	SC
Old Toy Trains	Miller, Roger	45-365	OZP
Old Violin	Paycheck, Johnny	22-45	CB
Old Weakness (Comin' On Strong)	Tucker, Tanya	25-529	MM
Old Weakness (Comin' On Strong)	Tucker, Tanya	18-805	ST
Old Weakness (Coming On Strong)	Tucker, Tanya	32-194	THM
Older Than My Years	Cherie	20-546	PHM
Older The Violin, Sweeter the Music	Thompson, Hank	19-333	CB
Older Women	McDowell, Ronnie	8-211	CB
Older Women	McDowell, Ronnie	13-499	P
On A Bus To St. Cloud	Yearwood, Trisha	3-628	SC
On A Carousel	Hollies	44-362	LG
On A Clear Day	Monro, Matt	9-231	PS
On A Clear Day	Sinatra, Frank	12-552	P
On A Clear Day You Can See Forever	Streisand, Barbra	48-783	MM
On A Day Like Today	Adams, Bryan	14-289	MM
On A Good Night	Hayes, Wade	7-272	MM
On A Good Night	Hayes, Wade	4-370	SC
On A Good Night	Hayes, Wade	22-896	ST
On A High	Sheik, Duncan	25-314	MM
On A Mission	Trick Pony	33-181	CB
On A Mission	Trick Pony	25-359	MM
On A Mission	Trick Pony	18-206	ST
On A Night Like This	Trick Pony	34-347	CB
On A Night Like This	Trick Pony	15-190	ST
On A Slow Boat To China	Standard	17-160	DK
On A Slow Boat To China	Standard	13-632	SGB
On A Snowy Christmas	Presley, Elvis	45-758	CB

SONG TITLE	ARTIST	#	TYPE
Night			
On Again Off Again	Byrd, Tracy	8-222	CB
On Again Tonight	Willmon, Trent	29-204	CB
On And On	Badu, Erykah	33-363	CB
On And On	Badu, Erykah	25-685	MM
On And On	Bishop, Stephen	9-787	SAV
On Bended Knee	Boyz II Men	28-400	DK
On Bended Knee	Boyz II Men	16-632	MM
On Bended Knee	Boyz II Men	2-464	SC
On Bended Knee	Boyz II Men	29-122	ST
On Broadway	Benson, George	18-61	MM
On Broadway	Benson, George	13-152	P
On Broadway	Drifters	33-239	CB
On Broadway	Drifters	12-360	DK
On Down The Line	Loveless, Patty	1-713	CB
On Down the Line	Loveless, Patty	6-626	MM
On Eagles Wings	Amerson, Steve	49-716	VH
On Eagles Wings	Bondi, Renee	49-715	VH
On London Bridge	Stafford, Jo	15-541	CMC
On Moonlight Bay	Day, Doris	48-145	SFM
On My Father's Wings	Corrs	49-194	SC
On My Knees	Rich & Fricke	13-479	P
On My Knees	Rich & Fricke	5-439	SC
On My Knees	Velasquez, Jaci	35-316	CB
On My Own	LaBelle & McDonald	16-725	DK
On My Own	LaBelle & McDonald	12-832	P
On My Own	McEntire, Reba	1-784	CB
On My Own	McEntire, Reba	7-80	MM
On My Own	McEntire, Reba	3-535	SC
On My Own	Peach Union	7-691	PHM
On My Word Of Honor	Platters	45-74	DCK
On Our Last Date	Twitty, Conway	49-301	LOU
On Second Thought	Rabbitt, Eddie	33-100	CB
On Second Thought	Rabbitt, Eddie	11-703	DK
On Second Thought	Rabbitt, Eddie	2-388	SC
On Tap In The Can Or In The Bottle	Thompson, Hank	19-331	CB
On The Amazon	McLean, Don	47-250	SFM
On the Atchison Topeka & the Santa Fe	Garland, Judy	48-271	KV
On The Border	Eagles	44-94	ZMP
On the Coast of Somewhere Beautiful	Chesney, Kenny	49-786	TU
On The Dark Side	Cafferty, John	19-127	KC
On The Dark Side	Cafferty, John	17-489	LC
On The Evening Train	Cash, Johnny	45-715	VH
On The Floor - duet	Lopez & Pitbull	40-11	CB
On The Good Ship Lollipop	Temple, Shirley	12-547	P
On The Other Hand	Travis, Randy	1-392	CB
On The Other Hand	Travis, Randy	17-408	DK
On The Radio	Furtado, Nelly	21-649	CB
On The Radio	Furtado, Nelly	25-144	MM
On The Radio	Parnell, Lee Roy	2-344	SC
On The Radio	Summer, Donna	15-206	LE
On The Radio	Summer, Donna	16-153	SC
On The Road Again	Nelson, Willie	1-627	CB

SONG TITLE	ARTIST	#	TYPE
On The Road Again	Nelson, Willie	16-843	DK
On The Road Again	Nelson, Willie	13-350	P
On The Side Of Angels	Rimes, LeAnn	1-290	CB
On The Side Of Angels	Rimes, LeAnn	22-659	ST
On The Street Where You Live	Damone, Vic	11-574	DK
On The Street Where You Love	Williams, Andy	49-44	ZVS
On The Sunny Side Of The Street	Day, Doris	12-527	P
On The Sunny Side Of The Street	Laine, Frankie	3-879	PS
On The Sunny Side Of The Street	Standard	12-13	DK
On The Verge	Raye, Collin	14-652	CB
On The Verge	Raye, Collin	22-405	CHM
On The Way Down	Cabrera, Ryan	20-548	PHM
On The Way Down	Cabrera, Ryan	48-711	SC
On the Wings of a Nightingale	Everly Brothers	38-19	SF
On The Wings Of Love	Osborne, Jeffrey	27-239	DK
On The Wings Of Love	Osborne, Jeffrey	13-148	P
On The Wings Of Love	Osborne, Jeffrey	2-279	SC
On This Side Of The Moon	Alabama	24-90	SC
On Top Of Old Smoky	Standard	27-461	DK
On Your Way Home	Loveless, Patty	36-369	CB
On Your Way Home	Loveless, Patty	19-691	ST
Once	Husky, Ferlin	22-261	CB
Once A Day	Smith, Connie	15-542	CMC
Once A Day	Smith, Connie	20-288	SC
Once Bitten Twice Shy	Great White	23-48	MH
Once Bitten Twice Shy	Great White	13-281	P
Once Bitten Twice Shy	Great White	5-602	SC
Once I Was The Light Of Your Life	Bentley, Stephanie	7-329	MM
Once I Was The Light Of Your Life	Bentley, Stephanie	4-886	SC
Once In A Blue Moon	Conley, Earl Thomas	9-565	SAV
Once In A Blue Moon	Conley, Earl Thomas	5-153	SC
Once In A Lifetime	Urban, Keith	30-104	CB
Once In A Lifetime	Urban, Keith	30-95	PHM
Once In A Lifetime Love	Walker, Clay	14-96	CB
Once In A While	Chimes	7-67	MM
Once More	Harris, EmmyLou	1-235	CB
Once More With Feeling	Lewis, Jerry Lee	47-197	CB
Once Upon A Christmas	Parton & Rogers	46-98	DCK
Once Upon A December	Carter, Deana	22-762	ST
Once Upon A Dream	Fury, Billy	10-660	SF
Once Upon A Lifetime	Alabama	1-20	CB
Once Upon A Lifetime	Alabama	12-172	DK
Once Upon A Lifetime	Alabama	6-126	MM
Once Upon A Time	Rochelle & Candles	25-551	MM
Once You've Had The Best	Jones, George	8-347	CB
Once You've Loved Somebody	Dixie Chicks	15-543	SGB
One	Bee Gees	48-683	DFK

198

SONG TITLE	ARTIST	#	TYPE
One	Blige & U2	30-757	SF
One	Hill, Faith	32-243	THM
One	Metallica	13-625	LE
One	Three Dog Night	33-268	CB
One	Three Dog Night	11-595	DK
One	Three Dog Night	13-301	P
One	U2	13-276	P
One	U2	30-77	SC
One And Only	Adele	40-35	ZM
One And Only Love	Taff, Russ	2-699	SC
One Bad Apple	Osmonds	33-276	CB
One Bad Apple	Osmonds	17-66	DK
One Belief Away	Raitt, Bonnie	5-277	SC
One Believer	Diamond Rio	22-316	CB
One Black Sheep	Kearney, Mat	48-401	DCK
One Bourbon One Scotch One Beer	Hooker, John Lee	20-143	KB
One Bourbon One Scotch One Beer	Thorogood, George	2-566	SC
One Boy	Sommers, Joanie	19-111	SAV
One Boy One Girl	Raye, Collin	1-132	CB
One Boy One Girl	Raye, Collin	26-530	DK
One Boy One Girl	Raye, Collin	6-843	MM
One Boy One Girl	Raye, Collin	3-434	SC
One Boy Two Little Girls	Presley, Elvis	25-497	MM
One Broken Heart For Sale	Presley, Elvis	8-584	CB
One Broken Heart For Sale	Presley, Elvis	7-130	MM
One Bud Wiser	Wilson, Gretchen	29-372	CB
One By One	Cher	24-48	SC
One By One	Wells & Foley	6-4	SC
One By One - duet	Foley, Red & Kitty Wells	43-356	CB
One By One - duet	Wells & Foley	48-200	CB
One Call Away	Puth, Charlie	47-577	BKD
One Clear Voice	Cetera, Peter	24-178	SC
One Day At A Time	Carter, Deana	22-320	CB
One Day At A Time	Lane, Christy	12-69	DK
One Day At A Time - Gospel	Gospel	33-203	CB
One Day Closer To You	Johnson, Carolyn D.	18-128	ST
One Day I'll Fly Away	Crawford, Randy	11-24	PX
One Day Left To Live	Kershaw, Sammy	1-480	CB
One Day Left To Live	Kershaw, Sammy	22-691	ST
One Day You Will	Lady Antebellum	40-48	DFK
One Dyin' And A Buryin'	Miller, Roger	22-278	CB
One Emotion	Black, Clint	1-833	CB
One Emotion	Black, Clint	30-429	THM
One Fine Day	Chiffons	27-531	DK
One Fine Day	Chiffons	6-161	MM
One Fine Day	Chiffons	13-63	P
One Fine Day	King, Carole	24-73	SC
One Fine Day	Midler, Bette	45-918	KV
One Fine Wire	Cailliat, Colbie	48-217	KV
One Flight Down	Jones, Norah	19-191	Z
One For My Baby	Sinatra, Frank	21-223	SGB
One For My Baby (Live)	Midler, Bette	45-360	KV

SONG TITLE	ARTIST	#	TYPE
One Friend	Seals, Dan	48-106	SC
One Good Love	Diamond & Jennings	7-235	MM
One Good Love	Diamond & Jennings	4-199	SC
One Good Love	Rascal Flatts	22-7	CB
One Good Love - duet	Diamond & Jennings	45-172	SC
One Good Man	Joplin, Janis	46-307	SC
One Good Man	Wright, Michelle	6-612	MM
One Good Man	Wright, Michelle	3-541	SC
One Good Reason	McCloud, Nicole	21-732	TT
One Good Well	Williams, Don	20-21	SC
One Great Mystery - duet	Lady Antebellum	48-445	KCD
One Hand One Heart	Diamond, Neil	10-24	SC
One Has My Name, One Has My..	Reeves, Jim	44-264	TU
One Has My Name, Other My Heart	Wakely, Jimmy	19-839	CB
One Has My Name, Other My Heart	Wakely, Jimmy	5-218	SC
One Hell Of A Woman	Davis, Mac	23-510	CB
One Hell Of A Woman	Davis, Mac	47-595	CB
One Hell Of An Amen	Gilbert, Brantley	45-448	SSC
One Honest Heart	McEntire, Reba	8-945	CB
One Honest Heart	McEntire, Reba	7-865	CHT
One Hundred And Two	Judds	12-2	DK
One Hundred And Two	Judds	19-295	MH
One Hundred And Two	Judds	9-537	SAV
One Hundred Ways	Ingram, James	9-55	MM
One I Gave My Heart To	Aaliyah	9-96	PS
One I Love the	Gray, David	29-319	PHM
One I Loved Back Then the	Jones, George	4-653	SC
One In A Million	Lee, Johnny	4-544	SC
One In A Million	McCready, Mindy	10-192	SC
One in A Million You	Graham, Larry	6-556	MM
One In A Million You	Graham, Larry	13-306	P
One In A Million You	Graham, Larry	2-278	SC
One In The Middle the	Johns, Sarah	30-480	CB
One In The Middle the	Jones, Sarah	30-480	CB
One Kiss From You	Spears, Britney	15-811	CB
One Kiss To Many	Arnold, Eddy	19-642	CB
One Last Breath	Creed	18-419	MM
One Last Chance	Morrison, James	38-271	ZM
One Last Good Hand	McEntire, Reba	24-246	SC
One Last Kiss	Craddock, Billy C	45-830	VH
One Last Kiss	J. Geils Band	46-328	LE
One Last Thrill	Cyrus, Billy Ray	2-743	SC
One Last Time	Drake, Dusty	25-565	MM
One Last Time	Drake, Dusty	19-52	ST
One Less Bell To Answer	5th Dimension	15-544	MM
One Less Bell To Answer	Fifth Dimension	33-249	CB
One Less Lonely Girl	Bieber, Justin	36-59	ASK
One Less Set Of Footsteps	Croce, Jim	19-352	PS

SONG TITLE	ARTIST	#	TYPE
One Love At A Time	Tucker, Tanya	16-341	CB
One Love At A Time	Tucker, Tanya	5-58	SC
One Man Band	Sayer, Leo	47-481	SF
One Man Woman	Judds	2-369	SC
One Mic	Nas	25-464	MM
One Minute Past Eternity	Lewis, Jerry Lee	47-196	CB
One Mississippi	Eldridge, Brett	45-278	BKD
One Moment In Time	Houston, Whitney	33-331	CB
One Moment In Time	Houston, Whitney	6-357	MM
One Moment In Time	Houston, Whitney	12-874	P
One More Chance	Iglesias, Julio Jr.	47-562	PS
One More Day	Brice, Lee	41-74	PHN
One More Day	Diamond Rio	33-134	CB
One More Day	Diamond Rio	22-461	ST
One More Drinking Song	Niemann, Jerrod	37-221	CB
One More Goodbye	Randy Rogers Band	30-340	CB
One More Last Chance	Gill, Vince	26-313	DK
One More Last Chance	Gill, Vince	6-392	MM
One More Minute	Authority Zero	32-107	THM
One More Night	Collins, Phil	20-296	CB
One More Night	Collins, Phil	24-70	SC
One More Night	Maroon 5	39-108	PHM
One More Payment	Black, Clint	1-113	CB
One More Time	Price, Ray	3-783	CB
One More Time	Price, Ray	22-255	SC
One More Try	Michael, George	33-380	CB
One More Try	Michael, George	11-676	DK
One Night	Corrs	49-200	SF
One Night	Domino, Fats	47-805	SRK
One Night	Presley, Elvis	15-545	MM
One Night	Presley, Elvis	14-751	THM
One Night A Day	Brooks, Garth	6-575	MM
One Night A Day	Brooks, Garth	12-482	P
One Night At A Time	Strait, George	14-650	CB
One Night At A Time	Strait, George	7-605	CHM
One Night In Bangkok	Head, Murray	17-467	SC
One Night In Bangkok	Murray Head	29-16	MH
One Night In New Orleans	Blackhawk	17-575	ST
One Of A Kind	Wynette, Tammy	29-625	CB
One Of A Kind Love Affair	Spinners	16-560	P
One Of a Kind Pair Of Fools	Mandrell, Barbara	9-632	SAV
One Of The Boys	Wilson, Gretchen	30-444	CB
One Of The Guys	Clark, Terri	23-393	CB
One Of These Days	Harris, EmmyLou	15-76	CB
One Of These Days	McGraw, Tim	8-474	CB
One Of These Days	McGraw, Tim	7-741	CHM
One Of These Nights	Eagles	7-556	BS
One Of These Nights	Eagles	2-253	SC
One Of Those Days	Houston, Whitney	32-52	THM
One Of Those Days	Martin, Brad	19-66	ST
One Of Those Nights	Brokup, Lisa	2-737	SC
One Of Those Nights	McGraw, Tim	43-257	ASK
One Of Those Nights Tonight	Morgan, Lorrie	22-418	ST

SONG TITLE	ARTIST	#	TYPE
One Of Those Things	Tillis, Pam	1-452	CB
One Of Us	Abba	19-79	MM
One Of Us	Osborne, Joan	19-580	MH
One Of Us	Osborne, Joan	10-240	PS
One Of Us	Osborne, Joan	15-546	THM
One Of You	Strait, George	38-147	CB
One On One - WN	Hall & Oates	48-68	LC
One On The Right Is On The Left	Cash, Johnny	14-247	CB
One On The Right Is On The Left..	Cash, Johnny	5-203	SC
One Owner Heart	Sheppard, T.G.	43-322	CB
One Part Two Part	McGraw, Tim	38-258	PHN
One Piece At A Time	Cash, Johnny	14-242	CB
One Piece At A Time	Cash, Johnny	2-513	SC
One Promise Too Late	McEntire, Reba	34-273	CB
One Second Chance	Bates, Jeff	30-83	CB
One Small Miracle	White, Bryan	8-148	CB
One Small Miracle	White, Bryan	22-753	ST
One Song Away	Cash, Tommy	47-756	SRK
One Step Ahead Of The Storm	Lawrence, Tracy	48-383	MM
One Step At A Time	Jewell, Buddy	20-476	ST
One Step At A Time	Sparks, Jordin	36-471	CB
One Step Forward	Desert Rose Band	5-770	SC
One Summer Night	Danleers	6-263	MM
One Sweet Day	Carey & Boyz II	15-547	THM
One Sweet Love	Bareilles, Sara	37-22	PS
One That Got Away the	Owen, Jake	39-21	ASK
One That You Love the	Air Supply	11-324	DK
One That You Love the	Air Supply	4-324	SC
One the	Allan, Gary	25-127	MM
One the	Allan, Gary	16-326	ST
One the	Backstreet Boys	33-385	CB
One the	Backstreet Boys	29-177	MH
One the	Backstreet Boys	13-839	PHM
One the	Backstreet Boys	14-468	SC
One the	Backstreet Boyz	30-633	THM
One the	Bonham, Tracy	24-230	SC
One the	Foo Fighters	18-298	CB
One the	John, Elton	12-243	DK
One the	John, Elton	13-308	P
One the	John, Elton	9-837	SAV
One the	Shakira	20-468	CB
One The Wings Of Love	Osborne, Jeffrey	6-562	MM
One Thing	Finger Eleven	19-852	PHM
One Thing	One Direction	39-41	ASK
One Thing Leads To Another	Fixx	29-8	MH
One Thing Leads To Another	Fixx	3-135	SC
One Time	Bieber, Justin	36-60	ASK
One Time Around	Wright, Michelle	6-119	MM
One Tin Soldier	Coven	9-356	MG
One Tin Soldier	Coven	9-11	MH
One Toke Over The Line	Brewer & Shipley	10-362	KC
One Track Heart	Presley, Elvis	25-499	MM

SONG TITLE	ARTIST	#	TYPE
One Two I Love You	Walker, Clay	1-101	CB
One Two I Love You	Walker, Clay	10-86	SC
One Voice	Gilman, Billy	14-726	CB
One Voice	Gilman, Billy	19-250	CSZ
One Voice	Manilow, Barry	46-305	SC
One Way Or Another	Blondie	12-144	DK
One Way Or Another	Blondie	4-533	SC
One Way Out	Allman Brothers	9-374	AH
One Way Out	Allman Brothers	15-28	SC
One Way Out	Allman Brothers	13-769	SGB
One Way Ticket	Rimes, LeAnn	1-287	CB
One Way Ticket	Rimes, LeAnn	7-449	MM
One Way Ticket	Rimes, Leann	4-496	SC
One Way Ticket (Radio Version)	Darkness	29-245	SC
One Way Ticket To The Blues	Sedaka, Neil	9-167	SO
One Week	Barenaked Ladies	7-773	PHT
One Week	Barenaked Ladies	30-614	RS
One Who Really Loves You	Wells, Mary	6-559	MM
One Who Really Loves You the	Wells, Mary	49-479	MM
One Wing In The Fire	Tomlinson, Trent	30-26	CB
One Wing In The Fire	Tomlinson, Trent	30-103	PHM
One Woman Man	Turner, Josh	44-297	BKD
One You Love the	Frey, Glenn	15-712	LE
One You Love The Most	Confederate RR	4-587	SC
One's On The Way	Lynn, Loretta	4-741	SC
Ones You Love the	Astley, Rick	18-483	NU
Oney	Cash, Johnny	29-571	CB
Oney	Cash, Johnny	5-207	SC
Online	Paisley, Brad	30-528	CB
Only A Dream	Carpenter, M C	47-668	SC
Only A Lonely Heart Now	Mandrell, Barbara	5-247	SC
Only A Woman Like You	Bolton, Michael	25-202	MM
Only Believe	Presley, Elvis	25-504	MM
Only Daddy That'll Walk The Line	Jennings, Waylon	22-140	CK
Only Daddy That'll Walk The Line	Jennings, Waylon	5-91	SC
Only Girl In The World	Rihanna	37-270	PHM
Only God (Could Stop Me Lovin...)	Emerson Drive	25-574	MM
Only GOD Could Love You More	Niemann, Jerrod	39-72	PHN
Only God Could Stop Me Loving You	Emerson Drive	19-6	ST
Only God Knows Why	Kid Rock	14-180	CB
Only God Knows Why	Kid Rock	15-326	PHM
Only God Knows Why	Kid Rock	5-894	SC
Only Happy When It Rains	Garbage	4-668	SC
Only If	Enya	18-530	TT
Only In America	Brooks & Dunn	33-152	CB
Only In America	Brooks & Dunn	15-184	ST
Only In America	Jay & Americans	14-378	PS

SONG TITLE	ARTIST	#	TYPE
Only In My Dreams	Gibson, Debbie	12-754	P
Only In My Mind	McEntire, Reba	5-131	SC
Only In Your Heart	America	46-418	CB
Only Lonely	Hootie & Blowfish	7-791	PHT
Only Lonely Me	Trevino, Rick	8-154	CB
Only Love	Judd, Wynonna	1-651	CB
Only Love	Judd, Wynonna	6-405	MM
Only Love	Judds	12-484	P
Only Love Can Break A Heart	Pitney, Gene	7-262	MM
Only Love Can Break A Heart	Pitney, Gene	22-444	SC
Only Love Can Break A Heart	Pitney, Gene	9-180	SO
Only Love Is Real	King, Carole	43-447	CB
Only Make Believe	Presley, Elvis	18-441	KC
Only On Days That End In "Y"	Walker, Clay	22-895	ST
Only On Days That End In Y	Walker, Clay	7-248	MM
Only On Days That End In Y	Walker, Clay	4-361	SC
Only One Love In My Life	Milsap, Ronnie	19-438	SC
Only One Road	Dion, Celine	15-109	BS
Only One Woman	Bee Gees	9-781	SAV
Only One You	Sheppard, T.G.	5-558	SC
Only Prettier	Lambert, Miranda	37-224	KS
Only Sixteen	Cooke, Sam	46-637	LE
Only Sixteen	Dr. Hook	47-41	SFG
Only the	Static X	19-857	PHM
Only The Good Die Young	Joel, Billy	12-280	DK
Only The Good Die Young	Joel, Billy	16-143	LE
Only The Good Die Young	Joel, Billy	6-550	MM
Only The Lonely	Motels	19-361	DK
Only The Lonely	Motels	5-148	SC
Only The Lonely	Orbison, Roy	16-772	DK
Only The Lonely	Orbison, Roy	3-319	MH
Only The Lonely	Orbison, Roy	12-730	P
Only The Lonely	Orbison, Roy	9-493	SAV
Only The Lonely	Orbison, Roy	29-837	SC
Only The Lonely	Orbison, Roy	10-555	SF
Only The Lonely	Orbison, Roy	9-183	SO
Only The Strong Survive	Butler, Jerry	4-706	SC
Only The Wind	Dean, Billy	13-491	P
Only Thing That Looks Good On Me..	Adams, Bryan	23-446	CB
Only Thing That Looks Good...	Adams, Bryan	4-683	SC
Only Time	Enya	33-405	CB
Only Time	Enya	16-302	PHM
Only Time	Enya	23-93	SC
Only Time (Radio Version)	Enya	21-520	SGB
Only Time Will Tell	Asia	5-689	SC
Only U	Ashanti	22-347	CB

SONG TITLE	ARTIST	#	TYPE
Only Waiting For You - WN	Crosby Stills & Nash	48-71	SC
Only Wanna Be With You	Hootie & Blowfish	18-251	DK
Only Wanna Be With You	Hootie & Blowfish	3-427	SC
Only Way I Know the	Aldean, Jason	45-857	SBI
Only When I Love	Dunn, Holly	34-269	CB
Only When I Love	Dunn, Holly	5-617	SC
Only Women Bleed	Alice Cooper	14-566	AH
Only Women Bleed	Alice Cooper	20-361	SC
Only Yesterday	Carpenters	44-352	MFK
Only You	Lee, Brenda	45-881	VH
Only You	Platters	11-20	PX
Only You	Yoakam, Dwight	49-696	SRK
Only You (And You Alone)	Platters	25-175	MM
Only You And You Alone	Platters	13-43	P
Only You And You Alone	Tritt, Travis	4-157	SC
Only You Can Love Me This Way	Urban, Keith	36-311	PHM
Only You Know And I Know	Clapton, Eric	13-802	SGB
Ooby Dooby	Orbison, Roy	9-195	SO
Ooh Baby	O'Sullivan, Gilbert	24-198	SC
Ooh Baby Baby	Jana	10-186	SC
Ooh Baby Baby	Robinson, Smokey	16-861	DK
Ooh Baby Baby	Ronstadt, Linda	10-366	KC
Ooh Child	5 Stairsteps	25-276	MM
Ooh It's Kinda Crazy	Jana	12-389	PHM
Ooh Poo Pah Doo	Hill, Jordan	11-468	DK
Ooh!	Blige, Mary J.	19-650	CB
Ooh!	Blige, Mary J.	32-419	THM
Oops (Oh My) **	Tweet	25-218	MM
Oops I Did It Again	Spears, Britney	13-562	LE
Oops I Farted Again (Parody)	Parody	15-338	MM
Oops Upside Your Head	Gap Band	16-372	SF
Open Arms	Journey	10-360	KC
Open Arms	Journey	3-484	SC
Open Arms	Raye, Collin	22-648	ST
Open Invitation	Santana	9-377	AH
Open My Heart	Adams, Yolanda	20-619	CB
Open My Heart	Madonna	14-44	THM
Open The Door	Magnapop	24-118	SC
Open Up Your Eyes	Tonic	5-284	SC
Open Up Your Heart	Owens, Buck	4-808	SC
Open Your Heart	Madonna	15-548	CMC
Open Your Heart	Madonna	19-555	SC
Operator	Croce, Jim	33-285	CB
Operator	Croce, Jim	2-555	SC
Operator	Manhattan Transfer	7-472	MM
Ophelia	Lumineers	48-403	DCK
Opposites Attract	Abdul, Paula	18-241	DK
Opticon	Orgy	15-305	THM
Optimistic	Davis, Skeeter	43-327	CB
Orange Blossom Special	Cash, Johnny	14-246	CB
Orange Blossom Special	Cash, Johnny	21-585	SC

SONG TITLE	ARTIST	#	TYPE
Orange Colored Sky	Cole, Natalie	15-549	MM
Orchids Mean Goodbye	Smith, Carl	22-112	CB
Ordinary	Train	23-559	MM
Ordinary Average Guy	Walsh, Joe	15-709	LE
Ordinary Day	Carlton, Vanessa	25-341	MM
Ordinary Girl	Richie, Lionel	24-175	SC
Ordinary Life	Brock, Chad	8-854	CB
Ordinary Life	Brock, Chad	7-857	CHT
Ordinary Life	Brock, Chad	22-732	ST
Ordinary Love	Minor, Shane	10-210	SC
Ordinary Love	Minor, Shane	22-491	ST
Ordinary Miracle	McLachlan, Sarah	43-5	PHM
Ordinary Miracles	Streisand, Barbra	49-570	PS
Ordinary People	Legend, John	30-135	PT
Ordinary People	Walker, Clay	1-104	CB
Ordinary People	Walker, Clay	22-800	ST
Organ Grinder's Swing	Four Preps	9-824	SAV
Original Of The Species	U2	29-213	PHM
Osama Yo Mama	Stevens, Ray	16-338	ST
Other Guy the	Little River Band	18-306	SC
Other Side	McCready, Mindy	34-329	CB
Other Side of Me the	Montana, Hannah	36-68	WD
Other Side Of This Kiss the	McCready, Mindy	8-727	CB
Other Side Of This Kiss the	McCready, Mindy	5-295	SC
Other Side Of This Kiss the	McCready, Mindy	22-802	ST
Other Woman the	Parker, Ray Jr.	25-273	MM
Other Woman the	Price, Ray	45-882	VH
Otherside	Red Hot Chili Peppe	13-843	PHM
Oughta Be A Law	Parnell, Lee Roy	49-272	CB
Our Bed Of Roses	Jones, George	49-350	CB
Our Country	Mellencamp, John	30-205	CB
Our Country	Mellencamp, John	30-205	CB
Our Country	Mellencamp, John	45-418	CB
Our Day Will Come	Carpenters	44-355	SKG
Our Day Will Come	Romantics	4-37	SC
Our Day Will Come	Ruby & Romantics	35-50	CB
Our Day Will Come	Ruby & Romantics	11-599	DK
Our Day Will Come	Ruby & Romantics	19-617	MH
Our Day Will Come	Valli, Frankie	49-472	MM
Our House	Crosby Stills & Nash	2-779	SC
Our House	Madness	28-367	DK
Our House	Madness	29-5	MH
Our Kind Of Love - duet	Lady Antebellum	37-336	CB
Our Lips Are Sealed	Go-Go's	13-213	P
Our Lips Are Sealed	Go-Go's	4-539	SC
Our Love	Cole, Natalie	24-342	SC
Our Love Is Here To Stay	Connick, Harry Jr.	3-126	KB
Our Love Is Here To Stay	Connick, Harry Jr.	19-714	PS
Our Love Is On The Fault Line	Gayle, Crystal	9-519	SAV
Our Song	Swift, Taylor	30-548	CB
Ourbound Plane	Bogguss, Suzy	6-192	MM
Ours	Swift, Taylor	44-271	KV
Out Behind The Barn	Dickens, Little	45-334	CK

SONG TITLE	ARTIST	#	TYPE
	Jimmy		
Out Here In The Water	Howard, Rebecca L	6-62	SC
Out Here On My Own	Cara, Irene	17-428	KC
Out Here On My Own	Cara, Irene	12-759	P
Out Last Night	Chesney, Kenny	37-38	CB
Out Of Control	Eagles	44-93	LG
Out Of Control	Hoobastank	23-271	THM
Out Of Control Raging Fire	Loveless & Tritt	16-43	ST
Out Of Goodbyes - duet	Maroon 5 & Lady Antebellum	38-239	CB
Out Of Hand	Stewart, Gary	20-287	SC
Out Of My Bones	Travis, Randy	49-378	CB
Out Of My Bones	Travis, Randy	22-785	ST
Out Of My Head	Fastball	7-805	PHT
Out Of My Head & Back In My Bed	Lynn, Loretta	47-625	CB
Out Of My Head & Back In My Bed	Lynn, Loretta	46-194	SC
Out Of My Heart	BB Mak	25-312	MM
Out Of Sight And On My Mind	Royal, Billy Joe	47-370	SC
Out Of The Blue	Arnold, Eddy	4-476	SC
Out Of The Blue Clear Sky	Strait, George	1-263	CB
Out Of The Rain - duet	Jennings & Colter	45-183	DCK
Out Of The Woods	Swift, Taylor	48-428	MRH
Out Of Touch - WN	Hall & Oates	48-65	CB
Out Of Your Shoes	Morgan, Lorrie	1-332	CB
Out Of Your Shoes	Morgan, Lorrie	6-745	MM
Out On The Parking Lot - duet	Paisley & Jackson	48-495	CKC
Out With A Bang	Murphy, David Lee	7-170	MM
Out With A Bang	Murphy, David Lee	3-657	SC
Outbound Plane	Bogguss, Suzy	1-558	CB
Outbound Plane	Bogguss, Suzy	13-489	P
Outbound Plane	Bogguss, Suzy	2-329	SC
Outland Women	Williams, Hank Jr.	49-18	KV
Outlaw's Prayer the	Paycheck, Johnny	22-32	CB
Outside	Lewis & Durtz	16-480	MH
Outside	Lewis & Durtz	15-459	PHM
Outside My Window	Buxton, Sarah	36-314	PHM
Outside Of Heaven	Fisher, Eddie	49-47	ZVS
Outside the	Swift, Taylor	36-84	BM
Outside Woman Blues	Clapton, Eric	13-792	SGB
Outside Woman Blues	Cream	19-801	SGB
Outsiders	Church, Eric	46-617	ASK
Outstanding In Our Field	Paisley, Brad	40-53	ASK
Outta Here	Chesney, Kenny	48-83	CB
Outta My Head	Campbell, Craig	45-390	ASK
Outta My Head	Campbell, Craig	44-195	ASK
Outta State, Outta Mind - duet	Vallejo, Al & Kendall Beard	42-10	PHN
Outtathaway	Vines	23-152	PHM
Over	Lohan, Lindsay	22-363	CB
Over	Shelton, Blake	39-38	ASK
Over & Over	Nelly & McGraw	22-350	CB
Over And Over	Dave Clark Five	45-77	CB

SONG TITLE	ARTIST	#	TYPE
Over And Over	Johnson, Puff	4-603	SC
Over And Over	Nelly w/McGraw	20-190	PHM
Over It	McPhee, Katherine	30-490	CB
Over My Head	Fleetwood Mac	47-909	LE
Over My Head	Lit	15-644	THM
Over My Head	Steve Miller Band	4-874	SC
Over My Head (Cable Car)	Fray	30-149	PT
Over My Shoulder	Berry, John	8-107	CB
Over My Shoulder	Mike & Mechanics	14-883	SC
Over The Mountain	Osbourne, Ozzy	21-754	SC
Over The Mountain, Across the Sea	Johnnie & Joe	7-263	MM
Over The Rainbow	Garland, Judy	11-170	DK
Over The Rainbow	Garland, Judy	12-511	P
Over The Rainbow	Harris, Sam	7-478	MM
Over The Rainbow	McBride, Martina	29-542	CB
Over The Rainbow	McPhee, Katharine	30-156	PT
Over The Rainbow	McPhee, Katherine	30-156	PT
Over The Rainbow (Live Version)	McBride, Martina	23-38	SC
Over When It's Over	Church, Eric	46-615	ASK
Over You	Daughtry	38-138	CB
Over You	Lambert, Miranda	45-64	BKD
Over You	Pope, Cassadee	49-671	SBI
Over You	Puckett & Union Gap	3-15	SC
Overkill	Men At Work	18-499	SAV
Overnight	Zac Brown Band	49-13	KV
Overnight	Zac Brown Band	46-72	KV
Overnight Male	Strait, George	2-812	SC
Overnight Success	Strait, George	1-253	CB
Overnight Success	Strait, George	5-133	SC
Overnight Success	Strait, George	8-597	TT
Overprotected	Spears, Britney	25-207	MM
Owner Of A Lonely Heart	Yes	11-698	DK
Oxygen	Caillat, Colbie	37-19	PS
Oye Mi Canto (Radio Vers)	NORE, Nina Sky & Daddy Yankee	37-107	SC
P.I.M.P. (Radio Verson) **	50 Cent	21-792	SC
P.I.M.P. (Remix	50 Cent	32-381	THM
P.S. I Love You	Beatles	29-334	SC
Pac-Man Fever	Buckner & Garcia	37-84	SC
Pacific Coast Party	Smash Mouth	33-392	CB
Pacific Coast Party	Smash Mouth	25-40	MM
Pacific Coast Party	Smash Mouth	16-79	ST
Padre	Robbins, Marty	48-21	CB
Pagan Baby	CCR	48-371	KV
Pageant Material	Musgraves, Kacey	45-320	KV
Pain	Jimmy Eat World	30-822	PHM
Pain Killer	Little Big Town	45-362	BKD
Paint It Black	Rolling Stones	19-753	LE
Paint Me A Birmingham	Lawrence, Tracy	19-679	ST
Painted On My Heart	Cult	15-436	PHM
Palisades Park	Cannon, Freddie	17-50	DK
Pamala Brown	Hall, Tom T.	45-669	DCK
Panama	Van Halen	13-620	LE

203

SONG TITLE	ARTIST	#	TYPE
Panama	Van Halen	20-45	SC
Pancho & Lefty	Haggard, Merle	43-56	CB
Pancho & Lefty	Nelson & Haggard	22-236	CB
Pancho & Lefty	Nelson & Haggard	13-411	P
Pancho & Lefty - duet	Haggard & Nelson	33-78	CB
Pandora's Box	Aerosmith	10-487	DA
Papa Bear	Harling, Keith	8-95	CB
Papa Bear	Harling, Keith	22-805	ST
Papa Can You Hear Me	Streisand, Barbra	9-49	MM
Papa Don't Preach	Madonna	11-586	DK
Papa Don't Preach	Madonna	21-157	LE
Papa Don't Preach	Madonna	12-817	P
Papa Loved Mama	Brooks, Garth	6-281	MM
Papa Loved Mama	Brooks, Garth	2-681	SC
Papa Loves Mambo	Como, Perry	20-782	PS
Papa Noel	Lee, Brenda	45-903	CB
Papa Oo Mau Mau	Rivingtons	6-651	MM
Papa Was A Rollin' Stone	Temptations	7-101	MM
Papa Was A Rolling Stone	Temptations	35-112	CB
Papa Was A Rolling Stone	Temptations	11-269	DK
Papa's Got A Brand New Bag	Brown, James	29-143	LE
Papa's Got A Brand New Bag	Brown, James	10-254	SS
Papa's Got A Brand New Bag	Redding, Otis	47-360	LE
Paparazzi	Lady Gaga	38-192	CB
Paper Angels	Wayne, Jimmy	22-96	CB
Paper Angels	Wayne, Jimmy	23-32	SC
Paper Angels	Wayne, Jimmy	19-769	ST
Paper Boy	Orbison, Roy	47-336	BAT
Paper In Fire	Mellencamp, John	21-422	SC
Paper Planes	MIA	36-230	PHM
Paper Roses	Osmond, Marie	11-826	DK
Paper Roses	Osmond, Marie	13-427	P
Paper Roses	Osmond, Marie	5-125	SC
Paper Rosie	Watson, Gene	14-666	CB
Paper Rosie	Watson, Gene	5-619	SC
Paper Walls	Cohn, Mark	24-19	SC
Paperback Writer	Beatles	18-116	DK
Parachute	Stapleton, Chris	49-10	KV
Paradise	Anderson, John	22-453	SC
Paradise	Coldplay	48-258	MRH
Paradise	Morgan, Craig	14-81	CB
Paradise	Prine, John	23-531	CB
Paradise	Sade	14-869	PS
Paradise - Duet	LL Cool J & Amerie	32-86	THM
Paradise By The Dashboard Lights	Meat Loaf	9-348	AH
Paradise By The Dashboard Lights	Meat Loaf	26-328	DK
Paradise By The Dashboard Lights	Meat Loaf	20-315	MH
Paradise By The Dashboard Lights	Meat Loaf	2-31	SC
Paradise City	Guns & Roses	10-504	DA
Paradise City	Guns & Roses	17-22	DK
Paradise City	Guns & Roses	13-278	P
Paralized	Presley, Elvis	14-776	THM
Paralyzer	Finger Eleven	48-603	DK
Paranoid	Black Sabbath	20-363	SC
Paranoid/War Pigs LIVE	Black Sabbath	13-656	SGB
Pardon Me	Moorer, Allison	8-919	CB
Parents Just Don't Understand	DJ Jazzy Jeff & Fresh Prince	34-137	CB
Parking Lot Party	Brice, Lee	43-255	ASK
Parody - 50 Ways To Get Bin Laden	Parody	49-307	RD
Parody - Big Sweet John	Colter, Ben	45-287	BS
Parody - Cats In The Kettle	Parody	46-567	RDK
Parody - Dirty Deeds Done With Sheep	Rivers, Bob	45-933	ZP
Parody - Girls In Leather Have Fun	Parody	49-309	WMP
Parody - Hair Keeps Falling Off My Head	Parody	47-614	WMP
Parody - What If Eminem Did Jingle...	Rivers, Bob	45-931	SC
Parody - What If God Smoked Cannibus	Rivers & Twisted Radio	45-934	SC
Parody - When A Man Loves A Chicken	Parody	49-308	RD
Parody - Wreck The Malls - duet	Rivers & Twisted Radio	45-932	SC
Parody - You Don't Smell Like Flowers	Parody	45-288	BS
Part Time Lover	Wonder, Stevie	20-304	CB
Part Time Lover	Wonder, Stevie	11-749	DK
Particle Man	They Might B Giants	5-641	SC
Partridge Family	TV Themes	2-153	SC
Party	Presley, Elvis	25-109	MM
Party All The Time	Murphy, Eddie	6-518	MM
Party Crowd	Murphy, David Lee	35-406	CB
Party Crowd	Murphy, David Lee	2-667	SC
Party Doll	Knox, Buddy	33-237	CB
Party Doll	Knox, Buddy	3-294	MM
Party Doll	Knox, Buddy	3-468	SC
Party For Two	Twain & Currington	21-164	CB
Party Lights	Brown, Junior	40-78	CB
Party Lights	Clark, Claudine	6-648	MM
Party On	McCoy, Neal	8-470	CB
Party People	Florida Georgia Line	43-459	ASK
Party People	Florida Georgia Line	40-23	PHN
Party Time	Sheppard, T.G.	3-379	SC
Party Train	Gap Band	18-361	AH
Party's Over the	Nelson, Willie	5-703	SC
Party's Over the (Turn Out The Lights)	Denver, Mike	45-807	KV
Pass It On Down	Alabama	1-15	CB
Pass Me By	Jones, George	47-741	SRK
Pass Me By If You're Only Passing T	Rodriguez, Johnny	14-256	SC
Pass You By	Boyz II Men	23-261	HS

SONG TITLE	ARTIST	#	TYPE
Passenger Seat the	SheDaisy	20-171	ST
Passionate Kisses	Carpenter, M C	1-423	CB
Passionate Kisses	Carpenter, M C	34-303	CB
Passionate Kisses	Carpenter, M C	6-132	MM
Passionate Kisses	Carpenter, M C	12-435	P
Passionate Kisses	Carpenter, M C	9-633	SAV
Passionate Kisses	Carpenter, M C	15-154	THM
Passionate Kisses	Carpenter, M C	8-594	TT
Password	Wells, Kitty	4-739	SC
Past The Point Of Rescue	Ketchum, Hal	4-150	SC
Patch It Up (Live)	Presley, Elvis	49-919	KVD
Patches	Carter, Clarence	17-144	DK
Patience	Guns & Roses	12-766	P
Patriotic - America the Beautiful	Standard	34-436	CB
Patriotic - America Will Always Stand	Travis, Randy	34-383	CB
Patriotic - America Will Survive	Williams, Hank Jr.	34-365	CB
Patriotic - Americans the	Mellencamp, John	30-451	CB
Patriotic - An American Child	Vassar, Phil	34-381	CB
Patriotic - Courtesy of the...	Keith, Toby	33-164	CB
Patriotic - Freedom Isn't Free	Ricochet	36-342	CB
Patriotic - God Bless America	Standard	33-209	CB
Patriotic - Have You Forgotten	Worley, Darryl	34-407	CB
Patriotic - Homeland	Rogers, Kenny	36-337	CB
Patriotic - I Believe In America	LeDoux, Chris	34-360	CB
Patriotic - I Raq & Roll	Black, Clint	34-410	CB
Patriotic - In America	Charlie Daniels Band	34-240	CB
Patriotic - It's America	Atkins, Rodney	36-261	PHM
Patriotic - Made In America	Keith, Toby	38-165	PHM
Patriotic - Star Spangled Banner	Standard	33-210	CB
Patriotic - Sunday Morning In Amer	Anderson, Keith	30-443	CB
Patriotic - That's An American	Blount, Benton	39-67	PHN
Patriotic - There's A Hero	Gilman, Billy	33-146	CB
Patriotic - This Is My Country	Ford, Tenn Ernie	34-438	CB
Patriotic - Where the Stars & Stripes	Tippin, Aaron	33-158	CB
Patriotic - You're a Grand Old Flag	Standard	34-440	CB
Pay Me My Money Down	Springsteen, Bruce	36-178	PHM
Payback	Rascal Flatts	45-280	BKD
Paycheck Woman	Judd, Cledus T.	23-388	SC
Paying For That Back Street Affair	Wells, Kitty	48-205	SSK
Paying The Cost to Be	King, B.B.	14-602	SC

SONG TITLE	ARTIST	#	TYPE
The Boss			
PayPhone	Boyce Avenue	46-279	KV
Peace (Where the Heart Is)	Brickman, Raye, Ashton	32-391	THM
Peace In The Valley	Foley, Red	8-669	SAV
Peace In The Valley	Presley, Elvis	30-374	SC
Peace Of Mind	Boston	5-73	SC
Peace Train	Stevens, Cat	23-650	BS
Peace Train	Stevens, Cat	13-578	NU
Peaceful Easy Feeling	Eagles	7-563	BS
Peaceful Easy Feeling	Eagles	2-252	SC
Peaceful World	Mellencamp, John	16-80	ST
Peaceful World	Mellencamp&India.Ar	25-24	MM
Peaceful World	Mellencamp&India.Ar	23-97	SC
Peacekeeper	Fleetwood Mac	25-577	MM
Peacekeeper	Fleetwood Mac	32-207	THM
Peach	Prince	49-824	KV
Peaches	Presidents of USA	13-595	P
Peaches & Cream	112	23-591	PHM
Peaches & Cream	112	16-394	SGB
Peanut Butter	Marathons	6-517	MM
Pearl's A Singer	Brooks, Elkie	11-21	PX
Pearls	Brown, Shannon	29-369	CB
Pearly Shells	Shaffer, Charlie	6-829	MM
Pearly Shells (Popo O Ewa)	Ives, Burl	43-441	CB
Pecos Promenade	Tucker, Tanya	38-15	CB
Peel Me A Grape	Krall, Diana	23-341	MM
Peel Me A Nanner	Drusky, Roy	20-748	CB
Peg	Steely Dan	15-391	RS
Peg O' My Heart	Reminiscing Series	3-31	SC
Peggy Sue	Holly, Buddy	11-218	DK
Peggy Sue	Holly, Buddy	3-216	LG
Peggy Sue	Holly, Buddy	12-735	P
Peggy Sue	Holly, Buddy	11-40	PX
Peggy Sue Got Married	Holly, Buddy	3-214	LG
Pencil Necked Geek	Blassie, Freddie	37-85	SC
Pencil Thin Mustache	Buffett, Jimmy	46-141	SC
Pennies From Heaven	Crosby, Bing	29-478	LE
Pennies From Heaven	Crosby, Bing	12-546	P
Pennies From Heaven	Lee, Brenda	48-577	DK
Pennies From Heaven	Lee, Brenda	45-906	DKM
Pennies From Heaven	Standard	11-301	DK
Pennsylvania Polka	Polka Favorites	29-811	SSR
Pennsylvania Polka - w/Words	Polka Favorites	29-865	SSR
Penny Arcade	Orbison, Roy	38-60	SF
Penny Lane	Beatles	16-799	DK
Penny Lane	Beatles	13-179	P
Penny Lane	Beatles	7-524	SAV
Penny Lover	Richie, Lionel	35-178	CB
Penny Lover	Richie, Lionel	10-389	LE
Pensylvania 6-5000	Andrew Sisters	46-434	KV
People	Streisand, Barbra	45-52	AHM
People	Streisand, Barbra	16-804	DK

SONG TITLE	ARTIST	#	TYPE
People Are Crazy	Currington, Billy	37-30	CB
People Are Crazy	Currington, Billy	47-558	SC
People Are People	Depeche Mode	5-385	SC
People Are Strange	Doors	4-699	SC
People Are Strange	Doors	18-648	SO
People Back Home	Florida Georgia Line	43-130	ASK
People Get Ready	Impressions	27-234	DK
People Get Ready	Impressions	13-100	P
People Get Ready	Stewart, Rod	4-291	SC
People Got To Be Free	Rascals	26-370	DK
People Got To Be Free	Rascals	12-871	P
People Like Us	Tippin, Aaron	22-587	ST
People Like Us	Tippin, Aaron	15-217	THM
People Loving People	Brooks, Garth	48-347	KV
People Say	Dixie Cups	47-25	SC
People That We Love	Bush	16-323	TT
Peppermint Twist	Dee & Starlighters	11-508	DK
Peppermint Twist - DANCE #	Dee & Starlighters	22-394	SC
Perfect	Evans, Sara	29-547	CB
Perfect	Evans, Sara	19-530	ST
Perfect	Fairground Attracti	10-527	SF
Perfect	One Direction	48-260	SBI
Perfect	Simple Plan	20-232	MM
Perfect Kiss the	Midler, Bette	45-942	PS
Perfect Love	Yearwood, Trisha	8-233	CB
Perfect Way	Seritti Politti	29-14	MH
Perfect World	Claypool, Philip	46-626	CB
Perfect World	Lewis & The News	11-393	DK
Perfect World	Sawyer Brown	14-76	CB
Perfectly Good Heart	Swift, Taylor	36-92	BM
Perfidia	Cole, Nat "King"	46-357	KV
Perfume	Spears, Britney	43-159	PHM
Perhaps Love	Denver, John	15-615	THM
Perhaps Perhaps Perhaps	Day, Doris	48-133	SFM
Personal Jesus	Cash, Johnny	43-398	KV
Personal Jesus	Depeche Mode	21-410	SC
Personal Jesus	Marilyn Manson	30-820	PHM
Personality	Price, Lloyd	17-361	DK
Personality	Price, Lloyd	10-702	JVC
Personality	Price, Lloyd	12-536	P
Personality	Price, Lloyd	10-609	SF
Personally	McDowell, Ronnie	47-226	CB
Peter Cottontail	Autry, Gene	45-660	DCK
Peter Pan	Ballerini, Kelsea	45-457	BKD
Peter The Meter Reader **	Wilson, Meri	15-2	SC
Petticoat Junction	TV Themes	2-154	SC
Pfft You Were Gone	Owens, Buck	40-49	SRK
Philadelphia Freedom	John, Elton	17-555	DK
Philadelphia Freedom	John, Elton	6-554	MM
Philadelphia Freedom	John, Elton	17-459	SC
Phones Are Ringing All Over Town	McBride, Martina	7-228	MM
Phony Calls	Yankovic, Weird Al	49-850	SGB
Photograph	Def Leppard	46-166	SC

SONG TITLE	ARTIST	#	TYPE
Photograph	Malibu Storm	20-452	ST
Photograph	Nickelback	30-131	PT
Photograph	Starr, Ringo	49-780	SC
Photograph	Verve Pipe	24-111	SC
Photographs & Memories	Croce, Jim	5-601	SC
Physical	Newton-John, Olivia	17-57	DK
Physical	Newton-John, Olivia	5-147	SC
Physical Attraction	Madonna	18-375	AH
Piano Has Been Drinking the	Waite, Tom	7-407	MM
Piano In The Dark	Russel, Brenda	11-533	DK
Piano Man	Joel, Billy	34-62	CB
Piano Man	Joel, Billy	12-276	DK
Piano Man	Joel, Billy	16-148	LE
Piano Man	Joel, Billy	6-541	MM
Piano Roll Blues	Cramer, Floyd	47-523	VH
Pick Me Up On Your Way Down	Cline, Patsy	22-197	CB
Pick Me Up On Your Way Down	Haggard & Nelson	49-816	KV
Pick Me Up On Your Way Down	Haggard, Nelson & Price	44-87	KV
Pick Me Up On Your Way Down	Walker, Charlie	8-776	CB
Pick Me Up On Your Way Down	Walker, Charlie	14-329	SC
Pick Me Up On Your Way Down - duet	Haggard, Merle	49-168	KV
Pick Of The Week	Drusky, Roy	20-756	CB
Pick The Wildwood Flower	Watson, Gene	14-670	CB
Pick The Wildwood Flower	Watson, Gene	5-812	SC
Pickin' Up Strangers	Lee, Johnny	47-175	SC
Pickin' Wildflowers	Anderson, Keith	23-4	CB
Pickup Man	Diffie, Joe	1-281	CB
Pickup Man	Diffie, Joe	2-458	SC
Picky	Montana, Joey	49-924	KVD
Picture	Crow, Sheryl & Kid Rock	32-10	THM
Picture	Kid Rock & Crow	18-433	CB
Picture	Kid Rock & Crow	29-666	RS
Picture	Kid Rock & Crow	32-10	THM
Picture Of Me Without You	Jones, George	12-191	DK
Picture Of Me Without You	Morgan, Lorrie	1-337	CB
Picture Of Me Without You	Morgan, Lorrie	26-583	DK
Picture Of Me Without You	Morgan, Lorrie	13-531	P
Picture Of Me Without You	Morgan, Lorrie	9-609	SAV
Picture Of You	Brown, Joe	11-52	PX
Picture Of You	Brown, Joe	10-558	SF
Picture Perfect	Sky Kings	7-244	MM
Picture Perfect (Radio Version)	Via, Angela	14-473	SC

SONG TITLE	ARTIST	#	TYPE
Picture Postcards From LA	Kadison, Joshua	2-469	SC
Picture This	Blondie	49-135	LG
Picture To Burn	Swift, Taylor	36-390	CB
Pictures	Montgomery, J M	34-371	CB
Pictures And Memories	Alabama	46-247	SC
Pictures Of Lily	Who	28-147	DK
Pictures Of Lily	Who	19-737	LE
Pictures Of You	Last Goodnight	49-912	SC
Piece By Piece	Clarkson, Kelly	48-653	DCK
Piece Of Me	Spears, Britney	36-524	CB
Piece Of Mind	Strait, George	38-148	CB
Piece Of My Heart	Etheridge, Melissa	47-69	RSZ
Piece Of My Heart	Hill, Faith	15-688	CB
Piece Of My Heart	Hill, Faith	6-467	MM
Piece Of My Heart	Hill, Faith	2-317	SC
Piece Of My Heart	Joplin, Janis	14-641	SC
Piece Of My Heart	Joplin, Janis	28-201	SF
Piece of My Heart	Knight, Beverly	30-756	SF
Piece Of My Heart	Tedeschi, Susan	17-455	AMS
Piece Of Sky	Streisand, Barbra	48-424	IDM
Piece Of Sky a	Streisand, Barbra	49-575	PS
Piece Of Work - duet	Buffett & Keith	38-168	SC
Piece Of Work - duet	Keith & Buffett	40-17	SC
Pieces	Allan, Gary	43-258	KCDC
Pieces Of April	Three Dog Night	4-329	SC
Pieces Of Me	Simpson, Ashlee	23-567	MM
Pied Piper	St. Peters, Crispian	10-669	SF
Pig In The Pen	Stanley Brothers	8-260	CB
Pilgrim Chapter 33	Kristofferson, Kris	45-205	DCK
Pill the	Lynn, Loretta	47-630	CB
Pillow Talk	Day, Doris	48-134	ZMP
Pillow Talk	Sylvia	2-847	SC
Pimpin' All Over The World	Ludacris	30-144	PT
Pinball Wizard	Who	19-730	LE
Pink Cadillac	Cole, Natalie	9-220	PT
Pink Cadillac	Cole, Natalie	3-552	SC
Pink Cadillac	Springsteen, Bruce	17-430	KC
Pink Cadillac	Springsteen, Bruce	17-621	LE
Pink Flamingos	Byrd, Tracy	20-110	CB
Pink Houses	Mellencamp, John	35-167	CB
Pink Houses	Mellencamp, John	21-429	LE
Pink Houses	Mellencamp, John	5-471	SC
Pink Shoelaces	Stevens, Dodie	6-857	MM
Pink Shoelaces	Stevens, Dodie	5-231	SC
Pioneer	Band Perry	40-42	ASK
Pirate Flag	Chesney, Kenny	44-327	SSC
Pirate Looks At 40 a	Buffett, Jimmy	46-138	SC
Pissin' In The Wind **	Walker, Jerry Jeff	30-664	RSX
Pistol Packin' Mama	Al Dexter & Troopers	8-769	CB
Place In The Sun a	McGraw, Tim	14-150	CB
Place In The Sun the	Wonder, Stevie	15-715	LE
Place In This World	Smith, Michael W	35-317	CB
Place In This World a	Swift, Taylor	36-82	BM

SONG TITLE	ARTIST	#	TYPE
Place To Fall Apart a	Fricke, Janie	12-411	P
Place To Fall Apart a	Haggard, Merle	49-817	PS
Places I've Never Been	Wills, Mark	7-637	CHM
Places I've Never Been	Wills, Mark	22-606	ST
Places That Belong To You	Streisand, Barbra	49-621	SC
Planet Of Love	Barnett, Mandy	7-622	CHM
Planets Of The Universe	Nicks, Stevie	47-897	MM
Plantation Rock the	Presley, Elvis	45-617	HM
Plastic Saddle	Stuckey, Nat	47-730	SRK
Platinum	Lambert, Miranda	46-271	SSC
Play	Lopez, Jennifer	16-124	PRT
Play Born To Lose Again	Milsap, Ronnie	47-280	VH
Play Guitar Play	Twitty, Conway	43-196	CB
Play It Again	Bryan, Luke	43-147	ASK
Play Me	Diamond, Neil	7-541	AH
Play Me	Diamond, Neil	18-694	PS
Play Me	Diamond, Neil	24-694	SC
Play Me	Diamond, Neil	30-508	THM
Play Something Country	Brooks & Dunn	23-143	CB
Play That Country Music	Chuck Wagon&Wheels	14-163	CB
Play That Funky Music	Wild Cherry	26-295	DK
Play That Funky Music	Wild Cherry	10-528	SF
Play The Game Tonight	Kansas	17-528	SC
Play The Song - duet	Joey & Rory	45-813	BKD
Play With Fire	Rolling Stones	18-17	LE
Play Your Part	Cox, Deborah	32-277	THM
Playboys of the Southwestern World	Shelton, Blake	25-649	MM
Playboys of the Southwestern World	Shelton, Blake	19-266	ST
Playboys Of The Southwestern World	Shelton, Blake	32-343	THM
Playground In My Mind	Newton, Wayne	47-309	LE
Playing For Keeps	King, Elle	46-122	ASK
Playing With Fire	Curfman, Shannon	14-485	SC
Pleasant Valley Sunday	Monkees	9-711	SAV
Please	Braxton, Toni	29-314	PHM
Please	Isaak, Chris	14-283	MM
Please	Isaak, Chris	7-784	PHT
Please	Kinleys	12-931	CB
Please	Kinleys	7-683	CHM
Please	Kinleys	22-661	ST
Please	Tillis, Pam	22-590	ST
Please	U2	48-314	SFG
Please Baby Please	Yoakam, Dwight	14-421	SC
Please Baby Please Don't Go	Morrison, Van	15-723	SI
Please Be Kind	Sinatra, Frank	25-262	MM
Please Call Home	Allman Brothers	21-811	SC
Please Come To Boston	Loggins, Dave	9-325	AG
Please Come To Boston	McEntire, Reba	15-550	SC
Please Don't Ask About Barbara	Vee, Bobby	49-66	ZVS
Please Don't Bury Me	Prine, John	23-526	CB
Please Don't Go	Immature	4-340	SC
Please Don't Go	KC & Sunshine	24-333	SC

SONG TITLE	ARTIST	#	TYPE
	Band		
Please Don't Go	Tank	30-491	CB
Please Don't Let Me Love You	Williams, Don	45-222	CB
Please Don't Stop Loving Me	Wagoner & Parton	5-442	SC
Please Don't Talk About Me When...	Martin, Dean	23-88	MM
Please Don't Tell Me How The Story	Bare, Bobby	18-274	CB
Please Don't Tell Me How The Story.	Milsap, Ronnie	4-638	SC
Please Forgive Me	Adams, Bryan	23-442	CB
Please Forgive Me	Adams, Bryan	2-116	SC
Please Forgive Me	Adams, Bryan	8-606	TT
Please Help Me I'm Falling	Locklin, Hank	8-650	SAV
Please Help Me I'm Falling	Locklin, Hank	2-634	SC
Please Let Me Love You	Paragons & Jesters	25-552	MM
Please Love Me Forever	Jackson, Wanda	47-797	SRK
Please Love Me Forever	Vinton, Bobby	7-264	MM
Please Make Up Your Mind	Williams, Hank Sr.	37-187	CB
Please Mister Please	Newton-John, Olivia	4-380	SC
Please Mr. Postman	Carpenters	44-346	CBE
Please Mr. Postman	Marvalettes	7-72	MM
Please Mr. Postman	Marvalettes	12-640	P
Please Mr. Sun	Ray, Johnnie	18-624	PS
Please Please Me	Beatles	16-872	DK
Please Please Me	Beatles	13-119	P
Please Please Me	Beatles	7-523	SAV
Please Please Me	Beatles	29-338	SC
Please Please Please	Brown, James	29-150	LE
Please Please Please	Brown, James	14-589	SC
Please Read The Letter - duet	Plant & Krauss	49-905	SC
Please Remember Me	Crowell, Rodney	2-745	SC
Please Remember Me	McGraw, Tim	8-955	CB
Please Remember Me	McGraw, Tim	7-860	CHT
Please Remember Me	Rimes, LeAnn	14-134	CB
Plush	Stone Temple Pilots	13-749	SGB
PMS Blues	Parton, Dolly	3-648	SC
Po' Folk	Anderson, Bill	46-211	CK
Pocket Full Of Gold	Gill, Vince	1-588	CB
Pocket Full Of Gold	Gill, Vince	6-207	MM
Pocket Of A Clown	Yoakam, Dwight	6-608	MM
Pocket Of A Clown	Yoakam, Dwight	2-313	SC
Pocketful Of Sunshine	Bedingfield, Natasha	36-456	CB
Podunk	Anderson, Keith	30-105	CB
Poem	Taproot	32-68	THM
Poems Prayers And Promises	Denver, John	48-411	DFK
Poetry In Motion	Tillotson, Johnny	11-116	DK
Poetry In Motion	Tillotson, Johnny	4-3	SC
Poetry Man	Snow, Phoebe	2-778	SC
Point At You	Moore, Justin	43-308	ASK
Point Of Light	Travis, Randy	9-533	SAV

SONG TITLE	ARTIST	#	TYPE
Poison	Bell Biv Devoe	25-478	MM
Poison Heart	Ramones	45-86	DCK
Poison Ivy	Coasters	11-509	DK
Poison Ivy	Coasters	10-697	JVC
Poison Ivy	Coasters	6-160	MM
Poison Whiskey	Lynyrd Skynyrd	5-260	SC
Poison Whiskey	Lynyrd Skynyrd	19-812	SGB
Poisoning Pigeons In The Park	Lehrer, Tom	23-29	SC
Poker Face	Lady Gaga	38-193	CB
Policy of Truth	Depeche Mode	16-524	P
Politically Uncorrect - duet	Haggard & Wilson	49-424	ST
Politics Religion And Her	Kershaw, Sammy	24-647	SC
Politics Religion And Her	Kershaw, Sammy	22-919	ST
Polk Salad Annie	Presley, Elvis	18-440	KC
Polka - E I E I O Polka	Polka Favorites	29-804	SSR
Polka - In Heaven There Is No Beer	Polka Favorites	29-806	SSR
Polka - Just Because Polka	Polka Favorites	29-805	SSR
Polka - Pennsylvania Polka	Polka Favorites	29-811	SSR
Polka - Roll Out The Barrel	Polka Favorites	29-809	SSR
Polka - Too Fat Polka	Polka Favorites	29-808	SSR
Polka - Who Stole The Keishka	Polka Favorites	29-807	SSR
Polka - Grab Your Balls We're Going	Polka Favorites	29-812	SSR
Polka Dots & Moonbeams	Standard	15-551	SGB
Polka Dots And Moonbeams	Lettermen	48-522	L1
Polka Your Eyes Out	Yankovic, Weird Al	49-749	KV
Pon De Replay	Rihanna	36-93	CB
Pon De Replay (Radio Vers)	Rihanna	37-101	SC
PONTOON	Little Big Town	39-39	ASK
Pontoon	Little Big Town	47-403	BKD
Pontoon	Little Big Town	47-402	MRH
Pontoon	Little Big Town	47-404	SRK
Pony Time	Checker, Chubby	11-564	DK
Pool Shark the	Dudley, Dave	43-289	CB
Poor Boy	Presley, Elvis	8-578	CB
Poor Boy	Presley, Elvis	14-777	THM
Poor Boy Blues	Atkins & Knopfler	44-80	KV
Poor Boy Blues	Atkins, Chet	46-447	KV
Poor Boy Shuffle	Tractors	45-859	VH
Poor Little Fool	Nelson, Ricky	21-704	CB
Poor Little Fool	Nelson, Ricky	2-51	SC
Poor Little Rich Girl	Lawrence, Steve	29-490	LE
Poor Man's Roses a	Cline, Patsy	22-183	CB
Poor Man's Roses a	Cline, Patsy	6-726	MM
Poor Man's Son	Robison, Charlie	9-404	CB
Poor Me	Diffie, Joe	1-285	CB
Poor Me	Diffie, Joe	22-679	ST

SONG TITLE	ARTIST	#	TYPE
Poor Poor Pitiful Me	Clark, Terri	7-387	MM
Poor Poor Pitiful Me	Clark, Terri	4-595	SC
Poor Poor Pitiful Me	Ronstadt, Linda	9-634	SAV
Poor Side Of Town	Rivers, Johnny	11-130	DK
Poor Side Of Town	Rivers, Johnny	4-39	SC
Pop	N'Sync	20-431	CB
Pop	N'Sync	18-572	TT
Pop A Top	Brown, Jim Ed	8-805	CB
Pop A Top	Brown, Jim Ed	5-432	SC
Pop A Top	Jackson, Alan	19-204	CB
Pop A Top	Jackson, Alan	5-807	SC
Pop A Top	Jackson, Alan	22-372	ST
Pop Life	Prince	23-330	CB
Pop Muzik	M	6-519	MM
Pop Muzik	M	22-931	SC
Popsicles and Icicles	Murmaids	3-586	SC
Porcelain	Moby	15-649	THM
Porch People	Borrowed Blue	39-64	PHN
Pork And Beans	Weezer	36-470	CB
Portland Oregon - duet	Lynn & Jack White	48-251	SC
Portrait Of My Love	Lawrence, Steve	15-552	MM
Portrait Of My Love	Lettermen	48-521	L1
Portrait Of My Love	Monro, Matt	9-247	PS
Positively 4th Street	Dylan, Bob	29-96	CB
Possession	McLachlan, Sarah	14-190	CB
Postcard From Paris	Band Perry	39-46	ASK
Postmarked Birmingham	Blackhawk	22-664	ST
Pour Me	Trick Pony	14-153	CB
Pour Me	Trick Pony	22-593	ST
Pour Me	Trick Pony	16-274	TT
Pour Me A Vacation	Great Divide	8-194	CB
Pour Me Another Tequila	Rabbitt, Eddie	14-310	SC
Pour Some Sugar On Me	Def Leppard	13-744	SGB
Powder Your Face With Sunshine	Martin, Dean	23-83	MM
Power Of Goodbye	Madonna	21-152	LE
Power Of Love	Dion, Celine	15=113	BS
Power Of Love	Dion, Celine	14-196	CB
Power Of Love	Dion, Celine	26-340	DK
Power Of Love	Dion, Celine	9-266	SC
Power Of Love	Lewis & The News	20-301	CB
Power Of Love	Lewis & The News	11-136	DK
Power Of Love	Lewis & The News	12-836	P
Power Of Love	Vandross, Luther	16-404	PR
Power Of Love (Love Power)	Vandross, Luther	33-337	CB
Power Of Love the	Lewis, Huey	48-573	DK
Power Of Love the	Parnell, Lee Roy	49-305	SC
Power Of One	Bomshel	30-551	CB
Power Of Positive Drinkin'	Janson, Chris	49-654	KV
Power Of Positive Drinking	Gilley, Mickey	16-179	THM
Power Of The Dream the	Dion, Celine	4-661	SC
Power Of Two the	Indigo Girls	14-873	SC
Power the	Cher	47-676	PS
Power To The People	Lennon, John	30-289	RS

SONG TITLE	ARTIST	#	TYPE
Power Windows	Berry, John	5-805	SC
Power Windows	Berry, John	22-522	ST
Powerful Stuff	Fabulous T-Birds	48-612	PCD
Powerful Thing	Yearwood, Trisha	8-866	CB
Powerful Thing	Yearwood, Trisha	10-164	SC
Powerful Thing	Yearwood, Trisha	22-698	ST
Powerless (Say What You Want)	Furtado, Nelly	19-665	CB
Practice Life	Griggs w/McBride	18-328	ST
Practice Life	Griggs, Andy	25-355	MM
Practice Life	Griggs, Andy	32-5	THM
Praise Chorus a	Jimmy Eat World	23-148	PHM
Pray For The Fish	Travis, Randy	19-367	ST
Prayer	Dion, Celine	19-22	PS
Prayer For The Dying	Seal	6-636	MM
Prayer the	Dion, Celine	15-119	BS
Prayin' For Daylight	Rascal Flatts	13-828	CHM
Praying For Time	Michael, George	17-93	DK
Preachin' Prayin' Singin'	Flatt & Scruggs	49-329	CB
Precious & Few	Climax	27-597	DK
Precious & Few	Climax	2-839	SC
Precious Declaration	Collective Soul	34-55	CB
Precious Thing	Charles, Ray	46-577	KV
Precious Thing	Wariner, Steve	1-498	CB
Precious Things	Amos, Tori	5-744	SC
Pressure	Joel, Billy	5-379	SC
Pretend	Cole, Nat "King"	29-459	LE
Pretend	Cole, Nat "King"	5-229	SC
Pretender the	Foo Fighters	37-118	SC
Pretty Baby	Carlton, Vanessa	25-430	MM
Pretty Baby	Carlton, Vanessa	32-97	THM
Pretty Blue Eyes	Lawrence, Steve	5-517	SC
Pretty Flamingo	Mann, Manfred	10-579	SF
Pretty Fly (For A White Guy)	Offspring	7-790	PHT
Pretty Good At Drinkin' Beer	Currington, Billy	37-205	AS
Pretty Hurts	Beyonce	48-388	KV
Pretty In Pink	Psychedelic Furs	13-33	P
Pretty In Pink	Psychedelic Furs	21-619	SF
Pretty Little Adriana	Gill, Vince	1-596	CB
Pretty Little Adriana	Gill, Vince	7-391	MM
Pretty Little Adriana	Gill, Vince	24-651	SC
Pretty Little Angel Eyes	Lee, Curtis	6-685	MM
Pretty Little Angel Eyes	Lee, Curtis	10-383	SS
Pretty Paper	Orbison, Roy	9-187	SO
Pretty Woman	Orbison, Roy	9-184	SO
Pretty Woman	Van Halen	13-616	LE
Pretty Young Thing	Jackson, Michael	11-462	DK
Price Of Love the	Everly Brothers	10-575	SF
Price To Pay	Staind	32-288	THM
Priceilla	Lambert, Miranda	44-305	BKD
Pride	Price, Ray	22-246	SC
Pride (In The Name of Love)	U2	30-72	SC
Pride And Joy	Vaughn, Stevie Ray	7-211	MM
Pride And Joy	Vaughn, Stevie Ray	15-317	SC

SONG TITLE	ARTIST	#	TYPE
Pride And Passion	Cafferty, John	45-158	SB
Pride In The Name Of Love	U2	13-275	P
Primal Scream **	Motley Crue	21-773	SC
Primrose Lane	Wallace, Jerry	29-620	CB
Primrose Lane	Wallace, Jerry	20-61	SC
Princess In Rags	Pitney, Gene	47-528	ZM
Princess Princess	Tillotson, Johnny	46-592	DCK
Prisoner Of Hope	Lee, Johnny	5-538	SC
Prisoner Of Love	Brown, James	29-141	LE
Prisoner Of Love **	Bob & Tom Band	37-87	SC
Private Dancer	Turner, Tina	10-418	LE
Private Dancer	Turner, Tina	16-525	P
Private Emotion	Martin, Ricky	15-325	PHM
Private Emotion	Martin, Ricky	9-137	PS
Private Emotion	Martin, Ricky	13-738	SGB
Private Eyes	Hall & Oates	35-152	CB
Private Eyes	Hall & Oates	4-87	SC
Private Idaho	B-52's	46-457	SC
Probably Wouldn't Be This Way	Rimes, LeAnn	22-328	CB
Problems	Everly Brothers	38-23	CB
Problems At Home	Shelton, Blake	47-764	SRK
Promiscuous	Furtado & Timbaland	30-146	PT
Promiscuous	Furtado&Timbaland	30-146	PT
Promiscuous - duet	Furtado & Timbaland	48-605	DK
Promise	Ciara	30-270	CB
Promise	Clara	30-270	CB
Promise	Jagged Edge	15-435	PHM
Promise Ain't Enough - WN	Hall & Oates	48-69	MM
Promise Me You'll Try	Lopez, Jennifer	23-326	CB
Promise Me You'll Try	Lopez, Jennifer	23-577	MM
Promise This	Adele	40-36	SF
Promise This (Live Version)	Adele	47-432	KV
Promise To Remember	Lymon, Frankie	30-524	LE
Promise, the	Chapman, Tracy	44-185	KV
Promised Land the	Berry, Chuck	46-228	THM
Promises	Basia	14-863	PS
Promises	Clapton, Eric	5-477	SC
Promises	Def Leppard	46-170	SC
Promises	Travis, Randy	20-651	SC
Promises In The Dark	Benatar, Pat	20-93	SC
Promises Promises	Anderson, Lynn	47-638	CB
Promises Promises	Naked Eyes	21-406	SC
Prop Me Up Beside The Jukebox	Diffie, Joe	1-278	CB
Prop Me Up Beside The Jukebox	Diffie, Joe	12-138	DK
Prop Me Up Beside The Jukebox	Diffie, Joe	6-380	MM
Proud Mary	CCR	11-353	DK
Proud Mary	CCR	12-924	P
Proud Mary	CCR	5-348	SC
Proud Mary	Turner, Ike & Tina	7-35	MM

SONG TITLE	ARTIST	#	TYPE
Proud Mary	Turner, Tina	47-405	CB
Proud Mary	Turner, Tina	10-428	LE
Proud Mary	Turner, Tina	47-406	SC
Proud Of The House We Built	Brooks & Dunn	30-468	CB
Proud One the	Osmonds	47-866	ZP
Prove Your Love	Dayne, Taylor	28-291	DK
Prove Your Love	Fleetwood Mac	11-680	DK
Ps I Love You	Beatles	11-682	DK
Psychedelic Shack	Temptations	34-34	CB
Psychedelic Shack	Temptations	17-395	DK
Psycho	Puddle Of Mud	36-438	CB
Psycho Circus	Kiss	10-38	SC
Pua Carnation	Ho, Don	6-837	MM
Pub With No Beer	Dusty, Slim	47-490	ARC
Puff The Magic Dragon	Kids	12-264	DK
Puff The Magic Dragon	Peter, Paul & Mary	33-442	CB
Puff The Magic Dragon	Peter, Paul & Mary	11-174	DK
Puff The Magic Dragon	Peter, Paul & Mary	9-123	PS
Pump It (Radio Vers) **	Black Eyed Peas	37-117	SC
Pump Up The Jam	Technotronic	14-642	SC
Pumpin' Up The Party	Montana, Hannah	36-63	WD
Punk Rock Girl	Dead Milkmen	21-408	SC
Puppet On A String	Presley, Elvis	8-588	CB
Puppet On A String	Presley, Elvis	7-124	MM
Puppy Love	Anka, Paul	35-42	CB
Puppy Love	Anka, Paul	27-501	DK
Puppy Love	Anka, Paul	9-176	SO
Puppy Love	Osmond, Donny	13-316	P
Puppy Love	Pitney, Gene	47-536	SO
Pure Bred Redneck	Brown, Cooter	4-93	SC
Pure Love	Milsap, Ronnie	1-436	CB
Pure Love	Milsap, Ronnie	5-251	SC
Pure Pleasere Seeker	Melako	20-9	SGB
Purest Of Pain (A Puro Dolor)	Son By Four	30-645	THM
Purple Haze	Hendrix, Jimi	2-758	SC
Purple Haze	Hendrix, Jimi	28-196	SF
Purple People Eater	Wooley, Sheb	4-2	SC
Purple People Eater	Wooley, Sheb	16-288	TT
Purple Rain	Prince	11-642	DK
Purple Rain	Prince	12-756	P
Purple Rain	Prince	8-609	TT
Purple Rain	Rimes, LeAnn	8-861	CB
Purpose	Bieber, Justin	49-721	KV
Push	Matchbox 20	10-108	SC
Push	McLachlan, Sarah	29-242	ZM
Push It	Garbage	5-275	SC
Push It **	Salt 'N Pepa	2-720	SC
Pusher the	Steppenwolf	2-757	SC
Pushin' Me Away	Linkin Park	16-321	TT
Pushing Me Away	Jonas Brothers	36-508	CB
Pushing Up Daisies	Brooks, Garth	48-356	SC
Pussycat **	Elliot, Missy	21-793	SC
Pussycat Song the **	Vannett, Connie	30-669	RSX
Pussycat Song the **	Vannett, Connie	5-553	SC
Pussywillows Cat Tails	Lightfoot, Gordon	43-495	SK

SONG TITLE	ARTIST	#	TYPE
Put A Girl In It	Brooks & Dunn	36-406	CB
Put A Lid On It	Squirrel Nut Zipper	13-695	SGB
Put A Little Holiday In Your Heart	Rimes, Lee Ann	45-787	SC
Put A Little Love In Your Heart	DeShannon, Jackie	11-402	DK
Put A Little Love In Your Heart	Lennox & Green	6-336	MM
Put A Little Love In Your Heart	Lennox & Green	18-379	SAV
Put A Little Love In Your Heart	Lennox, Annie	49-462	MM
Put Another Log On The Fire	Glaser, Tompall	8-446	CB
Put It Off Until Tomorrow	Kendalls	9-604	SAV
Put It On	Marley, Bob	25-380	MM
Put Me Out Of My Misery	McPotts	4-405	SC
Put On A Happy Face	Bennett, Tony	43-227	CB
Put On A Happy Face - show	Bye Bye Birdie	48-786	MM
Put Some Drive In Your Country	Tritt, Travis	1-673	CB
Put Some Drive In Your Country	Tritt, Travis	34-286	CB
Put That Woman First	Jaheim	20-525	CB
Put That Woman First	Jaheim	32-274	THM
Put You In A Song	Urban, Keith	46-156	PHN
Put Your Best Dress On	Holy, Steve	43-266	CB
Put Your Best Dress On	Holy, Steve	20-390	ST
Put Your Clothes Back On	Stampley, Joe	43-299	CB
Put Your Dreams Away	Gilley, Mickey	22-213	CB
Put Your Dreams Away	Sinatra, Frank	49-485	MM
Put Your Hand In Mind	Byrd, Tracy	14-704	CB
Put Your Hand In Mine	Byrd, Tracy	19-233	SC
Put Your Hand In Mine	Byrd, Tracy	22-379	ST
Put Your Hand In The Hand	Murray, Anne	11-8	PL
Put Your Hand In The Hand	Ocean	17-27	DK
Put Your Hand In The Hand	Ocean	24-61	SC
Put Your Hands Where My Eyes Can	Busta Rhymes	14-449	SC
Put Your Head On My Shoulder	Anka, Paul	12-11	DK
Put Your Head On My Shoulder	Anka, Paul	2-206	SC
Put Your Head On My Shoulder	Anka, Paul	9-175	SO
Put Your Head On My Shoulder	Lettermen	48-525	L1
Put Your Heart In To It	Austin, Sherrie	8-307	CB
Put Your Heart Into It	Austin, Sherrie	22-789	ST
Put Your Lights On	Santana & Everlast	9-338	PS
Put Your Lights On	Santana & Everlast	10-218	SC
Put Your Lights On	Santana & Everlast	19-824	SGB
Put Your Records On	Rae, Corinne Bailey	36-182	PHM
Put Yourself In My Shoes	Black, Clint	1-111	CB

SONG TITLE	ARTIST	#	TYPE
Put Yourself In My Shoes	Black, Clint	12-398	P
Put Yourself In My Shoes	Black, Clint	30-430	THM
Puttin' On The Ritz	Standard	10-472	MG
Puttin' On The Ritz	Taco	4-842	SC
Quando Quando Quando	Humperdinck, E.	15-850	MM
Quando Quando, Quando	Humperdinck, E.	34-6	CB
Quarter To Three	Bonds, Gary U.S.	10-742	JVC
Quarter To Three	Bonds, Gary U.S.	12-648	P
Quarter To Three	Bonds, Gary U.S.	10-252	SS
Que Sera Sera	Day, Doris	11-578	DK
Que Sera Sera	Day, Doris	3-354	MH
Que Sera Sera	Day, Doris	12-513	P
Que Sera Sera	Day, Doris	9-90	PS
Que Sera Sera	Day, Doris	2-240	SC
Queen Bee	Streisand, Barbra	45-796	SBI
Queen Of Hearts	Newton, Juice	35-161	CB
Queen Of Hearts	Newton, Juice	11-107	DK
Queen Of Hearts	Newton, Juice	13-440	P
Queen Of Hop	Darin, Bobby	5-511	SC
Queen Of Memphis	Confederate RR	34-304	CB
Queen Of Memphis	Confederate RR	10-754	JVC
Queen Of Memphis	Confederate RR	6-307	MM
Queen Of Memphis	Confederate RR	12-458	P
Queen Of Memphis	Confederate RR	2-707	SC
Queen Of My Double-Wide Trailer	Kershaw, Sammy	1-469	CB
Queen Of My Double-Wide Trailer	Kershaw, Sammy	3-637	SC
Queen Of The Broken Hearts	Loverboy	37-77	SC
Queen Of The Hop	Darin, Bobby	47-12	SC
Queen Of The House	Miller, Jodi	20-638	SC
Queen Of The Reich	Queensyrche	21-758	SC
Queen Of The Silver Dollar	Holly, Doyle	8-630	SAV
Queen Of The Slip Stream	Morrison, Van	23-606	BS
Queen Of The Slip Stream	Morrison, Van	15-732	SI
Questions	Tamia	20-569	CB
Quiet Your Mind	Zac Brown Band	46-67	KV
Quinn The Eskimo	Dylan, Bob	13-177	P
Quit Playing Games With My Heart	Backstreet Boys	18-709	MM
Quit Playing Games With My Heart	Backstreet Boys	21-549	PHM
Quits	Stewart, Gary	14-423	SC
Quittin' Kind the	Diffie, Joe	14-699	CB
Quittin' Kind the	Diffie, Joe	19-231	SC
Quittin' Kind the	Diffie, Joe	22-506	ST
Quittin' Time	Carpenter, M C	1-432	CB
Quittin' Time	Carpenter, M C	15-157	THM
Quizas, Quizas, Quizas	Cole, Nat "King"	46-369	SAV
R.O.C.K. In The USA	Mellencamp, John	21-431	LE
R.O.C.K. In The USA	Mellencamp, John	19-88	PS

SONG TITLE	ARTIST	#	TYPE
R.O.C.K. In The USA	Mellencamp, John	21-420	SC
Race Among The Ruins	Lightfoot, Gordon	43-483	SK
Race Is On the	Jones, George	8-265	CB
Race Is On the	Jones, George	17-290	NA
Race Is On the	Jones, George	13-472	P
Race Is On the	Jones, George	9-506	SAV
Race With The Devil	Vincent, Gene	49-233	DFK
Race You To The Bottom	Dean, Billy	23-304	CB
Radar	Spears, Britney	36-303	PHM
Radar Love	Golden Earring	2-146	SC
Radio	Corrs	49-197	SF
Radio	Rucker, Darius	41-49	ASK
Radio	Rucker, Darius	44-334	SSC
Radio Free Europe	REM	21-404	SC
Radio Heart	McClain, Charley	5-244	SC
Radio Waves	Eli Young Band	47-58	CB
Radioactive	Firm	5-476	SC
Rag Doll	Aerosmith	24-199	SC
Rag Doll	Four Seasons	34-16	CB
Rag Doll	Four Seasons	11-701	DK
Raggae Nights	Cliff, Jimmy	46-631	XPK
Ragged Old Flag	Cash, Johnny	29-566	CB
Rags To Riches	Bennett, Tony	49-213	MM
Rain	Beatles	20-205	SC
Rain	Breaking Benjamin	30-222	PHM
Rain	Glover, Dana	20-516	CB
Rain	Grover, Dana	25-588	MM
Rain	Madonna	21-159	LE
Rain	Madonna	6-372	MM
Rain	Madonna	13-24	P
Rain Is A Good Thing	Bryan, Luke	45-96	CB
Rain On Me	Ashanti	32-386	THM
Rain On The Roof Of This Car	James-Decker, Jessie	48-458	BKD
Rain On The Scarecrow	Mellencamp, John	21-428	LE
Rain On The Scarecrow	Mellencamp, John	45-416	SC
Rain Or Shine	5 Star	30-790	SF
Rain Rain Rain	Laine, Frankie	10-597	SF
Rain Tax (It's Inevitable)	Dion, Celine	19-29	PS
Rain The Park And Other Things	Cowsills	12-46	DK
Rain Through The Roof	Montana, Billy	7-29	MM
Rainbow At Midnight	Tubb, Ernest	19-636	CB
Rainbow In The Rain	Black, Clint	23-419	CB
Rainbow In The Rain	Black, Clint	29-612	ST
Rainbow Man	Bates, Jeff	19-533	ST
Rainbow Stew	Haggard, Merle	37-176	CB
Rainbow Stew	Haggard, Merle	5-41	SC
Raindrops	Clark, D	35-35	CB
Raindrops	Clark, Dee	6-679	MM
Raindrops Keep Fallin' On My Head	Thomas, B.J.	16-852	DK
Raindrops Keep Fallin' On My Head	Thomas, B.J.	36-151	LE
Raindrops Keep Fallin' On My Head	Thomas, B.J.	12-686	P
Rainin' In My Heart	Williams, Hank Jr.	37-298	CB

SONG TITLE	ARTIST	#	TYPE
Raining In Baltimore	Counting Crows	18-699	CB
Raining In My Heart	Holly, Buddy	3-219	LG
Raining In My Heart	Holly, Buddy	11-30	PX
Raining In My Heart	Roe, Tommy	48-112	CB
Raining On Our Love	Twain, Shania	7-446	MM
Raining On Sunday	Urban, Keith	34-373	CB
Raining On Sunday	Urban, Keith	25-445	MM
Raining On Sunday	Urban, Keith	18-589	ST
Raining On Sunday	Urban, Keith	32-81	THM
Rainy Day In June	Jackson, Alan	45-339	LM
Rainy Day In June	Jackson, Alan	47-745	SRK
Rainy Day People	Lightfoot, Gordon	43-484	SK
Rainy Day Woman	Jennings, Waylon	22-139	CK
Rainy Day Woman	Jennings, Waylon	4-733	SC
Rainy Day Woman #12 & 35	Dylan, Bob	29-97	CB
Rainy Day Woman #12 & 35	Dylan, Bob	12-190	DK
Rainy Day Women #12 & 35	Dylan, Bob	2-747	SC
Rainy Days & Mondays	Carpenters	16-856	DK
Rainy Days & Mondays	Carpenters	12-687	P
Rainy Days & Mondays	Carpenters	2-437	SC
Rainy Dayz	Blige & Ja Rule	18-220	CB
Rainy Night In Georgia	Benton, Brook	17-143	DK
Rainy Night In Georgia	Benton, Brook	13-18	P
Raise 'Em Up	Urban, Keith	45-62	SBI
Raise The Barn - duet	Urban & Dunn	42-27	CB
Raise Your Hands	Bon Jovi	21-782	SC
Raised On Rock	Presley, Elvis	9-723	SAV
Raised On Rock	Presley, Elvis	14-826	THM
Rake And Ramblin' Man	Williams, Don	45-227	CB
Rama Lama Ding Dong	Edsels	6-861	MM
Ramble On	Led Zeppelin	5-71	SC
Ramblin' Fever	Haggard, Merle	8-281	CB
Ramblin' Fever	Haggard, Merle	17-401	DK
Ramblin' Fever	Haggard, Merle	8-644	SAV
Ramblin' Gamblin' Man	Seger, Bob	46-338	SC
Ramblin' Man	Allman Brothers	18-154	CB
Ramblin' Man	Allman Brothers	16-787	DK
Ramblin' Man	Allman Brothers	12-777	P
Ramblin' Man	Allman Brothers	2-524	SC
Ramblin' Rose	Cole, Nat "King"	11-97	DK
Ramblin' Rose	Cole, Nat "King"	29-452	LE
Ramblin' Rose	Cole, Nat "King"	2-197	SC
Ramblin' Rose	Cole, Nat "King"	17-327	SS
Rambling Rose	Cole, Nat "King"	33-212	CB
Random Act Of Senseless Kindness	South Sixty Five	10-161	SC
Randy Scouse Git	Monkees	47-287	EZ
Rank Stranger	Stanley Brothers	38-28	CB
Raped And Freezing	Alice Cooper	16-444	SGB
Rapid Roy (That Stock Car Boy)	Croce, Jim	48-461	CB
Rapper's Delight	Sugarhill Gang	15-805	SC
Rapture	Blondie	11-823	DK
Rapture	Blondie	13-34	P

SONG TITLE	ARTIST	#	TYPE
Raspberry Beret	Prince	13-287	P
Rated X	Lynn, Loretta	4-740	SC
Rave On	Holly, Buddy	3-218	LG
Rave On	Holly, Buddy	11-34	PX
Ravishing Ruby	Hall, Tom T.	3-752	CB
Ravishing Ruby	Hall, Tom T.	5-821	SC
Rawhide	Blues Brothers	29-152	ZM
Rawhide	Laine, Frankie	12-893	P
Rawhide	Laine, Frankie	19-112	SAV
Rawhide	TV Themes	2-158	SC
Ray Of Light	Madonna	21-149	LE
Ray Ray's Juke Joint	Johnson, Jamey	48-508	KVD
Raymond	Eldridge, Brett	46-591	FTX
Re-Arranged	Limp Bizkit	5-781	SC
Reach Out & Touch Somebody	Ross, Diana	11-808	DK
Reach Out I'll Be There	Bolton, Michael	6-95	MM
Reach Out I'll Be There	Four Tops	11-142	DK
Reach Out In The Darkness	Friend & Lover	6-781	MM
Reaching Out To Hold You	West, Dottie	15-232	CB
Read Me My Rights	Gilbert, Brantley	46-159	BKD
Read My Lips	Osmond, Marie	47-852	SC
Read My Mind	McEntire, Reba	1-797	CB
Read My Mind	McEntire, Reba	17-226	NA
Read This Letter	Reeves, Jim	49-798	VH
Reading My Heart	Morgan, Lorrie	47-782	SRK
Ready	Stevens, Cat	23-651	BS
Ready	Stevens, Cat	13-579	NU
Ready For Love	India.Arie	25-689	MM
Ready For The Times To Get Better	Gayle, Crystal	29-782	CB
Ready Or Not	After 7	11-820	DK
Ready Set Roll	Rice, Chase	44-199	ASK
Ready Set Roll	Rice, Chase	49-662	KCD
Ready To Go	Republica	24-235	SC
Ready To Go Home	Williams, Hank Sr.	45-703	CB
Ready To Love Again	Lady Antebellum	44-127	KV
Ready To Rock	Tippin, Aaron	30-81	CB
Ready To Roll	Shelton, Blake	47-446	KV
Ready To Run	Dixie Chicks	8-974	CB
Ready To Run	Dixie Chicks	30-606	RS
Ready To Run	Dixie Chicks	10-61	SC
Ready To Run	Dixie Chicks	22-426	ST
Ready To Take A Chance Again	Manilow, Barry	12-123	DK
Ready To Take A Chance Again	Manilow, Barry	15-840	MM
Ready Willing and Able	Day, Doris	48-139	ZMP
Ready Willing And Able	White, Lari	4-22	SC
Real	Goo Goo Dolls	36-238	PHM
Real Bad Mood	Marie Sisters	16-702	ST
Real Deal	Gattis, Keith	4-417	SC
Real Fine Place To Start a	Evans, Sara	23-121	CB
Real Fine Place To Start a	Evans, Sara	23-377	SC

SONG TITLE	ARTIST	#	TYPE
Real Good Man	McGraw, Tim	29-513	CB
Real Good Man	McGraw, Tim	25-640	MM
Real Good Man	McGraw, Tim	19-170	ST
Real Good Man	McGraw, Tim	32-299	THM
Real Life (I Never Was The Same..)	Carson, Jeff	29-354	CB
Real Life (I Never Was The Same)	Carson, Jeff	15-607	ST
Real Live Girl	Monro, Matt	18-105	PS
Real Live Woman	Yearwood, Trisha	34-336	CB
Real Live Woman	Yearwood, Trisha	23-365	SC
Real Live Woman	Yearwood, Trisha	22-472	ST
Real Love	Blige, Mary J.	34-111	CB
Real Love	Blige, Mary J.	28-223	SF
Real Love	Blige, Mary J.	32-204	THM
Real Love	Doobie Brothers	29-91	CB
Real Love	Lightman, Toby	20-559	PHM
Real Love	Parton, Dolly	13-394	P
Real Love	Watley, Jodi	11-532	DK
Real Love	Watley, Jodi	16-519	P
Real Love the	Seger, Bob	46-344	SC
Real Man	Dean, Billy	8-752	CB
Real Me the	Grant, Natalie	36-177	PHM
Real Me the	Jennings, Shooter	49-637	PHN
Real Men Love Jesus	Ray, Michael	48-700	KCA
Real Slim Shady **	Eminem	25-469	MM
Real Slim Shady (Parody)	Parody	15-345	MM
Real Slim Shady (Radio Version) **	Eminem	14-480	SC
Real Slim Shady **	Eminem	19-827	SGB
Real World	Matchbox 20	21-555	PHM
Reality	Chesney, Kenny	44-380	BKD
Realize	Caillat, Colbie	36-459	CB
Realize	Caillat, Colbie	37-18	PS
Reason the	Dion, Celine	14-192	CB
Reason the	Hoobastank	20-352	PHM
Reason To Believe	Stewart, Rod	14-857	LE
Reason To Believe	Stewart, Rod	6-363	MM
Reason To Believe	Stewart, Rod	29-640	SC
Reason Why the	Gill, Vince	30-117	CB
Reason Why the - duet	Little Big Town	38-220	CB
Reasons To Quit	Haggard, Merle	29-437	DK
Reasons To Quit	Nelson & Haggard	11-436	DK
Reasons Why	Nickel Creek	14-709	CB
Rebecca Lynn	White, Bryan	3-625	SC
Rebel Yell	Joel, Billy	47-145	DM
Rebel Yell	Joel, Billy	47-150	SC
Rebel, Johnny Yuma the	Cash, Johnny	46-34	SSK
Rebelicious	Johnson, Jamey	29-577	CB
Recipe For Love	Connick, Harry Jr.	19-720	PS
Reckless	Alabama	6-401	MM
Reckless	Alabama	2-331	SC
Red	Swift, Taylor	43-148	ASK
Red Bandana	Haggard, Merle	37-182	CB
Red Dirt	Smith, Granger	47-487	PHN
Red Dirt Road	Brooks & Dunn	34-400	CB

SONG TITLE	ARTIST	#	TYPE
Red Dirt Road	Brooks & Dunn	25-612	MM
Red Dirt Road	Brooks & Dunn	19-47	ST
Red Dirt Road	Brooks & Dunn	32-266	THM
Red Dress	Sharp, Maia	29-320	PHM
Red High Heels	Pickler, Kellie	30-173	CB
Red House	Hendrix, Jimi	9-380	AH
Red House	Hendrix, Jimi	15-318	SC
Red Light	Nail, David	45-559	AC
Red Light Special	TLC	16-629	MM
Red Neckin' Love Makin' Night	Twitty, Conway	1-165	CB
Red Neckin' Love Makin' Night	Twitty, Conway	4-774	SC
Red Rag Top	McGraw, Tim	29-515	CB
Red Rag Top	McGraw, Tim	32-1	THM
Red Ragtop	McGraw, Tim	25-347	MM
Red Ragtop	McGraw, Tim	18-326	ST
Red Red Wine	Diamond, Neil	7-542	AH
Red Red Wine	Diamond, Neil	13-295	P
Red Red Wine	UB40	7-418	MM
Red Red Wine (Slower Version)	Diamond, Neil	30-688	LE
Red Red Wine (Slower Version)	Diamond, Neil	24-701	SC
Red Red Wine & Cheatin' Songs	Stuart, Marty	8-966	CB
Red Red Wine & Cheatin' Songs	Stuart, Marty	10-190	SC
Red Right Hand	Nick Cave & the Badseeds	43-79	SF
Red River Valley	Robbins, Marty	48-32	KV
Red River Valley	Robbins, Marty	47-765	SRK
Red River Valley	Standard	11-487	DK
Red Rose Cafe the	Fureys	44-109	KV
Red Rose From The Blue Side Of Town	Reeves, Jim	8-568	CB
Red Rose From the Blue Side/Town	Morgan, George	29-630	CB
Red Roses	McEntire, Reba	1-785	CB
Red Roses For A Blue Lady	Newton, Wayne	21-19	CB
Red Roses For A Blue Lady	Williams, Andy	16-845	DK
Red Roses For A Blue Lady	Williams, Andy	13-551	LE
Red Roses For My Lady	Humperdinck, E.	49-248	DFK
Red Rubber Ball	Cyrkle	7-62	MM
Red Rubber Ball	Cyrkle	3-21	SC
Red Sails In The Sunset	Platters	11-302	DK
Red Sails In The Sunset	Platters	9-555	SAV
Red Skies	Fixx	21-409	SC
RED SOLO CUP	Keith, Toby	38-155	AT
Red Strokes the	Brooks, Garth	17-260	NA
Red the	Chevelle	23-161	PHM
Red Umbrella	Hill, Faith	30-575	CB
Red White & Blue Collar	Gibson Miller Band	17-228	NA
Red White And Blue	Lynn, Loretta	48-252	THM
Red Wine And Blue Memories	Stampley, Joe	43-300	CB

SONG TITLE	ARTIST	#	TYPE
Redeemer	Mullen, Nicole C	35-318	CB
Redneck Christmas	Stevens, Ray	46-289	CB
Redneck Crazy	Farr, Tyler	49-704	KV
Redneck Crazy	Farr, Tyler	44-332	SSC
Redneck Girl	Bellamy Brothers	13-391	P
Redneck Girl	Bellamy Brothers	5-26	SC
Redneck Radio	Farris, Matt	41-75	PHN
Redneck Son	England, Ty	4-206	SC
Redneck Woman	Wilson, Gretchen	35-438	CB
Redneck Woman	Wilson, Gretchen	20-254	PHM
Redneck Woman	Wilson, Gretchen	20-324	ST
Redneck Yacht Club	Morgan, Craig	23-136	CB
Rednecks White Sock & Blue Ribbon	Russell, Johnny	5-623	SC
Reelin' In The Years	Steely Dan	12-818	P
Reelin' In The Years	Steely Dan	15-381	RS
Reeling And A-Rocking	Berry, Chuck	11-48	PX
Reet Petite	Wilson, Jackie	11-45	PX
Reflex the	Duran Duran	17-97	DK
Reflex the	Duran Duran	21-739	MH
Refried Dreams	McGraw, Tim	1-530	CB
Refried Dreams	McGraw, Tim	4-71	SC
Refried Dreams	McGraw, Tim	22-870	ST
Refugee	Petty & Heartbreake	16-62	SC
Rehab	Winehouse, Amy	48-596	DK
Reindeers Are Better Than People	Frozen	46-379	DIS
Relatively Speaking	Denver, John	15-617	THM
Relax	Frankie Goes Hollyw	29-13	MH
Relax	Frankie Goes Hollyw	5-117	SC
Relax Take It Easy	Mika	37-115	SC
Release Me	Humperdinck, E.	37-157	CB
Release Me	Humperdinck, E.	16-859	DK
Release Me	Humperdinck, E.	12-497	P
Release Me	Humperdinck, E.	2-196	SC
Release Me	Price, Ray	45-630	SV
Release Me	Wilson Phillips	28-411	DK
Release Me	Wilson Phillips	13-248	P
Remedy	Adele	49-790	BKD
Remedy	Adele	46-8	DCK
Remedy	Mraz, Jason	25-545	MM
Remedy the	Abandoned Pools	32-175	THM
Remedy the	Black Crowes	13-279	P
Remedy the	Black Crowes	19-340	STP
Remedy the (I Won't Worry)	Mraz, Jason	34-177	CB
Remember	Disturbed	23-146	PHM
Remember Me	Anthony, Marc	17-737	PS
Remember Me	Hoobastank	18-829	THM
Remember Me	Journey	13-707	SGB
Remember Me	Nelson, Willie	38-73	CB
Remember Me	Osmonds	47-869	ZP
Remember Me This Way	Hill, Jordan	3-429	SC
Remember That	Simpson, Jessica	36-242	PHM
Remember The Ride	Perfect Stranger	4-205	SC
Remember The Time	Jackson, Michael	33-355	CB
Remember Then	Earls	7-68	MM

SONG TITLE	ARTIST	#	TYPE
Remember Walking In The Rain	Shangri-Las	6-646	MM
Remember Walking In The Rain	Shangri-Las	9-708	SAV
Remember When	Jackson, Alan	19-673	ST
Remember When	Newton, Wayne	47-315	LE
Remember When	Platters	49-664	DCK
Remember When	Vega, Ray	7-404	MM
Remember When It Rained	Groban, Josh	20-547	PHM
Remember You're Mine	Boone, Pat	48-775	P
Remind Me - duet	Paisley & Underwood	37-355	CB
Reminiscing	Holly, Buddy	48-673	DCK
Reminiscing	Holly, Buddy	47-884	ZM
Reminiscing	Little River Band	19-130	KC
Reminiscing	Little River Band	18-305	SC
Renegade	Daughtry	38-263	PHM
Renegade	Styx	4-559	SC
Renegades Rebels & Rogues	Lawrence, Tracy	6-596	MM
Renegades Rebels & Rogues	Lawrence, Tracy	2-318	SC
Reno	Supernaw, Doug	6-528	MM
Repetitive Regret	Rabbitt, Eddie	48-38	CB
Rescue	Uncle Kracker	23-553	MM
Rescue Me	Bass, Fontella	35-77	CB
Rescue Me	Bass, Fontella	19-618	MH
Rescue Me	Bass, Fontella	6-557	MM
Rescue Me	Bass, Fontella	9-230	PT
Rescue Me	Buckcherry	48-473	CB
Respect	Franklin, Aretha	17-48	DK
Respect	Franklin, Aretha	36-169	JT
Respect	Franklin, Aretha	10-735	JVC
Respect	Franklin, Aretha	13-74	P
Respect	Franklin, Aretha	9-225	PT
Respect	Franklin, Aretha	9-286	SC
Respect	Redding, Otis	47-355	KV
Respect	Train	37-319	PHM
Respect Yourself	Staple Singers	27-259	DK
Respect Yourself	Staple Singers	12-920	P
Respect Yourself	Willis, Bruce	49-730	KVD
Rest In Pieces	Saliva	25-663	MM
Rest Of Mine the	Adkins, Trace	22-630	ST
Rest Of My Life	Unwritten Law	23-166	PHM
Rest Your Love On Me	Twitty, Conway	5-864	SC
Restless	Krauss, Alison	23-13	CB
Restless	Krauss, Alison	23-384	SC
Restless Kind the	Yearwood, Trisha	48-333	C2C
Return To Me	Martin, Dean	10-402	LE
Return To Me	Martin, Dean	7-192	MM
Return To Me	Robbins, Marty	48-17	CB
Return To Sender	Presley, Elvis	8-582	CB
Return To Sender	Presley, Elvis	11-152	DK
Return To Sender	Presley, Elvis	12-895	P
Return To Sender	Presley, Elvis	2-595	SC
Return To Sender	Presley, Elvis	14-761	THM
Reunited	Peaches & Herb	13-150	P

SONG TITLE	ARTIST	#	TYPE
Reunited - duet	Peaches & Herb	35-158	CB
Rev It Up And Go	Stray Cats	48-168	SS
Revenge Of A Middle Aged Woman	Byrd, Tracy	22-78	CB
Revolution	Beatles	16-857	DK
Revolution	Beatles	13-178	P
Revolution	Rascal Flatts	30-546	CB
Rewind	Rascal Flatts	43-133	PHN
Rhiannon	Fleetwood Mac	10-30	SC
Rhinestone Cowboy	Campbell, Glen	8-358	CB
Rhinestone Cowboy	Campbell, Glen	15-275	DK
Rhinestone Cowboy	Campbell, Glen	9-635	SAV
Rhumba Boogie the	Snow, Hank	22-124	CB
Rhumba Boogie the	Snow, Hank	5-425	SC
Rhythm Dancer	Jackson, Janet	15-420	PS
Rhythm Divine	Iglesias, Enrique	17-540	SC
Rhythm Is A Dancer	Snap	6-410	MM
Rhythm Is Gonna Get You	Estefan & Miami Sound	34-82	CB
Rhythm Is Gonna Get You the	Estefan, Gloria	17-739	PT
Rhythm Of Life	Adams, Oleta	46-388	PS
Rhythm Of My Heart	Stewart, Rod	14-856	LE
Rhythm Of The Night	DeBarge	28-348	DK
Rhythm Of The Night	DeBarge	4-884	SC
Rhythm Of The Rain	Cascades	12-659	P
Ribbon In The Sky	Wonder, Stevie	10-363	KC
Ribbon Of Darkenss	Smith, Connie	8-391	CB
Ribbon Of Darkness	Robbins, Marty	8-369	CB
Ribbon Of Darkness	Robbins, Marty	4-801	SC
Ribbon Of Darkness	Smith, Connie	6-779	MM
Rich Girl	Hall & Oates	11-83	DK
Rich Girl	Hall & Oates	4-851	SC
Rich Girl	Stefani & Eve	22-357	CB
Ricky	Yankovic, Weird Al	49-839	SC
Riddle	En Vogue	33-282	CB
Riddle (Radio Version)	En Vogue	14-467	SC
Ride	McBride, Martina	36-258	PHM
Ride - duet	Rice & Malloy	48-3	BKD
Ride Away	Orbison, Roy	9-196	SO
Ride Captain Ride	Blues Image	9-360	MG
Ride Captain Ride	Blues Image	3-472	SC
Ride Like The Wind	Cross, Christopher	11-330	DK
Ride Like The Wind	Cross, Christopher	14-646	SC
Ride the	Coe, David Allan	18-310	CB
Ride The Wild West	Wood, David	38-214	PHN
Ride This Train	McDaniel, Mel	49-121	SHER
Ride With Me	Nelly	18-573	TT
Riders On The Storm	Doors	33-280	CB
Riders On The Storm	Doors	18-649	SO
Ridin'	Buckcherry	48-477	SC
Ridin'	Buckcherry	15-299	THM
Ridin' My Thumb To Mexico	Rodriguez, Johnny	22-48	CB
Ridin' Out The Heartache	Tucker, Tanya	16-578	SC
Ridin' The Rodeo	Perfect Stranger	45-209	CZC

SONG TITLE	ARTIST	#	TYPE
Riding For A Fall	LeDoux, Chris	24-89	SC
Riding On A Railroad	Taylor, James	45-536	OZP
Riding With Private Malone	Ball, David	33-151	CB
Riding With Private Malone	Ball, David	25-6	MM
Riding With Private Malone	Ball, David	15-857	ST
Right As Rain	Adele	36-292	PHM
Right Back Atcha Babe	McGraw, Tim	39-51	ASK
Right Back Where We Started	Nightingale, Maxine	2-502	SC
Right Down The Line	Rafferty, Gerry	15-742	SC
Right Down Through The Middle Of Us	Coty, Neal	29-351	CB
Right From The Start	Conley, Earl Thomas	29-64	CB
Right From The Start	Conley, Earl Thomas	5-134	SC
Right Hand Man	Osborne, Joan	10-241	PS
Right Here	Cyrus, Miley	36-76	WD
Right Here	Staind	30-223	PHM
Right Here	Staind	30-223	PHM
Right Here	Staind	30-157	PT
Right Here (Departed)	Brandy	36-500	CB
Right Here Right Now	Jones, Jesus	12-38	DK
Right Here Right Now	Jones, Jesus	5-345	SC
Right Here Waiting	Marx, Richard	33-332	CB
Right Here Waiting	Marx, Richard	6-348	MM
Right In Front Of You	Dion, Celine	19-18	PS
Right In The Wrong Direction	Gosdin, Vern	47-118	CB
Right Kind Of Wrong the	Rimes, LeAnn	14-137	CB
Right Left Hand the	Jones, George	8-338	CB
Right Man For The Job	Robison, Charlie	25-13	MM
Right Man For The Job	Robison, Charlie	16-337	ST
Right Now	Al B. Sure!	9-854	SAV
Right Now	Brooks, Garth	5-792	SC
Right Now	Carpenter, M C	1-433	CB
Right Now	Carpenter, M C	15-162	THM
Right Now	SR-71	15-788	THM
Right Now	Van Halen	5-740	SC
Right On The Money	Jackson, Alan	8-219	CB
Right On The Money	Jackson, Alan	22-681	ST
Right Or Wrong	Jackson, Wanda	8-781	CB
Right Or Wrong	Jackson, Wanda	12-409	P
Right Or Wrong	Strait, George	9-170	CB
Right Place Wrong Time	Dr. John	4-89	SC
Right Round - duet	Flo Rida	45-649	B
Right Thing To Do	Simon, Carly	49-150	CB
Right Thurr	Clingy	32-313	THM
Right Thurr **	Chingy	25-713	MM
Right Thurr ** (Radio Version)	Chingy	21-789	SC
Right Time Of The Night	Warnes, Jennifer	4-377	SC
Right Time the	Corrs	49-193	SC
Right To Be Wrong	Stone, Joss	43-118	ASK
Right To Be Wrong	Stone, Joss	22-367	CB
Right Where I Need To Be	Allan, Gary	14-715	CB

SONG TITLE	ARTIST	#	TYPE
Right Where I Need To Be	Allan, Gary	10-259	SC
Right Where I Need To Be	Allan, Gary	22-579	ST
Right Where You Want Me	McCartney, Jesse	30-62	PHM
Righteously	Williams, Lucinda	25-629	MM
Righteously	Williams, Lucinda	32-381	THM
Rikki Don't Lose That Number	Steely Dan	17-337	DK
Rikki Don't Lose That Number	Steely Dan	15-386	RS
Ring A Ding Ding	Sinatra, Frank	49-491	MM
Ring My Bell	Ward, Anita	2-492	SC
Ring Of Fire	Cash, Johnny	3-159	CB
Ring Of Fire	Cash, Johnny	11-435	DK
Ring Of Fire	Cash, Johnny	8-662	SAV
Ring Of Fire	Cash, Johnny	21-591	SC
Ring Of Fire	Jackson, Alan	49-179	CB
Ring Of Fire	Yoakam, Dwight	49-703	SRK
Ring Of Fire (Faster Version)	Cash, Johnny	29-753	CB
Ring On Her Finger	McEntire, Reba	1-782	CB
Ring On Her Finger	McEntire, Reba	7-172	MM
Ring On Her Finger	McEntire, Reba	3-622	SC
Ring On Her Finger Time On Her Hand	Greenwood, Lee	17-294	NA
Ring Ring	Abba	19-77	MM
Ring Them Bells	Minelli, Liza	49-219	LG
Ringo	Greene, Lorne	5-845	SC
Rings Of Gold	Gibson, Don	43-286	CB
Rio	Duran Duran	34-80	CB
Rio	Duran Duran	17-462	SC
Rio	Nesmith, Michael	30-761	SF
Riot	Three Days Grace	36-484	CB
Riot In Cell Block No. 9	Blues Brothers	38-36	LE
Rip Her To Shreds	Blondie	49-137	SC
Rip It Up	Presley, Elvis	14-778	THM
Rip Off The Knob	Bellamy Brothers	6-753	MM
Ripple	Grateful Dead	29-263	SC
Ripples	4 Runner	4-124	SC
Rise	Robbie Seay Band	49-913	SC
Rise Above This	Seether	36-506	CB
Riser	Bentley, Dierks	44-146	BKD
Rising the	Springsteen, Bruce	25-305	MM
River	Merchant, Natalie	18-37	PS
River And The Highway the	Tillis, Pam	1-460	CB
River And The Highway the	Tillis, Pam	4-159	SC
River Bank	Paisley, Brad	44-132	ASK
River Deep Mountain High	Turner, Tina	10-417	LE
River Lea	Adele	46-4	DCK
River Of Dreams	Joel, Billy	12-270	DK
River Of Dreams	Joel, Billy	16-137	LE
River Of Dreams	Joel, Billy	6-361	MM
River Of Dreams	Joel, Billy	2-230	SC

SONG TITLE	ARTIST	#	TYPE
River of Love	Strait, George	38-149	CB
River Road	Gayle, Crystal	47-755	SRK
River the	Brooks, Garth	6-283	MM
River the	Brooks, Garth	2-682	SC
River the	McLachlan, Sarah	43-1	ST
River the	Springsteen, Bruce	20-237	LE
River the	Wright, Chely	23-492	CB
River the	Wright, Chely	29-614	ST
Riverbank	Bates, Jeff	36-618	CB
Riverboat	Young, Faron	20-737	CB
Road Dogs	Charlie Daniels Band	14-729	CB
Road Dogs	Charlie Daniels Band	43-274	CB
Road I'm On the	3 Doors Down	32-215	THM
Road Less Traveled the	Strait, George	38-150	CB
Road Runner	Diddley, Bo	11-46	PX
Road Runner	Diddley, Bo	10-248	SS
Road Song	Rich, Charlie	8-452	CB
Road That I Walk	Twitty, Conway	49-125	SBI
Road the	Browne, Jackson	23-609	BS
Road Trippin'	Wariner, Steve	8-739	CB
Road You Leave Behind the	Murphy, David Lee	7-321	MM
Road You Leave Behind the	Murphy, David Lee	4-894	SC
Roadhouse Blues	Doors	18-652	SO
Roadhouse Blues	Jeff Healy Band	47-724	KV
Roam	B-52's	12-786	P
Roar	Perry, Katy	44-309	SBI
Robot Man	Francis, Connie	29-814	SF
Rock 'N Me	Steve Miller Band	3-483	SC
Rock 'N Roll (I Gave You The Best..	Davis, Mac	23-515	CB
Rock & Roll Party Queen	St. Louis, Louis	10-10	SC
Rock & A Hard Place	Rolling Stones	20-194	SC
Rock & Roll	Led Zeppelin	11-499	DK
Rock & Roll	Led Zeppelin	13-224	P
Rock & Roll All Night	Kiss	9-349	AH
Rock & Roll All Night	Kiss	10-40	SC
Rock & Roll Band	Boston	4-564	SC
Rock & Roll Christmas	Thorogood, George	45-763	CB
Rock & Roll Dreams Come…	Meat Loaf	2-107	SC
Rock & Roll Heaven	Righteous Brothers	2-444	SC
Rock & Roll Hoochie Koo	Derringer, Rick	17-120	DK
Rock & Roll Is Here To Stay	Danleers	6-653	MM
Rock & Roll Lullaby	Thomas, B.J.	21-807	SC
Rock & Roll Music	Beach Boys	5-505	BS
Rock & Roll Music	Beatles	7-511	SAV
Rock & Roll Music	Berry, Chuck	27-485	DK
Rock & Roll Music	Berry, Chuck	7-290	MM
Rock & Roll Waltz the	Starr, Kay	5-15	SC
Rock & Roll Waltz the	Starr, Kay	10-598	SF
Rock & Rye	Ritter, Tex	20-715	CB

SONG TITLE	ARTIST	#	TYPE
Rock A Billy	Bellamy Brothers	47-807	SRK
Rock A Bye Heart	Holy, Steve	25-527	MM
Rock A Bye Heart	Holy, Steve	18-797	ST
Rock A Bye Heart	Holy, Steve	32-154	THM
Rock A Bye Your Baby	Garland, Judy	2-237	SC
Rock And Roll Hoochie Koo	Winter, Johnny	49-373	CB
Rock And Roll Is Here To Stay	Grease	49-429	SDK
Rock And Roll Lullaby	Thomas, B.J.	36-156	LE
Rock And Roll Music	Beach Boys	34=65	CB
Rock And Roll Music	Checker, Chubby	46-611	DKM
Rock And Roll Never Forgets	Seger, Bob	46-339	AH
Rock And Roll Part 2	Glitter, Gary	49-143	SC
Rock Around The Clock	Haley & Comets	12-119	DK
Rock Around The Clock	Haley & Comets	12-728	P
Rock Around The Clock	Haley & Comets	49-534	SC
Rock Around With Ollie Vee	Holly, Buddy	47-881	ZM
Rock Bottom	Judd, Wynonna	6-497	MM
Rock Bottom	Judd, Wynonna	12-413	P
ROCK In The USA	Mellencamp, John	33-293	CB
Rock Is My Life & This Is My Song	BTO	46-549	CB
Rock Island Line	Cash, Johnny	45-35	CBE
Rock Lobster	B-52's	11-714	DK
Rock Me	Abba	19-83	MM
Rock Me	Great White	6-19	SC
Rock Me Baby	King, B.B.	15-20	SC
Rock Me Gently	Kim, Andy	27-576	DK
Rock Me Gently	Kim, Andy	3-608	SC
Rock Me My Baby	Holly, Buddy	48-674	DCK
Rock Me Right	Tedeschi, Susan	17-453	AMS
Rock Me Right	Tedeschi, Susan	15-25	SC
Rock Me Tonight	Fountains of Wayne	48-570	DK
Rock Me Tonight	Jackson, Freddie	17-132	DK
Rock My Baby	Shenandoah	1-488	CB
Rock My World Little Country Girl	Brooks & Dunn	1-86	CB
Rock My World Little Country Girl	Brooks & Dunn	6-464	MM
Rock My World Little Country Girl	Brooks & Dunn	2-92	SC
Rock Of Ages	Def Leppard	46-167	SC
Rock On	Essex, David	34-61	CB
Rock On	Essex, David	4-762	SC
Rock On Baby	Lee, Brenda	30-331	CB
Rock Show	Blink 182	16-385	SGB
Rock Steady	Franklin, Aretha	36-170	JT
Rock Steady	Franklin, Aretha	19-559	SC
Rock Steady - duet	Adams & Raitt	35-314	CB
Rock That Body	Black Eyed Peas	46-189	BHK
Rock The Boat	Hues Corporation	16-824	DK
Rock The Boat	Hues Corporation	13-132	P
Rock The Casbah	Clash	11-752	DK
Rock The Casbah	Clash	5-137	SC
Rock This Country	Twain, Shania	5-408	SC

SONG TITLE	ARTIST	#	TYPE
Rock This Country	Twain, Shania	22-533	ST
Rock This Town	Stray Cats	13-4	P
Rock This Town	Stray Cats	5-142	SC
Rock This Town	Stray Cats	13-698	SGB
Rock Wit U (Awww Baby)	Ashanti	25-723	MM
Rock Wit U (Awww Baby)	Ashanti	32-308	THM
Rock With You	Jackson, Michael	36-122	JTG
Rock With You	Jackson, Michael	12-700	P
Rock You Baby	Keith, Toby	34-389	CB
Rock You Baby	Keith, Toby	25-517	MM
Rock You Baby	Keith, Toby	38-167	SC
Rock You Baby	Keith, Toby	18-782	ST
Rock You Baby	Keith, Toby	32-118	THM
Rock You Like A Hurricane	Scorpions	17-335	DK
Rock You Like A Hurricane	Scorpions	23-62	MH
Rock Your Baby	McCrae, George	33-251	CB
Rock Your Baby	McCrae, George	11-409	DK
Rock Your Body	Timberlake, Justin	20-513	CB
Rock Your Body	Timberlake, Justin	25-579	MM
Rock Your Body	Timberlake, Justin	19-336	STP
Rock Your Body	Timberlake, Justin	32-205	THM
Rock-A-Bye Your Baby	Jolson, Al	29-467	LE
Rock-A-Bye Your Baby With A Dixie	Jolson, Al	15-836	MM
Rock-A-Bye Your Baby With A Dixie	Jolson, Al	12-940	PS
Rockabilly Blues	Cash, Johnny	43-414	SRK
Rocket	Def Leppard	46-171	SC
Rocket 2 You	Jets	11-282	DK
Rocket Man	John, Elton	34-41	CB
Rocket Man	John, Elton	17-404	DK
Rocket Man	John, Elton	16-399	PR
Rockin' All Over The World	Fogerty, John	48-651	DCK
Rockin' Around The Christmas Tree	Gilley, Mickey	45-757	CB
Rockin' Chair	Mills Brothers	47-264	LRT
Rockin' Chair Money	Williams, Hank Sr.	45-699	CB
Rockin' Down The Highway	Doobie Brothers	29-84	CB
Rockin' In The Free World	Young, Neil	46-337	SC
Rockin' Me	Miller, Steve	23-622	BS
Rockin' My Life Away	Lewis, Jerry Lee	47-201	CB
Rockin' Pneumonia & Boogie Woogie	Rivers, Johnny	26-445	DK
Rockin' Pneumonia & Boogie Woogie	Rivers, Johnny	2-54	SC
Rockin' Robin	Jackson, Michael	12-60	DK
Rockin' Robin	Jackson, Michael	13-136	P
Rockin' Santa - xmas	Wiggles	45-237	WIG
Rockin' The Beer Gut	Trailor Choir	45-369	BKD
Rockin' The Beer Gut	Trailor Choir	37-62	CB
Rockin' The Rock	Stewart, Larry	2-744	SC
Rockin' With The	Judds	1-148	CB

SONG TITLE	ARTIST	#	TYPE
Rhythm of the Rain			
Rockin' With the Rhythm of the Rain	Judds	6-628	MM
Rockin' With the Rhythm of the Rain	Judds	5-16	SC
Rockin' Years	Parton&VanShelton	8-116	CB
Rockin' Years	Parton&VanShelton	2-300	SC
Rockin' Years - duet	Parton & Van Shelton	49-338	CB
Rocking Around the Christmas Tree	Lee, Brenda	35-324	CB
Rocking The Country	Gregory, Clinton	8-979	CB
Rocks In Your Shoes	West, Emily	36-578	CB
Rocks That You Can't Move	Greenwood, Lee	32-47	THM
Rockstar	Nickelback	30-64	PHM
Rocky Mountain High	Denver, John	16-358	CB
Rocky Mountain High	Denver, John	36-144	LE
Rocky Mountain High	Denver, John	9-38	MM
Rocky Mountain High	Denver, John	13-369	P
Rocky Mountain Music	Rabbitt, Eddie	8-449	CB
Rocky Mountain Way	Walsh, Joe	12-695	P
Rocky Top	Anderson, Lynn	47-650	P
Rocky Top	Osbourne Brothers	8-47	CB
Rocky Top	Osbourne Brothers	12-96	DK
Rocky Top	Standard	13-416	P
Rocky Top	Standard	2-34	SC
Rodeo	Brooks, Garth	6-282	MM
Rodeo	Brooks, Garth	2-683	SC
Rodeo Man	Reeves, Ronna	4-409	SC
Rodeo Or Mexico	Brooks, Garth	18-14	CB
Rodeo Song **	Lee, Gary & Sundown	2-181	SC
Rodeo Song the **	Gary Lee & Showdowns	30-659	RSX
Rodeo Song the **	Lee & Showdown	30-659	RSX
Roll Back The Rug And Dance	Lee, Scooter	45-855	VH
Roll In My Sweet Baby's Arms	Flatt & Scruggs	8-255	CB
Roll In My Sweet Baby's Arms	Russell, Leon	4-631	SC
Roll Me Away	Seger, Bob	17-527	SC
Roll Me Up And Smoke Me When I Die	Nelson, Willie	45-18	KV
Roll Muddy River	Wilburn Brothers	33-14	CB
Roll On	Kid Rock	49-319	CB
Roll On Big Mama	Stampley, Joe	8-838	CB
Roll On Big Mama	Stampley, Joe	9-598	SAV
Roll On Down The Highway	BTO	5-600	SC
Roll On Eighteen Wheeler	Alabama	4-447	BS
Roll On Eighteen Wheeler	Alabama	1-6	CB
Roll On Eighteen Wheeler	Alabama	11-720	DK
Roll On Mississippi	Pride, Charley	38-123	CB
Roll Out The Barrel	Andrew Sisters	46-436	SC

SONG TITLE	ARTIST	#	TYPE
Roll Out The Barrel	Polka Favorites	29-809	SSR
Roll Out The Barrel - w/Words	Polka Favorites	29-863	SSR
Roll Over Beethoven	Beatles	29-332	SC
Roll Over Beethoven	Berry, Chuck	35-8	CB
Roll Over Beethoven	Berry, Chuck	12-103	DK
Roll Over Beethoven	Berry, Chuck	5-87	SC
Roll To Me	Amitri, Del	48-575	DK
Roll To Me	Del Amitri	28-420	DK
Roll Wit MVP	Stagga Lee	32-271	THM
Roll With It	Corbin, Easton	45-391	CB
Roll With It	Corbin, Easton	44-209	CB
Roller Coaster	Bryan, Luke	44-111	KV
Roller Derby Queen	Croce, Jim	48-462	CB
Rollin'	Brooks, Garth	7-171	MM
Rollin' (Ballad - Rap Style)	Big & Rich	23-46	SC
Rollin' (Ballad of Big&Rich)	Big & Rich	23-45	SC
Rollin' & Ramblin'	Harris, EmmyLou	16-356	CB
Rollin' & Tumblin'	Muddy Waters	14-593	SC
Rollin' In My Sweet Baby's Arms	Owens, Buck	8-617	SAV
Rollin' In The Deep	Adele	38-181	CB
Rollin' Stoned	Great White	21-781	SC
Rollin' With The Flow	Chesnutt, Mark	30-542	CB
Rollin' With The Flow	Rich, Charlie	8-459	CB
Rollin' With The Flow	Rich, Charlie	5-209	SC
Rollover DJ	Jet	20-549	PHM
Roly Poly	Dixie Chicks	16-654	RS
Roly Poly	Wills, Bob	9-460	SAV
Romeo	Parton, Dolly	8-545	CB
Romeo	Parton, Dolly	17-388	DK
Romeo	Parton, Dolly	12-404	P
Romeo & Juliet	Earl & Stacy	9-855	SAV
Romeo's Tune	Forbert, Steve	16-243	AMS
Roni	Brown, Bobby	29-287	SC
Ronnie	Four Seasons	43-385	LG
Rooftops (A Liberation Broadcast)	Lostprophets	30-725	SF
Room Full Of Roses	Gilley, Mickey	22-215	CB
Room Full Of Roses	Gilley, Mickey	12-428	P
Room Full Of Roses	Morgan, George	5-577	SC
Rooms On Fire	Nicks, Stevie	47-895	LE
Roots Of My Raising the	Haggard, Merle	37-169	CB
Rope The Moon	Montgomery, J M	2-210	SC
Rosa Rio	Reeves, Jim	44-231	SRK
Rosalee	Campbell, Stacy D.	20-116	CB
Rosalita	Al Dexter & Troopers	38-38	CB
Rosalita Come Out Tonight	Springsteen, Bruce	20-236	LE
Rosalita Come Out Tonight	Springsteen, Bruce	21-513	SC
Rosanna	Toto	16-523	P
Rosanna's Going Wild	Cash, Johnny	29-740	CB
Rose Bouquet	Vassar, Phil	22-591	ST
Rose Colored Glasses	Conlee, John	33-44	CB

SONG TITLE	ARTIST	#	TYPE
Rose Colored Glasses	Conlee, John	9-529	SAV
Rose Garden	Anderson, Lynn	8-24	CB
Rose Garden	Anderson, Lynn	17-4	DK
Rose Garden	Anderson, Lynn	13-431	P
Rose Garden	Lee, Brenda	45-909	IDM
Rose Garden	McBride, Martina	36-371	SC
Rose Garden (I Never Promised...)	McBride, Martina	23-414	CB
Rose In Paradise	Jennings, Waylon	5-393	SC
Rose Is A Rose a	Edwards, Meredith	14-793	ST
Rose Is A Rose a	Edwards, Meredith	15-197	THM
Rose Is Still A Rose a	Franklin, Aretha	36-159	JT
Rose Is Still A Rose a	Franklin, Aretha	9-95	PS
Rose Of Cimarron	Poco	49-236	DFK
Rose Of My Heart	Cash, Johnny	45-664	DCK
Rose Of San Antone	Cline, Patsy	45-503	KV
Rose the	Midler, Bette	11-85	DK
Rose the	Midler, Bette	10-529	SF
Rose the	Twitty, Conway	48-238	CB
Rose the (Faster Version)	Midler, Bette	13-2	P
Rose the (Slow Version)	Midler, Bette	13-1	P
Rose the (With Harmonies)	Midler, Bette	9-636	SAV
Roses	Reeves, Jim	44-254	DFK
Roses Are Red My Love	Vinton, Bobby	11-778	DK
Rosie	Browne, Jackson	23-610	BS
Rough & Ready	Adkins, Trace	20-338	ST
Rough Water	Mraz, Jason	43-167	ASK
Roun' The Globe	Nappy Roots	32-348	THM
Round & Round	Ratt	12-5	DK
Round & Round	Ratt	3-616	SC
Round About Way	Strait, George	8-231	CB
Round About Way	Strait, George	7-721	CHM
Round and Round	Como, Perry	13-548	LE
Round And Round	Como, Perry	20-773	PS
Round And Round	Prince	12-762	P
Round And Round	Ratt	23-57	MH
Round Here	Counting Crows	18-697	CB
Round Here	Counting Crows	2-466	SC
Round Here	Florida Georgia Line	47-93	ASK
Round Here	Sawyer Brown	7-180	MM
Round Here	Sawyer Brown	3-662	SC
Round Midnight	Ronstadt, Linda	10-705	JVC
Route 66	Asleep at the Wheel	15-75	CB
Route 66	Asleep at the Wheel	43-18	CB
Route 66	Berry, Chuck	46-230	SRK
Route 66	Cole, Nat "King"	46-355	DK
Route 66	Standard	26-487	DK
Roxanne	Police	2-140	SC
Rub A Dub Dub	Thompson, Hank	19-326	CB
Rub A Dub Dub	Thompson, Hank	5-370	SC
Rub A Dubbin'	Mellons, Ken	3-664	SC
Rub It In	Craddock, Billy C	2-133	SC
Rub It In	King, Matt	5-731	SC
Rub Me In The Right Way	Martin, Brad	18-459	ST

SONG TITLE	ARTIST	#	TYPE
Rub Me The Right Way	Martin, B	32-3	THM
Rub Me The Right Way	Martin, Brad	32-3	THM
Rub You The Right Way	Gill, Johnny	28-426	DK
Rub You The Right Way	Gill, Johnny	16-556	P
Rubber Ball	Vee, Bobby	49-67	ZVS
Rubber Band Man **	T.I.	23-251	THM
Rubber Biscuit	Blues Brothers	38-29	SC
Rubber Neckin'	Presley, Elvis	8-592	CB
Rubberband	Worsham, Charlie	42-4	PHN
Rubberband Man	Spinners	7-477	MM
Rubberband Man	Spinners	9-767	SAV
Rubberband Man	Spinners	4-295	SC
Rubberneckin'	Presley & Oakenfold	32-427	THM
Ruby	Charles, Ray	46-585	PS
Ruby (Are You Mad at Your Man)	Owens, Buck	39-8	CB
Ruby Ann	Robbins, Marty	15-79	CB
Ruby Baby	Craddock, Billy C	35-374	CB
Ruby Baby	Dion & Belmonts	47-21	SC
Ruby Brown	Carter, Deana	22-518	ST
Ruby Don't Take Your Love To Town	Rogers, Kenny	8-38	CB
Ruby Don't Take Your Love To Town	Rogers, Kenny	11-616	DK
Ruby Don't Take Your Love To Town	Rogers, Kenny	10-518	SF
Ruby Tuesday	Rolling Stones	18-19	LE
Rueben James	First Edition	9-732	SAV
Rueben James	Rogers, Kenny	5-35	SC
Rum And Coca Cola	Andrew Sisters	46-424	KV
Rum Is The Reason	Keith, Toby	45-388	BKD
Rumor Has It	McEntire, Reba	6-624	MM
Rumor Has It	Walker, Clay	14-661	CB
Rumor Has It	Walker, Clay	7-591	CHM
Rumor Has It	Walker, Clay	7-422	MM
Rumour Has it	Adele	38-232	PHM
Rump Shaker	Wreckx-N-Effect	14-437	SC
Run	Collective Soul	7-810	PHT
Run	Strait, George	25-47	MM
Run	Strait, George	16-3	ST
Run Around	Blues Traveler	9-322	AG
Run Around	Blues Traveler	3-431	SC
Run Away	McAnally, Shane	14-88	CB
Run Away Little Tears	Smith, Connie	48-96	CB
Run Away With You	Big & Rich	48-710	BKD
Run Daddy Run	Lambert, Miranda	39-47	ASK
Run It!	Brown, Chris	30-153	PT
Run On	Presley, Elvis	25-501	MM
Run Run Run	Tyler, Ryan	19-371	ST
Run Samson Run	Sedaka, Neil	45-358	CB
Run Through The Jungle	CCR	5-359	SC
Run To Him	Vee, Bobby	4-253	SC
Run To You	Adams, Bryan	23-435	CB
Run To You	Houston, Whitney	6-416	MM
Run Woman Run	Wynette, Tammy	6-86	SC
Runaround Sue	Dion	7-288	MM
Runaround Sue	Dion	12-908	P

SONG TITLE	ARTIST	#	TYPE
Runaround Sue	Dion	9-17	PS
Runaround Sue	Dion & Belmonts	29-840	SC
Runaway	Bon Jovi	21-717	CB
Runaway	Bon Jovi	23-50	MH
Runaway	Bon Jovi	5-491	SC
Runaway	Bon Jovi	13-665	SGB
Runaway	Cher	47-673	CB
Runaway	Corrs	49-190	MM
Runaway	Del Shannon	35-36	CB
Runaway	Del Shannon	26-356	DK
Runaway	Del Shannon	3-290	MM
Runaway	Del Shannon	2-58	SC
Runaway	Jackson, Janet	15-421	PS
Runaway	Jefferson Starship	20-75	SC
Runaway	Love And Theft	37-46	CB
Runaway	Raitt, Bonnie	33-305	CB
Runaway	Raitt, Bonnie	10-769	JVC
Runaway	Tedeschi, Susan	17-456	AMS
Runaway (Live)	Presley, Elvis	25-748	MM
Runaway Boys	Stray Cats	48-165	EK
Runaway Child Running Wild	Temptations	11-756	DK
Runaway Train	Cam	49-535	KVD
Runaway Train	Cash, Roseanne	11-788	DK
Runaway Train	Cash, Roseanne	13-332	P
Runaway Train	John, E & Clapton	24-25	SC
Runaway Train	Sears, Dawn	6-582	MM
Runaway Train	Sears, Dawn	13-20	P
Runaway Train	Soul Asylum	35-206	CB
Runaway Train	Soul Asylum	28-440	DK
Runaway Train	Soul Asylum	6-366	MM
Runnin' Away With My Heart	Lonestar	22-899	ST
Runnin' Behind	Lawrence, Tracy	1-573	CB
Runnin' Behind	Lawrence, Tracy	2-796	SC
Runnin' Down A Dream	Petty & Heartbreake	24-204	SC
Runnin' Out Of Air	Love And Theft	39-81	PHN
Runnin' Outta Moonlight	Houser, Randy	45-404	BKD
Runnin' Through The Fire	Cafferty, John	45-160	KV
Runnin' With The Devil	Van Halen	4-563	SC
Running	No Doubt	20-462	CB
Running	No Doubt	32-168	THM
Running Away	Hoobastank	35-270	CB
Running Bare	Nesbitt, Jim	15-143	SC
Running Bear	James, Sonny	15-91	CB
Running Bear	James, Sonny	10-738	JVC
Running Bear	Preston, Johnny	12-310	DK
Running Bear (Faster Version)	James, Sonny	19-466	CB
Running From Me	TRUST Company	32-105	THM
Running Gun	Robbins, Marty	48-30	VH
Running In The Family	Level 42	44-184	ZMH
Running Kind	Foster, Radney	47-97	SC
Running Kind	Haggard, Merle	49-815	KV
Running On Empty	Browne, Jackson	23-608	BS
Running On Empty	Browne, Jackson	17-181	SC

220

SONG TITLE	ARTIST	#	TYPE
Running On Faith	Clapton, Eric	4-272	SC
Running On Faith	Clapton, Eric	13-798	SGB
Running Out Of Reasons To Run	Trevino, Rick	4-593	SC
Running Scared	Orbison, Roy	5-235	SC
Running Scared	Orbison, Roy	9-188	SO
Running With The Night	Richie,, Lionel	47-465	SFM
Running With The Wind	Rabbitt, Eddie	48-37	CB
Runway Lights	Cyrus, Billy Ray	38-91	PHM
Rush	Aly & AJ	30-160	PT
Rusty Cage	Cash, Johnny	43-410	KCA
Rusty Old Halo	Axton, Hoyt	44-64	SRK
Rye Whiskey	Ritter, Tex	20-713	CB
S'Posin'	Sinatra, Frank	49-493	MM
S'Wonderful	Reese, Della	15-839	MM
Sacrifice	John, Elton	13-313	P
Sacrifice	John, Elton	2-377	SC
Sad	Maroon 5	39-118	PHM
Sad But True	Metallica	47-260	SC
Sad Cafe the	Eagles	44-106	ZMP
Sad Caper	Hootie & Blowfish	24-373	SC
Sad Eyes	Iglesias, Enrique	14-23	THM
Sad Eyes	John, Robert	35-157	CB
Sad Eyes	John, Robert	11-410	DK
Sad Lisa	Leace, Donal	21-612	SF
Sad Lookin' Moon	Alabama	7-608	CHM
Sad Movies	Thompson, Sue	5-82	SC
Sad Songs (Say So Much)	John, Elton	30-3	DK
Sad Songs Say So Much	John, Elton	13-311	P
Sad Songs Say So Much	John, Elton	2-385	SC
Saddest Song the	Ataris	32-443	THM
Safe In The Arms Of Love	McBride, Martina	1-380	CB
Safe In The Arms Of Love	McBride, Martina	7-22	MM
Safe Place From The Storm	Bolton, Michael	5-278	SC
Safety Line	Sixpence None The	39-131	PHM
Saga Begins the	Yankovic, Weird Al	49-841	SC
Saginaw Michigan	Frizzell, Lefty	19-482	CB
Saginaw Michigan	Frizzell, Lefty	7-111	MM
Said I Loved You But I Lied	Bolton, Michael	2-108	SC
Sail Away	Oak Ridge Boys	47-327	ASK
Sail On	Richie, Lionel	10-394	LE
Sail On Sailor	Beach Boys	15-746	SC
Sailing	Cross, Christopher	17-118	DK
Sailing	N'Sync	15-780	BS
Sailing	N'Sync	20-440	CB
Saint Cecilia	Foo Fighters	48-416	BKD
Saints And Angels	Evans, Sara	29-552	CB
Saints And Angels	Evans, Sara	25-10	MM
Saints And Angels	Evans, Sara	15-671	ST
Saints' Rock & Roll the	Haley & Comets	12-551	P
Sally Was A Good Old Girl	Jennings, Waylon	45-182	DCK
Salt In My Tears the	Parton, Dolly	8-855	CB

SONG TITLE	ARTIST	#	TYPE
Salty Dog	Flatt & Scruggs	8-248	CB
Salty Dog	Flogging Molly	48-616	KV
Salvation	Cranberries	7-570	THM
Salvation Song	Cranberries	13-602	P
Sam Hall	Cash, Johnny	47-811	SRK
Sam Stone	Prine, John	23-532	CB
Sam, You Made the Pants Too Long	Streisand, Barbra	49-560	LG
Sam's Place	Owens, Buck	5-702	SC
Sam's Song	Martin, Dean & ?	23-89	MM
Same Ol' Love	Skaggs, Ricky	12-439	P
Same Old Me the	Price, Ray	3-781	CB
Same Old Me the	Price, Ray	4-798	SC
Same Old Saturday Night	Sinatra, Frank	49-488	MM
Same Old Side Road	Whitley, Keith	49-400	CB
Same Old Song	Sev	23-157	PHM
Same Old Song And Dance	Aerosmith	12-771	P
Same Old Song And Dance	Aerosmith	5-885	SC
Same Old Story	Brooks, Garth	48-353	PT
Same Old You	Lambert, Miranda	45-952	KV
Same Thing Happened To Me	Prine, John	45-873	VH
San Angelo	Robbins, Marty	47-749	SRK
San Antonio Rose	Cline, Patsy	22-190	CB
San Antonio Rose	Price, Ray	45-628	P
San Antonio Rose	Wills, Bob	20-690	CB
San Antonio Rose	Wills, Bob	17-384	DK
San Antonio Rose	Wills, Bob	13-356	P
San Antonio Stroll	Tucker, Tanya	8-451	CB
San Antonio Stroll	Tucker, Tanya	6-770	MM
San Antonio Stroll - DANCE #	Tucker, Tanya	22-385	SC
San Franciscan Nights	Animals	15-52	LE
San Franciscan Nights	Clapton, Eric	15-555	LE
San Francisco (Be Sure To Wear..)	McKenzie, Scott	12-922	P
San Francisco Bay Blues	Standard	12-180	DK
San Francisco Bay Blues	Standard	47-722	DKM
San Isabella	Great Divide	8-952	CB
San Isabella	Great Divide	14-614	SC
San Quentin	Cash, Johnny	21-614	SF
Sandman	America	46-416	CB
Sandy	Travolta, John	10-13	SC
Sangria	Shelton, Blake	45-948	KV
Santa Claus And Popcorn - xmas	Haggard, Merle	45-247	CB
Santa Done Got Hip - xmas	Marquees	45-244	CB
Santa Lucia	Standard	27-449	DK
Santa Monica	Everclear	4-673	SC
Santa's Got A Brand New Bag - xmas	SheDaisy	45-246	CB
Santa's Got A Semi - xmas	Harling, Keith	45-243	CB

221

SONG TITLE	ARTIST	#	TYPE
Santabilly Boogie - xmas	Blue Moon Boys	46-287	CB
Santeria	Sublime	30-215	PHM
Sara	Fleetwood Mac	3-528	SC
Sara	Jefferson Starship	12-354	DK
Sara Smile	Hall & Oates	13-667	SGB
Satin Doll	Ellington, Dale	10-704	JVC
Satin Doll	Standard	27-420	DK
Satin Doll	Standard	13-635	SGB
Satin Sheets	Pruett, Jeannie	13-371	P
Satin Sheets	Pruett, Jeannie	8-680	SAV
Satisfaction	Rolling Stones	19-126	KC
Satisfaction	Rolling Stones	19-746	LE
Satisfaction	Rolling Stones	14-390	PT
Satisfied	Marx, Richard	13-663	SGB
Satisfied	Monroe, Ashley	29-210	CB
Satisfied Mind	Foley, Red	43-365	CB
Satisfied Mind	Wagoner, Porter	19-308	CB
Satisfied Mind	Wagoner, Porter	8-668	SAV
Saturday Afternoon	Wicks, Chuck	48-456	KCD
Saturday In The Park	Chicago	34-25	CB
Saturday in The Park	Chicago	17-78	DK
Saturday In The Park	Chicago	13-218	P
Saturday In The Park	Chicago	4-286	SC
Saturday Love	Cherrelle	12-372	DK
Saturday Night	Bay City Rollers	11-267	DK
Saturday Night	Eagles	49-84	ZPA
Saturday Night	Lonestar	8-917	CB
Saturday Night	Lonestar	22-727	ST
Saturday Night At The Movies	Drifters	45-892	MFK
Saturday Night Is The Lonliest Nigh	Sinatra, Frank	9-252	PT
Saturday Night Special	Lynyrd Skynyrd	5-264	SC
Saturday Night's Alright For Fighting	John, Elton	11-525	DK
Saturday Night's Alright For Fighting	John, Elton	13-137	P
Save A Horse Ride A Cowboy	Big & Rich	20-387	ST
Save All Your Kisses For Me	Brotherhood Of Man	47-587	P
Save All Your Kisses For Me	Brotherhood Of Man	47-588	ZM
Save It For A Rainy Day	Bishop, Stephen	9-789	SAV
Save It For A Rainy Day	Bishop, Stephen	46-516	SAV
Save It For A Rainy Day	Bishop, Stephen	21-511	SC
Save It For A Rainy Day	Chesney, Kenny	45-135	KRG
Save It For Me	Four Seasons	43-433	LG
Save Me	Fleetwood Mac	47-915	SBI
Save Me	Once Blue	24-236	SC
Save Me	Shinedown	29-256	SC
Save Me	Zero, Remy	30-655	THM
Save Me San Francisco	TRain	38-200	PHM
Save Room	Legend, John	37-114	SC
Save Room	Legend, John	46-322	SC
Save The Best For Last	Williams, Vanessa	26-279	DK
Save The Best For Last	Williams, Vanessa	19-575	MH
Save The Best For Last	Williams, Vanessa	36-364	SC

SONG TITLE	ARTIST	#	TYPE
Save the Last Dance For Me	Buble, Michael	38-171	SC
Save The Last Dance For Me	Diamond, Neil	47-422	PS
Save The Last Dance For Me	Drifters	16-770	DK
Save The Last Dance For Me	Drifters	13-256	P
Save The Last Dance For Me	Drifters	2-852	SC
Save The Last Dance For Me	Gates, David	2-738	SC
Save The Last Dance For Me	Harris, EmmyLou	1-238	CB
Save The Last Dance For Me	Parton, Dolly	45-346	KV
Save This One For Me	Trevino, Rick	7-85	MM
Save Tonight	Eagle Eye Cherry	15-629	PHM
Save Up All Your Tears	Cher	15-123	SGB
Save You **	Pearl Jam	23-164	PHM
Save Your Heart For Me	Lewis & Playboys	6-59	SC
Save Your Sadness	Cross, Christopher	14-871	SC
Saved By The Bell	Gibb, Robin	10-630	SF
Saved By The Bell	Gibb, Robin	49-26	SF
Savin' Me	Nickelback	30-161	PT
Savin' Me	Nickelback	30-276	SC
Saving All My Love For You	Houston, Whitney	20-303	CB
Saving All My Love For You	Houston, Whitney	15-556	CMC
Saving Forever For You	Shanice	17-389	DK
Sawdust On Her Halo	Lawrence, Tracy	22-83	CB
Sawmill	Tillis, Mel	19-453	CB
Sawmill	Tillis, Mel	5-814	SC
Say (All I Need)	OneRepublic	36-517	CB
Say (All I Need)	OneRepublic	47-331	CB
Say A Little Prayer	Franklin, Aretha	10-593	SF
Say Anything	McAnally, Shane	8-377	CB
Say Goodbye To Hollywood	Joel, Billy	12-802	P
Say Goodnight	Eli Young Band	47-56	ASK
Say Hello To Heaven	Slocum, Jamie	30-344	CB
Say I	Alabama	1-25	CB
Say I	Alabama	7-281	MM
Say I	Alabama	22-897	ST
Say If You Feel Alright	Crystal Waters	10-686	HH
Say It	Voices of Theory	15-631	PHM
Say It Again	Williams, Don	4-770	SC
Say It Isn't So	Bon Jovi	20-1	SGB
Say It Isn't So	Weezer	5-737	SC
Say It Isn't So - WN	Hall & Oates	48-72	SC
Say It Loud (I'm Black & Proud)	Brown, James	29-144	LE
Say It Right	Furtado, Nelly	30-265	CB
Say Love	JoJo	48-397	DCK
Say My Name	Destiny's Child	14-171	CB
Say My Name	Destiny's Child	13-565	LE
Say My Name	Destiny's Child	15-329	PHM
Say No More	Walker, Clay	30-32	CB

SONG TITLE	ARTIST	#	TYPE
Say No More	Walker, Clay	9-865	ST
Say Say Say	McCartney, Paul	15-557	CMC
Say Si Si (Para Vigo Me Voy)	Andrew Sisters	46-433	KV
Say Somethin'	Carey, Mariah	30-717	SF
Say Somethin'	Carey, Mariah w Snoop Dogg	30-717	SF
Say Something	Carey&Snoop Dogg	23-310	CB
Say Something	Great Big World & Aguilera	43-252	BKD
Say Something	Great Big World & Aguilera	43-253	SBI
Say Something	James	30-772	SF
Say When	Lonestar	8-308	CB
Say When	Lonestar	7-766	CHM
Say When	Lonestar	22-769	ST
Say Yes	Burnin' Daylight	10-100	SC
Say Yes	Drake, Dusty	30-342	CB
Say Yes	Floetry	25-684	MM
Say Yes	Floetry	32-270	THM
Say You Do	Bentley, Dierks	48-741	BKD
Say You Do	Bentley, Dierks	46-233	SSC
Say You Love Me	Crowell, Rodney	29-60	CB
Say You Love Me	Fleetwood Mac	17-392	DK
Say You Love Me	Fleetwood Mac	4-527	SC
Say You Say Me	Richie, Lionel	11-535	DK
Say You Say Me	Richie, Lionel	10-390	LE
Say You Say Me	Richie, Lionel	13-202	P
Say You Say Me	Richie, Lionel	4-288	SC
Say You Will	Fleetwood Mac	25-658	MM
Say You Will	Fleetwood Mac	32-354	THM
Say You Will	Foreigner	5-140	SC
Say You Will	Isley Brothers	11-679	DK
Say You'll Be Mine	Grant, Amy	29-134	ST
Say You'll Be There	Spice Girls	28-186	SF
Scar Tissue	Red Hot Chili Peppe	8-510	PHT
Scarborough Fair	Simon & Garfunkel	4-714	SC
Scarlet Fever	Rogers, Kenny	4-777	SC
Scarlet Ribbons	Browns	9-605	SAV
Scarlet Ribbons For Her Hair	Browns	47-543	SAV
Scary Old World	Foster, Radney	19-12	ST
Scenes From An Italian Restaurant	Joel, Billy	16-135	LE
Scenes From An Italian Restaurant	Joel, Billy	20-367	SC
Schism	Tool	16-378	SGB
School Days	Berry, Chuck	43-389	CBEP
School's Out	Alice Cooper	17-355	DK
Scientist the	Coldplay	20-233	MM
Scientist the	Coldplay	32-295	THM
Scotch & Soda	Kingston Trio	2-415	SC
Scotch & Soda	Standard	13-638	SGB
Scratch My Back	Presley, Elvis	47-768	SRK
Scratch My Back/Whisper In My Ear	Bailey, Razzy	29-386	CB
Scream	Joel, Billy	47-146	LE

SONG TITLE	ARTIST	#	TYPE
Scream	McCready, Mindy	14-169	CB
Scream	McCready, Mindy	22-594	ST
Sea Cruise	Dion & Belmonts	47-22	BC
Sea Cruise	Ford, Frankie	35-34	CB
Sea Cruise	Ford, Frankie	6-145	MM
Sea Cruise	Ford, Frankie	12-904	P
Sea Cruise	Ford, Frankie	2-50	SC
Sea Of Cowboy Hats	Wright, Chely	4-107	SC
Sea Of Cowboy Hats	Wright, Chely	22-875	ST
Sea Of Heartbreak	Buffett & Strait	20-498	ST
Sea Of Heartbreak	Cash, Johnny	45-92	KV
Sea Of Heartbreak	Gibson, Don	34-200	CB
Sea Of Heartbreak	Gibson, Don	2-629	SC
Sea Of Love	Honeydrippers	12-192	DK
Sea Of Love	Honeydrippers	6-163	MM
Sea Of Love	Phillips & Twilight	10-335	KC
Seagull	Bad Company	15-753	AMS
Sealed With A Kiss	Hyland, Bryan	35-51	CB
Sealed With A Kiss	Hyland, Bryan	11-692	DK
Sealed With A Kiss	Hyland, Bryan	7-265	MM
Sealed With A Kiss	Vinton, Bobby	49-89	FH
Search Is Over the	Survivor	16-155	SC
Searchin'	Coasters	11-412	DK
Searchin'	Coasters	10-694	JVC
Searchin'	Lynyrd Skynyrd	19-811	SGB
Searchin' For A Rainbow	Marshall Tucker Band	47-223	CB
Searchin' For Some Kind of Clue	Royal, Billy Joe	47-372	SC
Searchin' My Soul	Shepard, Vonda	16-223	PHM
Searchin' My Soul	Shepard, Vonda	5-271	SC
Searching For Someone Like You	Wells, Kitty	5-571	SC
Searching For The Missing Peace	Raybon, Marty	14-75	CB
Seashores Of Old Mexico	Strait, George	29-197	CB
Seashores Of Old Mexico	Strait, George	29-843	SC
Season's Change	Expose	12-374	DK
Seasons In The Sun	Jacks, Terry	29-633	SC
Seasons In The Sun	Jacks, Terry	10-547	SF
Seasons Of My Heart	Cash, Johnny	29-725	CB
Second Chance	38 Special	16-246	AMS
Second Fiddle To An Old Guitar	Shepard, Jeanne	15-89	CB
Second Hand Flowers	Hall, Tom T.	45-716	VH
Second Hand Heart	Morris, Gary	20-25	SC
Second Hand News	Fleetwood Mac	47-916	SC
Second Hand Rose	Drusky, Roy	20-746	CB
Second Hand Rose	Streisand, Barbra	18-60	MM
Second Hand Rose	Streisand, Barbra	49-538	MM
Second Time Around	Sinatra, Frank	12-49	DK
Second Time Around	Sinatra, Frank	12-503	P
Second Time Around the	Shalamar	25-274	MM
Second Time Around the	Streisand, Barbra	49-606	PS
Second Wind	Worley, Darryl	15-213	NSC
Second Wind	Worley, Darryl	15-99	ST

223

SONG TITLE	ARTIST	#	TYPE
Secong Chance	Shinedown	36-22	PT
Secret	Madonna	2-465	SC
Secret Agent Man	Rivers, Johnny	11-447	DK
Secret Agent Man	TV Themes	2-175	SC
Secret Garden	Springsteen, Bruce	17-618	LE
Secret Garden	Springsteen, Bruce	14-878	SC
Secret Love	Bee Gees	48-693	ZMP
Secret Love	Day, Doris	11-577	DK
Secret Love	Emilio	4-350	SC
Secret Love	Fender, Freddie	37-360	CK
Secret Lovers	Atlantic Star	2-845	SC
Secret Of Life the	Hill, Faith	14-622	SC
Secret Smile	Semisonic	7-809	PHT
Secret Valentine	We the Kings	36-268	PHM
Secrets	OneRepublic	44-140	BKD
See About A Girl	Brice, Lee	39-54	PHN
See My Friend	Kinks	48-170	LE
See Rock City	Trevino, Rick	8-128	CB
See Rock City	Trevino, Rick	22-638	ST
See Ruby Fall	Cash, Johnny	45-88	DFK
See See Rider	Animals	43-422	DKM
See See Rider	Willis, Chuck	49-733	P
See The Day	Mitchell, Ross	21-618	SF
See Ya Later Alligator	Haley & Comets	33-228	CB
See You Again	Cyrus, Miley	36-71	WD
See You Again	Underwood, Carrie	40-50	ASK
See You Again (Piano Version)	Puth, Charlie	47-575	KV
See You In September	Happenings	10-365	KC
See You In September	Happenings	7-39	MM
See You Later Alligator	Haley & Comets	11-44	PX
See You Later Alligator	Haley & Comets	3-465	SC
See You Tonight	McCreery, Scotty	44-2	BKD
See You Tonight	McCreery, Scotty	43-139	KCD
See You When I See You	Aldean, Jason	48-670	KV
See You When You're 40	Dido	29-236	ZM
Seeing Is Believing	Presley, Elvis	25-502	MM
Seek And Destroy	Metallica	47-284	SC
Seeker the	Parton, Dolly	49-334	CB
Self Control	Branigan, Laura	16-639	MM
Self Control	Branigan, Laura	24-425	SC
Self Made Man	Montgomery Gentry	9-414	CB
Self Made Man	Montgomery Gentry	13-853	CHM
Self Made Man	Montgomery Gentry	22-548	ST
Sell A Lot Of Beer	Warren Brothers	47-504	SC
Sell A Lot Of Beer	Warren Brothers	20-511	ST
Semi Charmed Life	Third Eye Blind	30-213	PHM
Seminole Wind	Anderson, John	34-302	CB
Seminole Wind	Anderson, John	2-398	SC
Send A Message	Paige, Allison	20-219	CB
Send A Message To My Heart	Yoakam & Loveless	49-689	CB
Send Down An Angel	Moorer, Allison	14-83	CB
Send For Me	Cole, Nat "King"	46-351	CB
Send In The Clowns	Collins, Judy	12-517	P
Send In The Clowns	Streisand, Barbra	49-552	FH
Send In The Clowns	Streisand, Barbra	49-567	PS

SONG TITLE	ARTIST	#	TYPE
Send Me A Lover	Dion, Celine	4-610	SC
Send Me An Angel	Scorpions	49-98	KVD
Send Me Down To Tucson	Tillis, Mel	19-461	CB
Send Me Some Lovin'	Cooke, Sam	12-897	P
Send Me Some Loving	Holly, Buddy	45-585	OZP
Send Me The Pillow	Locklin, Hank	8-777	CB
Send Me The Pillow	Locklin, Hank	8-651	SAV
Send Me The Pillow	Locklin, Hank	19-392	SC
Send Me The Pillow That You Dream..	Martin, Dean	23-85	MM
Send My Love (To Your New Girlfriend)	Adele	46-7	DCK
Send The Pain Below	Chevelle	32-180	THM
Send Your Love	Sting	20-230	MM
Sending Me Angels	McClinton, Delbert	8-302	CB
Senor Santa Claus - xmas	Reeves, Jim	45-268	DFK
Senorita	Timberlake, Justin	32-355	THM
Sensitivity	Tresvant, Ralph	28-404	DK
Sentimental	Orbison, Roy	47-341	DCK
Sentimental Journey	Day, Doris	35-27	CB
Sentimental Journey	Day, Doris	16-827	DK
Sentimental Journey	Day, Doris	12-496	P
Sentimental Journey	Day, Doris	2-239	SC
Sentimental Me	Presley, Elvis	25-93	MM
Sentimental Ol' You	McClain, Charley	5-862	SC
Separate Lives	Collins & Martin	20-306	CB
Separate Lives	Collins & Martin	6-235	MM
Separate Ways	Presley, Elvis	9-730	SAV
Separate Ways	Trevino, Rick	30-320	CB
Separate Ways (Worlds)	Journey	4-885	SC
Separte Lives (Acoustic Version)	Bishop, Stephen	46-517	SBI
September	Earth Wind & Fire	27-319	DK
September	Earth Wind & Fire	15-698	LE
September Morn	Diamond, Neil	7-543	AH
September Morn	Diamond, Neil	30-689	LE
September Morn	Diamond, Neil	4-298	SC
September Song	Houston, Walter	15-558	CMC
September When It Comes	Cash, Johnny & Roseann	43-460	CB
September When It Comes - duet	Cash, J. & Cash, R.	37-252	CB
Sequel	Chapin, Harry	21-509	SC
Serenade	Miller, Steve	23-623	BS
Serves You Right	Richie, Lionel	47-460	LE
Set 'Em Up Joe	Gosdin, Vern	15-822	CB
Set Adrift On Memory Bliss	Backstreet Boys	18-704	MM
Set Fire To The Rain	Adele	38-182	PHM
Set Him Free	Davis, Skeeter	43-325	CB
Set Me Free	Kinks	48-172	LE
Set The Night To Music	Flack & Priest	6-226	MM
Set This Circus Down	McGraw, Tim	29-520	CB
Set You Free	Moorer, Allison	8-188	CB
Settin' The Woods On Fire	Williams, Hank Sr.	14-221	CB

SONG TITLE	ARTIST	#	TYPE
Settin' The Woods On Fire	Williams, Hank Sr.	19-399	SC
Settle For A Slowdown	Bentley, Dierks	29-188	CB
Settle For A Slowdown	Bentley, Dierks	29-852	SC
Settle For A Slowdown	Bentley, Dierks	29-707	ST
Settle Me Down	Zac Brown Band	46-68	KV
Settlin'	Sugarland	30-197	CB
Seven	Bowie, David	19-826	SGB
Seven Bridges Road	Eagles	7-565	BS
Seven Days A Thousand Times	Brice, Lee	39-95	PHN
Seven Deadly Sins	Flogging Molly	48-615	KV
Seven Lonely Days	Cline, Patsy	45-501	LE
Seven Nation Army	White Stripes	19-604	CB
Seven Nation Army	White Stripes	19-545	SC
Seven Nation Army	White Stripes	32-218	THM
Seven Spanish Angels	Nelson, Willie	9-469	SAV
Seven Whole Days	Braxton, Toni	18-819	PS
Seven Wonders	Fleetwood Mac	48-908	LE
Seven Year Ache	Cash, Roseanne	8-266	CB
Seven Year Ache	Cash, Roseanne	13-366	P
Seven Years	Jones, Norah	19-183	Z
Seven Years	Merchant, Natalie	18-38	PS
Seventeen	McGraw, Tim	8-971	CB
Seventeen	Winger	6-20	SC
Seventeen Forever	Metro Station	36-248	PHM
Seventh Son	Rivers, Johnny	10-496	DA
Seventy Six Trombones	Preston, Robert	12-137	DK
Sex (I'm A ...) **	Berlin	30-671	RSX
Sex (I'm a...)	Berlin	19-550	SC
Sex & Candy	Marcy Playground	5-191	SC
Sex As A Weapon	Benatar, Pat	46-126	SC
Sex Farm	Spinal Tap	37-83	SC
Sex Machine	Brown, James	27-278	DK
Sex Machine	Brown, James	29-137	LE
Sex On Fire	Kings Of Leon	36-270	PHM
Sexual Healing	Gaye, Marvin	11-370	DK
Sexual Healing	Gaye, Marvin	36-117	JTG
Sexual Healing	Gaye, Marvin	12-888	P
Sexuality	Bragg, Billy	30-778	SF
Sexuality	Lang, k.d.	47-172	SC
Sexy & 17	Stray Cats	3-446	SC
Sexy Eyes	Dr. Hook	9-690	SAV
Sh-Boom	Bennett, Tony	11-602	DK
Sh-Boom	Chords	27-507	DK
Sh-Boom Life Could Be A Dream	Chords	12-658	P
Sh's Got To Be A Saint	Price, Ray	5-869	SC
Sha La La	Shirelles	48-377	RB
Sha La La La Lee	Small Faces	10-578	SF
Shackles & Chains	Robbins, Marty	47-729	SRK
Shaddap A You Face	Dolce, Joe	6-522	MM
Shaddap A You Face	Dolce, Joe	16-375	SF
Shades Of Cool	Del Rey, Lana	45-283	BKD
Shadow	Caillat, Colbie	38-209	PHM
Shadow Boxer	Apple, Fiona	33-357	CB
Shadow Dancing	Gibb, Andy	11-105	DK

SONG TITLE	ARTIST	#	TYPE
Shadow Dancing	Gibb, Andy	5-474	SC
Shadow Land	Williams, Don	10-75	SC
Shadow Of A Doubt	Conley, E.T.	47-600	CB
Shadow Of Your Smile	Bennett, Tony	16-755	DK
Shadow Of Your Smile	Bennett, Tony	12-515	P
Shadow Of Your Smile	Bennett, Tony	19-782	SGB
Shadowboxer	Apple, Fiona	24-549	SC
Shadows	Yates, Billy	48-713	CB
Shadows In The Moonlight	Murray, Anne	33-311	CB
Shadows In The Moonlight	Murray, Anne	29-660	SC
Shadows Of The Night	Benatar, Pat	19-560	SC
Shadows Of The Night	Benatar, Pat	19-163	SGB
Shake	Redding, Otis	47-363	SC
Shake A Hand	Adams, Faye	10-225	SS
Shake A Tail Feather	Charles, Ray	46-568	AH
Shake A Tail Feather	Purify,James&Bobby	22-399	SC
Shake It	Metro Station	36-30	PT
Shake It Off	Swift, Taylor	48-307	KV
Shake It Up	Cars	17-75	DK
Shake Me	Cinderella	21-772	SC
Shake Me Wake Me (When It's Over	Four Tops	43-427	CB
Shake Rattle & Roll	Haley & Comets	11-668	DK
Shake Rattle & Roll	Haley & Comets	11-49	PX
Shake Rattle & Roll	Haley & Comets	2-47	SC
Shake Rattle And Roll	Cline, Patsy	45-511	DIG
Shake Shake Shake	KC & Sunshine Band	4-60	SC
Shake the	Cooke, Sam	46-638	LE
Shake the	McCoy, Neal	1-841	CB
Shake the	McCoy, Neal	7-654	CHM
Shake the	McCoy, Neal	22-609	ST
Shake The Sugar Tree	Tillis, Pam	1-455	CB
Shake The Sugar Tree	Tillis, Pam	10-763	JVC
Shake The Sugar Tree	Tillis, Pam	12-423	P
Shake The Sugar Tree	Tillis, Pam	2-792	SC
Shake Up Christmas	Train	45-774	KV
Shake Ya Tail Feather - Duet	Nelly, P. Diddy, Lee	32-344	THM
Shake Ya Tail Feathers **	Nelly & P Diddy	25-711	MM
Shake Ya Tailfeather (Radio Version	Kelly&P Diddy&Les	21-790	SC
Shake You Down	Abbott, Gregory	18-493	SAV
Shake You Down	Abbott, Gregory	29-641	SC
Shake Your Bon Bon	Martin, Ricky	29-181	MH
Shake Your Bon Bon	Martin, Ricky	9-136	PS
Shake Your Bon Bon	Martin, Ricky	13-739	SGB
Shake Your Groove Thing	Peaches & Herb	2-498	SC
Shake Your Groove Thing	Peaches & Herb	15-37	SS
Shake Your Money Maker	James, Elmore	20-141	KB
Shake Your Tailfeather	Blues Brothers	29-157	ZM

225

SONG TITLE	ARTIST	#	TYPE
Shake Your Thang (It's Your Thing)	Salt 'N Pepa	49-320	CB
Shake, Rattle & Roll	Presley, Elvis	43-249	MM
Shakedown	Seger, Bob	24-71	SC
Shakin'	Money, Eddie	14-644	SC
Shakin'	Money, Eddie	13-662	SGB
Shakin' All Over	Kid & Pirates	10-551	SF
Shaky Town	Browne, Jackson	23-613	BS
Shambala	Three Dog Night	4-49	SC
Shame	King, Evelyn C.	17-135	DK
Shame	King, Evelyn C.	5-110	SC
Shame About That	Evans, Sara	8-310	CB
Shame About That	Evans, Sara	10-123	SC
Shame On Me	Fargo, Donna	29-699	SC
Shame On Me	Wilkinsons	14-711	CB
Shame On The Moon	Seger, Bob	11-540	DK
Shame On The Moon	Seger, Bob	3-477	SC
Shame On You	Cooley, Spade	38-39	CB
Shame On You	Foley, Red	43-354	CB
Shameless	Brooks, Garth	1-215	CB
Shameless	Brooks, Garth	6-274	MM
Shameless	Brooks, Garth	2-676	SC
Shameless	Joel, Billy	48-10	SC
Shang A Lang	Bay City Rollers	45-943	KV
Shanghai Breezes	Denver, John	15-614	THM
Shania I'm Broke	Judd, Cledus T.	16-509	CB
Shape I'm In the	Nichols, Joe	47-320	CB
Shape Of My Heart	Backstreet Boys	35-203	CB
Shape Of My Heart	Backstreet Boys	23-260	HS
Shape Of My Heart	Backstreet Boys	16-478	MH
Shape Of My Heart	Backstreet Boys	14-38	THM
Shapes Of Things	Yardbirds	6-56	SC
Sharing The Night Together	Dr. Hook	47-38	SC
Sharing You	Vee, Bobby	49-68	ZVS
Sharp Dressed Man	ZZ Top	12-814	P
Shatterday	Vendetta Red	32-332	THM
Shattered Dreams	Johnny Hates Jazz	3-444	SC
Shattered Glass	Paisley, Brad	45-347	KV
Shaving Cream	Bell, Benny	5-632	SC
Shaving Cream **	Bell, Benny	30-668	RSX
She	Costello&Bacharach	13-784	SGB
She	Monkees	47-291	SC
She Ain't Hooked On Me No More	Keith & Haggard	49-778	SC
She Ain't Hooked On Me No More	Keith, Toby	47-152	AMM
She Ain't Right	Brice, Lee	45-383	ST
She Ain't Right For You	Gray, Macy	19-601	CB
She Ain't The Girl For You	Kinleys	9-395	CB
She Ain't The Girl For You	Kinleys	13-826	CHM
She Ain't Worth It	Maderios, Glenn	33-330	CB
She Ain't Your Ordinary Girl	Alabama	6-823	MM
She Ain't Your Ordinary Girl	Alabama	3-413	SC

SONG TITLE	ARTIST	#	TYPE
She Always Talked About Mexico	Ball, David	16-694	ST
She And I	Alabama	1-12	CB
She Bangs	Martin, Ricky	34-151	CB
She Bangs	Martin, Ricky	23-256	HS
She Bangs	Martin, Ricky	14-42	THM
She Believes In Me	Rogers, Kenny	3-166	CB
She Believes In Me	Rogers, Kenny	26-467	DK
She Believes In Me	Rogers, Kenny	13-445	P
She Believes In Me	Rogers, Kenny	9-794	SAV
She Blinded Me With Science	Dolby, Thomas	18-364	AH
She Blinded Me With Science	Dolby, Thomas	29-9	MH
She Blinded Me With Science	Dolby, Thomas	30-781	SF
She Bop	Lauper, Cyndi	3-476	SC
She Called Me Baby	Rich, Charlie	8-292	CB
She Called Me Baby	Rich, Charlie	9-586	SAV
She Came From Fort Worth	Mattea, Kathy	1-189	CB
She Came From Fort Worth	Mattea, Kathy	19-304	MH
She Came In Through The Bathroom	Cocker, Joe	5-683	SC
She Can Put Her Shoes Under My…	Duncan, Johnny	29-774	CB
She Can Put Her Shoes Under My…	Duncan, Johnny	5-758	SC
She Can't Save Him	Brokop, Lisa	4-29	SC
She Can't Say I Didn't Cry	Trevino, Rick	6-611	MM
She Can't Say I Didn't Cry	Trevino, Rick	3-44	SC
She Can't Say That Anymore	Conlee, John	47-619	CB
She Can't Love You	Boy Howdy	3-545	SC
She Caught The Katy	Blues Brothers	19-805	SGB
She Caught The Katy	Blues Brothers	29-160	ZM
She Couldn't Change Me	Montgomery Gentry	30-30	CB
She Couldn't Change Me	Montgomery Gentry	14-792	ST
She Cranks My Tractor	Lynch, Dustin	44-153	BKD
She Cried	Jay & Americans	14-376	PS
She Cried	Lettermen	48-532	L1
She Didn't Have Time	Clark, Terri	23-303	CB
She Didn't Have Time	Clark, Terri	29-610	ST
She Doesn't Dance	McGuinn, Mark	25-69	MM
She Doesn't Dance	McGuinn, Mark	16-34	ST
She Don't Believe In Fairy Tales	Randall, Jon	10-168	SC
She Don't Know She's Beautiful	Kershaw, Sammy	1-468	CB
She Don't Know She's Beautiful	Kershaw, Sammy	6-305	MM
She Don't Love You	Paslay, Eric	45-16	BKD
She Don't Tell Me To	Montgomery Gentry	29-17	CB
She Don't Tell Me To	Montgomery Gentry	29-507	SC
She Don't Tell Me To	Montgomery Gentry	23-451	ST
She Don't Use Jelly	Flaming Lips	5-750	SC

SONG TITLE	ARTIST	#	TYPE
She Dreams	Chesnutt, Mark	6-610	MM
She Dreams	Chesnutt, Mark	2-569	SC
She Drew A Broken Heart	Loveless, Patty	1-733	CB
She Drew A Broken Heart	Loveless, Patty	7-582	CHM
She Drives Like Crazy	Yankovic, Weird Al	49-847	SGB
She Drives Me Crazy	Fine Young Cannibal	33-333	CB
She Drives Me Crazy	Fine Young Cannibal	18-253	DK
She Drives Me Crazy	Fine Young Cannibal	6-169	MM
She Drives Me Crazy	Fine Young Cannibal	5-136	SC
She Even Woke Me Up To Say Goodbye	Lee, Johnny	9-491	SAV
She Even Woke Me Up To Say Goodbye	Lewis, Jerry Lee	47-198	CB
She Feels Like A Brand New Love	Tippin, Aaron	2-664	SC
She Get Me High	Bryan, Luke	44-270	SSC
She Gets That Way	Chesney, Kenny	1-328	CB
She Gets That Way	Chesney, Kenny	48-86	CB
She Got Gold Mine I Got The Shaft	Reed, Jerry	13-461	P
She Got Gold Mine I Got The Shaft	Reed, Jerry	9-463	SAV
She Got Gold Mine I Got The Shaft	Reed, Jerry	20-726	SC
She Got The Goldmine I Got..	Reed, Jerry	33-76	CB
She got What She Deserved	Frazier River	7-203	MM
She Hates Me	Puddle Of Mud	25-340	MM
She Is	Ashton, Susan	19-372	ST
She Is	Ketchum, Hal	15-104	ST
She Is His Only Need	Judd, Wynonna	1-646	CB
She Is His Only Need	Judd, Wynonna	6-198	MM
She Is His Only Need	Judd, Wynonna	13-336	P
She Is His Only Need	Judd, Wynonna	2-801	SC
She Just Started Liking Cheatin Songs	Jackson, Alan	40-97	CB
She Keeps The Home Fires Burnin'	Milsap, Ronnie	4-482	SC
She Keeps the Home Fires Burning	Milsap, Ronnie	34-264	CB
She Knows Why	King, Claude	47-922	SSK
She Left Love All Over Me	Bailey, Razzy	29-381	CB
She Let Herself Go	Strait, George	23-464	CB
She Likes It In The Morning	Walker, Clay	36-428	CB
She Loved A Lot In Her Time	Jones, George	8-346	CB
She Loves Me Not	Papa Roach	18-429	CB
She Loves To Hear Me Rock	Nichols, Turner	17-248	NA
She Loves You	Beatles	16-813	DK
She Loves You	Beatles	12-738	P

SONG TITLE	ARTIST	#	TYPE
She Loves You	Beatles	29-344	SC
She Misses Him	Rushlow, Tim	34-343	CB
She Misses Him	Rushlow, Tim	22-467	ST
She Moves In Her Own Way	Kooks	30-733	SF
She Needs Someone To Hold Her	Twitty, Conway	14-427	SC
She Needs Someone To Hold Her..	Twitty, Conway	1-153	CB
She Never Cried In Front Of Me	Keith, Toby	47-163	CB
She Never Cries In Front Of Me	Keith, Toby	36-609	CB
She Never Cries In Front of Me	Keith, Toby	36-204	PHM
She Never Got Me Over You	Chesnutt, Mark	37-48	CB
She Never Knew Me	Williams, Don	29-702	SC
She Never Lets It Go To Her Heart	McGraw, Tim	1-534	CB
She Never Looks Back	Supernaw, Doug	7-200	MM
She Never Looks Back	Supernaw, Doug	4-228	SC
She Never Spoke Spanish To Me	Texas Tornados	49-750	KV
She Only Smokes When She Drinks	Nichols, Joe	25-607	MM
She Only Smokes When She Drinks	Nichols, Joe	19-60	ST
She Only Smokes When She Drinks	Nichols, Joe	32-268	THM
She Really Loves Me	Miller, Lance	30-350	CB
She Runs Away	Shiek, Duncan	10-95	SC
She Said Yes	Akins, Rhett	3-575	SC
She Sells Sanctuary	Cult	21-767	SC
She Talks To Angels	Black Crowes	13-280	P
She Thinks His Name Was John	McEntire, Reba	1-820	CB
She Thinks His Name Was John	McEntire, Reba	6-599	MM
She Thinks His Name Was John	McEntire, Reba	2-455	SC
She Thinks I Still Care	Jones, George	8-339	CB
She Thinks I Still Care	Jones, George	11-818	DK
She Thinks I Still Care	Jones, George	8-631	SAV
She Thinks I Still Care	Presley, Elvis	25-103	MM
She Thinks I Still Care	Presley, Elvis	14-827	THM
She Thinks My Tractor's Sexy	Chesney, Kenny	19-195	CB
She Thinks My Tractor's Sexy	Chesney, Kenny	5-803	SC
She Thinks My Tractor's Sexy	Chesney, Kenny	22-374	ST
She Thinks She Needs Me	Griggs, Andy	35-447	CB
She Thinks She Needs Me	Griggs, Andy	20-173	ST
She Used To Be Mine	Bareillas, Sara	48-211	KV
She Used To Be Mine	Brooks & Dunn	1-84	CB
She Used To Be Mine	Brooks & Dunn	26-561	DK
She Used To Be Mine	Brooks & Dunn	10-774	JVC

SONG TITLE	ARTIST	#	TYPE
She Used To Be Mine	Brooks & Dunn	6-379	MM
She Used To Be Somebody's Baby	Gatlin, Larry	47-102	CB
She Used To Love Me A Lot	Coe, David Allan	14-250	SC
She Wants To Be Wanted Again	Herndon, Ty	7-402	MM
She Wants To Be Wanted Again	Herndon, Ty	24-660	SC
She Wants You	Billie	10-183	SC
She Was	Chesnutt, Mark	34-374	CB
She Was	Chesnutt, Mark	25-131	MM
She Was	Chesnutt, Mark	16-333	ST
She Was Only 17 (He Was 1 Yr More)	Robbins, Marty	48-13	CB
She Wears My Ring	King, Solomon	10-631	SF
She Wears My Ring	Presley, Elvis	25-764	MM
She Went Out For Cigarettes	Wright, Chely	14-719	CB
She Went Out For Cigarettes	Wright, Chely	22-547	ST
She Will Be Loved	Maroon 5	46-206	SC
She Won't Be Lonely Long	Parnell, Lee Roy	49-271	CB
She Wore A Yellow Ribbon	Miller, Mitch	43-396	SAV
She Wore Red Dresses	Yoakam, Dwight	49-702	SRK
She Works Hard For The Money	Summer, Donna	11-524	DK
She Wouldn't Be Gone	Shelton, Blake	36-203	PHM
She'd Rather Be With Me	Turtles	3-457	SC
She'll Be Comin' 'Round the Mtn	Standard	23-228	SM
She'll Go On You	Turner, Josh	18-212	ST
She'll Leave You With A Smile	Strait, George	25-349	MM
She'll Leave You With A Smile	Strait, George	18-324	ST
She's A Bad Mama Jama	Carlton, Carl	18-367	AH
She's A Fool	Gore, Lesley	5-168	SC
She's A Hottie	Keith, Toby	36-388	CB
She's A Lady	Jones, Tom	33-281	CB
She's A Lady	Jones, Tom	12-149	DK
She's A Miracle	Exile	11-741	DK
She's A Miracle	Exile	9-516	SAV
She's A Miracle	Exile	5-628	SC
She's A Woman	Beatles	11-199	DK
She's A Woman	Beatles	29-337	SC
She's Actin' Single	Stewart, Gary	4-571	SC
She's Acting Single	Dunn, Ronnie	42-26	PHN
She's All I Ever Had	Martin, Ricky	35-221	CB
She's All I Ever Had	Martin, Ricky	29-180	MH
She's All I Ever Had	Martin, Ricky	8-501	PHT
She's All I Ever Had	Martin, Ricky	9-127	PS
She's All I Ever Had	Martin, Ricky	13-740	SGB
She's All Lady	Nichols, Joe	47-572	PS
She's All That	Raye, Collin	22-459	ST
She's All Woman	Houston, David	48-190	CB
She's Always A Woman	Joel, Billy	12-281	DK

SONG TITLE	ARTIST	#	TYPE
She's Always A Woman	Joel, Billy	6-549	MM
She's Always Right	Walker, Clay	8-928	CB
She's Always Right	Walker, Clay	7-887	CHT
She's Always Right	Walker, Clay	22-728	ST
She's Been Good To Me	Anthony, Marc	17-731	PS
She's Comin' Back To Stay	Rabbitt, Eddie	5-324	SC
She's Country	Aldean, Jason	45-458	CB
She's Every Woman	Brooks, Garth	7-76	MM
She's Everything	Paisley, Brad	29-201	CB
She's Everything	Paisley, Brad	30-101	PHM
She's Getting There	Sawyer Brown	24-159	SC
She's Give Anything	Boy Howdy	6-463	MM
She's Going Home With Me	Tritt, Travis	7-610	CHM
She's Gone	Clapton, Eric	5-282	SC
She's Gone	Hall & Oates	20-76	SC
She's Gone	Ricochet	14-114	CB
She's Gone Gone Gone	Campbell, Glen	48-493	CKC
She's Gone Gone Gone	Frizzell, Lefty	20-642	SC
She's Gonna Make It	Brooks, Garth	8-300	CB
She's Got A Butt Bigger Than The..	Judd, Cledus T.	16-507	CB
She's Got A Mind Of Her Own	Bonamy, James	4-105	SC
She's Got A Single Thing In Mind	Twitty, Conway	11-780	DK
She's Got It All	Chesney, Kenny	1-324	CB
She's Got It All	Chesney, Kenny	7-662	CHM
She's Got It All	Chesney, Kenny	22-616	ST
She's Got That Look In Her Eyes	Alabama	8-407	CB
She's Got That Look In Her Eyes	Alabama	22-766	ST
She's Got The Rhythm	Jackson, Alan	1-40	CB
She's Got The Rhythm	Jackson, Alan	6-114	MM
She's Got The Rhythm	Jackson, Alan	12-436	P
She's Got The Rhythm	Jackson, Alan	2-424	SC
She's Got You	Cline, Patsy	17-9	DK
She's Got You	Cline, Patsy	13-373	P
She's Got You	Roberts, Emily Ann	47-401	BKD
She's In Love	Wills, Mark	19-206	CB
She's In Love	Wills, Mark	10-195	SC
She's In Love With A Rodeo Man	Williams, Don	47-761	SRK
She's In Love With The Boy	Yearwood, Trisha	1-631	CB
She's In Love With The Boy	Yearwood, Trisha	13-524	P
She's In Love With The Boy	Yearwood, Trisha	9-637	SAV
She's In the Bedroom Crying	Wiggins, J & A	2-573	SC
She's Inflatable	Judd, Cledus T.	16-504	CB
She's Just an Old Love Turned Memor	Pride, Charley	3-797	CB
She's Just An Old Love Turned Memor	Pride, Charley	5-751	SC
She's Just My Style	Lewis & Playboys	3-459	SC

SONG TITLE	ARTIST	#	TYPE
She's Leaving	Rascal Flatts	39-48	ASK
She's Leaving Home	Beatles	17-61	DK
She's Like The Wind	Swayze, Patrick	6-449	MM
She's More	Griggs, Andy	22-531	ST
She's My Girl	Gilman, Billy	15-189	ST
She's My Girl	Turtles	6-51	SC
She's My Kind Of Rain	McGraw, Tim	29-514	CB
She's My Kind Of Rain	McGraw, Tim	25-516	MM
She's My Kind Of Rain	McGraw, Tim	18-783	ST
She's My Kind Of Rain	McGraw, Tim	32-149	THM
She's My Rock	Jones, George	8-343	CB
She's No Lady	Lovett, Lyle	12-136	DK
She's Not Cryin' Anymore	Cyrus, Billy Ray	26-543	DK
She's Not Cryin' Anymore	Cyrus, Billy Ray	6-304	MM
She's Not Just A Pretty Face	Twain, Shania	20-269	SC
She's Not Just A Pretty Face	Twain, Shania	19-528	ST
She's Not Really Cheatin'	Bandy, Moe	19-500	CB
She's Not Really Cheatin'	Bandy, Moe	5-668	SC
She's Not The Cheatin' Kind	Brooks & Dunn	1-88	CB
She's Not The Cheatin' Kind	Brooks & Dunn	26-560	DK
She's Not The Cheatin' Kind	Brooks & Dunn	6-667	MM
She's Not The Cheatin' Kind	Brooks & Dunn	2-477	SC
She's Not There	Zombies	17-42	DK
She's Not There	Zombies	13-71	P
She's Not There	Zombies	5-456	SC
She's Not There	Zombies	10-656	SF
She's On Fire	Train	18-290	CB
She's On Fire	Train	25-200	MM
She's On Fire	Train	37-320	PHM
She's Out Of My Life	Groban, Josh	48-49	KVD
She's Out Of My Life	Jackson, Michael	25-278	MM
She's Pretty	De Azlan, Star	36-565	CB
She's Pulling Me Back Again	Gilley, Mickey	16-177	THM
She's Really Something To See	Murphy, David Lee	22-917	ST
She's Single Again	Fricke, Janie	13-537	P
She's So California	Allan, Gary	36-243	PHM
She's So Cold	Rolling Stones	20-199	SC
She's So Cold	Rolling Stones	47-871	SC
She's Sure Taking It Well	Sharp, Kevin	14-657	CB
She's Sure Taking It Well	Sharp, Kevin	22-400	CHM
She's Taken A Shine	Berry, John	7-577	CHM
She's Taken A Shine	Berry, John	22-913	ST
She's Taking Him Back Again	Morgan, Lorrie	49-115	CB
She's Too Good To Be True	Pride, Charley	6-89	SC
Shed A Little Light	Taylor, James	45-539	CB

SONG TITLE	ARTIST	#	TYPE
Sheena Is A Punk Rocker	Ramones	45-87	SC
Sheila	Roe, Tommy	6-794	MM
Shelf In The Room	Days Of The New	5-279	SC
Shelly's Winter Love	Haggard, Merle	45-722	VH
Shenandoah	Standard	11-486	DK
Sherry	Four Seasons	35-49	CB
Sherry	Four Seasons	11-214	DK
Sherry	Four Seasons	13-85	P
Sherry	Four Seasons	19-113	SAV
Sherry Frazier	Marcy Playground	16-213	MM
Shift Work - Duet	Chesney & Strait	30-585	CB
Shilo	Diamond, Neil	18-687	PS
Shilo	Diamond, Neil	24-695	SC
Shilo	Diamond, Neil	30-509	THM
Shimmy Shimmy Ko Ko Bop	Little Anthony	30-516	LE
Shimmy Shimmy Ko Ko Bop	Little Anthony	5-637	SC
Shine	Messina, Jo Dee	37-37	CB
Shine On	Carson, Jeff	8-740	CB
Shine On	Dean, Billy	29-53	CB
Shine On Harvest Moon	Miller, Mitch	23-547	CB
Shine On You Crazy Diamond	Pink Floyd	36-125	SGB
Shine Shave Shower It's Sat Nite	Frizzell, Lefty	3-734	CB
Shine Shine Shine	Raven, Eddy	20-289	SC
Shine Them Buckles	Bellamy Brothers	4-414	SC
Shinin' On Me	Niemann, Jerrod	44-150	BKD
Shining Star	Earth Wind & Fire	27-321	DK
Shining Star	Earth Wind & Fire	16-554	P
Shining Star	Manhattans	35-131	CB
Shining Star	Manhattans	17-101	DK
Shiny Happy People	REM	33-346	CB
Shiny Happy People	REM	28-437	DK
Shiny Happy People	REM	12-806	P
Shiny Happy People	REM	5-337	SC
Ships	Manilow, Barry	29-118	CB
Ships	Manilow, Barry	6-552	MM
Ships that Don't Come In	Diffie, Joe	1-275	CB
Shiver	O'Neal, Jamie	25-7	MM
Shiver	O'Neal, Jamie	15-679	ST
Shock The Monkey	Gabriel, Peter	21-403	SC
Shock To The System	Joel, Billy	47-149	NT
Shoe Box	Barenaked Ladies	30-616	CB
Shoe Box	Barenaked Ladies	30-616	RS
Shoe Was On The Other Foot	LaBelle, Patti	9-101	PS
Shoebox the	Young, Chris	48-736	KV
Shoes	Twain, Shania	23-465	CB
Shoes You're Wearing	Black, Clint	1-834	CB
Shoes You're Wearing	Black, Clint	7-743	CHM
Shoo Be Doo Be Doo Da Da	Wonder, Stevie	15-717	LE
Shoo Shoo Baby	Andrew Sisters	46-432	KV
Shoop	Salt 'N Pepa	16-573	SC
Shoop Shoop Song	Cher	11-643	DK

229

SONG TITLE	ARTIST	#	TYPE
Shoop Shoop Song	Cher	19-128	KC
Shoop Shoop Song	Cher	14-64	RS
Shoop Shoop Song	Cher	15-124	SGB
Shoot Straight From Your Heart	Gill, Vince	14-785	ST
Shoot Straight From Your Heart	Gill, Vince	15-196	THM
Shoot The Moon	Jones, Norah	19-187	Z
Shooting Star	Bad Company	5-588	SC
Shop Around	Captain & Tennille	46-553	CB
Shop Around	Miracles	11-141	DK
Shop Around	Miracles	3-292	MM
Shop Around	Robinson, Smokey	36-109	JTG
Short Dick Man **	20 Fingers	2-723	SC
Short Fat Fannie **	Williams, Larry	5-519	SC
Short People	Newman, Randy	35-144	CB
Short People	Newman, Randy	26-263	DK
Short People	Newman, Randy	5-475	SC
Short Shorts	Royal Teens	29-830	SC
Short Skirt Long Jacket	Cake	16-393	SGB
Short Sweet Ride	Jackson, Alan	47-747	SRK
Shortenin' Bread	Tractors	8-399	CB
Shortenin' Bread	Tractors	10-157	SC
Shortnin' Bread	Standard	47-838	SDK
Shot Gun Boogie	Ford, Tenn Ernie	22-204	CB
Shot Gun Boogie	Ford, Tenn Ernie	4-865	SC
Shot In The Dark	Osbourne, Ozzy	5-487	SC
Shot Of Poison	Ford, Lita	19-556	SC
Shot Of Rhythm And Blues a	Beatles	45-610	OZP
Shotgun	Walker & All Stars	3-22	SC
Shotgun Rider	McGraw, Tim	47-246	KVD
Shotgun Wedding	Clark, Roy	10-620	SF
Should I Come Home	Watson, Gene	14-663	CB
Should I Stay Or Should I Go	Clash	27-196	DK
Should I Stay Or Should I Go	Clash	12-800	P
Should I Stay Or Should I Go	Clash	10-530	SF
Should've Asked Her Faster	England, Ty	20-396	MH
Should've Asked Her Faster	England, Ty	6-821	MM
Should've Asked Her Faster	England, Ty	3-419	SC
Should've Been	Lopez, Jennifer	23-325	CB
Should've Been A Cowboy	Keith, Toby	1-698	CB
Should've Been A Cowboy	Keith, Toby	26-554	DK
Should've Been A Cowboy	Keith, Toby	6-397	MM
Should've Been A Cowboy	Keith, Toby	12-452	P
Should've Been A Cowboy	Keith, Toby	2-29	SC
Should've Been Us	Kelly, Tori	48-647	BKD
Should've Never	Lopez, Jennifer	23-578	MM

SONG TITLE	ARTIST	#	TYPE
Should've Ran After You	Swindell, Cole	45-394	DCK
Should've Ran After You (Inst)	Swindell, Cole	49-760	BKD
Should've Said No	Swift, Taylor	36-596	CB
Shoulda Known	Lil Mo	32-385	THM
Shoulda Woulda Coulda	McKnight, Brian	20-517	CB
Shoulda Woulda Coulda	McKnight, Brian	25-581	MM
Shoulda Woulda Coulda	McKnight, Brian	32-197	THM
Shoulder To Cry On a	Pride, Charley	14-251	SC
Shout	Day, Otis & Knights	2-35	SC
Shout	Isley Brothers	11-791	DK
Shout	Isley Brothers	12-891	P
Shout	Isley Brothers	11-23	PX
Shout	Tears For Fears	26-348	DK
Shout At The Devil	Motley Crue	5-481	SC
Shout It Out Loud	Kiss	10-34	SC
Shout Shout	Maresca, Ernie	3-577	SC
Show - 42nd Street	42nd Street	2-293	SC
Show - Adelaide's Lament	Guys & Dolls	7-364	MM
Show - All I Ask Of You	Phantom Of Opera	6-316	MM
Show - All I Ask Of You	Phantom Of Opera	9-141	PS
Show - All I Care About	Chicago - Show	19-515	STS
Show - All That Jazz	Chicago - Show	25-590	MM
Show - All That Jazz	Chicago - Show	18-809	PS
Show - All That Jazz	Chicago - Show	19-511	STS
Show - All Time High	James Bond Movies	18-85	SC
Show - Almost Like Being In Love	Brigadoon	12-290	DK
Show - Almost Like Being In Love	Brigadoon	18-813	PS
Show - Am I Blue	Funny Lady - Streisand	49-585	PS
Show - Am I Blue	Waters, Ethyl	12-286	DK
Show - America	Almost Famous	18-677	PS
Show - Another Day	Rent	17-635	SSR
Show - Another Suitcase In Another	Evita	15-243	PS
Show - Anthem	Chess	15-239	PR
Show - Anthem	Chess	17-697	PS
Show - Any Dream Will Do	Joseph & Amazing	10-374	KC
Show - Any Dream Will Do	Joseph & Amazing	5-659	SC
Show - Any Dream Will Do	Joseph & Amazing	18-631	STS
Show - Anyone Can Whistle	Sondheim, Stephen	17-777	PS
Show - Anything Goes	Sinatra, Frank	12-296	DK
Show - Anything You Can Do	Annie Get Your Gun	19-585	SC
Show - Arthur's Theme	Cross, Christopher	16-812	DK
Show - As Long As He Needs Me	Oliver	27-385	DK
Show - As Long As He Needs Me	Oliver	48-788	MM
Show - As Long As He Needs Me	Oliver	18-811	PS
Show - At The Beginning	Anastasia	17-652	PR

230

SONG TITLE	ARTIST	#	TYPE
- Duet			
Show - Back In The Saddle Again	Autry, Gene	12-284	DK
Show - Ball And Chain - Nashville	Britton & Chase	45-476	KVD
Show - Banana Boat Song (Day-O)	Belafonte, Harry	6-330	MM
Show - Bare Necessities	Jungle Book	20-179	Z
Show - Begin The Beguine	Bye Bye Birdie	27-423	DK
Show - Believe In Yourself	The Wiz	49-434	SDK
Show - Bella Notte	Lady Is A Tramp	20-181	Z
Show - Benjamin Calypso	Joseph & Amazing	18-640	STS
Show - Best Of Times	La Cage Au Folle	6-245	MM
Show - Best That You Can Do	Arthur's Theme	6-889	MM
Show - Best That You Can Do	Arthur's Theme	12-877	P
Show - Big Rock Candy Mountain	O Brother Where	18-661	KB
Show - Black Roses - Nashville	Bowen, Clare	45-461	BKD
Show - Blackbird	I Am Sam	18-672	PS
Show - Born Free	Born Free	12-30	DK
Show - Born To Hand Jive	Grease	49-425	SDK
Show - Brand New Day	The Wiz	49-433	SDK
Show - Bring Him Home	Les Miserables	17-643	PR
Show - Bring Him Home	Les Miserables	18-186	PS
Show - Broadway Baby	Dames At Sea	48-784	MM
Show - Buenos Aires	Evita	15-240	PS
Show - Bushel And A Peck	Guys And Dolls	49-773	PS
Show - Cabaret	Cabaret	16-45	MM
Show - Cabaret	Minelli, Liza	18-233	DK
Show - Can You Feel the Love Tonite	Lion King	20-185	Z
Show - Castle On A Cloud	Les Miserables	17-644	PR
Show - Castle On A Cloud	Les Miserables	18-89	PS
Show - Cell Block Tango	Chicago - Show	19-513	STS
Show - Change Is Gonna Come a	Ali	18-676	PS
Show - Chitty Chitty Bang Bang	Chitty Chitty Bang	9-809	SAV
Show - Cindy	O Brother Where	18-659	KB
Show - Circle Of Life	Lion King	20-186	Z
Show - Class	Chicago - Show	19-523	STS
Show - Climb Every Mountain	Sound Of Music	10-48	SC
Show - Close Every Door To Me	Joseph & Amazing	18-636	STS
Show - Close Every Door To Me	Joseph & Amazing..	18-195	PS
Show - Cockeyed Optimist	South Pacific	17-710	SC
Show - Colours of the	Pocohontas	20-189	Z

SONG TITLE	ARTIST	#	TYPE
Wind			
Show - Come Rain Or Come Shine	St. Louis Blues	12-295	DK
Show - Come What May	Moulin Rouge	19-121	PR
Show - Come What May	Moulin Rouge	18-664	PS
Show - Comedy Tonight	Sondheim, Stephen	17-775	PS
Show - Coming Of Age	Damn Yankees	5-66	SC
Show - Could I Leave You	Sondheim, Stephen	17-771	PS
Show - Da-Doo	Lil' Shop of Horror	17-680	PS
Show - Damned For All Time	Jesus Christ Supers	15-256	PS
Show - Dance Ten Looks Three	Chorus Line	7-371	MM
Show - Day By Day	Godspell	18-201	PS
Show - Deadwood Stage the	Calamity Jane	49-852	SGB
Show - Dentist	Lil' Shop of Horror	7-362	MM
Show - Dentist	Lil' Shop of Horror	17-684	PS
Show - Diamonds Are Forever	James Bond Movies	18-87	SC
Show - Ding Dong the Witch Is Dead	Wizard Of Oz	33-219	CB
Show - Ding Dong the Witch is Dead	Wizard Of Oz	9-815	SAV
Show - Disappear - Nashville	Panettiere, Hayden	45-466	BKD
Show - Do I Hear A Waltz	Sondheim, Stephen	17-773	PS
Show - Do You Love Me - duet	Fiddler On The Roof	19-586	SC
Show - Do You Want To Build A Snowman	Bell, Kristen	43-186	ASK
Show - Do-Re-Mi	Sound Of Music	11-796	DK
Show - Do-Re-Mi	Sound Of Music	10-44	SC
Show - Dominique - The Singing Nun	Reynolds, Debbie	45-70	CB
Show - Don Quixote	Man of La Mancha	18-808	PS
Show - Don't Cry For Me Argentina	Evita	15-246	PS
Show - Don't Cry For Me Argentina	Evita	2-288	SC
Show - Don't Feed The Plants	Lil' Shop of Horror	17-690	PS
Show - Don't Nobody Bring Me No Bad..	The Wiz	49-438	SDK
Show - Don't Rain On My Parade	Funny Girl	49-440	MM
Show - Don't Tell Mama	Cabaret	16-46	MM
Show - Dreamgirls	Dreamgirls	2-294	SC
Show - Dulcenia	Man of La Mancha	5-656	SC
Show - Ease On Down The Road	The Wiz	49-435	SDK
Show - Edelweiss	Sound Of Music	10-45	SC
Show - Elephant Love Medley	Moulin Rouge	19-120	PR
Show - Empty Chairs at Empty Tables	Les Miserables	17-649	PR
Show - Evergreen	Star Is Born a - Streisand	49-568	PS
Show - Evergreen	Streisand, Barbra	16-736	DK

SONG TITLE	ARTIST	#	TYPE
Show - Every Road Leads Back To U	Midler, Bette	12-285	DK
Show - Every Which Way But Loose	Every Which Way But	6-890	MM
Show - Everybodys' Out to Have/Maid	Sondheim, Stephen	17-772	PS
Show - Everything's Allright	Jesus Christ Supers	15-253	PS
Show - Everything's Coming Up Roses	Gypsy	5-646	SC
Show - Eye Of The Tiger	Rocky	6-876	MM
Show - Fade Into You - Nashville	O'Connor & Scott	45-469	KVD
Show - Feed Me (Get It)	Lil' Shop of Horror	17-685	PS
Show - Feed The Birds	Mary Poppins	20-183	Z
Show - Fernando	Muriel's Wedding	6-900	MM
Show - Fixer Upper - Frozen	Frozen	46-381	DIS
Show - For The First Time In Forever	Frozen	46-377	DIS
Show - For Your Eyes Only	For Your Eyes Only	6-881	MM
Show - For Your Eyes Only	James Bond Movies	18-86	SC
Show - From Russia With Love	James Bond Movies	18-79	SC
Show - Funny Honey	Chicago - Show	16-48	MM
Show - Funny Honey	Chicago - Show	19-512	STS
Show - Gee Officer Krupke	West Side Story	7-369	MM
Show - Get Me to the Church on Time	My Fair Lady	6-882	MM
Show - Get Me To the Church on Time	My Fair Lady	18-200	PS
Show - Get Me To The Church on Time	My Fair Lady	2-289	SC
Show - Getting To Know You	King And I, the	6-249	MM
Show - Getting To Know You	King And I, the	2-286	SC
Show - Girl That I Marry the	Annie Get Your Gun	18-197	PS
Show - Give Me Forever I Do	Tesh & Ingram	17-654	PR
Show - Give My Regards To Broadway	Yankee Doodle Dandy	49-442	MM
Show - Go Go Joseph	Joseph & Amazing	18-637	STS
Show - Goldeneyes	James Bond Movies	18-84	SC
Show - Goldfinger	Bassey, Shirley	19-106	SAV
Show - Goldfinger	James Bond Movies	18-76	SC
Show - Good Morning Starshine	Oliver	11-346	DK
Show - Goodnight And Thank You	Evita	15-241	PS
Show - Grease	Grease	16-761	DK
Show - Greased Lightnin'	Grease	49-430	SDK
Show - Grow For Me	Lil' Shop of Horror	17-681	PS
Show - Grow For Me	Lil' Shop of Horror	5-658	SC
Show - Hair	Mills, Frank	49-264	SC

SONG TITLE	ARTIST	#	TYPE
Show - Halloween	Rent	17-640	SSR
Show - Halloween - Rent	Rent	45-122	PS
Show - Hard Candy Christmas	Best Little Whorehs	6-252	MM
Show - Have You Ever Really Loved..	Don Juan De Marco	6-899	MM
Show - He's A Tramp	Lady Is A Tramp	20-182	Z
Show - He's The Wizard	The Wiz	49-436	SDK
Show - Heart	Damn Yankees	7-375	MM
Show - Heat Is On the	Beverly Hills Cop	6-887	MM
Show - Heaven Help My Heart	Chess	17-698	PS
Show - Heaven On Their Minds	Jesus Christ Supers	15-252	PS
Show - Hello Dolly	Armstrong, Louis	9-561	SAV
Show - Hello Dolly	Hello Dolly	6-247	MM
Show - High Enough	Damn Yankees	9-668	SAV
Show - High Flying Adored	Evita	15-247	PS
Show - Highest Judge Of All	Carousel	14-386	PS
Show - Hold On	Good Charlotte	19-660	CB
Show - Hold On	Secret Garden	10-373	KC
Show - Home	The Wiz	49-432	SDK
Show - Honey Bun	South Pacific	17-709	SC
Show - Hooray For Hollywood	Hooray For Hollywoo	6-871	MM
Show - Hopelessly Devoted To You	Grease	49-427	SDK
Show - Hosanna	Jesus Christ Supers	15-254	PS
Show - Hot Patootie	Rocky Horror Pictur	15-352	MM
Show - How Do I Live	Con Air	18-180	DK
Show - I Am A Man Of Constant Sorro	O Brother Where	18-656	KB
Show - I Am Changing	Dreamgirls	10-375	KC
Show - I Am What I Am	La Cage Au Folle	10-371	KC
Show - I Believe I Can Fly	Space Jam	18-178	DK
Show - I Believe In You And Me	Preacher's Wife	18-183	DK
Show - I Cain't Say No	Oklahoma	7-370	MM
Show - I Could Write A Book	Pal Joey	6-875	MM
Show - I Could've Danced All Night	My Fair Lady	17-804	PS
Show - I Could've Danced All Night	My Fair Lady	2-296	SC
Show - I Don't Know How To Love Him	Jesus Christ Supers	6-327	MM
Show - I Don't Know How to Love Him	Jesus Christ Supers	15-255	PS
Show - I Dreamed A Dream	Les Miserables	6-318	MM
Show - I Dreamed A Dream	Les Miserables	17-645	PR
Show - I Dreamed A Dream	Les Miserables	18-88	PS
Show - I Enjoy Being A Girl	Flower Drum Song	17-801	PS
Show - I Feel Pretty	West Side Story	6-251	MM

SONG TITLE	ARTIST	#	TYPE
Show - I Feel Pretty	West Side Story	5-647	SC
Show - I Finally Found Someone	Up Close&Personal	18-184	DK
Show - I Found a Million Dollar Baby	Funny Lady - Streisand	49-583	PS
Show - I Got A Feeling I'm Falling	Ain't Misbehavin'	6-329	MM
Show - I Got A Feeling I'm Falling	Ain't Misbehavin'	48-790	MM
Show - I Hate You Then I Love You	Dion & Pavaratti	17-655	PR
Show - I Have Confidence	Sound Of Music	10-46	SC
Show - I Have Dreamed	King And I, the	18-193	PS
Show - I Know Him So Well	Chess	17-701	PS
Show - I Only Have Eyes For You	Garfunkel, Art	12-287	DK
Show - I Only Want To Say	Jesus Christ Supers	15-258	PS
Show - I Stand All Alone	Quest for Camelot	17-668	PR
Show - I Wanna Be Like You	Jungle Book	20-180	Z
Show - I Will Fall - Nashville - duet	Scott & O'Connor	45-477	KVD
Show - I Will Never Let You Know	Bowen & Palladio	45-467	BKD
Show - I Wish I Didn't Love You So	Perils Of Pauline	12-288	DK
Show - I Won't Send Roses	Mack & Mabel	17-796	PS
Show - I'd Be Surprisingly Good	Evita	15-242	PS
Show - I'd Do Anything	Oliver	6-250	MM
Show - I'll Cover You	Rent	17-636	SSR
Show - I'll Cover You - Duet	Rent	15-263	MM
Show - I'll Fly Away	O Brother Where	18-658	KB
Show - I'll String Along With You	Broadway Arrangemen	19-777	SGB
Show - I'm A Believer	Shrek	18-669	PS
Show - I'm A Mean Ol' Lion	The Wiz	49-437	SDK
Show - I'm Gonna Wash That Man...	South Pacific	7-372	MM
Show - I'm Gonna Wash That Man...	South Pacific	17-705	SC
Show - I'm In Love w/Wonderful Guy	South Pacific	17-712	SC
Show - I'm Looking Through You	I Am Sam	18-674	PS
Show - I'm On My Way	Shrek	18-670	PS
Show - I'm Outta Love	Anastasia	13-842	PHM
Show - I'm Still Here	Sondheim, Stephen	17-774	PS
Show - I've Never Been In Love Befo	Guys & Dolls	18-194	PS
Show - I've Never Been In Love Befo	Guys & Dolls	19-584	SC
Show - If Ever I Would Leave You	Camelot	12-294	DK
Show - If Ever I Would	Camelot	18-187	PS

SONG TITLE	ARTIST	#	TYPE
Leave You			
Show - If He Walked Into My Life	Mame	6-253	MM
Show - If He Walked Into My Life	Mame	17-799	PS
Show - If I Didn't Know Better - duet	Bowen & Palladio	45-472	KVD
Show - If I Love Again	Funny Lady - Streisand	49-586	PS
Show - If I Only Had A Brain	Wizard Of Oz	9-813	SAV
Show - If I Were A Rich Man	Fiddler On The Roof	6-246	MM
Show - If I Were A Rich Man	Fiddler On The Roof	18-192	PS
Show - If I Were A Rich Man	Fiddler On The Roof	5-654	SC
Show - If My Friends Could See Me..	Sweet Charity	6-244	MM
Show - Iko Iko	Rainman	6-885	MM
Show - Impossible Dream the	Man of La Mancha	12-87	DK
Show - Impossible Dream the	Man of La Mancha	6-326	MM
Show - Impossible Dream the	Man of La Mancha	15-235	PR
Show - Impossible Dream the	Man of La Mancha	2-285	SC
Show - In My Father's Wings	Quest for Camelot	17-666	PR
Show - In My Life	Les Miserables	6-242	MM
Show - In Summer - Frozen	Frozen	46-380	DIS
Show - In The Jailhouse Now	O Brother Where	18-660	KB
Show - Isn't This Better	Funny Lady - Streisand	49-584	PS
Show - It Ain't Necessarily So	Porgy & Bess	14-383	PS
Show - It Might As Well Be Spring	State Fair	27-398	DK
Show - It Might Be You	Bishop, Stephen	13-187	P
Show - It Only Takes A Moment	Hello Dolly	18-199	PS
Show - It's A Mad Mad Mad World	Glaser, Tompall	9-811	SAV
Show - It's The Hard Knock Life	Annie	6-880	MM
Show - Jacob & Sons	Joseph & Amazing	18-632	STS
Show - Jesus Christ Superstar	Jesus Christ Supers	15-260	PS
Show - John 19:41	Jesus Christ Supers	15-261	PS
Show - Joseph's Coat	Joseph & Amazing	18-633	STS
Show - Journey To The Past	Anastasia	17-653	PR
Show - June Is Busting Out All Over	Carousel	6-874	MM
Show - Just Around the River Bend	Pocohontas	20-188	Z
Show - Just Blew In From the Windy City	Day, Doris (Calamity Jane)	48-143	SBI

233

SONG TITLE	ARTIST	#	TYPE
Show - Kids	Bye Bye Birdie	12-291	DK
Show - Kids	Bye Bye Birdie	7-363	MM
Show - King Herod's Song	Jesus Christ Supers	15-259	PS
Show - Ladies Who Lunch the	Sondheim, Stephen	17-779	PS
Show - Lady Marmalade	Moulin Rouge	18-665	PS
Show - Lament	Evita	15-250	PS
Show - Last Night Of The World	Miss Saigon	10-378	KC
Show - Last Night of the World	Miss Saigon	17-650	PR
Show - Last Supper the	Jesus Christ Supers	15-257	PS
Show - Le Jazz Hot	Victor Victoria	10-372	KC
Show - Let It Flow	Waiting To Exhale	18-821	PS
Show - Let It Go - Frozen	Frozen	46-378	DIS
Show - Let It Go - Frozen	Mendel, Idina	45-459	ASK
Show - Let Me Entertain You	Gypsy	6-241	MM
Show - License To Kill	James Bond Movies	18-83	SC
Show - Light My Candle	Rent	15-149	MM
Show - Little Bit Of Good a	Chicago - Show	19-516	STS
Show - Little Fall Of Rain a	Les Miserables	17-648	PR
Show - Live And Let Die	James Bond Movies	18-77	SC
Show - Living Daylights the	James Bond Movies	18-82	SC
Show - Lola	Damn Yankees	10-370	KC
Show - Look At Me I'm Sandra Dee	Grease	6-878	MM
Show - Looking for A Place To Shine	Bowen, Clare	45-475	KVD
Show - Looking Thru Your Eyes	Quest for Camelot	17-664	PR
Show - Looking Thru Your Eyes (Duet	Corrs & White	17-667	PR
Show - Losing My Mind	Sondheim, Stephen	17-776	PS
Show - Lots Of Living Left To Do	Bye Bye Birdie	6-872	MM
Show - Love Changes Everything	Aspects Of Love	6-255	MM
Show - Love Has Come Of Age	Jekyll & Hyde	16-51	PS
Show - Love Is An Open Door - Frozen	Bell & Fontana	43-189	SBIG
Show - Love Like Mine - Nashville	Panettiere, Hayden	45-464	BKD
Show - Loving You	Sondheim, Stephen	17-785	PS
Show - Luck Be A Lady	Guys & Dolls	27-397	DK
Show - Luck Be A Lady	Guys & Dolls	10-377	KC
Show - Luck Be A Lady	Guys & Dolls	5-655	SC
Show - Luck Be A Lady	Guys And Dolls - Streisand	49-563	PS
Show - Lullaby	Chess	17-703	PS
Show - Makes No Sense At All - Nashville	Peeples, Audrey	45-462	BKD
Show - Man Of La Mancha	Man of La Mancha	5-660	SC
Show - Man With The	James Bond Movies	18-80	SC

SONG TITLE	ARTIST	#	TYPE
Golden Gun			
Show - Maniac	Flashdance	11-696	DK
Show - Maria	West Side Story	12-31	DK
Show - Maria	West Side Story	5-657	SC
Show - Master Of The House	Les Miserables	7-368	MM
Show - Matchmaker	Fiddler On The Roof	48-785	MM
Show - Maybe	Annie	5-650	SC
Show - Maybe This Time	Cabaret	10-381	KC
Show - Maybe This Time	Rent	15-267	MM
Show - Me An My Shadow	Funny Lady - Streisand	49-587	PS
Show - Me And My Baby	Chicago - Show	19-520	STS
Show - Mean Green Mother From...	Lil' Shop of Horror	17-689	PS
Show - Meek Shall Inherit the	Lil' Shop of Horror	17-688	PS
Show - Mein Herr	Cabaret	15-720	MM
Show - Memory	Cats	6-319	MM
Show - Men In Black	Men In Black	18-181	DK
Show - Merry Old Land Of Oz the	Wizard Of Oz	9-816	SAV
Show - Mighty Quinn the	Quinn The Eskimo	6-897	MM
Show - Miracle Of Miracles	Fiddler On The Roof	14-381	PS
Show - Money Makes the World Go..	Cabaret	10-369	KC
Show - Moon River	Breakfast at Tiffan	6-879	MM
Show - More Than You Know	Funny Lady - Streisand	49-582	PS
Show - Mr. Cellophane	Chicago - Show	16-50	MM
Show - Music Of The Night	Phantom Of Opera	6-322	MM
Show - Music Of The Night	Phantom Of Opera	9-133	PS
Show - Musiq	Madonna	20-3	SGB
Show - My Favorite Things	Andrews, Julie	12-534	P
Show - My Favorite Things	Sound Of Music	27-381	DK
Show - My Favorite Things	Sound Of Music	10-47	SC
Show - My Girl Back Home	South Pacific	17-708	SC
Show - My Heart Will Go On	Titanic	18-177	DK
Show - My Man	Funny Girl	49-441	MM
Show - My Man	Funny Girl	48-789	MM
Show - My Own Best Friend	Chicago - Show	19-519	STS
Show - N.Y. N.Y. What a Wonderful	On The Town	10-379	KC
Show - Nature Boy	Moulin Rouge	18-666	PS
Show - New Argentina a	Evita	15-245	PS
Show - New Life a	Jekyll & Hyde	16-56	PS
Show - No Contest	Chess	17-699	PS
Show - No One Knows Who I Am	Jekyll & Hyde	16-55	PS
Show - No One Will Ever Love You	James & Claybourne	45-473	KVD

234

SONG TITLE	ARTIST	#	TYPE
Show - Nobody Does It Better	James Bond Movies	18-73	SC
Show - Nobody's Side	Chess	17-696	PS
Show - Nothing	Chorus Line	5-649	SC
Show - Nowadays	Chicago - Show	19-524	STS
Show - Nowhere Man	I Am Sam	18-673	PS
Show - Oh What a Beautiful AM	Oklahoma	14-382	PS
Show - Oh What A Beautiful AM	Oklahoma	2-283	SC
Show - Oh What A Beautiful Morning	Oklahoma	27-383	DK
Show - Oklahoma	Oklahoma	27-384	DK
Show - Oklahoma	Oklahoma	2-292	SC
Show - Old Man River	Show Boat	27-447	DK
Show - On A Clear Day	On A Clear Day	6-883	MM
Show - On My Own	Les Miserables	17-646	PR
Show - On My Own	Les Miserables	9-94	PS
Show - On The Street Where U Live	My Fair Lady	27-390	DK
Show - On the Street Where U Live	My Fair Lady	18-185	PS
Show - Once Upon A December	Anastasia	17-651	PR
Show - Once Upon A Dream	Jekyll & Hyde	17-656	PS
Show - Once Upon A Dream (Reprise)	Jekyll & Hyde	17-663	PS
Show - One	Chorus Line	6-243	MM
Show - One	Chorus Line	15-237	PR
Show - One Day I'll Fly Away	Moulin Rouge	19-119	PR
Show - One Day In Your Life	Anastasia	25-252	MM
Show - One Day In Your Life	Anastasia	21-731	TT
Show - One More Angel In Heaven	Joseph & Amazing	18-634	STS
Show - One Night In Bangkok	Chess	17-694	PS
Show - One Song Glory	Rent	17-633	SSR
Show - Otto Titsling	Beaches	7-361	MM
Show - Out Tonight	Rent	15-265	MM
Show - Out Tonight	Rent	17-634	SSR
Show - Over The Rainbow	Wizard Of Oz	9-812	SAV
Show - Peron's Last Flame	Evita	15-244	PS
Show - Phantom Of The Opera	Phantom Of Opera	18-94	PS
Show - Pity The Child	Chess	17-702	PS
Show - Potiphar	Joseph & Amazing	18-635	STS
Show - Prayer the	Quest for Camelot	17-665	PR
Show - Prologue	Joseph & Amazing	18-630	STS
Show - Prologue	Lil' Shop of Horror	17-678	PS
Show - Put On A Happy Face	Bye Bye Birdie	48-786	MM
Show - Put The Blame On Mama	Broadway Arrangemen	19-783	SGB
Show - Putting It	Sondheim, Stephen	17-782	PS

SONG TITLE	ARTIST	#	TYPE
Together			
Show - Rainbow Connection the	Muppet Movie	6-325	MM
Show - Rainbow Tour	Evita	15-248	PS
Show - Raindrops Keep Falling On...	Butch Cassidy/Sunda	6-892	MM
Show - Razzle Dazzle	Chicago - Show	16-47	MM
Show - Razzle Dazzle	Chicago - Show	19-522	STS
Show - Reindeers Are Better Than People	Frozen	46-379	DIS
Show - Rent	Rent	17-632	SSR
Show - Rent - Duet	Rent	15-264	MM
Show - Rock And Roll Is Here To Stay	Grease	49-429	SDK
Show - Roxie	Chicago - Show	19-518	STS
Show - Sadder But Wiser Girl the	Music Man	18-198	PS
Show - Sadie Sadie	Funny Girl	7-365	MM
Show - Salty Dog	O Brother Where	18-662	KB
Show - Say Darlin' Say	O Brother Where	18-663	KB
Show - Seasons Of Love	Rent	15-30	MM
Show - Seasons Of Love	Rent	12-486	P
Show - Seasons Of Love	Rent	18-814	PS
Show - Seasons Of Love	Rent	17-637	SSR
Show - Seasons Of Love - Movie Vers	Rent	29-247	SC
Show - Second Hand Rose	Funny Girl	10-375	KC
Show - Seventy-Six Trombones	Music Man	27-388	DK
Show - Seventy-Six Trombones	Music Man	6-895	MM
Show - Seventy-Six Trombones	Music Man	2-295	SC
Show - Shipoopi	Music Man	14-388	PS
Show - Show Me	My Fair Lady	5-651	SC
Show - Sixteen Going on Seventeen	Sound Of Music	10-41	SC
Show - Skid Row - Downtown	Lil' Shop of Horror	17-679	PS
Show - So Long Farewell	Sound Of Music	10-43	SC
Show - Some Enchanted Evening	South Pacific	27-400	DK
Show - Some Enchanted Evening	South Pacific	17-707	SC
Show - Some Fun Now	Lil' Shop of Horror	17-683	PS
Show - Someone Else's Story	Chess	17-798	PS
Show - Someone Like You	Jekyll & Hyde	16-53	PS
Show - Something In The Air	Almost Famous	18-679	PS
Show - Something's Coming	West Side Story	6-877	MM
Show - Somewhere That's Green	Lil' Shop of Horror	17-682	PS
Show - Song For Mama	Soul Food	18-182	DK
Show - Song Of The King	Joseph & Amazing	18-638	STS
Show - Sound Of Music	Sound Of Music	27-379	DK

SONG TITLE	ARTIST	#	TYPE
the			
Show - Sound Of Music the	Sound Of Music	10-42	SC
Show - Sparkling Diamonds	Moulin Rouge	19-117	PR
Show - Sparkling Diamonds	Moulin Rouge	18-668	PS
Show - Speak Softly Love	Godfather Theme	12-121	DK
Show - Stand By Your Man	Sleepless In Seattl	6-894	MM
Show - Stars	Les Miserables	17-647	PR
Show - Stars	Les Miserables	18-90	PS
Show - Story Of Chess	Chess	17-691	PS
Show - Stranger In Paradise	Kismet	18-188	PS
Show - Suddenly Seymour	Lil' Shop of Horror	17-686	PS
Show - Suddenly Seymour - (best)	Lil' Shop of Horror	19-590	SC
Show - Summer Nights - duet	Grease	49-426	SDK
Show - Sunrise Sunset	Fiddler On The Roof	6-321	MM
Show - Supercalifragilisticexpea lido...	Mary Poppins	49-851	SGB
Show - Superstar Overture	Jesus Christ Supers	15-251	PS
Show - Suppertime	Lil' Shop of Horror	17-687	PS
Show - Surrey With the Fringe/Top	Oklahoma	12-292	DK
Show - Sweet Transvestite	Rocky Horror Pictur	7-367	MM
Show - Take A Look Around (M-2)	Limp Bizkit	14-494	SC
Show - Take Me Or Leave Me	Rent	15-266	MM
Show - Take Me Or Leave Me	Rent	17-638	SSR
Show - Take My Breath Away	Top Gun	6-873	MM
Show - Take My Breath Away	Top Gun	13-193	P
Show - Talk To The Animals	Newley, Anthony	9-817	SAV
Show - Terrace Dust	Chess	17-695	PS
Show - Thank Heaven for Little Girl	Annie	6-898	MM
Show - There Are Worse Things I ...	Grease	6-891	MM
Show - There Are Worse Things I...	Channing, Stockard	10-9	SC
Show - There Is Nothing Like a Dame	South Pacific	7-373	MM
Show - There Is Nothing Like a Dame	South Pacific	17-706	SC
Show - There's a Boat Dat's Leavin'	Porgy & Bess	14-387	PS
Show - There's No Busines Like Show	Annie Get Your Gun	2-282	SC
Show - There's No	Annie Get Your Gun	6-886	MM

SONG TITLE	ARTIST	#	TYPE
Business Like Sho			
Show - They Say It's Wonderful	Annie Get Your Gun	17-800	PS
Show - Think Of Me	Phantom Of Opera	6-248	MM
Show - Think Of Me	Phantom Of Opera	18-93	PS
Show - This Is Halloween	Nightmare B4 Christmas	45-196	HM
Show - This Is The Moment	Jekyll & Hyde	10-382	KC
Show - This Is The Moment	Jekyll & Hyde	15-236	PR
Show - This Is The Moment	Jekyll & Hyde	18-189	PS
Show - This Nearly Was Mine	South Pacific	18-196	PS
Show - This Nearly Was Mine	South Pacific	17-711	SC
Show - This Town - Nashville	Esten, Charles	45-478	KVD
Show - Those Canaan Days	Joseph & Amazing	18-639	STS
Show - Through The Eyes Of Love	Ice Castles	6-320	MM
Show - Through The Eyes Of Love	Ice Castles	13-147	P
Show - Thunderball	James Bond Movies	18-75	SC
Show - Till There Was You	Music Man	6-884	MM
Show - Till You Came Into My Life	Jekyll & Hyde	17-660	PS
Show - Time Heals Everything	Mack & Mabel	17-797	PS
Show - Time Warp	Rocky Horror Pictur	2-141	SC
Show - Time Warp	Rocky Horror Pictur	16-293	TT
Show - Tiny Dancer	Almost Famous	18-678	PS
Show - Tomorrow	Annie	33-220	CB
Show - Tomorrow	Annie	26-507	DK
Show - Tomorrow	Annie	6-328	MM
Show - Tomorrow	Annie	13-196	P
Show - Tomorrow Never Dies	James Bond Movies	18-81	SC
Show - Tonight	West Side Story	27-377	DK
Show - Tonight	West Side Story	6-254	MM
Show - Tonight	West Side Story	19-587	SC
Show - Too Much Love To Care	Sunset Boulevard	19-591	SC
Show - Truly Scrumptious	Chitty Chitty Bang	9-810	SAV
Show - Two Lost Souls	Damn Yankees	19-589	SC
Show - Two Of Us	I Am Sam	18-671	PS
Show - Undermine - Nashville	Esten, Charles	45-474	KVD
Show - Unexpected Song	Song And Dance	18-812	PS
Show - Until	Kate & Leopold	18-680	PS
Show - View To A Kill	Duran Duran	18-234	DK
Show - View To A Kill	James Bond Movies	18-74	SC
Show - Waltz For Eva & Che	Evita	15-249	PS
Show - We Are Water -	Panettiere, Hayden	45-468	BKD

SONG TITLE	ARTIST	#	TYPE
Nashville			
Show - We Both Reached For The...	Chicago - Show	19-517	STS
Show - We Go Together	Grease	49-431	SDK
Show - We Need a Little Christmas	Mame	12-283	DK
Show - We're Off to See the Wizard	Wizard Of Oz	33-221	CB
Show - We're Off To See the Wizard	Wizard Of Oz	9-814	SAV
Show - We're In The Money	42nd Street	2-291	SC
Show - What A Wonderful World	Armstrong, Louis	6-323	MM
Show - What I Did For Love	Chorus Line	12-282	DK
Show - What I Did For Love	Chorus Line	6-324	MM
Show - What You Own	Rent	17-641	SSR
Show - When I Fall In Love	Sleepless In Seattle	48-787	MM
Show - When the Right One Comes Along	Bowen & Palladio	45-471	KVD
Show - When the Right One Comes Along	Nashville Cast	45-465	AHN
Show - When You Wish Upon a Star	Pinocchio	20-184	Z
Show - When You're Good To Mama	Chicago - Show	16-49	MM
Show - When You're Good To Mama	Chicago - Show	19-514	STS
Show - Where I Want To Be	Chess	17-692	PS
Show - Where Is Love	Oliver	17-805	PS
Show - Where Or When	Connick, Harry Jr.	12-293	DK
Show - Who Are You Now	Funny Girl - Streisand	49-581	PS
Show - Who Will Love Me As I Am	Side Show	18-807	PS
Show - Whole New World a	Aladdin	20-187	Z
Show - Why Do I Love You	Show Boat	17-803	PS
Show - Why God Why	Miss Saigon	18-191	PS
Show - Wishing You Were Here Again	Phantom Of Opera	9-163	PS
Show - With A Little Bit Of Luck	My Fair Lady	5-653	SC
Show - With One Look	Sunset Blvd - Streisand	49-566	PS
Show - With One Look	Sunset Boulevard	10-380	KC
Show - With One Look	Sunset Boulevard	17-802	PS
Show - Without You	Rent	17-639	SSR
Show - World's Greatest Hero the	Ali	18-675	PS
Show - Wouldn't It Be Loverly	My Fair Lady	6-893	MM
Show - Wrong Song - duet - Nashville	James & Barnes	45-470	KVD
Show - Y'All Got It	The Wiz	49-439	SDK
Show - You And I	Chess	15-238	PR

SONG TITLE	ARTIST	#	TYPE
Show - You And I	Chess	17-700	PS
Show - You And I (Reprise)	Chess	17-704	PS
Show - You Are My Home	Scarlet Pumpernel	18-810	PS
Show - You Are My Sunshine	O Brother Where	18-657	KB
Show - You Gotta Have Heart	Damn Yankees	6-896	MM
Show - You Must Love Me	Evita	18-179	DK
Show - You Only Live Twice	James Bond Movies	18-78	SC
Show - You'll Never Walk Alone	Carousel	2-284	SC
Show - You're The One	Anything Goes	19-588	SC
Show - You're The One That I Want	Grease	49-428	SDK
Show - Younger Than Springtime	South Pacific	27-399	DK
Show - Younger Than Springtime	South Pacific	14-380	PS
Show - Your Eyes	Rent	17-642	SSR
Show - Your Feet's Too Big	Ain't Misbehavin'	7-366	MM
Show - Your Song	Moulin Rouge	19-118	PR
Show - Your Song	Moulin Rouge	18-667	PS
Show - Yours Forever - Perfect Storm	Mellencamp, John	45-417	SC
Show - Yours Forever (Perfect Storm	Mellencamp, John	14-502	SC
Show -Look At Me I'm Sandra Dee	Channing, Stockard	9-279	SC
Show – Broadway Baby	Dames At Sea	7-374	MM
Show – Mr. Cellophane	Chicago - Show	19-521	STS
Show And Tell	Wilson, Al	35-120	CB
Show And Tell	Wilson, Al	11-673	DK
Show And Tell	Wilson, Al	7-479	MM
Show Biz Kids	Steely Dan	15-385	RS
Show Is Over the	Bassey, Shirley	46-483	SBI
Show Me Love	Robyn	7-698	PHM
Show Me Love	Robyn	5-333	SC
Show Me The Meaning of Being Lonely	Backstreet Boys	18-715	MM
Show Me The Meaning Of Being Lonely	Backstreet Boys	5-886	SC
Show Me The Meaning of Being Lonely	Backstreet Boys	30-405	THM
Show Me The Meaning of...	Backstreet Boys	35-213	CB
Show Me The Way	Frampton, Peter	12-698	P
Show Me The Way	Frampton, Peter	5-872	SC
Show Me The Way	Styx	47-377	CB
Show Me What I Am Looking For	Carolina Liar	36-290	PHM
Show Must Go On the	Sayer, Leo	47-480	SF
Show Mw How To Live	Audio Slave	32-325	THM
Show Them To Me	Carrington, Rodney	30-358	CB
Show Up Naked Bring Beer	Jones, Kacey	47-501	KAC

237

SONG TITLE	ARTIST	#	TYPE
Show You Off	Dan + Shay	44-284	KCD
Shower Me With Your Love	Surface	34-100	CB
Shower Me With Your Love	Surface	9-683	SAV
Shower The People	Taylor, James	10-71	SC
Shriner's Convention	Stevens, Ray	16-494	CB
Shut Up	Black Eyed Peas	47-584	MRH
Shut Up	Simple Plan	47-583	CB
Shut Up And Dance	Ryan, Derek	45-25	KVD
Shut Up And Dance	Walk The Moon	47-585	MRH
Shut Up And Drive	Rihanna	30-570	CB
Shut Up And Drive	Wright, Chely	7-669	CHM
Shut Up And Drive	Wright, Chely	4-835	SC
Shut Up And Drive	Wright, Chely	22-621	ST
Shut Up And Fish	Maddie & Tae	47-927	BKD
Shut Up And Fish	Maddie & Tae	49-642	KV
Shut Up And Fish - instrumental	Maddie & Tae	48-745	BKD
Shut Up And Hold On	Keith, Toby	43-94	HM
Shut Up And Kiss Me	Carpenter, M C	1-427	CB
Shut Up and Kiss Me	Carpenter, M C	17-245	NA
Shut Up And Kiss Me	Carpenter, M C	2-456	SC
Shut Up And Kiss Me	Carpenter, M C	15-151	THM
Shut Up And Let Me Go	Ting Tings	47-586	MRH
Shut Up Train	Little Big Town	47-205	KV
Shut Your Mouth	Made In London	21-634	SGB
Shutters And Boards	Pride, Charley	38-137	DFK
Sic 'Em On A Chicken	Zac Brown Band	43-465	KV
Sick And Tired	Cross Can Ragweed	20-175	ST
Sick Cycle Carousel	Lifehouse	18-574	TT
Sick Things	Alice Cooper	16-451	SGB
Side By Side	Miller, Mitch	23-539	CB
Side By Side	Starr, Kay	11-312	DK
Side By Side	Starr, Kay	15-845	MM
Side By Side	Starr, Kay	4-348	SC
Side Of A Bullet	Nickelback	30-569	CB
Sidewalks Of New York the	Standard	27-444	DK
Sideways	Bentley, Dierks	37-26	CB
Sideways	Worley, Darryl	25-53	MM
Sideways	Worley, Darryl	16-11	ST
Sierra	Maddie & Tae	48-502	KVD
Sign O' The Times	Prince	23-331	CB
Sign Of The Times the	Clark, Petula	9-86	PS
Sign the	Ace Of Base	12-245	DK
Sign the	Ace Of Base	19-573	MH
Sign the	Ace Of Base	13-604	P
Sign the	Ace Of Base	8-604	TT
Sign Your Name	D'Arby, Terrance T.	18-490	SAV
Sign Your Name	D'Arby, Terrence T.	5-614	SC
Signed Sealed Delivered	Wonder, Stevie	34-31	CB
Signed Sealed Delivered I'm Yours	Wonder, Stevie	11-776	DK
Signs	Five Man Elec Band	12-778	P
Signs	Five Man Elec Band	5-311	SC
Signs Of Love Makin'	Tyrese	32-420	THM

SONG TITLE	ARTIST	#	TYPE
Silence Is Golden	Tremeloes	10-592	SF
Silence Of Selling Yourself Short the	Less Th	32-367	THM
Silence On The Line	LeDoux, Chris	14-107	CB
Silent All These Years	Amos, Tori	10-691	HH
Silent Lucidity	Queensryche	13-599	P
Silent Lucidity	Queensyrche	18-378	SAV
Silent Night	Streisand, Barbra	49-545	PS
Silhouettes	Herman's Hermits	4-515	SC
Silhouettes	Rays	11-510	DK
Silhouettes	Rays	25-177	MM
Silly Love Songs	McCartney, Paul	16-782	DK
Silly Love Songs	McCartney, Paul	14-645	SC
Silly Me	McEntire, Reba	1-786	CB
Silly Me	McEntire, Reba	24-12	SC
Silver And Gold	Parton, Dolly	34-291	CB
Silver And Gold	Parton, Dolly	17-215	NA
Silver Bells	Lady Antebellum	45-776	KV
Silver Bells - Xmas	Reeves, Jim	44-252	STTW
Silver Dew On the Blue Grass Tonight	Asleep At The Wheel	46-216	VH
Silver Haired Daddy Of Mine	Autry, Gene	45-657	TB
Silver Lining	Musgraves, Kacey	45-311	KV
Silver Lining	Raitt, Bonnie	25-313	MM
Silver Springs	Fleetwood Mac	7-685	PHM
Silver Spurs (On Golden Stairs)	Autry, Gene	22-178	CB
Silver Threads & Golden Needles	Wynette & Parton	6-476	MM
Silver Threads And Golden Needles	Ronstadt, Linda	29-622	CB
Silver Thunderbird	Cohn, Marc	47-702	DCK
Silver Thunderbird	Messina, Jo Dee	8-977	CB
Silver Tongue And Gold Plated Lies	Oslin, K.T.	4-451	SC
Silver Tounged Devil And I	Kristofferson, Kris	45-198	ASK
Silver Wings	Haggard, Merle	8-39	CB
Similar Features	Etheridge, Melissa	24-564	SC
Simon Says	1910 Fruitgum Co.	11-419	DK
Simon Says	1910 Fruitgum Co.	16-668	LC
Simon Smith & His Amazing Dancing	Burns, George	21-603	SF
Simple I Love You a	Barnett, Mandy	4-427	SC
Simple Kind Of Life	No Doubt	14-483	SC
Simple Kind Of Life	No Doubt	15-785	THM
Simple Life	Carpenter, M C	47-663	CB
Simple Life	John, Elton	6-92	MM
Simple Life	John, Elton	9-673	SAV
Simple Life	Johnson, Carolyn D.	20-264	SC
Simple Life	Johnson, Carolyn D.	19-689	ST
Simple Little Words	Lane, Christy	20-657	SC
Simple Love	Krauss, Alison	30-477	CB
Simple Man	Charlie Daniels Band	35-394	CB
Simple Man	Charlie Daniels Band	20-281	SC

SONG TITLE	ARTIST	#	TYPE
Simple Man a	Lobo	46-335	ZP
Simple Things	Brickman, Jim	23-96	SC
Simply Irresistible	Palmer, Robert	11-391	DK
Simply Irresistible	Palmer, Robert	16-537	P
Simply Irresistible	Palmer, Robert	14-634	SC
Simultaneous **	Chef	13-715	SGB
Sin City	Brooks, Meredith	13-682	SGB
Sin For A Sin	Lambert, Miranda	46-257	KV
Sin Wagon	Dixie Chicks	14-703	CB
Sin Wagon	Dixie Chicks	30-607	RS
Sin Wagon	Dixie Chicks	22-460	ST
Sin Wagon	Dixie Chicks	14-37	THM
Since I Don't Have You	Guns 'N Roses	48-54	SC
Since I Don't Have You	Milsap, Ronnie	1-449	CB
Since I Don't Have You	Skyliners	17-418	DK
Since I Don't Have You	Skyliners	6-261	MM
Since I Fell For You	Rich, Charlie	9-513	SAV
Since I Fell For You	Welch, Larry	6-256	MM
Since I Gave My Heart Away	Isaacs, Sonya	14-721	CB
Since I Lost My Baby	Temptations	14-894	DK
Since I Lost My Baby	Vandross, Luther	48-290	LE
Since I Met You Baby	Fender, Freddie	37-358	CK
Since I Met You Baby	Hunter, Ivory Joe	3-508	SC
Since I Met You Baby	James, Sonny	4-856	SC
Since I've Seen You Last	Janet, Joanna	16-693	ST
Since You've Been Gone	Clarkson, Kelly	22-349	CB
Since You've Been Gone	Outfield	45-373	KV
Since You've Been Gone	Vandross, Luther	48-297	SC
Sincerely	Lettermen	48-536	L1
Sincerely	McGuire Sisters	46-198	SC
Sincerely	Moonglows	7-311	MM
Sing	Carpenters	13-140	P
Sing	Judd, Wynonna	49-419	BKD
Sing	Judd, Wynonna	48-316	CB
Sing A Rainbow	Lee, Peggy	49-933	KV
Sing A Sad Song	Haggard, Merle	49-814	VH
Sing A Song	Earth Wind & Fire	34-419	CB
Sing About Love	Anderson, Lynn	47-644	CB
Sing Along	Atkins, Rodney	30-37	CB
Sing Along	Atkins, Rodney	17-572	ST
Sing Cause I Love To	Howard, Rebecca L	36-216	PHM
Sing Me An Old Fashioned Song	Spears, Billie Jo	47-593	P
Sing Me Back Home	Haggard, Merle	8-323	CB
Sing Me Back Home	Haggard, Merle	4-734	SC
Sing Me Home	McGraw, Tim	47-243	CB
Sing Sing Sing	Andrew Sisters	9-564	SAV
Sing Sing Sing (I'm Gonna	Williams, Hank Sr.	37-293	CB
Singin' In The Rain	Kelly, Gene	11-816	DK
Singin' In The Rain	Kelly, Gene	25-266	MM
Singin' In The Rain	Kelly, Gene	12-508	P
Singin' The Blues	Robbins, Marty	3-234	CB
Singin' The Blues	Robbins, Marty	13-376	P
Singin' The Blues	Robbins, Marty	3-601	SC
Singing In My Sleep	Semisonic	14-286	MM

SONG TITLE	ARTIST	#	TYPE
Singing In The Rain	Crosby, Bing	29-479	LE
Singing My Song	Wynette, Tammy	4-747	SC
Singing The Blues	Mitchell, Guy	33-231	CB
Singing The Blues	Mitchell, Guy	45-68	CB
Singing Tree	Presley, Elvis	25-767	MM
Single	Everything B T Girl	4-611	SC
Single	New Kids On Block w Ne-Yo	36-501	CB
Single	New Kids On Block w Ne-Yo	36-235	PHM
Single Father	Kid Rock	20-484	ST
Single For The Rest Of My Life	Isyss	32-55	THM
Single Ladies	Beyonce	36-489	CB
Single White Female	Wright, Chely	8-953	CB
Single White Female	Wright, Chely	7-869	CHT
Single White Female	Wright, Chely	14-604	SC
Single Women	Parton, Dolly	45-667	DCK
Sink The Bismarck	Horton, Johnny	18-626	PS
Sink The Bismarck	Horton, Johnny	4-145	SC
Sinking In	Presley, Lisa Marie	25-660	MM
Sinking In	Presley, Lisa Marie	19-541	SC
Sinners And Saints	Jones, George	14-706	CB
Sinners Like Me	Church, Eric	30-21	CB
Sippin' On Fire	Florida Georgia Line	45-156	DCK
Sir Duke	Wonder, Stevie	15-559	CMC
Sir Duke	Wonder, Stevie	27-262	DK
Sirens	Cher	47-681	KV
Sissy's Song	Jackson, Alan	37-27	CB
Sister	Nixons	4-665	SC
Sister Christain	Night Ranger	16-244	AMS
Sister Golden Hair	America	11-138	DK
Sister Golden Hair	America	9-788	SAV
Sisters - duet	Clooney, Rosemary & Betty	49-768	MM
Sisters - duet	Midler & Ronstadt	45-914	HSW
Sisters Are Doing It For Themselves	Eurythmics&Franklin	16-637	MM
Sit Down I Think I Love You	Springfield, Dusty	9-726	SAV
Sit Down You're Rockin' The Boat	Henley, Don	48-152	MM
Sit Still Look Pretty	Daya	49-861	DCK
Sittin' And Thinkin'	Price, Ray	46-30	SSK
Sittin' On Go	White, Bryan	14-656	CB
Sittin' On Go	White, Bryan	7-609	CHM
Sittin' On The Dock Of The Bay	Redding, Otis	14-550	SC
Sittin' On Top Of The World	Lonesome River Road	49-326	CB
Sittin' Up In My Room	Brandy	4-166	SC
Sitting	Stevens, Cat	23-653	BS
Sitting	Stevens, Cat	13-581	NU
Sitting In The Balcony	Cochran, Eddie	16-863	DK
Sitting Pretty	Yoakam, Dwight	49-688	CB
Sitting Pretty	Yoakam, Dwight	17-590	ST
Six Days On The Road	Dudley, Dave	8-271	CB
Six Days On The Road	Dudley, Dave	12-17	DK

SONG TITLE	ARTIST	#	TYPE
Six Days On The Road	Dudley, Dave	8-626	SAV
Six Days On The Road	Earle, Steve	46-179	CB
Six Days On The Road	Sawyer Brown	7-611	CHM
Six Foot Deep, Six Foot Down	Jones, George	47-752	SRK
Six Pack Summer	Vassar, Phil	15-187	ST
Six Pack To Go	Russell, Leon	2-407	SC
Six Pack To Go	Thompson, Hank	19-329	CB
Six White Horses	Jennings, Waylon	45-184	DCK
Sixteen Candles	Crests	11-149	DK
Sixteen Candles	Crests	10-323	KC
Sixteen Candles	Crests	25-171	MM
Sixteen Candles	Crests	13-56	P
Sixteen Candles	Crests	9-20	PS
Sixteen Candles	Crests	4-696	SC
Sixteen Going On Seventeen	Sound Of Music	10-41	SC
Sixteen Tons	Ford, Tenn Ernie	15-827	CB
Sixteen Tons	Ford, Tenn Ernie	16-862	DK
Sixteen Tons	Ford, Tenn Ernie	7-117	MM
Sixteen Tons	Ford, Tenn Ernie	13-320	P
Sixteen Tons	Ford, Tenn Ernie	18-616	PS
Sixteen Tons	Ford, Tenn Ernie	9-495	SAV
Sixteen Tons	Platters	9-556	SAV
Size I Wear the	Keith, Toby	47-165	KV
Size Matters (Someday)	Nichols, Joe	29-186	CB
Size Matters (Someday)	Nichols, Joe	29-849	SC
Size Matters (Someday)	Nichols, Joe	29-709	ST
Sk8er Boi	Lavigne, Avril	33-448	CB
Sk8er Boi	Lavigne, Avril	25-334	MM
Sk8er Boy	Lavigne, Avril	18-339	PHM
Skeleton Dance - Halloween	Halloween Songs	45-101	KV
Skid Row Joe	Wagoner, Porter	19-317	CB
Skillz - She's Got	All-4-One	13-307	P
Skin	Rascal Flatts	22-313	CB
Skinny Dippin'	Duncan, Whitney	37-52	CB
Skinny Minnie	Haley & Comets	49-532	DCK
Skip A Rope	Cargill, Henson	10-745	JVC
Skip A Rope	Cargill, Henson	4-868	SC
Skoal Ring	Wilson, Gretchen	29-511	SC
Sky	Sonique	18-531	TT
Sky Is Crying the	Moore, Gary	19-792	SGB
Sky Is Crying the	Vaughn, Stevie Ray	20-132	KB
Sky Is Crying the	Vaughn, Stevie Ray	15-17	SC
Sky Pilot	Animals	43-424	SC
Skyfall	Adele	44-178	MRH
Slave To The Heart	Minor, Shane	8-944	CB
Sledge Hammer	Gabriel, Peter	2-556	SC
Sleep Tonight	McGraw, Tim	49-787	TU
Sleepin' With The Radio On	McClain, Charley	8-201	CB
Sleeping Satellite	Archer, Tasmin	18-387	SAV
Sleeping Single In A Double Bed	Mandrell, Barbara	8-27	CB
Sleeping Single In A Double Bed	Mandrell, Barbara	26-465	DK
Sleeping Single In A	Mandrell, Barbara	13-442	P

SONG TITLE	ARTIST	#	TYPE
Double Bed			
Sleeping With A Friend	Neon Trees	43-165	ASK
Sleeping With The Telephone	McEntire & Hill	36-548	CB
Sleepwalking	Blindside	32-184	THM
Sleepy Joe	Herman's Hermits	47-142	ZM
Sleigh Ride	Carpenters	45-805	SF
Slice	Five For Fighting	42-30	PHM
Slide	Goo Goo Dolls	14-282	MM
Slide	Goo Goo Dolls	7-782	PHT
Slide	Goo Goo Dolls	13-676	SGB
Slide Along Side	Shifty	20-545	PHM
Slide Off Of Your Satin Sheets	Paycheck, Johnny	22-38	CB
Slide Off Of Your Satin Sheets	Paycheck, Johnny	14-309	SC
Slip Away **	Carter, Clarence	5-521	SC
Slip Slidin' Away	Simon & Garfunkel	23-638	BS
Slip Slidin' Away	Simon & Garfunkel	15-560	DM
Slippin' And Slidin'	Little Richard	10-198	SS
Slippin' Around	Whiting & Wakely	19-640	CB
Slippin' Around	Whiting & Wakely	6-3	SC
Slippin' Away	Bellamy Brothers	45-300	DCK
Slippin' Away	Shepard, Jeanne	8-786	CB
Slipping Around	Tubb, Ernest	22-300	CB
Sloop John B	Beach Boys	5-506	BS
Sloop John B	Beach Boys	46-596	CB
Sloop John B	Beach Boys	46-597	LE
Sloop John B	Beach Boys	46-595	SC
Sloop John B	Kingston Trio	7-360	MM
Sloop John B	Standard	27-368	DK
Sloop John B.	Folk Standard	18-169	DK
Slow	Minogue, Kylie	20-571	CB
Slow An' Easy	Whitesnake	6-18	SC
Slow Burn	Sheppard, T.G.	33-85	CB
Slow Burning Fire	Wynette, Tammy	47-783	SRK
Slow Burning Memory	Gosdin, Vern	47-117	CB
Slow Dance More	Rogers, Kenny	19-235	SC
Slow Dancin' Swayin' To The Music	Rivers, Johnny	35-149	CB
Slow Dancing With The Moon	Parton, Dolly	24-249	SC
Slow Down	LeDoux, Chris	2-772	SC
Slow Down	Nesler, Mark	8-217	CB
Slow Hand	Pointer Sisters	27-293	DK
Slow Hand	Pointer Sisters	9-222	PT
Slow Hand	Pointer Sisters	19-557	SC
Slow Hand	Twitty, Conway	8-200	CB
Slow Hand	Twitty, Conway	9-436	SAV
Slow Hand	Twitty, Conway	4-266	SC
Slow It Down	Lumineers	48-420	SBI
Slow Me Down	Evans, Sara	43-154	ASK
Slow Me Down	Lynne, Shelby	6-815	MM
Slow Motion	Adams, Oleta	46-385	PS
Slow Poke	King, Pee Wee	8-721	CB
Slow Ride	Foghat	3-610	SC
Slow Twistin'	Checker, Chubby	46-610	CB

SONG TITLE	ARTIST	#	TYPE
Slowly	Pierce, Webb	29-403	CB
Slowly But Surely	Presley, Elvis	25-492	MM
Slummin' In Paradise	Moore, Mandy	37-24	PS
Smack	3 Doors Down	47-660	SBI
Smackwater Jack	King, Carole	5-681	SC
Small Stuff	Alabama	5-806	SC
Small Stuff	Alabama	22-378	ST
Small Town	Anderson, John	8-134	CB
Small Town	Anderson, John	22-665	ST
Small Town	Mellencamp, John	21-435	LE
Small Town	Mellencamp, John	19-90	PS
Small Town	Mellencamp, John	21-417	SC
Small Town Girl	Wariner, Steve	5-321	SC
Small Town Jerico	Sugarland	30-239	RS
Small Town Saturday Night	Jackson, Alan	43-64	CB
Small Town Saturday Night	Ketchum, Hal	13-470	P
Small Town Southern Man	Jackson, Alan	36-435	CB
Small Town Throwdown	Gilbert, Moore & Rhett	44-274	KCD
Small Town USA	Moore, Justin	43-309	CB
Small Wonders	Dog's Eye View	24-547	SC
Smaller Pieces	Drake, Dusty	19-369	ST
Smells Like Nirvana	Yankovic, Weird Al	15-344	MM
Smells Like Teen Spirit	Anka, Paul	49-245	DFK
Smile	Allen, Lily	30-732	SF
Smile	Cole, Nat "King"	29-453	LE
Smile	Lettermen	48-520	L1
Smile	Lonestar	10-230	SC
Smile	Lonestar	22-501	ST
Smile	Vitamin C	10-202	SC
Smile a Little Smile For Me	Flying Machine	4-713	SC
Smile Like Yours a	Cole, Natalie	10-105	SC
Smiley Faces	Barkley, Gnarls	30-728	SF
Smilin'	McGraw, Tim	29-524	CB
Smiling Bill McCall	Cash, Johnny	29-572	CB
Smiling Faces Sometimes	Undisputed Truth	24-339	SC
Smoke	Thousand Horses	45-27	BKD
Smoke (Inst)	Thousand Horses	49-665	BKD
Smoke & Ashes	Chapman, Tracy	24-639	SC
Smoke A Little Smoke	Church, Eric	37-61	CB
Smoke Along The Track	Yoakam, Dwight	49-693	DFK
Smoke Break	Underwood, Carrie	45-348	BKD
Smoke From A Distant Fire	Sandford/Townsend	21-505	SC
Smoke Gets In Your Eyes	Platters	35-17	CB
Smoke Gets In Your Eyes	Platters	11-310	DK
Smoke Gets In Your Eyes	Platters	13-59	P
Smoke Gets In Your Eyes	Streisand, Barbra	49-596	PS
Smoke In Her Eyes	England, Ty	3-626	SC

SONG TITLE	ARTIST	#	TYPE
Smoke On The Water	Deep Purple	34-56	CB
Smoke On The Water	Deep Purple	11-772	DK
Smoke On The Water	Deep Purple	15-167	MH
Smoke On The Water	Foley, Red	34-185	CB
Smoke Rings In The Dark	Allan, Gary	5-734	SC
Smoke Rings In The Dark	Allan, Gary	22-504	ST
Smoke Smoke Smoke That Cigarette	Williams, Tex	19-632	CB
Smoke Smoke Smoke That Cigarette	Williams, Tex	19-405	SC
Smokestack Lightning	Howlin' Wolf	14-588	SC
Smokey Joe's Café	Robins	6-676	MM
Smokey Mountain Boogie	Ford, Tenn Ernie	22-208	CB
Smokey Mountain Memories	Sparks, Larry	36-352	CB
Smokin'	Boston	5-874	SC
Smokin' And Drinkin'	Lambert, Miranda	45-19	KV
Smokin' Grass	Lawson, Shannon	20-348	ST
Smokin' In The Boy's Room	Motley Crue	2-558	SC
Smokin' In The Boys Room	Motley Crue	35-182	CB
Smoking Cigarettes	Tweet	32-19	THM
Smoking Gun	Cray, Robert	15-311	SC
Smoking Gun	Cray, Robert	19-803	SGB
Smoky Mountain Rain	Milsap, Ronnie	1-443	CB
Smoky The Bar	Thompson, Hank	19-332	CB
Smoky The Bar	Thompson, Hank	5-854	SC
Smooth	Santana & Thomas	30-207	PHM
Smooth	Santana & Thomas	8-499	PHT
Smooth Criminal	Alien Ant Farm	35-255	CB
Smooth Criminal	Alien Ant Farm	25-22	MM
Smooth Criminal	Alien Ant Farm	16-395	SGB
Smooth Operator	Sade	17-111	DK
Smooth Operator	Sade	13-182	P
Smooth Operator	Sade	14-866	PS
Smooth Up In Ya	Bulletboys	21-763	SC
Snake Eyes	Mumford & Sons	48-427	MRH
Snakes Crawl At Night the	Pride, Charley	8-440	CB
Snakes On A Plane - duet	Cobra Starship & Gym...	30-65	PHM
Snap Your Fingers	Milsap, Ronnie	1-446	CB
Snapback	Old Dominion	48-4	KCD
Snapshot	Sylvia	5-776	SC
Sneaky Snake	Hall, Tom T.	45-837	VH
Snoopy VS The Red Baron	Royal Guardsmen	15-140	SC
Snoopy Vs. The Red Baron	Royal Guardsmen	6-520	MM
Snoopy's Christmas	Royal Guardsmen	45-742	SC
Snortin' Whiskey	Travers, Pat	40-32	KV
Snow Fall On The Sand	Wariner, Steve	18-790	ST
Snowbird	Murray, Anne	17-124	DK
Snowbird	Murray, Anne	13-354	P
Snowbird	Murray, Anne	8-622	SAV

241

SONG TITLE	ARTIST	#	TYPE
Snowbird	Presley, Elvis	25-750	MM
Snowblind	Styx	47-386	SC
Snowflake	Reeves, Jim	45-258	CKC
So Am I	Willmon, Trent	30-115	CB
So Amazing	Vandross, Luther	48-287	KV
So Close	Hall & Oates	9-198	SO
So Cold	Breaking Benjamin	30-821	PHM
So Damn Beautiful	Chris Weaver Band	41-64	PHN
So Doggone Lonesome	Cash, Johnny	29-760	CB
So Doggone Lonesome	Cash, Johnny	5-572	SC
So Emotional	Houston, Whitney	11-318	DK
So Emotional	Hues Corporation	27-313	DK
So Far Away	King, Carole	33-256	CB
So Far Away	King, Carole	12-878	P
So Far Away	King, Carole	9-715	SAV
So Far Away	King, Carole	4-843	SC
So Far Away	Staind	20-229	MM
So Far Away	Staind	32-329	THM
So Glad You're Mine	Presley, Elvis	14-828	THM
So Gone	Jewell, Buddy	23-490	CB
So Gone	Monica	34-174	CB
So Gone	Monica	32-273	THM
So Gone (Radio Version)	Monica	21-788	SC
So Good	Destiny's Child	19-823	SGB
So Help Me Girl	Barlow, Gary	7-699	PHM
So Help Me Girl	Diffie, Joe	1-282	CB
So Help Me Girl	Diffie, Joe	4-69	SC
So Help Me Girl	Diffie, Joe	22-871	ST
So High	Presley, Elvis	25-508	MM
So I Need You	3 Doors Down	47-657	CB
So In Love With Two	Mikaila	34-167	CB
So In Love With Two	Mikalia	15-432	PHM
So Into You	Atlanta Rhythm Sec	7-56	MM
So Into You	Atlanta Rhythm Sec	3-481	SC
So Long	Abba	19-86	MM
So Long Farewell	Big Bad Voodoo Dadd	15-210	AMS
So Long Pal	Al Dexter & Troopers	46-404	CB
So Many Ways	Braxtons	24-238	SC
So Much For Pretending	White, Bryan	4-420	SC
So Much In Love	All-4-One	49-481	MM
So Much In Love	Tymes	25-166	MM
So Much Like My Dad	Strait, George	6-185	MM
So Much To Say	Dave Matthews Band	24-107	SC
So Pure	Morrisette, Alanis	8-311	PHT
So Rare	Sinatra, Frank	25-269	MM
So Round So Firm So Fully Packed	Travis, Merle	19-633	CB
So Sad (To Watch Good Love...)	Everly Brothers	38-24	CB
So Sad To Say	Mighty Bosstones	14-489	SC
So Small	Underwood, Carrie	30-545	CB
So So Long	McEntire, Reba	1-812	CB
So What	Cochran, Tammy	14-115	CB
So What	Pink	36-505	CB

SONG TITLE	ARTIST	#	TYPE
So Wrong	Cline, Patsy	22-196	CB
So Wrong	Cline, Patsy	16-588	MM
So Yesterday	Duff, Hilary	32-357	THM
So Yesterday	Duff, Hillary	21-632	CB
So You Don't Have to Love Me...	Jackson, Alan	38-256	PHN
So You Want To Be A Rock N Roll...	Byrds	20-57	SC
So You Want To Touch Me	Glitter, Gary	49-146	SF
So Young	Corrs	49-188	LG
Soak Up The Sun	Crow, Sheryl	18-350	CB
Soak Up The Sun	Crow, Sheryl	25-201	MM
Soak Up The Sun	Crow, Sheryl	29-665	RS
Sober	Clarkson, Kelly	30-571	CB
Sober	Little Big Town	40-3	ASK
Sock It To Me Santa - xmas	Seger, Bob	46-288	CB
Soft Place To Fall a	Moorer, Allison	8-735	CB
Soft Rain	Price, Ray	3-780	CB
Softly As I Leave You	Monro, Matt	18-99	PS
Softly As I Leave You	Monro, Matt	11-54	PT
Softly As I Leave You	Sinatra, Frank	49-486	MM
Softly Softly	Murray, Ruby	10-604	SF
Sold	Boy George	46-521	KV
Sold	Montgomery, J M	14-209	CB
Sold	Montgomery, J M	6-796	MM
Sold	Montgomery, J M	2-739	SC
Soldier	Destiny's Child	20-24	PHM
Soldier	Destiny's Child&Lil	22-343	CB
Soldier Boy	Shirelles	17-316	SS
Soldier Comin' Home	O'Neal, Jamie	36-319	PHM
Soldier Of Love	Osmond, Donny	47-853	SFM
Soldier's Last Letter	Haggard, Merle	37-183	CB
Soldier's Last Letter	Tubb, Ernest	8-796	CB
Soldier's Prayer a	Raye, Collin	30-463	CB
Soldier's Wife a	Dean, Roxie	23-403	CB
Soldier's Wife a	Dean, Roxie	20-483	ST
Solid Ground	Anderson, John	4-147	SC
Solid Ground	Skaggs, Ricky	4-28	SC
Solitaire	Aiken, Clay	36-322	PS
Solitaire	Branigan, Laura	34-63	CB
Solitaire	Branigan, Laura	3-617	SC
Solitaire	Carpenters	44-351	LG
Solitary Man	Cash, Johnny	43-408	KCA
Solitary Man	Diamond, Neil	7-544	AH
Solitary Man	Diamond, Neil	18-691	PS
Solitary Man	Diamond, Neil	24-703	SC
Solitary Man	Isaak, Chris	24-26	SC
Solitary Thinkin'	Womack, Lee Ann	37-43	CB
Some Beach	Shelton, Blake	23-392	CB
Some Beach	Shelton, Blake	30-10	SC
Some Beach	Shelton, Blake	20-492	ST
Some Broken Hearts	Bellamy Brothers	45-298	KVD
Some Broken Hearts Never Mend	Williams, Don	34-227	CB
Some Broken Hearts Never Mend	Williams, Don	13-465	P

SONG TITLE	ARTIST	#	TYPE
Some Broken Hearts Never Mend	Williams, Don	5-128	SC
Some Change	Scaggs, Boz	24-27	SC
Some Days You Gotta Dance	Dixie Chicks	8-904	CB
Some Days You Gotta Dance	Dixie Chicks	25-60	MM
Some Days You Gotta Dance	Dixie Chicks	30-608	RS
Some Days You Gotta Dance	Dixie Chicks	15-855	ST
Some Enchanted Evening	Como, Perry	11-303	DK
Some Enchanted Evening	Como, Perry	13-544	LE
Some Enchanted Evening	Como, Perry	20-777	PS
Some Enchanted Evening	Crosby, Bing	9-548	SAV
Some Enchanted Evening	Jay & Americans	14-379	PS
Some Enchanted Evening	Streisand, Barbra	49-574	PS
Some Folks	Alice Cooper	16-449	SGB
Some Fools Never Learn	Wariner, Steve	4-824	SC
Some Girls	Racey	48-756	P
Some Girls	Rolling Stones	49-775	SC
Some Girls Do	Sawyer Brown	33-109	CB
Some Girls Do	Sawyer Brown	12-417	P
Some Guys Have All The Luck	Little Texas	12-401	P
Some Guys Have All The Luck	Stewart, Rod	11-285	DK
Some Guys Have All The Luck	Stewart, Rod	25-604	MM
Some Hearts	Underwood, Carrie	30-124	AS
Some Hearts	Underwood, Carrie	29-61	CB
Some Hearts	Underwood, Carrie	29-504	SC
Some Hearts	Underwood. Carrie	30-124	AS
Some Kind Of Lover	Watley, Jodi	11-316	DK
Some Kind Of Miracle	Clarkson, Kelly	47-698	SC
Some Kind Of Trouble	Tucker, Tanya	16-344	CB
Some Kind Of Trouble	Tucker, Tanya	19-303	MH
Some Kind Of Trouble	Tucker, Tanya	6-111	MM
Some Kind Of Wonderful	Drifters	12-359	DK
Some Kind Of Wonderful	Grand Funk RR	4-77	SC
Some Kind Of Wonderful	Lewis & The News	24-143	SC
Some Like It Hot	Cafferty, John	45-159	KV
Some Like It Hot	Power Station	34-52	CB
Some Like It Hot	Power Station	21-747	MH
Some Memories Just Won't Die	Robbins, Marty	5-825	SC
Some People	Rimes, LeAnn	30-25	CB
Some People Change	Chesney, Kenny	48-87	CB
Some Such Foolishness	Roe, Tommy	48-116	CB
Some Things Are Meant To Be	Davis, Linda	3-666	SC
Some Things I Know	Womack, Lee Ann	8-962	CB
Some Things Never	Evans, Sara	36-414	CB

SONG TITLE	ARTIST	#	TYPE
Change			
Some Things Never Change	McGraw, Tim	9-411	CB
Some Things Never Change	McGraw, Tim	13-817	CHM
Some Things Never Change	McGraw, Tim	22-541	ST
Some Type Of Love	Puth, Charlie	49-656	KV
Some Velvet Morning - duet	Sinatra, N. & Hazelwood	47-513	VH
Somebody	McEntire, Reba	19-765	ST
Somebody Else's Fire	Frickie, Janie	49-810	CB
Somebody Else's Moon	Raye, Collin	1-127	CB
Somebody Help Me	Spencer Davis Grp	10-643	SF
Somebody Lied	VanShelton, Ricky	8-562	CB
Somebody Lied	VanShelton, Ricky	13-502	P
Somebody Lied	VanShelton, Ricky	8-703	SAV
Somebody Like Me	Arnold, Eddy	19-40	CB
Somebody Like You	Urban, Keith	33-180	CB
Somebody Like You	Urban, Keith	25-292	MM
Somebody Like You	Urban, Keith	18-127	ST
Somebody Loves You	Gayle, Crystal	8-454	CB
Somebody Loves You	Gayle, Crystal	5-51	SC
Somebody Must Be Praying	McGraw, Tim	8-967	CB
Somebody New	Cyrus, Billy Ray	12-167	DK
Somebody New	Cyrus, Billy Ray	17-167	JVC
Somebody New	Cyrus, Billy Ray	17-231	NA
Somebody New	Cyrus, Billy Ray	2-802	SC
Somebody Paints The Wall	Lawrence, Tracy	2-815	SC
Somebody Said A Prayer	Cyrus, Billy Ray	36-217	PGM
Somebody Should Leave	McEntire, Reba	13-402	P
Somebody Should Leave	McEntire, Reba	3-376	SC
Somebody Slap Me	Anderson, John	7-666	CHM
Somebody Slap Me	Anderson, John	4-839	SC
Somebody Somewhere	Lynn, Loretta	4-743	SC
Somebody Special	Fargo, Donna	48-664	SC
Somebody Stand By Me	Hill, Faith	15-689	CB
Somebody To Love	Bieber, Justin	36-61	ASK
Somebody To Love	Bogguss, Suzy	8-99	CB
Somebody To Love	Bogguss, Suzy	7-767	CHM
Somebody To Love	Bogguss, Suzy	22-815	ST
Somebody To Love	Jefferson Airplane	11-185	DK
Somebody To Love	Jefferson Airplane	3-265	SC
Somebody To Love	Michael, G & Queen	4-279	SC
Somebody To Love	Musgraves, Kacey	45-317	KRG
Somebody To Love	Queen	18-261	DK
Somebody To Love You	Judd, Wynonna	22-916	ST
Somebody Touched Me	Dillards	36-356	CB
Somebody Wants Me Out Of The Way	Jones, George	47-731	SRK
Somebody Who Would Die For You	Dean, Tyler	29-54	CB
Somebody Will	River Road	10-125	SC
Somebody's Always Saying Goodbye	Murray, Anne	46-14	SC
Somebody's Baby	Browne, Jackson	5-306	SC

SONG TITLE	ARTIST	#	TYPE
Somebody's Been Sleeping	100 Proof Aged in S	15-9	SC
Somebody's Callin'	Chesney, Kenny	1-319	CB
Somebody's Child	Staley, Karen	8-245	CB
Somebody's Crying	Isaak, Chris	3-493	SC
Somebody's Doing Me Right	Whitley, Keith	33-111	CB
Somebody's Gonna Love You	Greenwood, Lee	9-477	SAV
Somebody's Gonna Pay	James, Mickie	40-22	PHN
Somebody's Heartbreak	Hayes, Hunter	38-254	PHN
Somebody's Hero	O'Neal, Jamie	22-333	CB
Somebody's Knockin'	Gibb, Terri	13-529	P
Somebody's Needin' Somebody	Twitty, Conway	4-494	SC
Somebody's Out There Watching	Kinleys	19-564	CB
Somebody's Out There Watching	Kinleys	22-689	ST
Somebody's Watching Me	Rockwell	12-143	DK
Someday	Azar, Steve	7-210	MM
Someday	Carey, Mariah	21-461	CB
Someday	Cline, Patsy	6-722	MM
Someday	Gill, Vince	25-575	MM
Someday	Gill, Vince	19-7	ST
Someday	Gill, Vince	32-261	THM
Someday	Glass Tiger	24-200	SC
Someday	Jackson, Alan	3-40	SC
Someday	Nickelback	19-653	CB
Someday	Nickelback	20-227	MM
Someday	Nickelback	23-173	PHM
Someday	Thomas, Rob	47-610	CB
Someday	Warden, Monte	8-940	CB
Someday Never Comes	CCR	48-367	SC
Someday Soon	Bogguss, Suzy	1-557	CB
Someday Soon	Bogguss, Suzy	13-507	P
Someday Soon	Collins, Judy	11-439	DK
Someday We'll Be Together	Ross, Diana	15-353	LE
Someday We'll Be Together	Supremes	14-886	DK
Someday We'll Look Back	Haggard, Merle	49-339	CB
Someday When Things Are Good	Haggard, Merle	16-664	CB
Someday When Things Are Good	Jackson, Alan	1-36	CB
Someday You'll Call My Name	Williams, Hank Sr.	45-701	CB
Someday You'll Want Me To Want U	Autry, Gene	22-181	CB
Someday You'll Want Me To Want U	Martin, Dean	23-91	MM
Somedays Are Diamonds	Denver, John	4-488	SC
Somedays Are Diamonds	Denver, John	15-619	THM
Someone	Clarkson, Kelly	48-438	KCD

SONG TITLE	ARTIST	#	TYPE
Someone	Mathis, Johnny	29-462	LE
Someone Could Lose A Heart Tonite	Rabbitt, Eddie	8-203	CB
Someone Could Lose A Heart Tonite	Rabbitt, Eddie	5-669	SC
Someone Else Calling You Baby	Bryan, Luke	45-32	CB
Someone Else's Dream	Hill, Faith	15-690	CB
Someone Else's Dream	Hill, Faith	4-198	SC
Someone Else's Star	White, Bryan	6-845	MM
Someone Else's Star	White, Bryan	2-775	SC
Someone Else's Turn To Cry	Tennison, Chalee	8-477	CB
Someone Else's Turn To Cry	Tennison, Chalee	14-617	SC
Someone Like You	Adele	38-183	PHM
Someone Like You	Eder, Linda	16-718	PS
Someone Like You	Ingram, James	4-277	SC
Someone Loves You Honey	Pride, Charley	40-112	CB
Someone Loves You Honey	Pride, Charley	9-856	SAV
Someone Loves You Honey	Pride, Charley	5-624	SC
Someone Must Feel Like A Fool Tonit	Rogers, Kenny	24-15	SC
Someone Somewhere Tonight	Pickler, Kellie	41-71	PHN
Someone To Call Me Darlin'	Morgan, Lorrie	49-117	CB
Someone To Call My Lover	Jackson, Janet	18-398	MM
Someone To Call My Lover	Jackson, Janet	18-532	TT
Someone To Give My Love To	Paycheck, Johnny	22-34	CB
Someone To Give My Love To	Paycheck, Johnny	5-165	SC
Someone To Lay Down Beside Me	Ronstadt, Linda	20-101	SC
Someone To Love	Jon B with Babyface	3-436	SC
Someone To Share It With	Atkins, Rodney	30-41	CB
Someone To Share It With	Atkins, Rodney	20-342	ST
Someone To Watch Over Me	Ronstadt, Linda	7-186	MM
Someone To Watch Over Me	Sinatra, Frank	4-353	SC
Someone To Watch Over Me	Standard	27-430	DK
Someone To Watch Over Me	Streisand, Barbra	49-620	SC
Someone You Used To Know	Raye, Collin	8-157	CB
Someplace Far Away	Ketchum, Hal	24-354	SC
Somethin' 'Bout A Sunday	Peterson, Michael	8-949	cB
Somethin' 'Bout A Truck	Moore, Kip	45-352	KST
Somethin' In The Water	Steele, Jeffrey	25-5	MM

SONG TITLE	ARTIST	#	TYPE
Somethin' Like This	Diffie, Joe	22-623	ST
Somethin' Stupid	Sinatra, Frank	27-565	DK
Something	Beatles	7-513	SAV
Something	Lasgo	18-610	PHM
Something	Lasgo	32-101	THM
Something About A Woman	Owen, Jake	36-420	CB
Something About A Woman	Owen, Jake	49-899	SC
Something About The Way	John, Elton	7-686	PHM
Something About You	Four Tops	43-426	CB
Something About You	Level 42	15-793	SC
Something About You I Love	Paycheck, Johnny	22-42	CB
Something About You I Love	Paycheck, Johnny	5-819	SC
Something Bad - Duet	Lambert & Underwood	44-278	PHN
Something Beautiful Remains	Turner, Tina	24-286	SC
Something Blue	Diamond, Neil	46-593	DCK
Something Happened on/to Heaven	Collins, Phil	24-256	SC
Something I Need	OneRepublic	47-333	KV
Something In Red	Morgan, Lorrie	1-343	CB
Something In Red	Morgan, Lorrie	6-115	MM
Something In Red	Morgan, Lorrie	2-13	SC
Something In The Water	Steele, Jeffrey	15-861	ST
Something In The Way She Moves	Taylor, James	45-541	RSZ
Something Like A Broken Heart	Hanna-McEuen	22-324	CB
Something Like That	McGraw, Tim	19-194	CB
Something Like That	McGraw, Tim	22-486	ST
Something More	Sugarland	23-115	CB
Something More	Sugarland	30-231	RS
Something More	Sugarland	23-382	SC
Something More	Train	25-41	MM
Something More	Train	37-321	SC
Something Of A Dreamer	Carpenter, M C	1-430	CB
Something Of A Dreamer	Carpenter, M C	15-161	THM
Something Real	Petrone, Shawna	5-802	SC
Something So Right	Yearwood, Trisha	48-331	CB
Something So Strong	Crowded House	7-492	MM
Something So Strong	Crowded House	12-808	P
Something So Strong	Crowded House	15-797	SC
Something Stronger Than Me	Tritt, Travis	30-582	CB
Something Stupid	Sinatra, Frank	11-466	DK
Something Stupid	Sinatra, Frank	49-492	MM
Something Stupid	Sinatra, Frank	21-225	SGB
Something That We Do	Black, Clint	1-835	CB
Something That We Do	Black, Clint	7-682	CHM
Something That We Do	Black, Clint	22-629	ST
Something To Be Proud Of	Montgomery Gentry	23-130	CB
Something To Believe In	Eder, Linda	16-713	PS
Something To Believe In	Poison	24-682	SC

SONG TITLE	ARTIST	#	TYPE
Something To Believe In	Poison	13-758	SGB
Something To Do With My Hands	Rhett, Thomas	43-12	ASK
Something To Do With My Hands	Rhett, Thomas	45-407	BKD
Something To Talk About	Raitt, Bonnie	11-803	DK
Something To Talk About	Raitt, Bonnie	10-764	JVC
Something To Talk About	Raitt, Bonnie	9-264	SC
Something To Write Home About	Morgan, Craig	6-75	SC
Something To Write Home About	Morgan, Craig	22-553	ST
Something Worth Leaving	Womack, Lee Ann	17-565	ST
Something Worth Leaving Behind	Womack, Lee Ann	25-289	MM
Something You Should've Said	Clark, Terri	7-327	MM
Something's Burning	First Edition	9-731	SAV
Something's Goin' On	UNV	13-21	P
Something's Got A Hold Of My Heart	Pitney, Gene	47-530	ZM
Something's Gotta Give	Davis, Sammy Jr.	7-195	MM
Something's Gotta Give	Rimes, LeAnn	29-34	CB
Something's Happening	Herman's Hermits	47-139	SF
Sometime Around Midnight	Airborne Toxic Event	36-380	SC
Sometimes	Anderson, Bill	46-212	CB
Sometimes	Davidson, Clay	14-790	ST
Sometimes	Lee, Johnny	47-787	SRK
Sometimes	Lee, Johnny	45-841	VH
Sometimes	Leigh, Danni	16-692	ST
Sometimes	Spears, Britney	13-561	LE
Sometimes	Spears, Britney	8-160	PHT
Sometimes	Spears, Britney	13-700	SGB
Sometimes - duet	Anderson & Turner	40-69	CB
Sometimes I Cry - live	Stapleton, Chris	49-651	KV
Sometimes I Dream	Groban, Josh	48-52	PSJT
Sometimes I Forget	Stone, Doug	7-25	MM
Sometimes I Forget	Stone, Doug	3-537	SC
Sometimes I Get Lucky & Forget	Watson, Gene	14-674	CB
Sometimes It's Just Your Time	Heatherly, Eric	18-471	ST
Sometimes It's Only Love	Vandross, Luther	24-264	SC
Sometimes Love Just Ain't Enough	Smyth & Henley	6-229	MM
Sometimes Love Just Ain't Enough	Smyth & Henley	9-674	SAV
Sometimes When We Touch	Hill, Dan	16-66	SC
Sometimes When We Touch	West, Dottie	49-774	SC
Sometimes You Can't Make It On Your Own	U2	48-313	ST
Somewhere	Streisand, Barbra	33-322	CB

SONG TITLE	ARTIST	#	TYPE
Somewhere Along The Line	Reeves, Jim	44-235	DCK
Somewhere Along The Way	Cole, Nat "King"	46-348	CB
Somewhere Between	Bogguss, Suzy	1-566	CB
Somewhere Between	Haggard, Merle	44-59	KV
Somewhere Between	Haggard, Merle	46-22	SSK
Somewhere Between Right & Wrong	Conley, Earl Thomas	13-538	P
Somewhere Between Right & Wrong	Conley, Earl Thomas	14-420	SC
Somewhere Between TX & Mexico	Green, Pat	23-140	CB
Somewhere Down In Texas	Strait, George	38-154	SC
Somewhere I Belong	Linkin Park	32-214	THM
Somewhere In Love	Wiggins, J & A	10-83	SC
Somewhere In My Broken Heart	Dean, Billy	35-401	CB
Somewhere In My Broken Heart	Dean, Billy	17-351	DK
Somewhere in My Car	Urban, Keith	45-625	SSC
Somewhere In The Night	Manilow, Barry	6-544	MM
Somewhere In The Sun	Chesney, Kenny	48-82	CB
Somewhere In The Vicinity/Heart	Shenandoah/Krauss	17-259	NA
Somewhere In The Vicinity/Heart	Shenandoah/Krauss	2-822	SC
Somewhere My Love	Jones, Jack	19-785	SGB
Somewhere My Love	Snow, Hank	48-581	DK
Somewhere My Love	Williams, Andy	11-305	DK
Somewhere My Love	Williams, Andy	13-549	LE
Somewhere On A Beach	Bentley, Dierks	48-747	BKD
Somewhere On A Beach	Bentley, Dierks	47-700	DCK
Somewhere On A Beach (Inst)	Bentley, Dierks	49-411	BKD
Somewhere Only We Know	Keane	21-687	Z
Somewhere Other Than The Night	Brooks, Garth	6-271	MM
Somewhere Other Than The Night	Brooks, Garth	2-686	SC
Somewhere Out There	Our Lady Peace	25-401	MM
Somewhere Out There	Ronstadt & Ingram	11-805	DK
Somewhere Out There	Ronstadt & Ingram	6-335	MM
Somewhere Out There	Ronstadt & Ingram	13-185	P
Somewhere Out There	Ronstadt & Ingram	9-205	SO
Somewhere There's A Someone	Martin, Dean	23-87	MM
Somewhere Tonight	Highway 101	13-497	P
Somewhere With You	Chesney, Kenny	37-233	CB
Son Of A Gun	Jackson & Elliot	16-75	ST
Son Of A Preacher Man	Austin, Sherrie	20-481	ST
Son Of A Preacher Man	Springfield, Dusty	21-196	DK
Son Of A Preacher Man	Springfield, Dusty	10-732	JVC
Son Of A Preacher Man	Springfield, Dusty	6-785	MM
Son Of A Preacher Man	Springfield, Dusty	17-312	NA
Son Of A Rotten Gambler	Murray, Anne	38-7	PHM

SONG TITLE	ARTIST	#	TYPE
Son Of A Rotten Gambler	Murray, Anne	11-14	PL
Son Of A Son Of A Sailor	Buffett, Jimmy	42-16	SC
Son Of Hickory Holler's Tramp	Smith, O.C.R.	10-632	SF
Song About A Girl	Paslay, Eric	44-275	PHN
Song And Dance Man	Paycheck, Johnny	22-36	CB
Song And Dance Man	Paycheck, Johnny	5-625	SC
Song Bird	Streisand, Barbra	49-541	MM
Song For A Winter's Night	Lightfoot, Gordon	43-485	SK
Song For Mama	Boyz II Men	5-182	SC
Song For The Dumped **	Ben Folds Five	37-86	SC
Song For The Life	Jackson, Alan	1-49	CB
Song For The Life	Jackson, Alan	2-653	SC
Song For The Lonely	Cher	25-141	MM
Song For The Lonely	Cher	21-733	TT
Song For You a	Aguilera & Hancock	29-280	PHM
Song For You a	Buble, Michael	38-177	ZM
Song Is You the	Standard	15-561	SGB
Song Of Joy	Captain & Tennille	46-558	CB
Song Of The South	Alabama	4-448	BS
Song Of The South	Alabama	1-13	CB
Song Remembers When the	Yearwood, Trisha	1-636	CB
Song Remembers When the	Yearwood, Trisha	2-349	SC
Song Sung Blue	Darin, Bobby	49-722	KV
Song Sung Blue	Diamond, Neil	7-545	AH
Song Sung Blue	Diamond, Neil	13-298	P
Song Sung Blue	Diamond, Neil	16-409	PR
Song Sung Blue	Diamond, Neil	24-697	SC
Songs About Me	Adkins, Trace	23-1	CB
Songs About Rain	Allan, Gary	20-268	SC
Songs About Rain	Allan, Gary	19-847	ST
Songs Of Life	Diamond, Neil	18-692	PS
Sonnet	Verve	8-514	PHT
Soolaimon	Diamond, Neil	18-693	PS
Soolaimon	Diamond, Neil	30-510	THM
Soon	Rimes, LeAnn	25-20	MM
Soon	Rimes, LeAnn	15-673	ST
Soon	Tucker, Tanya	1-611	CB
Soon	Tucker, Tanya	6-378	MM
Soon And Very Soon	Crouch, Andre	13-83	P
Sooner Or Later	Breaking Benjamin	48-544	DK
Sooner Or Later	Fastball	47-87	CB
Sooner Or Later	Grass Roots	11-545	DK
Sooner Or Later	Grass Roots	9-719	SAV
Sooner Or Later	James, Duncan	30-720	SF
Sooner Or Later	Sondheim, Stephen	17-784	PS
Soorry I Ran All The Way Home	Impalas	6-683	MM
Sorrow On The Rocks	Wagoner, Porter	19-315	CB
Sorry	Buckcherry	36-461	CB
Sorry 2004	Studdard, Ruben	20-538	CB
Sorry 2004	Studdard, Ruben	36-327	PS
Sorry For Love	Dion, Celine	19-27	PS

SONG TITLE	ARTIST	#	TYPE
Sorry For The Stupid Things	Babyface	29-318	PHM
Sorry Seems To Be The Hardest...	John, Elton	34-45	CB
Sorry Seems To Be The Hardest...	John, Elton	2-386	SC
Sorry Suzanne	Hollies	44-367	ZM
Sorry You Asked	Yoakam, Dwight	7-245	MM
Sorry You Asked?	Yoakam, Dwight	22-890	ST
Sorta Fairytale a	Amos, Tori	25-393	MM
Sorta Fairytale a	Amos, Tori	18-606	PHM
SOS	Abba	7-503	MM
SOS	Jonas Brothers	30-592	PHM
SOS	Rihanna	30-150	PT
SOS (Rescue Me)	Rihanna	36-96	CB
Soul & Inspiration	Righteous Brothers	11-237	DK
Soul & Inspiration	Righteous Brothers	3-331	PS
Soul & Inspiration	Righteous Brothers	2-46	SC
Soul Drifter	Buckingham,Lindsey	24-258	SC
Soul Man	Blues Brothers	29-154	ZM
Soul Man	Sam & Dave	12-92	DK
Soul Man	Sam & Dave	12-711	P
Soul Song	Stampley, Joe	5-537	SC
Sound A Dream Makes the	Heartland	39-55	PHN
Sound Of A Million Dreams	Nail, David	45-558	ZP
Sound Of Goodbye	Gayle, Crystal	45-832	VH
Sound Of Silence	Disturbed	49-1	DCK
Sound Of Silence	Simon & Garfunkel	23-639	BS
Sound Of Silence	Simon & Garfunkel	17-174	SC
Sounds Like Love	Lee, Johnny	5-861	SC
Sounds So Good	Shepherd, Ashton	36-604	CB
South City Midnight Lady	Doobie Brothers	29-87	CB
South Of Santa Fe	Brooks & Dunn	7-881	CHT
South Of Santa Fe	Brooks & Dunn	14-631	SC
South Of Santa Fe	Brooks & Dunn	22-747	ST
South Of The Border	Cline, Patsy	22-191	CB
South Of The Border	Sinatra, Frank	28-505	DK
South Of The Border	Sinatra, Frank	12-499	P
South Of The Border	Standard	11-298	DK
South Side	Moby	16-259	TT
South the	Cadillac Three	48-457	ASK
South, The	Cadillac 3, FGL, etc	44-290	KC
South's Gonna Do It Again	Charlie Daniels Band	2-17	SC
Southbound	Kershaw, Sammy	1-473	CB
Southbound	Kershaw, Sammy	6-716	MM
Southbound	Kershaw, Sammy	17-272	NA
Southbound	Kershaw, Sammy	2-539	SC
Southern Boy	Charlie Daniels/Tri	18-802	ST
Southern Boy - duet	Charlie Daniels & Tritt	34-357	CB
Southern Fried	Anderson, Bill	5-40	SC
Southern Girl	Cagle, Chris	41-63	PHN
Southern Girl	McGraw, Tim	45-402	BKD

SONG TITLE	ARTIST	#	TYPE
Southern Grace	Little Texas	6-802	MM
Southern Grace	Little Texas	2-767	SC
Southern Lovin'	Brown, Jim Ed	46-536	SSK
Southern Man	Young, Neil	10-502	DA
Southern Nights	Campbell, Glen	11-618	DK
Southern Nights	Campbell, Glen	13-426	P
Southern Nights	Campbell, Glen	8-658	SAV
Southern Nights	Campbell, Glen	5-126	SC
Southern Rains	Tillis, Mel	19-463	CB
Southern Rains	Tillis, Mel	13-521	P
Southern Star	Alabama	4-449	BS
Southern Streamline	Fogerty, John	47-734	SRK
Southern Style	Rucker, Darius	49-783	SSC
Southern Voice	McGraw, Tim	47-237	CB
Souvenirs	Bogguss, Suzy	6-670	MM
Souvenirs	Bogguss, Suzy	2-427	SC
Souvenirs	Buffett, Jimmy	46-131	SC
Souvenirs	Prine, John	23-527	CB
Sowin' Love	Overstreet, Paul	29-771	CB
Space Between	Dave Matthews Band	33-418	CB
Space Between	Dave Matthews Band	16-390	SGB
Space Between	Dave Matthews Band	16-324	TT
Space Oddity	Bowie, David	14-567	AH
Space Oddity	Bowie, David	30-741	SF
Space Truckin'	Deep Purple	13-756	SGB
Spaceman	4 Non Blondes	46-236	KRG
Spaceman	Killers	36-385	SC
Spam	Yankovic, Weird Al	49-840	SC
Spanish Eyes	Humperdinck, E.	37-155	CB
Spanish Eyes	Humperdinck, E.	9-315	STR
Spanish Eyes	Martin, Ricky	9-138	PS
Spanish Eyes	Martin, Ricky	13-741	SGB
Spanish Eyes	Martino, Al	18-238	DK
Spanish Eyes	Martino, Al	29-497	LE
Spanish Eyes	Martino, Al	4-356	SC
Spanish Eyes	Martino, Al	19-786	SGB
Spanish Eyes	Presley, Elvis	25-91	MM
Spanish Eyes	Standard	10-465	MG
Spanish Fire Ball	Snow, Hank	22-133	CB
Spanish Fireball	Stevens, Ray	6-766	MM
Spanish Harlem	Drifters	45-890	LE
Spanish Harlem	King, Ben E.	22-443	SC
Spanish Harlem	Mamas & Papas	47-216	KV
Spanish Nights	Orbison, Roy	47-337	BAT
Spanish Pipedream	Prine, John	23-533	CB
Sparks Are Gonna Fly	Catherine Wheel Th	15-791	THM
Sparks Fly	Swift, Taylor	38-206	AS
Speak	Nickel Creek	19-56	ST
Speak Low	Streisand, Barbra	15-292	PS
Speak Of The Devil	Pirates Of Mississippi	47-565	CB
Speak Softly (You're Talking To My.	Watson, Gene	14-672	CB
Speak To Me Pretty	Lee, Brenda	45-452	EZC

247

SONG TITLE	ARTIST	#	TYPE
Speakin' Of The Devil	Beard, Jan	24-355	SC
Special	Garbage	13-786	SGB
Special	Wilshire	32-322	THM
Special Lady	Ray/Goodman/Brown	2-561	SC
Speed	Montgomery Gentry	34-380	CB
Speed	Montgomery Gentry	25-453	MM
Speed	Montgomery Gentry	18-591	ST
Speed	Montgomery Gentry	32-117	THM
Speed Of Life	Sugarland	30-238	RS
Speed Of Sound	Coldplay	23-316	CB
Speed Of Sound	Coldplay	30-140	PT
Speedball Tucker	Croce, Jim	48-464	CB
Speedo	Cadillacs	25-554	MM
Speedy Gonzales	Boone, Pat	13-446	P
Spend My Time	Black, Clint	19-680	ST
Spend The Night	Earth Wind & Fire	4-284	SC
Spice Up Your Life	Spice Girls	7-702	PHM
Spicks And Specks	Bee Gees	48-691	ZMP
Spiders & Snakes	Stafford, Jim	8-450	CB
Spiders & Snakes	Stafford, Jim	11-347	DK
Spiderwebs	No Doubt	24-110	SC
Spill The Wine	Burdon, Eric & War	15-51	LE
Spill The Wine	Burdon, Eric & War	7-57	MM
Spill The Wine	Burdon, Eric & War	3-132	SC
Spilled Perfume	Tillis, Pam	2-211	SC
Spin	Lifehouse	25-344	MM
Spinning Wheel	Blood Sweat &Tears	16-800	DK
Spinning Wheel	Blood Sweat &Tears	12-859	P
Spinout	Presley, Elvis	8-590	CB
Spirit In The Sky	Greenbaum, Norman	35-102	CB
Spirit In The Sky	Greenbaum,Norman	12-132	DK
Spirit In The Sky	Greenbaum,Norman	5-149	SC
Spirit In The Sky	Kentucky HH	49-706	KV
Spirit Of A Boy Wisdom Of A Man	Travis, Randy	22-674	ST
Splish Splash	Darin, Bobby	11-628	DK
Splish Splash	Darin, Bobby	10-326	KC
Spoken Like A Man	Larsen, Blaine	30-252	CB
Spooky	Classics IV	34-47	CB
Spooky	Classics IV	26-343	DK
Spooky	Classics IV	6-688	MM
Spooky	Classics IV	16-289	TT
Spooky	Springfield, Dusty	48-585	DK
Spotlight	Hudson, Jennifer	36-498	CB
Spotlight	Hudson, Jennifer	38-203	PHM
Spring Affair	Summer, Donna	15-205	LE
Spring Can Really Hang You Up...	Streisand, Barbra	49-599	PS
Springsteen	Church, Eric	43-11	ASK
Squaws Along The Yukon	Thompson, Hank	19-324	CB
Squeeze Box	Who	35-122	CB
Squeeze Box	Who	19-744	LE
Squeeze Box	Who	2-721	SC
Squeeze Me In	Brooks & Yearwood	18-12	CB
Squeeze Me In	Brooks & Yearwood	25-121	MM

SONG TITLE	ARTIST	#	TYPE
Squeeze Me In	Brooks & Yearwood	16-108	ST
St. Elmo's Fire	Parr, John	20-374	SC
St. Elmo's Fire	Parr, John	10-520	SF
St. Louis Blues	Jazz Standard	47-522	VH
St. Louis Blues	Standard	12-14	DK
St. Louis Blues	Wills, Bob	20-700	CB
St. Theresa	Osborne, Joan	10-239	PS
Stacy's Mom	Fountains of Wayne	35-292	CB
Stacy's Mom	Fountains of Wayne	20-226	MM
Stacy's Mom	Fountains of Wayne	23-183	PHM
Stagger Lee	Price, Lloyd	35-1	CB
Stagger Lee	Price, Lloyd	11-384	DK
Stagger Lee	Price, Lloyd	10-700	JVC
Stagger Lee	Price, Lloyd	4-701	SC
Stairway Of Love	Robbins, Marty	48-12	CB
Stairway To Heaven	Led Zeppelin	11-771	DK
Stairway To Heaven	Led Zeppelin	13-225	P
Stake the	Miller, Steve	23-625	BS
Stampede	LeDoux, Chris	5-840	SC
Stan **	Eminem	21-643	TT
Stan **	Eminem & Dido	25-465	MM
Stand	Jewel	20-235	MM
Stand	Jewel	32-433	THM
Stand	Rascal Flatts	30-307	CB
Stand	REM	12-799	P
Stand Back	Nicks, Stevie	16-638	MM
Stand Back	Nicks, Stevie	16-130	SC
Stand Back	Quayle, Stephanie	41-91	PHN
Stand Back Up	Sugarland	23-480	CB
Stand Back Up	Sugarland	30-241	RS
Stand Beside Me	Messina, Jo Dee	8-214	CB
Stand Beside Me	Messina, Jo Dee	22-688	ST
Stand By Me	Gilley, Mickey	8-36	CB
Stand By Me	Gilley, Mickey	16-170	THM
Stand By Me	King, Ben E.	11-372	DK
Stand By Me	King, Ben E.	10-736	JVC
Stand By Me	King, Ben E.	12-626	P
Stand By Me	King, Ben E.	2-81	SC
Stand By Me	Lennon, John	30-300	RS
Stand By Me	Redding, Otis	47-353	KV
Stand By My Woman Man	Milsap, Ronnie	4-572	SC
Stand By You (Instrumental Version)	Platten, Rachel	48-147	BKD
Stand By Your Man	Wynette, Tammy	11-427	DK
Stand By Your Man	Wynette, Tammy	13-343	P
Stand By Your Man	Wynette, Tammy	9-614	SAV
Stand On It	McDaniel, Mel	49-123	DFK
Stand Or Fall	Fixx	16-68	SC
Stand Up	McDaniel, Mel	2-125	SC
Standing In Line	Chris Weaver Band	39-62	PHN
Standing In The Shadows	Four Tops	16-764	DK
Standing Knee Deep In A ...	Mattea, Kathy	2-716	SC
Standing On The Corner	Bennett, Tony	10-406	LE
Standing On The Corner	Four Lads	21-536	SC

248

SONG TITLE	ARTIST	#	TYPE
Standing On The Corner	Martin, Dean	23-81	MM
Standing On The Edge Of Goodbye	Berry, John	2-657	SC
Standing On The Edge Of Love	Gregory, Clinton	24-255	SC
Standing Outside a Broken Phone Boo	Primitive Radio God	24-113	SC
Standing Outside The Fire	Brooks, Garth	6-466	MM
Standing Outside The Fire	Brooks, Garth	3-37	SC
Standing Right Next To Me	Bonoff, Karla	2-229	SC
Standing Room Only	Mandrell, Barbara	48-694	CB
Standing Still	Clark Family Exp.	15-332	CB
Standing Still	Clark Family Exp.	15-194	ST
Standing Still	Jewel	25-42	MM
Standing Still	Jewel	16-78	ST
Standing Tall	Morgan, Lorrie	4-123	SC
Stanger In Your Eyes	Mellons, Ken	7-283	MM
Star	Adams, Bryan	23-447	CB
Star Spangled Banner	Houston, Whitney	20-158	BCI
Star Spangled Banner	Patriotic	44-35	PT
Star Spangled Banner	Standard	12-106	DK
Star Spangled Banner	Standard	12-614	P
Star Spangled Banner - Patriotic	Standard	33-210	CB
Star Star	Rolling Stones	20-204	SC
Stardust	Cole, Nat "King"	43-226	CB
Stardust	Crosby, Bing	29-419	CB
Stardust	Nelson, Willie	38-80	CB
Stardust	Standard	27-54	DK
Stardust	Ward & Dominos	12-528	P
Starry Starry Nights (Vincent)	Denver, John	48-488	CKC
Stars Fell On Alabama	Sinatra, Frank	19-790	SGB
Stars On The Water	Strait, George	18-208	ST
Stars Over Texas	Lawrence, Tracy	1-583	CB
Stars Over Texas	Lawrence, Tracy	7-339	MM
StarShine	Sweetwater Rain	39-59	PHN
Start All Over	Cyrus, Miley	36-72	WD
Start Me Up	Rolling Stones	18-22	LE
Start Over Georgia	Raye, Collin	10-208	SC
Start Over Georgia	Raye, Collin	22-428	ST
Start The Car	Tritt, Travis	14-613	SC
Startin' Over Blues	Diffie, Joe	24-356	SC
Startin' With Me	Owen, Jake	30-175	CB
Starting Over Again	McEntire, Reba	1-790	CB
Starting Over Again	McEntire, Reba	4-204	SC
Starting Over Again	Parton, Dolly	8-542	CB
Starting Today	Presley, Elvis	25-95	MM
Starts With Goodbye	Underwood, Carrie	30-125	AS
Starwood In Aspen	Denver, John	49-250	DFK
State Fair	Supernaw, Doug	2-321	SC
State Of Mind	Black, Clint	1-120	CB
State Of Mind	Black, Clint	6-456	MM
State Of Mind	Black, Clint	30-431	THM
Statesboro Blues	Allman Brothers	15-312	SC

SONG TITLE	ARTIST	#	TYPE
Statue	Low Millions	29-322	PHM
Statue Of A Fool	Greene, Jack	43-342	CB
Statue Of A Fool	VanShelton, Ricky	8-555	CB
Statue Of A Fool	VanShelton, Ricky	17-288	NA
Statue Of A Fool	VanShelton, Ricky	2-621	SC
Statues Without Hearts	Gatlin, Larry	34-226	CB
Stay	Browne, Jackson	23-617	BS
Stay	Eternal	15-759	NU
Stay	Florida Georgia Line	43-95	HM
Stay	Hollies	44-371	ZM
Stay	Rihanna	45-8	ASK
Stay	Sugarland	30-452	CB
Stay	Williams, Maurice	34-1	CB
Stay	Williams, Maurice	17-106	DK
Stay	Williams, Maurice	6-654	MM
Stay (Faraway So Close)	Al B. Sure!	18-475	NU
Stay (I Missed You)	Loeb & Nine Stories	4-666	SC
Stay (I Missed You)	Loeb, Lisa	14-198	CB
Stay (I Missed You)	Loeb, Lisa	6-631	MM
Stay A Little Longer	Brothers Osborne	49-785	SS
Stay A Little Longer	Wills, Bob	20-703	CB
Stay A Little Longer	Wills, Bob	6-6	SC
Stay Away From The Apple Tree	Spears, Billie Jo	49-377	CB
Stay Away Joe	Presley, Elvis	25-108	MM
Stay Beautiful	Swift, Taylor	36-86	BM
Stay By Me	Eurythmics	47-113	SFG
Stay Forever	Ketchum, Hal	2-652	SC
Stay Gone	Wayne, Jimmy	34-368	CB
Stay Gone	Wayne, Jimmy	25-521	MM
Stay Gone	Wayne, Jimmy	18-804	ST
Stay Gone	Wayne, Jimmy	32-187	THM
Stay In My Corner	Dells	25-169	MM
Stay On These Roads	A-Ha	46-238	KV
Stay Out Of My Arms	Strait, George	4-119	SC
Stay The Night	Zedd feat Hayley Williams	43-158	PHM
Stay The Same	McEntire, Joey	7-844	PHM
Stay There Til I Get There	Anderson, Lynn	47-643	CB
Stay Together For the Kids	Blink 182	36-138	SGB
Stay Together For The Kids	Blink 182	16-322	TT
Stay Up Late	Newfield, Heidi	38-221	CB
Stay With Me (Brass Bed)	Gracin, Josh	23-122	CB
Stay With Me Tonight	Osborne, Jeffrey	25-283	MM
Stay Young	Williams, Don	9-437	SAV
Stay Young	Williams, Don	5-556	SC
Stayin' Alive	Bee Gees	18-111	DK
Stayin' Alive	Bee Gees	17-497	LE
Stayin' Alive	Bee Gees	2-499	SC
Stays In Mexico	Keith, Toby	23-394	CB
Stays In Mexico	Keith, Toby	30-12	SC
Stays In Mexico	Keith, Toby	20-487	ST
Steady As She Goes	Collie, Mark	3-631	SC
Steady At The Wheel	Jennings, Shooter	29-47	CB

SONG TITLE	ARTIST	#	TYPE
Steal Away	Dupree, Robbie	14-568	AH
Steal Away	Dupree, Robbie	28-323	DK
Steal Away	Whitesnake	48-568	DK
Steal My Kisses	Harper, Ben	13-840	PHM
Steal My Kisses (Radio Version)	Harper& Innocent Cr	14-465	SC
Steal My Sunshine	Len	8-497	PHT
Steal My Sunshine	Len	10-205	SC
Steal My Sunshine - duet	Len	33-407	CB
Stealin'	Uriah Heep	19-138	SGB
Stealing Cinderella	Wicks, Chuck	30-580	CB
Stealing Kisses	Hill, Faith	29-591	CB
Steam	Brooks, Garth	48-359	THM
Steam	Herndon, Ty	14-694	CB
Steam	Herndon, Ty	5-732	SC
Steam	Herndon, Ty	22-507	ST
Steamroller (Live)	Taylor, James	14-600	SC
Steamroller Blues	Presley & Philharmonics	49-653	KV
Steamroller Blues	Presley, Elvis	18-446	KC
Steamroller Blues	Taylor, James	11-278	DK
Steamroller Blues	Taylor, James	10-68	SC
Steamy Windows	Turner, Tina	9-685	SAV
Steelo	702	24-371	SC
Stella By Starlight	Sinatra, Frank	28-498	DK
Stella By Starlight	Standard	15-562	SGB
Stellar	Incubus	15-643	THM
Step Aside	Young, Faron	45-729	VH
Step By Step	Crests	7-266	MM
Step By Step	Houston, Whitney	49-311	BC
Step By Step	New Kids On Block	33-347	CB
Step By Step	New Kids On Block	11-531	DK
Step By Step	Rabbitt, Eddie	13-455	P
Step In The Name Of Love	Kelly, R.	49-520	SC
Step Off	Musgraves, Kacey	45-313	KV
Step Right Up	Cactus Choir	8-309	CB
Step That Step	Sawyer Brown	20-15	SC
Steppin' Out	Jackson, Joe	28-369	DK
Steppin' Out (Gonna Boogie Tonight)	Orlando & Dawn	49-323	CB
Steppin' Out With My Baby	Bennett, Tony	18-246	DK
Stepping Stone	White, Lari	8-495	CB
Stepping Stone	White, Lari	22-806	ST
Steve McQueen	Crow, Sheryl	18-428	CB
Steve McQueen	Crow, Sheryl	25-343	MM
Steve McQueen	Crow, Sheryl	29-676	RS
Stewball	Peter, Paul & Mary	5-237	SC
Sticks And Stones	Lawrence, Tracy	1-571	CB
Sticks And Stones	Lawrence, Tracy	10-786	JVC
Stiletto	Joel, Billy	5-687	SC
Still	98 Degrees	15-373	SKG
Still	Anderson, Bill	20-783	CB
Still	Anderson, Bill	12-308	DK
Still	Commodores	26-472	DK
Still	Commodores	14-355	MH

SONG TITLE	ARTIST	#	TYPE
Still	Gray, Macy	23-263	HS
Still	McGraw, Tim	47-239	CB
Still	McKnight, Brian	25-83	MM
Still	Richie, Lionel	10-396	LE
Still A Lot Of Chicken Left On That Bone	Morgan, Craig	48-280	CB
Still Crazy After All These Years	Simon, Paul	46-128	SC
Still Doin' Time	Jones, George	8-205	CB
Still Doin' Time	Jones, George	4-731	SC
Still Frame	Trapt	23-179	PHM
Still Got The Blues	Moore, Gary	14-594	SC
Still Got This Thing	Miles, Alannah	48-507	KVD
Still Holding On	Black & McBride	1-840	CB
Still Holding On	Black & McBride	7-639	CHM
Still Holding On	Black, Clint	22-598	ST
Still Holding Out For You	SheDaisy	15-96	ST
Still In Love With You	Jonas Brothers	36-543	WD
Still In Love With You	Tritt, Travis	8-144	CB
Still In Love With You	Tritt, Travis	22-420	ST
Still Lovin' You	Kershaw, Sammy	4-25	SC
Still Lovin' You	Scorpions	5-494	SC
Still Lovin' You	Scorpions	49-95	SC
Still Loving You	Luman, Bob	5-778	SC
Still On My Brain	Timberlake, Justin	19-656	CB
Still On My Brain	Timberlake, Justin	32-384	THM
Still On Your Side	BB Mak	14-40	THM
Still Smokin'	Clark, Jameson	16-695	ST
Still Standing	Roys	39-76	PHN
Still Standing Tall	Seals, Brady	48-98	MM
Still Taking Chances	Murphy, Michael M	5-539	SC
Still The One	Orleans	16-405	PR
Still The One	Orleans	22-923	SC
Still The Same	Seger, Bob	10-172	UK
Still Thinkin' 'Bout You	Craddock, Billy C	5-663	SC
Still Waiting	Sum 41	23-160	PHM
Still Water	Four Tops	43-425	CB
Stillness Of Heart	Kravitz, Lenny	18-289	CB
Stir It Up	LaBelle, Patti	49-240	DFK
Stir It Up	Marley, Bob	12-797	P
Stitches	Mendes, Shawn	48-439	KCD
Stole	Rowland, Kelly	35-267	CB
Stole	Rowland, Kelly	32-15	THM
Stole My Heart	One Direction	39-112	PHM
Stomp	Brothers Johnson	15-45	SS
Stomp Them Grapes	Tillis, Mel	19-456	CB
Stone Cold Country	Gibson Miller Band	47-872	NT
Stone Cold Sober	Gilbert, Brantley	49-371	BKD
Stone the	Berry, John	8-135	CB
Stone the	Berry, John	22-652	ST
Stoned	Dido	29-234	ZM
Stoned Soul Picnic	5th Dimension	11-288	DK
Stoned Soul Picnic	5th Dimension	9-703	SAV
Stones	Diamond, Neil	47-419	MM
Stones In The Road	Carpenter, M C	47-669	SC
Stones In The Road	Walker, Mike	17-606	CB
Stoney	Lobo	46-334	MDG

250

SONG TITLE	ARTIST	#	TYPE
Stoney End	Streisand, Barbra	11-735	DK
Stood Up	Nelson, Ricky	21-705	CB
Stood Up	Nelson, Ricky	20-39	SC
Stop	Brooks, Meredith	16-227	PHM
Stop	Spice Girls	10-141	SC
Stop	Spice Girls	21-594	SF
Stop & Stare	OneRepublic	49-855	SC
Stop And Smell The Roses	Davis, Mac	23-514	CB
Stop And Smell The Roses	Davis, Mac	4-330	SC
Stop And Stare	OneRepublic	36-457	CB
Stop And Stare	OneRepublic	44-107	SC
Stop Complainint	Roe, Tommy	48-117	CB
Stop Draggin' My Heart Around	Nicks & Petty	13-199	P
Stop Drop And Roll	Lawrence, Tracy	44-182	ASK
Stop In The Name Of Love	Ross, Diana	15-357	LE
Stop In The Name Of Love	Supremes	29-842	SC
Stop Look & Listen	Presley, Elvis	25-114	MM
Stop Look And Listen	Cline, Patsy	45-490	CB
Stop Stop Stop	Hollies	44-359	LG
Stop The World	Cline, Patsy	45-509	CB
Stop The World	Yoakam, Dwight	49-694	DCK
Stop The World And Let Me Off	Nerney, Declan	45-852	VH
Stop To Love	Vandross, Luther	12-78	DK
Stop Your Sobbing	Kinks	48-185	ZMJ
Stop! In The Name Of Love	Supremes	11-173	DK
Stop! In The Name Of Love	Supremes	12-631	P
Stop! In The Name Of Love	Supremes	9-23	PS
Storm In The Heartland	Cyrus, Billy Ray	17-269	NA
Storm In The Heartland	Cyrus, Billy Ray	2-542	SC
Storm Is Over the	Kelly, R.	16-260	TT
Storm Warning	Hayes, Hunter	39-53	ASK
Storm Warning	Hayes, Hunter	38-249	PHN
Storms Never Last	Dr. Hook	47-50	ZM
Storms Never Last - Duet	Colter & Jennings	44-66	KV
Storms Never Last - duet	Jennings & Colter	45-185	DCK
Stormy	Classics IV	6-789	MM
Stormy Monday	Walker, T-Bone	15-321	SC
Stormy Monday Blues	Allman Brothers	11-296	DK
Stormy Monday Blues	Allman Brothers	7-222	MM
Stormy Monday Blues	Bland, Bobby Blu	47-725	KV
Stormy Weather	Horne, Lena	2-242	SC
Story Of My Life	Diamond, Neil	47-413	DKM
Story Of My Life	Williams, Don	45-219	SFM
Story Of My Life the	Robbins, Marty	3-237	CB
Story Of My Life the	Robbins, Marty	4-862	SC
Story Of My Life the	Robbins, Marty	10-599	SF
Story Of Us	Swift, Taylor	37-357	CB
Story Untold	Nutmegs	25-550	MM

SONG TITLE	ARTIST	#	TYPE
Storyline	Hayes, Hunter	45-460	BKD
Straight From The Heart	Adams, Bryan	23-434	CB
Straight Life the	Goldsboro, Bobby	45-877	TB
Straight Lines	Silverchair	37-122	SC
Straight On	Heart	24-424	SC
Straight Talk	Parton, Dolly	8-546	CB
Straight Talk	Parton, Dolly	4-478	SC
Straight Tequila	Triggs, Trini	8-179	CB
Straight Tequila Night	Anderson, John	13-527	P
Straight Tequila Night	Anderson, John	9-539	SAV
Straight Tequila Night	Anderson, John	2-635	SC
Straighten Up And Fly Right	Cole, Nat "King"	12-574	P
Strange	Cline, Patsy	6-723	MM
Strange	McEntire, Reba	49-421	KV
Strange Brew	Cream	12-327	DK
Strange Days	Doors	18-654	SO
Strange Magic	ELO	3-130	SC
Strange Way	Firefall	16-406	PR
Stranger	Kristofferson, Kris	45-206	OZP
Stranger (What Doesn't Kill You)	Clarkson, Kelly	39-49	ASK
Stranger In A Strange Land	Streisand, Barbra	49-623	ST
Stranger In My Arms	Cline, Patsy	45-505	LE
Stranger In My Hometown	Presley, Elvis	25-120	MM
Stranger In My House	Milsap, Ronnie	8-684	SAV
Stranger In My House	Milsap, Ronnie	14-425	SC
Stranger In My House	Tamia	12-388	PHM
Stranger In My Mirror	Travis, Randy	8-929	CB
Stranger In My Mirror	Travis, Randy	7-888	CHT
Stranger In My Mirror	Travis, Randy	22-729	ST
Stranger In My Place a	Murray, Anne	11-17	PL
Stranger In Paradise	Bennett, Tony	10-412	LE
Stranger In Paradise	Bennett, Tony	10-606	SF
Stranger In The Crowd	Presley, Elvis	25-749	MM
Stranger Just A Friend, A	Reeves, Jim	44-261	OZP
Stranger the	Joel, Billy	48-11	SC
Stranger Things Have Happened	Milsap, Ronnie	2-521	SC
Strangers In The Night	Sinatra, Frank	11-568	DK
Strangers In The Night	Sinatra, Frank	10-723	JVC
Strangers In The Night	Sinatra, Frank	12-520	P
Strangers In The Night	Sinatra, Frank	9-251	PT
Stranglehold	Nugent, Ted	36-129	SGB
Stranglers In The Night	Parody	47-878	ADU
Strarting Over	Lennon, John	9-650	SAV
Straw Hat And Old Dirty Hank	Barenaked Ladies	30-618	RS
Strawberry Fair	Newley, Anthony	29-819	SF
Strawberry Fields Forever	Beatles	11-234	DK
Strawberry Fields Forever	Beatles	12-926	P
Strawberry Fields Forever	Beatles	7-527	SAV

SONG TITLE	ARTIST	#	TYPE
Strawberry Wine	Carter, Deana	4-422	SC
Stray Cat Strut	Stray Cats	35-168	CB
Stray Cat Strut	Stray Cats	2-32	SC
Stray Cat Strut	Stray Cats	13-697	SGB
Streak the	Stevens, Ray	16-489	CB
Streak the	Stevens, Ray	2-179	SC
Street Fighting Man	Rolling Stones	18-21	LE
Street Fighting Man	Rolling Stones	14-404	PT
Street Life	Crawford, Randy	11-18	PX
Street Symphony	Monica	8-356	PHT
Streetcorner Symphony	Thomas, Rob	47-608	SC
Streets Of Bakersfield	Yoakam, Dwight	49-679	STT
Streets Of Bakersfield - duet	Yoakam & Owens	49-686	CB
Streets Of Baltimore	Pride, Charley	47-442	KV
Streets Of Baltimore the	Bare, Bobby	3-708	CB
Streets Of Baltimore the	Bare, Bobby	5-367	SC
Streets Of Heaven	Austin, Sherrie	34-421	CB
Streets Of Heaven	Austin, Sherrie	25-648	MM
Streets Of Heaven	Austin, Sherrie	19-178	ST
Streets Of Heaven	Austin, Sherrie	32-342	THM
Streets Of Laredo	Arnold, Eddy	7-355	MM
Streets Of Laredo	Robbins, Marty	8-436	CB
Streets Of Laredo	Standard	27-445	DK
Streets Of Philadelphia	Springsteen, Bruce	17-617	LE
Strength Of A Woman	Shaggy	32-93	THM
Strength Of A Woman the	Claypool, Philip	4-127	SC
Strength Of A Woman the	Shaggy	25-399	MM
Stricken	Disturbed	29-249	SC
Strip It Down	Bryan, Luke	45-30	BKD
Stripper the	David Rose Band	2-76	SC
Stroke the **	Squier, Billy	2-726	SC
Strokin' **	Carter, Clarence	30-665	RSX
Strokin' **	Carter, Clarence	2-188	SC
Stroll the	Diamonds	27-490	DK
Stroll the - DANCE #	Diamonds	22-396	SC
Strong Enough	Cher	33-375	CB
Strong Enough	Cher	8-34	PHT
Strong Enough	Cher	14-53	RS
Strong Enough	Cher	10-182	SC
Strong Enough	Cher	13-701	SGB
Strong Enough	Crow, Sheryl	29-674	RS
Strong Enough	Crow, Sheryl	10-53	SC
Strong Enough	Jackson, Alan	49-181	KV
Strong Enough To Be Your Man	Tritt, Travis	34-392	CB
Strong Enough To Be Your Man	Tritt, Travis	18-129	ST
Strong Enough To Bend	Tucker, Tanya	16-339	CB
Strong Enough To Bend	Tucker, Tanya	11-719	DK
Strong Heart	Sheppard, T.G.	5-673	SC
Strong One the	Black, Clint	30-479	CB
Strong One the	Mason, Mila	8-483	CB
Strong Strong Wind	Air Supply	46-402	SBI
Stronger	Spears, Britney	33-435	CB

SONG TITLE	ARTIST	#	TYPE
Stronger	Spears, Britney	15-427	PHM
Stronger Beer	Hicks, Tim	47-498	DFK
Stronger Than I Am	Womack, Lee Ann	48-483	CKC
Strut	Easton, Sheena	17-510	SC
Strutter	Kiss	10-35	SC
Struttin' My Stuff	Bishop, Elvin	46-518	CB
Stubborn Love	Lumineers	48-419	SBI
Stuck	Orrico, Stacie	34-176	CB
Stuck	Orrico, Stacie	20-379	HP
Stuck	Orrico, Stacie	25-631	MM
Stuck	Orrico, Stacie	20-625	NS
Stuck	Orrico, Stacie	32-208	THM
Stuck In A Moment You Can't Get..	U2	15-817	CB
Stuck In Love	Judds	13-820	CHM
Stuck In The Middle With You	Stealers Wheel	2-151	SC
Stuck On You	Caldwell, Bobby	9-384	AH
Stuck On You	Presley, Elvis	11-605	DK
Stuck On You	Presley, Elvis	13-264	P
Stuck On You	Presley, Elvis	2-601	SC
Stuck On You	Presley, Elvis	14-762	THM
Stuck On You	Richie, Lionel	10-388	LE
Stuck On You	Richie, Lionel	16-161	SC
Stuck On You	Rogers, Kenny	45-611	OZP
Stuck With You	Lewis & The News	15-563	CMC
Stuck With You	Lewis & The News	17-112	DK
Stuck With You	Lewis & The News	21-741	MH
Stuff	Diamond Rio	14-713	CB
Stuff Like That There	Midler, Bette	45-935	KV
Stuff That Dreams Are Made Of	Simon, Carly	49-148	CB
Stupid	McLachlan, Sarah	20-574	CB
Stupid	Musgraves, Kacey	45-434	KVD
Stupid Boy	Urban, Keith	30-244	CB
Stupid Cupid	Cline, Patsy	45-516	MM
Stupid Cupid	Francis, Connie	10-332	KC
Stupid Cupid	Francis, Connie	4-694	SC
Stupid Girl	Cold	19-602	CB
Stupid Girl	Cold	32-221	THM
Stupid Girl	Garbage	24-115	SC
Stupid Things	Cook, Elizabeth	18-601	ST
Stutter	Joe & Mystikal	15-457	PHM
Stutter	Joe & Mystikal	18-576	TT
Style	Swift, Taylor	48-304	KV
Substitute	Who	28-148	DK
Substitute	Who	19-743	LE
Subterranean Homesick Blues	Dylan, Bob	29-106	CB
Subterranean Homesick Blues	Dylan, Bob	18-175	DK
Success	Lynn, Loretta	47-632	CB
Such A Fool	Drusky, Roy	20-754	CB
Such An Easy Question	Presley, Elvis	8-589	CB
Sucked Out	Superdrag	24-228	SC
Sucu Sucu	Johnson, Lonnie	29-821	SF
Suddenly	Ocean, Billy	6-570	MM

SONG TITLE	ARTIST	#	TYPE
Suddenly	Ocean, Billy	2-277	SC
Suddenly	Rimes, LeAnn	25-569	MM
Suddenly	Rimes, LeAnn	18-806	ST
Suddenly	Soraya	24-49	SC
Suddenly I See	Tunstall, K.T.	30-267	CB
Suddenly Last Summer	Motels	19-360	DK
Suddenly Last Summer	Motels	24-569	SC
Suddenly Single	Clark, Terri	4-403	SC
Suds In The Bucket	Evans, Sara	29-543	CB
Suds In The Bucket	Evans, Sara	20-383	ST
Suffocate	Holiday, J.	36-460	CB
Suffocate **	Cold	23-181	PHM
Sugar	Maroon 5	48-434	KCD
Sugar	Nettles, Jennifer	49-784	SS
Sugar And Spice	Spears, Billie Jo	10-565	SF
Sugar Moon	Boone, Pat	47-792	SRK
Sugar Moon	Wills, Bob	19-634	CB
Sugar Shack	Gilmer, Jimmy	12-115	DK
Sugar Sugar	Archies	35-67	CB
Sugar Sugar	Archies	27-521	DK
Sugar Sugar	Archies	13-113	P
Sugar Sugar	Archies	9-697	SAV
Sugar Town	Sinatra, Nancy	12-719	P
Sugar Town	Sinatra, Nancy	6-49	SC
Sugar Walls **	Easton, Sheena	15-4	SC
Sugar We're Goin' Down	Fall Out Boy	30-137	PT
Sugar We're Goin' Out	Fall Out Boy	45-447	EZH
Sugarbush	Day, Doris	48-140	ZMP
Sugarfoot Rag	Foley, Red	5-213	SC
Sugarland	Earle, Steve	46-180	KV
Sugartime	McGuire Sisters	2-247	SC
Suite Judy Blue Eyes	Crosby Stills & Nash	3-447	SC
Suite Madam Blue	Styx	47-376	AH
Sukiyaki	4 PM	12-196	DK
Sukiyaki	Taste Of Honey	13-290	P
Sultans Of Swing	Dire Straits	11-645	DK
Summer (The First Time)	Goldsboro, Bobby	45-876	SF
Summer Breeze	Mraz, Jason	47-299	KV
Summer Breeze	Seals & Croft	29-634	SC
Summer Buddies	Kelly, R.	49-705	KV
Summer Country Friday Night	Brice, Lee	38-92	PHM
Summer Girl	Andrews, Jessica	23-294	CB
Summer Girls	LFO	10-203	SC
Summer Holiday	Cliff, Richard	48-752	P
Summer In Dixie	Confederate RR	17-262	NA
Summer In The City	Lovin' Spoonful	35-61	CB
Summer In The City	Lovin' Spoonful	11-647	DK
Summer Is Over - duet	McLaughlin & Bareilles	48-734	PHM
Summer Knows the	Streisand, Barbra	12-887	P
Summer Means Fun	Jan & Dean	49-36	SHER
Summer Night City	Abba	19-80	MM
Summer Nights	Rascal Flatts	37-49	CB
Summer Nights	Travolta & Newton-John	12-95	DK

SONG TITLE	ARTIST	#	TYPE
Summer Nights	Travolta & Newton-John	13-142	P
Summer Nights	Travolta & Newton-John	9-277	SC
Summer Nights	Travolta & Newton-John	10-531	SF
Summer Nights - duet	Grease	49-426	SDK
Summer Nights - duet	Newton-John & Travolta	33-253	CB
Summer Of ' 69	Adams, Bryan	23-437	CB
Summer Of ' 69	Adams, Bryan	7-487	MM
Summer Of ' 69	Adams, Bryan	16-527	P
Summer Of Love	Steps	20-5	SGB
Summer Place a	Lettermen	48-527	L1
Summer Rain	Carlisle, Belinda	21-599	SF
Summer Rain	Rivers, Johnny	47-367	RSX
Summer Rain	Thomas, Carl	14-20	THM
Summer Side of Life	Lightfoot, Gordon	43-481	SK
Summer Song	Orbison, Roy	38-65	PS
Summer Sunshine	Corrs	23-565	MM
Summer Wind	Buble, Michael	30-183	LE
Summer Wind	Sinatra, Frank	34-15	CB
Summer Wind	Sinatra, Frank	20-763	KB
Summer Wind	Sinatra, Frank	12-558	P
Summer Wind	Sinatra, Frank	9-256	PT
Summer Wind	Sinatra, Frank	2-204	SC
Summer Wine	Sinatra, N & Hazelwood	44-322	DFK
Summer's Comin'	Black, Clint	1-836	CB
Summer's Comin'	Black, Clint	2-824	SC
Summerfling	Lang, k.d.	47-168	MM
Summertime	Chesney, Kenny	29-573	CB
Summertime	Chesney, Kenny	37-311	SC
Summertime	Cooke, Sam	46-635	KV
Summertime	Joplin, Janis	15-224	LE
Summertime	New Kids on Block	36-441	CB
Summertime	Standard	13-637	SGB
Summertime	Stewart, Billy	11-224	DK
Summertime	Stewart, Billy	3-318	MH
Summertime	Stewart, Billy	7-71	MM
Summertime - Duet	Armstrong & Fitzgerald	44-112	KV
Summertime Blues	Brian Setzer Orch	46-532	KV
Summertime Blues	Cochran, Eddie	11-188	DK
Summertime Blues	Jackson, Alan	1-46	CB
Summertime Blues	Jackson, Alan	20-401	MH
Summertime Blues	Jackson, Alan	6-601	MM
Summertime Blues	Jackson, Alan	17-218	NA
Summertime Blues	Jackson, Alan	2-312	SC
Summertime Blues	Who	13-222	P
Summertime Girls	Y & T	6-24	SC
Summertime Sadness	Del Rey, Lana	43-81	MRH
Summerzcool	Buffett, Jimmy	46-149	PS
Sun Ain't Gonna Shine Anymore	Walker Brothers	3-127	SC
Sun Always Shines On TV	A-Ha	46-237	CK
Sun Daze	Florida Georgia Line	45-155	BKD

253

SONG TITLE	ARTIST	#	TYPE
Sun King	Beatles	44-122	KV
Sun the	Maroon 5	21-686	Z
Sunday And Me	Jay & Americans	14-369	PS
Sunday Bloody Sunday	U2	16-71	SC
Sunday Girl	Blondie	10-549	SF
Sunday In New York	Darin, Bobby	47-9	MM
Sunday Kind Of Love	McEntire, Reba	1-816	CB
Sunday Kind Of Love a	Harptones	25-180	MM
Sunday Kind Of Love a	James, Etta	25-667	MM
Sunday Mornin' Comin' Down	Cash, Johnny	8-423	CB
Sunday Mornin' Comin' Down	Cash, Johnny	9-601	SAV
Sunday Mornin' Comin' Down	Cash, Johnny	5-196	SC
Sunday Mornin' Comin' Down	Kristofferson, Kris	45-204	DCK
Sunday Morning	Maroon 5	22-344	CB
Sunday Morning	Maroon 5	21-683	Z
Sunday Morning In America	Anderson, Keith	30-443	CB
Sunday Morning Sunshine	Chapin, Harry	46-566	KV
Sunday Sunrise	Lee, Brenda	9-615	SAV
Sundown	Lightfoot, Gordon	9-319	AG
Sundown	Lightfoot, Gordon	43-26	CB
Sundown	Lightfoot, Gordon	4-379	SC
Sundown	Lightfoot, Gordon	43-488	SK
Sunglasses At Night	Hart, Corey	14-569	AH
Sunglasses At Night	Hart, Corey	5-382	SC
Sunny	Hebb, Bobby	35-60	CB
Sunny	Hebb, Bobby	17-133	DK
Sunny	Hebb, Bobby	6-266	MM
Sunny	Hebb, Bobby	13-52	P
Sunny Afternoon	Kinks	48-179	LE
Sunny Afternoon	Kinks	3-726	SC
Sunny Afternoon	Kinks	10-668	SF
Sunny And 75	Nichols, Joe	42-34	ASK
Sunny And 75	Nichols, Joe	44-329	SSC
Sunny Came Home	Colvin, Shawn	16-398	PR
Sunny Came Home	Colvin, Shawn	15-564	SC
Sunny In Seattle	Shelton, Blake	47-445	FTX
Sunrise	Jones, Norah	20-537	CB
Sunrise	Simply Re	32-392	THM
Sunrise Sunset	Fiddler On The Roof	6-321	MM
Sunset	Orbison, Roy	38-66	PS
Sunset Grill	Henley, Don	48-155	ZMP
Sunshine	Aerosmith	16-83	ST
Sunshine	Edwards, Jonathan	7-58	MM
Sunshine	Edwards, Jonathan	2-780	SC
Sunshine	Keane	21-691	Z
Sunshine	Rogers, Kenny	9-364	MG
Sunshine (Radio Version)	Aerosmith	16-88	SC
Sunshine And Summertime	Hill, Faith	30-85	CB
Sunshine And Whiskey	Ballard, Frankie	49-757	BKD
Sunshine Girl	Herman's Hermits	47-141	ZM

SONG TITLE	ARTIST	#	TYPE
Sunshine Lollipops And Rainbows	Gore, Lesley	47-111	SBI
Sunshine Of Your Love	Cream	3-128	SC
Sunshine On My Shoulder	Denver, John	11-613	DK
Sunshine On My Shoulder	Denver, John	36-143	LE
Sunshine Superman	Donovan	27-108	DK
Sunshine Superman	Donovan	3-463	SC
Sunshine Superman	Donovan	30-763	SF
Sunspot Baby	Seger, Bob	19-282	SGB
Suntan City	Bryan, Luke	45-856	KCD
Super Bad	Brown, James	29-138	LE
Super Duper Love	Stone, Joss	43-120	ZPA
Super Kind Of Woman	Hart, Freddie	29-649	SC
Super Love	Exile	17-347	DK
Super Trouper	Abba	7-507	MM
Supercalifragilisticexpea lidocious	Mary Poppins	49-851	SGB
Superfly	Mayfield, Curtis	28-110	DK
Superfreak	James, Rick	15-700	LE
Superman	Black Lace	49-52	ZVS
Superman	Eminem	32-198	THM
Superman	Fargo, Donna	8-837	CB
Superman	Five For Fighting	15-812	CB
Superman	Five For Fighting	20-378	HP
Superman	Five For Fighting	18-401	MM
Superman	Streisand, Barbra	45-867	VH
Superman Inside	Clapton, Eric	15-302	THM
Superman's Dead	Our Lady Peace	6-37	SC
Supermassive Black Hole	Muse	30-721	SF
Supersonic Rocket Ship	Kinks	48-177	LE
Superstar	Carpenters	11-733	DK
Superstar	Stewart, Rod	16-219	MM
Superstar	Studdard, Ruben	36-326	PS
Superstar	Studdard, Ruben	19-543	SC
Superstition	Wonder, Stevie	12-26	DK
Superstition	Wonder, Stevie	25-282	MM
Superwoman	White, Karyn	19-359	DK
Suppose	Presley, Elvis	25-96	MM
Sure Be Cool If You Did	Shelton, Blake	42-32	ASK
Sure Feels Like Love	Gatlin, Larry	47-108	CB
Sure Feels Real Good	Peterson, Michael	8-973	CB
Sure Feels Real Good	Peterson, Michael	22-509	ST
Sure Feels Real Good	Peterson, Michael	16-198	THM
Sure Gonna Miss Her	Lewis & Playboys	14-464	SC
Sure Thing	Foster & Lloyd	5-867	SC
Surf City	Jan & Dean	33-246	CB
Surf City	Jan & Dean	15-565	DK
Surfer Girl	Beach Boys	12-670	P
Surfin' Safari	Beach Boys	46-492	LE
Surfin' USA	Beach Boys	5-507	BS
Surfin' USA	Beach Boys	16-776	DK
Surfin' USA	Beach Boys	3-324	MH
Surfin' USA	Beach Boys	12-733	P
Surprise	Stone, Doug	9-421	CB

SONG TITLE	ARTIST	#	TYPE
Surrender	Cheap Trick	17-81	DK
Surrender	Cheap Trick	4-566	SC
Surrey With The Fringe On	Oklahoma	12-292	DK
Survivor	Destiny's Child	15-453	PHM
Survivor	Destiny's Child	18-534	TT
Susie Darling	Roe, Tommy	48-118	CB
Susie Q	CCR	5-349	SC
Suspended Animation	Hollies	44-378	ZM
Suspicion	Presley, Elvis	18-523	KC
Suspicion	Presley, Elvis	14-779	THM
Suspicion	Stafford, Terry	11-530	DK
Suspicion	Stafford, Terry	7-69	MM
Suspicions	McGraw, Tim	30-440	CB
Suspicions	Rabbitt, Eddie	33-56	CB
Suspicions	Rabbitt, Eddie	9-572	SAV
Suspicions	Rabbitt, Eddie	4-641	SC
Suspicious Minds	Presley, Elvis	16-851	DK
Suspicious Minds	Presley, Elvis	13-40	P
Suspicious Minds	Presley, Elvis	2-588	SC
Suspicious Minds	Presley, Elvis	14-780	THM
Suspicious Minds	Yoakam, Dwight	49-680	SC
Sussuidio	Collins, Phil	20-299	CB
Suzie-Q	CCR	33-255	CB
Swalbr	Clapton, Eric	13-794	SGB
Swamp Music	Lynryd Skynyrd	5-266	SC
Swamp Music	Lynyrd Skynyrd	19-819	SGB
Swamp Witch	Stafford, Jim	47-521	VH
Swanee	Crosby, Bing	9-549	SAV
Swanee	Garland, Judy	7-194	MM
Swanee	Jolson, Al	29-468	LE
Swanee	Jolson, Al	12-941	PS
Swanee River (Old Folks At Home)	Standard	27-457	DK
Sway	Buble, Michael	30-184	LE
Sway	Martin, Dean	7-182	MM
Sway	Rydell, Bobby	47-476	SF
Swayin To The Music	Rivers, Johnny	21-512	SC
Swear It Again	Westlife	16-233	PHM
Sweat (A la la la la lon...)	Inner Circle	6-365	MM
Sweet	Keith, Toby	47-159	CB
Sweet & Wild	Bentley, Dierks	36-247	PHM
Sweet Adeline	Miller, Mitch	23-550	CB
Sweet And Innocent	Osmond, Donny	47-851	SBI
Sweet Annie	Zac Brown Band	43-89	HM
Sweet Baby James	Taylor, James	2-560	SC
Sweet By And By	Lambert, Miranda	48-749	BKD
Sweet By And By (Inst)	Lambert, Miranda	49-414	BKD
Sweet Caroline	Diamond, Neil	7-546	AH
Sweet Caroline	Diamond, Neil	30-686	LE
Sweet Caroline	Diamond, Neil	30-511	THM
Sweet Cherry Wine	James & Shondells	3-466	SC
Sweet Child O' Mine	Crow, Sheryl	8-247	PHT
Sweet Child O' Mine	Crow, Sheryl	29-679	RS
Sweet Child O' Mine	Crow, Sheryl	10-55	SC
Sweet Child O' Mine	Guns & Roses	11-320	DK
Sweet Child O' Mine	Guns & Roses	12-765	P

SONG TITLE	ARTIST	#	TYPE
Sweet City Woman	Stampeders	9-367	MG
Sweet City Woman	Stampeders	5-381	SC
Sweet Country Music	Atlanta	5-419	SC
Sweet Desire	Kendalls	5-403	SC
Sweet Dream Baby	Orbison, Roy	9-194	SO
Sweet Dreams	Air Supply	46-395	CB
Sweet Dreams	Cline, Patsy	11-203	DK
Sweet Dreams	Cline, Patsy	12-415	P
Sweet Dreams	La Bouche	4-336	SC
Sweet Dreams	Young, Faron	20-734	CB
Sweet Dreams Are Made Of This	Eurythmics	11-207	DK
Sweet Dreams Are Made Of This	Eurythmics	13-242	P
Sweet Dreams Are Made Of This	Lennox, Annie	17-726	PS
Sweet Dreams Ladies, Forward March	Boxtops	46-520	SC
Sweet Emotion	Aerosmith	12-773	P
Sweet Emotion	Aerosmith	16-154	SC
Sweet Georgia Brown	Fitzgerald, Ella	15-837	MM
Sweet Georgia Brown	Torme, Mel	9-802	SAV
Sweet Gypsy Rose	Orlando & Dawn	7-103	MM
Sweet Hitch-Hiker	CCR	48-364	CB
Sweet Home Alabama	Lynyrd Skynyrd	12-355	DK
Sweet Home Alabama	Lynyrd Skynyrd	12-693	P
Sweet Home Alabama	Lynyrd Skynyrd	5-265	SC
Sweet Home Alabama	Lynyrd Skynyrd	13-773	SGB
Sweet Home Chicago	Blues Brothers	9-382	AH
Sweet Home Chicago	Blues Brothers	20-134	KB
Sweet Home Chicago	Blues Brothers	19-791	SGB
Sweet Home Chicago	Blues Brothers	29-159	ZM
Sweet Home Chicago	Johnson, Robert	7-225	MM
Sweet Jane	Reed, Lou	21-810	SC
Sweet Jane	Reed, Lou	19-283	SGB
Sweet Lady	Tyrese	7-834	PHM
Sweet Leilani	Standard	47-831	SC
Sweet Little Rock N' Roller	Dolan, Joe	49-142	SRK
Sweet Little Sixteen	Berry, Chuck	12-140	DK
Sweet Little Sixteen	Berry, Chuck	4-7	SC
Sweet Little Sixteen	Checker, Chubby	48-559	DK
Sweet Little Somethin'	Aldean, Jason	49-21	SSC
Sweet Little You	Sedaka, Neil	45-354	CB
Sweet Lorraine	Cole, Nat "King"	46-356	KV
Sweet Love	Baker, Anita	12-628	P
Sweet Magnolia Blossom	Craddock, Billy C	5-399	SC
Sweet Music Man	McEntire, Reba	25-123	MM
Sweet Music Man	McEntire, Reba	16-98	ST
Sweet Music Man	Rogers, Kenny	4-768	SC
Sweet Nothins'	Lee, Brenda	30-322	CB
Sweet Nothins'	Lee, Brenda	3-293	MM
Sweet Nothins'	Lee, Brenda	11-26	PX
Sweet Nothins'	Lee, Brenda	4-6	SC
Sweet Pea	Roe, Tommy	35-88	CB
Sweet Pea	Roe, Tommy	6-790	MM
Sweet Pea	Roe, Tommy	21-540	SC

SONG TITLE	ARTIST	#	TYPE
Sweet Sacrifice	Evanescence	30-492	CB
Sweet Sacrifice	Evanescence	30-492	CB
Sweet Seasons	King, Carole	33-261	CB
Sweet Seasons	King, Carole	43-122	SC
Sweet Sexy Thing	Nu Flavor	10-96	SC
Sweet Sixteen	Joel, Billy	47-151	ZM
Sweet Someone	Ho, Don	6-835	MM
Sweet Southern Comfort	Jewell, Buddy	22-13	CB
Sweet Southern Comfort	Jewell, Buddy	19-677	ST
Sweet Sue Just You	Reeves, Jim	47-841	DCK
Sweet Sue Just You	Reeves, Jim	44-242	DCK
Sweet Summer	Diamond Rio	15-97	ST
Sweet Summer Rain	Rushlow	20-389	ST
Sweet Surrender	Bread	46-529	PR
Sweet Surrender	Denver, John	5-528	SC
Sweet Surrender	McLachlan, Sarah	14-188	CB
Sweet Sweet Smile	Carpenters	44-356	TB
Sweet Talkin' Guy	Chiffons	10-330	KC
Sweet Talkin' Guy	Chiffons	6-561	MM
Sweet Talkin' Guy	Chiffons	4-33	SC
Sweet Talkin' Woman	ELO	5-593	SC
Sweet Thing	Khan, Chaka	27-296	DK
Sweet Thing	Morrison, Van	23-598	BS
Sweet Thing	Morrison, Van	15-725	SI
Sweet Thing	Rufus&Chaka Kahn	5-108	SC
Sweet Thing	Urban, Keith	36-257	PHM
Sweet Violets	Miller, Mitch	23-551	CB
Sweet Woman Like You	Tex, Joe	17-317	SS
Sweeter Than Fiction	Swift, Taylor	42-23	ASK
Sweeter Than Fiction	Swift, Taylor	44-310	SBI
Sweetest Days the	Williams, Vanessa	9-270	SC
Sweetest Days the	Williams, Vanessa	29-124	ST
Sweetest Devotion	Adele	46-88	DCK
Sweetest Gift	Yearwood, Trisha	48-341	SC
Sweetest Goodbye	Maroon 5	21-685	Z
Sweetest Of All	Dr. Hook	47-42	SFG
Sweetest Sin	Simpson, Jessica	32-359	THM
Sweetest Taboo	Sade	14-868	PS
Sweetest Taboo the	Sade	29-632	SC
Sweetest Thing	U2	16-211	MM
Sweetest Thing	U2	7-818	PHM
Sweetest Thing the	Newton-John, Olivia	8-198	CB
Sweetest Thing the	Newton-John, Olivia	45-9	MM
Sweetest Thing the	Newton, Juice	6-738	MM
Sweetest Thing the	Newton, Juice	2-837	SC
Sweetest Thing the	Refugee Camp	10-111	SC
Sweetheart	Humperdinck, E.	37-164	CB
Sweetness	Jimmy Eat World	18-417	MM
Swimming In Champagne	Heatherly, Eric	14-120	CB
Swimming In Champagne	Heatherly, Eric	10-260	SC
Swing	Adkins, Trace	29-588	CB
Swing Down Sweet Chariot	Presley, Elvis	30-380	SC
Swing Life Away	Rise Against	30-228	PHM
Swing Swing	All American Reject	32-147	THM

SONG TITLE	ARTIST	#	TYPE
Swing Swing	All American Rejects	32-147	THM
Swing Swing	All-American Reject	23-165	PHM
Swing the	Bonamy, James	7-612	CHM
Swing the	Bonamy, James	10-84	SC
Swing the	Bonamy, James	22-610	ST
Swingin'	Anderson, John	8-16	CB
Swingin'	Anderson, John	17-419	DK
Swingin'	Anderson, John	6-758	MM
Swingin'	Anderson, John	13-466	P
Swingin' Doors	McBride, Martina	1-385	CB
Swingin' Doors	McBride, Martina	4-433	SC
Swinging Doors	Haggard, Merle	8-318	CB
Swinging Doors	Haggard, Merle	6-772	MM
Swinging Doors	Haggard, Merle	8-645	SAV
Swinging Doors	Haggard, Merle	4-723	SC
Swinging For The Fence	Dean, Billy	29-600	CB
Swinging On A Star	Crosby, Bing	29-414	CB
Swinging On A Star	Crosby, Bing	17-379	DK
Swinging On A Star	Crosby, Bing	29-475	LE
Swinging On A Star	Crosby, Bing	15-844	MM
Swinging On A Star	Irwin, B.	29-825	SF
Swinging School	Rydell, Bobby	47-474	PS
Swings & Waterslides	Beach, Viola	49-932	MRH
Swingtown	Miller, Steve	23-619	BS
Swingtown	Steve Miller Band	5-309	SC
Switch	TLC	15-424	CB
Switch Into Glide	Kings	13-661	SGB
Sylvia's Mother	Dr. Hook	5-598	SC
Sympathy	Goo Goo Dolls	25-587	MM
Sympathy	Goo Goo Dolls	19-341	STP
Sympathy	Goo Goo Dolls	32-217	THM
Sympathy For The Devil	Rolling Stones	19-748	LE
Sympathy For The Devil - WN	Guns 'N Roses	48-66	KV
T Is For Texas	Lynyrd Skynyrd	19-808	SGB
T-Shirt	Rhett, Thomas	49-368	BKD
T-Shirt	Shontelle	48-698	PHM
T-U-R-T-L-E Power	Partners In Kryme	18-389	SAV
Table For Two	Lynn, Loretta	43-235	CB
Tailgate	McCoy, Neal	30-27	CB
Tailor Made Woman	Ford, Tenn Ernie	22-212	CB
Tainted Love	Soft Cell	11-655	DK
Tainted Love	Soft Cell	29-3	MH
Take A Back Road	Atkins, Rodney	38-118	CB
Take A Bow	Madonna	21-150	LE
Take A Bow	Madonna	9-267	SC
Take A Bow	Madonna	29-123	ST
Take A Bow	Rihanna	36-102	CB
Take A Chance On Me	Abba	7-509	MM
Take A Chance On Me	Abba	4-317	SC
Take A Giant Step	Monkees	47-289	EZ
Take A Letter Maria	Greaves, R. B.	27-548	DK
Take a Letter Maria	Shay, Sam	17-34	DK
Take A Little Ride	Aldean, Jason	39-25	ASK
Take A Little Trip	Alabama	1-19	CB
Take A Little Trip	Alabama	6-183	MM

256

SONG TITLE	ARTIST	#	TYPE
Take A Long Line	Angels	46-437	CDA
Take A Look	Cole, Natalie	24-267	SC
Take A Look At My Heart	Prine, John	23-536	CB
Take A Message	Shand, Remy	18-229	CB
Take A Message	Shand, Remy	25-222	MM
Take A Message To Mary	Everly Brothers	38-20	CB
Take A Picture	Filter	34-143	CB
Take A Picture	Filter	16-184	PHM
Take A Picture	Filter	5-888	SC
Take A Picture	Jepsen, Carly Rae	49-127	BKD
Take An Old Cold Tater And Wait	Melancholy Ramblers	45-682	VH
Take Another Road	Buffett, Jimmy	45-847	VH
Take Away	Elliott&Tweet&Ginuw	20-614	CB
Take Good Care Of Her	James, Sonny	19-470	CB
Take Good Care Of My Baby	Vee, Bobby	11-361	DK
Take Good Care Of My Baby	Vee, Bobby	7-267	MM
Take Good Care Of My Baby	Vee, Bobby	13-258	P
Take Good Care Of My Baby	Vee, Bobby	9-713	SAV
Take Good Care Of My Baby	Vinton, Bobby	35-46	CB
Take It All	Adele	44-172	KV
Take It All Out On Me	Wills, Mark	30-318	CB
Take It Back	J. Geils Band	46-327	LE
Take It Back	McEntire, Reba	1-805	CB
Take It Back	McEntire, Reba	6-215	MM
Take It Back	McEntire, Reba	2-5	SC
Take It Back	McEntire, Reba	8-593	TT
Take It Back	Pink Floyd	24-260	SC
Take It Easy	Eagles	7-557	BS
Take It Easy On Me	Little River Band	18-301	SC
Take It From Me	Brandt, Paul	10-98	SC
Take It Like A Man	BTO	46-544	CB
Take It Like A Man	Wright, Michelle	35-399	CB
Take it Like A Man	Wright, Michelle	6-535	MM
Take It Like A Man	Wright, Michelle	12-480	P
Take It Like A Man	Wright, Michelle	2-103	SC
Take It Off	Donnas	25-543	MM
Take It Off	Donnas	23-171	PHM
Take It Off	Donnas	23-336	SC
Take It Off	Nichols, Joe	37-356	CB
Take It On Back	Bryant, Chase	45-398	BKD
Take It On Home	Rich, Charlie	5-206	SC
Take It On The Run	REO Speedwagon	7-98	MM
Take It On The Run	REO Speedwagon	13-288	P
Take It On The Run	REO Speedwagon	3-612	SC
Take It Out On Me	Florida Georgia Line	44-313	SBI
Take It Outside	Gilbert, Brantley	44-159	BKD
Take It Slow	O''Ryan	30-810	PHM
Take It Slow	O'Ryan	30-810	PHM
Take It To The Limit	Bogguss, Suzy	6-470	MM
Take It To The Limit	Eagles	7-558	BS
Take It To The Limit	Eagles	6-425	MM

SONG TITLE	ARTIST	#	TYPE
Take It To The Limit	Eagles	2-265	SC
Take Me	Jones, George	8-345	CB
Take Me	White, Lari	22-677	ST
Take Me - duet	Wynette & Jones	49-358	CB
Take Me As I Am	Dylan, Bob	45-840	VH
Take Me As I Am	Hill, Faith	15-695	CB
Take Me As I Am	Hill, Faith	2-399	SC
Take Me As I Am	Price, Ray	48-409	DFK
Take Me Away (Remix Edit)	Lifehouse	32-211	THM
Take Me Away From Here	McGraw, Tim	47-242	CB
Take Me Back	Little Anthony	30-518	LE
Take Me Back To Tulsa	Strait, George	38-151	CB
Take Me Back To Tulsa	Wills, Bob	20-696	CB
Take Me Down	Alabama	9-509	SAV
Take Me Home	Cher	14-66	RS
Take Me Home	Collins, Phil	44-13	PSJT
Take Me Home Country Roads	Denver, John	17-30	DK
Take Me Home Country Roads	Denver, John	36-145	LE
Take Me Home Country Roads	Denver, John	12-827	P
Take Me In Your Arms (Rock Me)	Doobie Brothers	29-88	CB
Take Me In Your Arms And Hold Me	Reeves, Jim	45-264	BSP
Take Me Out To The Ballgame	Standard	12-609	P
Take Me Out To The Ballgame	Standard	23-220	SM
Take Me There	Backstreet & Mia	7-816	PHM
Take Me There	Rascal Flatts	30-531	CB
Take Me To Texas	Strait, George	47-400	BKD
Take Me To The Country	McDaniel, Mel	49-124	DFK
Take Me To The Mardi Gras	Simon & Garfunkel	49-764	LG
Take Me To The River	Talking Heads	12-795	P
Take Me To Your Lovin' Place	Gatlins	4-489	SC
Take Me To Your Loving Place	Gatlin, Larry	47-106	CB
Take Me To Your World	Wynette, Tammy	4-744	SC
Take Me With You When You Go	Byrd, Tracy	14-116	CB
Take My Breath Away	98 Degrees	15-380	SKG
Take My Breath Away	Berlin	12-377	DK
Take My Drunk Ass Home	Bryan, Luke	43-262	BFK
Take My Drunk Ass Home	Bryan, Luke	43-270	KV
Take My Hand	Tillis & Bryce	5-448	SC
Take My Hand Precious Lord	Presley, Elvis	30-386	SC
Take My Ring Off Your Finger	Smith, Carl	46-29	SSK
Take On Me	A-Ha	20-302	CB
Take On Me	A-Ha	28-340	DK

SONG TITLE	ARTIST	#	TYPE
Take On Me	A-Ha	13-249	P
Take On Me	A-Ha	20-82	SC
Take That	Brokop, Lisa	17-261	NA
Take That	Brokop, Lisa	2-570	SC
Take The A-Train	Ellington, Dale	10-707	JVC
Take The Long Way Home	Supertramp	17-515	SC
Take The Money And Run	Miller, Steve	23-621	BS
Take The Money And Run	Steve Miller Band	4-90	SC
Take The Skinheads Bowling **	VanBeethoven,Camper	23-22	SC
Take These Chains From My Heart	Charles, Ray	46-580	LE
Take These Chains From My Heart	Parnell w/Brooks&D	2-326	SC
Take These Chains From My Heart	Williams, Hank Sr.	34-190	CB
Take These Chains From My Heart	Williams, Hank Sr.	8-642	SAV
Take This Job And Shove It	Paycheck, Johnny	22-31	CB
Take This Job And Shove It	Paycheck, Johnny	26-200	DK
Take This Job And Shove It	Paycheck, Johnny	15-341	MM
Take This Job And Shove It	Paycheck, Johnny	12-429	P
Take This Job And Shove It	Paycheck, Johnny	8-681	SAV
Take You Down	Brown, Chris	36-479	CB
Take You High	Clarkson, Kelly	48-437	KCD
Take You Home	Martinez & Kelis	32-125	THM
Take You Home	Rhett, Thomas	43-182	ASK
Take You Out	Vandross, Luther	48-294	MM
Take Your Mama	Scissor Sisters	23-561	MM
Take Your Mama	Scissor Sisters	29-225	ZM
Take Your Memory With You	Gill, Vince	17-391	DK
Take Your Time	Holly, Buddy	47-892	ZM
Take Your Time	Hunt, Sam	45-22	KVD
Take Your Time	S.O.S. Band	18-373	AH
Take Your Time	Tre	10-688	HH
Takes A Little Time	Grant, Amy	7-684	PHM
Takes A Little Time	Grant, Amy	18-763	PS
Takes A Lot To Rock You	Yoakam, Dwight	49-690	CB
Takin' Care Of Business	BTO	11-332	DK
Takin' Care Of Business	BTO	13-170	P
Takin' It Easy	Dalton, Lacy J.	9-566	SAV
Takin' It Easy	Dalton, Lacy J.	5-245	SC
Takin' It To The Streets	Doobie Brothers	29-81	CB
Takin' Off This Pain	Shepherd, Ashton	36-417	CB
Takin' The Country Back	Anderson, John	8-303	CB
Takin' The Country Back	Anderson, John	22-790	ST
Taking A Chance On Love	Sinatra, Frank	14-278	MM
Taking A Chance On	Sinatra, Frank	21-216	SGB

SONG TITLE	ARTIST	#	TYPE
Love			
Taking Back My Brave	Johnson, Carolyn D.	30-116	CB
Taking Chances	Dion, Celine	49-914	SC
Taking Everything	Levert, Gerald	7-819	PHM
Taking You Home	Henley, Don	30-643	THM
Tales Of Brave Ulysses	Cream	19-279	SGB
Tales Of Great Ulysses	Clapton, Eric	13-791	SGB
Taliban Song the	Keith, Toby	20-267	SC
Talk	Coldplay	29-248	SC
Talk Back Trembling Lips	Ashworth, Ernie	15-84	CB
Talk Back Trembling Lips	Ashworth, Ernie	4-302	SC
Talk Back Trembling Lips	Hobbs, Becky	9-492	SAV
Talk Dirty To Me	Poison	23-53	MH
Talk Is Cheap	Jackson, Alan	45-108	KV
Talk To Me	Estefan, Gloria	6-371	MM
Talk To Me	Fender, Freddie	48-499	CKC
Talk To Me	Gilley, Mickey	22-219	CB
Talk To Me	Nicks, Stevie	16-636	MM
Talk To Me	Nicks, Stevie	16-129	SC
Talk To Me	Sinatra, Frank	10-718	JVC
Talk To Me Texas	Whitley, Keith	49-396	CB
Talkin' 'Bout A Revolution	Chapman, Tracy	24-570	SC
Talkin' 'Bout A Revolution	Chapman, Tracy	44-194	SCB
Talkin' In Your Sleep	Gayle, Crystal	15-830	CB
Talkin' In Your Sleep	Gayle, Crystal	13-375	P
Talkin' In Your Sleep	Gayle, Crystal	10-515	SF
Talkin' In Your Sleep	Presley, Elvis	43-250	PSJT
Talkin' Song Repair Blues	Jackson, Alan	22-326	CB
Talkin' Song Repair Blues the	Jackson, Alan	23-383	SC
Talkin' To Me	Amerie	32-14	THM
Talkin' To The Moon	Gatlin, Larry	47-109	CB
Talkin' To The Wall	Anderson, Lynn	47-647	CB
Talking In Your Sleep	Romantics	14-570	AH
Talking In Your Sleep	Romantics	21-744	MH
Talking Walls	Reeves, Jim	47-728	SRK
Talking Walls, The	Reeves, Jim	44-236	DCK
Talking Walls, The	Reeves, Jim	44-233	SRK
Tall Tall Trees	Jackson, Alan	3-634	SC
Talladega	Church, Eric	46-622	SBI
Tallahassee Lassie	Cannon, Freddie	6-677	MM
Talula	Amos, Tori	24-745	SC
Tammy	Reynolds, Debbie	5-11	SC
Tangerine	Dorsey, Jimmy	47-30	PS
Tangerine	Jazz Standard	47-715	KV
Tangerine	Sinatra, Frank	9-243	PT
Tangerine Speedo (Radio Version)	Caviar	23-30	SC
Tangled And Dark	Raitt, Bonnie	10-766	JVC
Tangled Mind	Snow, Hank	22-134	CB
Tangled Mind	Snow, Hank	37-302	SC
Tangled Up	Currington, Billy	30-478	CB

SONG TITLE	ARTIST	#	TYPE
Tangled Up In Blue	Dylan, Bob	29-105	CB
Tangled Up In Texas	Frazier River	7-322	MM
Tangled Up In Texas	Frazier River	4-396	SC
Tapestry	King, Carole	43-449	KV
Taste Of Your Love	Due West	39-82	PHN
Tattoo	Hayes, Hunter	45-95	ASK
Tattoo	Sparks, Jordin	30-588	PHM
Tattoo Rose	Griggs, Andy	30-474	CB
Tattoo's On This Town	Aldean, Jason	45-429	BKD
Taxi	Chapin, Harry	9-350	AH
Taxi	Chapin, Harry	29-294	SC
Tea For Two	Day, Doris	11-798	DK
Tea For Two	Day, Doris	12-537	P
Teach Me To Forget	Haggard, Merle	45-712	VH
Teach Your Children	Byrds	47-556	SC
Teach Your Children	Crosby Stills & Nash	3-480	SC
Teach Your Children	Crosby, Stills, Nash & Young	34-35	CB
Teacher's Pet	Day, Doris	9-92	PS
Tear Fell a	Craddock, Billy C	46-646	CB
Tear Stained Letter	Loveless, Patty	7-427	MM
Teardrops	Andrews & Hearts	49-456	MM
Teardrops In My Heart	Sons Of The Pioneers	45-708	VH
Teardrops On My Guitar	Swift, Taylor	30-312	CB
Teardrops Will Fall	Mellencamp, John	19-696	ST
Tearin' It Up & Burnin' It Down	Brooks, Garth	8-872	CB
Tearin' It Up & Burnin' It Down	Brooks, Garth	10-153	SC
Tearin' It Up & Burnin' It Down	Brooks, Garth	22-699	ST
Tearin' Up My Heart	N'Sync	15-775	BS
Tearin' Up My Heart	N'Sync	20-429	CB
Tearin' Up My Heart	N'Sync	29-166	MH
Tears Are Falling	INXS	11-790	DK
Tears Are Falling	Kiss	21-774	SC
Tears Dry On Their Own	Winehouse, Amy	30-590	PHM
Tears In Heaven	Clapton, Eric	11-79	JTG
Tears In Heaven	Clapton, Eric	15-59	LE
Tears Of A Clown	Robinson, Smokey	35-103	CB
Tears Of A Clown	Robinson, Smokey	4-849	SC
Tears Of A Clown	Robinson, Smokey	9-313	STR
Tears Of The Lonely	Gilley, Mickey	22-224	CB
Tears On My Pillow	Little Anthony	12-12	DK
Tears On My Pillow	Little Anthony	30-513	LE
Tears On My Pillow	Little Anthony	6-269	MM
Teddy Bear	Presley, Elvis	9-885	DK
Teddy Bear	Presley, Elvis	3-325	MH
Teddy Bear	Presley, Elvis	12-732	P
Teddy Bear	Presley, Elvis	2-593	SC
Teddy Bear	Presley, Elvis	14-752	THM
Teddy Bear	Sovine, Red	8-276	CB
Teddy Bear Song	Fairchild, Barbara	8-17	CB
Teddy Bear Song	Fairchild, Barbara	8-623	SAV
Teddy Bear Song	Fairchild, Barbara	4-784	SC
Tee Na Na - Cajun	Cajun	49-293	GS

SONG TITLE	ARTIST	#	TYPE
Teen Angel	Dinning, Mark	35-39	CB
Teen Angel	Dinning, Mark	11-507	DK
Teen Angel	Dinning, Mark	10-743	JVC
Teen Angel	Dinning, Mark	4-695	SC
Teenage Daughters	McBride, Martina	37-222	CB
Teenage Dirtbag	Wheatus	15-447	PHM
Teenage Idol	Nelson, Ricky	21-706	CB
Teenage Life	Daz Sampson	30-695	SF
Teenage Life	Sampson, Daz	30-695	SF
Teenage Love Affair	Keys, Alicia	36-507	CB
Teenager In Love	Dion	11-96	DK
Teenager In Love	Dion	7-296	MM
Teenager In Love	Dion	12-906	P
Teenager In Love	Dion	9-895	SAV
Teenager's Romance a	Nelson, Ricky	21-707	CB
Telefone	Easton, Sheena	5-690	SC
Telephone - duet	Lady Gaga & Beyonce	38-194	CB
Telephone Man **	Wilson, Meri	2-182	SC
Tell Her	Lonestar	14-139	CB
Tell Her	Lonestar	13-855	CHM
Tell Her	Lonestar	19-216	CSZ
Tell Her	Lonestar	10-262	SC
Tell Her About It	Joel, Billy	35-170	CB
Tell Her About It	Joel, Billy	16-145	LE
Tell Her About It	Joel, Billy	16-516	P
Tell Her About It	Joel, Billy	21-615	SF
Tell Her No	Zombies	11-555	DK
Tell Her No	Zombies	14-460	SC
Tell Him	Dion, Celine	15-115	BS
Tell Him	Exciters	18-250	DK
Tell Him	Exciters	6-659	MM
Tell Him	Exciters	13-72	P
Tell Him	Exciters	3-587	SC
Tell Him	Midler, Bette	45-917	KV
Tell Him	Streisand & Dion	7-693	PHM
Tell Him	Streisand & Dion	10-118	SC
Tell It Like It Is	Heart	46-117	SC
Tell It Like It Is	Neville, Aaron	12-100	DK
Tell It Like It Is	Neville, Aaron	6-563	MM
Tell It Like It Is	Neville, Aaron	3-263	SC
Tell It Like It Is	Royal, Billy Joe	33-92	CB
Tell It Like It Is	Royal, Billy Joe	4-657	SC
Tell It To Me Brother	Rogers, Kenny	48-123	SC
Tell It To My Heart	Dayne, Taylor	11-497	DK
Tell It To My Heart	Dayne, Taylor	12-815	P
Tell It To The Rain	Four Seasons	43-432	CBE P
Tell Laura I Love Her	Peterson, Ray	2-53	SC
Tell Laura I Love Her	Valens, Richie	10-552	SF
Tell Lorrie I Love Her	Whitley, Keith	49-395	JER
Tell Mama	James, Etta	21-697	PS
Tell Me	Groove Theory	4-686	SC
Tell Me	Hill, Dru	24-544	SC
Tell Me	Owen, Jake	45-666	CB
Tell Me 'Bout It	Stone, Joss	30-566	CB
Tell Me (What's Goin'	Smilez & Southstar	32-128	THM

259

SONG TITLE	ARTIST	#	TYPE
On)			
Tell Me A Lie	Fricke, Janie	8-210	CB
Tell Me A Lie	Fricke, Janie	7-152	MM
Tell Me A Lie	One Direction	39-109	PHM
Tell Me About It	Tucker & McClinton	8-112	CB
Tell Me About It	Tucker & McClinton	6-527	MM
Tell Me About It	Tucker & McClinton	2-338	SC
Tell Me Baby	Red Hot Chili Peppe	30-722	SF
Tell Me How	Brock, Chad	16-169	CB
Tell Me How	Brock, Chad	25-12	MM
Tell Me How	Brock, Chad	15-676	ST
Tell Me How You Like It	Florida Georgia Line	45-153	ASK
Tell Me I Was Dreaming	Tritt, Travis	2-732	SC
Tell Me I'm Not Dreaming	Jackson, Janet	11-590	DK
Tell Me My Lying Eyes Are Wrong	Jones, George	6-90	SC
Tell Me Something	Gray, David	29-220	PHM
Tell Me Something Bad About Tulsa	Strait, George	25-609	MM
Tell Me Something Bad About Tulsa	Strait, George	19-45	ST
Tell Me Something Bad About Tulsa	Strait, George	32-228	THM
Tell Me Something Good	Rufus	4-52	SC
Tell Me Something I Don't Know	Major, Charlie	4-630	SC
Tell Me What It's Like	Lee, Brenda	30-333	CB
Tell Me Where It Hurts	Steiner, Tommy S.	25-298	MM
Tell Me Where It Hurts	Steiner, Tommy S.	17-586	ST
Tell Me Why	Expose	13-194	P
Tell Me Why	Expose	18-501	SAV
Tell Me Why	Hollister, Dave	20-527	CB
Tell Me Why	Judd, Wynonna	1-650	CB
Tell Me Why	Judd, Wynonna	18-249	DK
Tell Me Why	Judd, Wynonna	6-314	MM
Tell Me Why	Judd, Wynonna	12-412	P
Tell Me Why	Judd, Wynonna	2-818	SC
Tell Me Why	Presley, Elvis	25-765	MM
Tell Me Why	Swift, Taylor	43-170	ASK
Tell Me Why	Wynonna	34-308	CB
Tell Me You Get Lonely	Ballard, Frankie	49-758	CB
Tell Me You're Coming Back	Rolling Stones	18-26	LE
Telling Stories	Chapman, Tracy	44-187	SC
Telluride	McGraw, Tim	29-521	CB
Telluride	McGraw, Tim	15-195	ST
Temptation	Everly Brothers	38-25	ZM
Temptation Eyes	Grass Roots	4-55	SC
Tempted	Squeeze	29-4	MH
Tempted	Squeeze	2-562	SC
Tempted	Stuart, Marty	9-538	SAV
Ten Days	Dion, Celine	19-24	PS
Ten Feet Away	Whitley, Keith	49-398	CB
Ten Feet Tall & Bulletproof	Tritt, Travis	1-674	CB
Ten Guitars	Humperdinck, E.	48-392	LE
Ten Pound Hammer	Mandrell, Barbara	24-130	SC
Ten Rounds With Jose	Byrd, Tracy	33-182	CB

SONG TITLE	ARTIST	#	TYPE
Quervo			
Ten Rounds With Jose Quervo	Byrd, Tracy	25-189	MM
Ten Rounds With Jose Quervo	Byrd, Tracy	16-433	ST
Ten Thousand Angels	McCready, Mindy	4-232	SC
Ten Times Crazier	Shelton, Blake	41-50	ASK
Ten With A Two	Chesney, Kenny	48-89	CB
Tender Feeling	Presley, Elvis	25-318	MM
Tender Lie a	Restless Heart	1-411	CB
Tender Love	Force M.D.'s	11-281	DK
Tender Moment	Parnell, Lee Roy	49-277	CB
Tender Moment	Parnell, Lee Roy	6-394	MM
Tender Trap the	Sinatra, Frank	9-255	PT
Tender Trap the	Sinatra, Frank	21-214	SGB
Tender When I Wanna Be	Carpenter, M C	8-888	CB
Tender When I Wanna Be	Carpenter, M C	17-273	NA
Tender When I Wanna Be	Carpenter, M C	2-580	SC
Tender When I Wanna Be	Carpenter, M C	15-165	THM
Tender Years	Jones, George	4-725	SC
Tenderly	Cole, Nat "King"	46-370	SAV
Tenderness	General Public	29-262	SC
Tennessee	Armed Development	18-383	SAV
Tennessee	Sugarland	30-234	RS
Tennessee	Wreckers	30-361	CB
Tennessee Birdwalk	Blanchard&Morgan	8-716	CB
Tennessee Border #2	Tubb & Foley	22-302	CB
Tennessee Border No. 2	Foley, Red	43-358	CB
Tennessee Flat Top Box	Cash, Roseanne	12-426	P
Tennessee Flat Top Box	Cash, Roseanne	9-638	SAV
Tennessee Girl	Kershaw, Sammy	30-92	CB
Tennessee Homesick Blues	Parton, Dolly	49-335	CB
Tennessee Local	Ford, Tenn Ernie	8-817	CB
Tennessee Local	Ford, Tenn Ernie	18-620	PS
Tennessee Mojo	Cadillac Three	44-312	SBI
Tennessee Moon	Diamond, Neil	7-197	MM
Tennessee River	Alabama	4-450	BS
Tennessee River	Alabama	13-471	P
Tennessee River Run	Worley, Darryl	25-645	MM
Tennessee River Run	Worley, Darryl	19-264	ST
Tennessee River Run	Worley, Darryl	32-374	THM
Tennessee Saturday Night	Foley, Red	19-641	CB
Tennessee Saturday Night	Foley, Red	6-10	SC
Tennessee Stud	Arnold, Eddy	19-38	CB
Tennessee Waltz	Francis, Connie	8-810	CB
Tennessee Waltz	King, Pee Wee	15-825	CB
Tennessee Waltz	Page, Patti	11-150	DK
Tennessee Waltz	Page, Patti	13-353	P
Tennessee Whiskey	Coe, David Allan	18-315	CB
Tennessee Whiskey	Jones, George	34-260	CB
Tennessee Whiskey	Jones, George	14-321	SC

SONG TITLE	ARTIST	#	TYPE
Tennessee Whiskey	Stapleton, Chris	45-439	KV
Tenth Avenue Freezeout	Springsteen, Bruce	17-616	LE
Tenth Avenue Freezeout	Springsteen, Bruce	13-671	SGB
Tequila	Champs, T.	12-120	DK
Tequila Makes Her Clothes Fall Off	Nichols, Joe	23-410	CB
Tequila On Ice	Worley, Darryl	36-228	PHM
Tequila Sheila	Bare, Bobby	44-71	SRK
Tequila Sheila	Flynnville Train	30-577	CB
Tequila Sunrise	Eagles	2-258	SC
Tequila Sunrise	Jackson, Alan	1-45	CB
Tequila Talkin'	Lonestar	7-88	MM
Tequila Talkin'	Lonestar	3-656	SC
Terry	Twinkle	10-662	SF
Test the	White, Lari	4-230	SC
Testify To Love	Avalon	46-450	SC
Testify To Love	Judd, Wynonna	48-320	SC
Texarkana	Arnold, Eddy	19-840	CB
Texas	Charlie Daniels Band	45-690	BAT
Texas	Strait, George	23-292	CB
Texas Fiddle Man	Asleep At The Wheel	45-864	VH
Texas Flood	Vaughn, Stevie Ray	15-26	SC
Texas In My Rear View Mirror	Davis, Mac	23-516	CB
Texas in My Rear View Mirror	Davis, Mac	4-542	SC
Texas Plates	Coffey, Kelly	19-538	ST
Texas Size Heartache	Diffie, Joe	8-468	CB
Texas Tattoo	Gibson Miller Band	6-398	MM
Texas Tattoo	Gibson Miller Band	12-459	P
Texas Tornado	Lawrence, Tracy	1-580	CB
Texas Tornado	Lawrence, Tracy	2-765	SC
Texas When I Die	Tucker, Tanya	17-309	NA
Texas When I Die	Tucker, Tanya	9-478	SAV
Texas Women	Williams, Hank Jr.	37-305	CB
Texas Women Don't Stay Lonely Long	Brooks & Dunn	4-113	SC
Text Me Texas	Young, Chris	45-54	VH
Thank God And Greyhound	Clark, Roy	4-580	SC
Thank God For Believers	Chesnutt, Mark	4-826	SC
Thank God For Believers	Chesnutt, Mark	22-618	ST
Thank God For Kids	Oak Ridge Boys	23-499	CB
Thank GOD For The Radio	Jackson, Alan	44-125	KV
Thank God For The Radio	Kendalls	29-654	SC
Thank GOD For You	Sawyer Brown	34-306	CB
Thank God For You	Sawyer Brown	2-515	SC
Thank God I Found You	Carey&Joe&98 Degree	16-183	PHM
Thank God I Found You	Carey&Joe&98 Degree	17-542	SC
Thank God I'm A Country Boy	Dean, Billy	20-350	ST
Thank God I'm A Country Boy	Denver, John	8-19	CB
Thank God I'm A	Denver, John	11-615	DK

SONG TITLE	ARTIST	#	TYPE
Country Boy			
Thank God I'm A Country Boy	Denver, John	36-147	LE
Thank God I'm A Country Boy	Denver, John	13-450	P
Thank God I've Got You	Statler Brothers	19-388	CB
Thank U	Morrisette, Alanis	7-780	PHT
Thank You	Dido	35-240	CB
Thank You	Dido	16-121	PRT
Thank You	Dido	18-535	TT
Thank You	Sly & Family Stone	27-344	DK
Thank You	Sly & Family Stone	14-360	MH
Thank You	Sly & Family Stone	7-40	MM
Thank You	Sly & Family Stone	5-458	SC
Thank You Baby (For Makin' Some...	Twain, Shania	23-432	CB
Thank You For Loving Me	Bon Jovi	30-216	PHM
Thank You For Loving Me	Bon Jovi	18-577	TT
Thank You For The Feelin'	BTO	46-541	CB
Thank You For The Music	Abba	7-504	MM
Thanks A Lot	Cash, Johnny	29-569	CB
Thanks A Lot	Tubb, Ernest	22-305	CB
Thanks For The Memories	Fall Out Boy	48-606	DK
Thanks For The Memories	Sinatra, Frank	15-567	MM
Thanks For The Memory	Hope, Bob	21-13	SC
Thanks For The Memory	Hope, Bob & ?	11-457	DK
Thanks That Was Fun	Barenaked Ladies	18-296	CB
Thanks To You	Harris, EmmyLou	16-591	MM
Thanks To You	Stuart, Marty	4-430	SC
That Ain't My Truck	Akins, Rhett	35-407	CB
That Ain't My Truck	Akins, Rhett	3-418	SC
That Ain't No Way To Go	Brooks & Dunn	1-87	CB
That Ain't No Way To Go	Brooks & Dunn	2-212	SC
That Do Make It Nice	Arnold, Eddy	19-44	CB
That Don't Impress Me Much	Twain, Shania	8-860	CB
That Don't Impress Me Much	Twain, Shania	10-162	SC
That Don't Impress Me Much	Twain, Shania	22-695	ST
That Don't Make Me A Bad Guy	Keith, Toby	47-164	CB
That Evil Child	Watson, Gene	45-869	VH
That Girl	Houston, M.	32-163	THM
That Girl	Nettles, Jennifer	43-92	HM
That Girl	Priest, Maxi&Shaggy	25-379	MM
That Girl Is A Cowboy	Brooks, Garth	48-355	PHN
That Good (Wanna Get To Know You	Twain, Shania	23-428	CB
That Just About Does It	Gosdin, Vern	16-354	CB
That Kind Of Day	Buxton, Sarah	30-343	CB
That Lady	Isley Brothers	16-877	DK
That Lady	Kravitz, Lenny	48-555	DK

SONG TITLE	ARTIST	#	TYPE
That Last Mile	Carson, Jeff	24-155	SC
That Lonesome Road	Taylor, James	45-522	SC
That Look	Watson, Aaron	49-406	BKD
That Look (Inst)	Watson, Aaron	49-407	BKD
That Lucky Old Sun	Laine, Frankie	3-875	PS
That Lucky Old Sun - duet	Chesney & Nelson	36-241	PHM
That Ol' Wind	Brooks, Garth	1-216	CB
That Ol' Wind	Brooks, Garth	7-384	MM
That Old Black Magic	Davis, Sammy Jr.	47-15	PS
That Old Black Magic	Prima, Louis	12-178	DK
That Old Black Magic	Prima, Louis	12-531	P
That Old Black Magic	Sinatra, Frank	21-217	SGB
That Old Devil Called Love	Moyet, Allison	11-22	PX
That Old Feeling	Standard	47-518	VH
That Old Feeling	Stewart, Rod	25-596	MM
That Old Gang Of Mine	Miller, Mitch	23-549	CB
That Old Pair Of Jeans	Fatboy Slim	30-707	SF
That Road Not Taken	diffie, Joe	6-852	MM
That Rock Won't Roll	Restless Heart	13-539	P
That Rock Won't Roll	Restless Heart	5-404	SC
That Scares Me	Van Zant	30-448	CB
That Smell	Lynyrd Skynyrd	5-259	SC
That Smile	Dean, Tyler	38-247	PHN
That Song In My Head	Hough, Julianne	36-429	CB
That Song Is Driving Me Crazy	Hall, Tom T.	3-753	CB
That Song Is Driving Me Crazy	Hall, Tom T.	6-2	SC
That Summer	Brooks, Garth	6-388	MM
That Summer	Brooks, Garth	2-677	SC
That Summer Song	Blue County	22-335	CB
That Sunday That Summer	Cole, Nat "King"	45-875	DCK
That Thing You Do	Wonders	24-542	SC
That Train Don't Run	Berg, Martraca	22-650	ST
That Was A River	Raye, Collin	1-128	CB
That Was Him	4 Runner	7-319	MM
That Was Him	4 Runner	4-413	SC
That Was Us	Brock, Chad	19-13	ST
That Was Us	Brock, Chad	32-191	THM
That Was Yesterday	Fargo, Donna	48-663	CB
That Way Again	Brice, Lee	39-85	PHN
That Way Again	Brice, Lee	45-381	PHN
That Woman Of Mine	McCoy, Neal	1-852	CB
That Woman Of Mine	McCoy, Neal	22-915	ST
That'd Be Alright	Jackson, Alan	25-449	MM
That'd Be Alright	Jackson, Alan	18-781	ST
That'd Be Alright	Jackson, Alan	32-113	THM
That'll Be The Day	Holly, Buddy	15-281	DK
That'll Be The Day	Holly, Buddy	11-33	PX
That'll Be The Day	Holly, Buddy	29-841	SC
That'll Be The Day	Ronstadt, Linda	34-36	CB
That'll Be The Day	Ronstadt, Linda	10-7	SC
That's A No No	Anderson, Lynn	47-639	CB
That's A Plan	McGuinn, Mark	15-609	ST

SONG TITLE	ARTIST	#	TYPE
That's A Woman	Wills, Mark	22-6	CB
That's A Woman	Wills, Mark	20-262	SC
That's A Woman	Wills, Mark	19-848	ST
That's All	Darin, Bobby	23-358	PS
That's All	Genesis	15-737	SC
That's All I'll Ever Need	Wayne, Jimmy	30-168	CB
That's All Right	Presley, Elvis	11-610	DK
That's All Right	Presley, Elvis	21-569	SAV
That's All Right Mama	Presley, Elvis	14-782	THM
That's All She Wrote	Nelson, Ricky	47-842	DCK
That's All That Matters	Gilley, Mickey	22-221	CB
That's All That Matters	Gilley, Mickey	5-246	SC
That's All That Matters	Gilley, Mickey	16-172	THM
That's All You Gotta Do	Lee, Brenda	47-726	SRK
That's Amore	Martin, Dean	28-517	DK
That's Amore	Martin, Dean	23-64	MM
That's Amore	Martin, Dean	4-351	SC
That's An American - Patriotic	Blount, Benton	39-67	PHN
That's Another Song	White, Bryan	7-378	MM
That's Another Song	White, Bryan	4-596	SC
That's As Close As I'll Get	Tippin, Aaron	7-82	MM
That's As Close As I'll Get	Tippin, Aaron	3-539	SC
That's Cool	Blue County	20-388	ST
That's Enough Of That	Mason, Mila	7-405	MM
That's Enough Of That	Mason, Mila	4-428	SC
That's Entertainment	Garland, Judy	48-275	PS
That's How Country Boys Roll	Currington, Billy	36-44	PT
That's How I Got To Memphis	Bare, Bobby	5-817	SC
That's How I Got To Memphis	Dodd, Deryl	7-397	MM
That's How I Got To Memphis	Dodd, Deryl	24-654	SC
That's How Love Moves	Hill, Faith	6-74	SC
That's How Much I Love You	Arnold, Eddy	17-631	THM
That's How They Do It In Dixie	Williams, w/Wilson.	29-363	CB
That's How Things Go Down	King, Carole	43-442	CB
That's How You Know	White, Lari	8-882	CB
That's How You Know It's Love	Carter, Deana	24-652	SC
That's How You Know When You're..	White, Lari	6-712	MM
That's How You Know When You're...	White, Lari	17-281	NA
That's How You Know When...	Wariner & Larson	5-443	SC
That's Important To Me	Joey & Rory	45-818	BKD
That's It, I Quit, I'm Movin' On	Adele	44-175	KV
That's Just About Right	Blackhawk	2-740	SC
That's Just Jessie	Denney, Kevin	33-186	CB
That's Just Jessie	Denney, Kevin	25-71	MM

SONG TITLE	ARTIST	#	TYPE
That's Just Jessie	Denney, Kevin	16-105	ST
That's Just That	Diamond Rio	17-602	CB
That's Just That	Diamond Rio	25-54	MM
That's Just That	Diamond Rio	16-5	ST
That's Life	Sinatra, Frank	11-184	DK
That's Life	Sinatra, Frank	12-523	P
That's Me	McBride, Martina	1-383	CB
That's Me	McBride, Martina	6-182	MM
That's My Baby	White, Lari	19-300	MH
That's My Baby	White, Lari	16-592	MM
That's My Desire	Dion & Belmonts	25-549	MM
That's My Desire	Laine, Frankie	21-639	PS
That's My Job	Twitty, Conway	4-769	SC
That's My Kind Of Night	Bryan, Luke	45-31	SBI
That's My Story	Raye, Collin	1-129	CB
That's My Story	Raye, Collin	26-354	DK
That's My Story	Raye, Collin	6-453	MM
That's My Story	Raye, Collin	2-6	SC
That's Okay	Anthony, Marc	17-735	PS
That's Old Fashioned	Everly Brothers	38-26	CB
That's So You	Rushlow Harris	30-253	CB
That's Someone You Never Forget	Presley, Elvis	25-320	MM
That's The Beat Of A Heart	Warren Brothers	9-393	CB
That's The Beat Of A Heart	Warren Brothers	13-862	CHM
That's The Beat Of A Heart	Warren Brothers	19-251	CSZ
That's The Kind Of Love I'm In	Everett, Jace	23-296	CB
That's The Kind Of Love I'm In	Mason, Mila	16-579	SC
That's The Kind Of Mood I'm In	Loveless, Patty	14-77	CB
That's The Kind Of Mood I'm In	Loveless, Patty	13-846	CHM
That's The Thing About Love	Williams, Don	4-766	SC
That's The Truth	Brandt, Paul	14-616	SC
That's The Way	Katrina & Waves	9-857	SAV
That's The Way	Messina, Jo Dee	9-420	CB
That's The Way	Messina, Jo Dee	13-849	CHM
That's The Way Boys Are	Gore, Lesley	5-88	SC
That's The Way I Like It	KC & Sunshine Band	15-568	CMC
That's The Way I Like It	KC & Sunshine Band	17-129	DK
That's The Way I've Always...	Simon, Carly	2-559	SC
That's The Way It Is	Dion, Celine	15-293	CB
That's The Way It Is	Dion, Celine	8-525	PHT
That's The Way It Is	Dion, Celine	17-539	SC
That's The Way Love Goes	Haggard, Merle	1-366	CB
That's The Way Love Goes	Haggard, Merle	9-466	SAV
That's The Way Love	Haggard, Merle	22-382	ST

SONG TITLE	ARTIST	#	TYPE
Goes			
That's The Way Love Goes	Rodriguez, Johnny	22-49	CB
That's The Way Love Goes	Rodriguez, Johnny	20-282	SC
That's the Way Love Goes - duet	Haggard & Jewel	49-809	CB
That's The Way Love Moves	Midler, Bette	45-940	MM
That's The Way Of The World	Earth Wind & Fire	16-555	P
That's the Way the World Goes...	Lambert, Miranda	38-222	CB
That's What Breakin' Hearts Do	Strait, George	41-100	PHN
That's What Brothers Do	Confederate RR	25-14	MM
That's What Brothers Do	Confederate RR	16-10	ST
That's What Friends Are For	Multi-Voice	18-683	PR
That's What Friends Are For	Warwick & Friends	9-876	DK
That's What Friends Are For	Warwick & Friends	17-421	KC
That's What Friends Are For	Warwick & Friends	6-343	MM
That's What Happens When I Hold U	Tippin, Aaron	7-428	MM
That's What I Get	Ketchum, Hal	2-799	SC
That's What I Get For Loving You	Arnold, Eddy	45-573	OZP
That's What I Get For Loving You	Diamond Rio	1-174	CB
That's What I Like About You	Montgomery, J M	14-783	ST
That's What I Like About You	Yearwood, Trisha	1-633	CB
That's What I Like About You	Yearwood, Trisha	6-186	MM
That's What I Like About You	Yearwood, Trisha	13-337	P
That's What I Like About You	Yearwood, Trisha	2-327	SC
That's What I Love About Sunday	Morgan, Craig	22-101	CB
That's What It's All About	Brooks & Dunn	30-800	PHM
That's What It's All About	Brooks & Dunn	20-486	ST
That's What Love Demands	Isaacs, Sonya	14-910	CB
That's What Love Is For	Grant, Amy	18-762	PS
That's What She Gets For Loving Me	Brooks & Dunn	20-167	ST
That's What They Said About the Buffalo	Peterson, Michael	49-107	CDG
That's What They Say	Holly, Buddy	48-675	DCK
That's What You Do When You're In	Forrester Sisters	20-682	SC
That's What You Get	Paramore	36-526	CB
That's What Your Love Does	Harvick, Kerry	23-288	CB

263

SONG TITLE	ARTIST	#	TYPE
That's What Your Love Does To Me	Kendall, Jeannie	20-218	CB
That's When I Love You	Vassar, Phil	17-604	CB
That's When I Love You	Vassar, Phil	25-65	MM
That's When I Love You	Vassar, Phil	16-6	ST
That's When I See The Blues	Reeves, Jim	44-249	SRK
That's When You Came Along	Hart, Tara Lyn	14-714	CB
That's When You Know It's Over	Brice, Lee	41-51	ASK
That's When You Know It's Over	Brice, Lee	39-74	PHN
That's Where You're Wrong	Singletary, Daryle	8-475	CB
That's Why	Wilson, Jackie	7-300	MM
That's Why God Made Mexico	McGraw, Tim	49-76	ZPA
That's Why I Fell In Love	Rabbitt, Eddie	12-72	DK
That's Why I'm Here	Chesney, Kenny	8-234	CB
That's Why I'm Here	Chesney, Kenny	7-746	CHM
That's Why I'm Here	Chesney, Kenny	22-773	ST
The "F" Word - duet	Williams & Kid Rock	45-133	SC
Theme From Exodus	Williams, Andy	13-554	LE
Theme From Mahogany	Ross, Diana	14-891	DK
Theme From The Monkees	Monkees	6-858	MM
Then	Paisley, Brad	37-36	CB
Then Again	Alabama	1-18	CB
Then Again	Alabama	9-530	SAV
Then And Only Then	Smith, Connie	5-756	SC
Then Came You	Warwick, Dionne	26-394	DK
Then He Kissed Me	Crystals	3-291	MM
Then He Kissed Me	Crystals	10-652	SF
Then I Kissed Her	Beach Boys	46-503	ZM
Then It's Love	Williams, Don	5-866	SC
Then The Morning Comes	Smash Mouth	35-256	CB
Then The Morning Comes	Smash Mouth	8-524	PHT
Then The Morning Comes	Smash Mouth	5-789	SC
Then They Do	Adkins, Trace	25-572	MM
Then They Do	Adkins, Trace	19-8	ST
Then They Do	Adkins, Trace	32-265	THM
Then What	Walker, Clay	8-226	CB
Then What	Walker, Clay	7-720	CHM
Then What	Walker, Clay	22-757	ST
Then Who Am I	Pride, Charley	43-207	CB
Then You Can Tell Me Goodbye	Arnold, Eddy	17-629	THM
Then You Can Tell Me Goodbye	Campbell, Glen	9-523	SAV
Then You Can Tell Me Goodbye	Casinos	6-267	MM
Then You Can Tell Me Goodbye	Casinos	2-844	SC
Then You Can Tell Me Goodbye	McCoy, Neal	7-276	MM

SONG TITLE	ARTIST	#	TYPE
There Ain't no Easy Run	Dudley, Dave	43-295	CB
There Ain't No Future In This	McEntire, Reba	14-426	SC
There Ain't No Good Chain Gang	Cash & Jennings	29-562	CB
There Ain't No Good Chain Gang	Cash & Jennings	20-663	SC
There Ain't Nothin' Wrong W/Radio	Tippin, Aaron	6-201	MM
There Ain't Nothin' Wrong W/Radio	Tippin, Aaron	2-24	SC
There Are The Days	Lamar, Holly	18-453	ST
There For Awhile	Wariner, Steve	1-499	CB
There Goes	Jackson, Alan	1-56	CB
There Goes	Jackson, Alan	7-657	CHM
There Goes Another Love	Outlaws	7-463	MM
There Goes Another Love	Outlaws	2-522	SC
There Goes My Baby	Drifters	12-357	DK
There Goes My Baby	Drifters	5-452	SC
There Goes My Baby	Yearwood, Trisha	1-643	CB
There Goes My Baby	Yearwood, Trisha	7-761	CHM
There Goes My Everything	Greene, Jack	8-774	CB
There Goes My Everything	Greene, Jack	8-671	SAV
There Goes My Everything	Humperdinck, E.	49-45	ZVS
There Goes My Everything	Murray, Anne	11-6	PL
There Goes My Everything	Whittaker, Roger	13-588	PL
There Goes My First Love	Drifters	45-893	MFK
There Goes My Heart	Mavericks	2-490	SC
There Goes My Life	Chesney, Kenny	22-2	CB
There Goes My Life	Chesney, Kenny	19-674	ST
There Goes The Neighborhood	Crow, Sheryl	7-800	PHT
There Goes The Neighborhood	Crow, Sheryl	29-678	RS
There Goes The Neighborhood	Harling, Keith	8-915	CB
There He Goes	Cline, Patsy	22-192	CB
There I've Said It Again	Monroe, Vaughn	4-195	SC
There I've Said It Again	Vinton, Bobby	4-720	SC
There Is	Box Car Racer	32-71	THM
There Is No Arizona	O'Neal, Jamie	14-100	CB
There Is No Greater Love	Cole, Nat "King"	46-368	PS
There Is No War	Chapman, Donovan	19-690	ST
There Is No Xmas Like A Home Xmas	Como, Perry	45-748	CB
There Must Be An Angel	Eurythmics	47-74	EZ
There Must Be More To Love Than This	Lewis, Jerry Lee	47-199	CB
There She Goes	Sixpence None The	8-502	PHT
There She Goes	Smith, Carl	22-117	CB
There Stands The Glass	Pierce, Webb	8-392	CB
There There	Radiohead	32-292	THM

SONG TITLE	ARTIST	#	TYPE
There Will Come A Day	Hill, Faith	20-587	CB
There Will Come A Day	Hill, Faith	16-303	PHM
There Will Come A Day	Hill, Faith	22-569	ST
There Will Never Be Another You	Standard	15-569	SGB
There Won't Be Anymore	Rich, Charlie	13-481	P
There Won't Be Anymore	Rich, Charlie	5-204	SC
There You Are	McBride, Martina	9-423	CB
There You Are	McBride, Martina	13-823	CHM
There You Are	McBride, Martina	22-545	ST
There You Go	Cash, Johnny	29-746	CB
There You Go	Cash, Johnny	5-214	SC
There You Go	Pink	14-179	CB
There You Go Again	Rogers, Kenny	14-787	ST
There You Go Again	Rogers, Kenny	15-215	THM
There You Go Again	Rogers, Kenny	16-275	TT
There You Have It	Blackhawk	8-181	CB
There You'll Be	Hill, Faith	33-445	CB
There You'll Be	Hill, Faith	15-182	ST
There You'll Be	Hill, Faith	18-537	TT
There'll Be No Teardrops Tonight	Nelson, Willie	47-524	VH
There'll Be Sad Songs (To Make U Cr	Ocean, Billy	25-285	MM
There'll Be Sad Songs To...	Ocean, Billy	35-205	CB
There's A Ghost In My House	Taylor, Dean	30-792	SF
There's A Ghost In My House	Taylor, R. Dean	30-792	SF
There's A Girl In Texas	Adkins, Trace	7-280	MM
There's A Heartache Following Me	Reeves, Jim	3-840	LG
There's A Hero - Patriotic	Gilman, Billy	36-339	CB
There's A Honky Tonk Angel	Twitty, Conway	29-617	CB
There's A Kind Of Hush	Carpenters	44-347	DK
There's A Kind Of Hush	Herman's Hermits	16-880	DK
There's A Kind Of Hush	Herman's Hermits	12-921	P
There's A Kind Of Hush	Herman's Hermits	5-465	SC
There's A Moon Out Tonight	Capris	6-264	MM
There's A Moon Out Tonight	Capris	13-271	P
There's A Moon Out Tonight	Capris	5-240	SC
There's A New Moon Over My Shoulder	Ritter, Tex	20-706	CB
There's A Rainbow 'Round My Shoulder	Darin, Bobby	47-6	KV
There's A Stranger In My House	Tamia	18-538	TT
There's A Tear In My Beer	Williams, Hank Jr.	7-420	MM
There's A Tear In My Beer	Williams, Hank Jr/S	9-449	SAV
There's A Whole Lot About A Woman	Greene, Jack	43-348	CB
There's Always Me	Reeves, Jim	45-265	BSP

SONG TITLE	ARTIST	#	TYPE
There's Always Something	Shapiro, Helen	10-611	SF
There's Been A Change In Me	Arnold, Eddy	45-572	CKC
There's Been A Change In Me	Reeves, Jim	44-267	CKC
There's Got To Be More To Life	Orrico, Stacie	19-645	CB
There's More To Me Than That	Andrews, Jessica	25-446	MM
There's More To Me Than You	Andrews, Jessica	34-356	CB
There's More To Me Than You	Andrews, Jessica	18-595	ST
There's More To Me Than You	Andrews, Jessica	32-119	THM
There's More Where That Came From	Womack, Lee Ann	29-499	SC
There's No Business Like Show...	Merman, Ethel	12-571	P
There's No Business Like Show...	Merman, Ethel	2-244	SC
There's No Getting Over Me	Milsap, Ronnie	1-444	CB
There's No Getting Over Me	Milsap, Ronnie	11-619	DK
There's No Getting' Over Me	Milsap, Ronnie	13-423	P
There's No Limit	Carter, Deana	34-349	CB
There's No Limit	Carter, Deana	25-422	MM
There's No Limit	Carter, Deana	18-468	ST
There's No Limit	Carter, Deana	32-41	THM
There's No Love In Tennessee	Mandrell, Barbara	5-59	SC
There's No Stoppin Your Heart	Osmond, Marie	4-795	SC
There's No Way	Alabama	1-9	CB
There's Only One Way To Rock	Hagar, Sammy	21-768	SC
There's Only You	Sharp, Kevin	8-149	CB
There's Only You	Sharp, Kevin	22-415	ST
There's Poison In Your Heart	Wells, Kitty	47-391	CB
There's Still A Place For That	Riggs, Levi	39-68	PHN
There's Your Trouble	Dixie Chicks	8-466	CB
There's Your Trouble	Dixie Chicks	7-742	CHM
There's Your Trouble	Dixie Chicks	10-57	SC
These Are Days	10,000 Maniacs	13-237	P
These Are My People	Atkins, Rodney	30-354	CB
These Are The Days	O-Town	25-404	MM
These Are The Days	O-Town	32-61	THM
These Are The Days Of Our Lives	Stansfield & Mic	18-235	DK
These Are The Good Old Days	Otto, James	36-263	PHM
These Are The Times	Hill, Dru	13-674	SGB
These Arms	Yoakam, Dwight	16-662	CHT
These Arms Of Mine	Redding, Otis	33-244	CB
These Arms Of Mine	Rimes, LeAnn	8-485	CB

265

SONG TITLE	ARTIST	#	TYPE
These Arms Of Mine	Rimes, LeAnn	22-701	ST
These Boots Are Made For Walkin'	Bardo, Sharie	14-46	THM
These Boots Are Made For Walkin'	Sinatra, Nancy	17-47	DK
These Boots Are Made For Walkin'	Sinatra, Nancy	10-730	JVC
These Boots Are Made For Walkin'	Sinatra, Nancy	13-96	P
These Days	Alien Ant Farm	23-178	PHM
These Days	Rascal Flatts	34-384	CB
These Days	Rascal Flatts	25-294	MM
These Days	Rascal Flatts	17-581	ST
These Days	Rascal Flatts	32-75	THM
These Days (Album Version)	Alien Ant Farm	32-362	THM
These Dreams	Heart	35-192	CB
These Eyes	Guess Who	9-355	MG
These Eyes	Guess Who	7-269	MM
These Foolish Things	Stewart, Rod	25-592	MM
These Hands	Cash, Johnny	48-432	VH
These Hard Times	Matchbox 20	36-481	CB
These Lips Don't Know How To Say	Stone, Doug	12-160	DK
These Lips Don't Know How To Say..	Stone, Doug	20-593	CB
These Lips Don't Know How To Say..	Stone, Doug	6-625	MM
These Walls	Geiger, Teddy	36-186	PHM
They All Laughed	Sinatra, Frank	49-499	MM
They All Went To Mexico	Santana	44-68	KV
They Asked About You	McEntire, Reba	1-809	CB
They Asked About You	McEntire, Reba	6-457	MM
They Asked About You	McEntire, Reba	2-425	SC
They Call It Fallin' For A Reason	Yearwood, Trisha	36-611	CB
They Call It Fallin' For A Reason	Yearwood, Trisha	36-210	PHM
They Call The Wind Maria	Kingston Trio	7-350	MM
They Call You Gigolette	Orbison, Roy	38-61	AT
They Can't Take That Away	Sinatra, Frank	9-240	PT
They Can't Take That Away	Sinatra, Frank	21-221	SGB
They Can't Take That Away From Me	Stewart, Rod	25-595	MM
They Don't Make 'Em Like My Daddy Anymore	Lynn, Loretta	8-368	CB
They Don't Make 'Em Like...	Boy Howdy	6-593	MM
They Don't Understand	Sawyer Brown	23-481	CB
They Don't Understand	Sawyer Brown	29-615	ST
They Just Can't Stop It	Spinners	17-142	DK
They Just Can't Stop It	Spinners	9-667	SAV
They Never Made It To Me	Newton, Juice	14-732	CB
They Say Vision	RES	17-599	PHM
They Still Play Country Music In Texas	Dunn, Ronnie	45-234	VH

SONG TITLE	ARTIST	#	TYPE
They're Coming To Take Me Away	Napoleon XIV	6-860	MM
They're Coming To Take Me Away	Napoleon XIV	5-631	SC
They're Coming To Take Me Away	Napoleon XIV	16-291	TT
They're Playing Our Song	McCoy, Neal	1-853	CB
They're Playing Our Song	McCoy, Neal	6-798	MM
They're Playing Our Song	McCoy, Neal	2-823	SC
Thicker Than Blood	Brooks, Garth	25-290	MM
Thicker Than Blood	Brooks, Garth	17-579	ST
Thicker Than Water	Brooks, Garth	18-13	CB
Thieves In The Temple	Prince	23-333	CB
Thin Line Between Love & Hate	Lennox, Annie	19-554	SC
Thin Line Between Love & Hate	Pretenders	13-285	P
Thing About You	Hayes, Hunter	44-315	SBI
Thing Called Love	Raitt, Bonnie	33-334	CB
Thing Called Love	Raitt, Bonnie	10-771	JVC
Thing Called Love a	Cash, Johnny	29-561	CB
Thing Called Love a	Cash, Johnny	20-650	SC
Thing Called Love a	Presley, Elvis	25-505	MM
Things	Darin, Bobby	21-531	SC
Things A Mama Don't Know	Roberts, Mica & Keith	36-585	CB
Things Are Tough All Over	Lynne, Shelby	7-161	MM
Things Aren't Funny Anymore	Haggard, Merle	8-324	CB
Things Can Only Get Better	Jones, Howard	16-641	MM
Things Change	McGraw, Tim	10-269	CB
Things Change	McGraw, Tim	22-465	ST
Things Change	Yoakam, Dwight	22-804	ST
Things Have Gone To Pieces	Haggard, Merle	49-813	DCK
Things I Miss The Most	Van Zant	29-580	CB
Things That Make You Go Hmmm	C&C Music Factory	27-331	DK
Things That Never Cross a Man's Min	Pickler, Kellie	30-586	CB
Things That You Do the	Thompson, Gina	24-52	SC
Things To Do In Wichita	Chesnutt, Mark	48-706	BKD
Things We Did Last Summer	Lettermen	48-528	L1
Things We Do For Love	10CC	15-806	SC
Things We Do For Love	Brown, Horace	24-233	SC
Things We Do the	Morgan, Lorrie	49-113	CB
Think	Franklin, Aretha	33-245	CB
Think	Franklin, Aretha	11-810	DK
Think	Franklin, Aretha	3-357	MH
Think	Franklin, Aretha	12-718	P
Think About A Lullaby	Haggard, Merle	49-807	CB
Think About A Lullaby	Haggard, Merle	49-343	CB
Think About You	Vandross, Luther	23-248	THM

SONG TITLE	ARTIST	#	TYPE
Think I'm In Love	Money, Eddie	47-282	LC
Think It Over	Holly, Buddy	3-209	LG
Think It Over	Holly, Buddy	11-41	PX
Think It Over	Moorer, Allison	49-346	SC
Think It Over	Moorer, Allison	49-226	SC
Think Of The Good Times	Jay & Americans	14-368	PS
Think Of The Good Times	Jay & Americans	45-168	PS
Think Of Tomorrow	Isaak, Chris	4-614	SC
Think Of You - duet	Young & Pope	48-2	BKD
Think Twice	Dion, Celine	6-645	MM
Think Twice	Eve 6	32-333	THM
Thinkin' About You	Yearwood, Trisha	1-637	CB
Thinkin' About You	Yearwood, Trisha	6-709	MM
Thinkin' About You	Yearwood, Trisha	17-285	NA
Thinkin' About You	Yearwood, Trisha	22-866	ST
Thinkin' Of A Rendezvous	Duncan, Johnny	5-533	SC
Thinkin' Problem	Ball, David	34-310	CB
Thinkin' Problem	Ball, David	6-587	MM
Thinkin' Problem	Ball, David	2-319	SC
Thinkin' Strait	McCready, Rich	7-255	MM
Thinking About Leaving	Yoakam, Dwight	14-698	CB
Thinking About You	Presley, Elvis	25-104	MM
Thinking Of You	Perry, Katy	38-198	CBE
Thinking Over	Glover, Dana	32-26	THM
Third Rate Romance	Kershaw, Sammy	1-472	CB
Third Rate Romance	Kershaw, Sammy	17-230	NA
Third Rate Romance	Kershaw, Sammy	2-798	SC
Third Rock From The Sun	Diffie, Joe	1-280	CB
Third Rock From The Sun	Diffie, Joe	6-614	MM
Third Rock From The Sun	Diffie, Joe	2-478	SC
Thirty Nine & Holding	Lewis, Jerry Lee	33-69	CB
Thirty Nine & Holding	Lewis, Jerry Lee	13-496	P
This Ain't A Love Song	Bon Jovi	3-435	SC
This Ain't A Scene it's An Arms Race **	Fall Out Boy	48-607	DK
This Ain't Dallas	Williams, Hank Jr.	14-432	SC
This Ain't My First Rodeo	Gosdin, Vern	29-648	SC
This Ain't No Rag It's A Flag	Charlie Daniels Band	16-31	ST
This Ain't No Rag It's A Flag	Charlie Daniels Band	20-579	CB
This Ain't No Thinkin' Thing	Adkins, Trace	7-421	MM
This Ain't Nothin'	Morgan, Craig	37-227	CB
This Ain't Tennessee	Brooks, Garth	8-750	CB
This Bitter Earth	Washington, Dinah	23-354	MM
This Bottle In My Hand	Coe & Jones	18-322	CB
This Bottle In My Hand - duet	Coe & Jones	48-425	CB
This Boy	Beatles	29-343	SC
This Cat's On A Hot Tin Roof	Brian Setzer Orch	13-688	SGB

SONG TITLE	ARTIST	#	TYPE
This Could Take All Night	Marshall, Amanda	19-157	SGB
This Crazy Love	Oak Ridge Boys	47-329	SC
This Diamond Ring	Lewis & Playboys	35-56	CB
This Diamond Ring	Lewis & Playboys	11-90	DK
This Diamond Ring	Lewis & Playboys	10-328	KC
This Door Swings Both Ways	Herman's Hermits	45-599	OZP
This Everyday Love	Rascal Flatts	14-126	CB
This Everyday Love	Rascal Flatts	14-14	CHM
This Everyday Love	Rascal Flatts	19-224	CSZ
This Far Gone	Hanson, Jennifer	20-220	CB
This Far Gone	Hanson, Jennifer	19-49	ST
This Far Gone	Hanson, Jennifer	32-262	THM
This Feels a Lot Like Love	Corbin, Easton	40-20	PHN
This Girl Is A Woman Now	Puckett & Union Gap	34-18	CB
This Golden Ring	Fortunes	45-600	OZP
This Guy's In Love With You	Albert, Herb	35-100	CB
This Guy's In Love With You	Albert, Herb	11-594	DK
This Guy's In Love With You	Albert, Herb	19-110	SAV
This Heart	Mason, Mila	8-763	CB
This Heartache Never Sleeps	Chesnutt, Mark	7-886	CHT
This Heartache Never Sleeps	Chesnutt, Mark	14-610	SC
This Heartache Never Sleeps	Chesnutt, Mark	22-742	ST
This I Gotta See	Griggs, Andy	23-290	CB
This I Promise You	N'Sync	20-434	CB
This I Promise You	N'Sync	16-484	MH
This I Promise You	N'Sync	16-115	PRT
This I Promise You	N'Sync	14-507	SC
This I Promise You	N'Sync	14-19	THM
This I Swear	Skyliners	18-66	MM
This Is A Call	Foo Fighters	48-230	SC
This Is All I Ask Of You	Cole, Nat "King"	46-367	PS
This Is God	Vassar, Phil	25-518	MM
This Is God	Vassar, Phil	18-785	ST
This Is God	Vassar, Phil	32-121	THM
This Is Gonna Hurt	Hoobastank	39-121	PHM
This Is How A Heart Breaks	Thomas, Rob	23-314	CB
This Is How We Do It	Jordan, Montell	49-446	MM
This Is How We Do It	Perry, Katy	46-186	MRH
This Is How We Party	S.O.A.P.	16-225	PHM
This Is How We Party	S.O.A.P.	10-138	SC
This Is How We Roll	Florida Georgia Line	43-123	ASK
This Is It	Loggins, Kenny	34-67	CB
This Is It	Loggins, Kenny	14-577	SC
This Is It	Reeves, Jim	8-809	CB
This Is It	Reeves, Jim	4-799	SC
This Is Me	Dream	18-539	TT
This Is Me	Travis, Randy	6-666	MM

SONG TITLE	ARTIST	#	TYPE
This Is Me Leaving You	Carpenter, M C	29-359	CB
This Is Me Missing You	House, James	6-817	MM
This Is Me Missing You	House, James	2-770	SC
This Is Me You're Talking To	Yearwood, Trisha	36-411	CB
This Is My Country	Ford, Tenn Ernie	34-438	CB
This Is My Country	Ford, Tenn Ernie	21-11	SC
This Is My Country	Patriotic	44-44	PT
This Is My Life	Bassey, Shirley	46-484	SBI
This Is My Life	Vassar, Phil	30-461	CB
This Is My Now	Sparks, Jordin	30-563	CB
This Is My Song	Clark, Petula	10-589	SF
This Is My Song	Humperdinck, E.	48-391	KV
This Is Our Moment	Chesney, Kenny	37-330	CB
This Is Something For The Radio	Biz Markie	28-224	SF
This Is The Last Time	Keane	21-692	Z
This Is The Life	Dean, Billy	23-129	CB
This Is The Life	Montana, Hannah	36-69	WD
This Is The Night	Aiken, Clay	25-651	MM
This Is The Night	Aiken, Clay	19-540	SC
This Is The Night	Aiken, Clay	32-316	THM
This Is What Makes Us Girls	Del Rey, Lana	48-506	KVD
This Is Where I Came In	Bee Gees	48-686	EG
This Is Why I'm Hot **	Mims	48-604	DK
This Is Your Brain	Diffie, Joe	7-626	CHM
This Is Your Brain	Diffie, Joe	10-74	SC
This Is Your Night	Amber	24-554	SC
This Is Your Time	Smith, Michael W.	9-334	PS
This Is Your Time	Smith, Michael W.	14-488	SC
This Kind Of Town	Moore, Justin	45-645	BKD
This Kiss	Hill, Faith	15-691	CB
This Kiss	Hill, Faith	7-731	CHM
This Kiss	Hill, Faith	22-767	ST
This Kiss	Jepsen, Carly Rae	49-109	BKD
This Kiss (Pop Version)	Hill, Faith	15-624	PHM
This Land Is Your Land	Christy Minstrels	7-349	MM
This Land Is Your Land	Guthrie, Woody	35-33	CB
This Land Is Your Land	Guthrie, Woody	26-322	DK
This Land Is Your Land	Patriotic	44-45	PT
This Land Is Your Land	Standard	20-159	BCI
This Little Girl Of Mine	Young, Faron	5-816	SC
This Love	Maroon 5	20-561	CB
This Love	Maroon 5	21-681	Z
This Love	Rimes, LeAnn	20-273	SC
This Love	Rimes, LeAnn	19-698	ST
This Love	Swift, Taylor	48-305	KV
This Love Of Mine	Sinatra, Frank	49-490	MM
This Magic Moment	Drifters	35-43	CB
This Magic Moment	Drifters	11-219	DK
This Magic Moment	Drifters	12-656	P
This Magic Moment	Drifters	9-838	SAV
This Magic Moment	Drifters	17-328	SS
This Magic Moment	Jay & Americans	26-387	DK
This Magic Moment	Jay & Americans	14-377	PS
This Masquerade	Benson, George	16-785	DK

SONG TITLE	ARTIST	#	TYPE
This Masquerade	Benson, George	14-353	MH
This Masquerade	Benson, George	16-536	P
This Masquerade	Carpenters	44-354	SFG
This Missin' You Heart Of Mine	Sawyer Brown	19-442	SC
This Moment	Etheridge, Melissa	23-558	MM
This Night Won't Last Forever	Sawyer Brown	7-671	CHM
This Nightlife	Black, Clint	1-837	CB
This Ol' Guitar	Denver, John	15-621	THM
This Old Heart Of Mine	Isley Brothers	27-334	DK
This Old Heart Of Mine	Shepard, Vonda	48-556	DK
This Old Heart Of Mine	Stewart, Rod	14-847	LE
This Old Heart Of Mine	Stewart, Rod	6-233	MM
This Old House	Brian Setzer Orch	13-699	SGB
This Old House	Brian Setzer Orch	46-535	SGB
This Old Town	River City Gang	38-213	PHN
This Ole Boy	Morgan, Craig	48-284	CB
This Ole Boy	Nichols, Joe	47-322	KV
This Ole House	Clooney, Rosemary	2-241	SC
This One's For The Children	New Kids On Block	9-859	SAV
This One's For The Girls	McBride, Martina	29-528	CB
This One's For The Girls	McBride, Martina	25-637	MM
This One's For The Girls	McBride, Martina	19-169	ST
This One's For The Girls	McBride, Martina	32-335	THM
This One's For You	Manilow, Barry	29-117	CB
This Pretender	Diffie, Joe	25-195	MM
This Pretender	Diffie, Joe	16-686	ST
This Romeo Ain't Got Julie Yet	Diamond Rio	1-172	CB
This Romeo Ain't Got Julie Yet	Diamond Rio	6-532	MM
This Romeo Ain't Got Julie Yet	Diamond Rio	2-821	SC
This Shirt	Carpenter, M C	8-887	CB
This Side	Nickel Creek	18-337	ST
This Song Will Last Forever	Rawls, Lou	10-500	DA
This Song's For You - duet	Joey & Rory	45-815	CB
This Summer's Gonna Hurt Like A...	Maroon 5	48-443	KCD
This Thing Called Wantin' & Havin'	Sawyer Brown	7-21	MM
This Time	Jennings, Waylon	45-193	VH
This Time	Moman, Chips	16-649	JTG
This Time	Petrone, Shawna	16-195	THM
This Time	Sawyer Brown	17-257	NA
This Time	Sawyer Brown	2-540	SC
This Time Around	Cross Can Ragweed	29-582	CB
This Time Around	Eder, Linda	17-440	PS
This Time Around	Hanson	29-172	MH
This Time Around	Hanson	16-240	PHM
This Time Around	Yankee Grey	14-90	CB
This Time Around	Yankee Grey	22-560	ST
This Time I Almost Made It	Wynette, Tammy	49-366	CB

268

SONG TITLE	ARTIST	#	TYPE
This Time I Know It's For Real	Summer, Donna	15-199	LE
This Time I Know It's For Real	Young Divas	47-675	SFK
This Time I've Hurt Her More Than..	Twitty, Conway	8-363	CB
This Time I've Hurt Her More Than..	Twitty, Conway	13-513	P
This Time The Dream's On Me	Standard	15-570	SGB
This Town	Musgraves, Kacey	45-375	KV
This Town - Nashville	Esten, Charles	45-478	KVD
This Train Don't Stop	John, Elton	25-138	MM
This Used To Be My Playground	Madonna	9-675	SAV
This Very Moment	K-Ci & JoJo	20-467	CB
This Very Moment	K-Ci & JoJo	32-87	THM
This Way	Jewel	18-432	CB
This White Circle On My Finger	Wells, Kitty	47-392	CB
This Will Be	Cole, Natalie	34-71	CB
This Woman And This Man	Walker, Clay	1-96	CB
This Woman And This Man	Walker, Clay	17-284	NA
This Woman And This Man	Walker, Clay	22-865	ST
This Woman Needs	SheDaisy	19-232	SC
This Woman Needs	SheDaisy	22-500	ST
This World Is Not My Home	Reeves, Jim	44-244	DCK
Thistlehair The Christmas Bear	Alabama	45-755	CB
Thong Song the	Sisquo	29-171	MH
Thorn In My Side	Eurythmics	47-72	DMG
Those Lazy Hazy Crazy Days Of Summer	Cole, Nat "King"	35-19	CB
Those Lazy Hazy Crazy Days Of Summer	Cole, Nat "King"	11-304	DK
Those Lazy Hazy Crazy Days Of Summer	Cole, Nat "King"	29-456	LE
Those Magic Changes	Sha-Na-Na	10-11	SC
Those Oldies But Goodies	Little Caesar&Roman	3-584	SC
Those Sweet Words	Jones, Norah	22-351	CB
Those Three Words	Hill, Ingram	39-58	PHN
Those Were The Days	Hopkins, Mary	12-193	DK
Those Were The Days	Hopkins, Mary	7-34	MM
Those Were The Days	Hopkins, Mary	10-587	SF
Those Were The Words We Said	Richey, Kim	3-567	SC
Those Words He Said	Yearwood, Trisha	48-335	SC
Thou Swell	Standard	15-571	SGB
Thoughts Of A Fool	Strait, George	4-144	SC
Thousand Miles a	Carlton, Vanessa	33-429	CB
Thousand Miles a	Carlton, Vanessa	25-204	MM
Thousand Miles From Nowhere	Yoakam, Dwight	9-623	SAV
Thousand Miles From Nowhere	Yoakam, Dwight	2-371	SC

SONG TITLE	ARTIST	#	TYPE
Thousand Stars a	Young, Kathy	30-760	SF
Thousand Stars In The Sky	Young, Kathy	7-306	MM
Thousand Times A Day	Loveless, Patty	1-728	CB
Thousand Times A Day	Loveless, Patty	7-253	MM
Thousand Times A Day a	Loveless, Patty	22-884	ST
Three Bells the	Browns	22-450	SC
Three Chords and The Truth	Evans, Sara	4-833	SC
Three Chords And The Truth	Evans, Sara	22-636	ST
Three Chords Country & American	Anderson, Keith	30-18	CB
Three Cigarettes In An Ashtray	Cline, Patsy	22-193	CB
Three Coins In A Fountain	Williams, Andy	34-7	CB
Three Corn Patches	Presley, Elvis	45-614	HM
Three Days	Green, Pat	16-437	ST
Three Days	lang, k.d.	18-31	CB
Three Good Reasons	Frances, Connie	45-871	VH
Three Good Reasons	Gayle, Crystal	24-250	SC
Three Hearts In A Tangle	Drusky, Roy	20-745	CB
Three Little Teardrops	Keller, Joanie	9-398	CB
Three Marlenas	Wallflowers	7-694	PHM
Three Minute Up Tempo Love Song	Jackson, Alan	49-173	ASK
Three Mississippi	Clark, Terri	20-217	CB
Three Mississippi	Clark, Terri	25-571	MM
Three Mississippi	Clark, Terri	19-2	ST
Three Mississippi	Clark, Terri	32-267	THM
Three Steps To Heaven	Cochran, Eddie	10-550	SF
Three Time Loser	Seals, Dan	48-107	SC
Three Times A Lady	Commodores	35-145	CB
Three Times A Lady	Commodores	7-470	MM
Three Times A Lady	Commodores	21-617	SF
Three Times A Lady	Richie, Lionel	16-821	DK
Three Times A Lady	Richie, Lionel	17-423	KC
Three Times A Lady	Richie, Lionel	10-393	LE
Three Wooden Crosses	Travis, Randy	34-378	CB
Three Wooden Crosses	Travis, Randy	25-525	MM
Three Wooden Crosses	Travis, Randy	18-594	ST
Three Wooden Crosses	Travis, Randy	32-223	THM
Three Words Two Hearts One Night	Collie, Mark	6-848	MM
Three's Company	TV Themes	2-174	SC
Thrill Is Gone the	King, B.B.	12-94	DK
Thrill Is Gone the	King, B.B.	20-140	KB
Thrill Is Gone the	King, B.B.	12-666	P
Thrill Is Gone the	King, B.B.	14-590	SC
Thriller	Jackson, Michael	16-865	DK
Thriller	Jackson, Michael	16-292	TT
Through His Eyes	Martin, Marilyn	2-654	SC
Through The Eyes Of Love	Manchester,Melissa	26-366	DK
Through The Rain	Carey, Mariah	25-426	MM
Through The Rain	Carey, Mariah	18-584	NS
Through The Rain	Carey, Mariah	32-100	THM

SONG TITLE	ARTIST	#	TYPE
Through The Years	Rogers, Kenny	3-172	CB
Through The Years	Rogers, Kenny	6-444	MM
Through The Years	Rogers, Kenny	12-471	P
Through The Years	Rogers, Kenny	2-3	SC
Through Your Hands	Henley, Don	48-154	SC
Throw The Roses Away - WN	Hall & Oates	48-70	SC
Thru' These Walls	Collins, Phil	44-33	SBI
Thumbelina	Kaye, Danny	48-429	VH
Thump Factor	Smokin' Armadillos	7-278	MM
Thunder	Boys Like Girls	36-531	CB
Thunder In My Heart	Sayer, Leo	30-739	SF
Thunder Road	Springsteen, Bruce	17-619	LE
Thunder Road	Springsteen, Bruce	17-177	SC
Thunder Rolls the	Brooks, Garth	6-276	MM
Thunder Rolls the	Brooks, Garth	2-678	SC
Thunderball	Jones, Tom	9-59	SC
Tic Tac Toe	Kyper	2-187	SC
Tic Toc	Rimes, LeAnn	36-365	CB
Tick-Tock	Vaughn, Stevie Ray & Jimmie	48-509	KVD
Ticket Out Of Kansas	Simpson, Jenny	8-216	CB
Ticket To Heaven	3 Doors Down	47-661	SBI
Ticket To Ride	Beatles	11-91	DK
Ticket To Ride	Carpenters	44-353	MFK
Tickets	Maroon 5	39-132	PHM
Ticks	Paisley, Brad	30-351	CB
Tico Tico	Andrew Sisters	46-431	KV
Tide Is High the	Blondie	33-314	CB
Tide Is High the	Blondie	17-65	DK
Tide Is High the	Blondie	13-15	P
Tide Is High the (Get The Feeling)	Atomic Kid	32-324	THM
Tie A Yellow Ribbon	Orlando & Dawn	12-128	DK
Tie A Yellow Ribbon	Orlando & Dawn	3-246	LG
Tie A Yellow Ribbon	Orlando & Dawn	6-353	MM
Tie It Up	Clarkson, Kelly	43-151	BKD
Tie Me Kangaroo Down Sport	Harris, Rolf	26-339	DK
Tie Me Kangaroo Down Sport	Harris, Rolf	9-826	SAV
Tie Me Kangaroo Down Sport	Harris, Rolf	37-80	SC
Tie Our Love In A Double Knot	Parton, Dolly	9-470	SAV
Tie Your Mother Down	Queen	4-569	SC
Tied Together With a Smile	Swift, Taylor	36-85	BM
Ties That Bind	Williams, Don	45-226	CB
Tiger Woman	King, Claude	47-919	SSK
Tight Fittin' Jeans	Twitty, Conway	8-41	CB
Tight Fittin' Jeans	Twitty, Conway	2-640	SC
Tight Rope	Russell, Leon	47-473	SC
Til I Can Make It On My Own	McBride, Martina	30-28	CB
Til I Was A Daddy Too	Lawrence, Tracy	36-408	CB
Til It's Gone	Chesney, Kenny	45-128	BKD
Til My Last Day	Moore, Justin	43-307	ASK

SONG TITLE	ARTIST	#	TYPE
Til Santa's Gone (Milk & Cookies) - xmas	Black, Clint	45-242	BS
Til The End	Gosdin, Vern	47-121	SC
Til Then	Mills Brothers	47-262	AH
Till	Angels	5-79	SC
Till A Tear Becomes A Rose	Whitley & Morgan	8-118	CB
Till A Tear Becomes A Rose	Whitley & Morgan	2-302	SC
Till A Tear Becomes A Rose	Whitley, Keith	6-616	MM
Till A Woman Comes Along	Janson, Chris	45-370	BKD
Till I Can Make It On My Own	Rogers & West	15-234	CB
Till I Can Make It On My Own	Wynette, Tammy	8-371	CB
Till I Gain Control Again	Harris, EmmyLou	45-717	VH
Till I Get It Right	Wynette, Tammy	35-367	CB
Till I Get It Right	Wynette, Tammy	4-746	SC
Till I Get Over You	Branch, Michelle	20-539	CB
Till I Get Over You	Branch, Michelle	20-358	PHM
Till I Kissed Ya	Everly Brothers	35-14	CB
Till I Kissed Ya	Everly Brothers	7-286	MM
Till I Kissed Ya	Everly Brothers	3-335	PS
Till I Loved You - duet	Streisand & Johnson	49-539	CB
Till I Was Loved By You	Wright, Chely	2-550	SC
Till I'm Too Old To Die Young	Bandy, Moe	19-503	CB
Till I'm Too Old To Die Young	Bandy, Moe	9-446	SAV
Till I'm Too Old To Die Young	Bandy, Moe	5-811	SC
Till It Shines	Seger, Bob	10-177	UK
Till Love Comes Again	McEntire, Reba	14-683	CB
Till Love Comes Again	McEntire, Reba	9-522	SAV
Till Nothing Comes Between Us	Montgomery Gentry	25-447	MM
Till Nothing Comes Between Us	Montgomery, J M	33-188	CB
Till Nothing Comes Between Us	Montgomery, J M	18-138	ST
Till Nothing Comes Between Us	Montgomery, J M	19-350	THM
Till Summer Comes Around	Urban, Keith	37-323	SF
Till The End Of Time	Como, Perry	11-575	DK
Till The End Of Time	Como, Perry	20-775	PS
Till The Rivers All Run Dry	Williams, Don	5-202	SC
Till Then	Classics	7-312	MM
Till Then	Lettermen	48-538	L1
Till Then	Standard	10-473	MG
Till There Was You	Beatles	11-451	DK
Till We Meet Again	Crosby, Bing	29-418	CB
Till We Meet Again	Miller, Mitch	23-552	CB
Till You Come Back To Me	Eder, Linda	17-448	PS
Till You Come Back To	Franklin, Aretha	10-478	DA

SONG TITLE	ARTIST	#	TYPE
Me			
Till You Do Me Right	After 7	3-433	SC
Till You Love Me	McEntire, Reba	2-486	SC
Till You're Gone	Mandrell, Barbara	5-57	SC
Tim McGraw	Swift, Taylor	30-23	CB
Timber	Pitbull & KeSha	43-192	PHM
Timber I'm Falling	Husky, Ferlin	22-263	CB
Timber I'm Falling In Love	Loveless, Patty	1-710	CB
Timber I'm Falling In Love	Loveless, Patty	2-342	SC
Time	Alan Parsons Projec	16-241	AMS
Time	Hootie & Blowfish	21-138	CB
Time	Hootie & Blowfish	24-747	SC
Time	Pink Floyd	19-275	SGB
Time	Richie, Lionel	47-461	MM
Time (Clock Of The Heart)	Culture Club	46-649	SBI
Time After Time	INOJ	14-292	MM
Time After Time	INOJ	15-627	PHM
Time After Time	Lauper, Cyndi	17-37	DK
Time After Time	Lauper, Cyndi	4-754	SC
Time Ago	Black Lab	16-228	PHM
Time And Tide	Basia	14-864	PS
Time And Time Again	Papa Roach	18-830	THM
Time Changes Everything	Wills, Bob	20-695	CB
Time Changes Everything	Wills, Bob	8-646	SAV
Time For Action	Secret Affair	30-785	SF
Time For Me To Fly	Parton, Dolly	24-358	SC
Time For Me To Ride	Keith, Toby	38-161	SC
Time Has Come the	McBride, Martina	6-189	MM
Time Has Come Today	Chambers Brothers	14-451	SC
Time In a Bottle	Croce, Jim	13-133	P
Time Is Love	Turner, Josh	39-22	ASK
Time Is Love	Turner, Josh	44-148	BKD
Time Is On My Side	Rolling Stones	11-397	DK
Time Is On My Side	Rolling Stones	19-749	LE
Time Is On My Side	Rolling Stones	14-392	PT
Time Love & Tenderness	Bolton, Michael	34-107	CB
Time Love And Money	Milsap, Ronnie	14-72	CB
Time Marches On	Lawrence, Tracy	1-582	CB
Time Marches On	Lawrence, Tracy	7-205	MM
Time Marches On	Lawrence, Tracy	22-881	ST
Time Of My Life the	Cook, David	36-492	CB
Time Of My Life the	Medley & Warnes	6-333	MM
Time Of The Season	Zombies	11-554	DK
Time Of The Season	Zombies	12-651	P
Time On My Hands	Dodd, Deryl	8-103	CB
Time Out Of Mind	Steely Dan	15-387	RS
Time Passages	Stewart, Al	21-508	SC
Time Passes By	Mattea, Kathy	1-192	CB
Time Time Time	Sugarland	30-240	RS
Time To Get A Gun	Lambert, Miranda	45-34	ASK
Time Warp	Rocky Horror Pictur	2-141	SC
Time Warp	Rocky Horror Pictur	16-293	TT

SONG TITLE	ARTIST	#	TYPE
Time Won't Let Me	Outsiders	6-48	SC
Time's A Wastin' - duet	Cash & Carter	49-294	HKC
Timeless	Clarkson & Guari	25-633	MM
Times Like These	Foo Fighters	32-140	THM
Times Like These (Acoustic Version)	Foo Fighers	25-625	MM
Times They Are A-Changin'	Dylan, Bob	29-100	CB
Times They Are A-Changin'	Dylan, Bob	18-174	DK
Tin Cup Chalace	Buffett, Jimmy	46-148	SBI
Tin Man	America	33-295	CB
Tin Man the	Chesney, Kenny	1-318	CB
Tin Man the	Chesney, Kenny	15-603	ST
Ting A Ling	Holly, Buddy	48-676	DCK
Tiny Bubbles	Ho, Don	6-826	MM
Tiny Dancer	John, Elton	6-542	MM
Tiny Dancer	John, Elton	2-374	SC
Tiny Dancer	McGraw, Tim	18-602	ST
Tiny Dancer	McGraw, Tim	32-80	THM
Tiny Town	Byrd, Tracy	22-322	CB
Tiny Town	Fairchild, Shelly	22-23	CB
Tip It On Back	Bentley, Dierks	39-23	ASK
Tip It On Back	Bentley, Dierks	45-50	SBI
Tip Toe Through The Tulips	Miller, Mitch	34-444	CB
Tippy Toeing	Lynn, Lorretta	45-709	VH
Tips Of My Fingers	Clark, Roy	19-393	SC
Tips Of My Fingers	Drusky, Roy	20-749	CB
Tips Of My Fingers	Wariner, Steve	1-501	CB
Tips Of My Fingers	Wariner, Steve	17-254	NA
Tipsy **	J-Kwon	23-252	THM
Tiptoe Through The Tulips With Me	Tiny Tim	9-839	SAV
Tiptoe Through The Tulips With Me	Tiny Tim	5-645	SC
Tired	Adele	46-1	SBI
Tired Of Being Alone	Green, Al	12-717	P
Tired Of Being Sorry	Ringside	30-227	PHM
Tired Of Loving This Way	Raye & Eakes	14-82	CB
Tired Of Waiting For You	Kinks	10-663	SF
Tisket A Tasket a	Fitzgerald, Ella	16-414	PR
Title	Trainor, Meghan	45-149	KJ
Titty's Beer	Ford, Colt	47-508	KST
TLCASAP	Alabama	1-22	CB
TLCASAP	Alabama	6-460	MM
To All The Girls I've Loved Before	Nelson & Iglesias	16-848	DK
To All The Girls I've Loved Before	Nelson & Iglesias	13-183	P
To All The Girls I've Loved Before	Nelson & Iglesias	9-204	SO
To All the Girls I've Loved... - duet	Iglesias & Nelson	35-333	CB
To Be Loved By You	Judd, Wynonna	1-655	CB
To Be Loved By You	Judd, Wynonna	4-126	SC
To Be Loved By You	Wynonna	35-408	CB

271

SONG TITLE	ARTIST	#	TYPE
To Be With You	Mavericks	7-725	CHM
To Be With You	Mavericks	22-775	ST
To Be With You	Mr. Big	6-170	MM
To Be With You	Stewart, Rod	16-261	TT
To Daddy	Harris, EmmyLou	13-342	P
To Daddy	Parton, Dolly	8-547	CB
To Do What I Do	Jackson, Alan	46-309	SC
To Each His Own	America	46-419	CB
To Each His Own	Platters	45-73	DCK
To Find Where I Belong	Gregg, Ricky Lynn	2-733	SC
To Get Me To You	McCann, Lila	8-193	CB
To Get To You	Morgan, Lorrie	49-114	CB
To Have You Back Again	Loveless, Patty	8-301	CB
To Heck With Ole Santa Claus - xmas	Lynn, Loretta	46-49	SSK
To Know Her Is To Love Her	Lettermen	48-530	L1
To Know Him Is To Love Him	Parton, Harris & Ronstadt	49-353	CB
To Know Him Is To Love Him	Teddy Bears	19-622	MH
To Know Him Is To Love Him	Teddy Bears	22-446	SC
To Love A Woman	Richie, Lionel	47-464	SF
To Love Somebody	Bee Gees	17-494	LE
To Love Somebody	Bolton, Michael	24-137	SC
To Love You More	Dion, Celine	15-114	BS
To Love You More	Dion, Celine	21-554	PHM
To Make You Feel My Love	Brooks, Garth	8-484	CB
To Make You Feel My Love	Brooks, Garth	7-759	CHM
To Me	Greenwood&Mandrell	2-307	SC
To Me You're Everything	98 Degrees	15-376	SKG
To Quote Shakespeare	Clark Family Exp.	17-605	CB
To Quote Shakespeare	Clark Family Exp.	16-14	ST
To Remember	Kelley, Josh	36-255	PHM
To Say Goodbye	Joey & Rory	45-814	BKD
To See My Angel Cry	Twitty, Conway	22-251	SC
To Sir With Love	Lulu	11-359	DK
To Sir With Love	Lulu	10-724	JVC
To Sir With Love	Lulu	12-885	P
To Tell You The Truth I Lied	Nichols, Joe	47-323	SC
To The Aisle	Five Satins	2-862	SC
To The Moon And Back	Savage Garden	21-545	PHM
To Where You Are	Groban, Josh	35-307	CB
To Where You Are	Groban, Josh	18-415	MM
To Where You Are	Groban, Josh	17-592	PHM
To Zion	Hill, Lauryn	19-727	CB
Tobacco Road	Nashville Teens	10-655	SF
Today	Allan, Gary	38-127	CB
Today	Allan, Gary	36-318	PHM
Today	Denver, John	15-616	THM
Today All Over Again	McEntire, Reba	1-787	CB
Today I Started Loving You Again	Haggard, Merle	8-425	CB

SONG TITLE	ARTIST	#	TYPE
Today I Started Loving You Again	Haggard, Merle	11-125	DK
Today My World Slipped Away	Strait, George	1-254	CB
Today My World Slipped Away	Strait, George	22-626	ST
Today Tomorrow & Forever	Presley, Elvis	25-756	MM
Today Was A Fairytale	Swift, Taylor	36-53	PT
Today's Lonely Fool	Lawrence, Tracy	1-572	CB
Today's Teardrops	Orbison, Roy	47-735	SRK
Toes	Zac Brown Band	36-315	PHM
Toes (Female Version)	Zac Brown Band	49-287	CK
Together (Wherever We Go)	Lawrence & Gorme	25-257	MM
Together Again	Harris, EmmyLou	46-195	SC
Together Again	Jackson, Janet	7-709	PHM
Together Again	Jackson, Janet	9-100	PS
Together Again	Owens, Buck	15-829	CB
Together Again	Owens, Buck	17-18	DK
Together Again	Owens, Buck	8-616	SAV
Together Forever	Astley, Rick	11-261	DK
Together You And I	Parton, Dolly	49-740	CB
Tom Dooley	Kingston Trio	35-11	CB
Tom Dooley	Kingston Trio	27-370	DK
Tom Dooley	Kingston Trio	7-346	MM
Tom Dooley	Standard	18-171	DK
Tom Sawyer	Rush	4-567	SC
Tomb Of Unknown Love	Rogers, Kenny	5-243	SC
Tomorrow	Cranberries	38-250	PHM
Tomorrow	SR-71	18-828	THM
Tomorrow	Streisand, Barbra	49-571	PS
Tomorrow	Young, Chris	37-207	AS
Tomorrow - Show	Annie	33-220	CB
Tomorrow Never Comes	Dickens, Little Jimmy	45-576	SSK
Tomorrow Never Comes	Presley, Elvis	25-747	MM
Tomorrow Never Comes	Zac Brown Band	46-77	BKD
Tomorrow Never Dies	Crow, Sheryl	9-65	SC
Tomorrow Night	Johnson, Lonnie	10-399	SS
Tomorrow's Girls	Fagen, Donald	16-631	MM
Tonight	Evans, Sara	22-99	CB
Tonight	Jonas Brothers	36-523	CB
Tonight	Kinder, Ryan	41-99	PHN
Tonight	New Kids On Block	9-682	SAV
Tonight	West Side Story	19-587	SC
Tonight	Wood & Beymer	11-795	DK
Tonight (I'm Loving You)	Iglesias, Enrique	49-70	ZPC
Tonight (Radio Version)	Evans, Sara	21-665	SC
Tonight Carmen	Robbins, Marty	3-239	CB
Tonight Carmen	Robbins, Marty	5-847	SC
Tonight I Celebrate My Love - duet	Bryson & Flack	35-311	CB
Tonight I Celebrate My Love For U	Bryson & Flack	6-228	MM
Tonight I Celebrate My Love For U	Bryson & Flack	9-208	SC
Tonight I Climbed The	Jackson, Alan	12-462	P

272

SONG TITLE	ARTIST	#	TYPE
Wall			
Tonight I Climbed The Wall	Jackson, Alan	2-417	SC
Tonight I Fell In Love	Tokens	25-547	MM
Tonight I Wanna Be Your Man	Griggs, Andy	33-153	CB
Tonight I Wanna Be Your Man	Griggs, Andy	25-132	MM
Tonight I Wanna Be Your Man	Griggs, Andy	16-328	ST
Tonight I Wanna Cry	Urban, Keith	29-36	CB
Tonight I'm Getting Over You	Jepsen, Carly Rae	49-110	KCD
Tonight I'm Yours	Stewart, Rod	14-860	LE
Tonight I'm Yours (Don't Hurt Me)	Stewart, Rod	24-68	SC
Tonight I'm Yours Don't Hurt Me	Steward, Rod	48-215	LE
Tonight Is Right For Loving **	Chef & Meatloaf	13-720	SGB
Tonight Looks Good On You	Aldean, Jason	45-368	BKD
Tonight My Baby's Comin' Home	Mandrell, Barbara	20-689	SC
Tonight She's Gonna Love Me	Bailey, Razzy	29-383	CB
Tonight The Bottle Let Me Down	Mavericks	44-115	KV
Tonight The Heartache's On Me	Dixie Chicks	8-862	CB
Tonight The Heartache's On Me	Dixie Chicks	7-862	CHT
Tonight The Heartache's On Me	Dixie Chicks	22-737	ST
Tonight The Heartaches On Me	Dixie Chicks	10-64	SC
Tonight Tonight	Mellokings	6-265	MM
Tonight We Just Might Fall In Love	Ketchum, Hal	6-590	MM
Tonight We Just Might Fall In Love	Ketchum, Hal	17-222	NA
Tonight You Belong To Me	West, Dottie	15-230	CB
Tonight You Belong To Me	West, Dottie	47-816	SRK
Tonight, Tonight, Tonight	Collins, Phil	44-29	BS
Tonight's Not The Night	Randy Rogers Band	22-321	CB
Tonight's The Night	Shirelles	48-375	MM
Tonight's The Night	Stewart, Rod	25-601	MM
Tonight's The Night	Stewart, Rod	2-859	SC
Too Bad	Nickelback	30-648	THM
Too Bad You're No Good	Yearwood, Trisha	48-336	SC
Too Busy Being In Love	Stone, Doug	20-599	CB
Too Busy Being In Love	Stone, Doug	6-218	MM
Too Busy Being In Love	Stone, Doug	2-710	SC
Too Busy Thinking About My Baby	Gaye, Marvin	12-10	DK
Too Busy Thnking About My Baby	Gaye, Marvin	2-84	SC

SONG TITLE	ARTIST	#	TYPE
Too Close	Next	21-561	PHM
Too Close For Comfort	Davis, Sammy Jr.	47-17	PS
Too Cold At Home	Chesnutt, Mark	1-346	CB
Too Cool To Dance	Eden Xo	48-400	DCK
Too Drunk To Fish	Stevens, Ray	47-846	FMG
Too Drunk To Karaoke - duet	Keith & Buffett	41-44	ASK
Too Far From Texas	Nicks with Dixie Chicks	47-901	TU
Too Far Gone	Wynette, Tammy	49-361	CB
Too Fat Polka	Polka Favorites	29-808	SSR
Too Fat Polka - w/Words	Polka Favorites	29-862	SSR
Too Funky	Michael, George	12-837	P
Too Funky	Michael, George	5-746	SC
Too Gone Too Long	En Vogue	7-690	PHM
Too Gone Too Long	Travis, Randy	1-398	CB
Too Gone Too Long	Travis, Randy	9-498	SAV
Too Gone Too Long	Travis, Randy	3-380	SC
Too Good To Be True	Peterson, Michael	8-240	CB
Too Good To Be True	Peterson, Michael	7-738	CHM
Too Good To Last	Rivers, Johnny	47-369	DFK
Too Hot	Kool & The Gang	49-475	MM
Too Late	Lopez, Jennifer	23-323	CB
Too Late	Lopez, Jennifer	23-579	MM
Too Late For Goodbyes	Lennon, Julian	5-682	SC
Too Late For Love	Def Leppard	46-169	SC
Too Late To Turn Back Now	Cornelius & Rose	16-566	P
Too Late To Turn Back Now	Cornelius & Rose	5-376	SC
Too Late To Turn Back Now	Williams, Don	48-552	DK
Too Late To Worry Too Blue To Cry	Milsap, Ronnie	47-275	CB
Too Late To Worry, Too Blue to Cry	Al Dexter & Troopers	34-181	CB
Too Late Too Soon	Secada, Jon	10-687	HH
Too Lazy To Work, Nervous to Steal	BR5-49	17-477	TT
Too Lazy To Work/Nervous to Steal	BR5-49	29-356	CB
Too Legit To Quit	Hammer, MC	12-126	DK
Too Legit To Quit	Hammer, MC	25-484	MM
Too Many Fish In The Sea	Midler, Bette	45-938	KV
Too Many Highways	England, Tyler	5-834	SC
Too Many Lovers	Gayle, Crystal	48-497	CKC
Too Many Rivers	Lee, Brenda	30-324	CB
Too Many Rivers	Lee, Brenda	45-449	CB
Too Many Walls	Dennis, Cathy	9-684	SAV
Too Marvelous For Words	Sinatra, Frank	9-254	PT
Too Much	Dave Mattherw Band	34-125	CB
Too Much	Presley, Elvis	2-585	SC
Too Much	Presley, Elvis	14-764	THM
Too Much	Spice Girls	7-713	PHM
Too Much	Spice Girls	5-185	SC
Too Much Fun	Singletary, Daryle	35-413	CB

273

SONG TITLE	ARTIST	#	TYPE
Too Much Fun	Singletary, Daryle	7-167	MM
Too Much Fun	Singletary, Daryle	4-19	SC
Too Much Heaven	Bee Gees	17-496	LE
Too Much Heaven	Bee Gees	21-808	SC
Too Much In Love To Care	Sunset Boulevard	19-591	SC
Too Much Love	Bread	46-527	CB
Too Much Month at the End of/Money	Stuart, Marty	19-706	ST
Too Much Of A Good Thing	Jackson, Alan	20-442	ST
Too Much On My Heart	Statler Brothers	19-385	CB
Too Much On My Heart	Statler Brothers	11-722	DK
Too Much On My Heart	Statler Brothers	5-527	SC
Too Much Time On My Hands	Styx	20-88	SC
Too Much To Lose	Kentucky HH	14-147	CB
Too Much Too Little Too Late	Mathis & Williams	35-309	CB
Too Much Too Little Too Late	Mathis & Williams	11-460	DK
Too Much Too Little Too Late	Mathis & Williams	6-341	MM
Too Much Too Little Too Late	Mathis & Williams	13-156	P
Too Much Too Little Too Late	Mathis, Johnny	29-464	LE
Too Old To Play Cowboy	Bailey, Razzy	29-391	CB
Too Shy	Kajagoogoo	21-401	SC
Too Soon To Know	Gibson, Don	8-821	CB
Too Soon To Tell	Raitt, Bonnie	10-770	JVC
Too Young	Cole, Nat "King"	12-526	P
Too Young To Fall In Love	Motley Crue	6-23	SC
Toot Toot Tootsie	Jolson, Al	29-471	LE
Toot Toot Tootsie Goodbye	Jolson, Al	12-943	PS
Toot Toot Tootsie Goodbye	Jolson, Al	21-1	SC
Toot Toot Tootsie Goodbye	Newton, Wayne	47-317	LE
Toot Toot Tootsie Goodbye	Standard	35-26	CB
Top Of The World	Anderson, Lynn	47-649	KT
Top Of The World	Carpenters	12-688	P
Top Of The World	McGraw, Tim	45-38	BKD
Tore Up From The Floor Up	Hayes, Wade	8-351	CB
Tore Up From The Floor Up	Hayes, Wade	22-722	ST
Torn	Imbruglio, Natalie	8-513	PHT
Torn	Imbruglio, Natalie	13-713	SGB
Torn Between Two Lovers	MacGregor, Mary	22-928	SC
Tornado	Little Big Town	40-4	ASK
Toss A Little Bone	Confederate RR	14-105	CB
Tossin' And Turnin'	Lewis, Bobby	11-565	DK
Tossin' And Turnin'	Lewis, Bobby	10-741	JVC
Tossin' And Turnin'	Lewis, Bobby	6-147	MM

SONG TITLE	ARTIST	#	TYPE
Tossin' And Turnin'	Lewis, Bobby	13-122	P
Tossin' And Turnin'	Lewis, Bobby	3-254	SC
Total Eclipse Of The Heart	French, Nicki	3-434	SC
Total Eclipse Of The Heart	Tyler, Bonnie	14-571	AH
Total Eclipse Of The Heart	Tyler, Bonnie	18-231	DK
Total Eclipse Of The Heart	Tyler, Bonnie	9-16	MH
Touch And Go Crazy	Greenwood, Lee	46-113	SC
Touch It	Monifah	7-799	PHT
Touch Me **	Doors	2-727	SC
Touch Me **	Doors	18-650	SO
Touch Me **	Fox, Samantha	5-554	SC
Touch Me In The Morning	Ross, Diana	16-741	DK
Touch Me In The Morning	Ross, Diana	15-356	LE
Touch Me In The Morning	Ross, Diana	9-657	SAV
Touch Me In The Morning	Ross, Diana	4-752	SC
Touch Me When We're Dancing	Alabama	4-818	SC
Touch Me When We're Dancing	Carpenters	44-345	CBE
Touch My Body	Carey, Mariah	36-440	CB
Touch My Heart	Price, Ray	3-778	CB
Touch Of Grey	Grateful Dead	3-522	SC
Touch The Hand	Twitty, Conway	1-156	CB
Touch The Hand	Twitty, Conway	13-518	P
Touch The Morning	Gibson, Don	5-130	SC
Touched By The Sun	Simon, Carly	24-29	SC
Tough	Morgan, Craig	30-309	CB
Tough	Pickler, Kellie	38-227	FTX
Tough Little Boys	Allan, Gary	25-643	MM
Tough Little Boys	Allan, Gary	19-173	ST
Tough Little Boys	Allan, Gary	32-336	THM
Tougher Than Nails	Diffie, Joe	30-8	SC
Tougher Than Nails	Diffie, Joe	20-177	ST
Tougher Than The Rest	Springsteen, Bruce	17-614	LE
Town Without Pity	Pitney, Gene	6-442	MM
Town Without Pity	Pitney, Gene	9-177	SO
Toxic	Anderson, Jordin	41-66	PHN
Toxic	Spears, Britney	20-535	CB
Toy Soldier	Martika	7-102	MM
Toy Soldier	Martika	21-601	SF
Toys In The Attic	Aerosmith	4-561	SC
Tra Le La Le La Triangle	Cline, Patsy	5-697	SC
Traces	Classics IV	12-319	DK
Traces/Memories	Lettermen	48-524	L1
Tracks Of My Tears	Rivers, Johnny	47-364	CB
Tracks Of My Tears	Robinson, Smokey	16-806	DK
Tracks Of My Tears	Robinson, Smokey	12-638	P
Tracks Of My Tears	Robinson, Smokey	2-91	SC
Trademark	Smith, Carl	22-113	CB
Traffic Jam (Live)	Taylor, James	45-523	SC

SONG TITLE	ARTIST	#	TYPE
Tragedy	Anthony, Marc	25-27	MM
Tragedy	Bee Gees	11-415	DK
Tragedy	Bee Gees	17-493	LE
Tragedy	Bee Gees	9-784	SAV
Tragedy	Steps	15-331	PHM
Tragedy	Wayne, Thomas	20-31	SC
Trail Of Broken Hearts	lang, k.d.	8-890	CB
Trail Of Tears	Cyrus, Billy Ray	4-431	SC
Trail Of The Lonesome Pines	Laurel & Hardy	47-592	P
Trailer Song the	Musgraves, Kacey	45-276	BKD
Trailerhood	Keith, Toby	38-158	PHM
Train	3 Doors Down	47-655	CB
Train In Vain	Lennox, Annie	17-725	PS
Train Kept A Rollin'	Aerosmith	13-757	SGB
Train Of Memories	Mattea, Kathy	5-530	SC
Train Train	Blackfoot	18-158	CB
Train Train	Blackfoot	2-531	SC
Train Without A Whistle	Tillis, Pam	47-795	SRK
Train Wreck	McLachlan, Sarah	29-243	ZM
Trains & Boats & Planes	Kramer & Dacotas	10-653	SF
Trainwreck Of Emotion	Morgan, Lorrie	1-333	CB
Tramp	Redding, Otis	47-358	LE
Tramp On The Street the	Williams, Hank Sr.	45-707	CB
Transcendental Blues	Earle, Steve	46-184	SC
Trashy Women	Confederate RR	6-403	MM
Travelin' Band	CCR	11-420	DK
Travelin' Band	CCR	5-355	SC
Travelin' Blues	Frizzell, Lefty	19-490	CB
Travelin' Man	Nelson, Ricky	21-701	CB
Travelin' Man	Nelson, Ricky	11-134	DK
Travelin' Man	Nelson, Ricky	13-261	P
Travelin' Man	Nelson, Ricky	9-499	SAV
Travelin' Man	Nelson, Ricky	29-839	SC
Travelin' On	Chris Weaver Band	42-1	PHN
Travelin' Shoes	Bishop, Elvin	46-519	CB
Travelin' Soldier	Dixie Chicks	34-333	CB
Travelin' Soldier	Dixie Chicks	25-186	MM
Travelin' Soldier	Dixie Chicks	16-439	ST
Travelin' Soldier	Dixie Chicks	32-115	THM
Traveller	Stapleton, Chris	45-438	BKD
Travellin' Light	Cliff, Richard	48-768	P
Treasure	Mars, Bruno	47-220	KV
Treat Her Like A Lady	Cornelius & Rose	9-722	SAV
Treat Her Like A Lady	Cornelius & Rose	2-858	SC
Treat Her Like A Lady	Temptations	15-699	LE
Treat Her Right	Head, Roy	7-33	MM
Treat Her Right	Sawyer Brown	7-231	MM
Treat Her Right	Sawyer Brown	22-889	ST
Treat Me Nice	Presley, Elvis	14-765	THM
Treat Me Right	Benatar, Pat	18-243	DK
Treat Me Right	Benatar, Pat	5-145	SC
Treat U Rite	Winbush, Angela	15-761	NU
Tree Of Hearts	White, Bryan	8-746	CB
Tree Of Hearts	White, Bryan	22-833	ST
Tribute **	Tenacious D	37-90	SC
Trickle Trickle	Videos	20-67	SC

SONG TITLE	ARTIST	#	TYPE
Tricky Tricky	Bega, Lou	9-340	PS
Tricky Tricky	Bega, Lou	5-891	SC
Triflin' Gal	Al Dexter & Troopers	46-406	CB
Trip Around The Sun	Buffett & McBride	21-168	CB
Trip Around The Sun	Buffett & McBride	30-7	SC
Trip Around The Sun	Buffett & McBride	20-506	ST
Trip Around The Sun	Buffett, Jimmy	46-135	ASK
Trolley Song the	Garland, Judy	12-540	P
Trolley Song the	Garland, Judy	9-822	SAV
Tropical Depression	Jackson, Alan	40-98	CB
Troubadour	Strait, George	36-593	CB
Trouble	Chesnutt, Mark	7-147	MM
Trouble	Chesnutt, Mark	3-542	SC
Trouble	Coldplay	48-254	SC
Trouble	Pink	19-644	CB
Trouble	Presley, Elvis	14-781	THM
Trouble	Tritt, Travis	1-675	CB
Trouble	Tritt, Travis	6-538	MM
Trouble	Tritt, Travis	13-526	P
Trouble	Tritt, Travis	2-102	SC
Trouble In Amen Corner	Reeves, Jim	49-300	LDK
Trouble In Mind	Cash, Johnny	46-35	SSK
Trouble In Mind	Lewis, Jerry Lee	45-731	VH
Trouble In Paradise	Lynn, Loretta	8-813	CB
Trouble Is A Woman	Reeves, Jim	44-262	SC
Trouble Is A Woman	Reeves, Julie	8-479	CB
Trouble Me	10,000 Maniacs	29-286	SC
Trouble On The Line	Sawyer Brown	2-340	SC
Trouble Sleeping	Rae, Corinne Bailey	30-716	SF
Trouble With Angels	Mattea, Kathy	9-409	CB
Trouble With Girls the	McCreery, Scotty	45-636	ASK
Trouble With Love Is the	Clarkson, Kelly	35-288	CB
Trouble With Never the	McGraw, Tim	8-960	CB
Trouble With The Truth	Loveless, Patty	1-734	CB
Trouble With The Truth	Loveless, Patty	7-618	CHM
Troublemaker	Weezer	36-521	CB
Truck Driver's Blues	Haggard, Merle	4-374	SC
Truck Drivin' Man	Dudley, Dave	8-390	CB
Truck Drivin' Son Of A Gun	Dudley, Dave	43-294	CB
Truck Drivin' Song	Yankovic, Weird Al	44-82	KV
Truck Driving Man	Owens, Buck	46-100	KWD
Truck Driving Song	Yankovik, Weird Al	46-281	KV
Truck Yeah	McGraw, Tim	39-26	ASK
Trudy	Charlie Daniels Band	49-372	CB
True	Cabrera, Ryan	22-362	CB
True	Cabrera, Ryan	21-163	PHM
True	Spandau Ballet	7-105	MM
True	Strait, George	1-269	CB
True	Strait, George	22-807	ST
True Believer	Milsap, Ronnie	47-278	SC
True Believers	Rucker, Darius	40-44	PHN
True Blue	Madonna	15-573	CMC
True Colors	Collins, Phil	16-221	MM
True Colors	Lauper, Cyndi	11-244	DK

275

SONG TITLE	ARTIST	#	TYPE
True Colors	Lauper, Cyndi	12-684	P
True Companion	Cohn, Marc	29-323	PS
True Faith	New Order	21-596	SF
True Fine Love	Miller, Steve	23-624	BS
True Friends	Curfman, Shannon	5-900	SC
True Love	Benatar, Pat	46-124	SC
True Love	Crosby, Bing	29-480	LE
True Love	John, E & Dee, Kiki	24-148	SC
True Love	Myles, Heather	8-195	CB
True Love	Williams, Don	22-288	CB
True Love Ways	Gilley, Mickey	22-223	CB
True Love Ways	Gilley, Mickey	5-132	SC
True Love Ways	Gilley, Mickey	16-171	THM
True Love Ways	Holly, Buddy	11-31	PX
True Nature	Jane's Addiction	19-853	PHM
True To His Word	Boy Howdy	24-123	SC
Truly	Richie, Lionel	10-385	LE
Truly	Richie, Lionel	12-889	P
Truly Madly Deeply	Deep Blue Something	13-683	SGB
Truly Madly Deeply	Savage Garden	7-705	PHM
Truly Madly Deeply	Savage Garden	10-119	SC
Trust In Me	James, Etta	21-694	PS
Trust In Me	Washington, Dinah	23-353	MM
Truth About Men the	Byrd, Griggs, Shelton, Mont	34-406	CB
Truth About Men the	Byrd, Griggs, Shelton, Mont	32-226	THM
Truth About Men the	Byrd, Tracy	25-563	MM
Truth About Men the	Byrd, Tracy	19-4	ST
Truth Is	Barrino, Fantasia	22-345	CB
Truth No. 2	Dixie Chicks	36-368	CB
Truth No. 2	Dixie Chicks	19-59	ST
Truth the	India.Arie	32-200	THM
Truth'll Set You Free	Mother's Finest	24-557	SC
Truthfully	Loeb, Lisa	14-200	CB
Try	Cailliat, Colbie	45-10	BKD
Try	Furtado, Nelly	20-564	CB
Try A Little Kindness	Campbell, Glen	33-24	CB
Try A Little Kindness	Campbell, Glen	9-619	SAV
Try A Little Kindness	Campbell, Glen	14-328	SC
Try A Little Tenderness	Redding, Otis	35-75	CB
Try A Little Tenderness	Redding, Otis	12-713	P
Try Again	Aaliyah	35-224	CB
Try Again	Aaliyah	15-632	THM
Try Again	Aaliyah	18-540	TT
Try Honesty	B Talent	32-406	THM
Try Honesty	Talent, Billy	23-182	PHM
Try It On My Own	Houston, Whitney	34-178	CB
Try It On My Own	Houston, Whitney	25-537	MM
Try It On My Own	Houston, Whitney	32-240	THM
Try Just a Little Bit Harder	Joplin, Janis	5-676	SC
Try Me Again	Yearwood, Trisha	48-338	SC
Try Me I Know We Can Make It	Summer, Donna	15-202	LE
Try Me One More Time	Tubb, Ernest	22-301	CB

SONG TITLE	ARTIST	#	TYPE
Try Not To Look So Pretty	Yoakam, Dwight	3-36	SC
Try Our Love Again	McKnight, Brian	19-672	CB
Try To Remember	Brothers Four	27-530	DK
Try To Remember	Holmes, Rupert	11-212	DK
Tryin' To Forget The Blues	Wagoner, Porter	19-312	CB
Tryin' To Get Over You	Gill, Vince	1-600	CB
Tryin' To Get Over You	Gill, Vince	6-468	MM
Tryin' To Get Over You	Gill, Vince	2-97	SC
Tryin' To Get The Feeling Again	Manilow, Barry	29-114	CB
Tryin' To Hide A Fire In The Dark	Dean, Billy	6-530	MM
Tryin' To Live My Life Without You	Seger, Bob	46-362	LG
Trying To Find Atlantis	O'Neal, Jamie	22-78	CB
Trying To Find Atlantis	O'Neal, Jamie	21-659	SC
Trying To Love Two Women	Oak Ridge Boys	33-61	CB
Trying To Love Two Women	Oak Ridge Boys	13-476	P
Trying To Love You	Yearwood, Trisha	29-27	CB
Trying To Love You	Yearwood, Trisha	23-455	ST
Trying To Stop Your Leaving	Bentley, Dierks	36-400	CB
Tu Compania	Urban, Keith	36-597	CB
Tubthumping	Chumbawamba	30-214	CB
Tubthumping	Chumbawamba	7-692	PHM
Tubthumping	Chumbawamba	10-116	SC
Tucker's Town	Hootie & Blowfish	21-133	CB
Tuesday Afternoon	Moody Blues	28-138	DK
Tuesday Afternoon	Moody Blues	10-358	KC
Tuesday's Gone	Lynyrd Skynyrd	19-821	SGB
Tuesday's Gone	Williams, Hank Jr.	16-673	C2C
Tuff Enuff	Fabulous T-Birds	35-186	CB
Tuff Enuff	Fabulous T-Birds	7-215	MM
Tulsa Telephone Book	Hall, Tom T.	45-926	VH
Tulsa Time	Clapton, Eric	15-61	LE
Tulsa Time	McHayes	20-455	ST
Tulsa Time	Williams, Don	17-289	NA
Tumbleweed	Sylvia	14-431	SC
Tumbling Dice	Rolling Stones	18-28	LE
Tumbling Tumbleweeds	Sons Of Pioneers	35-341	CB
Tumbling Tumbleweeds	Sons Of Pioneers	17-348	DK
Tunbling Tumbleweeds	Sons Of Pioneers	5-369	SC
Tunnel Of Love	Springsteen, Bruce	20-238	LE
Tupelo Honey	Morrison, Van	17-464	SC
Turkey In The Straw	Standard	47-839	SDK
Turn Around Look At Me	Campbell, Glen	48-491	CKC
Turn Around Look At Me	Vogues	11-560	DK
Turn Back The Hands Of Time	Big Twist	19-802	SGB
Turn Back The Hands Of Time	Davis, Tyrone	10-670	HE
Turn Back The Hands Of Time	Davis, Tyrone	5-390	SC
Turn Back Time	Aqua	5-276	SC

276

SONG TITLE	ARTIST	#	TYPE
Turn It Loose	Judds	1-149	CB
Turn It On Turn It Up Turn Me Loose	Yoakam, Dwight	34-294	CB
Turn It On Turn It Up Turn Me Loose	Yoakam, Dwight	4-143	SC
Turn Me Loose	Fabian	3-469	SC
Turn Me On	Jones, Norah	19-669	CB
Turn Me On	Jones, Norah	25-666	MM
Turn Me On	Jones, Norah	19-188	Z
Turn Off The Lights	Furtado, Nelly	15-820	CB
Turn Off The Lights	Furtado, Nelly	18-403	MM
Turn Off The Lights	Furtado, Nelly	23-587	PHM
Turn On Your Love Light	Bland, Bobby	21-574	SC
Turn On Your Love Light	Bland, Bobby	10-246	SS
Turn Out the Light & Love Me...	Williams, Don	34-216	CB
Turn Out The Lights & Love Me...	Williams, Don	8-364	CB
Turn That Radio On	Milsap, Ronnie	16-363	CB
Turn The Beat Around	Robinson, Vicki Sue	35-127	CB
Turn The Beat Around	Robinson, Vicki Sue	9-15	MH
Turn The Cards Slowly	Cline, Patsy	45-513	MM
Turn The Page	Metallica	7-796	PHT
Turn The Page	Seger, Bob	19-122	KC
Turn The Page	Seger, Bob	10-169	UK
Turn The World Around	Arnold, Eddy	19-42	CB
Turn To Stone	ELO	20-85	SC
Turn Turn Turn	Byrds	35-95	CB
Turn Turn Turn	Byrds	26-323	DK
Turn Turn Turn	Byrds	15-574	MM
Turn Your Love Around	Benson, George	35-164	CB
Turn Your Love Around	Benson, George	12-791	P
Turn Your Love Around	Benson, George	15-798	SC
Turn Your Radio On	Stevens, Ray	16-497	CB
Turnin' Off A Memory	Haggard, Merle	37-177	CB
Turning Away	Gayle, Crystal	38-42	CB
Turning Home	Nail, David	45-560	CB
Turning Japanese	Vapors	21-399	SC
Turning Tables	Adele	38-187	CB
Turtle Blues	Joplin, Janis	49-748	KV
Tush	ZZ Top	33-303	CB
Tush	ZZ Top	2-728	SC
Tutti Frutti	Little Richard	11-220	DK
Tutti Frutti	Little Richard	13-42	P
Tutti Frutti	Little Richard	3-257	SC
Tuxedo Junction	Andrew Sisters	46-435	KV
TV - Ballad Of Jed Clampett	Flatt & Scruggs	33-222	CB
TV Theme - Archies the	Archies	46-440	SC
TV Theme - Meet The Flintstones	B-52's	46-458	KV
TV Themes - Big Bang Theory	Barenaked Ladies	49-751	KV
Twang	Strait, George	49-524	BKD
Twelfth Of Never	Mathis, Johnny	10-462	MG
Twelfth Of Never	Mathis, Johnny	18-47	MM
Twelfth Of Never	Mathis, Johnny	2-860	SC
Twelfth Of Never	Mathis, Johnny	19-787	SGB

SONG TITLE	ARTIST	#	TYPE
Twelfth Of Never	Mathis, Johnny`	35-9	CB
Twelfth Of Never the	Mathis, Johnny	29-463	LE
Twelfth Of Never the	Presley, Elvis	25-330	MM
Twelve Pains Of Christmas - xmas	Rivers, Bob	45-252	SC
Twentieth Century	Alabama	23-364	SC
Twentieth Century	Alabama	22-539	ST
Twenty Foreplay	Jackson, Janet	4-174	SC
Twenty Four Hours From Tulsa	Pitney, Gene	46-118	SC
Twenty Four Sycamore	Pitney, Gene	47-535	SFM
Twenty Years & Two Husbands Ago	Womack, Lee Ann	29-40	CB
Twenty Years Ago	Rogers, Kenny	9-639	SAV
Twenty Years Ago	Rogers, Kenny	5-122	SC
Twilight On The Trail	Autry, Gene	8-818	CB
Twilight Time	Platters	12-364	DK
Twilight Time	Platters	2-88	SC
Twilight Zone Music	Golden Earring	15-794	SC
Twinkle Twinkle Lucky Star	Haggard, Merle	1-369	CB
Twinkle Twinkle Lucky Star	Haggard, Merle	11-747	DK
Twist & Shout	Beatles	16-835	DK
Twist & Shout	Beatles	3-323	MH
Twist & Shout	Beatles	7-516	SAV
Twist & Shout	Beatles	2-55	SC
Twist & Shout	Beatles	29-341	SC
Twist And Crawl	Beat	49-108	CDG
Twist the	Checker, Chubby	26-498	DK
Twist the	Checker, Chubby	3-316	MH
Twist the	Checker, Chubby	2-41	SC
Twisted Transistor	Korn	29-253	SC
Twistin' The Night Away	Cooke, Sam	10-244	SS
Two	Adams, Ryan	30-596	PHM
Two Black Cadillacs	Underwood, Carrie	39-33	ASK
Two Car Garage	Thomas, B.J.	20-673	SC
Two Divided By Love	Grass Roots	17-523	SC
Two Doors Down	Parton, Dolly	8-539	CB
Two Doors Down	Parton, Dolly	13-372	P
Two Dozen Roses	Shenandoah	1-482	CB
Two Faces Have I	Christie, Lou	43-213	MM
Two Feet Of Topsoil	Paisley, Brad	45-578	OZP
Two Fine People	Stevens, Cat	23-649	BS
Two Fine People	Stevens, Cat	13-577	NU
Two Hearts	Collins, Phil	44-8	LG
Two Hearts	Springsteen, Bruce	20-242	LE
Two Kinds Of Teardrops	Del Shannon	29-813	SF
Two Less Lonely People In The World	Air Supply	46-397	CB
Two Little Sisters	Simon, Carly	49-156	DCK
Two Lonely People	Bandy, Moe	19-506	CB
Two Lovers	Wells, Mary	6-565	MM
Two More Bottles Of Wine	Harris, EmmyLou	1-239	CB
Two More Bottles Of Wine	Harris, EmmyLou	6-741	MM
Two More Bottles Of	Harris, EmmyLou	13-477	P

SONG TITLE	ARTIST	#	TYPE
Wine			
Two More Bottles Of Wine	Harris, EmmyLou	5-127	SC
Two Of A Crime	Lambert, Miranda	45-408	BKD
Two Of A Kind Working On A Full	Brooks, Garth	13-326	P
Two Of A Kind Working On A Full	Brooks, Garth	2-679	SC
Two Of a Kind Working On A Full..	Brooks, Garth	12-146	DK
Two Of A Kind Working On A Full...	Brooks, Garth	6-284	MM
Two Of Hearts	Q, Stacey	24-550	SC
Two Of Us	Carpenters	44-339	OZP
Two Out Of Three Ain't Bad	Meat Loaf	6-481	MM
Two Out Of Three Ain't Bad	Meat Loaf	22-920	SC
Two People	Turner, Tina	10-422	LE
Two People Fell In Love	Paisley, Brad	33-156	CB
Two People Fell In Love	Paisley, Brad	9-864	ST
Two People Fell In Love	Paisley, Brad	16-276	TT
Two Pina Coladas	Brooks, Garth	1-221	CB
Two Pina Coladas	Brooks, Garth	7-730	CHM
Two Pina Coladas	Brooks, Garth	22-779	ST
Two Pink Lines	Church, Eric	30-246	CB
Two Princes	Spin Doctors	12-74	DK
Two Princes	Spin Doctors	5-375	MM
Two Princes	Spin Doctors	12-782	P
Two Rings Shy	Lambert, Miranda	46-269	KV
Two Shadows On Your Window	Reeves, Jim	44-260	DFK
Two Six Packs Away	Dudley, Dave	47-54	CB
Two Sleepy People	Martin & Renaud	23-76	MM
Two Sparrows In A Hurricane	Tucker, Tanya	1-610	CB
Two Sparrows In A Hurricane	Tucker, Tanya	6-213	MM
Two Sparrows In A Hurricane	Tucker, Tanya	12-416	P
Two Steps Behind	Def Leppard	6-373	MM
Two Teardrops	Wariner, Steve	8-923	CB
Two Teardrops	Wariner, Steve	7-866	CHT
Two Tickets To Paradise	Money, Eddie	4-382	SC
Two-Step	Bundy, Laura Bell	47-507	KV
Tyler	Daniel, Davis	4-477	SC
Typical Male	Turner, Tina	10-421	LE
U & Ur Hand **	Pink	48-598	DK
U Can't Touch This	Hammer, MC	33-439	CB
U Can't Touch This	Hammer, MC	25-472	MM
U Can't Touch This	Hammer, MC	24-138	SC
U Don't Have To Call	Usher	35-271	CB
U Don't Have To Call	Usher	25-212	MM
U Don't Know Me Like U Used To	Brandy	5-788	SC
U Got It Bad	Usher	33-422	CB
U Got It Bad	Usher	25-82	MM
U Got The Look	Prince	49-829	LG
U Got The Look	Prince & Easton	23-332	CB

SONG TITLE	ARTIST	#	TYPE
U Make Me Wanna	Jadakiss & Carey	20-192	PHM
U Remind Me	Usher	15-814	CB
U Remind Me	Usher	23-588	PHM
U Remind Me	Usher	16-386	SGB
U S of A	Fargo, Donna	8-365	CB
U Should've Known Better	Monica	20-541	CB
U Smile	Bieber, Justin	36-62	ASK
Ugly Duckling - kids	Kaye, Danny	48-466	SBI
Ugly Girl	Fleming & John	10-220	SC
Uh Huh	B2K	17-597	PHM
Ullo John Got A New Motor	Unknown	21-605	SF
Ultimate Love	Vassar, Phil	19-174	ST
Um Um Um Um Um Um	Fontana, Wayne	10-572	SF
Uma Thurman	Fall Out Boy	45-655	SBI
Umbrella	Rihanna	30-493	CB
Umbrella (So Ho Mix)	Swift, Taylor	48-608	DK
Unanswered Prayers	Brooks, Garth	6-277	MM
Unanswered Prayers	Brooks, Garth	2-680	SC
Unbeautiful	Roy, Lesley	36-252	PHM
Unbelievable	Diamond Rio	1-179	CB
Unbelievable	Diamond Rio	22-686	ST
Unbelievable	EMF	21-453	CB
Unbelievable	EMF	5-341	SC
Unbelievable	EMS	34-106	CB
Unbreak My Heart	Braxton, Toni	33-360	CB
Unbreak My Heart	Braxton, Toni	18-815	PS
Unbreak My Heart	Braxton, Toni	24-374	SC
Unbreakable Heart	Andrews, Jessica	8-910	CB
Unbreakable Heart	Andrews, Jessica	22-479	ST
Unbreakable Heart	Carter, Carlene	24-131	SC
Unbroken	McGraw, Tim	29-518	CB
Unbroken	McGraw, Tim	25-288	MM
Unbroken	McGraw, Tim	17-566	ST
Unbroken Ground	Nichols, Gary	30-89	CB
Unchain My Heart	Charles, Ray	12-148	DK
Unchain My Heart	Cocker, Joe	34-53	CB
Unchain My Heart	Cocker, Joe	21-436	LE
Unchained	Van Halen	23-110	SC
Unchained Melody	Presley, Elvis	18-423	KC
Unchained Melody	Righteous Brothers	11-549	DK
Unchained Melody	Righteous Brothers	6-148	MM
Unchained Melody	Righteous Brothers	13-38	P
Unchained Melody	Righteous Brothers	3-329	PS
Unchained Melody	Righteous Brothers	14-555	SC
Unchained Melody	Rimes, LeAnn	1-293	CB
Unchained Melody	Rimes, LeAnn	7-576	CHM
Uncharted	Bareillas, Sara	48-207	CB
Uncle Albert/Admiral Halsey	McCartney, Paul	20-49	SC
Uncle Tom's Cabin	Warrant	5-69	SC
Uncloudy Day	Nelson, Willie	38-74	CB
Unconditional	Collins, Simon	36-232	PHM
Unconditional	Davidson, Clay	14-184	CB
Unconditional	Davidson, Clay	19-244	CSZ
Unconditional	Davidson, Clay	23-370	SC

SONG TITLE	ARTIST	#	TYPE
Unconditional Love	Summer, Donna	17-59	DK
Unconditionally	Perry, Katy	43-156	PHM
Under Attack	Abba	46-221	FUN
Under My Thumb	Rolling Stones	18-27	LE
Under My Thumb	Rolling Stones	21-243	SC
Under My Wheels	Alice Cooper	16-442	SGB
Under The Boardwalk	Drifters	17-103	DK
Under The Boardwalk	Drifters	3-328	MH
Under The Boardwalk	Drifters	2-90	SC
Under The Boardwalk	Mellencamp, John	45-423	KV
Under The Bridge	Red Hot Chili Peppe	6-167	MM
Under The Bridges Of Paris	Martin, Dean	49-48	ZVS
Under The Influence	King, Elle	49-927	KVD
Under The Water	Bainbridge, Merrill	10-690	HH
Under The Water	Bainbridge, Merrill	10-89	SC
Under This Old Hat	LeDoux, Chris	4-108	SC
Under Your Spell Again	Owens, Buck	8-386	CB
Under Your Spell Again	Owens, Buck	8-618	SAV
Under Your Spell Again	Owens, Buck	4-261	SC
Undercover Angel	O'Day, Allan	4-385	SC
Undercover Of The Night	Rolling Stones	21-628	SC
Underdog	Loeb, Lisa	25-435	MM
Undermine - Nashville	Esten, Charles	45-474	KVD
Underneath It All	No Doubt	18-434	CB
Underneath It All	No Doubt&Lady Saw	25-403	MM
Underneath The Stars	Carey, Mariah	24-632	SC
Underneath The Tree	Clarkson, Kelly	45-773	KV
Underneath Your Clothes	Shakira	18-294	CB
Underneath Your Clothes	Shakira	25-209	MM
Understand Your Man	Cash, Johnny	14-244	CB
Understand Your Man	Cash, Johnny	21-592	SC
Understanding	Xscape	17-407	DK
Undiscovered	Morrison, James	38-276	SF
Undo It	Underwood, Carrie	36-45	PT
Undo The Right	Nelson, Willie	46-48	SSK
Undun	Guess Who	26-508	DK
Uneasy Rider	Charlie Daniels Band	43-276	CB
Uneasy Rider	Charlie Daniels Band	2-533	SC
Unfaithful	Rihanna	36-98	CB
Unfaithful	Rihanna	30-729	SF
Unfinished Sympathy	Massive Attack	30-749	SF
Unforgettable	Cole, Nat "King"	7-187	MM
Unforgettable	Cole, Nat & Natalie	12-127	DK
Unforgiven	Lawrence, Tracy	48-384	MM
Unforgiven	Lawrence, Tracy	14-796	ST
Unforgiven the	Metallica	13-621	LE
Unglamorous	McKenna, Lori	36-558	CB
Uninvited	Morrisette, Alanis	13-684	SGB
Union City Blue	Blondie	49-136	LG
United States Of Whatever	Lynch, L.	32-259	THM
United We Stand - duet	Brotherhood Of Man	33-271	CB
Unleash The Dragon	Sisquo	19-822	SGB

SONG TITLE	ARTIST	#	TYPE
Unlove You	Nettles, Jennifer	49-660	BKD
Unnamed Feeling	Metallica	47-254	PHR
Unpretty	TLC	8-295	PHT
Unsent	Morrisette, Alanis	16-202	PHT
Unsent	Morrisette, Alanis	13-680	SGB
Unskinny Bop	Poison	5-493	SC
Unstable	Adema	23-180	PHM
Unsung Hero	Clark, Terri	10-193	SC
Until I Fall Away	Gin Blossoms	6-644	MM
Until I Met You	Rodman, Judy	29-658	SC
Until It Sleeps	Metallica	7-569	THM
Until It's Time For You To Go	Diamond, Neil	47-417	PS
Until It's Time For You To Go	Presley, Elvis	18-579	KC
Until My Dreams Come True	Greene, Jack	43-341	CB
Until We Fall Back In Love Again	Carson, Jeff	25-193	MM
Until We Fall Back In Love Again	Carson, Jeff	16-691	ST
Until You Come Back To Me	Franklin, Aretha	34-44	CB
Until You Come Back To Me	Franklin, Aretha	36-173	JT
Unto Us This Holy Night - xmas	Wiggles	45-240	WIG
Untold Stories	Mattea, Kathy	1-185	CB
Untouchable	Swift, Taylor	37-334	CB
Untouched	Veronicas	36-251	PHM
Unusual Way	Eder, Linda	17-449	PS
Unusually Unusual	Lonestar	34-377	CB
Unusually Unusual	Lonestar	25-351	MM
Unusually Unusual	Lonestar	15-606	ST
Unwell	Matchbox 20	35-295	CB
Unwell	Matchbox 20	25-536	MM
Unwell	Matchbox 20	20-632	NS
Unwell	Matchbox 20	32-172	THM
Unwound	Strait, George	38-152	SC
Unwritten	Bedingfield, Natasha	30-146	PT
Unwritten	Bedingfield,Natasha	29-255	SC
Up	Twain, Shania	34-363	CB
Up	Twain, Shania	25-454	MM
Up	Twain, Shania	18-590	ST
Up	Twain, Shania	32-112	THM
Up & Down (In & Out)	Cox, Deborah	32-17	THM
Up Against The Wall	Walker, Jerry Jeff	15-15	SC
Up All Night	Pardi, John	41-57	PHN
Up All Night	Slaughter	23-60	MH
Up All Night	Willis, Matt	49-731	KVD
Up And Gone	McCarter Sisters	14-691	CB
Up Around The Bend	CCR	5-354	SC
Up North	Hayes, Wade	6-61	SC
Up On Cripple Creek	Band	46-467	MM
Up On The Housetop	Autry, Gene	45-662	SY
Up On The Housetop - Xmas	Arnold, Eddy	44-224	SC
Up On The Ridge	Bentley, Dierks	45-163	CB

SONG TITLE	ARTIST	#	TYPE
Up On The Roof	Drifters	16-834	DK
Up On The Roof	Drifters	12-672	P
Up On The Roof	Taylor, James	45-538	RSZ
Up The Ladder To The Roof	Ross, Diana	48-549	DK
Up The Ladder To The Roof	Supremes	17-340	DK
Up This High	Moorer, Allison	49-207	CB
Up To Him	Lawrence, Tracy	48-381	CB
Up Up and Away	5th Dimension	11-526	DK
Up Where We Belong	Cocker & Warnes	6-227	MM
Up Where We Belong	Cocker & Warnes	13-190	P
Up Where We Belong	Mellencamp & ?	21-437	LE
Upper Middle Class White Trash	Brice, Lee	36-610	CB
Upper Middle Class White Trash	Brice, Lee	36-202	PHM
Upside Down	Johnson, Jack	29-214	PHM
Upside Down	Johnson, Jack	30-769	SF
Upside Down	Ross, Diana	16-730	DK
Upside Down	Ross, Diana	9-658	SAV
Upside Of Being Down the	Britt, Catherine	23-397	CB
Upside Of Being Down the	Britt, Catherine	20-509	ST
Upstairs Downtown	Keith, Toby	1-699	CB
Upstairs Downtown	Keith, Toby	6-719	MM
Upstairs Downtown	Keith, Toby	17-271	NA
Upstairs Downtown	Keith, Toby	2-575	SC
Uptight Everything Is Alright	Wonder, Stevie	17-377	DK
Uptight Everything Is Alright	Wonder, Stevie	13-138	P
Uptown	Crystals	9-701	SAV
Uptown	Orbison, Roy	38-50	PS
Uptown	Stranglers	11-675	DK
Uptown Down-Home Good Ol' Boy	Brooks, Garth	8-730	CB
Uptown Funk	Mars, Bruno	45-15	KV
Uptown Girl	Joel, Billy	34-75	CB
Uptown Girl	Joel, Billy	12-272	DK
Uptown Girl	Joel, Billy	21-750	MH
Ur So Gay	Perry, Katy	46-190	KV
Us Against The World	Milian, Christina	36-285	PHM
Us And Them	Pink Floyd	19-280	SGB
USA Today	Jackson, Alan	23-406	CB
Use Me	Hinder	36-514	CB
Use Me	Withers, Bill	16-159	SC
Use Mine	Wood, Jeff	10-76	SC
Use Somebody	Kings Of Leon	36-18	PT
Use Ta Be My Girl	O'Jays	17-139	DK
Use Ta Be My Girl	O'Jays	24-340	SC
Use Your Heart	SWV	24-169	SC
Used To Be's the	Singletary, Daryle	10-77	SC
Used To Blue	Sawyer Brown	5-762	SC
Used To Love Her	Guns & Roses	21-766	SC
Used To Love You Sober	Brown, Kane	49-627	DCK
Used To The Pain	Lawrence, Tracy	23-305	CB

SONG TITLE	ARTIST	#	TYPE
Used To The Pain	Lawrence, Tracy	29-608	ST
Used To The Pain	Nesler, Mark	5-299	SC
Ute Me	Kernaghan, Lee	39-98	PHN
Vacation	Francis, Connie	16-364	CB
Vacation	Go-Go's	28-278	DK
Vacation	Go-Go's	5-109	SC
Vacation	Rhett, Thomas	45-441	BKD
Valentine	McBride, Martina	8-133	CB
Valentine	McBride, Martina	22-768	ST
Valerie	Zutons	30-723	SF
Valleri	Monkees	11-231	DK
Valley Of Tears	Holly, Buddy	47-890	ZM
Valley Of The Dolls	Warwick, Dionne	5-233	SC
Valley Road the	Hornsby, Bruce	12-176	DK
Vaya Con Dios	Fender, Freddie	48-500	CKC
Vaya Con Dios	Paul & Ford	5-516	SC
Vaya Con Dios	Paul, Les & Ford, Mary	34-3	CB
Vehicle	Ides Of March	19-132	KC
Vehicle	Ides Of March	3-550	SC
Veil Of Tears	Ketchum, Hal	3-633	SC
Venom Wearin' Denim	Brown, Junior	7-320	MM
Venom Wearing Denim	Brown, Junior	40-80	CB
Ventura Highway	America	33-288	CB
Ventura Highway	America	13-305	P
Ventura Highway	America	4-54	SC
Venus	Avalon, Frankie	11-365	DK
Venus	Avalon, Frankie	13-86	P
Venus	Lettermen	48-529	L1
Venus	Shocking Blue	3-475	SC
Venus In Blue Jeans	Clanton, Jimmy	5-14	SC
Vertical Expression (of Horizontal)	Bellamy Brothers	44-77	KV
Vertigo	U2	22-341	CB
Very Special Love Song a	Rich, Charlie	8-833	CB
Very Special Love Song a	Rich, Charlie	13-517	P
Very Thought Of You the	Cole, Nat "King"	16-413	PR
Very Thought Of You the	Cole, Nat "King"	46-365	PS
Very Thought Of You the	Cole, Natalie	15-575	MM
Very Thought Of You the	Standard	47-828	PS
Viagra Song	Moore, Seamus	49-203	KWD
Vibeology	Abdul, Paula	18-390	SAV
Victim Of Love	Eagles	7-561	BS
Victims	Culture Club	47-2	SF
Vidalia	Kershaw, Sammy	1-476	CB
Vidalia	Kershaw, Sammy	7-273	MM
Vidalia	Kershaw, Sammy	4-425	SC
Video	India.Arie	18-354	CB
Video	India.Arie	25-149	MM
Video Killed The Radio Star	Buggles	11-672	DK
Vienna	Eder, Linda	17-435	PS
Vienna	Joel, Billy	9-385	AH
View To A Kill	Duran Duran	4-387	SC
Village	Cam	49-755	KVD

SONG TITLE	ARTIST	#	TYPE
Vincent (Starry Starry Night)	McLean, Don	16-152	SC
Vincent (Starry Starry Night)	Groban, Josh	43-303	CB
Vino Dinero Y Amor	Presley, Elvis	25-493	MM
Violet Hill	Coldplay	36-533	CB
Virginia Bluebell	Lambert, Miranda	46-264	KV
Vision Of Love	Carey, Mariah	21-237	SC
Visit the	Brock, Chad	14-909	CB
Visit the	Brock, Chad	13-861	CHM
Visit the	Brock, Chad	19-221	CSZ
Visit the	Brock, Chad	22-555	ST
Visit the	Brock, Chad	14-34	THM
Viva La Vida	Coldplay	36-490	CB
Viva Las Vegas	Presley, Elvis	8-586	CB
Vogue	Madonna	19-579	MH
Vogue	Madonna	6-175	MM
Vogue	Madonna	12-854	P
Voice Inside My Head	Dixie Chicks	36-176	PHM
Voices	Young, Chris	47-932	CB
Voices Carry	Til Tuesday	4-875	SC
Voices That Care	Multi-Voice	18-682	PR
Volare	Martin & Modugno	26-344	DK
Volare	Martin, Dean	35-13	CB
Volare	Martin, Dean	23-63	MM
Volare	Sinatra, Frank	48-586	DK
Volcano	Buffett, Jimmy	6-432	MM
Voodoo Child	Rogue Traders	30-788	SF
Voulez Vous	Abba	19-87	MM
Vows Go Unbroken the	Rogers, Kenny	1-765	CB
Wabash Blues	Wills, Bob	20-704	CB
Wabash Cannonball	Acuff, Roy	21-635	CB
Wabash Cannonball	Acuff, Roy	12-302	DK
Wabash Cannonball	Acuff, Roy	3-605	SC
Wagon Wheel	Rucker, Darius	40-43	ASK
Wagon Wheels	Arnold, Eddy	19-32	CB
Wait	White Lion	5-64	SC
Wait For Me	Seger, Bob	46-346	SC
Wait For The Light To Shine	Gospel	49-713	VH
Wait For You	Yamin, Elliott	49-901	SC
Wait Till The Sun Shines	Reminiscing Series	3-33	SC
Waiter! Bring Me Water!	Twain, Shania	23-433	CB
Waitin' In Your Welfare Line	Owens, Buck	15-88	CB
Waitin' In Your Welfare Line	Owens, Buck	4-870	SC
Waitin' On A Woman	Paisley, Brad	36-602	CB
Waitin' On A Woman	Paisley, Brad	36-194	PHM
Waitin' On Joe	Azar, Steve	18-134	ST
Waitin' On Sundown	Griggs, Andy	14-102	CB
Waitin' On Sundown	Griggs, Andy	13-854	CHM
Waitin' On The Wonderful	Lines, Aaron	23-9	CB
Waiting For A Girl Like You	Foreigner	11-121	DK
Waiting For A Girl Like You	Foreigner	4-764	SC

SONG TITLE	ARTIST	#	TYPE
Waiting For A Train	Haggard, Merle	46-24	SSK
Waiting For Superman	Daughtry	43-160	PHM
Waiting For Tonight	Lopez, Jennifer	23-324	CB
Waiting For Tonight	Lopez, Jennifer	23-581	MM
Waiting For Tonight	Lopez, Jennifer	8-518	PHT
Waiting For You	Seal	32-429	THM
Waiting In The Lobby Of Your Heart	Thompson, Hank	19-325	CB
Waiting On A Sunny Day	Springsteen, Bruce	25-540	MM
Waiting On Joe	Azar, Steve	34-387	CB
Waiting On The World To Change	Mayer, John	36-184	PHM
Waiting the	Petty & Heartbreake	5-469	SC
Wake Me Up Before You Go Go	Wham!	35-176	CB
Wake Me Up Before You Go-Go	Wham!	16-777	DK
Wake Me Up Before You Go-Go	Wham!	12-760	P
Wake Me Up Before You Go-Go	Wham!	10-532	SF
Wake Up	Duff, Hilary	35-302	CB
Wake Up	Haggard, Merle	49-812	DFK
Wake up And Smell The Whiskey	Miller, Dean	8-414	CB
Wake Up Irene	Thompson, Hank	19-322	CB
Wake Up Little Susie	Everly Brothers	11-448	DK
Wake Up Little Susie	Everly Brothers	13-78	P
Wake Up Little Susie	Everly Brothers	3-336	PS
Wake Up Little Susie	Everly Brothers	29-828	SC
Wake Up Lovin' You	Campbell, Craig	45-399	BKD
Wake Up Lovin' You	Morgan, Craig	44-155	BKD
Wake Up Make A Move	Lostprophets	30-818	PHM
Wake Up Older	Roberts, Julie	22-25	CB
Wake Up Wendy	John, Elton	13-719	SGB
Waking In L.A.	Missing Persons	24-433	SC
Waking Up In Vegas	Perry, Katy	38-199	CB
Wal-Mart Parking Lot	Cagle, Chris	29-206	CB
Walk A Little Straighter	Currington, Billy	25-618	MM
Walk A Little Straighter	Currington, Billy	19-175	ST
Walk A Little Straighter	Currington, Billy	32-373	THM
Walk A Mile In My Shoes	Presley, Elvis	6-795	MM
Walk A Mile In My Shoes	Presley, Elvis	14-829	THM
Walk A Mile In My Shoes	South, Joe	10-753	JVC
Walk Away	Clarkson, Kelly	30-152	PT
Walk Away	Clarkson, Kelly	30-703	SF
Walk Away	Davis, Linda	24-161	SC
Walk Away	Davis, Linda	22-918	ST
Walk Away	James Gang	3-609	SC
Walk Away	Walsh, Joe	15-711	LE
Walk Away Renee	Four Tops	2-80	SC
Walk Away Renee	Left Banke	18-237	DK
Walk Down Your Street	Bangles	46-470	JVC
Walk In The Country	Urban, Keith	46-153	CAP
Walk In The Sun	Hornsby, Bruce	3-495	SC
Walk Like A Man	Four Seasons	27-142	DK
Walk Like A Man	Valli, Frankie	4-34	SC
Walk Like An Egyptian	Bangles	7-104	MM

281

SONG TITLE	ARTIST	#	TYPE
Walk Like An Egyptian	Bangles	4-294	SC
Walk Like An Eqyptian	Bangles	17-412	DK
Walk Me Down The Middle	Band Perry	44-391	KV
Walk Of Life	Dire Straits	6-487	MM
Walk Of Life	Dire Straits	12-803	P
Walk Of Life	Dire Straits	4-845	SC
Walk Of Life	Jennings, Shooter	49-638	ST
Walk On	McEntire, Reba	11-704	DK
Walk On	McEntire, Reba	17-249	NA
Walk On	McEntire, Reba	2-517	SC
Walk On	Orbison, Roy	38-49	PS
Walk On	Ronstadt, Linda	2-825	SC
Walk On	U2	30-76	SC
Walk On By	Van Dyke, Leroy	8-780	CB
Walk On By	Van Dyke, Leroy	12-474	P
Walk On By	Van Dyke, Leroy	4-310	SC
Walk On By	Warwick, Dionne	11-793	DK
Walk On By	Warwick, Dionne	14-341	SC
Walk On Faith	Reid, Mike	13-487	P
Walk On Faith	Reid, Mike	9-532	SAV
Walk On Faith	Reid, Mike	2-391	SC
Walk On The Rocks	Jackson, Alan	49-185	SC
Walk On The Wild Side	Reed, Lou	2-717	SC
Walk On Water	Money, Eddie	47-281	KV
Walk Right Back	Everly Brothers	43-22	CB
Walk Right Back	Everly Brothers	9-640	SAV
Walk Right Back	Murray, Anne	46-89	OZP
Walk Right In	Rooftop Singers	21-16	CB
Walk Right In	Rooftop Singers	12-141	DK
Walk Right In	Rooftop Singers	7-352	MM
Walk Softly	Dixie Chicks&Skaggs	14-158	CB
Walk Softly On This Heart Of Mine	Kentucky HH	6-765	MM
Walk Softly On This Heart Of Mine	Kentucky HH	17-310	NA
Walk Softly On This Heart Of Mine	Kentucky HH	2-619	SC
Walk the	Sawyer Brown	12-56	DK
Walk The Dinosaur	Was (Not Was)	34-101	CB
Walk The Llama Llama	Rascal Flatts	14-791	ST
Walk The Way The Wind Blows	Mattea, Kathy	1-182	CB
Walk The Way The Wind Blows	Mattea, Kathy	5-135	SC
Walk This Way	Aerosmith	35-137	CB
Walk This Way	Aerosmith	16-601	MM
Walk This Way	Run DMC	13-282	P
Walk Through This World With Me	Jones, George	8-340	CB
Walk Through This World With Me	Jones, George	4-256	SC
Walk To The Light	Messina, Jo Dee	7-247	MM
Walkashame	Musgraves, Kacey	45-955	KV
Walkaway Joe	Yearwood & Diffie	8-121	CB
Walkaway Joe	Yearwood, Trisha	10-758	JVC
Walkaway Joe	Yearwood, Trisha	6-211	MM

SONG TITLE	ARTIST	#	TYPE
Walkaway Joe	Yearwood, Trisha	12-477	P
Walkaway Joe	Yearwood, Trisha	9-676	SAV
Walkin'	Francis, Cleve	24-252	SC
Walkin' A Broken Heart	Williams, Don	5-622	SC
Walkin' After Midnight	Cline, Patsy	16-823	DK
Walkin' After Midnight	Cline, Patsy	13-415	P
Walkin' After Midnight	Cline, Patsy	9-484	SAV
Walkin' Away	Black, Clint	1-109	CB
Walkin' Away	Black, Clint	12-169	DK
Walkin' Away	Black, Clint	30-433	THM
Walkin' Away	Diamond Rio	4-101	SC
Walkin' Back To Happiness	Shapiro, Helen	10-556	SF
Walkin' Blues	Royal Crown Revue	15-211	AMS
Walkin' Good	Heart	48-162	PHM
Walkin' In The Rain	Jay & Americans	14-370	PS
Walkin' In The Rain	Ronnettes	11-639	DK
Walkin' In The Sunshine	Miller, Roger	22-282	CB
Walkin' My Baby Back Home	Cole, Nat "King"	15-576	MM
Walkin' My Baby Back Home	Ray, Johnnie	18-623	PS
Walkin' On Broken Glass	Lennox, Annie	17-729	PS
Walkin' On The Sun	Smash Mouth	30-211	CB
Walkin' On The Sun	Smash Mouth	7-687	PHM
Walkin' Talkin' Cryin' Barely...	Highway 101	2-514	SC
Walkin' Talkin' Cryin' Barely......	Highway 101	17-332	DK
Walkin' The Floor Over You	Jackson, Alan	47-748	SRK
Walkin' The Floor Over You	Lewis, Jerry Lee	46-41	SSK
Walking After Midnight	Brooks, Garth	48-345	JVC
Walking After You	Foo Fighters	21-557	PHM
Walking Away	David, Craig	18-347	CB
Walking Away	David, Craig	25-221	MM
Walking Away	David, Craig	17-598	PHM
Walking Away A Winner	Mattea, Kathy	1-193	CB
Walking Away A Winner	Mattea, Kathy	10-784	JVC
Walking Away A Winner	Mattea, Kathy	12-455	P
Walking Away A Winner	Mattea, Kathy	2-215	SC
Walking Contradiction	Green Day	4-675	SC
Walking In Jerusalem Just Like John	Monroe, Bill	47-298	CB
Walking In Memphis	Cher	47-684	MRE
Walking In Memphis	Cohn, Mark	17-460	SC
Walking In Memphis	Lonestar	25-699	MM
Walking In Memphis	Lonestar	19-364	ST
Walking In Memphis	Lonestar	32-409	THM
Walking In The Sunshine	Miller, Roger	16-646	JVC
Walking Man	Taylor, James	45-542	RSZ
Walking On A Thin Line	Lewis & The News	47-191	SC
Walking On Broken Glass	Eurythmics	47-79	SFG
Walking On Broken Glass	Lennox, Annie	12-246	DK
Walking On Broken	Lennox, Annie	13-243	P

SONG TITLE	ARTIST	#	TYPE
Glass			
Walking On Broken Glass	Lennox, Annie	5-338	SC
Walking On Sunshine	Katrina & Waves	3-607	SC
Walking Piece Of Heaven	Robbins, Marty	20-649	SC
Walking Shoes	Tucker, Tanya	16-350	CB
Walking Shoes	Tucker, Tanya	26-579	DK
Walking Shoes	Tucker, Tanya	9-454	SAV
Walking Shoes	Tucker, Tanya	2-352	SC
Walking The Dog	Thomas, Rufus	17-134	DK
Walking The Floor Over You	Tubb, Ernest	22-292	CB
Walking The Floor Over You	Tubb, Ernest	11-709	DK
Walking The Floor Over You	Tubb, Ernest	8-661	SAV
Walking To Jerusalem	Byrd, Tracy	20-107	CB
Walking To Jerusalem	Byrd, Tracy	6-803	MM
Walking To New Orleans	Domino, Fats	10-250	SS
Wall In Your Heart	Lynne, Shelby	25-43	MM
Walls	Petty & Heartbreake	24-56	SC
Walls Can Fall	Jones, George	24-11	SC
Walls Have Ears the	Presley, Elvis	47-769	SRK
Waltz - Blue Skirt Waltz	Waltz Favorites	29-810	SSR
Waltz Across Texas	Tubb, Ernest	33-2	CB
Waltz Across Texas	Tubb, Ernest	4-864	SC
Waltz Of The Wind	Robbins, Marty	48-24	DFK
Waltz You Saved For Me the	Husky, Ferlin	45-344	BSP
Waltzing Matilda	Standard	47-835	SDK
Wanderer the	Dion	11-656	DK
Wanderer the	Dion	10-334	KC
Wanderer the	Dion	6-159	MM
Wanderer the	Dion	12-892	P
Wanderer the	Dion	9-26	PS
Wanderer the	Rabbitt, Eddie	48-33	CB
Wandering Eyes	McDowell, Ronnie	4-823	SC
Wang Dang Doodle	Taylor, Koko	15-310	SC
Wanna Be	Adams, Oleta	46-389	ESS
Wanna Get To know You That Good	Twain, Shania	45-531	CB
Wanna Take You Home	Gloriana	49-862	DCK
Wannabe	Spice Girls	16-44	SC
Want A Million Years	Grass Roots	20-95	SC
Want Ads	Honey Cone	35-108	CB
Want Ads	Honey Cone	17-375	DK
Want To	Sugarland	30-44	CB
Want To	Sugarland	30-96	PHM
Wanted	Hayes, Hunter	39-50	ASK
Wanted	Jackson, Alan	1-32	CB
Wanted	Martino, Al	29-498	LE
Wanted Dead Or Alive	Bon Jovi	11-770	DK
Wanted Dead Or Alive	Bon Jovi	20-308	MH
Wanted Man	Cash, Johnny	43-411	KCA
Wanted Man	Cash, Johnny	44-4	VH
Wanted Me Gone	Thompson, Josh	45-564	BKD
Wanted You More - duet	Lady Antebellum	46-81	BKD

SONG TITLE	ARTIST	#	TYPE
Wanting Out	Branch, Michelle	32-390	THM
War	Springsteen, Bruce	20-250	LE
War	Temptations	11-380	DK
War Is Hell On The Home Front Too	Sheppard, T.G.	4-481	SC
War Paint	Clarkson, Kelly	47-696	KV
War Paint	Morgan, Lorrie	49-118	SC
War Pigs	Black Sabbath	10-477	DA
Warm Love	Morrison, Van	23-599	BS
Warm Love	Morrison, Van	15-726	SI
Warm Machine	Bush	14-484	SC
Warmth Of The Sun	Beach Boys	46-498	NT
Warning	Incubus	18-225	CB
Warning Labels	Stone, Doug	20-598	CB
Warning Labels	Stone, Doug	2-351	SC
Warning Sign	Rabbitt, Eddie	5-327	SC
Warning Signs	Engvall & Montgomer	12-932	CB
Warrior the	Scandal	4-531	SC
Was It Something I Didn't Do	98 Degrees	15-374	SKG
Was That My Life	Messina, Jo Dee	34-358	CB
Was That My Life	Messina, Jo Dee	25-519	MM
Was That My Life	Messina, Jo Dee	18-780	ST
Was That My Life	Messina, Jo Dee	32-120	THM
Wasn't Expecting That	Lawson, Jamie	47-704	BKD
Wasn't Expecting That	Lawson, Jamie	48-447	KCD
Wasn't That A Party	Paxton & Clancy Bro	18-172	DK
Wasn't Through Loving You Yet	Alabama	49-672	KCD
Waste Of Good Whiskey	Stampley, Tony	17-577	ST
Wasted	Underwood, Carrie	30-127	AS
Wasted	Underwood, Carrie	30-245	CB
Wasted Days & Wasted Nights	Fender, Freddie	8-49	CB
Wasted Days & Wasted Nights	Fender, Freddie	18-240	DK
Wasted Days & Wasted Nights	Fender, Freddie	13-45	P
Wasted Days & Wasted Nights	Fender, Freddie	9-599	SAV
Wasted On The Way	Crosby Stills & Nash	3-517	SC
Wasted Time	Eagles	44-91	ZMP
Wasted Time	Fuel	36-485	CB
Wasted Time	Skid Row	23-101	SC
Wasted Time	Urban, Keith	49-639	DCK
Wasteland	10 Years	30-230	PHM
Wasteland	10 Years	30-285	SC
Wasting All These Years	Pope, Cassadee	49-670	SSC
Wasting My Time	Default	25-147	MM
Wasting Time	Kid Rock	15-429	PHM
Watch Me	Morgan, Lorrie	1-339	CB
Watch Me	Morgan, Lorrie	6-750	MM
Watch Me	Morgan, Lorrie	13-401	P
Watch the	Emerick, Scotty	43-264	CB
Watch the	Emerick, Scotty	20-394	ST
Watch The Wind Blow By	McGraw, Tim	22-4	CB

SONG TITLE	ARTIST	#	TYPE
Watch The Wind Blow By	McGraw, Tim	19-687	ST
Watch This	Walker, Clay	1-102	CB
Watch This	Walker, Clay	22-617	ST
Watchin' The Wheels	Lennon, John	30-299	RS
Watching Airplanes	Allan, Gary	30-538	CB
Watching Girls Go By	McDowell, Ronnie	34-253	CB
Watching My Baby Not Comin' Back	Ball, David	14-632	SC
Watching Scotty Grow	Davis, Mac	23-517	CB
Watching Scotty Grow	Goldsboro, Bobby	4-639	SC
Watching The Wheels	Lennon, John	29-261	SC
Watching You	Atkins, Rodney	30-111	CB
Water	Paisley, Brad	38-132	CB
Water Runs Dry	Boyz II Men	29-131	ST
Water Runs Dry	Boyz II Men	33-374	CB
Water Tower	Aldean, Jason	44-293	BKD
Water Tower Town	McCreary, Scotty	39-40	ASK
Water Tower Town	McCreery, Scotty	45-637	ASK
Water Under The Bridge	Adele	46-9	DCK
Water Under The Bridge (Inst)	Adele	49-410	BKD
Waterfalls	Midler, Bette	45-936	KV
Waterfalls	TLC	14-904	SC
Waterloo	Abba	11-519	DK
Waterloo	Abba	7-510	MM
Waterloo	Jackson, Stonewall	8-779	CB
Waterloo	Jackson, Stonewall	4-859	SC
Waterloo Sunset	Kinks	48-173	LE
Watermelon Crawl	Byrd, Tracy	1-543	CB
Watermelon Crawl	Byrd, Tracy	2-576	SC
Watermelon Time In Georgia	Frizzell, Lefty	47-812	SRK
Wave	Standard	15-577	SGB
Wave On Wave	Green, Pat	25-646	MM
Wave On Wave	Green, Pat	19-68	ST
Wax Ecstatic	Sponge	24-106	SC
Way Back Texas	Green, Pat	30-475	CB
Way Down	Oak Ridge Boys	47-328	NS
Way Down	Pinson, Bobby	29-28	CB
Way Down	Presley, Elvis	14-830	THM
Way Down Deep	Gosdin, Vern	47-116	CB
Way Down Yonder In New Orleans	Cannon, Freddie	4-248	SC
Way Down Yonder In New Orleans	Cannon, Freddie	10-622	SF
Way He Makes Me Feel the	Streisand, Barbra	17-786	PS
Way I Am the	Haggard, Merle	46-25	SSK
Way I Am the	Haggard, Merle	45-719	VH
Way I Am the	Michaelson, Ingrid	36-519	CB
Way I Are the - duet	Timbaland & Hilson	37-152	SC
Way I Feel the	Shand, Remy	20-519	CB
Way I Love You the	Swift, Taylor	43-171	ASK
Way It Is the	Hornsby & Range	5-478	SC
Way It Used To Be the	Humperdinck, E.	37-165	CB
Way It Was In '51 the	Haggard, Merle	46-44	SSK
Way Of Love the	Cher	14-51	RS

SONG TITLE	ARTIST	#	TYPE
Way Of The World	Turner, Tina	10-432	LE
Way Old Friends Do the	Abba	46-223	KV
Way Out Here	Thompson, Josh	45-562	CB
Way Over Yonder	King, Carole	43-448	CBE
Way Past My Beer Time	Dugger, Tim	38-261	PHN
Way She Loves Me the	Marx, Richard	6-633	MM
Way She Loves Me the	Marx, Richard	2-462	SC
Way She's Looking the	Raybon Brothers	12-929	CB
Way That I Want To Touch You the	Captain & Tennille	46-551	CB
Way the	Aiken, Clay	36-323	PS
Way the	Fastball	33-394	CB
Way the	Fastball	5-281	SC
Way To Survive a	Price, Ray	45-880	VH
Way Too Deep	Sixwire	25-418	MM
Way Too Deep	Sixwire	18-470	ST
Way We Were the	Streisand, Barbra	18-124	DK
Way We Were the	Streisand, Barbra	6-354	MM
Way We Were the	Streisand, Barbra	12-512	P
Way You Do The Things You Do	Temptations	11-175	DK
Way You Like It the	Adema	30-654	THM
Way You Look Tonight the	Lettermen	48-516	THM
Way You Look Tonight the	Sinatra, Frank	49-498	MM
Way You Look Tonight the	Standard	13-629	SGB
Way You Look Tonight the	Stewart, Rod	25-593	MM
Way You Love Me the	Hill, Faith	23-366	SC
Way You Love Me the	Hill, Faith	22-470	ST
Way You Make Me Feel the	Anka, Paul	49-247	DFK
Way You Make Me Feel the	Jackson, Michael	11-768	DK
Way You Make Me Feel the	Jackson, Michael	13-214	P
Wayfaring Stranger	Harris, EmmyLou	1-240	CB
Waymore's Blues	Jennings, Waylon	45-189	SRK
Ways Of A Woman In Love the	Cash, Johnny	29-763	CB
Ways Of A Woman In Love the	Cash, Johnny	5-427	SC
Ways To Love A Man the	Wynette, Tammy	9-618	SAV
Ways To Love A Man the	Wynette, Tammy	20-639	SC
Wayward Wind the	Arnold, Eddy	7-359	MM
Wayward Wind the	Cline, Patsy	22-194	CB
Wayward Wind the	Grant, Gogi	3-514	SC
We All Fall Down	Diamond Rio	19-764	ST
We All Get Lucky Sometime	Parnell, Lee Roy	4-497	SC
We All Sleep Alone	Cher	14-50	RS
We Are All Made Of Stars	Moby	35-277	CB
We Are All Made Of Stars	Moby	25-205	MM
We Are All One	Cliff, Jimmy	46-629	SC
We Are Family	Sister Sledge	26-371	DK

284

SONG TITLE	ARTIST	#	TYPE
We Are Family	Sister Sledge	9-6	MH
We Are Family	Sister Sledge	13-5	P
We Are Family	Sister Sledge	9-218	PT
We Are Family	Sister Sledge	2-33	SC
We Are In Love	Connick, Harry Jr.	30-189	LE
We Are In Love	Connick, Harry Jr.	19-718	PS
We Are Never Ever Getting Back...	Swift, Taylor	39-24	ASK
We Are The Champions	Queen	35-140	CB
We Are The Champions	Queen	12-185	DK
We Are The Champions	Queen	15-181	MH
We Are the People Our Parents Warned..	Buffett, Jimmy	44-69	KV
We Are The World	USA For Africa	20-297	CB
We Are The World	USA For Africa	19-124	KC
We Are Water - Nashville	Panettiere, Hayden	45-468	BKD
We Are Young	Boyce Avenue	45-11	KV
We Are Young	Fun.	39-116	SF
We Believe In Happy Endings	Rodriguez, Johnny	22-58	CB
We Belong	Benatar, Pat	11-661	DK
We Belong	Benatar, Pat	9-691	SAV
We Belong Together	Carey, Mariah	30-136	PT
We Belong Together	Los Lobos	13-102	P
We Belong Together	Robert & Johnny	25-555	MM
We Belong Together	Valens, Richie	45-432	KV
We Both Walk	Morgan, Lorrie	1-336	CB
We Built This City	Starship	20-305	CB
We Built This City	Starship	17-76	DK
We Built This City	Starship	7-60	MM
We Bury The Hatchet	Brooks, Garth	17-217	NA
We Can	Rimes, LeAnn	19-599	CB
We Can	Rimes, LeAnn	25-665	MM
We Can	Rimes, LeAnn	19-542	SC
We Can Work it Out	Beatles	11-210	DK
We Can't Go On Living Like This	Rabbitt, Eddie	48-35	CB
We Can't Love Like This	Alabama	2-461	SC
We Care A Lot	Faith No More	30-783	SF
We Could	Pride, Charley	40-117	CB
We Danced	Paisley, Brad	14-913	CB
We Danced	Paisley, Brad	19-211	CSZ
We Danced	Paisley, Brad	22-558	ST
We Danced Anyway	Carter, Carlene	7-578	CHM
We Dared The Lightning	Bellamy Brothers	3-658	SC
We Didn't Start The Fire	Joel, Billy	34-97	CB
We Didn't Start The Fire	Joel, Billy	12-267	DK
We Didn't Start The Fire	Joel, Billy	16-142	LE
We Didn't Start The Fire	Joel, Billy	14-579	SC
We Do It In The Field	Smith, Granger	39-56	PHN
We Don't Have To Do This	Tucker, Tanya	6-462	MM
We Don't Love Here Anymore	Lawrence, Tracy	48-378	CB
We Don't Need Another Heartache	Turner, Tina	10-430	LE
We Don't Talk Anymore	Cliff, Richard	48-758	P
We Don't Talk Anymore	Richards, Cliff	21-804	SC

SONG TITLE	ARTIST	#	TYPE
We Fit Together	O-Town	25-44	MM
We Go Together	Grease	49-431	SDK
We Go Together	Little Big Town	40-5	PHM
We Go Together	Travolta & Newton-John	6-869	MM
We Got Love	Rydell, Bobby	47-477	SRI
We Got The Beat	Go-Go's	11-228	DK
We Got The Beat	Go-Go's	16-548	P
We Got The Beat	Go-Go's	9-773	SAV
We Got The Love	Restless Heart	1-418	CB
We Gotta Get Out Of This Place	Animals	11-275	DK
We Gotta Get Out Of This Place	Animals	15-47	LE
We Gotta Get Out Of This Place	Animals	9-704	SAV
We Have All the Time In the World	Armstrong, Louis	46-441	SF
We Just Disagree	Dean, Billy	6-458	MM
We Just Disagree	Dean, Billy	2-25	SC
We Just Disagree	Mason, Dave	9-331	AG
We Just Disagree	Mason, Dave	26-341	DK
We Like To Party	Venga Boys	7-838	PHM
We Like To Party	Venga Boys	13-785	SGB
We Live	Bosson	14-475	SC
We Live For Love	Benatar, Pat	46-512	MH
We Loved It Away	Jones & Wynette	49-374	CB
We Made Love	Alabama	9-427	CB
We Made Love	Alabama	22-552	ST
We May Never Pass This Way Again	Seals & Croft	3-456	SC
We Must Be Loving Right	Streisand, Barbra	15-290	PS
We Never Really Say Goodbye	Captain & Tennille	46-557	CB
We Never Touch At All	Haggard, Merle	49-806	CB
We Never Touch At All	Haggard, Merle	49-342	CB
We Owned The Night	Lady Antebellum	38-114	CB
We Really Shouldn't Be Doin' This	Strait, George	8-494	CB
We Ride	Rihanna	36-106	CB
We Ride	Rihanna	30-57	PHM
We Rode In Trucks	Bryan, Luke	36-556	CB
We Shall Be Free	Brooks, Garth	20-590	CB
We Shall Overcome	Baez, Joan	46-460	MIK
We Shall Overcome	Jackson, Mahalia	33-211	CB
We Shook Hands (Man To Man)	Tebey	25-448	MM
We Shook Hands (Man to Man)	Tebey	18-600	ST
We Shook Hands (Man to Man)	Tebey	32-158	THM
We Should Be Together	Williams, Don	45-224	CB
We Sure Can Love Each Other	Wynette, Tammy	49-365	CB
We Tell Ourselves	Black, Clint	1-115	CB
We Tell Ourselves	Black, Clint	6-116	MM
We Tell Ourselves	Black, Clint	30-434	THM
We Thank Thee (VR)	Reeves, Jim	44-243	DCK

SONG TITLE	ARTIST	#	TYPE
We The People	Cyrus, Billy Ray	20-583	CB
We To Together	Travolta & Newton-John	10-12	SC
We Went	Houser, Randy	49-369	BKD
We Were In Love	Keith, Toby	1-700	CB
We Were In Love	Keith, Toby	7-661	CHM
We Were In Love	Keith, Toby	22-603	ST
We Were Us	Urban & Lambert	43-87	PHN
We Were Us - duet	Lambert & Urban	46-249	ASK
We Weren't Crazy	Gracin, Josh	36-434	CB
We Will Meet Again	Adams, Oleta	23-344	MM
We Will Rock You	Queen	17-84	DK
We Will Rock You	Queen	12-776	P
We'll Burn That Bridge When We...	Brooks & Dunn	1-82	CB
We'll Burn That Bridge When We...	Brooks & Dunn	2-335	SC
We'll Sing In The Sunshine	Garnett, Gale	11-449	DK
We'll Sing In The Sunshine	Garnett, Gale	3-253	SC
We're An American Band	Grand Funk RR	17-89	DK
We're An American Band	Grand Funk RR	4-753	SC
We're Goinna Go Fishin'	Locklin, Hank	40-8	CB
We're Gonna Hold On	Jones & Wynette	8-122	CB
We're In This Love Together	Jarreau, Al	18-48	MM
We're In This Love Together	Jarreau, Al	18-504	SAV
We're Makin' Up	Hot Apple Pie	29-20	CB
We're Not Gonna Take It	Twisted Sister	23-61	MH
We're Not Makin' Love Anymore	Simon, Carly	49-158	MM
We're Not Makin' Love Anymore	Streisand, Barbra	6-441	MM
We're Off To See The Wizard - Show	Wizard Of Oz	33-221	CB
We're Over	Rodriguez, Johnny	22-53	CB
We're So Good Together	McEntire, Reba	14-734	CB
We're So Good Together	McEntire, Reba	13-860	CHM
We're Through	Hollies	44-369	ZM
We're Young And Beautiful	Underwood, Carrie	30-128	AS
We're Young And Beautiful	Underwood, Carrie	37-13	CB
We've Got A Groovy Thing Going	Simon & Garfunkel	49-766	LG
We've Got It Goin' On	Backstreet Boys	34-157	CB
We've Got It Goin' On	Backstreet Boys	30-414	THM
We've Got It Going On	Backstreet Boys	18-702	MM
We've Got It Made	Greenwood, Lee	47-129	CB
We've Got To Keep On Meeting	Overstreet, Paul	4-128	SC
We've Got Tonight	Rogers & Easton	15-578	MM
We've Got Tonight	Seger, Bob	34-70	CB
We've Got Tonight	Seger, Bob	6-446	MM
We've Only Just Begun	Carpenters	18-112	DK
We've Only Just Begun	Carpenters	12-689	P
We've Only Just Begun	Streisand, Barbra	9-879	DK

SONG TITLE	ARTIST	#	TYPE
We've Tried Everything	Tillis, Pam	6-507	MM
Weak And Powerless	Perfect Circle	23-184	PHM
Wealth Won't Save Your Soul	Williams, Hank Sr.	45-706	CB
Wear My Ring Around Your Neck	Presley, Elvis	2-589	SC
Wear My Ring Around Your Neck	Presley, Elvis	14-766	THM
Wear Your Love Like Heaven	Donovan	27-111	DK
Wearin' Of The Green	Standard	12-142	DK
Weary Blues From Waitin'	Williams, Hank Sr.	45-702	CB
Weather Is Here With You	Buffett, Jimmy	46-140	SC
Weathered	Creed	32-108	THM
Wedding Bell Blues	5th Dimension	35-74	CB
Wedding Bell Blues	5th Dimension	11-289	DK
Wedding Bell Blues	5th Dimension	2-865	SC
Wedding Bells	Williams, Hank Sr.	14-222	CB
Wedding Bells	Williams, Hank Sr.	17-307	NA
Wedding Bells	Williams, Hank Sr.	5-373	SC
Wedding March the	Standard	49-465	MM
Wedding Song	Chapman, Tracy	44-191	MM
Wedding Song the	Captain & Tennille	49-324	CB
Wedding Song the	Captain & Tennille	46-561	CB
Wedding Song the	Standard	2-67	SC
Wednesday's Child	Monro, Matt	18-108	PS
Weed With Willie	Keith, Toby	20-274	SC
Week In A Country Jail a	Hall, Tom T.	18-281	CB
Weekend In New England	Manilow, Barry	9-82	PS
Weekend In New England	Manilow, Barry	16-64	SC
Weekend the	Wariner, Steve	5-320	SC
Weep No More My Baby	Lee, Brenda	49-241	DFK
Weight the	Band	6-482	MM
Weight the	Band	13-235	P
Welcome Back	Lovin' Spoonful	47-211	LE
Welcome Home	Littrell, Brian	36-187	PHM
Welcome Home	Parton, Dolly	46-202	SC
Welcome Home Baby	Shirelles	48-376	RB
Welcome To Burlesque	Cher	47-683	KV
Welcome To My Life	Simple Plan	22-346	CB
Welcome To My Life	Simple Plan	30-817	PHM
Welcome To My Nightmare	Alice Cooper	19-288	SGB
Welcome To My World	Arnold, Eddy	12-304	DK
Welcome To My World	Arnold, Eddy	8-660	SAV
Welcome To My World	Reeves, Jim	8-571	CB
Welcome To My World	Reeves, Jim	40-121	CK
Welcome To My World	Reeves, Jim	3-828	LG
Welcome To My World	Reeves, Jim	6-788	MM
Welcome To My World	Reeves, Jim	5-212	SC
Welcome To The Fishbowl	Chesney, Kenny	48-76	BKD
Welcome To The Future	Paisley, Brad	36-312	PHM
Welcome To The Jungle	Guns & Roses	17-21	DK

SONG TITLE	ARTIST	#	TYPE
Welcome To The Jungle	Guns & Roses	13-277	P
Well Alright	Holly, Buddy	47-880	CB
Well Respected Man	Kinks	48-171	LE
Wendy	Beach Boys	46-495	NT
Were You Really Livin'	Brother Phelps	24-127	SC
Werewolves Of London	Zevon, Warren	17-466	SC
Werewolves Of London	Zevon, Warren	16-296	TT
West End Girls	Pet Shop Boys	5-388	SC
Western Movies	Olympics	6-682	MM
Western Movies	Olympics	5-463	SC
Western Union	Five Americans	16-667	LC
Wet Dream **	Addotta, Kip	23-19	SC
Wha't Going On In Your World	Strait, George	1-243	CB
Whan Mama Ain't Happy	Byrd, Tracy	1-555	CB
What A Beautiful Day	Cagle, Chris	34-355	CB
What A Beautiful Day	Cagle, Chris	25-444	MM
What A Beautiful Day	Cagle, Chris	18-467	ST
What A Beautiful Day	Cagle, Chris	32-82	THM
What A Cryin' Shame	Mavericks	12-451	P
What A Cryin' Shame	Mavericks	2-516	SC
What A Difference A Day Makes	Washington, Dinah	19-614	MH
What A Difference A Day Makes	Washington, Dinah	5-451	SC
What A Difference You've Made..	Milsap, Ronnie	11-710	DK
What A Difference You've Made...	Milsap, Ronnie	1-441	CB
What A Difference You've Made…	Milsap, Ronnie	13-475	P
What A Fool Believes	Doobie Brothers	29-83	CB
What A Fool Believes	Doobie Brothers	11-247	DK
What A Fool Believes	Doobie Brothers	13-129	P
What A Girl Wants	Aguilera, Christina	13-569	LE
What A Good Boy	Barenaked Ladies	30-621	RS
What A Man My Man Is	Anderson, Lynn	34-222	CB
What A Man My Man Is	Anderson, Lynn	7-108	MM
What A Man My Man Is	Anderson, Lynn	5-562	SC
What A Memory	Lawrence, Tracy	16-438	ST
What A Shame	Howard, Rebecca L	25-704	MM
What A Shame	Howard, Rebecca L	19-272	ST
What a Woman Feels	Burnette, Billy	10-270	CB
What A Woman Knows	Tyler, Kris	10-127	SC
What A Woman Knows	Tyler, Kris	22-421	ST
What A Woman Wants	White, Lari	10-787	JVC
What A Wonderful Life	Presley, Elvis	25-490	MM
What A Wonderful World	Armstrong, Louis	9-351	AH
What A Wonderful World	Armstrong, Louis	18-242	DK
What A Wonderful World	Armstrong, Louis	6-323	MM
What A Wonderful World	Armstrong, Louis	9-562	SAV
What A Wonderful World	Armstrong, Louis	10-585	SF
What A Wonderful World	Herman's Hermits	47-135	LE
What A Wonderful World - duet	Bennett & Lang	45-518	SC
What About Georgia	Lambert, Miranda	46-250	CB
What About Love	Heart	11-280	DK
What About Me	Moving Pictures	21-801	SC

SONG TITLE	ARTIST	#	TYPE
What About Now	Daughtry	36-26	PT
What About Now	Lonestar	9-416	CB
What About Now	Lonestar	13-807	CHM
What About Now	Lonestar	22-543	ST
What About Us	Brandy	25-219	MM
What About You	Sons Of The Desert	8-918	CB
What About You	Sons of the Desert	43-7	SC
What About You	Sons Of The Desert	22-749	ST
What About Your Friends	TLC	35-204	CB
What Am I Doin' Loving You	Lynns	8-747	CB
What Am I Doing Hangin' Around	Monkees	47-290	EZ
What Am I Gonna Do	Stewart, Rod	14-854	LE
What Am I Gonna Do (With The Rest...)	Haggard, Merle	46-32	SSK
What Am I Gonna Do About You	McEntire, Reba	11-740	DK
What Am I Gonna Do About You	McEntire, Reba	12-438	P
What Am I Living For	Willis, Chuck	49-728	CB
What Are We Doin' In Love	Rogers & West	5-436	SC
What Are We Doin' Lonesome	Gatlin, Larry	47-107	CB
What Are You Doing The Rest Of …	Streisand, Barbra	15-848	MM
What Are You Doing The Rest Of…	Streisand, Barbra	12-575	P
What Are You Listening To	Stapleton, Chris	45-437	BKD
What Are You Waiting For	Grant, Natalie	29-55	CB
What Becomes of the Broken Hearted	Ruffin, Jimmy	35-84	CB
What Becomes Of The Broken Hearted	Ruffin, Jimmy	12-157	DK
What Can I Do	Corrs	49-187	LG
What Child Is This	Mathis, Johnny	45-782	SBI
What Child Is This	Underwood, Carrie	45-786	KV
What Children Believe	Shenandoah	14-106	CB
What Comes Over You	Brandt, Paul	22-764	ST
What Did I Have That I Don't Have..	Streisand, Barbra	15-847	MM
What Do I Care	Cash, Johnny	29-762	CB
What Do I Have To Do	Stabbing Westward	4-669	SC
What Do I Know	Ricochet	4-153	SC
What Do Ya Think About That	Montgomery Gentry	30-532	CB
What Do You Do	Troys	32-249	THM
What Do You Know About Love	Yoakam, Dwight	14-149	CB
What Do You Know About Love	Yoakam, Dwight	10-261	SC
What Do You Know About Love	Yoakam, Dwight	22-575	ST
What Do You Mean	Bieber, Justin	48-620	BKD
What Do You Say	McEntire, Reba	19-240	SC
What Do You Say	McEntire, Reba	22-373	ST

287

SONG TITLE	ARTIST	#	TYPE
What Do You Say To That	Strait, George	5-729	SC
What Do You Say To That	Strait, George	22-429	ST
What Do You Want	Faith, Adam	48-755	P
What Do You Want From Me	Foster & Lloyd	5-766	SC
What Do You Want From Me	Niemann, Jerrod	37-209	AS
What Do You Want From Me	Yates, Billy	14-795	ST
What Do You Want The Girl To Do	Scaggs, Boz	46-320	SC
What Do You Want With Him	Ball, David	6-808	MM
What Do You Want With Him	Ball, David	2-769	SC
What Does It Take	Davis, Skeeter	43-330	CB
What Does It Take	Davis, Skeeter	5-848	SC
What Does It Take To Win Your Love	Walker, Junior	17-376	DK
What Have I Done To Deserve This	Pet Shop Boys	17-529	SC
What Have They Done To The Rain	Peter, Paul & Mary	9-124	PS
What Have You Done For Me Lately	Jackson, Janet	27-305	DK
What Have You Done For Me Lately	Jackson, Janet	12-824	P
What Hurts The Most	Rascal Flatts	29-185	CB
What Hurts The Most	Rascal Flatts	29-705	ST
What Hurts The Most (Radio Vers)	Cascada	49-904	SC
What I Can't Put Down	Pardi, Jon	47-409	ASK
What I Cannot Change	Rimes, LeAnn	36-617	CB
What I Cannot Change	Rimes, LeAnn	36-218	PHM
What I Did For Love	Groban, Josh	48-51	KVD
What I Did Last Night	Britt, Catherine	30-308	CB
What I Did Right	Sons Of The Desert	14-845	ST
What I Didn't Do	Wariner, Steve	4-656	SC
What I Didn't Know	Athenaeum	7-776	PHT
What I Go To School For	Busted	20-556	PHM
What I Like About You	Romantics	9-352	AH
What I Like About You	Romantics	2-45	SC
What I Meant To Say	Hayes, Wade	3-624	SC
What I Meant To Say	Osmond, Donny	47-862	ZP
What I Need	Raye, Collin	16-435	ST
What I Need To Do	Chesney, Kenny	29-428	CB
What I Need To Do	Chesney, Kenny	13-812	CHM
What I Need To Do	Chesney, Kenny	22-529	ST
What I Need To Do (Radio Version)	Chesney, Kenny	23-375	SC
What I Really Meant To Say	Thompson, Cyndi	33-172	CB
What I Really Meant To Say	Thompson, Cyndi	15-105	ST
What I Tell Myself	Tennison, Chalee	14-912	CB
What I Wanna Be	Twain, Shania	45-532	CB
What I Want	Daughtry	30-558	CB

SONG TITLE	ARTIST	#	TYPE
What I'd Say	Conley, Earl Thomas	5-394	SC
What I'm For	Green, Pat	47-123	CB
What I've Got In Mind	Spears, Billie Jo	8-359	CB
What If	Creed	5-889	SC
What If	McEntire, Reba	8-150	CB
What If	McEntire, Reba	22-754	ST
What If	Studdard, Ruben	36-328	CB
What If	Studdard, Ruben	36-328	PS
What If Eminem Did Jingle Bells**	Rivers, Bob	45-931	SC
What If God Smoked Cannibus	Rivers & Twisted Radio	45-934	SC
What If I	Trainor, Meghan	45-644	KV
What If I Came Knocking	Mellencamp, John	24-261	SC
What If I Do	McCready, Mindy	8-127	CB
What If I Do	McCready, Mindy	22-643	ST
What If I Said	Cochran & Wariner	8-143	CB
What If I Said	Cochran & Wariner	22-761	ST
What If I Wanna Kiss You Tomorrow	Trainor, Meghan	45-147	KCD
What If It All Goes Right	Lawson, Melissa	36-246	PHM
What If It's Me	Day, Jennifer	9-386	CB
What If It's You	McEntire, Reba	1-823	CB
What If It's You	McEntire, Reba	7-681	CHM
What If It's You	McEntire, Reba	22-628	ST
What If Jesus Comes Back Like That	Raye, Collin	7-177	MM
What If Jesus Comes Back Like That	Raye, Collin	4-23	SC
What If She's An Angel	Steiner, Tommy S.	33-190	CB
What If She's An Angel	Steiner, Tommy S.	25-124	MM
What If She's An Angel	Steiner, Tommy S.	16-103	ST
What In The World	Supernaw, Doug	4-201	SC
What Is It To Burn	Finch	32-181	THM
What Is Life	Harrison, George	5-686	SC
What Is Life Without Love	Arnold, Eddy	19-635	CB
What Is Truth	Cash, Johnny	29-734	CB
What Is Truth	Cash, Johnny	29-698	SC
What It Ain't	Turner, Josh	20-343	ST
What It's Like	Everlast	7-803	PHT
What Kind Of A Woman Would I Be	Cochran, Tammy	19-55	ST
What Kind Of Fool	Streisand & Gibb	15-579	MM
What Kind Of Fool	Streisand, Barbra	49-556	KKS
What Kind Of Fool - duet	Streisand & Gibb	49-608	PS
What Kind Of Fool Am I	Newley, Anthony	27-382	DK
What Kind Of Fool Am I	Standard	47-824	DK
What Kind Of Fool Do You Think I Am	Parnell, Lee Roy	48-332	CB
What Kind Of Fool Do You Think I Am	Tams	6-787	MM
What Kind Of Girl Do You Think I Am	Lynn, Loretta	43-234	CB
What Kind Of Man Would I Be	Mint Condition	24-293	SC
What Kind Of Woman Would I Be	Cochran, Tammy	25-616	MM
What Kinda Gone	Cagle, Chris	30-536	CB

SONG TITLE	ARTIST	#	TYPE
What Locks The Door	Green, Al	48-5	KCD
What Locks The Door	Greene, Jack	43-339	CB
What Made Milwaukee Famous..	Lewis, Jerry Lee	3-375	SC
What Made You Change Your Mind	Coe, David Allan	18-318	CB
What Made You Say That	Twain, Shania	19-289	MH
What Made You Say That	Twain, Shania	16-658	THM
What Makes You Beautiful	One Direction	39-42	ASK
What Mattered Most	Herndon, Ty	2-658	SC
What Might Have Been	Little Texas	2-115	SC
What More Do You Want From Me	Vincent, Rhonda	4-240	SC
What My Woman Can't Do	Jones, George	46-282	KV
What Now My Love	Bassey, Shirley	46-486	SF
What Now My Love	Lettermen	19-108	SAV
What Now My Love	Sinatra & Franklin	15-580	MM
What One Man Can Do	Denver, John	15-622	THM
What Part Of No	Morgan, Lorrie	1-340	CB
What Part Of No	Morgan, Lorrie	6-130	MM
What Say You	Tritt & Mellencamp	20-510	ST
What Say You	Tritt, Travis	22-63	CB
What She Is (Is A Woman In Love)	Conley, E.T.	47-604	CB
What She's Doing Now	Brooks, Garth	6-285	MM
What She's Doing Now	Brooks, Garth	2-674	SC
What The Cowgirl's Do	Gill, Vince	2-479	SC
What The Cowgirls Do	Gill, Vince	1-594	CB
What The Cowgirls Do	Gill, Vince	20-411	MH
What The Cowgirls Do	Gill, Vince	6-607	MM
What The Heart Wants	Raye, Collin	7-672	CHM
What The Hell Happened To Me **	Sandler, Adam	5-555	SC
What The Hell Happened To Me **	Sandler, Adam	13-727	SGB
What The World Needs	Judd, Wynonna	25-606	MM
What The World Needs	Judd, Wynonna	19-69	ST
What The World Needs	Wynonna	34-403	CB
What The World Needs	Wynonna	32-263	THM
What The World Needs Now	DeShannon, Jackie	11-528	DK
What They're Talkin' About	Akins, Rhett	6-714	MM
What This Country Needs	Tippin, Aaron	5-826	SC
What This Country Needs	Tippin, Aaron	22-519	ST
What Time Do You Have To Be Back	Bailey, Razzy	29-389	CB
What To Do	Holly, Buddy	47-887	ZM
What U Do 2 Me	Boomcat	32-319	THM
What Was I Thinkin'	Bentley, Dierks	34-412	CB
What Was I Thinkin'	Bentley, Dierks	25-614	MM
What Was I Thinkin'	Bentley, Dierks	19-57	ST
What Was I Thinkin'	Bentley, Dierks	32-264	THM
What We Ain't Got	Owen, Jake	45-640	SSC
What We're Fighting For	Dudley, Dave	43-290	CB

SONG TITLE	ARTIST	#	TYPE
What We're Gonna Do About It	Steiner, Tommy S.	18-460	ST
What Will Mary Say	Mathis, Johnny	29-461	LE
What Will You Do With M-E	Western Flyer	4-892	SC
What Would Happen	Brooks, Meredith	7-704	PHM
What Would Happen	Brooks, Meredith	10-113	SC
What Would Willie Do	Robison, Bruce	17-603	CB
What Would You Do	City High	18-541	TT
What Would You Do	Isley Brothers & Mr. Biggs	32-235	THM
What Would You Do	Reeves, Jim	49-801	VH
What Would You Say	Dave Matthews Band	3-441	SC
What Would You Say	Trailor Choir	37-44	CB
What Would You Say To Me	Carpenter, M C	49-332	CB
What Would You Say To Me	Carpenter, M C	47-664	CB
What Would Your Memories Do	Gosdin, Vern	47-119	CB
What Ya Gonna Do	Hinder	48-632	CB
What You Ain't Gonna Get	Lucas, Lauren	23-125	CB
What You Do To Me	Dan + Shay	44-379	BKD
What You Give	Tesla	6-21	SC
What You Give Away	Gill, Vince	30-365	CB
What You Need	Inxs	33-317	CB
What You Won't Do For Love	Caldwell, Bobby	17-409	DK
What You Won't Do For Love	Caldwell, Bobby	25-286	MM
What You're Doing	Beatles	44-124	KV
What'd I Say	Charles, Ray	16-798	DK
What'd I Say	Charles, Ray	12-664	P
What'd I Say	Charles, Ray	4-5	SC
What'd I Say	Lewis, Jerry Lee.	29-820	SF
What'd I Say	Presley, Elvis	8-587	CB
What'll I Do	Bellamy Brothers	45-305	CB
What'll I Do	Ronstadt, Linda	15-582	MM
What'll You Do About Me	Supernaw, Doug	6-718	MM
What'll You Do About Me	Supernaw, Doug	17-277	NA
What'll You Do About Me	Supernaw, Doug	22-863	ST
What's A Guy Gotta Do	Nichols, Joe	22-91	CB
What's a Guy Gotta Do	Nichols, Joe	23-41	SC
What's A Memory Like You Doing...	Schneider, John	20-291	SC
What's a Memory Like You...	Schneider, John	33-90	CB
What's Come Over You	Brandt, Paul	8-306	CB
What's Forever For	Murphy, Michael M	13-486	P
What's Forever For	Murphy, Michael M.	34-251	CB
What's Goin' On	All Star Tribute	25-45	MM
What's Goin' On	All Star Tribute	16-300	PHM
What's Goin' On	All Star Tribute	16-81	ST
What's Goin' On	Gaye, Marvin	11-371	DK
What's Goin' On	Gaye, Marvin	13-144	P
What's Goin' On	Gaye, Marvin	4-290	SC
What's Going On In Your	Strait, George	14-688	CB

289

SONG TITLE	ARTIST	#	TYPE
World			
What's Going On In Your World	Strait, George	5-121	SC
What's Going On?	Gaye, Marvin	36-116	JTG
What's Happened To Blue Eyes	Colter, Jessi	5-397	SC
What's He Doin' In My World	Arnold, Eddy	19-35	CB
What's He Doin' In My World	Arnold, Eddy	5-99	SC
What's He Doin' In My World	Arnold, Eddy	17-623	THM
What's In It For Me	Berry, John	17-252	NA
What's In It For Me	Berry, John	2-483	SC
What's In It For Me	Hill, Faith	14-151	CB
What's In It For Me	Tritt, Travis	6-668	MM
What's It Gonna Be	McKnight, Brian	18-357	CB
What's It To You	Walker, Clay	2-804	SC
What's Left Of Me	Lachey, Nick	30-159	PT
What's Left Of The Flag	Flogging Molly	48-617	KV
What's Love Got To Do With It	Turner, Tina	10-420	LE
What's Love Got To Do With It	Turner, Tina	12-678	P
What's My Age Again	Blink 182	8-512	PHT
What's My Age Again	Blink 182	19-828	SGB
What's New Pussycat	Jones, Tom	12-488	P
What's New Pussycat	Jones, Tom	4-44	SC
What's On Your Mind	Information Society	21-405	SC
What's Simple Is True - (Radio Ver)	Jewel	17-543	SC
What's The Colour Of Money	Hollywood Beyond	9-800	SAV
What's The Matter With You Baby	Church, Claudia	8-331	CB
What's The Matter With You Baby	Church, Claudia	22-735	ST
What's This Life For	Creed	7-777	PHT
What's Up	4 Non Blondes	28-431	DK
What's Up	4 Non Blondes	6-419	MM
What's Up With That	Emerick, Scotty	29-597	CB
What's Up With That	ZZ Top	24-362	SC
What's Your Flava?	David, Craig	32-54	THM
What's Your Mama's Name	Tucker, Tanya	8-42	CB
What's Your Mama's Name	Tucker, Tanya	5-52	SC
What's Your Name	Don & Juan	7-301	MM
What's Your Name	Lynyrd Skynyrd	12-356	DK
What's Your Name	Lynyrd Skynyrd	5-268	SC
Whatcha Gonna Do	Pablo Cruise	15-735	SC
Whatcha Gonna Do With A Dog Like That	Raye, Susan	45-687	VH
Whatcha Goona Do With A Cowboy	Ledoux & Brooks	6-181	MM
Whatcha Reckon	Turner, Josh	49-105	CDG
Whatcha See Is Whatcha Get	Dramatics	25-280	MM
Whatchalookinat	Houston, Whitney	18-426	CB

SONG TITLE	ARTIST	#	TYPE
Whatchalookinat	Houston, Whitney	32-202	THM
Whatever Comes First	Sons Of The Desert	10-73	SC
Whatever Gets You Thru the Night	Lennon, John	30-288	RS
Whatever Happened to Old Fashioned Love	Thomas, B.J.	44-323	DFK
Whatever Happened To The Blues	Jennings, Waylon	45-188	SRK
Whatever It Is	Zac Brown Band	37-33	CB
Whatever It Takes	Chesney, Kenny	45-130	CB
Whatever It Takes	Coffey, Kelly	25-522	MM
Whatever It Takes	Coffey, Kelly	18-795	ST
Whatever It Takes	Coffey, Kelly	32-192	THM
Whatever It Takes	Grant, Amy	18-767	PS
Whatever It Takes	Lifehouse	36-477	CB
Whatever Lola Wants	Vaughn, Sarah	23-347	MM
Whatever Lola Wants	Vaughn, Sarah	3-503	SC
Whatever She's Got	Nail, David	43-146	ASK
Whatever She's Got	Nail, David	45-400	BKD
Whatever She's Got	Nail, David	44-335	SSC
Whatever We Imagine	Ingram, James	9-212	SO
Whatever We Wanted	Mellencamp, John	19-95	PS
Whatever You Like	TI	36-6	PT
Whatever You Need	Turner, Tina	14-477	SC
Whatever You Say	McBride, Martina	8-947	CB
Whatever You Say	McBride, Martina	7-828	CHT
Whatever You Want	Dayne, Taylor	21-734	TT
Whatta Man	Salt 'N Pepa	2-109	SC
Wheel Of Fortune	Starr, Kay	4-182	SC
Wheels	Hometown News	18-334	ST
Wheels	Restless Heart	34-283	CB
Wheels	Restless Heart	5-252	SC
When	Skaggs, Ricky	24-162	SC
When	Twain, Shania	1-525	CB
When	Twain, Shania	22-550	ST
When A Child Is Born	Mathis, Johnny	45-781	ZM
When A Man Loves A Chicken	Parody	49-308	RD
When A Man Loves A Woman	Bolton, Michael	21-467	CB
When A Man Loves A Woman	Sledge, Percy	17-40	DK
When A Man Loves A Woman	Sledge, Percy	12-712	P
When A Man Loves A Woman	Sledge, Percy	2-274	SC
When A Woman Loves A Man	Parnell, Lee Roy	7-84	MM
When A Woman Loves A Man	Parnell, Lee Roy	3-570	SC
When A Woman's Fed Up	Kelly, R.	49-519	PS
When All Is Said And Done	Abba	46-222	KV
When And Where	Confederate RR	6-804	MM
When Autumn Comes	Eder, Linda	17-450	PS
When Boy Meets Girl	Clark, Terri	7-169	MM
When Boy Meets Girl	Clark, Terri	3-665	SC
When Can I See You	Babyface	34-114	CB

SONG TITLE	ARTIST	#	TYPE
When Can I See You	Babyface	12-184	DK
When Children Rule The World	Osmond, Donny	47-848	BSP
When Cowboys Didn't Dance	Lonestar	4-503	SC
When Did You Stop Loving Me	Jones, George	45-711	VH
When Did You Stop Loving Me	Strait, George	8-172	CB
When Did You Stop Loving Me	Strait, George	24-248	SC
When Doves Cry	Prince	16-775	DK
When Doves Cry	Prince	12-843	P
When God Fearin' Women Get The	McBride, Martina	15-601	ST
When God Fearing Women Get The..	McBride, Martina	29-529	CB
When Hell Freezes Over	McCready, Rich	4-891	SC
When I Call Your Name	Gill, Vince	1-586	CB
When I Call Your Name	Gill, Vince	9-444	SAV
When I Close My Eyes	Chesney, Kenny	1-323	CB
When I Close My Eyes	Chesney, Kenny	15-583	RIS
When I Come Back	Holland, Greg	2-581	SC
When I Could Come Home To You	Wariner, Steve	2-507	SC
When I Die	No Mercy	21-551	PHM
When I Dream	Gayle, Crystal	4-791	SC
When I Dream At Night	Anthony, Marc	14-503	SC
When I Fall	Barenaked Ladies	30-619	RS
When I Fall In Love	Cole, Nat "King"	29-455	LE
When I Fall In Love	Cole, Nat & Natalie	24-548	SC
When I Fall In Love	Day, Doris	33-218	CB
When I Fall In Love	Day, Doris	9-91	PS
When I Fall In Love	Dion & Griffin	12-239	DK
When I Fall In Love	Dion & Griffin	6-331	MM
When I Fall In Love	Standard	12-838	P
When I Fall In Love - show	Sleepless In Seattle	48-787	MM
When I Get Through With You	Cline, Patsy	45-504	CB
When I Get Where I'm Going	Paisley, Brad	23-485	CB
When I Grow Up	Daniels, Clint	8-224	CB
When I Grow Up	Pussycat Dolls	36-502	CB
When I Grow Up To Be A Man	Beach Boys	46-491	LE
When I Kissed The Teacher	Abba	46-224	KV
When I Look Into Your Eyes	Firehouse	23-107	SC
When I Look Into Your Heart	Gill & Grant	9-871	ST
When I Look To The Sky	Train	19-662	CB
When I Look To The Sky	Train	37-322	SC
When I Looked At Him	Expose	12-758	P
When I Looked At Him	Expose	18-491	SAV
When I Need You	Sayer, Leo	35-150	CB
When I Need You	Sayer, Leo	29-642	SC
When I Need You	Sayer, Leo	10-536	SF

SONG TITLE	ARTIST	#	TYPE
When I Said Goodbye	Steps	19-658	SGB
When I Said I Do	Black, Clint	19-236	SC
When I Said I Do	Black, Clint	22-498	ST
When I Said I Do - Duet	Black & Hartman	30-420	THM
When I See This Bar	Chesney, Kenny	45-127	BKD
When I See This Bar	Chesney, Kenny	44-333	SSC
When I See U	Fantasia	30-572	CB
When I See You	Gray, Macy	25-544	MM
When I See You Smile	Bad English	13-215	P
When I See You Smile	Bad English	15-740	SC
When I Stop Leaving I'll Be Gone	Pride, Charley	40-114	CB
When I Think About Angels	O'Neal, Jamie	33-169	CB
When I Think About Angels	O'Neal, Jamie	9-867	ST
When I Think About Cheating	Wilson, Gretchen	22-84	CB
When I Think About Leaving	Chesney, Kenny	29-436	CB
When I Think Of You	Jackson, Janet	27-303	DK
When I Think Of You	Jackson, Janet	4-854	SC
When I'm 64	Beatles	17-62	DK
When I'm 64	Beatles	13-68	P
When I'm Away From You	Bellamy Brothers	5-159	SC
When I'm Back On My Feet	Bolton, Michael	17-91	DK
When I'm Gone	3 Doors Down	35-279	CB
When I'm Gone	3 Doors Down	25-425	MM
When I'm Gone	3 Doors Down	18-826	THM
When I'm Gone	Cyrus, Billy Ray	24-4	SC
When I'm Gone	Simple Plan	36-474	CB
When I'm Gone - duet	Joey & Rory	45-817	BKD
When I'm With You	Sheriff	21-751	MH
When Irish Eyes Are Smiling	Various	48-583	DK
When It All Goes South	Alabama	22-457	ST
When It Comes To You	Anderson, John	20-115	CB
When It Comes To You	Anderson, John	24-359	SC
When It Rains	Eli Young Band	47-57	CB
When It Rains	Wilson, Gretchen	23-138	CB
When It Rains It Pours	Haggard, Merle	49-808	CB
When It Rains It Pours	Haggard, Merle	49-344	CB
When It's Just You & Me	West, Dottie	15-228	CB
When It's Over	Sugar Ray	35-259	CB
When It's Springtime In Alaska	Horton, Johnny	5-435	SC
When It's Love	Van Halen	13-614	LE
When Johnny Comes Marching Home	Folk Standard	18-170	DK
When Johnny Comes Marching Home	Patriotic	44-49	PT
When Love And Hate Collide	Def Leppard	46-168	SC
When Love Comes Around The Bend	Seals, Dan	48-105	SC
When Love Fades	Keith, Toby	5-796	SC
When Love Fades	Keith, Toby	22-380	ST

SONG TITLE	ARTIST	#	TYPE
When Love Finds You	Gill, Vince	1-599	CB
When Love Finds You	Gill, Vince	2-457	SC
When Love Starts Talkin'	Judd, Wynonna	8-130	CB
When Love Starts Talkin'	Judd, Wynonna	22-654	ST
When Mama Ain't Happy	Byrd, Tracy	7-827	CHT
When Mama Ain't Happy	Byrd, Tracy	22-718	ST
When My Blue Moon Turns To Gold	Haggard, Merle	44-61	KV
When My Dreamboat Comes Home	Cline, Patsy	45-512	MM
When My Dreams Come True	Howard, Rebecca L	8-987	CB
When My Little Girl Is Smiling	Drifters	45-885	VH
When My Little Girl Is Smiling	Justice, Jimmy	10-623	SF
When My Ship Comes In	Black, Clint	1-117	CB
When My Ship Comes In	Black, Clint	6-127	MM
When My Ship Comes In	Black, Clint	12-479	P
When My Ship Comes In	Black, Clint	30-435	THM
When October Goes	Manilow, Barry	9-80	PS
When Rita Leaves	McClinton, Delbert	17-478	TT
When She Cries	Restless Heart	1-409	CB
When She Cries	Restless Heart	6-217	MM
When She Says Baby	Aldean, Jason	43-140	ASK
When She Was My Girl	Four Tops	43-387	CB
When She Was My Girl	Four Tops	43-431	SF
When Smokey Sings	ABC	18-388	SAV
When Somebody Knows You	Shelton, Blake	20-327	ST
When Somebody Knows You...	Shelton, Blake	39-1	CB
When Somebody Loves You	Jackson, Alan	40-101	CB
When Somebody Loves You	Jackson, Alan	14-834	ST
When Somebody Loves You	Jackson, Alan	15-218	THM
When Somebody Loves You	Restless Heart	1-410	CB
When Something Is Wrong	Sam & Dave	12-27	DK
When Sunny Gets Blue	Mathis, Johnny	15-584	MM
When The Bartender Cries	Peterson, Michael	8-490	CB
When The Bartender Cries	Peterson, Michael	5-287	SC
When The Bartender Cries	Peterson, Michael	22-801	ST
When The Children Cry	White Lion	23-56	MH
When The Children Cry	White Lion	24-684	SC
When The Fallen Angels Fall	Loveless, Patty	20-13	SC
When The Going Gets Tough	Ocean, Billy	48-574	DK
When The Grass Grows Over Me	Jones, George	8-348	CB
When The Heartache is Over	Turner, Tina	5-892	SC
When The Last Curtain	Jones, George	49-349	CB

SONG TITLE	ARTIST	#	TYPE
Falls			
When The Last Time **	Clipse	32-130	THM
When The Lights Go Down	Hill, Faith	25-441	MM
When The Lights Go Down	Hill, Faith	18-466	ST
When The Lights Go Down	Hill, Faith	32-77	THM
When The Man Comes Around	Cash, Johnny	43-417	SRK
When The Music's Over	Doors	18-651	SO
When The Night Comes	Cocker, Joe	5-339	SC
When The Red Red Robin Comes...	Miller, Mitch	23-545	CB
When The Red Red Robin Goes...	Reminiscing Series	3-27	SC
When The Right One Comes Along - duet	Bowen & Palladio	45-471	KVD
When The Right One Comes Along - show	Nashville Cast	45-465	AHN
When the Right One Comes...	Nashville Cast	39-91	PHN
When The Saints Go Marching In	Armstrong, Louis	10-708	JVC
When The Saints Go Marching In	Armstrong, Louis	46-442	LE
When The Saints Go Marching In	Kingston Trio	7-354	MM
When The Saints Go Marching In	Standard	34-439	CB
When The Stars Go Blue	Corrs & Bond	18-413	MM
When The Stars Go Blue	McGraw, Tim	29-365	CB
When The Sun Goes Down	Chesney, Kenny	20-165	ST
When The Sun Goes Down	Milsap, Ronnie	47-267	CB
When the Sun Goes Down - duet	Chesney & Uncle Kracker	35-445	CB
When The Thought Of You Catches...	Ball, David	17-232	NA
When The Thought Of You Catches...	Ball, David	21-299	NA
When The Thought Of You Catches...	Ball, David	2-447	SC
When The Tingle Becomes A Chill	Lynn, Loretta	4-750	SC
When The Wrong One Loves U Right	Dion, Celine	19-23	PS
When The Wrong One Loves U Right	Hayes, Wade	8-100	CB
When Two Worlds Collide	Miller, Roger	22-284	CB
When Two Worlds Collide	Reeves, Jim	3-831	LG
When U Think About Me	One Voice	9-335	PS
When We All Sang Along	Orbison, Roy	47-349	KV
When We All Sang Along	Orlando & Dawn	49-33	SHER
When We Get Married	Dreamlovers	2-853	SC
When We Make Love	Alabama	9-439	SAV
When We Were Young	Adele	46-3	DCK

292

SONG TITLE	ARTIST	#	TYPE
When Will I Be Loved	Everly Brothers	38-27	CB
When Will I Be Loved	Everly Brothers	45-294	ZMP
When Will I Be Loved	Ronstadt, Linda	16-766	DK
When Will I Be Loved	Ronstadt, Linda	9-7	MH
When Will I Be Loved	Ronstadt, Linda	12-639	P
When Will I Be Loved	Ronstadt, Linda	10-1	SC
When Will I See You Again	Three Degrees	35-117	CB
When Will I See You Again	Three Degrees	12-104	DK
When Will I See You Again	Three Degrees	24-345	SC
When Will You Say I Love You	Fury, Billy	10-619	SF
When You Are Gone	Reeves, Jim	44-237	DCK
When You Are Gone	Reeves, Jim	44-247	SRK
When You Believe	Carey & Houston	7-787	PHT
When You Believe	Carey, Mariah	35-218	CB
When You Believe	Carey, Mariah	16-397	PR
When You Come Around	Rutan, Deric	19-368	ST
When You Come Back Down	Nickel Creek	17-479	TT
When You Come Back To Me Again	Brooks, Garth	14-720	CB
When You Come Back To Me Again	Brooks, Garth	19-252	CSZ
When You Come Back To Me Again	Brooks, Garth	22-544	ST
When You Cry	Hill, Faith	8-983	CB
When You Feel Like You're In Love	Smith, Carl	43-281	SC
When You Get To Be You	Brokop, Lisa	8-857	CB
When You Get To Be You	Brokop, Lisa	10-159	SC
When You Got A Good Thing	Lady Antebellum	44-128	KV
When You Hurt I Hurt	McDowell, Ronnie	47-232	CB
When You Kiss Me	Twain, Shania	20-446	ST
When You Kiss Me	Twain, Shania	32-83	THM
When You Leave Don't Slam The Door	Ritter, Tex	20-711	CB
When You Leave That Way	Confederate RR	2-567	SC
When You Lie Next To Me	Coffey, Kelly	33-150	CB
When You Lie Next To Me	Coffey, Kelly	25-73	MM
When You Lie Next To Me	Coffey, Kelly	16-329	ST
When You Look At Me	Milian, Christina	21-735	TT
When You Look Me In The Eyes	Jonas Brothers	36-451	CB
When You Love A Woman	Journey	24-375	SC
When You Love Me	McBride, Martina	29-540	CB
When You Love Me	Rushlow, Tim	9-396	CB
When You Love Someone	Kershaw, Sammy	22-487	ST
When You Need A Laugh	Cline, Patsy	45-506	OZP

SONG TITLE	ARTIST	#	TYPE
When You Need My Love	Worley, Darryl	9-394	CB
When You Need My Love	Worley, Darryl	13-852	CHM
When You Need My Love	Worley, Darryl	19-248	CSZ
When You Need My Love	Worley, Darryl	22-551	ST
When You Said You Loved Me	Carson, Jeff	30-319	CB
When You Say Love	Luman, Bob	5-865	SC
When You Say Nothing At All	Krauss, Alison	2-656	SC
When You Say Nothing At All	Whitley, Keith	35-395	CB
When You Say Nothing At All	Whitley, Keith	2-99	SC
When You Say You Love Me	Groban, Josh	43-306	CB
When You Tell Me That You Love Me	Iglesias & Parton	29-327	PS
When You Tell Me That You Love Me	Iglesias & Parton	49-771	PS
When You Tell Me That You Love Me	Ross, Diana	24-263	SC
When You Think Of Me	Wills, Mark	34-404	CB
When You Think Of Me	Wills, Mark	25-528	MM
When You Think Of Me	Wills, Mark	18-794	ST
When You Think Of Me	Wills, Mark	32-190	THM
When You Walk In The Room	Searchers	9-700	SAV
When You Walk In The Room	Tillis, Pam	26-573	DK
When You Walk In The Room	Tillis, Pam	6-606	MM
When You Walk In The Room	Tillis, Pam	17-225	NA
When You Walk In The Room	Tillis, Pam	2-454	SC
When You Wasn't Famous **	Streets	30-693	SF
When You Were Mine	Shenandoah	1-487	CB
When You Were Sweet Sixteen	Como, Perry	12-68	DK
When You Wish Upon A Star	Armstrong, Louis	21-14	CB
When You Wore A Tulip	Reminiscing Series	3-34	SC
When You're Hot You're Hot	Reed, Jerry	13-504	P
When You're Hot You're Hot	Reed, Jerry	20-720	SC
When You're In Love (That's What..)	Forrester Sisters	19-443	SC
When You're In Love With A Beautiful Woman	Dr. Hook	13-130	P
When You're In Love With A Beautiful Woman	Dr. Hook	15-741	SC
When You're Lonely	Kramer, Jana	48-196	PHN
When You're Smiling	Garland, Judy	17-420	DK
When You're Smiling	Garland, Judy	12-543	P
When You're Smiling	Garland, Judy	4-359	SC
When You're Smiling	Sinatra, Frank	21-12	CB
When You're Young	3 Doors Down	37-266	CB
When You've Been	LaBelle, Patti	24-270	SC

SONG TITLE	ARTIST	#	TYPE
Blessed			
Whenever Forever Comes	Parton & Raye	2-310	SC
Whenever God Shines His Light	Morrison, Van	23-605	BS
Whenever God Shines His Light On..	Morrison, Van	15-731	SI
Whenever I Call You Friend	Loggins & Nicks	11-292	DK
Whenever I Call You Friend	Loggins & Nicks	13-159	P
Whenever Wherever	Shakira	25-77	MM
Whenever You Come Around	Gill, Vince	1-593	CB
Whenever You Come Around	Gill, Vince	6-571	MM
Whenever You Come Around	Gill, Vince	2-213	SC
Whenever You're Near Me	Ace Of Base	14-284	MM
Where Are You	Simpson & Lachey	20-127	PHM
Where Are You Going	Dave Matthews Band	33-411	CB
Where Are You Now	Black, Clint	1-114	CB
Where Are You Now	Black, Clint	12-397	P
Where Are You Now	Black, Clint	30-436	THM
Where Are You Now	Yearwood, Trisha	14-71	CB
Where Are You Now	Yearwood, Trisha	13-847	CHM
Where Corn Don't Grow	Tritt, Travis	7-584	CHM
Where Corn Don't Grow	Tritt, Travis	7-399	MM
Where Corn Don't Grow	Tritt, Travis	24-659	SC
Where Could I Go	Presley, Elvis	14-831	THM
Where Could I Go But To The Lord	Presley, Elvis	30-379	SC
Where Did I Go Wrong	Wariner, Steve	1-496	CB
Where Did I Go Wrong	Wariner, Steve	5-328	SC
Where Did My Heart Go	Ingram, James	24-252	SC
Where Did Our Love Go	Supremes	16-727	DK
Where Did Our Love Go	Supremes	19-616	MH
Where Did Our Love Go	Supremes	12-629	P
Where Did Our Love Go	Supremes	4-31	SC
Where Did We Go Right	Dalton, Lacy J.	45-820	DCK
Where Do Broken Hearts Go	Houston, Whitney	27-314	DK
Where Do Broken Hearts Go	Houston, Whitney	8-613	TT
Where Do I Begin	Williams, Andy	11-308	DK
Where Do I Fit In The Picture	Walker, Clay	1-92	CB
Where Do I Fit In The Picture	Walker, Clay	2-820	SC
Where Do I Go To Start All Over	Hayes, Wade	4-459	SC
Where Do I Put Her Memory	Pride, Charley	40-108	CB
Where Do We Go From Here	Cox, Deborah	24-60	SC
Where Do You Go	No Mercy	24-299	SC
Where Do You Go To My Lovely?	Sarstedt, Peter	10-633	SF

SONG TITLE	ARTIST	#	TYPE
Where Do You Start	Streisand, Barbra	49-595	PS
Where Does It Hurt	Warren Brothers	15-192	ST
Where Does My Heart Beat	Dion, Celine	15-110	BS
Where Does My Heart Beat	Dion, Celine	33-336	CB
Where Does My Heart Beat	Dion, Celine	28-407	DK
Where Have All The Cowboys Gone	Cole, Paula	10-689	HH
Where Have All The Cowboys Gone	Cole, Paula	24-638	SC
Where Have All The Flowers Gone	Kingston Trio	18-163	DK
Where Have All The Flowers Gone	Kingston Trio	7-356	MM
Where Have All The Flowers Gone	Peter, Paul & Mary	12-495	P
Where I Belong	Proctor, Rachel	22-71	CB
Where I Belong	Proctor, Rachel	30-8	SC
Where I Come From	Jackson, Alan	33-155	CB
Where I Come From	Jackson, Alan	15-604	ST
Where I Ought Not To Be	Davis, Skeeter	43-328	CB
Where I Stood	Rimes, LeAnn	41-93	PHN
Where I Used To Have A Heart	McBride, Martina	1-384	CB
Where I Used To Have a Heart	McBride, Martina	2-671	SC
Where I Used To Have A Heart	McBride, Martina	22-874	ST
Where I'm From	Carroll. Jason M.	36-265	PHM
Where Is The Love	Black Eyed Peas	19-594	CB
Where Is The Love	Black Eyed Peas	25-714	MM
Where Is The Love	Black Eyed Peas	32-360	THM
Where Is The Love	Flack, Roberta	47-89	LE
Where It's At (Yep, Yep)	Lynch, Dustin	44-204	KCDC
Where Love Begins	Watson, Gene	14-668	CB
Where Love Begins	Watson, Gene	29-697	SC
Where Love Used To Live	Houston, David	48-189	CB
Where My Girls' At	702	8-378	PHT
Where Or When	Dion & Belmonts	25-556	MM
Where Or When (Live at Sands)	Sinatra, Frank	49-494	MM
Where The Blacktop Ends	Urban, Keith	34-350	CB
Where The Blacktop Ends	Urban, Keith	9-862	ST
Where The Blue And Lonely Go	Drusky, Roy	20-753	CB
Where The Boat Leaves From	Zac Brown Band	46-63	FTX
Where The Boys Are	Francis, Connie	11-251	DK
Where The Boys Are	Francis, Connie	9-24	PS
Where The Grass Don't Grow	Judd, Cledus T.	16-508	CB
Where The Green Grass Grows	McGraw, Tim	8-753	CB
Where The Green Grass	McGraw, Tim	22-823	ST

SONG TITLE	ARTIST	#	TYPE
Grows			
Where The Sidewalk Ends	Strait, George	45-363	DFK
Where The Stars&Stripes&Eagle Flys	Tippin, Aaron	20-580	CB
Where The Stars&Stripes&Eagle Flys	Tippin, Aaron	25-46	MM
Where The Stars&Stripes&Eagle Flys	Tippin, Aaron	16-7	ST
Where The Streets Have No Name	U2	30-74	SC
Where There's Smoke	Archer & Park	24-133	SC
Where U At Rock **	Kid Rock	36-348	SC
Where We Both Say Goodbye	Britt, C & John, E	23-135	CB
Where We Both Say... - duet	Britt & Elton John	36-379	SC
Where We Come From	Phillips, Phillip	39-100	ASK
Where Were You	Jackson, Alan	20-578	CB
Where Were You	Jackson, Alan	25-62	MM
Where Were You	Jackson, Alan	16-38	ST
Where Were You On Our Wedding..	Price, Lloyd	10-701	JVC
Where Were You When I Was Falling...	Lobo	46-331	SC
Where Would You Be	McBride, Martina	29-532	CB
Where Would You Be	McBride, Martina	25-234	MM
Where Would You Be	McBride, Martina	16-698	ST
Where You Are	El DeBarge	14-872	SC
Where You Are	Simpson & Lachey	14-183	CB
Where You Are	Simpson, Jessica	15-330	PHM
Where You At	Hudson, Jennifer	37-267	CB
Where You Lead	King, Carole	43-4	CB
Where You Lead	Streisand, Barbra	49-551	PS
Where Your Road Leads	Brooks & Yearwood	22-667	ST
Where Your Road Leads	Yearwood, Trisha	8-185	CB
Where'd You Get Your Cheatin' From	Highway 101	7-209	MM
Where'm I Gonna Live	Cyrus, Billy Ray	33-114	CB
Where'm I Gonna Live	Cyrus, Billy Ray	6-220	MM
Where'm I Gonna Live	Cyrus, Billy Ray	3-381	SC
Where's My Beer	Emerick, Scotty	47-497	CB
Where's The Love	Hanson	15-585	SC
Where've You Been	Mattea, Kathy	14-679	CB
Where've You Been	Mattea, Kathy	9-452	SAV
Wherever I May Roam	Metallica	13-623	LE
Wherever She Is	VanShelton, Ricky	2-489	SC
Wherever You Are	Carpenter, M C	47-667	MM
Wherever You Are	Chesnutt, Mark	10-150	SC
Wherever You Are	Chesnutt, Mark	22-675	ST
Wherever You Are	Ingram, Jack	29-30	CB
Wherever You Go	Black, Clint	1-839	CB
Wherever You Go	Black, Clint	16-400	PR
Wherever You Will Go	Boyce Avenue	46-94	KV
Wherever You Will Go	Calling	33-424	CB
Wherever You Will Go	Calling	20-375	HP

SONG TITLE	ARTIST	#	TYPE
Wherever You Will Go	Calling	25-25	MM
Which Bridge To Cross	Gill, Vince	4-75	SC
Which Bridge To Cross	Gill, Vince	22-850	ST
While My Guitar Gently Weeps	Healy, Jeff	36-126	SGB
While Strolling Thru The Park 1 Day	Miller, Mitch	23-546	CB
While The Feeling's Good	Rogers, Kenny	15-77	CB
While You Loved Me	Rascal Flatts	9-866	ST
While You Loved Me	Rascal Flatts	16-277	TT
While You See A Chance	Winwood, Steve	7-483	MM
While You Sleep	Lawrence, Tracy	22-831	ST
Whip It	Devo	26-357	DK
Whip It	Devo	29-12	MH
Whip It	Devo	13-217	P
Whipping Post	Allman Brothers	2-526	SC
Whiskey	Kramer, Jana	47-578	ASK
Whiskey Ain't Workin' Anymore	Tritt & Stuart	12-442	P
Whiskey Ain't Workin' Anymore	Tritt & Stuart	2-410	SC
Whiskey Ain't Workin' Anymore	Tritt, Travis	7-413	MM
Whiskey And You	Stapleton, Chris	48-679	KVD
Whiskey Bent & Hell Bound	Williams, Hank Jr.	16-669	C2C
Whiskey Bent & Hell Bound	Williams, Hank Jr.	5-151	SC
Whiskey Chasin'	Stampley, Joe	45-843	VH
Whiskey Girl	Keith, Toby	20-253	PHM
Whiskey Girl	Keith, Toby	20-326	ST
Whiskey If You Were A Woman	Highway 101	29-65	CB
Whiskey If You Were A Woman	Highway 101	19-297	MH
Whiskey If You Were A Woman	Highway 101	13-395	P
Whiskey If You Were A Woman	Highway 101	8-695	SAV
Whiskey In My Water	Farr, Tyler	43-179	ASK
Whiskey in The Jar	Metallica	7-812	PHT
Whiskey Lullaby	Paisley & Krauss	20-323	ST
Whiskey River	Nelson, Willie	1-628	CB
Whiskey River	Nelson, Willie	7-406	MM
Whiskey River	Nelson, Willie	2-639	SC
Whiskey Rock A Roller	Lynyrd Skynyrd	19-813	SGB
Whiskey Sunday	Livewire	41-79	PHN
Whiskey Trip	Stewart, Gary	29-691	SC
Whiskey Under The Bridge	Brooks & Dunn	7-149	MM
Whiskey Under The Bridge	Brooks & Dunn	3-532	SC
Whiskey's Gone	Zac Brown Band	43-468	KV
Whisper	Dalton, Lacy J.	45-824	SC
Whisper	Rice, Chase	48-394	DCK
Whisper A Prayer	Paris, Mica	24-268	SC
Whisper My Name	Travis, Randy	20-409	MH
Whisper My Name	Travis, Randy	6-598	MM

295

SONG TITLE	ARTIST	#	TYPE
Whisper My Name	Travis, Randy	17-236	NA
Whisper My Name	Travis, Randy	2-323	SC
Whisper Your Name (If I Could)	Connick, Harry Jr.	30-187	LE
Whispering Pines	Horton, Johnny	3-894	PS
Whispering Wind Blows On & On	Barnett, Mandy	5-728	SC
Whistle	Flo Rida	45-651	MRH
Whistlin' Dixie	Houser, Randy	45-554	CB
White Christmas	Brooks, Garth	45-794	PS
White Christmas	Clarkson, Kelly	45-793	KV
White Christmas	Drifters	45-897	SBI
White Christmas	Midler, Bette	45-779	PS
White Christmas	Presley, Elvis	45-760	CB
White Christmas	Swift, Taylor	45-791	KV
White Christmas - duet	Buble & Twain	45-792	KV
White Christmas Makes Me Blue	Travis, Randy	45-790	CB
White Flag	Dido	19-652	CB
White Flag	Dido	20-225	MM
White Flag	Dido	32-356	THM
White Flag	Dido	29-233	ZM
White Horse	Swift, Taylor	43-175	CB
White Houses	Carlton, Vanessa	20-555	PHM
White Liar	Lambert, Miranda	36-39	PT
White Light'nin'	Diffie, Joe	4-146	SC
White Light'nin'	Jones, George	3-602	SC
White Lightning	Cadillad Three	48-444	KCD
White Limousine	Sheik, Duncan	29-282	PHM
White Limozeen	Parton, Dolly	49-337	CB
White Line Fever	Dudley, Dave	46-27	SSK
White Rabbit	Jefferson Airplane	17-121	DK
White Rabbit	Jefferson Airplane	12-917	P
White Rabbit	Jefferson Airplane	2-753	SC
White Red & Beautiful	Kaperton, Kaley	41-59	PHN
White Room	Clapton & Cream	15-60	LE
White Room	Cream	11-650	DK
White Room	Cream	12-855	P
White Sport Coat a	Robbins, Marty	8-40	CB
White Sport Coat a	Robbins, Marty	13-364	P
White Sport Coat a	Robbins, Marty	10-595	SF
White Tees	Dem Franchize Boyz	30-811	PHM
White Trash Wedding	Dixie Chicks	20-215	CB
White Wedding	Idol, Billy	2-854	SC
Whiter Shade Of Pale	Lennox, Annie	17-727	PS
Whiter Shade Of Pale	Procol Harem	49-450	MM
Who Am I	Andrews, Jessica	14-167	CB
Who Am I	Presley, Elvis	30-383	SC
Who Am I To Say	Statler Brothers	19-381	CB
Who Am I To Say	Statler Brothers	14-261	SC
Who Are They	McGraw, Tim	49-78	ZPA
Who Are You	Who	19-740	LE
Who Are You	Who	5-596	SC
Who Are You When I'm Not Looking	Nichols, Joe	47-569	PS
Who Are You When I'm Not Looking	Shelton, Blake	37-234	CB

SONG TITLE	ARTIST	#	TYPE
Who Can Explain	Lymon, Frankie	30-525	LE
Who Can I Count On	Cline, Patsy	45-500	ABA
Who Can I Turn To	Bennett, Tony	10-416	LE
Who Can I Turn To	Roar of the Greasep	27-389	DK
Who Can I Turn To	Standaed	47-825	DK
Who Can It Be Now	Men At Work	33-310	CB
Who Can It Be Now	Men At Work	16-878	DK
Who Can It Be Now	Men At Work	16-550	P
Who Can It Be Now	Men At Work	4-846	SC
Who Cares	Gibson, Don	5-853	SC
Who Did They Think He Was	Twitty, Conway	48-248	THM
Who Divided	Osborne, Joan	30-254	CB
Who Do U Love	Cox, Deborah	4-171	SC
Who Do You Love	Thorogood, George	46-208	SC
Who Do You Think You Are	Spice Girls	9-99	PS
Who I Am	Andrews, Jessica	33-147	CB
Who I Am	Andrews, Jessica	22-462	ST
Who I Am With You	Young, Chris	43-259	ASK
Who Invited You	Donnas	32-256	THM
Who Knew	Pink	48-597	DK
Who Knew	Pink	49-884	SC
Who Knew	Pink	30-714	SF
Who Left The Door To Heaven Open	Thompson, Hank	21-637	CB
Who Let In The Rain	Lauper, Cyndi	24-24	SC
Who Let The Dogs Out	Baha Men	14-7	PHM
Who Loves You	Four Seasons	43-384	CB
Who Makes You Feel	Dido	29-238	ZM
Who Needs Pictures	Paisley, Brad	8-927	CB
Who Needs Pictures	Paisley, Brad	22-748	ST
Who Needs You	Brokop, Lisa	3-534	SC
Who Needs You Baby	Walker, Clay	1-95	CB
Who Needs You Baby	Walker, Clay	7-77	MM
Who Needs You Baby	Walker, Clay	3-538	SC
Who Put All My Ex's In Texas	Nelson, Willie	46-91	SSK
Who Put The Bomp	Mann, Barry	6-652	MM
Who Put The Bomp	Mann, Barry	12-903	P
Who Put The D### On The Snowman **	Carrington, Rodney	44-95	SC
Who Said	Montana, Hannah	36-64	WD
Who Says There Ain't No Santa	Brooks & Dunn	49-367	CB
Who Says You Can't Go Home - duet	Nettles & Bon Jovi	30-242	RS
Who Says You Can't Have It All	Jackson, Alan	1-43	CB
Who Says You Can't Have It All	Jackson, Alan	6-477	MM
Who Says You Can't Have It All	Jackson, Alan	2-106	SC
Who Says You Can't Go Home	Bon Jovi & Nettles	30-242	RS
Who Stole The Keishka	Polka Favorites	29-807	SSR
Who Stole The Keishka - w/Words	Polka Favorites	29-861	SSR
Who Will Buy	Oliver	12-197	DK

SONG TITLE	ARTIST	#	TYPE
Who Will Buy The Wine	Walker, Charlie	5-426	SC
Who Will Save Your Soul	Jewel	4-345	SC
Who Wouldn't Wanna Be Me	Urban, Keith	25-639	MM
Who Wouldn't Wanna Be Me	Urban, Keith	32-340	THM
Who Wouldn't Wanna Be Me	Urban, Keith	19-171	ST
Who You Are	Pearl Jam	24-231	SC
Who You Gonna Blame It On	Gosdin, Vern	5-398	SC
Who You'd Be Today	Chesney, Kenny	23-479	CB
Who'll Stop The Rain	CCR	35-93	CB
Who'll Stop The Rain	CCR	5-352	SC
Who's Cheatin' Who	Jackson, Alan	1-55	CB
Who's Cheatin' Who	Jackson, Alan	7-604	CHM
Who's Cheatin' Who	McClain, Charley	2-131	SC
Who's Crying Now	Journey	4-51	SC
Who's Gonna Fill Their Shoes	Jones, George	33-69	CB
Who's Gonna Fill Their Shoes	Jones, George	4-729	SC
Who's Gonna Love You	Highway 101	24-360	SC
Who's Gonna Mow Your Grass	Owens, Buck	46-103	VH
Who's In The Strawberry Patch	Orlando & Dawn	3-242	LG
Who's Julie	Tillis, Mel	45-730	VH
Who's Lonely Now	Highway 101	14-689	CB
Who's Making Love	Blues Brothers	29-158	ZM
Who's Making Love	Taylor, Johnnie	12-158	DK
Who's Making Love	Taylor, Johnnie	26-234	DK
Who's Making Love	Taylor, Johnnie	15-13	SC
Who's Sorry Now	Francis, Connie	19-608	MH
Who's Sorry Now	Francis, Connie	7-292	MM
Who's Sorry Now	Francis, Connie	4-693	SC
Who's Sorry Now	Francis, Connie	10-514	SF
Who's That Girl	Bentley, Stephanie	4-155	SC
Who's That Girl	Eurythmics	34-83	CB
Who's That Girl	Eurythmics	47-81	SFM
Who's That Knocking	Genies	49-454	MM
Who's That Man	Keith, Toby	1-704	CB
Who's That Man	Keith, Toby	17-241	NA
Who's That Man	Keith, Toby	2-482	SC
Who's To Bless And Who's To Blame	Kristofferson, Kris	45-202	DCK
Who's Your Daddy	Keith, Toby	33-184	CB
Who's Your Daddy	Keith, Toby	25-350	MM
Who's Your Daddy	Keith, Toby	18-204	ST
Who's Your Daddy	Walker, Mike	17-486	CB
Who's Zoomin' Who	Franklin, Aretha	36-174	JT
Whoever You Are	Tah, Geggy	24-370	SC
Whoever's In New England	McEntire, Reba	13-339	P
Whoever's In New England	McEntire, Reba	8-693	SAV
Whoever's In New England	McEntire, Reba	22-780	ST
Whole Lot Of Things To	Pride, Charley	40-120	CB

SONG TITLE	ARTIST	#	TYPE
Sing About			
Whole Lotta Gone	Diffie, Joe	4-412	SC
Whole Lotta Hurt	Seals, Brady	8-856	CB
Whole Lotta Love	Led Zeppelin	17-85	DK
Whole Lotta Love	Led Zeppelin	12-768	P
Whole Lotta Loving	Domino, Fats	4-707	SC
Whole Lotta Shakin' Goin' On	Lewis, Jerry Lee	3-320	MH
Whole Lotta Shakin' Goin' On	Lewis, Jerry Lee	13-55	P
Whole Lotta Woman	Rainwater, Marvin	10-605	SF
Whole New World a	Aladdin	20-187	Z
Whole New World a	Bryson & LaBelle	17-424	KC
Whole New World a	Bryson & LaBelle	9-208	SC
Whole World Comes To Me the	Greene, Jack	43-346	CB
Whoomp! There It Is	Tag Team	12-133	DK
Whose Bed Have Your Boots Been	Twain, Shania	17-276	NA
Whose Bed Have Your Boots Been	Twain, Shania	16-657	THM
Whose Bed Have Your Boots Been..	Twain, Shania	7-438	MM
Whose Bed Have Your Boots Been...	Twain, Shania	1-512	CB
Why	Aldean, Jason	29-39	CB
Why	Aldean, Jason	29-502	SC
Why	Aldean, Jason	23-454	ST
Why	Avalon, Frankie	4-215	SC
Why	Lennox, Annie	12-247	DK
Why	Lennox, Annie	13-244	P
Why	Lennox, Annie	17-723	PS
Why	Osmond, Donny	47-857	ZM
Why	Richie, Lionel	47-463	SBI
Why	Walters, Jamie	3-490	SC
Why Ain't I Running	Brooks, Garth	18-9	CB
Why Ain't I Running	Brooks, Garth	25-524	MM
Why Ain't I Running	Brooks, Garth	18-796	ST
Why Ain't I Running	Brooks, Garth	32-188	THM
Why Are We Still Friends	98 Degrees	18-353	CB
Why Baby Why	Jones, George	4-726	SC
Why Baby Why	Locklin, Hank	44-215	CB
Why Baby Why	Pierce, Webb	29-402	CB
Why Baby Why	Pride, Charley	3-799	CB
Why Can't He Be You	Cline, Patsy	6-727	MM
Why Can't I	Phair, Liz	19-654	CB
Why Can't I	Phair, Liz	25-626	MM
Why Can't I	Phair, Liz	32-287	THM
Why Can't it Wait 'Till Morning	Collins, Phil	44-34	SBI
Why Can't This Be Love	Van Halen	9-379	AH
Why Can't This Be Love	Van Halen	13-613	LE
Why Can't This Be Love	Van Halen	13-755	SGB
Why Can't We All Just Get A Longneck	Williams, Hank Jr.	45-520	SC
Why Can't We All Just Get/Longneck	Williams, Hank Jr.	20-258	PHM
Why Can't We All Just	Williams, Hank Jr.	20-176	ST

SONG TITLE	ARTIST	#	TYPE
Get/Longneck			
Why Can't We Be Friends	War	12-166	DK
Why Can't We Be Friends	War	15-800	SC
Why Can't You	Stewart, Larry	7-324	MM
Why Can't You	Stewart, Larry	4-411	SC
Why Didn't I Think Of That	Stone, Doug	20-601	CB
Why Didn't I Think Of That	Stone, Doug	2-626	SC
Why Didn't You Call Me	Gray, Macy	14-497	SC
Why Didn't You Call Me	Gray, Macy	19-830	SGB
Why Didn't You Call Me	Gray, Macy	30-639	THM
Why Do Fools Fall In Love	Avalon, Frankie	46-451	KBA
Why Do Fools Fall In Love	Lymon & Teenagers	33-232	CB
Why Do Fools Fall In Love	Lymon & Teenagers	12-150	DK
Why Do Fools Fall In Love	Lymon & Teenagers	12-660	P
Why Do Fools Fall In Love	Lymon, Frankie	30-527	LE
Why Do Fools Fall In Love	Ross, Diana	15-355	LE
Why Do People Fall In Love	Eder, Linda	17-439	PS
Why Do You Have To Be So Hard To	Adams, Bryan	29-283	PHM
Why Does It Always Rain On Me	Travis	15-789	THM
Why Does It Have To Be ...	Restless Heart	1-419	CB
Why Does It Have to Be Wrong or...	Restless Heart	34-277	CB
Why Does Love Got To Be So Sad	Clapton, Eric	13-800	SGB
Why Does My Heart Feel So Bad	Moby	16-262	TT
Why Don't That Telephone Ring	Byrd, Tracy	20-105	CB
Why Don't We Get Drunk & Screw **	Buffett, Jimmy	9-353	AH
Why Don't We Get Drunk & Screw **	Buffett, Jimmy	7-411	MM
Why Don't We Get Drunk & Screw **	Buffett, Jimmy	2-177	SC
Why Don't We Just Dance	Turner, Josh	46-299	BKD
Why Don't We Just Dance	Turner, Josh	36-34	PT
Why Don't You & I	Santana & Band	32-321	THM
Why Don't You & I	Santana & Kroeger	25-657	MM
Why Don't You & I	Santana feat Alex Band	35-285	CB
Why Don't You Believe Me	James, Joni	5-85	SC
Why Don't You Do Right	Lee, Peggy	25-677	MM
Why Don't You Love Me	Williams, Hank Sr.	4-869	SC
Why Don't You Spend	Milsap, Ronnie	47-269	CB

SONG TITLE	ARTIST	#	TYPE
The Night			
Why Georgia	Mayer, John	25-535	MM
Why Georgia	Mayer, John	19-343	STP
Why Georgia	Mayer, John	32-246	THM
Why Have You Left The One You Left Me For	Gayle, Crystal	33-36	CB
Why Have You Left The One You Left Me For	Gayle, Crystal	13-341	P
Why Haven't I Heard From You	McEntire, Reba	1-810	CB
Why Haven't I Heard From You	McEntire, Reba	2-214	SC
Why I Love You So Much	Monica	7-572	THM
Why I Sing The Blues	King, B.B.	15-320	SC
Why I'm Walkin'	Jackson, Stonewall	5-433	SC
Why Lady Why	Alabama	1-2	CB
Why Lady Why	Alabama	4-552	SC
Why Me	Lost Trailers	30-113	CB
Why Me Lord	Cash, Johnny	43-421	SF
Why Me Lord	Kristofferson, Kris	8-682	SAV
Why Not Me	Judd, Wynonna	13-396	P
Why Not Me	Judds	1-141	CB
Why Not Me	Judds	9-467	SAV
Why They Call It Falling	Womack, Lee Ann	33-185	CB
Why They Call It Falling	Womack, Lee Ann	9-863	ST
Why Walk When You Can Fly	Carpenter, M C	8-886	CB
Why Walk When You Can Fly	Carpenter, M C	3-635	SC
Why We Said Goodbye	McGraw, Tim	29-526	CB
Why Why	Smith, Carl	22-119	CB
Why Why Why	Currington, Billy	29-209	CB
Why Won't You Give Me Your Love	Zutons	30-751	SF
Why Would I Say Goodbye	Brooks & Dunn	14-658	CB
Why Would I say Goodbye	Brooks & Dunn	7-606	CHM
Why Ya Wanna?	Kramer, Jana	43-280	BKD
Why'd You Come In Here Lookin'...	Parton, Dolly	33-58	CB
Why'd You Come In Here Lookin'...	Parton, Dolly	10-778	JVC
Why'd You Come In Here Lookin'...	Parton, Dolly	2-98	SC
Wichita Jail	Charlie Daniels Band	43-273	CB
Wichita Lineman	Campbell, Glen	8-286	CB
Wichita Lineman	Campbell, Glen	12-298	DK
Wichita Lineman	Campbell, Glen	10-744	JVC
Wichita Lineman	Campbell, Glen	13-454	P
Wichita Lineman	Campbell, Glen	5-216	SC
Wichita Lineman	Hayes, Wade	22-637	ST
Wicked Game	Isaak, Chris	12-147	DK
Wicked Game	Isaak, Chris	12-807	P
Wide Open Spaces	Dixie Chicks	8-155	CB
Wide Open Spaces	Dixie Chicks	10-58	SC
Wide Open Spaces	Dixie Chicks	22-828	ST
Wig Wam Bam	Sweet	49-56	ZVS

SONG TITLE	ARTIST	#	TYPE
Wild And Blue	Anderson, John	5-156	SC
Wild And Lonesome	Jennings, Shooter	41-56	PHN
Wild And Wooly	LeDoux, Chris	24-13	SC
Wild Angels	McBride, Martina	1-381	CB
Wild Angels	McBride, Martina	7-176	MM
Wild Angels	McBride, Martina	3-663	SC
Wild As The Wind	Brooks & Yearwood	8-871	CB
Wild As The Wind	Brooks & Yearwood	10-165	SC
Wild As The Wind	Brooks, Garth	7-822	CHT
Wild At Heart	Gloriana	37-29	CB
Wild At Heart	White, Lari	7-284	MM
Wild Blue Yonder	Diamond Rio	4-470	SC
Wild Blue Yonder	Patriotic	44-40	PT
Wild Child - duet	Chesney & Potter	45-46	BKD
Wild Horses	Brooks, Garth	10-268	CB
Wild Horses	Brooks, Garth	22-583	ST
Wild Horses	Rolling Stones	19-757	LE
Wild In The Country	Presley, Elvis	25-94	MM
Wild In Your Smile	Lynch, Dustin	47-929	ASK
Wild Is The Wind	Simone, N.	23-355	MM
Wild Is The Wind	Streisand, Barbra	49-602	PS
Wild Man	VanShelton, Ricky	8-556	CB
Wild Man	VanShelton, Ricky	2-713	SC
Wild Mountain Honey	Miller, Steve	23-632	BS
Wild Night	Mellencamp, John	19-89	PS
Wild Night	Mellencamp&Ndege'o	21-423	SC
Wild Night	Morrison, Van	23-604	BS
Wild Night	Morrison, Van	15-730	SI
Wild One	Hill, Faith	15-692	CB
Wild One	Hill, Faith	2-20	SC
Wild One	Rydell, Bobbie	13-73	P
Wild Rose	Reeves, Jim	47-739	SRK
Wild Rose	Reeves, Jim	44-248	SRK
Wild Side Of Life	Pirates Of Mississippi	47-566	KV
Wild Side Of Life - duet	Jennings & Colter	45-195	SSK
Wild Side Of Life the	Thompson, Hank	19-320	CB
Wild Side Of Life the	Thompson, Hank	9-607	SAV
Wild Thing	Troggs	11-246	DK
Wild Thing	Troggs	13-164	P
Wild Thing	Troggs	16-297	TT
Wild Thing (Rock Version)	Kinison, Sam	21-770	SC
Wild Thing the	Tone-Loc	12-154	DK
Wild Week End	Anderson, Bill	20-788	CB
Wild West Show	Big & Rich	22-8	CB
Wild West Show	Big & Rich	19-772	ST
Wild Wild Life	Talking Heads	14-572	AH
Wild Wild West	Escape Club	35-217	CB
Wild Wild West	Escape Club	11-640	DK
Wild Wild West	Escape Club	5-378	SC
Wild Wild West	Smith, Will	7-891	PHT
Wild Wild West	Smith, Will	13-781	SGB
Wild World	Cliff, Jimmy	46-632	HSG
Wild World	Mr. Big	23-112	SC
Wild World	Stevens, Cat	9-317	AG

SONG TITLE	ARTIST	#	TYPE
Wild World	Stevens, Cat	23-644	BS
Wild World	Stevens, Cat	13-572	NU
Wild World	Stevens, Cat	15-801	SC
Wildest Dreams	Swift, Taylor	48-309	MRH
Wildfire	Murphy, Michael M	17-562	PR
Wildfire	Murphy, Michael M	2-788	SC
Wildfire	Murphy, Michael M.	34-319	CB
Wildflower	Skylark	7-466	MM
Wildflower	Skylark	3-482	SC
Wildflower	Skylark	13-668	SGB
Wildwood Frower	Carter Family	34-198	CB
Wildwood Weed	Stafford, Jim	2-134	SC
Will He Ever Go Away	McEntire, Reba	24-84	SC
Will It Go Round In Circles	Preston, Billy	11-443	DK
Will The Circle Be Unbroken	Lynn, Loretta	47-636	CB
Will the Circle be Unbroken - Gospel	Martin, Jimmy	33-204	CB
Will You Be Here	Cochran, Anita	8-96	CB
Will You Be There	Jackson, Michael	6-374	MM
Will You Be There In The Mornin'	Heart	2-114	SC
Will You Love Me Tomorrow	Shirelles	11-129	DK
Will You Love Me Tomorrow	Shirelles	3-286	MM
Will You Love Me Tomorrow	Shirelles	12-714	P
Will You Love Me Tomorrow	Shirelles	4-9	SC
Will You Marry Me	Alabama	15-98	SC
Will You Marry Me	Alabama	16-278	TT
Will You Still Love Me Tomorrow	King, Carole	42-36	SC
Will Your Lawyer Talk To My Lawyer	Wells, Kitty	4-742	SC
Willie & The Hand Jive	Clapton, Eric	26-360	DK
Willie & The Hand Jive	Clapton, Eric	15-62	LE
Willie The Wimp	Vaughn, Stevie Ray	45-361	KV
Willie Waylon And Me	Coe, David Allan	18-314	CB
Willin'	Carlton, Carl	17-357	DK
Willin'	Little Feat	37-75	SC
Willin' To Walk	Foster, Radney	2-668	SC
Willing To Forgive	Franklin, Aretha	6-635	MM
Willing To Forgive	Franklin, Aretha	15-762	NU
Willingly - duet	Nelson & Collie	38-96	CB
Willow Weep For Me	Standard	12-50	DK
Willy Nilly	Thomas, Rufus	47-612	RB
Win	McKnight, Brian	25-29	MM
Winchester Cathedral	New Vaudeville Band	27-112	DK
Winchester Cathedral	New Vaudeville Band	3-582	SC
Wind Beneath My Wings	Midler, Bette	26-367	DK
Wind Beneath My Wings	Midler, Bette	6-356	MM
Wind Beneath My Wings	Midler, Bette	2-61	SC
Wind Beneath My Wings	Morris, Gary	9-440	SAV
Wind Changes the	Cash, Johnny	45-689	BAT

SONG TITLE	ARTIST	#	TYPE
Wind Cries Mary the	Hendrix, Jimi	28-197	SF
Wind It Up	Stefani, Gwen	30-266	CB
Wind the	Zac Brown Band	44-151	BKD
Windflowers	Seals & Croft	47-485	KKS
Windmills Of Your Mind	Jones, Jack	12-487	P
Window Up Above the	Jackson, Wanda	8-792	CB
Window Up Above the	Jones, George	4-730	SC
Winds Of Change	Scorpions	7-493	MM
Winds Of Change	Scorpions	8-611	TT
Windy	Association	35-64	CB
Windy	Association	17-117	DK
Wine After Whiskey	Underwood, Carrie	47-579	KV
Wine Colored Roses	Jones, George	8-335	CB
Wine Into Water	Brown, T. Graham	10-146	SC
Wine Into Water	Brown, T. Graham	22-707	ST
Wine Me Up	Young, Faron	20-741	CB
Wine Women And Song	Al Dexter & Troopers	19-626	CB
Wine, Women & Song	Lynn, Loretta	43-232	CB
Wingman	Currington, Billy	43-314	CB
Wings Of A Butterfly	him	30-274	SC
Wings Of A Dove	Husky, Ferlin	8-366	CB
Wings Of A Dove	Husky, Ferlin	3-604	SC
Wings Of A Dove	Lynn, Loretta	43-230	CB
Wings Upon Your Horns	Lynn, Loretta	45-683	VH
Wink	McCoy, Neal	1-843	CB
Wink	McCoy, Neal	6-581	MM
Wink	McCoy, Neal	12-450	P
Winner At A Losing Game	Rascal Flatts	36-549	CB
Winner Takes All	Abba	19-73	MM
Winner the	Bare, Bobby	15-146	SC
Winning	Santana	29-264	SC
Winter Time	Miller, Steve	23-630	BS
Winter World Of Love	Humperdinck, E.	35-105	CB
Winterwood	McLean, Don	47-249	SFM
Wipe Out	Beach Boys	11-769	DK
Wipe Out	Fat Boys/Beach Boys	28-395	DK
Wire	Nixons	24-109	SC
Wish I Could Fly	Roxette	14-27	THM
Wish I Didn't Have To Miss You	Greene & Seely	5-444	SC
Wish I Didn't Have To Miss You	Greene, Jack	43-344	CB
Wish I Didn't Know Now	Keith, Toby	1-701	CB
Wish I Didn't Know Now	Keith, Toby	12-454	P
Wish I Didn't Know Now...	Keith, Toby	2-359	SC
Wish I Didn't Miss You	Stone, Angie	18-222	CB
Wish I Didn't Miss You	Stone, Angie	33-449	CB
Wish You Were Here	Mandrell, Barbara	48-695	CB
Wish You Were Here	Pink Floyd	10-476	DA
Wish You Were Here	Pink Floyd	36-141	SGB
Wish You Were Here	Wills, Mark	8-374	CB
Wish You Were Here	Wills, Mark	7-829	CHT
Wish You Were Here	Wills, Mark	22-717	ST
Wishes	Morris, Nathan	24-177	SC

SONG TITLE	ARTIST	#	TYPE
Wishes	White, Lari	4-469	SC
Wishful Thinking	Little Anthony	30-519	LE
Wishin' And Hopin'	Springfield, Dusty	10-731	JVC
Wishing	Holly, Buddy	3-221	LG
Wishing And Hoping	Warwick, Dionne	34-135	CB
Wishing I Was There	Imbruglio, Natalie	15-623	PHM
Wishing On A Star	Cover Girls	24-141	SC
Wishlist	Pearl Jam	33-367	CB
Witch Doctor	Seville, David	33-238	CB
Witch Doctor	Seville, David	6-856	MM
Witch Doctor	Seville, David	16-298	TT
Witchcraft	Sinatra, Frank	20-771	KB
Witchcraft	Sinatra, Frank	12-559	P
Witchy Woman	Eagles	7-564	BS
Witchy Woman	Eagles	2-262	SC
With A Girl Like You	Troggs	37-274	ZM
With A Little Help From My Friends	Beatles	13-167	P
With A Little Help From My Friends	Cocker, Joe	33-320	CB
With A Little Help From My Friends	Cocker, Joe	17-60	DK
With A Little Help From My Friends	Cocker, Joe	21-441	LE
With A Little Love	McCartney, Paul	48-564	DK
With A Little Luck	McCartney & Wings	12-82	DK
With Arms Wide Open	Creed	30-208	PHM
With Arms Wide Open	Creed	16-120	PRT
With Arms Wide Open	Creed	14-474	SC
With Bells On	Rogers & Parton	18-759	CB
With Bells On	Rogers & Parton	3-394	SC
With Every Beat Of My Heart	Dayne, Taylor	11-713	DK
With Every Beat Of My Heart	Dayne, Taylor	12-757	P
With Heaven On Our Side	Foreigner	24-16	SC
With Me	Lonestar	25-2	MM
With Me	Lonestar	15-667	ST
With One Exception	Houston, David	22-249	SC
With One Look	Streisand, Barbra	49-557	KKS
With Or Without You	U2	12-341	DK
With Or Without You	U2	13-273	P
With Or Without You	U2	30-79	SC
With Pen In Hand	Goldsboro, Bobby	45-878	TB
With These Hands	Jones, Tom	18-262	DK
With These Hands	Jones, Tom	15-586	PS
With This Ring	Brown, T. Graham	47-547	CB
With This Ring	Platters	2-856	SC
With You	Brown, Chris	36-442	CB
With You	McCann, Lila	8-332	CB
With You	McCann, Lila	7-854	CHT
With You	McCann, Lila	22-734	ST
With You	Simpson, Jessica	35-291	CB
With You	Something/People	24-57	SC
With You I'm Born Again	Preston & Syretta	12-23	DK
With You I'm Born Again	Preston & Syretta	10-675	HE
Withdrawals	Farr, Tyler	45-673	SBI

SONG TITLE	ARTIST	#	TYPE
Without Love	Cash, Johnny	43-405	KC
Without Love	Lewis, Donna	24-643	SC
Without Love (There Is Nothing)	Presley, Elvis	7-135	MM
Without Me **	Eminem	25-466	MM
Without Me **	Eminem	18-143	PHM
Without Me Around	Strait, George	4-479	SC
Without The Love	Lovato, Demi	48-654	DCK
Without You	Badfinger	17-524	SC
Without You	Carey, Mariah	2-119	SC
Without You	Dixie Chicks	20-212	CB
Without You	Dixie Chicks	13-856	CHM
Without You	Dixie Chicks	30-609	RS
Without You	Dixie Chicks	30-609	RS
Without You	Doobie Brothers	29-89	CB
Without You	Hinder	36-254	PHM
Without You	Motley Crue	12-775	P
Without You	Nillson	13-221	P
Without You	Tillotson, Johnny	20-32	SC
Without You	Urban, Keith	37-235	CB
Without You What Do I Do With Me	Tucker, Tanya	16-346	CB
Without Your Love	Daltry, Roger	16-242	AMS
Without Your Love	Tippin, Aaron	4-99	SC
Without Your Love I'm Going Nowhere	Judd, Wynonna	14-80	CB
Wives And Lovers	Jones, Jack	29-487	LE
Wives And Lovers	Newton, Wayne	47-312	LE
Wives And Lovers	Sinatra, Frank	21-228	SGB
Wives Do It All The Time	Judd, Cledus T.	16-503	CB
WKRP In Cincinatti	TV Themes	2-164	SC
Woke Up In Love	Exile	33-86	CB
Woke Up In Love	Exile	11-433	DK
Woke Up This Morning	A3	16-238	PHM
WOLD	Chapin, Harry	21-515	SC
Wolf Call	Presley, Elvis	25-110	MM
Wolf Creek Pass **	McCall, C.W.	23-24	SC
Wolverton Mountain	King, Claude	8-709	CB
Wolverton Mountain	King, Claude	22-447	SC
Wolves	Brooks, Garth	17-227	NA
Woman	Lennon, John	17-372	DK
Woman	Lennon, John	30-297	RS
Woman Always Knows	Houston, David	5-254	SC
Woman Before Me the	Yearwood, Trisha	1-634	CB
Woman Before Me the	Yearwood, Trisha	19-290	MH
Woman Before Me the	Yearwood, Trisha	6-200	MM
Woman Down	Morrisette, Alanis	39-130	PHM
Woman From Tokyo	Deep Purple	5-871	SC
Woman Gets Lonely a	Angelle, Lisa	14-97	CB
Woman He Loves the	Alabama	16-9	ST
Woman I Never had	Williams, Hank Jr.	16-670	C2C
Woman In Love	Streisand, Barbra	28-286	DK
Woman In Love	Streisand, Barbra	18-72	MM
Woman In Love	Streisand, Barbra	8-612	TT
Woman In Love a	Milsap, Ronnie	47-279	SC
Woman In Me the	Heart	2-231	SC
Woman In Me the	Twain, Shania	1-514	CB

SONG TITLE	ARTIST	#	TYPE
Woman In Me the	Twain, Shania	7-450	MM
Woman In My Life the	Vassar, Phil	30-53	CB
Woman In The White House	Crow, Sheryl	46-298	BKD
Woman Knows a	Anderson, John	30-315	CB
Woman Like You a	Brice, Lee	45-61	BKD
Woman Like You a	Brice, Lee	45-382	SBI
Woman Lives For Love a	Jackson, Wanda	45-592	OZP
Woman Loves a	Wariner, Steve	1-502	CB
Woman Of The World	Lynn, Loretta	43-231	CB
Woman Sensuous Woman	Chesnutt, Mark	6-504	MM
Woman Sensuous Woman	Chesnutt, Mark	2-220	SC
Woman Sensuous Woman	Gibson, Don	35-362	CB
Woman Sensuous Woman	Gibson, Don	5-392	SC
Woman the	Franklin, Aretha	36-171	JT
Woman To Woman	Judd, Wynonna	8-186	CB
Woman To Woman	Judd, Wynonna	22-680	ST
Woman To Woman	Lynns	8-415	CB
Woman To Woman	Lynns	22-791	ST
Woman Tonight	America	46-417	CB
Woman Walk The Line	Yearwood, Trisha	24-253	SC
Woman With The Blues	Thorogood, George	48-406	DFK
Woman With You the	Chesney, Kenny	22-66	CB
Woman With You the	Chesney, Kenny	20-499	ST
Woman Woman	Puckett & Union Gap	20-68	SC
Woman's Love a	Jackson, Alan	30-243	CB
Woman's Touch a	Keith, Toby	7-333	MM
Woman's Touch a	Keith, Toby	4-418	SC
Woman's Word	Cher	47-682	KV
Woman's Worth a	Keys, Alicia	33-390	CB
Woman's Worth a	Keys, Alicia	25-31	MM
Womanhood	Wynette, Tammy	49-360	CB
Womanizer	Spears, Britney	36-522	CB
Women I've Never Had	Williams, Hank Jr.	37-299	SC
Won't Back Down	Fuel	32-144	THM
Won't Be Lonely Long	Thompson, Josh	38-107	CB
Won't Get Fooled Again	Who	19-732	LE
Won't Go Home Without You	Maroon 5	36-444	CB
Won't Let Go	Berg, Martraca	2-314	SC
Won't Let You Fall	Fergie	48-236	KV
Won't You Come Home Bill Bailey	Standard	11-483	DK
Won't You Forgive	Robbins, Marty	48-26	DCK
Won't You Ride In My Little Red Wagon	Nelson, Willie	46-92	SSK
Wonder	Merchant, Natalie	19-572	MH
Wonder	Merchant, Natalie	18-36	PS
Wonder	Merchant, Natalie	4-663	SC
Wonder Of You the	Presley, Elvis	11-450	DK
Wonder Of You the	Presley, Elvis	2-596	SC
Wonder Of You the	Presley, Elvis	14-763	THM
Wonder Who's Kissing	Combo Oldies	16-415	PR

SONG TITLE	ARTIST	#	TYPE
Her Now			
Wonderful	Everclear	35-235	CB
Wonderful	Everclear	15-441	PHM
Wonderful	Everclear	20-8	SGB
Wonderful	Go, Gary	36-308	PHM
Wonderful (Radio Version)	Everclear	14-499	SC
Wonderful Tonight	Clapton, Eric	15-57	LE
Wonderful Tonight	Clapton, Eric	6-436	MM
Wonderful Tonight	Clapton, Eric	28-203	SF
Wonderful Tonight	Kersh, David	8-482	CB
Wonderful Wonderful	Mathis, Johnny	18-55	MM
Wonderful World	Cooke, Sam	21-240	SC
Wonderful World	Morrison, James	38-275	EK
Wonderful World	Presley, Elvis	45-615	HM
Wonderful World Beautiful People	Cliff, Jimmy	46-627	MFK
Wonderful World Of Christmas	Presley, Elvis	45-759	CB
Wondering	Pierce, Webb	8-772	CB
Wonderland	Swift, Taylor	48-302	KV
Wonderwall	Oasis	30-219	PHM
Wooden Heart	Presley, Elvis	10-553	SF
Wooden Heart	Presley, Elvis	14-767	THM
Wooden Ships - duet - WN	Crosby Stills & Nash	48-56	SC
Woodpecker Song the	Andrew Sisters	9-820	SAV
Woodstock	Crosby Stills & Nash	12-910	P
Wooly Bully	Sam The Sham & Pharoahs	16-836	DK
Wooly Bully	Sam The Sham & Pharoahs	6-136	MM
Wooly Bully	Sam The Sham & Pharoahs	13-64	P
Wooly Bully	Sam The Sham & Pharoahs	10-533	SF
Word Up	Cameo	11-516	DK
Word Up	Cameo	16-543	P
Word Up	Cameo	16-69	SC
Wordplay	Mraz, Jason	44-385	CB
Words	Bee Gees	17-505	LE
Words	Bee Gees	6-50	SC
Words	Horton, Johnny	45-574	SSK
Words	Missing Persons	24-559	SC
Words	Monkees	47-288	EZ
Words By Heart	Cyrus, Billy Ray	6-475	MM
Words By Heart	Cyrus, Billy Ray	3-41	SC
Words Get In The Way	Estefan, Gloria	17-748	PT
Words In Your Eyes the	Everly, Phil	47-810	SRK
Words Of Love	Beatles	11-270	DK
Words Of Love	Elliot, Cass	49-473	MM
Words Of Love	Holly, Buddy	3-211	LG
Words Of Love	Mamas & Papas	9-119	PS
Words Of Love	Mamas & Papas	5-228	SC
Work Hard Play Harder	Wilson, Gretchen	37-225	CB
Work In Progress	Jackson, Alan	40-103	CB
Work In Progress	Jackson, Alan	25-291	MM
Work In Progress	Jackson, Alan	17-580	ST

SONG TITLE	ARTIST	#	TYPE
Work It	Elliot, Missy	32-91	THM
Work It (Remix)	Nelly w/Timberlake	20-353	PHM
Work It **	Elliot, Missy	25-456	MM
Work It Out	Beyonce	48-386	SC
Work It Out	Monet, J	32-199	THM
Work This Out	Ingram, Jack	9-419	CB
Work To Do	Average White Band	2-564	SC
Work To Do	Williams, Vanessa	18-384	SAV
Workin' At The Car Wash Blues	Croce, Jim	19-353	PS
Workin' For MCA	Lynyrd Skynyrd	5-258	SC
Workin' For MCA	Lynyrd Skynyrd	19-818	SGB
Workin' For The Weekend	Mellons, Ken	2-695	SC
Workin' It Out	Singletary, Daryle	7-254	MM
Workin' Man Can't Get Nowhere Today	Haggard, Merle	8-823	CB
Workin' Man's Blues	Diamond Rio	2-643	SC
Workin' Man's Blues	Diamond Rio	22-862	ST
Workin' Man's Blues	Haggard, Merle	6-776	MM
Working Class Hero	Lennon, John	30-301	RS
Working For A Living	Lewis & The News	47-188	JVC
Working For The Man	Orbison, Roy	47-345	KVD
Working For The Weekend	Loverboy	28-351	DK
Working For The Weekend	Loverboy	4-389	SC
Working Girl	Cher	47-679	SC
Working In A Coal Mine	Devo	12-896	P
Working In A Coal Mine	Dorsey, Lee	5-174	SC
Working Man	Conlee, John	47-621	CB
Working Man's PHD	Tippin, Aaron	20-405	MH
Working Man's PHD	Tippin, Aaron	17-233	NA
Working My Way Back To You	Four Seasons	35-160	CB
Working My Way Back To You	Four Seasons	22-445	SC
Working On A Tan	Paisley, Brad	49-231	DFK
Working On The Building	Presley, Elvis	25-507	MM
Working On The Building	Presley, Elvis	30-385	SC
World	Five For Fighting	43-6	PHM
World Is Round the	Drusky, Roy	20-752	CB
World Of Make Believe	Anderson, Bill	20-794	CB
World Of Our Own	Seekers	49-61	ZVS
World Of Our Own	Westlife	18-343	PHM
World Of Our Own a	James, Sonny	19-467	CB
World Of Our Own a	Presley, Elvis	25-322	MM
World On Fire	McLachlan, Sarah	48-187	MM
World the	Paisley, Brad	29-362	CB
World Without Love	Peter & Gordon	33-248	CB
World Without Love	Peter & Gordon	11-195	DK
World Without Love	Peter & Gordon	10-357	KC
World Without Love	Peter & Gordon	19-114	SAV
World Without Love	Peter & Gordon	5-172	SC
World You Left Behind, The	Reeves, Jim	44-255	DFK

SONG TITLE	ARTIST	#	TYPE
World's Apart	Gill, Vince	7-343	MM
World's Apart	Gill, Vince	4-897	SC
World's Greatest	Kelly, R.	33-413	CB
World's Greatest the	Kelly, R.	49-510	PHM
Worst That Could Happen	Brooklyn Bridge	3-583	SC
Worst That Could Happen	Maestro, J.	9-357	MG
Worth The Fall	James, Brett	4-130	SC
Would I	Travis, Randy	4-507	SC
Would I Lie To You	Charles & Eddie	24-144	SC
Would I Lie To You	Eurythmics	11-94	DK
Would I Lie To You	Eurythmics	13-245	P
Would I Lie To You	Eurythmics	4-534	SC
Would Jesus Wear A Rolex	Stevens, Ray	47-905	VH
Would These Arms Be In Your Way	Whitley, Keith	49-399	CB
Would U Be Mine	Grace, Stephanie	39-93	PHN
Would You Be Happier	Corrs	49-192	SBI
Would You Catch A Falling Star	Anderson, John	5-767	SC
Would You Go With Me	Turner, Josh	29-601	CB
Would You Hold It Against Me	West, Dottie	6-1	SC
Would You Lay With Me	Tucker, Tanya	1-603	CB
Would You Take Another Chance On Me	Lewis, Jerry Lee	47-200	CB
Wouldn't It Be Nice	Beach Boys	5-508	BS
Wouldn't It Be Nice	Beach Boys	17-545	DK
Wouldn't It Be Nice	Beach Boys	12-913	P
Wound Time Can't Erase a	Jackson, Stonewall	5-693	SC
Wrangler Butts	Moore, Jeff	49-205	CB
Wrap It Up	Fabulous T-Birds	7-216	MM
Wrapped	Strait, George	30-352	CB
Wrapped Around	Paisley, Brad	33-161	CB
Wrapped Around	Paisley, Brad	25-3	MM
Wrapped Around	Paisley, Brad	15-672	ST
Wrapped Around Your Finger	Police	46-115	SC
Wrapped Up In You	Brooks, Garth	17-601	CB
Wrapped Up In You	Brooks, Garth	25-48	MM
Wrapped Up In You	Brooks, Garth	16-1	ST
Wreck Of The Day	Nalick, Anna	36-193	PHM
Wreck Of The Edmond Fitzgerald	Lightfoot, Gordon	5-301	SC
Wreck Of The John B.	Standard	47-823	DK
Wreck Of The Old ' 97 the	Cash, Johnny	29-570	CB
Wreck On The Highway	Acuff & Nitty Gritty Dirt Band	46-242	CB
Wreck On The Highway	Acuff, Roy	38-67	CB
Wreck The Malls - duet	Rivers & Twisted Radio	45-932	SC
Wreckin' Crew	Triggs, Trini	14-733	CB
Wreckin' Crew	Triggs, Trini	6-65	SC
Wrecking Ball	Cyrus, Miley	42-19	ZM
Wreckoning the **	Boomkat	20-630	NS

SONG TITLE	ARTIST	#	TYPE
Wrinkles	Diamond Rio	25-702	MM
Wrinkles	Diamond Rio	19-261	ST
Wrinkles	Diamond Rio	32-410	THM
Write It In Stone	Harling, Keith	8-870	CB
Write It In Stone	Harling, Keith	10-156	SC
Write This Down	Strait, George	19-197	CB
Write This Down	Strait, George	7-884	CHT
Write This Down	Strait, George	22-738	ST
Writing On The Wall	Jones, George	8-344	CB
Written In The Stars	John, E & Rimes	16-204	PHT
Written In The Stars	John, E & Rimes	13-713	SGB
Wrong	Everything B T Girl	4-335	SC
Wrong	Jennings, Waylon	16-586	MM
Wrong	Locke, Kimberly	20-560	PHM
Wrong Again	McBride, Martina	8-183	CB
Wrong Again	McBride, Martina	10-149	SC
Wrong Again	McBride, Martina	22-671	ST
Wrong Baby Wrong Baby Wrong	McBride, Martina	37-326	CB
Wrong Five O'Clock	Heatherly, Eric	22-466	ST
Wrong Girl	Womack, Lee Ann	35-425	CB
Wrong Girl the	Womack, Lee Ann	20-169	ST
Wrong Ideas	Lee, Brenda	30-329	CB
Wrong Impression	Imbruglia, Natalie	33-450	CB
Wrong Impression	Imbruglio, Natalie	18-288	CB
Wrong Impression	Imbruglio, Natalie	25-137	MM
Wrong Mr. Right Again the	Martin, Dusty	4-480	SC
Wrong Night	McEntire, Reba	8-851	CB
Wrong Night	McEntire, Reba	22-684	ST
Wrong Place Wrong Time	Chesnutt, Mark	1-359	CB
Wrong Place Wrong Time	Chesnutt, Mark	22-905	ST
Wrong Side Of Love	Allen, Deborah	4-138	SC
Wrong Side Of Memphis	Yearwood, Trisha	1-635	CB
Wrong Side Of Memphis	Yearwood, Trisha	12-445	P
Wrong Side Of Memphis	Yearwood, Trisha	2-800	SC
Wrong Side Of Sober - duet	Ryan & Daniels	49-920	KVD
Wrong Song - duet - Nashville	James & Barnes	45-470	KVD
Wrong Way	Sublime	7-689	PHM
Wrong's What I Do Best	Jones, George	24-83	SC
Wrote A Song For Everyone	CCR	48-370	KV
Wurlitzer Prize	Jennings, Waylon	35-377	CB
Wurlitzer Prize the	Jennings, Waylon	8-267	CB
Wurlitzer Prize the	Jennings, Waylon	4-728	SC
Wuthering Heights	Bush, Kate	48-760	P
Www.Memory	Jackson, Alan	14-123	CB
Www.Memory	Jackson, Alan	19-215	CSZ
Www.Memory	Jackson, Alan	22-570	ST
Www.Memory	Jackson, Alan	14-30	THM
Wynona's Big Brown Beaver **	Primus	5-542	SC
X	Liberty X	30-719	SF
X-Offender	Blondie	49-138	SF

SONG TITLE	ARTIST	#	TYPE
Xmas - All I Want For Christmas	Carey, Mariah	7-8	MM
Xmas - All I Want For Christmas	Carey, Mariah	3-383	SC
Xmas - All I Want For Christmas Is You	Mandrell, Louise	45-256	CB
Xmas - All I Want For Xmas Is My Tw	Christmas	14-517	SC
Xmas - All I Want For Xmas Is My Tw	Jones, Spike	5-713	SC
Xmas - All I Want For Xmas Is You	Stone, Doug	18-757	CB
Xmas - All I Want For Xmas Is You	Vance & Valients	8-93	CB
Xmas - All I Want For Xmas Is You	Vance & Valients	5-711	SC
Xmas - All Wrapped Up In Christmas	Lawrence, Tracy	48-382	CB
Xmas - And So This Is Christmas	Lennon, John	7-15	MM
Xmas - Angels From The Realms/Glory	Christmas	10-257	SC
Xmas - Angels We Have Heard On High	Christain Christmas	10-448	BF
Xmas - Angels We Have Heard on High	Christmas	14-419	SC
Xmas - Another Rock & Roll Christmas	Glitter, Gary	45-780	SF
Xmas - Ave Maria (in Latin)	Christmas	22-289	TT
Xmas - Away In A Manger	Cash, Johnny	30-389	SC
Xmas - Away In A Manger	Cash, Johnny	45-37	SC
Xmas - Away In A Manger	Christian Christmas	10-443	BF
Xmas - Away In A Manger	Christmas	25-365	MM
Xmas - Away In A Manger	Christmas	14-409	SC
Xmas - Away In A Manger	Jennings, Waylon	8-66	CB
Xmas - Away In A Manger	Wiggles	45-241	WIG
Xmas - Baby it's Cold Outside	Lady Antebellum	45-775	KV
Xmas - Baby It's Cold Outside	Martin, Dean	14-301	MM
Xmas - Bad Little Boy	Stevens, Ray	47-903	CB
Xmas - Be Bop Santa Claus	Gonzales, Babs	45-245	CB
Xmas - Beautiful Star Of Bethlehem	Judds	15-652	THM
Xmas - Blame It On The Mistletoe	Keith, Toby	48-486	CKC
Xmas - Blue Christmas	Christmas	12-583	P
Xmas - Blue Christmas	Female Country	15-660	THM
Xmas - Blue Christmas	Gilley, Mickey	33-205	CB
Xmas - Blue Christmas	Presley, Elvis	7-1	MM
Xmas - Blue Christmas	Presley, Elvis	41-17	PR
Xmas - Blue Christmas	Presley, Elvis	14-537	SC

SONG TITLE	ARTIST	#	TYPE
Xmas - Blue Christmas	Presley, Elvis	22-849	ST
Xmas - Blue Christmas	Presley, Elvis	14-797	THM
Xmas - Boogie Woogie Santa Claus	Page, Patti	45-248	CB
Xmas - C-H-R-I-S-T-M-A-S	VanShelton, Ricky	8-60	CB
Xmas - Candy Cane Christmas	Rucker, Darius	45-769	CK
Xmas - Carol Of The Bells	Christmas	45-747	CB
Xmas - Carol Of The Bells	Country Christmas	18-738	CB
Xmas - Carol Of The Bells	Standard	41-7	CB
Xmas - Chasin' That Neon Reindeer	Reddmann	18-724	CB
Xmas - Chipmunk Christmas Song	Chipmunk Christmas	18-733	CB
Xmas - Christ Was Born On Xmas Day	Christmas	25-368	MM
Xmas - Christ Was Born on Xmas Day	Country Christmas	18-734	CB
Xmas - Christ Was Born on Xmas Day	Standard	41-3	CB
Xmas - Christmas At Ground Zero	Yankovic, Weird Al	5-715	SC
Xmas - Christmas At Our House	Mandrell, Barbara	15-650	THM
Xmas - Christmas Blues	Canned Heat	45-762	CB
Xmas - Christmas by the old Corral	Ritter, Tex	20-719	CB
Xmas - Christmas Card a	Stone, Doug	45-751	CB
Xmas - Christmas Carol	Ewing, Skip	22-291	CB
Xmas - Christmas Carol a	Lehrer, Tom	5-710	SC
Xmas - Christmas Cookies	Strait, George	45-754	CB
Xmas - Christmas Guest	Grandpa Jones	45-789	DW
Xmas - Christmas Guest	McEntire, Reba	45-767	CB
Xmas - Christmas In Dixie	Alabama	4-437	BS
Xmas - Christmas In Dixie	Alabama	8-51	CB
Xmas - Christmas In Dixie	Alabama	14-544	SC
Xmas - Christmas In Heaven	McCreery, Scotty	45-638	KV
Xmas - Christmas In Killarney	Day, Dennis	45-771	THX
Xmas - Christmas In My Hometown	Pride, Charley	3-404	SC
Xmas - Christmas In My Hometown	Tritt, Travis	18-754	CB
Xmas - Christmas In Prison	Prine, John	46-284	CB
Xmas - Christmas Island	Buffett, Jimmy	45-251	SC
Xmas - Christmas Letter a	McEntire, Reba	8-59	CB
Xmas - Christmas Like Mama Used To...	Byrd, Tracy	45-768	CB
Xmas - Christmas Long	Echelons	45-766	CB

SONG TITLE	ARTIST	#	TYPE
Ago			
Xmas - Christmas Lullaby	Streisand, Barbra	49-588	PS
Xmas - Christmas Memories	Streisand, Barbra	49-589	PS
Xmas - Christmas Rock	Keith, Toby	45-752	CB
Xmas - Christmas Shoes	Newsong	34-434	CB
Xmas - Christmas Song the	Christmas	6-292	MM
Xmas - Christmas Song the	Christmas	12-591	P
Xmas - Christmas Song the	Cole, Nat "King"	14-539	SC
Xmas - Christmas Song the	Travis, Randy	30-394	SC
Xmas - Christmas Time	Anderson, John	18-755	CB
Xmas - Christmas Time Is Coming	Reed, Jerry	8-56	CB
Xmas - Christmas Time Is Here	Christmas	25-372	MM
Xmas - Christmas Time Is Here	Standard	41-19	PR
Xmas - Christmas To Remember a	Rogers & Parton	18-721	CB
Xmas - Christmas Waltz	Standard	41-18	PR
Xmas - Christmas Wish	Vee, Bobby	45-788	TB
Xmas - Christmas Without You	Parton & Rogers	8-85	CB
Xmas - Christmas Wrapping	Waitresses	14-304	MM
Xmas - Christmas Wrapping	Waitresses	45-743	SC
Xmas - Daddy Stuff	Kershaw, Sammy	8-88	CB
Xmas - Daddy's Drinking Up Our Xmas	Trailor Choir	46-286	CB
Xmas - Deck The Halls	Boxcar Willie	8-74	CB
Xmas - Deck The Halls	Christain Christmas	10-436	BF
Xmas - Deck The Halls	Christmas	17-206	CMC
Xmas - Deck The Halls	Christmas	11-728	DK
Xmas - Deck The Halls	Christmas	21-273	NCG
Xmas - Deck The Halls	Christmas	14-407	SC
Xmas - Deck The Halls	Cole, Nat "King"	14-298	MM
Xmas - Ding Dong Merrily On High	Christmas	45-14	KV
Xmas - Do They Know It's Christmas	Band Aid	14-527	SC
Xmas - Do You Hear What I Hear	Christmas	25-366	MM
Xmas - Do You Hear What I Hear	Christmas	10-253	SC
Xmas - Do You Hear What I Hear	Country Christmas	18-744	CB
Xmas - Do You Hear What I Hear	Houston, Whitney	7-14	MM
Xmas - Do You Hear What I Hear?	Standard	41-13	CB
Xmas - Driving Home For Christmas	Rea, Chris	45-778	ZM
Xmas - Every Year Every Christmas	Vandross, Luther	45-772	KV

SONG TITLE	ARTIST	#	TYPE
Xmas - Father Christmas	Kinks	45-250	SC
Xmas - Feliz Navidad	Christmas	6-297	MM
Xmas - Feliz Navidad	Feliciano, Jose	14-538	SC
Xmas - First Noel the	Anderson, Bill	8-79	CB
Xmas - First Noel the	Christian Christmas	10-442	BF
Xmas - First Noel the	Christmas	17-202	CMC
Xmas - First Noel the	Christmas	6-288	MM
Xmas - First Noel the	Christmas	21-269	NCG
Xmas - First Noel the	Christmas	12-585	P
Xmas - First Noel the	Christmas	10-251	SC
Xmas - First Noel the	Presley, Elvis	49-876	MM
Xmas - First Noel the	Underwood, Carrie	45-783	KV
Xmas - Friendly Beast the	Christmas	45-12	KV
Xmas - Friendly Beasts the	Male Country	15-661	THM
Xmas - Frosty The Snowman	Autry, Gene	45-659	DKM
Xmas - Frosty The Snowman	Christmas	17-210	CMC
Xmas - Frosty The Snowman	Christmas	11-239	DK
Xmas - Frosty The Snowman	Christmas	21-277	NCG
Xmas - Frosty The Snowman	Christmas	12-577	P
Xmas - Frosty The Snowman	Christmas	14-513	SC
Xmas - Gift the	Brooks, Garth	30-390	SC
Xmas - Go Santa Go	Wiggles	45-239	WIG
Xmas - God Rest Ye Merry Gentlemen	Christian Christmas	10-449	BF
Xmas - God Rest Ye Merry Gentlemen	Christmas	17-204	CMC
Xmas - God Rest Ye Merry Gentlemen	Christmas	21-271	NCG
Xmas - God Rest Ye Merry Gentlemen	Christmas	14-418	SC
Xmas - Good Christain Friends Rejoi	Christmas	10-243	SC
Xmas - Grandma Got Run Over By..	Elmo & Patsy	8-55	CB
Xmas - Grandma Got Run Over By..	Elmo & Patsy	3-390	SC
Xmas - Grandma Got Run Over By...	Elmo & Patsy	6-291	MM
Xmas - Greatest Gift Of All	Rogers & Parton	22-847	ST
Xmas - Grown-Up Christmas List	Streisand, Barbra	49-591	PS
Xmas - Hairy Christmas - duet	Robertson & Bryan	43-82	ASK
Xmas - Hallelujah	Gayle, Crystal	45-254	CB
Xmas - Happy Christmas (War/Over)	Lennon, John	3-389	SC
Xmas - Happy Holiday	Williams, Andy	18-745	CB
Xmas - Happy Holiday	Williams, Andy	14-302	MM
Xmas - Happy Holidays/Holiday Season	Williams, Andy	41-14	CB
Xmas - Happy Xmas The	Lennon, John	30-305	RS

SONG TITLE	ARTIST	#	TYPE
War Is Over			
Xmas - Hard Candy Christmas	Parton, Dolly	8-54	CB
Xmas - Hard Candy Christmas	Parton, Dolly	3-396	SC
Xmas - Hark The Herald Angels Sing	Christian Christmas	10-447	BF
Xmas - Hark The Herald Angels Sing	Christmas	25-363	MM
Xmas - Hark The Herald Angels Sing	Christmas	14-443	SC
Xmas - Hark The Herald Angels Sing	Robbins, Marty	48-23	CB
Xmas - Hark The Herald Angels Sing	Underwood, Carrie	45-784	KV
Xmas - Have Yourself A Merry Little	Christmas	12-500	P
Xmas - Have Yourself A Merry Little	Como, Perry	14-534	SC
Xmas - Have Yourself A Merry Little	Garland, Judy	11-241	DK
Xmas - Have Yourself A Merry Little	Gayle, Crystal	18-756	CB
Xmas - Have Yourself A Merry Little	McBride, Martina	30-387	SC
Xmas - Have Yourself A Merry Little	Pretenders	14-296	MM
Xmas - Have Yourself A Merry...	Carpenters	44-338	CB
Xmas - Here Come The Reindeer	Wiggles	45-238	WIG
Xmas - Here Comes Santa Claus	Autry, Gene	45-661	KKS
Xmas - Here Comes Santa Claus	Christmas	14-524	SC
Xmas - Here Comes Santa Claus	Presley, Elvis	33-206	CB
Xmas - Here Comes Santa Claus	Presley, Elvis	7-5	MM
Xmas - Here Comes Santa Claus	Presley, Elvis	49-870	MM
Xmas - Here Comes Santa Claus	Presley, Elvis	14-799	THM
Xmas - Here Comes Santa Claus	Yoakam, Dwight	30-393	SC
Xmas - Holly Jolly Christmas	Christmas	6-298	MM
Xmas - Holly Jolly Christmas	Ives, Burl	35-322	CB
Xmas - Holly Jolly Christmas	Ives, Burl	14-540	SC
Xmas - Holly Leaves & Xmas Trees	Presley, Elvis	49-867	MM
Xmas - Holly Leaves And Christmas Trees	Presley, Elvis	45-777	CB
Xmas - Holy Is The Lamb	Adams, Oleta	46-391	PR
Xmas - Home For The Holidays	Male Country	15-666	THM
Xmas - Home For The Holidays	Williams, Andy	18-746	CB
Xmas - How Do I Wrap	Travis, Randy	8-62	CB

SONG TITLE	ARTIST	#	TYPE
My Heart Up			
Xmas - I Am Santa Claus	Rivers, Bob	45-745	SC
Xmas - I Believe In Santa Claus	Parton & Rogers	8-73	CB
Xmas - I Believe In Santa Claus - duet	Rogers & Parton	48-122	CB
Xmas - I Heard the Bells On Xmas Day	Gatlin, Larry	47-100	CB
Xmas - I Heard The Bells On Xmas Day	Gatlin, Larry	45-253	CB
Xmas - I Heard The Bells On Xmas..	Christmas	25-373	MM
Xmas - I Only Want You For Xmas	Jackson, Alan	8-52	CB
Xmas - I Saw Mommy Kissing Santa	Christmas	17-53	DK
Xmas - I Saw Mommy Kissing Santa	Christmas	12-593	P
Xmas - I Saw Mommy Kissing Santa Claus	Ronettes	47-589	ZM
Xmas - I Saw Mommy Kissing Santa..	Christmas	6-295	MM
Xmas - I Saw Mommy Kissing Santa..	Christmas	14-516	SC
Xmas - I Saw Three Ships	Christmas	45-13	KV
Xmas - I Want A Hippopatamus For..	Bartels, Joanie	14-303	MM
Xmas - I Want A Hippopatamus For..	Peevey, Gayla	5-712	SC
Xmas - I Wonder As I Wander	Christmas	14-414	SC
Xmas - I'll Be Home For Christmas	Bogguss, Suzy	18-752	CB
Xmas - I'll Be Home For Christmas	Christmas	12-579	P
Xmas - I'll Be Home For Christmas	Christmas	14-541	SC
Xmas - I'll Be Home For Christmas	Grant, Amy	7-3	MM
Xmas - I'll Be Home For Christmas	Presley, Elvis	25-770	MM
Xmas - I'll Be Home For Christmas	Presley, Elvis	14-802	THM
Xmas - I'll Be Home For Xmas	Streisand, Barbra	49-590	PS
Xmas - I'm A Lonely Jew	South Park	5-709	SC
Xmas - If Every Day Was Like Xmas	Presley, Elvis	7-9	MM
Xmas - If Every Day Was Like Xmas	Presley, Elvis	49-877	MM
Xmas - If Every Day Was Like Xmas	Presley, Elvis	3-399	SC
Xmas - If Every Day Was Like Xmas	Presley, Elvis	14-803	THM
Xmas - If I Get Home On Christmas Day	Presley, Elvis	45-761	CB
Xmas - If I Get Home On Xmas Day	Presley, Elvis	49-872	MM
Xmas - If We Make It Thru December	Haggard, Merle	8-67	CB

SONG TITLE	ARTIST	#	TYPE
Xmas - If We Make It Thru December	Haggard, Merle	14-548	SC
Xmas - It Came Upon A Midnight Clea	Anderson, Bill	8-71	CB
Xmas - It Came Upon a Midnight Clea	Christain Christmas	10-437	BF
Xmas - It Came Upon A Midnight Clea	Christmas	25-364	MM
Xmas - It Came Upon a Midnight Clea	Christmas	14-413	SC
Xmas - It Just Don't Feel Like...	Rihanna	36-95	CB
Xmas - It Must Have Been The Mistletoe	Streisand, Barbra	48-514	KVD
Xmas - It Wasn't His Child	Yearwood, Trisha	18-749	CB
Xmas - It Wasn't His Child	Yearwood, Trisha	7-6	MM
Xmas - It Wasn't His Child	Yearwood, Trisha	15-656	THM
Xmas - It Won's Seem Like Christmas..	Presley, Elvis	49-871	MM
Xmas - It Won't Be Christmas Without You	Brooks & Dunn	45-749	CB
Xmas - It Won't Seem Like Christmas	Presley, Elvis	18-735	CB
Xmas - It Won't Seem Like Xmas w/o You	Standard	41-4	CB
Xmas - It's Beginning To Look A Lot	Christmas	10-456	BF
Xmas - It's Beginning To Look A Lot	Christmas	6-299	MM
Xmas - It's Beginning To Look A Lot	Christmas	12-582	P
Xmas - It's Beginning To Look A Lot	Christmas	14-510	SC
Xmas - It's Christmas	Milsap, Ronnie	45-756	CB
Xmas - It's Gonna Be a Cold Cold Xmas	Dana	45-591	OZP
Xmas - It's The Most Wonderful Time	Williams, Andy	14-305	MM
Xmas - Jingle Bell Rock	Christmas	27-469	DK
Xmas - Jingle Bell Rock	Christmas	12-589	P
Xmas - Jingle Bell Rock	Helms, Bobby	35-323	CB
Xmas - Jingle Bell Rock	Helms, Bobby	3-408	SC
Xmas - Jingle Bell Rock	Lee, Brenda	45-904	DMG
Xmas - Jingle Bell Rock	Travis, Randy	22-845	ST
Xmas - Jingle Bells	Christmas	10-450	BF
Xmas - Jingle Bells	Christmas	17-209	CMC
Xmas - Jingle Bells	Christmas	11-238	DK
Xmas - Jingle Bells	Christmas	6-286	MM
Xmas - Jingle Bells	Christmas	21-276	NCG
Xmas - Jingle Bells	Christmas	12-642	P
Xmas - Jingle Bells	Christmas	14-514	SC
Xmas - Jingle Bells	Thomas, B.J.	46-96	CB
Xmas - Jolly Old Saint Nicholas	Chicago	45-255	SC
Xmas - Jolly Old St. Nicholas	Christmas	14-512	SC
Xmas - Jolly Old St. Nicholas	Hall, Tom T.	8-77	CB
Xmas - Joy To The World	Christain Christmas	10-435	BF
Xmas - Joy To The World	Christmas	17-199	CMC
Xmas - Joy To The World	Christmas	27-474	DK
Xmas - Joy To The World	Christmas	25-369	MM
Xmas - Joy To The World	Christmas	21-266	NCG
Xmas - Joy To The World	Christmas	10-249	SC
Xmas - Joy To The World	Gilley, Mickey	8-65	CB
Xmas - Joy To The World	Weaver, Patty	33-207	CB
Xmas - Joy To The World	Willie, Boxcar	45-257	CB
Xmas - Last Christmas	Wham!	11-725	DK
Xmas - Leroy the Redneck Reindeer	Diffie, Joe	18-720	CB
Xmas - Let It Be Christmas	Jackson, Alan	30-396	SC
Xmas - Let It Snow	Boyz II Men	22-835	ST
Xmas - Let It Snow	Buble, Michael	45-739	Zp
Xmas - Let It Snow	Christmas	6-290	MM
Xmas - Let It Snow	Christmas	12-588	P
Xmas - Let It Snow	Horne, Lena	14-518	SC
Xmas - Let It Snow	Lady antebellum	45-741	KVD
Xmas - Let It Snow	Nichols, Joe	45-740	CB
Xmas - Let It Snow	Sinatra, Frank	45-738	SFX
Xmas - Let It Snow	Thomas, B.J.	45-737	CB
Xmas - Let There Be Peace On Earth	Christmas	10-245	SC
Xmas - Let There Be Peace On Earth -duet	Gill, Vince	41-35	CB
Xmas - Let's Make A Baby King	Judd, Wynonna	15-662	THM
Xmas - Little Christmas Tree	Jackson, Michael	47-478	DCK
Xmas - Little Drummer Boy	Christmas	26-358	DK
Xmas - Little Drummer Boy	Christmas	6-294	MM
Xmas - Little Drummer Boy	Christmas	12-578	P
Xmas - Little Drummer Boy	Country Christmas	18-739	CB
Xmas - Little Drummer Boy	Murray, Anne	30-392	SC
Xmas - Little Drummer Boy	Seger, Bob	41-40	CB
Xmas - Little Drummer Boy	Seger, Bob	46-343	SC
Xmas - Little Saint Nick	Beach Boys	33-208	CB
Xmas - Little Saint Nick	Beach Boys	3-401	SC
Xmas - Little Saint Nick	Beach Boys	22-840	ST
Xmas - Mama	Frizzell, Lefty	46-51	SSK
Xmas - Marshmallow	Martin, Dean	46-277	KV

SONG TITLE	ARTIST	#	TYPE
World a			
Xmas - Marvelous Little Boy	Country Christmas	18-740	CB
Xmas - Mary's Little Boy Child	Country Christmas	18-741	CB
Xmas - May The Good Lord Bless &...	Female Country	15-654	THM
Xmas - Meet Me Under the Mistletoe	Travis, Randy	15-651	THM
Xmas - Mele Kalikimaka	Buffett, Jimmy	5-716	SC
Xmas - Merry Christmas Alabama	Buffett, Jimmy	46-145	TU
Xmas - Merry Christmas Baby	Berry, Chuck	7-11	MM
Xmas - Merry Christmas Baby	Presley, Elvis	14-807	THM
Xmas - Merry Christmas Baby	Springsteen, Bruce	41-39	CB
Xmas - Merry Christmas Baby	Springsteen, Bruce	22-839	ST
Xmas - Merry Christmas Darling	Carpenters	3-406	SC
Xmas - Merry Christmas Darling	Carpenters	22-841	ST
Xmas - Merry Christmas Everybody	Slade	45-770	SF
Xmas - Merry Christmas From The Family	Montgomery Gentry	45-750	CB
Xmas - Merry Christmas Polka	Reeves, Jim	49-288	CON
Xmas - Merry Christmas To Me	Jackson, Alan	49-177	CB
Xmas - Merry Christmas Wherever You Are	Strait, George	45-765	CB
Xmas - Merry Xmas Strait To You	Strait, George	18-760	CB
Xmas - Miss You Most At Christmas Time	Carey, Mariah	45-799	SBI
Xmas - Mistletoe	Bieber, Justin	48-625	KVD
Xmas - Mistletoe And Holly	Christmas	6-296	MM
Xmas - My Christmas Wish	Montgomery, J M	45-753	CB
Xmas - My Favoirite Things	Standard	41-1	CB
Xmas - My Favorite Things	Country Christmas	18-732	CB
Xmas - Night Before Christmas the	Keith, Toby	30-388	SC
Xmas - Nuttin' For Christmas	Country Christmas	18-742	CB
Xmas - Nuttin' For Christmas	Freberg, Stan	14-297	MM
Xmas - Nuttin' For Christmas	Freberg, Stan	5-708	SC
Xmas - Nuttin' For Christmas	Standard	41-11	CB
Xmas - O Come All Ye Faithful	Presley, Elvis	49-873	MM
Xmas - O Holy Night	Underwood, Carrie	45-785	KV
Xmas - O Little Town Of	Presley, Elvis	49-868	MM

SONG TITLE	ARTIST	#	TYPE
Bethlehem			
Xmas - O White Christmas	Little People the	45-795	SC
Xmas - Oh Christmas Tree	Christmas	14-406	SC
Xmas - Oh Christmas Tree	Hall, Tom T.	8-70	CB
Xmas - Oh Come All Ye Faithful	Christian Christmas	10-439	BF
Xmas - Oh Come All Ye Faithful	Christmas	25-376	MM
Xmas - Oh Come All Ye Faithful	Christmas	14-410	SC
Xmas - Oh Come All Ye Faithful	Evans, Sara	30-395	SC
Xmas - Oh Come All Ye Faithful	Jennings, Waylon	8-78	CB
Xmas - Oh Come Oh Come Emmanuel	Christian Christmas	10-444	BF
Xmas - Oh Come Oh Come Emmanuel	Christmas	14-412	SC
Xmas - Oh Holy Night	Campbell, Tevin	22-836	ST
Xmas - Oh Holy Night	Christian Christmas	10-434	BF
Xmas - Oh Holy Night	Christmas	17-208	CMC
Xmas - Oh Holy Night	Christmas	25-370	MM
Xmas - Oh Holy Night	Christmas	21-275	NCG
Xmas - Oh Holy Night	Christmas	14-415	SC
Xmas - Oh Holy Night	Christmas	22-290	TT
Xmas - Oh Holy Night	Gatlins	8-75	CB
Xmas - Oh Little Town of Bethlehem	Christian Christmas	10-440	BF
Xmas - Oh Little Town of Bethlehem	Christmas	17-205	CMC
Xmas - Oh Little Town Of Bethlehem	Christmas	25-367	MM
Xmas - Oh Little Town of Bethlehem	Christmas	21-272	NCG
Xmas - Oh Little Town of Bethlehem	Christmas	12-594	P
Xmas - Oh Little Town Of Bethlehem	Christmas	10-255	SC
Xmas - Oh Little Town of Bethlehem	Gilley, Mickey	8-68	CB
Xmas - Oh Little Town of Bethlehem	Harris, EmmyLou	30-400	SC
Xmas - Oh Tannenbaum	Christmas	12-592	P
Xmas - Oh What A Silent Night	Travis, Randy	15-659	THM
Xmas - Old Christmas Card	Reeves, Jim	8-58	CB
Xmas - Old Hippie Christmas	Bellamy Brothers	45-306	CB
Xmas - Old Man's Back In Town the	Brooks, Garth	18-731	CB
Xmas - Old Man's Back In Town the	Brooks, Garth	7-2	MM
Xmas - Old Man's Back In Town the	Brooks, Garth	15-657	THM
Xmas - Old Time Christmas	Strait, George	45-764	CB
Xmas - On A Snowy	Presley, Elvis	45-758	CB

SONG TITLE	ARTIST	#	TYPE
Christmas Night			
Xmas - On A Snowy Xmas Night	Presley, Elvis	49-874	MM
Xmas - On This Day	McEntire, Reba	18-723	CB
Xmas - On This Day	McEntire, Reba	15-658	THM
Xmas - Once Upon A Christmas	Parton & Rogers	46-98	DCK
Xmas - One Bright Star	Gill, Vince	18-729	CB
Xmas - One Bright Star	Gill, Vince	22-846	ST
Xmas - Papa Noel	Lee, Brenda	45-903	CB
Xmas - Peace On Earth/Little Drummer - duet	Crosby & David Bowie	41-42	CB
Xmas - Please Come Home For Christmas	Bon Jovi, Jon	41-41	CB
Xmas - Please Come Home For Xmas	Eagles	7-4	MM
Xmas - Please Come Home For Xmas	Eagles	14-533	SC
Xmas - Please Come Home For Xmas	VanShelton, Ricky	18-750	CB
Xmas - Pretty Paper	Nelson, Willie	8-61	CB
Xmas - Pretty Paper	Nelson, Willie	14-546	SC
Xmas - Put A Little Holiday In Your...	Rimes, Lee Ann	45-787	SC
Xmas - Redneck 12 Days Of Xmas	Foxworthy, Jeff	18-719	CB
Xmas - Redneck Christmas	Stevens, Ray	46-289	CB
Xmas - Rock & Roll Christmas	Thorogood, George	45-763	CB
Xmas - Rockin' Around The Christmas Tree	Gilley, Mickey	45-757	CB
Xmas - Rockin' Around the Xmas Tree	Christmas	12-590	P
Xmas - Rockin' Around The Xmas Tree	Lee, Brenda	8-53	CB
Xmas - Rockin' Around the Xmas Tree	Lee, Brenda	11-729	DK
Xmas - Rockin' Around the Xmas Tree	Lee, Brenda	6-300	MM
Xmas - Rockin' Around The Xmas Tree	Lee, Brenda	3-398	SC
Xmas - Rockin' Little Christmas	Allen, Deborah	8-57	CB
Xmas - Rockin' Santa	Wiggles	45-237	WIG
Xmas - Rudolph the Red-Nosed Rein	Autry, Gene	14-511	SC
Xmas - Rudolph the Red-Nosed Rein	Christmas	10-453	BF
Xmas - Rudolph The Red-Nosed Rein	Christmas	11-727	DK
Xmas - Run Rudolph Run	Berry, Chuck	5-717	SC
Xmas - Same Old Lang Syne	Fogelberg, Dan	14-532	SC
Xmas - Santa Baby	Madonna	6-289	MM
Xmas - Santa Baby	Madonna	14-530	SC
Xmas - Santa Bring My Baby Back..	Presley, Elvis	14-808	THM
Xmas - Santa Bring My	Presley, Elvis	7-12	MM

SONG TITLE	ARTIST	#	TYPE
Baby Back...			
Xmas - Santa Claus And Popcorn	Haggard, Merle	45-247	CB
Xmas - Santa Claus Boogie	Tractors	3-392	SC
Xmas - Santa Claus Is Back In Town	Presley, Elvis	49-875	MM
Xmas - Santa Claus is Back in Town	Yearwood, Trisha	18-728	CB
Xmas - Santa Claus Is Back In Town	Yoakam, Dwight	15-653	THM
Xmas - Santa Claus Is Comin' To...	Springsteen, Bruce	34-433	CB
Xmas - Santa Claus is Coming/Town	Christmas	10-457	BF
Xmas - Santa Claus is Coming/Town	Christmas	12-266	DK
Xmas - Santa Claus Is Coming/Town	Christmas	12-580	P
Xmas - Santa Claus Is Coming/Town	Christmas	14-515	SC
Xmas - Santa Claus Is Coming/Town	Springsteen, Bruce	7-7	MM
Xmas - Santa Claus Is Coming/Town	Yoakam, Dwight	7-10	MM
Xmas - Santa Claus Is Watching You	Stevens, Ray	16-500	CB
Xmas - Santa Claus is Watching You	Stevens, Ray	5-707	SC
Xmas - Santa Done Got Hip	Marquees	45-244	CB
Xmas - Santa Got Lost In Texas	Carson, Jeff	8-81	CB
Xmas - Santa I'm Right Here	Keith, Toby	8-89	CB
Xmas - Santa Looked a Lot Like Dadd	Brooks, Garth	7-13	MM
Xmas - Santa Looked A Lot Like Dadd	Brooks, Garth	22-843	ST
Xmas - Santa Looked A Lot Like Dadd	Owens, Buck	8-64	CB
Xmas - Santa Looked a Lot Like Dadd	Owens, Buck	14-543	SC
Xmas - Santa's Gonna Come/Pickup	Jackson, Alan	18-717	CB
Xmas - Santa's Gonna Come/Pickup	Jackson, Alan	22-842	ST
Xmas - Santa's Gonna Come/Pickup...	Jackson&Chipmunks	8-80	CB
Xmas - Santa's Got A Brand New Bag	SheDaisy	45-246	CB
Xmas - Santa's Got A Semi	Harling, Keith	45-243	CB
Xmas - Santabilly Boogie	Blue Moon Boys	46-287	CB
Xmas - Senor Santa Claus	Elmo & Patsy	3-388	SC
Xmas - Senor Santa Claus	Reeves, Jim	45-268	DFK
Xmas - Shake Up Christmas	Train	45-774	KV

SONG TITLE	ARTIST	#	TYPE
Xmas - Silent Night	Christain Christmas	10-438	BF
Xmas - Silent Night	Christmas	17-200	CMC
Xmas - Silent Night	Christmas	25-362	MM
Xmas - Silent Night	Christmas	21-267	NCG
Xmas - Silent Night	Christmas	12-586	P
Xmas - Silent Night	Christmas	14-408	SC
Xmas - Silent Night	Streisand, Barbra	49-545	PS
Xmas - Silent Night	Wilson Phillips	22-838	ST
Xmas - Silver Bells	Christmas	14-522	SC
Xmas - Silver Bells	Crosby, Bing	11-242	DK
Xmas - Silver Bells	Crosby, Bing	29-482	LE
Xmas - Silver Bells	Lady Antebellum	45-776	KV
Xmas - Silver Bells	Presley, Elvis	49-866	MM
Xmas - Silver Bells	Reeves, Jim	44-252	STTW
Xmas - Silver Bells	Williams, Andy	14-300	MM
Xmas - Sleigh Bells	Christmas	10-454	BF
Xmas - Sleigh Ride	Carpenters	45-805	SF
Xmas - Sleigh Ride	Christmas	27-471	DK
Xmas - Sleigh Ride	Christmas	12-581	P
Xmas - Sleigh Ride	Diamond, Neil	14-295	MM
Xmas - Sleigh Ride	Mathis, Johnny	14-521	SC
Xmas - Snoopy's Christmas	Royal Guardsmen	45-742	SC
Xmas - Sock It To Me Santa	Seger, Bob	46-288	CB
Xmas - Star the	Mattea, Kathy	18-758	CB
Xmas - Step Into Christmas	John, Elton	13-314	P
Xmas - Step Into Christmas	John, Elton	14-531	SC
Xmas - Sweet Little Jesus Boy	Murray, Anne	11-5	PL
Xmas - Sweetest Gift the	Yearwood, Trisha	30-398	SC
Xmas - Take A Walk Thru Bethlehem	Yearwood, Trisha	15-664	THM
Xmas - Tennessee Christmas	Grant, Amy	8-50	CB
Xmas - Thank God For Kids	Oak Ridge Boys	14-547	SC
Xmas - There Is No Xmas Like A Home...	Como, Perry	45-748	CB
Xmas - There's A New Kid In Town	Strait, George	15-655	THM
Xmas - There's A New Kid In Town	Whitley, Keith	18-753	CB
Xmas - There's A New Kid In Town	Yearwood, Trisha	22-844	ST
Xmas - There's No Place Like Home..	Como, Perry	14-294	MM
Xmas - This Christmas	Hathaway, Donny	41-38	CB
Xmas - Thistlehair The Christmas Bear	Alabama	45-755	CB
Xmas - Til Santa's Gone (Milk & Cookies)	Black, Clint	45-242	BS
Xmas - Till Santa's Gone	Black, Clint	8-63	CB
Xmas - To Heck With Ole Santa Claus	Lynn, Loretta	46-49	SSK
Xmas - Twas the Night Before Xmas	Country Christmas	18-737	CB

SONG TITLE	ARTIST	#	TYPE
Xmas - Twas The Night Before Xmas	Country Christmas	15-665	THM
Xmas - Twas the Night Before Xmas	Standard	41-6	CB
Xmas - Twelve Days Of Christmas	Christmas	10-455	BF
Xmas - Twelve Days Of Christmas	Christmas	17-207	CMC
Xmas - Twelve Days Of Christmas	Christmas	17-54	DK
Xmas - Twelve Days Of Christmas	Christmas	6-287	MM
Xmas - Twelve Days Of Christmas	Christmas	21-274	NCG
Xmas - Twelve Days Of Christmas	Christmas	12-587	P
Xmas - Twelve Days Of Christmas	Christmas	14-405	SC
Xmas - Twelve Days Of Christmas	Sherman, Allen	5-714	SC
Xmas - Twelve Pains Of Christmas	Rivers, Bob	45-252	SC
Xmas - Two-Step 'Round the Xmas Tree	Standard	41-16	PR
Xmas - Underneath The Tree	Clarkson, Kelly	45-773	KV
Xmas - Unto Us This Holy Night	Wiggles	45-240	WIG
Xmas - Up On The Housetop	Arnold, Eddy	14-519	SC
Xmas - Up On The Housetop	Autry, Gene	45-662	SY
Xmas - Up On The Housetop	Boxcar Willie	8-69	CB
Xmas - Walkin' Round in Women's...	Rivers, Bob	5-706	SC
Xmas - We Need A Little Christmas	Country Christmas	18-736	CB
Xmas - We Need A Little Christmas	Standard	41-5	CB
Xmas - We Three Kings	Christian Christmas	10-445	BF
Xmas - We Three Kings	Christmas	25-374	MM
Xmas - We Three Kings	Christmas	14-417	SC
Xmas - We Three Kings	Country Christmas	18-743	CB
Xmas - We Three Kings	Standard	41-12	CB
Xmas - We Wish You A Merry Xmas	Boone, Pat	14-306	MM
Xmas - We Wish You A Merry Xmas	Christian Christmas	10-441	BF
Xmas - We Wish You A Merry Xmas	Christmas	17-203	CMC
Xmas - We Wish You A Merry Xmas	Christmas	17-52	DK
Xmas - We Wish You A Merry Xmas	Christmas	21-270	NCG
Xmas - We Wish You A Merry Xmas	Christmas	12-584	P
Xmas - We Wish You a Merry Xmas	Christmas	14-525	SC
Xmas - We Wish You A Merry Xmas	Rabbitt, Eddie	18-761	CB

SONG TITLE	ARTIST	#	TYPE
Xmas - We Wish You A Merry Xmas	Wagoner, Porter	8-76	CB
Xmas - What A Merry Christmas This	Strait, George	18-748	CB
Xmas - What Are You Doing NYE	Wilson, Nancy	14-307	MM
Xmas - What Are You Doing NYE	Womack, Lee Ann	30-401	SC
Xmas - What Child Is This	Christian Christmas	10-446	BF
Xmas - What Child Is This	Christmas	17-201	CMC
Xmas - What Child Is This	Christmas	25-371	MM
Xmas - What Child Is This	Christmas	21-268	NCG
Xmas - What Child Is This	Christmas	14-416	SC
Xmas - What Child Is This	Gayle, Crystal	8-72	CB
Xmas - What Child Is This	Gill, Vince	30-397	SC
Xmas - What Child Is This	Judds	30-391	SC
Xmas - What Child Is This	Mathis, Johnny	45-782	SBI
Xmas - What Child Is This	Underwood, Carrie	45-786	KV
Xmas - What Child Is This	Williams, Vanessa	22-837	ST
Xmas - What If Jesus Comes Back	Raye, Collin	18-747	CB
Xmas - When A Child Is Born	Mathis, Johnny	45-781	ZM
Xmas - When God Made You	Moffats	18-727	CB
Xmas - When It's Xmas Time in Texas	Strait, George	18-751	CB
Xmas - White Christmas	Brooks, Garth	45-794	PS
Xmas - White Christmas	Christmas	12-576	P
Xmas - White Christmas	Clarkson, Kelly	45-793	KV
Xmas - White Christmas	Crosby, Bing	11-726	DK
Xmas - White Christmas	Crosby, Bing	29-483	LE
Xmas - White Christmas	Crosby, Bing	14-536	SC
Xmas - White Christmas	Crosby, Bing	22-848	ST
Xmas - White Christmas	Drifters	45-898	SBI
Xmas - White Christmas	Midler, Bette	45-779	PS
Xmas - White Christmas	Presley, Elvis	45-760	CB
Xmas - White Christmas	Presley, Elvis	49-865	MM
Xmas - White Christmas	Swift, Taylor	45-791	KV
Xmas - White Christmas - duet	Buble & Twain	45-792	KV
Xmas - White Christmas Makes Me Blue	TRavis, Randy	45-790	CB
Xmas - White Xmas Makes Me Blue	Travis, Randy	15-663	THM
Xmas - Who Says There Ain't No Santa	Brooks & Dunn	49-367	CB
Xmas - Who'd Be a Turkey at Xmas	John, Elton	5-720	SC

SONG TITLE	ARTIST	#	TYPE
Xmas - Winter Wonderland	Christmas	10-452	BF
Xmas - Winter Wonderland	Christmas	14-523	SC
Xmas - Winter Wonderland	Grant, Amy	14-299	MM
Xmas - Winter Wonderland	Lonestar	30-399	SC
Xmas - Winter Wonderland	Presley, Elvis	49-869	MM
Xmas - With Bells On	Rogers & Parton	18-759	CB
Xmas - With Bells On	Rogers & Parton	3-394	SC
Xmas - Wonderful Christmastime	McCartney, Paul	34-431	CB
Xmas - Wonderful World Of Christmas	Presley, Elvis	45-759	CB
Xmas - Wonderful World of Xmas the	Presley, Elvis	49-878	MM
Xmas - Year Without A Santa Claus	Heat Miser/Snow Miser	45-249	SC
Xmas - You're a Mean One Mr Grinch	How Grinch Stole...	5-719	SC
Xmas - Zat You Santa Claus	Armstrong, Louis	45-744	SC
XO	Ballerini, Kelsea	47-396	BKD
XXL	Anderson, Keith	36-374	SC
XXL - (Double XL)	Anderson, Keith	23-412	CB
XXX's And OOO's	Yearwood, Trisha	1-638	CB
XXX's And OOO's	Yearwood, Trisha	12-183	DK
XXX's And OOO's	Yearwood, Trisha	6-588	MM
XXX's And OOO's	Yearwood, Trisha	17-211	NA
XXX's And OOO's	Yearwood, Trisha	12-481	P
XXX's And OOO's	Yearwood, Trisha	2-452	SC
Y Viva Espana	Sylvia	16-370	SF
Y'All Come	Wagoner, Porter	19-305	CB
Y'All Come Back Saloon	Oak Ridge Boys	23-502	CB
Y'All Got It	The Wiz	49-439	SDK
Ya Ya	Dorsey, Lee	6-864	MM
Ya'll Come Back Saloon	Oak Ridge Boys	2-402	SC
Yakety Yak	Coasters	35-12	CB
Yakety Yak	Coasters	26-144	DK
Yakety Yak	Coasters	10-696	JVC
Yankee Doodle Boy	Patriotic	44-47	PT
Yankee Doodle Dandy	Patriotic	44-46	PT
Yankee Doodle Dandy	Standard	23-230	SM
Yankee Rose	Roth, David Lee	47-466	SC
Yard Sale	Kershaw, Sammy	1-467	CB
Yard Sale	Kershaw, Sammy	3-372	SC
Yeah	Usher/Lil Jon/Ludac	23-263	THM
Yeah Boy	Ballerini, Kelsea	45-387	BKD
Yeah Buddy	Carson, Jeff	2-735	SC
Yeah!	Nichols, Joe	44-133	ASK
Yeah!	Nichols, Joe	43-256	BKD
Year At A Time a	Denney, Kevin	19-681	ST
Year Of The Cat the	Stewart, Al	2-785	SC
Year That Clayton Delany Died	Hall, Tom T.	8-283	CB
Year That Clayton Delany Died	Hall, Tom T.	4-308	SC

SONG TITLE	ARTIST	#	TYPE
Year Without A Santa Claus - xmas	Heat Miser/Snow Miser	45-249	SC
Years	Mandrell, Barbara	15-587	DK
Years After You	Conlee, John	47-616	CB
Years From Here	Baker & Myers	4-133	SC
Years From Here	Baker, Anita	7-237	MM
Years From Now	Dr. Hook	47-47	SFM
Years May Come Years May Go	Herman's Hermits	47-143	ZM
Yee-Haw	Owen, Jake	29-374	CB
Yellow	Coldplay	21-640	TT
Yellow Brick Road	Frazier, Morgan	39-96	PHN
Yellow Ledbetter	Pearl Jam	9-294	RS
Yellow Rose Of Texas	Miller, Mitch	43-224	CB
Yellow Rose Of Texas - duet	Lee & Brody	49-645	VH
Yellow Rose Of Texas the	Miller & Orchestra	11-762	DK
Yellow Rose Of Texas the	Miller & Orchestra	3-515	SC
Yellow Rose Of Texas the	Standard	23-226	SM
Yellow Roses	Parton, Dolly	17-315	NA
Yellow Roses	Parton, Dolly	4-66	SC
Yellow Submarine	Beatles	11-109	DK
Yes (Hex Hector Mix)	Amber	21-736	TT
Yes I Am	Etheridge, Melissa	47-68	RSZ
Yes I Guess They Oughta Name A Drin	Prine, John	23-535	CB
Yes I Will	Hollies	44-361	EK
Yes I'm Ready	Desario & KC	12-384	DK
Yes I'm Ready - duet	Desario & KC	35-79	CB
Yes Mr. Peters	Drusky & Mitchell	20-742	CB
Yes Mr. Peters	Drusky & Mitchell	9-611	SAV
Yes Sir That's My Baby	Standard	35-31	CB
Yes Sir! That's My Baby	Cantor, Eddie	43-216	CB
Yes We Can Can	Pointer Sisters	9-729	SAV
Yes We Have No Bananas	Jones, Spike	17-417	DK
Yes!	Brock, Chad	13-822	CHM
Yes!	Brock, Chad	6-72	SC
Yester Me Yester You Yesterday	Wonder, Stevie	49-476	MM
Yesterday	Beatles	11-100	DK
Yesterday	Charles, Ray	46-578	KV
Yesterday (Guitar Version)	Clark, Roy	45-656	TBR
Yesterday Has Gone	Cupids Inspiration	10-634	SF
Yesterday Man	Andrews, Chris	10-576	SF
Yesterday Once More	Carpenters	34-23	CB
Yesterday Once More	Carpenters	11-235	DK
Yesterday When I Was Young	Clark, Roy	8-290	CB
Yesterday When I Was Young	Clark, Roy	10-752	JVC
Yesterday When I Was Young	Clark, Roy	4-264	SC
Yesterday's Girl	Thompson, Hank	45-726	VH
Yesterday's Song	Diamond, Neil	30-685	LE

SONG TITLE	ARTIST	#	TYPE
Yesterday's Wine	Haggard & Jones	22-242	CB
Yesterday/Something	Monro, Matt	11-58	PT
Yippy Ky Yay	McCann, Lila	8-731	CB
Yippy Ky Yay	McCann, Lila	22-819	ST
YMCA	Village People	18-363	AH
YMCA	Village People	9-216	PT
Yoda	Yankovic, Weird Al	15-351	MM
You	Carpenters	44-340	OZP
You	Duarte, Ryan	20-536	CB
You	Dyllon, Marshall	15-214	THM
You	Powell, Jesse	7-833	PHM
You	Raitt, Bonnie	6-634	MM
You & Me & The Bottle Makes Three	Big Bad Voodoo Dadd	15-208	AMS
You & Me & The Bottle Makes Three	Big Bad Voodoo Dadd	13-687	SGB
You 2-Timed Me 1 Time Too Often	Ritter, Tex	20-708	CB
You Ain't Dolly & You Ain't Porter	Shelton & Monroe	49-522	BKD
You Ain't Dolly & You... (Inst)	Shelton & Monroe	49-523	BKD
You Ain't Going Nowhere	Byrds	47-552	KV
You Ain't Hurt Nothin' Yet	Anderson, John	9-417	CB
You Ain't Just Whistlin' Dixie	Bellamy Brothers	4-644	SC
You Ain't Much Fun	Keith, Toby	1-702	CB
You Ain't Much Fun	Keith, Toby	3-370	SC
You Ain't Seen Nothin' Yet	B.T.O.	13-171	P
You Ain't Seen Nothin' Yet	B.T.O.	4-760	SC
You Ain't Seen Nothing Yet	BTO	46-542	CB
You Ain't That Lonely Yet	Big House	16-581	SC
You Ain't Woman Enough	Lynn, Loretta	15-835	CB
You Ain't Woman Enough	Lynn, Loretta	13-474	P
You Ain't Woman Enough	McBride, Martina	29-599	CB
You Almost Slipped My Mind	Pride, Charley	40-111	CB
You Always Come Back To Hurtin' Me	Rodriguez, Johnny	22-47	CB
You Always Come Back To Hurting Me	Rodriguez, Johnny	5-405	SC
You And I	Lady Gaga	38-202	SF
You And I	Rabbitt & Gayle	8-109	CB
You And I	Rabbitt & Gayle	26-369	DK
You And I	Rabbitt & Gayle	6-231	MM
You And I	Rabbitt & Gayle	13-197	P
You And I	Rabbitt & Gayle	2-306	SC
You And I	Scorpions	49-100	KVD
You And I (Nobody In The World)	Legend, John	45-808	KV
You And I Both	Mraz, Jason	44-387	SC

SONG TITLE	ARTIST	#	TYPE
You And Me	Alice Cooper	15-750	AMS
You And Me	Lifehouse	30-142	PT
You And Me	Watkins, Sara	41-73	PHN
You And Me	Wynette, Tammy	12-408	P
You And Me - duet	Foley, Red & Kitty Wells	43-363	CB
You And Me - duet	Wells & Foley	48-202	CB
You And Me Against The World	Reddy, Helen	12-45	DK
You And Only You	Berry, John	2-579	SC
You And Tequila	Chesney, Kenny	37-217	CB
You And The Mona Lisa	Colvin, Shawn	7-696	PHM
You And You Alone	Gill, Vince	7-668	CHM
You And Your Sweet Love	Smith, Connie	48-94	CB
You Are	Brock, Chad	19-708	ST
You Are	Richie, Lionel	34-81	CB
You Are	Wayne, Jimmy	30-804	PHM
You Are	Wayne, Jimmy	20-329	ST
You Are Everything	Hill, Dru	28-225	SF
You Are Everything	Stylistics	9-760	SAV
You Are Everything	Stylistics	24-332	SC
You Are Everything - duet	Ross & Gaye	49-69	ZVS
You Are In Love	Swift, Taylor	48-303	KV
You Are Loved (Don't Give Up)	Groban, Josh	48-44	CB
You Are My Destiny	Anka, Paul	9-553	SAV
You Are My Destiny	Anka, Paul	3-511	SC
You Are My Destiny	Anka, Paul	9-172	SO
You Are My Lady	Jackson, Freddie	15-721	LE
You Are My Love	Reeves, Jim	49-799	VH
You Are My Number One	Smash Mouth	25-654	MM
You Are My Sunshine	Autry, Gene	8-437	CB
You Are My Sunshine	Charles, Ray	46-584	LE
You Are My Sunshine	Crosby, Bing	29-476	LE
You Are My Sunshine	Crosby, Bing	9-550	SAV
You Are My Sunshine	Miller, Mitch	43-223	CB
You Are My Sunshine	Standard	26-413	DK
You Are My Sunshine/Open Up Your Heart	Murray, Anne	45-950	KV
You Are My Treasure	Greene, Jack	43-340	CB
You Are Not Alone	Jackson, Michael	36-124	JTG
You Are So Beautiful	Cocker, Joe	26-277	DK
You Are So Beautiful	Cocker, Joe	21-443	LE
You Are So Beautiful	Cocker, Joe	13-131	P
You Are So Good To Me	Third Day	34-422	CB
You Are The One	A-Ha	46-239	KV
You Are The One	Smith, Carl	22-118	CB
You Are The One	Smith, Carl	22-253	SC
You Are The Sunshine Of My Life	Wonder, Stevie	27-256	DK
You Are The Sunshine Of My Life	Wonder, Stevie	14-367	MH
You Are The Woman	Firefall	2-842	SC
You Are What I Am	Lightfoot, Gordon	43-480	SK
You Asked Me To	Jennings, Waylon	45-179	ASK

SONG TITLE	ARTIST	#	TYPE
You Be Illin'	Run DMC	14-444	SC
You Beat Me To The Punch	Wells, Mary	12-66	DK
You Believed In Me	Bonoff & Nitty Grit	4-373	SC
You Belong To Me	Doobie Brothers	47-28	PS
You Belong To Me	Duprees	15-589	MM
You Belong To Me	Martin, Dean	23-82	MM
You Belong To Me	Simon, Carly	49-154	CB
You Belong To Me	Stafford, Jo	11-576	DK
You Belong To Me	Standard	47-817	DK
You Belong To The City	Frey, Glenn	15-713	LE
You Belong With Me	Swift, Taylor	37-213	AS
You Belong With Me	Swift, Taylor	36-21	PT
You Better Run	Benatar, Pat	24-565	SC
You Better Run	Rascals	10-494	DA
You Better Sit Down Kids	Cher	14-54	RS
You Better Think Twice	Gill, Vince	6-799	MM
You Better Think Twice	Gill, Vince	2-830	SC
You Better Think Twice	Poco	49-265	DFK
You Better Wait	Perry, Steve	6-638	MM
You Better You Bet	Who	19-739	LE
You Better You Bet	Who	5-877	SC
You Brought A New Kind Of Love	Sinatra, Frank	9-235	PT
You Can Always Come Home	Jackson, Alan	45-340	KV
You Can Call Me Al	Simon & Garfunkel	23-640	BS
You Can Call Me Al	Simon & Garfunkel	15-590	DM
You Can Close Your Eyes	Taylor, James	49-2	DCK
You Can Depend On Me	Lee, Brenda	45-451	CBE
You Can Depend On Me	Restless Heart	1-420	CB
You Can Do Magic	America	34-74	CB
You Can Do Magic	America	18-265	DK
You Can Do Magic	America	18-500	SAV
You Can Dream Of Me	Wariner, Steve	20-17	SC
You Can Feel Bad	Loveless, Patty	1-727	CB
You Can Feel Bad	Loveless, Patty	4-104	SC
You Can Get It If You Really Want	Dekker & the Aces	25-378	MM
You Can Have Her	Jennings, Waylon	14-258	SC
You Can Have Her	Jones & Paycheck	9-584	SAV
You Can Have Her - duet	Paycheck & Jones	45-214	SAV
You Can Leave Your Hat On	Cocker, Joe	21-438	LE
You Can Let Go	Shawanda, Crystal	36-583	CB
You Can Let Go	Shawanda, Crystal	36-226	PHM
You Can Look But You Better Not...	Springsteen, Bruce	20-244	LE
You Can Make History Young Again	John, Elton	24-368	SC
You Can Say That Again	Rodriguez, Johnny	24-157	SC
You Can Sleep While I Drive	Etheridge, Melissa	19-547	SC
You Can Sleep While I Drive	Yearwood, Trisha	6-801	MM
You Can Sleep While I Drive	Yearwood, Trisha	2-693	SC

SONG TITLE	ARTIST	#	TYPE
You Can Still Rock In America	Night Ranger	37-64	SC
You Can't Always Get What U Want	Rolling Stones	19-125	KC
You Can't Always Get What U Want	Rolling Stones	19-747	LE
You Can't Be A Beacon	Fargo, Donna	13-495	P
You Can't Be a Beacon...	Fargo, Donna	35-365	CB
You Can't Count Me Out Yet	Tritt, Travis	18-593	ST
You Can't Get There From Here	Parnell, Lee Roy	22-622	ST
You Can't Give Up On Lovin'	Jackson, Alan	2-431	SC
You Can't Have Your Kate & Edith To	Statler Brothers	19-386	CB
You Can't Hide Beautiful	Lines, Aaron	25-415	MM
You Can't Hide Beautiful	Lines, Aaron	18-214	ST
You Can't Hide Redneck	Lawrence, Tracy	48-380	CB
You Can't Hurry Love	Collins, Phil	44-24	SF
You Can't Hurry Love	Dixie Chicks	30-610	RS
You Can't Hurry Love	Midler, Bette	45-937	KV
You Can't Hurry Love	Supremes	16-794	DK
You Can't Hurry Love	Supremes	4-719	SC
You Can't Lose Me	Hill, Faith	15-693	CB
You Can't Lose Me	Hill, Faith	19-291	MH
You Can't Lose Me	Hill, Faith	7-344	MM
You Can't Lose Me	Hill, Faith	4-407	SC
You Can't Make A Heart Love Some-..	Strait, George	1-261	CB
You Can't Make A Heart Love Some-..	Strait, George	17-274	NA
You Can't Make A Heart Love Some-.d	Strait, George	22-851	ST
You Can't Make Old Friends	Rogers & Parton	49-23	KV
You Can't Read My Mind	Keith, Toby	47-166	KV
You Can't Rollerskate In A Buffalo	Miller, Roger	8-811	CB
You Can't Run From Love	Rabbitt, Eddie	5-322	SC
You Can't Stop Love	Stuart, Marty	7-401	MM
You Can't Stop Love	Stuart, Marty	24-658	SC
You Can't Stop Me	Eldridge & Rhett	45-349	BKD
You Can't Take It With You	Vincent, Rhonda	19-682	ST
You Can't Take It With You...	Vincent, Rhonda	36-370	CB
You Can't Take The Honky Tonk Out..	Brooks & Dunn	19-675	ST
You Can't Win	Clarkson, Kelly	48-505	KVD
You Can't Wrap Your Arms/Memory	Brown, Marty	24-653	SC
You Caught Me At A Bad Time	Keith, Toby	36-378	SC
You Cheated You Lied	Shields	25-546	MM
You Comb Her Hair	Jones, George	20-643	SC
You Could Be Mine	Guns & Roses	21-769	SC
You Could Know As Much About...	Watson, Gene	14-669	CB

SONG TITLE	ARTIST	#	TYPE
You Could've Had Me	Lace	9-406	CB
You Da Man	Clark, J	32-8	THM
You Da Man	Clark, Jameson	18-335	ST
You Da Man	Clark, Jameson	32-6	THM
You Decorated My Life	Rogers, Kenny	3-174	CB
You Decorated My Life	Rogers, Kenny	9-567	SAV
You Didn't Have To Be So Nice	Lovin' Spoonful	6-46	SC
You Didn't Miss A Thing	Gregory, Clinton	2-665	SC
You Do Something To Me	Sinatra, Frank	9-805	SAV
You Do Your Thing	Montgomery Gentry	30-802	PHM
You Do Your Thing	Montgomery Gentry	20-488	ST
You Don't Bring Me Flowers	Diamond&Streisand	30-512	THM
You Don't Bring Me Flowers	Streisand&Diamond	7-547	AH
You Don't Bring Me Flowers	Streisand&Diamond	18-51	MM
You Don't Bring Me Flowers	Streisand&Diamond	9-206	SO
You Don't Even Know Who I Am	Loveless, Patty	1-725	CB
You Don't Even Know Who I Am	Loveless, Patty	2-687	SC
You Don't Have To Be A Baby To Cry	Caravelles	3-591	SC
You Don't Have To Be A Star	McCoo & Davis Jr.	17-140	DK
You Don't Have To Go Home	Wilson, Gretchen	30-564	CB
You Don't Have To Remind Me	Jordan, Sass	24-556	SC
You Don't Have To Say You Love Me	Presley, Elvis	18-444	KC
You Don't Have To Say You Love Me	Springfield, Dusty	19-615	MH
You Don't Have To SayYou Love Me	Presley, Elvis	25-768	MM
You Don't Hear	Wells, Kitty	4-738	SC
You Don't Know	Shapiro, Helen	19-109	SAV
You Don't Know A Thing	Azar, Steve	30-93	CB
You Don't Know Her Like I Do	Gilbert, Brantley	42-25	ASK
You Don't Know Jack	Bryan, Luke	38-101	PHM
You Don't Know Love	Fricke, Janie	14-429	SC
You Don't Know Me	Arnold, Eddy	19-31	CB
You Don't Know Me	Arnold, Eddy	13-530	P
You Don't Know Me	Arnold, Eddy	17-630	THM
You Don't Know Me	Cassidy & Gray	25-673	MM
You Don't Know Me	Charles, Ray	17-305	NA
You Don't Know Me	Gilley, Mickey	22-225	CB
You Don't Know Me	Gilley, Mickey	16-174	THM
You Don't Know Me At All	Henley, Don	48-159	ZMP
You Don't Know What Love Is	Standard	13-641	SGB
You Don't Know What Love Is	White Stripes	49-908	SC
You Don't Lie Here	Fairchild, Shelly	22-80	CB

SONG TITLE	ARTIST	#	TYPE
Anymore			
You Don't Lie Here Anymore	Fairchild, Shelly	23-39	SC
You Don't Love Me Anymore	Rabbitt, Eddie	48-41	CB
You Don't Love Me Anymore	Yankovic, Weird Al	49-836	SC
You Don't Mess Around With Jim	Croce, Jim	19-354	PS
You Don't Need Me Now	Black, Clint	8-397	CB
You Don't Need Me Now	Black, Clint	7-855	CHT
You Don't Need Me Now	Black, Clint	22-725	ST
You Don't Need Me Now	Black, Clint	30-421	THM
You Don't Own Me	Gore, Lesley	19-621	MH
You Don't Own Me	Gore, Lesley	5-80	SC
You Don't Own Me	Midler, Bette	45-919	KV
You Don't Seem To Miss Me	Loveless, Patty	1-735	CB
You Don't Seem To Miss Me	Loveless, Patty	22-641	ST
You Don't Smell Like Flowers - parody	Parody	45-288	BS
You Don't Own Me	Gore, Lesley	11-527	DK
You Done Me Wrong	Nelson, Willie	38-81	PS
You Done Me Wrong	Yearwood, Trisha	6-210	MM
You Drive Me Crazy	Spears, Britney	13-558	LE
You Drive Me Crazy	Spears, Britney	10-200	SC
You Dropped A Bomb On Me	Gap Band	16-643	MM
You Found Me	Fray	36-266	PHM
You Gave Her Your Name	Daniel, Dale	24-254	SC
You Gave Me A Mountain	Watson, Gene	24-353	SC
You Get Used To Somebody	McGraw, Tim	29-527	CB
You Get What You Give	New Radicals	7-788	PHT
You Give Good Love	Houston, Whitney	11-461	DK
You Give Good Love	Houston, Whitney	13-189	P
You Give Love A Bad Name	Bon Jovi	12-59	DK
You Give Me Love	Hill, Faith	15-694	CB
You Give Me Something	Morrison, James	38-272	SF
You Go First (Do You Wanna Kiss)	Andrews, Jessica	22-489	ST
You Go To My Head	Sinatra, Frank	49-497	MM
You Go To My Head	Standard	19-784	SGB
You Go To My Head	Stewart, Rod	25-591	MM
You Go To My Head	Streisand, Barbra	49-384	PS
You Gonna Fly	Urban, Keith	45-624	ASK
You Got Gold	Prine, John	23-530	CB
You Got It	N'Sync	15-771	BS
You Got It	Orbison, Roy	9-524	SAV
You Got It	Orbison, Roy	4-289	SC
You Got It	Orbison, Roy	9-186	SO
You Got It (The Right Stuff)	New Kids On Block	16-867	DK
You Got It (The Right Stuff)	New Kids On Block	9-694	SAV

SONG TITLE	ARTIST	#	TYPE
You Got It All	Grams, Shannon	17-73	DK
You Got Lucky	Petty & Heartbreake	20-74	SC
You Got Me	Cailliat, Colbie	48-218	KV
You Got Me Rocking	Rolling Stones	20-202	SC
You Got Me Runnin'	Reed, Jimmy	7-223	MM
You Got That Right	Lynyrd Skynyrd	5-261	SC
You Got The Love	Source	30-736	SF
You Got What It Takes	Johnson, Mary	6-568	MM
You Gotta Fight For Your Right...	Beastie Boys	34-87	CB
You Gotta Fight for Yr Right/Party	Beastie Boys	10-499	DA
You Gotta Love That	McCoy, Neal	1-854	CB
You Gotta Love That	McCoy, Neal	4-129	SC
You Had Me	Stone, Joss	21-162	PHM
You Had Me From Hello	Chesney, Kenny	19-207	CB
You Had Me From Hello	Chesney, Kenny	7-885	CHT
You Had Me From Hello	Chesney, Kenny	14-623	SC
You Had Me From Hello	Chesney, Kenny	22-750	ST
You Had To Be There	McGraw, Tim	44-164	BKD
You Have Killed Me	Morrissey	30-698	SF
You Have The Right to Remain Silent	Perfect Stranger	7-89	MM
You Have The Right To Remain Silent	Perfect Stranger	3-426	SC
You Have The Right To Remain Silent	Stone, Doug	6-818	MM
You Haven't Left Me Yet	Strait, George	8-496	CB
You Haven't Seen The Last Of Me	Cher	47-672	CB
You Hear A Song	Pope, Cassadee	49-667	SBI
You Just Can't Quit	Nelson, Ricky	47-843	DCK
You Just Get One	Wood, Jeff	7-426	MM
You Just Stepped In (From Stepping Out)	Lynn, Loretta	47-628	CB
You Just Watch Me	Tucker, Tanya	6-505	MM
You Just Watch Me	Tucker, Tanya	2-430	SC
You Keep Me Hangin' On	Supremes	11-178	DK
You Keep Me Hangin' On	Wilde, Kim	6-491	MM
You Keep Me Hanging On	Supremes	35-89	CB
You Know I'm No Good	Winehouse, Amy	36-476	CB
You Know Me Better Than That	Strait, George	8-169	CB
You Know Me Better Than That	Strait, George	12-441	P
You Know Me Better Than That	Strait, George	2-702	SC
You Know What's Up	Jones, Donell	9-339	PS
You Know You're Right	Nirvana	25-405	MM
You Know You're Right	Nirvana	18-823	THM
You Lay A Whole Lot Of Love On Me	Twain, Shania	16-659	THM
You Learn	Morrisette, Alanis	10-682	HE
You Learn	Morrisette, Alanis	39-128	SC
You Learn	Morrisette, Alanis	19-159	SGB
You Left The Water Running	Amazing Rhythm Aces	47-789	SRK
You Lie	Band Perry	37-203	AS

315

SONG TITLE	ARTIST	#	TYPE
You Lie	McEntire, Reba	16-587	MM
You Light Up My Life	Boone, Debbie	12-42	DK
You Light Up My Life	Rimes, LeAnn	8-894	CB
You Light Up My Life	Rimes, LeAnn	7-678	CHM
You Look Good In My Shirt	Urban, Keith	23-396	CB
You Look Like I Need A Drink	Moore, Justin	45-619	DCK
You Look So Good In Love	Strait, George	1-256	CB
You Look So Good In Love	Strait, George	6-759	MM
You Look So Good In Love	Strait, George	4-648	SC
You Love Keeps Working	Watley, Jodi	15-763	NU
You Love Me	Clarkson, Kelly	47-694	KV
You Love The Thunder	Browne, Jackson	23-611	BS
You Made A Wanted Man Out Of Me	McDowell, Ronnie	47-227	CB
You Made Me Love You	Cline, Patsy	45-481	ABA
You Made Me Love You	Cline, Patsy	45-507	KVD
You Made Me Love You	Garland, Judy	33-215	CB
You Made Me Love You	Garland, Judy	15-846	MM
You Made Me Love You	Harry James Orchestra	43-218	CB
You Made Me Love You	James & Orchestra	21-7	CB
You Made Me Love You	Standard	15-598	DK
You Made Me That Way	Griggs, Andy	14-140	CB
You Made Me That Way	Griggs, Andy	14-11	CHM
You Made Me That Way	Griggs, Andy	10-265	SC
You Made Me That Way	Griggs, Andy	22-576	ST
You Make It Seem So Easy	Kinleys	8-751	CB
You Make Loving Fun	Fleetwood Mac	12-352	DK
You Make Loving Fun	Fleetwood Mac	10-25	SC
You Make Me Feel Brand New	Flack, Roberta	24-269	SC
You Make Me Feel Brand New	Stylistics	11-213	DK
You Make Me Feel Brand New	Stylistics	7-480	MM
You Make Me Feel Brand New	Stylistics	9-757	SAV
You Make Me Feel Like a Natural...	Franklin, Aretha	36-175	JT
You Make Me Feel Like Dancing	Groove Generation	17-38	DK
You Make Me Feel Like Dancing	Sayer, Leo	33-304	CB
You Make Me Feel Like Dancing	Sayer, Leo	29-298	SC
You Make Me Feel Mighty Real	Sylvester	15-701	LE
You Make Me Feel So Young	Sinatra, Frank	9-246	PT
You Make Me Feel So Young	Sinatra, Frank	21-222	SGB
You Make Me Sick	Pink	21-642	TT
You Make Me Wanna	Usher	7-701	PHM

SONG TITLE	ARTIST	#	TYPE
You Make Me Wanna	Usher	5-285	SC
You Make Me Want To Make You...	Newton, Juice	34-257	CB
You Make Me Want To Make You...	Newton, Juice	38-133	SC
You Make My Dreams	Hall & Oates	21-737	MH
You May Be Right	Joel, Billy	16-146	LE
You May Be Right	Joel, Billy	6-546	MM
You May See Me Walkin'	Skaggs, Ricky	5-856	SC
You Mean Everything To Me	Sedaka, Neil	45-353	CB
You Mean More To Me	Richie, Lionel	47-459	LE
You Mean The World To Me	Braxton, Toni	2-222	SC
You Mean The World To Me	Braxton, Toni	8-615	TT
You Mean The World To Me	Houston, David	9-606	SAV
You Mean The World To Me	Houston, David	5-105	SC
You Might Think	Cars	20-51	SC
You Move Me	Brooks, Garth	8-176	CB
You Must Believe In Spring	Streisand, Barbra	49-600	PS
You Must Love Me	Madonna	4-609	SC
You Must've Been A Beautiful Baby	Crosby, Bing	21-5	CB
You Must've Been A Beautiful Baby	Crosby, Bing	12-545	P
You Must've Been A Beautiful Baby	Darin, Bobby	18-43	MM
You Must've Been A Beautiful Baby	Darin, Bobby	4-15	SC
You Must've Been A Beautiful Baby	Darin, Bobby	9-312	STR
You Need A Man Around Here	Paisley, Brad	44-89	SRK
You Need A Man Around Here	Paisley, Brad	45-59	TBR
You Need A Woman Tonight	Captain & Tennille	46-560	CB
You Need To Be With Me	Tedeschi, Susan	17-452	AMS
You Needed Me	Monro, Matt	11-62	PT
You Needed Me	Murray, Anne	16-838	DK
You Needed Me	Murray, Anne	13-81	P
You Needed Me	Murray, Anne	11-1	PL
You Needed Me	Murray, Anne	9-451	SAV
You Never Can Tell	Berry, Chuck	43-437	LG
You Never Can Tell (C' Est La Vie)	Harris, EmmyLou	14-249	SC
You Never Cry Like A Lover	Eagles	44-104	ZMP
You Never Done It Like That	Captain & Tennille	46-555	CB
You Never Even Called Me By My..	Coe, David Allan	18-309	CB
You Never Even Called Me By My..	Coe, David Allan	13-414	P
You Never Even Called Me By My...	Coe, David Allan	17-243	NA

316

SONG TITLE	ARTIST	#	TYPE
You Never Gave Up On Me	Gayle, Crystal	9-490	SAV
You Never Know	Jackson, Alan	48-512	KVD
You Never Know Just How Good You've..	Jones, George	49-348	CB
You Never Miss A Real Good Thing	Gayle, Crystal	8-834	CB
You Never Remind Me	Eder, Linda	17-438	PS
You Never Take Me Dancing	Tritt, Travis	30-465	CB
You Only Live Twice	Sinatra, Nancy	9-62	SC
You Only Live Twice	Sinatra, Nancy	30-791	SF
You Only Want Me For My Body	Dickens, Little Jimmy	45-330	BSP
You Only Want Me For My Body	Dickens, Little Jimmy	45-681	VH
You Ought To Be With Me	Potentials	17-394	DK
You Oughta Know	Morrisette, Alanis	18-40	PS
You Oughta Know	Morrisette, Alanis	3-487	SC
You Oughta Know	Morrisette, Alanis	19-153	SGB
You Put A Move On My Heart	Jones, Quincy	21-145	SC
You Raise Me Up	Groban, Josh	20-354	PHM
You Really Got A Hold On Me	Robinson, Smokey	15-282	DK
You Really Got A Hold On Me	Robinson, Smokey	36-110	JTG
You Really Got A Hold On Me	Robinson, Smokey	6-564	MM
You Really Got Me	Kinks	13-223	P
You Really Got Me	Kinks	3-266	SC
You Really Got Me	Van Halen	13-751	SGB
You Really Had Me Going	Dunn, Holly	17-221	NA
You Really Had Me Going	Dunn, Holly	12-443	P
You Really Had Me Going	Dunn, Holly	3-374	SC
You Remain	Nelson, Willie	45-327	DCK
You Remind Me Of Something	Kelly, R.	49-518	CB
You Rock My World	Jackson, Michael	25-16	MM
You Rock My World	Jackson, Michael	16-306	PHM
You Rubbed It In All Wrong	Craddock, Billy C	34-224	CB
You Rubbed It In All Wrong	Craddock, Billy C	20-278	SC
You Said	Mona Lisa	24-50	SC
You Sang To Me	Anthony, Marc	16-236	PHM
You Sang To Me	Anthony, Marc	17-730	PS
You Save Me	Chesney, Kenny	30-56	CB
You Say You Will	Yearwood, Trisha	6-312	MM
You Say You Will	Yearwood, Trisha	2-817	SC
You See The Trouble With Me	White, Barry	15-696	LE
You Send Me	Cooke, Sam	43-21	LEG
You Send Me	Cooke, Sam	21-236	SC
You Send Me	Cooke, Sam	10-188	SS
You Sexy Thing	Hot Chocolate	11-381	DK

SONG TITLE	ARTIST	#	TYPE
You Sexy Thing	Hot Chocolate	5-380	SC
You Sexy Thing	Hot Chocolate	10-543	SF
You Shook Me	Dixon, Willie	14-592	SC
You Shook Me All Night Long	AC/DC	9-354	AH
You Shook Me All Night Long	Big & Rich	30-482	CB
You Should Be Dancing	Bee Gees	11-414	DK
You Should Be Dancing	Bee Gees	17-502	LE
You Should Be Dancing	Bee Gees	9-776	SAV
You Should Be Dancing	Bee Gees	2-500	SC
You Should Be Here	Swindell, Cole	48-742	BKD
You Should Be Here	Swindell, Cole	46-97	DCK
You Should Be Here (Inst)	Swindell, Cole	49-416	BKD
You Should've Told Me	Price, Kelly	20-622	CB
You Shouldn't Kiss Me Like This	Keith, Toby	14-157	CB
You Shouldn't Kiss Me Like This	Keith, Toby	14-18	CHM
You Shouldn't Kiss Me Like This	Keith, Toby	22-458	ST
You Shouldn't Kiss Me Like This	Keith, Toby	16-279	TT
You Show Me Yours & I'll Show You Mine	Kristofferson, Kris	45-197	JBK
You Showed Me	Turtles	5-175	SC
You Smile	Gregory, Clinton	41-82	PHN
You Sound Good To Me	Hale, Lucy	43-239	ASK
You Stay With Me	Martin, Ricky	9-129	PS
You Stay With Me	Martin, Ricky	13-742	SGB
You Stepped Out Of A Dream	Cole, Nat "King"	46-361	MM
You Stepped Out Of A Dream	Standard	15-591	SGB
You Still Got Me	Supernaw, Doug	4-97	SC
You Still Move Me	Seals, Dan	5-671	SC
You Still Own Me	Emerson Drive	30-535	CB
You Still Shake Me	Carter, Deana	8-330	CB
You Still Shake Me	Carter, Deana	7-826	CHT
You Still Shake Me	Carter, Deana	22-716	ST
You Still Take Me There	Raye, Collin	14-840	ST
You Still Take Me There	Raye, Collin	15-219	THM
You Suck **	Murmurs	5-739	SC
You Take Me For Granted	Haggard, Merle	22-240	CB
You Take My Breath Away	Smith, Margo	8-272	CB
You Take My Breath Away	Smith, Rex	5-684	SC
You Talk Too Much	Jones, Joe	3-285	MM
You Talk Too Much	Jones, Joe	3-578	SC
You Took Advantage Of Me	Day, Doris	48-131	KV
You Took Advantage Of Me	Standard	15-592	SGB
You Took Him Off My Hands	Cline, Patsy	22-195	CB
You Took Him Off My	Cline, Patsy	6-734	MM

SONG TITLE	ARTIST	#	TYPE
Hands			
You Took The Words Right Out..	Meat Loaf	6-494	MM
You Turn Me On Like A Radio	Bruce, Ed	4-490	SC
You Turned The Tables On Me	Standard	15-593	SGB
You Two-Timed Me One Time Too...	Ritter, Tex	5-368	SC
You Walked In	Lonestar	22-631	ST
You Wanna What	Elliott, Alecia	9-389	CB
You Wanted More	Tonic	8-508	PHT
You Wear It Well	Stewart, Rod	25-603	MM
You Wear It Well	Stewart, Rod	3-526	SC
You Were Always There	Fargo, Donna	39-9	CB
You Were Always There	Fargo, Donna	4-787	SC
You Were Made For Me	Freddie & Dreamers	10-566	SF
You Were Meant For Me	Jewel	19-576	MH
You Were Meant For Me	Jewel	4-601	SC
You Were Mine	Dixie Chicks	8-876	CB
You Were Mine	Dixie Chicks	10-59	SC
You Were Mine	Dixie Chicks	22-697	ST
You Were On My Mind	We Five	16-881	DK
You Were Only Fooling	Cline, Patsy	45-499	ABA
You Will	Loveless, Patty	6-465	MM
You Will	Loveless, Patty	2-95	SC
You Will Be My Music	Sinatra, Frank	49-504	MM
You Will Have To Pay	Ritter, Tex	20-709	CB
You Win Again	Bee Gees	48-685	P
You Win Again	Carpenter, M C	1-431	CB
You Win Again	Carpenter, M C	15-160	THM
You Win Again	Lewis, Jerry Lee	34-196	CB
You Win Again	Lewis, Jerry Lee	47-194	CB
You Win Again	Pride, Charley	43-209	CB
You Win Again	Williams, Hank Sr.	14-223	CB
You Win Again	Williams, Hank Sr.	8-643	SAV
You Win My Love	Twain, Shania	1-515	CB
You Win My Love	Twain, Shania	7-448	MM
You With Me	Cochran, Anita	14-103	CB
You Won't Be Lonely Now	Cyrus, Billy Ray	14-98	CB
You Won't Be Lonely Now	Cyrus, Billy Ray	19-222	CSZ
You Won't Be Lonely Now	Cyrus, Billy Ray	22-564	ST
You Won't Be Lonely Now	Cyrus, Billy Ray	14-29	THM
You Won't Ever Be Lonely	Griggs, Andy	7-859	CHT
You Won't See Me	Murray, Anne	38-6	PS
You Won't See Me Cry	Wilson Phillips	6-370	MM
You Wouldn't Know Love	Bolton, Michael	14-587	SC
You Wouldn't Say That To A Stranger	Bogguss, Suzy	6-576	MM
You'd Be So Nice To Come Home To	Sinatra, Frank	17-158	DK
You'd Be So Nice To Come Home To	Sinatra, Frank	10-713	JVC

SONG TITLE	ARTIST	#	TYPE
You'd Be So Nice To Come Home To	Sinatra, Frank	14-269	MM
You'd Be So Nice To Come Home To	Standard	47-820	DK
You'd Make An Angel Want To Cheat	Kendalls	20-675	SC
You'd Think He'd Know Me	Cryner, Bobbie	4-165	SC
You'd Think He'd Know Me Better	Morgan, Lorrie	8-741	CB
You'll Accomp'ny Me	Seger, Bob	10-175	UK
You'll Always Be Loved By Me	Brooks & Dunn	9-387	CB
You'll Always Be Loved By Me	Brooks & Dunn	13-819	CHM
You'll Always Be Loved By Me	Brooks & Dunn	19-247	CSZ
You'll Always Be My Baby	Evans, Sara	30-55	CB
You'll Always Be My Baby	Evans, Sara	30-102	PHM
You'll Be Back	Statler Brothers	6-83	SC
You'll Be In My Heart	Collins, Phil	11-68	JTG
You'll Be In My Heart	Collins, Phil	13-783	SGB
You'll Be Mine (Party Time)	Estefan, Gloria	24-180	SC
You'll Be There	Strait, George	22-337	CB
You'll Be There	Strait, George	23-385	SC
You'll Have To Swing It	Fitzgerald, Ella	46-274	KV
You'll Lose A Good Thing	Fender, Freddie	37-359	CK
You'll Lose A Good Thing	Fender, Freddie	20-290	SC
You'll Lose A Good Thing	Lynn, Barbara	7-307	MM
You'll Never Be Alone	Anastacia	32-59	THM
You'll Never Be Alone	Anastasia	32-59	THM
You'll Never Be Sorry	Bellamy Brothers	45-302	KV
You'll Never Be Sorry	Bellamy Brothers	47-771	SRK
You'll Never Find Another Love Like	Buble, Michael	30-185	LE
You'll Never Find Another Love Like	Rawls, Lou	17-141	DK
You'll Never Find Another Love Like	Rawls, Lou	17-433	KC
You'll Never Find Another Love Like	Rawls, Lou	4-293	SC
You'll Never Know	McCready, Mindy	8-239	CB
You'll Never Miss A Real Good Thing	Gayle, Crystal	5-53	SC
You'll Never Never Know	Platters	12-362	DK
You'll Never Walk Alone	Presley, Elvis	30-372	SC
You'll Never Walk Alone	Streisand, Barbra	49-619	PS
You'll See	Madonna	21-151	LE
You'll See	Madonna	15-594	THM
You'll Think Of Me	Presley, Elvis	25-97	MM
You'll Think Of Me	Urban, Keith	19-699	ST
You're A God	Vertical Horizon	15-645	THM
You're A God (Radio Version)	Vertical Horizon	14-500	SC

318

SONG TITLE	ARTIST	#	TYPE
You're A Grand Old Flag	Patriotic	44-50	PT
You're A Grand Old Flag - Patriotic	Standard	34-440	CB
You're All I Need To Get By	Gaye & Terrell	11-829	DK
You're Always On My Mind	SWV	12-249	DK
You're An Ocean	Fastball	15-449	PHM
You're Beautiful (Radio Version)	Blunt, James	29-258	SC
You're Beginning To Get To Me	Walker, Clay	8-156	CB
You're Driving Me Crazy	Temperance Seven	10-654	SF
You're Easy On The Eyes	Clark, Terri	8-158	CB
You're Free To Go	Reeves, Jim	44-238	DCK
You're Getting To Be A Habit w/Me	Krall, Diana	23-346	MM
You're Gone	Diamond Rio	1-178	CB
You're Gone	Diamond Rio	5-290	SC
You're Gone	Diamond Rio	22-811	ST
You're Gonna Be	McEntire, Reba	23-471	CB
You're Gonna Change Or I'm Gonna Le	Williams, Hank Sr.	14-231	CB
You're Gonna Hear From Me	Streisand, Barbra	49-607	PS
You're Gonna Lose That Girl	Beatles	28-471	DK
You're Gonna Lose That Girl	Terry Baxter Orch.	16-783	DK
You're Gonna Love Me	Young, Chris	30-362	CB
You're Gonna Love Yourself	Rich, Charlie	9-581	SAV
You're Gonna Miss Me When I'm Gone	Brooks & Dunn	3-412	SC
You're Gonna Miss This	Adkins, Trace	36-424	CB
You're Gonna Ruin My Bad Reputation	McDowell, Ronnie	11-742	DK
You're Having My Baby	Anka, Paul	15-595	DK
You're In My Head	McComas, Brian	19-534	ST
You're In My Heart	Stewart, Rod	25-600	MM
You're In My Heart	Stewart, Rod	9-652	SAV
You're Invited (...Friend Can't Come)	Neil, Vince	21-775	SC
You're Just Another Beer Drinking Song	Watson, Gene	47-492	CB
You're Like Coming Home	Lonestar	23-281	CB
You're Lookin' At Country	Lynn, Loretta	8-294	CB
You're Lookin' At Country	Lynn, Loretta	5-413	SC
You're Lucky I Love You	Ashton, Susan	8-968	CB
You're Lucky I Love You	Ashton, Susan	22-492	ST
You're Makin' Me High	Braxton, Toni	18-818	PS
You're Makin' Me High	Braxton, Toni	4-677	SC
You're Makin' Me High	Braxton, Toni	7-568	THM
You're More Than A Number	Drifters	45-899	SF
You're Moving Out	Sager, Carole Bayer	30-794	SF

SONG TITLE	ARTIST	#	TYPE
Today			
You're My Best Friend	Queen	12-336	DK
You're My Best Friend	Queen	13-7	P
You're My Best Friend	Williams, Don	8-628	SAV
You're My Bestest Friend	Davis, Mac	23-512	CB
You're My Bestest Friend	Davis, Mac	4-487	SC
You're My Better Half	Urban, Keith	22-92	CB
You're My Better Half	Urban, Keith	21-664	SC
You're My Jamaica	Pride, Charley	40-110	CB
You're My Man	Anderson, Lynn	47-640	CB
You're My Soul & Inspiration	Oak Ridge Boys	23-501	CB
You're My Soul & Inspiration	Righteous Brothers	35-97	CB
You're My World	Black, Cilla	10-581	SF
You're Nearer	Garland, Judy	48-277	PS
You're No Good	Ronstadt, Linda	35-123	CB
You're Nobody 'Til Somebody Loves U	Martin, Dean	15-596	MM
You're Nobody Til Somebody Loves	Martin, Dean	34-9	CB
You're Nobody Till Somebody...	Buble, Michael	40-90	PS
You're Not Alone	Joe And Jake	49-882	SF
You're Not Alone	Miller, Marie	40-21	PHN
You're Not Easy To Forget	West, Dottie	15-227	CB
You're Not In Kansas Anymore	Messina, Jo Dee	7-332	MM
You're Not In Kansas Anymore	Messina, Jo Dee	4-900	SC
You're Not My Darlin' Anymore	Autry, Gene	22-180	CB
You're Not Sorry	Swift, Taylor	36-382	SC
You're Not the Best	Robison, Charlie	8-986	CB
You're Only Lonely	Souther, J.D.	21-802	SC
You're Out Doing What I'm Doing Without	Watson, Gene	14-673	CB
You're Pretty When I'm Drunk	Bloodhound Gang	47-582	KV
You're Sixteen	Starr, Ringo	33-296	CB
You're Sixteen	Starr, Ringo	9-840	SAV
You're So Good When You're Bad	Pride, Charley	3-801	CB
You're So Good When You're Bad	Pride, Charley	34-249	CB
You're Something Special To Me	Strait, George	4-647	SC
You're Still Beautiful To Me	White, Bryan	22-432	ST
You're Still Here	Hill, Faith	34-352	CB
You're Still Here	Hill, Faith	25-608	MM
You're Still Here	Hill, Faith	19-63	ST
You're Still Here	Hill, Faith	32-269	THM
You're Still Mine	Young, Faron	20-733	CB
You're Still On My Mind	Jones, George	49-90	YBK
You're Still The One	Twain, Shania	35-416	CB

SONG TITLE	ARTIST	#	TYPE
You're Still The One	Twain, Shania	8-304	CB
You're Still The One	Twain, Shania	7-712	PHM
You're Still The One	Twain, Shania	22-765	ST
You're Stronger Than Me	Cline, Patsy	6-728	MM
You're The Best Break This Heart..	Bruce, Ed	12-449	P
You're The Best Thing That Ever...	Price, Ray	8-800	CB
You're The Devil In Disguise	Presley, Elvis	43-251	PSJT
You're The First The Last My Everyt	White, Barry	17-99	DK
You're The First Time I Thought...	McEntire, Reba	1-788	CB
You're The First Time I Thought...	McEntire, Reba	4-788	SC
You're The Inspiration	Chicago	2-857	SC
You're The Last Thing I Needed...	Schneider, John	5-675	SC
You're The Nearest Thing To Heaven	Cash, Johnny	29-743	CB
You're The One	Anything Goes	29-588	SC
You're The One	Carpenters	44-341	OZP
You're The One	Oak Ridge Boys	23-503	CB
You're The One	Yoakam, Dwight	26-540	DK
You're The One	Yoakam, Dwight	20-665	SC
You're The One For Me - Pt. 1	D-Train	15-34	SS
You're The One For Me - Pt. 2	D-Train	15-35	SS
You're The One That I Want	Grease	49-428	SDK
You're The One That I Want	Travolta & Newton-John	11-172	DK
You're The One That I Want	Travolta & Newton-John	6-339	MM
You're The One That I Want	Travolta & Newton-John	9-280	SC
You're The Only Good Thing..	Reeves, Jim	3-838	LG
You're The Only One	Mena, Maria	23-562	MM
You're The Only One	Parton, Dolly	8-541	CB
You're The Only World I Know	James, Sonny	19-478	CB
You're The Only World I Know	James, Sonny	4-262	SC
You're The Part Of Me	Brown, Jim Ed	45-714	VH
You're The Power	Mattea, Kathy	6-79	SC
You're The Reason	Locklin, Hank	44-214	CB
You're The Reason	Tillotson, Johnny	49-286	CAK
You're The Reason God Made OK	Frizzell & West	8-120	CB
You're The Reason God Made OK	Frizzell & West	13-523	P
You're The Reason God Made OK	Frizzell & West	2-311	SC
You're The Reason I'm Living	Darin, Bobby	47-13	SC
You're The Reason Our Kids R Ugly	Jones & McClinton	14-160	CB

SONG TITLE	ARTIST	#	TYPE
You're The Top	Streisand, Barbra	49-542	MM
You're The World	Bellamy Brothers	45-307	KV
You're Where I Belong	Yearwood, Trisha	9-403	CB
You're Where I Belong	Yearwood, Trisha	22-528	ST
You've Got A Friend	Flack, Roberta	47-88	KV
You've Got A Friend	King, Carole	43-443	CB
You've Got A Friend	Taylor, James	11-86	DK
You've Got A Friend	Taylor, James	10-67	SC
You've Got A Good Love Comin'	Greenwood, Lee	47-126	CB
You've Got A Way	Troccoli, Kathy	6-177	MM
You've Got A Way	Twain, Shania	22-424	ST
You've Got A Way - Pop Mix	Twain, Shania	8-108	PHT
You've Got Another Thing Comin'	Judas Priest	23-55	MH
You've Got Possibilities	Monro, Matt	18-106	PS
You've Got The Magic Touch	Platters	12-365	DK
You've Got The Magic Touch	Platters	22-438	SC
You've Got The Touch	Alabama	29-76	CB
You've Got The Touch	Alabama	11-429	DK
You've Got The Touch	Alabama	13-347	P
You've Got To Hide Your Love Away	Beatles	11-551	DK
You've Got To Hide Your Love Away	Vedder, Eddie	25-140	MM
You've Got To Stand For Something	Tippin, Aaron	20-576	CB
You've Got To Stand For Something	Tippin, Aaron	8-599	TT
You've Got To Talk To Me	Womack, Lee Ann	22-413	ST
You've Got Your Troubles	Blanchard&Morgan	9-590	SAV
You've Got Your Troubles	Fortunes	48-751	P
You've Gotta Have Boobs **	Wallis, Ruth	30-670	RSX
You've Lost That Lovin' Feelin'	Righteous Brothers	16-850	DK
You've Lost That Lovin' Feelin'	Righteous Brothers	6-448	MM
You've Lost That Lovin' Feelin'	Righteous Brothers	3-330	PS
You've Made Me So Very Happy	Blood Sweat & Tears	48-587	DK
You've Never Been This Far Before	Twitty, Conway	15-72	CB
You've Never Been This Far Before	Twitty, Conway	4-780	SC
You've Really Got A Hold On Me	Gilley, Mickey	22-218	CB
You've Really Got A Hold On Me	Miracles	49-478	MM
You're No Good	Ronstadt, Linda	10-6	SC
You're Sixteen	Starr, Ringo	11-145	DK
You're So Vain	Simon, Carly	11-198	DK
You're So Vain	Simon, Carly	13-181	P

SONG TITLE	ARTIST	#	TYPE
You're So Vain	Simon, Carly	10-537	SF
You're Still You	Groban, Josh	18-776	PHM
You're The One	Vogues	5-512	SC
Young	Chesney, Kenny	29-427	CB
Young	Chesney, Kenny	25-122	MM
Young	Chesney, Kenny	16-325	ST
Young Americans	Bowie, David	21-407	SC
Young And Beautiful	Del Rey, Lana	46-188	BHK
Young And Crazy	Ballard, Frankie	49-745	KRG
Young And Foolish	Standard	15-597	SGB
Young And The Hopeless	Good Charlotte	34-175	CB
Young And The Hopeless	Good Charlotte	32-328	THM
Young At Heart	Sinatra, Frank	12-524	P
Young At Heart	Sinatra, Frank	9-232	PT
Young Blood	Bad Company	24-202	SC
Young Blood	Coasters	11-413	DK
Young Blood	Coasters	10-695	JVC
Young Blood	Coasters	12-905	P
Young Girl	Puckett & Union Gap	33-259	CB
Young Girl	Puckett & Union Gap	11-556	DK
Young Girl	Puckett & Union Gap	13-267	P
Young Girl	Puckett & Union Gap	10-586	SF
Young Girls	Mars, Bruno	43-161	PHM
Young Love	Air Supply	46-396	CB
Young Love	Carter's Chord	36-567	CB
Young Love	James, Sonny	19-480	CB
Young Love	James, Sonny	27-233	DK
Young Love	James, Sonny	7-114	MM
Young Love	James, Sonny	3-506	SC
Young Love	Judds	1-150	CB
Young Love	Judds	6-775	MM
Young Love	Judds	9-450	SAV
Young Love	Lettermen	48-535	L1
Young Love	Moore, Kip	49-204	BKD
Young Love	Moore, Kip	49-37	SBI
Young Love	Osmond, Donny	47-855	ZM
Young Man's Town	Gill, Vince	19-683	ST
Young Turks	Stewart, Rod	14-861	LE
Young Turks	Stewart, Rod	25-602	MM
Young Volcanoes	Fall Out Boy	45-444	SFK
Young World	Nelson, Ricky	21-712	CB
Young World	Nelson, Ricky	5-238	SC
Younger Girl	Lovin' Spoonful	47-214	PS
Your Body Is A Wonderland	Mayer, John	25-338	MM
Your Body Is A Wonderland	Mayer, John	18-342	PHM
Your Body Is An Outlaw	Tillis, Mel	19-462	CB
Your Cheatin' Heart	Cline, Patsy	45-497	PS
Your Cheatin' Heart	Williams, Hank Sr.	16-809	DK
Your Cheatin' Heart	Williams, Hank Sr.	13-345	P
Your Everything	Urban, Keith	35-424	CB

SONG TITLE	ARTIST	#	TYPE
Your Everything	Urban, Keith	13-824	CHM
Your Everything	Urban, Keith	6-68	SC
Your Eyes Open	Keane	21-689	Z
Your Good Girl's Gonna Go Bad	Wynette, Tammy	8-278	CB
Your Good Girl's Gonna Go Bad	Wynette, Tammy	17-13	DK
Your Good Girl's Gonna Go Bad	Wynette, Tammy	14-324	SC
Your Guardian Angel	Red Jumpsuit Apparatus	30-594	PHM
Your Heart's In Good Hands	Green, Al	4-173	SC
Your Heart's Not In It	Fricke, Janie	4-782	SC
Your Kind Of Love	Dunn, Ronnie	42-28	PHN
Your Life Is Now	Mellencamp, John	14-285	MM
Your Little Secret	Etheridge, Melissa	47-70	SC
Your Love	Outfield	45-374	PHM
Your Love Amazes Me	Berry, John	35-403	CB
Your Love Amazes Me	Berry, John	6-502	MM
Your Love Amazes Me	Berry, John	2-491	SC
Your Love Had Taken Me That High	Twitty, Conway	48-237	CB
Your Love Has Lifted Me Higher	Hunter Sisters	17-114	DK
Your Love Is A Miracle	Chesnutt, Mark	1-349	CB
Your Love Keeps Lifting Me Higher	Hunter Sisters	35-87	CB
Your Love's On The Line	Conley, E.T.	47-602	CB
Your Loving Arms	Martin, Billie Ray	24-171	SC
Your Mama Don't Dance	Loggins & Messina	11-137	DK
Your Mama Don't Dance	Loggins & Messina	13-139	P
Your Man	Turner, Josh	23-418	CB
Your Man	Turner, Josh	29-846	SC
Your Man Loves You Honey	Hall, Tom T.	18-284	CB
Your Nobody Till Somebody Loves You	Sinatra, Frank	48-580	DK
Your Old Love Letters	Reeves, Jim	49-802	VH
Your Old Love Letters	Wagoner, Porter	19-314	CB
Your Old Used To Be	Young, Faron	20-739	CB
Your Own Little Corner Of My Heart	Blackhawk	8-376	CB
Your Own Little Corner Of My Heart	Blackhawk	22-733	ST
Your Plan	Lynch, Dustin	47-931	PHN
Your Secret Love	Vandross, Luther	24-292	SC
Your Side Of The Bed	Little Big Town	41-45	ASK
Your Side Of Town	Maddie & Tae	45-112	KVD
Your Smiling Face	Taylor, James	6-427	MM
Your Smiling Face	Taylor, James	10-70	SC
Your Song	John, Elton	11-103	DK
Your Song	John, Elton	3-240	LG
Your Song	John, Elton	12-691	P
Your Song	John, Elton	2-383	SC
Your Squaw Is On The Warpath	Lynn, Loretta	4-736	SC
Your Tattoo	Kershaw, Sammy	7-83	MM
Your Time's Comin'	Young, Faron	46-58	VH

SONG TITLE	ARTIST	#	TYPE	SONG TITLE	ARTIST	#	TYPE
Your Woman	White Town	10-685	HH				
Your Woman	White Town	10-94	SC				
Yours	Dorsey, Jimmy	47-35	PS				
Yours	Henderson, Ella	48-327	MRH				
Yours Forever	Mellencamp, John	45-417	SC				
Youth Gone Wild	Skid Row	5-67	SC				
Youth Of The Nation	POD	30-650	THM				
Yummy Yummy Yummy	Ohio Express	22-439	SC				
Yup	Corbin, Easton	48-452	KCD				
Zabadak	Davy Dee Dozy Bee	10-612	SF				
Zat You Santa Claus	Armstrong, Louis	45-744	SC				
Zephyr Song the	Red Hot Chili Peppe	25-397	MM				
Ziggy Stardust	Bowie, David	13-752	SGB				
Zing! Went the Strings of My Heart	Garland, Judy	43-378	PSJT				
Zip Gun Bop	Royal Crown Revue	13-694	SGB				
Zombie	Cranberries	16-633	MM				
Zoo the	Scorpions	21-756	SC				
Zoot Suit Riot	Cherry Poppin Daddy	21-562	PHM				
Zoot Suit Riot	Cherry Poppin Daddy	5-283	SC				
Zoot Suit Riot	Cherry Poppin Daddy	13-690	SGB				

Made in the USA
Las Vegas, NV
22 January 2023